Ferozsons

URDU — ENGLISH

DICTIONARY

A COMPREHENSIVE DICTIONARY OF CURRENT VOCABULARY

(Revised Edition)

★

FEROZSONS (Pvt.) LTD.
LAHORE-RAWALPINDI-KARACHI

FEROZSONS'
Urdu-English Dictionary

آ

آ *ā*, Lengthened form of Alif. Alif is the first letter of the Arabic, Persian and Urdu alphabets and, in *abjad*, it stand for number one.

آ آ *ā ā, v. (Lit.)* Come, come; bird call for pigeons, hens, etc.

آبننا *ā ban-nā, v.* To happen (to); to befall; to be involved in trouble.

آ بیل مجھے مار *ā bail mujhe mār, prov.* To ask for or to invite or court trouble.

آ پڑنا *ā paṛnā, v.* To befall; to come or fall (upon); to fall (to); to descend (upon).

آ پکڑنا *ā pakaṛnā, v.* To overtake; to seize.

آ پہنچنا *ā pahuṅchnā, v.* To appear suddenly; to draw near; to arrive.

آ جانا *ā jānā, v.* To come (suddenly); to happen to come; to arrive; to befall.

آ دھمکنا *ā dhamaknā, v.* To make a sudden appearance; to come uninvited.

آ رھنا *ā rehnā, v.* To como and reside; to dwell (in) (despite opposition); to fall down.

آ گرنا *ā girnā, v.* To fall down; to make a rush (at or upon); to fall upon others (for sustenance).

آ گھیرنا *ā ghernā, v.* To surround; to besiege; to encircle; to press to do a thing.

آ لگنا *ā lagnā, v.* To touch the shore (boat); to catch (disease); to be hit (by stone, bullet etc.); to be close at hand

آ لینا *ā lenā, v.* To overtake; to reach.

آ ملنا *ā milnā, v.* To join (with); to meet happily (in reconciliation).

آ نکلنا *ā nikalnā, v.* To come by chance; to come suddenly or unexpectedly; to turn up.

آب *āb* (P) *n.m.* Water. *n.f.* Splendour; elegance; polish; magnificence; water or lustre (in gems); temper (of steel); sharpness (of sword); brightness.

آب آب کرنا *āb āb karnā, v.* To reproach; to put to shame; to discredit; to ask for water.

آب آب ھونا *āb āb honā, v.* To be drenched with prespiration; to be thoroughly ashamed.

آب آتش رنگ، *āb-ĕ ātish rang,* آب آتش مزاج، *āb-ĕ ātishmizāj,* آب آتشناک، *āb-ĕ ātishnāk,* آب آتشیں *ab-ĕ ātishiṅ,* } *n.m.* Wine; liquor; bitter tears.

آب آ جانا *āb ā jānā, v.* To get polished; to shine; to become sharp.

آب آمد ، تیمم برخاست *āb āmad tayammum barkhāst, prov.* John goes when Jesus comes.

آب آھک *āb-ĕ āhak, n.m.* Lime-water.

آب آھن *āb-ĕ āhan, n.f.* Temper of steel.

آب آھن تاب *āb-ĕ āhantāb, n.m.* Water in which red-hot iron is dipped.

آب آئینہ *āb-ĕ ā'inah, n.f.* Lustre or polish of a mirror.

آب احمر،آب ارغوانی *āb-ĕ aḥmar, āb-ĕ arghawānī, n.m.* Wine; liquor.

آب اڑنا، آب اترنا، آب بگڑنا *āb uṛnā, āb utarnā, āb bigaṛnā, vo* To lose lustre; to become dull or blunt (sword).

آب استادہ *eb-ĕ istāda n.m.* Still water.

آب انار āb-ĕ anār, n.m. Pomegranate juice; red wine.

آب انفعال āb-ĕ infiʻāl, n.m. Sweat caused by remorse or shame.

آب انگور āb-ĕ angūr, n.m. Grape-juice; wine.

آب باران āb-ĕ bārāṅ, n.m. Rain-water.

آب بستہ āb-ĕ bastah, n.m. Ice; hailstone.

آب بقا āb-ĕ baqā, n.m. Water conferring immortality.

آب بینی āb-ĕ bīnī, n.m. Mucus from the nose; nasal discharge.

آب پاش āb pāsh, n.m. Watering-can.

آب پاشی āb pāshī, n.f. Irrigation; sprinkling water.

آب پشت āb-ĕ pusht, n.m. Semen.

آب پیکان āb-ĕ paikāṅ, n.f. Sharpness of the arrow.

آب تلخ āb-ĕ talkh, n.m. Bitter water; wine; tears.

آب تیغ āb-ĕ tegh, n.f. Sharpness of sword.

آب جاری āb-ĕ jārī, n.m. Running water; a rivulet; tears streaming down the cheek.

آب جاودان āb-ĕ jāwidāṅ, n.m. Immortalizing water, fluid or syrup.

آب جو āb-ĕ jau, n.m. Barley-water; beer.

آبجو ābjū, n.f. A stream; a rivulet.

آب جوش āb josh, n.m. Broth; gravy; juice of cooked meat; boild water.

آب‌چڑھانا āb charhānā, v. To polish; to temper; to whet; to sharpen.

آب چشم āb-ĕ chashm, n.m. Tears.

آب حرام āb-ĕ harām, n.m. Wine; liquor; unclean or forbidden water.

آب حیات ، آب حیوان ، آب خضر ، آب زندگی āb-ĕ hayāt, āb-ĕ haiwāṅ, āb-ĕ khizr, āb-ĕ zindagī, n.m. Water giving immortality; a fabulous spring containing the water of immortality.

آب خاصہ āb-ĕ khāṣah, n.m. Special drinking water for nobles and kings.

آب خجالت āb-ĕ khijālat, n.m. Sweat caused by shame or bashfulness.

آبخورہ āb khorah, n.m. Earthen tumbler.

آبخورے بھرنا ābkhore bharnā, v. To offer cups of sherbet or milk.

آبدار ābdār, n.m. The person having charge of the drinking water. adj. Brilliant, polished, bright (as gems); well-tempered (as steel); sharp (as a sword).

آبدار خانہ ābdār khānah, n.m. A repository for drinking water.

آبداری ābdārī, n.f. Brilliance (of gems); temper or polish (of steel); sharpness (of sword).

آب دست āb dast, n.f. Washing of the private parts after evacuation.

آب دست کرنا āb dast karnā, v. To lave; to clean oneself after evacuation.

آب دندان āh-ĕ dandāṅ, n.f. Polish of the teeth; a species of pear; a kind of pomegranate.

آب دہن āb-ĕ dahan, n.m. Saliva; spittle.

آب دیدہ āb-ĕ dīdah, n.m. Tears.

آبدیدہ āb dīdah, adj. Weeping; in tears.

آبدیدہ ہونا āb dīdah honā, v. To weep; to be in tears; to shed tears.

آب دینا āb denā, v. To polish; to sharpen.

آب رحمت āb-ĕ rahmat, n.m. Rain water; mercy; pity; kindness.

آب روان āb-ĕ rawāṅ, n.m. Running water; a kind of fine muslin.

آب ریز āb rez, n.m. A drain; a tap; a watering-can.

آب زر āb-ĕ zar, n.m. Gold water; gold reduced to a liquid state.

آب زلال āb-ĕ zulāl, n.m. Pure, clear water; decanted water.

آب زمزم āb-ĕ zamzam, n.m. Water of the well in Mecca called Zamzam.

آب شور āb-ĕ shor, n.m. Sea water; salt water.

آب شیرین āb-ĕ shīrīṅ, n.m. Sweet water.

آب عشرت āb-ĕ ʻishrat, n.m. Wine.

آب کار āb kār, n.m. A distiller or seller of wine; a wine merchant.

آب کاری āb kārī, n.f. Distillery; liquor shop; excise duty; Excise Department.

آب کش āb kash, n.m. A water-carrier; a strainer; one who draws water from a well.

آب کشی āb kashi, n.f. Drawing water from a well.

آب کوثر āb-ĕ kauṣar, n.m. The water of the river Kauṣar flowing in Paradise.

آب گلگوں āb-e gulgūṅ, n.m. Rose-red wine.

آب گوشت āb-e gosht, n.m. Soup; gravy; broth

آب گوں āb gūṅ, adj. Of the colour of water, sky, glass, snow or ice; shining (sword).

آب لیموں āb-e lemūṅ, n.m. Lemon water.

آب مروارید āb-e marwārid, n.f. Lustre of a gem; a particular disease of the eye; cataract.

آب مقطر āb-e muqattar, n.m. Distilled water.

آب ندامت āb-e nadāmat, n.m. Sweat caused by repentance; contrition.

آب نقره āb-e nuqrah, n.m. Liquid silver used for silver-plating

آب نیسان āb-e naisān, n.m. Spring rains; the rainfall during the month of Naisāṅ, the seventh month of the Romans corresponding to the month of March.

آب و تاب āb-ŏ tāb, n.f. Lustre; dignity; beauty; grandeur; magnificence.

آب و رنگ āb-ŏ rang, n.m. Glory.

آب و دانه āb-ŏ dānā, n.m. Subsistence.

آب و دانه اٹھنا āb-ŏ dānah uṭhnā, v. To be transferred from a place; cessation of a source of income; to be about to die.

آب‌ودانه حرام هونا āb-ŏ dānah ḥarām ḥonā, v. To be tired of life; to be fed up with life.

آب و دانے کا زور هونا āb-ŏ dāne kā zor honā, v. To be driven or attracted to a place by the subsistance in store for one at that place; to be attracted by fate.

آب و گل āb-ŏ gil, n.f. Disposition; temperament; matter; the elemen employed in the creation of the universe. (Lit.) Water and clay.

آب و نان āb-ŏ nān n.m. Food.

آب و نمک āb-ŏ namak, n.m. Taste; savour; relish.

آب و هوا āb-ŏ hawā, n.f. Climate.

آب و هوا بدل جانا āb-ŏ-hawā badal janā, v. To change (climate).

آب و هوا تبدیل کرنا āb-ŏ hawā tabdīl karnā, v. To go for a change of climate.

آب و هوا راس نه آنا āb-ŏ hawā rās nah ānā, v. To be unsuitable (climate).

آب و هوا موافق آنا āb-ŏ hawā muwāfiq ānā, v. To be agreeable (climate).

آباد ābād (P) adj. Inhabited; populated; peopled; cultivated; flourishing; prosperous; happy.

آباد کار ābād kār, n.m. A settler on waste land; a cultivator.

آباد کاری ābād kārī, n.f. Settlement; habitation; populating; cultivating.

آباد کرنا ābād karnā, v. To populate; to cultivate; to inhabit; to settle.

آبادانی ābādānī (P) n.f. Population; cultivation; habitation; abundance; prosperity.

آبادی ābādi (P) n.f. Population; prosperity; a village site; the people living in a place.

آبان ābān (P) n.m. The eighth month of the Persian year; tenth day of that month.

آباء ābā' (A) n.m. (plu. of اب ab) Fathers; fore-fathers.

آباء و اجداد abā'ŏ ajdād, n.m. Ancestors; fore-fathers.

آبائے شہر *ābā-ĕ shahr*, *n.m.* City fathers; municipal commissioners; councillors.

آبائے علوی *ābā-ĕ 'ulwī*, *n.m.* People of high rank.

آبائی *ābā'ī* (A) *adj.* Ancestral.

آبرو *ābrū* (P) *n.f.* Brightness of face; honour; character; good name; fame; rank; dignity; chastity.

آبرو اتارنا ، آبرو بگاڑنا ، آبرو لینا *ābrū utārnā, ābrū bigārnā, ābrū lenā, v.* To bring into disrepute; to dishonour; to disgrace; to violate the chastity of.

آبرو بچانا *ab·ū bachānā, v.* To save one's honou·.

آبرو بخشنا *ıbrū bakhshnā, v.* To confer hono ır.

آبرو برباد کرنا، آبرو پر پانی پھیر دینا، آبرو خاک میں ملانا *ābrū barbād karnā, ābrū par pām pher denā, ābrū khāk meṅ milānɔ, v.* To destroy one's honour, self-respect or reputation.

آبرو بڑھنا *ābrū barhnā, v.* To gain more honour.

آبرو بنانا *ābrū banānā, v.* To acquire honour or reputation.

آبرو پانا، آبرو پیدا کرنا، آبرو حاصل کرنا *ābrū pānā, ābrū paidā karnā, ābrū ḥāṣil karnā, v.* To gain renown, rank or dignity.

آبرو پر حرف آنا *ābrū par ḥarf ānā, v.* To be disgraced; to lose reputation.

آبرو رکھنا *ābrū rakhnā, v.* To uphold one's respect, honour or reputation; to save from dishonour.

آبرو ریزی *ābrū rezī, n.f.* Slander; calumny; defamation; vilification; violation of chastity; rape.

آبرو ریزی کرنا *ābrū rezi karnā, v.* To slander; to defame; to rape; to calumniate; to violate the chastity of.

آبرو کا لاگو ہونا، آبرو کے پیچھے پڑنا *ābrū kā lāgū honā, ābrū ke pīchhe parnā, v.* To be bent upon ruining one's honour, character or reputation.

آبرو کھونا *ābrū khonā, v.* To lose respect.

آبرو گئی پھر نہیں آتی *ābrū ga'ī phir nahin ātī, prov.* Lost reputation is seldom regained; credit lost is like a Venice glass which when broken cannot be soldered.

آبرو موتی کی سی آب ہے *ābrū matī kī sī āb hai, prov.* Hohnour is like the lustre of a pearl.

آبرو میں بٹا لگنا، آبرو میں فرق آ جانا *ābrū meṅ baṭṭā lagnā, ābrū meṅ farq ā jānā, v.* To bring slur on character or reputation; to lose confidence or good name.

آبستنی *ābistanī* (P) *n.f.* A pregnant woman; a kind of musical instrument.

آبشار *ābshār* (P) *n.f.* Waterfall; cataract; cascade.

آبگینہ *ābgīnah* (P) *n.m.* Crystal glass; mirror; a lover's wine glass.

آبلہ *āblah* (P) *n.m.* Blisters; boils.

آبلہ پا *āblah pā, adj.* Having blisters on the feet; tired; fatigued; exhausted.

آبلہ پائی *āblah pā'ī, n.f.* State of being tired; helplessness.

آبلہ فرنگ *ālbah-ĕ farang n.m.* Syphilis.

آبنائے *ābnāi* (P) *n.f.* (*Geog.*) A strait.

آبنوس *ābnūs* (P) *n.m.* Ebony.

آبنوسی *ābnūsī* (P) *adj.* Made of ebony; of ebony colour; black; ebonized.

آبی *ābī* (P) *adj.* Watery; aquatic; moist; aqueous.

آبیاری *ābyārī* (P) *n.f.* Irrigation; watering.

آبیانہ *ābyānah* (P) *n.m.* Water tax; water rate.

آپ *āp* (H) *pro.* Self; selves; you; yourself; you sir (used when addressing a superior).

آپ آپ کرنا *āp āp karnā, v.* To flatter; to be selfish.

آپ بھاتی *āp bhātī, adv.* According to one's own pleasure.

آپ بھلے تو جگ بھلا *āp bhale to jag bhalā, prov.* Good mind good find.

آپ بیتی *āp bitī, n.f.* The story of one's own experience; autobiography.

آپ جانیں آپ کا کام āo jāneṅ āp kā kām. Manage your own affairs; do as you like.

آپ ڈال ڈال میں پات پات āp ḍāl ḍāl, maiṅ pāt pāt, prov. I am cleverer than you.

آپ ڈوبے تو جگ ڈوبا ، آپ موے تو جگ موا āp ḍūbe to jag ḍūbā, āp mue to jag muā, prov. Death's day is dooms-day.

آپ ڈوبے تو ڈوبے ، اور کو بھی لے ڈوبے āp ḍūbe to ḍūbe au. ko bhī le ḍūbe, prov. To ruin others along with oneself.

آپ سے ابے هونا āp se abe honā, v. To have one's position lowered; to be disgraced; to be degraded; to be undervalued.

آپ سے آپ āp se āp, adv. Of one's own accord; voluntarily; spontaneously.

آپ فضیحت اوروں کو نصیحت āp fazīhat, auroṅ ko naṣīhat, prov. He plucks out the teeth of a dog and barks himself; bell calls others to church, but goes not itseif.

آپ کا پاس هے ، آپ کا منه هے āp kā pās hai, ap kā muṅh hai. It is out of regard for you.

آپ کاج ، مہا کاج āp kāj mahā kāj, prov. Self done well done; one's own business is the most important.

آپ کا کیا بگڑتا هے ؟ āp kā kiyā bigaṛtā hai? You won't lose anything.

آپ کو آسمان پر کھینچنا ، آپ کو شاخ زعفران سمجھنا āp ko āsmān par kheṅchnā, āp ko shākh-ĕ z'afrān samajhnā, v. To put on airs; to be proud.

آپ کو بھول جانا āp ko bhūl jānā, v. To forget one's past.

آپ کو پانا āp ko pānā, v. To estimate one's correct value.

آپ کو دور کھینچنا āp ko dūr kheṅchnā, v. To keep oneself aloof (from); to think too much of one's self.

آپ کو ڈبونا āp ko ḍabonā, v. To ruin oneself.

آپ کو کھونا āp ko khonā, v. To forget oneself.

آپ کھائے بلی کو بتائے āp khāe billi ko batāe, prov. Blaming others for one's own fault.

آپ هی آپ āp hī āp, adv. Spontaneously; alone.

آپا āpā (T) n.f. An elder sister; a nurse.

آپا āpā (H) n.m. Self.

آپا دھاپی āpā dhāpi, n.f. A race for self; selfishness.

آپے سے باهر هونا āpe se bāhar honā, v. To be beside oneself (with joy or anger); to be in a rapture; to be in a fury.

آپے میں آنا āpe meṅ ānā, v. To come to one's senses.

آپے میں هونا āpe meṅ honā, v. To be in one's senses.

آپس āpas, adv. One another; each other; together.

آپس داری āpas dārī, n.f. Brotherhood; relationship.

آپس کی بات āpas kī bāt, n.f. Between ourselves; a private or family affairs.

آپس کی پھوٹ āpas kī phūṭ, v. Internal discord or dissension; quarrel between husband and wife.

آپس میں āpas meṅ, adv. Mutually; a matter between friends or relatives.

آپس میں رهنا āpas meṅ rehnā, v. To live together; to maintain good relations with neighbours.

آتا ātā (H) n.m. That which is due to one; dues; debts.

آتا جاتا ata jātā (H) n.m. A traveller; a passer-by.

آتا نه چھوڑیے ، جاتا نه موڑیے ātā nah chhoṛiye, jātā nah moṛiye, prov. Take what comes your way, pursue not the evanescent.

آتش ātish (P) n.f. Fire.

آتش انداز ātish āndāz, adj. & n.m. Casting out fire; one who kindles fire.

آتش انگیز ātish āngez, *adj.* Kindling or stirring up fire. *n.m.* One who kindles fire; firebrand; a seditious person; an incendiary.

آتش بار ātish bār, *adj.* Raining fire; fiery; explosive. *n.m.* A musket; a tinder box.

آتش باز ātish bāz, *n.m.* A maker of fireworks; pytrotechnist.

آتش بازی ātish bāzi *n.f.* Fireworks; pyrotechnics.

آتش بیان ātish bayān, *adj.* Fiery speaker.

آتش بے دود ātish-ĕ be dūd, *n.f.* Wine; liquor; anger; sun.

آتش پارہ ātish pārah, *n.m.* A spark; a lighted coal; a very beautiful person; a provoker of quarels. *adj.* Quarrelsome.

آتش پرست ātish parast, *adj.* A worshipper of fire; a guebre; a follower of Zoroaster.

آتش پرستی ātish parasti, *n.f.* Fire worship.

آتش پیما ātish paimā, *n.m.* Pyrometer.

آتش تر ātish-ĕ tar, *n.f.* Wine.

آتش خاموش ātish-ĕ khāmosh, *n.f.* Wine.

آتش خانہ ātish khānah, *n.m.* A fire temple; a fire place; a powder magazine.

آتش خو ātish khū, *adj.* A firebrand.

آتش خوار ātish khwār, *adj.* A fire-eater; a salamander; a worm born in fire.

آتش دان ātish dān, *n.m.* Fireplace; any receptacle for fire; a grate; a chafing dish.

آتش رخ ātish rukh, *adj.* Red-faced; rosy-cheeked.

آتش زبان ātish zobān, *adj.* A firebrand; an eloquent speaker.

آتش زدگی ātish zadagi, *n.f.* Arson; combustion; breaking out of fire.

آتش زنی ātish zani, *n.f.* Act of setting on fire; arson.

آتش سیال ātish-ĕ sayyāl, *n.f.* Wine.

آتش طبع ātish ṭab', *adj.* Hot-tempered; passionate.

آتش فشاں ātish fishāṅ, *adj.* Fire ejector. *n.m.* A volcano.

آتش کا پرکالہ ātish kā parkālah, *n.m.* A very astute and wicked person; a very beautiful person.

آتش کدہ ātish kadah, *n.m.* A fire-temple; furance; grate.

آتش گیر ātish gir, *adj.* Combustible. *n.m.* Tongs.

آتش مزاج ، آتش ناک ātish mizāj, ātsh nāk, *adj.* Fiery-tempered; ill-tempered.

آتش موسیٰ ātish-ĕ Moosā, *n.f.* Light that Moses saw at Mount Senai.

آتش نفس ātish-ĕ nafs, *n.f.* Lust; lasciviousness.

آتش نمرد ātish-ĕ namrud, *n.f.* Pyre made by Namrud to throw Prophet Abraham in.

آتشک ātishak (P) *n.f.* Syphilis (a venereal disease).

آتشی ātishi (P) *adj.* Fiery; hot; irascible; belonging to fire.

آتشی شیشہ ātishī shīshah, *n.m.* A glass which can burn by focussing the rays of the sun; a magnifying glass.

آتشیں ātishiṅ (P) *adj.* Resembling fire.

آتشیں خو atishiṅ khū *adj.* Passionate; irascible.

آتما ātmā (S) *n.f.* Soul; spirit; mind; the reasoning faculty; the understanding; appetite; belly.

آٹا āṭā (H) *n.m.* Flour; meal.

آٹا کرنا āṭā karnā, v. To reduce to powder

آٹا گیلا ہونا āṭā gilā honā, v. To be plunged into difficulties; to get into hot water.

آٹے دال کا بھاؤ کھلنا āṭe dāl kā bhāo khulnā v. To find oneself in hot water; to become conscious of one's miserable state.

آٹے کی آپا āṭe kī āpā, *adj.* Fool; a simpleton.

آٹے کے ساتھ گھن بھی پس جاتا ھے āṭe ke sāth ghun bhī pis jātā hai, *prov.* The innocent also get punished with the guilty.

آٹے میں نون یا نمک āṭe men nūn yā namak, *adj.* Not much; very little; mite in the cheese.

آٹھ āṭh (H) *adj.* Eight.

آٹھ آٹھ آنسو رلانا āṭh āṭh ānsū rulānā, v. To cause to weep bitterly.

آٹھ آٹھ آنسو رونا āṭh āṭh ānsū ronā, *v.* To weep bitterly; to shed a flood of tears.

آٹھ پہر āṭh pahr, *n.m. & adv.* All the twenty-four hours; day and night; constantly.

آٹھواں āṭhwāṅ (H) *adj.* Eighth.

آٹھوں āṭhoṅ (H) *adj* All the eight.

آٹھوں گانٹھ کمیت āṭhoṅ gāṅṭh kumait, *adj.* Clever; shrewd; cunning; cute; (*Lit.*) a bay horse with all the eight joints marked reddish-brown, *viz.*, the four knees and the four ankles.

آثار āsār (A) *n.m.* (*plu. of* اثر āsar) Symptoms; signs; tokens; traces; footprints; effects; relics; impressions; basis; the breadth of a wall; historical traditions; foundation of a building.

آثارالصنادید āsār-us-ṣanādīd, *n.m.* Relics of ancient people.

آثار شریف āsār-ĕ sharīf, *n.m.* Tombs of saints; sacred relics of prophets.

آثار قدیمہ āsār-ĕ qadīmah, *n.m.* Ancient relics; archaeological monuments.

آثم āsim (A) *n.m.* A sinner; a culprit.

آج āj (H) *n.m.* Today; this day.

آج تک āj tak, *adv.* Uptil now; upto this day.

آج کا کام کل پر چھوڑنا āj kā kām kal par chhoṛnā, *v.* To put off today's work till tomorrow.

آج کرے گا، کل پائے گا āj karegā kal pāegā, *prov.* As you sow, so shall you reap.

آج کل āj kal, *adv.* Now-a-days; in a day or two; recently; of late; today or tomorrow.

آج کل کرنا āj kal karnā, v. To procrastinate; to delay; to evade.

آج مرے کل دوسرا دن āj mare kal dūsrā din, *prov.* Dead persons are soon forgotten.

آچا āchā (P) *n.m.* Father; paternal or maternal grandfather; an old servant.

آختہ ākhtah (*defective form*) See اختہ akhtah.

آخ تھو ākh thū, *interj.* Tush! pooh! pshaw! fie!

آخر ākhir (A) *adj.* Last; hindmost; later; final. *n.m.* Termination; conclusion; issue.

آخرالامر ākh-ul amr, *adv.* At last; finally; after all; ultimately; eventually.

آخرالزمان ākhir-uz-zamān, *adj.* The last of of all; an epithet of the Holy Prophet of Islam.

آخربیں ākhir bīn, *adj.* Far-sighted.

آخر شب ākhir-ĕ shab, *n.f.* Before morning; the close of the night.

آخر کار ākhir-ĕ kār, *adv.* At last; eventually; in the end; at length.

آخر کرنا ākhir karnā, *v.* To finish; to close; to put an end to; to conclude.

آخر وقت ākhir waqt, *n.m.* The last breath; just before the end.

آخر ھونا ākhir honā, *v.* To end; to close; to die.

آخرت ākhirat (A) *n.f.* The life hereafter; the life to come.

آخرت بگاڑنا ākhirat bigāṛnā, *v.* To spoil or mar one's life to come.

آخرت بنانا، سنوارنا ākhirat banānā, sanwārnā, *v.* To do good deeds; to ensure one's good in the life to come.

آخرش ākhirash (P) *adv.* At last; finally; afterall.

آخری ākhirī (A) *adj.* Last; latter; final; extreme.

آخری چہار شنبہ ākhiri chahār shambah, n.m. The last Wednesday of the month of Safar which is observed by Muslims with solemnity and rejoicing in memory of the recovery of the Holy Prophet from a very severe illness.

آخریں ākhirīn (P) adj. Last; final.

آخور akhor (P) n.f. Sweepings; scourings; entrails; filth; stable; refuse; offals; litter.

آخور کی بھرتی ākhor kī bharti, n.f. Gathering of scraps; odds and ends; insertion of irrelevant and useless matter in composition.

آخون ، آخوند ākhūn, ākhūnd (P) n.m. School-master; teacher, tutor; theology-teacher.

آداب ādāb (A) n.m. (plu. of ادب adab), Good-breeding; good manners; etiquette; politeness; forms of address in writing and speaking; salutation; respects; elegant manners; rules; ceremonies.

آداب بجالانا ādāb bajā lānā, v. To pay homage or respects (to); to say good-bye; to wish (time).

آداب و القاب ādāb-ŏ alqāb, n.m. Designation; title; forms of address; appellation.

آداب و تسلیمات ādāb-ŏ taslīmāt, n.m. Best compliments; best respects.

آدم ādam (A) n.m. Adam, the first man; father of mankind.

آدم ثانی ādam-ĕ ṣāni, n.m. The epithet of Prophet Noah.

آدم خور ādam khor, adj. Man eater; cannibal.

آدم زاد ādam zād, cdj Born of Adam; human race; mankind.

آدم شناس ādam shinās, adj. One who finds out the sort of person one is; one gifted to evaluate human beings; acute person.

آدمی ādamī (P) n.m. An offspring of Adam; an individual person; (metaph.) a husband; a sevant.

آدمی آدمی انتر ، کوئی هیرا کوئی کنکر ādami ādamī antar, ko'i hirā ko'ī kankar, prov. All are not alike; man differs from man; no two persons are alike.

آدمی بن جانا ādami ban jānā, v. To learn good manners; to be civilized; to attain sense of responsibility.

آدمی بنانا ādami banānā, v. To teach one good manners; to civilize; to humanise.

آدمی صحبت سے پہچانا جاتا ھے ādamī ṣuḥbat se pahchānā jātā hai, prov. Man is known by the company he keeps.

آدمی نے آخر تو کچادودھ پیا ھے ādamī ne ākhir to kachchā dūdh piyā hai, prov. To err is human.

آدمیت ādamiyyat (A) n.f. Humanity; human nature; fellow feeling; civility; courtesy; goodmanners.

آدمیت اٹھ جانا ādamiyyat uṭh jānā, v. To be bereft of sympathy and courtesy; to become devoid of civility and good manners.

آدمیت پکڑنا ādamiyyat pakaṛnā, v. To become civilized; to learn good manners; to come to one's self; to recover one's senses.

آدمیت سکھانا ādamiyyat sikhānā, v. To teach good manners; to render humane; to polish; to civilize; to discipline; to chasten.

آدمیت سے گزر جانا adamiyyat se guzar jānā, v. To behave improperly; to act savagely.

آدھا ، آدھی ādhā, ādhi (H) adj. Half.

آدھا آدھا ādhā ādhā, adj. Fifty fifty; half and half; divided into two equal parts.

آدھا تیتر آدھا بٹیر ādhā tītar, ādhā baṭer, prov. Neither fish nor flesh nor good red herring (applied to a confused or jumbled state of things).

آدھا کرنا ādhā karnā, v. To bisect; to halve; to divide into two equal parts,

آدھا ھونا ādhā honā, v. To be very much reduced; to decrease in size; to grow lean.

آدھی چھوڑ ساری کو جاوے (دھاوے) آدھی رہے نہ ساری پاوے ādhī chhoṛ sārī ko jāve (dhāwe), ādhī rahe nah sārī pāwe, prov. Run after the whole and lose all; catch at the shadow and lose the substance.

آدینہ ādinah (P) n.m. Friday.

آڈٹ āḍit (E) n.m. Audit.

آڈیٹر āḍiṭar (E) n.m. Auditor.

آذار āẕār (A) n.m. Sixth month of the Greek or Syrian year corresponding to the month of March.

آذر āẕar (P) n.m. Fire; the ninth solar month, corresponding to the middle of December to the middle of January.

آر ār (H) n.f. An awl; cobbler's needle.

آرا ārā (P) adj. Embellishing; adorning (used in comps. as in جہاں آرا jahāṅ ārā, that which embellishes the world).

آرا ārā, n.m. A saw.

آرا سر پر چل جانا ārā sar par chal jānā, v. To be tortured; to be put to excruciating pain.

آرا کش ārā-kash, n.m. A sawyer.

آراستگی ārāstagī (P) n.f. Preparation; decoration; embellishment; arrangement; adornment; order; regularity.

آراستہ ārāstah (P) adj. Prepared; decorated; arranged; equipped.

آرام ārām (P) n.m. Rest; repose; respite; relief; ease; health; comfort; alleviation; convenience.

آرام پانا ārām pānā, v. To get rest; to regain health; to get all sorts of comfort.

آرام تلخ ھونا ārām talkh honā, v. To be put to discomfort.

آرام دینا ārām denā, v. To solace; to comfort; to ease; to relieve; to allay; to repose; to heal.

آرام طلب ، آرام پسند ārām ṭalab, ārām pasand, adj. Idle; lazy; indolent; slothful; inert; lotus-eater.

آرام کرسی ārām kursī, n.f. Easy chair.

آرام کرنا ārām karnā, v. To rest; to recline; to go to bed.

آرام گاہ ārām gāh, n.f. Bed-chamber; a resting place.

آراء ārā' (A) n.f. (plu. of رائے rā'e) Views; opinions.

آرائش ārā'ish (P) n.f. Decoration; adornment; embellishment; dressing; beauty.

آر پار ār pār (H) adj. Through and through; from one side to the other (as a hole); pierced through; across.

آرپن ārpan (H) n.m. An offering; a trust.

آرتی ārtī (H) n.f. A religious ceremony among Hindus.

آرٹ ārṭ (E) n.m. Art.

آرٹسٹ ārṭisṭ (E) n.m. Artist.

آرد ārad (P) n.m. Flour; meal.

آرڈر ārḍar (E) n.m. Order.

آرڈر بک ārḍar buk n.f. Order-book.

آرڈر دینا ārḍar denā, v. To place order (with a firm).

آرزو ārzū (P) n.f. Yearning; longing; desire; wish; hope; inclination; solicitude; love; request; entreaty; trust; expectation.

آرزو بر آنا ārzū bar ānā, v. Fulfilment of a desire.

آرزو خاک میں مل جانا ārzū khāk meṅ mil jānā, v. To be disappointed; to be frustrated.

آرزو کرنا ārzū karnā, v. To desire; to long for; to yearn.

آرزو مند ārzū mand, adj. Wishing; desirous; eager; longing; aspiring; intent on.

آرزو مندی ārzū mandī, n.f. Eagerness; desire; yearning; wishfulness.

آرسی ārsī (H) n.f. A thumb ring with mirror (set in place of a stone) worn by women; a looking glass; a mirror.

آروغ ārogh (P) n.m. A belching; eructation.

آری ārī (H) n.f. A small saw; a hand-saw.

آریا ، آریہ āryā, aryah(S) n.m. An Aryan.

آرے āre (P) adv. Yes; yea.

آرے بلے کرنا āre bale karnā. To evade.

آڑ āṛ (H) n.f. A covering; concealment; shelter; defence; buttress; a bar; a wall; a curtain; protection; prevention; interception; impediment.

آڑ پکڑنا āṛ pakaṛnā, v. To take shelter; to lie in ambush.

آڑ کرنا āṛ karnā, v. To screen; to shelter; to conceal.

آڑ لینا āṛ lenā, id. To be behind the screen; to get behind a shelter.

آڑ میں āṛ men, adv. Behind; under cover of; under the pretence of; lying in ambush.

آڑا ، آڑی āṛā, āṛi (H) adj. Inclined; bent; athwart; diagonal; transverse; cross; oblique.

آڑے آنا āṛe ānā, v. To come between; to protect; to shield; to interpose; to stand in good stead.

آڑے ھاتھوں لینا āṛe hāthon lenā, v. To chide; to scold; to upbraid; to take one to task.

آڑو āṛū (H) n.m. Peach.

آڑھت āṛhat (H) n.f. Agency; brokerage; commission depot.

آڑھتی āṛhati (H) n.m. A commission agent; a broker.

آز āz (P) n.f. Ardent desire; greed; lust; avarice; covetousness.

آزاد āzād (P) adj. Free; unrestrained; independent; unchained; liberated. n.m. A freeman.

آزاد رائے āzād rāe, adj. Holding an unbiased opinion; holding an independent view.

آزاد رو āzād rau, adj. Fearless; unbigoted; bold.

آزاد طبع ، آزاد منش āzād ṭaba', āzād manish, adj. Of fearless disposition; dauntless.

آزاد کرنا āzād karnā, v. To liberate; to set free; to unfetter; to discharge.

آزاد مرد āzād mard, n.m. A bold and fearless person; carefree.

آزادانہ āzādānah (P) adv. Freely; independently.

آزادی āzādi (P) n.f. Freedom; liberty; emancipation; liberation.

آزادی خواہ āzādi khwāh, adj. A lover of freedom.

آزار āzār (P) n.m. Illness; ailment; malady; woe; injury; disease.

آزار دہ āzār deh, adj. Annoying; irksome; teasing; troublesome.

آزار دھی āzār dehī, n.f. Vexation; affliction.

آزار دینا āzār denā, v. To torment; to annoy; to gall.

آزار لگنا āzār lagnā, v. To catch a disease.

آزر āzar (A) n.m. Name of Prophet Abraham's father, more correct form than آذر; an idolater.

آزردگی āzardagi (P) n.f. Woe; grief; calamity; distress; dissatisfaction; trouble; displeasure; affliction; sorrow.

آزردہ āzardah (P) adj. Annoyed; dejected; dissatisfied; troubled; uneasy; sorry; gloomy; sad.

آزردہ دل āzardah dil, adj. Dejected; worried; sad.

آزردہ خاطر āzardah khāṭir, adj. Annoyed; displeased; sorrowful; vexed; disgusted.

آزردہ کرنا āzardah karnā, v. To displease; to annoy; to afflict; to trouble.

آزمانا āzmānā, v. To put to test; to scrutinise; to try; to make experiments.

آزمائش āzmā'ish (P) n.f. Trial; test; experiment; assay; examination.

آزمودہ āzmūdah (P) adj. Experienced; tried; tested; proved.

آزمودہ کار āzmūdah kār, adj. Skilled; practised; experienced in business.

آزوقہ ، آزقہ āzūqah, āzuqah (A) n.m. Meagre diet or income; food of birds.

آس ās (H) n.f. Longing; desire; hope; expectation; faith; assurance; confidence; protection; shelter; refuge; support; mainstay.

آس اولاد ās aulād, n.f. Offspring; progeny.

آس باندھنا ās bandhnā, v. To entertain hope.

آس پوری ہونا ās pūri honā, v. To have one's desire fulfilled; to be gratified.

آس توڑنا ās toṛnā, v. To disappoint; to lose hope; to despond.

آس جاتی رہنا ās jātī rehnā, v. Vanishing of hope.

آس دینا ās denā, v. To give hope or solace; to encourage.

آس سے ہونا ās se honā, v. To be in the family way; to be pregnant.

آس لگی ہونا ās lagī honā, v. To pin hope on(person, etc.)

آس ās (P) n.f. Grind stone.

آسا āsā (H) n.f. Hope; confidence. (P) adj. Like; resembling.

آسا جیے نراسا مرے āsā jiye, nirāsā mare, prov. Hope keeps one alive, despondence kills.

آسان āsān (P) adj. Light; easy; facile; convenient.

آسان کرنا āsān karnā, v. To render easy; to facilitate; to disentangle; to make convenient.

آسانی āsānī (P) n.f. Ease; facility; smoothness; convenience.

آسائش āsā'ish (P) n.f. Respite; ease; comfort; calmness; facility; repose; tranquility.

آس پاس ās pās, adv. Near, in the neighbourhood.

آستان ، آستانہ āstān, āstānah (P) n.m. Threshhold; entrance; tomb of a saint.

آستاں بوسی āstān bosī, n.f. A visit to a great or a religious person; paying one's respects.

آستین āstin (P) n.f. A sleeve.

آستین پکڑنا āstin pakaṛnā, v. To compel one to do a thing; to force one (to); to insist ; to detain; to kick up a row.

آستین جھاڑنا āstin jhāṛnā, v. To renounce the world; to give in charity all one has.

آستین چڑھانا āstin chaṛhānā, v. To turn up the sleeves; to be ready to fight; to menace; to threaten; to be ready to undertake a job; to shoulder a responsibility.

آستین کا سانپ āstin kā sānp, n.m. A snake in the grass; a hidden enemy; an enemy in the guise of a friend.

آستین میں چھری رکھنا āstin men chhurī rakhnā, v. To be prepared for attack; to be ready for all eventualities.

آسرا āsrā (H) n.m. Means of subsistance; means of protection; confidence; support; faith; assurance; expectation; sanctuary; retreat; refuge; shelter; abode; prop.

آسرا تکنا ، آسرا ڈھونڈنا āsrā taknā, āsrā ḍhūnḍnā, v. To look for help or support (from); to seek succour from.

آسرا دینا āsrā denā, v. To rouse hope; to raise expectation; to reassure; to extend support.

آسکت askat (H) n.f. Idleness; indolence; laziness; stretching of the limbs.

آسمان āsmān (P) n.m. Sky; firmament; heaven.

آسمان پر اڑنا āsmān par urnā, v. To be very conceited; to boast; to brag; to fly high in the air.

آسمان پر تھوکا منہ پر آوے āsmān par thūkā munh par āwe, prov. He that blow into the dust fills his own eye.

آسمان پر چڑھانا āsmān par chaṛhānā, v. To fawn upon; to wheedle; to praise highly; to cajole.

آسمان پر دماغ ہونا āsmān par dimāgh honā, v. To be very vain or proud.

آسمان ٹوٹ پڑنا ، آسمان پھٹ پڑنا āsmān ṭūṭ paṛnā, āsmān phaṭ paṛnā, v. To be overwholmed with trouble; to be completely destroyed.

آسمان جاہ āsmān jāh, adj. Of exalted rank or dignity; of elevated position.

آسمان زمین ایک کر دینا āsmān zamin ek kar denā, v. To leave no stone unturned; to move heaven and earth; to do one's very best.

آسمان سر پر ٹوٹ پڑنا āsmān sar par ṭūṭ paṛnā, v. To suffer very greatly; to be overwhelmed with misfortunes.

آسمان سے باتیں کرنا āsmān se bāten karnā, v. To be very haughty.

آسمان سے گرا ، کھجور میں اٹکا āsmān se girā khajūr men aṭkā, prov. Out of the frying pan into the fire.

آسمان سے گرنا āsmān se girnā, v. To come as a windfall; to come to utter ruin.

آسمان کی خبر لانا āsmān ki khabar lānā, v. To achieve something very great; to fly very high.

آسمان کے تارے توڑنا āsmān ke tāre toṛnā, v. To be expert at anything; to accomplish the most difficult task.

آسمانی āsmāni (P) adj. Celestial; heavenly; divine; unexpected; azure; blue.

آسمانی بلا گرنا āsmāni balā girnā, v. To be overtaken by misfortunes; a bolt from the blue.

آسمانی پلانا āsmāni pilānā, v. To make (a person) intoxicated (specially with potion made from hemp-leaves).

آسمانی کتاب āsmāni kitāb, n.f. A revealed book.

آسمانی گولا āsmāni golā, n.m. A bolt from the blue.

آسن āsan (H) n.m. Sitting posture peculiar to Jogis; a seat; a small carpet; mattress or deer-skin on which Hindus sit during prayer; the inner or upper part of the thigh; the sixth Hindi month corresponding with September and October.

آسن جوڑنا ، آسن مارنا āsan joṛnā, āsan mārnā, v. To sit firmly; to sit on the thighs like Jogis; to sit firmly on horse-back.

آسن جمانا āsan jamānā, v. To sit on the ground like a Jogi; to sit firmly on horse-back; to stay at a place.

آسن لگانا āsan lagānā, v. To establish; to stay; to sit stubbornly in a given posture till one's object is gained.

آسودگی āsūdagi (P) n.f. Easy circumstances; ease; contentment; prosperity; comfort; opulence.

آسودہ āsūdah (P) adj. Opulent; rich; contented; satisfied; satiated; at ease.

آسودہ حال āsūdah ḥāl, adj. Well-to-do; in easy circumstance; opulent; wealthy.

آسودہ دل āsūdah dil, adj. Of composed mind; calm.

آسیا āsiyā (P) n.f. A mill.

آسیب āseb (P) n.m. Demon; evil spirit; one that haunts.

آسیب اتارنا āseb utārnā, v. To exorcise; to conjure; to drive away an evil spirit.

آسیب زدہ āseb zadah, adj. Under the influence of an evil spirit; haunted.

آش āsh (P) n.m. Soup; broth; pottage; gruel.

آش جو āsh-ē jau, n.m. Barley water; gruel.

آشا āshā (S) n.f. Desire; longing; hope; confidence; expectation.

آشام āshām (P) adj. Drinking (*used in comps.*). n.m. A kind of diet.

آشتی āshti (P) n.m. Peace; concord; reconcilement.

آشرم ، آسرم āshram, āsram (H) n.m. Hermitage; the abode of a hermit; a Hindu religious training centre or institution.

آشفتگی āshuftagi (P) n.f. Uneasiness; perturbation; distraction.

آشفتہ āshuftah (P) adj. Distracted; confused; weary; careworn; perplexed.

آشفته حال āshuftah ḥāl, *adj.* In afflicted condition; distressed.

آشفته خاطر، آشفته دل، آشفته طبع āshuftah khāṭir; āshuftah dil, āshuftah ṭaba', *adj.* Disturbed in mind; uneasy; depressed; worried.

آشفته دماغ، آشفته سر āshuftah dimāgh, āshuftah sar, *adj.* Of unsound mind; having a deranged mind.

آشکار، آشکارا āshkār, āshkārā (P) *adj.* Apparent; manifest; clear; evident; open; known; public.

آشنا āshnā (P) *n.m.* Acquaintance; comrade; friend; lover; paramour.

آشنا بھی نہیں آتے برے وقت میں کام āshnā bhī nahīn āte bure waqt men kām, *prov.* Poverty parts friends.

آشنا ہونا āshnā honā, *v.* To become very friendly.

حرف آشنا harf āshnā, *n.m.* A beginner.

صورت آشنا ṣūrat āshnā, *n.m.* One known by sight only.

آشنائی āshnā'ī (P) *n.f.* Friendship; intimacy; acquaintance; illicit connection.

آشنائی کرنا āshnā'ī karnā, *v.* To make friends; to associate; to be intimate.

آشوب āshob (P) *n.m.* Tumult; clamour; uproar; disturbance; revolution; mutiny.

آشوب چشم āshob-ĕ chashm, *n.m.* Conjunctivitis; inflammation of the eyes.

آشوب روزگار āshob-ĕ rozgār, *n.m.* Upheaval of the age; sweetheart.

آشوب محشر āshob-ĕ maḥshar, *n.m.* Tumult of the Day of Resurrection; great disturbance.

آشیاں، آشیانہ āshiyān, ashyānah (P) *n.m.* Nest; house; residence.

آشیاں اٹھانا āshiyān uṭhānā, *v.* To abandon one's residence.

آشیاں بنانا āshyān banānā, *v.* To build a nest or a house; to take up abode.

آشیر باد āshīr bād (H) *n.f.* Blessing; benediction; greetings.

آغا āghā (T) *n.m.* Leader; master; ruler; chieftian; elder brother.

آغاز ākhāz (P) *n.m.* Beginning: commencement; origin; outset.

آغاز کرنا āghāz karnā, *v.* To start; to make a beginning.

آغشته āghashtah (P) *adj.* Wet; moistened; mixed; polluted.

آغوش āghosh (P) *n.f./m.* Embrace; lap; bosom.

آغوش گرم کرنا āghosh garm karnā, *v.* To take someone in the lap; to embrace.

آغوش لحد میں جا گرنا āghosh-ĕ laḥad men jā girnā, *v.* To die.

آغوش میں آ جانا āghosh men ā jānā, *v.* To fall in the lap (of).

آفات āfāt (A) *n.f.* (*plu.* of آفت āfat) Misfortunes; evils; accidents; calamities; dangers.

آفات ارضی āfāt-ĕ arẓī, *n.f.* Calamities pertaining to the Earth; epidemics; pestilence.

آفات سماوی āfāt-ĕ samāvī, *n.f.* Bolts from the blue; sudden calamities.

آفاق āfāq (A) *n.m.* (*plu.* of افق ufaq) Horizons; the world.

آفاقی āfāqi, *adj.* Universal; global; cosmopolitan.

آفت āfat (A) *n.f.* Evil; disaster; misfortune; misery; calamity; hardship; catastrophe; wicked; famine.

آفت اٹھانا، آفت جھیلنا āfat uṭhānā, āfat jhelnā, *v.* To suffer from pain, sorrow or misery; to bear adversity.

آفت آنا، آفت ٹوٹنا āfat ānā, āfat ṭūṭnā, *v.* Coming of misfortune or trouble; befalling of a calamity.

آفت توڑنا āfat toṛnā, *v.* To terrorise; to tyrannise.

آفت جاں āfat-ĕ jān, *adj.* Torturer; tormentor, (metaphorically) a beloved.

آفت ڈھانا یا مچانا āfat ḍhānā yā machānā, *v.* To raise a tumult; to create miseries and troubles.

آفت رسیدہ یا زدہ *āfat rasidah yā zadah, adj.* Oppressed by adversity; involved in misfortune; miserable; unlucky.

آفت کا پرکالہ *āfat kā parkālah, n.m.* A mischievous person; a sharp astute fellow; (metaphorically) a beloved.

آفت مول لینا *āfat mol lenā, v.* To court calamity; to invite trouble.

آفت میں پڑنا یا پھنسنا *āfat men paṛnā yā phansnā, v.* To be overwhelmed with affliction; to be overtaken by calamity or disaster; to be entangled in difficulties.

آفتاب *āftāb* (P) *n.m.* The sun.

آفتاب آمد دلیل آفتاب *āftāb āmad dalil-ĕ āftab, prov.* A self-evident truth needs no proof.

آفتاب اقبال غروب ہونا *āftāb-ĕ iqbāl ghurub honā, v.* Not to remain in luck's way; to meet one's downfall.

آفتاب بین *āftāb bin, n.m.* Helioscope.

آفتاب پرست *āftāb parast, n.m.* Sun-worshipper.

آفتاب سر پر آنا *āftāb sar par ānā, v.* To be midday.

آفتاب سوا نیزے پر آنا *āftāb sawā neze par ānā, v.* To have a very hot day; to be in hot waters; to be overwhelmed with trouble.

آفتاب عالم تاب *āftāb-ĕ 'ālamtāb, n.m.* The world-illuminating sun; the sun; beautiful person.

آفتاب کو چراغ دکھانا *āftāb ko chirāgh dikhānā, v.* To hold a candle to the sun (used to acknowledge one's scholarship and greatness); trying to instruct one already well-versed in a thing.

آفتاب گیر *āftāb gir, n.m.* Parasol; a sun shade; an umbrella.

آفتاب لب بام *āftāb-ĕ lab-ĕ bām, n.m.* The setting sun; an old man on the verge of death.

آفتاب محشر *āftāb-ĕ meḥshār.* The sun on the Day of Resurrection; a charming beauty.

آفتاب نیم شب *āftāb-ĕ nim shab, n.m.* The midnight sun.

آفتابہ *āftābah* (P) *n.m.* A small vessel for holding water; an ewer.

آفتابی *āftābi* (P) *adj.* Of the sun; like the sun; solar; prepared by exposure to the sun; gold coloured. *n.f.* A sunshade; a kind of firework.

آفتابی چہرہ *āftābi chehrā, n.m.* A bright round face.

آفتابی غسل *āftābi ghusl, n.m.* A sun bath.

آفریدگار ، آفرینندہ *āfridgār, āfrinindah* (P) *n.m.* The creator.

آفریدہ *āfridah* (P) *adj.* Created; creature.

آفریدی *āfridi* (P) *n.m.* A clan of Pathans living in the northern part of West Pakistan.

آفریں *āfrin* (P) *n.f.* Praise; commendation; acclamation. *adj.* Creating (used in *comp.* as in جہاں آفریں *jahān āfrin*, creator of the world). *intj.* Well done! bravo!

آفریں کہنا *āfrin kahnā, v.* To applaud; to commend; to Praise.

آفرینش *āfrinish* (P) *n.f.* Creation.

آفس *āfis* (E) *n.m.* Office.

آقا *āqā* (P) *n.m.* Lord; master; owner; employer.

آک *āk* (H) *n.m.* Swallow-wort; a wild shrub.

آکاس ، آکاش *ākās, ākāsh* (H) *n.m.* Sky; space.

آکاس بیل *ākās bel, n.f.* Air-creeper or dodder; a parasite.

آگ *āg* (H) *n.f.* Fire; flame; heat. *Fig.* Anger; passion; love; lust; hatred; deep red; glitter.

آگ ببولا یا بھبوکا یا بگولا ہونا *āg babūlā yā babhūkā yā bagūlā honā, v.* To foam with rage or fury.

آگ بجھانا *āg bujhānā, v.* To extinguish fire; to satisfy hunger or lust; to put down a disturbance; to quell a tumult.

آگ برسانا *āg barsānā, v.* To fire a volley; to cannonade; to bombard.

آگ برسنا *āg barasnā, v.* To be extremely hot; heavy bombing or shelling.

آگ بن جانا *āg ban jānā, v.* To rage with anger.

آگ پانی کا بیر، آگ پھونس کا بیر *āg pāni kā bair, āg phūns kā bair.* Antagonism like that of fire and water or dry grass; natural antagonism; avowed enmity.

آگ پانی کا سنجوگ *āg pāni kā sanjog.* Union of two opposites.

آگ پر تیل چھڑکنا *āg par tel chhiṛaknā, v.* To fan the flame; to provoke or to excite trouble.

آگ پر لوٹنا *āg par loṭnā, v.* To be restless with anguish; to be consumed with jealousy.

آگ دبانا *āg dabānā, v.* To control or quell anger, passion, or rebellion; to cover embers with ashes.

آگ دینا ، دکھانا *āg denā , dikhānā, v.* to burn a corpse; to kindle; to set fire to.

آگ روک پتھر *āg rok patthar, n.m.* Firestone.

آگ سے پانی ہوجانا *āg se pāni ho jānā, v.* To sober down; to lose the heat of passion; to recover from a violent fit of temper.

آگ کا پتلا *āg kā putlā, n.m.* A very diligent and agile person; a sharp person.

آگ کا جلا آگ ہی سے اچھا ہو ، آگ کو آگ مارتی ہے *āg kā jalā āg hi se achchhā ho, āg ko āg mārti hai, prov.* Diamond cuts diamond; like cures like; measure for measure.

آگ کے مول *āg ke mol, adj.* Scarce; very dear; high priced.

آگ لگا کے پانی کو دوڑنا *āg lagā ke pānī ko dauṛnā, v.* To pretend to appease a quarrel which one has purposely excited; to play tricks; to deceive.

آگ لگانا *āg lagānā, v.* To burn; to foment a quarrel; to sow strife; to provoke; to inflame; to make mischief; to dissipate.

آگ لگاؤ *āg lagāū, adj.* Inflammable; combustible. *n.m.* A fire-brand; mischief maker; a rebel.

آگ لگنا *āg lagnā, v.* To catch fire; to be set on fire; to burn with envy or rage; to be incensed; to be consumed with love or envy; to be very hungry.

آگ لگے *āg lage, intj.* May it perish! to hell with it.

آگ لگے پر کنواں کھودنا *āg lage par kūṅwāṅ khodnā, Lit.* To dig a well after fire has broken out. *prov.* To shut the stable door after the horse is stolen.

آگ لینے آنا *āg lene ānā, v.* To pay a flying visit; to pay a doctor's visit.

آگ میں جھونک دینا *āg meṅ jhoṅk denā, v.* To fling into the fire; to burn to ashes.

آگ میں گرنا *āg men girnā, v.* To fall in the flame.

آگ میں لوٹنا *āg meṅ loṭnā, v.* To be afflicted with sorrow; to be consumed with jealousy.

آگ ہونا *āg honā, v.* To become exceedingly hot; to be inflamed; to be incensed; to burn with rage.

آگا *āgā* (H) *n.m.* Front; fore-part; forehead; face; the front of a house; the fore part of the body or dress; the future.

آگا بھاری ہونا *āgā bhāri honā, v.* To be pregnant.

آگا پیچھا *āgā pīchhā, n.m.* Front and rear; the beginning and the end.

آگا پیچھا دیکھنا ، سوچنا *āgā pichhā dekhnā, sochnā, v.* To look before and behind; to be cautious; to consider the *pros* and *cons*; to deliberate.

آگا تاگا لینا *āgā tāgā lenā, v.* To pry into the affairs or secrets of another person; to look minutely; to doubt.

آگا سنبھالنا، آگا لینا *āgā sambhālnā, āgā lenā*, *v.* To advance; to go forward; to take the lead.

آگاہ *āgāh* (P) *adj.* Apprised; informed; acquainted; knowing; conversant.

آگاہ کرنا *āgāh karnā*, *v.* To acquaint with; to inform; to warn.

آگاہی *āgāhi* (P) *n.f.* Awareness; knowledge; information; intelligence; cognition; insight; vigilance.

آگہی *āgahi* (P) *n.f.* Contraction of آگاہی *āgāhi*.

آگے *āge* (H) *adv.* Before; in front; in the presence of; face to face; in sight; in advance; ahead; hereafter; in future; beyond; formerly.

آگے آگے *āge āge*, *adv.* In advance, ahead; by and by; hereafter.

آگے آنا *āge ānā*, *v.* To approach; to advance; to come near; to challenge; to come about; to take place; to befall.

آگے بڑھنا *āge baṛhnā*, *v.* To proceed; to press forward; to go ahead; to go forth; to outdo; to surpass; to press forward; to improve.

آگے پیچھے *āge pichhe*, *adv.* One after the other; in front and in the rear; in a line; in process of time; sooner or later; unmethodically; confusedly; fore and aft.

آگے خدا کا نام ہے *āge khudā kā nām hai.* This is the end of it; so far and no further.

آگے دوڑ پیچھے چھوڑ *age dauṛ pichhe chhoṛ.* Leaving a task incomplete; passing on from one job to another without completing either.

آگے دیکھنا *āge dekhnā*, *v.* To be vigilant; to be cautious; to look to the future.

آگے سے *āge se*, *adv.* Beforehand; in anticipation; previously; in future.

آگے نکل جانا *āge nikal jānā*, *v.* To excel; to take the lead; to surpass; to outstrip.

آگے ہی *āge hi*, *adv.* Already.

آگیا *āggyā* (H) *n.f.* Command; behest; mandate; order; permission.

آگیا پالنا *āggyā pālnā*, *v.* To obey orders (of); to submit without demand.

آگیں *āgiṅ* (P) *adj.* Full (used in *comp.* as نیاز آگیں *niāz āgiṅ*, full of longing or desire).

آل *āl* (A) *n.f.* Children and grand-children; progeny.

آل اولاد *āl aulād*, *n.f.* Offspring; progeny; descendants; race; family; kindred· dynasty.

آل رسول *āl-ĕ rasūl*, *n.f.* The daughter of the Prophet of Islam, Hazrat Fatimah and his children.

آل عبا *āl-ĕ ʻabā*, *n.f.* Stands for Hazrat Fatimah, Hazrat Ali, Imam Hasan and Imam Husain.

آلاپ *ālāp* (H) *n.f.* Conversation; discourse; talk; communication; tuning the voice preparatory to singing.

آلاپنا *ālāpnā* (H) *v.* To tune the voice; to run over the different notes previous to singing; to sing.

آلات *ālāt* (A) *n.m.* (*plu.* of آلہ *ālah*) Instruments; tools; implements; apparatus.

آلات حرب *ālāt-ĕ ḥarb*, *n.m.* Arms; munition.

آلات کشا ورزی *ālāt-ĕ kashāwarzi*, *n.m.* Agricultural implements.

آلام *ālām* (A) *n.m.* (*plu.* of الم *alam*) Pains; griefs; afflictions; misfortunes.

آلائش *ālā'ish* (P) *n.f.* Filth; pollution; refuse; pus; lumber.

آلت *ālat* (A) *n.m.* Tool; apparatus; utensil; rigging; penis.

آلتی پالتی *ālti pālti* (H) *n.f.* The posture of sitting upon the hams; squat.

آلتی پالتی مارنا *ālti pālti mārnā*, *v.* To squat; to squat in the manner of a Jogi.

آلس ، آلکس ، آلکسی ālas, ālkas, ālkasi (H) *n.f.* Idleness; laziness; inactivity.

آلسانا ālsānā (H) *v.* To doze; to be drowsy; to slacken.

آلسی ālsi (H) *adj.* Indolent; lazy; sleepy; drowsy.

آلن ālan (H) *n.m.* Straw mixed with mud used for brick-making or plastering, etc.; mixture of *dāl* and dough.

آلو ālū, *n.m.* Potato.

آلو بخارا ālū bukhārā (P) *n.m.* A Persian plum; prune; damson.

آلوچہ ālūchah (P) *n.m.* Plum.

آلودگی ālūdagi (P) *n.f.* Contamination; pollution; impurity; foulness; taint.

آلود ، آلودہ ālūd, ālūdah (P) *adj.* Polluted; soiled; unclean; foul; impure.

آلہ ālah (P) *n.m.* Tool; implement; weapon; instrument.

آلۂ تناسل ālah-ĕ tanāsul, *n.m.* Male progenitive organ; penis.

آلۂ حرارت ālah-ĕ harārat, *n.m.* Thermometer.

آلۂ کار ālah-ĕ kār, *n.m.* Means; a useful tool or support.

آلۂ مہلک ālah-ĕ mohlik, *n.m.* Deadly weapon.

آم ām (H) *n.m.* Mango.

آم ٹپکنا ām ṭapaknā, *v.* Dropping of ripe mangoes from trees.

آم کھانے سے کام پیڑ گننے سے نہیں ām khāne se kām peṛ gin-ne se nahiṅ, *prov.* I would have the fruit, not the basket.

آم کے آم گٹھلیوں کے دام ām ke ām, guṭhliyoṅ ke dām, *prov.* To kill two birds with one stone; a bargain without any loss.

آم میں مور آنا ām meṅ maur ānā, *v.* Blossoming of mango trees.

آماج ، آماج گاہ āmāj, āmājgāh (P) *n.m./f.* Target; a mark to fire at for practice; object of desire or ambition.

آمادگی āmādagi (P) *n.f.* Readiness; alertness; preparedness; inclination.

آمادہ āmādah (P) *adj.* Prepared; ready.

آماس āmās (P) *n.m.* Swelling; tumour.

آمد āmad (P) *n.f.* Advent; arrival; revenue; income; (*Poet.*) Inspiration.

آمد آمد āmad āmad, *n.f.* Approach; announcement of an arrival.

آمدم بر سر مطلب āmdam bar sar-ĕ matlab. Reverting to the subject; coming to the point.

آمد و خرچ āmad-ŏ kharch, *n.m.* Income and expenditure; receipts and disbursement.

آمد و رفت ، آمد و شد āmad-ŏ raft, āmad ŏ shud (P) *n.f.* Ingress and egress; communication; traffic.

آمدنی āmadni (P) *n.f.* Income; revenue; profit;; resources.

آمر āmir (A) *n.m.* A ruler; a commander; a dictator.

آمرزش āmurzish (P) *n.f.* Forgiveness; grace; pardon of sins (by God).

آمرزگار āmurzgār (P) *adj.* Forgiver; he who pardons; an epithet of Merciful God.

آمریت āmiriyyat (A) *n.f.* Dictatorship.

آملہ āmlah (P) *n.m.* A kind of myrobalan; a fruit used, while green, for making pickles.

آملہ (آنولا) سار گندھک āmlah (aonlā) sār gandhak, *n.f.* Purified sulphur.

آمنا سامنا āmnā sāmnā, *n.m.* Confronting; front.

آمنا و صدقنا āmannā wa saddaqnā (A). We believe in and testify to the truth.

آمنے سامنے āmne sāmne, *adv.* Face to face; over against; opposite.

آموختہ āmokhtah (P) *adj.* Taught; learnt. *n.m.* An old lesson.

آموزش āmozish (P) *n.f.* Education; teaching.

آموزش گاہ āmozish gāh, *e.f.* A school

آمیختہ āmekhtah (P) *adj.* Mixed.

آميزش āmezish (P) *n.f.* Mixture; sociableness; intercourse; temperament; adulteration; association.

آمين āmin (A) *n.f.* & *intj.* Amen; so be it.

آن ān (A) *n.f.* Time; second; moment; instant.

آن کا مہمان *ān kā mehmān*, *n.m.* On the verge of death.

آن کی آن میں ، آن واحد میں *ān ki ān meṅ*, *ān-ĕ wāḥid meṅ*, *adv.* In an instant; immediately; in a moment.

آن ān (H) *n.f.* Bashfulness; modesty; shame.

آن ān (P) *n.f.* Manner; style; behaviour; beauty; a graceful attitude; affectation; an affected gait; pride; dignity.

آن بان *ān bān*, *n.f.* Pomp & show; splendour.

آن بان سے رہنا *ān bān se rahnā*, *v.* To live handsomely; to lead an elegant life.

آن توڑنا *ān toṛnā*, *v.* To break one's promise; to go back on one's oath; to go against custom.

آن ماننا *ān mān-nā*, *v.* To acknowledge the superiority of; to admit defeat; to feel helpless.

آن نکلنا *ān nikalnā*, *v.* To acquire the elegance or grace of the beloved; blossoming of one's beauty.

آن و ادا *ān-ŏ adā*, *n.f* Loveliness; beauty; dignity; honour; pride; obstinacy; stubbornness.

آنا (آنہ) *ānā* (*ānah*), *n.m.* The sixteenth part of a rupee; an anna.

آنا *āṇā* (H) *v.* To come; to approach; to reach; to be possible; to be; to become; to pass; to appear; to arrive; to happen.

آناً فاناً *ānan̲ fānan̲* (A) *adv.* At once; suddenly; instantly; forthwith.

آنا کانی *ānā kāni* (H) *n.f.* Turning a deaf ear; purposely neglecting; overlooking; disregarding; trifling with, connivance.

آنت *āṅt* (H) *n.f.* Entrails; guts; intestines.

آنت اترنا *āṅt utarnā*, *v.* Protrusion of intestine into the testicle; to suffer from hernia.

آنتوں کا قل ھو اللہ پڑھنا *āṅtoṅ kā qul huwallā paṛhnā*, *v.* To feel very hungry.

آنتوں کے بل کھلنا *āṅtoṅ ke bal khulnā*, *v.* To eat well; to feel hungry.

آنتیں سوکھنا *āṅteṅ sūkhnā*, *v.* To be very hungry.

آنتیں گلے آنا (پڑنا) *āṅteṅ gale ānā* (*paṛnā*), *v.* To be distressed; to suffer; to become entangled in some calamity.

آنتیں منہ کو آنا *āṅteṅ muṅh ko ānā*, *v.* To be greatly worried; to feel suffocated.

آنٹ *āṅt*, *n.f.* Twist; a knot; envy; malice; enmity.

آنٹ سانٹ *āṅt sāṅt*, *n.f.* Conspiracy; plot; intrigue; unlawful partnership; alliance; reconciliation.

آنٹی *āṅṭi* (H) *n.f.* Knot; a bundle of wood or grass, a skein of thread; a leg trick in wrestling.

آنٹی دینا (لگانا) *āṅṭi denā* (*lagānā*), *v.* To throw across the hip; to employ a leg trick; to trip one up.

آنچ *āṅch* (H) *n.f.* Flame, fire; blaze; heat; warmth; fervour; loss; grief.

آنچ آنا (پہنچنا) *āṅch ānā* (*pahuṅchnā*), *v.* To suffer a loss; to be in trouble.

آنچ کھانا *āṅch khānā*, *v.* To be heated in fire; to melt.

آنچل *āṅchal* (H) *n.m.* The corner of a sheet (called دوپٹا *ḍopaṭṭā*) used by women to cover the upper portions of the body, particularly head and breast.

آنچل پلو *āṅchal pallū*, *n.m.* The border of a *ḍopaṭṭā* embroidered (particularly in Benaras).

آنچل ڈالنا *āṅchal ḍālnā*, *v.* To throw the veil over the face; to marry.

آنچل میں گرہ دینا *āṅchal meṅ girah denā*, *v.* To tie a knot in the corner of a *ḍopaṭṭā*, this is usually done to remind oneself of an errand or a task one has agreed to attend to.

آندھی *āṅdhī* (H) *n.f.* Dust-storm; hurricane; tempest.

(چلنا) آندھی آٹھنا ãndhī uṭhnā (chalnā), v. Blowing of a hurricane or dust-storm.

آندھی کی طرح آنا ãndhī kī ṭarah ānā, v. To come suddenly like a dust-storm; to blow over like a hurricane.

آندھی کی طرح آنا بگولے کی طرح جانا ãndhī kī ṭarah ānā bagūle kī ṭarah jānā, (Lit.) To come like hurricane and blow like a whirl-wind. id. To come suddenly and leave abruptly.

آندھی کے آم ãndhī ke ām, n.m. A windfall; a very cheap thing; anything obtained without effort.

آنڈ ãnḍ (H) n.m. Testicle.

آنڈو ãnḍū (H) adj. Having large testicles.

آنسو ãnsū (H) n.m. A tear; tears.

آنسو آنا ، آنسو بھر آنا ãnsū ānā, ãnsū bhar ānā, v. To have tears in the eyes; to weep; to have the eyes filled with tears.

آنسو پونچھنا ãnsū ponchhnā, v. To wipe one's eyes; to dry one's tears; to console; to comfort; to soothe.

آنسو پی جانا ãnsū pī jānā, v. To suppress one's tears; to control (one's emotion); to bear.

آنسو ٹپکنا ، آنسو پھوٹ بہنا ، آنسوؤں سے منہ دھونا ãnsū ṭapaknā, ãnsū phūṭ behnā, ãnsūon se munh dhona, v. To weep; to burst into tears; to weep excessively.

آنسوؤں کا تار بندھنا، آنسوؤں کی جھڑی لگنا ãnsūon kā tār bandhna, ãnsūon kī jharī lagnā, v. To weep bitterly; to weep excessively.

آنک ãnk (H) n.f. A letter; dot; test; examination.

آنکڑا ãnkṛā (H) n.m. An iron rod with a curved end (used to pluck fruit or leaves from trees); the barb of an arrow; a fishing hook.

آنکس ãnkas (H) n.m. A hook or iron with which an elephant is driven; a goad.

آنکس مارنا ãnkas mārnā, v. To goad; to reduce to submission.

آنکنا ãnknā (H) v. To evaluate; to appraise; to rate; to measure; to examine.

آنکھ ãnkh, n.f. Eye.

آنکھ آجانا ãnkh ā jānā, v. To have an inflammation of the eyes; to have a sore-eye; to suffer from ophthalmia.

آنکھ آٹھا کر نہ دیکھنا ãnkh uṭhā kar nah dekhnā, v. To be abashed; to feel ashamed; not to care for; to disregard; to slight; to avoid noticing; to feel angry or displeased.

آنکھ اوجھل پہاڑ اوجھل ãnkh ojhal pahāṛ ojhāl, prov. Out of sight, is out of mind.

آنکھ اونچی نہ کرنا ، نہ ہونا ãnkh ūnchī nah karnā, nah honā, v. To be unable to raise one's eyes or to look anyone in the face (through respect or shame).

آنکھ بچا جانا ãnkh bachā jānā, v. To steal away secretly or unseen; to avoid the glance of; to pass without taking notice of.

آنکھ بچا کے نکل جانا ãnkh bachā ke nikal jānā, v. To slip away unnoticed; to slink away.

آنکھ بچی مال دوستوں کا ãnkh bachī, māl doston kā, prov. Eye withdrawn, property gone.

آنکھ بدلنا ãnkh badalnā, v. To withdraw one's favour or affection from anyone; to be fickle or inconsistent.

آنکھ برابر نہ کر سکنا ãnkh barābar nah kar saknā, v. Not to be able to look into another's face; to be ashamed.

آنکھ بند کر لینا ãnkh band kar lenā, v. To shut the eyes; to sleep; to die; to take no notice of; to treat one with neglect; to be afraid.

آنکھ بند کئے چلے جانا ãnkh band kiye chale jānā, v. To go forward without fear.

آنکھ بھر کے دیکھنا ãnkh bhar ke dekhnā, v. To look till one's curiosity is satisfied; to look intently.

آنکھ بہہ جانا ānkh bah jānā, v. To become blind; to lose eyesight.

آنکھ (آنکھیں) پتھرانا ānkh (ānkhen) pathrānā, v. To be about to breathe one's last; (also used when) eyes become dim with long expectation or constant gazing.

آنکھ پر چڑھنا ānkh per charhnā, v. To have a special liking for a thing.

آنکھ (آنکھیں) پھاڑ پھاڑ کے دیکھنا ānkh (ānkhen) phār phār ke dekhnā, v. To gaze with eager eyes; to strain one's eye; to look at with wonder; to observe with eagerness and love.

آنکھ پھڑکنا ankh pharaknā, v. To feel a pulsation in the eye (regarded as a premonition).

آنکھ پھوٹنا ānkh phūtnā, v. To lose one's sight; to be blind.

آنکھ پھوٹی ، پیڑ گئی ānkh phūti, pir ga'i, prov. Better the eye out than constant pain.

آنکھ پھوڑنا ānkh phornā, v. To hit one on the eye; to make one blind.

آنکھ پھیر لینا ānkh pher lenā, v. To turn away the eyes (as from grief, displeasure, etc.); to refrain; to show aversion (after friendship); to die.

آنکھ (آنکھیں) ٹھنڈی کرنا ānkh (ānkhen) thandi karnā, v. To get consolation; to fresh the eye; to be glad.

آنکھ جھپکنے میں ānkh japakne men, adv. In the twinkling of an eye.

آنکھ چرانا ānkh churāna, v. To avert the eyes through shame, pride, dislike, ect.; to avoid anyone.

آنکھ چڑھانا ānkh charhānā, v. To be angry; to be drunk.

آنکھ چڑھنا ānkh charhnā, v. To have eyes heavy from intoxication, headache or other causes; to have eyes turned up while dying.

آنکھ چمکانا ānkh chamkānā, v. To make the eyes flash; to move one's eyes in anger or as a blandishment.

آنکھ دکھانا ānkh dikhānā, v. (Lit.) To get the eyes examined for treatment. id. To stare defiantly; to frighten; to overawe; to bully; to look daggers.

آنکھ دکھنا ānkh dukhnā, v. To suffer from sore eyes.

آنکھ دوڑانا ānkh daurānā, v. To look around, as if in search of something; to look for a support.

آنکھ دھوئی دھائی ānkh dho'i dhāi, n.f. Shamelessness; unashamed of one's conduct; impudence.

آنکھ ڈبڈبانا ānkh dubdubānā, v. To have the eyes full of tears; to be ready to weep; to feel sad or grieved.

آنکھ (آنکھیں) روشن کرنا ānkh (ānkhen) raushan karnā, v. To delight the eyes (by the sight of).

آنکھ (آنکھیں) روشن ہونا ānkh (ānkhen) raushan honā, v. To be delighted on meeting someone; to have children.

آنکھ (آنکھیں) سرخ کرنا ānkh (ānkhen) surkh karnā, v. Ta be angry.

آنکھ سے دیکھ کے ānkh se dekh ke, adv. Knowingly; with one's eye open.

آنکھ (آنکھیں) سینکنا ānkh (ānkhen) senknā, v. To feast the eyes on; to delight or refresh the eyes by the sight of; to admire the beauty of.

آنکھ کا پانی مرنا ānkh kā pāni marnā, v. To become wanton and daring; to abandon modesty.

آنکھ کا تارا ānkh kā tārā, adj. Darling; pet; favourite, beloved.

آنکھ کھلنا ānkh khulnā, v. To get up from sleep; to be born; to become aware (of); to be alive (to).

آنکھ کھولنا ānkh kholnā, v. To open one's eyes; to acquaint; to impart knowledge or wisdom.

آنکھ کی پتلی ānkh ki putli, n.f. The pupil of the eye; favourite.

آنکھ کے سامنے ānkh ke sāmne, *adv.* Before one's eyes; under one's nose; in the presence of.

آنکھ (آنکھیں) لڑانا ānkh (ānkheṅ) larāna, *v.* To make love (with the eyes); to cast wanton glaces; to face or oppose someone.

آنکھ لڑنا āṅkh larnā, *v.* To meet the eye of; to exchange amorous glances; to take a fancy to; to set one's affection on.

آنکھ لگانا ānkh lagānā, *v.* To contract friendship or affection for someone; to fall in love; to wait for someone; to doze off; to sleep.

آنکھ لگنا ānkh lagnā, *v.* To fall asleep; to doze off; to be in love.

آنکھ مارنا ānkh mārnā, *v.* To wink at; to drop a hint by a movement of the eye; to attract someone's attention; to cast amorous glances.

آنکھ مچولی ānkh micholi, *n.f.* Blind man's buff; bo-peep; hide and seek.

آنکھ ملانا ānkh milānā, *v.* To gaze; to exchange glances; to contract friendship; to compete with.

آنکھ موند کے ānkh mūnd ke, *adv.* Precipitately; blindly; inconsiderately; with eyes shut.

آنکھ موندنا ānkh mundnā, *v.* To shut the eyes; to take no notice of; to die.

آنکھ میلی کرنا ānkh maili karnā, *v.* To look angry; to scowl; to frown.

آنکھ نہ ٹھہرنا ānkh nah thahernā, *v.* To be unable to fix the gaze (on); to be dazzled (by).

آنکھوں پر بٹھانا ānkhoṅ par biṭhānā, *v.* To treat with respect; to receive or treat warmly or cordially; to hold dear; to love; to adore.

آنکھوں پر پردہ پڑنا ānkhoṅ par pardah parnā, *v.* To be deceived; to be misled.

آنکھوں پر ٹھیکری رکھ لینا ānkhoṅ par thikrī rakh lenā, *v.* To be blind to all shame; to have no feeling (for); to behave in an unfriendly manner.

آنکھوں پر چربی چڑھنا ānkhon par charbi charhnā, *v.* To be wilfully blind; to pretend from pride not to know one's old acquaintances; to become shameless.

آنکھوں پر رکھنا ānkhoṅ par rakhna, *v.* To treat with veneration or respect, to hold dear.

آنکھوں دیکھا مانا ' سنا نہ مانا ānkhon dekha mānā, sunā nah mānā, *prov.* Seeing is believing.

آنکھوں سے بجا لانا ānkhoṅ se bajā lānā, *v.* To obey willingly and cheerfully.

آنکھوں سے گر جانا ānkhoṅ se gir jānā, *v.* To lose favour; to be degraded.

آنکھوں کا کاجل چرانا ānkhoṅ kā kājal churānā, *v.* To be a very expert thief; to steal the teeth out of one's mouth; to cheat.

آنکھوں کے اندھے نام نین سکھ ānkhoṅ ke andhe, nām nain sukh, *prov.* To call a black man Mr. White.

آنکھوں میں پھرنا (بسنا) ānkhoṅ meṅ phirnā (basnā), *v.* To be ever present in one's mind; to be agreeable or liked.

آنکھوں میں خار ھونا ānkhoṅ meṅ khār honā, *v.* To be an eyesore; to be ugly; to be an enemy.

آنکھوں میں خاک ڈالنا (جھونکنا) ānkhoṅ meṅ khāk ḍālnā (jhoṅknā), *v.* To throw dust in one's eyes; to cheat; to pilfer something quickly and stealthily; to sell deceitfully wares of inferior quality.

آنکھوں میں رات کاٹنا ānkhoṅ meṅ rāt kāṭnā *v.* To keep awake the whole night to have sleepless night.

آنکھوں میں سرسوں پھولنا ānkhoṅ meṅ sarsoṅ phūlnā, *v.* To see yellow on all sides; to feel happy.

آنکھوں میں کھٹکنا ānkhoṅ meṅ khatakṅā, *v.* To be looked upon with jealousy and aversion.

آنکھیں چار ہونا *ānkheṅ chār honā, v.* To meet; to fall in love.

آنکھیں چھت سے لگنا *ānkheṅ chhat se lagnā, v.* To be dying.

آنکھیں سفید ہونا *ānkheṅ sufed honā, v.* To become blind (with weeping or vain expectation).

آنکھیں نکالنا *ānkheṅ nikālnā, v.* To remove the eyeballs; to deprive one of sight; to look menacingly at.

آنکھیں نیلی پیلی کرنا *ānkhen nīlī pīlī karnā, v.* To be very angry; to show or express anger.

آنگن *āṅgan* (H) *n.m.* Courtyard.

آنند *ānand* (H) *n.m.* Happiness; pleasure; delight.

آنند کرنا ، آنند کے تار بجانا *ānand karnā, ānand ke tār bajānā, v.* To enjoy; to rejoice.

آنولا *ānolā* (H) See آملہ *āmlāh.*

آنول نال *ānol nāl* (H) *n.f.* The navel string.

آنی جانی *ānī jānī* (H) *adj.* Unsteady; transitory; mortal; groundless.

آوا *āvā* (H) *n.m.* A potter's kiln; a furnace for melting glass; a kiln (for bricks, etc.).

آوے کا آوا ہی بگڑا ہوا ہے *āve kā āvā hī bigṛā hūā hai, prov.* Chips of the same block; whole the system from top to bottom is rotten.

آوا جاوا ، آوا جائی *āvā jāvā, āvā jā'i* (H) *n.f.* Unnecessary coming and going; intercourse; intercharge of visits.

آوارگی *āwāragī* (P) *n.f.* Wandering; vagrancy; profligacy.

آوارہ *āwārah* (P) *adj. n.m.* Without hearth and home; a wanderer; a vagabond; malefactor; characterless.

آوارہ گرد *āwārah gard, adj.* A profligate; dissolute; without house and home; vagrant; abandoned; lost, destitute of name or character.

آوارہ مزاج *āwārah mizāj, adj.* Careless; thoughtless; dissolute.

آوارہ وطن *āwārah waṭan, adj. n.m.* A stranger; a foreigner; a person away from his motherland; a traveller.

آواز *āwāz* (P) *n.f.* Sound; voice; cry; shout; noise; tinkling; echo.

آواز اٹھانا *āwāz uṭhānā, v* To raise one's voice; to spread a report (against); to protest.

آواز بدل جانا ، آواز بگڑ جانا ، آواز بھاری ہونا، آواز بھرانا، آواز بیٹھنا *āwāz badal jānā, āwāz bigaṛ jānā, āwāz bhārī honā, āwāz bharrānā, āwāz baiṭhnā, v.* To become hoarse; to lose voice; suppression of voice from hoarseness.

آواز بلند *āwāz-ĕ buland, n.f.* Loud voice.

آواز بلند کرنا *āwāz buland karnā, v.* To raise one's voice; to cry; to protest against.

آواز جرس *āwāz-ĕ jaras, n.f.* Sound of a bell (usually rung to warn the members that the caravan is about to leave).

آواز دینا *āwāz denā, v.* To call aloud; to shout; to cry out.

آواز سے آواز ملنا *āwāz se āwāz milnā, v.* Harmony of one voice or tone with the other; to have the same voice or tone; to sing in harmony.

آواز صور *āwāz-ĕ ṣūr, n.f.* A clarion call; the sound of the trumpet which *Isrāfīl* will blow on the day of Resurrection.

آواز غیب *āwāz-ĕ ghaib, n.f.* A voice from heaven; mysterious voice; a revelation.

آواز کا آتار چڑھاؤ *āwāz kā utār chaṛhāo, n.m.* Rise and fall of voice.

آواز کرنا *āwāz karnā, v.* To call aloud; to let a gun or pistol go off; to cry for alms (like a beggar).

آواز کھل جانا *āwāz khul jānā, v.* To have voice cleared; to recover voice.

آواز میں لوچ ہونا *āwāz meṅ loch honā, v.* To have a soft and melodious voice.

آواز میں نمک ہونا *āwāz meṅ namak honā, v* To have a pathetic or an appealing voice.

آوازہ *āwāzah* (P) *n.m.* Report; rumour; fame; reputation.

آوازہ بلند ہونا *āwāzuh buland honā, v.* To have a good reputation.

آوازہ کسنا (مارنا) *āwāzah kasnā (mārnā), v.* To make insinuations (about); to jeer (at); to taunt.

آواگون *āwāgaun* (H) *n.m.* Transmigration of soul; metempsychosis.

آورد *āward* (P) *n.f.* Writing of poetry with special effort. *adj.* Not natural; artificial; assumed.

آوردہ *āwardah,* (P) *adj. & n.m.* That which is brought over (accounts); one who is favoured; a protege.

آویختہ ' آویزاں *āwek͟htah, āwezāṅ* (P) *adj.* Suspended; hanging; pendulous; pendant; attached.

آویزاں کرنا *āwezāṅ karnā, v.* To hang; to hook up; to fix; to attach; to suspend.

آویزہ *āwezah* (P) *n.m.* An ear-ring; a pendant; appendix.

آہ *āh n.f.* A sigh. *inter.* Alas! Oh dear! Ah!

آہ بھرنا ' آہ کرنا ' آہ مارنا *āh bharnā, āh karnā, āh mārnā, v.* To sigh; to give or draw a sigh; to lament.

آہ پڑنا *āh paṛnā, v.* Repercussions on the oppressor of the patient endurance of the tyranny and suffering borne by the oppressed.

آہ جانکاہ *āh-ĕ jāṅkāh, n.f.* A heart-rending sigh.

آہ جگر سوز *āh-ĕ jigarsoz, n.f.* A heart-burning sigh.

آہ سرد *āh-ĕ sard, n.f.* A deep sigh.

آہ لینا *āh lenā, v.* To bear the repercussions of evil done to another; to oppress.

آہ نیم شب *āh-ĕ nīm-shab, n.f.* A midnight sigh or lamentation; midnight prayer or supplication.

آہ و بکا ' آہ و زاری ' آہ و فغاں *āh-ŏ bukā, āh-ŏ zārī, āh-ŏ fug͟hāṅ, n.f.* Lamentation; complaint; cry of pain or distress; groaning; wailing.

آہا *āhā, inter.* Oh! An exclamation of delight or wonder.

آہٹ *āhaṭ* (H) *n.f.* Sound; sound of soft footsteps.

آہٹ لیتے رہنا *āhaṭ lete rahnā, v.* To be on the alert; to be on the *qui vive* for the sound of footsteps, etc.

آہستگی *āhistagī* (P) *n.f.* Slowness; tardiness; delay; softness; tenderness; gentleness; mildness.

آہستہ *āhistah* (P) *adv.* Slowly; softly; tenderly; leisurely; by degrees. *adj.* Slow; slack; lazy; soft

آہستہ رو *āhistah rau, adj.* Slow-paced.

آہن *āhan* (P) *n.m.* iron.

آہن ربا *āhan rubā, n.m.* A loadstone; magnet.

آہن گر *āhan gar, n.m.* Blacksmith.

آہن گری *āhan garī, n.f.* The profession of a blacksmith.

آہنی ' آہنیں *āhanī, āhanīṅ* (P) *adj.* Made of iron; irony; ferric; strong; hard.

آہنگ *āhaṅg* (P) *n.m.* Design; intention; purpose; way; mode. *n.f.* Sound; harmony; music; melody.

آہو *āhū* (P) *n.m.* A deer; antelope; vice; fault; defect.

آہو چشم *āhū chashm, adj.* Having eyes like those of a deer; gazelle-eyed (beloved).

آہوئے حرم *āhū-ĕ ḥaram, n.m.* A deer living in the vicinity of *k͟hānah-ĕ kā'ba*; (it is not permissible to hunt such game owing to the sanctity of the *ḥaram*). *Fig.* A beloved who is beyoned one's reach.

آہوئے فلک āhū-ĕ falak, n.m. The sun.

آئنہ āi'nah, See آئینہ āinah.

آؤ بھگت āo-bhagat (H) n.f. Civil reception; courteous welcome; courtesy; civility.

آؤ دیکھا نہ تاؤ āodekhā nah tāo, id. To do something in great hurry and spoil it eventually.

آئی a'ī, n.f. Doom; death; calamity.

آئی نہیں ٹلتی ā'i nahin ṭaltī, say. The inevitable must happen.

آئی بلا سر سے ٹالنا ā'i balā sar se ṭālnā, v. To avoid misfortune; to avoid getting into trouble.

آئی گئی ہو جانا ā'i ga'i ho jānā, v. To get finished; to come to an end; to be lost; to be forgotten.

آئین ā'īn (P) n.m. Law; regulation; constitution; statute; rules; custom; etiquette.

آئین داد رسی ā'in-ĕ dād-rasi, n.m. Principles of trial; trial procedure.

آئین پارلیمان ā'in-ĕ parlīmān, n.m. Statutory rule of procedure of law making body.

آئین تحریری ā'in-ĕ taḥriri, n.m. Written law.

آئین دیوانی ā'in-ĕ diwānī, n.m. Civil law.

آئین رواجی ā'in-ĕ riwāji, n.m. Customary law.

آئین فوجداری ā'in -ĕ faujdārī, n.m. Criminal law.

آئین مال ā'in-ĕ māl, n.m. Revenue law.

آئین عدالت ā'in-ĕ 'adālat n.m. Judiciary law.

آئین غیر نوشتہ ā'n-ĕ ghair nawishtah, n.m. Unwritten law.

آئین نامہ ā'īn nāmah, n.m. Manual of rules and regulations.

آئیں بائیں شائیں ā'īn-ba'īn-shā'in, n.f. Irrelevant or meaningless talk.

آئینہ ā'īnah (P) n.m. A mirror; looking-glass.

آئینہ اندھا ہو جانا ā'inah andhā ho jānā, v. Blinding of the mirror.

آئینہ باطن ā'inah-ĕ bāṭin, n.m. Clear conscience; a pure-heart; enlightened person; clairvoyant.

آئینہ بنانا ā'inah banānā, v. To make or manufacture a mirror; to lose one's senses; to be bewildered.

آئینہ بندی ā'inah bandī, n.f. Decorating or adorning with mirrors.

آئینہ خانہ ā'inah khānah, n.m. Glass house; a chamber whose walls are recovered with mirrors.

آئینہ دار ā'inah-dār, n.m. A person who holds the mirror (when one makes one's toilet); a barber (as he holds the mirror before the person he dresses). adj. Holding identical views.

آئینہ دکھانا ā'īnah dikhānā, v. To show a mirror; to show the pros and cons (of); to expose one's faults or defects.

آئینہ رخ (رو) ā'inah-rukh (rū), adj. Fair-faced; having a bright face like a mirror.

آئینہ ساز ā'īnah-sāz, adj. A mirror-maker; a glazier.

آئینہ سامنے سے نہ ہٹنا ā'inah sāmne se nah haṭnā, v. To be constantly paying attention to one's face; wasting time on make-up.

آئینہ سکندری ā'inah-ĕ sikandarī, n.m. A mirror of polished steel, attributed to Alexander; a magic mirror; the mirror of King Rynce.

آئینہ سیما ā'inah simā, adj. Mirror-like beauty; handsome; beloved.

آئینہ کر دینا ā'īnah kar denā, v. To make absolutely clear; to cause to glitter.

آئینہ مجوف ā'inah-ĕ mujawwaf, n.m. A concave mirror.

آئینہ میں بال ā'inah men bāl, n.m. A crack in the glass or mirror.

آیا āyā (H) n.f. Nurse; lady's maid. interrog. particle. Whether or not; whether.

آیا گری āyā gari, n.f. Midwifery.

آیا گیا āyā gayā (H) (Lit) Came and gone; past; done with. n.m. A visitor.

آیت āyat (A) n.f. A mark; a sign; a verse of the Quran (plu. آیات āyāt).

آینده āyandah (P) adj. Coming in future; hereafter; next; ensuing; subsequent. adv. In future; again; afterwards.

آینده رونده āyandah rawindah, n.m. A passer-by; a person coming and going; a traveller.

ا

ا—Alif, the first letter of the Arabic, Persian and Urdu alphabets.

اب ab (H) adv. Now; presently; just now.

اب بھی ab bhi, adv. Even now; still; yet; as yet.

اب پچھتائے کیا ہوت ہے جب چڑیاں چگ گئیں کھیت ab pachhtāe kyā hovat hai jab chiryān chug ga'in khet, prov. There is no use crying over spilt milk.

اب تب ab tab, adv. Now and then; occasionally.

اب تب کرنا ab tab karnā, v. To evade; to delay; to shuffle.

اب تک ab tak, adv. Till now; hitherto; yet; still.

اب تو ' اب سے ab to, ab se, adv. Henceforth; from now on; henceforward; in future.

اب سے دور ab se dur. (Lit). Away from now, id. Heaven protect us (from the recurrence of a past misfortune).

اب کے ' اب کی بار ab ke, ab ki bar, adv. This time; now; next time.

اب ab (A) n.m. Father; superior.

ابا abbā, n.m. Father.

ابا جان (جی) abbā jān (ji), n.m. Father; dear father.

ابابیل abābil (A) n.f. A swallow.

ابال ubāl (H) n.m. Boiling; fury; rage; anger; ebullition.

ابال آنا (اٹھنا) ubāl ānā (uthānā), v. To start boiling; to get into a state of boiling.

ابالنا ubālnā (H) v. To boil; to cause to boil.

ابتداء ibtidā' (A) n.f. Beginning; commencement; source; origin.

ابتداء کرنا ibtidā' karnā, v. To begin; to start; to commence.

ابتداً ibtidā-an (A) adv. In the beginning; at first; originally; firstly; in the first place.

ابتدائی ibtidā'i (A) adj. Preliminary; introductory; elementary; primary.

ابتدائی تعلیم ibtidā'i t'alim, n.f. Primary education.

ابتدائی حروف ibtidā'i ḥurūf, n.m. Initial letters; initials.

ابتدائی رسوم ibtibā'i rusūm, n.f. Initiatory rites.

ابتدائی ڈگری ibtidā'i ḍigri, n.f. Elementary degree.

ابتر abtar (A) adj. Issueless; destitute of good qualities. (P) Ruined; spoiled; scattered; confused; disordered; worthless; uncultured.

ابتر ہونا abtar honā, v. To be ruined; to be spoiled.

ابتری abtarı (P) n.f. Deterioration; ruin; worthlessness; poverty; disorder; confusion; bad management.

ابتسام ibtisām (A) n.m. Smile; cheerfulness; gaiety.

ابتلا ibtilā (A) n.m. Trial; misfortune; affliction; suffering.

ابٹن ' ابٹنا ubtan, ubtanā (H) n.m. A cosmetic; a mixture of prefumes, oil, flour, etc., which is rubed on the body (particularly of the bride and bridegroom) to make skin soft and clean.

ابجد abjad (A) n.m. An arrangement of the letters of the Arabic alphabet in which they were originally set. The letters so arranged have been assigned numerical value.

ابجد خواں abjad-khwān, adj. A beginner; one who is learning the alphabet.

ابخره abkhirah (A) n.m. (plu. of بخار bukhār) Vapours; fumes; steam; exhalations.

ابخل abkhal (A) adj. (sup. of بخیل bakhīl) More or most miserly or covetous; very avaricious.

ابد abad (A) n.f. Eternity; time without end.

ابدالاباد abad-ul-ābād, adj. Eternal; for ever and ever; perpetual.

ابداع ibdā' (A) n.m. Invention; the production of something new; innovation.

ابدال abdāl (A) n.m. (plu. of بدل badal or badil): Devotees; religious persons; saints not known to the public moving from place to place occasionally, in the interest of divine administration.

ابدالی abdālī (P) n.m. A clan of the Pathans.

ابدی abadi (A) adj. Eternal; immortal; perpetual.

ابر abr (P) n.m. A cloud.

ابر بہار abr-ĕ bahār, n.m. A spring cloud.

ابر بہمن abr-ĕ Bahman n.m. Bahman is a Persian month corresponding to March, hence a spring cloud.

ابر تر ، ابر باراں abr-ĕ tar, abr-ĕ bārāṅ, n.m. The rain cloud; nimbus.

ابر تنک abr-ĕ tunuk, n.m. A light cloud.

ابر چھانا abr chhānā, v. To be cloudy; to be overcast with clouds.

ابر دریا بار abr-ĕ daryā-bār, n.m. Rain soaked clouds; cloud saturated with water vapour.

ابر رحمت یا کرم abr-ĕ raḥmat ya karam, n.m. A cloud of God's mercy or grace.

ابر سیاہ abr-ĕ siyah, n.m. A dark cloud; a black cloud.

ابر عالمگیر abr-ĕ 'ālamgir, n.m. Clouds covering a large part of the country; wide-spread rain.

ابر غلیظ abr-ĕ ghalīẓ, n.m. A thick cloud.

ابر کھلنا abr khulnā, v. Dispersion of clouds after rain; clearing of the sky after rain.

ابر مردہ abr-ĕ murdah, n.m. A sponge.

ابر نیساں abr-ĕ naisāṅ n.m. Spring clouds; the vernal cloud or rain.

ابرا abrā (P) n.m. The outer fold of a double garment distinguished from استر astar, the lining.

ابرار abrār (A) n.m. (plu. of بر barr) Holy or pious men; saints.

ابراھیم Ibrāhim (A) n.m. Prophet Abraham.

ابراھیم ادھم Ibrāhīm Adham (A) n.m. Ibrahim, son of Adham, a saint who gave up his throne for a religious life.

ابرش abrash (A) n.m. Piebald (horse) marked with spots of various colour or shades of a colour.

ابرص abraṣ (A) adj. Leprous; having leprosy.

ابرق abraq (A) }
ابرک abrak (H) } n.m.) Mica; talc.

ابرو abrū (P) n.m. Eyebrow.

ابرو پر گرہ مارنا abru par girah mārnā, v. To knit the brow; to frown.

ابرو پر میل نہ آنا abrū par mail nah ānā, v. To be firm against heavy odds; to be steadfast.

ابروے پیوستہ abrū-ĕ paiwastah, n.m. Close and thick eyebrows.

ابروے فلک abrū-ĕ falak, n.m. Crescent.

ابری abri (P) adj. Clouded; variegated; mottled. n.f. A kind of thick and shining paper resembling overspread clouds, often used as a covering for books.

ابریشم abresham (P) n.m. A cocoon; raw silk; silk.

اُبسانا ubsana (H) v. To cause to rot; to cause to ferment.

اُبسنا ubasna (H) v. To putrefy; to become fetid; to give offensive smell (meat or food); to become musty.

ابصار abṣār (A) n.m. (plu. of بصر baṣr) Eyes.

ابطال ibṭāl (A) n.m. Confutation; refutation; proving a thing to be false; act of abolishing or destroying.

ابعد ab'ad (A) adj. (sup. of بعید ba'id) Further; furthest; most distant or remote.

ابکار **abkār** (A) *n.f.* (*plu.* of بکر *bikr*) Virgins; (*plu.* of بکرہ *bukrah*) mornings; dawns; day-breaks.

آبکائی **ubkā'i** (H) *n.f.* The act of vomiting; nausea.

آبل پڑنا **ubal paṛnā** (H) *v.* To boil over; to be angry; a burst out.

ابلاغ **iblāgh** (A) *n.m.* Causing to arrive; sending; conveying; communication.

ابلق **ablaq** (A) *adj.* Piebald (horse); black and white; mottled; parti-coloured; pepper and salt; hypocrite.

ابلق ایام **ablaq-ĕ ayyām**, *n.m.* Days and nights.

ابلق چشم **ablaq chashm**, *adj.* (A person) having beautiful eyes.

آبلنا **ubalnā**(H) *v.* To boil; to boil over; to flow over; to burst forth; to swell with pride or rage.

ابلہ **ablah** (A) *n.m.* Simpleton; silly; stupid; artless; foolish; ignorant.

ابلہ فریب **ablah fareb**, *n.m.* A wily knave; an imposotor; a cheat.

ابلہی **ablahi** (A) *n.f.* Foolishness; silliness; folly.

ابلیس **iblīs** (A) *n.m.* The devil; satan.

ابن **ibn** (A) *n.m.* A son; a child.

ابن السبیل **ibn-us-sabīl**, *n.m.* A traveller.

ابن الغرض **ian-ul-gharaẓ**, *n.m.* A selfish person.

ابن الغیب **ibn-ul-ghaib**, *n.m.* A man whose parentage is not known; an upstart.

ابن الوقت **ibn-ul-waqt**, *n.m.* A time-server.

ابناء **abnā'** (A) *n.m.* (*plu.* of ابن *ibn*) Sons; peoples; tribes.

ابنائے جنس **abnā-ĕ-jins**, *n.m.* People of the same kind or class, quality or rank; companions; equals.

ابو **abū** (A) *n.m.* Father; lord or master.

ابوالبشر **Abū-ul-Bashar**, *n.m.* The father of the human race; Adam.

ابوالفضل **Abū-ul-Faẓl**, *n.m.* Father of excellence; a courtier of Emperor Akbar.

ابو بکر **Abu Bakr**, *n.m.* The name of the father-in-law and first successor of the Holy Prophet.

ابو تراب **Abū Turāb**, *n.m.* Father of dust; appellation of Hazrat Ali.

ابو جہل **Ahū-Jahl**, *n.m.* Father of ignorance; an uncle and bitterest enemy of the Holy Prophet.

ابو علی سینا **Abū 'Ali Sinā**, *n.m.* The name of the celebrated sage and physician.

ابوہریرہ **Abū Hurairah**, *n.m.* Father of the cat; the family name of one of the companions of the Holy Prophet.

ابواب **abwāb** (A) *n.m.* (*plu.* of باب *bāb*) Doors; gates; chapters; sections; cesses; taxes; charges levied by government.

آبھار **ubhār** (H) *n.m.* Swelling; plumpness; acquiring fullness; budding; development of breasts (in women); excitation; persuasion; the act of stirring up.

آبھارنا **ubhārnā** (H) *v.* To raise up; to lift; to induce; to excite; to persuade.

ابھاگی **abhāgī** (H) *adj.* Unfortanate; a poor wretch.

ابہام **ibhām** (A) *n.m.* The thumb; confusion; ambiguity; suspicion.

آبھرنا **ubharnā** (H) *v.* To rise; to grow; to come to the surface of water after a dive; to swell; to overflow; to give oneself airs; to become famous.

ابھی **abhī** (H) *adv.* This very moment; immediately; just now; instantly; already.

ابے **abe**, *interj.* (In contempt) Hallo! you fellow! you rascal!

ابے تبے کرنا ، ابے تبے سے پیش آنا **abe tabe karnā, abe tabe se pesh ānā**, *v.* To be rude in speech; to address one with undue familiarity; to speak with contempt.

ابیات **abyāt** (A) *n.m.* (*pl.* of بیت *bait*), Houses. *n.f.* Verses; distiches.

ابیض abyaẓ (A) adj. White; very splendid or shining.

اپاہج apāhaj (H) adj. Cripple; a lazy or an indolent person; a useless or worthless person.

آپدش updesh (H) n.m. Advice; counsel; sermon; admonition; instruction; exhortation.

آپدیشک updeshak (H) adj. & n.m. Preacher, instructor; adviser; admonisher; teacher.

اپریل aprail (E) n.m. The fourth month of the English calendar; April.

اپریل فول aprail ful, n.m. April fool; one sent upon a bootless errand on the 1st of April, by way of joke.

آپلا uplā (H) n.m. Dried cakes of cow-dung used as fuel.

اپنا ، اپنی apnā, apni (H) pron. & adj. Of or belong to self; one's own; personal; individual; exclusive; dear one; relative.

اپنا اپنا apnā apnā, adj. Each his own; respective; personal.

اپنا آلو سیدھا کرنا apnā ullū sidha karnā, v. To fool others to achieve one's own purpose; to gain one's object.

اپنا بیگانہ یا پرایا apnā begānah yā praya, n.m. Relatives and strangers; friends and foes.

اپنا ٹھکانا کرنا apnā thikānā karnā, v. To make one's own arrangements; to find an bode for oneself; to search for a house or employment.

اپنا جوہر دکھانا apnā jauhar dikhānā, v. To show one's worth or skill; to achieve something praiseworthy.

اپنا راستہ لینا apnā rāstah lenā, v. To mind one's own business.

اپنا سا منہ لے کر رہ جانا apnā sā munh le kar rah jānā, v. To hang down one's head through shame; to fail to come up to one's pretentions; to be unsuccessful.

اپنا سر پیٹنا apnā sar piṭnā, v. To be sorry for what one has done; to receive the punishment of one's own faults.

اپنا سر کھاؤ apnā sar khāo. Do as you please.

اپنا کیا پانا apnā kiyā pānā, v. To suffer the consequences of one's own deeds.

اپنا گھر بھرنا apnā ghar bharnā, v. To fill one's own pocket; to get hold of what belongs to another.

اپنا لہو پینا apnā lahū pinā, v. To be greatly vexed; to suffer distress.

اپنا منہ دیکھو apnā munh dekhū. Weigh your own worth.

اپنا ہی رونا رونا apnā hi ronā ronā, v. To talk incessantly of one's own woes and troubles.

اپنی اپنی بولی بولنا apni apni boli bolnā, v. Every one giving his own suggestion; each one pressing his own views or demand.

اپنی اپنی پڑنا apni apni parnā. v. To be anxious about one's own interests; everyone thinking of self.

اپنی بات پر اڑ جانا apni bāt par aṛ jānā, v. To persist in one's own view.

اپنی چال سے نہ چوکنا apni chāl se nah chūknā, v. Not to give up one's (undesirable) habits.

اپنی کرنی بھرنی apni karni bharni, prov. To reap the fruit of one's own misdeeds.

اپنی کھال میں مست ہونا apni khāl men mast hona, v. To be content with one's poverty; to be happy with one's circumstances.

اپنی گانا apni gānā, v. To sing one's own praises; to egotize; to boast; to brag; to talk big.

اپنی گوں کا یار apni gaun kā yār, n.m. A self-interested or a selfish person; a time-server.

اپنی نیند سونا apni nind sonā, v. To be care-free; to be one's own master.

اپنے آپ apne āp, adv. By oneself; voluntarily; automatically.

اپنے پاؤں میں آپ کلہاڑی مارنا apne pāoṅ meṅ āp kulhāṛī mārnā, v. To dig one's own grave; to be one's own enemy or assassin; to be cause of one's own ruin.

اپنے جامے سے باہر ہونا apne jāme se bāhar honā, v. To be unable to restrain or control oneself; to be beside oneself with anger or joy; to live beyond one's means.

اپنے حال میں مست ہونا apne hāl meṅ mast honā, v. To be self-complacent.

اپنے ڈھب کا apne ḍhab kā, adj. Of one's own liking; of the same temperament; a man of his own type.

اپنے سائے سے ڈرنا apne sā'e se ḍarnā, v. To be mightily afraid; to show extreme cowardice; to be extremely superstitious.

اپنے کام سے کام رکھنا apne kām se kām rakhnā, v. To mind one's own business.

اپنے کیے پر پچھتانا apne kiye par pachhtānā, v. To grieve over one's misdeeds; to regret over one's actions.

اپنے کیے کی سزا پانا apne kiye ki sazā pānā, v. To suffer for one's own doings.

اپنے گریبان میں منہ ڈالنا apne garebān meṅ muṅh ḍālnā, v. To look within oneself; to confess and be ashamed of one's conduct; to be conscious of one's short-comings.

اپنے منہ میاں مٹھو apne muṅh miāṅ mittū, prov. Self-praise is no recommendation.

اپنے منہ پر طمانچہ مارنا apne muṅh par tamānchah mārnā, v. To reproach oneself for bad conduct.

اپنانا apnānā, v. To make a thing one's cwn; to appropriate something to one's wn use; to adopt.

اپنایت apnāyat, n.f. Family; relationship; kindred; adoption.

اپھر جانا ، اپھرنا aphar jānā, apharnā (H) v. To swell out (the stomach); to be overloaded; to be overfull with food; to boast; to be puffed up with pride; to go to extreme.

اپیل apīl (E) n.f. An appeal.

اپیل داخل کرنا apīl dākhil karnā, v. To file an appeal.

اپیل کرنا apīl karnā, v. To prefer an appeal.

اپیل منظور کرنا apīl manzūr karnā, v. To allow an appeal; to accept an appeal.

اتا atā (T) n.m. Father.

اتاترک atāturk, n.m. Father of the Turks; an appellation given to Ghazi Mustafa Kamal Pasha.

اتابک atābak (P) n.m. A master; teacher; an appellation given to kings or prime ministers in Iran; name of a family of the kings of Iran.

آتار utār (H) n.m. Descent; slope; fall; decrease; declination; a reduction in price; ebb-tide.

آتار چڑھاؤ utār charhāo, n.m. Descent and ascent; ups and downs; the vicissitudes of life; ebb and flow; loss and gain.

آتار دینا utār denā, v. To take off; to put down; to pull down; to disgrace; to give old clothes to servants or menials.

آتار لینا utār lenā, v. To cause to alight; to trace out; to make copy (of); to succeed in taking off or bringing down.

آتارا utārā (H) n.m. A slope; a wharf; a halting place; ransom; duplicate copy; cast-off clothes; an offering (flowers or sweetmeats, etc., passed a certain number of times from head to foot of a sick person under the belief that evil spirit is thus transferred from the sick person to the utārā).

آتارا آتارنا utārā utārnā, v. To dispossess an evil spirit by means of the utārā.

آتارنا utārnā (H) v. To cause to alight; to bring down; to take across the river; to disembark; to land; to unload; to cause to dismount; to lower; to disgrace; to degrade; to tear off; to cut off; to take off; to cast off; to lay (in the grave).

اتالیق atāliq (T) n.m. A teacher; a private tutor; an instructor; a preceptor.

اتالیقی atāliqi, n.f. Private tuition; instruction; tutorship; preceptorship.

اتائی atā'ī (H) n.m. & adj. A self taught artist, singer or musician; one who has not had any formal training in an art.

اتباع ittiba' (A) n.m. Compliance; following; obedience; obeying.

اتحاد ittiḥād (A) n.m. Union; alliance; concord; amity; friendship; conformity; treaty.

اتحاد ثلاثہ ittiḥād-ĕ ṣalāṣh, n.m. Triple alliance.

اتحادی ittiḥādi (A) n.m. Allies; leaguers.

آتر uttar (H) n.m. The north.

اترانا itrānā (H) v. To show off; to be conceited; to give oneself airs; to behave in a boastful and arrogant way; to act coquettishly.

آترائی utrā'ī (H) n.f. Descent; slope; coming down (from hills); repayment; ferriage; payment for unloading goods.

آترتا چاند utartā chand, n.m. Last phase of the moon; the waning moon.

اترسوں atarson, adv. & n.m. The day following the day after to-morrow.

آترن utran (H) n.f. Old clothes; used clothes.

آترنا utarnā (H) v. To alight; to get down; to dismount; to halt; to lodge; to land; to disembark; to cross; to fall off; to fade; to decrease; to abate; to forget; to dislocate (a limb); to flag; to be relieved of responsibility; to fall in value or dignity; to become insipid; to grow old; to become pale; to grow thin; to die.

آتروانا utarwānā (H) v. To cause to descend or alight; to cause to be taken off.

اتصال ittiṣāl (A) n.m. Conjunction; contact; adhesion; union; neighbourhood; contiguity; confluence.

اتفاق ittifāq (A) n.m. Agreement; concord; coincidence; amity alliance; friendship; harmony; unity; union; consent; similarity of views; chance; event; opportunity; probability.

اتفاق پڑنا ittifāq paṛnā, v. To occur; to come to pass; to happen.

اتفاق حسنہ irtifāq-ĕ ḥasanah, n.m. Unexpected good fortune; good luck; favourable opportunity; auspicious occasion.

اتفاق رائے ittifāq-ĕ rāe, n.m. Holding the same views; unanimity; general concurrence.

اتفاق رکھنا ittifāq rakhnā, v. To live in harmony; to be on good terms.

اتفاق کرنا ittifāq karnā, v. To agree; to unite; to form a friendship; to concur.

اتفاق ہونا ittifāq honā, v. To have unanimity or harmony; to happen.

اتفاقاً ittifāqan (A) adv. Accidentally; by chance; occasionally.

اتفاقات ittifāqāt (A) n.m. (plu. of اتفاق ittifāq) Accidents; occurrences; events; surprises; unforeseen happenings.

اتفاقی ، اتفاقیہ ittifaqi ittifāqiyah, adj. Accidental; casual; fortuitous; concurring.

اتفاقی اخراجات ittafāqi akhrājāt, n.m. Contingent expenditure; incidental charges.

اتقاء ittiqā' (A) n.m. Piety; abstaining from evil; shunning; avoiding; living in accordance with Islamic law.

اتقیاء atqiyā' (A) adj. (plu. of تقی taqi) The pious; devot; the righteous; the virtuous. n.m. Religious men; devotees.

اتکاء ittikā' (A) n.m. Dependence; reliance.

اتلاف *itlāf* (A) *n.m.* Loss; decay; ruin; destruction.

اتم *atamm* (A) *adj.* (*sup.* of تام *tām*) The most perfect or complete.

آتم *uttam* (H) *adj.* Highest; best; first; chief; most excellent.

آتم کھیتی مدھم بان ، نکھد چاکری بھیک ندان *uttam kheti maddham bān, nakhid chākrī bhīk nadān, prov.* Agriculture is the best occupa ion, trade is second best, service is bad and beggary worse.

آتم گانا ، مدھم بجانا *uttam gānā, maddham bajānā, prov.* Singing is best and instrumental music is second best.

اتمام *itmām* (A) *n.m.* Completion; accomplishment; perfection.

اتنا ، اتنی *itna, itni* (H) *adj.* As much as this; this much; so much; thus far; up to this place.

اتنا ہی *itnā hi, adj.* Exactly this much.

اتنی سی جان ، گز بھر کی زبان *Itnī sī jān, gaz bhar ki zabān, prov.* To be too impudent for one's years.

اتنی عقل بھی اجیرن ہوتی ہے *itni 'aql bhi ajiran hotī hai, prov.* Too much wisdom is also harmful.

اتنے سے اتنا ہونا *itne se itnā honā, v.* To rise from poverty to wealth; to rise from log cabin to White House.

اتنے میں *itne meṅ, adj.* Meanwhile; in the meantime.

آتنا ، آتنی *ūtnā, utni, adj.* That much.

آتو *uttū* (P) *n.m.* Needlework; embroidery; plaiting; gathering cloth into ornamental folds.

آتو بنانا *uttū banānā, v.* To streak; to mark; to beat severely.

آتو کرنا *uttū karnā, v.* To plait; to mark; to crimp; to make a fool of one; to vilify.

آتو کش ، آتو ساز ، آتو گر *uttū kash, uttū sāz, uttū gar, n.m.* One who makes ornamental folds in cloth; a plaiter.

اتوار *itwār* (H) *n.m.* Sunday.

اتہام *ittihām* (A) *n.m.* Suspicion, imputation; censure; accusation; impeachment; blame.

اتہام بیجا *ittihām-ĕ bejā, n.m.* A false accusation.

اتھاہ *athāh* (H) *adj.* Very deep; unfathomable; bottomless; unfordable.

آتھل پتھل *ūthal puthal* (H) *adj.* Upset; topsy-turvy; in complete disorder.

اٹ جانا یا اٹنا *at jānā yā atnā* (H) *v.* To be choked with (mud).

اٹرنی *atarnī* (E) *n.m.* Attorney; one legally authorised to act for another; one legally qualified to manage a case in a court of law.

اٹ سٹ *at sat* (H) *n.f.* Close alliance; close attachment; conspiracy; treachery.

اٹک *atak* (H) *n.f.* Obstruction; obstacle; restraint; entanglement; interruption.

اٹکانا *atkānā* (H) *v.* To obstruct; to hinder; to impede; to restrain; to prevent; to detain; to get one a job; to embroil.

اٹکاؤ *atkā'o* (H) *n.m.* Hindrance; detention; restraint; prevention; postponement.

اٹکل *atkal* (H) *n.f.* Guess; supposition; conjecture; opinion; rough computation or estimate; knack; discernment.

اٹکل باز *atkal bāz, adj.* Good guesser; an appraiser.

اٹکل پچو *atkal pachchū, n.m.* Random guess; mere conjecture; random. *adj.* Uncertain. *adv.* At random.

اٹکل سے *atkal se, adv.* Approximately; by conjecture.

اٹکنا *ataknā* (H) *v.* To stop; to hesitate; to falter; to be entangled; to be prevented; to adhere; to stammer.

اٹکھیلی *atkheli* (H) *n.f.* Coquetry; affected gait; playfulness; gambol; flirtation; toying; blandishment. (*plu.* اٹکھیلیاں *atkheliyāṅ*).

اٹل *atal* (H) *adj.* Unavertible; firm; stationary; unchangeable; determined; of a determined resolution; inevitable.

آٹنگن uṭaṅgan (H) n.m. A species of nettle, the seeds of which are used by physicians as an aphrodisiac.

اٹھا aṭṭhā (H) n.m. Eighth of a suit of cards.

اٹھا بیٹھی uṭṭhā baiṭhi, n.f. Frequently rising up and sitting down; agitation; uneasiness; a kind of exercise among athletes.

اٹھا رکھنا uṭhā rakhnā (H) v. To assume (responsibility for); to take upon oneself a burden; to put by something for the future.

اٹھارہ aṭṭārah (H) adj. Eighteen.

اٹھارہ گوٹی aṭṭhārah goṭī, n.f. A game played with eighteen small pieces of stones.

اٹھاسی aṭhāsi (H) adj. Eighty-eight.

اٹھا لے جانا uṭhā le jānā (H) v. To run away with; to kidnap; to abduct; to carry off.

اٹھا لینا uṭhā lenā (H) v. To lift up; to pick up; to remove (from); to undertake (to do something).

اٹھان uṭhān (H) n.f. Act of rising; ascent; ascention; elevation; height; size; growth; bloom of life; beginning of youth; developing of breasts in girls; expenses.

اٹھانا uṭhānā (H) v. To lift; to raise up; to hoist; to build; to awaken; to excite; to bear; to carry; to abolish; to eject.

اٹھانوے aṭṭhānawe (H) adj. Ninety-eight.

اٹھاون aṭṭhāwan (H) adj. Fifty-eight.

اٹھاؤ چولھا uṭhāū chūlhā, adj. A wanderer; a vagabond; a gypsey.

اٹھائیس aṭṭhā'is (H) adj. Twenty-eight.

اٹھائی گیرا uṭhā'i girā, n.m. A pilferer; a petty thief; a purloiner; a wicked or immoral person.

اٹھ بیٹھنا uṭh baiṭhnā, v. To get up; to wake up; to get well; to recover; to revive.

اٹھتا بیٹھتا uṭhtā baiṭhtā, adv. Walking and resting; with difficulty.

اٹھتر aṭhattar (H) adj. Seventy-eight.

اٹھتی جوانی uṭhti jawānī, n.f. Bloom of life; the beginning of youth.

اٹھتے بیٹھتے uṭhte baiṭhte, adv. Constantly; every time; with difficulty; by-degrees.

اٹھ جانا uṭh jānā, v. To come to an end; to die; to disappear; to go away.

اٹھک بیٹھک uṭṭhak baiṭhak, n.f. Sitting and standing.

اٹھ کھڑا ہونا uṭh khaṛā honā, v. To rise up; to recover from illness.

اٹھلانا ithlānā, athlānā (H) v. To walk affectedly or coquettishly; to sturt; to give oneself airs.

اٹھنا uṭhnā (H) v. To get up; to rise up; to stand up; to awake; to grow; to be spent; to be abolished; to ply; to recover from illness; to ferment (as leaven); to be occupied; to proceed; to quit; to begin (pain or disease).

اٹھنا بیٹھنا uṭhnā baiṭhnā, n.m. Deportment; manners; etiquette; association. v. To sit and stand frequently.

اٹھوارا aṭhwārā (H) n.m. A week; a period of eight days; the eighth day.

اٹھوانا uṭhwānā (H) v. To cause to lift; to cause to be removed or abolished.

اٹھوانسا aṭhwāṅsā (H) n.m. A child born in the eighth instead of the ninth month; octagonal; a plot of land which is under sugarcane cultivation for eight months.

اٹی aṭṭi (H) n.f. Twine or skein of thread; bundle of thread; a plait; a sheaf.

اٹیرن aṭeran (H) n.m. A reed on which thread is wound before spinning; a winder; a reel; a skein of thread; the circle in which a horse is trained.

اٹیرن کر دینا aṭeran kar denā, v. To reduce one to a skeleton; to puzzle; to confuse.

اٹیرنا aṭernā (H) v. To wind thread into hanks or skeins; to reel; to train a horse in the manege.

اثاث ، اثاث البیت ، اثاثہ asās, asās-ul-bait, asāsah (A) n.m. Household furniture or property; wealth; cattle; goods; effects.

اثبات iṣbāt (A) n.m. Corroboration; affirmation; positiveness; proof; verification; certain knowledge.

اثبات جرم iṣbāt-ĕ jurm, n.m. Establishment of guilt; conviction.

اثبات حقیقت iṣbāt-ĕ ḥaqiqat, n.m. Proof of the truth.

اثر aṣar (A) n.m. Footprint; mark; sign; trace; impression; effect; influence; consequence; a kind of Hadis (tradition of the Prophet of Islam).

اثر پذیر aṣar pazīr, adj. Taking effect; susceptible to impression; impressionable.

اثر ہونا aṣar honā, v. To have effect or impression on; to be influenced.

اثر قانون aṣar-ĕ qānūn, n.m. The effect of law.

اثم iṣm (A) n.m. Sin.

اثمار aṣmār (A) n.m. (plu. of ثمر ṣamar) Fruits of all kinds.

اثناء aṣnā' (A) n.m. Interval; midst; middle; interim period.

اثنائے حال aṣnā-ĕ ḥāl, adv. In the midst of a certain state or condition.

اثناء میں aṣnā' meṅ, adv .Meanwhile; during the interval.

اثنا عشر iṣnā 'ashar (A) adj. Twelve. metaph. The twelve Imams.

اثنا عشری iṣnā 'ashari (A) n.m. A sect of the Shia community who follow the twelve Imams.

اجابت ijābat (A) n.f. Answering (of prayer or petition); consent; compliance; a favourable reply; acceptance of a request; action of the bowls; motion; stool.

اجارہ ijārah (A) n.m. Letting land on lease; hire; rent; lease; monopoly.

اجارے کا پٹا ijāre kā paṭṭā, n.m. A deed of lease; agreement; title-deed.

اجارہ دار ijārah dār, n.m. A lease-holder; lessee; a tenant; a farmer; the holder of a monopoly; proprietor.

اجارہ داری ijārah dāri, n.f. Having or establishing a monopoly; obtaining on rent.

اجارہ نامہ ijārah nāmah, n.m. A lease; a title-deed.

اُجاڑ ujāṛ (H) adj. Ruined; devastated; deserted: waste; uninhabited; abandoned.

اُجاڑنا ujāṛnā (H) v. To uproot; to destroy; to desolate; to lay waste; to plunder; to ravage; to depopulate; to ruin; to expose to loss; to demolish.

اُجاڑو ujāṛū, adj. Squander; waster; spendthrift; destroyer.

اجازت ijāzat (A) n.f. Permission; leave; sanction; authority to do something; licence; passport; permit.

اجازت تبنیت ijāzat-ĕ tabniyat, n.f. Authority to adopt a son.

اجازت چاھنا ijāzat chāhnā, v. To ask for leave; to seek permission.

اجازت خواہ ijāzat khwāh, n.m An applicant; a petitioner; one who seeks permission.

اجازت نامہ ijāzat nāmah, n.n. A written authority; a licence: a permit.

اجازتی احکام ijāzati aḥkām, n.m. Consent orders.

اُجاگر ujāgar (H) adj. Bright; luminous; splendid; conspicuous; manifest.

اُجالا ujālā (H) n.m. Light; day light; sunshine; day-break; dawn: glory; splendour.

اُجالا ہونا ujālā honā, v. To be lighted; to dawn; to be lit up.

اجتماع ijtimā' (A) n.m. Act of assembling; agreeing together; congregation; assemblage; afflux; (Astro.) conjunction.

اجتماع ضدین ijtimā'-ĕ ẓiddain, n.m. Combination of the two opposites.

اجتماع کرنا ijtimā' karnā, v. To gather together; to assemble; to combine; to league.

اجتماعی ijtimā'i (A&P) adj. Social; congregational; collective; the whole; aggregate.

اجتماعی حقوق ijtimā'i ḥuqūq, n.m. Social rights.

اجتناب ijtināb (A) n.m. Turning aside (from); keeping aloof; shunning; refraining from; avoiding; hatred; abstinence; self-denial; austerity; asceticism.

اجتہاد ijtihād (A) n.m. Exerting the faculties to the utmost; utmost endeavour; earnest effort; solving a problem after deep thought; interpretation or re-interpretations of Islamic law.

اجداد ajdād (A) n.m. (plu. of جد jadd) Ancestors; forefathers.

اُجڈ ujaḍḍ (H) adj. Ill-mannered; uncouth; obstinate; unlettered; extremely ignorant; rude; unmannerly; clownish; idiot; an arrant blockhead; a lout.

اجر ajr (A) n.m. Reward of good or bad actions; recompense; remuneration; compensation; wages; retribution.

اجر جائز ajr-ĕ jā'iz, n.m. A legal remuneration.

اجر دینا ajr denā, v. To remunerate; to recompense; to reward.

اجرام ajrām (A) n.m. (plu. of جرم jirm) Bodies.

اجرام فلکی ijrām-ĕ falaki, n.m. The heavenly bodies.

اجراء ijrā' (A) n.m. Putting into execution or circulation; service; issue.

اجراء کرنا ijrā' karnā, v. To issue; to set on foot; to execute; to perform; to carry out.

اجرائے تعمیل ijrā-ĕ ta'mil, n.m. Execution.

اجرائے حکمنامہ ijrā-ĕ hukmnāmah, n.m. Writ (petition).

اُجرت ujrat (A) n.f. Wages; fare; fee; remuneration.

اُجڑا پجڑا ، اُجڑی پجڑی ujṛā pujṛā, ujṛi pujṛi (H) adj. In ruins; desolate.

اُجڑنا ujaṛnā (H) v. To become desolate; to be utterly destroyed; to be ruined; to be ravaged or plundered; to be deprived of habitation; to die out.

اُجڑوانا ujaṛwānā (H) v. To cause to be laid waste.

اجزاء ajzā' (A) n.m. (plu. of جز juz) Parts; portions; members; ingredients; (Chem.) constituents; elements.

اجزائے ترکیبی ajzā-ĕ tarkibi, n.m. Component parts; composite parts.

اجزائے متناسبہ ajzā-ĕ mutanāsibah, n.m. Proportionate parts.

اجساد ajsād (A) n.m. (plu of جسد jasad) Bodies (animated).

اجسام ajsām (A) n.m. (plu. of جسم jism) Bodies; bulk; solid substances.

اجل ajal (A) n.f. Death; the term of life; destiny; fate; appointed time; delay; period for the payment of a debt.

اجل رسیدہ ajal rasidah, adj. Overtaken by fate; doomed; on the point of death.

اجل گرفتہ ajal giriftah, adj. Seized by fate; in the jaws of death; on the point of death.

اجل ajall (A) adj. (sup. of جلیل jalīl) Greatest (man); most glorious.

اُجلا ، اُجلی ujlā, ujli (H) adj. White; clean; clear; bright; luminous; radiant; pure.

اُجلا آدمی ujlā ādmi, n.m. A man dressed in clean white clothes; a respectable man.

اُجلا پن ujlā pan, n.m. Whiteness; cleanliness; brightness.

اُجلا منہ کرنا ujlā munh karnā, v. To exculpate; to clear one's reputation.

اُجلا ہونا ujlā honā, v. To be dressed in clean clothes; to be polished or polite.

اُجلی سمجھ ujli samajh, n.f. Intelligence.

اُجلی گزران ujli guzrān, n.f. Being well-to-do; doing well; in an opulent state.

اجلاس ijlās (A) n.m. Session; meeting; the sitting of a court of justice.

اجلاس فرما ijlās-farmā, adj. Presiding.

اجلاس کامل ijlās-ĕ kāmil, n.m. A full bench.

اجلاس کرنا ijlās karnā, v. To preside; to sit in court.

اجلاس منقسم ijlās-ĕ munqasim, n.m. Division bench.

اجلال ijlāl (A) n.m. Magnificence; honour; glory; exaltation; greatness.

اجماع ijmā' (A) n.m. A unanimity; general agreement.

اجماع اُمت ijmā-ĕ ummat, n.m. General agreement of the followers of the Holy Prophet; unanimous consent of great religious leaders on certain points of law.

اجمال ijmāl (A) n.m. Sum and substance; an abstract; compendious account; epitome; synopsis.

اجمالی ijmālī, adj. Brief; abriged.

اجمالی خاندان ijmālī khāndān, n.m. A joint family.

اجمالی محال ijmālī maḥāl, n.m. An undivided estate.

اجمل ajmal (A) adj. (sup. of جمیل jamil). Most beautiful.

اجمعین ajma'īn (A) adj. (plu. of اجمع ajma') The whole; all together.

اجناس ajnās (A) n.f. (plu. of جنس jins) Kinds; sorts; species; goods; chattels; commodities; merchandise.

اجنبی ajnabī (A) n.m. A stranger; an alien; a foreigner; an unknown person adj. Foreign; new; strange.

اجنبیت ajnabiyyat (A) n.f. Strangeness; the state of being an alien.

اجوائن ajwā'in (H) n.f. The seed of a plant of the dill kind; a species of aniseed having the flavour of caraways.

اجوائن خراسانی ajwā'in khurāsānī, n.f. Black henbane seed.

اجورہ ujūrah (A) n.m. Wages; reward; remuneration.

اجورہ دار ujūrah dār, adj. A labourer on hire; a hireling.

اجہل ajhal (A) adj. (sup. of جاہل jāhil) Very ignorant; a block-head.

اجی ajī, intj. Hallo! Sir! I say (a particle used to call attention or to express surprise).

اجیت ajīt (H) adj. Unconquered; unsubdued; impregnable; invincible.

اجیر ajīr (A) n.m. Hireling; hired servant; a hired workman.

اجیرن ajīran (H) adj. Distasteful; disagreeable; vexatious; wearisome; burdensome; oppressive.

اجیرن ہونا ajīran honā, v. To be sickening; to be nauseating.

اُچاپت uchāpat (H) n.f. Buying goods on credit; knavish tricks; fraud.

اُچاٹ uchāṭ (H) adj. Dissatisfied; disgusted; sad; sorrowful; weary; dull; offended; tired; downcast.

اُچاٹ ہونا uchāṭ honā, v. To be dissatisfied; to grow weary; to be disgusted; to be tired.

اچار achār (H) n.m. Pickles.

اچانک achānak (H) adv. Suddenly; unawares; by chance; unknowingly; all of a sudden; at once.

اُچٹنا uchaṭnā (H) v. To be disheartened; to be discouraged; to weary; to fail; to miss (an aim).

اچرج acharj (H) n.m. A wonder; marvel; miracle; bewilderment. adj. Astonishing; wonderful; marvellous; uncommon; novel.

اُچکا uchakkā (H) n.m. One who suddenly snatches a thing and makes off with it; a shop-lifter; a pick-pocket; a swindler; a sharper.

اُچکا پن uchakkāpan, n.m. Thieving; pilfering; fraud; knavery; swindling.

اُچکی uchakkī (H) n.f. A woman thief or pick-pocket.

اچکن achkan, n.f. A long coat having buttons in front.

اُچکنا uchaknā (H) v. To leap; to run away with; to carry off; to pounce upon.

اچنبھا achambhā (H) *n.m.* A wonderful thing; a marvel; a prodigy; astonishment.

اچنبھا کرنا *achambhā karnā, v.* To wonder; to be astonished.

اچنبھے میں آنا *achambhe men ānā, v.* To be lost in amazement; to be perplexed; to be bewildered.

اچھا *achchhā* (H) *adv.* Well; very good; yes; no matter; granted. *intj.* Bravo! Well-done! Fine!

اچھا ، اچھی *achchhā, achchhī* (H) *adj.* Good; right; excellent; sound; pleasing; agreeable; appropriate; righteous; healthy; pure; correct; genuine; happy; lovely; delicious; useful; precious; benevolent; clever (workman).

اچھا کرنا *achchhā karnā, v.* To cure; to recover; to do good.

اچھا کہنا *achchhā kahnā, v.* To say yes; to speak well of.

اچھا لگنا *achchhā lagnā, v.* To be pleasing; to be agreeable; to appear pretty; to afford pleasure; to relish; to prove beneficial.

اچھا ہونا *achchhā honā, v.* To be cured; to recover; to be in sound health.

اچھی طرح سے *achchhī ṭaraḥ se, adv.* Carefully; suitably; thoroughly; fully; plentifully; satisfactorily; well.

اچھی کہی *achchhī kahī, inter.* Well said! What next!

اُچھالنا *uchhālnā* (H) *v.* To throw up; to toss up; to bring to light; to make known.

اچھل پڑنا *uchhal paṛnā, v.* To jump; to leap; to fly into a passion; to be startled.

اُچھل کود *uchhal kūd, n.f.* Hopping and skipping; leaping and jumping; revelry.

اُچھلنا *uchhalnā* (H) *v.* To leap; to rejoice; to gush out; to spurt out; to assume airs.

اُچھو *uchchhū* (H) *n.m.* Suffocation; choking.

اُچھو لگنا، ہونا *uchchhū lagnā, honā, v.* To be suffocated in the act of swallowing.

اچھوانی *achhwānī* (H) *n.f.* Caudle (usually given to women after child birth).

اچھوتا ، اچھوتی *achhūtā, achhūtī* (H) *adj.* Unique; untouched; unpolluted; un-used.

احادیث *aḥādīṡ* (A) *n.f.* (*plu.* of حدیث *ḥadīṡ*) Traditions, particularly the traditions or sayings of the Holy Prophet.

احاطہ *iḥāṭah* (A) *n.m.* An enclosure; fence; premises; precincts; boundary; circuit; circle; compound; area; territory; a province; comprehension.

احاطہ کرنا *iḥāṭah karnā, v.* To surround; to fence; to besiege; to blockade; to limit; to confine; to encircle; to comprehend.

احباب ، احباء *aḥbāb, aḥibbā'* (A) *n.m.* (*plu.* of حبیب *ḥabīb*). Friends; lovers; relatives; dear ones.

احبار *aḥbār* (A) *n.m.* (*plu.* of حبر *ḥibr*) Wise men; priests of Jews.

احتجاج *iḥtijāj* (A) *n.m.* Protest; objection.

احتراز *iḥtirāz* (A) *n.m.* Guarding against; abstaining from improper action; controlling the passions; abstinence; forbearance.

احتراز کرنا *iḥtirāz karnā, v.* To abstain or protect oneself (from); to avoid; to refrain (from); to be on one's guard (against).

احترام *iḥtirām* (A) *n.m.* Honour; veneration; treating with respect; holding in veneration; act of honouring; reverence.

احترام کرنا *iḥtirām karnā, v.* To respect; to venerate.

احتساب *iḥtisāb* (A) *n.m.* Making up accounts; reckoning; computing; administration of the police; inhibition.

احتشام *iḥtishām* (A) *n.m.* Having many followers or dependents; retinue; pomp; magnificence; ostentation.

احتلام *iḥtilām* (A) *n.m.* Nocturnal emission; night discharge; wet dream.

احتمال iḥtimāl (A) n.m. Supposition; probability; conjecture; likelihood; doubt; uncertainty; fear; apprehension; bearing; supporting.

احتمال قانونی ihtimāl-ĕ qānūni, n.m. A legal presumption.

احتمال کرنا iḥtimāl karnā, v. To suppose; to presume; to suspect; to impute.

احتمال ہونا iḥtimāl honā, v. To be likely; to be probable; to be allowable.

احتمالی iḥtimālī (A) adj. Problematical; conjectural; probable; likely; doubtful; hypothetical.

احتیاج iḥtiyāj (A) n.f. Want; need; necessity; indigence; urgency; exigence; scarcity.

احتیاط iḥtiyāṭ (A) n.f. Caution; care; foresight; vigilance; circumspection; scrupulousness; precaution.

احتیاط سے iḥtiyāṭ se, adv. Carefully; cautiously.

احتیاط کرنا ، احتیاط رکھنا iḥtiyāṭ karnā, iḥtiyāṭ rakhnā, v. To exercise care; to guard (against); to take precautions.

احتیاطاً iḥtiyāṭan (A) adv. Carefully; cautiously; watchfully; prudently; circumspectly.

احتیاطی iḥtiyāṭī, adj. Precautionary; preventive.

احتیاطی ذخیرہ iḥtiyāṭī zakhīrah, n.m. Buffer stock.

احد aḥad (A) n.m. One; unity; unique.

احدی aḥadi (P) n.m. An idle person; a body of soldiers in the reign of Akbar who were paid but were liable to be called only in an emergency; sluggard.

احدیت aḥdiyyat (A) n.f. Unity; oneness; individuality; harmony; alliance.

احرار aḥrār (A) adj. (plu. of حر ḥur) The free born; the liberal; the generous; the noble.

احرام iḥrām (A) n.m. Two unsitched pieces of white cloth wrapped down the body by male pilgrims during Haj (pilgrimage to k'abah); a white scarf tied round the head and hair by woman pilgrims during Haj.

احرام باندھنا iḥrām bāndhnā, v. To wear pilgrim's dress preparatory to entering precincts of Mecca and making the pilgrim's vow.

احزاب aḥzāb (A) n.m. (plu of حزب ḥizb) Armies; groups; parties.

احزان aḥzān (A) n.m. (plu of حزن ḥuzn) Sorrow; afflictions.

احساس iḥsās (A) n.m. Perception; feeling; apprehension.

احسان iḥsān (A) n.m. Doing good; beneficence; kindness; favour; good offices; obligation; conferred benevolence; benevolent actions.

احسان جتانا iḥsān jatānā, v. To speak or boast of favours conferred.

احسان فراموش iḥsān farāmosh, adj. Ungrateful; ingrate; forgetting favours and benefits received.

احسان کرنا iḥsān karnā, v. To oblige; to do acts of kindness; to benefit; to confer favour or benefit (upon).

احسان لینا iḥsān lenā, v. To be under obligation (to).

احسان ماننا iḥsān mān-nā, v. To be thankful; to acknowledge kindness (of or from).

احسان مند iḥsā mand, adj. Grateful; thankful; obliged.

احسان مندی iḥsān mandi, n.f. Gratitude; thankfulness.

احسن aḥsan (A) adj. (sup. of حسن hasan) Better; best; most lovely; preferable.

احسنت aḥsant (A) inter (Lit. You have done well); Bravo! Well done!

احضار iḥẓār (A) n.m. Attendance; appearance; summoning; summons.

احضار بالجبر iḥẓār biljabr, n.m. Compulsory attendance.

احقر aḥqar (A) adj. (sup. of حقیر ḥaqir) Lowest; most mean; most contemptible; your most unworthy slave (a self-humiliating expression).

احکام aḥkām (A) n.m. (plu. of حکم ḥukm) Orders; commands; instructions; injunctions; decrees.

احمد Aḥmad (A) adj. Most commendable or praiseworthy. n.m. Name of the Holy Prophet.

احمد کی پگڑی محمود کے سر aḥmad ki pagṛi mbḥmūd ke sar, prov. To rob peter, to pay paul.

احمدیه aḥmadiyah, n.m. The religion of Mirza Ghulam Ahmad Qadiyani, who claimed to be a prophet.

احمر aḥmar (A) adj. Red.

احمق aḥmaq (A) adj. Foolish; stupid. n.m. Fool; dunce; blockhead; idiot.

احمق الناس aḥmaq-uń-nās, n.m. The biggest fool.

احمق بنانا aḥmaq banānā, v. To make a fool of; to cheat.

احمق پن aḥmaq-pan, n.m. Stupidity; blockheadedness; idiocy; folly.

احمقانه aḥmaqānah, adj. Foolishly; stupidly.

احناف aḥnāf (A) n.m. (plu. of حنفی ḥanafi) A sect among the Muslims, following the school of Imam Abu Hanifa.

احوال aḥwāl (A) n.m (plu. of حال ḥāl) State; condition; narrative; accounts; circumstances; affairs; incidents; events; occurrences.

احوال بتانا aḥwāl batānā, v. To state one's condition; to tell the story (of); to give an account (of).

احوال پرسی aḥwāl pursi, n.f. Enquiry after one's health, affairs, etc.

احول aḥwal (A) adj. Squint-eyed.

احیاناً aḥyānan̲ (A) adv. Occasionally; now and then; sometimes; from time to time; once in a way.

احیاء iḥyā' (A) n.m. Restoring the dead to life; reviving; giving life; preserving; vivification.

اخ akh̲ (A) n.m. A brother.

اخاه akh̲khāh, int. A exclamation of wonder or suprise; Ha!

اخبار akh̲bār (A) n.m. (plu. of خبر kh̲abar) News; newspaper; a gazette.

اخبار نویس akh̲bār-navis, n.m. News-writer; an editor (of a paper).

اخبث akh̲bas̱ (A) adj. (sup. of خبیث kh̲abīs̱) Most mean; most contemptible.

اخت ukh̲t (A) n.f. Sister.

اختتام ikh̲titām (A) n.m. Termination; end; conclusion; completion; expiry; fulfilment.

اختر akh̲tar (A) n.m. A star; a constellation; good omen; good luck; good fortune.

اختر شماری akh̲tar-shumāri, n.f. Passing night in anxiety; employing oneself in loneliness in counting stars.

اختر شناسی akh̲tār-shināsi, n.f. The calculation of one's horoscope; astrology.

اختراع ikh̲tirā' (A) n.m. Invention; devising; contrivance.

اختراع کرنا ikh̲tirā' karnā, v. To invent; to create; to contrive; to devise.

اختر بختر akh̲tar bakh̲tar, n.m. Household effects; chattels.

اختصار ikh̲tiṣār (A) n.m. Abbreviation; brevity; curtailment; synopsis; summary; abridgment; conciseness; compendium; contraction; reduction.

اختصار کرنا ikh̲tiṣār karnā, v. To abstract; to epitomize; to reduce; to curtail; to abridge; to summarize; to abbreviate.

اختصاص ikh̲tiṣāṣ (A) n.m. Speciality; peculiarity; characteristic; appropriation.

اختلاج ikh̲tilāj (A) n.m. Palpitation; moving speedily and quickly; restlessness; fluttering.

اختلاج قلب ikh̲tilāj-ĕ qalb, n.m. Palpitation of heart; irregular action of the heart caused by excitement or excessive exertion.

اختلاط ikh̲tilāṭ (A) n.m. The state of being mixed; amalgamation; cross; friendship; amity; intimacy; warmth; concord; unison; intercourse; warm attachment.

اختلاف i<u>kh</u>tilāf (A) *n.m.* Difference; discord; opposition; dissension; misunderstanding; variation; disagreement; breach.

اختلاف رائے i<u>kh</u>tilāf-ĕ rāe, *n.m.* Difference of opinion; dissent; disagreement.

اختلال i<u>kh</u>tilāl (A) *n.m.* Disorder; hindrance; interruption; obstacle.

اختہ a<u>kh</u>tah (P) *adj.* Castrated.

اختیار i<u>kh</u>tiyār (A) *n.m.* Choice; option; discretion; control; will; jurisdiction; authority; power; influence; competency; permission; dominion; (*plu.* اختیارات i<u>kh</u>tiyārāt).

اختیار تمیزی i<u>kh</u>tiyār-ĕ tamīzī, *n.m.* Discretion.

اختیار جائز i<u>kh</u>tiyār-ĕ jā'iz, *n.m.* Legal authority.

اختیار حکومت i<u>kh</u>tiyār-ĕ ḥukūmat, *n.m.* Jurisdiction.

اختیار خصوصی i<u>kh</u>tiyār-ĕ <u>kh</u>uṣūṣī, *n.m.* Special powers.

اختیار دست اندازی i<u>kh</u>tiyār-ĕ dast-andāzī, *n.m.* Power to take cognizance of.

اختیار دینا i<u>kh</u>tiyār denā, *v.* To authorize; to give permission to act.

اختیار رکھنا i<u>kh</u>tiyār rakhnā, *v.* To be entitled to; to have a claim upon; to have discretion (in).

اختیار سرسری i<u>kh</u>tiyār-ĕ sarsarī, *n.m.* Summary powers.

اختیار سماعت i<u>kh</u>tiyār-ĕ samā'at, *n.m.* Jurisdiction.

اختیار شوہری i<u>kh</u>tiyār-ĕ shauharī, *n.m.* Marital authority.

اختیار مطلق i<u>kh</u>tiyār-ĕ muṭlaq, *n.m.* Absolute authority.

اختیار مقامی i<u>kh</u>tiyār-ĕ maqāmī, *n.m.* Local authority.

اختیار ملنا i<u>kh</u>tiyār milnā, *v.* To be invested with power to act.

اختیار میں ہونا i<u>kh</u>tiyār men̐ honā, *v.* To be in one's power; to be dependent on.

اختیار ناجائز i<u>kh</u>tiyār-ĕ nājā'iz, *n.m.* Illegal authority or power.

اختیاری i<u>kh</u>tiyārī, *adj.* Optional; voluntary; in on's power; at one's disposal.

اخذ a<u>kh</u>ẕ (A) *n.m.* Grasping; seizing; adoption; inference.

اخذ کرنا a<u>kh</u>ẕ karnā, *v.* To take away; to exact; to seize; to assume; to adopt; to infer.

اخراج i<u>kh</u>rāj (A) *n.m.* Expulsion; eviction; evacuation; deportation; extradition; rejection; extraction; discharge; elimination; removal; derivation; expenses; cost.

اخراجات i<u>kh</u>rājāt (A) *n.m.* (*plu.* of خرج <u>kh</u>arj or اخراج i<u>kh</u>rāj) Expenses; costs; disbursement; charges.

اخراجات عدالت i<u>kh</u>rājāt-ĕ 'adālat, *n.m.* Judicial costs.

اخروٹ a<u>kh</u>roṭ, *n.m.* A walnut.

اُخروی u<u>kh</u>rawī (A & P) *adj.* Pertaining to the next world; concerning hereafter.

اخضر a<u>kh</u>ẓar (A) *adj.* Green.

اخفاء i<u>kh</u>fā (A) *n.m.* Concealment; hiding.

اخفا کرنا i<u>kh</u>fā karnā, *v.* To conceal; to hide; to cover.

اخفائے جرم i<u>kh</u>fā-ĕ jurm, *n.m.* Concealment of an offence.

اخفش a<u>kh</u>fash (A) *adj.* Weak-sighted; dim-sighted; having small eyes; seeing better at night than in day time. *n.m.* Title of Abul Hasan Sa'eed, a well known grammarian.

اخگر a<u>kh</u>gar (P) *n.m.* Ember; a spark of fire.

اخلاص i<u>kh</u>lāṣ (A) *n.m.* Sincerity; purity; love; tenderness; pure friendship; great affection; selfless adoration or worship.

اخلاص جوڑنا i<u>kh</u>lāṣ joṛnā, *v.* To cement an intimacy; to contract friendship.

اخلاص مند i<u>kh</u>lāṣ mand, *adj.* Sincere; true; affectionate; intimate; genuinely; friendly.

اخلاص مندی *ikhlāṣ mandī, n.f.* Sincerity; friendliness; affection; intimacy; love.

اخلاط *akhlāṭ* (A) *n.m.* (*plu.* of خلط *khilṭ*) Mixtures; the humours of human body.

اخلاط اربعه *akhlāṭ-ĕ arba'h, n.m.* The four humours of human body, *viz.*, blood, phlegm, choler (yellow bile) and melancholy (black bile).

اخلاق *akhlāq* (A) *n.m.* (*plu.* of خلق *khulq*) Morals; virtues; good qualities; manners; affability; politeness; morality; ethics.

اخلاقیات *akhlāqiyyāt* (A) *n.m.* Ethics; code of morality.

اخوان *ikhwān* (A) *n.m.* (*plu.* of اخ *akh*) Brothers; brethren; friends.

اخوان الزمان *ikhwān-uz-zamān, n.m.* People of the same time; contemporaries.

اخوان الشیاطین *ikhwān-ush-shayāṭīn, n.m.* Wicked people; followers of the devil.

اخوان الصفا *ikhwān-uṣ-ṣafā, n.m.* Sincere friends; righteous people.

آخوت *ukhuwwat* (A) *n.f.* Brotherhood.

اخون ، اخوند *akhūn, akhūnd* (P) *n.m.* Teacher; instructor; preceptor.

اخیار *akhyār* (A) *adj.* (*plu.* of خیر *khair*) The good and excellent people; the righteous people.

اخیافی *akhyāfī* (A) *adj.* Brothers or sisters by the same mother, but by a different father.

اخیر *akhīr* (A) *adj.* Last; final. *n.f.* The moment of death; the end.

ادا *adā* (A) *n.f.* Payment or discharge of debt; fulfilment; acquittance; settlement.

ادا کرنا *adā karnā, v.* To make payment; to comply; to accomplish; to defray; to repay; to pronounce; to utter; to express.

ادا ہونا *adā honā, v.* To be performed satisfactorily; to be discharged (a debt); to be re-paid (a sum of money); to be expressed intelligibly.

ادائے شہادت *adā-ĕ shahādat, n.m.* Deposition; giving of evidence.

ادائے مالگزاری *adā-ĕ mālguzārī, n.m.* Payment of revenue.

ادا *adā* (P) *n.f.* Grace; elegance; charm; fascination; blandishment; coquetry; expression; acting.

ادا دکھانا *adā dikhānā, v.* To show blandishments; to behave as a coquet.

ادا شناس *adā shinās, adj.* One who understands amorous signs; one who readily takes a hint; a clever person.

ادا فہم *adā fahm, adj.* One skilled in the art of understanding blandishment.

ادا فہمی *adā-fahmī, n.f.* Understanding of amorous signs or of the arts of coquetry.

اداکار *adā kār, n.m. & n.f.* An actor; an actress.

ادارت *idārat* (A) *n.f.* Editorship of a newspaper or a journal; compilation of book.

ادارہ *idārah* (A) *n.m.* Department; office; management; organisation; institute; administration.

اداریہ *idāriyah, n.m.* Editorial; leading article; a leader.

اُداس *udās* (H) *adj.* Lonely; forlorn; dejected; sorrowful; sad; unsettled in mind; apathetic.

اُداسی *udāsī* (H) *n.f.* Sadness; despondency; dullness; loneliness; dejection. *n.m.* A hermit; a class of faqirs.

اُداسی چھانا *udāsī chhānā, v.* To be clouded with sorrow; to become dull or sad.

ادام اللہ *adām allah* (A) *intrej.* May God preserve you!

ادائی *adā'ī, n.f.* Performance (of a duty); payment of debt; uttered or expressed in an intelligible manner.

ادب *adab* (A) *n.m.* Elegant manners; decorum; respect; courtesy; civility; politeness; good breeding; urbanity; etiquette; literature.

ادب کرنا *adab karnā*, *v.* To show respect; to regard with esteem; to respect; to venerate; to behave politely.

اُدباء *udabā'* *n.m.* (A) (*plu.* of ادیب *adib*) Men of letters; teachers of good manners.

ادبار *idbār* (A) *n.m.* Calamity; bad luck; mishap; affliction; penury; misfortune; adversity; ruin.

ادبار آنا *idbār ānā*, *v.* To be overtaken by misfortune; to have bad luck.

ادخال *idkhāl* (A) *n.m.* Introduction; insertion; entry; admission; ingress.

ادخال خون *idkhāl-ĕ khūn*, *n.m.* Blood transfusion.

ادرار *idrār* (A) *n.m.* Flowing freely of milk, urine, &c.; hard rain; munificence.

ادراک *idrāk* (A) *n.m.* Perception; comprehension; sagacity; understanding.

ادرک *adrak*, *n.f.* Ginger, in the undried state.

ادرکی *adrakī*, *n.f.* Pieces of green ginger coated over with sugar.

ادریس *Idrīs* (A) *n.m.* Prophet Enoch.

ادعاء *iddi'ā* (A) *n.m.* Demanding one's rights; claim; pretension.

ادعیه *ad'iyah* (A) *n.f.* (*plu.* of دعا *du'ā*) Prayers; benedictions.

ادغام *idghām* (A) *n.m.* Duplication of a letter by *tashdid*; contraction of one letter into another similar; merger.

ادق *adaqq* (A) *adj.* (*sup.* of دقیق *daqīq*) Most abstruse or difficult; very subtle; very obscure; very minute.

ادل بدل ، ادلا بدلا *adal badal*, *adlā badlā*, *n.m.* Alteration; commutation; exchange; barter.

ادل بدل کرنا *adal badal karnā*, *v.* To interchange; to exchange; to barter; to transform; to shift; to commute.

ادنیٰ *adnā* (A) *adj.* (*sup.* of دنی *dani*) Inferior; petty; scanty; base; trivial; insignificant; unimportant; vile; menial; baseborn; lowest; meanest. *n.m.* A low, common, obscure person.

ادنیٰ ملازمین *adnā mulāzimīn*, *n.m.* Inferior servants; menial staff.

ادنیٰ و اعلیٰ *adnā-ŏ a'lā*, *n.m.* High and low people; prince and peasant; the high-born and the low-born.

ادوان ، ادوائن *adwān*, *adwā'in*, *n.f.* Strings at the foot of a bed-stead for tightening its tape.

ادوائن کھینچنا *adwā'in khenchnā*, *v.* To tighten the strings of a bed-stead.

ادویه *adwiyah* (A) *n.f.* (*plu.* of دوا *dawā*) Medicines; drugs.

ادویاتی *adwiyātī*, *adj.* Medicinal.

ادھ *adh* (H) *adj.* Half.

ادھ بیچ *adh bich*, *n.f.* Half-way; middle.

ادھ پکا *adh-pakkā*, *adj.* Half-ripe; half-cooked; immature.

ادھ جلا *adh-jalā*, *adj.* Half-burnt.

ادھ کچا *adh-kachchā*, *adj.* Half-ripe; unripe; half-baked.

ادھ کھلا *adh-khilā*, *adj.* Half-bloomed (flower).

ادھ کھلا *adh-khulā*, *adj.* Half-open.

ادھ موا *adh-mūā*, *adj.* Half-dead.

ادھا *addhā* (H) *n.m.* Half of anything; half-bottle.

ادھار *adhār* (H) *n.m.* Food; victuals; nutriment; nourishment; sustenance; subsistence.

اُدھار *udhār* (H) *n.m.* Loan; debt or cradit; advance.

اُدھار دینا *udhār denā*, *v.* To lend or give on credit.

اُدھار کھانا *udhār khānā*, *v.* To live on credit.

اُدھار کھائے بیٹھے ھیں *udhār khāe baiṭhe hain*, To be ready or prepared (for any eventuality); to be determined to oppose under all circumstances.

اُدھار لینا *udhār lenā*, *v.* To borrow; to buy on credit.

ادھر *idhar* (H) *adv.* Here; hither; on this side; this way.

آدھر udhar (H) adv. There; thither; on that side.

ادھر آدھر idhar udhar, adv. This way and that; here and there; right and left; around; scattered.

ادھر آدھر کی باتیں idhar udhar kī bāteṅ, n.f. Unimportant talk; useless talk.

آدھر سے udhar se, adv. From that side or place; from that direction.

ادھر سے آدھر کر دینا idhar se udhar kar denā, v. To conceal; to steal; to misplace.

ادھر سے آدھر ہونا idhar se udhar bonā, v. To be lost, gone or made away with.

ادھر کی آدھر لگانا idhar ki udhar lagānā, v. To backbite; carrying tales.

ادھر کی دنیا آدھر ہو جانا idhar kī dunyā udhar ho jānā, v. To be topsy turvy; to be turned upside down.

ادھر یا آدھر ہونا idhar yā udhar honā, v. Deciding a definite course of action in a crisis; recovery or death of a patient; settlement of a dispute.

آدھڑنا udhaṛnā, (H) v. To be undone; to be unrolled or untwisted; to be peeled off.

آدھل جانا udhal jānā (H) v. To be carried off; to be beside oneself (under emotional stress); to be spoiled; to be dissipated.

ادھم adham (A) n.m. Dark bay; a black horse; a dark coloured horse.

آدھم udham, n.m. (H) Tumult; uproar; disturbance.

آدھم مچانا ūdham machānā, v. To create a disturbance; to make a noise; to kick up a row.

ادھنا ، ادھنی adhannā, adhanni, n.m./n.f. Half an anna; six pies.

ادھورا ، ادھوری adhūrā, adhūri (H) adj. Half-prepared; half-dressed; half-ready; immature; incomplete; imperfect; unfinished.

ادھوڑی adhaūri (H) n.f. A hide; the coarsest and thickest sort of leather generally used for the soles of shoes.

ادھی addhi (H) n.f. One eighth of a pice; a kind of fine thin cotton cloth.

ادھی ادھی پر جان دینا addhi addhi par jān denā, v. To be a skin-flint; to be a miser or a niggard.

ادھی ادھی کا حساب کرنا addhi addhi kā ḥisāb karnā, v. To be very cautious in doing accounts.

ادھیڑ adheṛ (H) adj. Just past the prime of life; middle-aged.

آدھیڑ بن udheṛ bun (H) n.f. Reflection; deliberation; meditation; anxious thought; perplexity.

آدھیڑنا udheṛnā (H) v. To unsew; to undo (sewing); to rip up; to open; to pluck out; to flay.

ادھیلا adhelā, n.f. Half a pice.

ادھیلا نہ دے ادھیلی دے adhelā nah de adheli de, prov. Penny wise, pound foolish.

ادھیلی adheli, n.f. Half a pice.

ادیان adyān (A) n.m. (plu. of دین din) Religions.

ادیب adib (A) n.m. A teacher of refined manners; a writer; an author.

ادیم adim (A) n.m. Scented or tanned leather (brought from Arabia); surface of the earth or sky.

ادیم السما adim-us-samā, n.m. The expanse of the sky.

اڈا aḍḍā, n.m. A pigeon-house; a dove-cote; a frame for embroidery or lace work; a tonga or motor stand; weaver's stool; a meeting place of idlers; house of ill fame.

اڈی aḍḍi (H) n.f. Heel; the portion of the shoe round the heel.

اڈیشن aḍishan (E) n.m. Copies of a book or newspaper printed at one time.

اڈیٹر aḍiṭar (E) n.m. On who conducts a newspaper; editor.

اذان azān (A) n.f. The Muslim call to prayers (generally proclaimed from the minarets or towers of a mosque).

اذعان iz'ān (A) n.m. Obedience; submission; confidence; belief; admission.

اذکار aẓkār (A) n.m. (plu. of ذکر ẓikr) Praises; praises of God; recitals; commemorations; narrations; narratives.

اذکیاء aẓkiyā' (A) n.m. (plu. of ذکی ẓakī) People of discernment; the intelligent; the ingenious; the shrewd.

اذل aẓall (A) adj. (sup. of ذلیل ẓalīl) Most vile, base or abject; most despicable; most contemptible.

اذن iẓn (A) n.m. Leave; permission; consent of two contracting parties (as in marriage).

اذن عام iẓn-ĕ 'ām, n.m. General permission.

اذہان aẓhān (A) n.m. (plu. of ذہن ẓihn) Geniuses; intellects; wits; capacities.

اذیت aẓiyyat (A) n.f. Wanton injury; molestation; oppression; distress; vexation; trouble; suffering; torment; annoyance; loss.

اذیت دینا aẓiyyat denā, v. To harm; to injure; to harass; to molest; to persecute; to tease; to trouble.

ارانا arrāṭā (H) n.m. A loud and prolonged sound as from the discharge of artillery, or the fall of a building; continuous loud cry of a child.

ارادت irādat (A) n.f. Belief; faith; goodwill.

ارادتاً irādatan̲ (A) adv. Intentionally; deliberately.

ارادہ irādah (A) n.m. Will; intention; aim; object; purpose; determination.

اراروٹ arāroṭ (E) n.m. Arrowroot.

اراضی arāẓī (A) n.f. (plu. of ارض arẓ) Lands; cultivated lands; fields.

اراضی آبادی arāẓī-ĕ ābādī, n.f. Village sites.

اراضی اُفتادہ arāẓī-ĕ uftādah, n.f. Barren lands; uncultivated lands.

اراضی باغ arāẓī-ĕ bāgh, n.f. Garden lands.

اراضی خراج arāẓī-ĕ k͟hirāj, n.f. Rent-paying lands.

اراضی دار arāẓīdār, n.m. Landholder.

اراضی مالگزاری arāẓī-ĕ mālguzārī, n.f. Revenue-paying lands.

اراضی وقف arāẓī-ĕ waqf, n.f. Endowed lands.

اراضیات arāẓiyāt, n.f. Lands; estates.

اراکین arākīn (A) n.m. (plu. of ارکان arkān).

ارب arb (H) adj. One hundred millions.

ارب کھرب arb kharb, adj. Innumerable; countless; numberless; incalculable.

ارباب arbāb (A) n.m. (plu. of رب rabb). Lords; masters, possessors; friends; supporters.

ارباب بصیرت arbāb-ĕ basīrat, n.m. Prudent, sagacious, intelligent people.

ارباب جاہ arbāb-ĕ jāh, n.m. Persons of rank, position or dignity.

ارباب دانش و فہم arbāb-ĕ dānish-ŏ fahm, n.m. The intelligent; the wise.

ارباب سخن arbāb-ĕ suk͟han, n.m. Orators; eloquent speakers; poets; masters of language.

ارباب شرع arbāb-ĕ shar', n.m. Persons, well-versed in Islamic law.

ارباب عدالت arbāb-ĕ 'adālat, n.m. Officers of the court.

ارباب نشاط arbāb-ĕ nishāṭ, n.m. Dancers, singers and musicians.

ارباب ہمت arbāb-ĕ himmat, n.m. Men of courage; men of high spirit.

اربع ، اربعہ arba', arba'h (A) adj. Four.

اربعہ عناصر arba'ah anāṣir, n.m. The four elements, earth, air, fire and water.

اربعہ متناسبہ arba'ah mutanāsibah, n.m. A rule in Arithmetic according to which from three given ratios the fourth is found.

اربعون ، اربعین arba'ūn, arba'īn (A) adj. Forty.

ارتباط irtibāṭ (A) n.m. Alliance; connection; close friendship; familiarity; affinity.

ارتحال irtiḥāl (A) n.m. Death; demise; departure.

ارتداد irtidād (A) n.m. Apostasy; retraction.

ارتفاع irtifā' (A) n.m. Altitude; elevation; exaltation; height; ascent; eminence; grandeur.

ارتقاء Irtiqā' (A) n.m. Evolution; rules of growth or promotion.

ارتکاب irtikāb (A) n.m. Commission or perpetration (of sin or crime); undertaking (of an enterprise).

ارتکاب جرم irtikāb-ĕ jurm, n.m. Commission of a crime.

ارتھ arth (H) n.m. Import; significance; interpretation; design; purpose.

ارتھی arthī (H) n.f. A bier on which a Hindu corpse is conveyed to the pyre.

ارث irs (A) n.f. Inheritance; heritage.

ارجمند arjmand (P) adj. Honourable; noble; worthy; blessed; possessing dignity; dear.

ارجل arjal (A) n.m. Horse having one foot white and the other three of some other colour (which is regarded as a serious blemish).

ارجن arjun (H) n.m. An archer; a Hindu warrior and wrestler; name of one of the five Pāṅdu brothers.

ارحام arḥām (A) n.m. (plu. of رحم riḥm) Wombs; matrices; relations by the mother's side.

ارحم arḥam (A) adj. (sup. of راحم rāḥim) Most merciful; most compassionate.

ارحم الراحمین arḥam-ur-rāḥimin, adj. The most merciful of the merciful (an attribute of God).

آرد urd (H) n.m. A kind of vetch.

آرد پڑھ کر مارنا urd paṛh kar mārnā, v. To enchant.

آرد پر سفیدی urd par safedi, id. The least bit; the smallest particle; not a bit.

آردا بیگنی urdā-begani (T) n.f. A female armed attendant or guard in a royal ḥarem.

اردب ardab (P) n.m. Middleman; an intervener; (in chess) a piece moved to save the king from check-mate.

ارد گرد irdgird, adv. All around; round about; on all sides.

اردلی ardali (corr. from English). n.m. An orderly; a peon in regular attendance on an official.

اردلی بازار ardalī bāzār, n.m. A shop in attendance of the officers or kings on tour for the supply of rations to them.

آردو urdū (T) n.f. Army; camp; encampment or market of a camp; Urdu language.

آردو بازار urdū bāzār, n.m. A market near an encampment; a bāzār in cantonment.

آردوئے معلی urdū-ĕ mu'allā, n.f. The standard Urdu language spoken in Delhi Fort during the time of the last Mughal Emperor, Bahadurshah Zafar; a collection of the letters of poet Ghalib.

آردی ، آردی بہشت urdi, urdi bihisht (P) n.m. The second month of the Persian calendar corresponding to April; a Persian festival.

ارزاں arzāṅ (P) adj. Low-priced; cheap.

ارزانی arzānī (P) n.f. Low price; cheapness.

ارزانی ہونا arzānī honā, v. To be conferred; to be bestowed; cheapness and abundance.

ارژنگ arzhang (P) n.m. The picture gallery of the famous Chinese painter, Mani; a picture gallery or album.

ارسال irsāl (A) n.m. Remittance; act of sending; despatching; remitting.

ارسال کرنا irsāl karnā, v. To send; to despatch; to remit.

ارسطو arasṭū (ارسطاطالیس Arasṭāṭālis) (G) n.m. Aristotle (a famous Greek philosopher).

ارسلاں arsalāṅ (T) n.m. Lion.

ارشاد irshād (A) n.m. Instruction; command; behest; order; direction; will; pleasure.

ارشاد بجا لانا irshād bajā lānā, v. To obey or carry out instruction or command.

ارشاد فرمانا (کرنا) irshād farmānā (karnā), v. To command; to desire; to direct; to bid; to enjoin.

ارشد arshad (A) adj. (sup. of رشید rashīd) Most honest; most upright; well-guided (person).

ارشمیدس arshamīdas (G) n.m. Archimedes (a Greek philosopher).

ارض arẓ (A) n.f. The earth; land; region; country.

ارض مقدس arẓ-ĕ muqaddas, n.f. Palestine; (Lit.) a sacred land.

ارض و سماء arẓ-ŏ samā', n.m. Earth and sky.

ارضی arẓi (A) adj. Relating to the earth; earthly; terrestrial.

ارضیات arẓiyyāt (A) n.m. Geology; geognosy.

ارغن ، ارغنون arghan, arghnūn (P) n.m. Organ; a musical instrument.

ارغوان arghawān (P) n.m. A plant whose flowers and fruits are of purple colour.

ارغوانی arghawāni (P) adj. Purple; crimson; of red colour.

ارفع arfa' (A) adj. (sup. of رفیع raf'i) Most exalted; most elevated; most high; sublime.

ارقام arqām (A) n.m./f. (plu. of رقم raqam) Figures; numbers.

ارقام irqām (A) n.m. Writing; act of writing.

ارکان arkān (A) n.m. (plu. of رکن rukn) Pillars; columns; props; supports; members of a body or association; (Chem.) ingredients; component parts.

ارکان دولت (سلطنت) arkān-ĕ daulat (salṭanat), n.m. Pillars of state; ministers of Government; members of a cabinet; nobles; courtiers; grandees.

ارم iram (A) n.m. A famous garden in Arabia designed and built on the model of Paradise by Shaddad, an ancient King of Yemen; Paradise.

ارمان armān (P) n.m. Wish; desire; longing; yearning.

ارمان رہ جانا armān rah jānā, v. To be disappointed about the fulfilment of one's wish or desire.

ارمان نکالنا armān nikālnā, v. To satisfy one's desires; to gratify one's wishes.

ارمغان armughān (A) n.m. Gift; present; rarity; curiosity.

ارمن arman (P) n.m. Armenia.

ارمنی armanī (P) adj. Armenian.

ارنا arnā (H) n.m. A wild buffalo; a fat black man.

ارنڈ aranḍ (H) n.m. The tree from which castor oil is prepared.

ارنڈ خربوزہ aranḍ kharbūzah, n.m. A fruit called papita; the papita(carica papaya)

ارنڈی کا تیل aranḍi kā tel, n.m. Castor-oil.

ارنی arini (A) Show me [O God, show me Thyself; this was the earnest desire (prayer) expressed by Moses on Mount Senai.

ارنی arnī (H) n.f. A female wild buffalo; a reed of which a pipe or flute is made.

ارواح arwāḥ (A) n.f. (plu of روح rūḥ) Spirits; souls.

اروڑا aroṛā (H) n.m. A caste of Hindu shop-keepers.

اروگ arogi (H) n.m. Free from disease; quite healthy.

اروی arwi (H) n.f. A species of arum, the root of which is used as a vegetable.

ارهر arhar (H) n.f. A species of pulse.

ارے ، اری are, ari, inter. Ho; O! Hear you! Hollo! (used in calling or addressing generally in a disrespectful way); are is used for men and ari for women.

آریب ureb, adj. Crooked; slanting; sloping; crafty.

اڑ ar (H) n.f. Obstinacy; obduracy; stubbornness; contention; dispute; contrariety.

اڑ بیٹھنا ar baithnā, v. To persist in solicitation; to be obdurate or stubborn.

اڑان uṛān, (H) n.f. Act of flying; flight.

اڑان گھائی بتانا uṛān ghā'i batānā, v. To deceive; to circumvent; to make a trick.

اڑانا arānā (H) v. To cause to stop; to obstruct; to impede; to entangle or fasten one thing to another; to ram; to plug; to thrust.

اڑانا uṛānā (H) v. To cause to fly; to let fly; to squander; to fritter away; to rob; to pilfer; to allure; to blow up; to explode; to efface; to befool; to deceive.

اڑاؤ uṛāū, n.m. A spend-thrift; a squanderer; a prodigal; an extravagant person.

اڑبنگا aṛbangā (H) adj. Crooked; rough; ragged; uneven. n.m. Obstacle; impediment.

اڑ بھاگنا uṛ bhāgnā, v. To run away quickly; to escape.

اڑتالیس aṛtālis (H) adj. Forty-eight.

اڑتیس aṛtis (H) adj. Thirty-eight.

اڑ جانا uṛ jānā, v. To vanish; to disappear; to be spent; to depart suddenly; to fly away.

اڑ چلنا uṛ chalnā, v. To assume airs; to feel proud; to live beyond one's means or status: to be immoral.

آڑتی تول uṛti tol, n.f. Weighing less.

آڑتی چڑیا پہچاننا uṛti chiṛiyā pahchān-nā, v. To know a crook at sight; to be intelligent or clever.

آڑتی خبر uṛti khabar, n.f. Rumour; hearsay; an unreliable news or report.

اڑسٹھ aṛsaṭh (H) adj. Sixty-eight.

آڑن uṛan (H) adj. Flying; on the wing.

آڑن بیماری uṛan bimāri, n.f. An infectious disease.

آڑن چھو ہو جانا uṛān chhū ho jānā, v. To fly way; to disappear; to vanish.

آڑن کھٹولا uṛan khaṭolā, n.m. Flying throne of fairy tales, or of Solomon.

اڑنا aṛnā (H) v. To stop; to come to a standstill; to get entangled; to be obstinate; to gib (as a horse); to be restive; to hesitate.

آڑنا uṛnā (H) v. To take to flight; to fly; to soar; to disappear; to be cut off; to fade; to vanish; to spread (rumour or report); to become current; to be worn out.

اڑنگا aṛangā (H) n.m. A hindrance; an obstruction; an obstacle; impediment; a leg trick in wrestling.

اڑنگے پر چڑھانا aṛange par chaṛhānā, v. To have an advantage over a person; (in wrestling) to have an adversary in such a position that it is easy to throw him down.

اڑوس پڑوس aṛos paṛos, n.m. Neighbourhood; vicinity. adv. Near.

آڑھانا uṛhānā (H) v. To cause to dress; to cover a person with a sheet or mantle; to help to dress.

اڑھائی aṛhā'ī (H) adj. Two and a half.

اڑیل aṛyal (H) adj. Obstinate; perverse; mulish; restive; headstrong.

از az (P) prep. From; than; by; of; out of.

از بر az bar, adv. By rote; by heart; by memory.

از بس az bas, adv. Extremely necessary; sufficiently; enormous.

از جانب az jānib, adv. From; by; in behalf of.

از حد az ḥad, adj. Unlimited; indefinite; immeasurable; infinite; beyond description.

از خود az khud, adv. Of one's own accord; voluntarily; spontaneously; suo moto.

از خود رفتہ ، از خویش رفتہ az khud raftah, az khwesh raftah, adv. Out of one's mind; distracted; absent minded; cracked; beside oneself.

از راہ az rāh, adv. By way of; apropos.

از روے az rūe, adv. By virtue of; by reason of; under the circumstances.

از سر تا پا az sar tā pā, adv. From head to foot; completely perfectly; wholly.

از سر نو az sar-ĕ nau, adv. Anew; afresh; over again; de novo.

از غیب az ghaib, adj. Providential; God sent.

ازار izār (A) n.f. & n.m. Trousers; drawers.

ازار بند azār bañd, n.m. The string with which trousers are tied.

ازار بندی رشته azār-bañdi rishtah, n.m. Connection through wife; relatives of the wife; petti-coat interest.

ازاله izālah (A) n.m. Removal; annulling; revocation; abolition; purification; (in grammar) elision of a letter or of a vowel point from a word.

ازالۂ حیثیت عرفی izālah-ĕ ḥaiṣiyyat-ĕ 'urfi, n.m Robbing one of good name; defamation; libel.

ازاله کرنا izālah karnā, v. To remove one's difficulty; to compensate.

ازاں azāñ (P) adv. Thence; from among.

ازاں جمله azāñ jumlah, adv. Of that number; out of that whole; from among.

ازدحام izdiḥām (A) n.m. A concourse; a throng; a crowd; rushing together of people.

ازدواج izdiwāj (A) n.m. Matrimony; marriage; wedding.

ازدیاد izdiyād (A) n.m. Increase; enlargement; augmentation; extension.

ازرق azraq (A) adj. (wrongly spelt as ارزق arzaq) Blue; cerulean; blue-eyed; azure.

ازرق چشم azraq chashm, adj. Blue-eyed; having eyes like cat's.

ازل azal (A) n.f. Beginning; source; origin; eternity; without beginning.

ازلی azali (A) adj. Eternal; perpetual; from eternity.

ازلیت azaliyyat, (A) n.f. Eternal existence.

ازمنه azminah (A) n.m. (plu. of زمان zamān) Times; periods; ages.

ازمنه ثلاثه azminah-ĕ salāsah, n.m. The three times viz., the present, past and future.

ازواج azwāj (A) n.f. (plu. of زوج zauj) Spouses; couples; wives.

ازهر azhar (A) adj. Very bright or brilliant; a university in Egypt called jāmi'ah-ĕ Azhar.

اژدر ، اژدها azhdar, azhdahā (P) n.m. A dragon; a (winged) serpent; a large serpent; a boa.

اژدهات azhdhāt (P) n.f. Bell-metal; mixed metal.

اس is, pron. This.

اس اثنا میں is asnā meñ, adv. Meanwhile; in the meantime.

اس پر is par, adv. Upon this; on this.

اس پر بهی is par bhi, adv. Still; yet; notwithstanding; even on this; moreover.

اس دم is dam, adv. Presently; forthwith; immediately; directly.

اس طرح is ṭarah, adv. So; thus; in this manner.

اس قدر is qadr, adj. To this degree; as much as this; this much; so many; to this extent.

اس لئے is liye, conj. Hence; therefore; for this reason; so.

آس us, pron. That; it.

اساتذه asātizah (A) n.m. (plu. of أستاذ ustāz) Teachers; instructors; masters; lecturers.

اساڑه asāṛh (H) n.m. The third solar month of the Hindus corresponding to June-July.

اساڑهی asāṛhi (H) n.f. The summer harvest; day of the full moon in asāṛh.

اساس asās (A) n.f. Foundation; base; pedestal.

اساسی asāsi (A) adj. Basic; fundamental; essential.

اساطیر asāṭir (A) n.f. (plu. of اسطاره asṭārah or اسطوره asṭūrah) Stories; tales; fables.

اساطیرالاولین asāṭir-ul-awwalin, n.f. Stories of the ancient peoples.

اساطین asāṭin (A) n.m. (plu. of آسطوانه usṭuwānah) Pillars.

اسافل asāfil (A) adj. (plu. of اسفل asfal) Most mean; very mean (fellows).

اسالیب asālib (A) n.m. (plu. of اسلوب uslūb) Ways; styles; forms; modes.

اسامی **asāmī** (A) *n.f.* (*plu.* of اسم *ism*) Names; appointment; post; cultivator; tenant; customer; client.

اسامی دخیل کار **asāmī-ĕ dak͟hīl-ĕ kār**, *n.f.* An occupancy tenant.

اسامی شکمی **asāmī-ĕ shikamī**, *n.f.* A sub-tenant; a subordinate cultivator.

اسامی موروثی **asāmi-ĕ maurūṣī**, *n.f.* A hereditary tenant.

اساوری **asāwarī** (H) *n.f.* A musical tune. *n.m.* A kind of pigeon; a kind of silk and silver cloth.

اسباب **asbāb** (A) *n.m.* (*plu.* of سبب *sabab*). Causes; motives; means; reasons; goods and chattels; effects; baggage; luggage.

اسباب جنگ **asbāb-ĕ jang**, *n.m.* Causes of war; arms and ammunition; armament.

اسباب خانه داری **asbāb-ĕ k͟hānahdārī**, *n.m.* Household effects.

اسباط **asbāṭ** (A) *n.m.* (*plu.* of سبط *sibṭ*) Grandchildren; tribes (especially of Israel).

اسپ **asp** (P) *n.m.* A horse; the knight at chess.

اسپی طاقت **aspi ṭāqat**, *n.f.* Horse power.

اسپات **aspāt**, *n.m.* Steel

اسپتال **aspatāl**, *n.m.* (*corr.* from English) Hospital.

اسپغول **ispag͟hol** (P) *n.m.* Seeds of fleawort or plantain.

اسپنج **ispanj** (E) *n.m.* Sponge.

اسپند **ispand** (P) *n.m.* Seeds of wild rue, burnt on ceremonial occasions (to drive away evil spirits).

آستاد **ustād** (P) *n.m.* Teacher; tutor; instructor; a preceptor; an expert; an adept; an artist; a clever or cunning person.

استادگی **istādagī** (P) *n.f.* Standing; rising; erection; resistance; firmness.

استاده **istādah** (P) *adj.* Standing; erected; set up; a prop for supporting the door of a tent.

آستادی **ustādī** (P) *n.f.* Instruction; training; tutorship; skilfulness; ingenuity; mastery; dexterity; skill; workmanship; tactics.

استنبول، استامبول **istāmbol, istanbol** (T) *n.m.* Constantinople.

آستانی **ustānī**, *n.f.* Woman teacher; a mistress; wife of a teacher.

استبداد **istibdād** (A) *n.m.* Tyranny; absolute dominion; despotism; insisting upon a thing being done.

استثناء **istiṣnā'** (A) *n.m.* Exception; exclusion; exemption.

استثنائی **istiṣnā'ī** (A&P) *adj.* Exceptional.

استحاله **istiḥālah** (A) *n.m.* Change of state; undergoing a change; being impossible or absurd.

استحباب **istiḥbāb** (A) *n.m.* Contracting friendship; an action, the performance of which is meritorious but the omission of it is not an offence; work of supererogation.

استحسان **istiḥsān** (A) *n.m.* Approval; praising; taking or considering as a favour.

استحصال **istiḥṣāl** (A) *n.m.* Acquisition; desire to gain or acquire.

استحصال بالجبر **istiḥṣāl biljabr**, *n.m.* Extortion; unlawful exaction.

استحقاق **istiḥqāq** (A) *n.m.* Right; demanding as a right; due; title; merit; ability.

استحقاق امتناع **istiḥqāq-ĕ imtinā'**, *n.m.* A right of veto.

استحقاق انفکاک رهن **istiḥqāq-ĕ infikāk-ĕ rihn**, *n.m.* Right of redemption of a mortgage.

استحقاق ترکه **istiḥqāq-ĕ tarkah**, *n.m.* Right of succession or inheritance.

استحقاق حفاظت خود اختیاری **istiḥqāq-ĕ ḥifāẓat-ĕ k͟hud ik͟htiyārī**, *n.m.* Right of self-defence or protection.

استحقاق حین حیات **istiḥqāq-ĕ ḥīn-ĕ ḥayāt**, *n.m.* A life interest.

استحقاق دائمی **istiḥqāq-ĕ dā'imī**, *n.m.* A permament right or tenure.

استحقاق ذاتی **istiḥqāq-ĕ ẕātī**, *n.m.* Personal interest or privilege.

استحقاق شفع *istiḥqāq-ĕ shufa'*, *n.m.* A pre-emption right or title.

استحقاق قبضه *istiḥqāq-ĕ qabẓah*, *n.m.* Right of ownership or possession.

استحقاق مالكانه *istiḥqāq-ĕ mālikānah*, *n.m.* Proprietory right.

استحقاق مرتهنی *istiḥqāq-ĕ murtahinī*, *n.m.* A mortgage right or title.

استحقاق نالش *istiḥqāq-ĕ nālish*, *n.m.* A right to sue.

استحقاق وراثت *istiḥqāq-ĕ wirās̤at*, *n.m.* Right to inheritance.

استحکام *istiḥkām* (A) *n.m.* Stability; strengthening; fastness; strength; firmness.

استخاره *istik͟hārah* (A) *n.m.* Seeking to obtain the divine favour; looking into the Holy Book for a good augury; judging from omens.

استخراج *istik͟hrāj* (A) *n.m.* Expulsion; banishment; extradition; ejection; taking out; removal; drawing forth.

استخفاف *istik͟hfāf* (A) *n.m.* Holding in contempt; despising; vilifying; making light of.

استخلاص *istik͟hlāṣ* (A) *n.m.* Liberation; release; freedom; liberty; discharge.

اُستخوان *ustuk͟hwān* (P) *n.m.* A bone; the stone of fruits.

استدراج *istidrāj* (A) *n.m.* An abnormal or unusual action performed by an unscrupulous person or an infidel.

استدراک *istidrāk* (A) *n.m.* Comprehension; comprehending; understanding.

استدعاء *istid'ā'* (A) *n.f.* Request; prayer; petition; entreaty; solicitation; supplication; desire.

استدلال *istidlāl* (A) *n.m.* Proof; argument; reasoning; demonstration.

استدلال کرنا *istidlāl karnā*, *v.* To argue; to reason out; to prove.

استر *astar* (P) *n.m.* Lining.

استر کاری *astar kārī*, *n.f.* Coating; plastering.

استر کاری کرنا *astar kārī karnā*, *v.* To coat; to plaster.

استراحت *istirāḥat* (A) *n.f.* Peace; relief; repose; sleep; rest; ease; tranquility.

استرداد *istirdād* (A) *n.m.* Rejection; annulling; reversal; revocation; repeal; setting aside.

استرداد نیلام *istirdād-ĕ nilām*, *n.m.* Setting aside an auction.

استرضاء *istirẓā'* (A) *n.f.* Assent; willingness; consent; alacrity.

اُستره *ustarah* (P) *n.m.* A razor.

استری *istrī* (H) *n f.* Woman; wife.

استری *istrī*, *n.f.* A smoothing iron.

استری کرنا *istrī karnā*, *v.* To smooth with an iron; to iron.

استسقاء *istisqā'* (A) *n.m.* Dropsy; a disease in which water fluid collects in cavities or tissues of the body.

استشهاد *istishhād* (A) *n.m.* Summoning witnesses; producing evidence or proof; sacrificing life for religion; martyrdom.

استصواب *istiṣwāb* (A) *n.m.* Consulting regarding what is right or proper; consultation; reference; referendum.

استصواب کرنا *istiṣwāb karnā*, *v.* To make an enquiry; to consult; to refer.

استطاعت *istiṭā'at* (A) *n.f.* Competency; power; ability; potentiality.

استعاره *isti'ārah* (A) *n.m.* A metaphor; figurative expression; using a word metaphorically.

استعانت *isti'ānat* (A) *n.f.* Praying for help; soliciting aid; assistance; succour.

استعجاب *isti'jāb* (A) *n.m.* Surprise; wonder; astonishment.

استعداد *isti'dād* (A) *n.m.* Capacity; qualification; competency; talent; ability; readiness; proficiency; aptitude; dexterity.

استعفاء *isti'fā'* (A) *n.m.* Resignation; asking pardon or forgiveness.

استعفاء دینا *isti'fā' denā*, *v.* To resign (an office).

استعلاء *isti'lā'* (A) *n.m.* Superiority; exaltation; supremacy; seeking promotion.

استعمار *isti'mār* (A) *n.m.* Colonization; settlement.

استعماری *isti'māri, adj. & n.m.* Colonial; colonist.

استعماری طاقتیں *isti'māri ṯāqateṅ, n.f.* Colonial powers.

استعماریت *isti'māriyyat* (A) *n.f.* Colonialism.

استعمال *isti'māl* (A) *n.m.* Use; application; exercise; custom; usage.

استعمال کرنا *isti'māl karnā, v.* To make use of; to employ.

استغاثہ *istighāṣah* (A) *n.m.* Demanding justice or help; suit; complaint.

استغاثہ دائر کرنا *istighāṣah dā'ir karnā, v.* To file a suit.

استغراق *istighrāq* (A) *n.m.* Absorption; engrossment; īmmersion; drowning.

استغفار *istighfār* (A) *n.m.* Asking forgiveness; craving grace or mercy; begging pardon; penitence.

استغفار کرنا *istighfār karnā, v.* To seek forgiveness of God; to beg pardon; to crave mercy.

استغفراللہ *astaghfirullah* (A) *int.* I ask forgiveness of God; May God forgive me! (an expression signifying negation: God forbid!).

استغناء *istighnā'* (A) *n.m.* Above want; content; self-sufficiency; freedom from care.

استفادہ *istifādah* (A) *n.m.* Seeking gain or advantage: attainment; profit; gain; advantage.

استفتاء *istiftā'* (A) *n.m.* Seeking legal advice (in religious matters); consulting a lawyer or a learned man.

استفسا *istifsār* (A) *n.m.* Searching for information; inquiry; reference; interrogation.

استفسار کرنا *istifsār karnā, v.* To call for information; to interrogate; to make a reference; to inquire; to ask.

استفہام *istifhām* (A) *n.m.* Seeking information; demanding an explanation; desiring to understand; enquiry; investigation; (*Tech.*) a sign of interrogation(?)

استفہامیہ *istifhāmiyyah* (A) *adj.* Interrogative.

استقامت *istiqāmat* (A) *n.f.* Standing straight or erect; uprightness; rectitude; steadiness; stability; firmness; constancy; residence.

استقبال *istiqbāl* (A) *n.m.* Reception; welcoming a visitor; future (tense); futurity.

استقبال کرنا *istiqbāl karnā, v.* To receive; to welcome.

استقرار *istiqrār* (A) *n.m.* Settlement; establishment; stopping of a place.

استقرارحقیت *istiqrār-ē ḥaqqiyyat, n.m.* Declaration of title.

استقراء *istiqrā'* (A) *n.m.* Searching; following; reasoning from induction.

استقلال *istiqlāl* (A) *n.m.* Steadfastness; constancy; stability; steadiness; fortitude; resolution; firmness; self-determination; preservance; absolute power; sovereignity; independence.

استکبار *istikbār* (A) *n.m.* Haughtiness; vainglory; presumption; pride; conceit.

استکراہ *istikrah* (A) *n.m.* Dislike; aversion; repugnance; abhorrence; reluctance.

استکشاف *istikshāf* (A) *n.m.* Disclosure; revelation; manifestation or exposition (of anything).

استماع *istimā'* (A) *n.m.* Hearing; listening (to music); listening.

استمداد *istimdād* (A) *n.m.* Soliciting aid; asking help; begging assistance.

استمرار *istimrār* (A) *n.m.* Continuance; repetition; perpetuity; uninterrupted possession; perseverance.

استمراردار *istimrār dār, n.m.* Permanent tenure-holder; the holder of a perpetual lease.

استمراری *istimrāri* (A) *adj.* Uninterrupted; lasting; perpetual; continuative.

استمراری بندوبست *istimrāri bandobast, n.m.* Permanent settlement.

استمراری پٹا **istimrārī paṭṭā, n.m.** A perpetual lease.

استمراری جمع **istimrārī jam', n.f.** Fixed assessment of rent.

استنباط **istimbāṭ (A) n.m.** Deduction; drawing out; extraction; selection.

استنباط کرنا **istimbāṭ karnā, v.** To draw forth; to extract; to deduce.

استنجاء **istinjā' (A) n.m.** Washing or cleaning the private parts after a natural evacuation.

استنشاق **istinshāq (A) n.m.** Smelling (odours, etc.); sniffing water up the nostrils when performing *wuẓū* (ablutions for prayers).

استواء **istiwā' (A) n.m.** Parity; equality.

آستوار **ustuwār (P) adj.** Strong; powerful; solid; compact; stable; firm.

آستواری **ustuwārī (P) n.f.** Strength; firmness; stability; permanence.

استهان **asthān (H) n.m.** Place; abode; situation; a hermit's residence.

استهزاء **istihzā' (A) n.m.** Laughing at; derision; ridicule, mockery; scorn; scoff; jest; joke.

استهزاء کرنا **istihzā' karnā, v.** To laugh at; to mock; to deride.

استیصال **istiṣāl (A) n.m.** Uprooting; eradication; demolition; destruction; devastation; extermination.

استیلاء **istilā' (A) n.m.** Domination; mastery; superiority; supermacy; predominence.

اسٹیشن **isteshun (E) n.m.** Station (as a railway or police station).

اسٹام ، اشٹام **isṭām, ishṭām, n.m.** (*corr.* from English). A non-judicial stamped paper.

اسحاق **Isḥāq (A) n.m.** Isaac the Prophet.

اسد **asad (A) n.m.** Lion; (*Astro.*) Leo, the fifth sign of the zodiac.

اسداللہ **Asadullah, n.m.** The lion of God; an appellation of Hazrat Ali.

اسرار **asrār (A) n.m.** (*plu.* of سر *sirr*) Secrets; hidden or mysterious matter.

اسراف **isrāf (A) n.m.** Waste; extravagance; abuse of wealth; squandering; prodigality; dissipation; profusion.

اسرافیل **isrāfīl (A) n.m.** Name of an angel who will sound the last trumpet on the Day of Resurrection.

اسرائیل **isrā'īl (A) n.m.** (*Lit.* One chosen by God), a servant of God; the surname of Jacob, the Prophet; Isreal.

اسرائیلی **Isrā'īlī (A) n.m. & adj.** The Jews; followers of Moses; descendants of Jacob; concerning Isreal.

آسطرلاب **usṭarlāb (G) n.m.** An astrolabe; instruments for taking altitudes.

آسطوخودوس **usṭūkhūd-dūs (G) n.m.** A kind of grass whose flowers are used as medicine:

اسفار **asfār (A) n.m.** (*plu.* of سفر *safar*) Voyages; travels; advantures.

اسفل **asfal (A) adj.** (*sup.* of سافل *sāfil*) Very mean; very low; very inferior; nethermost.

اسفل السافلین **asfal-us-sāfilīn, n.f.** The lowest hell; inferno.

اسفنج **isfanj.** See اسپنج *ispanj*.

اسفندیار **Isfandyār (P) prop. n.** Name of the son of *Gushtāsp*, a Persian King, whose body was supposed to be hard like steel.

اصفہان **Iṣfahān (P) n.m.** Ispahan, a city of Iran (Persia)—the capital of Persian Iraq (the ancient Parthia).

اسقاط **isqāṭ (A) n.m.** Causing to fall; miscarriage; abortion; procuring an abortion; elimination.

اسقام **asqām (A) n.m.** (*plu.* of سقم *suqm*) Weaknesses; defects; evils.

آسقف **usquf (A) n.m.** A bishop.

اسکندر **iskandar (A) n.m.** Alexander.

اسکول **iskūl (E) n.m.** School.

اسلاف **aslāf (A) n.m.** (*plu.* of سلف *salaf*) Forefathers; ancestors; people of past time; ancients.

اسلام **Islām (A) n.m.** (*Lit.* Submission to God); the Muslim religion; Islam.

اسلامی **Islāmī (A) adj.** Concerning Islam; Muslim.

اسلحہ **aslihah** (A) *n.m.* (*plu.* of سلاح *silāḥ*). Arms; armour; weapons of war.

اسلحہ خانہ *aslihah-khānah*, *n.m.* Arsenal; armoury; a magazine.

اسلم **aslam** (A) *n.m.* (*sup.* of سالم *sālim*) Very safe; snake-bitten.

آسلوب **uslūb** (A) *n.m.* Way; style; manner; mode; method; form; shape; arrangement; order.

آسلوباً **uslūban** (A) *adj.* Methodically.

اسم **ism** (A) *n.m.* Name; denomination; appellation; (*Gram.*) a noun.

اسم استفہام *ism-ĕ istifhām* *n.m.* (*Gram.*) Interrogative Pronoun.

اسم اشارہ *ism-ĕ ishārah* *n.m.* (*Gram.*) Demonstrative Pronoun.

اسم اعظم *ism-ĕ a'zam*, *n.m.* Name of the Almighty God (regarded as the greatest name or attribute of God); one of the ninety-nine names or attributes of God the utterance of which casts an irresistible spell over evil spirits.

اسم بامسمیٰ *ism bā musammā*, *n.m.* A name fully denoting the qualities of the named person.

اسم تفضیل *ism-ĕ tafẓil*, *n.m.* An objective in comparative or superlative degree.

اسم جامد *ism-ĕ jāmid*, *n.m.* (*Gram.*) A Primitive Noun.

اسم جلالی *ism-ĕ jalāli*, *n.m.* The glorious name (of God).

اسم جنس *ism-ĕ jins*, *n.m.* (*Gram.*) Generic Noun; Noun Appellative..

اسم حالیہ *ism-ĕ ḥāliyyah*, *n.m.* (*Gram.*) The Present Participle.

اسم صفت *ism-ĕ ṣifat*, *n.m.* (*Gram.*) An Adjective.

اسم ضمیر *ism-ĕ ẓamir*, *n.m.* (*Gram.*) Personal Pronoun.

اسم فاعل *ism-ĕ fā'il*, *n.m.*(*Garm.*)The subject.

اسم فرضی *ism-ĕ farẓi*, *n.m.* Nom de plume; assumed name; fictitious name.

اسم معرفہ *ism-ĕ ma'rifah*, *n.m.* (*Gram.*) Proper Noun.

اسم مفعول *ism-ĕ maf'ūl*, *n.m.* (*Gram.*) The Passive Participle; the object.

اسم موصول *ism-ĕ mauṣūl*, *n.m.* (*Gram.*) Relative Pronoun.

اسم نکرہ *ism-ĕ nakrah*, *n.m.* (*Gram.*) Common Noun.

اسم نویسی *ism. nawisi*, *n.f.* A list or roll of names; a catalogue; enrolment; a register of entering names.

اسم وار *ism wār*, *adv.* Entry according to the order of individual names.

اسماء **asmā'** (A) *n.m.* (*plu.* of اسم *ism*) Names.

اسماء الرجال *asmā'-ur-rijāl*, *n.m.* Names of prominent men; names of persons who reported the Tradition of Prophet Muhammad; the art determining the authenticity of the persons reporting the Tradition.

اسماء حسنہ *asmā'-ĕ ḥasanah*, *n.m.* The ninety-nine names or attributes of God.'

اسمار **asmār** (A) *n.m.* (*plu.* of سمر *samar*) Tales related at night; nightly conversations.

اسماعیل **Ismā'il** (A) *n.m.* Ismael, the Prophet, son of Abraham.

اسماعیلیہ **Ismā'iliyyah** (A) *n.m.* A sect founded by Hasan bin Sabbah.

اسناد **asnād** (A) *n.m.* (*plu.* of سند *sanad*) Certificates; warrants; documents; testimonials; characters; deeds.

اسوج **asūj** (H) *n.m.* The sixth solar month of Hindus.

اسود **aswad** (A) *n.m.* Very black.

اسود و احمر *aswad-ŏ-aḥmar*, *n.m.* The Arabs and non-Arabs; the Black and the Red Seas.

آسوہ **uswah** (A) *n.m.* Model; example.

اسہال **ishāl** (A) *n.m.* Purging; looseness (of the bowels); diarrhoea.

اسہال دموی *ishāl-ĕ damvi*, *n.m.* Bloody flux; stools with blood.

اسہام ishām (A) n.m. Throwing of arrows to foretell events.

اسہل ashal (A) n.m. (sup. of سہل sahl) The easiest.

اسی assi (H) adj. Eighty.

اسیاف asyāf (A) n.m. (plu. of سیف saif) Swords. (plu. of سیف sif) Banks; shores.

اسیر asīr (A) n.m. Prisoner; captive.

اسیر سلطانی asīr-ĕ sulṭānī, n.m. A State prisoner.

اسیری asīrī (A&P) n.f. Imprisonment; captivity; incarceration.

اسیسر asesar (E) n.m. Assessor, one who gives his opinion in a criminal case before the Sessions Judge.

اسیس asīs (H) n.f. Blessing; prayer; benediction.

اشارات ishārāt (A) n.m. (plu. of اشارہ ishārah) Notes; hints; clues; signs; symbols.

اشارات میزانیہ ishārāt-ĕ mīzāniyyah, n.m. Budget notes.

اشارہ ishārah (P) n.m. Sign; gesture; token; symbol; wink; hint; suggestion; indication; gesticulation; signal; allusion.

اشارہ کرنا ishārah karnā, v. To make a sign; to beckon; to nod; to wink; to suggest; to indicate; to hint.

اشاری کارڈ ishārī cārḍ, n.m. Index card.

اشارے پر چلنا ishāre par chalnā, v. To be under one's control; to be at one's beck and call; to follow signs.

اشاریہ ishāriyyah (A) n.m Index.

اشاعت ishā'at (A) n.f. Circulation; publication; diffusion; propagation; dissemination; publicity; edition.

اشاعت العلوم ishā'at-ul-'ulūm, n.f. The diffusion of knowledge.

اشتباہ ishtibāh (A) n.m. Suspicion; doubt; ambiguity; distrust; scruple; mistake.

اشتداد ishtidād (A) n.m. Excess in violence; being hard on; abundance; plenty.

اشتر ushtur (P) n.m. A camel.

اشتراک ishtirāk (A) n.m. Partnership; company; fellowship; participation.

اشتراکی ishtirākī, n.m. A communist. adj. Communistic.

اشتراکیت ishtirākiyyat (A) n.f. Communism.

اشتراء ishtirā' (A) n.m. Buying and selling.

اشتعال ishti'āl (A) n.m. Provoking; inciting; provocation; inflaming; fomenting; exciting; instigating a quarrel; burning; blazing.

اشتعال طبع ishti'āl-ĕ ṭaba', n.m. Provocation.

اشتعالک ishti'ālak (A&P) n.f. A small blaze or flame; brawl; excitement; a quarrel.

اشتعالک دینا ishti'ālak denā, v. To foment (quarrels); to incite to bad actions; to instigate; to excite; to provoke.

اشتغال ishtighāl (A) n.m. Occupation; employment; avocation; pursuit; business.

اشتقاق ishtiqāq (A) n.m. Etymology; derivation (of one word from another).

اشتمال ishtimāl (A) n.m. Inclusion; comprising; containing.

اشتمال اراضی ishtimāl-ĕ arāẓī, n.m. Consolidation of land.

اشتمال بے جا ishtimāl-ĕ bejā, n.m. Misjoinder.

اشتمال بے جا الزامات ishtimāl-ĕ bejā ilzāmāt, n.m. Misjoinder of charges.

اشتمال دعوی ishtimāl-ĕ dā'wā, n.m. Joinder of causes of action.

اشتہار ishtihār (A) n.m. Notification; advertisement; announcement; proclamation; publication; notice; placard; poster; reputation; renown.

اشتہار آویزاں کرنا ishtihār āwezāṅ karnā, v. To put up or affix a placard; to Paste a notice on the board.

اشتہار دینا ishtihār denā, v. To advertise; to make known; to publish; to propagate; to circulate; to notify.

اشتہار قرق ishtihār-ĕ qurqī, n.m. Notice of attachment.

اشتہاری ishtihārī (A) adj. Pertaining tonotification, proclamation, etc. proclaimed (as an offender). n.m. An offender who has absconded; one who advertises (as a quack).

اشتہاء ishtihā' (A) n.m. Appetite; desire; wish; longing; hunger.

اشتیاق ishtiyāq (A) n.m. Longing; craving; yearning; desire; liking; fondness; eagerness; strong inclination.

اشٹمی ashṭamī (H) n.f. The eighth day of every lunar month.

اشجار ashjār (A) n.m. (plu. of شجر shajar) Trees.

اشخاص ashkhāṣ (A) n.m. (plu. of شخص shakhṣ) Persons; people; men.

اشد ashadd (A) adj. (sup. of شدید shadīd) Extreme; severe; violent; excessive; most vehement.

اشد ضروری ashadd ẓurūrī, adj. Most urgent.

اشد ضرورت ashadd ẓurūrat, n.f. Stark necessity.

اشدھ ashudh (S) adj. Unholy; corrupt; contaminated; not pure; opposite of شدھ shudh, holy.

اشر asharr (A) adj. (sup. of شریر sharīr) Very wicked; vicious; atrocious; flagitious.

اشر الناس ashar-run-nās, adj. The most wicked of men.

اشرار ashrār (A) n.m. (plu. of شریر sharīr) The wicked; criminal or seditious people.

اشراف ashrāf (A) n.m. (plu. of شریف sharīf) Noble men; gentlemen; men of high birth; men of culture.

اشرافیہ ashrāfiyah (A) n.f. Aristocracy.

اشراق ishrāq (A) n.m. Dawn; day break; lustre; brilliance; radiance.

نماز اشراق namāz-ĕ ishrāq, n.f. Prayer offered after day-break.

اشراقی ishrāqī (A) adj. Of or pertaining to sunrise; eastern; oriental; having the radiance of the east.

اشراقین ishrāqiyyīn (A) n.m. A sect of learned hermits who could impart education to their pupils from a distance by means of kashf (purification of heart from evil by austerity and devotion).

اشرف ashraf (A) adj. (sup. of شریف sharīf) Most noble; most distinguished; most eminent. n.m. A person of noble birth; a nobleman; a gentleman.

اشرف المخلوقات ashraf-ul-makhlūqāt, n.m. The most eminent of created things; men; mankind.

اشرف الناس ashraf-un-nās, n.m. Noblest of men; the Holy Prophet.

اشرفی ashrafī (P) n.f. A gold coin (once a legal tender in Indo-Pakistan sub-continent worth about Rs. 15/-); a guinea.

اشعار ash'ār (A) n.m. (plu. of شعر shi'r) Verses; couplets; distiches.

اشعاع ish'ā' (A) n.m Spreading the rays (sun).

اشعاعی علاج ash'ā'ī 'ilāj, n.m. Radiotherapy.

اشعریہ ash'ariyyah (A) n.m. A school of Islamic philosophers; the Asharites.

اشعہ ashi'ah (A) n.m. (plu. of شعاع shu'ā') Beams; rays of light.

اشعاعیات ash'ā'iyāt (A) n.f. Radiology.

اشعاعیات دان ash'ā'iyāt dān, n.m. Radiologist.

اشغال ashghāl (A) n.m. (plu. of شغل shughl) Engagement; occupations; employments; recreations.

اشفاق ashfāq (A) n.m. (plu. of شفق shafaq) Favours; kindnesses.

اشفاق ishfāq (A) n.m. Compassion; kindness; tenderness.

اشقیاء ashqiyā' (A) n.m. (plu. of شقی shaqī) Cruel; heartless; miserable; wretched.

اشک ashk (P) n.m. A tear; tears.

اشک افشاں ashk afshān, adj. Shedding tears.

اشک بار ashk bār, adj. Weeping; shedding tears.

اشک باری ashk bāri, *n.f.* Weeping.

اشک شوئی ashk sho'ī, *n.f.* Wiping away tears; consoling; comforting; soothing.

سیل اشک sail-ĕ ashk, *n.m.* A flood of tears.

اشکال ashkāl (A) *n.f.* (*plu.* of شکل shakl) Forms; shapes; likeness; appearanceses. (*Math.*) Figures; propositions.

اشکال ishkāl (A) *n.m.* Ambiguity; difficulty; perplexity; obstruction.

اشکالی ishkāli, *adj.* Creating doubts or difficulties.

اشلوک ashlok (H) *n.m.* Verse; distich; couplet; poem.

اشنان ashnān (H) *n.m.* Bathing; ablution; purification; a bathing fair.

اشوک ، اشوکا Ashok, Ashokā (S) *adj.* At ease; unmolested. *n.m.* Ease; peace; cheerfulness; tranquillity; name of a plant (jonesia asoca); a famous Buddhist King of India.

اشوکا اشٹمی Ashokā ashtamī, *n.m.* The eighth day in the first half of the month of *Chait*, when a festival in honour of Vishnu is observed and water is drunk with the buds of Asoka (jonesia asoca) in it.

اشہاد ashhād (A) *n.m.* (*plu.* of شاہد shāhid) Witnesses; eye-witnesses; deponents; those who were present at a transaction.

اشہاد ishhād (A) *n.m.* Bringing proof; producing evidence; taking (some one) to witness.

اشہب ashhab (A) *adj.* Dull grey; dun coloured; drab; of dull black and white colour in which the white prevails. *n.m.* A dun coloured horse, camel or mule.

اشہد ashhadu (A) *v.* (Ist per. pres. tense) I bear witness; I testify; I declare.

اشہد ان لا الہ الا اللہ ashhadu ān lā ilāhā illallāh. I bear witness (or I declare) that there is no God except Allah.

اشہر ashhar (A) *adj.* (*sup.* of شہیر shahir) More or most celebrated or known. *n.m.* (*plu.* of شہر shahr) Months.

اشیاء ashyā' (A) *n.f.* (*plu.* of شے shai) Goods; things; chattels; articles.

اشیاء خورد و نوش ashyā'-ĕ khūrd-ŏ nosh, *n.f.* Provisions; eatables.

اشیاء آبکاری ashyā'-ĕ ābkārī. Excisable articles.

اشیاء صرف ashyā'-ĕ ṣarf, *n.m.* Consumer's goods.

اصابت iṣābat (A) *n.f.* Access; approach; maturity; solidity.

اصالت iṣālat (A) *n.f.* Soundness; integrity; genuineness; stability; nobleness; purity of blood; effect of heredity, origin or root.

اصالتاً iṣālatan (A) *adv.* Originally; primarily; in person; radically; firmly; entirely; absolutely.

اصح aṣaḥḥ (A) *adj.* (*sup.* of صحیح ṣaḥih) Most correct.

اصحاب aṣḥāb (A) *n.m.* (*plu.* of صاحب ṣāḥib) Companions; friends; comrades; lords; masters; apostles.

اصحاب علم aṣḥāb-ĕ 'ilm, *n.m.* Learned people.

اصحاب فیل aṣḥāb-ĕ fil, *n.m.* Masters of elephants; (refers to) the army of Abraha-bin-Sabah, ruler of Yaman, which came on elephants to attack Mecca and to destroy Kaaba, but Divine punishment annihilated them all.

اصحاب کہف aṣḥāb-ĕ kahf, *n.m.* Companions of the cave; (refers to) a number of pious men (five, seven or nine) still sleeping in the den of the Pamir Desert, to save themselves from the tyranny of the heretic ruler and fell asleep there.

اصحاب نبی aṣḥāb-ĕ nabi, *n.m.* Companions of the Holy Prophet.

اصرار iṣrār (A) *n.m.* Obduracy; persistence; perseverance, especially in something (bad); obstinacy.

اصراف aṣrāf (A) n.m. (plu. of صرف ṣarf) Lavish expenditure.

اسراف iṣrāf (A) n.m. Expense; expenditure.

اصطباغ iṣṭibāgh (A) n.m. Colouring; imbuing; staining; dipping; immersion; baptism.

اصطبل aṣṭabal (A) n.m. A stable.

اصطرلاب uṣṭarlāb (G) n.m. An astrolabe; an instrument for measuring altitudes and distances of the sun and stars now superseded by Hadley's quadrant and sextant.

اصطفاء iṣṭifā' (A) n.f. Selection; choice; choosing.

اصطلاح iṣṭilāḥ (A) n.f. Technical term; phrase; idiom; conventional meaning.

اصطلاحات iṣṭilāḥāt (A) n.f. (plu. of اصطلاح iṣṭilaḥ) Technical terms; phraseology; terminology; idioms.

اصطلاحی iṣṭilāḥi (A) adj. Idiomatical; technical; phraseological.

اصطلاحی معنی iṣṭilāḥī ma'na, n.m. Idiomatic meanings; conventional or secondary meaning.

اصغر asghar (A) adj. (sup. of صغیر ṣaghīr) Smallest; youngest.

اصفار aṣfār (A) n.m. (plu. of صفر ṣifr) Ciphers; zeros.

اصفر aṣfar (A) adj. Yellow; saffron-coloured.

اصفیاء aṣfiyā' (A) adj. (plu. of صفی ṣafi) The pure; the holy; the elect; the saints.

اصل aṣl (A) n.f. Root; origin; foundation; cause; essence; reality; fact; race; lineage; stock; capital; principal sum; stock in trade. adj. Essential; vital; fundamental; important.

اصل اخراجات aṣl ikhrājāt, n.m. Actual expenses.

اصل اصول aṣl-ĕ uṣūl, n.m. The fundamental principal; basic laws.

اصل السوس aṣl-us-sūs, n.f. Root of liquorice.

اصل مع سود aṣl m'a sūd, n.m. Principal with interest.

اصل نفع aṣ! nafa', n.m. Net profit.

اصل و فرع aṣl-ŏ fara', n.m. Root and branch; cause and effect.

اصلا ، اصلاً aṣlā, aṣlan (A) adv. In reality; somehow; ever; always; just a little; nominal; entirelly; wholly.

اصلاً مطلقاً aṣlan muṭlaqan, adv. By no means; never; not at all.

اصلاح Iṣlāḥ (A) n.f. Rectification; amendment; revision; correction; mending; improvement; trimming the beard.

اصلاح پذیر iṣlāḥ pazīr, adj. Capable of being set right; remediable.

اصلاح دینا یا کرنا iṣlāḥ denā yā karnā, v. To correct; to amend; to reform; to rectify; to make better; to revise.

اصلاح مذہبی iṣlāḥ-ĕ mazhabi, n.f. Religious reformation.

اصلح aṣlaḥ (A) adj. (sup. of صالح ṣāliḥ) Best; most virtuous or righteous; most correct; most advisable.

اصلی aṣli (A) adj. Original; actual; primordial; fundamental; unmixed; natural; real; right; genuine; radical; noble; of good or noble breed.

اصلیت aṣliyyat (A) n.f. Origin; purity; genuineness; authenticity; actuality.

اصمعی aṣm'ai (A) n. prop. The famous Arab writer, whose name was Abu Said Abdul Malak-bin-Qarib.

اصناف aṣnāf (A) n.f. (plu. of صنف ṣinf) Kinds; species; varieties.

اصنام aṣnām (A) n.m. (plu. of صنم ṣanam) Idols.

اصوات aṣwāt (A) n.f. (plu. of صوت ṣaut) Voices; sounds; noises.

آصول uṣūl (A) n.m. (plu. اصل aṣl) Roots; fundamentals; principles; rules; laws; doctrines.

اصول متعارفہ uṣūl-ĕ muta'ārifah, n.m. Self-evident truths; axioms.

اصول موضوعہ uṣūl-ĕ mauẓū'ah, n.m. Postulates; self-evident problems; accepted facts.

اصول و فروع uṣūl-ŏ furū', n.m. Roots and branches; causes and effects.

اصیل aṣil (A) *adj.* Of good stock; of good family; well-born; noble; genuine. *n.f.* A maid-servant.

اضافت iẓāfat (A) *n.f.* Addition; reference; adjunct; (*Gram.*) prefixing a noun to a noun so that the former governs the latter in the genetive case e.g., غلام زید *ghulām-ĕ Zaīd*, the slave of Zaīd.

اضافه iẓāfah (A) *n.m.* Addition; annexation; augmentation; enlargement; enhancement; excess; increment.

اضافه لگان *iẓāfah-ĕ lagān*, *n.m.* Enhancement of revenue or rent.

اضافی iẓāī (A) *adj.* Additional; relative; (*Gram*) Relative pronoun.

اضافی پولیس *iẓāfī polīs*, *n.f.* Additional police.

اضافیه iẓāfiyyah (A) *n.m.* Addendum.

اضحیٰ aẓḥā (A) *n.f.* Sacrifice.

اضحوکه uẓḥūkah (A) *n.m.* A laughing-stock; comical thing.

اضداد aẓdād (A) *n.f.* (*plu.* of ضد *ẓid*) Opposites.

اضطراب iẓṭirāb (A) *n.m.* Restlessness; distraction; perturbation; chagrin; disturbance; commotion; vexation; anxiety.

اضطرار iẓṭirār (A) *n.m.* Helplessness; constraint; perturbation; agitation.

اضعاف iẓ'āf (A) *n.m.* Multiplying; doubling.

اضعف aẓ'af (A) *adj.* (*sup.* of ضعیف *ẓa'īf*) Very feeble; very weak or helpless.

اضغاث aẓghāṣ (A) *n.m.* Bundles of vegetables.

اضغاث احلام *aẓghāṣ-ĕ aḥlām*, *n.m.* Bad dreams having no interpretation or explanation; meaningless nightmares.

أضلاع aẓlā' (A) *n.m.* (*plu.* of ضلع *ẓil'a*) Districts; division of land; (*Anat.*) ribs; (*Math.*) sides (of a figure).

اضمار iẓmār (A) *n.m.* Use of pronoun in place of noun.

اضمار قبل الذکر *iẓmār qabl-uẓ-ẓikr*, *n m.* Use of a pronoun before the noun is mentioned.

اضمحلال iẓmiḥlāl (A) *n.m.* Weakness; dejection; depression; prostration; indolence.

اطاعت iṭā'at (A) *n.f.* Obedience; submission; subordination; reverence; worship; homage.

اطاعت کرنا *iṭā'at karnā*, *v.* To obey; to submit; to serve; to serve; to pay homage (to); to worship.

اطال الله عمره ' aṭal-allaho 'umrahu (A) *interj.* May he live long; may God grant him long life.

اطالیه Aṭālīyah (A) *n.m.* Italy.

اطباء aṭibbā' (A) *n.m.* (*plu.* of طبیب *ṭabīb*) Physicians; doctors.

اطراف aṭrāf (A) *n.f.* (*plu.* of طرف *ṭaraf*) Sides; ends; environs; confines; outskirts; limits; suburbs; extremities; outposts; boundaries; borders.

اطراف و اکناف *aṭrāf-ō aknāf*, *n.f.* All sides; all over.

اطراف شهر *aṭrāf-ĕ shehr*, *n.f.* Suburbs; outskirts; environs of a city or town.

اطریفل iṭrīfal (A) *n.m.* A compound medicine made with *haṛ*, *baheṛā* and *āmlah*.

اطفال aṭfāl (A) *n.m.* (*plu.* of طفل *ṭifl*) Children; offspring; issues

اطلاع iṭṭilā' (A) *n.f.* Notice; information; communication; report; notification; announcement.

اطلاع حاضری *iṭṭilā'-ĕ ḥāẓirī*, *n.f.* Joining report.

اطلاع دینا یا کرنا *iṭṭilā' denā yā karnā*, *v.* To intimate; to communicate; to apprize; to acquaint; to report; to inform.

اطلاع موصولی *iṭṭilā'-ĕ mauṣūlī*, *n.f.* Acknowledgment of receipt or intimation.

اطلاع نامه *iṭṭilā' namah*, *n.m.* A written notice; summons or citation; notification.

اطلاع یابی *iṭṭilā' yābī*, *n.f.* The act of receiving information; receipt or acknowledgment of notice, &c.

اطلاعاً iṭṭilā'ṉ (A) *adv.* By way of intimation or notification; by way of notice.

اطلاق iṭlāq (A) n.m. Application; reference; setting at liberty; freedom; disengagement.

اطلاق کرنا iṭlāq karnā, v. To apply (to); to use (in a particular sense); to appertain.

اطلس aṭlas (A) n.f. Satin.

اطلسی aṭlasi, adj. Made of satin.

اطمینان iṭmīnān (A) n.m. Quiet; comfort; repose; tranquillity; calmness; composure; satisfaction; consolation; contentment; security.

اطمینان خاطر یا قلب iṭmīnān-ĕ khāṭir yā qalb, n.m. Peace of mind; thorough satisfaction.

اطمینان کرنا iṭmīnān karnā, v. To satisfy; to feel assured; to get assurance.

اطناب iṭnāb (A) n.m. Profuseness of speech.

اطنه aṭnah (G) n.m. Athens; the capital of Greece.

اطوار aṭwār (A) n.m. (plu. of طور ṭaur) Manners; modes; behaviour; habits; ways; conduct; deportment.

اطهر aṭhar (A) adj. (sup. of طاهر ṭāhir) Very pious.

اظلم aẓlam (A) adj. (sup. of ظالم ẓālim) Most cruel; very tyranical.

اظهار iẓhār (A) n.m. Disclosure; proclamation; deposition; testimony; manifestation; demonstration; publication; display; declaration; expression; statement.

اظهار حلفی iẓhār-ĕ ḥalfi, n.m. A deposition on oath; evidence on oath.

اظهار دینا iẓhār denā, v. To make a deposition or a statement; to depose; to swear; to give evidence.

اظهار کرنا iẓhār karnā, v. To give expression (to); to unfold; to announce; to disclose; to reveal; to notify; to declare.

اظهار لینا iẓhār lenā, v. To examine; to put one in the witness box.

اظهار نامه iẓhār nāmah, n.m. Notification; an announcement; manifesto.

اظهار نویس iẓhār nawis, n.m. A statement writer; a deposition writer.

اظهر aẓhar (A) adj. (sup. of ظاهر ẓāhar) Very clear; very evident; very plain; most apparent.

اظهر من الشمس aẓhar min-ash-shams, adj. Absolutely clear; (Lit. As clear as the sun).

اعاده i'ādah (A) n.m. Doing a thing second time; repetition; return; revising.

اعانت i'ānat (A) n.f. Help; aid; assistance; support; patronage.

اعانت مجرمانه i'ānat-ĕ mujrimānah, n.f. Abetment of an offence.

اعانت بمشوره i'ānat bamashwarah, n.f. Abetment by conspiracy.

اعتبار i'tibār (A) n.m. Confidence; trust; faith; belief; credence; reliance; respect; esteem.

اعتبار رکھنا یا کرنا i'tibār rakhnā yā karnā, v. To believe; to trust; to rely (on); to confide in; to give credit to.

اعتبار کھونا i'tibār khonā, v. To lose credit or confidence.

اعتباری i'tibārī, adj. Trustworthy, worth of confidence; creditable; reliable.

اعتدال i'tidāl (A) n.m. Moderation; temperateness; equilibrium; mean.

اعتدال پر رهنا i'tidāl par rahnā, v. To observe moderation; to follow the happy mean.

اعتذار i'tizār (A) n.m. Apology; excuse.

اعتذار نامه i'tizār nāmah, n.m. A letter of apology.

اعتراض i'tirāẓ (A) n.m. Objection; fault finding; criticism; protest; resistance; opposition; refusing assent; animadversion.

اعتراض رفع کرنا i'tirāẓ rafa' karnā, v. To dispose of an objection.

اعتراض ضابطه i'tirāẓ-ĕ ẓābṭah, n.m. A technical objection.

اعتراض قانونی i'tirāẓ-ĕ qānūnī, n.m. A legal objection.

اعتراض کرنا *i'tirāẓ karnā*, *v.* To object; to criticise; to protest (against); to take exception (to); to urge an objection; to dispute; to call in question; to lodge an objection.

اعتراف *i'tirāf* (A) *n.m.* Confession; acknowledgement; avowal; recognition; admission.

اعتراف کرنا *i'tirāf karnā*, *v.* To acknowledge; to avow; to confess; to admit; to own.

اعتزال *i'tizāl* (A) *n.m.* Secession; abdication; abjuration; withdrawing from office.

اعتصام *i'tiṣām* (A) *n.m.* Abstaining from sin in obedience to God's will; refraining from what is illegal; grasping; clawing; catching hold of anything for defence.

اعتقاد *i'tiqād* (A) *n.m.* Faith; belief; confidence; credence; trust.

اعتقاد رکھنا *i'tiqād rakhnā*, *v.* To place confidence in; to keep faith; to believe (in).

اعتقاد لانا *i'tiqād lānā*, *v.* To evince faith in; to believe; to become convert (to).

اعتقادی *i'tiqādī* (A) *adj.* Pertaining to faith.

اعتکاف *i'tikāf* (A) *n.m.* Retirement to a mosque for a continuing prayer; retirement for God worship; restraining passions from religious motives; self-control.

اعتماد *i'timād* (A) *n.m.* Reliance; trust; dependence; confidence; faith.

اعتماد رکھنا یا کرنا *i'timād rakhnā yā karnā*, *v.* To place confidence in; to rely on; to depend upon.

اعتمادی *i'timādī*, *adj.* Trustworthy (person); one in whom confidence is placed; reliable (person).

اعتناء *i'tinā'* (A) *n.f.* Solicitude; uneasiness; care; taking pains; heed; sympathy; concern.

اعجاز *i'jāz* (A) *n.m.* Miracle; astonishment; marvel; wonder.

اعجاز بیانی *i'jāz bayānī*, *n.f.* Eloquence; fluency of speech.

اعجاز مسیحائی *i'jāz-ě masīḥāī'*, *n.m.* A wonderful cure; a cure as miraculous as the cures of the Messiah.

اعجوبہ *u'jūbah* (A) *n.m.* Wonder; miracle; prodigy; a marvel.

اعداء *a'dā'* (A) *n.m.* (*plu.* of عدو *'adū*) Enemies.

اعداد *a'dād* (A) *n.m.* (*plu.* of عدد *'adad*) Numbers; figures.

اعداد و شمار *a'dād-ŏ shumār*, *n.m.* Statistics.

اعدل *a'dal* (A) *adj.* (*sup.* of عادل *'ādil*) Very just.

اعراب *a'rāb* (A) *n.m.* (*plu.*) Beduoins; nomadic tribes of Arabia; Arabs.

اعراب *i'rāb* (A) *n.m.* The vowel or diacritical points.

اعرابی *a'rābī* (A) *n.m.* A bedouin; an Arab of the desert.

اعراض *i'rāẓ* (A) *n.m.* Turning away (from); avoidance; shunning; aversion; dislike.

اعراض کرنا *i'rāẓ karnā*, *v.* To turn away from; to avoid; to dislike.

اعراف *a'rāf* (A) *n.m.* Purgatory; (according to Muslims) a place intervening between heaven and hell.

اعزاز *ī'zāz* (A) *n.m.* Exalting; honouring; esteem; respect; honour.

اعزازی *i'zāzī*, *adj.* Honorary; complimentary.

اعزازیہ *i'zāziyah*, *n.m.* Honorarium; a party held in honour (of).

اعزہ *a'izzah* (A) *n.m.* (*plu.* of عزیز *'aziz*) Relatives; dear ones; most dear.

اعصاب *a'ṣāb* (A) *n.m.* (*plu.* of عصب *'aṣab*) Muscles; nerves.

اعضاء *a'ẓā'* (A) *n.m.* (*plu.* of عضو *'uẓv*) Limbs; members of the body; organs.

اعضاء رئیسہ *a'ẓā'-ě ra'īsah*, *n.m.* The principal parts of the body; vital parts (i.e., heart, brain, liver, etc.); organs.

اعضاء شکنی *a'ẓā' shikanī*, *n.f.* Fatigue.

اعطاء i'ṯā' (A) n.m. To give; to grant; to bestow upon.

اعظم a'ẕam (A) adj. (sup. of عظیم 'aẕim) Greatest; very great.

اعلام a'lām (A) n.m. (plu. of علم 'alam) Flags; banners.

اعلام i'lām (A) n.m. Announcing; informing; revealing; notification.

اعلامیه i'lāmmiyah (A) n.m. Press communique; press statement; declaration.

اعلان i'lān (A) n.m. Announcement; communique; manifesto; proclamation; advertisement; notification; notice.

اعلیٰ a'lā (A) adj. (sup. of عالی 'āli) Superior; higher; most dignified; elevated; supreme; top-most; first rate.

اعلیٰ علیین a'lā 'illiyyin, n.f. The most sublime paradise.

اعم a'amm (A) adj. (sup. of عام a'ām) Very common.

اعمال a'māl (A) n.m. (plu. of عمل 'amal) Actions; behaviour; conduct; deeds.

اعمال نامه a'māl nāmah, n.m. A character book or sheet; character roll.

اعمیٰ a'mā (A) adj. Blind; born blind.

اعوان a'wān (A) n.m. (plu. of عون 'aūn) Helpers; a clan of Rajputs.

اعیان a'yān (A) n.m. (plu. of عین 'ain) Eyes; peers, noblemen, ministers (who are so to say the eyes of the State).

اغراض aghrāẓ (A) n.m. & n.f. (plu. of غرض gharaẓ) Motives; aims; purposes.

اغذیه aghẕiyyah (A) n.f. (plu. of غذا ghiẕā) Foods; eatables; diets; aliments; provisions.

اغلاط aghlāṯ, n.f. (plu. of غلط ghalaṯ) Mistakes.

اغلاق ighlāq (A) n.m. Impediment; incomprehensibleness.

اغلام ighlām (A) n.m. Sodomy.

اغلام باز ighlām bāz, n.m. Sodomite.

اغلب ighlab (A) adj. (sup. of غالب ghālib) Stronger; superior. adv. Most likely; most probably.

اغل بغل aghal baghal, adv. On all sides; right and left; in this direction or that.

اغماز ighmāz. (A) n.m. Coquetry; ogling; haughtiness; superciliousness,

اغماض ighmāẓ (A) n.m. Overlooking; connivance; carelessness.

اغماض کرنا ighmāẓ karnā, v. To overlook; to neglect; to connive at.

اغنیاء aghniyā' (A) n.m. (plu. of غنی ghani) The rich; moneyed people.

اغواء ighwā' (A) n.m. Seduction; inducement; enticement; abduction; elopement.

اغواء کرنا ighwā' karnā, v. To seduce; to tempt; to entice; to instigate; to abduct; to allure; to elope with.

اغیار aghyār (A) n.m. (plu. of غیر ghair) Strangers; unfamiliar persons; unknown persons; rivals.

آف uff (A) int. Fy! oh! alas.

آف نه کرنا uff nah karnā, v. To suffer without complaint.

آف نه کهنا uff nah kahnā, v. To endure in silence.

افاده ifādah (A) n.m. Benefitting; instructing; benefit; gain.

افاده عام ifādah-ĕ a'ām, n.m. General welfare.

افادیت ifādiyyat (A) n.f. Benefit; usefulness.

افاغنه afāghinah (A) n.m. (plu. of افغان afghān) Pathans.

افاقه ifāqah (A) n.m. Relief; recovery from a disease; convalescence.

آفتاد uftād (P) n.f. Misery; distress; accident; chance; mishap; disposition; foundation.

آفتادگی uftādagi (P) n.f. Helplessness; supplication; selfabasement; humbleness.

آفتاده uftādah (P) adj. Waste (land); fallow (land); fallen; useless; miserable; powerless.

آفتان و خیزان uftān-ŏ khezān (P) adj. With much ado; helter-skelter; in a state of consternation; (Lit.) falling and getting up.

افتتاح iftitāḥ (A) n.m. Opening; inauguration; exposing.

افتتاحی *iftitāḥī* (A&P) *adj.* Beginning; opening.

افتتاحیه *iftitāḥiyyah* (A&P) *n.m.* Editorial note.

افتخار *iftikhār* (A) *n.m.* Honour; grace; glory; distinction; credit; repute.

افتراء *iftirā'* (A) *n.m.* Calumny; false accusation; imputation; scandal; slander.

افتراء باندھنا *iftirā' bāndhnā, v.* To accuse unjustly; to impute falsely; to slander.

افتراء پرداز *iftirā' pardāz, adj.* Accuser; scandale-monger.

افتراء پردازی *iftirā' pardāzī, n.f.* Accusation; slandering.

افتراق *iftirāq* (A) *n.m.* Division; separation; disunity.

افتیمون *aftīmūn* (A) *n.f.* A rootless shrub; a parasite.

افراتفری *afrātafrī, n.f.* Uproar; tumult; disorder; hurly-burly; hurry-scurry; confusion; dismay; panic; turmoil.

افراد *afrād* (A) *n.m.* (*plu.* of فرد *fard*) Individuals; persons.

افراز *afrāz* (P) *adj.* Elevating; commending; exalting; lifting (*used in comps.*)

افراط *ifrāṭ* (A) *n.f.* Excess; exuberance; abundance; plenty; surplus.

افراط و تفریط *ifrāṭ-ŏ tāfrīṭ, n.f.* Excess and deficiency; abnormal condition.

افرنگی *afrangī* (P) See *farangī*.

افروخته *afrokhtah* (P) *adj.* Lighted; ignited; set on fire; angry; furious.

افروخته کرنا *afrokhtah karnā, v.* To incite; to excite; to enrage.

افروز *afroz* (P) *adj.* Inflaming; enkindling; igniting (*used in comp*).

افریقه *Afrīqah* (A) *n.m.* Name of a continent in the south of Europe and west of Asia; Africa.

افزا *afzā* (P) *adj.* Augmenting; increasing; adding (*used in comp*).

افزائش *afzā'ish* (P) *n.f.* Increase; augmentation; breeding.

افزائش نسل *afzā'ish-ĕ nasl, n.f.* Live-stock breeding.

افزود *afzūd* (P) *n.m.* Increase; addition; enlargement; augmentation; plenty; excess.

افزوں *afzūṅ* (P) *adj.* Increasing; augmenting; numerous; manifold; much.

افزوں ہونا *afzūṅ honā, v.* To increase; to enlarge; to be of higher price.

افزونی *afzūnī* (P) *n.f.* Increase; excess; plenty; rise (in price).

افسانه *afsānah* (P) *n.m.* A tale; a legend; a story; fiction.

افسانه گو *afsānah go, n.m.* A story-teller.

افسر *afsar* (P) *n.m.* An officer; one who possesses authority.

افسر بالا دست *afsar-e bālādast, n.m.* A superior officer; chief authority.

افسر بحالیات *afsar-ĕ baḥāliyāt, n.m.* Rehabilitation officer.

افسر تخمینه *afsar-ĕ takhmīnah, n.m.* Estimating officer.

افسر ترقیات *afsar-ĕ taraqqiyāt, n.m.* Development officer.

افسر حصول اراضی *afsar-ĕ ḥuṣūl-ĕ arāẓī, n.m.* Land-acquisition officer.

افسر خزانه *afsar-ĕ khazānah, n.m.* Treasury officer.

افسر مال *afsar-ĕ māl, n.m.* Revenue assistent or officer.

افسر مختار *afsar-ĕ mukhtār, n.m.* Controlling officer.

افسر نو آبادی *afsar-nauābādī, n.m.* Colonization officer.

افسردگی *afsurdagī* (P) *n.f.* Melancholy; dejection; depression of spirits; frigidity.

افسرده *afsurdah* (P) *adj.* Depressed; dispirited; frigid; melancholy.

افسرده خاطر یا دل *afsurdah khāṭir yā dil, adj.* Afflicted; distressed; cast down; down-hearted; dispirited; dejected.

افسوس *afsos* (P) *n.m.* Regret; sorrow; distress; repentance; remorse; dejection *interj.* Ah! Alas!

افسوس کرنا *afsos karnā, v.* To grieve; to lament; to repent; to deplore; to express sorrow; to regret; to mourn.

افسون **afsūṅ** (P) *n.m.* Charm; spell; magic; pretence; witchery; sorcery; artifice, deceit.

افسون سازی **afsūṅ sāzī**, *n.f.* Enchantment; witchery; use of spells or charm.

افسون گر **afsūṅ gar**, *n.m.* A magician; conjurer; sorcerer; wizard.

افشاء **ifshā'** (A) *n.m.* Divulgence; disclosure.

افشائے راز **ifshā-ĕ rāz**, *n.m.* Disclosure of a secret.

افشائے راز کرنا **ifshā-ĕ rāz karnā**, *v.* To disclose a secret; to lay bare; to divulge.

افشان **afshān** (P) *adj.* Dispersing; diffusing; spreading; sprinkling; pouring out; scattering; strewing; shedding (used in *comp.*). *n.f.* Strips of tinsel pasted on women's cheeks and forehead as decoration.

افشانی **afshānī** (P) *n.f.* Diffusion; scattering strewing; sprinkling.

افشانی کاغذ **afshāni kāghaẕ** *n.f.* Paper studded or spangled or sprinkled over with gold dust, used in writing to persons of distinctions.

افشردہ **afshurdah** (P) *adj.* Pressed; squeezed; filtered; stained. *n.m.* Squash.

افصح **afṣaḥ** (A) *adj.* (*sup.* of فصیح **faṣīḥ**) Very eloquent; rhetorical.

افضال **afẓāl** (A) *n.m.* (*plu.* of فضل **faẓl**) Kindnesses; graces; favours; virtues.

افضال **ifẓāl** (A) *n.m.* Causing to excel; causing to increase; benefitting.

افضل **afẓal** (A) *adj.* (*sup.* of فاضل **fāẓil**) Most excellent; prominent, most venerable.

افضل المرسلین **afẓal-ul-mursalīn**, *n.m.* The most distinguished of the Prophets; an epithet of the Holy Prophet.

افضلیت **afẓaliyyat** (A) *n.f.* Greatness; excellence; pre-eminence.

افطار **iftār** (A) *n.m.* Breaking a fast; a light breakfast.

افطار کرنا **iftār karnā**, *v.* To break one's fast at due time (sunset).

افطاری **iftārī**, *n.f.* Things to be eaten on breaking a fast.

افعال **af'āl** (A) *n.m.* (*plu.* of فعل **fi'l**). Actions; deeds; conduct.

افعال الادویہ **af'āl-ul-adwiyyah**, *n.m.* Pharmacology.

افعی **af'ī** (A) *n.m.* A serpent; basilisk; asp; adder; viper.

افغان **afghān** (P) *n.m.* A Pathan, an inhabitant of Afghanistan. *n.f.* Lamentation; complaint; wail.

اُفق **ufaq** (A) *n.m.* Horizon.

اُفقی **ufaqī** (A) *adj.* Horizontal.

افکار **afkār** (A) *n.m.* (*plu.* of فکر **fikr**) thoughts; meditations; ideas; notions.

افگار **afgār** (P) *adj.* Wounded; lacerated.

افگن **afgan** (P) *adj.* (used in *comp.*) Throwing down; hurling; overthrowing.

افگندگی **afgandagī** (P) *n.f.* Overthrowing; throwing down; flinging.

افگندہ **afgandah** (P) *adj.* Thrown; humble; down trodden.

افلاس **iflās** (A) *n.m.* Poverty; need; want; necessity; penury; indigence.

افلاطون **Aflātūn** (G) *n.m.* Plato, the famous Greek philosopher.

افلاک **aflāk** (A) *n.m.* (*plu.* of فلک **falak**) Sky; the heavens; the firmament.

افواج **afwāj** (A) *n.f.* (*plu.* of فوج **fauj**) Armies; soldiery.

افواج بری **afwāj-ĕ barrī**, *n.f.* Land forces.

افواج بحری **afwāj-ĕ baḥrī**, *n.f.* The navy.

افواج ہوائی **afwāj-ĕ hawā'ī**, *n.f.* Air forces.

افواج شیاطین **afwāj-ĕ shayaṭīn**, *n.f.* (*Lit.*) A host of satins; (*Met.*) a host of children.

افواج قاہرہ **afwāj-ĕ qāhirah**, *n.f.* A victorious army; the imperial forces.

افواہ **afwāh** (A) *n.f.* (*plu.* of فوہ **fūh**) Rumour; report; gossip; hearsay; common talk; fame.

افواہ اڑانا **afwāh uṛānā**, *v.* To spread a rumour; to broadcast a false report.

افواهاً afwāhan (A) adv. As a rumour.

افواهی afwāhi, adj. Reported; rumoured; talked about; famed.

افہام ifhām (A) n.m. Making one understand; informing.

افہام و تفہیم ifhām-ō tafhīm n.m./f. Understanding; comprehending.

افیم ' افیون afīm (U) afyūn (A) n.f. Opium.

افیون کشی afyūn kashi, n.f. Opium smoking.

افیمچی ' افیمی ' افیونی afīmchi, affīmi, afyūni, n.m. An opium-eater; an opium addict.

افیمن afīman, n.f. A woman opium-eater.

اقارب aqārib (A) n.m. (plu. of قریب qarib) Relations; kindred.

اقالیم aqālim (A) n.f. (plu. of اقلیم aqlim) Countries; states; tracts; regions.

اقامت iqāmat (A) n.f. Staying; dwelling; lodging; abode; resting place; residence.

اقامت کرنا iqāmat karnā, v. To reside; to stay; to take an abode.

اقامت گاہ iqāmat gāh, n.f. Resting place; a boarding house.

اقانیم ثلاثہ aqānim-ĕ salāsah (A) n.m. Trinity.

اقبال iqbāl (A) n.m. Prosperity; good fortune; luck; success; felicity; name of the great philosopher-poet of Indo-Pakistan subcontinent who was the first to conceive the idea of a separate homeland (Pakistan) for Musalmans of united India; (Law) admission; confession; avowing; owing; acceptance.

اقبال دعویٰ iqbāl-ĕ da'wā, n.m. Acknowledgment of a claim; cognovit.

اقبال سکندری iqbāl-ĕ sikandari, n.m. Good luck; good fortune.

اقبال کرنا iqbāl karnā, v. To confess; to admit.

اقبال مند iqbāl mand, adj. Fortunate; lucky; auspicious; thriving; prosperous.

اقبالی iqbāli, n.m., One who confesses; a confessant. adj. Confessional.

اقتباس iqtibās (A) n.m. Borrowing (fire or light from another); selection; quotation; extract; excerpt; acquiring (acknowledge); gaining.

اقتباس کرنا iqtibās karnā, v. To obtain; to borrow; to extract.

اقتدار iqtidār (A) n.m. Power; authority; influence; eminence; dignity; rank.

اقتدار جائز iqtidār-ĕ jā'iz, n.m. Lawful authority; legal rights.

اقتداء iqtidā' (A) n.f. Following as an example; imitation.

اقتصاد iqtiṣād (A) n.m. Moderation; operating economically.

اقتصادی iqtiṣādi (A) adj. Economic (condition).

اقتصادیات iqtiṣādiyyāt (A) n.f. Economics; political economy.

اقتضاء iqtiẓā' (A) n.m. Requirement; demand; need; requisition; necessity.

اقتضاء مصلحت iqtiẓā'-ĕ maṣlaḥat, n.m. Expedient.

اقدام iqdām (A) n.m. Going ahead or forward; boldness; courage; valour; intrepidity; attempt; effort; endeavour; spirit; resolution; firmness; intention.

اقدام خود کشی iqdām-ĕ khūd kushi, n.m. Intention to commit suicide.

اقدام قتل iqdām-ĕ qatl, n.m. Intention to commit murder.

اقدام قتل عمد iqdām-ĕ qatl-ĕ 'amd, n.m. Preplanned intention to commit murder.

اقدام جرم iqdām-ĕ jurm, n.m. Attempt to commit a crime.

اقدام کرنا iqdām karnā, v. To make an attempt; to take steps.

اقدس aqdas (A) adj. (plu. of قدس qudus) Most holy; very sacred.

اقرار iqrār (A) n.m. Promise; agreement; pledge; acknowledgement; corroboration; engagement; confession; assent; declaration; acceptance; covenant; contract.

اقرار کرنا *iqrār karnā*, *v.* To affirm; to promise; to accept; to admit; to assent; to own; to confess; to undertake.

اقرار صالح *iqrār-ĕ ṣāliḥ*, *n.m.* A solemn affirmation or declaration.

اقرار نامہ *iqrār nāmah*, *n.m.* Written bond; agreement; contact; an indenture; declaration.

اقرار نامہ بندوبست *iqrār nāmah-ĕ bandobast*, *n.m.* Administration papers; settlement with Government by the *mālguzār* and coparceners of a village.

اقرار نامہ ثالثی *iqrār nāmah-ĕ ṣāliṣi*, *n.m.* Arbitration agreement.

اقراری *iqrāri*, *n.m.* One who confesses or acknowledges; one who assents; a confessor. *adj.* Confessional.

اقرب *aqrab* (A) *adj.* (*sup.* of قریب *qarib*) Very near; nearest.

اقرباء *aqribā'* (A) *n.m.* (*plu.* of قریب *qarib*) Relatives; kins; friends; allies.

اقساط *aqsāṭ* (A) *n.f.* (*plu.* of قسط *qisṭ*) Parts; portions; instalments.

اقسام *aqsām* (A) *n.f.* (*plu.* of قسم *qism*) Kinds; sets; species; sorts.

اقصیٰ *aqṣā* (A) *adj.* (*sup.* of قاص *qāṣṣ*) Very far; most distant; most extreme.

اقطار *aqṭār* (A) *n.m.* (*plu.* of قطر *quṭr*) Diameters; regions.

اقطاع *aqṭā'* (A) *n.m.* (*pul.* of قطع *qiṭa'*) Tracts of land; estates.

اقل *aqall* (A) *adj.* (*plu.* of قلیل *qalil*) Least; very little; insignificant.

اقل درجہ *aqall darjah*, *n.m.* The least quantity; a minimum.

اقلیت *aqalliyyat* (A) *n.f.* Minority.

اقلیدس *uqlidas* (G) *n.m.* (*Math*) The science of mathematics taught by the Greek mathematician, Euclid.

اقلیم *aqlim* (A) *n.f.* Country; state; region; zone.

اقنوم *uqnūm* (A) *n.m.* One of the Trinity (Father, Son and the Holy Ghost); the true basis or reality of a thing.

اقوال *aqwāl* (A) *n.m.* (*plu.* of قول *qaul*) Truths; sayings.

اقوام *aqwām* (A) *n.f.* (*plu.* of قوم *qaum*) Nations; peoples; tribes; clans; races.

اقوام متحدہ *aqwām-ĕ muttaḥidah*, *n.f.* The United Nations.

اک *ik* (H) *adj.* (Contraction of ایک) One.

اکبار یا اکبارگی *ikbār yā ikbārgi*, *adv.* Once; instantly; immediately; all at once; suddenly.

اک پیچا *ik pechā*, *n.m.* A kind of turban; a kind of Indian smoking pipe.

اکتارا *iktārā*, *n.m.* Very fine cloth; a single-stringed musical instrument; a string of single thread.

اکجا *ik jā*, *adv.* At one place; together.

اک دم *ik dam*, *adv.* At once; without loss of time; immediately.

اک رخی *ik rukhī*, *adj.* One sided.

اک رخی تصویر *ik rukhī taṣvīr*, *n.f.* A profile; one sided picture.

اکسار ، اکساں *iksār*, *iksāṅ*, *adj.* Alike; similar; of the same kind.

اک گونہ *ik gūnah*, *adv.* Somewhat; of a kind; a little.

اک لڑا *ik laṛā*, *n.m.* One stringed (necklace).

اکا *ikkā* (H) *adj.* One; single; superfine; none such; unequalled; unique. *n.m.* A two-wheeled cheap conveyance; the ace (at cards or dice).

اکا دکا *ikkā dukkā*, *adj.* One or two; just a few; very few.

اکابر *akābir* (A) *adj.* & *n.m.* (*plu.* of اکبر *akbar*). Greatest (men); nobles; men of distinction.

اکابر و اصاغر *akābir-ŏ aṣāghir*, *n.m.* Great and small; rich and poor.

اکادشی *ikādshī* (H) *n.f.* Eleventh day of the solar or lunar month.

اکادمی akadmi (E) n.f. Academy.

اکارت akārat (H) adj. Unprofitable; unserviceable; unavailing; ineffectual; fruitless; vain; useless; worthless.

اکارت جانا akārat jānā, v. To serve no purpose; to be of no avail; to be wasted; to be in vain; to be useless; to be profitless.

اکاسرہ akāsirah (A) n.m. (plu. of کسریٰ kisrā) An epithet of the emperors of Persia.

اکاسی ikāsī (H) adj. Eighty-one.

اکانوے ikānawe (H) adj. Ninety-one.

اکاون ikāwan (H) adj. Fifty-one.

اکاؤنٹ ikāunṭ (E) n.m. Account.

اکاؤنٹنٹ ikāunṭanṭ (E) n.m. An accontant.

اکاؤنٹنٹ جنرل ikāunṭanṭ jeneral, n.m. Accountant General.

اکائی ikā'ī (H) n.f. Unit; (Math.) any digit from one to nine.

اکبر akbar (A) adj. (sup. of کبیر kabīr) Greater; greatest. n.m. An epithet of the famous third Moghal emperor of India named Jalal-ud-Din.

اکبری akbari, n.f. Name of a sweetmeat; name of a gold mohr. adj. Belonging to Jalal-ud-Din Akbar, the emperor of India.

اکبری نورتن akbari nauratan, n.m. The nine gems, i.e. the nine famous courtiers of Akbar (1) Mirza Abdur Rahim Khan Khan-i-Khanan; (2) Mirza Aziz Kokaltash, Khan-i-Azam; (3) Abdul Fatah Gilani; (4) Allama Abul Faiz Faizi, the Poet Laureate, (5) Abul Fazl Mutamemud Dolah; (6) Hakim Hammam; (7) Raja Todar Mal; (8) Raja Bir Bal; (9) Raja Man Singh.

آکتا جانا uktā jānā, v. To tire; to be fed up; to grow weary; to be disgusted.

اکتالیس iktālis (H) adj. Fourty-one.

آکتانا uktānā (H) v. To be tired of; to be weary (of); to tire; to be sad or sorrowful; to be dejected; to feel dull or downcast.

اکتساب iktisāb (A) n.m. Acquiring after hard work; attainment; acquisition; earning.

اکتشاف iktishāf (A) n.m. Exposure; discovery.

اکتفاء iktifā' (A) n.f. Adequacy; sufficiency; satisfaction; contentment.

اکتفاء کرنا iktifā' karnā, v. To be satisfied; to be content.

اکتوبر actūbar (E) n.m. October.

اکتیس ikattis (H) adj. Thirty-one.

اکٹھا ، اکٹھی ikatthā, ikatthi (H) adj. United; collected; assembled; crowded; together; in one place; in a bulk or lump.

اکثر akṣar (A) adj. (sup. of کثیر kaṣir) Most;; much; very many; frequent. adv. Mostly; generally; chiefly; frequently; usually; often.

اکثر اوقات akṣar auqāt, adv. Very often; at most time; commonly; usually; ordinarily.

اکثریت akṣariyyat (A) n.f. Majority.

اکرام ikrām (A) n.m. Honouring; treating with attention and ceremony; esteem; veneration; respect; deference; kindness; favour.

اکراہ ikrāh (A) n.m. Dislike; disgust; aversion; abhorrence; detestation; horror; extortion.

اکرم akram (A) adj. (sup. of کریم karim) Most gracious; most merciful; benevolent; very liberal; charitable; bountiful; very kind.

اکڑ akaṛ (H) n.f. Stiffness; rigidity; firmness; pride; conceit; vanity; airs; haughtiness; ill-temper; strut; crookedness.

اکڑ باز akaṛ bāz, n.m. A coxcomb; a fop; a swaggerer; an affected person.

اکڑ بازی akaṛ bāzi, n.f. Affectation; swaggering; airs; ostentation; conceit.

اکڑنا akaṛnā (H) v. To strut; to give oneself airs; to look defiantly at; to be ready to pick a quarrel; to be cramped; to be convulsed; to stiffen.

آکڑوں ukṛūn (H) adj. The posture of sitting on the hams with the soles of the feet on the ground; squatting.

آکسانا uksānā (H) v. To raise the wick of a lamp; to lift; to stir up; to rouse; to impel; to excite; to encourage; to instigate; to fan a flame; to urge; to provoke.

آکساهٹ uksāhaṭ (H) n.f. Inducement; excitement; stimulation.

اکسٹھ iksaṭh (H) adj. Sixty-one.

اکسیر iksīr (A) n.f. An elixir; a medicine said to be capable of converting other metals to gold or silver; alchemy; a sovereign remedy; a penacea.

اکسیر گر iksīr gar, n.m. An alchemist.

اکل و شرب akl-ō shurb (A) n.m. Eatables; eating and drinking.

اکلوتا ، اکلوتی iklautā, iklautī (H) adj. The only child; sole; single; alone.

اکمل akmāl (A) adj. (sup. of کامل kāmil) Most perfect; complete in every respect.

اکناف aknāf (A) n.m. (plu. of کنف kanaf) Borders; confines; suburbs; sides; environs.

اکنون aknūn (P) adv. Now; at present.

آکھاڑ ukhāṛ (H) n.f. Rooting up; extermination; eradication; devastation.

اکھاڑا akhāṛā (H) n.m. A palaestra; arena; wrestling pit; circus; a bevy of beautiful women.

آکھاڑنا ukhāṛnā (H) v. To exterminate; to uproot; to dig up; to tear up; to disjoint; to pull out; to dislocate; to waste; to ravage; to demolish; to destroy.

اکھتر ikhattar (H) adj. Seventy-one.

اکہرا ، اکہری ikahrā, ikahrī (H) adj. Of single fold.

اکھڑ akhkhaṛ, adj. Uncivilised; rough; rude; undisciplined; obstinate; conceited; quarrelsome; haughty. n.m. A hard-hearted person; a boar; a lout.

اکھڑ پن akhkhaṛ pan, n.m. Rudeness; roughness; obstinacy; haughtiness.

آکھڑنا ukhaṛnā (H) v. To be eradicated; to be uprooted; to be destroyed; to be torn asunder; to be displaced.

آکھڑوانا ukhaṛwānā (H) v. To cause to be uprooted; to have something pulled out.

اکھلی ukhlī. See اوکھلی ūkhlī.

اکھولا akholā (H) n.m. The top shoot of the sugarcane.

اکھنڈ akhanḍ (S) adj. Undivided; unbroken; whole; entire.

اکیاسی ikkiyāsī (H) adj. Eighty-one.

اکیاون ikkyāwan (H) adj. Fifty-one.

اکیس ikkīs (H) adj. Twenty-one.

اکیلا ، اکیلی akelā, akelī (H) adj. Alone; single; lonely; solitary; unique; peerless.

اگاڑی agāṛī (H) n.f. The front; forepart; the ropes with which a horse's fore-feet are tied. adv. Ahead; further on; in front; forward.

اگاڑی پچھاڑی لگانا agāṛī pichhāṛī lagānā, v. To confine a horse; to tie the fore and hind feet of a horse.

اگاڑی مارنا agāṛī mārnā, v. To attack the vanguard; to defeat an hostile army; to attack in front.

آگال ugāl (H) n.m. That which is spit out after chewing.

آگال دان ugāl dān, n.m. A spittoon; a vessel for spitting in.

آگالنا ugālnā, v. To throw out; to spit out.

آگانا ugānā (H) v. To cause to grow; to raise.

آگاهنا ugāhnā (H) v. To pile up; to recover; to collect; to levy; to realize (debt); to gather.

آگاهی ugāhī (H) n.f. Realisation of lent money by instalments; collection of rent or revenue; proceeds.

اگر agar, n.m. Wood of aloes; a kind of wood which gives scent when burnt.

اگردان agar dān, n.m. A pot to burn wood of aloes.

اگر کی بتی agar kī battī, n.f. Essence of a scented wood pasted on sticks.

اگر agar (P) conj. If; in case; in the event of.

اگرچه agarchih, conj. Although; though; even if.

اگر مگر **agar magar**, *n.f.* If and if not; hesitation; finding excuses.

اگروال **aggarwāl** (H) *n.m.* A caste of Hindu merchants.

اگڑ بگڑ ، اگڑم بگڑم **agaṛ bagaṛ, agṛam bagṛam**, *n.m.* Confusion; mess; disorder; nonsense; odds and ends; tresh; trifles.

اگست **agast** (E) *n.m.* August.

اگلا ، اگلی **aglā, aglī** (H) *adj.* Foremost; first; previous; former; forerunner; the past; the future.

اگلا جنم **aglā janam**, *n.m.* (According to Hindu belief) Former or future life or existence.

اگلا پچھلا ، اگلی پچھلی **aglā pichhlā, aglī pichhlī** *adj.* First and last; the whole lot; the past and the present.

آگلنا **ugalnā** (H) *v.* To throw-out; to spit out; to vomit; to disclose a secret.

اگن ، اگنی **agan, agni** (H) *n.f.* Fire.

اگن بوٹ **agan boat**, *n.f.* A steamship.

اگن کنڈ **agan kunḍ**, *n.m.* Fire pit for burning dead bodies.

اُگنا **ugnā** (H) *v.* To germinate; to sprout; to spring up; to grow; to rise.

اگولا **agolā**. See اکھولا **akholā**.

اُگھاڑا **ughāṛā** (H) *adj.* Unclothed; nude; bare; undressed; unveiled; divulged; apparent.

اگھن **aghan** (H) *n.m.* The eighth month of Hindus (November-December).

ال **al** (A) *art.* The.

الامان **al amān**, *int.* God preserve us! God have mercy! God help us!

الآن **alān**, *adv.* Now; at present.

الحاج **al-Hājj**, *n.m.* A person who has performed pilgrimage (to Mecca).

الحاصل **alḥāṣil**, *adv.* In short; briefly.

الحال **alḥāl**, *adv.* Now; at present; at this moment; just now.

الحذر **alḥaẕar**, *intj.* God forbid! God preserve us!

الحفیظ **alḥafiẓ**, *int.* Heaven defend us!

الحق **alḥaqq**, *adv.* Really; in truth; certainly; in reality; indeed.

الحمد للہ **alḥamd-ŏ lillah**, *int.* God be praised!

السلام علیکم **assalām-ŏ 'alaikum**, *sal.* Peace be on you; safety attend you.

العبد **al'abd**, *n.m.* Your servant; yours obediently; the signature of the writer of a letter or article; the undersigned.

العطش **al'aṭash**, *n.f.* Intense thrist. *intj.* Cry for water for quenching thirst.

العظمت للہ **al'aẓmat-ŏ lillah**, *int.* God is great; all greatness is for God.

الغرض **algharaẓ**, *adv.* Briefly; in short; on the whole.

الغیاث **alghayāṣ** *intj.* Appeal or cry for injustice; imploring help; help! help!

القصہ **alqiṣṣah**, *adv.* Briefly; in a word; in short.

المضاعف **almuẓā'af**, *adj.* Double; twice as big.

المنت للہ **alminnat-ŏ lillah**, *int.* God be praised.

الوداع **al widā'**, *int.* Good-bye; adieu; farewell.

الا **illā** (A) *adv.* If not; else; except; besides; otherwise.

الا ماشا اللہ **illā māshā allah.** Except what God wills.

الاپ **alāp** (H) *n.f.* See آلاپ **ālāp**.

الاپنا **alāpnā** (H) *v.* See آلاپنا **ālāpnā**.

الاچی ، الائچی **ilāchī, ilā'ichī**, *n.f.* Cardamoms.

الائچی دانہ **ilā'ichī dānah**, *n.m.* Cardamom seeds; cardamoms coated with sugar.

اُلار **ulār** (H) *adj.* Liable to be upset when heavily laden at the back (a cart).

الاؤ **alāo** (H) *n.m.* A bonfire; a fire (in the open) round which the villagers sit for a pastime.

الاونس **alāuns** (E) *n.m.* Allowance.

اُلاہنا **ulāhnā** (H) *n.m.* Taunt; wickedness; complaint; reproach; infamy.

آلانگنا ulāngnā (H) v. To jump over (a thing); (in horse-breeder's terminology) to ride the horse for the first time.

الباب albāb (A) n.m. (plu. of لب lubb) Hearts; minds; wisdom; intelligence.

البتہ albattah (A) adv. Certainly; surely; decidedly; positively; of course.

البرز Alburz (P) n.m. Name of celebrated mountain between Pakistan and Persia.

البم album (E) n.m. Album; a blank book for insertion of photographs, etc.

البیلا albelā, adj. Playful; wanton; wayward; lively; gay; blithe; frivolous; care-free; smart; showy; foppish. n.m. A fop; a beau; a dandy; a coxcomb.

البیلا پن albelā pan, n.m. Playfulness; dandyism; gaiety; frolic; smartness; airs; foppishness; charm; coquetry; beauty; elegance.

البیلی albeli, n.f. A belle; a gay young girl.

الپاکا alpākā (E) n.m. Name of an animal found in Africa; a kind of cloth made from the wool of alpākā.

التباس iltibās (A) n.m. Resemblance; similarity; similarity of two words in sound but having entirely different meaning; vagueness.

التجاء iltijā' (A) n.f. Fleeing to someone for relief or protection; entreaty; prayer; supplication; solicitation; petition.

التجاء کرنا iltijā' karnā, v. To beg; to solicit; to entreat; to request; to beseech.

التزام iltizām (A) n.m. Being necessary or expedient; taking on oneself.

التفات iltifāt (A) n.f. Regard; attention; kindness; courtesy; con ideration; friendship; inclination.

التفات کرنا iltifāt karnā, v. To have respect for; to show regard (for).

التماس altimās (A) n.f. Petition; prayer; application; request; supplication; entreaty.

التماس کرنا iltimās karnā, v. To petition; to beseech; to request; to supplicate; to represent humbly.

التمش altmash (T) n.m. An advance guard of the army; vanguard; title of Sultan Shams-ud-Din, the slave King of Delhi.

التمغا altamghā (T) n.m. The royal seal; royal insignia; a permanent royal grant; medal.

التواء iltiwā' (A) n.m. Postponement; deferring; delaying; holding in abeyance; adjournment; stay.

التواء جنگ iltiwā-ĕ jang, n.m. Cessation of hostilities; truce.

اُلٹ ulat (H) n.m. Reversing; overturning; upsetting; inversion; reverse; the wrong side; the opposite; contrary.

اُلٹ پڑنا ulat parnā, v. To attack; to change direction; to change direction of attack; to change side.

اُلٹ پلٹ ہونا ulat pulat honā, v. To be upside down; to be in a state of confusion; to be topsy-turvy.

اُلٹ پھیر ulat pher, n.m. Embarrassment; perplexity; knot; mess; entanglement; deception; trickery.

اُلٹ کے کروٹ نہ لینا ulat ke karwat nah lenā, v. To neglect; to forget altogether about a matter; not to pay any attention.

اُلٹ کے کہنا ulat ke kahnā, v. To say in reply; to repeat; to say a thing over again.

اُلٹا ulṭā (H) adj. Reversed; inverted; topsy-turvy; opposite; perverse. adv. On the contrary; on the other hand; notwithstanding.

اُلٹا بھاگنا ulṭā bhāgnā, v. To turn or flee back; to turn and run away.

اُلٹا پلٹا ulṭā pulṭā, adj. Inverted; topsy-turvy; confused; jumbled; upside down.

اُلٹا پھرنا ulṭā phirnā, v. To turn or go back; to return; to retrace one's steps.

اُلٹا توا ulṭā tawā, adj. Coal-black; jet black; very black; (Lit.) an inverted iron pan on which bread is baked.

اُلٹا جواب ulṭā jawāb, n.m. A retort; an impertinent reply; a crooked answer.

اُلٹا چور کوتوال کو ڈانٹے ultā chor kotwāl ko ḍānṭe, *prov.* The thief turns round and threatens the police officer; a criminal intimidating the judge; the sinner lording over the innocent.

اُلٹا سمجھنا ultā samajhnā, *v.* To misunderstand; to misapprehend.

اُلٹانا ulṭānā (H) *v.* To upset; to pervert; to thwart; to reverse; to convert; to modify; to turn upside down; to overturn; to overset.

اُلٹانا پلٹانا ulṭānā pulṭānā, *v.* To reverse; to modify; to mix together.

اُلٹ دینا، اُلٹنا ulaṭ denā, ulṭnā (H) *v.* To overturn; to upset; to pervert; to thwart; to overthrow; to empty; to turn over (leaves of a book); to refute; to cancel; to counteract; to tilt over; to be turned over.

اُلٹی ulṭi (H) *adj.* Feminine form of اُلٹا ulṭā. *n.f.* Vomit.

اُلٹی آنا ulṭi ānā, *v.* To feel nausea; to vomit.

اُلٹی پٹی پڑھانا ulṭi paṭṭi paṛhānā, *v.* To mislead; to set against; to poison the mind.

اُلٹی تقریر ulṭi taqrir, *n.f.* Inconsistent speech; a perverted declaration.

اُلٹی ریت ulṭi rīt, *n.f.* A wrong course; an improper custom.

اُلٹی سمجھ ulṭī samajh, *n.f.* Perverted understanding; erroneous view.

اُلٹی سیدھی سنانا ulṭi sīdhi sunānā, *v.* To scold roundly; to abuse; to insult.

اُلٹی کرنا ulṭi karnā, *v.* To vomit.

اُلٹی کھوپڑی اندھا گیان ulṭi khopṛi andhā gyān, *prov.* A crooked mind; wrong-headed; stupid.

اُلٹی مالا پھیرنا ulṭi mālā phernā, *v.* To invoke a curse; to do some thing contrary to accepted cuctom; (*Lit.*) to count one's beads backwards.

اُلٹی ہوا ulṭi havā, *n.f.* Contrary wind; unexpected happening.

اُلٹے پاؤں پھرنا nlṭe pāon phirnā, *v.* To retrace one's steps; to go back immediately; to go back from a place immediately after arriving.

الجبرا aljabrā (E) *n.m.* Algebra.

اُلجھانا uljhānā (H) *v.* To entangle; to complicate; to reveal; to involve; to entwine; to disarrange; to confuse; to entrap; to embroil; to ensnare; to make intricate; to mislead; to deceive.

اُلجھاؤ، اُلجھن uljhāo, uljhan, *n.m., n.f.* Entanglement; intricacy; perplexity; confusion; disorder; derangement; complication; difficulty; embarrassment; a complex.

اُلجھ پڑنا ulajh paṛnā, *v.* To quarrel; to wrangle with; to fall foul (of).

اُلجھ جانا ulajh janā, *v.* To be entangled; be delayed or detained.

اُلجھنا ulajhnā (H) *v.* To be entangled; to be involved (in a quarrel or difficulty); to quarrel; to cavil; to fret; to prevent or hinder.

اُلجھیڑا uljherā (H) *n.m.* Entanglement; intricacy; difficulty; quarrel; broil.

الحاد ilḥād (A) *n.m.* Apostasy; irreligion; heresy; atheism; disbelief; (*Lit.*) Deviation from the right path.

الحاق ilḥāq (A) *n.m.* Annexation; joining together; addition; contiguity.

الحان ilḥān (A) *n.m.* Tune; notes; melodies; modulation; an air in music; reciting baeutifully or in a beautiful voice.

الخ alakh (A) (Abr. of الی آخرہ ilā ākhirihi) To the end of it; et cetra, et cetra.

الزام ilzām (A) *n.m.* Censure; blame; reproof; accusation; charge; allegation; imputation.

الزام لگانا ilzām lagānā, *v.* To accuse; to charge; to blame.

السانا alsānā (H) *v.* See آلسانا ālsānā.

السنہ alsinah (A) *n.f.* (*plu.* of لسان lisān) Tongues; languages.

السی alsi (H) *n.f.* Linseed.

السیٹ alseṭ (H) *n.f.* Deception; fraud; knavery; duplicity; difference; quarrel; obstruction.

السیٹیا alsetyā (H) n.m. Deceiver; quarrelsome.

الغوزہ alghozah (P) n.m. A flageolet; a whistle; a flute.

الطاف altāf (A) n.m. (plu. of لطف lutf) Kindness; graces; favours.

الف لیلہ alf lailah (A) n.f. One thousand nights; Arabian Nights.

الف alif (A) adj. One; alone; unmarried. n.m. The first letter of the Arabic, Persian and Urdu alphabets.

الف بے alif be, n.f. The alphabet.

الف ہونا alif honā, v. To rear (as a horse); to be naked or nude.

الفاظ alfāz (A) n.m. (plu. of لفظ lafz) Words; terms.

اُلفت ulfat (P) n.f. Friendship; intimacy; love; attachment; affection; familiarity.

اُلفت کا بندہ ulfat kā bandah, n.m. Slave of love and friendship; very sincere and loving friend.

اُلفت کرنا ulfat karnā, v. To make love; to be intimate; to be familiar with; to make friends with.

الفتہ aliftah, n.m. Vagabond; a bad character; profligate.

الفی alfi, n.f. A kind of long shirt worn by fakirs; a shirt without sleeves and open at the sides.

القاء alqā' (A) n.m. Inspiration.

القاب alqāb (A) n.m. (plu. of لقب laqab) Titles; honorary names; forms of address in letters; epithets; surnames.

القاب و آداب alqāb-ō ādāb, n.m. Forms of address.

الکس ، الکسی alkas, alkasi, See آلکسی alkasi.

الکسانا alkasanā, See السانا alsānā.

الکلی alkalī (E) n.f. Alkali; (Chem.) Series of compounds called bases, including soda, potash, and amonia; (Commerce.) caustic soda, caustic potash, etc.

الگ alag (H) adj. Detached; loose; apart; distinct; separate; aloof; asunder; isolated; alone.

الگ الگ alag alag, adv. Separately; individually; apart; one by one; severally.

الگ تھلگ alag thalag, adj. Apart; having no connection.

الگ رہنا alag rehnā, v. To shun society; to live apart; to refrain from; to live alone.

الگ کرنا alag karnā, v. To separate; to disjoin; to part; to dismiss; to set apart; to divide; to remove; to unravel; to dispose of.

الگنی algani, n.f. A cord or line for hanging clothes on.

الالٹپ alaltap, adv. Speaking at random; at random.

اللذی نہ اللذی illallazī nah ullāllazī, adj. A soft eared person; wavering; suffering from indecision.

اللہ Allah (A) n.m. God.

اللہ اکبر Allah-ō-akbar. God is great.

اللہ اللہ Allah Allah, int. Excellent! Good God! My goodness! Good Gracious.

اللہ اللہ خیر سلا Allah Allah ghair sallā. Thank God, it is all over.

اللہ اللہ کر کے Allah Allah kar ke, adv. With great difficulty; after waiting a long time.

اللہ آمین Allah amīn, intj. God grant it; it be so; so it be!

اللہ بخشے Allah bakhshe, God bless his soul.

اللہ بیلی ، اللہ نگہبان Allah beli; Allah nigahbān, Good-bye; God be with you.

اللہ رے Allah re, intj. O God! Good God!

اللہ کا نام لینا Allah kā nām lenā, v. To take the name of God; to have the fear of God (said to one who tries to deceive a person by telling a lie).

اللہ لوگ Allah log, n.m. Holy men; good men; simple and guileless people.

الله مارا *Allah mārā, adj* Unfortunate, a term used in abhorrence for a wretched person.

الله میاں *Allah miāṅ, n.m.* God; the Supreme Lord.

اللے تللے *alalle talalle, n.m.* Profligacy; extravagance; sensual enjoyment.

الم *alam* (A) *n.m.* Agony; affliction; pain; torment; grief; anguish.

الم ناک *alam nāk, adj.* Full of grief; painful; afflicted.

الماری *almārī, n.f.* A chest of drawers; a cabinet; almirah; a book case.

الماس *almās* (P) *n.m.* A diamond; adamant.

الماس تراش *almās trāsh, n.m.* Diamond-cutter; diamond dust. *adj.* Cut into facets like a diamond.

الماسی *almāsī* (P) *adj.* Cut into angles or facets.

الست *almast, adj.* Intoxicated; drunk; inebriated; mad; insane.

الم غلم *allam ghallam, n.m.* Nonsense; idle talk; rubbish.

الم غلم بکنا *allam ghallam baknā, v.* To talk nonsense; to talk at random.

الم نشرح *alam nashraḥ* (A) (*Lit.*) "Have we not opened (thy breast)"; opening words and the name of a chapter of the Holy Quran. *adj.* Clear; evident; well-known.

آلو *ullū* (H) *n.m.* An owl; a fool; an idiot; a stupid fellow; a blockhead.

آلو بنانا *ullū banānā, v.* To befool; to make a fool of; to cheat.

آلو پھانسنا *ullū phāṅsnā, v.* To beguile a green or inexperienced fellow.

الواح *alwāḥ* (A) *n.m.* (*plu.* لوح *lauḥ*) Tablets; planks; tables.

الوان *alwān* (A) *n.m.* (*plu.* of لون *laun*) Colours; sorts; kinds.

الوان نعمت *alwān-ĕ ni'mat, n.m.* Blessing of various kinds; dishes of various kinds.

الوپ *alūp* (H) *adj.* Concealed; hidden; imperceptible; invisible; unseen.

الوپ مایا *alūp māyā, n.f.* The secrets of Nature; the imperceptible power in Nature; mysteries of Nature.

الوپ ہونا *alūp honā, v.* To be invisible; to disappear.

الول *alol* (H) *n.f.* Gambol; playsomeness; frolic.

الول کلول کرنا *alol kalol karnā, v.* To gambol; to caper; to frolic.

الونا *alonā, alūnā* (H) *adj.* Without salt; savourless; insipid; tasteless.

الوہیت *ulūhiyyat* (A) *n.f.* Divinity; godhead; the divine essence.

اله *ilah* (A) *n.m.* God; deity.

الہام *ilhām* (A) *n.m.* Inspiration; revelation.

الھڑ *allhaṛ* (H) *adj.* Inexperienced; childish.

آلہنا *ulahnā* (H) *n.m.* Accusation; charge; taunt; calumny.

آلہنا دینا *ulahnā denā, v.* To reproach; to charge; to complain; to accuse.

الہی *Elāhī* (A) *n.m.* God; Lord. *adj.* Divine; celestial; heavenly; of God. *intj.* O God!

الہی سن *elāhī san, n.m.* The era instituted by the Emperor Akbar in the 24th year of his reign beginning from 1556 A.D.

الہی گز *elāhī gaz, n.m.* The yard of 41 inches instituted by Akbar.

الہیات *elāhiyyāt* (A) *n.f.* Metaphysics.

الیاس *ilyās* (A) *n.m.* Elias; name of a Prophet.

الیم *alīm* (A) *adj.* Painful; torturing; excruciating.

اُم *umm* (A) *n.f.* Mother.

اُم الامراض *umm-ul-amrāẓ, n.f.* Mother of diseases; (*Met.*) cold; bronchitis.

اُم الخبائث *umm-ul-khabā'is, n.f.* Mother of evils; (*Met.*) liquor.

اُم الصبیان *umm-uṣ-ṣibyān, n.f.* Epilepsy (of children).

ام العلو *umm-ul-'ulūm, n.f.* Etymology.

ام القریٰ *umm-ul-qurā, n.f.* Mother of cities; Mecca.

ام الکتاب *Umm-ul-kitāb, n.f.* Mother of book; al-Quran.

ام الولد *umm-ul-walad, n.f.* Mother of the child; a slave girl who gives birth to a child from her master.

اما *ammā* (A) *conj.* But; nevetheless; however; yet.

اما بعد *ammā ba'd, adj.* Hereafter; after that; after which; then.

امارت *imārat* (A) *n.f.* Possession of command or authority; the office of a governor; being rich.

امارہ *ammārah* (A) *adj.* Domineering; imperious; headstrong; wilful; obstinate.

اماکن *amākin* (A) *n.m.* (*plu.* of مکان *makān*) Houses; places; habitations.

امام *imām* (A) *n.m.* Spiritual or religious leader (of Muslims); a prelate; partiarch; chief; a large bead in the rosary.

امام باڑہ *imām bāṛah, n.m.* A place where functions connected with *Muharram* are celebrated.

امام ضامن *imām ẓāmin, n.m.* The guardian saint; the protecting *imām*, named Ali Bin Musa al-Kazim.

امامت *imāmat* (A) *n.f.* Leadership; guidance; the office of an *imam*.

امامیہ *imāmiyah* (A) *n.m.* The Shia sect of Muslims.

اماں *ammāṅ, n.f.* Mother.

اماں *amān* (A) *n.f.* Safety; security; immunity; quarter; grace; mercy; protection.

امانت *amānat* (A) *n.f.* A thing or property committed to the trust and care of a person; anything given in trust; charge; guartrust; security; deposit.

امانت‌دار *amānat dār, n.m. & adj.* Trustee; dian, faithful; honest.

امانت داری *amānat dārī, n.f.* Trustworthiness; trust; deposit; charge; guardianship; faithfulness.

امانت رکھنا *amānat rakhnā, v.* To deposit; to leave in trust; to entrust.

امانت گزار *amānat guzār, n.m.* One who deposits a security.

امانت میں خیانت *amānat meṅ khiyānat, n.f.* Breach of trust.

امانت نامہ *amānat nāmah, n.m.* A trust or deposit deed.

امانی *amānī* (A) *n.f.* Security; trust; charge; deposit; land held or work done under owner's or government supervision.

اماوس *amāwas* (H) *n.f.* (*Astro.*) The last day of the dark fortnight; the night of the new moon; the conjunction of the sun and moon.

امبولنس *ambūlans* (E) *n.f.* Ambulance.

امبیا *ambiā, n.f.* A small unripe mango; diminutive of آم *ām* (mango).

امپائر *ampā'ir* (E) *n.m.* Umpire.

امت *ummat* (A) *n.f.* Followers; adherents; disciples; men of the same faith; caste; sect; nation.

امتثال *imtiṣāl* (A) *n.m.* Relating a story; quoting a proverb or a parable; obedience.

امتثال امر *imtiṣāl-ĕ amr, n.m.* Compliance of order; execution of orders.

امتحان *imtiḥān* (A) *n.m.* Examination; investigation; test; trial; proof; experiment.

امتحان دینا *imtiḥān denā, v.* To take an examination; to undergo a test.

امتحان پاس کرنا *imtiḥān pās karnā, v.* To pass a test; to go through an examination.

امتحان کرنا یا لینا *imtiḥān karnā yā lenā, v.* To test; to examine; to experiment; to try.

امتداد *imtidād* (A) *n.m.* Prolongation; protraction; period; time.

امتزاج *imtizāj* (A) *n.m.* Mixture; union; mingling.

امتزاج کیمیائی *imtizāj-ĕ kimyā'ī, n.m.* Chemical mixture.

امتلاء *imtilā'* (A) *n.m.* Repletion; indigestion; feeling sick.

امتناع imtināʻ (A) n.m. Prohibition; restriction; restraint.

آمتی ummati (A) n.m. Followers of a religious order.

امتیاز imtiyāz (A) n.m. Discrimination; discernment; discretion; pre-eminence; distinction; preference.

امتیاز کرنا imtiyāz karnā, v. To distinguish; to discriminate; to treat with distinction; to discern.

امتیازی imtiyāzi, adj. Of distinction; distinguished.

امتیازی اوصاف imtiyāzi auṣāf, n.m. Distinctive features.

امتیازی حقوق imtiyāzi ḥuqūq, n.m. Preferential rights; privileges.

امٹ amiṭ (H) adj. Ineffaceable; indestructible; unalterable; steady; indelible; fixed.

امثال amṣāl (A) n.m. (plu. of مثل maṣal) Narration; proverb; maxim; fables; examples; sayings; adages.

امثله amṣilah (A) n.f. (plu. of مثال miṣāl) Examples.

ام جانا am jānā (H) v. To be exhausted, fatigued, tired or worn out.

امجد amjad (A) n.m. (sup. of ماجد mājid) Most glorious; most noble, most venerable.

امچور amchūr (H) n.m. Mango parings dried in the sun.

امداد imdād (A) n.f. Aiding; assistance; help; support; relief; subsidy.

امداد باہمی imdād-ĕ bāhami, n.f. Cooperation; mutual help.

امداد دینا imdād denā, v. To give relief; to help; to assist.

امداد مالی imdād-ĕ māli, n.f. Financial help or assistance.

امدادی imdādi (A) adj. Co-operative; subsidiary; reserve.

امر amr (A) n.m. Order; command; behest; affair; business; matter; thing; point; (Gram.) the imperative mood.

امر تجویز شده amr-ĕ tajwiz shudah, n.m. Res judicata.

امر تنقیح طلب amr-e tanqiḥ ṭalab, n.m. A point for determination; issue.

امر مستفسره amr-ĕ mustafsirah, n.m. The point or matter referred to.

امر و نہی amr-ŏ nahi, n.m. Commands and prohibitions; orders and counter-orders; (Gram.) positive and negative.

امر amar (H) adj. Immortal; imperishable.

امر بیل amar bel, n.f. Dodder; air-plant.

امراض amrāz (A) n.m. (plu. of مرض maraẓ) Diseases; sicknesses.

امراء umarā' (H) n.m. (plu. of امیر amir) Rich poeple; nobles; grandees; lords.

امرت amrit (H) n.m. Nectar; water of life; ambrosia.

امرتی amriti (H) n.f. A kind of sweetmeat made of pulse.

امرد amrad (A) n.m. Young beardless lad; a handsome youth.

امرد پرست amrad parast, n.m. A sodomite.

امرس amras (H) n.m. Mango juice; thickened juice of mango.

امرود amrūd (P) n.m. Guava.

امروز imroz, imruz (P) adv. Today.

امروز و فردا imroz-ŏ fardā, n.m. Today and tomorrow; anon; prevarication.

امزجه amzijah (A) n.m. (plu. of مزاج mizāj) Temperaments; dispositions.

آمس umas (H) n.f. Sultriness; stuffiness; intense heat.

امساک imsāk (A) n.m. Holding; retention; parsimony; miserliness; drought; delaying emission; prolongation of sexual pleasure.

امساک باراں imsāk-ĕ bārān, n.m. Dearth of rain; drought.

امسال imsāl (P) adv. This year; the current year.

امشب imshab (P) adv. To-night.

امصار amṣār (A) n.m. (plu. of مصر miṣr) Towns; cities.

امکا ڈھمکا amkā ḍhamkā, n.m. This one and that one; small and great; a no body; a person of little importance; trifling.

امکان imkān (A) n.m. Possibility; potentiality. contingent existence; power; might.

امکانی imkāni (A) adj. Potential; possible; contingent.

امل amal (A) n.m. Hope; expectation; wish; desire.

امل amal (H) n.m. Intoxication.

املا imlā (A) n.m. Orthography; dictation; writing correctly.

املا نویس imlā nawis (P) adj. & n.m. One who takes dictation; calligrapher.

املاک amlāk (A) n.f. (plu. of ملک milk) Possessions; estates; property; lands.

املاک غیر منقولہ amlāk-ĕ ghair manqūlah, n.f. Immovable property.

املاک منقولہ amlāk-ĕ manqūlah, n.f. Movable property.

املتاس amaltās (H) n.m. A fruit used as a purgative; cassia fistula.

املی imlī (H) n.f. Tamarind tree or its fruits.

اُمم umam (A) n.f. (plu. of اُمت ummat) Nations; races.

امن amn (A) n.m. Peace; security; safety; tranquillity.

امن چین amn chain, n.m. Peace; comfort; rest.

امن و امان amn-ŏ aman, n.m. Safety and peace.

اُمنڈنا umanḍnā (H) v. To overflow; to swell; to gush out; to be touched or moved; to fall (as tears).

اُمنگ umang (H) n.f. Longing; excessive desire; ambition; eagerness; ardour; passion.

اموات amwāt (A) n.f. (plu. of موت maut) Deaths.

امواج amwāj (A) n.f. (plu. of موج mauj) Waves; surges; billows.

اموال amwāl (A) n.m. (plu. of مال māl) Riches; wealth; effects; goods; chattels; property.

اُمور umūr (A) n.m. (plu. of امر amr) Things; affairs; business; matters; actions; commands; questions; orders.

امور حوالہ umūr-ĕ ḥawālah, n.m. Terms of reference.

امور مشابہت umūr-ĕ mushābahat, n.m. Points of similarity.

امور ملکی umūr-ĕ mulkī, n.m. Political affairs; affairs of the State.

امول amol (H) adj. Invaluable; inestimable; priceless; (same as ان مول anmol).

اُمہات ummahāt (A) n.f. (plu. of اُم umm) Mothers.

اُمہات المومنین ummahāt-ul-mominīn, n.f. Mothers of the faithful (wives of the Holy Prophet).

امی ammī, n.f. Mother.

اُمی ummī (A) adj. Not knowing how to read or write; illiterate; uneducated.

اُمید ummīd (P) n.f. Hope; expectation; trust; pregnancy.

اُمید رکھنا ummīd rakhnā, v. To hope; to expect; to trust.

اُمید سے ummīd se, adj. Pregnant.

اُمیدوار ummīd wār, adj. Hopeful; expectant. n.m. An expectant; dependent; candidate; petitioner; apprentice; probationer.

اُمیدوار ہونا ummīd wār honā, v. To expect; to work as an apprentice; to be a candidate or applicant for a post; to hope.

اُمیدواری ummīd wārī, n.f. Hope; hopefulness; expectation; dependence; apprenticeship; candidateship.

امیر amīr (A) n.m. Commander; chieftain; ruler; governor; a rich man; a grandee; a nobleman.

امیر الامراء amīr-ul-umarā', n.m. Leader of the nobles; lord of lords.

امیر البحر amīr-ul-bhr, n.m. Admiral.

امیر زادہ amīr zādah, n.m. Nobly born; a prince; son of a wealthy man.

امیرالملک amir-ul-mulk, n.m. Governor-General.

امیر المومنین amir-ul-mominin, n.m. Commander of the faithful; a title of the caliph.

امیرانہ Amirānah, adj. Princely; lordly.

امیری amiri (A) n.f. Sovereignty; lordship; wealthiness; riches.

امین amīn (A) adj. Trustworthy; faithful; confidential. n.m. Trustee; guardian; a commissioner; arbitrator; law officer.

امینی amini, n.f. The office of an amin; guardianship; custody.

ان an (H) A negative prefix (equivalent to the English un or in).

ان بن an ban, n.f. Discord; disagreement.

ان پڑھ an paṛh, adj. Uneducated; illiterate.

ان دیکھا ، ان دیکھی an dekhā, an dekhi, adj. Unseen; invisible.

ان تھک an thak, adj. Untiring; diligent.

ان جان an jān, adj. Not knowing; ignorant; unacquainted.

ان جان بننا ، ہونا an jan bannā, honā, v. To feign ignorance or to be ignorant.

ان جانا ، ان جانی an jānā, an jāni, adj. Not known; unacqainted.

ان گنت an ginat, adj. Countless; innumerable.

انمل anmil, adj. Unsociable; remaining aloof; ill-assorted; disjointed.

انمول anmol, adj. Priceless; invaluable; precious.

انمیل anmel, adj. Discordant; unsuitable; not harmonizing; heterogeneous.

ان ann (S) n.m. Food; grain; corn; victuals.

ان پانی ، ان جل ann pāni, ann jal, n.m. Food and drink; victuals.

ان داتا ann dātā, n.m. Food-giver; supporter; master.

ان کا کیڑا ann kā kiṛā, n.m. Human being; man; which lives on food.

ان in (H) pron. These (by way of politeness also used for a single superior person).

ان دنوں in dinoṅ, adv. Now-a-days; at present.

اُن un (H) pron. Those; (by way of politeness also used for a single superior person).

انا anā (A) pro. & n.f. I; ego; self.

انا پرست anā parast, adj. Egoist; selfish.

انا annā (H) n.f. A wet-nurse.

انابت inābat (A) n.f. Return to the true faith; conversion to God's faith; penitence; repentance; representation.

انابیب anābīb (A) n.f. (plu. of انبوب unbūb) Water pipes; tubes.

انابیب شعری anābib-ĕ shiʻri, n.f. Capillary tubes or canals; a tube with a bore as fine as a hair; the minute vessels that unite the veins and arteries in animals.

اناپ شناپ anāp shanāp (H) adj. Meaningless; indiscriminate; foolish; nonsense; preposterous.

اناج anāj (H) n.m. Grain; corn.

اناجیل anājil (A) n.f. (plu. of انجیل injīl) Gospels; The New Testament.

انار anār (P) n.m. A pomegranate; a kind of fireworks shaped like a pomegranate.

انار دانہ anār dānah, n.m. Dried seeds of sour pomegranate.

انار بے دانہ anār-ĕ be danah, n.m. A superior species of pomegranate having no seeds.

انارکی ānārki (E) n.f. Anarchy.

اناڑ پن anāṛ pan (H) n.m. Rawness; clumsiness; ignorance.

اناڑی anāṛi (H) adj. Unskilful; inapt; inexpert; inexperienced; clumsy; green; artless; n.m. Novice; blockhead; idiot; bungler; sloven.

آناسی unāsi (H) adj. Seventy-nine.

انام anām (A) n.m. Created beings; creatures; creation; mankind.

انامل anāmil (A) n.f. (plu. of انملہ anmilah) Fingers; tips of fingers.

انانیت anāniyyat (A) n.f. Egotism; arrogance; self-conceit; self-praise; boasting.

انبار ambār (P) n.m. Heap; lump; pile; collection; store; stock; hoard; stack.

انبار خانہ ambār khānah, n.m. Store-house; warehouse; magazine.

انبساط imbisāt (A) n.m. Gladness; joy; delight; cheerfulness; merriment; mirth.

انبوہ amboh (P) n.m. A crowd; multitude; mob; concourse; throng; great quantity; abundance.

انبہ ambah (P) n.m. Mango.

انبیاء Ambiyā' (A) n.m. (plu. of نبی nabi) Prophets.

انت ant (S) n.m. End; completion; termination; conclusion; end of life; death. adv. After all; at last; in the end.

انت کال ant kāl, n.m. Dying moment; last moment.

اُنتالیس untālis (H) adj. Thirty-nine.

انتباہ intibāh (A) n.m. Alarm; caution; warning.

انتخاب intikhāb (A) n.m. Selection; choice; election; extract (from books).

انتخاب کرنا intikhāb karnā, v. To select; to elect; to extract; to choose; to pick up; to compile.

انتڑی antṛi (H) n.f. Entrails; bowels; intestines

انتڑی کا بل کھولنا antṛi kā bal kholnā, v. To eat a bellyful after starving.

انتڑیاں جلنا، انتڑیونکا قل ھو اللہ پڑھنا ، انتڑیوں میں آگ لگنا antṛiyāṅ jalnā, antṛiyoṅ kā qul hu-wallah paṛhnā, antṛiyoṅ meṅ āg lagnā, v. To be very hungry.

انتساب intisāb (A) n.m. Dedication; being related to; relation; connection; engagement.

انتشار intishār (A) n.m. Spreading abroad; scattering; dispersion; confusion; anxiety.

انتظار intizār (A) n.m. Waiting anxiously (for); looking out for; expectation.

انتظار دیکھنا intizār dekhnā, v. To be on the look out for.

انتظار کرنا intizār karnā, v. To expect; to look out for; to await.

انتظار کش intizār kash, adj. Expecting; waiting anxiously; looking out for.

انتظام intizām (A) n.m. Management; regulation; order; method; administration; arrangement; organization.

انتظام خانگی intizām-ĕ khānagi, n.m. Domestic management; private arrangement.

انتظام رکھنا intizām rakanā, v. To keep order; to maintain order and discipline.

انتظام کرنا intizām karnā, v. To arrange; to manage; to regulate; to plan.

انتظامی intizāmi, adj. Administrative.

انتظامیہ inttizāmiyah (A) n.f. Executive; administration.

انتقال intiqāl (A) n.m. Transfer; conveyance; alienation; assignment; transmission; migration; transportation; travelling; deparature; death.

انتقال اراضی intiqāl-ĕ arāzi, n.m. Transfer of land held jointly; alienation or mutation of land.

انتقال برق intiqāl-ĕ barq, n.m. Transmission of electricity.

انتقال جائداد intiqāl-ĕ jā'idād, n.m. Transfer of property.

انتقال جائز intiqāl-ĕ jā'iz, n.m. Legal or valid transfer.

انتقال حرارت intiqāl-ĕ ḥarārat, n.m. Conduction (of heat).

انتقال حقیت intiqqāl-ĕ ḥaqqiyat, n.m. Transfer of rights.

انتقال دائمی intiqāl-ĕ da'imi, n.m. Permanent alienation.

انتقال رسوم intiqāl-ĕ rusūm, n.f. Transfer of property fees.

انتقال رہن intiqāl-ĕ rahn, n.m. Transfer of mortgage.

انتقال کرنا intiqāl karnā, v. To transfter; to assign; to shift; to transport; to die.

انتقال کنندہ *intiqāl kunindah, n.m.* An aliener; one who conveys; transferor.

انتقال نامہ *intiqāl nāmah, n.m.* Deed of transfer or conveyance.

انتقام *intiqām* (A) *n.m.* Revenge; vengeance; retaliation; reprisal.

انتقام لینا *intiqām lenā, v.* To take revenge; to revenge oneself; to avenge; to retaliate.

انتہا *intihā* (A) *n.f.* Termination; close; finish; utmost limit; extremity; completion; end.

انتہا کا *intihā kā, adj.* Extreme; utmost; perfect; consummate.

اُنتیس *untis* (H) *adj.* Twenty-nine.

انٹا *anṭā* (H) *n.m.* A ball; a marble; the billiard ball; a large shell.

انٹا گھر *anṭā ghar, n.m.* A billiard room.

انٹی *anṭi* (H) *n.f.* A reel or frame on which thread is wound; a skein of thread; a bundle of grass; a handful; a small fagot; a leg trick in wrestling.

اُنثیٰ *unsā* (A) *n.f.* Female; woman.

انجام *anjām* (A) *n.m.* Termination; end; accomplishment; conclusion; performance; result; issue.

انجام بخیر ہونا *anjām bakhair honā, v.* To have a good ending.

انجام پانا *anjām pānā, v.* To be performed; to be completed; to be brought to an end or to a close.

انجام دینا *anjām denā, v.* To accomplish; to complete; to bring to an end; to manage; to comply with; to discharge.

انجام سوچنا *anjām sochnā, v.* To exercise discretion; to be prudent or far sighted; to have an eye on the end; to provide against.

انجام کار *anjām kār, adv.* Eventually; at last; in the end.

انجبار *anjabār* (P) *n.m.* A creeper or shrub used in preparation of some medicines.

انجذاب *injizāb* (A) *n.m.* To absorb; to draw.

انجر پنجر *anjar panjar, n.m.* Limbs; joints; organs.

انجر پنجر ڈھیلا ہونا *anjar panjar ḍhilā honā, v.* Loosening or weakening of limbs and joints of the body (as on account of fatigue).

انجم *anjum* (A) *n.m.* (*plu.* of نجم *najm*) Stars.

انجماد *injimād* (A) *n.m.* Freezing; condensation; congealing; curdling.

انجمن *anjuman* (P) *n.f.* Assembly; congregation; union; society; association; meeting.

انجمن اتحاد مزدوران *anjuman-ĕ ittihād-ĕ mazdūrān, n.f.* Labour union; workers' union.

انجن *anjan* (H) *n.m.* Antimony; collyrium.

انجن *Injan* (E) *n.m.* Engine; locomotive.

انجیر *anjir* (P) *n.m.* A fig.

انجیل *Injil* (A) *n.f.* The New Testament; the Gospel.

انچ *inch* (E) *n.m.* An inch.

اُنچاس *unchās* (H) *adj.* Forty-nine.

انحراف *inhirāf* (A) *n.m.* Deflection; turning away (from); deviation; revolt; rebillion; swerving from allegiance; disobediance; opposition; declination (in *Astro.*)

انحراف کرنا *inhirāf karnā, v.* To deviate; to turn against; to repudiate; to recant; to revolt; to rebel.

انحصار *inhiṣār* (A) *n.m.* Being surrounded; encircled; reliance; dependence.

انحطاط *inhiṭāṭ* (A) *n.m.* Descent; decline, degradation; reduction; decrease; deterioration.

انداز *andāz* (P) *n.m.* Way; manner; method; style; measure; degree. *adj.* Throwing; putting (in order); firing (a gun) (*used in comp.*)

اندازہ *andāzah* (P) *n.m.* Measurment; weight; valuation; conjecture; guess; forecast; rough estimate; tune in music.

اندازۂ فصل *andāzah-ĕ faṣl, n.m.* Crop forecast.

اندازہ کرنا یا لگانا *andāzah karnā yā lagānā, v.* To make rough estimate; to judge; to conjecture; to weigh; to guess; to measure.

اندازاً andāzan adv. By way of guess; approximately; conjecturally; roughly; moderately.

اندام andam (P) n.m. Body; stature; figure.

اندام نہانی andām-ĕ nihāni, n.f. Private part (of the body).

اندر andar (P) prep. Within; inside;

اندر سے andar se, adv. Internally.

اندر کرنا andar karna, v. To drive in; to bring in; to put within; to send behind the bars; to send to jail.

اندر indara (S) n.m. King of the gods; thunderer; the Jove of Hindu mythology; god of rain.

اندراج indirāj (A) n.m. Insertion; entry; registration; record.

اندرائن کا پھل indrā'in ka phal (H) n.m. Wild gourd; colocynth; a fruit of beautiful appearance but bitter taste. (Met.) An ill-natured or hot-tempered person; a mischief-maker.

اندرجو indar jau (H) n.m. The seed of a certain medicinal plant (nerium antidysentricum).

اندرسا andrasā, n.m. A sweetmeat made of rice flour and sugar fried in ghee.

اندرون andarūn (P) adj. Within; interior; inside. n.m. Inner apartments.

اندری indri (H) n.f. An organ of sense or perception; the organs of action; the male or female genital organ.

اندک andak (P) adj. Little; small; few; slight.

اندمال indimāl (A) n.m. Healing of a wound; getting better; recovery; satisfaction.

اندوختہ andokhtah (P) adj. Gained; saved; hoarded. n.m. Savings.

اندوز andoz (P) adj. Acquiring; gaining (used in comp.).

اندوہ andoh (P) n.m. Grief; sorrow; anxiety; care.

اندوہ گین ، اندوہ ناک andohgīn, andohnāk, adj. Full of grief; sorrowful; sad; afflicted.

اندھا andhā, adj. Blind; stone-blind; undiscerning; headless; thoughtless. n.m. A blind man.

اندھا بانٹے ریوڑیاں ، اپنوں ھی کو دے andhā bānte reweriyān, apnon hi ko de, prov. A mother's bowel yearns towards her own child.

اندھا پن andhā pan, n.m. Blindness; obscurity; folly.

اندھا خرچ andhā kharch, n.m. Profuse expenditure; prodigality; extravagance.

اندھا دھند andhā dhund, adj. In the manner of a blind person; indiscriminate; excessive; careless; wild; dark. adv. Blindly; wildly; indiscriminately.

اندھا دھند لٹانا andhā dhund lutānā, v. To squander; to spend extravagantly.

اندھا کرنا andhā karnā, v. To blind; to dupe; to defraud; to befool; to deceive; to throw dust in one's eyes.

اندھا کنواں andhā kunwān, n.m. A dry well.

اندھا ھونا andhā honā, v. To lose sight; to become blind; to go astray; to behave rashly.

اندھی andhi (H) adj. & n.f. Blind; thoughtless; a blind woman.

اندھیر andher (H) n.m. Darkness; oppression; violence; tyranny; anarchy; disorder; tumult; misrule; deceit; iniquity; injustice; outrage.

اندھیر کرنا andher karnā, v. To do wrong (to); to oppress; to tyrannise (over); to outrage.

اندھیر کھاتا andher khātā, n.m. Unfairness in accounts or dealings.

اندھیرا andherā (H) n.m. Darkness; dusk; obscurity; gloom. adj. Dark; gloomy; dusky; obscure.

اندھیرا کرنا *andherā karnā, v.* To darken; to obscure; to overcast; to put out (a light).

اندھیرا گھپ *andherā ghup, n.m.* Utter darkness.

اندھیرے گھر کا اُجالا *andhere ghar kā ujālā, n.m.* The only son; a very dear child.

اندھیرے منہ *andhere muṅh, adv.* Very early in the morning; at dawn.

اندھیری *andherī* (H) *n.f.* Darkness; blinkers for a horse. *adj.* Dark; dusky.

اندھیری کوٹھڑی *andherī koṭhṛī, n.f.* A dark room; a prison cell; black-hole; (*Met.*) the belly; womb.

اندیش *andesh* (P) *adj.* Thinking; considering; meditating; reflecting (*used in comp.* as بد اندیش *bad andesh*, evil-minded; harmful).

اندیشہ *andeshah* (P) *n.m.* Thought; deliberation; reflection meditation; suspicion; dread; fear; anxiety; concern.

اندیشہ کرنا *andeshah karnā, v.* To reflect; to fear; to feel anxiety or concern (for); to feel anxious (about); to be apprehensive (of).

اندیشہ ناک (اندیشناک) *andeshah nāk (andeshnāk), adj.* Fearful; dreadful; sad; thoughtful.

انڈا *anḍā* (H) *n.m.* Egg.

انڈا دینا *anḍā denā, v.* To lay an egg.

انڈا گندہ ہونا *anḍā gandah honā, v.* Egg turning bad; to become addled.

انڈوں پر ہونا *anḍoṅ par honā, v.* To hatch; to sit on eggs.

انڈے بچے *anḍe bachche, n.m.* Kiddies; children.

انڈے سینا *anḍe sainā, v.* To sit on eggs; to hatch eggs; to brood; to lead a retired life.

انڈے کا شہزادہ *anḍe kā shahzādah, n.m.* An inexperienced person; a simpleton; a greenhorn.

اُنڈیلنا *unḍelnā* (H) *v.* To pour out; to empty; to discharge.

انزال *inzāl* (A) *n.m.* Causing to come down; getting down; emission; seminal discharge.

انس *ins* (A) *n.m.* Man; mankind.

اُنس *uns* (A) *n.m.* Attachment; friendship; love; affection; fellowship.

انساب *ansāb* (A) *n.m.* (*plu.* of نسب *nasab*) Genealogies; generations; races; families.

انسان *insān* (A) *n.m.* Man; human being; mankind.

انسان بنانا *insān banānā, v.* To civilize; to educate; to polish; to humanize.

انسان ہی تو ہے *insān hī to hae, id.* He is but human; man is fallible.

انسانی *insānī* (A) *adj.* Concerning humanity; relating to man; human.

انسانیت *insāniyyat* (A) *n.f.* Humanity; human nature; civility; affability; human kindness; politeness.

انسب *ansab* (A) *adj.* Most suitable; convenient; worthy; very proper.

اُنسٹھ *unsaṭh* (H) *adj.* Fifty-nine.

انسداد *insidād* (A) *n.m.* Prevention; check; bar; hindrance; obstacle; management; arrangement.

انسدادی *insidādī* (A) *adj.* Preventive.

انشاء *inshā'* (A) *n.f.* Writing; composition; style; diction; (*Lit.*) creating.

انشاء پردازی *inshā' pardāzī, n.f.* Writing; composition; authorship; letter-writing; elegance of composition.

انشاء اللہ *inshā' Allah* (A) *adv.* God willing.

انشاء اللہ تعالیٰ *inshā' Allah t'ālā, adv.* If God, the most high, willeth.

انشائیہ *inshā'iyah* (A) *n.m.* A sentence which deals with futurity or shows uncertainty of action; a sentence which may be true and false; an essay.

انشراح *inshirāḥ* (A) *n.m.* Laying open; making clear; manifestation; explanation.

انصار anṣār (A) n.m. (plu. of ناصر nāṣir) Assistants; helpers; friends; the Musalmans of Medina who extended every help to the Holy Prophet and his companions on their migration to Medina.

انصاری anṣārī (A) adj. Related to the Anṣārs.

انصاف inṣāf (A) n.m. Justice; fairplay; impartiality; equity; (Lit.) dividing into two equal parts.

انصاف چاهنا inṣāf chāhnā, v. To seek jusitce; to demand fairplay; to seek redress.

انصاف کرنا inṣāf karnā, v. To do justice; to be partial.

انصاف کا خون کرنا inṣāf kā khūn karnā, v. To be unjust; to be partial; to be cruel.

انصرام inṣirām (A) n.m. Accomplishment; completion; performance; administration; management (of an estate); termination; conclusion.

انضباط inẓibāṭ (A) n.m. Being bound or regulated; the act of regulating; restraint; self-control; discipline; (Lit.) strengthening.

انضباط اوقات inẓibāṭ-ĕ auqāt, n.m. A time-table; a routine.

انطباع inṭibā' (A) n.m. The being stamped, impressed or printed; impression.

انطباق inṭibāq (A) n.m. Coincidence.

انعام in'ām (A) n.m. A present; gift; prize; gratuity; reward; largess; favour; grant.

انعام و اکرام in'ām-ŏ ikrām, n.m. Gifts and honours; an honourable gift.

انعام دینا in'ām denā, v. To award a prize; to give a reward.

انعام تقسیم کرنا in'ām taqsīm karnā, v. To give away prizes; to distribute prizes.

انعامی in'āmī, adj. Prize; presentable.

انعامی رقم in'āmī raqm, n.f. Gratuity; honorarium.

انعقاد in'iqād (A) n.m. Taking place; holding; celebrating.

انعکاس in'ikās (A) n.m. Inversion; reflection (as from a mirror).

انفاس anfās (A) n.m. (plu. of نفس nafas) Breaths.

انفرادی infirādī (A) adj. Individually; pertaining to an individual, existing separately; subsisting as one.

انفصال infiṣāl (A) n.m. Division; separation; decision (of a case or matter); settlement,

انفعال infi'āl (A) n.m. Abashment; repentance; contrition; bashfulness; shame; modesty.

انفکاک infikāk (A) n.m. Redemption; dislocation (of a bone); release.

انفکاک رهن infikāk-ĕ rahn, n.m. Redemption of mortgage.

انقباض inqibāẓ (A) n.m. Contraction; detention; restraint; constipation.

انقره anqrah (T) n.m. Ankara (capital of Turkey).

انقسام inqisām (A) n.m. Division; partition; assignment; apportionment; distribution.

انقضاء inqiẓā' (A) n.m. Expiry (of a term); lapse (of a period); termination; completion; extinction.

انقضاء منظوری inqiẓā'-ĕ manẓūrī, n.m. Lapse of a sanction.

انقطاع inqiṭā' (A) n.m. Being cut or broken off; amputation; separation; discontinuance.

انقلاب inqilāb (A) n.m. Revolution; vicissitude (of time); change; alteration.

انقیاد inqiyād (A) n.m. Obedience; subjection. submission; compliance; docility; restriction.

انکار inkār (A) n.m. Denial; disavowal; disallowance; contradiction; declining; refusal; negation; opposition.

انکار کرنا inkār karnā, v. To refuse; to disown; to disallow; to disavow; to deny; to disagree.

انکس aṅkas (H) See آنکس āṅkas.

انکسار inkisār (A) n.m. Humility; humbleness; meekness; modesty.

انکساری **inkisārī**, *n.f.* See انکسار *inkisār*.

انکساف **inkisāf** (A) *n.m.* Solar eclipse.

انکشاف **inkishāf** (A) *n.m.* Disclosure; detection; revelation; exposition.

انکھڑیاں **ankhṛiyāṅ** (H) *n.f.* Eyes (diminutive form).

انکھیارا ، انکھیاری **aṅkhyārā, aṅkhyārī** (H) *adj.* Having eyes.

انگ **aṅg** (H) *n.m.* Body; limb; organ; breasts.

انگ لگانا **aṅg lagānā**, *v.* To embrace; to clasp; to wear; to give in marriage; to be nourished.

انگا **aṅgā** (H) *n.m.* A long coat or tunic.

انگارا **aṅgārā** (H). *n.m.* Burning charcoal; sparks remaining in ashes; embers; bright red.

انگاروں پر لوٹنا **aṅgāroṅ par loṭnā**, *v.* To be on thorns; to be agitated or troubled; to burn with rage, envy or jealousy.

انگارے برسنا **aṅgāre barasnā**, *v.* To rain fire (excessive heat).

انگبین **aṅgbīn** (P) *n.m.* Honey.

انگرکھا **aṅgrakhā** (H) *n.m.* Long coat, worn by men.

انگریز **aṅgrez**, *n.m.* Englishman.

انگریزی **aṅgrezī**, *n.f.* The English language. *adj.* Of England; pertaining to England.

انگڑائی **aṅgṛā'ī** (H) *n.f.* Stretching the limbs; yawning.

انگڑائی لینا **aṅgṛā'ī lenā**, *v.* To yawn; to stretch the limbs; to oscitate.

انگشت **aṅgusht** (P) *n.f.* A finger.

انگشت حیرت دانتوں میں رکھنا **āngusht-ĕ ḥairat dāṅtoṅ meṅ rakhnā**, *v.* To express surprise; to bite the finger.

انگشت شناسی **aṅgusht shināsī**, *n.f.* Dactyloscopy.

انگشت شہادت **aṅgusht-ĕ shahādat**, *n.f.* The forefinger.

انگشت نر **angusht-ĕ nar**, *n.f.* The thumb; the great toe.

انگشتانہ **aṅgushtānah** (P) *n.m.* A thimble.

انگشتری **aṅgushtrī** (P) *n.f.* A finger-ring.

آنگل **ungal**, *n.m.* A finger; a finger's breadth; a digit; a measure.

آنگلانا **unglānā**, *v.* To tease; to chaff; to annoy; to goad.

انگلستان **inglistān**, *n.m.* England.

آنگلی **unglī**, *n.f.* A finger.

آنگلی دھرنا ، آنگلی رکھنا **unglī dharnā, unglī rakhnā**, *v.* To criticize; to find fault (with); to take into possession; to bring under control; to develop friendship.

آنگلی نہ لگانا **unglī nah lagānā**, *v.* Not to touch at all; to show complete indifference towards anything.

آنگلیاں اٹھانا **ungliyāṅ uṭhānā**, *v.* To point towards an undesirable and notorious man; to ridicule; to look down upon.

آنگلیاں توڑنا **ungliyāṅ toṛnā**, *v.* To pass time aimlessly; to snap (the fingers).

آنگلیاں چٹخانا **uṅgliyāṅ chaṭkhānā**, *v.* To snap the fingers.

آنگلیاں نچانا **ungliyāṅ nachānā**, *v.* To move fingers or hands aimlessly.

آنگلیوں پر نچانا **ungliyoṅ par nachānā**, *v.* To harass; to do as one pleases with a (person); to trifle with; to make a fool of.

انگنائی **aṅgnā'ī**, *n.f.* The inner court; courtyard.

انگوٹھا **aṅgūṭhā** (H) *n.m.* Thumb; the great toe.

انگوٹھا چوسنا **aṅgūṭhā chūsnā**, *v.* To suck the thumb.

انگوٹھا چومنا **aṅgūṭhā chūmnā**, *v.* To flatter; to show great love.

انگوٹھا دکھانا **aṅgūṭhā dikhānā**, *v.* To mock; to jeer; to irritate; to refuse point blank.

انگوٹھی **aṅgūṭhī** (H) *n.f.* Ring.

انگوچھا aṅgochhā (H) n.m. A towel; a handkerchief; a piece of cloth which Hindus wrap round their waists when bathing and afterwards wipe their body with it.

انگور aṅgūr (P) n.m. Grapes; granulation in a healing wound; scab of a sore.

انگوری سرکہ aṅgūrī sirkah, n.m. Vinegar.

انگوری شراب aṅgūrī sharāb, n.f. Wine distilled from grapes.

انگیا aṅgiyā (H) n.f. Bodice; corset; stays.

انگیٹھی aṅgīṭhī (H) n.f. Grate; stove. brazier.

انگیز aṅgez (P) adj. (used in comp.). Exciting; rousing; causing; fomenting; raising.

اناس anannās, n.m. A pine-apple.

انوار anwār (A) n.m. (plu. of نور nūr) Light; brightness; lustre.

انواع anwā' (A) n.f. (plu. of نوع nau') Varieties; species; kinds; sorts.

انواع و اقسام anwā'-ŏ aqsām, n.f. Of all sorts and kinds.

انوپ anūp (H) adj. Incomparable; unique; matchless; peerless.

انور anwar (A) adj. Very brilliant; very splendid; resplendent; beautiful.

انوکھا ، انوکھی anokhā, anokhī, adj. Singular; uncommon; unusual; curious; extraordinary; rare.

انہار anhār (A) n.f. (plu. of نہر nahr) Streams; canals.

اُنہتر unhattar (H) adj. Sixty-nine.

انہدام inhidām (A) n.m. Demolition; destruction; extermination.

انہماک inhimāk (A) n.m. Concentration; absorption; engagement.

انہیں ، اُنہیں inheṅ, unheṅ (H) pron. Them.

انیس anīs (A) n.m. A companion; a comrade; an associate.

اُنیس unnīs (H) adj. Nineteen.

اُنیس بیس unnīs bīs, adj. Slightly different; almost equal.

انیسوں anisūṅ (Gr.) n.m. Anise seed; (Pimpinella anisum).

اُنیسواں unnīswāṅ (A) adj. Nineteenth.

او O (H) The vocative interjection; O.

اواخر awākhir (A) n.m. (plu. of آخر ākhir) Ends; latter parts; extremes.

اوامر awāmir (A) n.m. (plu. of امر amr) Orders; commands.

اوائل awā'il (A) n.m. (plu. of اول awwal) Beginning; commencement; early portion or period.

اوائل عمر awā'il-ĕ 'umr, n.f. Beginning of life; early youth; childhood; early age.

اوباش aubāsh (A) n.m. Vagabond; dissolute; debauchee; a rake; voluptuary; libertine; profligate. adj. Gallant; licentious; dissolute; rakish.

اوباشانہ aubāshānah, adj. Like a rake; depraved; vagabondish.

اوباشی aubāshī (A) n.f. Depravity; debauchery; dissipation; dissoluteness; rakishness.

اُوپر ūpar (H) adv. Up; on; at; high; aloft; above; upon; over.

اُوپر آنا ūpar ānā, v. To come up; to rise; to ascend.

اُوپر اُوپر ūpar ūpar, adv. Over and above one's head; secretly.

اُوپر اُوپر سے ūpar ūpar se, adv. Superficially; showingly.

اُوپر اُوپر کا ūpar ūpar kā, adj. Superior; excellent; best.

اُوپر تلے ūpar tale, adv. On upon another; in succession; continuously.

اُوپر تلے کے بچے ūpar tale ke bachche, n.m. Child born in succession.

اُوپر سے ūpar se, adv. From above, overhead; in addition to; over and above.

اُوپر کی آمد ūpar kī āmad, n.m. Present; bribe; unearned emoluments; perquisites.

اُوپر کے دم بھرنا ūpar ke dam bharnā, v. To gasp; to be at the point of death.

اوپر والا ūpar wālā, n.m. God Almighty; new moon; crescent.

اوپر والیاں ūpar wāliyān, n.f. Fairies; evil spirits; nurses; female servants.

اوپر والے ūpār wāle, n.m. Officers; residents of the upper storey; stars; heavenly bodies; male servants; strangers; other persons.

اوپر ہی اوپر ūpar hī ūpar, adv. Secretly; apart.

اوپر کا کام ūpar kā kām, n.m. Miscellaneous work; extra work.

اوپری ūpri (H) adj. Foreigners; tranger; unknown; superficial; artificial.

اوت ūt (H) n.m. One who dies without leaving an issue; issuless; a stupid person; blockhead; dunce; an ill-omened person.

اوتاد autād (A) n.m. (plu. of وتد watad) Pegs; a body of saints, whose number at one time in the world is just four.

اوتار autār (S) n.m. Descent (especially of a deity from heaven); incarnation; prophet; messengar (of God); holy person; spiritual guide or teacher; (Iron.) wicked; depraved.

اوٹ oṭ (H) n.f. A covering; screen; curtain; veil; mask; protection; shelter; refuge; concealment.

اوٹ کرنا oṭ karnā, v. To conceal; to screen; to hide; to shield; to cover.

اوٹ ہونا oṭ honā, v. To be concealed; to be hid.

اوٹا oṭā (H) n.m. A partition-wall; a screen; one who separates the seeds from cotton.

اوٹ پٹانگ ūṭ paṭāng, adj. Senseless; meaningless; nonsense; absurd; ridiculous; disjointed.

اوٹ پٹانگی ūṭ paṭāngī, adj. One who speaks inconsiderately or senselessly.

اوٹنا oṭnā (H) v. To separate seeds from cotton; to gin.

اوٹنی oṭnī (H) n.f. An instrument for separating the seeds from cotton.

اوج auj (A) n.m. Highest point; summit; top; zenith; the highest apsis of a planet; highest position or dignity.

اوجھ ojh (H) n.m. Stomach or guts of an animal,

اوجھڑی ojhaṛī (H) n.f. Stomach of an animal.

اوجھل ojhal (H) adj. Invisible; hidden; concealed.

اوجھل کرنا ojhal karnā, v. To hide; to screen; to conceal.

اوجھل ہونا ojhal honā, v. To be invisible; to be concealed; to be screened.

اوچھا ، اوچھی ochhā, ochhī (H) adj. Frivolous; shallow; petty; trivial; paltry; mean; of little importance; contemptible; low-bred; fickle; capricious.

اوچھا پن ochhā pan, n.m. Shallowness; absurdity; meanness; capriciousness.

اوچھا ہاتھ ocbhā hāth, n.m. Light grip.

اوچھا ہونا ochhā honā, v. To be shallow; to be mean; to be fickle.

اود ، اود بلاؤ ūd, ūd-bilāo' (H) n.m. Otter.

اودا ، اودی ūdā, ūdi (H) adj. Purple; azure.

اوداھٹ ūdāhaṭ, n.f. Being of purple colour.

اودھم ūdham. See ادھم ūddham.

اور aur (H) conj. And; also. adj. More; not this; different; else.

اور ایک aur ek, adj. Another; one more; different.

اور سنو aur suno, intj. Just listen! ridiculous! how ridiculous!

اور کیا aur kyā, adv. Indeed; besides this; what else.

اور نہیں تو aur nahīn tau; adv. And if not, then; and otherwise.

اور ہی aur hi. Quite different; quite changed.

اوراد aurād (A) n.m. (plu. of ورد wird) Daily recitation of a sacred phrase or verse.

اوراق aurāq (A) n.m. (plu. of ورق waraq) Leaves of a book or of a tree.

اورنگ **aurang** (P) *n.m.* A throne; places where goods are manufactured for sale; a kind of flower; intellect; understanding.

اورنگ زیب **Aurangzeb**, *n.m.* The appellation of Alamgir, the Mughal Emperor of Hindustan *adj.* Adorner of the throne.

اورنگ زیبی **aurangzebī**, *n.f.* A kind of cloth.

اورنگ زیبی پھوڑا **aurangzebī phoṛā**, *n.m.* A dangerous sore; carbuncle.

اورنگ شاهی **aurang shāhī**, *n.m.* A kind of silk.

اوڑھنا **oṛhnā** (H) *v.* To cover the head or body with a sheet; to cover. *n.m.* A sheet used by a woman to cover her head and breast; a stole.

اوڑھنا بچھونا **oṛhnā bichhonā**, *n.m.* Covering and bedding; small savings or income.

اوڑھنا آتارنا **oṛhnā utārnā**, *v.* To remove the sheet (from the head); to disgrace; to expose; to defame.

اوڑھنی **oṛhni** (H) *n.f* A smaller sheet used by a girl to cover her head.

اوزار **auzār** (A) *n.m.* (*plu.* of وزر *wizr*) Instruments; tools; apparatus; arms.

اوزان **auzān** (A) *n.m.* (*plu.* of وزن *wazn*) Weights; measures; metres.

اوس **os** (H) *n.f.* Dew.

اوس پڑنا **os paṛnā**, *v.* To despair; to feel disappointed; to fade.

اوسان **ausān** (H) *n.m.* Senses; self-possession; presence of mind; courage.

اوسان خطا هونا **ausān khaṭā honā**, *v.* To lose one's senses; to lose presence of mind; to be stunned or stupefied.

اوسر **ausar** (S) *n.m.* A turn; occasion; fit time; favourable opportunity.

اوسر چوکی ڈومنی گاوے تال بے تال **ausar chūki domnī gāwe tāl be tāl**, *prov.* A singer who loses the right opportunity sings out of tune.

اوسط **ausaṭ** (A) *adj.* & *n.f.* Average; middling; medium; mean.

اوسط تنخواہ **ausaṭ tankhwāh**, *n.f.* Average pay.

اوسط جمع بندی **ausaṭ jama' bandī**, *n.f.* Average revenue.

اوسط حسابی **ausaṭ-ĕ ḥisābī**, *n.f* Arithmetic mean.

اوسط نکالنا **ausaṭ nikālnā**, *v.* To strike an average.

اوسطی **ausaṭi** (A) *adj.* Moderate; middling; intermediate; pertaining to the average.

اوشدھ **aushadh** (S) *n.f.* A drug; a medicine; any herb or mineral used in medicine.

اوشدھالیہ **aushadhāliyah**, *n.m.* Dispensary; a drug-shop.

اوصاف **auṣāf** (A) *n.m.* (*plu.* of وصف *waṣf*) Qualities; properties; attributes; qualifications; praises; manners; morals; virtues; descriptions.

اوصاف حمیدہ **aūṣāf-ĕ ḥamidah**, *n.m.* Commendable attributes; noble properties.

اوصیا **auṣiyā** (A) *n.m.* (*plu.* of وصی *waṣī*) Executors or administrators (of the will).

اوقات **auqāt** (A) *n.m.* (*pl.* of وقت *waqt*) Times; hours. *n.f.* Status; position; resources.

اوقات بسری **auqāt basari**, *n.f.* Passing one's time; pastime; amusement; employment; livelihood; occupation.

اوقات بسری کرنا **auqāt basarī karnā**, *v.* To pass (one's times); to subsist; to earn one's living.

اوقات تلخ هونا **auqāt talkh honā**, *v.* To have a bad time; to lead an unhappy life.

اوقات ضائع کرنا **auqāt ẓā'i' karnā**, *v.* To waste time.

اوقاف **auqāf** (A) *n.m.* (*plu.* of وقف *waqf*) Charitable endowments.

اوک **ok** (H) *n.f.* The palm of the hand, contracted so as to hold water.

اوکھ ūkh (H) *n.f.* See ایکھ ikh.

آوک چوک ūk chūk (H) *n.f.* Error; slip; oversight.

اوکھلی ūkhli (H) *n.f.* A wooden mortar to pound grains (in).

اول awwal (A) *adj.* First; foremost; best; highest; excellent. *n.m.* The first or earlier part; commencement; beginning. *adv.* At first; in the first place.

اول خویش بعده درویش *awwal khesh ba'dohū darwesh, prov.* Charity begins at home.

اول درجے کا *awwal darje kā, adj.* First class; first rate.

اول دن سے *awwal din se, adv.* From the very first day; from the very beginning.

اول رہنا *awwal rehnā, v.* To stand first; to maintain the first place.

اولاً *awwalan* (A) *adv.* At first; in the first place; before all.

اولا *olā* (H) *n.m.* Hail.

اولا ہو جانا *olā ho jānā, v.* To become icy cold.

اولا مولا *aulā maulā, adj.* Good-for-nothing; unmannerly.

اولاد *aulād* (A) *n.f.* (*plu.* of ولد *walad*) Children; descendants; progeny; offsprings.

اولاد اناث *aulād-ĕ ināṣ, n.f.* Female children.

اولاد حلال *aulād-ĕ hilāl, n.m.* Legitimate children.

اولاد ذکور *aulād-ĕ ẕakūr, n.m.* Male childern.

آول جلول *ūl-jalūl, adj.* Ugly; stupid; untidy; unmannerly; awkward; clumsy; slovenly.

اولیٰ *ūlā* (A) *adj.* Better; best; preferable; capital; chief.

آولو، آولی *ūlū, ūlī* (A) *adj.* Possessed of; owners; possessing.

اولوالابصار *ūl-ul-abṣār, adj.* Discerning; cute; wise.

اولوالامر *ūl-ul-amr, adj.* Those who possess command or authority.

اولوالباب *ūl-ul-bāb, adj.* Person of understanding.

اولوالعزم *ūl-ul 'azm, adj.* Resolute; enterprising; ambitious.

اولوالعزمی *ūl-ul 'azmi, n.f.* Resolution; determination.

اولوالعلم *ūl-ul 'ilm, adj.* Those who possess knowledge; learned people.

اولیاء *Auliyā'* (A) *n.m.* (*plu.* of ولی *wali*) Friends (of God); saints; holy men; apostels; companions; friends; associates.

اولیائے آمور *auliyā'-ĕ umūr, n.m.* Authorities; administrative officers.

اولیت *awwaliyyat* (A) *n.f.* Priority; pre-eminence; excellence; superiority.

اولین *awwalin* (P) *adj.* The first; the ancients; the past time.

اولین و آخرین *awwalīn-ŏ ākhirīn, adj.* The ancients and the moderns.

اوم *Om* (S) The most sacred name of Hindu god, Ishwar; Amen.

آون *ūn* (H) *n.f.* Wool.

آونٹ *ūnṭ* (H) *n.m.* Camel.

آونٹ چڑھے کتا کاٹے *ūnṭ charhe kuttā kāṭe, prov.* The dog bites the one who is mounted on a camel, i.e., misfortune has long arms for the unfortunate.

آونٹ دیکھئے کس کل یا کروٹ بیٹھے *ūnṭ dekhye kis kal yā karwaṭ beṭhe, prov.* Let us see how the wind blows.

آونٹ کٹارا *ūnṭ kaṭārā, n.m.* Name of a thistle of which camels are fond.

آونٹ کے منہ میں زیرہ *ūnṭ ke munh men zīrah, prov.* A giant will strave on what surfeits a dwarf.

اونٹنا *aunṭnā* (H) *v.* To boil.

آونٹنی *ūnṭnī* (H) *n.f.* A female camel; dromedary.

آونچا ، آونچی *ūnchā, ūnchi* (H) *adj.* High; elevated; lofty; tall; precipitous.

آونچا بول بولنا *ūṅchā bol bolnā, v.* To speak in a loud voice: to talk proudly or boldly; to talk big; to brag.

آونچا سننا *ūṅchā sun-nā, v.* To be hard of hearing; to be deaf.

آونچا ہاتھ رکھنا *ūṅchā hāth rakhnā, v.* To have the upper hand; to excel; to be in a position always to give.

آونچی دکان *ūṅchī dokān, n.f.* A big shop.

آونچی دکان پھیکا پکوان *ūṅchī dokān phikā pakwān, prov.* Great cry little wool.

آونچے بول کا منہ نیچا *ūṅche bol kā muṅh nīchā, prov.* Pride goeth before a fall; the proud ones brought low.

آونچائی *ūṅcha'i* (H) *n.f.* Height; altitude; elevation; loftiness; tallness; steepness.

آونچ نیچ *ūṅch nīch* (H) *n.f.* Inequality; vicissitudes; ups and downs; profit and loss; good and bad.

اوندھا ، اوندھی *auṅdhā, auṅdhi* (H) *adj.* Upside down; inverted; subverted; topsy-turvy; stupid; foolish.

اوندھا بخت *auṅdhā bakht, adj.* Misfortune; bad luck.

اوندھا لیٹنا *auṅdhā leṭnā, v.* To lie face downward; to lie with the face or head down.

آونگنا *ūṅgnā* (H) *v.* To grease the axle of a carriage.

آونگھ *ūṅgh* (H) *n.f.* Dozing; drowsiness; sleepiness.

آونگھنا *ūṅghnā* (H) *v.* To nod; to doze.

اوں ھوں *ūṅhooṅ, intj.* Nay! never!

آونی *ūnī* (H) *adj.* Woollen.

اونے پونے *aune paune, adv.* More or less; irrespective of loss or profit; at a loss.

اوہام *auhām* (A) *n.m.* (*plu.* of وہم *wahm*) Whims; apprehension; fears; superstition.

اوھو *oho, int.* Ho! hey!

اویر سویر *awer sawer* (H) *adv.* Late and early; at all hours.

اہالی *ahālī* (A) *n.m.* (*plu.* of اہل *ahl*) Masters; owners; residents of a place; people; citizens; inhibitants.

اہالی موالی *ahālī-ŏ mawālī, n.m.* People in general; courtiers; retainers; retinue; train of followers; the rich and the poor; children.

اہانت *ihānat* (A) *n.f.* Contempt; scorn; slight; affront; insult; slander.

اہانت عدالت *ihānat-ĕ 'adālat, n.f.* Contempt of court.

اہانت کرنا *ihānat karnā, v.* To insult; to slight; to slander; to defame.

اہاہا *ahahā, int.* Used in praise; the expression of surprise, pain or pleasure.

اہتداء *ihtidā'* (A) *n.m.* Guidance; direction to the right path; conducting; leading.

اہتزاز *ihtizāz* (A) *n.m.* Blowing (wind); vibrating; rejoicing; being over-joyed.

اہتمام *ihtimām* (A) *n.m.* Management; administration; supervision; superintendence; effort.

اہرام *ahrām* (A) *n.m.* (*plu.* of ہرم *haram*) Pyramids of Egypt.

اہرمن *ahraman* (P) *n.m.* God of evil; the devil; satan.

اہرن *ahran* (H) *n.m.* An anvil.

اہل *ahl* (A) *n.m.* People; members of a family; citizens; inhabitants; followers; owners; lords; masters. *adj.* Fit; capable; worthy; suitable; deserving.

اہل اجتہاد *ahl-ĕ ijtihād, n.m.* Qualified jurists; people qualified to make legal investigations.

اہل اللہ *ahl ullah, n.m.* The people of God; pious people; dervishes.

اہل باطن *ahl-ĕ bāṭin, n.m.* Contemplative people; saints.

اہل بیت *ahl-ĕ bait, n.m.* People of a family or house; relatives; members of the family of the Holy Prophet, consisting of Hazrat Ali, Hazrat Fatima and their childern.

اهل تسنن ahl-ĕ tasannun, n.m. Members of the Sunni sect of Islam.

اهل تشیع ahl-ā tashayyo', n.m. The followers of Hazrat Ali; members of the Shia sect.

اهل تفسیر ahl-ĕ tafsir, n.m. Doctors of theology; commentators on theology.

اهل حرفه ahl-ĕ hirfah, n.m. Artisans; workmen; artificers.

اهل خانه ahl-ĕ khānah, n.m. Domestics; members of the household; owner or master of a house. n.f. Wife.

اهل خدمت ahl-ĕ khidmat, n.m. An officer; one in office under the government.

اهل خرد ahl-ĕ khirad, n.m. People endowed with wisdom; wise men; sages.

اهل دل ahl-ĕ dil, adj. Brave; spirited; courageous; liberal; generous.

اهل دلق ahl-ĕ dalq, n.m. Dervishes; mendicants; those who are devoted to God.

اهل دنیا ahl-ĕ dunyā, n.m. Worldly people; slaves of the world; those who seek to attain the best only in this world.

اهل دول یا دولت ahl-ĕ duwal yā daulat, n.m. Possessors of fortune; wealthy; rich; king.

اهل ذوق ahl-ĕ zauq, adj. Connoisseur; one having a literary or aesthetic taste.

اهل رزم ahl-ĕ razm, n.m. Combatants; warriors; soldiers.

اهل روزگار ahl-ĕ rozgār, adj. Knowing the world; skilful. n.m. Working men; servants.

اهل زبان ahl-ĕ zabān, n.m. Well-versed in one's mother tongue; expert or authority in a language.

اهل زمین ahl-ĕ zamīn, n.m. Inhabitants of the earth.

اهل زهد ahl-e zuhd, adj. Chaste; holy; religious; pious; continent; devout.

اهل سخن ahl-ĕ sukhan, n.m. Eloquent; orators; poets.

اهل سنت Ahl-ĕ sunnat, n.m. The followers of the Sunni sect; followers of Traditions.

اهل سیف ahl-ĕ saif, n.m. Swordsmen; warriors.

اهل شرع ahl-ĕ shara' n.m. A law-giver; a lawyer; a legislator; an observer of the laws of Islam.

اهل صفا ahl-ĕ ṣafā, n.m. Pious people; pure in heart.

اهل صنعت ahl-ĕ ṣan'at, n.m. Artisan; workman.

اهل صورت ahl-ĕ ṣūrat, adj. Lover of outward appearance; a superficial observer; one who takes things for what they seem.

اهل طاعت ahl-ĕ ṭā'at, n.m. Obedient; faithful to God.

اهل طریق یا طریقت ahl-ĕ ṭariq yā ṭariqat, n.m. An observer of the laws of Islam.

اهل ظرف ahl-ẓarf, adj. Great; noble; magnanimous.

اهل عرف ، اهل عرفان ahl-ĕ 'urf, ahl-ĕ 'irfān, adj. Learned men; well-informed; intelligent people.

اهل عقل ahl-ĕ 'aql, adj. Wise men; intelligent; sagacious.

اهل علم ahl-ĕ 'ilm, adj. Learned; erudite; well-informed.

اهل غرض ahl-ĕ gharaẓ, n.m. Interested persons; selfish; designing.

اهل فرنگ ahl-ĕ farang, n.m. Europeans.

اهل فضل ahl-ĕ fazl, adj. Good; righteous; erudite.

اهل فن ahl-ĕ fann, n.m. Artist; craftsman.

اهل فکر ahl-ĕ fikr, n.m. Thinkers; philosophers.

اهل قبله ahl-ĕ qiblah, n.m. Muslims; those who turn their faces to Mecca in prayer.

اهل قلم *ahl-ĕ qalam, n.m.* Man of letters; a literary man; a writer.

اهل قیافه *ahl-ĕ qayāfah, n.m.* Those who can judge character from face or form of body; physiognomists.

اهل کار *ahl kār, n.m.* Artisans; public servants; workmen; men of business.

اهل کتاب *ahl-ĕ kitāb, n.m.* People of the Book; persons who believe in revealed Books; followers of revealed religions having a Book.

اهل کرم *ahl-ĕ karam, adj.* Charitable; generous; liberal; pious.

اهل کسب *ahl-ĕ kasb, n.m.* Tradesmen; traders; dealers.

اهل لسان *ahl-ĕ lisān, n.m.* People skilled in a language.

اهل مجلس *ahl-ĕ majlis, n.m.* Members of a society or meeting; courtiers.

اهل مد *ahl-madd, n.m.* Person in charge of a branch or a department.

اهل مصارف *ahl-ĕ maṣārif, n.m.* An owner; one having authority to incur expenditure.

اهل معرفت *ahl-ĕ m'arafat, adj.* Knowing God; devout; pious.

اهل مقدمه *ahl-ĕ muqaddamah, n.m.* Party to a suit.

اهل منصب *ahl-ĕ manṣab, n.m.* A minister; an officer; a dignitary.

اهل نظر *ahl-ĕ naẓar, adj.* Discerning; penetrating; sharp-sighted; worshipper (of beauty).

اهل نفاق *ahl-ĕ nifāq, n.m.* Irreligious; ungodly; traitors; infidels; enemies; hypocrites.

اهل ورع *ahl-ĕ wara', adj.* Holy; godly; pious; religious.

اهل و عیال *ahl-ŏ 'ayāl, n.m.* Family; children.

اهل هنر *ahl-ĕ hunar, n.m.* Skilful; artisan.

اهلاً و سهلاً و مرحبا *ahlan-ŏ sahlan-ŏ marḥabā (A) int.* Welcome.

اهلیت **ahliyyat** (A) *n.f.* Worth; worthiness; capability; aptitude; skill; possession.

اهلیه **ahliyah** (A) *n.f.* Wife.

اهم **ahamm** (A) *adj.* Most important; very momentous; pressing; grave; significant; most difficult.

اهم امور *ahamm umūr, n.m.* More important matters or things.

اهمیت **ahammiyat** (A) *n.f.* Gravity; significance; importance.

آهو **oho**, *int.* Ah! oh! hallo! ha!

اهیر **ahīr** (S) *n.m.* A cowhered; a caste or tribe among Hindus whose business is to look after cows.

ائمه **a'immah** (A) *n.m.* (*plu.* of امام *imām*) Leaders; authorities in religious matters.

اے **ae** (S&P) *interj.* O; (used in calling or addressing).

اے کاش *ae kāsh, inter.* Would to God! O, how I wish!

ایاز **Ayyāz** (T) *n.m.* Name of the Turkish slave and favourite of Sultan Mahmud of Ghazni, afterwards Governor of Lahore.

ایال **ayāl** (P) *n.f.* Mane.

ایام **aiyyām** (A) *n.m.* (*plu.* of یوم *yaum*). Days; time; period; duration.

ایام اسود *aiyyām-ĕ aswad, n.m.* Dark days; the last three nights of a lunar month.

ایام بیض *aiyyām-ĕ bīẓ, n.m.* Brightest days; thirteenth, fourteenth and fifteenth nights of a lunar month.

ایام سے ہونا *aiyyām se honā, v.* To menstruate; to be having the menses.

ایام مستی *aiyyām-ĕ masti, n.m.* Heat period.

ایبک **aibak** (P) *n.m.* Beloved; a messenger; slave.

ایتام **aitām** (A) *n.m.* (*plu.* of یتیم *yatīm*) Orphans.

ایتلاف ، ائتلاف **itilāf, i'tilāf** (A) *n.m.* Familiarity; friendship; association; amity; connection; alliance.

ایثار **iṣār** (A) *n.m.* Sacrifice; selflessness.

ایجاب ijāb (A) *n.m.* Making necessary affirmation; assent; rendering necessary or incumbent; the first proposal made by one of the parties in negotiating or concluding a bargain.

ایجاب و قبول ijāb-ŏ qubūl, *n.m.* Proposal and consent (in a negotiation of marriage).

ایجاد ījād (A) *n.m.* Invention; creation; production; contrivance.

ایجاد کرنا ījād karnā, *v.* To invent; to create; to devise; to design; to originate.

ایچ پیچ ech pech, *n.m.* Entanglement; perplexity; deceit; fraud.

ایچ پیچ کی باتیں ech pech ki bātėn, *n.f.* Crooked or cross talks; deceitful dealings; double dealings.

ایچ پیچ نہ جاننا ech pech nah jānnā, *v.* To be straight forward; to have straight talk.

ایذاء īzā' (A) *n.f.* Annoyance; harm; pain; trouble; distress; vexation; affliction.

ایذاء دینا īzā' denā, *v.* To injure; to hurt; to pain; to vex; to afflict; to annoy.

ایذاء رساں īzā' rasāṅ, *adj.* Vexatious; troublesome

ایذاء رسانی īzā' rasāni, *n.f.* Causing trouble or injury.

ایرا پھیری erā pheri, *n.f.* Exchanging; interchange; barter; roaming or wandering to and fro.

ایرا غیرا airā ghairā, *n.m.* Anyone and everyone; an unknown person; a nobody-knows-who; Tom, Dick and Harry.

ایران īrān (P) *n.m.* Persia; Iran.

ایرانی īrānī (P) *adj.* Persian; Iranian.

ایڑ eṛ (H) *n.f.* Spur; spurring.

ایڑ مارنا eṛ mārnā, *v.* To spur.

ایڑی eṛi (H) *n.f.* The heel.

ایڑیاں رگڑنا eṛiyān ragarnā, *v.* To be in straitened circumstances; to be in distress or agony.

ایزد ezad (P) *n.m.* God.

ایزدی ezadi (P) *adj.* Divine; heavenly.

ایسا، ایسی aisā, aisī (H) *adj.* Such; like this; resembling like.

ایسا تیسا aisā taisā, *adj.* (used to express contempt). Mean; contemptible; despicable.

ایسا ویسا، ایسی ویسی aisā waisā, aisī waisī, *adj.* Ordinary; undesirable; inferior; indecent; this and that.

ایسی تیسی aisi taisi, *n.f.* A term of contempt; a polite term used for anything indecent.

ایسے ہی aise-hi, *adv.* So to speak; accidentally; casually.

ایشور īshwar (S) *n.m.* Ruler; chief master; Lord; God.

ایشیا eshiā (E) *n.m.* Asia.

ایشیائی eshiā'ī, *adj.* Asiatic.

ایصال īṣāl (A) *n.m.* Bringing together; conveying; conduction of something.

ایصال ثواب iṣāl-ĕ ṣawāb, *n.m.* Conveying reward of virtue.

ایصال حرارت iṣāl-ĕ ḥarārat, *n.m.* Conduction of heat.

ایضاً aiẕan (A) *adv.* Ditto; as above; the same.

ایفاء īfā' (A) *n.f.* Fulfilment; observance; paying.

ایفائے ڈگری ifā-ĕ ḍigri, *n.f.* Satisfaction of a decree; execution of a decree.

ایقان iqān (A) *n.m.* Knowing for a fact; knowing to be true; being certain (of).

ایک ek (H) *adj.* One; only; single; sole; a certain one; the one of its kind; unique; singular.

ایک آدھ ek ādh, *adj.* A half; a part; some; just a few.

ایک انار، سو بیمار ek anār, sau bimār, *prov.* One post and lots of candidates.

ایک انڈا، وہ بھی گندہ ek anḍā, woh bhi gandāh, *prov.* But one egg and that addled.

ایک بار ek bār, adv. Once; once upon a time; at one time.

ایک بارگی ek bārgī, adv. Suddenly; all at once.

ایک پاپی ناؤ کو ڈبوتا ھے ek pāpī nāo ko dabotā hai, prov. One rotten sheep infects the whole flock.

ایک پیٹ کے ek pet ke, adj. From he same mother; brother and sister.

ایک تال ek tāl, n.m. Harmony; unison,

ایک جان ek jān, adj. Of one mind; intimate.

ایک دل ek dil, adj. Unanimous; of one mind; of one accord.

ایک دم ek dam, adv. Instantly; forthwith; immediately.

ایک زبان ھونا ek zabān honā, v. To be of one accord; to be unanimous.

ایک سے دن نہیں رھتے ek se din nahīn rahte, say. Change of fortune or of circumstances from good to bad or vice versa.

ایک کی دس سنانا ek kī das sunānā, v. To give one more than he deserves; to give one a volley of abuse; to retaliate more sharply.

ایک ماں باپ کے ek māṅ bāp ke, adj. Born of the same parents; real brothers and sisters; have similar appearance or habits.

ایک مشت ek musht, adv. Entirely; wholly; in full payment.

ایک نہ ایک ek nah ek, adj. One or the other.

ایکا ekā (H) n.m. Union; combination; friendship; treaty.

ایکا ایکی ekā eki, adv. Suddenly; unexpectedly; unawares.

ایکٹ act (E) n.m. An act.

ایکھ ikh (H) n.f. Sugarcane (farm).

ایلچی elchi (T) n.m. An ambassador; emissary; representative; agent.

ایلوا elwa (H) n.m. Aloes.

ایما imā (A) n.m. Sign; hint; suggestion; intention.

ایمان imān (A) n.m. Belief; faith; creed; trustworthiness; credence; conscience; confidence.

ایمان بیچنا imān bechnā, v. To go against one's faith or religion; to betray truth for worldly gain.

ایماندار imāndār, adj. Faithful; conscientious; upright; trustworthy; true.

ایمانداری imāndārī, n.f. Faithfulness; constancy; honesty; consientiousness; uprightness; trustworthiness.

ایمان سے imān se, adv. Faithfully; honestly; conscientiously.

ایمان لانا īmān lānā, v. To believe; to put faith in; to accept the religion of.

ایمان میں خلل آنا imān meṅ khalal ānā, v. To have one's honesty shaken or disturbed; to prove faithless.

ایمن aiman (A) adj & n.m. Most happy or auspicious; right-hand side; the right-hand valley of the Mount Senai.

اینٹ īnṭ (H) n.f. A brick.

اینٹ کی چنائی īnṭ kī chunā'ī, n.f. Brickwork.

اینٹ سے اینٹ بجانا īnṭ se īnṭ bajānā, v. To destroy; to demolish; to ruin.

اینٹ کا جواب پتھر سے دینا īnṭ kā jawāb paththar se denā, v. To give blow for blow; to give tit for tat.

اینٹ کی خاطر مسجد ڈھانا īnṭ ki khāṭir masjid ḍhānā, v. To incur heavy loss for a small gain.

اینٹ گری īnṭ gari, n.f. Brick work.

اینٹھن ainthan (H) n.f. Contortion; gripe; colic; obstinacy; pride; arrogance.

اینٹھنا ainṭhna (H) v. To tighten; to writhe; to distort; to contort; to twist; to strut; to be offended.

اینچا تانی enchā tānī (obs.) n.f. Tug-of-war; struggle; stretching and straining repeated pulling.

اینچ پینچ ench pench. See ایچ پیچ ech pech.

ایندھن indhan (H) n.m. Fuel; firewood.

ایندھن ہو جانا indhan ho jānā, v. To become useless; to grow old and weak.

اینڈنا aindnā (H) v. To walk affectedly; to strut; to loll about; to swagger.

اینڈی بینڈی aindi baindi (H) adj. Crooked; rough; rude.

اینڈی بینڈی سنانا aindi baindi sunānā, v. To abuse; to call names.

ایوان aiwān (P) n.m. A hall; a gallery; a palace; chamber.

ایوب Ayyūb (A) n. prop. Job, the patriarch.

ایہام īhām (A) n m. Creating doubt; (Poetry) use of a word having double meanings.

ب be (called bā in Arabic) is the second letter of the Urdu, Arabic and Persian alphabets. In abjad ابجد it stands for number two.

ب bi (A) prep. (always prefixed to another word). By, with; from; in; into; near; on; according to; for; towards.

بالاتفاق bil-ittifāq, adv. Unanimously; with one voice.

بالا جمال bil-ijmāl, adv. Briefly; in brief.

بالارادہ bil-irādah, adv. Intentionally; deliberately.

بالتخصیص bit-takhsis, adv. Specially; particularly.

بالتصریح bittasrih adv. Expressly; distinctly; in detail.

بالتفصیل bittafsil, adv. Explicitly; in detail; at full length.

بالجبر bil-jabr, adv. Forcibly; violently.

بالجملہ bil-jumlah, adv. In short; on the whole; altogether; in a word.

بجنسہ bijinsihi, adj. Identical; the very same. adv. Exactly; precisely.

بالخیر bil-khair, adv. Happily; well; in a good manner.

بالضرور biz-zurūr, adv. Necessarily; inevitably; certainly.

بالعکس bil-'aks, adv. On the contrary; on the other hand.

بالعموم bil-'umūm, adv. Generally; commonly; universally.

بعینہ bi'ainihi, adv. The very same; precisely; exactly.

بالفرض bil-farz, adv. Supposing; granted that; admitting for the sake of argument.

بالفعل bil-f'il, adv. Now; at present; in fact; actually.

بالکل bil-kul, adv. Entirely; wholly; completely.

باللہ billah, adv. By God

بالمشافہ bil-mushāfah, adv. Face to face.

بالمقابلہ bil-muqābalah, adv. Face to face; in the presence of; as compared to.

ب ba (P) prep. (often prefixed to another word). With; by; for; from; in; into; to; upto; on; upon. When standing alone, it is written as بہ.

بافراط ba ifrāt, adv. In abundance; plentifully.

بپا bapā. See برپا barpā.

بتدریج batadrij, adv. By degrees; gradually.

بتصریحات bat-tasrihāt, adv. With remarks; with explanations.

بجواب bajawāb, adv. In response to.

بحساب bahisāb, adv. With the computation; according to; in the proportion of.

بحق bahaq, adv. In the matter of; in the case of; on account of; in the interest of; in favour of

بحق مدعا علیہ bahaq-ē mudd'ā 'alaih, adv. In the interest of the defendant; in favour of the defendant.

بحکم ba-hukam, adv. By command (of); by authority; under the order of.

بخلاف bakhilāf, adv. Contrary to; in opposition to.

بخوبی bakhūbī, adv. In a good manner; thoroughly; well.

بخوشی bakhūshi, adv. With pleasure; gladly; cheerfully.

بخیر bakhair, adv. Attended with good; in safety; well; in peace and safety.

بدرجہ badarjah, adv. In a degree; by many degrees; over so much; greatly.

بدستور badastūr, adv. As usual; according to custom; in the usual manner; customarily.

بدقت badiqqat, adv. Wtih difficulty.

بدل badil, adv. Heartily; with all one's heart.

بدولت badaulat, adv. By the kindness of; by the bounty (of); by means of.

بدون badun, prep. Without; besides; expect.

بزور ba-zor, adv. By force; perforce; forcibly; under-compulsion.

بسبب ba-sabab, adv. By reason of; on account of.

بسر و چشم basar-ō chashm, adv. Most willingly; by all means.

بسلسلہ basilsilah, adv. In continuation of.

بشرطیکہ bashartekeh, adv. Provided that; on condition that; with the proviso.

بصورت ba-ṣūrat, adv. In the manner (of); by way (of); in case of.

بصورت خلاف ورزی baṣūrat-ē khilāf warzi, In case of breach (of)

بصیغہ baṣighah, adv. In the form of; in the department of.

بصیغہ دیوانی baṣighah-ē diwānī, adv. Under civil jurisdiction or department.

بطور baṭaur, adv. After the manner of; by way of; as.

بطور خود baṭaur-ē khūd, adv. In one's own way; on one's own account; of one's own accord.

بظاہر baẓāhir, adv. Outwardly; apparently; ostensibly; in appearance.

بعوض ba'iwaẓ, adv. In lieu of; instead of; in place of; in exchange.

بعون ba'aun, adv. With the help of; by the assistance (of).

بغیر baghair, adv. Without; excluding; except.

بقدر baqadr, adv. To the extent or measure (of); according to; by the power (of).

بقول ba-qaul, adv. According to; according to the saying (of).

بکار ba-kār, adv. In use; for use; of use; serviceable.

بکثرت bakasrat, adv. In abundance; plentiful.

بمجرد bamujarrad, adv. Instantly; forthwith; immediately.

بمرتبہ bamartabah, adv, To a degree; in a degree; to some extent.

بمقتضاے bamuqtaẓāe, adv. In consequence of; according to the requirements of.

بمنزلہ bamanzilah, adv. In the place of; instead.

بموجب bamūjib, adv. By reason of; in pursuance of; in accordance with; in conformity with; as per; by; under.

بنام banām, adv. In the name of; to the address of.

بہ نسبت banisbat, adv. In respect of; with relation to; in comparison with.

بوجہ bawajh, adv. By reason of; for; in the mode or manner.

بہ یک کرشمہ دو کار bah yak karishamh do kār, To kill two birds with one stone.

با bā (P) prep. With; by; possessed of.

باآنکہ ، بااینکہ bā ānkeh, bā ínkeh, adv. Nevertheless; though; although; notwithstanding that.

بااثر bā aṣar, adj. Effectual; influential.

بااختیار bā ikhtiyār, adj. Holding authority or power.

بااخلاص bā ikhlāṣ, adj. Sincere; cordial.

با ادب bā adab, adj. Respectful; polite; having good manners.

با اندازہ bā-andāzah, adv. According to measure; moderately; proportionately.

با ایمان bā imān, adj. Religious; faithful; believing; pious; honest.

با این ہمہ bā in hamah, adv. With all that.

با تدبیر bā tadbir, adj. Prudent; with good council; discreet; wise.

با تمیز bā tamiz, adj. Polite; courteous; cultured; sensible; discreet; judicious.

با حیا bā ḥayā, adj. Bashful; modest.

با خبر bā khabar, adj. Informed; intelligent; expert.

با خدا bā khudā, adj. Pious; godly; religious.

با شعور bā shu'ūr, adj. Intelligent; sagacious; shrewd; wise.

با ضابطہ bā zābiṭah, adv. In accordance with law or rule; according to custom; formal.

با فراغت bā farāghat, adv. Satisfactorily; leisurely.

با قاعدہ bā qā'idah, adj. Regular; formal; correct.

باقرینہ bā qarinah, adj. Methodical; well-arranged; in order.

با مروت bā murawwat, adj. Humane; kind; obliging; generous.

با مزہ bā mazah, adj. Savoury; delicious; tasteful.

با نوا bā navā, adj. Wealthy; powerful; influential. n.m. A sect of Muslim beggars.

با وجود ، باوجودیکہ bā wujūd, bā wujūdekeh, adv. Notwithstanding; in spite of; although.

باوردی bā wardi, adj. In uniform.

با وصف bā waṣf, adv. With the attribute; nevertheless; notwithstanding.

با وضع bā waẓ', adj. Good mannered; cultured; polite; formal.

با وضو bā wuẓū, adj. Pure and clean; having performed ablutions.

با وفا bā wafā, adj. True; faithful.

باب bāb (A) n.m. Door; gate; section; chapter; division of a book; heading; affair; topic; subject; kind; in the matter (of); with regard to.

بابا bābā, n.m. Father; grandfather; sire; old man; (Urdu form of baby, usually used for) children of Europeans (often called بابا لوگ bābā log).

بابا جان bābā jān, n.m. Dear father; grandfather.

بابت bābat (A) n.f. & adv. Account; head; article; item; affair; matter; concerning; respecting; in the matter of; on account (of); as regards.

بابر Bābar (T) n.m. (corr. of ببر babar, a lion). Name of the first Mughal Emperor of India.

بابل bābul (H) n.m. Father.

بابل Bābil (A) n.m. A city in old Iraq, known for witchcraft; Babel or Babylon.

بابو bābū, n.m. A nobleman; a man of distinction; a title of respect, as Mr.; a clerk.

بابونہ bābūnah (P) n.m. Wild ivy; camomile.

بابی Bābi (P) n.m. A sect of Muslims in Persia.

باپ bap, n.m. Father; elder; superior.

باپ بنانا bāp banānā, v. To consider or regard one as a father.

باپ تک جانا bāp tak jānā, v. To go to the extent of abusing one's father.

باپ دادا bāp dādā, n.m. Ancestors; forefathers; pedigree.

باپ رے باپ bāp re bāp, int. (an exclamation of surprise, fear, etc.). O father! a cry for help or mercy.

باپ مارے کا بیر bāp māre kā bair, n.m. Family feud; long standing enmity; (Lit.) a feud caused by the murder of one's father.

بات bāt (H) n.f. Word; saying; discourse; speech; news; tale; story; talk; subject; question; account; business; affair; gossip; substance; matter; point; proposal; particular.

بات بات میں bāt bāt meṅ, adv. In every word; in every particular; on every occasion; every time.

بات بدلنا bāt badalnā, v. To depart from one's word; to deny an assertion; to say one thing and do another.

بات بڑھانا hāt baṛhānā, v. To prolong a dispute; to continue an altercation.

بات بگاڑنا bāt bigāṛnā, v. To mar one's plan; to ruin one's credit.

بات بنانا bāt banānā, v. To concoct a story; to make lame excuses; to tell tales; to boast.

بات بننا bāt bannā, v. To succeed; to prove a success; to prosper; to flourish.

بات پانا bāt pānā, v, To attain one's object; to understand the purport; to get to the bottom of a matter.

بات پچنا bāt pachnā, v. To keep a secret.

بات پر بات یاد آنا bāt par bāt yād ānā, v. To recollect a forgotten thing while talking of some unconnected matter.

بات پکڑنا bāt pakaṛnā, v. To criticise severely; to carp or cavil (at).

بات پکی کرنا bāt pakki karnā, v. To have a matter confirmed; to confirm a bargain; to covenant.

بات پوچھنا bāt puchhnā, v. To put a question to; to enquire after one's welfare; to evince concern (for); to respect; to welcome.

بات پھیرنا bāt phernā, v. To change the topic; to usẹ doubtful words in order to mislead; to equivocate.

بات پھیلانا bāt phailānā, v. To give currency to a report; to circulate a rumour; to spread the news.

بات پھیلنا bāt phailnā, v. (A matter) getting abroad; to become the talk of the town; to be talked about.

بات پھینکنا bāt phaiṅknā, v. To mock; to jeer.

بات پی جانا bāt pi jānā, v. To pocket or swallow (an insult); to control one's feelings; to bear in silence.

بات پیدا کرنا bāt paidā karnā, v, To create something new; to put a wrong interpretation (on something); to offer an excuse; to attain excellence.

بات ٹالنا bāt ṭālnā, v. To put off; to evade.

بات ٹھنڈی پڑنا bāt ṭhanḍī paṛnā, v. To allow a matter to be put in cold storage; to abate; to allow the matter to cool down.

بات ٹھہرانا bāt ṭhahrānā, v. To make a settlement; to arrive at a decision; to be engaged.

بات جانا bāt jānā, v. To lose one's credit; to be disgraced.

بات جمانا bāt jamānā, v. To drive home; to finalize a matter; to make some one agree to one's point of view.

بات چبا جانا bāt chabā jānā, v. To swallow one's word.

بات چبانا bāt chabānā, v. To change the topic (abruptly).

بات چلانا bāt chalānā, v. To start discussion on a subject; to engage in conversation.

بات چیت **bāt chit**, *n.f.* Conversation; discourse; talk.

بات چیت کرنا **bāt chit karnā**, *v.* To converse; to talk; to have a chat; to confabulate.

بات دھرانا **bāt dohrānā**, *v.* To recapitulate; to repeat a thing; to harp on a subject.

بات رھنا **bāt rahnā**, *v.* To make good one's words; to succeed; to get the better in argument; to prevail.

بات کا بتنگڑ بنانا **bāt kā batangaṛ banānā**, *v.* To multiply words; to talk much about little; to stretch a point; to make a mountain of a mole-hill; to exaggerate.

بات کا پکا، بات کا پورا، بات کا سچا **bāt kā pakkā, bāt kā pūrā, bāt kā sachchā**, *adj.* True to one's word; faithful to one's promise; trustworthy.

بات کاٹنا **bāt kāṭnā**, *v.* To interrupt; to speak when another is speeking; to cut in.

بات کا سر پیر نہ ہونا **bāt kā sar pair nah honā**, *v.* Not to be able to make head or tail; to take irrelevantly.

بات کان پڑنا **bāt kān paṛnā**, *v.* To come to learn of a matter; to be informed.

بات کرتے پتھر مارنا **bāt karte paththar mārnā**, *v.* To be harsh in one's talk; to talk rudely.

بات کو کھٹائی میں ڈالنا **bāt ko khaṭā'i men ḍālnā**, *v.* To dilly-dally; to procrastinate; to postpone; to defer a matter; to put the matter in cold storage.

بات کھلنا **hāt khulnā**, *v.* To be disclosed; to be laid bare; to be out (secret).

بات کھو دینا ، کھونا **bāt kho denā, khonā**, *v.* To lose credit; to lose one's respect.

بات کھولنا **bāt kholnā**, *v.* To have a plain or straight talk.

بات کہی پرائی ہوئی **bāt kahi parā'i ho'i**, *prov.* A word spoken is an arrow let fly; a word and a stone let go cannot be re-called.

بات کیے پھول جھڑنا **bāt kiye phūl jhaṛnā**, *v.* To be eloquent and sweet in speech.

بات کی بات خرافات کی خرافات **bāt ki bāt khurāfāt ki khurāfāt**, *prov.* Unmeaning commands are not obeyed; many a true word is spoken in jest.

بات گھڑنا **bāt ghaṛnā**, *v.* To concoct a story; to tell a tale; to spread a rumour.

بات لاکھ کی کرنی خاک کی **bāt lākh ki karni khāk ki**, *prov.* A long tongue has a short hand; great talkers are little doers.

بات ماننا **bāt mān-nā**, *v.* To accept a suggestion; to obey.

بات میں سے بات نکالنا **bāt men se bāt nikālnā**, *v.* To discuss the many sides of a matter; to bring out a new point; to criticise.

بات میں ف نکالنا **bāt men fi nikālnā**, *v.* To pick holes in an argument; to cavil (at).

بات ھلکی ھونا **bāt halki honā**, *v.* To be of little esteem.

باتوں میں آنا **bāton men ānā**, *v.* To be taken in; to be deceived.

باتوں میں آڑانا **bāton men uṛānā**, *v.* To talk a person out of his wits; to put off with a joke; to fool one by talk.

باتوں میں بہلانا **bāton men bahlānā**, *v.* To delude with fair words; to divert one's attention

باتوں میں لگانا **bāton men lagānā**, *v.* To engage a person in conversation; to occupy one's attention.

باتیں سنانا **bāten sunānā**, *v.* To revile; to abuse; to reproof; to repeat one's story; to relate one's adventure.

باتیں سننا **bāten sun-nā**, *v.* To hear attentively; to listen to a person; to receive abuse or harsh reproof; to bear unpleasant remarks.

باتون یا باتونی **batun ya batuni**, *adj* Talkative; a garrulous person.

باٹ **bāṭ** (H) *n.m.* A weight or measure of weight. *n.f.* Way; path; route; highway.

باٹ اور ترازو **bāṭ aur tarāzū**, *n.m.* Weights and scales.

باٹ چھپائی **bāṭ chhapā'ī**, *n.f.* Fee charged for stamping weights; stamping weights and measures.

باج **bāj** (P) *n.m.* A tax; duty; impost; cess; revenue; toll; tribute.

باج دار ، باج گیر **bāj dār, bāj gīr**, *n.m.* A tax or revenue collector.

باج گزار **bāj guzār**, *n.m.* A tax-payer; a tributary; a feudatory or dependent state.

باجا **bājā**, *n.m.* A musical instrument.

باجرا **bājrā** (H) *n.m.* Millet; a drizzle.

باجرا برسنا **bājrā barasnā**, *v.* Drizzling.

باجنا **bājnā** (H) *v.* To sound (as a musical instrument); to be well-known.

باجی **bāji** (T) *n.f.* Elder sister.

باچھ **bāchh** (H) *n.f.* Corner of the mouth.

باچھیں آنا **bāchheṅ ānā**, *v.* To have a pain or inflammation at the corners of the mouth.

باچھیں کھل جانا یا کھلنا **bāchheṅ khil jānā yā khilnā**, *v.* To laugh; to laugh loudly; to burst with joy; to be proud of; to feel proud.

باختہ **bākhtah** (P) *adj.* Beaten at play; lost (by gambling); played (used in *comp.*).

باد **bād** (P) *n.f.* Wind; air; breeze.

بادبان **bād bān** *n.m.* A sail.

باد پا **bād pā**, *adj.* Fast; swift; a swift horse.

باد پیما **bād paimā**, *adj.* Swift; fast; *n.m.* An aerometer; a swift horse; an idle talker; a liar.

باد تند **bād-ĕ tund**, *n.f.* A wind storm; a strong gale.

باد خور **bād khor**, *n.m.* A disease in horses from which their hairs falls off.

باد خورہ **bād khorah**, *adj.* Scald-headed.

باد رفتار **bād raftār**, *adj.* Swift as the wind; a very active and swift horse.

باد سموم **bād-ĕ samūm**, *n.f.* A hot pestilential wind; the simoom.

باد سنج **bād sanj**, *adj.* & *n.m.* Air gauge; vain; idly speculative; one who builds castles in the air.

باد شرط **bād-ĕ shurṭ**, *n.f.* A fair wind; a favourable wind.

باد صبا **bād-ĕ ṣabā**, *n.f.* Morning breeze; the zephyr; a refreshing wind.

باد فرنگ **bād-ĕ farang**, *n.f.* Syphilis; the pox.

باد فروش **bād farosh**, *n.m.* A talkative person; at flatterer; a minstrel.

باد کش **bād kash**, *n.m.* A ventilator.

باد گرد **bād gard**, *n.m.* Whirlwind.

باد مخالف **bād-ĕ mukhālif**, *n.f.* A contrary wind; an unfavourable wind.

باد مراد ، باد موافق **bād-ĕ murād, bād-ĕ muāfiq**, *n.f.* A fair or favourable wind.

باد نما **bād numā**, *n.m.* A weathercock.

بادام **bādām** (P) *n.m.* An almond.

بادامی **bādāmi**, *adj.* Of almond colour; light brown colour; composed of or containing almonds.

باد رنگ **bādrang** (P) *n.m.* Cucumber.

بادشاہ **bādshāh** (P) *n.m.* A king; a sovereign.

بادشاہ زادہ **bādshāh zādah**, *n.m.* A king's son; a prince.

بادشاہ زادی **bādshāh zādī**, *n.f.* A princess.

بادشاہ کشی **bādshāh kushi**, *n.f.* Murdering a king; regicide.

بادشاہ گر **bādshāh gar**, *adj.* King-maker.

بادشاہانہ **bādshāhānah** (P) *adj.* Imperial; kingly; royal. *adv.* Royally; princely; kingly.

بادشاہت **bādshāhat** (P) *n.f.* Kingdom; realm; empire.

بادشاہی **bādshāhī** (P) *adj.* Royal; regal; imperial. *n.f.* Empire; reign, rule; sovereignty.

بادشاهی سند bādshāhi sanad, n.f. Royal warrant; a royal document conveying lands or titles.

بادشاهی عدالت bādshāhi 'adālat, n.f. The royal court; court of chancery; his majesty's court.

بادل bādal (H) n.m. A cloud; clouds.

بادل چهانا bādal chhānā, v. To be cloudy.

بادل گرجنا bādal garajnā, v. Thundering of clouds.

بادلوں کا دیوتا bādaloṅ kā deotā, n.m. A god of clouds.

بادلا bādlā (H) n.m. Gold or silver thread or wire; brocade.

بادنجان bādanjān (A) n.m. Egg-plant; brinjal.

باده bādah (P) n.m. Wine; spirits.

باده پرست bādah parast, adj. Drunkard; addicted to wine.

باده کش bādah kash, adj. Drunkard; given to drinking wine.

باده نوش bādah nosh, adj. Wine-drinker; one who drinks wine.

بادی bādi (A) adj. & adv. Beginning; at first.

بادی النظر میں bādi-un-naẓar men, adv. At first sight; prima facie.

بادی bādi (P) adj. Flatulent; windy; rheumatic.

بادی بدن bādi badan, n.m. Bloated body; corpulence.

بادیان bādiyān (P) n.f. Anise seed.

بادیه bādiyah (A) n.m. A desert; a wilderness; a forest.

بادیه پیما bādiyah paimā, adj. A wanderer; a wayfarer.

بادیه bādiyah (P) n.m. A cup; a bowl; a goblet.

بار bār (H) n.m. Time; turn; chance; opportunity; occasion; delay; obstacle; a day of the week.

بار بار bār bār, adv. Again and again; repeatedly; often.

بار بٹائی bār baṭā'i, n.f. Division of the corp by sheaves before the corn is thrashed out.

بار bār (P) n.m. Burden; load; liability; threshold; admission; permission; leave; fruite; produce; difficulty; grief; pregnancy; heaviness; assembly; court; sitting of a sovereign to give audience.

بار آور bār āwar, adj. Bearing fruit; producing fruit; fructuous.

بار بردار bār bardār, n.m. A porter; a carrier; a beast of burden.

بار برداری bār bardāri, n.f. Mean of conveyance; cost of conveyance; beasts of burden; carriage; transport.

بار تردید bār-ĕ tardid, n m. The onus of rebutment; burden of disproving.

بار ثبوت bār ṣabūt, n.m. The onus or burden of proof.

بار خاص bār-ĕ k͟hās, n.m. Private court or hall of audience; privy counci chamber; special permission or audience.

بار خاطر bār-ĕ k͟hāṭir, adj. Unpleasant; disagreeable; offensive.

بار خانه bār k͟hānah, n.m. Godown.

بار خدایا bār-ĕ k͟hudāyā, intj. Great God! Lord God.

بار دار bār dār, adj. Pregnant; full of fruit; loaded; lucky; fortunate; rich.

بار دانه bār dānah, n.m. Supplies; provisions; forage, pots. utensils, bags, etc., in which provisions are kept.

بار عام bār-ĕ 'ām, n.m. Public audience.

بار کرنا bār karnā, v. To load.

بار کش bār kash, n.m. A load carrier; a cart or an animal for carrying loads.

بارگاه bārgāh, n.f. A court; a palace; place of audience.

بارور bārwar, adj. Fruitful; producing or having fruit; plentiful.

بار هونا bār honā, v. To be laden; to be a burden; to be a hinderance.

باریاب bāryāb, adj. Admitted at court or into company.

باریابی bāryābi n.f. Admittance at court; audience.

بارات bārāt (H) n.f. See برات barāt.

باران bārāṅ (P) n m. Rain; rainy season.. adj. Raining.

بارانی bārānī (P) adj. Relating to or depending on rain; of rain. n.f. A waterproof coat.

بار تنگ bārtang (P) n.m. A drug; seed of flewort.

بارد bārid (A) adj. Cold.

بارز bāriz (A) adj. Issuing forth; coming forth; manifest; apparent.

بارش bārish (P) n.f. Rain; shower.

بارک اللہ bārak allah (A) intj. God bless you! may you prosper!

بارود ، باروت bārūd, barut (T) n.f. Gunpowder.

بارود خانہ bārūd khānah, n.m. Powder magazine.

بارہ bārah (P) n.m. & adv. Time; turn; about; in respect (of); in regard (of).

بارے میں bāre meṅ, adv. In respect of; concerning.

بارہ bārah (H) adj. Twelve.

بارہ امام bārah imām, n.m. The twelve imāms (religious leaders) of the Shia sect; 1. Hazrat ‘Ali, 2. Imam Hasan, 3. Imam Hussian, 4. Imam Zainul-‘Abidin, 5. Imam Baqar, 6. Imam J‘afar Sadiq, 7. Imam Musa Kazim, 8. Imam Raza, 9. Imam Naqi, 10. Imam Taqi, 11. Imam Hasan ‘Askari, 12. Imam Mehdi, the would-be Imam.

بارہ باٹ ہونا bārah bāṭ honā, id. To become bewildred or perplexed; to be ruined or harassed; to be useless; to be dispersed.

بارہ پتھر bārah paththar, n.m. Boundry of a city or cantonment marked with twelve stone pillars.

بارہ دری bārah darī, n.f. A summer house with twelve doors (three on each side).

بارہ سنگھا bārah singhā, n.m. A stag (having twelve horns).

بارہ ماسہ bārah māsah, n.m Hindi verse of twelve stanzas describing the pain of separation from the husband, with the characteristic changes of the season and scenery and pastimes which distinguish each month of the year.

بارہ وفات bārah wafāt, n.f. First twelve days of Rabi‘ul-Awwal (the third month of the Islamic calendar), during which the Holy Prophet remained ill.

بارہا bār-hā, adv. Times out of number; often; frequently.

بارھواں bārhwāṅ (H) adj. Twelfth.

باری bārī (A) n.m. The deity; the creator.

باری تعالی Bārī T‘a’lā, n.m. The Most High God.

باری bāri (H) n.f. Time; turn of duty; turn.

باری کی تپ bārī kī tap, n.f. An intermittent fever.

باری باری bārī bārī, adv. In turn; each in due course.

باریک bārīk (P) adj. Fine; thin; delicate; slender; thread-like; minute; difficult; subtle.

باریک بات bārīk bāt, n.f. Nice point; subtle question; fine discrimination.

باریک بین ، باریک نظر bārīk bīn, bārik naẓar, adj. Penetrating; shrewd; sagacious; quick of apprehenison; intelligent.

باریکی bārīkī (P) n.f. Fineness; delicacy; subtlety; minuteness; discernment.

باریکیاں نکالنا bārīkiāṅ nikālnā, v. To discriminate; to find fault (with).

بارے bāre (P) adv. At last; in short.

باڑ ، باڑھ bāṛ, bāṛh (H) n.f. Border; fence. hedge; boundary. margin; edge of a weapon or tool; volley; a line of soldiers.

باڑ اڑانا ، باڑ مارنا ، باڑ جھاڑنا bāṛ uṛānā, bāṛ mārnā, bāṛ jhāṛnā, v. To fire a volley.

باڑ باندھنا یا لگانا bāṛ bāṅdhnā yā lagānā, v. To fence or enclose a field.

باڑ پر چڑھانا bāṛ par chaṛhānā, v. To sharpen; to grind; to whet; to animate; to incite; to stir up.

باڑ دینا ، رکھنا bāṛ denā, rakhnā, v. To sharpen.

باڑ ھی جب کھیت کو کھائے تو رکھوالی کون کرے bāṛ hī jab khet ko khāe to rakhwālī kaun kare, prov. A fox should not be a juror in a goose's trial; who will respect the law, when the law-makers themselves break it.

باڑا bāṛā (H) n.m. An enclosure; fence; hedge; alms or charity given at the time of Hindu marriage.

باڑی bāṛī (H) n.f. A garden; an orchard; an enclosure; an enclosed piece of ground; kitchen garden; cotton plant.

باز bāz (P) A particle affixed to nouns to denote an agent or doer, as, جوے باز jūe bāz, a gambler.

باز bāz (P) n.m. A hawk; a falcon.

بازدار bāzdār, n.m. One who is incharge of hawks or falcons; a falconer.

باز bāz (P) adv. & adj. Again; back; abstaining; refusing.

باز آ bāz ā, intj. Hold! stop!

باز آنا bāz ānā, v. To turn back from; to leave off; to decline; to abstain (from); to refuse; to abandon.

باز ادائی bāz adā'ī, n.f. Rebursement; repayment.

باز پرس bāz purs, n.f. Interrogation; cross-examination; investigation; detailed examination.

باز حراست bāz ḥirasat, n.f. Remand to custody.

باز خواست baz khwāst, n.f. Investigation; calling to account; enquiry.

باز خواہ bāz khwāh, adj. An investigator; an enquirer.

باز داشت bāz dāsht, n.f. Recovery or regaining.

باز رکھنا bāz rakhnā, v. To hold back; to disallow; to debar; to prohibit; to restrain from; to repress; to prevent; to dissuade.

باز رهنا bāz rahnā, v. To abstain from; to leave off; to desist; to refrain from; to cease; to forbear; to shun.

باز گشت bāz gasht, n.f. Returning; retreat; relapse; echo.

بازیاب bāz yāb, adj. Regaining; recovering.

بازیابی bāz yābi, n.f. Recovery.

باز یافت bāz yāft, n.f. Recovery; getting back; the act of resuming alienated lands.

بازار bāzār (P) n.m. A market; a bazar.

بازار بٹا bāzār baṭṭā, n.m. Discount; the market rate of exchange; commission.

بازار گرم ھونا bāzār garm honā, v. To be in great demand; to have a good sale.

بازار لگانا bāzār lagānā, v. To establish a market; to display one's wares; to gather a crowd.

بازار مندا یا سرد ھونا bāzār mandā yā sard honā, v. To be in little demand; having a dull market.

رشوت کا بازار گرم ھے rishwat kā bāzār garm hae. Bribery is the order of the day; bribery and corruption are rampant.

بازاری bāzārī (P) adj. Relating to the market; common; low; vulgar.

بازاری آدمی bāzāri ādamī, n.m. Common man; man in the street; not a respectable person.

بازاری عورت bāzārī 'aurat, n.f. A common woman; a prostitute; harlot.

بازاری گپ bāzārī gap, n.f. Street talk; a rumour; hearsay; an unconfirmed report.

بازاری نرخ bāzārī nirkh, n.m. Market rates.

بازو bāzū (P) n.m. The arm; the fold of a door; the side of a bedstead; a supporter; a companion; the flank (of an army); an accompanier; a repeater of the chorus of the مرثیہ marṣiyah (elegy).

بازو بند bāzū band, n.m. A bracelet; an ornament worn on the arm; an armlet; amulet.

بازو دینا **bāzū denā**, *v.* To assist, to help; to support; to lend a helping hand; to aid.

بازو پھڑکنا **bāzū pharaknā**, *v.* An arm vibrating with involuntary motion (regarded as an omen foretelling the meeting of a friend).

بازو دعویٰ **bāzū da'wā**, *n.m.* Claim for the restitution of conjugal rights.

بازی **bāzī** (P) *n.f.* Sport; game; play; a wager; a bet.

بازی دینا **bāzī denā**, *v.* To defeat; to beat; to win a·game; to checkmate.

بازی کھانا **bāzī khānā**, *v.* To lose; to be defeated; to be cheakmated.

بازی گاہ **bāzi gāh**, *n.f.* Place for play; a theatre or playground.

بازی گر **bāzi gar**, *n.m.* A rope-dancer; a conjurer; an acrobat; a juggler.

بازی گری **bāzi gari**, *n.f.* The art of a juggler; legerdemain.

بازی لگانا **bāzī lagānā**, *v.* To wager; to bet; to stake.

بازی لے جانا **bāzī lejānā**, *v.* To win; to overcome; to excel.

بازیچہ **bāzīchah** (P) *n.m.* Fun; play; sport; frolic; a toy; a plaything.

باس **bās** (H) *n.m.* Dwelling; lodging; residence; abode.

باس **bās** (H) *n.f.* Scent; odour; smell; offensive smell.

باسٹھ **bāsaṭh** (H) *adj.* Sixty-two.

باسط **bāsiṭ** (A) *adj.* Giver of prosperity; one of the attributes of God.

باسمتی **bāsmati** (H) *n.m.* A fine and fragrant kind of rice.

باسلیق **bāsaliq** (G) *n.f.* The great vein in the arm; (*vena basilica*).

باسن **bāsan** (H) *n.m.* A basin; a plate; dish; pot.

باسی **bāsi** (H) *adj.* Stale; fusty; food left over night. *n.m.* Dweller; inhabitant

باسی بچے نہ کتا کھائے **bāsi bache nah kuttā khāe**, *prov.* To spend everything; not to lay by a penny.

باسی تباسی **bāsī tibāsi**, *adj.* Two or three days' old stale food.

باسی عید **bāsi 'id**, *n.f.* The day after 'Id.

باسی کرنا **bāsi karnā**, *v.* To make stale; to make mouldy.

باسی کڑھی میں ابال آنا **bāsi karhī men ubāl ānā**, *id.* To storm after the event; to wish to be young in old age.

باسی منہ **bāsi munh**, *n.m.* Before one has taken breakfast.

باش **bāsh** (P) *adj.* (in *comp.*) Being; living. *intr.* Stop! stay.

باشندہ **bāshindah** (P) *n.m.* Inhabitant; resident.

باشہ **bāshah** (P) *n.m.* A hawk; a falcon.

باصر **bāṣir** (A) *adj.* One who sees; looker-on.

باصرہ **bāṣirah** (A) *n.f.* Sight; theksense of seeing.

باطل **bāṭil** (A) *adj.* False; null and void; futile; ineffectual; spurious; useless; unsound; fictitious; absurd.

باطل السحر **bāṭil-us-seḥr**, *adj.* Counteractor or neutralizer of enchantment.

باطل سمجھنا **bāṭil samajhnā**, *v.* To regard as false; to set at naught.

باطل کرنا **bāṭil karnā**, *v.* To vitiate; to falsify; to rescind; to revoke; to abolish; to cancel; to refute.

باطن **bāṭin** (A) *n.m.* The innermost part; the inside; the internal; the mind; the heart.

باطنی **baṭini** (A&P) *adj.* Internal; hidden; concealed; latent; intrinsic.

باعث **bā'iṣ** (A) *n.m.* Cause; occasion; reason; condition; ground; basis.

باغ **bāgh** (P) *n.m.* A garden; orchard; a grove.

باغ باغ ہونا **bāgh bāgh honā**, *id.* To rejoice greatly; to be over-joyed.

باغبان **bāgh bān**, *n.m.* Gardener.

باغبانی **bāgh bānī**, *n.f;* Gardening; horticulture.

باغ نباتات bāgh-ĕ nabātāt, n.m. A vegetable garden; botanical garden.

باغات bāghāt, n.m. Orchards; gardens.

باغیچہ bāghichah (P) n.m. A small grove or orchard.

باغی bāghi (A) n.m. A rebel; a traitor; a mutineer; an insurgent.

بافت bāft (P) n.f. Weaving; web; texture; tissue.

بافتگی bāftagi (P) n.f. Weaving; knitting.

بافتہ bāfatah (P) adj. Woven; knitted. n.m. A kind of silk cloth; a tissue.

بافندہ bāfindah (P) n.m. Weaver.

باقر bāqir (A) adj. Deeply learned; abounding in riches and knowledge.

باقر خانی bāqir khāni (T) n.f. A kind of crisp and sweatened bread made of butter and flour.

باقلا ، باقلہ bāqlā, bāqlah (A) n.m. A kind of bean; pea.

باقی bāqī (A) adj. Remaining; lasting; existing; perpetual. n.f. Residue; remainder; balance; arrears; outstandings; surplus.

باقی جمع bāqī jama', n.f. Unrealized assessments.

باقی حساب bāqi ḥisāb, n.f. Balance of an account.

باقی دار bāqi dār, n.m. Owning a balance; a defaulter; a debtor.

باقی رہنا bāqi rahnā, v. To remain (unpaid); to have a balance; to be left.

باقی غیر ممکن الوصول bāqi ghair mumkin-ul-wuṣūl, n.f. Irrecoverable balance.

باقی فرضی bāqī farẓī, n.f. A nominal balance.

باقی ماندہ bāqi māndah, adj. Remaining; residuary; residue; remainder.

باقی نکالنا bāqi nikālnā, v. To strike a balance; to find the difference between two numbers; to subtract.

باقیات bāqiyāt (A) adj. Remnant; arrears.

باک bāk (P) n.m. Fear; terror.

باکرہ bākirah (A) n f. A virgin.

باگ bāg (P) n.f. A rein; a bridle.

باگ اٹھانا bāg uṭhānā, v. To give a horse the rein; to set a horse at full gallop; to start (on a journey).

باگ ڈور bāg ḍor, n.f. A long rein with which horses are led; a halter.

باگ ڈھیلی کرنا bāg ḍhīlī karnā, v. To give a loose rein; to leave one free to act as he likes (used in bad sense).

باگ لینا bāg lenā, v. To take the reins; to gallop a horse; to start.

باگ موڑنا bāg moṛnā, v. To turn the reinso to turn the direction of a horse; t; turn away attention to something else.

باگ ہاتھ سے چھوٹنا bāg hāth se chhūṭnā, v. To allow the reins to slip from the hands; to lose a chance; to be out of control.

باگڑ بلا bagaṛ billā (H) n.m. A wildcat.

باگھ bāgh (H) n.m. A lion; a leopard.

باگیسری bāgesri (H) n.f. Name of a ragnī.

بال bāl (A) n.m. Heart; mind; state; power; condition.

بال bāl (P) n.m. A wing; a pinion.

بال bāl (H) n.m. Hair; a child; a boy under five years or a girl not above sixteen; an ear of corn; a crack in a glass or china.

بال آنا bāl ānā, v. To have hair on the chin or face; to have a crack (in); to be cracked (china).

بال اتارنا bāl utārnā, v. To shave off; to cut the hair.

بال بال bāl bāl, adv. Every hair; completely; altogether; clearly.

بال بال بچنا bāl bāl bachnā, v. To escape by a hair's breadth; to have a narrow escape.

بال باندھا غلام bāl bāndhā ghulām, n.m. A verp obedient servant.

بال باندھنا bāl bāṅdhnā, v. To set or braid the hair.

بال باندھی کوڑی مارنا bāl bāndhi kauṛī mārnā, v. To shoot without missing; to be a sure shot; to have a true aim; not to make a mistake.

بال بچے bāl bachche, n.m. Wife and children; family.

بال بدھ bāl budh, n.f. Child instinct; inexperience; puerility.

بال برابر bāl barābar, adj. Hair-like; fine like the hair; very thin; very little.

بال بکھرنا bāl bikharnā, v. To have dishevelled hair; to be in a state of perplexity.

بال بنانا bāl banānā, v. To do the hair; to dress the hair.

بال بیکا نہ ہونا bāl bikā nah honā, v. Not to receive the slightest injury or harm.

بال پکنا bāl paknā, v. To have the hair turned grey; to grow old; ripening of the fruit or corn.

بال توڑ bāl toṛ, n.m. A boil or sore caused by breaking of a hair.

بال تراش bāl tarāsh, n.m. Hair dresser.

بال جھڑنا bāl jhaṛnā, v. Falling off the hair.

بال چھڑ bāl chhaṛ, n.m. The hyacinth; spikenard.

بال دار bāl dār, adj. A cracked vessel (of china or glass, &c.).

بال رکھنا bāl rakhnā, v. To allow the hair to grow.

بال کمانی bāl kamāni, n.f. Hair spring (of a watch).

بال کھڑے ہونا bāl khaṛe honā, v. To feel cold; to be in terrible fright; to be terror-stricken.

بال کی بھیڑ بنانا bāl kī bheṛ banānā, v. To exaggerate; to make a mountain of a mole-hill.

بال کی کھال کھینچنا یا نکالنا bāl ki khāl kheṅchnā yā nikālnā, v. To split hairs; to be hypercritical; to investigate thoroughly.

بال لینا bāl lenā, v. To use a razor; to shave private parts.

بال والا bāl wālā, adj. Hairy.

بال و پر نکالنا bāl-ŏ par nikālnā, v. To be fledged; to start flying; to betray one's evil disposition; to show the cloven hoof; to oppose; to stand against.

بال ہٹ bāl haṭ, n.f. Childish obstinacy.

بالوں کا برش bāloṅ kā bursh, n.m. Hair brush.

بالوں کا تیل bāloṅ kā tel, n.m. Hair oil.

بالوں کا کپڑا bāloṅ kā kapṛā, n.m. Hair cloth.

بالوں کی رسی bāloṅ ki rassi, n.f. Hair line.

بالوں کی کثرت bāloṅ ki kas̤rat, n.f. Hairiness.

بالا bālā (P) prep. On; upon; above. adj. High; lofty; exalted; foregoing. n.m. Top; upper part; supra.

بالا بالا bālā bālā, adv. Secretly; apart; stealthily; privately; over and above the head of one.

بالا بتانا bālā batānā, v. To delude; to cheat; to deceive; to dupe; to circumvent.

بالا بند bālā band, n.m. A part of dress; a kind of turban; a particular kind of coat.

بالا پوش bālā posh, n.m. A coverlet; a quilt; an overcoat.

بالا خانہ bālā k͟hānah, n.m. An upper room; a balcony; an upper storey.

بالا دست bālā dast, adj. Having the upper hand; higher; superior.

بالا نشین bālā nashīn, adj. Seated aloft; occupying the chief seat.

بالا و پست bālā-o past, n.m. The heavens above and the earth below; the high and low.

بالا bālā (H) n.m. A child; a large ear-ring.

بالا پن bālā pan, n.m. Childhood; infancy.

بالائی bālā'i (P) adj. Over and above; extrenal; extraordinary; superficial. n.f. That which is on the surface; cream.

بالائی اخراجات **balā'ī ikhrājāt,** *n.m.* Overhead expenses.

بالائی یافت **balā'ī yāft,** *n.m.* Pre-requisites; picking; bribes.

بالٹی **bālṭi,** *n.f.* A pail or bucket.

بالش **bālish** (P) *n.f.* Pillow; cushion.

بالشت **bālisht** (P) *n.m.f.* A span.

بالشتیا **bālishtiyā,** *n.m.* A dwarf.

بالغ **bāligh** (A) *adj.* Having attained puberty; having reached the age of maturity. *n.m.* An adult.

بالک **bālak** (H) *n.m.* A young child; an infant.

بالکا **bālakā** (H) *n.m.* A disciple; a follower.

بالم **bālam** (S) *n.m.* A lover; a sweet-heart; husband.

بالو **bālū** (H) *n.f.* Sand.

بالو شاہی **bālū shāhi,** *n.f.* A kind of sweetmeat.

بالی **bālī** (H) *n.f.* A small girl; an ear-ring; a spike of corn.

بالی عمر **bāli 'umr,** *n.f.* Young age; prime of life.

بالیدگی **bālidagī** (P) *n.f.* Vegetation; growth; increase; development; expansion.

بالین **bālīn** (P) *n.f.m.* A pillow; a cushion; the head-side of a bedstead or tomb.

بام **bām** (P) *n.m.* An upper storey; the terrace or roof of a house; a balcony.

بامداد **bāmdād** (P) *n.m.* Morning; dawn; aurora.

بان **bān** (H) *n.f.* Disposition; nature; habit; quality; temper; manners. *n.m.* An arrow; a rope or string made of reeds or twisted grass (*mūnj*).

بان **bān** (A) *n.m.* Name of a tree which yields Benzoin; a tree called by the Persians *Bed-mushk*, the leaves and flowers of which are sweet-scented.

بان **bān** (P) (used as suffix) signifying keeper guardian, as دربان *darbān*—door-keeper.

باں باں کرنا **bāṅ bāṅ karnā,** *v.* To prate; to talk foolishly.

بانا **bānā** (H) *n.m.* Dress; a veil; garment; costume; the woof in weaving; a kind of weapon; fashion in dress peculiar to individuals or to bodies taken individually (so regimentals may be called *bana*-uniform) habit; appearance.

بانا باندھنا **bānā bāndhnā,** *v.* To be prepared; to be ready; to be determined.

بانا بدلنا **bānā badalnā,** *v.* To disguise oneself; to change oae's dress.

بانات **bānāt,** *n.f.* Broad-cloth.

بانبی **bāṅbi** (H) *n.f.* Ant-hill; snake's hole.

بانٹ **bāṅṭ** (H) *n.f.* Share; division; allotment; quotient; food given to a cow while milking her.

بانٹنا **bāṅṭnā** (H) *v.* To apportion; to divide; to allot; to dispose of; to share; to distribute.

بانجھ **bāṅjh,** *adj.* Barren (woman); sterile; unproductive.

باندھ **bāṅdh** (H) *n.f.* An embankment; imprisonment.

باندھنا **bāṅdhnā** (H) *v.* To tie; to fasten; to shut; to bind; to pack; to compose; to chain; to embank; to fetter; to captivate; to join together (in marriage); to construct (bridge); to levy (tax); to design; to plan.

باندی **bāṅdī** (H) *n.f.* A female servant; a female slave; a handmaid; a maid-servant.

بانڈی **bāṅḍi** (H) *n.f.* A short thick stick; a cudgel.

بانس **bāṅs** (H) *n.m.* A bamboo; a ten feet long measure.

بانس پر چڑھانا **bāṅs par chaṛhānā,** *v.* To hold up; to ridicule or disgrace; to dishonour; to defame; to praise an unworthy man.

بانس واڑی **bāṅs wāṛī,** *n.f.* A bamboo forest.

بانسوں اچھلنا یا کودنا *bāṅsoṅ uchhalnā yā kūdnā, v.* To be highly pleased; to be overjoyed.

بانسا *bāṅsā, n.m.* The bridge of the nose.

بانسا پھر جانا *bāṅsā phir jānā, v.* Turning of the bridge of the nose, which generally happens at the time of death.

بانسری ، بانسلی *bāṅrsī, bāṅslī* (H) *n.f.* A flute made of bamboo wood.

بانسی *bāṅsī* (H) *n.f.* The bamboo stick; a kind of stone having yellow white colour.

بانک *bāṅk* (H) *n.f.* Curvature; bend; hook; a reach or turning of a river; a crook; fault; offence; wickedness; a semi-circular ornament worn on arms or ankles; a kind of dagger; an exercise with the dagger.

بانکا *bāṅkā* (H) *adj.* Curved; crook; cunning; arrant; sly. *n.m.* A fop; a beau; a coxcomb; a bully; a kind of a knife to cut bamboo with.

بانکا چور *bāṅkā chor, n.m.* A beau; a coxcomb; an expert thief.

بانکپن *bāṅkpan, n.m.* Foppishness; smartness; gaiety; wantonness.

بانکی *bāṅkī*. The feminine form of بانکا *bāṅkā*.

بانگ *bāṅg* (P) *n.f.* A cry; a shout; the call to prayer; the crowing of a cock.

بانگ درا *hāṅg-ĕ darā, n.f.* Sound of a bell rung at the time of the march of a caravan; a collection of early Urdu poems of Doctor Iqbal.

بانگ دینا *bāṅg denā, v.* To summon Muslims to prayers; to crow.

بانگر *bāṅgar* (P) *n.f.* High-land; table-land; the land which can be cultivated without water.

بانگڑو *bāṅgṛū* (H) *adj.* A native of the high lands; rude; rough; ignorant; stupid.

بانگی *bāṅgī* (H) *n.f.* A model; a pattern; a sample.

بانو *bāno* (P) *n.f.* A lady; a princess; a gentlewoman.

بانوے *bānwe* (H) *adj.* Ninety-two.

بانہہ *bāṅh* (H) *n.f.* Arm; support.

بانی *bānī* (A) *n.m.* Founder; builder; architect; composer; inventor; originator; author.

بانی فساد *bānī-ĕ fasād, n.m.* Mischief-monger.

بانی *bāni* (H) *n.f.* Advice; saying; sound; verse; principle.

باوا *bāwā, n.m.* Father; superior; spiritual guide or teacher.

باوا آدم *bāwā ādam, n.m.* The first man; Adam.

باوا آدم نرالا ہونا *bāwā ādam nirālā honā, v.* Being a curious person; following one's own whims.

باوا کا *bāwā kā, adj.* Ancestral; hereditary; personal.

باور *bāwar* (P) *n.m.* Belief; faith; confidence; trust. *adj.* True; credible; trustworthy.

باور کرنا *bāwar karnā, v.* To believe; to trust; to credit.

باورچی *bāwarchi, n.m.* A cook.

باورچی خانہ *bāwarchī khānah, n.m.* A kitchen.

باون *bāwan* (H) *adj.* Fifty-two.

باون تولے پاؤ رتی *bāwan tole pāo' ratti, adv.* Precisely; exactly the same.

باون گز کا *bāwan gaz kā, adj.* Mischievous; tall; long.

باہ *bāh* (A) *n.f.* Lust; virility; venereal passion.

باہر *bāhir* (H) *n.m. & adv.* Out; outside; abroad; external; beyond; exceeding; away; without.

باہر باہر *bāhir bāhir, adv.* At a distance. *intj.* Keep away! cut away!

باہر جانا *bāhir jānā, v.* To go out; to g abroad.

باہر کا *bāhir kā, n.m.* An outsider; a foreigner.

باہر کرنا یا نکالنا bāhir karnā yā nikālnā, v. To exclude; to omit; to strike out; to turn out; to dismiss; to oust; to eject, to expel.

باہر لے جانا bāhir le jānā, v. To export; to take abroad; to take out (of).

(کہنے سے) باہر ہونا (kahne se) bāhir honā, Not to agree; not to listen; to disobey.

باہم bāham (P) adv. Together; conjointly; reciprocally; mutually.

باہم دگر bāham digar, adv. Together; by mutual endeavour.

باہمن bāhaman (H) n.m. A Brahman.

باہمنی bāhmani (H) n.f. Wife of a Brahman.

باہمی bahami, adj. Mutual, reciprocal.

بائع bāi' (A) n.m. A seller, a vendor; a merchant.

باؤ bā'o (H) n.f. Wind; air; flatulency; rheumatism.

باؤلا bā olā (H) adj. Mad; demented; crazy; insane. n.m. A mad man.

باؤلا پن bā'olā pan, n.m. Madness.

باؤلی bā'oli (H) n.f. A large well into which people descend by means of steps to get water; the drag (thing or animal) with which beasts and birds of prey are trained to hunt; a mad woman.

باؤنی bā'oni (H) n.f. Seed time; sowing.

بائی bā'i (H) n.f. Mistress; lady; dame; wife; woman; mother, nurse; dancing girl.

بائیس bā'is (H) adj. Twenty-two.

بایاں bāyan (H) adj. Left. n.m. (Music) the bass; left hand.

باید و شاید bāyad-ō shāyad (P) adj. Fit; proper; as it should be.

ببر babar (A) n.m. A lion.

ببول babūl, n.f. The acacia tree.

ببول کے پیڑ بونا babūl ke per bonā, v. To do something harmful or conducive to a bad end.

ببولا babūlā (H) n.m. See بگولا bagūlā.

ببی bibbi. n.f. A kiss.

بپتا biptā (H) n.f. Adversity; misfortune; calamity; distress.

بپتسمہ baptismah (G) n.m. Baptism.

بپھرنا bipharnā (H) v To become irritated or enraged; to be out of control; to be perverse, refractory, disobedient, cross or obstinate.

بت but (P) n.m. An idol; an image; a statue; a beloved. adj. Speechless; dumb; stupefied.

بت بننا but ban-nā, v To turn into a statue, to become rigid and speechless as a statue.

بت پرست but parast, n.m. & adj. An idolator; an iconolater.

بت پرستی but parasti, n.f. Idol worship; idolatry.

بت تراش būt tarāsh n.m. A sculptor; a carver of idols.

بت تراشی but tarāshī, n.f. Sculpture; statuary; the art of a sculptor.

بت خانہ but khānah, n.m. An idol-temple.

بت شکن but shikan, adj. & n.m. An iconoclast; an idol breaker.

بت کدہ but kadah. n.m. An idol temple.

بتا buttā (H) n.m. Pretext; evasion; fraud; trick, overreaching; deception.

بتا دینا buttā denā, v. To overreach; to defraud; to deceive.

بتاسا ' بتاشا batāsā, batāshā, n.m. A bubble: a kind of small sugar-cake; a puffed sugar drop; a kind of firework.

بتانا batānā (H) v. To tell; to point out; to show; to describe; to indicate; to explain; to teach; to acquaint.

بتلانا batlānā, v. To explain; to tell; to talk; to converse; to point out; to instruct; to impart.

بتنگڑ ' بتکڑ batangar, batkkar (H) n.m. Multiplication of words; an exaggerated or magnified version of a thing

بتول batūl (A) n.f. A virgin. a pure and chaste woman devoted to God (usually applied to the Virgin Mary and to Hazrat Fatimah).

بتی battī, n.f. A candle; a stick (of wax); a wick.

بتی جلانا batti jalānā, v. To light a candle or a lamp; to switch on a light.

بتی چڑھانا batti charhānā, v. To put a candle in the candle stick; to raise the wick (of a lamp).

بتی دکھانا batti dikhānā, v. To show a light.

بتی دینا batti denā, v. To kindle fire; to ignite; to fill a wound with guaze.

بتی کی طاقت batti ki ṭāqat, n.f. Candle power.

بتی گل کرنا batti gul karnā, v. To put out a lamp; to switch off light.

بتیس battis (H) adj. Thirty-two.

بتیس دانتوں میں زبان battis dānton meṅ zabān, prov. Encircled by enemies (like the tongue in thirty-two teeth).

بتیس دھار battis dhār, n.m. Mother's milk which is supposed to flow in 32 streams.

بتیسا battisā (H) n.m. A tonic composed of thirty-two ingredients given to women after child birth or to mares after foaling.

بتیسی battisi (H) n.f. A set of teeth; any collection consisting of thirty-two parts.

بتیسی دکھانا battisi dikhānā, v. To show the teeth (to); to laugh (aimlessly); to mock; to grin.

بتیسی بجنا battisi bajnā, v. Chattering of teeth; to shiver (with clod).

بٹ baṭ (H) n.f. A portion; a fold; a twist; a wrinkle or fold on the body (on account of obesity); a measure of weight; a by-path; a way; an Indian fig tree; a cast of Kashmiris.

بٹا baṭṭā (H) n.m. A measure of weight, exchange or discount; deficiency; loss; blemish; injury; a ball (of wood or stone); a casket.

بٹا لگانا baṭṭā lagānā, v. To raduce the value or price; to defame; to stigmatise.

بٹا لگنا daṭṭā lagnā, v. To lose reputation; to be defamed; to incur infamy; to suffer a loss.

بٹا کھاتا baṭṭā khātā, n.m. Irrecoverable balances; bad debts account.

بٹے باز baṭṭe bāz, n.m. A juggler; a swindlar; a cheat; a knave; artful; crafty.

بٹے پر baṭṭe par, adv. At a discount; at a reduction.

بٹانا baṭānā (H) v. To cause to divide; to help; to divert attention.

بٹائی baṭā'i (H) n.f. Wages paid for twisting ropes; division of the crop between the cultivator and the landlord.

بٹنا baṭnā (H) v. To twist; to form by twisting; to be diverted (attention); to divide; to share; to gain; to make profit. n.m. An instrument with which ropes are twisted; a cosmetic; a preparation for cleaning the pores of the body and beautifying the skin (same as اُبٹن ubṭan or اُبٹنا ubṭanā).

بٹنگ baṭang (H) n.m. A pear-like fruit.

بٹوا baṭwā (H) n.m. A purse; a money-bag; a brass utensil for dressing food.

بٹوارا batwārā (H) n.m. Partition; division of an estate; a share.

بٹوانا baṭwānā (H) v. To cause to twist; to cause to be separated or partitioned; to cause to be apportioned.

بٹورنا baṭornā (H) v. To gather up; to collect; to accumulate; to amass; to take by deceit.

بٹھا دینا ، بٹھانا biṭhā denā, biṭhānā (H) v. To cause one to sit down; to seat, to set or fix; to plant; to instal on a throne; to lay; to impress (on the mind).

بٹھا رکھنا biṭhā rakhnā, v. To keep seated; to keep one waiting; not to give in marriage (intentionally) a daughter who is major; torefuse to let a married daughter go to her husband.

بٹیا biṭiyā (H) n.f. Daughter; my little daughter.

بٹیر *baṭer* (H) *n.f.* The quail.

بجا *bajā* (P) *adj.* In place; fit; right; proper; opportune; suitable. *adv.* Properly; fitly; precisely.

بجا لانا *bajā lānā, v.* To perform; to execute; to comply with; to obey; to accomplish; to effect.

بجانا *bajānā* (H) *v.* To play upon a musical instrument; to beat (a drum).

بجائے *bajāe* (P) *adv.* Instead of; in place of.

بجرا *bajrā* (H) *n.m.* A boat commonly used for travelling; a large pleasure boat.

بجری *bajri* (H) *n.f.* Gravel; small hailstone.

بجز *bajuz* (P) *prep.* Besides; except; with the exception of; without.

بجلی *bijlī* (H) *n.f.* Thunderbolt; lightning; a sort of ear-ring; the kernel of a mango seed. *adj.* Active; smart.

بجلی چمکنا *bijli chamaknā, v.* Flashing of the lightning.

بجلی کی تلوار *bijlī ki talwār, n.m.* A sharp-edged sword.

بجلی کی کڑک *bijli kī kaṛak, n.f.* Thunder-clap.

بجلی گرنا *bijlī girnā, v.* To be struck by lightning; to be blasted.

بجنا *bajnā* (H) *v.* To sound; to strike (as a clock); to be played upon (as a musical instrument); to be rung (as a bell); to chatter (as teeth).

بجو *bijjū* (H) *n.m.* Badger. (*Fig.*) A cunning, sharp and evil-minded person.

بجوانا *bajwānā* (H) *v.* To cause to sound; to cause an instrument of music to be played on.

بجھانا *bujhānā* (H) *v.* To extinguish; to satiate; to slake (lime); to temper the steel; to disinfect water (by dipping heated iron into it); to smother anger; to repress; to damp or depress (the spirits); to quench; to make one understand (a riddle); to cause one to comprehend; to instruct; to teach; to explain; to cause to believe; to signify.

بجھنا *bujhnā* (H) *v.* To be extinguished; to be slaked; to be damped (the spirits); to be quenched (thirst).

بجھارت *bujhārat* (H) *n.f.* A riddle; a problem; a puzzle; adjustment of accounts.

بچی ' بچا *buchchā, buchchi* (H) *adj.* Having ears cut or lapped.

بچار *bichār* (H) *n.m.* Considration; reflection; judgment; opinion; apprehension; thought; will; discernment.

بچا کھچا *bachā khuchā, n.m.* Remainder; residue.

بچانا *bachānā* (H) *v.* To save; to preserve; to protect; to secure; to spare; to defend; to guard; to extricate; to help; to conceal.

بچاؤ *bachā'o* (H) *n.m.* Defence; protection; security; preservation; salvation; deliverance; rescue; liberation.

بچاؤ نکالنا *bachāo nikālnā, v.* To contrive escape or deliverance.

بچپن *bachpan* (H) *n.m.* Childhood; babyhood; infancy.

بچت *bachat* (H) *n.f.* Savings; surplus; gain; profit.

بچکانا *bachkānā, adj.* Pertaining to children; childish.

بچگان *bachagān* (P) *n.m.* (*plu. of* بچہ *bachchah*) Children; little ones.

بچلنا *bichalnā* (H) *v.* To slip; to go astray; to lose one's way; to be refractory; to be stubborn; to retreat or back out of a promise.

بچن *bachan* (S) *n.m.* Speech; talk; discourse; word of honour; pledge; promise; agreement.

بچنا *bachnā* (H) *v.* To save oneself; to escape from; to be spared; to avoid; to remain over or unspent; to recover; to survive.

بچو *bacho* (H) *intj.* Be out of the way! keep out of the way! take care! look out!

بچو *bachchū, int.* My dear! my boy! my son! a word of contempt used for the enemy.

بچولیا bicholiyā (H) n.m. One who interferes; intermeddler; a mediator; interposer; arbitrator; agent.

بچہ bachchah (P) n.m. A child; an infant; a babe; a lad; the young one of any creature; a young plant; a sapling; an inexperienced person; an innocent person.

بچہ بازی bachchah bāzi, n.f. Sodomy.

بچہ دان bachchah dān, n.m. The womb; uterus.

بچہ کشی bachchah kashi, n.f. Child-bearing; breeding.

بچہ کشی bachchah kushi, n.f. Infanticide.

بچوں کا کھیل bachchoṅ kā khel, n.m. Mere child's play; mere trifle; easy matter.

بچھا جانا bichhā jānā, v. To bow; to be extremely polite; to entertain; to be humble and meek; to make humble entreaty to.

بچھانا bichhānā (H) v. To spread; to extend; to knock down; to fell; to lay low.

بچھڑا bachhṛā (H) n.m. A calf.

بچھڑنا bichhaṛnā (H) v. To be separated or parted from.

بچھنا bichhnā (H) v. To be spread; to lie flat; to humble oneself; to show great regard (for).

بچھو bichchhū (H) n.m. A scorpion.

بچھوا bichhwā (H) n.m. A kind of dagger; an ornament worn on the toes; an iron claw or hook; a kind of pickle.

بچھوانا bichhwānā (H) v. To cause to spread.

بچھونا bichhaunā (H) n.m. Bedding; bedclothes; bed; carpet; carpeting.

بچھیا bachhiyā (H) n.f. A female calf.

بچھیرا bachherā (H) n.m. A colt.

بچھیری bachheri (H) n.f. A foal; a filly.

بچی bachchi, n.f. A little girl; a female child; a tuft of hair between the lower lip and the chin.

بحال bahāl (A) adj. In the usual state or condition; unaltered; *status quo*; flourishing; reinstated in office or work; restored to (health); refreshed; happy.

بحال رکھنا bahāl rakhnā, v. To keep in the same condition; to uphold a decision; to reinstate; to establish.

بحال کار bahāl kār, n.m. Restorer.

بحال کرنا bahāl karnā, v. To reinstate; to re-establish; to replace; to restore; to refresh; to confirm.

بحال ہونا bahāl honā, v. To be reinstated; to return to a former state or condition; to begin to flourish again.

بحالی bahāli, n.f. Restoration; reinstatement; return to (its) former state or condition; maintenance; recovery; rehabilitation; prosperity.

بحالی اراضی bahāli-ĕ arāzi, n.f. Land reclamation.

بحث bahṣ (A) n.f. (*Lit.* Digging); disputation; discussion; debate; dispute; altercation; controversy; argument; question.

بحثا بحثی bahṣā bahṣi, n.f. Controversy; discussion; argumentation.

بحث کرنا یا بحثنا bahṣ karnā yā bahṣnā, v. To argue; to discuss; to raise a question; to dispute; to debate.

بحر bahr (A) n.m. A sea; an ocean; n.f. Metre; verse; rhythm.

بحر کھلنا bahr khulnā, v. To deliver a speech fluently; to improve memory and intellect.

بحران buhrān (A) n.m. Crisis of a disease; the turning point; a critical moment.

بحور buhūr (A) n.m. (*plu.* of بحر bahr) Oceans; seas. n.f. Metres; verses.

بحری bahri (A) adj. Of or belonging to the sea; maritime; naval; marine; nautical.

بحریہ bahriyyah (A) n.m. Navy; Naval Department.

بحیرہ buhairah (A) n.m. (diminutive of بحر bahr) A small sea; a lake.

بخار bukhār (A) n.m. Heat; steam; vapour; fever; rage; grief; anguish.

بخار آنا bukhār ānā, v. To get fever; to suffer from fever.

بخار دل میں رکھنا *bukhār dil meṅ rakhnā*, *v.* To harbour animosity (against); to bear a grudge, against.

بخار نکالنا *bukhār nikālnā*, *v.* To appease one's anger; to vent one's rage; to let off steam.

بخارات *bukhārāt* (A) *n.m.* (*plu.* of بخار *bukhār*). Fumes; vapours; steam; mist.

بخاری *bukhārī*, *n.f.* A projection in a wall for storing grain; stove; fire-place; a collection of the Traditions of the Prophet (صحیح بخاری *Sahih Bukhārī*) called after the name of its editor *Imam Bukhārī*. *adj.* Belonging to *Bukhārā*.

بخت *bakht* (P) *n.m.* Good fortune; luck; prosperity; lot; portion.

بخت اڑ گئے بلندی رہ گئی *bakht uṛ gae bulandī reh gai*, *prov.* A man in poverty cherishes his one time big name; a pauper still dreaming of his past fortune.

بخت آزمائی *bakht āzmā'ī*, *n.f.* Trying one's luck; hazard; venture; effort.

بخت آور *bakht āwar*, *adj.* Fortunate; lucky.

بخت جلنا *bakht jalnā*, *v.* To be in bad luck; to be unfortunate.

بخت سیاہ یا تیرہ *bakht-ĕ siyāh yā tīrah*, *n.m.* Misfortune.

بخت خفتہ *bakht-ĕ khuftah*, *n.m.* Bad luck; misfortune; adversity.

بختیار *bakhtiyār*, *adj.* Fortunate; lucky.

بختی *bukhtī* (P) *n.f.* A quick paced camel (used for riding and not for loading); a dromedary.

بخرا *bakhrā* (P) *n.m.* Share; portion; lot; allotment.

بخش *bakhsh* (P) (used in *comp.*) Giving; imparting; bestowing; forgiving. *n.m.* Share; allotment; lot.

بخش دینا *bakhsh denā*, *v.* To bestow; to grant; to forgive.

بخشش *bakhshish* (P) *n.f.* Gift; donation; grant; reward; forgiveness; pardon; generosity; beneficence; boon.

بخشنا *bakhshnā*, *v.* To give; to grant; to bestow; to forgive; to pardon; to excuse; to absolve.

بخشندہ *bakhshindah* (P) *adj.* Giver; bestower; donor; pardoner.

بخشوانا *bakhshwānā*, *v.* To cause to give; to obtain pardon for another; to have one's sins or offence pardoned.

بخشی *bakhshī* (P) *n.m.* A ġeneral; a commander-in-chief; a paymaster; a disbursing officer.

بخشی الممالک *bakhshi-ul-mamālik*, *n.m.* Paymaster and commander-in-chief.

بخشی خانہ *bakhshī khānah*, *n.m.* The pay-office (of the army).

بخشی گری *bakhshī garī*, *n.f.* Office of a paymaster (in the army).

بخل *bukhl* (A) *n.m.* Avarice; stinginess; parsimony; niggardliness.

بخیل *bakhīl* (A) *adj.* A miser; niggard; stingy; avaricious.

بخیلی *bakhīlī*, *n.f.* Stinginess; parsimony; avarice; niggardliness.

بخیہ *bakhyah* (P) *n.m.* A kind of strong and fine stitching.

بخیہ لگانا *bakhyah lagānā*, *v.* To stitch.

بخیے ادھیڑنا *bakhiye udheṛnā*, *v.* To unsew; to expose (a person); to disclose the secrets of a person.

بد *bad* (P) *adj.* Bad; wicked; evil; naughty; mischievous.

بد اچھا بد نام برا *bad achchhā bad nām burā*, *prov.* The bad is better than the ill-known.

بد اختر *bad akhtar*, *adj.* Unfortunate; ill-starred; unlucky.

بد اخلاق *bad akhlāq*, *adj.* Of bad manners; impolished; ill-mannered; rude; coarse; immoral

بد اسلوب *bad uslūb*, *adj.* Ill-shaped; ill-made; inelegant; ill-behaved; of bad conduct.

بد اصل *bad aṣl*, *adj.* Low-born; base-born; vulgar.

بد اطوار **bad atwār**, *adj.* Of evil ways; ill-mannered; vulgar.

بد اعتقاد **bad i'tiqād**, *adj.* Faithless; lacking in faith or belief.

بد افعال **bad af'āl**, *adj.* Of wicked deeds; of bad habits.

بد آموز **bad āmoz**, *adj.* An evil teacher; one who instructs others in evil.

بد انتظامی **bad intizāmi**, *n.f.* Mismanagement; misrule; maladministration.

بد انجام **bad anjām**, *adj.* Having a bad end.

بد اندیش **bad andesh**, *adj.* Evil-minded; malicious; malevolent; inimical.

بد اندیشی **bad andeshi**, *n.f.* Malice; malignity; ill-will; malevolence.

بد باطن **bad bātin**, *adj.* Ill-natured; evil-minded; false-hearted; malicious.

بد باطنی **bad bātini**, *n.f.* Malice; ill-nature; evil mindedness.

بد بخت **bad bakht**, *adj.* Unlucky; unfortunate; wretched.

بد بختی **bad bakhti**, *n.f.* Misfortune; adversity; wretchedness.

بد بو **bad bū**, *n.f.* Bad smell; stink.

بد بین **bad bīn**, *adj.* One who sees (only) evil.

بد پرهیز **bad parhez**, *adj.* Intemperate; not controlling one's inclinations and passions; self-indulgent.

بد پرهیزی **bad parhezi**, *n.f.* Self-indulgence; intemperance; extravagance; carelessness.

بد تر **bad tar**, *adj.* Worse; inferior.

بد چشم **bad chashm**, *adj.* Malignant; envious; coveting other people's good fortune; evil-eyed; jealous.

بد چلن **bad chalan**, *adj.* Of bad conduct; ill-mannered; immoral.

بد حال **bad hāl**, *adj.* In bad circumstance; in evil plight.

بد حواس **bad hawās**, *adj.* Senseless; stupefied; confounded; bewildered; stunned; in consternation.

بد خصال ، بد خصلت **bad khisāl, bad khaslat**, *adj.* Of bad conduct or disposition; ill-disposed; ill-natured.

بد خط **bad khat**, *adj.* A bad or illegible writer; scrawler.

بد خطی **bad khati**, *n.f.* Illegible writing; scrawl.

بد خلق **bad khulq**, *adj.* Having a bad disposition; ill-tempered; ill-behaved.

بد خو **bad khū**, *adj.* Of bad habits; of evil disposition; evil-minded.

بد خواب **bad khwāb**, *n.m./f.* A bad dream. *adj.* Having a disturbing dream or a night-mare.

بد خوابی **bad khwābi**, *n.f.* A nightmare; wet dream; sleeplessness.

بد خواه **bad khwāh**, *adj.* Malevolent; malicious; malignant.

بد خواهی **bad khwāhi**, *n.f.* Ill-wishing; malevolence; enmity; hatred.

بد دعا **bad du'ā**, *n.f.* Curse; imprecation; malediction.

بد دل **bad dil**, *adj.* Suspicious; disheartened; hopeless; dejected.

بد دماغ **bad dimāgh**, *adj.* Peevish; fretful; proud; dissatisfied (with everything).

بد دماغی **bad dimāghi**, *n.f.* Peevishness; ill-will; showing displeasure; pride.

بد دیانت **bad diyānat**, *adj.* Dishonest; faithless; unreliable; cheat.

بد ذات **bad zāt**, *adj.* Low-born; of bad disposition; base; ill-bred; unprincipled; wicked; vicious; evil-minded.

بد ذائقه **had zā'iqah**, *adj.* Tasteless; unsavoury.

بد ذهن **bad zihn**, *adj.* Slow of apprehension; stupid; obtuse; blunt.

بد راه **bad rāh**, *adj.* Wicked; sinful; on the wrong path; astray.

بد رکاب **bad rakāb**, *adj.* Difficult to ride (horse); ill-paced.

بد رنگ **bad rang**, *adj.* Of bad colour; of another colour; discoloured; dull; faded.

بد رو **bad rū**, *adj.* Ugly; repulsive to sight.

بد زبان **bad zabān**, *adj.* Indecent (speaker); abusive; reviler; impertinent.

بد زبانی **bad zabānī**, *n.f.* Abuse; use of indecent and foul language; impertinence.

بد زیب **bad zeb**, *adj.* Ugly; graceless; ungraceful.

بد ساعت **bad sā'at**, *n.f.* An unlucky or unhappy moment; an unfortunate occasion.

بد سرشت **bad sarisht**, *adj.* Ill-disposed; ill-natured.

بد سگال **bad sigāl**, *adj.* Evil-minded; malevolent; malignant.

بد سلوکی **bad sulūki**, *n.f.* Misbehaviour; maltreatment.

بد سیرت **bad sirat**, *adj.* Ill-natured; ill-tempered; ill-disposed.

بد شکل **bad shakl**, *adj.* Ill-shaped; repulsive to sight; ugly; unbeautiful.

بد شگنی ، بد شگونی **bad shugnī, bad shugūnī**, *n.f.* Bad omen; inauspiciousness.

بد صورت **bad ṣūrat**, *adj.* Ill-shaped; ugly; ill-looking; unbeautiful.

بد طینت **bad ṭinat**, *adj.* Malevolent; evil-minded.

بد ظن **bad ẓan**, *adj.* Suspicious; mistrustful.

بد عہد **bad 'ahd**, *adj.* Faithless; treacherous; one who goes back upon his word or promise.

بد عہدی **bad 'ahdi**, *n.f.* Faithlessness; breach of promise; treachery; neglect of agreement or promise.

بد فعلی **bad fi'li**, *n.f.* Adultery; sodomy; misdeed; wickedness.

بد کار یا بد کردار **bad kār yā bad kirdār**, *adj.* Evil-doer; malefactor; sinful; wicked; bad character.

بدگمان **bad gumān**, *adj.* Suspicious; mistrustful.

بدگمانی **bad gumānī**, *n.f.* Suspicion; mistrust.

بد گو **bad go**, *adj.* Evil-speaker; calumniator; slanderer.

بد گوئی **bad go'ī**, *n.f.* Slander; evil-speaking.

بد گوہر **bad gouhar**, *adj.* Of bad origin; of evil nature; unprincipled.

بد لحاظ **bad liḥāẓ**, *adj.* Disrespectful; impudent; indecent; immodest; shameless; unmannerly.

بد لگام **bad lagām**, *adj.* Not obedient to the reins; hard mouthed (horse); uncontrollable; wilful; rude.

بد مزاج **bad mizāj**, *adj.* Ill-tempered; ill-natured; peevish.

بد مزاجی **bad mizāji**, *n.f.* Ill-temper; peevishness.

بد مزگی **bad mazagi**, *n.f.* Tastelessness; coolness between friends; unpleasantness; disagreement.

بد مزہ **bad mazah**, *adj.* Having a bad taste; unsavoury; ill-flavoured; insipid; tasteless; unpleasant.

بد مست **bad mast**, *adj.* Dead-drunk; inebriated; intoxicated; lustful; wicked.

بد معاش **bad m'āsh**, *adj.* Of a bad way of life; immoral; of an evil profession; roguish. *n.m.* A bad character; rascal; a blackguard; vagabond.

بد معاملہ **bad mu'āmalah**, *adj.* Unfair dealing; dishonest; fraudulent.

بد معاملگی **bad mu'āmalagi**, *n.f.* Unfair dealing; trickery; fraud.

بد نام **bad nām**, *adj.* Disreputable; infamous; ignominous; notorious.

بدنام کرنا **bad nām karnā**, *v.* To injure one's reputation; to defame; to vilify; to asperse.

بدنامی **bad nāmī**, *n.f.* Bad name; infamy; ignominy; dishonour.

بد نسل **bad nasl**, *adj.* Of a bad race or breed.

بد نصیب **bad naṣīb**, *adj.* Unfortunate; unlucky.

بد نما bad numā, adj. Ill-looking; ungraceful; inelegant; ugly; clumsy.

بد نمائی bad numā'i, n.f. Ungracefulness; inelegance; clumsiness; ugliness.

بد نہاد bad nihād, adj. Ill-disposed; ill-natured· Ill-intentioned.

بد نہادی bad nihādi, n.f. Ill-nature; badness of disposition.

بد نیت bad nivyat, adj. Ill-intentioned; ill-disposed; avaricious; inclined towards adultery or fornication.

بد نیتی bad niyyatı, n.f. Ill-will; malice; badness of intention or faith.

بد وضع bad waza', adj. Ill-shaped; ugly; Ill-mannered.

بد وضعی bad waza'i, n.f. Ugliness; evil disposition.

بد ہضمی bad hazmi, n.f. Indigestion.

بد ہیئت bad hai'at, adj. Ill-made; inelegant; unbeautiful.

بد یمن bad yumn, adj. Ill-omened; unpropitious; inauspicious.

بد یمنی bad yumni, n.f. Bad omen; bad luck.

بدا badā (S) n.m. Fate; fortune; destiny.

بدائع badā'e' (A) adj. (plu of بدیع badi') Curiosities; rare things; wonders; rarities.

بدایوں کے للا badāyūṅ ke lallā, n.m. A fool; a simpleton; stupid fellow.

بدر badr (A) n.m. The full moon.

بدر badar (P) adv. Out of doors; without; out; outside.

بدر کرنا badar karnā, v. To turn out; to expel; to eject; to banish.

بدر رو badar-rau (P) n.f. A drain; a sewer; outlet for water.

بدرقہ badraqah (P) n.m. A guide; an escort; a fellow-traveller; a convoy; a guard on the road; means; support.

بدعت bid'at (A) n.f. Innovation in religion; heresy; violence; oppression; wrong; schism.

بدعتی bid'ati (H) n.m. Innovator in religion; heretic; tyrant; oppressor.

بدل badal (A) n.m. Exchange; change; substitution.

بدل جانا badal jānā, v. To change; to back out.

بدل لینا badal lenā, v To exchange; to take.

بدلا badlā, n.m. Exchange; lieu; compensation; retaliation; revenge.

بدلا دینا badlā denā, v. To compensate; to indemnify; to requite.

بدلا لینا badlā lenā, v. To take revenge; to retaliate; to wreak vengeance on.

بدلانا badlānā, v. To exchange; to alter; to cause to change.

بدلائی badlā'i, n.f. Price of exchange; barter; something given in exchange.

بدلنا badalnā, v. To change; to exchange; to alter; to vary; to assume another form; to shift.

بدلی badlī, n.f. Transfer; substitution; change of guards.

بدلی badlı (H) n.f. A small cloud; cloudiness.

بدن badan (A) n.m. Body.

بدن ٹوٹنا badan ṭūṭnā, v. To suffer racking pains in the body.

بدن پھیکا ہونا badan phikā honā, v. To feel feverish; to have temperature.

بدن کے رونگٹے کھڑے ہونا badan ke rauṅgte khare honā, v. To have the hair of the body stand on end (on account of extreme fear or cold); to feel intense cold; to be terror-stricken.

بدنی badani (A) adj. Of or relating to the body; corporal.

بدنی سزا badani sazā, n.f. Corporal punishment; physical torture.

بدو baddū (A) n.m. Nomadic tribes of Arabia; forest.

بدوی badawi (A) adj.&n.m. Of the desert; an Arab of the desert; Bedouin.

بدھ budh (H) n.m. Sense; knowledge; wisdom; understanding; intellect; discretion; wise or learned man; a sage; Budha, the enlightened one, who is regarded as a incarnation of God, and is the founder of Budhism; the planet Mercury; Wednesday.

بدھو buddhū, n.m. A fool; a devoid of sense.

بدی badī (P) n.f. Badness; wickedness; evil; vice; mischief; enmity; backbiting.

بدی پر آترنا badī par utarnā, v. To be bent upon doing mischief; to be enimical; to be perverse.

بدی کرنا badī karnā, v. To do mischief; to harm a person; to backbite.

بدیس bades (H) n.m. A foreign country; an other land; abroad.

بدیسی badesī (H) adj. Of another country; from a foreign land; a foreigner; foreign.

بدیع badī' (A) adj. Novel; strange; extraordinary; wounderful; rare.

بدیع الجمال badī'-uj-jamāl, adj. Of rare or wonderful beauty; paragon of beauty.

بدیہہ badīh (A) adj. Evident; appropriate; opportune; apposite; apropos.

بدیہی badīhī (A) adj. Self-evident; axiomatic.

بدیہیات badīhiyyāt (A) n.f. Self-evident truths; axiom.

بڈھا buḍḍhā, adj. & n.m. An old man; aged.

بڈھا پھونس buḍḍhā phūṅs, adj. A very old man; a decrepit person.

بڈھی buḍḍhī (H) adj. & n.f. An old woman.

بذل bazl (A) n.m. Giving liberally; munificence; gift.

بذلہ bazlah (A) n.m. Witticism; joke; jest; raillery; fun; pleasantry.

بذلہ سنج bazlah sanj, adj. A witty person; one who indulges in jokes and jests.

بر barr (A) n.m. A dry land; a desert; jungle; land.

بر اعظم barr-ĕ a'ẓam, n.m. Continent.

بر bar (H) n.m. Bridegroom; wish; desire; prayer.

بر bar (P) prep. On; up; upon; above; at; (used as prefix as بر فلک bar-falak). adj. Bearer; carrier, e.g., نامہ بر nāmah-bar. n.f. Bosom; breast; the heart; fruit.

بر آنا bar ānā, v. To come forth; to bear fruit; to succeed; to be accomplished.

برپا bar pā, adv. On foot; standing; established.

برپا کرنا bar pā karnā, v. To set on foot; to cause to establish; to excite.

برپا ہونا bar pā honā, v. To happen; to take place; to befall; to be established.

برتر bartar, adj. Higher; superior; excellent; eminent.

برتری bartarī, n.f. Excellence; superiority.

برحق bar ḥaq, adj. Right; rightful; by right; justifiable; inevitable.

برخلاف ' برعکس bar khilāf, bar 'aks, adv. On the contrary; in opposition (to); at variance.

برخوردار bar khūrdār, adj. Obedient; happy; prosperous; enjoying long life and prosperity; (Lit.) enjoying the fruits of life. n.m. A male child; my son.

بر زبان تسبیح و در دل گاؤ خر bar zabān tasbīḥ-ŏ dar dil gāo' khar, prov. Being a hypocrite; double-dealing; to be a wolf in sheep'ss kin.

برطرف bar ṭaraf, adj. Dismissed; discharged; separated; aside; apart.

برطرف کرنا bar ṭaraf karnā, v. To dismiss; to discharge; to push or set aside; to get rid of.

برطرف ہونا bar ṭaraf honā, v. To be dismissed; to be discharged; to be cast aside; to be turned out.

برطرفی bar ṭarafī, n.f. Dismissal, discharge.

برقرار bar qarār, adj. Firm; established; fixed; extant; continuing as before.

برلانا bar lānā, v. To fulfil; to grant.

برمحل ' برموقع ' بروقت bar maḥal, bar mauqa', bar waqt, adj. Opportune; seasonable; in the nick of time; apposite; apropos.

برملا bar malā, adv. Openly; publicly; in the presence of everybody.

بر **birr** (A) *n.f.* A boon; a blessing; a gift.

برا **burā** (H) *n.m.* An enemy; opponent.

برا ' بری **burā, burī** (H) *adj.* Bad; wicked; mischievous; ungraceful; ill-mannered; ugly; worthless; faulty; defective.

برا بننا *burā bannā, v.* To be regarded as an enemy; to be accused of; to be condemned.

برا بھلا *burā bhalā, adj.* Good or bad; tolerable; passable; unbecoming. *n.m.* Reproach; abuses.

برا بھلا کہنا *burā bhalā kahnā, v.* To reproach; to revile; to abuse; to admonish.

برا حال کرنا *burā ḥāl karna, v.* To ill-treat; to chaff; to annoy; to ruin; to reduce to a bad condition.

برا کام *burā kām, n.m.* An evil deed; unbecoming or indecent action.

برا لکھا *burā likhkhā, n.m.* Ill-fate; bad luck.

برا لگنا *burā lagnā, v.* To be disagreeable; to be unpleasant.

برا ماننا *burā mānnā, v.* To take ill; to take as an affront; to be displeased.

برا وقت *burā waqt, n.m.* Evil days; hard time.

برے حالوں جینا *bure ḥāloṅ jīnā, v.* To lead a miserable life.

برے کی جان کو رونا *bure kī jān ko ronā, v.* To complain of tyranny.

برے وقت کا اللہ بیلی *bure waqt kā Allah belī, prov.* Man's extremity is God's opportunity.

برابر **barābar** (P) *adj.* Equal; abreast; even; level; plain; smooth; uniform; like; alike; on a par; side; near; opposite; over against; regular; continuous; exact; adequate; straight; accurate.

برابر برابر *barābar barādar, adv.* Side by side; shoulder to shoulder; continuously; regularly; half-by-half.

برابر کا *barābar kā, adj.* Of equal standing or strength; of the same age, size or kind.

برابر کا بیٹا *barābar kā beṭā, n.m.* Grown up son.

برابر کرنا *barābar karnā, v.* To equalise; to smooth; to level; to adjust; to assimilate; to match; to do continuously; to do unhesitatingly; to divide in halves; to destroy; to ruin; to waste.

برابر کی ٹکر کا *barābar kī ṭakkar kā, adj.* Of equal rank or standing or position; at par; equal.

برابر ہو جانا *barābar ho jānā, v.* To be level with; to be equal to; to balance; to be at par; to be up to the brim; to be spent up.

برابر ہونا *barābar honā, v.* To be equal; to be at par; to come abreast of; to come up to; to overtake; to end; to fit; to agree; to suit; to be spent up.

برابری **barābarī**, *n.f.* Equality; par; parity; competition; emulation; rivalry.

برابری کرنا *barābarī karnā, v.* To try to equal; to imitate; to insult; to vie with; to emulate; to rival.

برات **barāt** (H) *n.f.* A marriage procession; a multitude.

برات چڑھنا *barāt chaṛhnā, v.* The setting out of the bridegroom in procession to the bride's house; starting of a marriage procession.

براتی **barātī**, *n.m.* A member of the marriage procession; one who attends a marriage.

براجمان **birājmān** (H) *adj.* Brilliant; splendid. *n.m.* President.

براجنا **birājnā** (H) *v.* To grace; to adorn; to preside; to sit.

برادر **barādar** (P) *n.m.* Brother.

برادر اخیافی *barādar-ĕ akhyāfī, n.m.* Step-brothers (born from the same mother but having different fathers).

برادر توام *barādar-ĕ tau am, n.m.* Twin brothers.

برادر حقیقی *barādar-ĕ ḥaqīqī, n.m.* Real brothers.

برادر رضاعی barādar-ĕ razā'i, n.m. Foster brother (one who has suck milk from the breast of one's mothers).

برادر زاده barādar zādch, n.m. Brother's son; nephew.

برادر علاتی barādar-ĕ 'allātī, n.m. A step-brother (having the same father but different mother).

برادر کشی barādar kushī, n.f. Fractricide.

برادر نسبتی barādar-ĕ nisbatī, n.m. Brother-in-law (wife's brother or sister's husband).

برادرانہ barādarānah, adj. & adv. Brotherly; fraternal; like a brother.

برادری barādarī, n.f. Brotherhood; small community; fraternity; relationship; group.

برادہ burādah (P) n.m. Sawdust; powder; filings.

براز barāz (A) n.m. Stool; motion; faeces; excrement; (often used with بول baul as بول و براز baul-ŏ barāz).

برافروختہ barāfrokhtah (P) adj. Inflamed; enraged.

براق burāq (A) n.m. The horse-like animal on which the Holy Prophet ascended to Heaven.

براق barrāq (A) adj. Shining; flashing; brilliant; swift; skilled; sagacious.

برآمد barāmad (P) n.f. Coming up; coming or going out; egress; out-going; exist; issue; expenditure; export; land thrown up by a river; recovery of stolen property.

برآمدہ barāmdah (P) n.m. A verandah; balcony; gallery; piazza; the recovered property (goods); the property seized (by the police).

بران burrān (P) adj. Cutting; sharp.

برانا barrānā, v. To brag; to talk in one's sleep; to rave (in delirium).

برانگیختہ barāngekhtah (P) adj. Roused; enraged; excited; stirred up.

برانگیختہ کرنا barāngekhtah karnā, v. To excite; to stir up; to rouse; to anger.

براہمہ barāhimah (P) n.m. (plu. of براہمن brāhman) Hindu priests.

براہین burāhīn (A) n.f. (plu. of برہان burhān) Arguments; proofs; demonstrations.

برأت barā't (A) n.f. A warrant conferring immunity or exemption; warrant; acquittal.

برائی burā'ī (H) n.f. Badness; mischief; evil; wickedness; lie; backbiting; harm.

برائی ابد تک رہتی ہے burā'ī abad tak rehtī hae, say. Evil that men do lives after them.

برائی پر کمر باندھنا burā'ī par kamar bāndhnā, v. To be bent on doing mischief or harm.

برائے barā'e (P) adv. On account of; by reason of; for; for the sake of; in order to.

برائے بیت barā'e bait, adv. Only for the sake of composing a couplet; for the sake of rhyming; extra; unwanted.

برائے خدا barā'e khudā, adv. For God's sake.

برائے نام barā'e nām, adv. For name's sake; nominally.

برایا barāyā (A) n.f. (plu. of بریت bariyyat) Creation; universe; world.

برباد barbād (P) adj. Thrown to the wind; cast away; squandered; wasted; destroyed; laid waste; ruined; desolated.

برباد کرنا barbād karnā, v. To throw to the winds; to lose; to throw away; to squander; to waste; to ruin; to destroy; to ravage.

برباد ہونا barbad honā, v. To be thrown away; to be squandered; to be lost; to be wasted; to be ruined.

بربادی barbādī (P) n.f. Destruction; ruin; loss; waste; ravage.

بربرا burburā, adj. See بھربھرا bhurbhurā.

بربری barbarī (P) n.f. A kind of goat from Barbary; anything from Barbary.

بربط barbaṯ (P) n.m. A kind of harp.

برتا *birtā* (H) *n.m.* Ability; capacity; power; strength; courage; support; help.

برتے پر اچھلنا *birte par uchhalnā*, *v.* To pride oneself on the support (of).

برتانا *bartānā* (H) *v.* To distribute; to deal out; to apportion.

برتاؤ *bartāo* (H) *n.m.* Treatment; usage; practice; conduct; intimacy.

برتاؤ کرنا *bartāo karnā*, *v.* To behave (towards); to treat (with).

برتن *bartan* (H) *n.m.* Utensil; a vessel.

برتنا *bartnā* (H) *v.* To use; to make use of; to spend; to test; to experiment; to pull on (with).

برج *birj* (H) *n.m.* Enclosure; a cowshed; a part of Uttar Pardesh (India) extending over Mathura and Agra associated with the childhood of Krishna.

برج بھاکا یا بھاشا *birj bhākā yā bhāshā*, *n.f.* The dialect (Hindi) spoken in or round about *Birj* (Mathura).

برج *burj* (A) *n.m.* A bastion; a turret; a tower; a sign of the zodiac.

برجس *birjis* (corr. of English). *n.f.* Breeches.

برجستہ *barjastah* (P) *adj.* Befitting; proper; right; apportune; exact; prompt.

برجی *Burjī*, *n.f.* A small tower; a turret.

برچھا *barchhā* (H) *n.m.* A spear; a lance; a javelin; a dart.

برچھی *barchhī* (H) *n.f.* A small spear.

برخاست *barkhāst* (P) *n.f.* Rising up (of a court, etc.); recall or removal from the office; discharge; dismissal.

برخاست کرنا *barkhāst karnā*, *v.* To dismiss; to remove from office; to break up (a court).

برخاست ہونا *barkhāst honā*, *v.* To rise or break up (as an assembly); to be dismissed; to be deprived of office.

برخاستگی *barkhāstgī* (P) *n.f.* Dismissal; removal; recall; breaking up or dissolution of an assembly.

برد *burd* (P) *n.f.* Bearing or carrying off; acquisition; gain; profit; bribe; wager; a term used at chess to indicate a checkmate when the adversary has lost all the pieces except the king.

برد *burd* (A) *n.f.* A kind of sheet with stripes (especially manufactured in Yeman).

بردار *bardār* (P) *adj.* Bearer; carrier; (used as suffix as in حقہ بردار *ḥuqqah bardār*).

برداری *bardāri* (P) *n.f.* The act of bearing or carrying.

برداشت *bardāsht* (P) *n.f.* Endurance; patience; tolerance; resignation; buying goods on credit.

برداشت کرنا *bardāsht karnā*, *v.* To tolerate; to bear; to endure.

برداشت ہونا *bardāsht honā*, *v.* To be tolerable; to be endured.

برداشتہ *bardāshtah* (P) *adj.* Raised up; elevated.

برداشتہ خاطر ہونا *bardāshtah khāṭir honā*, *v.* To be disappointed; to be dejected; to be distressed; to be confused.

بردبار *burdbār* (P) *adj.* Tolerant; forbearing; enduring; patient.

بردباری *burdbārī* (P) *n.f.* Bearing of a burden; toleration; patience; forbearance; endurance.

بردہ *bardah* (P) *n.m.* A slave; a captive.

بردہ فروش *bardah farosh*, *n.m.* A slave-dealer; a slave merchant.

بردہ فروشی *bardah faroshī*, *n.f.* Slave trade.

برزخ *barzakh* (A) *n.m.* Interval between Death and Resurrection; the purgatory; partition; obstruction (between two thing); interference; isthmus.

برس *baras* (H) *n.m.* A year.

برسات *barsāt* (H) *n.f.* The rainy season; the rains.

برساتی *barsāti* (H) *adj.* & *n.f.* Pertaining to the rainy season; a water-proof coat; a mackintosh; a room on the top of the house for shelter from rain; a disease of horses.

برسانا barsānā (H) v. To cause to rain; to shower down; to pour down; to scatter; to winnow the grain.

برس پڑنا baras paṛnā, v. To begin raining; to pour out a torrent of invective; to give one a bit of one's mind.

برسنا barasnā (H) v. To rain; to be angry or in a passion (with).

برسی barsi (H) n.f. Annual ceremony in remembrance of a deceased relative.

برش burrish (P) n.f. Cutting; sharpness.

برش bursh (E) n.m. Brush.

برشگال (برشکال) barshagāl (barshakāl) (P) n.m. The season; rainy rain.

برص barṣ (A) n.m. Leprosy.

برف barf (P) n.f. Ice; snow. adj. Very cold; white.

برف پڑنا barf paṛnā, v. To snow.

برف ہونا barf honā, v. To be benumbed; to become very cold.

برفانی barfānī, adj. Icy; snowy; very cold.

برفی barfī (P) n.f. A kind of sweetmeat made of condensed milk and sugar.

برق barq (A) n.f. Lightning; electricity. adj. Clever; swift-footed.

برق آبی barq ābī, n.f. Hydro-electricity.

برق‌انداز (برقنداز) barqandāz, n.m. A musketeer; a matchlock man; a sentinal; a messenger.

برق پیما barq paimā, n.m. Electrometer.

برق زدہ barq zadah, adj. Struck with lightning.

برق گیر barq gir, n.m. A conductor.

برق نما barq numā, n.m. Electroscope.

برقع burqa' (A) n.m. A veil; a kind of mantle or veil covering the whole body from head to foot.

برقع پوش burqa' posh, adj. & n.f. A woman who wears burqa'; a veiled-woman.

برقی barqī, adj. Electric; electrical.

برقی رو barqī rau, n.f. Electric current; electro-motion.

برقی شعاع barqī sh'uā', n.f. Flash light.

برقی علاج barqī 'ilāj, n.m. Electropathy.

برقی قوت سے ہلاک کرنا barqī quwwat se halāk karnā, v. To electrocute.

برقی قوتیں barqī quwwateṅ, n.f. Electric powers.

برقی لیمپ barqī lemp, n.m. Electric lamp.

برقی مقناطیس barqī miqnāṭīs, n.m. Electromagnet.

برقی موٹر barqī moṭor, n.m. Electro-motor.

برقانا barqānā, v. To electrify; to electrize.

برقیات barqiyāt, n.f. Electricity; electrology.

برقیات دان barqiyāt dān, n.m. Electrician.

برقیہ barqiyyah (A) n.m. Electron.

برکات barakāt (A) n.f. (plu. of برکت barkat) Blessings; prosperity; auspiciousness; good fortune.

برکت barkat (A) n.f. Abundance; prosperity; auspiciousness; good fortune; blessing.

برکت دینا barkat denā, v. To bless; to bring good furtune.

برکھا barkhā (H) n.f. Rain; rainy season.

برگ barg (P) n.m. A leaf; provision for a journey.

برگ و بار barg-ō bār, n.m. Leaves and fruit.

برگد bargad (H) n.m. Banyan tree.

برگزیدہ bar-guzidah (P) adj. Chosen; selected; elect.

برگشتگی bargashtagī (P) n.f. Turning away from; turning back; apostacy; rebellion; mutiny.

برگشتہ bargashtah (P) adj. Turned back; changed; mutinied; rebellious; rebelled; reverted; apostate.

برما barmā (H) n.m. A gimlet; a drill; an auger.

برمانا barmānā, v. To bore hole with a gimlet.

برنج brinj (P) n.m. Rice; brass.

بروا barwā (H) n f. Name of a tune (rāgni) in music, by which deer and serpents are said to be tamed.

بروا **birwā** (H) *n.m.* A plant; a young tree; a lad; a promising youngman.

بروج **burūj** (A) *n.m.* (*plu. of* برج *burj*) Bastions; turrets; towers; signs of the zodaic.

برودت **burūdat** (A) *n.f.* Coldness; coolness; chilliness.

برومند **biromand** (P) *adj.* Fortunate; lucky.

برون **birūn** (P) *adv.* (abr. of بیرون *berūn*) Without; outside; externally.

بره **barrah** (P) *n.m.* Lamb; kid; fawn; the sign of Aries.

بره فلک **barrah-ĕ falak**, *n.m.* A sign of the zodaic—Aries.

برہان **burhān** (A) *n.f.* Argument; proof; demonstration; reason.

برہم ' برہما **brahm, brahmā** (S) *n.m.* The supreme deity of Hindus; God; the Creator.

برہم چاری **brahmchārī**, *n.m.* A student of Vedas (Hindu's religious books); an ascetic; a celibate.

برہم **barham** (P) *adj.* Angry; vexed; confused; jumbled together; entangled; inflamed; disordered.

برہمن **barhaman** (H) *n.m.* A Hindu priest; a high cast of Hindus.

برہمی **barahmī** (P) *n.f.* Anger; vexation; annoyance; displeasure; confusion; anarchy.

برہنگی **barahnagī** (P) *n.f.* Nakedness; nudity; bareness.

برہنہ **barahnah** (P) *adj.* Naked; nude; bare.

بری **barī** (H) *n.f.* Wedding gifts (clothes; ornaments etc.) given by the bridegroom to the bride.

بری **barī** (A) *adj.* Acquitted; guiltless; released; exonerated; exempt; innocent.

بری الذمہ **barī-uz-zimmah**, *adj.* Free from blame or obligation; absolved of responsibility; unaccountable.

بری **barrī** (A) *adj.* Belonging to or connected with land (in opposition to water).

بریان **biryān** (P) *adj.* Fried; roasted; broiled; parched; grilled.

بریانی **biryānī** (P) *n.f.* A dish of meat and rice.

بریت **bariyyat**, *n.f.* Exemption; release; exoneration. (A) *n.f.* Creation; world.

بریٹھا **bareṭhā** (H) *n.m.* A washerman; a launder.

بریٹھن **bareṭhan** (H) *n.f.* A washerwoman; a laundress.

برید **barīd** (P) *n.m.* A messenger; a courier; a runner; a postman.

برید فلک **barīd-ĕ falak**, *n.m.* The Moon; the planet Saturn.

بریں **barīṅ** (P) *adj.* Lofty; very high; sublime. *adv.* On this; thereupon.

بڑ **baṛ** (H) *n.m.* Banyan tree.

بڑ **baṛ** (H) *n.f.* Loquacity; nonsense; foolish talk.

بڑ بولا **baṛ bolā**, *n.m.* A boaster; a braggart; a noisy talkative person.

بڑ ھانکنا یا مارنا **baṛ hāṅknā yā mārnā**, *v.* To boast; to brag.

بڑا **baṛā** (H) *n.m.* Small cakes made of pulse, meal and spices, and fried in ghee or oil.

بڑا ' بڑی **baṛā, baṛī**, *adj.* Large; big; huge; elder, eldest; rich; grand; principal; superior; respectable; supreme; old.

بڑا بول آگے آتا ھے **baṛā bol āge ātā hae**, *prov.* Bragging often brings shame to a person.

بڑا بول بولنا **baṛā bol bolnā**, *v.* To brag; to boast.

بڑا دن **baṛā din**, *n.m.* The 25th of December when the day begins to lengthen; Christmas.

بڑا دیدہ ہونا **baṛā dīdah honā**, *v.* To be fearless; to be bold; to be enterprising; to be wanton-eyed; to have big eyes.

بڑا صاحب **baṛā ṣāhib**, *n.m.* A chief civil functionary; a big officer.

بڑا کوئی **baṛā ko'ī**, *adj.* Clever; skilful; sly; wicked.

بڑا گھر ***baṛā ghar, n.m.*** A spacious house; a well-to-do family; jail; prison.

بڑا گھرانا ***baṛā gharānā, n.m.*** A wealthy family; a noble or respectable family.

بڑا نام کرنا ***baṛā nām karnā, v.*** To acquire reputation; to win a great name.

بڑونکی بڑی بات ***baṛoṅ kī baṛī bāt.*** Great men have great views.

بڑے بول کا سر نیچا ***baṛe bol kā sar nīchā, prov.*** Pride goes before a fall.

بڑی بی ***baṛī bī, n.f.*** An old woman; a form of address indicating respect.

بڑے گھر پڑے اور پتھر ڈھو ڈھو مرے ***baṛe ghar parye aur paththar ḍho ḍho marye, prov.*** Marry above your rank and you get a master; he that marries wealth sells his liberty.

بڑے میاں ***baṛe miyāṅ, n.m.*** An old man; head of the family; master of the house; a form of address indicating respect, equivalent to sir or honoured.

بڑائی ***baṛā'ī*** (H) *n.f.* Largeness; bigness; greatness; excellence; superiority; exaltation; praise; bulk; old age; magnifying; vaunting; boasting.

بڑائی کرنا یا مارنا ***baṛā'ī karnā yā mārnā, v.*** To boast of superiority over others; to extol; to magnify; to vaunt.

بڑ بڑ ***baṛbaṛ, n.f.*** Foolish or light-hearted talk; loquacity.

بڑبڑ ***buṛbuṛ, n.f.*** Murmuring; muttering; grumbling.

بڑبڑانا ***baṛbaṛānā, v.*** To talk nonsense; to talk light-heartedly; to chatter; to rave.

بڑبڑانا ***buṛbuṛānā, v.*** To murmur; to mutter; to grumble.

بڑھاپا ***buṛhāpā*** (H) *n.m.* Old age; senility.

بڑھانا ***baṛhānā*** (H) *v.* To increase; to enlarge; to lengthen; to expand; to extend; to amplify; to promote; to exalt; to elevate; to aggrandize; to eulogize. *id.* To put out (lamp); to close (a shop); to remove the table-cloth.

بڑھاؤ ***baṛhā'o*** (H) *n.m.* Swell; excess; increase; expansion; prolongation; advancement; enlargement; over-hanging projection.

بڑھتی ***baṛhtī*** (H) *adj. & n.f.* More than usual; increase; augmentation; enhancement; excess; promotion; elevation; aggrandisement; progress; prosperity.

بڑھ کر بولنا ***baṛh kar bolnā, v.*** To be rude; to exceed limits in behaviour or talk; to raise the bid.

بڑھنا ***baṛhnā*** (H) *v.* To increase; to grow; to expand; to stretch; to swell; to be elevated or raised high; to go forward; to become rich; to advance; to attain higher social position; to prosper; to exceed; to surpass; to shut up (a shop); to put out (a lamp).

بڑھوتری ***baṛhotarī*** (H) *n.f.* Increase; addition; profit; interest; gain; advantage; increment; surplus; prosperity.

بڑھئی ***baṛha'ī*** (H) *n.m.* A carpenter.

بڑھیا ***baṛhiyā*** (H) *adj.* Superior; of good quality; high priced; expensive.

بڑھیا ***buṛhiyā*** (H) *n.f.* An old woman; mother.

بڑی ***baṛī*** (H) *n.f.* A small lump of powdered pulse dried in the sun before being cooked.

بز ***buz*** (P) *n.m.f.* A goat (male or female).

بزاخفش ***buz-ĕ akhfash, n.m.*** A brainless fellow; a dolt; a blockhead.

بز کوھی ***buz-ĕ kohī, n.m.*** Mountain goat.

بزدل ***buz dil. adj.*** Coward; faint-hearted (person).

بزدلی ***buz dilī, n.f.*** Timidity; cowardice; faint-heartedness.

بزاز ***bazāz*** (A) *n.m.* Cloth-merchant; a draper.

بزازا ***bazāzā, n.m.*** A cloth market.

بزازی ***bazāzī, n.f.*** The business of a cloth merchant; linen-drapery.

بزرگ ***buzurg*** (P) *adj.* Great; revered; venerable; noble; sensible; aged. *n.m.* A holy man; a saint; an elder; an ancestor; a wise man.

بزرگ زادہ ***buzurg zādah***, *n.m.* High born; of noble birth.

بزرگ منش ***buzurg manish***, *adj.* Noble-minded; magnanimous.

بزرگ منشی ***buzurg manishi***, *n.f.* Greatness of mind; magnanimity.

بزرگوار ***buzurgwār***, *adj.* Great (man); noble. *n.m.* Ancestor; elder; saint.

بزرگی ***buzurgi*** (P) *n.f.* Greatness; exaltation; eminence; grandeur; nobleness; respectability.

بزم ***bazm*** (P) *n.f.* Assembly; association; meeting; company (especially at a feast or entertainment).

بزن ***bizan*** (P) *imp.* Strike; slay.

بزن کرنا ***bizan karnā***, *v.* To slay; to put to sword; to behead.

بس ***bas*** (P) *adj.* Enough; sufficient; plenty; too much; very much. *adv.* And so; in short; *intj.* Enough! that will do! hold! stay!

بس بس ***bas bas***, *int.* Enough! stop, no more! enough of it!

بس حد ہو گئی ***bas ḥadd ho ga'ī***. Stop, this is the limit! has had a bad time.

بس دیکھ لیا ***bas dekh liyā***. Enough of it! no more; no need to test one (you) any more; you have been exposed.

بس کرنا ***bas karnā***, *v.* To stop; to cease; to have done; to close; to finish.

بس کہ ***bas kih***, *adv.* Although; whereas.

بس ***bas*** (S) *n.m.* Will; power; authority; sway; influence; control.

بس چلنا ***bas chalnā***, *v.* To avail against; to have power (over); to be able to control or influence.

بس میں آنا ، بس میں پڑنا ***bas meṅ ānā, bas meṅ paṛnā***, *v.* To fall into the power of; to be subdued.

بس میں رکھنا ***bas meṅ rakhnā***, *v.* To keep one under control; to hold one in check.

بس میں کرنا ***bas meṅ karnā***, *v.* To subdue; to subjugate; to get the better of one; to overpower; to fascinate.

بس ***bis*** (S) *n.m.* Poison; venom; anything bitter; dispute; disturbance.

بس آگلنا ***bis ugalnā***, *v.* To spit poison; to say spiteful things; to revile; to take revenge (by saying venomous things); to stir up a dispute or disturbance; to backbite.

بس بونا ***bis bonā***, *v.* To sow discord; to make mischief (between).

بس بھری ***bis bhari***, *adj.* Poisonous; soaked with poison; melicious or misvicious; mischief-maker; quarrelsome.

بس کی پڑیا یا گانٹھ ***bis ki puṛyā yā gāṅṭh***, *n.f.* Deadly poison; a melicious or mischievous person; devil.

بسا ***basā*** (P) *adj.* Much; many; more; very.

بسا اوقات ***basā auqāt***, *adv.* Generally; very often; frequently; mostly.

بسارنا ***bisārnā*** (H) *v.* To forget.

بساط ***bisāṭ*** (A) *n.f.* Bedding; bed; carpet; a chess board; extent; expanse; capacity; capital; stock.

بساطی ***bisāṭi***, *n.m.* A vender of small wares; a pedlar; haberdesher.

بسانا ***basānā*** (H) *v.* To colonise; to people; to inhabit; to settle (a country); to build (a city); to bring into cultivation; to cause to be scented.

بست ***bast*** (P) *n.m.* Obstacle; knot; embankment; asylum. (H) Household effects; thing; article.

بست و کشاد ***bast-ŏ kushād***, *n.f.* (Shut and opened) untying a knot; solution of a problem.

بستان ***bustān*** (P) *n.m.* (*abr.* of بوستان *bostān*) A garden.

بستر *bistar* (P) *n.m.* Bedding; mattress; carpet.

بستر بند *bistar band, n.m.* Straps or rope with which a bedding is tied; a hold-all.

بسترا *bistarā, n.m.* Bed; bedding peculiar to soldiers and fakirs.

بستگی *bastagī* (P) *n.f.* Contraction; constipation; obstruction.

بستنی *bastani* (P) *n.f.* A case or covering for cages or musical instruments.

بستہ *bastah* (P) *n.m.* A satchel. *adj.* Frozen; bound; tied; congealed.

بستہ بردار *bastah bardār, adj.* Record-carrier.

بستی *bastī* (H) *n.f.* A settlement; a village; a town; a city; population.

بسر *basar* (P) *n.f.* Living; livelihood; course of life.

بسر کرنا *basar karnā, v.* To bring to an end; to finish; to accomplish; to execute; to spend; to pass.

بسر ہونا *basar honā, v.* To be completed; to be finished; to be accomplished; to be spent; to be passed.

بسر *bisar* (H) *n.m.* Forgetfulness; oblivion.

بسر جانا *bisar jānā, v.* To forget; to be forgotten.

بسرانا *bisrānā* (H) *v.* To cause to forget; to put out of mind.

بسط *basṭ* (A) *n.m.* Commentary; detail; explanation; diffusiveness.

بسفائج *bisfā'ij* (A) *n.m.* A medicinal root; *polypody.*

بسم اللہ *Bismillah* (A) *adv.* In the name of God —a formula generally pronounced by Muslims at the beginning of any action or work. *n.f.* Beginning; commencement.

بسم اللہ کرنا *Bismillah karnā, v.* To pronounce the formula 'in the name of God' at the beginning of a work; to begin; to commence.

بسم اللہ کے گنبد میں بیٹھنا *Bismillah ke gumbad meṅ baiṭhnā, v.* To live at a place of safety; to live in peace; to live under protection.

بسمل *bismil* (P) *n.m.* A slaughtered animal; (an animal of) sacrifice; a lover.

بسمل کرنا *bismil karnā, v.* To immolate; to wound the heart of a lover; to sacrifice; to slaughter.

بسمل گاہ *bismil gāh, n.f.* Place o sacrifice.

بسنا *basnā* (H) *v.* To dwell; to ii habit; to settle; to reside; to abide; to become perfumed.

بسنت *basant* (H) *n.f.* The spring season; a spring festival; a musical mode.

بسنت پھولنا *basant phūlnā, v.* Blossoming of (yellow) flowers of *sarsoṅ* plants (a species of mustard).

آنکھوں میں بسنت پھولنا *āṅkhoṅ meṅ basant phūlnā, v.* To be dazzled; to be astonished or amazed.

بسنتی *basantī* (H) *adj.* Of yellow colour; yellow.

بسورنا *bisūrnā, v.* To put on a crying face; to prepare to weep; to cry slowly; to sob.

بسولا *basūlā* (H) *n.m.* A carpenter's axe; an adze.

بسولی *basūli* (H) *n.f.* A tool for cutting bricks.

بسوہ *biswah* (H) *n.m.* A land measure; the 20th part of a بیگھ *bighah.*

بسیار *bisyār* (P) *adj.* Much very; abundant; many.

بسیرا *baserā* (H) *n.m.* Roosting; a night's lodging; reposing; resting; an abode; the time in the evening when birds return to their nests; a bird's roost or perch.

بسیرا کرنا *baserā karnā, v.* To roost; to repose.

بسیرے کا وقت *basere kā waqt, n.m.* Roosting time.

بسیط *basiṭ* (A) *adj.* Simple; elementary; unmixed; extended; wide; superficial.

بشارت *bishārat* (A) *n.f.* Good news; glad tidings; revelation; inspiration.

بشارت دینا bishārat denā, v. To convey good news.

بشاش bashshāsh (A) adj. In good spirits; pleased; delighted; cheerful; blooming; gay; joyful, hilarious.

بشاشت bashāshat (A) n.f. Gaiety; liveliness; freshness; hilarity; cheerfulness; joy; pleasure.

بشر bashar (A) n.m. Man, a human being; mortal.

بشره bushrah (A) n.m. Face; countenance; visage; physiognomy.

بشری bashari (A) adj. Human; relating to man.

بشریت bashariyat (A) n.f. Human nature; humanness.

بشنو (وشنو) bishnu (wishnu) (H) n.m. One of the Hindus gods; the Preserver.

بشیر bashir (A) adj. A messenger of good news.

بصارت baṣārat (A) n.f. Sight; perceiving; insight; vision.

بصر baṣar (A) n.f. Sight; vision; the eye.

بصره Baṣrah (A) n.m. A city in Iraq, famous for its dates.

بصیر baṣir (A) adj. Seer; sage; wise; sagacious; an expert; an attribute of God.

بصیرت baṣīrat (A) n.f. Sight; insight; prudence; intelligence; discernment; skill.

بضاعت biẓā'at (A) n.f. Capital; stock in trade; wealth; property; power; effects; goods.

بط baṭ (A) n.f. A goose; a duck.

بط مے baṭṭ-ĕ mae, n.f. A kind of duck-shaped goblet for wine.

بطخ baṭṭakh (P) n.f. Duckling; a duck;

بطریق biṭriq (A) n.m. General of a Christian army; a bishop; wicked; a good for nothing fellow.

بطل baṭl (A) n.m. Brave; courageous; hero.

بطلان buṭlān (A) n.m. Refutation; falseness; insignificance; abolishing.

بطن baṭn (A) n.m. Belly; abdomen; the womb; the inside.

بطناً بعد بطن baṭnan ba'd-a baṭnin (A) adv. Generation after generation; hereditarily.

بطون buṭūn (A) n.m. (plu. of بطن baṭn) Interior parts; bellies.

بعث ba's (A) n.m. Sending (of) a messenger; excitement; resurrection; raising the dead to life.

بعثت bi'ṣat (A) n.f. Divine mission; apostleship; the period of an apostle, particulary that of the Prophet of Islam.

بعد ba'd (A) adv. After; subsequently; later.

بعد ازاں ba'd azāṅ, adv. After that; afterwards.

بعد از جنگ ba'd az jang, adv. After the war; post-war.

بعد از خرابی بسیار ba'd az kharābī-ĕ bisyār, adv. After great difficulty.

بعد از سلام ba'd az salām, adv. After salutation.

بعد از مرگ واویلا ba'd az marg wāwelā, prov. To cry over spilt milk.

بعد الموت ba'd-al-maut, adv. After death; post mortem.

بعده ba'duhu, adv. After that.

بعد bu'd (A) n.m. Distance; remoteness; difference.

بعد المشرقین bu'd-ul-mashriqain, n.m. The distance between the two poles; poles asunder.

بعض ba'z, (A) adj. Some; few; several; many.

بعید ba'id (A) adj. Far; remote; distant.

بعید العقل ba'īd-ul-'aql, adj. Far removed from reason; unreasonable; absurd; improbable.

بعید القیاس ba'īd-ul-qiās, adj. Inconceivable.

بعیدالوطن ba'īd-ul-waṭan, adj. Far from home.

بغاوت baghāwat (A) n.f. Revolt; rebellion; mutiny; disloyalty; disobedience.

بغتةً baghtatan (A) adv. All of a sudden; suddenly; all at once.

بغچه bughchah. See بقچه buqchah.

بغدا hughdā (P) n.m. A cleaver used by butchers; a big chopping knife.

بغض bughẓ (A) n.m. Malice; spite; hatred; hate; grudge; enmity.

بغل baghal (P) n.f. Armpit; side.

بغل پروردہ baghal parwardah, adj. A darling or favourite child.

بغل گرم ہونا یا کرنا baghal garm honā yā karnā, v. To embrace the beloved; to share a bed with the beloved; to take in one's lap.

بغل گند baghal gaṅd, n.f. Stinking armpits.

بغل گیر ہونا baghal gir honā, v. To embrace (by way of salutations); to clasp; to hug.

بغل میں دبانا baghal meṅ dabāna, v. To carry off something deceitfully; to conceal a thing under an armpit.

بغل میں لینا baghal meṅ lenā, v. To embrace; to hug; to be taller than another.

بغلیں بجانا baghleṅ bajānā, v. To be highly pleased; to be happy over another's downfall; to mock.

بغلیں جھانکنا baghleṅ jhāṅknā, v. To hide one's face through shame; to be ashamed; to look from side to side in discomfiture; to be non-plussed.

بغلول baghlol, n.m. A stupid fellow; a simpleton; a dullard.

بغلی baghli, adj. Axiliary; relating to the armpit; belonging to a side. n.f. A woman's handbag for keeping needle, thread and small articles of everyday use; a beggar's sack; trick in wrestling.

بغلی تکیہ baghli takiyah, n.m. A big and long pillow to recline on.

بغلی دشمن ، بغلی گھونسا baghlī dushman, baghli ghūṅsā, n.m. A hidden enemy; an enemy in disguise.

بغلی دینا baghli denā, v. A trick in wrestling; to break into a house by removing a portion of the wall and unbolting the door.

بغیچہ baghīchah, n.m. (abr. of باغیچہ bāghīchah) A small garden.

بقا baqā (A) n.f. Permanence; continuance; everlastingness; immortality.

بقال baqqāl (A) n.m. A grocer; a vegetable seller; a shop-keeper; a grain merchant.

بقایا baqāyā (A) n.f. (plu. of باقی bāqī) Dues; arrears; balances; remainders.

بقچہ buqchah (T) n.m. A small bundle of cloth; a knapsack.

بقر عید baqra'id (A) n.f. A Muslim festival of sacrifice on the 10th of the month of Zilḥij, held in commemoration of Ibraham's offering to sacrifice his son Ismāīl.

بقعہ buq'ah (A) n.m. A place distinguished from others; a prominent place; a monastery.

بقعۂ نور buq'ah-ĕ nūr, n.m. A place dazzling with light; a dazzling light.

بقل، بقلہ baql, baqlah (A) n.f. Spinach; potherb; vegetable.

بقلۃ الحمقا baqlah tul-ḥumaqā, n.f. (Lit. the stupid herbage); purslane.

بقیہ baqiyyah (A) n.m. Arrears; remainder; balance; dues.

بکا bukā (A) n.f. Weeping; lamentation; wailing.

بکارت bakārat (A) n.f. Virginity; maidenhood.

بکاؤ bikāū, adj. For or on sale.

بکاول bakāwal (P) n.m. A cook; a steward; a butler.

بکان یا بکائن bakān yā bakā'in (H) n.m. Name of a tree (melia semper-virens).

بک بک ، جھک جھک bak bak, jhak jhak, n.f. Babble; chatter; idle talk.

بک بک کرنا bak bak karnā, v. To chatter; to talk idly; to gabble; to prate; to babble.

بکتر baktar (P) n.m. A coat of mail; armour; a cuirass.

بکتر پوش baktar posh, adj. Clad in armour; a cuirassier.

بکتری baktarī, *adj.* An armourer.

بکٹ bikaṭ (H) *adj.* Terrible; perilous; difficult; ugly.

بکر bikr (A) *n.f.* Virginity; maidenhood.

بکرا bakrā (H) *n.m.* A he-goat.

بکری bakrī (H) *n.f.* A she-goat.

بکری bikrī (H) *n.f.* Sale; total sale.

بکس bakas, *n.m.* (*corr.* of English) Box.

بکسوا baksūā, *n.m.* (*corr.* of English). A buckle; the tongue of a buckle.

بکم bukm (A) *adj.* (*plu.* of ابکم abkum) Dumb; mute.

بکنا baknā (H) *v.* To prate; to chatter; to talk idly; to babble; to gabble; to jabber.

بکنا biknā (H) *v.* To be sold off; to be disposed of.

بکنی buknī (H) *n.f.* Powder.

بکنی کر ڈالنا buknī kar ḍālnā, *v.* To grind; to reduce to powder.

بکواس bakwās, *n.f.* Chatter; idle talk; garrulity; loquacity.

بکواسی bakwāsī, *adj.* An idler talker; gabbler

بکوانا bikwānā (H) *v.* To cause to be sold; to have a thing sold off.

بکوائی bikwā'ī (H) *n.f.* Fee for selling; salesman's commission.

بکھرنا bikharnā (H) *v.* To be scattered; to be dispersed; to be dishevelled (hair).

بکھیرنا bakhernā (H) *v.* To disperse; to scatter; to sow.

بکھیڑا bakheṛā (H) *n.m.* A troublesome or vexatious business; complicated matter; dispute; quarrel; imbroglio; uproar.

بکھیڑا چکانا bakheṛā chukānā, *v.* To settle a dispute; to stop a quarrel.

بکھیڑا ڈالنا bakheṛā ḍālnā, *v.* To complicate matter; to make difficult or troublesome; to create a difficulty; to raise a dispute.

بکھیڑیا bakheṛyā (H) *adj.* Quarrelsome; contentious. *n.m.* A brawler; a disputant; a mischief-monger; a wrangler; a rascal.

بکی bakkī, *adj.* A prater; a chatterer; a jabberer; talkative.

بگاڑ bigāṛ (H) *n.m.* Deterioration; corruption; defect; fault; damage; harm; quarrel; discord.

بگاڑ ڈال دینا bigāṛ ḍāl denā, *v.* To create unpleasantness; to sow seeds of discord or enmity.

بگاڑنا bigāṛnā (H) *v.* To spoil; to mar; to damage; to injure; to harm; to ruin; to bungle; to displease; to pollute; to cause misunderstanding between friends.

بگٹٹ bagṭuṭ (H) *adj.* With broken reins; without reins; at full gallop; very fast.

بگڑنا bigarnā (H) *v.* To be impaired; to be spoiled; to be damaged; to be disfigured; to lose modesty; to quarrel; to disagree; to be enraged; to go or turn bad; to be deteriorated; to go out of order; to become vicious; to rebel; to revolt.

بگلا baglā (H) *n.m.* A crane; a heron. *adj.* Very white.

بگلا بھگت baglā bhagat, *n.m.* A false devotee; a cunning or artful fellow; a hypocrite.

بگولا bagūlā (H) *n.m.* A whirlwind.

بگھار baghār (H) *n.m.* The act of seasoning (a dish with spices); seasoning condiments.

بگھارنا baghārnā (H) *v.* To season; to season a dish with spices and condiments by frying them in oil or ghee.

بگی ، بگھی bagghī, baggī, *n.f.* A gig; a light carriage; a buggy; a horse-fly.

بگھیلا ، بگھیل baghel, baghelā (H) *n.m.* A panther; a young tiger; name of a tribe of Rajputs living in Baghel Khand.

بل bal (H) *n.m.* Twist; convolution; coil; curl; wrinkle; contortion; convulsion.

بل پڑنا bal paṛnā, *v.* To be curved or twisted; to convulse; to have convulsion.

بل دار bal dār, *adj.* Curved; twisted; coiled; bent; crooked.

بل دینا bal ḍenā, v. To twist; to entwine; to coil.

بل کھانا bal khānā, v. To be entwined; to be twisted; to be angry.

بل نکالنا bal nikālnā, v. To remove coils; to punish; to set right; to correct.

بل bal (S) n.m. Power; strength; might; vigour; physical force; vanity; pride; sacrifice; a religious offering.

بل بوتا bal botā, n.m. Strength; well built body; courage; pride.

بل کرنا bal karnā, v. To show off strength; to be envious.

بل وان ، بل ونت bāl wān, bal want, adj. Stout; strong; powerful.

بل bil (H) n.m. A hole; a burrow; an opening.

بل ڈھونڈنا bil ḍhūnḍna, v. To seek a hiding place through fear or shame; to go underground.

بل bil (E) n.m. Bill; draft.

بل جاری کرنا bil jāri karnā, v. To issue a draft; to draw a bill.

بلا ballā, n.m. A long staff; a cricket bat.

بلا billā, n.m. A male-cat; a badge.

بلا balā (A) n.f. Trial; calamity; misfortune; evil; distress; spirit; fiend; an awful or terrible thing. adj. Awful; dreadful; enormous, excessive.

بلا بدتر balā badtar, n.f. Rubbish; worthless; useless.

بلا پیچھے لگانا balā pichhe lagānā, v. To be beset with affliction; to be involved in trouble.

بلا جانے balā jāne, id. The devil knows; what do I know; it is no concern of ours.

بلا زدہ balā zadah, adj. Overwhelmed with calamity; struck with misfortune.

بلا کا ، بلا کی balā kā, balā kī, adj. Most; excessive; intensive; severe.

بلا کش balā kash, adj. Afflicted; distressed.

بلا گردان balā gardān, adj. Warding off evil; what averts evil; one who offers oneself for sacrifice; sufferer.

بلا نوش balā nosh, adj. A great eater; a glutton.

بلائیں لینا balāeṅ lenā, v. Expressing extreme affection and concern for a dear one.

بلا bilā (P) prep. Without.

بلا اکرہ bilā ikrāh, adv. Without compulsion; voluntarily.

بلا تامل bilā tāammul, adv. Without hesitation; instantaneously; unhesitatingly; unthinkingly; recklessly; rashly.

بلا تحاشا bila taḥāshā, adv. See بے تحاشا be taḥāshā.

بلا تردد bilā taraddud, adv. Without hesitation; without reluctance.

بلا تصنع ، بلا تکلف bilā taṣanno', bilā takalluf, adv. Without embelishment; spontaneously; without formality; frankly; without hesitation.

بلا توقف bilā tawaqquf, adv. Without delay; without loss of time; speedily.

بلا ریب ، بلا شک bilā raib, bilā shak, adv. Without doubt or suspicion; unquestionably; doubtlessly.

بلا شرط bilā sharṭ, adv. Unconditionally; absolutely.

بلا ناغہ bilā nāghah, adv. Regularly; constantly; without intermission; daily.

بلا واسطہ bilā wāsṭah, adv. Without intermediary; directly.

بلا وجہ bilā wajh, adv. Without any cause or reason.

بلاد bilād (A) n.m. (plu. of بلد balad) Countries; towns; cities.

بلاغ balāgh (A) n.m. Communication or delivery of a message.

بلاغت balāghat (A) n.f. Eloquence; rhetoric; maturity.

بلاق bulāq (T) n.m. An ornament worn in nose.

بلانا bulānā (H) v. To call; to summon; to invite.

بلاوا bulāwā (H) n.m. Summons; call; invitation; bidding.

بلاؤ bilā'o (H) n.m. See بن بلاؤ ban bilā'o.

بلبل bulbul (P) n.f./m. A nightingale.

بلبلا bulbulā (H) n.m. A bubble.

بلبلانا balbalānā (H) v. The sound or cry of a camel; to burn with anger; to be in heat.

بلبلانا bilbilānā (H) v. To be restless; to lament; to be uneasy; to sob or cry bitterly; to be tormented with pain.

بلٹی bilṭī (corr. of E) n.f. Billet; a bill of lading; a receipt for the despatch of goods by rail or by ship.

بلد ، بلدہ balad, baldah (A) n.m. A city; a town; a village; a region.

بلدان buldān (A) n.m. (plu. of بلد balad) Countries; cities.

بلدیہ baldiyah (A) n.f. Municipality.

بلسان balasān (A) n.m. Balsam.

بلغم balgham (A) n.m. Phelgm---one of the humours of the body.

بلغمی balghamī (A) adj. Phlegmatic.

بلکنا bilaknā (H) v. To weep bitterly; to cry violently; to be restless or uneasy; to wish or desire earnestly.

بلکہ balkeh (P) conj. But; then; on the contrary.

بلم ballam (H) n.m. A lance; a short spear.

بلم بردار ballam bardār, n.m. A lancer; a spearman.

بلم ، بلما balam, balmā (H) n.m. A lover; a beloved; a husband.

بلند buland (P) adj. High; lofty; raised; elevated; sublime; exalted; tall; loud.

بلند آواز buland āwāz, n.f. Loud voice; loud sound; high note or tune.

بلند پایہ buland pāyah, adj. Of high rank; having an exalted position.

بلند پرواز buland parwāz, adj. Soaring high; having sublime or deep thoughts.

بلند پروازی buland parwāzī, n.f. High flight; high thinking.

بلند حوصلہ buland ḥauṣlah, adj. Courageous; brave; ambitious; aspiring; generous.

بلند کرنا buland karnā, v. To lift; to elevate; to exalt; to raise up.

بلند مرتبہ ، بلند رتبہ buland martabah, buland rutbah, adj. High in rank or dignity.

بلند نظر buland naẓar, adj. Magnanimous; aspiring.

بلندہمت buland himmat, adj. Magnanimous; ambitious; high-minded.

بلند ہمتی buland himmatī, n.f. Magnanimity; high-mindedness; ambition.

بلند ہونا buland honā, v. To ascend; to climb up.

بلندی bulandī (P) n.f. Height; elevation; loftiness; exaltation.

بلوا balwā (H) n.m. Riot; disturbance; tumult; insurrection.

بلوانا bulwānā (H) v. To send for; to summon.

بلور billaur (P) n.m. Crystal; crystal glass; very bright; transparent.

بلوری ، بلوریں billaurī, billaurīn, adj. Made of crystal or glass; clear and shining; transparent.

بلوط balūt (A) n.m. An acorn; an oak; a chestnut tree.

بلوغ ، بلوغت bulūgh, bulūghat (A) n.m./n.f. Puberty; maturity; attainment of a marriageable age.

بلونا bilonā (H) v. · To churn.

بلونی bilonī (H) n.f. A churning pot; a churn.

بلہاری balihārī (H) A word spoken to express extreme affection for a child or beloved; offering oneself as a sacrifice to ward off evil from the beloved.

بلی **balli** (H) *n.f.* A support or prop; a long wooden or bamboo post; a long pole or bamboo to steer or row a boat.

بلی مارنا **balli mārnā**, *v.* To steer.

بلی **billi** (H) *n.f.* A she-cat; the bolt or bar of a door.

بلیات **baliyyāt** (A) *n.f.* Evils; calamities; misfortunes.

بلیغ **baligh** (A) *adj.* Eloquent; learned.

بلی لوٹن **billi lotan** (H) *n.m.* A medicine; *valerian.*

بلیلہ **balelah** (P) *n.f.* A fruit used as medicine; *bellaric myrobalan.*

بم **bam**, *n.f.* Shafts of a carriage by which the horse is yoked; noise; tumult; clamour; a spring (of water).

بم **bam** (P) *n.f.* A bass part in music; a bass or lowest string or drum, having the deepest tone; deep sound (as that of the large pipes of an organ).

بم **bam**, *n.m.* (*corr.* of English). A bomb.

بمبا **bambā**, *n.m.* Fountain; source (of a river); canal; fire engine; postal letter box.

بمباری **bambārī**, *n.f.* Bombardment.

بن **ban** (H) *n.m.* Forest; jungle; a wood; desert.

بن باس **ban bās**, *n.m.* Exile; banishment.

بن بلاؤ **ban bilāo**, *n.m.* A wild cat.

بن کنڈا **ban kaṇḍā**, *n.m.* Cow-dung found in forests.

بن مانس **ban mānas**, *n.m.* A chimpanzee; guerilla; a wild man.

بن **bin** (A) *n.m.* (*contr.* of ابن *ibn*). A son.

بن یا بنا **bin yā binā** (H) *adv.* Without; except; unless.

بن آئی مرنا **bin ā'i marnā**, *v.* To die a sudden death; to be unjustly ruined.

بن جانے **bin jāne**, *adv.* Unknowingly, unwittingly.

بن داموں غلام **bin dāmoṅ ghulām**, *n.m.* One under heavy obligation; a very devoted person.

بن دانے پانی **bin dāne pāni**, *adv.* Without food and drink.

بن مارے شہید **bin māre shahīd**, *n.m.* False pretension to goodness or virtue.

بن مارے کی توبہ کرنا **bin māre ki taubah karnā**, *v.* To fear without a cause; to cry out before being hurt.

بن بلائے مہمان کی قدر نہیں ہوتی **bin bulāe mehmān kī qadr nahin hotī**, *prov.* An uninvited guest sits on thorns.

بن بلائے خدا کے ہاں بھی نہیں جائے **bin bulāe khudā ke haṅ bhi nahiṅ jāte**, *prov.* To a wedding or christening go not without an invitation.

بن روئے ماں بچے کو دودھ نہیں دیتی **bin ro'e māṅ bachche ko dūdh nahiṅ deti**, *prov.* A closed mouth catches no flies; nothing ask, nothing have; nothing venture, nothing win.

بنا **bannā** (H) *n.m.* A bridegroom.

بنا **binā** (A) *n.f.* Foundation; basis; root; cause; motive; origin.

بنا براں ، بنا بریں **binā barāṅ, binā bariṅ**, *adv.* On this account; therefore.

بنا کرنا **binā karnā**, *v.* To build; to lay the foundation of; to begin.

بنا بنایا **banā banāyā** (H) *adj.* Completed; finished; ready made.

بنات **banāt** (A) *n.f.* (*plu.* of بنت *bint*) Daughters.

بنات النعش **banāt-un-na'sh**, *n.f.* The constellation of the Great or Little Bear.

بناٹھنا ، بنی ٹھنی **banā ṭhanā, bani ṭhani**, *adj.* Fully adorned; bedecked; embellished.

بنا رہنا **banā rehnā**, *v.* To continue in good condition; to do well; to remain unaltered; to last long; to thrive; to prosper.

بناسپتی **banāspati** (S) *n.f.* Grass; blade of grass; herbage; vegetation. *adj.* Vegetable (oil).

بنا گوش bunāgosh (P) n.m. The lobe of the ear; the tip of the ear.

بنانا banānā (H) v. To make; to prepare; to form; to shape; to fabricate; to build; to compose; to acquire; to pluck (a fowl); to dress (food); to mend; to repair· to invent; to redicule; to mock.

بناوٹ banāwaṭ (H) n.f. Make; build; embellishment; form; figure; deceit; fabrication; shape; formation; show; display; affectation.

بناوٹ bunāwaṭ (H) n.f. The type of weaving or knitting; texture.

بناوٹی banāwaṭi (H) adj Artificial; fabricated.

بناؤ banā'o (H) n.m. Preparation; decoration; dressing; adornment; harmony; concord; reconciliation.

بناؤ سنگار کرنا banā'o singār karnā, v. To adorn; to bedeck; to decorate; to embellish.

بنت bint (A) n.f. Daughter.

بنت العنب bint-ul-'inab, n.f. Wine; (Lit.) daughter of the grape.

بنتی binti (H) n.f. Prayer; an apology; entreaty; imploration.

بنج banj (H) n.m. Trade; commerce; (commercial) transaction; profession.

بنجارا banjārā (H) n.m. A grain merchant; a roving trader carrying merchandise on his back.

بنجارن ، بنجاری banjāran, banjāri (H) n.f. The wife of a بنجارا banjārā.

بنجر bañjār (H) n.f. Waste land; barren or unproductive land; fallow (land).

بنجر توڑنا bañjar toṛnā, v. To cultivate a fallow land.

بنجر جدید bañjar jadid, n.f. A land lying fallow continuously for four years.

بنجر خارج الجمع bañjar khārij-uj-jam', n.f. Fallow land on which no revenue is charged.

بنجر قدیم bañjar qadim, n.f. A land lying fallow till the time of new settlement.

بند bañd (P) n.m. Joint; knuckle, knot; band; belt; string; a fastening; imprisonment; captivity; fetters; a dyke, dam or embankment; stanza; burden (of a song); agreement or pledge; mortgage. adj. Fastened; tied; bound; shut; stopped; barred; prevented; checked; closed; ceased; still.

بند باندھنا bañd bāndhnā, v. To construct a dam; to check an inundation with dykes; to tie a knot; to forestall; to plan; to manage.

بند بند bañd bañd, n.m. Every joint; every part. adj. Depressed; dejected.

بند بند ٹوٹنا bañd bañd ṭūṭnā, v. To be dead tired; to be exhausted; to feel pain in every joint.

بند بند جدا کرنا bañd bañd judā karnā, v. To cut into pieces; to put asunder all the joints.

بند بند ڈھیلے کر دینا bañd bañd ḍhile kar denā, v. To tire out; to exhaust (one) fully.

بند سوال bañd sawāl, n.m. A confidential query (sent by a court to a person).

بند کرنا bañd karnā, v, To shut; to close; to fasten; to stop; to prevent; to discontinue; to lock up; to confine; to imprison; to wind up an account.

بند ہونا bañd honā, v. To be closed; to be finished; to come to an end; to cease to exist; to be abolished.

بند ہیضہ bañd haizah, n.m. Choleraic diarrhoea.

بندا bundah (H) n.m. Ear-ring; pendant; ear drops.

بندر bai.dar (P) n.m. A harbour; a sea-port; a trading town on the sea shore to which a large number of foreign ships resort.

بندر bañdar (H) n.m. A monkey.

بندریا bandaryā (H) *n.f.* A female monkey.

بندش bandish (P) *n.f.* Composition; elegance of style; plan; contrivance; artifice; obstruction; prohibition; the act or state of tying or binding.

بندکی bundki, *n.f.* (*dim*. of بوند būnd) A dot; a tiny drop; a little spot; a light shower or drizzling.

بند کی دار bandki dār, *adj.* Dotted; spotted.

بندکی دار چھینٹ bundkī dār chhint, *n.f.* Spotted chintz.

بندگان bandagān (P) *n.m.* (*plu.* of بندہ bandah) Slaves; servants.

بندگی bandagī (P) *n.f.* Service; devotion; worship; compliment; a mode of salutation (among Hindus).

بندگی بجا لانا bandagī bajā lānā, *v.* To pay one's respects (to); to serve.

بندگی بیچارگی bandagi bechāragi. There is little to choose between service and servitude; service amounts to helplessness.

بندگی میں خدائی کرنا bandagī men khudā'i karnā, *v.* To affect authority while in servitude.

بندوبست bandobast (P) *n.m.* Settlement of (revenue); regulation; organization; management; method; order; system.

بندوبست استمراری bandobast-ĕ istimrāri, *n.m.* Permanent settlement.

بندوبست چند روزہ bandobast-ĕ chand rozah, *n.m.* Temporary settlement.

بندوق bandūq (A) *n.f.* A gun; a musket.

بندوق بھرنا bandūq bharnā, *v.* To load a gun or a musket.

بندوق چلانا bandūq chalānā, *v.* To fire a gun; to shoot (at); to fire.

بندوقچی bandūqchi, *n.m.* A musketeer.

بندہ bandah (P) *n.m.* A slave; a bondsman; a servant; an obedient person; an individual: a man.

بندہ بشر ہے bandah bashr hae, *prov.* To err is human.

بندہ پرور ، بندہ نواز bandah parwar, bandah nawāz, *adj.* Cherisher of servants; patron; a term of respect used in addressing a superior (as, your honour or my master).

بندہ پروری bandah parwarī, *n.f.* Cherishing of servants; a term expressing great kindness.

بندۂ درگاہ bandah-ĕ dargāh, *n.m.* A servant.

بندہ زادہ bandah zādah, *n.m.* A slave's son; the most humble servant.

بندھائی bandhā'i (H) *n.f.* The act of binding, tying or fastening; price paid for binding or fastening.

بندھن bandhan (H) *n.m.* Fastening; tying; knot; bandage; obstacle; imprisonment; hinderance; relationship; allowance; pay.

بندھوانا bandhwānā (H) *v.* To cause to be bound or tied or imprisoned; to blame; to accuse.

بندی bandi, *n.f.* A female slave or servant; obstacle; prohibition; an ornament worn (by Hindu women) on the forehead.

بندی bandı (P) *n.m.* A prisoner

بندی خانہ bandi khānah, *n.m.* A prison; a jail.

بندی bindi (H) *n.f.* A dot; a cypher; a coloured mark made by Hindus (usually women) on their forehead; a spangle (of crystal or metal) pasted on forehead by Hindu women.

بنڈی banḍi, *n.f.* A cotton stuffed waistcoat; a short woollen coat.

بنسی bansi (H) *n.f.* A flute; a pipe; a fishing hook.

بنفشہ banafshah (P) *n.f.&m.* The violet.

بنک bank (*corr.* of English) *n.m.* The bank.

بنگالی bangalī, *n.f.* The Bengali language. *adj.* Relating to Bengal; belonging to Bengal; of Bengal.

بنگلہ bańglah, adj. A bungalow; a thatched house; a summer-house made after the fashion of those made in Bengal. n.m. a kind of betel leaf. n.f. the Bengali language.

بننا bun-nā (H) v. To weave; to knite.

بننا ban-nā (H) v. To be made; to be prepared; to be built; to be cooked; to be mended; to be settled; to succeed.

بنوانا banwānā (H) v. To cause to be made, prepared or built.

بنوانا bunwānā (H) v. To cause to be woven or knitted; to get a thing woven or knitted.

بنوائی banwā'ī (H) n.f. Price paid for making a thing; the act of making or building etc.

بنوائی bunwā'ī (H) n.f. Price paid for weaving or knitting a thing; the act of weaving or knitting.

بنوٹ binnoṭ (H) n.f. Fighting iwth cudgels; a club-fight.

بنولا binaulā (H) n.m. Cotton seed.

بنی banī (H) n.f. A bride.

بنی banī (A) n.m. (plu. of ابن bin) Sons; children; descendant; race.

بنی آدم banī ādam, n.m. Sons or descendants of Adam; man.

بنی اسرائیل banī isrā'īl, n.m. Israelites; childern of Israel.

بنیا baniyā (H) n.m. A shopkeeper; a grain-seller; a merchant; a niggard; a timid man; a petty minded person.

بنیاد bunyād (P) n.f. Foundation; groundwork; basis; origin.

بنیاد ڈالنا bunyād ḍālnā, v. To found; to lay the foundation (of).

بنیان bunyān (A) n.f. Foundation; origin; basis.

بنیان banyān, n.f. A vest; a under-garment.

بنیٹی baneṭī (H) n.f. A torch lighted at both ends and whirled round so as to form a double circle of fire.

بو bū (P) n.f. Smell; odour; scent; stink.

بو آنا bū ānā, v. To stink; to emit bad smell; to smell.

بو bū (A) n.m. (Shortened form of ابو abū) father; possessed of; endowed with.

بوالعجب būl'ajab, adj. Wonderful; marvellous; foolish; conjurer.

بوالفضول būl-fūzūl, adj. Given to exaggeration or foolish talk; an idle talker.

بوالہوس būl-hawas, adj. Very greedy; avaricious; slave of passions.

بو الہوسی būl-hawasī, n.f. Greed; avarice; passion.

بو قلموں bū qalmūn, adj. Of various colours; variegated; chequered; wonderful.

بوا būā (H) n.f. Sister; father's sister; paternal aunt.

بواسیر bawāsīr (A) n.f Piles.

بوانا buwānā (H) v. To cause to be sown.

بوائی bawā'ī (H) n.f. A kibe; chilblain; an itching sore on foot through exposure to cold

جس کے نہ پھٹے بوائی وہ کیا جانے پیڑ پرائی jis ke nah phaṭe bawā'ī wuh kyā jāne pīṛ parā'ī, prov. One who has not suffered cannot understand the suffering of others.

بوائی buwā'ī (H) n.f. Sowing; the act of sowing; seed-time.

بو بو būbū (H) n.f. Sister; a respected old maid-servant who has served or brought up the children of a family.

بوتا būtā (H) n.m. Strength; power; capacity; status.

بوتل botal (corr. of English) n.f. A bottle.

بوتل میں بھرنا botal men bharnā, v. To bottle.

بوتہ būtah (T) n.m. A melting-pot; a crucible; a young camel.

بوتیمار būtimār (P) n.m. A heron.

بوٹ **būṭ** (E) *n.m.* Boot.

بوٹا **būṭā** (H) *n.m.* A bush; a shrub; a plant; a flower or flowery pattern worked on cloth or painted on paper.

بوٹا سا قد *būṭā sā qad, adj.* Of small and well proportioned stature.

بوٹا کاڑھنا *būṭā kāṛhnā, v.* To work flowers or flowery pattern on cloth; to embroider.

بوٹے دار *būṭe dār, adj.* Flowered; embroidered.

بوٹی **boṭi** (H) *n.f.* A small piece of flesh or meat.

بوٹی آتار لینا *boṭi utār lenā, v.* To bite off a piece of flesh.

بوٹی بوٹی پھڑکنا *boṭi boṭī pharaknā, v.* To throb in every vein; to be very lively, naughty and wanton.

بوٹیاں آڑانا *boṭiyāṅ uṛānā, v.* To beat black and blue; to cut into pieces.

بوٹیاں توڑنا یا کاٹنا یا نوچنا *boṭiyāṅ toṛnā yā kāṭnā yā nochnā, v.* To beat severely; to taunt.

بوٹی **būṭi** (H) *n.f.* Herbs; small flower; roots; hemp leaves (from which an intoxicating potion is made).

بوجھ **bojh** (H) *n.m.* Load; burden; debt; encumbrance.

بوجھ آتارنا *bojh utārnā, v.* To put down a load or burden; to discharge an obligation or responsibility; to throw off an encumbrance; to pay off a debt; to act carelessly; to compensate.

بوجھ آٹھانا *bojh uṭaānā, v.* To carry a load; to bear; to undertake a responsibility; to be under an obligation; to relieve one of responsibility.

بوجھ سر پر ھونا *bojh sar par honā, v.* To be under an obligation.

بوجھ **būjh** (H) *n.f.* Understanding; sagacity; perception; comprehension.

بوجھ بجھکڑ *būjh bujhakkaṛ, n.m.* A wise-care; a sententious dullard.

بوجھل **bojhal** (H) *adj.* Heavy; burdened; loaded; rich; respected.

بوجھنا **būjhnā** (H) *v.* To guess; to make out; to comprehend; to perceive; to conceive; to calculate; to presage.

بوچا ، بوچی **būchā, būchī** (H) *adj.* Ear-cropt; without ears; shameless.

بوچڑ **būchaṛ** (*corr.* of English) *n.m.* Butcher.

بوچھاڑ **būchhāṛ** (H) *n.f.* Driving rain; wind and rain; a heavy shower of rain; excess; abundance.

بوچھاڑ پڑنا *būchhāṛ paṛnā, v.* To face heavy shower of rain; to be severely criticised from all direction.

بوچھاڑ کرنا *būchhāṛ karnā, v.* To criticise severely; to scold bitterly; to spend lavishly; to squander; to talk unceasingly.

بود **būd** (P) *n.f.* Being; existence.

بود و باش *būd-ŏ bāsh, n.f.* Residence; abode; living.

بودا ، بودی **bodā, bodi** (H) *adj.* Weak; faint-hearted; low-spirited; feeble; timid; dull.

بودا کرنا *bodā karnā, v.* To weaken; to make one lose courage.

بودلا **bodlā** (H) *n.m.* A simpleton; a fool; an innocent person; a sect of faqirs.

بودلی **bodli** (H) *n.f.* A simple woman; a trollop; a woman who lives with a class of mendicants and dresses like a man.

بور **būr** (H) *adj.* Barren (land). *n.f.* Chaff; husk; sawdust.

بور کے لڈو *bur ke laḍḍū, n.m.* Sweetmeat shaped like balls made with the husk of grain; a person who holds out false hope; anything fair without and foul within; deceit.

بورا **baurā.** See باؤلا *ba'olā.*

بورا **būṛā** (H) *n.m.* Coarse sugar; sawdust; powder.

بورا **borā** (H) *n.m.* A canvas bag; a sack; a kind of bean like French beans; gunny bag.

بورق būraq (A) n.m. Borax.

بوریا boryā (P) n.m. A mat made of palm leaves.

بوڑھا būṛhā (H) adj. & n.m. Old man; aged.

بوڑھا بابا būṛhā bābā, n.m. Very old; reverend father; old man.

بوڑھا بالا برابر būṛhā bālā barābar, prov. Between an old man and a child there is little to choose; an old man is twice a child.

بوڑھا چونچلا būṛhā chonchlā, n.m. Practising affectations and blandishment of youth in old age.

بوڑھا ہونا buṛhā honā, v. To become old or aged.

بوڑھی būṛhī, adj. & n.f. Aged; old woman.

بوزہ bozah (P) n.m. Beer.

بوزہ گر bozah gar, adj. A brewer.

بوزہ خانہ bozah khānah, n.m. A beer-shop; a brewery.

بوزنہ būznah (P) n.m. A monkey.

بوس bos (P) part. Kissing. adj. Kissing (used in comp).

بوس و کنار bos-ŏ kinār, n.m. Kissing and embracing; dalliance; kissing and caressing.

بوستان bostān (P) n.m. A flower-garden; the title of a famous work by the Persian poet, Saadi.

بوسہ bosah (P) n.m. A kiss.

بوسہ بازی bosah bāzī, n.f. Kissing and toying.

بوسیدگی bosidagī (P) n.f. Rottenness; oldness; decay.

بوسیدہ bosidah (P) adj. Rotten; decayed.

بوکا bokā (H) n.m. Basket or leather bucket for drawing water from a well, etc.

بوکھلانا baukhlānā (H) v. To be upset; to be perturbed.

بوکھلاہٹ baukhalāhat (H) n.f. Perturbation; confusion.

بول baul (A) n.m. Urine.

بول دان baul dān, n.m. Chamber-pot.

بول bol (H) n.m. Speech; word; saying; burden of a song; utterance; taunt; jeer; melody; tune; fame; words of a song; verse.

بول اٹھنا bol uṭhnā, v. To speak out; to exclaim; to cry out.

بول بالا bol bālā, n.m. Success; prosperity.

بول بالا ہونا bol bālā honā, v. To prosper; to succeed; to be fortunate; to attain wealth and position; to become famous.

بول چال bol chāl, n.f. Talk; conversation; mode of speech; confabulation; dialect; diction; friendship; dispute.

بول سنانا bol sunānā, v. To sing verses or songs.

بول مارنا bol mārnā, v. To taunt; to ridicule; to turn one's bark on.

بولانا baulānā (H) v. To go mad; to become crazy; to lose one's wits or presence of mind.

بولنا bolnā (H) v. To speak; to talk; to utter; to say; to tell; to call; to chirp; to pronounce; to sound; to bid (at an auction).

بولنا چالنا bolnā chālnā, v. To converse; to talk.

بولی bolī (H) n.f. Speech; language; dialect; talk; conversation; bid; taunt; saying.

بولی بولنے والا boli bolne wālā, n.m. Bidder at an auction.

بولی دینا bolī denā, v. To bid at an auction.

بولی ٹھولی bolī ṭholī, n.f. Jeering; taunt; joke.

بولی ٹھولی سنانا bolī ṭholī sunānā, v. To reproach; to taunt; to joke; to blame.

بولیاں بولنا boliyāṅ bolnā, v. To speak in different tongues; to utter different sounds; many persons speaking at one and the same time; to give different and conflicting opinion; to babble; to make insinuations about; to taunt; to sing folk song.

بولیاں سننا boliyāṅ sun-nā, v. To hear taunts; to be reproached; to hear songs being sung.

بوم būm (P) n.m. An owl; earth; land.

بونا baunā (H) adj. Dwarfish. n.m. A dwarf; pygmy; the fifth incarnation of Vishnu.

بونا bonā (H) v. To sow; to plant; to cultivate; to have a cow or buffalo bulled.

بوند būṅd (H) n.f. A drop; a rain drop; blood; semen; a kind of spotted silk.

بوند بوند būṅd būṅd, adv. By drops; drop by drop.

بوندا باندی būṅdā bāṅdī, n.f. A slight drizzle; a light shower of rain; slight and interrupted rain; drizzling.

بوند بھر būṅd bhar, adj. Just a drop; very little.

بوند ٹپکنا bāṅd ṭapaknā, v. To trickle; to drip.

بوند چرانا būṅd churānā, v. To secrete semen; to conceive (a woman).

بوندی būṅdi (H) n.f. A kind of sweetmeat like drops.

بونڈی boṅḍī (H) n.f. The germ of a plant after the flower is shed.

بونگا bauṅgā (H) n.m. An awkward or rude fellow; a stupid person; one who talks nonsense.

بونی bauni (H) n.f. A female dwarf.

بونی boni (H) n.f. Season of sowing; seed-time.

بوھرا bauhrā (H) n.m. A class of village bankers or money-lenders; an individual of that class.

بوھنی bohnī (H) n.f. First sale for ready money in the morning; handsel.

بوئیا bo'iyā (H) n.m. A small basket; a work basket.

به bih (P) adj. Good.

بہتر bihtar, adj. (comp.) Better; superior.

بہتری bihtary, n.f. Welfare; betterment.

بہترین bihtarin, adj. (sup.) Best of all.

بہا bahā (P) n.m. Value; price; rate.

بھابی bhābi (H) n.f. A brother's wife; sister-in-law.

بھاپ bhāp (H) n.f. Steam; vapour; exhalation; hot breath.

بھاپ نکلنا bhāp nikalnā, v. Emission of steam or vapour.

بھات bhāt (H) n.m. Boiled rice.

بھاٹ bhāṭ (H) n.m. Name of a tribe; a bard; a minstrel.

بھاٹا bhāṭā (H) n.m. A current; a stream; ebb-tide.

بھاجی bhāji (H) n.f. Greens; fried or cooked vegetables; distribution of sweets among relatives and friends; sweets so distributed.

بہادر bahādur (P) adj. Brave; bold; courageous; valiant; high-spirited. n.m. Hero; champion; knight; a title equivalent to 'Honourable'.

بہادری bahāduri (P) n.f. Bravery; heroism; valour.

بھادوں bhādon (H) n.m. Name of the fifth month of the Hindus (August-September).

بھادوں کی بھرن bhādoṅ kī bharan, n.f. Heavy rain in August which fill the tanks and flood the fields.

بھادوں کے ڈونگرے bhādoṅ ke ḍūṅgre, n.m. Light showers in the month of Bhādoṅ (August-September).

بہار bahār (P) n.f. Spring; prime; bloom; beauty; glory; elegance; delight; enjoyment; flourishing state; fine landscape.

بہار پر آنا bahār par ānā, v. To blossom; to flourish.

بہار لوٹنا bahār lūṭnā, v. To derive pleasure or delight from; to revel in.

بهارستان Bahāristān, n.m. A lovely or beautiful spot; a place adorned with the bloom of spring; title of Persian work by jāmī.

بھارت bhārat (S) n.m. The epic describing the account of Yudhishtar's war; India (after partition).

بھارت ورش bhārat warsh, n.m. India proper; undivided India.

بهارن buhāran (H) n.f. Duster.

بهارنا buhārnā (H) v. To sweep; to dust; to clean.

بهارو ، بهاری buhāro, buhārī (H) n.f. A broom.

بھاری bhārī (H) adj. Heavy; weighty; important; valuable; large, fat; great; voluminous; valuable; costly; firm; strong; loud; troublesome; hard; difficult; ominous; slow; sluggish.

بھاری بھر کم bhārī bharkam, adj. Grave; solemn; serious; sober; patient; forbearing; respectable; trustworthy; fat.

بھاری پتھر چوم کر چھوڑ دینا bhārī patthar chūm kar chhoṛ denā, v. To withdraw from a difficult or impracticable undertaking.

بھاری لگنا bhārī lagnā, v. To weigh heavily (on); to find tedious or tiresome.

بھاری ہونا bhārī honā, v. To be heavy; to be cumbrous or cumbersome; to be dull or dejected; to be ominous.

بهاری bahārī (P) adj. Vernal; of the spring.

بھاڑ bhāṛ (H) n.m. Furnace; kiln; a fire place for parching grains; a large oven; the price of fornication.

بھاڑ جھونکنا bhāṛ jhonknā, v. To make a fire of dry leaves, &c. for parching grain; to make up a mean occupation; to learn no art or trade.

بھاڑ کھانا bhāṛ khānā, v, To live on the wages of a woman's prostitution; to be a pimp.

بھاڑ میں جھونکنا bhāṛ men jhonknā, v. To throw into the fire; to cast to the dogs; to waste; to destroy; to squander.

بھاڑا bhāṛā (H) n.m. Hire; fare; freight; rent; wages.

بھاڑے کا ٹٹو bhāṛe kā ṭaṭṭū, n.m. A hired pony; a hireling; a hack; a slave of necessity or habit; an object requiring constant repair; a person addicated to drugs.

بھاشا یا بھاکھا bhāshā yā bhākhā (S) n.f. Speech; language; dialect; the vernacular of any country.

بہاگ bihāg (H) n.m. Name of a rāgnī (a tune or musical mode).

بھاگ bhāg (H) n.m. Good fortune; luck; destiny; fate; lot; share; portion; division.

بھاگ پھوٹنا bhāg phūṭnā, v. To be unfortune.

بھاگ جاگنا ، بھاگ کھلنا ، بھاگ لگنا bhāg jāgnā, bhāg khulnā, bhāg lagnā, v. To be in luck; to be fortunate; to become rich; to receive an honour.

بھاگ وان bhāg wān, adj. Fortunate; lucky; rich; generous.

بھاگا بھاگ ، بھاگم بھاگ bhāgā bhāg, bhāgam bhāg, adv. Running at full speed; helter-skelter.

بھاگ جانا bhāg jānā (H) v. To run away; to flee; to abscond; to escape.

بھاگڑ bhāgaṛ (H) n.f. Flight; running helter-skelter; fright; tumult; defeat; escape from immediate danger.

بھاگنا bhāgnā (H) v. To run away; to flee; to escape; to abscond.

بھال bhāl (H) n.f. The point of an arrow or a bayonet; the blade of a spear or lance; search; supervision; investigation.

بھالا bhālā (H) n.m. Spear; lance.

بھالو bhālū (H) n.m. Bear.

بھان **bhān** (H) *n.m.* Change; lower coins given of higher ones.

بھانا **bhānā** (H) *v.* To be acceptable (to); to be pleasing; to suit; to fit; to be agreeable; to be approved of.

بہانا **bahānā** (H) *v.* To cause to flow; to set afloat or adrift; to float; to launch; to spill; to shed; to squander; to waste; to sell cheap.

بھانپنا **bhāṅpnā** (H) *v.* To divine; to guess; to see through; to make out; to perceive; to surmise.

بھانت **bhāṅt** (H) *n.f.* Sort; class; kind; manner; mode; method; style.

بھانت بھانت **bhāṅt bhāṅt**, *adj.* Of various kinds; of many sorts; various; diverse; multifarious.

بھانجا **bhāṅjā** (H) *n.m.* Sister's son; nephew.

بھانجی **bhāṅjī** (H) *n.f.* Sister's daughter; niece.

بھانجی **bhāṅjī** (H) *n.f.* Interruption; hindrance; defect; tale-bearing.

بھانجی خور **bhāṅjī khor**, *adj.* One who obstructs or pokes one's nose in another's affairs; backbiter.

بھانجی کھانا **bhāṅjī khānā**, *v.* To give malicious intelligence; to interfere; to obstruct.

بھانجی مار **bhāṅjī mār**, *adj.* Interrupter; a mar-plot.

بھانجی مارنا **bhāṅjī mārnā**, *v.* To interrupt; to interfere; to obstruct; to frustrate; to tell tales.

بھانڈ **bhāṅḍ** (H) *n.m.* A jester; a buffoon; a mimic; one who cannot keep a secret; a blab; a sycophant; a cavillar.

بھانڈا **bhāṅḍā** (H) *n.m.* A large earthen pot or vessel; a secret.

بھانڈا پھوٹنا **bhāṅḍā phūṭnā**, *v.* To be found out; disclosure of a secret; to lose one's character.

بھانڈا پھوڑنا **bhāṅḍā phoṛnā**, *v.* To disclose a secret; to point out a defect.

بھان متی **bhān matī** (H) *n.m.* A magician; a cheat.

بہانہ **bahānah** (P) *n.m.* Excuse; pretext; pretence; evasion; contrivance; affectation; deceit; feint; cause; reason; means.

بہانہ جو **bahānah jū**, *adj.* One seeking an excuse.

بہانہ خور **bahānah khor**, *adj.* One who pretends or feigns; a pretender; a cheat;

بہانہ ساز **bahānah sāz**, *adj.* An impostor; one who makes excuses.

بہانہ کرنا **bahānah karnā**, *v.* To make an excuse; to pretend; to evade.

بہائم **bahā'im** (A) *n.m.* (*plu.* of بہیمہ **bahimah**) Beasts; quadrupeds; animals.

بھاؤ **bhāo** (H) *n.m.* Price; value; rate; market price; state or condition; disposition; blandishment; coquetry; gesticulation; love; affection; mode of dancing; display; display of emotion through dancing.

بھاؤ بتانا **bhāŏ batānā**, *v.* To gesticulate in dancing; to express a state or condition; to represent passions in singing and dancing.

بہاؤ **bahāo** (H) *n.m.* Flow; flood; glide along; flux; fluidity.

بھاوج **bhāwaj** (H) *n.f.* Brother's wife; sister-in-law.

بھائی **bhā'ī** (H) *n.m.* Btother; comrade; companion; kinsman.

بھائی بند **bhā'ī band**, *n.m.* Brothers; kindred; relations; kinsmen; friends; belonging to same caste or nation.

بھائی بندی ، بھائی چارا **bhā'ī bandī, bhā'ī chārā**, *n.f.* & *n.m.* Brotherhood; fraternity; kinship; friendship; sharing one's joys and sorrows.

بھبک bhabak (H) n.f. A sudden bursting of flame; a sudden emission of offensive smell.

بھبکا bhabkā (H) n.m. A still; a blast from a furnace stinking smell; a kind of drinking vessel with a large mouth.

بھبکنا bhabaknā (H) v. To be enraged; to become hot; to catch fire; to burst into flame; to burn; to roar; to boil.

بھبکی bhabkī (H) n.f. Threat; menace;

بھبوت bhabūt (H) n.m. Ashes of cow-dung.

بہبود behbūd (P) n.f. Well-being; welfare; betterment.

بہبود خلائق behbūd-ĕ khəlā'iq, n.f. Public good; public welfare or benefit.

بھبوکا bhabūkā (H) n.m. Blaze; flame. adj. Ablaze; glowing; shining; bright; beautiful; hot; furious.

بھپارا bhapārā (H) n.m. Steam; vapour; exhalation.

بہت bahut (H) adj. Much; most; many; excessive; copious; abundant; plentiful; enough; sufficient. adv. Very much; largely; excessively; enormously; exceedingly.

بہت اچھا bahut achhā, adv. Very well; very good; accepted; agreed.

بہت ٹھیک bahut ṭhīk, adv. All right; quite true.

بہت سا bahut sā, adj. A great deal; too much; quite a bit.

بھتا bhattā (H) n.m. Travelling allowance; an allowance.

بہتات buhtāt (H) n.f. Abundance; excess; plenty.

بہتان buhtān (A) n.m. False accusation; calumny; aspersion; false imputation.

بہتان باندھنا buhtān bāndhnā, v. To bring a false accusation against; to slander; to calumniate.

بہتر bahattar (H) adj. Seventy-two.

بھتنا bhutnā (H) n.m. An evil spirit; an imp; a demon; a goblin; a ghost; an ugly person; one besmeared with mud and dirt.

بھتنی bhutnī (H) n.f. A female demon; an old hag; a very ugly woman.

بھتیانا bhutyānā (H) To be like a devil.

بہتے پانی میں ہاتھ دھونا bahte pānī meṅ hāth dhonā, id. To make hay while the sun shines.

بھتیجا bhatījā (H) n.m. Brother's son; nephew.

بھتیجی bhatījī (H) n.f. Brother's daughter; niece.

بہتیرا bahoterā (H) adj. Many; very much; quite sufficient; most; a great deal.

بھٹ bhaṭ (H) n.m. A pit; den.

بھٹا bhuṭṭā (H) n.m. Ear of Indian corn; ear of maize.

بھٹا سا اڑانا bhuṭṭā sā uṛānā, id. To cut off clean with one stroke.

بھٹا bhaṭṭā (H) n.m. An oven; a kiln; a furnace.

بھٹکا پھرنا bhaṭkā phirnā, v. To go wandering about; to roam about aimlessly; to lose the way; to go in search; to look out (for).

بھٹکانا bhaṭkānā (H) v. To mislead; to bewilder; to deceive; to cause to wander; to lead astray.

بھٹکنا bhaṭakā (H) v. To go astray; to wander about; to lose one's way; to miss the right path.

بھٹی bhaṭṭī (H) n.m. A grate or stove (as of a goldsmith); a furnace; a kiln; a distillery; washerman's cauldron for boiling clothes; name of a Rajput tribe.

بھٹی چڑھانا bhaṭṭī charhānā, v. To boil clothes for cleaning; to lit fire in the furnace.

بھٹیارا bhatyārā (H) n.m. One who prepares food for travellers in an inn; an attendant in an inn; one who looks after the requirements and comfort of residents of an inn.

بھٹیاری bhatyārī (H) n.f. Wife of a بھٹیارا bhatyārā.

بھٹیار خانہ bhatyār khānah, n.m. An inn; a carvanserai; a dwelling place of low type of people; slum.

بہہ جانا bah jānā (H) v. To flow; to glide away; to float with the stream; to be ruined; to be swept away.

بہجت bahjat (A) n.f. Joy; happiness; gladness; pleasure; freshness; grace; excellence.

بھجن bhajan (H) n.m. A sacred song; a hymn.

بھجنگ bhujang (S) n.m. A serpent; a black snake; a black man.

بھجنگا bhujangā (H) n.m. The king crow; a black man.

بھجوانا bhijwānā (H) v. To cause to be sent.

بھجیا bhujyā (H) n.f. Fried or cooked vegetables; fried rice.

بھچ جانا، بھچنا bhich jānā, bhichnā (H) v. To be crushed; to be squeezed; to be compressed; to feel shy or modest; to feel helpless.

بھد bhad (H) n.f. Sound of anything falling on soft ground; a thud; disgrace; insult.

بھد سے گرنا bhad se girnā, v. To fall with a thud.

بھدا ، بھدی bhaddā, bhaddī, adj. Awkward; clumsy; ill-shaped; ugly.

بہر bahr (P) prep. For; on account of; for the sake of.

بہر bahar (P) prep. In every; to every (used in Persian phrases).

بہر حال bahar hāl, adv. At any rate; anyhow; in any case.

بہر طور ، بہر صورت ، بہر کیف bahar taur, bahar sūrat, bahar kaif, adv. By all means; somehow or other; at all events.

بھر bhar (H) adj. (Used in comps.) Full; as much as; as far as; up to; all; whole.

بھر آنا bhar ānā, v. To heal up (sore or wound); to get filled to the brim.

بھر پانا bhar pānā, v. To be paid in full; to get one's deserts.

بھر پور bhar pūr, adj. Brimful; overflown; abundant; complete; replete prosperous; wealthy.

بھر جانا bhar jānā, v. To be filled.

بھر دینا bhar denā, v. To fill completely; to enrich; to pay; to compensate; to pay indemnity; to irr gate; to besmear.

بھر مار bhar mār, n.f. Abundance; excess; plenty.

بانس بھر bāns bhar, n.m. The ength of a bamboo.

دن بھر din bhar, adv. All the day long.

عمر بھر 'umar bhar, adv. During one's whole life; all lifetime.

کوس بھر kos bhar, n.m. A kos (about three mile).

مقدور بھر maqdūr bhar, adv. To the best of one's ability or power.

بھرا bharrā (H) n.m. Excitement; alarm; panic; incitement; provocation; deceit.

بھرا دینا bharrā denā, v. To incite; to deceive.

بھرے میں آنا bharre men ānā, v. To be decieve; to be panic-striken.

بہرا bahrā (H) n.m. Deaf; hard of hear ng; an heedless; inattentive; an attendant at the dining table.

بہرام Bahrām (P) n.m. The planet Mars appellation of several kings of Persia.

بھرانا bharānā (H) v. To cause to fill; to get covered (a cow or mare); feeding of their young one's by the birds.

بھرانا bharrānā (H) v. To become hoarse or husky.

بھرائی bharā'ī (H) n.f. The act of filling or stuffing; the wage paid for filling or stuffing or for watering the land; the fee paid for getting an animal covered.

بھر بھرا ، بھر بھری bhurbhurā, bhurbhuri (H) adj. Dry and powdery; crisp; crackling; light sandy (soil).

بھرت bhart (H) n.m. A mixed metal composed of copper, lead and zinc.

بھرتا bhurtā (H) n.m. Mash made of boiled or fried vegetables; mash.

بھرتا نکالنا یا کر دینا bhurtā nikālnā yā kar denā, v. To make a mash of; to beat to a pulp; to give a sound thrashing.

بھرتی bharti (H) n.f. Filling; stuffing; loading; completion; enrolment; enlistment; recruitment; insertion of irrelevant matter; fabrication; falsehood; lumber.

بھرتی کرنا bharti karnā, v. To load; to fill; to enlist; to fabricate.

بھرم bharam (H) n.m. Reputation; esteem; credit; trust; secret.

بھرم کرنا bharam karnā, v. To believe; to rely upon; to depend upon.

بھرم کھلنا bharam khulnā, v. To be exposed.

بھرم گنوانا bharam gaṅwānā, v. To lose one's reputation or credit.

بھرمانا bharmānā (H) v. To deceive; to mislead; to lead astray; to tempt.

بھرنا bharnā (H) v. To fill; to load; to stock; to fill up or heal (as a wound); to suffer; to pay indemnity; to enrage; to excite; to backbit; to irrigate; to obey; to stain or pollute.

بھرنا بھرنا bharnā bharnā, v. To pay debts or daily expenses; to have to pay the debts of another.

بہروپ bahrūp (H) n.m. Disguise; mimicry; deceit; cunning.

بہروپ بھرنا bahrūp bharnā, v. To disguise; to mimic.

بہروپیا bahrūpiā (H) n.m. A person assuming various characters or disguises; a mimic; an imitator; a cheat.

بھروسا bharosā (H) n.m. Reliance; trust; dependence; confidence; assurance; hope; expectation; faith; belief.

بھروسا کرنا bharosā karnā, v. To rely on; to confide (in); to hope; to trust.

بھروسا دینا bharosā denā, v. To give one hope; to reassure.

بہرہ bahrah (P) n.m. Share; portion; quota; destiny, profit; gain; fortune; benefit.

بہرہ مند ، بہرہ ور ، بہرہ یاب bahrah mand, bahrah war, bahrah yāb, adj. Prosperous; fortunate; lucky; happy; gainer.

بہرہ مندی bahrah mandi, n.f. Prosperity; happiness.

بھری bhari (H) n.f. The weight of one rupee, i.e. one tolah; a kind of grass which grows in the jungle; a (man-load) bundle of crop.

بہری bahri (H) n.f. A falcon; a female hawk; a deaf woman.

بھری برسات bhari barsāt, n.f. The rains in full swing; the rainy season.

بھری محفل bhari maḥfil, n.f. Full meeting; very big gathering.

بھڑ bhiṛ (H) n.f. A wasp; a hornet.

بھڑ کے چھتے میں ہاتھ ڈالنا bhiṛ ke chhatte meṅ hāth ḍālnā, id. To raise a hornets' nest round oneself; to stir up mischief or trouble.

سوتی بھڑوں کو جگانا soti bhiroṅ ko jagānā, id. To rouse a sleeping foe; to revive an old quarrel.

بھڑاس bharās (H) n.f. Rage; resentment; spleen; animosity; grude.

بھڑاس نکالنا bharās nikālnā, v. To vent one's rage or spleen.

بھڑانا bhirānā (H) v. To place in close contact; to bring into collision; to cause to fight.

بھڑ بھڑ bhar bhar, n.f. Sound of crackling fuel; crackle.

بھڑ بھڑ کرنا bhar bhar karnā, v. To burn fiercely; to roar; to crackle.

بھڑبھونجا bharbhūnjā (H) n.m. A man who parches grain; a cast of Hindus whose occupation is to parch grain; a dark ugly man.

بھڑبھونجن bharbūnjan (H) n.f. Wife of a بھڑبھونجا a woman who parches grain; a dark ugly woman.

بھڑک bharak (H) n.f. Splendour; glitter; flash; blaze; show; ostentation; rage; fury; agitation; shying (of a horse).

بھڑک دار bharak dār, adj. Splendid; shining; glittering; blazing; refulgent.

بھڑکانا bharkānā (H) v. To kindle; to inflame; to excite; to induce; to incite; to startle; to scare; to blow up into a flame.

بھڑکنا bharaknā (H) v. To burst forth into a flame; to blaze up; to flare up; to be very excited; to be enraged; to shy (a horse); to startle; to be alarmed.

بھڑکیلی ، بھڑکیلا bharkilā, bhirkilī (H) adj. Glittering; gorgeous; showy; splendid.

بھڑنا bhirnā (H) v. To come together; to close (as two armies); to come into collision; to clash; to fight; to be closed (a door).

بھڑوا bharvā (H) n.m. One who lives on the earnings of a prostitute; a pimp; a pander; procurer; a shameless person.

بھڑوائی bharwā'i (H) n.f. Pimping; the earning of prostitution.

بھس bhus (H) n.m. Husk; straw; chaff; bran.

بھس بھرنا bhus bharnā, v. To fill or stuff with chaff.

بھسم bhasam (H) n.f. Ashes; cinders.

بھسم کرنا bhasam karnā, v. To burn out; to reduce to ashes.

بھسم ہونا bhasam honā, v. To be reduced to ashes; to be utterly destroyed; to writhe in rage.

بہشت bihisht (P) n.f. The abode of the blessed; paradise; heaven.

بہشت کی ہوا bihisht kī hawā, n.f. Cool refreshing breeze.

بہشتی bihishtī (P) adj. Of or pertaining to paradise; celestial; virtuous; blessed. n.m. A water-carrier.

بھک bhak (H) n.f. Puff; blast; explosion (the sound of).

بھک سے اڑ جانا bhak se ur jānā, v. To explode; to fly off with a flap; to be cut clean off.

بھک سے اڑ جانے والا مادہ bhak se ur jāne wālā māddah, n.m. An explosive or combustible material.

بھکاری bhikāri (H) n.m. A beggar; a mendicant; a pauper.

بھکارن bhikāran (H) n.f. A beggar woman.

بہکانا bahkānā (H) v. To mislead; to deceive; to seduce; to cause one to err; to entice; to allure; to tempt; to instigate; to excite; to lead one to a sinful action.

بہکاوا bahkāwā (H) n.m. Deception; delusion; trick; intimidation.

بہکاوے میں آنا bahkāwe meṅ ānā, v. To be deceived (by); to be deluded (by); to fall into the snare or allurement (of); to be taken in (by).

بھک منگا bhik mangā. See بھکاری bhikārī..

بہکنا bahaknā (H) v. To be deceived; to be misled; to go astray; to stagger; to give oneself airs; to talk in a fit of fever or state of intoxication.

بھگا لے جانا bhagā le jānā (H) v. To run away with; to elope away; to drive off.

بھگانا bhagānā (H) v. To put to flight; to drive off; to cause to flee or escape; to defeat; to put to rout; to entice away; to gallop away (a horse).

بھگت bhagat (H) n.m. A righteous person; a devotee; pious or holy man.

بھگتان bhugtān (H) n.m. Full settlement; liquidation; punishment.

بھگتانا bhugtānā (H) v. To complete; to dispose of; to execute; to settle; to distribute; to liquidate; to adjust.

بھگتنا bhugatnā (H) v. To experience; to suffer; to bear; to pay the penalty; to settle with; to be requited for.

بھگدڑ bhagdaṛ (H) n.f. Stampede; sudden wild commotion; flight due to panic.

بھگندر bhagandar (H) n.m. Fistula in rectum; a boil in or close to the anus.

بھگوان bhagwān (H) n.m. The Supreme Being; God.

بھگو بھگو کے مارنا bhigo bhigo ke mārnā, id. To eulogise one mockingly or in fun; to shame a person thoroughly; to reproach one in a taunting manner.

بھگوت ، بھگونت bhagwat, bhagwant (H) adj. Divine.

بھگوت گیتا bhagwat Gītā, n.f. Name of a religious poem held in high esteem by the Hindus; the divine song.

بھگوڑا bhagoṛā (H) adj. & n.m. A fugitive; a deserter; a runaway.

بھگوڑی bhagoṛi. Feminine form of بھگوڑا bhagoṛā.

بھگونا bhigonā (H) v. To wet; to soak; to moisten.

بھلا ، بھلی bhalā, bhalī (H) adj. Good; excellent; virtuous; nice; fine; attractive; wonderful; healthy; auspicious; righteous; admirable.

بھلا چنگا bhalā changā, adj. In good health condition; healthy; hale and hearty.

بھلا لگنا bhalā lagnā, v. To appear or look pleasing or agreeable.

بھلا آدمی یا بھلا مانس bhalā ādmi yā bhalā mānis, n.m. A good man; a gentleman; a nobleman; a respectable person; courteous; humane.

بھلا کرنا bhalā karnā, v. To do good; to do a favour.

بھلانا bhulānā (H) v. To cause to forget; to (try to) forget.

بہلانا bahlānā (H) v. To amuse; to allure; to coax; to entertain; to cheer; to divert.

بھلاوا bhulāwā (H) n.m. Deception; fraud; misleading; misunderstanding; cheating.

بھلاوا دینا bhulāwā denā, v. To mislead; to deceive; to beguile; to play a trick on.

بہلاوا bahlāwā (H) n.m. Entertainment; amusement.

بھلائی bhalā'i (H) n.f. Good; goodness; excellence; kindness; virtue; gain; benefit; beneficence; welfare; prosperity.

بھلائی کرنا bhalā'i karnā, v. To show kindness (to); to do good.

بھلکڑ bhulakkaṛ (H) adj. Very forgetful; oblivious; dull.

بھلمنساہت ، بھلمنسائی bhalmansāhat, bhalmansā'i (H) n.f. Nobility; civility; politeness.

بہلنا bahalnā (H) v. To be amused; to be entertained; to be diverted.

بہلول bahlol (A) n.m. One who laughs heartily; a cheery person; a virtuous prince.

بہلی bahlī (H) n.f. A two-wheeled vehicle drawn by a pair of oxen.

بہم **baham** (P) *adv.* Together; one with another.

بہم آنا *baham ānā*, *v.* To be procured; to be acquired; to be obtained.

بہم پہنچانا *baham pahuṅchānā*, *v.* To supply; to provide; to procure; to acquire; to bring.

بہم پہنچنا *baham pahuṅchnā*, *v.* To be obtained, procured, supplied, or acquired; to arrive together; to come hand in hand.

بہم دگر *baham digar*, *adv.* Together; one with another.

بہم رسانی *baham rasānī*, *n.f.* Supply; procuration.

بھمبیری ، بھنبیری **bhambīrī**, **bhaṅbīrī** (H) *n.f.* A butterfly.

بھمبیری سا دوڑنا *bhambīrī sā dauṛnā*, *v.* To run swiftly (said of a child).

بہمن **bahman** (P) *adj./n.m.* Clever; intelligent; snow melting down from hills; eleventh month of the Persians; name of a herb.

بہن **bahan** (H) *n.f.* Sister.

بہنا **bahnā** (H) *v.* To flow; to float; to drift (with the stream); to be wasted; to melt; to dissolve; to run (as a sore).

بہناپا **bahnāpā** (H) *n.m.* Sisterhood; sisterly affection or kindness; sisterliness.

بھنانا **bhinnānā** (H) *v.* To have a ringing sound in the ears; to hum; to buzz; to be enraged; to be agitated.

بھنانا **bhunānā** (H) *v.* To cause to be fried or parched; to change a higher coin for lower ones; (same as بھنوانا *bhunwānā*).

بھنائی **bhunā'ī** (H) *n.f.* Price paid for parching; fee paid for exchange.

بھنبھنانا **bhiṅbhinānā** (H) *v.* To buzz; to hum; to speak through the nose.

بھنبھناہٹ **bhinbhināhaṭ** (H) *n.f.* Buzzing; humming; buzz.

بھنبھوڑنا **bhanbhoṛnā**, *v.* To gnaw; to bite; to devour.

بھنڈار **bhaṅḍār** (H) *n.m.* A storehouse; a water store; warehouse.

بھنڈارا **bhaṅḍārā** (H) *n.m.* Food given gratis; a feast of jogis, faqirs, &c.

بھنڈاری **bhaṅḍārī** (H) *n.m.* Owner of a storehouse; a storekeeper; a steward.

بھنڈی **bhiṅḍī** (H) *n.f.* A vegetable named lady's finger.

بھنک **bhanak** (H) *n.f.* A low distant sound; hum; an unauthentic news.

بھنک پڑنا *bhanak paṛnā*, *v.* To catch or hear the sound (of); to get wind of.

بھنکنا **bhinaknā**, *v.* To buzz; buzzing (of flies); to remain filthy; to sit idle.

بھنگ **bhaṅg** (H) *n.f.* Hemp; an intoxicating potion made from hemp-leaves.

بھنگا **bhungā** (H) *n.m.* An insect usually found in rainy season.

بھنگڑ **bhaṅgaṛ**, *n.m.* One addicted to drinking بھنگ *bhaṅg*; a talkative person.

بھنگڑا **bhaṅgaṛā**, **bhaṅgṛā** (H) *n.m.* Name of a herb; a wild care-free dance.

بھنگن **bhaṅgan** (H) *n.f.* A female sweeper; sweepress.

بھنگی **bhaṅgī** (H) *n.m.* A sweeper; a scavenger.

بہنگی **bahṅgī** (H) *n.f.* A thick bamboo stick, which is carried on the shoulder, with slings at both ends for carrying loads, as boxes, baskets, &c.

بھنوانا **bhunwānā** (H) *v.* To cause to be fried or parched; to have changed (money) (Same as بھنانا *bhunānā*).

بھنور **bhaṅwar** (H) *n.m.* A whirlpool; vortex; eddy; misfortune; grief.

بھنور جال *bhaṅwar jāl*, *n.m.* The world and its cares and snares.

بھنور میں پڑنا *bhaṅwar men paṛnā*, *v.* To be afflicted by misfortune or grief.

بہنوئی bahno'i (H) n.m. A brother-in-law (sister's husband).

بہنی buhnī. See بوھنی būhnī.

بہنیلا bahnelā (H) n.m. Sisterly affection; friendship among women.

بہنیلی bahnelī (H) n.f. A female friend (of a woman or a girl); an adopted sister.

بہو bahū (H) n.f. A daughter-in-law (son's wife); a bride; wife.

بہو بیٹیاں bahū beṭiyāṅ, n.f. Young female relatives as daughters; noble women; gentlewomen.

بھوانی bhawānī (S) n.f. A Hindu goddess; an epithet of the wife of Shiva.

بھو بھل bhūbhal (H) n.f. Hot ashes; embers.

بھوت bhūt (H) n.m. A demon; goblin; fiend; ghost; apparition; an evil spirit; an ugly or hideous looking person.

بھوت آتارنا bhūt utārnā, v. To exorcize; to drive away an evil spirit.

بھوت بننا ، چڑھنا یا سوار ھونا bhūt ban-nā, charhnā yā sawār honā, v. To behave like a devil; to be intoxicated; to be distracted with rage; to be enraged.

بھوت پریت bhūt paret, n.m. Ghosts and goblins.

بھوت ھونا bhūt honā, v. To look dirty or shabby; to behave like a devil.

بھوت ھو کر یا بن کر لپٹنا bhūt ho kar yā ban kar lipaṭnā, v. To cling (to one) like a devil or a ghost; to bore one to distraction.

بھوتنی bhūtnī. See بھتنی bhutnī.

بھوج bhoj (H) n.m. Eating; enjoying; feast; name of a tree.

بھوج پتر bhoj pattar, n.m. The leaf and the bark of a tree (a kind of birch) used for writing on, and making tubes and pipes for the huqqah.

بھوجن bhojan (H) n.m. Food; victuals; dish of food; meals; fried vegetables.

بھوچکا bhauchakkā. See بھونچکا baunchakkā.

بھور bhor (H) n.f. Dawn; day-break.

بھورا ، بھوری bhūrā, bhūrī (H) adj. Brown; auburn (as hair).

بھوسا bhūsā. See بھس bhus.

بھوسی bhūsī (H) n.f. Chaff; bran.

بھوک bhūk (H) n.f. Hunger; appetite; desire; need; want; lust.

بھوک پیاس مارنا bhūk pyās mārnā, v. To repress one's appetite; to mortify oneself.

بھوک مرنا bhūk marnā, v. To lose hunger or appetite.

بھوکوں مرنا bhūkoṅ marnā, v. To die of hunger; to famish; to starve to death

بھوکا ، بھوکی bhūkā, bhūki (H) adj. Hungry; famished; starving; needy; poor; fond; desirous.

بھوگنا bhognā (H) v. To enjoy; to bear; to suffer (con-equences of); to endure.

بھول bhūl (H) n.f. Forgetfulness; negligence; mistake; omission; oversight; fault; lapse.

بھول بھلیاں bhūl bhulayyāṅ, n.f. A labyrinth; a maze.

بھول چوک لینی دینی bhūl chūk leni deni. Errors and ommissions excepted.

بھول کے نہ کرنا bhūl ke nah karnā, v. Never to do a thing even by mistake or under any condition or circumstances.

بھولا ، بھولی bholā, bholī (H) adj. Simple; artless; undesigning; innocent; inexperienced; guileless.

بھولا پن یا بھولپن bholā pan yā bholpan, n.m. Simplicity; innocence; guilelessness; inexperience; innocent beauty.

بھولی باتیں bholi bāteṅ, n.f Simple or guileless talk or speech; innocent prattle.

بھولی صورت bholī ṣūrat, n.f. Simple or innocent face or looks.

بھولا بسرا ، بھولا چوکا ، بھولی بسری ، بھولی چوکی bhūlā bisrā, bhūlā chūkā, bhūlī bisrī, bhūlī chūkī (H) adj. Forgotten; gone astray; a cusual or chance visitor.

بھولا بھٹکا ، بھولی بھٹکی bhūlā bhaṭkā, bhūlī bhaṭkī (H) adj. One who has lost or missed the way.

بھولنا bhūlnā (H) v. To forget; to miss; to err; to be misled; to be deceived; to stray; to be deluded (by).

بھوم یا بھومی bhūm yā bhūmī (H) n.f. Land; the earh; site; place; country.

بھوں bhauṅ (H) n.f. The eyebrow.

بھویں تاننا ، چڑھانا bhaveṅ tān-na. charhānā, v. To raise the eyebrew; to knit the brow; to show anger.

بھون bhawan (S) n.m. A house; building; shrine.

بھونچال bhauṅchāl (H) n.m An earthquake.

بونچکا bhauṅchakkā (H) adj. Aghast; struck with amazement.

بھوندو bhoṅdū (H) adj. Simplton; artless; innocent; silly; stupid (fellow).

بھونڈا ، بھونڈی bhoṅḍā, bhoṅḍī (H) adj. Ugly; frightful; uncouth; misshaped; deformed; ill-looking.

بھونرا bhauṅrā (H) n.m. A large black bee enamoured of flowers; a moth.

بھونکنا bhauṅknā (H) v. To bark; to talk foolishly.

بھونکنا bhoṅknā (H) v. To thrust; to drive in; to pierce; to stab.

بھون کھانا bhūn khānā, v. To roast and eat; to squander; to waste money.

بھوننا bhūn-nā (H) v. To roast; to parch; to fry; to burn; to tease; to torment.

بھئی bha'ī, (Abbreviated form of بھائی) A mode of address.

بہی bahī (H) n.f. A ledger; a book of daily accounts; a diary.

بہی کھاتا bahī khātah, n.m. A ledger.

بہی پر چڑھانا bahī par charhānā, v. To enter in the account book.

بہی bihī (P) n.f. Quince; good; betterment.

بہی دانہ bihī dānah, n.m. Quince seed.

بہی خواہ bihī khwāh, adj. Well-wisher.

بھی bhī (H) adv. Also; too; even; moreover; likewise; as well as; as well.

بھیا bhayyā, n.m. Brother.

بھیانک bhayānak (H) adj. Frightful; formidable; terrible; dreadful; alarming; dismal; desolate.

بھیجا bhejā (H) n.m. The brain.

بھیجا کھانا bhejā khānā, id. To annoy or tease exceedingly; to bother one out of his patience.

بھیجا پک جانا bhejā pak jānā, id. To be bothered to the extent of head-ache.

بھیجنا bhejnā (H) v. To send; to remit; to despatch; to bestow; to grant; to utter; to transmit.

بھید bhed (H) n.m. A secret; secrecy; mystery; a clue; a riddle.

بھید پانا bhed pānā, v. To find out or discover a secret; to solve a mystery.

بھید دینا bhed denā, v. To give a clue; to betray a trust; to divulge a secret.

بھید رکھنا bhed rakhnā, v. To keep a secret.

بھید کھولنا bhed kholnā, v. To divulge a secret; to betray a confidence.

بھید لینا bhed lenā, v. To spy; to pry into; to find out a secret; to worm one-self into another's confidence.

بھیدی bhedī (H) adj.&n.m. One who knows a secret; a secret keeper; a confidant; a detective.

بھیروں bhairviṅ (H) n.f. A rāgni (tune) sung in the morning.

بھیڑ bhir (H) n.f. Crowd; multitude; press; throng.

بھیڑ بھاڑ، بھیڑ بھڑکا bhiṛ bhāṛ, bhīṛ bhrakkā, n.f./n.m. Mob; crowd; rush.

بھیڑ لگانا bhi ṛ lagānā, v. To collect people.

بھیڑ bheṛ (H) n.f. A sheep; an ewe.

بھیڑ چال bheṛ chāl, n.f. Following one another like sheep; blind imitation of another; blindly following another; blind following of custom.

بھیڑ کا گوشت bheṛ kā gosht, n.m. Mutton.

بھیڑا bheṛā (H) n.m. A ram.

بہیڑا baheṛā (H) n.m. Beleric myrobalan (see also بلیلہ balelah).

بھیڑیا bheryā (H) n.m. A wolf.

بھیس bhes (H) n.m. Appearance; form; air; feigned appearance; disguise; resemblance; guise; dress.

بھیس بدلنا bhes badalnā, v. To change one's appearance or garb; to counterfeit; to disguise oneself; to mimic.

بھیک bhīk (H) n.f. Charity; alms; begging.

بھیک کا ٹھیکرا bhīk kā thīkrā, n.m. Beggar's bowl.

بھیک مانگنا bhīk māṅgnā, v. To beg; to ask for alms.

بھیگنا bhīgnā (H) v. To be wet; to be drenched.

بھیل bhīl (H) n.m. The name of one aboriginal mountain tribe of India.

بھیلی bheli (H) n.f. A lump of گڑ gur.

بھیم bhīm (S) adj. Terrible; dreadful. n.m. The second brother of Yudhishtra.

بھینٹ bheṅṭ (H) n.f. Meeting; interview; a present; an offering; a sacrifice.

بھینچنا bhiṅchnā (H) v. To press; to crush; to squeeze; to force; to compel.

بھینس bhaiṅs (H) n.f. Buffalo (female).

بھینسا bhaiṅsā (H) n.m. Buffalo (male).

بھینسا داد bhaiṅsā dād, n.m. A kind of ring worm.

بھینگا bheṅgā, adj. & n.m. Squint-eyed; one who squints.

بھینگا پن bheṅgā pan, n.m. Squint.

بھینگی bheṅgi (H) Feminine form of بھینگا bheṅgā.

بی bī, n.f. (Abr. of بی بی) A lady; a vocative particle used in addressing females.

بی بی bī bī, n.f. A lady; a respectable woman; a virtuous woman; mistress of the house; a form of address used for mother, mother-in-law, sister or sister-in-law.

بے be. A vocative practicle used contemptuously for men; you fellow! you rascal.

بے be (P) A privative particle or preposition denoting "without" or "void of". When used as a prefix it forms compound words corresponding to the English words beginning with in; im; un; ir; etc., or ending with less.

بے آب be āb, adj. Without water; without lustre or temper.

بے آبرو be ābrū, adj. Dishonourable; shameless; disreputable.

بے آبروئی be ābrū'i, n.f. Disgrace; dishonour.

بے اتفاق be ittifāqī, n.f. Want of unity or harmony; discord.

بے اثر be āṣar, adj. Without impression or effect; ineffectual; inefficatious.

بے احتیاط be iḥtiyāṭ, adj. Incautious; indiscreet; improvident; imprudent; careless.

بے احتیاطی be iḥtiyāṭi, n.f. Incautiousness; improvidence; carelessness.

بے اختیار be ikhtiyār, adj. Without choice; involuntary; helpless; without control or authority.

بے اختیاری be ikhtiyāri, n.f. Helplessness; want of power; without choice.

بے ادب be adab, adj. Rude; unmannerly; impudent; disrespectful.

بے ادبی be adabi, n.f. Rudeness; impudence; disrespect.

بے آرام be ārām, adj. Restless; uneasy; uncomfortable.

بے اصل be aṣl, adj. Baseless; groundless; without foundation.

بے اعتبار be i'tibār, adj. Of no credit; not to be relied on; untrustworthy; unreliable.

بے اعتباری be i'tibāri, n.f. Discredit; mistrust; untrustworthiness.

بے اعتدال be i'tidāl, adj. Uneven; immoderate; intemperate.

بے اعتدالی be i'tidālī, n.f. Unevenness; immoderation; intemperance.

بے اعتقاد be i'tiqād, adj. Incredulous; faithless; disbelieving.

بے التفاتی be iltifātī, n.f. Want of regard; disregard; inconsiderateness; inattention; unconcern; indifference.

بے امتیاز be imtiyāz, adj. Indiscriminating; undistinguishing; rude; unmannerly.

بے امتیازی be imtiyāzi, n.f. Lack of discrimination; unmannerliless; incivility.

بے انتظامی be intiẓāmī, n.f. Mismanagement; misgovernment.

بے انتہا be intihā, adj. Infinite; endless; boundless.

بے اندازہ be aṅdāzah, adj. Unlimited; endless.

بے انصاف be inṣāf, adj. Unjust; unfair; iniquitous.

بے اولاد be aūlād, adj. Childless; issueless.

بے ایمان be imān, adj. Infidel; faithless; unprincipled; without conscience: dishonest; liar; cheat.

بے ایمانی کرنا be imānī karnā, v. To act dishonestly; to play false; to cheat; to misappropriate.

بے باق be bāq, adj. Leaving no arrears; paid up in full.

بے باق ہونا be bāq honā, v. To be paid in full; to be liquidated; settlement of accounts.

بے باک be bāk, adj. Fearless; bold; daring.

بے باکی be bāki, n.f. Boldness; temerity; fearlessness.

بے بال و پر be bāl-ŏ par, adj. Featherless; without resources; powerless; helpless; friendless; weak; pauper.

بے بدل be badal, adj. Matchless; unique; inestimable; incomparable.

بے بر be bar, adj Fruitless; barren.

بے برگ و بار be barg-ŏ bār, adj. Without leaves or fruit; destitute; fruitless.

بے بس be bas, adj. Without power or authority; helpless; weak.

بے بنیاد be bunyād, adj. Groundless; without foundation.

بے بہا be bahā, adj. Invaluable; very precious; unique; wonderful.

بے بہار be bahār, adj. Out of season.

بے بہرہ be bahrah, adj. Having no share or part; destitute; unfortunate; unsuccessful; deprived.

بے پایاں be pāyāṅ, adj. Boundless; very vast; endless.

بے پردگی be pardagī, n.f. Immodesty; unveiling; shamelessness; disclosure of a secret.

بے پردہ *be pardah, adj.* Unveiled; immodest; openly; exposed.

بے پروا *be parwā, adj.* Heedless; careless; improvident; above want; contented; thoughtless; unconcerned; indifferent.

بے پروائی *be parwā'i, n.f.* Carelessness; unconcern; indifference.

بے پیر *be pir, adj.* Unskilful; having no spiritual guide or leader; vicious; irreligious; non-believer; cruel; selfish.

بے تاب *be tāb, adj.* Powerless; restless; impatient.

بے تابانہ *be tābānah, adv.* Restlessly; unhesitatingly; hurriedly; impatiently.

بے تابی *be tābi, n.f.* Restlessness; impatience; agitation.

بے تاثیر *be tāṣir, adj.* Ineffectual; having no effect; useless.

بے تال *be tāl, adj.* Out of tune (*Music*); ill-timed.

بے تامل *be ta-ammul, adv.* Without deliberation; without hesitation; rashly; inconsiderate.

بے تحاشا *be taḥāshā, adv.* Rashly; recklessly; headlong; excessively.

بے تدبیر *be tadbir, adj.* Incautious; inconsiderate; without any plan; imprudent.

بے تعلق *be ta'lluq, adj.* Without connection; unconcerned.

بے تقصیر *be taqṣir, adj.* Innocent; blameless; faultless.

بے تکلف *be takalluf, adj.* Without ceremony; unceremonious; informal; frank.

بے تکلفی *be takallufi, n.f.* Frankness; informality; unceremonious.

بے تمیز *be tamiz, adj.* Lacking discrimination; indiscreet; unwise; rude; uncultured; incivil.

بے توجہ *be tawajjoh, adj.* Inattentive; inadvertent; unkind.

بے ٹھکانا *be ṭhikānā, adj.* Having no abode; wanderer; out of place; absurd; meaningless.

بے ثبات *be ṣabāt, adj.* Inconstant; unstable.

بے ثمر *be ṣamar, adj.* Fruitless; unfruitful; infructuous.

بے جا *be jā, adj.* Out of place; misplaced; improper; unlawful; unreasonable; useless; ill-timed.

بے جان *be jān, adj.* Lifeless; inanimate; rotten; dead.

بے جرم *be jurm, adj.* Innocent; faultless.

بے جوڑ *be jor, adj.* Disjointed; unmatched; unsuitable; inharmonious.

بے چارہ، بے چاری *be chārah, be chāri, adj.* Without remedy or resources; helpless; poor; miserable; unfortunate.

بے چراغ *be charāgh, adj.* Unlighted; dark; childless; desolate; unpopulated.

بے چون *be chūn, adj.* Matchless; unique.

بے چون و چرا *be chūn-ŏ chirā, adv.* Without any objection; without any hesitation; unwaveringly.

بے چین *be chain, adj.* Restless; uneasy.

بے چینی *be chaini, n.f.* Uneasiness; restlessness.

بے حال *be ḥāl, adj.* Out of condition; ill-circumstanced; unemployed; on the verge of death; indisposed; weary; miserable.

بے حالی *be ḥāli, n.f.* Badness of circumstances or condition; miserable plight.

بے حجاب *be ḥijāb, adj.* Unveiled; shameless; immodest; informal; open.

بے حجابانہ be ḥijābānah, *adv.* Openly; shamelessly; immodestly; informally.

بے حجابی be ḥijābi, *n.f.* Appearing unveiled; immodesty.

بے حد be ḥadd, *adj.* Boundless; endless.

بے حرکت be ḥarakat, *adj.* Immovable; immobile; motionless; still.

بے حرمت be ḥurmat, *adj.* Disgraced; molested.

بے حرمتی be ḥurmati, *n.f.* Disgrace; molestation.

بے حس be his, *adj.* Insensible; senseless.

بے حساب be ḥisāb, *adj.* Countless; beyond calculation; unlimited; excessive.

بے حوصلہ be ḥauṣalah, *adj.* Lacking ambition; dispirited; spiritless.

بے حیا be ḥayā, *adj.* Shameless; immodest; impudent; bare-faced.

بے خار be k͟hār, *adj.* Without thorns; without anxiety or fear; youngster; lad.

بے خان و مان be k͟hān-ŏ mān, *adj.* Having no abode; homeless; destitute.

بے خبر be k͟habar, *adj.* Uninformed; without notice; ignorant; stupid; negligent; neglectful; careless.

بے خطا be k͟haṭā, *adj.* Faultless; blameless; innocent.

بے خطر be k͟haṭar, *adj.* Free from danger; safe; fearless.

بے خواب be k͟hawāb, *adj.* Sleepless.

بے خوابی be k͟hwābī, *n.f.* Sleeplessness.

بے خود be k͟hud, *adj.* Beside one's self; out of one's mind; in ecstasy; enraptured; transported; delirious; senseless; intoxicated.

بے خودی be k͟hūdi, *n.f.* Ecstasy; rapture; delirium; senselessness.

بے داد be dād, *n.f.* Iniquity; injustice; oppression; violence. *adj.* Unjust; lawless; not doing justice

بے داغ be dāgh, *adj.* Spotless; without blemish; faultless; innocent.

بے دال کا بودم be dāl kā būdam, *n.m.* A fool; a blockhead; an idiot.

بے دانش be dānish, *adj.* Ignorant; idiot; foolish.

بے دانہ be dānah, *adj.* Seedless. *n.f.* Mulberry fruit.

بے دخل کرنا be dak͟hl karnā, *v.* To eject; to evict; to dispossess.

بے درد be dard, *adj.* Feelingless; void of compassion; pitiless; merciless.

بے درمان be darmān, *adj.* Incurable; having no remedy.

بے درنگ be drang, *adv.* Without delay; at once. *adj.* Clever.

بے دریغ be daregh, *adv.* Readily; rashly; ungrudgingly. *adj.* Without regret or hesitation; generous; bount ful.

بے دست و پا be dast-ŏ-pā, *adj.* Without hands or feet; crippled; helpless; without power or authority; resourceless.

بے دل be dil, *adj.* Dispirited; dissatisfied; displeased; dejected; sad; melancholy; fearless; crave.

بے دلی be dili, *n.f.* Dejection; dissatisfaction; heartlessness.

بے دم be dam, *adj.* Breathless; lifeless; very old; fatigued; indolent.

بے دماغ be dimāgh, *adj.* Ill-tempered; impatient; irritable; easily provoked; sensitive.

بے دوا be dawā, *adj.* Incurable; beyond cure or remedy.

بے دھڑک be dharak, *adv.* Readily; fearlessly; rashly. *adj.* Without fear or hesitation; fearless; bold.

بے دین be din, adj. Irreligious; without faith.

بے ڈول ba ḍaul, adj. Shapeless; ungainly; ugly; disproportionate; ill-bred; unpleasant.

بے ڈھب be dhab, adj. Ill-shaped; ugly; unmannerly; awkward.

بے ذوق be ẕaūq, adj. Without relish or desire for; having no appreciation or taste (for fine arts); inappreciative; tasteless; insipid.

بے ذوقی be ẕaūqi, n.f. Tastelessness; Insipidity.

بے راہ be rāh, adj. Erring; astray; unprincipled; dissolute.

بے ربط be rabṭ, adj. Irregular; contrary to rule; unconnected; inconsistant; incongruous; out of practice.

بے رحم be raḥm, adj. Merciless; pitiless; cruel.

بے رحمی be raḥmi, n.f. Cruelty; tyranny.

بے روک ٹوک be rok ṭok, adv. Without hindrance.

بے ریا be riyā, adj. Without guile; guileless, candid; sincere; without any show or formality.

بے ریائی be riyā'ī, n.f. Sincerity; candour.

بے ریش be rish, adj. Beardless; inexperienced; simpleton.

بے ریشہ be reshah, adj. Without fibre; fibreless.

بے زار be zār, adj. Disgusted; displeased; sick of

بے زبان be zabān, adj. Dumb; mute; quiet; speechless; modest; helpless.

بے زبانی be zabāni, n.f. Inability to speak; speechlessness; dumbness.

بے زر be zar, adj. Without money; destitute; poor.

بے زن و فرزند be zan-ŏ farzand, adj. Without wife and children; unmarried.

بے زور be zor, adj. Weak; impotent; powerless.

بے زیب و زینت be zeb-ŏ zinat, adj. Ugly and awkward; inelegant in dress and person.

بے زین be zin, adj. Unsaddled.

بے ساختگی be sākhtagi, n.f. Artlessness; simplicity; undisguised or unstudied conduct; straightforwardness.

بے ساختہ be sākhtah, adj. Plain; undisguised; unaffected; natural; artless. adv. Spontaneously; of its own accord; extempore; impromptu.

بے ساز be sāz, adj. Without apparatus, tools, &c.

بے سامانی be sāmāni, n.f. Want of apparatus or necessities; poverty.

بے سبب be sabab, adj. Without cause or reason.

بے سخن be sukhan, adj. Taciturn; quiet; unable to keep his word.

بے سرا be surā, adj. Out of tune.

بے سروپا be sar-ŏ-pā, adj. Without head or tale; absurd; baseless; helpless; friendless; unreliable.

بے سر و سامان be sar-ŏ sāmān, adj. Pauper; unprovided; helpless; destitute of necessities of life; without apparatus.

بے سلیقہ be saliqah, adj. Unmethodical; impolite; awkward; unmannerly.

بے شرم be sharm, adj. Shameless; immodest; impudent.

بے شعور be sho'ūr, adj. Blockhead; ignorant; stupid; unmannerly.

بے شک و شبہ be shak-ŏ shubah, adv. Undoubtedly; certainly.

بے شمار be shumār, adj. Countless; numberless; innumerable; much.

بے صبر be ṣabr, adj. Devoid of patience; impatient; restless.

بے صبری be ṣabri, n.f. Impatience; restlessness.

بے ضابطہ be ẓābiṭah, adj. Irregular; unlawful; unmethodical.

بے طاقت be ṭāqat, adj. Powerless; weak; without power of endurance.

بے طاقتی be ṭāqati, n.f. Weakness; inability to endure.

بے عدل be 'adl, adj. Unjust; partial.

بے عزت be 'izzat, adj. Without honour or respect; disgraceful.

بے عقل be aql, adj. Stupid; unwise; senseless.

بے علت be 'illat, adj. Without any cause; causeless.

بے عیب be 'aib, adj. Faultless; unblemished; pure.

بے غرض be gharaẓ, adj. Disinterested; selfless; impartial.

بے غل و غش be ghill-ō ghash, adv. Without trouble or anxiety; indifferently; blindly.

بے غم be gham, adj. Without sorrow or grief; happy.

بے غور و فکر be ghaur-o fikr, adv. Without consideration; without premeditation.

بے غیرت be ghairat, adj. Shameless; wanton; impudent.

بے فائدہ be fā'idah, adj. Unprofitable; useless; in vain; of no consequence.

بے فکر be fikr, adj. Free from care or anxiety; contented; thoughtless; unreflecting; inconsiderate.

بے فکری be fikri, n.f. Freedom from care; contentedness; unconcern.

بے فیض be faiẓ, adj. Unprofiting; ungiving; possessing but not bestowing; miserly.

بے قابو be qābū, adj. Out of one's power or reach; having no restraint or control over; uncontrollable.

بے قاعدہ be qā'idah, adj. Irregular; unarranged; ungrammatical; against rules or regulations.

بے قدر be qadr, adj. Worthless; unimportant; one not giving proper esteem; ungrateful.

بے قرار be qarār, adj. Uneasy; restless: anxious; disturbed in mind; unsettled; variable; impatient.

بے قصور be quṣūr. adj. Innocent; faultless; not guilty.

بے قیاس be qayās, adj. Inconceivable; contrary to common order of things; incomprehensible; immense; limitless.

بے کار be kār, adj. Unemployed; idle; useless; unserviceable.

بے کاری be kāri, n.f. Unemployment; idleness.

بے کار کرنا be kār karnā, v. To render useless or unserviceable.

بے کراں be karān, adj. Boundless; shoreless; immense; enormous.

بے کس be kas, adj. Friendless; lonely; forlorn; destitute.

بے کسی be kasi, n.f. Friendlessness; destitution; helplessness; loneliness.

بے کفن be kafan, adj. Without a shroud; unshrouded.

بے کل be kal, adj. Restless; uneasy; disturbed.

بے کم و کاست be kam-ō kāst, adj. Accurate; exact; without any decrease: without omission.

بے کھٹکے be khatke, adv. Without apprehension or doubt.

بے گمان be gumān, adj. Without doubt or suspicion; doubtless.

بے گناہ be gunāh, adj. Innocent; guiltless.

بے لحاظ be lihaz, adj. Shameless; indiscreet; unmannerly; impertinent.

بے لطف be lutf, adj. Without pleasure; insipid; flavourless; unpleasant.

بے لطفی be lutfi, n.f. Insipidness; unpleasantness.

بے لگام be lagām, adj. Unbridled (horse); licentious; intemperate.

بے لگاؤ be lagā'o, adj. Unconnected; independent; candid.

بے مایہ be māyah, adj. Without resources; poor.

بے مایگی be mayagi, n.f. Poverty; indigence.

بے مثل be m sl, adj. Unique; incomparable; unparalleled; unequalled.

بے محاسبہ be muhāsabah adj. Unaccountable; irresponsible; without calculation. adv. Unaccountably.

بے محل be mahal, adj. Out of place; improper.

بے مروت be murawwat, adj. Unkind; uncivil; inhuman; impolite.

بے مزا be mazā, adj. Tasteless; insipid.

بے معنی be ma'ni, adj. Meaningless; absurd; foolish.

بے مقدور be maqdūr, adj. Without authority; without resources; poor.

بے منت be minnat, adj. Independent; unwilling to incur obligation.

بے موسم be mausim, adj. Out of season; unseasonable.

بے موقع be mauqā', adj. Out of place; untimely; improper; inopportune; inconvenient.

بے مہر be mihr, adj. Unkind; unfriendly; wanting in affection.

بے نام be nām, adj. Without name, character or reputation; inglorious.

بے نام و نشان be nām-ŏ nishān, adj. Without name or identity; unknown.

بے نصیب be nasib, adj. Unfortunate; frustrated; deprived.

بے نصیبی be nasibi, n.f. Misfortune; bad luck.

بے نظیر be nazir, adj. Matchless; incomparable; unequalled; unique; peerless.

بے نمک be namak, adj. Without salt; saltless; insipid; unattractive; ordinary.

بے ننگ be nang, adj. Shameless; immodest.

بے ننگ و ناموس be nang-ŏ nāmūs, adj. Immodest; characterless; inglorious.

بے نوا be nawā, adj. Indigent; destitute; beggar.

بے نور be nūr, adj. Without light; dark.

بے نیاز be niyāz, adj. Without want; not in need of anything; independent; carefree.

بے وجہ be wajh, adj. Without cause.

بے وزن be wazn, adj. Unmeasured.

بے وطن be watan, adj. Without country; homeless.

بے وفا be wafā, adj. Faithless; perfidious; treacherous; ungrateful.

بے وفائی be wafā'i, n.f. Faithlessness; ingratitude.

بے وقار be waqār, adj. Undignified; dishonourable.

بے وقت be waqt, adj. Out of season; untimely; ill-timed.

بے وقوف be waqūf, adj. Foolish; stupid; dolt.

بے وقوف بنانا be waqūf banānā, v. To make a fool (of); to make fun (of); to ridicule.

بے وقوفی be waqūfi, n.f. Foolishness; stupidity; want of understanding.

بے همت be himmat, adj. Unambitious; unaspiring; indolent; lazy; slothful; coward; pusillanimous.

بے هنر be hunar, adj. Unskilful; unaccomplished; unskilled.

بے هنگم be hangam, adj. Unsuitable; ugly.

بے هودگی be hūdagi, n.f. Absurdity; foolishness; folly; frivolity; ill-manners.

بے هوده be hūdah, adj. Absurd; foolish; idle; frivolous; unprofitable; fruitless; vagabond; obscene,

بے هوده گو be hūdah go, adj. One who talks nonsense; uncultured; a foul-mouthed fellow; a babbler; an idle talker.

بے هوده گوئی be hūdah go'ī, n.f. Idle talk; talking nonsense; absurdity.

بے هوش be hosh, adj. Unconscious; senseless; insensible; stupefied.

بے هوشی be hoshi, Unconsciousness; senselessness.

بیا bayā, n.m. The weaver bird.

بیابان bayābān (P) n.m. Desert; wilderness.

بیابان گرد یا نورد bayābān gard yā navard, n.m. One traversing deserts; a wanderer.

بیابان قدس bayābān-ĕ quds, n.m. The desert of Jerusalem.

بیابانی bayābāni (P) adj. Of the desert; wild; a wanderer.

بیاج byāj (H) n.m. Interest; usury.

بیاج پر بیاج byāj par byāj, n.m. Compound interest.

بیاج خور byāj khor, n.m. A usurer; one who takes interest.

بیاج خوری byāj khori, n.f. Usury.

بیاسی byāsi (H) adj. Eighty-two.

بیاض bayāẓ (A) n.f. Whiteness; a note book; an account book; a commonplace book; a note book in which a poet writes his verses.

بیالیس byālis (H) adj. Forty-two.

بیان bayān (A) n.m. Statement; declaration; assertion; account; allegation; description.

بیان بدلنا bayān badalnā, v. To change one's statement; to prevaricate; to go back upon one's statement.

بیان دینا bayān denā, v. To make a statement; to declare.

بیان کرنا bayān karna, v. To relate; to describe; to recount; to state.

بیانا biyānā (H) v. To bring forth; to give birth to (applied to animals).

بیاہ biyāh (H) n.m. Marriage; wedlock.

بیاہ رچانا biyāh rachānā, v. To celebrate a marriage.

بیاہ کرنا biyāh karnā, v. To marry.

بیاہ لانا biyāh lānā, v. To bring home a wife.

بیاھا ' بیاھی biyāhā, biyāhī (H) adj. Married.

بیاھتا biyāhtā (H) n.f. Married woman; wife.

بیاھنا biyāhnā (H) v. To marry, to give in marriage.

بیت bait (A) n.m. Abode; house. n.f. A couplet or verse (in poetry).

بیت اللہ Baitullah, n.m. The House of Allah at Mecca.

بیت الحرام *Bait-ul-ḥarām, n.m.* The sacred House; the Ka'ba.

بیت الحزن *bait-ul-ḥuzn, n.m* House of Sorrow; the house in which Jacob used to bewail Joseph's separation.

بیت الخلا *bait-ul-khalā, n.m.* Water closet; a privy; a lavatory.

بیت السقر *bait-ul-saqar, n.m.* The infernal abode; hell.

بیت السلاح *bait-us-salāḥ, n.m.* Magazine; an armoury.

بیت الصنم *bait-uṣ-ṣanam, n.m.* An idol temple; (Met.) the abode of the beloved.

بیت العتیق *Bait-ul-'atiq, n.m.* The oldest House, the Ka'ba.

بیت العروس *bait-ul-'urūs, n.m.* Bride's house; a new house build for the bride.

بیت العلوم *bait-ul-'ulūm, n.m.* A college; a university.

بیت العنکبوت *bait-ul-'ankabūt, n.m.* A spider's web.

بیت العوام *bait-ul-'awām, n.m.* House of Commons.

بیت الامرا *bait-ul-umarā, n.m.* House of Lords.

بیت الغزل *bait-ul-ghazal, n.m.* The best verse of an ode.

بیت اللحم *Bait-ul-lahm, n.m.* The birth place of Christ.

بیت المال *bait-ul-māl, n.m.* Public exchequer; public treasury.

بیت المعمور *bait-ul-m'amūr, n.m.* An inhabited house; mosque in Heaven over the Ka'ba.

بیت المقدس *Bait-ul-muqaddas, n.m.* The temple of Jerusalem.

بیت بندی *bait bandi, n.f.* Versification.

بیتال *baitāl* (H) *n.m.* A ghost; a goblin; an evil spirit.

بیتال پچیسی *baitāl pachchisi, n.m.* A Hinid work containing twenty-five tales related by a goblin.

بیتنا *bitnā* (H) *v.* To happen; to elapse; to pass; to expire; to become a thing of the past; to befall.

بیٹ *bit* (H) *n.f.* Dung (of birds); a factitious salt containing sulphur.

بیٹا *beṭā* (H) *n.m.* A son; a child; a boy.

بیٹا بنانا ، بیٹا گود لینا *beṭā banānā, beṭā god lenā, v.* To adopt a son.

بیٹا بیٹی *beṭā beṭi, n.m.* Children; offspring.

بیٹے والا *beṭe wālā, n.m.* Father of the bridegroom.

بیٹھک *baiṭhak* (H) *n.f.* Act or state of sitting; posture; a seat; a room reserved for meeting people; a sitting room; an exercise; kind of a sitting of a committee.

بیٹھ جانا ، بیٹھنا *baiṭh jānā, baiṭhnā* (H) *v.* To sit down; to perch; to subside; to be idle; to be unemployed; to collaps (a house).

بیٹھواں *baiṭhwān, adj.* Flat; having a flat bottom.

بیٹھے بٹھائے ، بیٹھے بیٹھے *baiṭhe biṭhāe, baiṭhe baiṭhe, adv.* Suddenly; abruptly; unexpectedly; unjustly.

بیٹی *beṭi* (H) *n.f.* Daughter.

بیج *bīj* (H) *n.m.* Seed; germ; origin; source.

بیج بونا ، بیج ڈالنا *bij bonā, bij ḍālnā, v.* To sow seed; to sow the seed (of).

بیج دار ، بجیلا *bij dār, bijīlā, adj.* Seedy; full of seeds.

بیج مارنا *bij mārnā, v.* To destroy; to annihilate.

بیجنا *bijnā* (H) *n.m.* A fan.

بیچ bich (H) n.m. Middle; centre; midst; interval; average; difference; distance. adv. In; into; among; between; during.

بیچا بیچ bechā bich, adv. In the very middle; in the centre; in the midst of.

بیچ بچاؤ bich bachāo, n.m. Intervention; mediation; arbitration, interposition; settlement.

بیچ بچاؤ کرنا bich bachāo karnā, v. To intervene; to interpose; to mediate; to settle.

بیچ کا bich kā, adj. Central; middling; mean; average; medium.

بیچ میں پڑنا bich meṅ paṛnā, v. To act as an arbitrator; to take for responsibility; to be surety for; to intervene.

بیچ کی آنگلی bich kī uṅglī, n.f. Middle finger.

بیچک ، بیجک bichak, bījak (H) n.m. Invoice; a list of goods detailing rate, the price of each article, and the total amount.

بیچ کھانا bech khānā, v. To waste; to squander property.

بیچنا bechnā (H) v. To sell; to dispose of; to transfer.

بیچنے کے لائق bechne ke lā'iq, adj. Saleable; negotiable.

بیچنے والا bechne wālā, n.m. Seller; vendor.

بیخ bekh (P) n.f. Root; origin; foundation; lineage.

بیخ کن bekh kan, adj. One who roots out; an extirpator; an exterminator.

بیخ کنی bekh kanī, n.f. Extirpation; extermination; eradication.

بیخ کنی کرنا bekh kanı karnā, v. To root out; to extirpate; to extreminate; to eradicate.

بید baid. See وید waid.

بید bed. See وید wed.

بید bed (P) n.m. A cane; a willow.

بید باف bed bāf, n.m. A basket maker; weaver of bottoms of chairs.

بید کی طرح کانپنا bed kī ṭaraḥ kāṅpnā, v. To tremble with fear (like a willow).

بید مارنا bed mārnā, v. To cane; to beat with a cane; to flog.

بید مجنوں bed-ĕ mājnūṅ, n.m. A species of willow.

بید مشک bed mushk, n.m. Musk willow celebrated for its fragrance.

بیدار bedār (P) adj. Awake; watchful; wakeful; vigilant.

بیدار بخت bedār bakht, adj. Fortunate; lucky.

بیدار مغز bedār maghz, adj. Intelligent; clever; cute.

بیداری bedāri (P) n.f. Wakefulness; alertness.

بیدانت bedānt. See ویدانت vedānt.

بیدانتی bedāntī. See ویدانتی wedāntī.

بیدک baidak. See ویدک waidak.

بیدک bedak. See ویدک wedak.

بیر bīr (S) n.m. A hero. adj. Brave; gallant (same as ویر wir).

بیر bir (H) n.m. A brother.

بیر bair (S) n.m. Enmity; hostility; ill-will; malice; animosity; revenge.

بیر باندھنا ، کرنا یا رکھنا bair bāndhnā, karnā yā rakhnā, v. To have a grudge (against); to bear malice; to hate.

بیر لینا یا نکالنا bair lenā yā nikālnā, v. To take revenge; to retaliate.

بیر ber (H) n.m. A kind of fruit.

بیرا bairā (corr. of English) n.m. Bearer; table servant.

بیراگ bairāg (H) n.m. Act of renouncing pleasures of the world; seculsion from world; austerity; penance.

بیراگی bairagi (H) *n.m.* An ascetic; a devotee; a recluse; one who has subdued his worldly desires and passions.

بیر بہوٹی bir bahūṭi (H) *n.f.* An insect with a red velvet-like skin coat; scarlet or lady-fly.

بیرن bairan (H) *n.f.* A female enemy.

بیرنگ bairang (corr. of English) *adj.* Bearing; postage unpaid.

بیروں berūṅ (P) *prep.* Without; on the out-side; out.

بیروں جات berūṅ jāt, *n.m.* Suburbs; country side.

بیروں جاتی berūṅ jāti, *adj.* Rustic; rural; belonging to a village or to the country. *n.m.* A countryman.

بیرونی berūni (P) *adj.* Outer; external.

بیری bairī (H) *n.m.* Enemy; foe; adversary.

بیری beri (H) *n.m.* A kind of tree (jujube).

بیڑا beṛā (H) *n.m.* A big boat; fleet; enclosure; courtyard.

بیڑا پار لگانا beṛā pār lagānā, *v.* To ferry over a raft or boat; to relieve from distress; to remove difficulties.

بیڑا پار ہونا beṛā pār honā, *v.* Arrival of a boat or ship safely at its destination; to tide over a difficulty; to gain one's object or end.

بیڑا biṛā (H) *n.m.* A betel-leaf prepared with all its accessories (often exchanged amongst the Rajputs as a challenge).

بیڑا اٹھانا biṛā uṭhānā, *v.* To take up the gauntlet; to undertake to accomplish a business; to accept responsibility for.

بیڑا ڈالنا biṛā ḍālnā, *v.* To propose a premium for the performance of a difficult or hazardous task. The custom was to throw a *biṛā* in the midst of an assembly as an open invitation to any person to undertake some hazardous enterprise, and the person who picked up the *biṛā* was bound to perform that undertaking.

بیڑی beṛī (H) *n.f.* Irons fastened to the legs of criminals or to the legs of quadrupeds; fetters; a basket used to irrigate fields with; a boat.

بیڑیاں پڑنا beṛiyān paṛnā, *v.* To be put in irons; to be chained.

بیڑیاں ڈالنا beṛiyāṅ ḍālnā, *v.* To put in chains; to put fetters on.

بیڑیاں کاٹنا beṛiyāṅ kāṭnā, *v.* To take off the chains; to set free.

بیڑی biṛi (H) *n.f.* A piece of betel-leaf with all its accessories; a kind of inferior cigarette.

بیز bez (P) (in *comp.*). Sifting; dispersing; diffusing.

بیزار bezār (P) *adj.* Disgusted; out of humour; angry; displeased; sick.

بیزاری bezārī (P) *n.f.* Disgust; bad humour; anger; displeasure.

بیس bīs (H) *adj.* Twenty.

بیساکھ Baisākh (H) *n.m.* The first month of the Hindu calendar (April-May).

بیساکھی baisākhi, *n.f.* The fair held on the first day of *baisākh*.

بیستوں besutūṅ (P) *n.m.* Name of a famous mountain in Persia which *Farhād* excavated at the command of his mistress *Shiriṅ*.

بیسر besar (H) *n.f.* A small nose-ring.

بیسن besan, *n.m.* Flour of grams; meal of gram.

بیسنی روٹی besani roṭi, *n.f.* Bread made of wheat and gram flour proportionately mixed.

بیسوا beswā (H) *n.f.* Prostitute; harlot; whore

بیسواں biswāṅ (H) *adj.* Twentieth.

بیسوں bisoṅ (H) *adj.* Scores; endless number; countless.

بیسی bisi (H) *n.f.* A score; twenty; a measure for grain.

بیش besh (P) *adj.* More; better; superior; excellent; good.

بیش از بیش *besh az besh, adj.* Very much; a great deal.

بیش‌بہا یا بیش قیمت *besh bahā yā besh qīmat, adj.* Precious; costly.

بیشتر *beshtar, adj. & adv.* Mostly; often; for the most part; greater; better.

بیشہ *beshah* (P) *n.m.* A forest; a desert; wilderness.

بیشی *beshi* (P) *n.f.* Increase; surplus; excess.

بیشئ لگان *beshi-ĕ lagān, n.f.* Enhancement of rent (revenue).

بیض *baiẓ* (A) *n.m.* Signature; a mark fixed to public writings by the magistrate or any principal officer.

بیضا *baiẓā* (A) *adj.* White; bright.

بیضاوی *baiẓāwi* (A) *n.f.* Name of a book containing a commentary on the holy Quran and also the title of the author.

بیضوی *baiẓawi* (A) *adj.* Fashioned in the shape of an egg; oval.

خط بیضوی *khaṭ-ĕ baiẓawi, n.m.* A form of the Persian *nasta'liq* character in which the curved tails of letter are segments of an oval.

بیضہ *baiẓah* (A) *n.m.* An egg; a testicle.

بیطار *beṭār* (A) *n.m.* A farrier; a horse-doctor; a veterinary doctor.

بیع *bai'* (A) *n.f.* Sale; buying and selling.

بیع پٹا *bai' paṭṭā, n.m.* Lease or sub-lease obtained by (purchase).

بیع جائز *bai' jā'iz, n.f.* Valid sale.

بیع دار *bai' dār, n.m.* Proprietor by purchase; a possessor by purchase; a purchaser.

بیع سازشی *bai' sāzishi, n.f.* Collusive or deceitful sale.

بیع سلطانی *bai' sulṭāni, n.f.* Sale by order of government.

بیع فاسد *bai' fāsid, n.f.* Sale which is nul and void.

بیع کرنا *bai' karnā, v.* To sell; to transfer.

بیع مطلق *bai' mutlaq, n.f.* Absolute sale.

بیع ناقص *bai' nāqiṣ, n.f.* Imperfect sale.

بیع ناجائز *bai' nā jā'iz, n.f.* Illegal sale.

بیع نامہ *bai' nāmah, n.m.* Sale-deed.

بیعانہ *bai'ānah* (A & P) *n.m.* Earnest money in a sale transaction.

بیعت *bai'at* (A) *n.f.* Fealty; homage.

بیعت کرنا *bai'at karnā, v.* To become the disciple of a saint, etc.; to take the oath of allegiance.

بیگ *baig* (E) *n.m.* Bag.

بیگ *beg* (T) *n.m.* Mughal title corresponding to English "Lord"; master.

بیگار *begār* (H) *n.m.* Forced labour; compulsory labour with or without payment.

بیگار پکڑنا *begār pakaṛnā, v.* To compel one to serve with or without pay.

بیگار ٹالنا *begār ṭālnā, v.* To work in a perfunctory manner; to work carelessly.

بیگاری *begāri, n.m.* Forced labourer; one compelled to work without payment; one working carelessly or perfunctorily.

بیگانگی *begānagi* (P) *n.f.* Strangeness; irrelation; not being related or aquainted.

بیگانہ *begānah* (P) *adj.* A stranger; a foreigner; an alien; not related; allen; foreign.

بیگانہ خو begānah kho, adj. Of an unfriendly or callous disposition.

بیگانہ وار begānah wār, adj. Like a stranger or alien; rough; apathetic.

بیگانہ وضع begānah waẓa', adj. Having queer manners; strange-mannered.

بیگم begam (T) n.f. Lady; wife; queen; title of Mughal ladies.

بیگمی begamī, n.m. & adj. A kind of superior rice; a fine betel-leaf.

بیگھا bighā (H) n.m. A measure of land equal to 120 square feet.

بیل bel (P) n.m. A spade; a shovel; a mattock.

بیلدار bel dār, n.m. One who uses a spade; a digger.

بیل bel (H) n.f. A creeping plant; a creeper; climber; generation; descendants; offsprings; tape; embroidery; a tip given to dancing girls or singer.

بیل بوٹا bel būṭā, n.m. Shrubs and creepers; embroidery.

بیل دار bel dār, adj. Embroidered; engraved.

بیل منڈھے چڑھنا bel manḍhe chaṛhnā, id. To achieve one's object; to succeed; to flourish; to prosper.

بیل bail (H) n.m. A bull; bullock; an ox; a blockhead; a fool.

بیل گاڑی bail gāṛī, n.f. A bullock-cart.

بیلا belā (H) n.m. Land locked by water; a forest along the bank of a river; name of a musical instrument resembling a fiddle; a species of jesamine; money distributed among the poor, as charity on the occasion of a marriage.

بیلا بٹنا belā baṭnā, v. To give alms; to give charity to the poor.

بیلا بردار belā bardār, n.m. One of the retinue of a great man who distributes money among the poor.

بیلچہ belchah, n.m. A spade; a hoe; a mattock.

بیلن belan (H) n.m. A rolling pin; a roller.

بیلنا belnā (H) n.m. A rolling pin. v. To spread out; to roll the flour into a flat cake.

بیلنی belnī (H) n.f. A small rolling pin.

بیلی beli (H) n.m. Guardian; protector; helper; friend; companion.

بیم bim (P) n.m. Fear; terror; dread; danger.

بیمار bimār (P) adj. Sick; ill; ailing; indisposed; unwell. n.m. Sick person; a patient.

بیمار پرسی کرنا bīmār pursī karnā, v. Visiting the sick; enquiring after the sick.

بیمار خانہ bīmār khānah, n.m. Hospital; infirmary.

بیمار دار bīmār dār, n.m. A nurse; an attendant on the sick.

بیمار داری bīmār dārī, n.f. Nursing the sick person; attandance on the sick.

بیماری bimārī (P) n.f. Sickness; indisposition; illness; ailment; disease.

بیمہ bimah (P) n.m. Insurance; money paid for the insurance of goods; rate of insurance.

بیمہ بیچنے والا bimah bechne wālā, n.m. Insurer; underwriter.

بیمۂ بحری bimah-ĕ baḥrī, n.m. Marine insurance.

بیمۂ جان یا زندگی bīmah-ĕ jān yā zindagī, n.m. Life insurance.

بیمہ کرنا bimah karnā, v. To effect an insurance; to insure.

بیمہ کی سند bimah kī sanad, n.f. Policy of insurance.

بیمہ کی قسط bimah kī qisṭ, n.f. Premium.

بیں bīṅ (P) adj. (in comp.). Seeing; beholding; looking.

بین bīn (H) n.f. A flute made of dried gourd used by snake charmers; a wind instrument; a bag-pipe.

بین bain (...) n.m. Sound; word; lamentation; wailing (for the dead).

بین bain (A) prep. Among; between.

بین الاقوامی bain-al-aqwāmi, adj. International.

بین براعظمی bain-a barrĕa'zami, adj. Intercontinental.

بین بین bain bain, adj. Between good and evil; betwixt and between; middling; passable; tolerable.

بین السطور bain-as-saṭūr, n.m. Distance between two lines; between the lines.

بین المحکماتی bain-al-maḥkamāti, adj. Inter-departmental.

بین الممالک bain-al-mamālik, adj. Inter-dominions.

بین النجوم bain-nan-nujūm, adj. Inter-planetary.

بین bayyin (A) adj. Apparent; clear; lucid, well-exposed.

بینات bayyināt (A) n.m. (plu. of بینہ bayyinah) Clear arguments; clear proofs.

بینا bīnā (P) adj. Clear-sighted; discerning; observer; wise.

بینا کرنا bīnā karnā, v. To cause to see; to give sight to; to confer discernment to.

بینائی bīnā'ī (P) n.f. Sight; vision; eye-sight.

بیندھنا bindhnā (H) v. To bore; to perforate; to say cutting things to.

بینڈی binḍi (H) n.f. The hair twisted or plaited behind; braided hair.

بینش bīnish (P) n.f. Seeing; discernment.

بینگن baingan (H) n.m. The egg plant and its fruit; brinjal.

بیننا bīn-nā (H) v. To pick; to glean to gather; to select.

بینی bīnī (P) n.f. The nose; the guard of a sword.

بینی بریدہ bīnī buridah, adj. Having the nose cut; a nose-cliped person.

بیوپار beopār (H) n.m. Trade; business; traffic.

بیوپاری beopāri (H) n.m. Merchant; trader; dealer.

بیوت buyūt (H) n.m. (plu. of بیت bait) Houses.

بیونت biyont (H) n.m. The act of cutting out clothes; cut; shape; fashion; plan; agreement; economy.

بیونتنا biyontnā (H) v. To cut clothes.

بیوگی bevagī (P) n.f. Widowhood.

بیوہ bevah (P) n.f. A widow (plu. بیوگان bevagān, widows).

بیوی bīwī, n.f. Wife; married woman.

بیوی کا غلام bīwī kā ghulām, n.m. Henpecked; domineered over by one's wife.

بیہڑ behaṛ (H) n.m. Uncultivated and uneven land; rough or rugged land; sterile land; forest.

پ pe, is the third letter of Urdu and Persian alphabets. It does not occur in the Arabic alphabet, but the letter (ف fe) is generally substituted for it in Persian words adopted into the Arabic language, as fārsī for the word pārsī. In reckoning by 'abjad' pe is the same as ب and is equal to 2.

پا pā. A suffix denoting abstract quality, as بڑھاپا buṛhāpā, old age from بوڑھا būṛhā—old; موٹاپا moṭāpā—fatness, from موٹا moṭā—fat. In compound words it denotes permanency or continuity (as دیرپا derpā——permanent; lasting; continuing).

پا pā (P) n.m. Leg; foot; foot or root of a tree.

پا انداز pā andāz, n.m. A carpet spread at the entrance of a room for cleaning shoes on; a door-mat; a foot pad.

پابجولاں یا پا بزنجیر pā bajaūlān yā pā bazanjīr, adj. Fettered; in chains; helpless.

پابند pā band, n.f. A rope with which the forefeet of a horse are tied. adj. Fettered; bound; restrained; habituated; subjugated; obedient.

پابند رهنا pā band rahnā, v. To adhere to; to be bound by.

پابند کرنا pā band karnā, v. To check; to fetter; to employ as a servant.

پابند هونا pā-band honā, v. To be bound; to conform to; to observe; to follow.

پابندی pā bandi, n.f. Restraint; restriction; check; control; commitment; service; obedience.

پابوس pā bos, adj. Kissing the feet; worshipper; flatterer.

پابوسی pā bosi, n.f. Worship; adoration.

پابوسی کرنا pā bosi karnā, v. To worship; to adore; to revere.

پاپوش pā posh, n.f. Shoe.

پاپوش پر مارنا pā posh par mārnā, v. To treat with contempt; to make light of; to have no concern for.

پا پیادہ pā piyādah, adj. On foot; walking.

پاتابہ pā tābah, n.m. The straps of sandal.

پاجامہ pā jamah, n.m. Trousers; long drawers.

پاخانہ pā khānah, n.m. Lavatory; latrine; privy; stools; filth.

پا در رکاب pā dbr rikāb, adj. Having the foot in the stirrup; ready; alert.

پازیب pā zeb, n.f. An ornament worn on the feet or ankles.

پا شکستہ pā shikastah, adj. Broken footed; infirm; powerless; helpless.

پاشویہ pā shoyah, n.m. Washing of the feet with hot water.

پامال pā māl, adj. Trodden under foot; ruined.

پامالی pā māli, n.f. Destruction; devastation.

پامردی pā mardi, n.f. Resolution; valour.

پایاب pā yāb, adj. Within man's depth; fordable.

پاپ pāp (S) n.m. Sin; crime; vice; evil; guilt; transgression; fault; calamity; oppression.

پاپ کمانا یا مول لینا pāp kamānā yā mol lenā, v. To commit sin; to do wrong; to bring calamity upon.

پاپ کرنا pāp karnā v. To commit sin; to commit adultery.

پا پا pāpā (corr. of English) n.m. Papa; father; the Pope.

پاپڑ pāpaṛ (H) n.m. Thin crisp cake made of a pulse mixed with spices. adj. Thin (like a paper or leaf); very dry.

پاپڑ بیلنا pāpaṛ belnā, v. To roll out thin crisp cakes; to undergo great labour or pain; to live in poverty and suffering.

پاپڑا pāpṛā (H) n.m. A plant used as a medicine.

پاپن pāpan (H) n.f. A sinful or criminal woman; a wicked woman.

پاپی pāpi (H) n.m. A sinner; a criminal; a wicked man.

پات pāt (H) n.m. A leaf of a tree; any thin leaf or plate of metal; an ornament worn by women in the upper part of the ear.

پاتال pātāl (S) n.m. One of the seven regions under the earth (according to Hindus the abode of serpents and demons); hell.

پاتھنا pāthnā (H) v. To make up cow-dung into cakes for fuel.

پاٹ pāṭ (H) n.m. Breadth of a river; the width of a cloth; a throne; a seat; a board; a plank; fold of a door; mill-stone.

پاٹ رانی pāṭ rāni, n.f. Principal wife of a rāja; the ruling rāni.

پاٹنا pāṭnā (H) v. To roof; to cover; to fill up; to water; to irrigate; to accumulate; to pile; to give in abundance; to cross (a river); to conceal; to shut.

پاٹھ pāṭh (S) n.m. A lesson; reading; perusal; study; recital of sacred books; worship.

پاٹھ سالہ pāṭh sālah, n.m. Reading room; school; a college.

پاجانا pā jānā (H) v. To get; to receive; to understand; to come to know.

پاجی pāji (P) adj. Mean; low; base; vile; wicked; scoundrel; rascal.

پاجی پن pāji pan, n.m. Meanness; vileness; rascality.

پاجی مزاج pāji mizāj, adj. Mean-spirited; of a mean disposition.

پاچھ pāchh (H) n.m. Inoculation; the incision made in the poppy head for the opium to ooze out.

پاچھنا pāchhnā (H) v. To inoculate; to make an incision in.

پاد pād (H) n.m. A fart; passing of wind (from the anus).

پاداش pādāsh (P) n.m. Reward; recompense; requital; retaliation; retribution.

پادری pādri (Port.) n.m. Clergyman; priest; minister; caliph.

پادشاہ pādshah (P) n.m. See بادشاہ bādshāh.

پادشاھت pādshāhat (P) n.f. See بادشاھت bādshāhat.

پادشاھی pādshāhi (P) n.f. See بادشاھی bādshāhi.

پادنا pādnā (H) v. To fart; to pass wind; to lose heart; to flee; to turn back.

پار pār (H) n.m. The opposite bank or shore; the other side; the end; termination. adv. Over; across; on or to the other side; through; beyond. adj. Past; last.

پار آتارنا pār utārnā, v. To put or take across; to ferry over; to finish.

پار آترنا par utarnā, v. To cross the river; to get across; to gain one's end; to succeed; to get rid of; to die.

پار کرنا pār karnā, v. To cross; to ferry over; to get to the end of; to win; to bore.

پار لگانا pār lagānā, v. To carry across; to reach the shore; to achieve the end; to cause one to succeed.

پارا pārā (H) n.m. Quicksilver; mercury.

پارچہ pārchah (P) n.m. A piece of cloth; clothing; dress; fragment; piece.

پارچہ دوز pārchah doz, n.m. A ta lor; a dressmaker.

پارچہ فروش pārchah farosh, n.m. Cloth-merchant; draper.

پارچہ فروشی pārchah faroshi, n.f. Drapery.

پارس pāras (H) n.m. The philosopher's stone which according to Hindu legend immediately converts into gold any metal it touches; elixir.

پارس pārs, pāras, pāris (P) n.m. Persia; Iran.

پارسا pārsā (P) adj. Chaste; holy; vi tuous; abstenious.

پارسال pārsāl (P) n.m. & adv. Last year.

پارسائی pārsā'i (P) n.f. Chastity; abst:nence; purity; virtue; piety.

پارسل pārsal (E) n.m. Parcel.

پارسی pārsi (P) adj. Belonging to Persia. n.m. A native of Persia; a follower of Zoroaster. n.f. Persian language.

پارہ pārah (P) n.m. A piece; a bit; a fragment; a slice; a scrap.

پارہ پارہ کرنا parah pārah karnā, v. To tear to pieces.

پارہ دوز pārah doz, n.m. A patcher; a tailor; a cobler.

پارینہ pārīnah (P) adj. Old; ancient.

پارینہ دفتر pārīnah daftar, n.m. Ancient or old record.

پاژند pāzhand (P) n.f. A religious book of Pārsis.

پاس pās (P) n.m. Custody; observance; supervision; regard; consideration; a division of time consisting of three hours.

پاسبان pās bān, n.m. A watchman; a guard; a sentinel.

پاسبانی pās bānī, n.f. Watch; guard; guarding; the duty of a guard; protection.

پاس خاطر pās-ĕ khāṭir, n.m. In consideration or out of regard.

پاسداری pās dārī, n.f. Regard; favour; partiality; favouritism.

پاس pās (E) n.m. Passing; succeeding; getting through; a permit.

پاس کرنا pās karnā, v. To succeed; to get through; to get promotion; to approve; to take side.

پاس pās (H) adv. Alongside; near; about; at hand; close by.

پاس آنا pās ānā, v. To come near; to approach; to come up to.

پاس بیٹھنا pās beṭhnā, v. To sit near; to learn manners; to get training.

پاس بیٹھنے والا pās beṭhne wālā, n.m. Comrade; companion; a friend; a courtier.

پاس پاس pās pās, adv. Thereabout; approximately near; round about; in a row or line.

پاس پڑوس pās paṛos, n.m. Neighbourhood; round about.

پاس نہ پھٹکنا pās nah phaṭaknā, v. Not to approach; not to be near at hand; not to come near.

پاسا pāsā (H) n.m. A dice; a throw of dice; side.

پاسا پڑنا pāsā paṛnā, v. To be lucky in throwing dice; to win; to be fortunate.

پاسا پھینکنا pāsā pheṅknā, v. To throw the dice.

پاسا کھیلنا pāsā khelnā, v. To gamble with dice.

پاسنگ pāsang (P) n.m. A make-weight; something placed in one scale to balance the other; a balance; a small portion; a trifle.

پاش pāsh (P) (in comp.) Sprinkling; scattering.

پاش پاش pāsh pāsh (P) adj. Shivered in pieces; broken in pieces; shattered.

پاش پاش کرنا pāsh pāsh karnā, v. To break in pieces; to shatter; to shiver.

پاشا pāshā (T) n.m. A title of Turkish nobles or officers; governor; lord; head.

پاشی pāshī (P) n.f. Sprinkling (used in comp.).

پاک pāk (P) adj. Pure; clean; holy; innocent; spotless; immaculate; fair; sacred; undefiled; chaste; free; abbreviation of Pakistan.

پاک باز pāk bāz, adj. Undefiled; pure; honest; candid; sincere; chaste.

پاک بازی pāk bāzī, n.f. Purity; candour; sincerity.

پاک خصلت pāk khaṣlat, adj. Of chaste habits or disposition.

پاک دامن pāk dāman, adj. Pure; chaste; virtuous; modest; holy in life.

پاک دامنی pāk dāmanī, n.f. Purity of life; virtue; chastity; innocence; holiness.

پاک سیرت pāk sīrat, adj. Of spotless character; angelic.

پاک صاف *pāk ṣāf, adj.* Pure; chaste; clean; undefiled; unpolluted.

پاک صورت *pāk ṣūrat, adj.* Beautiful; lovely.

پاک کرنا *pāk karnā, v.* To purify; to clean; to wash; to square accounts.

پاکستان *Pākistān, n.m.* (*Lit.* it means holy land). In August 1947 the Muslim majority areas of India were separated to form an independent State. This new Muslim State is called the Islamic Republic of Pakistan.

پاکھنڈ *pākhanḍ* (H) *n.m.* Deceit; wickedness; hypocrisy; heresy.

پاکھنڈی *pākhanḍī* (H) *n.m. & adj.* Deceitful; hypocrite; heretic; imposter; pretender.

پاکی *pāki* (P) *n.f.* Cleanliness; purity; chastity.

پاکی لینا *pāki lenā, v.* To shave or remove hair from private parts.

پاکیزگی *pākizagī* (P) *n.f.* Cleanliness; purity; neatness; chastity.

پاکیزہ *pākizah* (P) *adj.* Neat; clean; pure; chaste.

پاگل *pāgal* (H) *adj.* Mad; insane; foolish; idiotic; distressed; worried. *n.m.* A fool; an idiot; a mad man; a lunatic.

پاگل خانہ *pāgal k͟hānah, n.m.* Lunatic asylum; mad-house; mental hospital.

پاگل ہونا *pāgal honā, v.* To go mad; to become over-zealous.

پال *pāl* (H) *n.f.* A dam; an embankment; a small tent; layers of straw, leaves, &c., between which raw fruits are placed to ripen.

پال کا پکا *pāl kā pakkā, adj.* Fruit ripened in straw.

پالا *pālā* (H) *n.m.* Frost; hoarfrost; snow; intense cold; intercourse; dealing; connection; brought up; amphitheatre; a line drawn by players to separate the two sides in a game of *kabaḍḍi*.

پالا پڑنا *pālā paṛnā, v.* To snow; to be intensely cold; to have to do with; to have dealing or intercourse with; to fall under one's power or influence.

پالاگن *pālāgan* (H) *n.m.* Obeisance by touching the feet.

پالان *pālān* (P) *n.m.* A pack saddle.

پالتو *pāltū* (H) *adj.* Pet.

پالتی *pālti* (H) *n.f.* A squatting posture.

پالتی مار کے بیٹھنا *pālti mār ke baiṭhnā, v.* To squat; to sit on one's hams.

پالک *pālak* (H) *n.f.* A potherb; a sort of spinach.

پالکی *pālkī* (H) *n.f.* A kind of litter or sedan; a palanquin.

پالن *pālan* (S) *n.m.* Bringing up; nourishing; cherishing; breeding; nursing; maintenance; protection; supervision.

پالن ہار *pālan hār, n.m.* God, who provides food to all creatures.

پالنا *pālnā* (H) *v.* To nourish; to foster; to maintain; to support. *n.m.* A cradle.

پالیز *pālez* (P) See فالیز *fālez*.

پام *pām* (H) *n.f.* Thread running along the edges of lace to prevent its revelling; a plant of the kind of date-palm or cocoanut tree.

پان *pān* (H) *n.m.* Betel-leaf; an embroidered work; starch used by weavers.

پان دان *pān dān, n.m.* A box in which betel leaves and its accessories are kept.

پان کھلائی *pān khilā'i, n.f.* Giving *pān* to eat; a betrothal ceremony.

پان لگانا یا بنانا *pān lagānā yā banānā, v.* To prapare betel-leaf with betel nuts, etc. for chewing.

جل پان کرنا *jal pān karnā, v.* To refresh oneself: to make a repast.

پانا pānā (H) v. To get; to obtain; to find.

پانچ pānch (H) adj. Five.

پانچ سات pānch sāt, n.m. Indifference.

پانچواں ' پانچویں bānchwāṅ, pānchwiṅ (H) adj. Fifth.

پانچوں pānchoṅ (H) adj. All five.

پانچوں انگلیاں برابرنہیں هوتیں pānchoṅ ungliāṅ brābar nahīṅ hotiṅ, prov. All are not alike in this world, some are born with a silver spoon and some with wooden ladle in their mouths.

پانچوں انگلیاں گھی میں pānchoṅ ungliāṅ ghi meṅ, prov. To make the best of an opportunity; to enjoy to hearts content.

پانچوں عیب شرعی pānchoṅ 'aib shar'i, n.m. The five sins prohibited by religion--stealing, adultery; falsehood, gambling and drinking.

پانچویں pānchweṅ (H) adv. Fifthly; in the fifth place.

پانچویں پنڈت چھٹے نارائن، پانچویں مولوی چھٹے ملا pānchweṅ panḍit chhaṭe nārā'in, pānchweṅ maulvi chhaṭe mullā, prov. He that reckons without his host, must reckon again; two hands are better than one.

پانڈو pāndo (S) n.m. The Pando dynasty (Yudhishtar and the other four Pando princes).

پانڈو pānḍū (H) n.f. Chalky earth or soil.

پانڈے pānḍe (H) n.m. A learned man; scholar; teacher; a school master, a title of Brahmans.

پانسو pānsau (H) adj. Five hundred.

پانی pāni (H) n.m. Water; rain water; lustre; polish; brightness; beauty; character; credit; reputation; honour.

پانی آنا pāni ānā, v. To rain; to be cloudy; to suffer from cataract; to suffer from leucorrhoea or whites.

پانی آترنا pāni utarnā, v. Decrease in the level of water; to suffer from cataract.

پانی برسنا pāni barasnā, v. To rain.

پانی بھرنا pāni bharnā, v. To draw water; to be humiliated or ashamed; to feel inferiority.

پانی بھر آنا (منہ میں) pāni bhar ānā (muṅh meṅ), v. To bring water to one's mouth; watering of the mouth.

پانی پانی کرنا pāni pāni karnā, v. To put one to shame; to cause one to perspire through shame.

پانی پانی هونا pāni pāni honā, v. To perspire with shame; to be overwhelmed with shame; to be flooded out.

پانی پھر جانا pāni phir jānā, v. To be disgraced; to be destroyed; to be polished; to be tinned; to gain lustre.

پانی پھیرنا pāni phernā, v. To undo; to destroy, to impart lustre; to polish; to guild.

پانی پی پی کر کوسنا pāni pī pi kar kosnā, v. To curse excessively; to heap curses upon.

پانی جانا یا چلنا pāni jānā yā chalnā, v. To be afflicted with the fluor albus; to be disgraced; to shed tears.

پانی دینا pāni denā, v. To water; to irrigate; to offer a libation of water.

پانی سا پتلا pāni sā patlā, adj. As thin as water; cheap; worthless.

پانی سر سے اونچا هونا pāni sar se ūnchā honā, v. To be in deep waters.

پانی سے پہلے پل باندھنا pāni se pahle pul bāndhnā, v. To call a surgeon before one is wounded.

پانی کا بلبلہ pāni kā bulbulah, n.m. A bubble of water. adj. Anything unstable; weak; frail.

پانی کاٹنا pāni kāṭnā, v. To turn off the water into another channel.

پانی کرنا pāni karnā, v. To liquefy.

پانی میں آگ لگانا pāni meṅ āg lagānā, v. To inflame one against another; to sow dissension; to do impossible.

پانی نہ مانگنا pāni nah māṅgnā, v. To die suddenly without having time to ask for water to cool one's dying lips.

پائندہ pā'indah (P) adj. Lasting; steady; durable.

پاؤ pāo (H) n.m. A quarter; a fourth part.

پاؤ بھر pāo bhar, adj. Quarter seer.

پاؤ روٹی pāo roti, n.f. A loaf of bread made in the European way and weighing about a pāo or quarter of a seer.

پاؤں pāoṅ (H) n.m. Foot; leg; root; basis.

پاؤں اترنا pāoṅ utarnā, v. Dislocating the foot.

پاؤں اڑانا pāoṅ aṛānā, v. To interfere or meddle with other people's affairs.

پاؤں اکھڑنا pāon ukhaṛnā, v. To lose footing; to be carried away by a stream; to run away; to be routed; to take to flight.

پاؤں بڑھانا pāon baṛhānā, v. To take the lead; to go ahead; to exceed bounds.

پاؤں بھاری ہونا pāon bhārī honā, v. To be in the family way; to be pregnant; to be with child

پاؤں پاؤں pāoṅ pāoṅ, adv. On foot.

پاؤں پر پاؤں رکھنا pāoṅ par pāoṅ rakhnā, v. To sit at ease; to sit cross legged; to walk in the steps of another.

پاؤں پڑنا pāoṅ paṛnā, v. To fall at the feet of; to entreat submissively; to implore; to beseach.

پاؤں پر کلھاڑی مارنا pāoṅ par kulhāṛī mārnā, v. To spoil one's own affair; to cut one's own throat.

پاؤں پسارنا pāon pasārnā, v. To stretch one's leg; to die; to insist; to be obstinate.

پاؤں پکڑنا pāoṅ pakaṛnā, v. To beseach submissively; to implore; to prevent one from proceeding further.

پاؤں پھٹنا pāoṅ phatnā, v. To have chilblains.

پاؤں پھیلا کر سونا pāon phailā kar sonā, v. To sleep with the legs stretched out; to sleep at ease; to be perfectly contented and happy.

پاؤں پھوک پھوک کر رکھنا pāoṅ phūk phūk kar rakhnā, v. To treat softly; to move cautiously; to be cautious.

پاؤں پیچھے ہٹنا pāoṅ pīchhe haṭnā, v. To beat retreat; to lose heart.

پاؤں تلے ملنا pāoṅ tale malnā, v. To crush under one's foot; to trample under foot.

پاؤں تلے سے زمین نکل جانا pāoṅ tale se zamīn nikal jānā, v. To feel the ground slipping from under one's feet; to be stunned or staggered.

پاؤں جمانا pāoṅ jamānā, v. To plant the feet firmly; to get a firm footing; to stand firmly.

پاؤں چھلنی ہونا pāoṅ chhalni honā, v. To get blisters on the feet.

پاؤں دھرنا یا رکھنا pāoṅ dharnā yā rakhnā, v. To set foot on; to step in; to enter; to begin.

پاؤں دھو دھو پینا pāoṅ dho dho pinā, v. To do honour or reverence to; to have perfect confidence in.

پاؤں رگڑنا pāoṅ ragaṛnā, v. To be in the agonies of death; to go about aimlessly and unprofitably.

پاؤں زمین پر نہ ٹھہرنا pāoṅ zamin par nah thehrnā, v. To be unsteady on the feet through joy; to be overjoyed.

پاؤں زمین پر نہ رکھنا *pāoṅ zamīn par nah rakhnā*, *v.* To walk like a swell; to be ostentatious; to be proud.

پاؤں سونا *pāoṅ sonā*, *v.* Benumbing of the foot; heaviness or sleeping of the foot.

پاؤں سے پاؤں باندھنا *pāoṅ se pāoṅ bāṅdhnā*, *v.* To watch one closely.

پاؤں کی آنگلی *pāoṅ kī uṅglī*, *n.f.* A toe.

پاؤں گاڑنا *pāoṅ gāṛnā*, *v.* To plant one's foot; to stand immovable.

پاؤں گور میں لٹکانا *pāoṅ gor meṅ laṭkānā*, *v.* To be advanced in years; to have one foot in the grave.

پاؤں گھسنا *pāoṅ ghisnā*, *v.* To undergo useless labour.

پاؤں میں مہندی لگانا *pāoṅ meṅ mehṅdī lagānā*, *v.* To be unable to set foot on the ground; to be unprepared to do a thing.

پائی *pā'ī* (H) *n.f.* A coin; third part of a pice; a pie.

پائے *pāe* (P) *n.m.* The foot; the leg; the stand of a table, chair, bedstead, &c; foundation.

پائے تخت *pāe takht*, *n.m.* The royal residence; the capital.

پائے ثبوت کو پہنچنا *pāe ṣabūt ko pahuṅchnā*, *v.* To be proved beyond doubt.

پائے جامہ *pāe jāmah*, *n.m.* See پاجامہ *pā jāmah*.

پائے دار *pāe dār*, *adj.* Having feet lasting; firm; steady; stable; durable; permanent.

پائے داری *pāe dārī*, *n.f.* Permanence; stability; durability; firmness.

پائے دان *pāe dān*, *n.m.* Running board; foot pad; door-mat.

پائے رفتن نہ جائے ماندن *pāe raftan nah jāe mandan*, *prov.* Utter helplessness.

پائے کوبی *pāe kobī*, *n.f.* Dancing; beating the feet in dancing.

پائے مال *pāe māl*. See پامال *pā māl*.

پائیں *pā'īṅ* (P) *adj.&adv.* Lower; back; beneath; under; lower part.

پائیں باغ *pā'īṅ bāgh*, *n.m.* A garden behind a palace.

پائینتی *pā'īntī* (H) *n.f.* Foot or bottom of a bed; foot of a bedstead.

پائینچہ *pāeṅchah*, *n.m.* One of the legs of a trousers.

پائینچہ بھاری کرنا *pāeṅchah bhārī karnā*, *v.* To make one's drawers heavy; to make a vow of rigid seclusion from women or take part in worldly affairs.

پایان *pāyān* (P) *n.f.* End; extremity; extreme; conclusion.

پایل *pāyal*, *n.f.* An anklet of gold or silver; a child born with feet first.

پایہ *pāyah* (P) *n.m.* Leg or foot; foundation; base; support; step; rank; dignity; the leg or foot of a table, chair etc.

پایہ تخت *pāyah takht*. See پائے تخت *pāe takht*

پپڑا ، پپڑی *papṛā*, *papṛī* (H) *n.m.* & *n.f.* Crust; incrustation; a scab; thin cakes of bread.

پپڑی جم جانا *papṛī jam jānā*, *v.* To form a crust; to crystallise.

پپڑیا کتھا *papṛiyā katthā*, *n.m.* A kind of white colour *katthā* or catechu.

پپوٹا *papoṭā* (H) *n.m.* Eyelid.

پپولنا *papolnā*, *v.* To munch; to masticate (like an old man without teeth).

پپیتا *papītā* (H) *n.m.* The papaya tree and its fruit.

پپیہا *papīhā* (H) *n.m.* The black and white crested cuckoo.

پت *pat* (H) *n.f.* Good name; honour; reputation; character. *n.m.* (*abr.* of پات *pāt*) A leaf.

پت جھڑ pat jhaṛ, n.m. Autumn.

پت جھڑ ہونا pat jhaṛ honā, v. To lose leaves in autumn; to decay (from old age).

پت pit (S) n.m. Bile; gall; anger.

پتا pitā (H) n.m. Father.

پتا pittā (H) n.m. Gall bladder; anger; passion; mental emotion; force of character.

پتا مارنا pittā mārnā, v. To control or subdue anger; to restrain one's passions.

پتا نکالنا pittā nikālnā, v. To chastise; to annoy; to harass.

پتا patā (H) n.m. Sign; symptom; clue; address to which a letter is directed; hint; token.

پتا دینا patā denā, v. To direct; to point; to give a clue.

پتا لگانا patā lagānā, v. To obtain a clue; to trace; to discover; to search out.

پتے کی کہنا pate kī kahnā, v. To tell the truth about a matter; to expose (one).

پتا pattā (H) n.m. A leaf; a card; a banner; trinket; a symbol; an ensign.

پتا کاٹنا paṭṭā kāṭnā, v. To dismiss; to dispose of; to discharge.

پتال patāl. See پاتال pātāl.

پتر pattar (H) n.m. A leaf; a letter; a sheet of metal.

پتری patrī (H) n.f. A letter; a note.

پتلا ' پتلی patlā, patlī (H) adj. Delicate; feeble; fine; lean; thin; narrow; sharp; meagre; meek.

پتلا حال patlā ḥāl, n.m. Straitened circumstances; a sad plight.

پتلا کرنا patlā karnā, v. To liquefy; to make thin; to sharpen or to point (a pencil).

پتلا putlā (H) n.m. A puppet; a large doll; idol; image; effigy.

عقل کا پتلا 'aql bā putlā, adj. Clever; skilful.

خاک کا پتلا k͟hāk kā putlā, n.m. Human body; human.

پتلی putlī (H) n.f. Pupil of the eye; puppet; a small idol; a doll; the frog of a horse's hoof; a slim delicate woman.

پتلی کا تارا putlī kā tārā, n.m. Dear as the pupil of the eye.

پتلی کا تماشا putlī kā tamāshā, n.m. Puppet show.

پتلیاں پھر جانا putliāṅ phir jānā, v. Turning of the eyes at the time of death.

پتنگ patang (H) n.f. Moth; a paper-kite.

پتنگا pataṅgā (H) n.m. A flying insect; moth; a spark (of fire).

پتھر patthar (H) n.m. A stone; rock-stone; hailstone; a gem. adj. Hard; cruel; heavy; difficult; inflexible.

پتھر برسنا patthar barasnā, v. To hail; to rain gravel.

پتھر بن جانا patthar ban jānā, v. To become as hard as stone; to be unmerciful.

پتھر پانی ہونا patthar pānī honā, v. Melting of a stony heart; to make a difficult task easy.

پتھر پڑنا patthar paṛna, v. To hail; to be overwhelmed with trouble; to be ruined.

پتھر پسیجنا patthar pasījnā, v. Softening of a stony heart.

پتھر چاٹا patthar chāṭā, n.m. A skinflint; a sort of a potherb. adj. One attached to the very stones of his house.

پتھر چھاتی پر رکھنا patthar chhātī par rakhnā, v. To suffer patiently; to be patient by compulsion or from being without remedy.

پتھر ڈھونا patthar ḍhonā, v. To carry stones; to work hard.

پتھر سا پھینک مارنا patthar sā phaiṅk marnā, v. To give a rude or sharp answer; to reply rashly without understanding the question.

پتھر کا چھاپا patthar kā chhāpā, n.m. Lithography; a lithograph.

پتھر کی لکیر patthar ki lakir, adj. Ineffaceable; unalterable.

پتھر مارنا patthar mārnā, v. To throw stones (on); to pelt stones.

پتھر نچوڑنا pitthar nichoṛnā, v. To expect mercy or leniency from a cruel person.

پتھرانا patthrānā, v. To be petrified; to become hard; to make callous or unfeeling.

پتھراؤ pathrā'o (H) n.m. Stoning; lapidation.

پتھراؤ کرنا pathrā'o karnā, v. To pelt stones; to lapidate.

پتھری patthri (H) n.f. Grit; gravel; the flint of musket; stone in the bladder.

پتھریلا ، پتھریلی patthrilā, patthrili, adj. Stony; rocky; gritty.

پتھواڑی patthwāṛi (H) n.f. Place for making or storing cow-dung cakes.

پتھیرا patherā (H) n.m. A brick-maker.

پتی patti (H) n.f. A leaf; a share; a thin plate of metal; hemp, of which intoxicating potion is made.

پتی دار patti dār, n.m. A shareholder.

پتیلا patilā, n.m. A kind of pan; a pot; a wide-mouthed cauldron.

پتیلی patili, n.f. A small pot or pan.

پٹ paṭ (H) n.m. A shutter; the valve of a folding door; a screen; a covering; a veil; sound of falling or beating; coarse cloth or canvas. adj. Upside down; overturned; flat.

پٹ بند کرنا paṭ band karnā, v. To shut or close the door.

پٹ کھولنا paṭ kholnā, v. To open the door; to take off the covering or veil.

پٹا paṭā (H) n.m. A wooden sword or foil; a cudgel.

پٹے باز paṭe bāz, n.m. A fencer; one who plays with foils or cudgels. n.f. A coquette; a wanton woman; a strumpet.

پٹا paṭṭā (H) n.m. Collar of a horse or of a dog; a horse's girth; strap and badge; a deed of lease.

پٹا آتارنا paṭṭā utārnā, v. To dismiss a person; to untie an animal.

پٹا تڑانا paṭṛā turānā, v. To break the collar and run off; to get loose; to run away.

پٹے دار paṭṭe dār, n.m. A lease-holder; a lessee.

پٹا رہن paṭṭā rahn, n.m. Mortgage-lease.

پٹاخا pāṭākhā, n.m. Cracker; fireworks; a squib; a gun cap.

پٹارا piṭārā (H) n.m. A large basket; a portmanteau; a box for clothes.

پٹاری piṭāri (H) n.f. A small basket, a betel box.

پٹاک یا پٹاخ paṭāk yā paṭākh, n.m. A loud sound; a crash; an explosion.

پٹخنا paṭakhnā, v. See پٹکنا paṭaknā.

پٹخنی paṭkhani. See پٹکنی paṭkani.

پٹڑا paṭṛā (H) n.m. A plank to sit on; a plank on which a washerman beats clothes; a plank used as harrow.

پٹڑا کر دینا paṭṛā kar denā, v. To deprive one of power or strength; to make one as flat as the ground; to render one absolutely powerless.

پٹڑی paṭri (H) n.f. A plank to sit on; an avenue; the bank of a canal or road; a footpath; a firm seat on horse back.

پٹ سن paṭ san (H) n.f. Jute.

پٹکا paṭkā (H) n.m. A cloth worn round the waist; a girdle; a turban.

پٹکا باندھنا paṭkā bāndhnā, v. To gird up the loins (for); to determine and be prepared for action; to put a girdle round the waist or to wear a turban.

پٹکا زری paṭkā zari, n.m. A golden girdle.

پٹکنا paṭaknā (H) v. To dash against; to throw on the ground with violence.

پٹکنی paṭkani (H) n.f. A throw; a fall; a knock down; a sharp blow; vengeance; divine wrath.

پٹکنی دینا paṭkani denā, v. To dash one on the ground with violence; to throw against anything with force.

پٹکنی کھانا paṭkani khānā, v. To be thrown down; to fall on the ground with force.

پٹنا paṭnā (H) v. To be roofed; to be settled; to be paid; to be in abundance; to be watered.

پٹنا piṭnā (H) v. To be beaten; to get a beating. n.m. A mallet; a wooden hammar used for pounding.

پٹو paṭṭū (H) n.m. A coarse woollen cloth.

پٹواری paṭwāri (H) n.m. A village registrar or accountant; a keeper of the records and accounts of lands; a land steward.

پٹوانا piṭwānā (H) v. To cause to be beaten.

پٹولی paṭolı (H) n.m. A man who strings pearls; a broider; a maker of fringe or tape.

پٹھ puṭh (H) n.f. Seasoning; sprinkling; excitement; flux; the flesh of the hip joint of an animal.

پٹھا puṭṭhā (H) n.m. The buttock; rump; hip.

پٹھے پر ھاتھ نہ رکھنے دینا puṭṭhe par hath nah rakhne denā, v. Not to allow any o to put a hand on the rump; not to bear being touched by any one; to be hard to get at; to be beyond reach.

پٹھا paṭṭhā (H) n.m. A young full-grown animal; a youth; a young wrestler; a nerve sinew; a tendon.

پٹھان paṭhān, n.m. Tribes inhabiting the north-west of West Pakistan; soldier; warrior.

پٹھو piṭṭhū (H) n.m. A follower; a comrade; a playmate; a supporter; a substitute in childern's game.

پٹھیا paṭhiyā (H) n.f. A young full-grown she-animal; a young hen.

پٹی paṭṭi (H) n.f. A bandage; a fillet; a strip of cloth used as a bandage; the side pieces of a bedstead; parting of the hair; a row; a side; a board to write on; a kind of sweetmeat; a lesson.

پٹی باندھنا paṭṭi bāndhnā, v. To dress; to apply a bandage.

پٹی دینا paṭṭi denā, v. To cheat; to deceive; to put one up to some trick.

پٹی پڑھانا paṭṭi paṛhānā, v. To advise; to counsel; to coax; to seduce.

پٹیاں جمانا paṭṭiāṅ jamānā, v. To paste the hair down on the temples.

پٹیل paṭel (H) n.m. Fencing with cudgels; cudgelling; the headman of a village; a title of Marhattas.

پٹین puṭin, n.f. (corr. of English) Pudding.

پجارن pujāran (H) n.f. A female worshipper; a priestess.

پجاری pujāri (H) n.m. A worshipper; a priest.

پجنا pujnā (H) v. To be worshiped.

پچ pach (H) n.m. Support; defence; protection; partisanship; prejudice.

پچ کرنا pach karnā, v. To defend; to support; to take one's side.

پچاس *pachās* (H) *adj.* Fifty.

پچاسواں *pachāswāṅ* (H) *adj.* Fiftieth.

پچاسی *pachāsi* (H) *adj.* Eighty-five.

پچانا *pachānā* (H) *v.* To digest; to assimilate.

پچانوے *pachānwe* (H) *adj.* Ninety-five.

پچاؤ *pachāo* (H) *n.m.* Digestion; assimilation.

پچ پچا *pach pachā* (H) *adj.* Soft; flabby; clammy; watery; moist.

پچپن *pachpan* (H) *adj.* Fifty-five.

پچر *pachchar* (H) *n.f.* A wedge; a slip of wood used to fill up a crack or opening.

پچر لگانا *pachchar lagānā*, *v.* To insert a slip of wood; to wedge in; to put in a wedge.

پچکارنا *puchkārnā* (H) *v.* To coax; to pat; to caress; to stroke.

پچکاری *puchkāri* (H) *n.f.* Patting; caressing.

پچکاری *pichkārī* (H) *n.f.* A syringe; a squirt.

پچکاری دینا *pichkāri denā*, *v.* To apply a clyster.

پچکاری لینا *pichkāri lenā*, *v.* To take an enema.

پچکاری مارنا *pichkārī mārnā*, *v.* To discharge water from a syringe.

پچکنا *pichaknā* (H) *v.* To be sequeezed; to be shrivelled.

پچنا *pachnā* (H) *v.* To be digested; to be consumed; to be assimilated.

پچھاڑ *pachhāṛ* (H) *n.f.* A fall on the back; falling back in a swoon; the act of winnowing; throwing down.

پچھاڑنا *pachhāṛnā* (H) *v.* To throw one down on the back; to give one a fall; to overcome; to subdue; to abase.

پچھاڑی *pichhāṛi* (H) *n.f.* The rear; the ropes by which a horse's hind legs are tied; heel ropes. *adv.* In the rear; behind.

پچھاڑی مارنا *pichhāṛī mārnā*, *v.* To kick with hind legs (horse); to attack from behind.

پچھتانا *pachhtānā* (H) *v.* To regret; to repent; to grieve; to rue.

پچھتاوا *pachhtāwā* (H) *n.m.* Repentance; remorse; regret; grief; sorrow; penitence; concern; compunction.

پچھتر *pachhattar* (H) *adj.* Seventy-five.

پچھڑنا *pachhaṛnā*, *v.* To fall back; to tumble down, to lag behind; to fail; to fall short (of).

پچھلا ، پچھلی *pichhlā*, *pichhli* (H) *adj.* Latter; last; past; succeeding; back; late; posterior; bygone; hindermost.

پچھلا پہر *pichhlā pahr*, *n.m.* The last quarter of the day or night; old age.

پچھلے پاؤں پھرنا *pichhle pāoṅ phirnā*, *v.* To retrace one's steps immediately; to return from a place the moment one reaches it.

پچھلے پاؤں ہٹنا *pichhle pāoṅ haṭnā*, *v.* To retreat; to back out of an agreement.

پچھل پائی *pichhal pā'ī* (H) *n.f.* A woman with inverted feet; a witch.

پچھم *pachchham* (H) *n.m.* West; countries situated in the west.

پچھمی *pachchhamī* (H) *adj.* Western.

پچھنا *pachhnā* (H) *n.m.* Tattooing; inoculating; scarifying; a scarificator (name of an instrument).

پچھوا ، پچھوائی *pachhwā pachhwāi* (H) *n.f.* Western wind.

پچھواڑا *pichhwāṛā* (H) *n.m.* The rear; the backpart; hind quarter; backyard; rearward.

پچھوانا *puchhwānā* (H) *v.* To cause to ask or make enquiry.

پچھوت *pichhūt* (H) *n.m.* A crop sown very late; back of a house. *adj.* Last; other. *adv.* Behind; afte rwards.

پچھیت *pachchhit* (H) *n.f.* The back of the house; a compound in the rear of the house.

پچی *pachchi* (H) *adj.* Attached; joined.

پچی کاری *pachchi kāri, n.f.* Mosaic work; patching or darning.

پچی کرنا *pachchi kāri, v.* To join; to fix.

پچی ہونا *pachchi honā, v.* To be stuck together as with a glue; to be in unison; to be strongly attached by love; to be joined; to adhere; to be sequeezed; to be wedged.

پچیس *pachchis* (H) *adj.* Twent-five.

پچیسواں *pachchiswāń* (H) *adj.* Twenty-fifth.

پچیسی *pachchisi* (H) *n.f.* A game played with کوڑی *cowṛi* instead of dice, and so named from the highest throw, which is twenty-five (now-a-days thirty).

پخ *pakh, n.f.* Difficulty; trouble; wrangle; hindrance; tumult; noise.

پخال *pakhāl* (H) *n.m.* A large leather bag for carrying water.

پختگی *pukhtagi* (P) *n.f.* Ripeness; maturity; firmness; strength; development.

پخت و پز *pukht-ŏ puz* (P) *n.f.* Complete settlement; full arrangement; concoction.

پختہ *pukhtah* (P) *adj.* Dressed; cooked; baked; strong; knowing; mature; expert; wise; solid; well made; matured.

پختہ کار *pukhtah kār, adj.* Experienced; strong; mature.

پختہ کاری *pukhtah kāri, n.f.* Solid workmanship; experience.

پختہ کرنا *pukhtah karnā, v.* To make strong; to ripen.

پختہ ہونا *pukhtah honā, v.* To be strong; to be definite.

پدا *piddā* (H) *n.m.* The brown-backed Indo-Pakistani robin.

پدر *pidar yā padar* (P) *n.m.* Father.

پدر سوختہ *pidar sokhtah, adj.* Rogue; scoundral.

پدر کشی *pidar kushi, n.f.* Patricide.

پدرم سلطان بود *pidram sultān būd, prov.* My father was a king (used when one boasts of having great ancestors).

پدرانہ *pidrānah* (P) *adj.* Father-like; paternal.

پدم *padam* (S) *adj.* & *n.m.* One thousand billions; the lotus flower.

پدمنی *padmani* (S) *n.f.* A woman of the most excellent order; a most beautiful and good woman.

پدو یا پدوڑا *paddū yā padoṛā* (H) *adj.* One addicted to farting; one easily frightened; a coward.

پذیر *pazir* (P) *adj.* Taking; receiving; admitting; liable; being possessed of; endowed with; susceptible (used in *comp.*).

پذیرائی *pazirā'i* (P) *n.f.* Acceptance; reception; entertainment.

پذیری *paziri* (P) *n.f.* (used in *comp.*) Taking; acceptance.

پر *par* (S) *adj.* Distant; remote; far; other; strange; beyond (used in *comp.* as, پرلوک *par lok*, the next world).

پر *par* (H) *prep.* On; upon; on the point of; above; through; after; at; by; for. *adv.* & *conj.* But; yet; however; still.

پر *par* (P) *n.m.* Feather; quill; wing; pinion.

پرافشاں *par afshān, adj.* Expanding or shaking the wings; anxious; perturbed; disturbed.

پر باندھنا *bar pāndhnā, v.* To bind the wings; to render helpless; to weaken; to withdraw help.

پر پرزوں سے درست ہونا *par purzon se durust honā, v.* To be ready; to be fully equipped.

پر ٹوٹنا یا جلنا par ṭūṭnā yā jalnā, v. To be without power, ability or help; to be rendered powerless; to be unable to have access (to).

پر جھاڑنا یا گرانا par jhāṛnā yā girānā, v. To shed feathers; to moult; to get new feathers after moulting.

پر دار par dār, adj Winged.

پر شکستہ par shikastah, adj. Distressed; afflicted; disabled.

پر قینچ کرنا par qaiṅch karnā, v. To cut off feathers; to disable; to render helpless; to compel.

پر کا قلم par kā qalam, n.m. A quill pen.

پر کا کوا بنا دینا par kā kawwā banā denā, v. To make a mountain out of a mole hill.

پر لگنا par lagnā, v. To be able to fly; to boast; to brag.

پر مارنا par mārnā, v. To flutter; to fly; to have access (to); to approach.

پر نکالنا یا پر پرزے نکالنا par nikālnā yā par purze nikālnā, v. To display hidden qualities; to give oneself airs; to display one's new feathers.

پر pur (P) adj. Full; complete; loaded; abounding in; quite (used at the beginning of compounds); charged.

پرپیچ pur pech, adj. Complicated; difficult.

پرتکلف pur takalluf, adj. Ceremonious; elaborated; sumptuous (feast).

پر خطر pur khaṭar, adj. Hazardous; risky.

پر درد pur dard, adj. Painful; sorrowful.

پرسوز pur soz, adj. Blazing; lighted; burning.

پر ملال pur malāl, adj Very sad; sorrowful; afflicting.

پرا parā (H) n.m. Rank; file; troops; a herd (of animals).

پرا باندھنا یا جمانا parā bāndhnā yā jamānā, v. To form a line; to draw up in line of battle.

پرات parāt (H) n.f. A large plate of brass; early morning; dawn.

پراٹھا parāṭhā (H) n.m. Bread made with butter or ghee, and of several lyers, like pie-crust.

پراچین parāchin (S) adj. Old; ancient; eastern; easterly.

پرارتھنا prārthanā (S) n.f. Prayer; supplication; request; petition.

پراکرت بھاشا prākrit bhāshā (S) n.f. A provincial dialect akin to Sanskrit; local dialect.

پراگندگی parāgandagi (P) n.f. Disturbance of mind; dispersion; separation.

پراگندہ parāgandah (P) adj. Scattered; dispersed; routed; dissipated; distracted; disturbed in mind.

پران purān (S) n.m. Legendary and traditionary ancient history; sacred works (eighteen in number supposed to have been compiled by the poet Vyasa).

پران parān or prān (S) n.m. Breath; soul; life; inspiration; spirit.

پران چھوٹنا parān chhūṭnā, v. To die; to be discouraged; to lose senses.

پران چھوڑنا parān chhoṛnā, v. To lose heart; to breathe one's last.

پرانا ، پرانی purānā, purānī (H) adj. Old; stale; time worn; ancient; experienced; antiquated; out of date.

پرانا خرانٹ یا گھاگ purānā kharrānṭ yā ghāg, adj. Experienced; crafty.

پرانے لوگ purāne log, n.m. Old people; old servants.

پرانے مردے اکھیڑنا purāne murde ukheṛnā, v. To bring forward old complaints.

پربال parbāl. See پروال parwāl.

پربت parbat (H) n.m. A mountain; a hill.

پربھو prabhū (S) n.m. Lord; master; principal.

پرتاپ partāp (S) n.m. Glory; majesty; splendour; dignity; magnanimity; generosity.

پرتو partau (P) n.m. Light; ray; reflection; beam; splendour; enlightenment.

پرتھی یا پرتھوری pirthī yā pirthwī (H) n.f. The earth; land; the world.

پرجا parjā (H) n.f. Off-spring; descendants; race; subjects; tenants.

پرچ pirch, n.f. Small plate; a saucer.

پرچار parchār (H) n.m. Publication; disclosure; propaganda; preaching.

پرچار کرنا parchār karnā, v. To preach; to publish; to make public; to propagate.

پرچانا parehānā (H) v. To make familiar; to tame; to domesticate; to practice upon; to kindle; to light.

پرچم parcham (P) n.m. A flag; a military ensign; a fringed tassel of a spear or lance; tassel.

پرچم اڑانا یا لہرانا parcham uṛānā yā lahrānā, v. To hoist a flag.

پرچنا parachnā (H) v. To be tamed; to become intimate; to be satisfied; to be consoled.

پرچول parchaul (H) n.f. Scrutiny; enquiry.

پرچون parchūn (H) n.m. Meal; flour; grocery; retail.

پرچونی parchūnī (H) n.f. Act of selling flour, meal, &c.; retail selling.

پرچونیا parchūniā (H) n.m. A grocer; a meal-merchant; a retailer.

پرچہ parchah (P) n.m. A slip of paper; newspaper; examination paper.

پرچہ چاک کرنا parchah chāk karnā, v. To commit an offender to trial; to send up a criminal case for trial; to re cord a preliminary report.

پرچہ دینا parchah denā, v. To give proof; to make a report; to set a question paper; to distribute question papers.

پرچہ' سزا parchah-ĕ sazā, n.m. Conviction slip.

پرچہ لینا parchah lenā, v. To test; to satisfy; to take an examination.

پرچہ نویس parchah nawis, n.m. A reporter; a spy; writer of a report.

پرچہ نویسی parchah nawisī, n.f. Espionage; reporting.

پرچھاواں parchhāṅwāṅ (H) n.m. Shadow; reflection; image; influence of an evil spirit; habit; effect.

پرچھاواں پڑنا parchhāṅwaṅ paṛnā, v. To be affected by an evil spirit; to be under the influence of an evil spirit.

پرچھائیں parchhā'iṅ (H) n.f. Shadow; reflection.

پرچھائیں سے بھاگنا parchhā'iṅ se bhāgnā, v. To be frightened of a shadow; to fly from the influence or nearness of an evil person.

پرچھتی parchhatī (H) n.f. A small thatch over mud walls.

پرخاش parkhash (P) n.f. War; battle; conflict; altercation; commotion; tumult; violence; oppression; severe inquisition; quarrel.

پرخچے parakhche, n.m. Pieces; bits.

پرخچے اڑانا parakhche uṛānā, v. To break into small pieces; to tear into bits; to beat severely.

پردادا pardādā (H) n.m. A great grand father (by the father's side); a forefather.

پرداز pardāz (P) adj. Performing; finishing; completing (used in comp.).

پردازی pardāzī (P) n.f. Performance; completion; elegance; ornament (chiefly used at the end of compounds as,

انشا پردازی inshā pardāzī, elegance of composition.

پردہ pardah (P) n.m. A curtain; a screen; a veil; a cover; secrecy; privacy; modesty; drum of the ear; surface of the earth; shelter; pretext; the frets of a guitar.

پردہ اٹھانا pardah uṭhānā, v. To lift or raise the curtain; to reveal; to expose.

پردہ پڑنا pardah paṛna, v. To be covered; to be screened; to be concealed.

پردہ پوش pardah posh, adj. A veiled person; one who connives at the faults of others.

پردہ پوشی pardah poshī, n.f. The act of concealing a blemish; conniving at a fault; keeping one's secret.

پردہ دار pardah dar, n.m. & adj. One who puts on the veil; confidential; a chamberlain.

پردہ در pardah dar, adj. One who rends the veil or exposes; an impru-dent or immodest man; a betrayer of secrets.

پردہ ڈالنا pardah ḍalnā, v. To draw the curtain; to connive at; to keep a secret.

پردہ رکھنا pardah rakhnā, v. To hide things (from); to give obscure hints; to relate a matter in such a way that it may be understood in part only.

پردہ غیب pardah-ĕ ghaib, n.m. Hidden or invisible world.

پردہ فاش کرنا pardah fāsh karnā, v. To betray secrets; to expose.

پردہ کرنا pardah karnā, v. To conceal; To hide oneself; to sit behind a curtain.

پردھان pardhān (H) n.m. Chief; leader; president; a minister or counsellor of state.

پردیس pardes (H) n.m. Foreign country.

پردیسی pardesi (H) n.m. & adj. Foreign; foreigner; stranger.

پرزہ purzah (P) n.m. A scrap of paper; a piece; a bit; a rag; a mop (of cloth); the down of birds.

پرزے اڑانا یا کرنا purze uṛānā yā karnā, v. To cut into pieces; to make mince-meat of; to hack.

پرزے ہونا purze honā, v. To be severely wounded; to be cut or haked to pieces.

چلتا پرزہ chaltā purzah, n.m. A sharp or cunning fellow.

پرس purs (P) Asking; questioning; enquiring (used at the end of comp.).

پرساد یا پرشاد parsād yā parshād (S) n.m. Food offered to a god; the remnants of food presented to an idol or a great man or spiritual guide.

پرسان pursān (P) adj. Asking; inquisitive; inquirer.

پرسان حال pursān-ĕ ḥāl, adj. Inquiring after one's condition or health.

پرست parast (P) adj. Worshipper; devoted to (used in comp. as, بت پرست but parast, an idolator).

پرستار parastār (P) n.m. A worshipper; an adorer; a devoted servant; a slave.

پرستاری parastārī, n.f. Worship; service; adoration.

پرستان paristāṅ, n.m. A fairy land.

پرستش parastish (P) n.f. Worship; devotion.

پرستش گاہ parastish gāh, n.f. A place of worship; mosque; temple; church.

پرسش pursish (P) n.f. Asking; questioning; enquiry; interrogation.

پرسش کرنا pursish karnā, v. To enquire; to make an enquiry; to interrogate.

پرسوت parsūt (S) n.m. The whites; flour albus; a disease with which newly delivered women sometimes suffer.

پرسوں parsoṅ (H) adv. The day before yesterdry; the day after to-morrow.

پرسیاوشاں parsiyāwushāṅ (P) n.m. The herb, maidenhair.

پرکار parkār (P) n.m. A pair of compasses.

پرکالہ parkālah (P) n.m. A spark; a pane of glass.

پرکھ parakh (H) n.f. Inspection; test; proof; scrutiny; examination; trial; experiment.

پرکھنا parakhnā (H) v. To examine; to test; to assay; to inspect; to prove; to try.

پرگنہ parganah (P) n.m. A sub-division of a district.

پرلا ' پرلی parlā, parlī (H) adj. Of the other side; the next in order. adv. On the other side; far beyond; a long way off.

پرلے درجے کا ' پرلے سرے کا parle darje kā, parle sire kā, adj. & adv. Of the highest order; great; thorough; in the extreme; utterly; thoroughly.

پرلی طرف parlī taraf, adv. On the other side.

پرلو parlo (H) n.f. A general destruction; destruction of the whole world; doomsday.

پرلوک parlok (S) n.m. Tne upper region; the next world.

پرلوک سدھارنا parlok sidhārnā, v. To die.

پرم آتما (پرماتما) parm ātmā (S) n.m. The Supreme Spirit; soul of the universe.

پرمل parmal (H) n.m. Parched rice. adj. Sweet-scented.

پرمیشور parmeshwar (S) n.m. The Supreme God.

پرنالہ parnālah (H) n.m. Outlet for water; conduit; gutter; a drain.

پرنالی parnāli (H) n.f. A small drain.

پرنانا parnānā (H) n.m. Maternal great grandfather.

پرنانی parnāni (H) n.f. Maternal great grandmother.

پرند ' پرندہ pariṅd, priṅdah (P) n.m. A winged creature; a bird. adj. Flying; winged.

پرنیاں parniyāṅ (P) n.m. A kind of fine painted silk (from China); garments made of this silk.

پروا parwā (P) n.f. Care; concern; anxiety; want; desire; inclination; affection; fear; terror.

پروا purwā (H) n.f. Easterly-wind.

پروار parwār (H) n.m. Dynasty; tribe; dependents; the next world.

پرواز parwāz (P) n.f. Flying; flight

پروازی parwāzi, n.f. Flying; (used at the end of comp. as, بلند پروازی buland parwāzi, lofty flight or thinking).

پروال parwāl (H) n.m. A disease of the eyelids in which the eye-lashes fall off and new crooked hair come out; stye.

پروان parwān (H) n.m. Fruit; result. adj. True; just; complete; successful

پروان چڑھنا parwān charhnā, v. To grow up; to increase; to thrive; to prosper; to be married.

پروانجات parwānajāt (P) n.m. (plu. of پروانہ parwānah) Orders; licences; royal grants; passes.

پروانگی parwānagī (P) n.f. Order; permission; leave; command.

پروانہ parwānah (P) n.m. A moth; a butterfly; a lover; a written order; a warrant; a writ; a licence; a pass; permission; command; a precept.

پروانہ' تلاشی parwānah-ĕ talāshī, n.m. A search warrant.

پروانہ' راہداری parwānah-ĕ rāhdāri, n.m. Passport; safe conduct; permit; pass.

پروانۂ گرفتاری *parwānah-ĕ giriftāri, n.m.* A warrant of arrest.

پروانه هونا *parwānah honā, v.* To be an ardent lover; to be desperately in love (with); to be an ardent lover (of).

پروتا *parotā* (H) *n.m.* Great-grandson; presents of food given to servants at marriages.

پرور *parwar* (P) *adj.* Nourisher; cherisher; protector; (used as the last member of compounds as, بنده پرور *bandah parwar*, cherisher of servant; my lord)

پروردگار *parwardigār* (P) *n.m.* The cherisher; Providence; an epithet of the Deity.

پرورده *pirwardah* (P) *adj.* & *n.m.* Fostered; brought up; nourished; reared; a slave; a domestic servant who has been brought up from babyhood.

پرورش *parwarish* (P) *n.f.* Fostering; rearing; nourishment; support; sustenance; patronising; educating; protecting.

پرورش کرنا *parwarish karnā, v.* To support; to nourish; to bring up; to patronise; to educate; to protect.

پرونا *pironā* (H) *v.* To pierce; to penetrate; to thread (a needle); to stringe (pearls).

پروهت *purohit* (H) *n.m.* A family priest.

پروین *parwin* (P) *n.m.* Plaiedes; cluster of small stars; brilliant group of persons or things.

پرهیز *parhez* (P) *n.m.* Abstinence; forbearance; abstaining or keeping aloof; control of passions; regimen; caution; sobriety; prevention; temperance.

پرهیز سب سے اچھا نسخه هے *parhez sab se achchhā nuskhah hai, prov.* Prevention is better than cure.

پرهیز کرنا *parhez karnā, v.* To abstain from; to keep aloof; to control one's passions; to be on one's guard (from); to avoid; to observe a regimen.

پرهیزی *parhezi, adj.* Fit for a person under a regimen.

پرهیزی کهانا *parhezi khānā, n.m.* Diet prescribed for a sick person.

پری *pari* (P) *n.f.* A fairy; a beautiful woman.

پری پیکر ، چهره ، رخسار ، رو *pari paikar, chehrah, rukhsār, rū, adj.* Fairy-faced; angelic; beautiful.

پری زاد *pari zād, n.m.* & *adj.* Born of a fairy; beautiful; lovely.

پری کا سایه هونا *pari kā sāyah honā, v.* To be possessed by a fairy.

پری وش *pari wash, adj.* Fairy-like; beautiful.

پرے *pare* (H) *adv.* Beyond; yonder; further off; at distance; on the other side; away.

پرے رهنا *pare rahnā, v.* To remain at a distance from; to keep away; not to mix with others.

پریت *prit* (S) *n.f.* Love; affection; amity; fondness; friendship.

پریت *pret* (S) *n.m.* A departed soul; spirit of the dead; ghost; evil spirit; a fiend.

پریتم *pritam* (H) *adj.* Dearest; most beloved. *n.m.* A lover; a husband.

پریشان *pareshān* (P) *adj.* Dispersed; perplexed; confused; troubled; dishevelled; distracted; distressed; deranged; ruined; wretched.

پریشان حال *pareshān ḥāl, adj.* Embarrassed; in a distressed condition.

پریشان خاطر یا دل *pareshān khātir yā dil*, Distressed in mind; troubled in mind.

پریشان کرنا *pareshān karnā, v.* To confound; to distract; to perplex; to trouble; to perturb; to derange; to harass.

پریشان گوئی pareshān go'ī, *n.f.* Confused or absurd talk.

پریشان نظری pareshān naẓarī, *n.f.* Confusion of sight.

پریشان ہونا pareshān honā, *v.* To be confused; to be distressed; to be perplexed.

پریشانی pareshānī (P) *n.f.* Confusion; distress; perplexity; dispersion; scattering; derangement; misery; distraction; perturbation; trouble.

پریم prem (S) *n.m.* Love; affection; kindness; friendship.

پریمی premī (S) *adj. & n.m.* Affectionate; loving; lover.

پڑا puṛā (H) *n.f.* A large parcel or packet.

پڑا پانا paṛā pānā *v.* To find something lying; to get easily or for nothing.

پڑا رہنا paṛā rahnā, *v.* To remain idle; to sleep or be idle all the time.

پڑاؤ paṛā'o (H) *n.m.* Halting place ; a camp ; encampment ; a camping ground ; an encamped army ; a crowd ; an assembly ; a stage.

پڑاؤ ڈالنا paṛā'o ḍālnā, *v.* To encamp.

پڑتا paṛtā (H) *n.m.* Share; portion; dividend; rate; rent.

پڑتال paṛtāl (H) *n.f.* Revision ; comparison ; survey ; remeasurement ; reweighing ; checking.

پڑتال کرنا paṛtāl karnā, *v.* To test ; to revise; to remeasure; to recount; to check; to audit.

پڑنا paṛnā (H) *v.* To fall; to lie down; to repose; to befall; to happen; to occur; to drop down; to be bed-ridden; to meddle; to hang or depend upon; to be bent upon.

پڑوس paṛos (H) *n.m.* Neighbourhood, vicinity.

پڑوسن paṛosan (H) *n.f.* A female neighbour.

پڑوسی paṛosī (H) *n.m.* A male neighbour.

پڑھا لکھا ، پڑھی لکھی paṛhā likkhā, paṛhī likkhī (H) *adj.* Educated ; learned.

پڑھانا paṛhānā (H) *v.* To teach; to instruct; to teach a bird to talk; to make one read or study.

پڑھائی paṛhā'ī, *n.f.* The act of reading or teaching; tuition; method of teaching.

پڑھ پتھر paṛh paththar (H) *adj. & n.m.* A learned fool.

پڑھن paṛhin (H) *n.f.* A mullet.

پڑھنا paṛhnā (H) *v.* To read; to recite; to repeate; to earn to read; to decipher; to speak.

پڑیا puṛyā (H) *n.f.* A small packet; anything wrapped up in paper or leaves; a powder; a dose of medicine.

پزاواہ pazāwah (P) *n.m.* A brick-kiln.

پژمردگی pazhmurdagī (P) *n.f.* Witheredness; fadedness; numbness; dejection; frozen state; rottenness.

پژمردہ pazhmurdah (P) *adj.* Withered; pallid; faded; decayed; drooping; blighted; sad.

پس pas (P) *adv. & prep.* After; behind; at length; then; therefore; finally; hence; so; consequently; wherefore.

پس انداز pas andāz, *n.m.* Savings; something laid by (for hard times).

پس پا pas pā, *adj.* Repulsed; driven back.

پس پا کرنا pas pā karnā, *v.* To repulse; to drive back.

پس پا ہونا pas pā honā, *v.* To retreat; to fall behind; to slink behind; to flee back; to desist from an attempt.

پس پشت pas-ĕ pusht *adv.* Behind one's back; in one's absence.

پس پشت ڈالنا pas-ĕ push˘ ḍālnā, *v.* To neglect; to postpone.

پس ماندہ *pas māndah, adj.* Remaining behind; survivor; surplus; backward.

پس منظر *pas manẓar, n.m.* Back-ground.

پس و پیش *pas-ŏ pesh, n.m.* Hesitation; indecision.

پس و پیش کرنا *pas-ŏ pesh karnā, v.* To doubt; to hesitate.

پس ورق *pas warq, adv.* Overleaf.

پسارنا *pasārnā* (H) *v.* To spread; to stretch out; to reach; to extend; to expand; to display; to distend.

پسانا *pisānā* (H) *v.* To cause to ground.

پسائی *pisā'i* (H) *n.f.* Price paid for grinding.

پست *past* (P) *adj.* Low; humble; mean; vile; lower; below; abject.

پست خیال *past khayāl, adj.* Having low ideas.

پست فطرت *past fitrat, adj.* Of inferior understanding; low natured; base.

پست قد *past qadd, adj.* Dwarf; low in stature; of small size.

پست و بلند *past-ŏ buland, n.m.* Ups and downs; vicissitudes.

پست همت *past himmat, adj.* Low-minded; mean-spirited; unambitious; coward.

پست همتی *past himmati, n.f.* Low-mindedness; mean-spiritedness; cowardice.

پست ہونا *past honā, v.* To be humbled; to be defeated; to be disgraced; to lag behind; to fall flat.

پستی *pastī* (P) *n.f.* Inferiority; lowness; humility.

پستان *pistān* (P) *n.m.* Breasts (of a woman); pap or dug.

پستول *pistaul* (corr. of English) *n.m.* Pistol.

پستہ *pistah* (P) *n.m.* Pistachio nut.

پستہ کتا *pistah kuttā, n.m.* A lap-dog.

پسر *pisar* (P) *n.m.* Son; boy; child; youth.

پسر خواندہ *pisar-ĕ khwāndah, n.m.* Adopted son.

پسر صلبی *pisar-ĕ ṣulbi, n.m.* One's own son; a son from one's own loins

پسرنا *pasarnā* (H) *v.* To be spread; to be stretched out; to be distended; to lie prostrate; to behave obstinately; to insist unduly.

پسلی *pasli* (H) *n.f.* A rib.

پسلی پھڑکنا *pasli pharaknā, v.* To feel a quivering sensation over the ribs which is regarded as a sign of an impending visit from an absent friend.

پسلی کا درد *paslī kā dard, n.m.* Pleurisy.

پسنا *pisnā* (H) *v.* To be ground; to be reduced to powder; to be ruined.

پسند، پسندیدگی *pasand, pasandīdagi* (P) *n.f.* Choice; approval; preference; discretion; approbation.

پسندا *pasandā, n.m.* Chopped or slashed meat.

پسندیدہ *pasandīdah* (P) *adj.* Chosen; liked; approved; desirable; pleasing; laudable; favourite.

پسو *pissū* (H) *n.m.* A flea.

پسوانا *piswāna* (H) *v.* See پسانا *pisānā.*

پسوائی *piswā'i* (H) *n.f.* See پسائی *pisā'ī.*

پسیجنا *pasījnā* (H) *v.* To perspire; to sweat; to melt (with pity); to soften; to regard or treat with compassion; to be touched.

پسینا *pasinā* (H) *n.m.* Prespiration; sweat.

پسینے پسینے ہونا *pasine pasine honā, v.* To break into violent perspiration (through shame); to be covered with sweat (through heat or toil); to be disturbed or alarmed.

پسینے میں ڈوبنا یا نہا جانا pasine men ḍūbnā yā nahā jānā, v. To be drenched in sweat.

پشت pusht (P) n.f. The back; support; generation; descent; progenitors; ancestry.

پشت بہ پشت یا پشت در پشت pusht bah pusht yā pusht dar pusht, adv. Generation after generation; with back to back joined.

پشت پر رهنا pusht par rahnā, v. To be at the back of; to back up; to support strongly.

پشت پناہ pusht panāh, n.f. Refuge; ally; support; patronage.

پشت دکھانا pusht dikhānā, v. To flee; to run away; to proceed on a journey.

پشت دینا pusht denā, v. To turn tail, to flee.

پشتارہ pushtārah (P) n.m. Burden; bundle; heap; load; mass.

پشتو pashto (P) n.f. The language of the Pathāns.

پشته pushtah (P) n.m. Prop; bank; dyke; buttress; quay; eminence; heap; dam.

پشته بندی pushtah bandi, n.f. Embankment.

پشتی pushti (P) n.f. Alliance, support; prop; the cover of a book.

پشتی بان pushti ban, n.m. Helper; supporter; ally; aider.

پشتی بانی pushti bāni, n.m. Support; alliance; aid.

پشتینی pushtini, adj. Hereditary; ancestral.

پشم pashm (P) n.f. Wool; fur; hair; any worthless thing.

پشم پر مارنا pashm par mārnā, v. To be perfectly contented and independent; to despise; to hate; to disregard entirely; to care not a fig.

پشمین pashmin (P) adj. Woollen; hairy.

پشمینه pashminah (P) n.m. Woollen cloth.

پشواز pishwāz, n.f. A gown worn by dancing girls.

پشه pashshah (P) n.m. A gnat.

پشیمان pashemān (P) adj. Penitent; sorrowful; repentant. ashamed; abashed; disgraced.

پشیمانی pashemāni (P) n.f. Repentance; penitence; regret; shame.

پطرس patras (L) n.m. A disciple of Christ; Peter.

پکا ، پکی pakkā, pakki (H) adj. Ripe; mature; baked; cooked; dressed; burnt (bricks); expert; strong; solid; firm; substantial; metalled (road); fast or lasting (colour); fearless; shrewd; resolute; cunning; instructed; permanent.

پکا پکایا ملنا pakkā pakāyā milnā, v. To get without toil or hardship; to achieve without undergoing much trouble.

پکا پھوڑا pakkā phoṛa, n.m. Suppurated boil; sad; distressed.

پکا کرنا pakkā karnā, v. To strengthen; to make sure; to corroborate; to verify; to establish a claim beyond dispute; to confirm.

پکا هونا pakkā honā, v. To be ripe; to be confirmed; to made permanent; to be established.

پکار pukār (H) n.f. Call; shout; cry; calling out aloud; complaint; summons; invitation; bawl.

پکارنا pukārnā (H) v. To call aloud; to bawl; to cry out; to exclaim; to shout.

پکانا pakānā (H) v. To ripen; to dress victuals; to cook; to bake.

پکاؤ pakā'o (H) n.m. Suppuration.

پکائی pakā'i (H) n.f. Ripeness; cooking; remuneration for cooking.

پکڑ pakaṛ (H) *n.f.* The act of seizing; seizure; capture; hold; grip; wrestling; clutch; grasp; criticism.

پکڑا دینا pakṛā denā (H) *v.* To cause one to be arrested; to hand over; to have one captured.

پکڑانا pakṛānā (H) *v.* To cause to be caught or seized or laid hold of: to make over; to deliver; to hand over

پکڑ دھکڑ pakaṛ dhakaṛ (H) *n.f.* Capture; seizure; arrest. general arrest.

پکڑ لانا pakaṛ lana (H) *v.* To lay hold (of): to arrest: to seize: to capture.

پکڑنا pakarna (H) *v.* To catch: to lay hold of; to arrest: to handle: to overtake; to detect; to discover; to seize; to apprehend: to pick holes in.

پکڑوانا pakarwana. See پکڑانا pakṛanā.

پکنا pakna (H) *v.* To be dressed or cooked; to ripen; to suppurate; to turn grey (hair).

پکوان pakwan (H) *n.m.* Cooked or dressed food; victuals fried in butter or oil; cakes; pastry.

پکوانا pakwāna (H) *v.* To cause to be cooked; to get one to cook; to cause to ripen.

پکوائی pakwā'ī (H) *n.f.* Price paid for cooking.

پکوڑا pakauṛā (H) *n.m.* Fried gram-flour paste mixed with onions and greens.

پکھال pakhāl. See پخال pakhal.

پکھراج pukhrāj (H) *n.m.* A topaz (a kind of precious stone).

پکھیرو pakherū (H) *n.m.* A bird; a fleet footed person.

پگ pag (H) *n.m.* Foot.

پگ ڈنڈی pag ḍanḍī, *n.f.* A footpath; pathway; track; a by-path.

پگاہ pagāh (P) *n.f.* Morning; dawn of day; twilight.

پگڑی pagṛī (H) *n.f.* A turban; black transaction; illegal payment.

پگڑی آتارنا pagṛī utarnā, *v.* To dishonour; to disgrace.

پگڑی اچھالنا pagṛī uchhālnā, *v.* To disgrace; to dishonour; to mock at.

پگڑی باندھنا pagṛī bāndhnā, *v.* To put on a turban; to be presented with a turban as a token of honour or headship; to mature.

پگڑی بدلنا pagṛī badalnā, *v.* To change turbans; to become intimate friends.

پگڑی پیروں پر رکھنا pagṛī pairon par rakhna, *v.* To place one's turban at the feet of another in token of extreme submission and humility; to ask for pardon with all humility.

پگلا pagla (H) *adj.* & *n.m.* Foolish; unwise; stupid; mad.

پگلانا ، پگھلانا piglānā, pighlānā (H) *v.* To melt; to dissolve, to soften; to assuage; to fuse; to mollify.

پگلنا ، پگھلنا pigalnā, pighalnā (H) *v.* To melt; to dissolve; to yield; to tone down; to fuse; to flow.

پگلی pagli. Faminine form of پگلا paglā.

پل pal (H) *n.m.* A moment; a particular measure of time round about a half second.

پل بھر میں pal bhar meṅ, *adv.* In an instant; in a moment; immediately; instantly; in the twinkling of an eye.

پل pul (H) *n.m.* A bridge; A cause-way.

پل باندھنا pul bāndhnā, *v.* To make a bridge; to raise a dam; to form a heap; to supply in abundance; to abound; to exaggerate.

پل صراط pul ṣirāṭ, *n.f.* According to Muslim, the bridge over which the righteous will pass into Paradise.

پلا palā (H) *n.m.* A large spoon for taking out oil; a ladle.

پلا pallā (H) n.m. Space; distance; one of a pair of scales; border of cloth; side; protection; assistance; one shutter or fold of a door.

پلا بھاری ہونا pallā bhārī honā, v. To be encumbered with a large family; to overwhelm; to have greater chances of success.

پلا چھڑانا pallā chhuṛānā, v. To get rid or quit (of).

پلے باندھنا palle bāndhnā, v. To preserve carefully; to marry; to take care; to remember.

پلے پڑنا palle paṛnā, v. To inherit; to be married (to); to be allotted (to).

پلے سے باندھنا palle se bāndhnā, v. To marry (a woman).

پلے ہونا palle honā, v. To possess money; to be wealthy.

پلا pillā (H) n.m. A puppy; a pup; a whelp.

حرامی پلا ḥarāmī pillā, adj. A bastard.

پلا پلایا ، پلی پلائی palā palāyā, pali palā'ī (H) adj. Well-fed; carefully or tenderly nurtured; grown up.

پلاس pilās (P) n.m. Very coarse canvas or cloth.

پلاس pilās (S) n.m. Name of a tree (ڈھاک dhāk).

پلانا pilānā (H) v. To give a drink of water or cause to drink; to suckle; to take an animal to water.

پلاؤ pulā'o (P) n.m. A dish made of rice boiled in soup with flesh, spices etc.

پلائی pilā'ī (H) n.f. Price paid for suckling; a wet-nurse.

پل پڑنا pil paṛnā (H) v. To attack suddenly; to give a thrashing; to jostle violently; to get to grips with work.

پلپلا ، پلپلی pilpilā, pilpilī (H) adj. Soft; flabby; flaccid; weak; feeble.

پلپلاھٹ pilpilāhaṭ (H) n.f. Softness; flabbiness.

پلٹا palṭā (H) n.m. Turning back; flight; retreat; turn; exchange; recompense; revenge; retaliation; an iron pan or ladle with a long handle.

پلٹا دینا palṭā denā, v. To send back; to turn over; to reverse.

پلٹا کھانا palṭā khānā, v. To turn over; to tilt over; to turn upside down; to overturn; to turn over head and heels.

پلٹانا palṭānā (H) v. To repel; to convert; to overturn.

پلٹس pulṭis (corr. of English) n.f. Poultice.

پلٹن palṭan (corr. of English) n.f. Platoon; regiment.

پلٹنا palaṭnā (H) v. To turn over; to retreat; to rebound; to suffer a turn of fortune; to exchange; to return.

پلٹی palṭī (H) n.f. A turn; repulsion; a somersault.

پلڑا palṛā (H) n.m. One side of a pair of scales.

پلستر palastar (corr. of English) n.m. Plaster.

پلک palak (H) n.f. The eyelashes; a moment; instant.

پلک جھپکنا palak jhapaknā, v. To wink; to twinkle.

پلک جھپکتے palak jhapakte, adv. In the twinkling of an eye; in a moment; in an instant.

پلک لگنا palak lagnā, v. To close the eyelids; to have a nap.

پلکوں سے زمین جھاڑنا pālkon se zamīn jhāṛnā, v. To welcome cordially; to show great respect.

پلکوں سے نمک چننا palkon se namak chun-nā, v. To undertake a very arduous task.

پلنا pilnā (H) v. To rush against; to attack; to assault; to be thrashed; to be crushed; to be trodden; to labour hard.

پلنا palnā (H) v. To be reared; to be nourished; to be fattened; to be fed; to thrive.

پلندا pulandā, n.m. A bundle; a parcel; a package.

پلنگ palang (H) n.m. A bed; a bedstead.

پلنگ پوش palang posh, n.m. A coverlet; a counterpane; a bed spread.

پلنگ کو لات مار کر کھڑے ہونا palang ko lāt mār kar khaṛe honā, v. To get rid of one's sickness; to regain health; to recover after severe illness.

پلنگڑی palangṛi (H) n.f. A small bedstead; a baby bed.

پلوانا pilwānā (H) v. To cause to be crushed.

پلوٹھا ' پلوٹھی کا palotthā, palotthī kā (H) adj. First born: the eldest child.

پلی palī (H) n.f. A sort of a ladle for taking out oil.

پلی پلی جوڑنا pali palı joṛnā, v. To collect by drops or little by little.

پلیا puliā (H) n.f. A small bridge; a culvert.

پلیتا palıta (P) n.m. A thick wick; a lighted roll of cotton or lint; the match of gun.

پلیتھن plethan (H) n.m. Dry; flour, used when rolling bread.

پلید palid (P) adj. Unclean; polluted; impure; nasty; defiled.

پلیدی palidi, n.f. Pollution; impurity; uncleanliness.

پن pun (S) n.m. Virtue; alms; charity; moral or religious merit.

پن کرنا pun karna, v. To give alms.

پن pan (H) A suffix denoting the abstract quality and equivalent to English termination (ship; hood; ness), as لڑکپن larakpan (childhood). Contraction of پانچ pānch (five), پانی pāni (water) and of پان pan (betel).

پن چکی pan chakkı, n.f. A water-mill.

پنسال pansal n.m. A water-gauge; a waterstand provided for passengers.

پنسال نویس pansāl nawis, n.m. A clerk who records the flow of water in a canal.

پن سیری pan seri, n.f. A weight of five seers.

پن گھٹ pan ghaṭ, n.m. A place for drawing water; well or tank from which water is drawn.

پن واڑی pan wāṛi, n.f. A betel-garden. n.m. A betel-seller.

پن pin (E) n.f. A knobbled needle; a peg or nail or pin.

پنا pannā (H) n.m. An emerald; a gold or silver leaf; page of a book; a sheet of metal.

پنا pinnā (H) n.m. A lump; a bail of thread; a real; oil-cake; a cake of mustard seed remaining after the extraction of oil and given to animals for food.

پنانا panānā (H) v. To cause the milk to come into the udder of animals.

پناہ panah (P) n.f. Protection; asylum; refuge; shade; shelter.

پناہ دینا panāh denā, v. To protect; to give shelter; to harbour.

پناہ گاہ panāh gāh, n.f. An asylum; a house of refuge.

پناہ گیر panāh gir, n.m. A refugee.

پناہ لینا panāh lenā, v. To take shelter.

پناہ مانگنا panāh māngnā, v. To seek protection; to seek refuge; to avoid; to shun.

پنبہ pambah (P) n.m. Cotton.

پنبہ دانہ pambah dānah, n.m. Cotton seed.

پنبہ دوز pambah doz, n.m. A cotton-carder.

پنبہ دھن pambah dahan, adj. Taciturn; silent in company.

پنپنا panapnā (H) v. To take root; to grow vigorously; to thrive; to prosper; to commence increasing in bulk.

پنتھ **panth** (H) *n.m.* A road; path; way; a path in morals or religion; a doctrine; a sect; a religious order.

پنتھی **panthi** (H) *n.m.* A traveller; a follower of any sect or party in religious matters.

پنج **panj** (P) *adj.* Five; five years old (a horse); cinque (in gambling).

(پنجاب) پنج آب **panjāb**, *n.m.* The land of five rivers; the Punjab; a former province of West Pakistan.

پنج آیت **panj āyat**, *n.f.* The five *sūrat* of the Quran which are read during the mourning of a Muslim.

پنج تن پاک **panj tan pāk**, *n.m.* Five holy persons, according to Muslims, the Holy Prophet, Hazrat Ali, Hazrat Fatimah, Imam Hasan and Imam Husain.

پنج روزہ **panj rozah**, *adj.* Of five days; a few days; a week constitutes seven days, deducting one day on which a person is born, and one day on which he is to die, the life consists of only five days.

پنج سالہ **panj sālah**, *adj.* Of five years; quinquennial.

پنج شاخہ **panj shākhah**, *n.m.* A lamp containing five candles; a hand made of ivory, &c. to scratch the back with.

پنج شنبہ **panj shambah**, *n.m.* Thursday.

پنج گانہ نماز **panj gānah namāz**, *n.f.* Five daily prayers.

پنج گوشہ **panj goshah**, *adj.* Having five angles; pentangular.

پنجابی **panjābi**, *n.m.* An inhabitant of the Punjab. *n.f.* The language spoken in the Punjab. *adj.* Relating to the Punjab.

پنجارا **pinjārā** (H) *n.m.* Cotton carder; one whose business is to beat or separate cotton.

پنجر **pinjar** (H) *n.m.* A skeleton; the ribs.

پنجر ہونا **pinjar honā**, *v.* To become a skeleton; to become thin or lean.

پنجرا **pinjrā** (H) *n.m.* A cage; a trap.

پنجم **panjum** (P) *adj.* Fifth.

پنجنی **pinjni** (P) *n.m.* A bow used for cleaning and beating cotton.

پنجہ **panjah** (P) *n.m.* The five of anything; an aggregate of five; the hand with fingers extended; claw; the forepart of a foot or shoe; clutch; grasp; the five of cards; a cast of five with dice; a torch having five branches.

پنجۂ آفتاب **panjah-ĕ āftāb**, *n.m.* Rays of the sun.

پنجۂ مریم **panjah-ĕ maryam** *n.m.* A kind of grass.

پنجہ پھیرنا **panjah phernā**, *v.* To overcome to over power; to twist round the hand of an adversary by interlocking fingers with him.

پنجہ کرنا یا لڑانا **panjah karnā yā laṛānā**, *v.* To interlock fingers with an adversary and endeavour to twist his hand or wrist.

پنجہ کش **panjah kash**, *n.m.* An iron instrument resembling a hand, with which wrestlers exerise themselves by locking their fingers into those of the instrument; a cake bearing the marks of five fingers.

پنجہ مارنا **panjah marnā**, *v.* To claw; to pounce upon; to snap at.

پنجوں کے بل چلنا **panjon ke bal chalnā**, *v.* To walk on tiptoe; to strut.

پنجے جمانا **panje jamānā**, *v.* To stabilize one's position; to take possession by force; to become firm.

پنجے جھاڑ کر پیچھے پڑ جانا **panje jhāṛ kar pichhe paṛ jānā**, *v.* To insist upon; to press hard; to tease.

پنجیری panjīrī (H) *n.f.* An invigorating preparation composed of five ingredients given to puerperal woman; a kind of sweetmeat composed of sugar, butter, flour, &c.

پنچ pańch (H) *adj.* Five. *n.m.* The member of a pańchāyat or an arbitrary committe consisting of five members.

پنچ پیریا pańch piriyā, *n.m.* Persons who worship five pirs of Muslims.

پنچ رتن pańch ratan, *n.m.* A collection of five jewels (gold, diamond, sapphre, ruby and pearl).

پنچایت pańchāyat (H) *n.f.* Meeting of any particular society; a native court of arbitration consisting of five or more members; a council; a jury; an inquest; a council of village elders.

پنچایت جوڑنا pańchāyat joṛnā, *v.* To call a meeting of the pańchāyat.

پنچایت نامه pańchāyat nāmah, *n.m.* Award of a court of arbitration.

پنچم pańcham (S) *adj.* Fifth. *n.m.* A musical note; the soprano.

پنچمی pańchamī (S) *n.f.* Fifth day of the lunar fortnight.

پنچھی pańchhī (H) *n.m.* A bird.

پند pańd (P) *n.m.* Advice; counsel; admonition; moral; maxim.

پند گو pańd go, *n.m.* An adviser; a monitor.

پندار pindār (P) *n.m.* Imagination; thought; notion; pride; arrogance; self-opinion; self-conceit.

پندره pańdrah (H) *adj.* Fifteen.

پندرهواڑه pańdarhwāṛah (H) *n.m.* Fifteen days; a fortnight.

پندرهواں pańdrahwāṅ (H) *adj.* Fifteenth.

پنڈ pińḍ (H) *n.m.* Body; person; a ball of flour or boiled rice.

پنڈ چھڑانا pińḍ chhuṛānā, *v.* To avoid; to escape.

پنڈ چھوٹنا pińḍ chhūṭnā, *v.* To be rid of.

پنڈا pińḍā (H) *n.m.* A lump; a ball of string; body; person; private part of a woman.

پنڈا پھیکا ہونا pińḍā phīkā honā, *v.* To feel feverish.

پنڈال pińḍāl (H) *n.m.* A canopy under which a meeting is held.

پنڈت pańḍit (S) *n.m.* A learned or wise man; a teacher; a learned Brahman. *adj.* Wise; learned.

پنڈتانی pańḍtānī, *n.f.* Wife of a pańḍit.

پنڈلی pińḍlī (H) *n.f.* Calf of the leg; the leg; the shin.

پنڈی pińḍī (H) *n.f.* A lump; a small ball of string.

پنس pinas. See پینس pīnas.

پنساری pansārī (H) *n.m.* A vendar of drugs, spices, herbs, &c., a druggist; a grocer.

پنشن pinshan (E) *n.f.* Pension; sinecure.

پنکھ pańkh (H) *n.m.* Feather; wing; pinion.

پنکھا pańkhā (H) *n.m.* A fan; a ventilator.

پنکھڑی pańkhṛī (H) *n.f.* A petal; a flower-leaf.

پنکھیا pańkhyā (H) *n.f.* A small fan. *n.m.* A kind of fakir who fans everybody.

پنک pinak (H) *n.f.* Intoxication from eating opium; drowsiness.

پنگوڑا pińgūṛā (H) *n.m.* A cradle.

پننا pinnā (H) *v.* To card or comb cotton.

پنوانا pinwānā (H) *v.* To have the cotton carded; to cause to be abused or reproached by another.

پنہاں pinhāṅ (P) *adj.* Concealed; hidden; secret.

پنی pinnī (H) *n.f.* A ball of sweetmeat made of rice, sugar and butter.

پنیر panir (P) *n.m.* Cheese.

پنیری paniri, *n.f.* Seedling; a young flowering plant.

پو pau (H) *n.f.* The one or ace in dice; dawn of the day.

پو بارہ pau bārah, *n.f.* The ace and the twelve in dice; success; triumph.

پو پھٹنا pau phaṭnā, *v.* To dawn.

پوا pawwā (H) *n.m.* A weight of a quarter of a seer; a quarter; a quarter of a full bottle.

پوپلا ، پوپلی poplā, popli (H) *adj.* Toothless person.

پوت pūt (H) *n.m.* A son.

پوت کے پاؤں پالنے میں نظر آجاتے ھیں pūt ke pāon pālne men nazar ā jāte hain, *prov.* Coming events cast their shadows before; childhood shows the man.

پوتا pota (H) *n.m.* Grandson; son's son; a whitewashing brush.

پوتڑا potṛā (H) *n.m.* Baby clouts.

پوتڑوں کے رئیس potṛon ke ra'is, *n.m.* Born with a silver spoon in the mouth.

پوتنا potnā (H) *v.* To besmear; to plaster.

پوتھی pothi (H) *n.f.* A book; a clove of garlic.

پوتی poti (H) *n.f.* Son's daughter; granddaughter.

پوٹ poṭ (H) *n.f.* A bundle; a bale; a package; margin.

پوٹا poṭā (H) *n.m.* The crop or craw of a bird; stomach; an unfledged bird; a bearded woman; capacity; ability; status.

پوٹا تر ھونا poṭā tar honā, *v.* To be wealthy; to be in possession of wealth; to be fully satisfied.

پوٹلی poṭli (H) *n.f.* A small bundle.

پوجا pūjā (H) *n.f.* Worship; veneration; respect; devotion; idolatory.

پوجا پاٹ pūjā pāṭ, *n.f.* Prayer; idol worship and study of religious books.

پوج بیٹھنا pūj baiṭhnā (H) *v.* To squander; to spend money uselessly.

پوجنا pūjnā (H) *v.* To worship; to adore; to honour; to venerate.

پوچ poch (P) *adj.* Absurd; obscene; useless; nonsense; injudicious; of no consequence; trifling; insignificant; petty; mean; vile.

پوچ گو poch go, *adj* One who talks nonsense; prater.

پوچ گوئی poch go'i, *n.f.* Prating; nonsensical talk.

پوچھ puchh (H) *n.f.* Inquiry; investigation; invitation; value.

پوچھ گچھ pūchh gachh, *n.f.* Interrogation; examination.

پوچھنا pūchhnā (H) *v.* To ask; to inquire (after); to question; to interrogate; to invite; to care about; to value.

پود pud (P) *n.m.* Woof; threads woven in the the cloth across the warp.

پود paud (H) *n.f.* Young plants; seedlings; off-spring; progeny; children.

پودا paudā (H) *n.m.* A young plant; a sapling.

پودا لگانا paudā lagānā, *v.* To plant a sapling.

پودنا podnā (H) *n.m.* A kind of a small bird which build a domed nest in the grass.

پودینہ podinah (P) *n.m.* Mint.

پودینہ کا ست podinah kā sat, *n.m.* Peppermint.

پور por (H) *n.f.* Space between two joints of of a body, a bamboo or sugarcane.

پورا porā (H) *n.m.* A joint or phalanx of the fingers.

پورا ، پوری pūra, puri (H) *adj.* Whole; entire; full; perfect; complete; exact; just; powerful; accomplished.

پورا آترنا pūra utarnā, v. To prove upto the mark; to succeed; to come upto the standard.

پورا پڑنا pūrā paṛna, v. To be sufficient; to be able to perform an engagement.

پورا کرنا pūra karna, v. To fill up; to complete; to make up; to carry out; to keep a promise; to reimburse; to fulfil; to accomplish.

پورا هونا pura hona, v. To be sufficient; to come to an end; to be fulfilled; to die.

پوری بات purī bat, n.f. A complete proposition; a complete thought.

پوری نه پڑنا pūri nah paṛnā, v. Inability to make the two ends meet; not to be sufficient.

پورب pūrab (H) n.m. The east; countries lying to the east; the orient.

پوربی pūrbi (H) adj. Eastern; oriental. n.f. the dialect of India's eastern districts; the name of a rāgnī sung before evening.

پوربیا pūrbiyā (H) n.m. A native of India's eastern districts.

پورن ماشی pūran māshi (H) n.f. The day of the full moon.

پوری pori (H) n.f. A joint or a piece of bamboo, sugarcane, &c.

پوری pūri (H) n.f. A thin cake of meal fried in butter.

پوڑا pūṛā (H) n.m. A kind of sweet bread made of meal.

پوس pūs (H) n.m. The tenth solar month of Hindus.

پوست post (P) n.m. Skin; rind; crust; shell; bark; layer; intoxicating drug; poppy head or capsule of poppy.

پوست کن post kan, n.m .A skinner; a flayer.

پوست کنده post kandah, adj. Having the skin peeled off; without reserve; exact; fully detailed.

پوست کھینچنا post kheṅchnā, v. To flay; to skin.

پوستی posti (P) n.m. One who habitually intoxicates himself with poppy-heads; a lazy indolent person; a sot.

پوستین postin (P) n.f. A fur or leather garment; a leathern coat.

پوستین دوز postin doz, n.m. A furrier; a maker of leathern garments.

پوسنا pusna (H) v. To nourish; to rear; to breed; to foster (generally used with پالنا palna).

پوش posh (P) adj. Covering; dressed in; wearing (used in comp. as in برقع پوش burq' posh, wearing a veil).

پوشاک poshāk (P) n.f. Dress; garment; clothes; attire; habit; vestments; raiment; accoutrement.

پوشش poshish (P) n.f. Dress; garment; covering; clothes; wear; vestment.

پوشیدگی poshidagī (P) n.f. Concealment; secrecy.

پوشیده poshīdah (P) adj. Concealed; hidden; covered.

پول pol, n.m. Emptiness; hollowness; flesh (butcher's term).

پول pol (E) n m. A pole (land measure=50 yards).

پولا ، پولی polā, poli (H) adj. Soft; hollow; spongy; empty.

پولیس polis (E) n.f. Police.

پولیس چوکی polis chauki, n.f. Police post.

پون paun (H) adj. Three-quarters.

پون pawan (H) n.f. Air; wind.

پونا paunā (H) n.f. A perforated iron ladle used by confectioners; strainer. adj. Three-quarters.

پونجی pūnjī (H) n.f. Funds; capital; principal sum; wealth.

پونچھ pūnchh (H) n.f. A tail.

پھاڑ کھانا phār khānā, v To tear to pieces; to worry; to bite and gnaw.

پہاڑی pahārī (H) n.f. A hill; a small mountain; a musical tune; adj. Hilly; mountainous.

پہاڑی کوا pahārī kawwā, n.m. A jackdaw; a mountain crow.

پہاڑیا pahāriyā, n.m. A mountaineer; a hillman.

پھاگ phāg (H) n.m. The festivities or sports of Holi, a Hindu festival.

پھاگ کھیلنا phāg khelnā; v. To throw coloured water at one another at the time of Holi; to revel.

پھاگن phāgun (H) n.m. The name of the 12th solar month of the Hindu calendar.

پھال phāl (H) n.f. A ploughshare; a lump of betelnut; a step.

پھانا phānā (H) n.m. A wedge; a slip of wood used to fill up an opening.

پھاند phand, n.m. Leap; spring; jump.

پھاندنا phāndnā, v. To jump; to spring over; to leap over.

پھانس phāns, n.f. A noose; a splinter.

پھانسنا phānsnā, v. To noose; to entrap; to ensnare; to catch; to involve.

پھانسی phānsi, n.f. A noose; a loop; strangulation; halter; execution.

پھانسی پانا phānsi pānā. v. To be hanged or executed.

پھانسی چڑھنا یا لگنا phansi charhnā yā lagnā, v. To mount the scaffold.

پھانسی دینا phānsī denā, v. To hang; to execute.

پھانک phānk (H) n.f. A piece; a flake; a slice; a mouthful (of parched grain).

پھانکنا phānknā, v. To chuck into the mouth from the palm of the hand; to squander.

پھانکی phānki (H) n.f. A mouthpul of grain; a slice or piece of fruit; an objection (in logic).

پھاوڑا phāorā (H) n.m. A mattcok; a spade; a hoe.

پھاوڑے سے دانت phāore se dānt. n.m. Long teeth.

پھاوڑی phāori (H) n.f. A shovel; a kind of crutch on which a jogi leans; an instrument for removing cattle's dung; a piece of wood or staff, with a support at each end, which is held in both hands and laid horizontally in performing the exercise of ڈنڈ dand.

پھاہا یا پھایا phāhā yā phāya (H) n.m. A flock of cotton used for scenting or as lint: a plaster; a pledget.

پھبتی phabti (H) n.f. Conjecturing how a person looks by his dress; pleasantry; fun; jest.

پھبتی اُڑانا - کہنا - کسنا phabtī urānā, kahnā, kasnā, v. To utter a jest; to say what is conjectured by one's dress.

پھبتی سوجھنا phabtī sūjhnā, v. To think of a suitable jest.

پھبن phaban (H) n.f. Embellishment; ornament; decoration; chirm; grace; beauty; loveliness.

پھبنا phabnā, v. To suit; to fit.

پھپھولا phapholā (H) n.m. A blister; vesicle; a bubble.

پھپھولے پھوٹنا phaphole phūtnā, v. To break a blister; to be satiated.

پھپھولے دل کے پھوڑنا phaphole dil ke phornā, v. To take revenge for a grudge; to appease one's wrath.

پھپوندی phapundı, n.m. Mildew; mouldiness.

پھپھیرا phupherā, adj. Descended from or related through a paternal aunt.

پھٹ پڑنا phat parnā, v. To burst; to become excessively fat; to be produced plentifully.

آسمان پھٹ پڑنا āsmān phat parnā, v. To have a cloud burst; to rain hard.

پھٹ ph't, n.m. Curse; malediction; inter. Fie; shame! curse on you!

پھٹ پھٹ کرنا phit phit karnā, v. To curse; to rail at; to treat with contempt.

پھٹا phaṭā, adj. Torn; cracked; broken; n.m. Crack; rent; fissure.

پھٹا پرانا phaṭā purānā, n.m. Cast-off clothes; rags.

پھٹے میں پاؤں اڑانا phaṭṭe men pāon arāna, v. To put one's finger in another's pie; to burn one's finger in another's quarrel; to meddle with unnecessarily.

پھٹکارنا phiṭkārna, v. To cry shame on; to curse; to turn away with contempt; to rail at; to scold; to chide; to revile.

پھٹکری phiṭkarī (H) n.f. Alum.

پھٹکل phuṭkal (H) adj. Odd; separated; sundry; miscellaneous; single.

پھٹکن phaṭkan, n.f. The chaff or husk; siftings.

پھٹکنا phaṭaknā, v. To winnow; to shake or knock off; to separate.

پھٹکی phuṭkī(H) n.f. An Indo-Pakistani tailor bird; a blot; a stain; a spot; the unsolved portion of any soluble matter.

پھٹنا phaṭnā (H) v. To be cracked; to be burst; to be dispersed; to turn or become sour; to be rent; to be broken up.

پھٹ سے phaṭ se, adv. Immediately; without hesitation.

پہچان pahchān (H) n.f. Acquaintance; knowledge; recognisance; sign; distinction.

پہچاننا pahchānnā, v. To recognise; to identify; to discriminate; to comprehend.

پھدکنا phudaknā (H) v. To jump; to leap; to hop (applied to small birds); to dance about in token of delight.

پھدکی phudki, n.f. Name of a bird; a jump; a hop.

پھر phurr (H) n.m. Noise made by a bird when suddenly taking wing or by the explosion of a little gunpowder; whir; whiz; a buzzing sound.

پھر سے اڑ جانا phurr se uṛ jānā, v. To take wing suddenly.

پھر phir, adv. & conj. Again; then; afterwards.

پھر آنا phir ānā, v. To come again; to return.

پھر بھی phir bhī, adv. Ever then; still; notwithstanding.

پھر پھر phir phir, adv. Over and over again.

پھر جانا phir jānā, v. To retract; to withdraw; to recant; to revoke; to warp.

پہر pahar (H) n.m. A division of time consisting of three hours; a watch; an eighth part of a day.

پہرا pahrā (H) n.m. Watch; guard; time; season.

پہرا بٹھانا pahrā biṭhanā, v. To place a guard over.

پہرا دینا pahrā denā, v. To keep a watch.

پھرانا phirānā, v. To cause to turn; to whirl; to wheel; to make something go round; to change; to roll; to shift; to wind.

پھراؤ phirāo (H) n.m. Return; restitution; rotation; turning; circuit.

پھرتی phurtī (H) n.f. Activity; quickness; briskness; alacrity; alertness; agility; promptness.

پھرتی کرنا phurtī karnā, v. To act briskly; to be quick.

پھرتیلا phurtīlā, adj. Quick; active; smart; expert; nimble; alert.

پھرچا pharchā (H) n.m. Clearance of the sky; decision; definitive sentence (of a judge).

پھرکی phirkī (H) n.f. A whirligig, anything turning on an axis.

پھرنا phirnā, v. To turn; to return; to walk about; to circulate; to roll; to whirl; to wheel; to wander; to travel; to ramble; to change; to deviate; to diverge; to back out.

پھریرا pharairā (H) n.m. A flag; a standard; a pennant.

پھریری phurairī (H) n.f. Trembling; shivering; shudder; a flock of cotton.

پھریری لینا *phurairī lenā, v.* To be excited; to bristle up through fear.

پھڑ پھڑانا *phaṛ phaṛānā v.* To flutter; to move with convulsive motion.

پھڑ پھڑاہٹ *pharpharāhat, n.f.* Agitation; disquietude; flutter; struggle.

پھڑک *pharak* (H) *n.f,* Flutter; palpitation; vibration; throbbing.

پھڑک جانا یا اُٹھنا *pharak jānā yā uṭhnā.* To be highly pleased; to be extremely fond of; to get the surprise of one's life.

پھڑکانا *pharkānā, v.* To cause to flutter; to cause convulsive motion in the muscles; to cause to throb; to make a display.

پھڑکنا *pharaknā, v.* To flutter; to twitch; to vibrate with involuntary motion (as eyelids); to palpitate; to writhe (the shoulders, &c.).

پھڑیا *pharyā* (H) *n.m.* A pedlar; a retailer; the keeper of a gambling den or dice table; a cheat; one who indulges in big talk.

پھڑیا *phuryā* (H) *n.f.* A small sore; a pimple; a bile.

پھس *phus, n.f.* Soft sound; whispering; a hissing sound.

پھس پھس *phus phus, n.f.* Whispering.

پھس پھسا *phusphusā, adj.* Flabby; loose; not rigid; spongy.

پھسڈی *phasaḍḍi* (H) *adj.* Lagging behind; late; last (in order, degree or time).

پھسر پھسر *phusar phusar* (H) *n.m.* Whispering.

پھسلانا *phislānā* (H) *v.* To cause to slip, slide or err.

پھسلاؤ یا پھسلاہٹ یا پھسلن *phislāo yā phislāhaṭ yā phislan, n.m.* Slipping; sliding; slip; slipperiness; error.

پھسلنا *phisalnā* (H) *v.* To slip; to slide; to incline towards; to err.

پھسلانا *phuslānā* (H) *v.* To coax; to wheedle; to cajole; to flatter; to instigate; to entice; to seduce; to amuse; to fondle.

پھسلاوا *phuslāwā, n.m.* Coaxing; wheedling; seduction; cajolery.

پھش *phish, interj.* Pish! pshaw! tush!

پھکڑ *phakkaṛ* (H) *n.m.* Raillery; wrangling; mutual abuse; brawl.

پھکڑ باز *phakkar bāz* (H) *n.m.* An abuser; an indecent prater; one who indulges in obscene language.

پھکنا *phuknā* (H) *v.* To be blown up into a flame; *n.m.* A bladder.

پھکنی *phukni* (H) *n. f.* A blow-pipe.

پہل *pahal* (H) *n.m.* A flock of cotton. *n.f.* Precedence; commencement; beginning; a side.

پہل کرنا *pahal karnā, v.* To begin; to precede.

پھل *phal* (H) *n.m.* Fruit; effect; advantage; children; progeny; produce; yield; harvest; profit; reward; result; a blade; the iron head of an arrow; ploughshare.

پھل آنا *phal ānā, v.* To bear fruit.

پھل پانا یا ملنا *phal pānā yā milnā, v.* To reap the reward of (good or bad actions).

پھل پھلاری *phal phalārī, n.f.* Fruits of various kinds.

پھل دار *phal dār, adj.* Fruitful; profitable.

پھل لگنا *phal lagnā, v.* To bear fruit; to reap the reward of; to bear a child.

پہلا *pahlā. adj.* The first; prior; original; primary; chief.

پہلا پھل *pahlā phal, n.m.* The first fruit; the first child.

پھلا *phalā* (H) *adj.* Abounding with fruits; *n.m.* Blade.

دو پھلا *do phalā, adj.* Two bladed.

پھلانا *phulānā, v.* To cause to swell; to fatten; to puff; to inflate; to distend; to make proud; to puff up with flattery.

پھلانگ phalāng (H) n.f A leap; a spring; a stride.

پھلانگنا phalāngnā (H) v. To spring; to jump; to leap.

پھلجھڑی phuljhaṛi, n.f. A kind of firework.

پھلکا phulkā (H) n.m. A small puffed up bread

پھلکاری phulkāri (H) n.f. Flowered cloth.

پھلنا phalnā, v. To bear fruit; to have issue; to prosper; to have blisters or eruptions.

پھلنا پھولنا phalnā phūlnā, v. To blossom; to prosper; to thrive.

پہلو pahlū (P) n.m. Side; the wing or flank of an army; advantage; point of view.

پہلو بچانا pahlū bachānā, v. To save one's skin; to keep aloof.

پہلو بسانا pahlū basānā, v. To live in the neighbourhood; to sit side by side; to embrace; to cling to.

پہلو تہی pahlū tihi, n.f. Evasion; shrinking.

پہلو تہی کرنا pahlū tihi karnā, v. To withdraw; to evade; to retreat; to refuse; to decline.

پہلو دار pahlū dār, adj. Having corners; having arms (chair); allusive.

پہلو دبانا pahlū dabānā, v. To overpower; to press; to conceal a fact.

پہلو گرم کرنا pahlū garm karnā, v. To enjoy the company of (a woman).

پہلو میں بیٹھنا pahlu men baithnā, v. To sit by the side of; to be in the company of.

ہم پہلو ham pahlū, adj. Equal in rank or dignity.

پہلو نشیں pahlū nashin, n. One who sits by the side; a companion.

پھلواڑی phulwāri (H) n.f. A flower garden; an orchard; children; off-spring.

پہلوان pahlwān (P) n.m. An athlete; a wrestler; a hero; a champion; a stout and sturdy fellow

پہلوانی pahlwāni (P) n.f. Heroism; athletic exercise.

پہلوٹا pahlautā (H) adj. & n.m. First born.

پھلی phali (H) n.f. A loop; a cod; a pod or seed of leguminous plant, particularly of peas or beans; a shield.

پھلی phulli (H) n.f. A white speck in the eye; an ornament of gold or silver worn in the nose or ear.

پہلی pahli (H) adj. First.

پہلی بار pahli bār, n.f. First time.

پہلے pahle (H) adv. At first; first; sooner; before; in the first place; chiefly; rather.

پہلے پہل pahle pahal, adv. At first; first of all; in the first instance.

پھلیانا phalyānā (H) v. To bear fruit.

پھلیل phulel (H) n.m. Oil impregnated with essence of flowers; essence (as a perfume); scented oil.

پھن phan (H) n.m The head of a snake; expanded hood or neck of a snake.

پھن پھنانا phan phanānā (H) v. To hiss (as a snake); to spread the hood (as a snake); to spring up quickly as snake or a fast growing plant; to move about briskly (as a playful child); to frisk.

پہنانا pahnānā, v. To clothe, to dress; to cause to put on.

پہناوا pahnāwā, n.m. Clothing; dress; garment.

پہنائی pahnā'i (P) n.f. Width; breadth.

پہنچ pahunch (H) n.f. Arrival; reach; admittance; penetration; capacity.

پہنچا pahunchā, n.m. The wrist, the fore-arm.

پہنچانا pahunchānā, v. To cause to arrive; to transmit; to convey; to conduct; to accompany; to carry; to cause to supply; to inflict.

پہنچا ہوا pahunchā huā, adj. Received; admitted; acknowledged; in the knowledge of; pious; chosen; saint.

پہنچنا pahuṅchnā, v. To arrive; to reach; to attain; to come (up to); to have access to; to befall to.

بہم پہنچنا baham pahuṅchnā, v To reach; to attain; to acquire; to be supplied with.

پہنچوانا pahuṅchwānā, v. To cause to be sent; to cause to be conveyed; to cause to arrive.

پہنچی pāhuṅchi (H) n.f. A kind of bracelet.

پھندا phandā (H) n.m. A net; a noose; a snare; grasp; clutches; perplexity; difficulty.

پھندا پڑنا یا لگنا phandā parnā yā lagnā, v. To get into knots (a string); to get entangled; to be noosed; to be strangled.

پھندا لگانا phandā lagānā, v. To set a snare; to entangle; to knot; to loop.

پھندے میں آنا یا پڑنا یا پھنسنا phande meṅ ānā yā parnā yā phaṅsnā, v. To fall into a trap; to be caught into a trap; to get into trouble.

پھندے میں پھانسنا phande meṅ phāṅsnā, v. To entrap; to ensnare; to drag into troubles.

پھندنا phuṅdnā (H) n.m. A tassel.

پھنساؤ phansāo (H) n.m. Entanglement; an ensnaring affair; a narrow place; a bottle neck; a sticking place as a bog.

پھنسنا phansnā, v. To be entangled; to be involved (in difficulty); to stick; to be ensnared; to be noosed; to be entrapped; to be caught.

پھنسوانا phaṅswānā, v. To cause to be entangled; to cause to be entrapped.

پھنسی phunsi (H) n.f. A pimple; a pustule; a small boil.

پھنکار phunkār (H) n.m. Hissing; hiss (of a snake).

پھنکارنا phunkārnā (H) v. To hiss (as a snake); hissing.

پھنکوانا phiṅkwānā, v. To cause to be flung or thrown away.

پھنکوانا phuṅkwānā, v. To cause to be set on fire; to have a thing set ablaze; to cause to be blown.

پھنگا phangā, (H) n.m. A grass-hopper.

پھوار phuwār (H) n.f. Small fine rain; a slight drizzle; mist; fog.

پھوپھا phūphā (H) n.m. Husband of father's sister.

پھوپھی phūphi, n.f. Father's sister; paternal aunt.

پھوٹ phūṭ (H) n.f. A kind of melon; difference of opinion; dissension; discord; split; quarrel; flaw; breach; break; crack; opening; gap.

پھوٹ بہنا phūṭ, bahnā v. To shed tears; to weep bitterly.

پھوٹ پڑنا phūṭ parnā, v., To arise dissension; to disclose a secret.

پھوٹ پھوٹ کر رونا phūṭ phūṭ kar ronā, v. To weep bitterly; to burst into tears; to cry excessively.

پھوٹ ڈالنا phūt ḍālnā, v. To sow dissension (between); to sow discord.

پھوٹ کر نکلنا phūt kar nikalnā, v. To erupt; to be afflicted with leprosy (used as a curse).

پھوٹ ہونا phūt honā, v. To be divided in opinion.

پھوٹے منہ سے phūṭe muṅh se, adv. With a distorted or wry face; even unwillingly.

پھوٹنا phūṭnā (H) v. To be broken; to be shattered; to be separated; to be impaired; to break; to burst; to split; to come out or sprout; to shoot up; to germinate; to bud; to get promotion or advancement.

پھوٹی قسمت یا تقدیر phūṭi qismat yā taqdir, n.f. Bad luck; ill fate.

پھوڑا phorā (H) n.m. A boil; a sore; an ulcer; an abscess; a tumour.

پھوڑا پھنسی phorā phunsi, n.m. Eruptions; small boils.

پھوڑنا phoṛnā (H) v. To break; to burst open; to divulge; to split; to shatter; to dissect.

پھوڑ ڈالنا phoṛ ḍālnā, v. See پھوڑنا phoṛnā.

پھوس یا پھونس phūs yā phūṅs (H) n.m. Dry grass or straw; anything weak, frail or decayed.

پھونس میں چنگاری ڈالنا phūṅs meṅ chingāṛī ḍālnā, v. To excite contention or strife; to throw a spark into the straw.

پھوسڑا phūsṛā (H) n.m. Rag; rubbish, tatters; shag or nap of a cloth.

پھوک phok (H) n. m. Dregs; sediment; refuse; dross; rubbish; hollowness. adj. Hollow.

پھوکا phokā, adj. Light; hollow; not solid; soft.

پھول phūl (H) n.m. Flower; blossom; bunch; spark; bell metal; rosette; bud; charred bones of a burnt corpse; the white marks of leprosy; a white opaque spot in the corner of the eye; any light thing.

پھول آنا phūl ānā, v. To blossom; to have the menses.

پھول اٹھنا phūl uṭhnā, v. To complete the forty days of mourning.

پھول پتی phūl pattī (H) n.f. Rosette; cockade; a knot of ribands.

پھول جانا phūl jānā, v. To swell; to be delighted; to be pleased; to become fat.

پھول جھڑنا phūl jhaṛnā, v. To speak eloquently; to drop flowers of rhetoric; fall of dried flowers from a tree.

پھول چڑھانا phūl chaṛhānā (H) v. To place wreaths of flowers on a grave; to offer or strew flowers at a shrine or tomb.

پھول سا phūl sā, adj. Like a flower; delicate as a flower.

پھول کترنا phūl katarnā, v. To snuff the wick.

پھول کھلنا phūl khilnā, v. To bloom; to flower.

پھول گوبھی phūl gobhī, n.f. A cauliflower.

پھولوں میں تلنا phūloṅ meṅ tulnā, v. To live in luxury; to be weighed in flowers; to be very light.

پھولا phūlā (H) adj. Swelled; swollen; puffed up; blossomed; having flowers.

پھولا پھرنا phūlā phirnā, v. To be unable to contain oneself; to be in spirits; to be puffed up.

پھولا پھلا phūlā phalā, adj. Developed; bloomy; prosprous.

پھولا نہ سمانا phūlā nah samānā, v. To be overjoyed; to exult; not to be able to contain oneself (from delight).

پھولنا phūlnā (H) v. To blossom; to blow; to flower; to be pleased; to be in health and spirits; to flourish; to swell; to be inflated; to be puffed up; to exult.

پھوں phuṅ, n.f. Swaggering; strutting; airs; hissing; snorting (of a dog).

پھوں پھوں کرنا phuṅ phuṅ karnā, v. To sniff; to snort; to swagger; to fret and fume.

پھوں پھاں کرنا phun phāṅ karnā, v. To brag; to boast.

پھونک phūṅk (H) n.f. Puff; blast; act of blowing up (fire); breath; blow; a charm.

پھونک دینا phūṅk denā, v. To blow up; to destroy by fire; to waste; to squander; to breathe into one's ears; to spread a report abroad.

پھونک پھونک کر قدم رکھنا phūṅk phūṅk kar qadam rakhnā, v. To walk or act carefully and cautiously.

پھونک مارنا phūṅk mārnā, v. To puff; to blow; to put out; to charm.

پھونک نکل جانا phūṅk nikal jānā, v. To die; to expire; to breathe one's last.

پھونکنا phunknā, v To below; to set on fire; to inflame; to kindle; to be lavish.

پھوھا یا پھویا (H) n.m. A nipple made of cotton; a flock of cotton.

پھوھڑ phūhar (H) adj. A bad houswife; undisciplined; uneducated; stupid; slovenly; foolish.

پھوھڑ پن phūhar pan, n.m. Stupidity; foolishness.

پھوئی pho'i, n.f. Mildew; small rain; drizzle.

پہیا pahiyā (H) n.m. A wheel.

پھیپھڑا phephra (H) n.m. The lungs.

پھیٹنا یا پھینٹنا phetnā yā phentna (H) v. To mix by trituration; to beat (eggs).

پھیر pher (H) n.m. Turning; turn; twist; winding; maze; meander; curvature; twisting; coil; fold; bend; crookedness; revolution; misfortune; dilemma.

ھیر پھیر her pher, n.m. Change; revolution; alternation; curvature; complication; deciet.

ھیر پھیر کرنا her pher karnā, v. To alternate; to make constant changes; to deceive.

پھیر دینا pher denā, v. To return; to restore; to refund; to turn.

پھیر میں آنا یا پڑنا pher meṅ ānā yā parnā, v. To fall into straits or difficulties; to be involved in difficulties.

پھیر میں ڈالنا pher men ḍālnā, v. To put obstacles (in the way of another); to place one in a dilemma; to mislead.

پھیر لینا pher lenā, v. To take back; to accept return (of).

پھیرا pherā (H) n.m. Turning; circuit; perambulation; a roll; a wooden frame with which lime, sand &c. is measured; walking of the bride and the bridegroom round the sacred fire.

پھیرا پھیری pherā pherī, n.f. Frequent change; interchange; alternation; going and coming repeatedly.

پھیرنا phernā, v. To turn over; to return; to give back; to reverse; to twist; to refund; to exercise or train a horse; to make one walk backwards and forwards; to plaster; to shift

ھاتھ پھیرنا hāth phernā, v. To caress; to stroke; to fondle.

پھیری pheri, n.f. Going round; rounds of a pedler; hawking; circumambulation.

ھیرا پھیری herā pheri, n.f. Coming and going; constant and repeated changes.

پھیری والا pheri wālā, n.m. A hawker; a pedlar.

پھیرے phere, n.m. Visits; walking of the bride and the bridegroom round the sacred fire.

پھیرے ڈالنا یا لینا phere ḍalnā yā lenā, v. To walk round the sacred fire (a marriage ceremony among the Hindus).

پھیکا phikā, adj. Insipid; tasteless; vapid; pale; light; weak; faint; dull; cheerless; sallow.

پھیلانا phailānā, v. To expand; to spread; to stretch; to multiply; to diffuse; to publish.

ھاتھ پھیلانا hāth phailānā, v. To beg; to ask humbly; to ask for alms.

پاؤں پھیلانا pāon phailānā, v. To insist; to persist; to stretch out legs; to rest.

پھیلاؤ phailāo, n.m. Spreading out; expansion; extent; diffusion; growth; breadth; publication.

پھیلاوا phailāwā, n.m. Expansion; breadth; prolixity.

پھیلنا phailnā (H) v. To expand; to spread; to grow luxuriantly; to become public; to be scattered; to be diffused.

پہیلی paheli (H) n.f. A riddle; an enigma.

پہیلی بوجھنا paheli būjhnā, v. To solve a riddle.

پھینٹ یا پھینٹا phent yā phentā, n.f. Waist band; a kind of small turban; a belt.

پھینٹا باندھنا phentā bāndhnā (H) v. To get ready; to resolve; to gird up the loins (for).

پھینٹی phenti (H) *n.f.* A skein (of thread).

پھینچنا phinchnā (H) *v.* To rinse; to wash; to squeeze.

پھینک phenk (H) *n.f.* Throw; cast; fling.

پھینک دینا phenk denā, *v.* To throw away; to cast away.

پھینکنا phenknā, *v.* To throw; to fling; to let fly (a hawk, &c., at game); to disregard; to waste; to hurl (spears, &c.) to squander; to spill.

پی pi (H) *n.m.* A husband; a lover; a sweetheart; *adj.* Beloved.

پے pai (P) *n.m.* The foot; footstep; mark; pursuit; nerve; sinew; *adv.* In the footstep of; in pursuit of; after; behind; on account of; therefore.

پے در پے یا پے بہ پے pai dar pai yā pai bah pai, *adv.* One after another; repeatedly; consecutively; incessantly.

در پے ہونا dar pai honā; *v.* To be after; to pursue.

پیا piyā (H) *n.m.* Husband; lover; sweetheart; *adj.* Beloved.

پیادہ piyādah (P) *n.m.* A footman; a foot-soldier; a pawn at chess.

پیادہ پا piyadah pā, *adj.* Afoot; on foot.

پیادۂ محاصل piādah-ĕ-mahāṣil, *n.m.* A peon appointed to compel defaulters to pay up arrears; bailiff.

پیار piyār (H) *n.m.* Love; affection; attachment; fondness; expression of love by kissing; friendship; kindness.

پیار کرنا piyār karnā, *v.* To love; to caress; to fondle.

پیارا piyārā (H) *adj.* Beloved; dear; favourite; charming; lovable; pleasing. *n.m.* A sweetheart.

پیاری piyāri, *adj.* Beloved; pleasant. *n.f.* A Sweatheart.

پیاز piyāz (P) *n.f.* Onion.

پیازی piyāzi, *n.f.* A kind of wild shrub; *adj.* Resembling an onion.

پیازی رنگ piyāzi rang, *n.m.* Crimson colour; pinkish.

پیاس piyās (H) *n.f.* Thirst; desire; craving.

پیاس بجھانا piyās bujhānā, *v.* To quench thirst.

پیاس لگنا piyās lagnā, *v.* To be thirsty.

پیاسا piyāsā (H) *adj.* Thirsty; thirsting for; longing for.

پیاسے مرنا piyāse marnā, *v.* To be very thirsty; to be dying of thirst.

پیاسی piyāsi (H) *n.f.* A species of fish; *adj.* Thirsty.

پیال payāl (H) *n.f.* Straw; dried grass; a fruit.

پیالہ piyālah (P) *n.m.* A cup; a firepan (of musket); a goblet; a funeral rite of Muslim mendicants.

پیالہ بھر جانا piyālah bhar jānā, *v.* To be puffed up with pride; the cup of one's life to be full; to die.

پیالہ پینا piyālah pinā, *v.* To drink the cup of; to become the disciple of.

ہم پیالہ ہم نوالہ ham piyālah ham niwālah, *n.* Very intimate friends; bosom friends.

پیالی piyāli, *n.f.* A small cup.

پیام payām (P) *n.m.* A message; news; intelligence; advice.

پیام بر payāmbar, *n.m.* A messenger; a prophet.

پیامی payāmi, *n.m.* A messenger.

پیپ pip (H) *n.f.* Pus; matter; purulent discharge.

پیپ پڑنا pip parnā, *v.* To become mattery.

پپیانا pipiyānā; *v.* To suppurate.

پیپا pipā (H) *n.m.* Cask; barrel; butt.

پیپل pipal (H) *n.m.* A tree; long pepper.

پیت pit (H) *n.f.* Love; affection.

پیت کی ریت نرالی ہے pit ki rit nirāli hai, *prov.* Strange are the ways of love.

پیت نہ جانے جات کجات pit nah jāne jāt kujāt, *prov.* Love is blind; love knows not rank or dignity.

پیت کریں سو باورے pit karen so bāwre, *prov.* No folly like being in love.

پیترا paitrā (H) *n.m.* The skilful movements at the time of wrestling; flourishing about before cudgelling.

پیترا بدلنا paitrā badalnā, *v.* To change tactics or skilful movements in order to win in cudgelling or wrestling.

پیتل pital (H) *n.m.* Brass; bronze.

پیتم pītam (H) *n.m.* Husband; lover; most beloved; a sweetheart.

پیٹ peṭ (H) *n.m.* Belly; stomach; womb; pregnancy, capacity; hunger; greediness; livelihood; interior of a thing; the bore of a gun; cavity.

ایک پیٹ کے ek peṭ ke, *adj.* Born of the same mother; uterine.

پیٹ اپھرنا peṭ apharnā, *v.* Swelling out of the belly.

پیٹ باندھنا peṭ bāndhnā, *v.* To eat less than one's appetite demands; to stint oneself of food.

پیٹ بجانا peṭ bajānā, *v.* To feel very happy.

پیٹ بھر peṭ bhar, *adv.* Bellyful.

پیٹ بھرنا peṭ bharnā, *v.* To fill belly; to be satisfied.

پیٹ بولنا peṭ bolnā, *v.* Rumbling of the stomach.

پیٹ بھاری ہونا peṭ bhārī honā, *v.* To suffer from indigestion; to be pregnant.

پیٹ بھرے کی باتیں کرنا peṭ bhare kī bāten karnā, *v.* To talk proudly; to talk like a rich man in a care-free manner.

پیٹ پالنا peṭ pālnā, *v.* To live from hand to mouth; to be selfish.

پیٹ پکڑے پھرنا peṭ pakṛe phirnā, *v.* To be in distress.

پیٹ پھولنا peṭ phūlnā, *v.* To burst with laughter; swelling of the belly; to be in the family way.

پیٹ پٹنا peṭ piṭnā, *v.* To be very hungry; to be greedy or impatient.

پیٹ چپاتی ہو جانا peṭ chapātī hojānā, *v.* To be awfully hungry.

پیٹ چلنا peṭ chalnā, *v.* To be purged; to have flux or diarrhoea.

پیٹ دکھانا peṭ dikhānā, *v.* To beg for food; to complain of hunger and poverty.

پیٹ رہنا peṭ rahnā, *v.* To be pregnant; to be conceived.

پیٹ سب رکھتے ہیں peṭ sab rakhte hain, *prov.* No food, no service; no supper, no song.

پیٹ سب کچھ سکھا لیتا ہے peṭ sab kuchh sikhā letā hai, *prov.* The belly teaches all arts.

پیٹ سے peṭ se, *adj.* Pregnant.

پیٹ سے ہونا peṭ se honā, *v.* To be pregnant; to be in the family way.

پیٹ سے پاؤں باہر نکالنا peṭ se pāon bāhar nikālnā, *v.* To show one's claws; to go beyond bounds.

پیٹ کاٹنا peṭ kāṭnā, *v.* To starve one's self; to pinch one's belly; to deprive one of livelihood.

پیٹ کا کتا peṭ kā kuttā, *n.m.* A greedy person.

پیٹ کا ہلکا peṭ kā halkā, *n.m.* One who is unable to keep a secret.

پیٹ کی آگ peṭ kī āg, *n.f.* Maternal affection; hunger.

پیٹ کی آگ بجھانا peṭ kī āg bujhānā, *v.* To eat something; to keep the wolf from the door.

پیٹ کے بال peṭ ke bāl, *n.m.* Hair on the head of a new born child.

پیٹ کی کھرچن peṭ ke khurchan, *n.f.* The last child of a woman.

پیٹ گرانا peṭ girānā, *v.* To cause an abortion.

پیٹ گرنا peṭ girnā, *v.* To miscarry; to abort.

پیٹ میں آنت نہ منہ میں دانت pet men ānt nah munh men dānt, n. An old frail person; old and decrepit.

پیٹ میں چوہے دوڑنا pet men chūhe daurnā, v. To be very hungry.

پیٹ والی pet wālī, n.f. Pregnant.

پیٹ پیٹ کر pit pit kar, adv. With great difficulty ; after a severe beating.

پیٹنا pītnā (H) v. To beat; to dash; to punish ; to pound ; to lament ; to mourn.

پیٹو petū (H) adj. Gluttonous ; epicurean. n. glutton ; gourmand ; epicure.

پیٹھ pith (H) n.f. The back ; the loins ; the back part ; support.

پیٹھ پر ھاتھ پھیرنا pīth par hāth phernā, v. To pat on the back ; to encourage.

پیٹھ پر ھونا pīth par honā, v. To support ; to aid.

پیٹھ پھیرنا pīth phernā, v. To turn back ; to withdraw ; to take flight ; to depart ; to flee.

پیٹھ پیچھے pīth pīchhe, adv. Behind one's back ; in the absence of.

پیٹھ پیچھے کہنا pīth pīchhe kahnā, v. To back-bite ; to talk against one behind one's back

پیٹھ ٹھوکنا pīth thoknā, v. To embolden; to encourage.

پیٹھ دکھانا pīt dikhānā, v. To turn tail ; to run away.

پیٹھ دینا pīth denā, v. To depart ; to shrink from ; to turn away in disgust.

پیٹھ لگانا pith lagānā, v. To throw down in wrestling.

پیٹھا pethā (H) n.m. A kind of sweet gourd.

پیٹی petī (H) n.f. Belly band ; belt ; a casket ; a portmanteau ; a box ; an iron safe.

پی جانا pī jānā, v. To drink ; to absorb ; to suppress anger ; to bear patiently ; to refrain from answering;

پیچ pech (P)n.m. A screw; twist ; perplexity; deceit ; a coil; a plait ; a fold ; maze ; difficulty ; trouble ; complication ; entanglement ; a trick in wrestling ; stratagem.

پیچ پڑنا pech parnā, v. To become intricate ; to occur as an obstacle ; to be entangled.

پیچ دار pech dār adj. Twisted ; coiled ; spiral; crooked; intricate ; winding ; ambiguous ; deceitful.

پیچ در پیچ pech dar pech, adv. Coil within coil ; complicated ; entangled ; complex ; intricate.

پیچ دینا pech denā, v. To twist ; to screw ; to circumvent ; to deceive.

پیچ ڈالنا pech ḍālnā, v. To throw obstacles in the way ; to entangle.

پیچ کرنا pech karnā, v. To deceive ; to trick ; to complicate ; to seize in wrestling ; to tangle.

پیچ کش pech kash, n.m. A screw-driver.

پیچ کھانا pech khānā, v. To coil ; to be perplexed ; to sustain a loss.

پیچ کھلنا pech khulnā, v. To be untwisted ; to be disentangled ; to be unscrewed ; to be unravelled (a mystery).

پیچ کھولنا pech kholnā, v. To untwist ; to unscrew ; to unravel.

پیچ کھیلنا pech khelnā, v. To deceive ; to play a trick (on).

پیچ لڑانا pech laṛānā, v. To entangle the string of an adversary's kite.

پیچ وتاب pech-ŏ tāb (P) n.m. Twisting and twining ; convolution ; perplexity ; agitation ; indignation ; vexation ; distress ; restlessness.

پیچ و تاب کھانا pech-ŏ tāb khānā, v. To writhe ; to be vexed ; to suffer distress ; to twist or twine.

پیچ و خم pech -ŏ kham, n.m. Perplexity ; difficulty ; trouble.

پیچش pechish (P) n.f. Twisting ; contortion ; gripes, colic pains; dysentery.

پیچک **pechak** (P) *n.f.* A ball; a skein of thread.

پیچوان **pechwān** (H) *adj.* Twisted; *n.m.* A kind of huqqa with flexible and twistable pipe; huqqa-snake.

پیچھ **pichh** (H) *n.f.* Rice gruel; water in which rice is bolied.

پیچھا **pichhā** (H) *n.m.* The hinder part; the rear; pursuit; persecution; following; absence.

پیچھا بھاری ہونا **pichhā bhāri honā**, *v.* To be pursued; to have an enemy in the rear; to belong to a wealthy and respectable family.

پیچھا پکڑنا **pichhā pakaṛnā**, *v.* To vex; to perplex; to follow; to dog.

پیچھا چھوٹنا **pichhā chhūṭnā**, *v.* To be rid (of); to be free.

پیچھا چھڑانا **pichhā chhuṛānā**, *v.* To get rid of; to shake off; to get away from

پیچھا چھوڑنا **pichhā chhoṛnā**, *v.* To let alone; to give over; to cease.

پیچھا کرنا **pichhā karnā**, *v.* To follow; to pursue; to press; to back (as a horse); to chase; to recoil (a gun).

پیچھا لینا **pichhā lenā**, *v.* To pursue; to dog; to vex; to pester.

پیچھا نہ چھوڑنا **pichhā nah chhoṛnā**, *v.* To pursue unremittingly; not to give up.

پیچھے **pichhe**, *adv.* In the absence of; behind; in the rear; astern; afterwards; subsequently; after the death of; in consequence of; for the sake of.

پیچھے آنا **pichhe ānā**, *v.* To follow; to ensue; to come late.

پیچھے پڑنا **pichhe paṛnā**, *v.* To persecute; to torment; to pursue doggedly.

پیچھے پیچھے **pichhe pichhe**, *adv.* Behind; one after another; in succession; in a row or series.

پیچھے چھوڑنا **pichhe chhoṛnā**, *v.* To leave behind.

پیچھے ڈالنا **pichhe ḍālnā**, *v.* To surpass; to out-strip; to leave behind.

پیچھے رہنا **pichhe rahnā**, *v.* To keep back; to fall back; to lag behind.

پیچھے لگنا **pichhe lagnā**, *v.* To follow; to pursue.

پیچھے لگا دینا **pichhe lagā denā**, *v.* To instigate against; to set some one after.

پیچھے ہو لینا **pichhe ho lenā**, *v.* To get behind; to keep back; to follow after.

پیچیدگی **pechidgi** (P) *n.f.* Twisting; winding; contortion.

پیچیدہ **pechidah** (P) *adj.* Twisted; coiled; complicated.

پیچیدہ معاملہ **pechidah mu'āmilah**, *n.m.* A difficult case; an intricate question.

پیخانہ **paikhānah** (P) *n.m.* A privy; a lavatory; filth.

پیدا **paidā** (P) *adj.* Born; produced; invented; manifest; discovered; exhibited; gained; acquired; *n.f.* Gain; profit; income; earning.

پیدا کرنا **paidā karnā**, *v.* To bring into being; to produce; to create; to gain; to earn; to invent; to breed; to hatch; to acquire; to find; to get; to procure.

پیدا ہونا **paidā honā**, *v.* To be born or created; to be produced; to be earned.

پیداوار **paidāwār**, *n.f.* Produce of a field; fruit; profit of trade: out-turn; income.

پیدائش **paidā'ish** (P) *n.f.* Birth; creation; production; earnings; produce; profit; in Bible the first book of the Old Testament, Genesis.

پیدائشی **paidā'ishi**, *adj.* Natural; inborn; innate; original.

پیدائشی حق **paidā'ishi ḥaq**, *n.m.* Birth right.

پیدل **paidal** (H) *adj.* On foot; *n.m.* Infantry; foot-soldier.

پیر pir (P) n.m. An old man; a saint; a spiritual guide; a holyman; Monday.

پیر بھائی pir bhāi, n.m. A fellow disciple.

پیر زادہ pir zadāh, n.m. The son of a saint.

پیر زال pir-ĕ zāl, n.f. An old woman.

پیر پکڑنا یا کرنا pir pakaṛnā yā karnā, v. To elect a spiritual leader.

پیر فرطوت pir-ĕ farṭūt, n.m. Old and decrepit person; a good-for-nothing fellow.

پیر مرد pir mard, n.m. An old man.

پیر مغاں pir-ĕ mughān, n.m. A tavern-keeper.

پیر نابالغ pir-ĕ nābaligh, n.m. An old fool.

پیر pair (H) n. m. The foot; footstep.

پیروں پڑنا pairoṅ paṛnā, v. To pay respects; to kiss the feet in token of respect; to supplicate.

پیروں میں سر دینا pairoṅ meṅ sar denā, v. To come under one's protection.

پیروں میں مہندی لگنا pairon meṅ mehndi lagnā, v. To bring forward a lame excuse.

پیراستہ pairāstah (P) adj. Decorated; adorned.

پیراک pairāk (H) n. A swimmer.

پیراکی pairāki, n.f. The act of swimming.

پیرانا pairānā, v. To cause to swin.

پیرانہ pirānah (P) adj. Elderly; like an old man; growing old; belonging to, connected with, or worthy of a saint.

پیراھن pairāhan (P) n.m. A long robe; a long shirt.

پیرایہ pairāyah (P) n.m. An ornament; a dress; manner; method; behaviour.

پیرو perū, n.m. A turkey fowl.

پیرو pairau (P) n. A follower; a disciple.

پیرو کار pairau kār (P) n. One engaged in a law suit.

پیروی pairavī (P) n.f. Following up; imitation; prosecution; pursuit; hunting after.

پیری piri (P) n.f. Old age; status of a saint.

پیڑ peṛ (H) n.m. A tree; a plant; a shrub.

پیڑا peṛā (H) n.m. A ball of dough or kneaded flour; a kind of sweetmeat.

پیڑھا piṛhā (H) n.m. A large stool or chair to sit on; a seat.

پیڑھی piṛhi (H) n.f. A small stool; generation; pedigree.

پیڑھی در پیڑھی piṛhi dar piṛhi, adv. Generation after generation; from age to age; for successive generations.

پیزار paizār (P) n.f. A slipper; a shoe.

پیزار پر مارنا paizār par mārnā, v. To look down upon; to despair; to condemn.

پیزار دکھانا paizār dikhānā, v. Not to regard or care for; to slight.

پیزار کھانا paizār khānā, v. To be beaten with shoes.

پیسا paisā (H) n.m. A copper coin equal to one-quarter of an anna; money; cash; wealth.

پیسا اڑانا paisā uṛānā, v. To spend money extravagantly; to run away with the money of another.

پیسا ڈبونا paisā ḍabonā, v. To sink money; to invest money without return.

پیسا کھانا paisā khānā, v. To take bribes; to embazzle; to waste.

پیسے والا paise wālā, adj. Moneyed; wealthy; rich.

پیسنا pisnā, v. To grind; to bruise; to powder; to gnash (the teeth). n.m. The corn or grain for grinding.

پیس ڈالنا pis ḍalnā, v. To cut to bits; to ruin; to grind; to powder.

پیش pesh (P) n.m. Front; fore-part; the vowal point. adj. Promoted; advanced; respected. prep. Before; in front of.

پیش آنا pesh ānā, v. To come to pass; to happen; to come before; to step forward; to behave; to negotiate.

پیش از مرگ واویلا pesh az marg wāwelā, prov. To call a surgeon before one is wounded.

پیش بند *pesh band, n.m.* The belt that passes over a horse's breast to prevent the saddle from slipping back; apron.

پیش بندی *pesh bandī, n.f.* Foresight; timely preparation.

پیش بین *bish bin, adj.* Prudent; circumspect; wise; provident.

پیش بینی *pesh benī, n.f.* Foresight; prudence.

پیش جانا *pesh jānā, v.* To go forth; to have effect.

پیش خیمہ *pesh khemah, n.m.* A tent or other baggage sent in advance; a prelude.

پیش دستی *pesh dastī, n.f.* Being beforehand; paying beforehand; anticipation; excelling; surpassing.

پیش دستی کرنا *pesh dastī karnā, v.* To make haste; to take the lead; to anticipate; to excel; to surpass.

پیش رو *pesh rau, n.m.* Forerunner; a leader; the advanced guard; precursor; predecessor; harbinger.

پیش روی *pesh rawi, n.f.* Act of preceding; advancing.

پیش قبض *pesh qabẓ, n.m.* A dagger.

پیش قدمی *pesh qadamī, n.f.* Stepping before or forward; outstripping; anticipation; alertness; activity; aggression.

پیش قدمی کرنا *pesh qadamī karnā, v.* To take the first step; to go before; to go in advance; to push forward.

پیش کار *pesh kār, n.m.* Agent; manager; deputy; a reader (to a magistrate).

پیش کرنا *pesh karnā, v.* To produce; to present; to submit; to put up.

پیش کش *pesh kash, n.f.* A present; a tribute.

پیش گوئی *pesh go'ī, n.f.* Prediction; foretelling; forecast.

پیش نظر *pesh-ĕ naẓar, prep. phr.* In view of (as an object or prospect).

پیش نماز یا امام *pesh namāz yā imām, n.m.* One who leads congregational prayers.

پیش نہاد *pesh nihād, n.m.* Example; custom; habit; mode; manner.

پیشگی *peshgi, n.f.* Earnest money; an advance of money.

پیشگی ادائگی *peshgi adāigi, n.f.* Advance payment.

پیشگی بلا سود *peshgi bilā sūd, n.f.* Advance not bearing interest.

پیشگی فیس نقل *peshgi fīs-ĕ naql, n.f.* Advance copying fee.

پیشوا *peshwā, (P) n.m.* A leader; a priest; a guide; the head of a party; the chief of a religious sect; a title of a *Marahatta* minister.

پیشوائی *peshwāī, n.f.* Guidance; leadership; reception of a visitor or guest.

پیشوائی کرنا *peshwāī karnā, v.* To receive; to welcome.

پیشہ *peshah, n.m.* Trade; profession; calling; office; custom; practice; habit.

پیشہ ور *peshah war, n.m.* An artisan; workman; tradesman.

پیشاب *peshāb (P) n.m.* Urine; piss.

پیشاب خطا ہونا *peshāb khaṭā honā, v.* To discharge urine (out of fear); to have very great fear.

پیشاب کرنا *peshāb karnā, v.* To make water.

پیشاب کی دھار پر مارنا *peshāb ki dhār par mārnā, v.* To condemn; to despise.

پیشاب نہ کرنا *peshāb nah karnā, v.* To despise; to hate; to condemn.

پیشانی *peshānī (P) n.f.* The forehead; brow; fate; heading; title.

پیشتر *peshtar (P) adv.* Before; formerly; prior to; sooner; heretofore; ago.

پیشی *peshī (P) n.f.* Presence; trial; coming before; being brought forward.

کچی پیشی *kachchi peshī, n.f.* Preliminary hearing.

پیشین peshin (P) adj. Ancient; former; the noon prayer.

پیشین گوئی peshin goi, n.f. Prophecy; prediction.

پیغام paighām (P) n.m. A message; mission; news; advice.

پیغام بر paighām bar (P) n.m. A messenger; an envoy; a prophet.

پیغامبری paighāmbarī (P) n.f. A mission; the office of a messenger; the act of carrying a message.

پیک paik (P) n.m. A courier; a messenger; a runner; an express.

پیک pik (H) n.f. The juice of the betel-leaf chewed and spit out.

پیک دان pīk dān, n.m. A vessel for holding the spittle; a spittoon.

پیکار paikār (P) n.f. Battle; contest; war.

پیکان paikān (P) n.m. The head of an arrow; any pointed missile.

پیکر paikar (P) n.m. Face; countenance; visage form; appearance; a portrait; a likeness; (used in comp. as پری پیکر very beautiful).

پیل pīl (P) n.m. Elephant; the bishop in chess.

پیل بان pīl bān, n.m. An elephant-keeper.

پیل بندی pilbandi, n.f. Mutual support of a bishop and of pawns at chess.

پیل پا pīl pā, n.f. Elephantiasis.

پیل پایہ pīl pāyā, A pillar; a column.

پیل تن pīl tan, adj. Gigantic; huge.

پیل مرغ pīl murgh, n.m. Turkey fowl.

پیلا pīlā (H) adj. Yellow; pale.

پیلا پن pīlā pan (H) n.m. Yellowness.

پیلنا pelnā (H) v. To shove; to push; to press; to thrust; to impel; to stuff; to crush.

پیلہ pīlah (P) n. The ball or cocoon which the silkworm forms round itself.

کرم پیلہ kirm pīlah, n.m. The silk-worm.

پیما paimā (P) adj. Measuring; measurer (used at the end of comp. as آب پیما āb paimā, water gauge. etc.).

پیمان paimān, (P) n.m. A promise; agreement; security; treaty; oath; confirmation; convention.

پیمانہ paimānah (P) n.m. A measure; a cup; a goblet; a bowl.

عمر کا پیمانہ بھرنا 'umr kā paimānah bharnā, v. Completing the allotted period of life; to approach the time of death.

پیمائش paimā'ish (P) n.f. Measurement; survey.

پیمائش کنندہ paimā'ish kunindah, n.m. A surveyer.

پیمائی paimāī, n.f. The act of measuring.

پیمک paimak (H) n.f. Gold or silver lace.

پینا pīnā, v. To drink; to imbibe; to quaff; to smoke; to suck; to absorb; to suppress one's feelings.

پینتالیس paintālīs (H) adj. & n. Forty-five.

پینتیس paintis (H) adj. & n. Thirty-five.

پینجنا painjnā (H) v. To clean cotton from the seeds.

پیندا peṅdā (H) n.m. The bottom of a vessel or a box or a pot.

پیندے کا ھلکا peṅde kā halkā, n.m. Untrustworthy; not faithful to one's promise.

پینس pinas (H) n.f. A palanquin; a litter.

پینسٹھ paiṅsath (H) adj. & n. Sixty-five.

پینک pīnak (H) n.f. Drowsiness and intoxication from opium.

پینگ paiṅg; n.m. The exertion to keep a swing going.

پینگ بڑھنا paiṅg baṛhnā, v. To be very intimate; to advance in intimacy.

پینگ چڑھانا paing chāṛhānā, v. To swing very high.

پیوست paiwast (P) adj. Joined. n.m. Conjunction; connection.

پیوستگی paiwastgi (P) n.f. Junction; connection; union; closeness; link.

پیوستہ paiwastah (P) adj. Joined; contiguous; absorbed; inseparable; sticking; close.

پیوند paiwand (P) n.m. A patch; junction; addition.

پیوند لگانا paiwand lagānā, v. To patch.

پیوندی paiwandi, adj. Patched; grafted. n.m. An engrafted tree.

پیوندی مونچھیں paiwandi munchhen, n.f. The whiskers joining the beard.

پیہم paiham (P) adv. Close together; successively.

ت

ت te Is the third letter of the Arabic and the fourth of the Persian and Urdu alphabets. When used numerically, it denotes 400, according to the 'Abjad'.

تا tā (P) adv. & conj. To; until; as far as; whilst; as long as; in order that; to the end that; since; interj. Behold! look! beware! n.m. A sheet of paper.

تابہ زیست یا تابہ‌حیات tā bah-zīst yā tā bah hayāt, adv. While life remains.

تا بہ کجا tā bah-kujā, adv. How far? whither? how long? till when.

تا بہ کے tā bah-kai, adv. Till what time? how long? when? how much? how many.

تاچند tā chand, adv. How many? how long? by how much?

تاحال tā ḥāl, adv. Yet; hitherto.

تا زندگی tā zindagī, adv. During life; till the end of life.

تاکہ tā keh, adv. So that; with the object that; until; so long.

تاہم tā hām, adv. Nevertheless; still; yet.

تاہنوز tā hanoz, adv. Yet; still; hitherto; till.

تاب tāb (P) n.f. Heat; power; endurance; courage; rage; fury; contortion. (part. in compos.); burning; inflaming; illuminating; shining.

تاب نہ لانا tāb nah lānā, v. To be unable to bear; to be powerless.

تاب و طاقت یا تاب و توان tāb-ŏ ṭaqat yā tāb-ŏ tawān, n.f. Ability; power; endurance.

تابان tābān (P) adj. Resplendent; splendid; glittering; refulgent; burning.

تابانی tābānī (P) n.f. Splendour; glitter; refulgence; light.

تاب تلی یا تاپ تلی tāb tillī yā tāp tillī (H) n. f. Enlargement of the spleen; spleenitis.

تابدار tāb dār (P) adj. Bright; luminous; warm.

تابدان tābdān (P) n.m. Window; a stove; a chimney; a lattice.

تابڑ توڑ tābaṛ toṛ, adv. Successively; repeatedly.

تابستان tābistān (P) n.m. The hot-weather; summer.

تابش tābish, n.f. Heat; splendour; brilliance; grief; sorrow.

تابع tābi' (A) adj. Following; dependent; subordinate; loyal.

تابعدار tābi'dār. (Common though ungrammatical). adj. Obedient; loyal; servant.

تابعداری tābi'dārī, n.f. Allegiance; obedience; fidelity; dependance; submission.

تابعین tābi'in (A) n.m. Followers; companions; attendants (esp. the successors of the companions of the Holy Prophet or their contemporaries whose sayings regarding the Prophet form part of the sunnat).

تابناک tābnāk (P) adj. Hot; passionate; bright; brilliant; shining; glowing.

تابندگی tābindagī, n.f. Splendour; brightness.

تابندہ tābindah (P) adj. Shining; bright; luminous.

تابوت tābūt (A) n.m. A coffin; a bier.

تاپ tāp (H) n.m. Warmth; heat; fever.

تاپنا tāpnā (H) v. To bask in the sun or before a fire; to warm oneself at or over a fire.

تاتار **tātār** (P) *n.m.* A Tatar.

تاثر **tāassur** (A) *v.* To take an impression. *n.m.* Impression; penetration.

تاثیر **tāsīr** (A) *v.* To make an impression; to influence. *n.f.* An effect; an impression; penetration.

تاج **tāj** (P) *n.m.* A crown; diadem; a high crowned cap; tiara plume; comb (of a cock).

تاج خروس **tāj-ĕ khros**, (P) *n.m.* The comb of a cock; a cock's comb flower.

تاجدار **tājdār**, *n.m.* Crowned head; a king; a prince.

تاجور **tājwar**, *n.m.* A king; a prince.

تاجوری **tājwarī**, *n.f.* Royalty; sovereignty; kingship.

تاجر **tājir** (A) *n.m.* A merchant; a trader.

تاجک **tājak** (A) *n.m.* One born in Arabia and brought up in Persia; a trader.

تاخت **tākht** (P) *n.f.* Assault; attack; incursion; inroad; invasion.

تاخت و تاراج کرنا **tākht-ŏ tārāj karnā**, *v.* To ruin; to ravage; to plunder; to devastate.

تاخر **tāakhur** (A) *n.m.* Delay; postponement.

تاخیر **tākhīr** (A) *n.f.* Delay; procrastination; impediment; postponement.

تاخیر کرنا **takhīr karnā**, *v.* To delay; to procrastinate; to postpone; to retard.

تادیب **tādīb** (A) *n.f.* Discipline; correction; chastisement; admonition; erudition.

تادیب خانہ **tādīb khānah**, *n.m.* Borstal institution; reformatory.

تار **tār** (P) *n.f.* A thread; a wire; the string of a musical instrument; chord; darkness; obscurity; the warp or threads placed lengthwise in weaving cloth; electric wire; telegram.

تار باندھنا **tār bāndhnā**, *v.* To continue or repeat an action without interruption.

تار برق **tār barqī**, *n.m.* Electric wire; telegram.

تار تار **tār tār**, *adj.* Tattered; torn to pieces; piecemeal.

تار تار کرنا **tār tār karnā** *v.* To tear; to cut to pieces.

تار ٹوٹنا **tār ṭūṭnā**, *v.* To be disjointed; to be separated; to be interrupted.

تار عنکبوت **tār-ĕ a'nkabūt** *n.m.* Cobweb.

تارکش **tār kash**, *n.m.* A wire-drawer; a drawer of gold or silver wire.

تارکشی **tār kashī**, *n.f.* A kind of needle-work; wire-drawing.

تار گھر **tār ghar**, *n.m.* Telegraph office.

تارا **tārā** (H) *n.m.* A star; the pupil of the eye.

تارا ٹوٹنا **tārā ṭūṭnā**, *v.* Falling of a meteor; shooting of a star.

تارا ہو جانا **tārā ho jānā**, *v.* To appear as small as a star; to attain to a great height.

تارے نظر آنا یا دکھائی دینا **tāre nazar ānā yā dikhāī denā**, *v.* To be perplexed; to be frightened; to see stars dancing before the eyes (as after a knock out blow or through debility.)

آنکھوں کا تارا **ānkhhoṅ kā tārā**, *n.m.* Dear as the apple of the eye; beloved.

تارے توڑنا **tāre toṛnā**, *v.* To do the impossible.

تارے گننا **tāre ginnā**, *v.* To count the stars; to get no sleep.

دمدار تارا **dumdār tārā**, *n.m.* Comet.

تاراج **tārāj** (P) *n.m.* Plunder; ruin; devastation.

تاراج کرنا **tārāj karnā**, *v.* To plunder; to devastate; to ruin; to spoil.

تارپین **tārpīn**, *n.m.* Turpentine.

تارک **tārik** (A) *adj.* Leaving; abandoning; relinquishing; deserting, *n.m.* A deserter.

تارک الدنیا *tārik ud-dunyā*, *adj.* Abandoning the world; sober; abstinent; chaste; recluse; hermit; *n.m.* Anchorite; a hermit.

تاریخ *tārikh* (A) *n.f.* Date; history; epoch; era; chronogram; annals.

تاریخ ارجاع *tārikh-e irja'*, *n.f.* Date of institution of a suit.

تاریخ انقضاے میعاد *tārikh-ĕ inqizā-ĕ-mi'ād*, *n.f.* The last day of limitation.

تاریخ حوالگی *tārikh-ĕ hawālgi*, *n.f.* Date of delivery.

تاریخ چڑھانا *tārikh charhānā*, *v.* To date; to copy the account of any date.

تاریخ وقوع *tārikh-ĕ waqū'*, *n.f.* Date of occurrence.

تاریخ وار *tārikh wār*, *adv.* According to date; datewise; daily.

تاریخ مقررہ *tārikh-ĕ muqārrarah*, *n.f.* Fixed date.

تاریک *tārik* (P) *adj.* Dark; obscure.

تاریکی *tāriki*, *n.f.* Darkness; obscurity.

تاریکی چھا جانا *tariki chhā jānā*, *v.* Spreading of darkness.

تاڑ *tāṛ* (H) *n.m.* A palm tree.

تاڑ *tāṛ* (H) *n.f.* Understanding; perception; cognizance.

تاڑ باز *tāṛ bāz*, *adj.* Intelligent; quick of apprehension.

تاڑنا ' تاڑجانا *tāṛnā*, *tāṛ jānā*, *v.* To understand; perceive; to make out; to fathom; to guess; to conjecture.

تاڑی *tāṛi* (H) *n.f.* Palm-juice or toddy; the hilt of a dagger.

تازگی *tāzgi* (P) *n.f.* Freshness; newness; greenness.

تازہ *tāzah* (P) *adj.* Fresh; new; recent; green; tender; happpy.

تازہ بتازہ *tāzah batāzah*, *adj.* Fresh and blooming; brand new; fresh; up-to-date.

تازہ خیال *tāzah khayāl*, *adj.* Imagining something new. *n.m.* A new idea.

تازہ دم *tāzah dam*, *adj.* Fresh; ready; prepared; fit; cheerful.

تازہ دم ہونا *tāzah dam honā*, *v.* To be refreshed; to be in good spirits; to be hale and hearty.

تازہ کرنا *tāzah karnā*, *v.* To renew; to refresh; to revive; to recreate; to change water of the *huqqa*.

تازہ وارد *tāzah wārid*, *n.* New-comer.

تازہ ہونا *tāzah honā*, *v.* To be refreshed; to be revived; to flourish.

تازی *tāzi* (P) *adj.* & *n.m.* Arabian; Arabic; fast running; an Arabic horse or dog.

تازی کتا *tāzi kuttā*, *n.m.* A grey-hound.

تازیانہ *tāziyānah* (P) *n.m.* A whip; flogging; a scourge.

تازیانہ مارنا یا لگانا *tāziyānah mārnā yā lagānā*, *v.* To whip; to flog; to scourge.

تاسف *tāassuf* (A) *n.m.* Grief; regret; remorse; pining; lamenting; brooding over affliction.

تاسف کرنا *tā'assuf karnā*, *v.* To regret; to lament; to sigh over; to grieve; to pine.

تاسیس *tāsis* (A) *n.f.* To lay foundation; to establish.

تاش *tāsh* (H) *n.m.* Brocade; playing crads; gold foil.

تاشا *tāshā*, *n.m.* A semi-spherical drum.

تافتہ *tāftah* (P) *n.m.* A kind of silk; a glassy cream colour in pigeons and horses; taffeta.

تاقی *tāqi* (T) *adj.* A horse having eyes of two different colours; a defective horse. *n.f.* A kind of hat.

تاک *tāk* (P) *n.f.* A vine; a grape; a creeper.

تاک *tāk*, *n.f.* Look; regard; glance; aim; lookout; view; the act of aiming.

تاک جھانک tāk jhāṅk, n.f. The act of peeping about; ogle.

تاک رکھنا tāk rakhnā, v. To keep in view.

تاک میں رھنا tāk meṅ rahnā, v. To be on the look out for; to lie in wait for.

تاک لگانا tāk lagānā, v. To look fixedly; to stare; to lie in wait for.

تاک کر مارنا tāk kar mārnā, v. To take aim at.

تاکنا tāknā, v. To stare at; to aim; to peep; to spy; to watch; to view; to behold; to look; to look for; to lie in ambush.

تاکید tākid (A) n.f. Stress; pressure; emphasis; confirmation; injunction; impressing; urging.

تاکید کرنا tākid karnā, v. To enjoin strictly; to urge; to press; to lay stress on; to insist.

تاکیداً takīdān, adv. Emphatically; positively; strictly; as a reminder.

تاکیدی tākīdī, adj. Emphatic; urgent; positive; peremptory.

تاگا tāgā (H) n.m. Thread; cord.

تاگا پرونا tāgā pironā, v. To thread a needle.

تاگا ڈالنا tāgā ḍālnā, v. To thread a needle; to put stitches in a quilt.

تاگڑی tāgṛi, n.m. The thread which Hindu children wear round their waist.

تال tāl (H) n.f. Rhythmic beating of the hands (in music); musical tune or measure; chime. n.m. A pond; a lake.

تال دینا tāl denā, v. To chime; to beat time in music.

تال بے تال ھونا یا تال سے بے تال ھونا tāl betāl honā yā tāl se betāl honā, v. To be out of tune.

تال میل tāl mel, n.f. Harmony; agreement; accord.

تالا tālā, n.m. A lock.

تالا لگانا tālā lagānā, v. To lock; to put a padlock on.

تالا کنجی tālā kunji, n.m. Lock and key.

تالاب tālāb (P&H) n.m. A tank; a pond; a pool; a reservoir of water.

تآلف tāalluf (A) n.m. Mutual love or friendship; intimacy; acquaintance.

تالم tāallum (A) n.m. Torment; sorrow; melancholy; grief; pain.

تالمکھانہ tālmakhānah (H) n.m. A medicinal herb; fruit of the lotus.

تالو tālū (S) n.m. The palate; the ridge or slit in the roof of the mouth; a disorder in horses.

تالو اٹھانا tālū uṭhānā, v. To raise the uvula of a new-born child.

تالو سے زبان نہ لگنا tālū se zubān nah lagnā, v. To talk unceasingly.

تالی tālī (H) n.f. A key; clapping of the hands together.

تالی بجانا tālī bajānā, v. To clap the hands; to applaud.

تالی پیٹنا tālī pīṭnā, v. To clap the hands (in delight or by way of censure and ridicule).

تالی ایک هاتھ سے نہیں بجتی tāli ek hāth se nahiṅ bajti, prov. It takes two to make a quarrel; it requires two hands to clap.

تالیف tālif (A) n.f. Compilation; composition; reconciling; joining in friendship; connecting.

تالیف قلوب talif-ĕ qulūb, n.f. Captivation of hearts; the art of winning friends.

تالیف کرنا tālif karnā, v. To compile; to join.

تام tām (A) adj. Complete; whole; perfect; entire; full.

تام چینی tām chīnī, n.f. Enamelled copper or iron.

تام جھام tām jhām (H) n.m. A rough palanquin; a rough kind of sedan chair with two poles at both ends and carried over two men's shoulders.

تامل tāammul (A) n.m. Careful consideration; meditation; hesitation; delay; disinclination; doubt; irresolution.

تامل کرنا tāammul karnā, v. To consider; to doubt; to hesitate; to meditate; to delibrate.

تان tān (H) n.f. A tune; a keynote in music; tension; knitting (the eye-brow); stretching; a kind of tree.

تان اڑانا tān uṛānā, v. To strike up a tune; to sing.

تان توڑنا tān toṛnā, v. To wind up a tune; to crack a joke; to drop a word.

تانا tānā (H) n.m. The warp. v. To heat.

تانابانا tānā bānā, n.m. Warp and woof.

تانبا tānbā (H) n.m. Copper.

تانبے کا تار نہ ہونا tānbe kā tār nah honā, Id. To possess not a single pice; to be utterly destitute.

تانت tānt (H) n.f. Catgut; sinew; the string of a musical intrument or bow; a loom.

تانت باجی راگ بوجھا tānt bāji rāg būjhā, prov. To understand from the very first word.

تانتا tāntā (H) n.m. Series; row; range; a line; a drove.

تانتا بندھ جانا tāntā bandh jānā, v. To have a constant coming and going of visitors.

تانگا tāngā (H) n.m. A small two wheeled carriage pulled by a horse.

تاننا tānnā, v. To stretch; to expand; to extend; to pull tight; to knit (the eye-brow); to string up; to encourage.

تانیث tānis (A) n.f. Feminine gender.

تاؤ tāo (H) n.m. Heat; passion; rage; strength; power; speed; a sheet of paper.

تاؤ آنا tāo ānā, v. To be heated; to be inflamed; to be enraged.

تاؤ پیچ tāo pech, n.m. Restlessness; perplexity; alarm; anger.

تاؤ دینا tāo denā, v. To heat; to melt; to fuze; to curl the moustache.

تاؤ کھانا یا تاؤ میں آنا tāo khānā yā tāo men ānā, v. To be heated; to be inflamed; to be enraged; to be angry.

تاوان tāwān (P) n.m. Penalty; fine; damages; compensation; retaliation; recompense; mulct.

تاوان دینا tāwān denā, v. To pay a penalty; to make amends.

تاوان لگانا tāwān lagānā, v. To fine; to amerce.

تاویل tāwīl (A) n.f. Explanation; elucidation; interpretation; paraphrase.

تاویل کرنا tāwīl karnā v. To interpret; to elucidate; to explain; to paraphrase; to give a different interpretation of an obvious meaning of a word.

تاہل tāahhul (A) n.m. Marriage; marrying; establishing a family.

تائب tā'ib (A) n.m. Repenting; penitent.

تائی tā'ī (H) n.f. Aunt; paternal uncle's wife.

تائید tā'īd (A) n.f Aid; support; corroboration; assistance.

تائید دعوی tā'īd-ĕ da'wā, n.f. Support of a claim.

تائید کردہ tā'īd kardah, adj. Sponsored.

تائید کرنا tā'īd karnā, v. To help; to support; to second; to corroborate; to justify; to confirm.

تائید کلام tā'īd-ĕ kalām, n.f. Support of a statement.

تایا tāyā (H) n.m. Father's elder brother.

تب tab (H) adv. Then; at that time; afterwards.

تب بھی tab bhī, adv. Even then; then too; still; nevertheless; notwithstanding.

تب تک tab tak, adv. Till then; so long; upto that time.

تب تو tab to, adv. In that case.

تب سے *tab se, adv.* Since that time ; thereafter ; thence.

تب ہی *tab hi, adv.* At that very moment ; there and then ; exactly then.

تب ہی تو *tab hi to, adv.* Then indeed; for that reason; then.

تب ہی سے *tab hī se, adv.* Thenceforth ; thence.

تبادلہ ، تبادل *tabādalah, tabādul* (A) *n.m.* Transfer ; change ; exchange; alternation.

تبادلہ خیالات کرنا *tabādalah-ĕ khayālāt karnā, v.* To exchange views.

تبار *tabār* (A) *n.m.* Family ; dynasty ; tribe ; people ; race.

تبارک *tabārak* (A) *adj.* Hallowed; to be magnified greatly.

تباشیر *tabāshir* (P) *n.f.* A medicinal sugar found between the joints of a bamboo.

تباہ *tabāh* (P) *adj.* Ruined ; spoiled ; depraved ; wretched.

تباہ حال *tabāh ḥāl, adj.* In bad condition ; ruined; miserably poor or wretched.

تباہی *tabāhi* (P) *n.f.* Destruction ; ruin ; wreck ; perdition ; wickedness ; depravity.

تباہی آنا *tabāhi ānā, v.* To be ruined ; to be wrecked.

تباہی کا مارا *tabāhī kā mārā, adj.* Wretched; afflicted ; ruined.

تبخیر *tabkhir* (A) *n.f* Evaporation; turning into vapour ; light fever.

تبدل *tabaddul* (A) *n.m.* Change; alteration ; difference; replacement; transfer.

تبدیل *tabdil* (A) *n.f.* Change; alteration; modification.

تبدیل آب و ہوا *tabdil-ĕ āb-ŏ hawā, n.f.* Change of climate.

تبدیل کرنا *tabdil karnā, v.* To change; to alter; to transfer.

تبدیل ہونا *tabdil honā, v.* To be transferred; to change.

تبدیل ہیت کرنا *tabdil-ĕ haiat karnā; v.* To disguise; to change the aspect.

تبدیلی *tabdili n.f.* Transfer; changing; alternation.

تبر *tabar* (P) *n.m.* An axe; a hatchet.

تبرا *tabarrā* (A) *n.m.* Curse; malediction; expressing disapproval or displeasure.

تبرا بھیجنا *tabarrā bhejnā, v.* To curse; to express displeasure.

تبرائی *tadarrā'i, n.m.* A Shia sect which considers cursing of certain companions of the Holy Prophet justified.

تبرک *tabarruk* (A) *n.m.* Benediction; blessing; a portion of presents (or what is left of food presented to great men) given to their dependents.

تبرکاً *tabarrukan, adv.* As a benediction; as a present; as a gift.

تبرید *tabrid* (A) *n.f.* Cooling; refreshing; a cooling and refreshing drink.

تبسم *tabassum* (A) *n.m.* Smiling; a smile.

تبصرہ *tābṣirah* (A) *n.m.* Review; criticism.

تبع *taba'* (A) *n.m.* Following; a follower.

تبع تابعین *taba' tābi'in, n.m.* The followers of the successors of the Holy Prophet's companions.

تبلیغ *tabligh* (A) *n.f.* Carrying the message of Islam to non-believers; preaching Islam.

تپ *tap* (P) *n.f.* Fever.

تپ اترنا *tap utarnā, v.* To get rid of fever; to shake off fever.

تپ چڑھنا *tap charhnā, v.* Getting fever.

تپ دق *tap-ĕ diq, n.f.* A hectic fever; a chronic fever; pulmonary tuberculosis.

تپ زرد *tap-ĕ zard, n.f.* Yellow fever.

تپ کا موت جانا *tap kā mūt jānā, v.* Breaking out of an eruption on the lips after fever.

تپ لرزہ *tap-ĕ larzah, n.f.* An ague.

تپ محرقہ *tap-ĕ moḥriqah, n.f.* An ardent or burning fever; Typhoid.

تپ نوبت *tap-ĕ naubat*, *n.f.* An intermittent fever.

تپاک *tapāk* (P) *n.m.* Affection; esteem; regard; love; zeal; cordiality; ardour; warmth; affliction; uneasiness

تپاں *tapāṅ* (P) *adj.* Growing hot; becoming agitated; palpitating.

تپانا *tapānā* (H) *v.* To heat; to warm; to cause to warm; to make something glow,

تپائی *tipā'i* (H) *n.f.* A tripod; a teapoy; a trivet.

تپڑ *tappar* (H) *n.m.* A matting (to sit on).

تپسیا *tapassiyā* (S) *n.f.* Austere devotion; religious penance; mortification of self.

تپش *tapish* (P) *n.f.* Heat; warmth; affliction; agitation.

تپنا *tapnā* (H) *v.* To be heated; to glow; to burn with pain or grief; to shine.

تپنچہ *tapanchah* (P) *n.m.* A pistol.

تتا *tattā* (H) *adj.* Hot; warm.

تتبع *tatabbo'* (A) *n.m.* Following after; pursuing; imitation.

تتبع کرنا *tatabbo' karnā*, *v.* To follow; to imitate; to ape.

تتر بتر *tittar bittar* (H) *adj.* Dispersed; scattered; out of order.

تتلانا *tutlānā* (H) *v.* To lisp; to speak indistinctly as a child; to stammer; to stutter.

تتلی *titlī* (H) *n.f.* A butterfly; a playful girl; a belle.

تتمہ *tatimmah* (A) *n.m.* A Supplement; an appendix.

تتمۂ خط *tatimmah-ĕ khaṭ*, *n.m.* Post-script of a letter.

تتمیم *tatmim* (A) *n.f.* Completion; accomplishment; consummation.

تتیا *tatayyā* (H) *n.f.* A kind of a wasp.

تثلیث *taṣlīṣ* (A) *n.f.* Trinity; division of Godhead into three personalities, the Father, the Son and the Holy Ghost; dividing into three parts; a trine (the aspect of the planets).

تثنیہ *taṣniyah* (A) *n.m.* Making two; doubling; the dual (number).

تج *taj* (S) *n.f.* The bay-tree or its bark; woody cassia; cinnamon; abandoning; forsaking.

تجار *tujjār* (A) *n.m.* (*plu.* of تاجر *tājir*). Merchants; the trading community.

ملک التجار *malik-ut-tujjār* (A) *n.m.* Chief merchant.

تجارب *tajārib* (A) *n.m.* (*plu.* of تجربہ *tajribah*) Experiences; experiments; trials.

تجارت *tijārat* (A) *n.f.* Trade; commerce; traffic.

تجارت کرنا *tijārat karnā*, *v.* To trade; to traffic; to deal in.

تجارت گاہ *tijārat gāh*, *n.f.* Place of trade or commerce; market.

تجارتی *tajārati*, *adj.* Mercantile; commercial.

تجاوز *tajāwuz* (A) *n.m.* Departing; passing; transgressing; surpassing; excess; deviation; offending.

تجاوز کرنا *tajāwuz karnā*, *v.* To exceed; to pass (beyond); to offend; to transgress; to err; to deviate; to stray; to trespass.

تجاہل *tajāhul* (A) *n.m.* Affected ignorance; apathy; connivance; indifference.

تجاہل عارفانہ کرنا *tājāhul-ĕ 'ārifānah karnā*, *v.* To pretend or to feign ignorance of a known thing.

تجربہ *tajribah* (A) *n.m.* Experience; experiment; trial; proof; assay; probation; test.

تجربہ کار *tajribah kār*, *adj.* Expert; experienced; skilful.

تجربہ کاری *tajribah kārī*, *n.f.* Experience; practical knowledge.

تجربہ کرنا *tajribah karnā*, *v.* To experince; to try; to experiment.

تجربات *tajribāt*, *n.* (*plu.* of تجربہ *tajribah*) Experiences; experiments.

تجرد *tajarrud* (A) *n.m.* Solitude; celibacy; bachelorhood; cutting oneself off from society.

تجرید tajrid (A) n.f. Separation; solitude; abstract.

تجزیہ tajziyah (A) n.m. Analysis.

تجسس tajassus (A) n.m. Curiosity; investigating; exploring; search; inquiry; inquisitiveness.

تجسس کرنا tajassus karnā, v. To search diligently; to explore; to pry into.

تجلی tajallī (A) n.f. Manifestation; splendour; brilliance; lustre; clearness; brightness; illumination.

تجمل tajammul (A) n.m. Dignity; pomp; parade; retinue; magnificence.

تجنا tajnā (H) v. To abandon; to desert; to quit; to divorce; to give up; to forsake.

تجنیس tajnis (A) n.f. Making of the same kind; resemblance; analogy; alliteration equivocation; pun.

تجنیس خطی tajnis-ĕ khaṭṭi, n.f. Using words written alike but with different vowel points, are pronounced differently; a sort of equivoque as pal, pil, pul.

تجوید tajwīd (A) n.f. Uttering of letters with reference to the organs of speech—lips, tongue, teeth, throat.

تجویز tajwīz (A) n.f. Opinion; judgment; resolution; scheme; plan; device; proposal; suggestion; contrivance; view; finding.

تجویز کرنا tajwīz karnā, v. To propose; to decide; to give judgment; to suggest; to plan; to estimate; to consider; to prescribe; to investigate; to inquire into; to contrive.

تجویز ہونا tajwiz honā, v To be contrived; to be ascertained.

زیرتجویز zer-ĕ tajwīz, adv. Under consideration; under investigation.

تجھ tujh (H) pron. Thee.

تجھے tujhe, pron. To thee.

تجھ کو پرائی کیا پڑی اپنی نبیڑ تو tujh ko parā'i kiyā parī apni nabeṛ tū, prov. Pry not into other peoples' affairs; mind of your own business; do not poke your nose into the affairs of others.

تجہیز tajhīz, n.f. Expediting; arranging; adorning; carrying to the grave; burial.

تجہیز و تکفین tajhīz-ŏ takfīn, n.f. Burial; interment.

تحائف tahā'if (A) n.m. (plu. of تحفہ toḥfah); Presents; curiosities; rarities.

تحت taht (A) n.m. The inferior or interior part; below; under; infra; after; subjection; possession; charge; control. prep. & adv. Beneath; in subjection to; under control of.

تحت الثرٰی tāhtaṣ-ṣarā, n.f. Under the earth; the nether regions.

تحت الشعور tāht-ash-sha'ūr, n.m. Subconsciousness.

تحت اللفظ taht-al-lafz, adj. Literal translation; verbal; interlinear. n.m. Recitation of verses without melody.

تحتانی taḥtānī (A) adj. Following; under mentioned; inferior; a letter of the alphabet having dots under it.

تحدی taḥaddī (A) n.f. Cry; challenge; threat.

تحریر taḥrīr, (A) n.f. Writing; description; composition; document; manumission; manuscript; fee for writing; lines.

تحریراً taḥrīran, adv. In writing; by writing.

تحریر اقلیدس tahrīr-ĕ uqledīs, n f. Euclids element.

تحریر بین السطور taḥrīr bain-ās-suṭūr, n.f. Writing between lines; interlineation.

تحریر ظہری tāhrīr-ĕ zahri, n.f. Endorsement; writing on the back.

تحریر کرنا taḥrīr karnā, v. To write; to record; to give in writing; to describe.

تحریر ہونا taḥrīr honā. To be written; to be recorded.

تحریری tahrīrī, *adj.* Documentary; in writing.

تحریص *tahriṣ* (A) *n.f.* Greediness; instigation; stimulation; temptation.

تحریف *tahrīf* (A) *n.f.* Transposition of words or letters so as to change the meaning; an anagram; clerical error; deliberate alteration of a word or words to change the meaning; distortion; tampering (with).

تحریک *tahrīk* (A) *n.f.* Movement; agitation; incitement; stimulation; excitement; instigation; temptation; encouragement; motion; broaching of a subject.

تحریک کرنا *tahrīk karnā, v.* To urge; to instigate; to move; to excite; to put in motion; to tempt.

تحریم *tahrīm* (A) *n.f.* Saying *Allah-o-Akbar* 'God is great' at the commencement of the prayer; assumption of a pilgrim's garb; honour; forbidding; prohibition.

تحسین *tahsīn,* (A) *n.f.* Approbation; applause; acclamation; cheers.

تحسین تلفظ *tahsīn-ĕ talaffuẓ, n.f.* Euphony.

تحسین کرنا *tahsīn karnā, v.* To praise; to applaud; to approve.

تحصیل *tahṣīl* (A) *n.f.* Getting; acquiring; collecting; gain; acquisition; education; attainment; profit; learning; collection (of revenue); office of the tax-collector; the area administered by a *tahṣildar.*

تحصیلی اخراجات *tahṣīlī ikhrājāt, n.m.* Collection charges.

تحصیل حاصل *tahṣīl-ĕ ḥāṣil, n.f.* Trying to gain what one already has; useless attempt.

تحصیلدار *tahṣīldār. n.m.* A collector; a tax-collector.

تحصیلداری *tahṣīldārī, n.f.* Collectorship; tax-collecting.

تحصیلات *tahṣīlāt, n.f.* Collections; acquisitions.

تحصیل کرنا یا تحصیلنا *tahṣīl karnā yā tahṣīlnā, v.* To acquire; to gain; to collect a tax; to learn; to receive education; to oppress; to afflict.

تحصیل مالگزاری *tahṣīl-ĕ mālguzārī, n.f.* Collection of revenue.

تحفظ *tahaffuẓ* (A) *n.m.* Preservation; conservation.

تحفظ اثمار *tahaffuẓ-ĕ aṣmār, n.m.* Fruit preservation.

تحفظ اراضی *tahaffuẓ-ĕ arāzī, n.m.* Soil conservation.

تحفظ اشجار و شکار *tahaffuẓ-ĕ ashjār-ŏ shikār, n.m.* Preservation of fauna and flora.

تحفہ *tohfah* (A) *n.m.* A present. *adj.* Rare; uncommon; excellent; admirable; nice; beautiful; wonderful.

تحقق *tahaqquq* (A) *n.m.* Proving to be truth, reality or fact; ascertainment; certain knowledge; certainty.

تحقیر *tahqīr* (A) *n.m.* Despising; scorn; neglect; disdain; contempt.

تحقیر عدالت *tahqīr-ĕ 'dālat, n.f.* Contempt of court.

تحقیق *tahqīq* (A) *n.f.* Ascertaining; ascertainment; investigation; verification; exactness; precision; research; inquiry; improvement; truth; certainty; fact. *adj.* Authentic; ascertained; actual; real; apparent; certain. *adv.* Truly; indeed.

تحقیقات *tahqīqāt, n.f.* Investigation; inquiry; research.

تحکم *tahakkum* (A) *n.m.* Command; ruling; dominion; power; authority.

تحکم کرنا *tahakkum karnā, v.* To command; to rule; to exercise control or authority.

تحلیف *tahlīf, n.f.* Administering an oath.

تحلیل *tahlīl,* (A) *n.f.* Dissolving; digestion; concoction; solubility; making lawful.

تحلیل کرنا *tahlīl karnā, v.* To digest; to dissolve; to assimilate.

تحمل *tahammul* (A) *n.m.* Patience; endurance; forbearance; toleration.

تحمل کرنا taḥammul karna, v. To forbear; to bear; to be patient; to endure.

تحمید taḥmid (A) n.f. Praise of God.

تحویل taḥwīl (A) n.f. Changing; transfering; renovation; passing of the sun, moon or a planet from one sign to another; trust; charge.

تحویل تصرف taḥwīl-ĕ taṣarruf, n.m. Misappropriation of a trust; embezzlement.

تحویلدار taḥwildār, n.m. A treasurer; a trustee.

تحویلداری taḥwildāri, n.f. Office of a treasurer.

تحیر taḥaiyur (A) n.m. Amazement; astonishment; wonder.

تخالف takhāluf (A) n.m. Mutual opposition; contention; enmity.

تخت takht (P) n.m. A throne; a low seat; a chair of state; a bed.

تخت بخت takht bakht, n.m. Throne and fortune; wedlock and wealth.

تخت پر بٹھانا takht par biṭhānā, v. To enthrone.

تخت پر بیٹھنا takht par baithnā, v. To occupy the throne; to enthrone; to reign; to govern; to be a king.

تخت پوش takht posh, n.m. A covering for a throne or seat; a wooden seat.

تخت چھوڑنا takht chhoṛnā, v. To abdicate a throne

تخت رواں takht-ĕ rawān, n.m. A travelling throne; a throne on which a king is carried.

تخت سلیمان takht-ĕ sulemān, n.m. The flying sedan of Solomon.

تخت سے آتارنا takht se utārnā, v. To dethrone.

تخت طاؤس takht-ĕ ṭāus, n.m. The Peacock throne of Shahjahan.

تخت گاہ takht gāh, n.m. Capital; metropolis; the royal residence.

تخت نشینی takht nashīnī, n.f. Accession to the throne; coronat on; reigning.

تخت یا تختہ takht yā takhtah, prov. Either a throne or a bier (spoken when engaging in a desperate enterprise); a do or die situation.

تختہ takhtah (P) n.m. A plank; a board; a stool; a bench; a bier; a sheet of paper; a bed of flowers; deck (of a ship); a sign board; drawbridge.

تختہ اُلٹنا takhtah ulaṭnā, v. To ruin; to destroy; to devastate; to overthrow (the government).

تختۂ برق takhtah-ĕ barqi, n.m. Electric board; switch-board.

تختہ بندی takhtah bandi, n.f. Boarding; wainscot; arranging flower beds.

تختہ بندی کرنا takhtah bandi karnā, v. To board; to plank; to floor with boards; to arrange flower beds.

تختہ پل takhtah pūl, n.m. A drawbridge.

تختۂ تابوت takhta-ĕ tābūt, n.m. Bier; a carriage or frame of wood for carrying the dead to the grave.

تختۂ سیاہ takhta-ĕ siyāh, n.m. Black-board.

تختۂ مشق takhta-ĕ mashq, n.m. Being frequently experimented on; a plaything; a prey; a victim; a practicing board; a little board like a slate which children write on.

تختۂ نرد takhtah-ĕ nard, n.m. Chess board; backgammon.

تختہ ہو جانا takhtah ho jānā, v. To become stiff; to become hard (a body).

تختی takhti (P) n. f. Tablet; a small board for children to write on; a small plank.

تخریب takhrib (A) n.f. Devastation; destruction; razing; subversion.

تخصیص takhṣiṣ, (A) n.f. Peculiarity; particularity; speciality; specification; reservation.

تخفیف takhfīf (A) n.f. Making light; alleviating; relieving: abbreviating; curtailing; abatement; relief; remission; abridgement; mitigation; extenuation; decrease; diminution; reduction; retrenchment.

تخفیف قیمت takhfīf-ĕ-qimat, n.f. Devaluation.

تخفیف کرنا takhfif karnā, v. To lessen; to reduce; to relax; to mitigate; to curtail; to deduct; to retrench.

تخفیف میں لانا takhfīf meṅ lānā, v. To abolish; to retrench; to reduce; to do away (with).

تخلخل takhalkhul (A) n.m. Hollowness.

تخلص takhalluṣ (A) n.m. The titular name assumed by poets; poetic name; nom de plume; pen-name.

تخلیہ takhliyah (A) n.m. Private room; privacy.

تخم tukhm (P) n.m. Seed; egg; sperm; a testicle; origin; progeny.

تخم بالنگوہ tukhm-ĕ bālangūh, n.m. A seed of cooling quality; the seed of the mountain balm.

تخم چشم tukhm-ĕ chashm, n. m. The eye ball.

تخم بد یا تخم حرام tukhm-ĕ-bad yā tukhm-ĕ ḥarām, adj. Low-bred fellow; bastard.

تخم ریحان tukhm-ĕ raiḥān, n.m. Seed of acymum pilosam; purslane.

تخم ریزی tukhm rezi, n.f. Sowing; scattering seed.

تخم کتان tukhm-ĕ-katān, n.m. Linseed.

تخمیر takhmir (A) n.f. Fermentation; forming into leaven.

تخمین takhmin (A) n.m. Estimate; calculation.

تخمیناً takhminan (A) adv. By guess; by conjecture; by appraisement; approximately; about.

تخمینہ takhminah (A) n.m. Estimate; guess; appraisement; conjecture; valuation.

تخویف takhwif (A) n.f. Putting in fear; threat; intimidation; terrifying; threatening.

تخویف مجرمانا takhwif-ĕ mujrimānah (A) n.f. Criminal intimidation.

تخیل takhaiyyul (A) n.m. Fancy; imagination; supposition.

تدارک tadāruk (A) n.m. (Lit. to get back a thing lost). Reparation; remedy; chastisement; precaution; preparation (to obtain justice); the instruments and means used to obtain justice (as writings, lawyers, witnesses, &c.).

تدارک کرنا tadāruk karnā, v. To guard against; to take precautions; to make preparation; to redress; to oppose; to provide against.

تداول tadāwūl (A) n.m. (Lit. passing from one to another); Tradition; handing from one to another.

تدبر tadabbur (A) n.m. Foresight; prudence.

تدبیر tadbir (A) n.f. Deliberation; counsel; contrivance; opinion; advice; arrangement; order; management; policy; prudence.

تدبیر سلطنت tadbir-ĕ salṭanat, n.f. Politics; political economy.

تدبیر منزل tadbir-ĕ-manzil, n.f. Domestic economy; policies of State.

تدریج tadrij (A) n.f. Gradation; scale.

بتدریج ba-tadrij, adv. By degrees; gradually.

تدریس tadris (A) n.f. Teaching; lecturing; giving lectures or lessons; instruction by means of reading.

تدفین tadfin (A) n.f. Burial; funeral; interment;

تدقیق tadqiq (A) n.f. Deep thought; close attention; pounding; grinding; bray.

تدوین tadwin (A) n.f. Compilation; collection; putting together.

تدین tadaiyyun (A) n.m. Religiousness; constancy in religion.

تذبذب tazabzub (A) n.m. Vacillation; suspension of judgment; ambiguity; wavering; perplexity; uncertainty; doubt.

تذکار tazkār (A) n.m. Explanation; account; a reminder; a memorandum; a note; description of the holiness of God.

تذکرہ tazkirah (A) n.m. Mention; a memoir; a biography; biographical memoirs.

تذکیر *tazkir* (A) *n.f.* Masculine gender; commemoration; bringing to memory; mentioning; recording; admonishing.

تذلیل *tazlil* (A) *n.f.* Abasement; debasement; degradation; humiliation.

تر *tar* (P) *adj.* Moist; damp; wet; fresh; green; young; juicy; saturated; greasy; rich; refreshed; the termination of comparative degree in Persian.

تر بتر *tar batar*, *adj.* Completely wet; saturated; covered (with water or blood).

تر دامن *tar daman*, *adj.* Guilty; sinful.

تر دامنی *tar dāmani*, *n.f.* Guilt; sinfulness; neglect of the laws of morality and religion.

تر کرنا *tar karna*, *v.* To wet; to saturate.

تر لقمہ یا تر مال یا تر نوالہ *tar luqmah yā tar māl yā tar niwālah*, *adj.* Delicious food; tasty morsel, easy; not difficult.

تر و تازہ *tar-ŏ tāzah*, *adj.* Fresh and tasty; ripe and fresh.

تراب *turāb* (A) *n.m.* Earth; ground; dust.

ترابی *turābi* (A) *adj.* Earthen.

تراجم *tarājim* (A) *n.m.* (*plu.* of ترجمہ) translations.

ترارا، تراڑا *tarārā*, *tarāṛā* (H) *n.m.* Quickness; rapidity; flow; stream.

ترارا بھرنا *tarārā bharnā*, *v.* To gallop; to run.

ترازو *tarāzū* (P) *n.f.* A scale; a balance.

ترازو ہو جانا *tarāzu ho jānā*, *v.* To be evenly balanced; to be counter-balanced.

تراسی *tirāsī* (H) *n.* & *adj.* Eighty-three.

تراش *tarāsh* (P) (*in comp.*). Cutting; cutter; carver. *n.f.* Cutting; shape; form; fashion (of clothes); make; build.

تراش خراش *tarāsh kharash*, *n.f.* Shape; neatness of form; shaping and fashioning (dress); elegantly; elegance in dress.

بت تراش *but tarāsh*, *n.m.* Image-carver; a sculptor.

تراشنا *tarāshnā*, *v.* To cut; to clip; to prune; to shave; to shape; to cut out; to slice.

تراشہ *tarashah* (P) *n.m.* A cutting; a chip; a scrap splinter; shred.

ترانوے *tirānwe* (H) *n.* & *adj.* Ninety-three.

ترانہ *taranah* (P) *n.m.* Harmony; symphony; voice; song; melody; trill; tune; quaver; a kind of song.

تراوٹ *tarawat* (H) *n.f.* Freshness; greenness; juiciness; humidity; dampness.

تراویح *tarāwiḥ* (A) *n.f.* Special prayers offered by Muslims in the month of *Ramaẓān* at night.

تراہا *tirāhā*, (H) *n.m.* Junction of three roads.

تربت *turbat* (A) *n.f.* A tomb; a grave; a sepulchre.

تربد *turbud* (P) *n.m.* A purgative Indian root.

تربوز *tarbūz*, *n.m.* A water-melon.

تر بھون یا ترلوک *tirbhuwan yā tarlok* (S) *n.m.* The three worlds (heaven; earth and infernal regions); the universe.

تربیت *tarbiyat* (A) *n.f.* Education; instruction; tuition; bringing up; breeding; training.

تربیت پذیر *tarbiat pazir*, *adj.* Docile; tractable.

تربیت کرنا یا دینا *tarbiat karnā yā denā*, *v.* To educate; to instruct; to bring up; to rear.

ترپال *tirpāl* *n.m.* (corr. of English) Tarpaulin.

ترپائی *turpā'i* (H) *n.f.* Stitching; hemming.

ترپن *turpan* (H) *n.f.* A kind of stitch.

ترپنا *turapnā* (H) *v.* To stitch; to darn; to hem.

ترپھلا *tirphalā* (H) *n.m.* A medicine composed of three myrobalans (*har*, *baheṛah* and *ānolah*).

ترت *turt* (H) *adv.* Instantly; quickly; hastily; directly; immediately.

ترت پھرت *turt phurt*, *n.f.* Quickness; promptness.

ترترا turturā (S) adj. Nimble; active; flippant; quick; sharp.

ترتیب tartib, n.f. Arrangement; disposition; order; method; formation; classification:

ترتیب تہجی tartib-ē tahajji, n.f. Alphabetical order.

ترتیب دینا tartib denā, v. To arrange; to set in order; to classify; to compose; to assort.

ترتیب سے یا ترتیب وار tartib se yā tartib wār, adv. Methodically; regularly; in proper order.

ترتیل tartil (A) n.f. Reciting the Quran in a clear and distinct manner.

ترجمان tarjuman (A) n.m. An interpreter.

ترجمہ tarjamah (A) n.m. Translation; interpretation.

ترجمہ کرنا tarjamah karnā, v. To translate; to interpret.

ترجمہ لفظی tarjamah-ē-lafzi, n.m. Literal translation.

ترجمہ با محاورہ tarjamah bā muhāwirah, n.m. Idiomatic translation.

ترجیح tarjih (A) n.f. Superiority; preference; pre-eminence; priority.

ترجیح دینا tarjih denā, v. To prefer; to give preference (over).

ترجیع tarji' (A) n.f. Repeating; getting back; returning.

ترجیع بند tarji' band, n.m. A stanza in which one line recurs at stated intervals.

ترچھا، ترچھی tirchhā, tirchhi (H) adj. Across; slanting; oblique; awry; askant; perverse; cross-wise.

ترچھا دیکھنا tirchhā dekhnā, v. To squint; to look askance.

ترچھی نگاہ سے دیکھنا tirchhi nigāh se dekhnā, v. To look angrily (at); to cast unkind looks.

ترچھی نظر tirchhi nazar, n.f. Leer; ogle; side-glance; squint.

ترحم tarahhum (A) n.m. Pity; compassion; kindness; mercy; lenity.

ترخیم tarkhim (A) n.f. Curtailing; (Gram.) apocope.

تردد taraddud (A) n.m. Irresolution; vacillation; indecision; hesitation; suspension of judgment; wavering; anxious consideration; anxiety; care.

تردید tardid (A) n.f. Repelling; refutation; repudiation; rebutment; contradiction.

تردید کرنا tardid karnā, v. To confute; to refute; to set aside; to repudiate; to contradict.

ترس tars (P) n.m. Fear; terror.

ترس (H) Compasion; pity; mercy.

ترس کھانا tars khāna, v. To pity; to compassionate.

ترسا tarsā (P) n.m. A Christian; a worshipper of fire. adj. Threatening, terrifying.

ترسا ترسا کر دینا tarsā tarsā kar dena, v. To give little by little merely to tease; to give piecemeal; to tantalize.

ترساں tarsān (P) adj, Fearful; timid; afraid; fearing.

ترسانا tarsānā (H) v. To cause to long for; to set agog; to tantalize; to tease.

ترسنا tarasna (H) v. To long for; to desire anxiously; to be agog; to be tantalized.

ترسول trisul (S) n.m. A trident; a three pointed pike or spear.

ترسوں tarson (H) adv. & n.m. The third day past or to come.

ترسیل tarsil (A) n.f. Transmission; sending; forwarding; conveyance; despatch.

ترسیل نمبر tarsil nambar, n.m. Despatch number.

ترسیل رجسٹر tarsil rajistar, n.m. Despatch register.

شعبہ ترسیل shu'bah-ē tarsil, n.m. Despatch branch.

ترش tursh (P) adj. Sour; acid; harsh; gruff; ill-tempered; crabbed.

ترش رو tursh rū, adj. Cynical; morose; surly; stern; cross; peevish.

ترش مزاج tursh mizaj, adj. Sour-tempered harsh; morose; crabbed.

ترشانا turshānā, v. To turn sour; to acidulate.

ترشح tarashshuḥ (A) n.m. Exuding; dropping; distilling; a drizzle. adj. Manifest; apparent.

ترشی turshī, n.f. Sourness; acidity.

ترصیع tarṣī' (A) n.f. Adorning with jewels; setting or fixing together; making the words of a rhyming prose or verse conformable and corresponding in their measures and agreeing with the corresponding words of the corresponding clause.

ترغیب targhīb (A) n.f. Exciting desire; incitement; instigation; inducement; temptation; stimulation.

ترغیب دینا targhīb denā, v. To stimulate; to excite; to incite; to tempt; to entice; to induce; to persuade.

ترقی taraqqī (A) n.f. Promotion; preferment; advancement; elevation; increase; improvement; development; making progress in learning; proficiency.

ترک turk (P) n.m. A Turk; a Turkish soldier; an inhabitant of Turkey; a beloved; a Muslim.

ترک تاز turk tāz, n.m. A soldier; a plunderer; onslaught; depredation; plundering; attack; inroad.

ترک چشم turk chashm, adj. Having a killing or captivating eye.

ترک tark (A) n.m. Abandonment; desertion; abdication; relinquishment.

ترک کرنا tark karnā, v. To abandon; to resign; to relinquish; to desist from; to forsake; to quit; to omit; to desert.

ترک وطن tark-ĕ-waṭan, n.m. Emigration.

ترکاری tarkārī, n.f. Esculent vegetables.

ترکش tarkash (P) n.m. A quiver.

ترکمان turkamān, n.m. A tribe inferior to Turks.

ترکہ tarkah (A) n.m. The estate of a deceased person; inheritance by bequest or succession; a legacy; bequest.

ترکہ بلا وصیت tarkah bilā waṣiyat, n.m. Intestate property; property left without a valid will.

ترکی turkī (P) adj. Of or belonging to a Turk Turkish; n.m. A country; a horse of Turkish breed; the Turkish language.

ترکی به ترکی جواب دینا turkī bah turkī jawāb denā, id. To give tit for tat; to pay in the same coin.

ترکی تمام ہونا turkī tamām honā, id. To be humbled or abased; to be all over (with).

ترکیب tarkīb (A) n.f. Composition; mixture; form; mechanism; plan; mode; construction; formation; structure; arrangement; method; parsing (grammar).

ترکیب بند tarkīb band, n.m. A particular kind of metrical composition; a stanza.

ترکیب سے چلنا tarkīb se chalnā, v. To be frugal; to work according to some principle or plan.

ترکیب کرنا tarkīb karnā, v. To parse; to organise; to devise.

کسی ترکیب سے kisī tarkīb se, adv. By some means; somehow or other; by whatever means possible.

ترکیبی tarkībī, adj. Composed; mixed; artful; artificial.

ترمرا tirmirā (H) n.m. A spot of oil swimming on water or other liquid; an ocular spectrum or spark appearing before the eye from the internal state of that organ.

ترمراہٹ tirmirāhaṭ (H) n.f. Vibration.

ترمیم tarmīm (A) n.f. Revision; amendment; improvement; modification.

ترمیم شدہ tarmīm shudah, adj. Modified; revised; improved; amended.

ترمیم کرنا tarmim karnā, v. To amend; to modify; to change; to improve.

ترنج turunj yā turanj (P) n.m. A citron; an orange; a lemon; an embroidered work.

ترنجبین turanjbin (P) n.m. Persian manna; honey mixed with lime-juice.

ترنگ tarang (S) n.f. Wave; billow; emotion; whim; conceit; fancy; caprice; ecstacy.

ترنگی tarangī (S) adj. Whimsical; braggart; fantastical.

ترنم tarannum (A) n.m. A kind of song; modulation.

ترویج tarwij (A) n.f. Currency; causing a thing to be in demand; circulation.

ترئی tura'i (H) n.f. A kind of cucumber.

تری tari (P) n.f. Moisture; freshness; dampness; marsh; swamp; river; sea; ocean.

تریا tiriyā or triyā (H) n.f. Female; a woman; a maid; a wife.

تریا چرتر tiriyā chartir, n.m. Woman's wiles; artfulness of women.

تریا راج tiriyā rāj, n.m. Woman's rule; Amazon country; petticoat government.

تریاهٹ tiriyāhat, n.f. Woman's persistency.

تریاق tiryāq (A) n.m. An antidote for snake-bites, poisons, &c.; Bezoar stone; sovereign remedy.

ترپن trepan (H) adj. & n. Fifty-three.

تریڑا tarerā (H) n.m. Falling of water from a spout or from height.

تریز tirez (P) n.f. Pieces in a vestment that are cut transversely or diagonally.

ترین tarin (P) Persian termination corresponding of the superlative degree.

تڑاک tarāk (H) n.m. The sound of beating; crack; crash; whack.

تڑاک پڑاک tarak parāk, adv. At once; without delay; quickly; one after another.

تڑاکا tarākā, n.m. Sound of striking; a blow; snap; smack; crash; rigour; violence; severity.

تڑاکے کا یا کی tarāke kā yā ki, adj. Intense; severe; bitter (as cold); violent (as sun).

تڑانا turānā (H) v. To break; to change (money).

تڑپ tarap (H) n.f. Tossing or rolling about restlessly; agitation; fury; leap; jump; a flash of lightning.

تڑپانا tarpānā (H) v. To put in great agitation; to render uneasy or restless; to cause to flutter or stumble.

تڑپنا tarapnā (H) v. To roll or toss about restlessly; to flutter; to palpitate; to flounce; to be agitated; to writhe; to wriggle; to quiver; to thirst after; to be anxiously eager for; to be dying for.

تڑخنا tarakhnā (H) v. To speak angrily; to be cracked.

تڑک tarak (H) n.f. Cracking; split; chink; fissure.

تڑکا tarkā, (H) n.m. Daybreak; dawn.

تڑکے tarke, adv. In the early morning; at dawn of day.

تڑکنا taraknā (H) v. To be cracked; to be split; to burst; to crack.

تڑوانا turwānā, v. To cause to break; to cause to change (money).

تزک tuzak yā tuzk (T) n.m. Pomp; dignity; retinue; memoirs.

تزکیہ tazkiyah (A) n.m. Purification; sanctification.

تزلزل tazalzul (A) n.m. Commotion; agitation; trepidation; wavering.

تزویج tazwij (A) n.f. Marrying; taking a wife.

تزویر tazwir, (A) n.f. Falsehood; lie; fraud; deceit; deception.

تزئین taz'in (A) n.f. Dressing oneself; decoration; ornament; honour; jewel.

تسالا *tisāla* (H) *adj.* Three years old.

تسامح *tasāmuh* (A) *n.m.* Mutual kindness and forgiveness; reciprocal indulgence or generosity; double meaning; connivance.

تساہل *tasāhul* (A) *n.m.* Conniving (at); carelessness; apathy; remissness; slowness; tardiness; laziness.

تساہل کرنا *tasāhul karnā, v.* To delay; to retard.

تسبیح *tasbih* (A) *n.f.* String of beads; a rosary; a chaplet of beads; the act of praising of God.

تسبیح پڑھنا یا پھیرنا *tasbih parhnā yā phernā, v.* To count the beads.

تسخیر *taskhir* (A) *n.f* Subduing; taking a strong-hold of; captivating; capture; subjection; subjugation; sorcery; imprisoning of an evil spirit.

تسخیر قلوب *taskhir-ě-qulūb, n.f.* Captivating of hearts; winning of hearts.

تسکین *taskin* (A) *n.f.* Consolation; comfort; pacifying; soothing; assuaging; appeasing; mitigation; satisfaction; ease; rest.

تسکین بخش *taskin bakhsh, adj.* Assuasive; consolatory; allaying; mitigating.

تسکین دینا *taskin denā, v.* To comfort; to calm; to appease; to tranquilize; to console; to pacify; to soothe.

تسکین ہونا *taskin honā, v.* To be consoled; to be comforted; to be satisfied; to be appeased.

تسلا *taslā* (H) *n.m.* Iron or brass vessel used as kneading trough or dressing victuals.

تسلسل *tasalsul* (A) *n.m.* Connecting like a chain; association (of ideas); sequence; series; succession.

تسلط *tasallut* (A) *n.m.* Domination; absolute rule; sway; command.

تسلی *tasalli* (A) *n.f.* Consolation; comfort; solace; satisfaction; contentment.

تسلی بخش *tasalli bakhsh, adj.* Consolatory; comforting.

تسلی دینا *tasalli denā, v.* To comfort; to console; to satisfy.

تسلی ہونا *tasalli honā, v.* To be consoled or comforted; to be satisfied; to derive comfort.

تسلیم *taslim* (A) *n.f.* Saluting most respectfully; homage; obeisance; salutation; greeting; compliments; surrender; resignation; acknowledging; accepting; recommending to the care or protection of another.

تسلیم کرنا *taslim karnā, v.* To salute respectfully; to do homage; to surrender; to admit; to confess.

تسلیم ہونا *taslim honā, v.* To be resigned; to be committed to surrender.

تسلیم یا تسلیمات بجا لانا *taslim yā taslimat baja lānā, v.* To make obeisance; to pay respects; to take leave (of); to bid adieu; to salute.

تسمہ *tasmah* (P) *n.m.* A thong; a strap of leather; latchet.

تسمیہ *tasmiyah* (A) *n.m.* Nomination; giving a name (to); pronouncing the name of God saying (بسم اللہ *Bismillah*, 'in the name of God').

تسنن *tasannun* (A) *n.m.* Following a *sunnat* and regulating life according to *Sunnah*; being or becoming *Sunni*.

تسنیم *tasnim* (A) *n.m.* A water or fountain of Paradise.

تسو *tassū* (H) *n.m.* One inch and a half; one eighth of a foot; 24th part of a yard.

تسوید *taswid* (A) *n.f.* Making black; rough draft (of a letter); sketch; a rough sketch; delineation.

تسویہ *tasviyah* (A) *n.m.* Adjustment.

تسہیل *tashil* (A) *n.f.* Facilitation; making easy.

تشابہ *tashābuh* (A) *n.m.* Resemblance; similitude; likeness.

تشاکل *tashākul* (A) *n.m.* Mutual resemblance.

تشبیہ *tashbih* (A) *n.f.* Simile; similitude; comparison; allegory; metaphor.

تشبیہ دینا *tashbih denā*, *v.* To assimilate (to); to liken; to compare (with).

تشت *tasht* (P) *n.m.* A platter; a large basin; a salver (see also طشت *ṭasht*)

تشت از بام ہونا *tasht az bām hona*, *v.* To come to be known; to come to light; to be revealed (a secret).

تشتت *tashattut* (A) *n.m.* Dispersion; distraction; separation; disunity.

تشتری *tashtari*, *n.f.* A solver; a small plate; a saucer; a small bowl; a dish.

تشخص *tashakh-khuṣ* (A) *n.m.* Discrimination appropriation; personality.

تشخیص *tashkhiṣ* (A) *n.f.* Ascertainment; ascertaining the diseases of a patient; diagnosis; discrimination; valuation; assessment.

تشخیص عام *tashkhis-ē-'am*, *n.f.* Rough estimate.

تشخیص کرنا *tashkhis karnā* *v.* To ascertain; to assess; to value; to appraise; to discriminate; to distinguish; to diagnose.

تشخیص گاہ *tashkhis gah*, *n.f.* Clinic.

تشدد *tashaddud* (A) *n.m.* Seizing or holding by force; aggravation; violence; intensity.

تشدید *tashdid* (A) *n.f.* Consolidating; corroborating; putting the orthographical mark *tashdid* (ّ) over letters to indicate that the letter is doubled; the *tashdid* mark itself.

تشریح *tashriḥ* (A) *n.f.* Explanation; exposition; elucidation; dissecting a body.

تشریح الابدان *tashrih-ul-abdan* (A) *n.m.* Anatomy.

تشریح کرنا *tashriḥ karna*, *v.* To explain; to elucidate; to give details.

تشریح وار *tashrih war*, *adv.* In detail; minutely; with full particulars.

تشریحی *tashrihi*, *adj.* Of or pertaining to anatomy; anatomical; explanatory; elucidative.

تشریحی یاد داشت *tashrihi yād dasht*, *n.f.* Explanatory memorandum.

تشریف *tashrif* (A) *n.f.* Honouring; exalting.

تشریف ارزانی فرمانا *tashrif arzāni farmana*, *v.* To be pleased to come; to be pleased to take a seat.

تشریف رکھنا *tashrif rakhnā*, *v.* To be pleased to sit down.

تشریف لانا *tashrif lānā*, *v.* To honour with one's presence; to come.

تشریف لے جانا *tashrif le jana*, *v.* To depart, to leave.

تشفی *tashaffi* (A) *n.f.* Consolation; satisfaction; calmness.

تشکک *tashakkuk* (A) *n.m.* Doubt; suspicion.

تشکیک *tashkik* (A) *n.f.* Raising suspicion; causing doubt; dubiousness; doubt; suspicion.

تشکیل *tashkil* (A) *n.f.* Formation; organisation.

تشنج *tashannuj* (A) *n.m.* Convulsion; spasm; cramp; twitching.

تشنگی *tishnagi* (P) *n.f.* Thirst; desire; longing; temptation.

تشنہ *tishnah* (P) *adj.* Thirsty; eagerly desiring; insatiable.

تشنہ کام *tishnah kam*, *adj.* Thirsty; unsuccessful; unfortunate.

تشنہ لب *tishnah lab*, *adj.* Having parched lips; thirsty.

تشنہ لبی *tishnah labi*, *n.f.* Thirstiness; state of having parched lips

تشویش *tashwish* (A) *n.f.* Confusion; distraction; apprehension; perplexity; anxiety; grief; disquietude.

تشہد *tashahhud* (A) *n.m.* Avowing belief in the unity of God and the mission of the Holy Prophet by reciting the formula "I bear witness that there is no god but God and that Muhammad is His servant and apostle"

تشہیر *tashhir* (A) *n.f.* Proclaiming; publishing; public exposure of an offender; reciting in public.

تشیع *tashaiyo'* (A) *n.m.* Proressing the Shia point of view.

تصادم *taṣādum* (A) *n.f.* Collision; clash; opposition; conflict.

تصانیف *taṣānif* (A) *n.f.* (*pl.* of تصنیف *taṣnif*). Literary works; literary compositions.

تصاویر *taṣāwir* (A) *n.f.* Pictures; paintings; photos; portraits (*pl.* of تصویر *taṣwir*).

تصحیح *taṣḥiḥ* (A) *n.f.* Rectification; correction; amendment; verification; illustration; attestation.

تصحیح کرنا *taṣḥiḥ karnā*, *v.* To correct; to amend; to rectify.

تصدق *taṣadduq* (A) *n.m.* Giving صدقہ *sadaqah* or alms; devotion; sacrifice; charity.

تصدق کرنا *taṣadduq karnā*, *v.* To sacrifice; to devote.

تصدیعہ *taṣdi'ah* (A) *n.m.* Headache; worry; affliction; trouble; annoyance; vexation toil; perplexity.

تصدیعہ آٹھانا *taṣdi'ah uṭhānā*, *v.* To take trouble; to worry (over); to be distressed; to be vexed.

تصدیق *taṣdiq* (A) *n.f.* Proving true; verifying; attesting; verification; attestation; authentication; affirmation.

تصدیق تعریفی *taṣdiq-ĕ t'arifi*, *n.f.* Commendation certificate.

تصدیق شدہ *taṣdiq shudah*, *adj.* Countersigned; verified; affirmed; certified; attested.

تصدیق کرنا *taṣdiq karnā*, *v.* To verify; to certify; to confirm; to attest; to affirm.

تصدیق نامہ *taṣdiq nāmah*, *n.m.* Certificate; a testimonial.

تصدیق نامۂ صحت *taṣdiq nāmah-ĕ ṣiḥhat*, *n.m.* Fitness certificate.

تصدیقی دستخط *tasdiqi dastk͟hāt* *n.m.* Countersignature

تصرف *taṣarruf* (A) *n.m.* Possession; use; sway; expenditure; disposal; embezzlement; extravagance.

تصرف بیجا *taṣarruf-ĕ be-jā*, *n.m.* Misappropriation of funds.

تصرفات *taṣarrufāt*, *n.m.* The sum-total of expenses.

تصریح *taṣriḥ* (A) *n.f.* Making clear; manifestation; narration; explanation; clarification.

تصریف *taṣrif* (A) *n.f.* Conjugation; declension; inflection (in grammar); changing; turning; converting.

تصغیر *taṣg͟hir* (A) *n.f.* Diminution.

اسم تصغیر *ism-ĕ-taṣg͟hir*, *n.m.* Diminutive noun.

تصفیہ *taṣfiyah* (A) *n.m.* Purifying (particularly, the mind from ill-will); purification; purgation; purity; reconciliation; settlement; adjustment; decision; disposal.

تصفیہ کرنا *taṣfiyah karnā*, *v.* To reconcile; to settle; to dispose of; to filter.

تصلیب *taṣlib* (A) *n.f.* Crucification.

تصنع *taṣanno'* (A) *n.m.* Making a show of art; showing a spacious exterior; spaciousness; hypocrisy.

تصنیف *taṣnif* (A) *n.f.* A literary composition; writing (of a book); compiling.

تصنیف کرنا *taṣnif karnā*, *v.* To compose; to write (a book, &c.).

حق تصنیف *ḥaqq-ĕ-taṣnif*, *n.m.* Copyright

تصور *taṣawwur* (A) *n.m.* Imagination; contemplation; meditation; reflection; fancy; idea; conception; preconception; apprehension.

تصور کرنا *taṣawwur karna*, *v.* To imagine; to fancy; to picture to oneself; to meditate.

تصوف *taṣawwuf* (A) *n.m.* Mysticism; the theology of the mystics of the East; contemplation; mystery.

تصویر *taṣwir* (A) *n.f.* A picture; a portrait; an image; photo; painting.

تصویر بن جانا *taṣwir ban jānā*, *v.* To be striken dumb; to be static.

تصویر خانہ taṣwīr khānah, n.m. Picture-gallery.

تصویر کا دوسرا رخ taṣwīr kā dūsrā rukh, n.m. The other side of the picture.

تصویر کھینچنا taṣwīr khaiṅchnā, v. To draw or paint a picture; to photograph; to portray.

عکسی تصویر 'aksī taṣwīr, n.f. A photograph.

تضاد taẓādd (A) n.m. Contradiction; inconsistency; contrast.

تضحیک taẓḥik (A) n.f. Mocking; derision; ridicule.

تضرع taẓarro' (A) n.m. Humility; self-abasement; supplication.

تضمین taẓmin (A) n.f. Giving satisfaction for an injury; comprehending or including one thing in another; introducing verses of another in one's own poem to complete or corroborate the meaning thereof; giving security or guarantee; entrusting with another.

تضمین کرنا taẓmin karnā, v. To insert the verses of another in one's own poem making the one correspond with the other.

تضیع taẓī' (A) n.f. Spoiling; wasting; destroying; idling away time.

تضیع اوقات taẓi'-ĕ auqāt, n.f. Wasting time; idling away time; weariness; ennui.

تطابق taṭābuq (A) n.m. Similarity; congruity; concurrence; conformity; coherence; cohesion.

تطبیق taṭbiq (A) n.f. Comparing; conforming; likening; drawing up two things face to face; causing to confront (as, two armies); reconciliation; similarity; congruity.

تطہیر taṭhir (A) n.f. Purification; purgation; sanctification.

تظلم taẓallum (A) n.m. Groaning under oppression; complaining of injustice; injustice; injury; oppression.

دست تظلم دراز کرنا dast-ĕ-taẓallum drāz karnā, v. To oppress; to be cruel and unjust.

تظہیر taẓhir (A) n.f. Endorsement; writing on the back of a document.

تظہیر کرنا taẓhīr karnā, v. To endorse.

تعارض ta'āruẓ (A) n.m. Quarrelling; disputing; confronting; contradiction; opposition.

تعارف ta'āruf (A) n.m. Mutual acquaintance; rule; fashion; custom; ceremonial courtesy.

تعاقب ta'āqub (A) n.m. Following; pursuit; chase; persecuting; alternate succession.

تعال الله ta'āl allah (A) inter. God be exalted; good God! bravo! well done!

تعالیٰ ta'ālā (A) adj. Most high; exalted (God).

تعاون ta'āwun (A) n.m. Assistance. mutual aid or help.

تعب ta'ab (A) n.m. Labour; toil; trouble; exertion; fatigue.

تعبیر ta'bīr (A) n.f. Explanation; interpretation (particularly of dreams); elucidation.

تعبیر گو ta'bīr go, n.m. An interpreter of dreams.

تعجب ta'ajjub (A) n.m. Wondering; admiration; wonder; astonishment; amazement; surprise.

تعجب کرنا ta'ajjub karnā, v. To wonder; to admire; to be surprised.

تعجیل ta'jīl (A) n.f. Haste; despatch; expedition; quickness; agility.

تعجیل کرنا ta'jil karnā, v. To expedite.

تعجیلی تار ta'jili tār, n.m Express telegram.

تعجیلی تقسیم ta'jīlī taqsim, n.f. Express delivery.

تعجیلی مراسلہ ta'jīlī marāsalah, n.f. Express letter.

تعداد ta'dād (A) n.f. Mumber; numbering; enumeration; computation; amount; sum; extent.

تعدد ta'addud (A) n.m. Frequency in number; more than one.

تعدد ازواج ta'addud-ĕ azwāj, n.m. Polygamy; having more wives than one.

تعدی ta'addi (A) n.f. Oppression; tyranny; violence; cruelty; wrongdoing; extortion; causation.

تعدیل ta'dil (A) n.f. Equalising; adjustment; correction.

تعدیل ارکان ta'dil-ĕ arkān (A) n.f. Correct performance of all postures in prayer.

تعرض ta'arruz (A) n.m. Resisting; preventing; hinderance; obstacle; opposition; impediment.

تعریض ta'riẓ (A) n.f. Enlarging; ambiguity in speech; hinting at a subject obscurely.

تعریف ta'rif (A) n.f. Explanation; description; praise; praising; assertion; definition; narration; admiration.

تعریف المجهول بالمجهول ta'riful-majhul, bil-majhul,n.f. Explaining in terms as little understood as the thing intended to be explained; explaining the unknown by the unknown.

تعریف کر کے منہ سو کھنا ta'rif karke munh sukhnā, v. To praise very highly; to fail in eulogizing adequately.

تعزیت ta'ziyat (A) n.f. Condolence; lementation; mourning.

تعزیت نامہ ta'ziyat namah, n.m. Letter of condolence.

تعزیر ta'zir (A) n.f. Punishment; correction; reproof; censure; reprimand; penalty.

تعزیری پولیس ta'ziri polis, n.f. Punitive police.

تعزیری چوکی ta'ziri chauki, n.f. Punitive post.

تعزیری قوانین ta'ziri qawānin; n.m. Penal laws.

تعزیری کارروائی ta'ziri kārrawāi, n.f. Punitive action or measure.

تعزیرات پاکستان ta'zirāt-ĕ Pākistān, n.f. Pakistan Penal Code.

تعزیہ ta'ziyah (A) n.m. A model of the tombs of Imam Hasan and Hussain carried in procession during Muharram.

تعزیہ اٹھانا ta'ziyah uṭhānā, v. To carry the ta'ziyah in procession.

تعزیہ ٹھنڈا کرنا ta'ziyah thanḍa karna, v. To bury a ta'ziyah or throw into the river after the observance of the anniversary of Muharram.

تعزیہ دار ta'ziyah dār, n.m. One who makes a ta'ziyah and observes mourning.

تعزیہ داری ta'ziyah dari, n.f. Observance of mourning in Muharram.

تعصب ta'aṣsub (A) n.m. Prejudice for or against; bigotry; prejudice; religious persecution.

تعطل ta'ṭṭul (A) n.m. Idleness; deadlock; suspension of work or activity.

تعطیل ta'til (A) n.f. A holiday; vacation; abandoning; neglecting; rendering useless; laying waste; suspension.

تعطیل منانا ta'til manana, v. To observe a holiday, to suspend work; to remain idle.

تعظیم ta'zim (A) n.f. Reverence; respect; honour; gentility; politeness; treating with ceremony and respect.

تعظیم بجا لانا ta'zim bajā lana, v. To show respect; to honour; to receive cordially; to salute.

تعظیم کرنا ta'zim karna, v. To honour; to respect.

تعفن ta'affun (A) n.m. Stink; fetidness; bad smell; offensive adour

تعلق ta'alluq (A) n.m. Connection; relation; concern; dependance; appertaining; consideration.

تعلق رکھنا ta'alluq rakhnā v. : To belong; to have connection with; to depend; to appertain; to be concerned with.

تعلقه ta'alluqah (A) n.m. Connection; possession; an estate; a division of a province.

تعلقه دار ta'alluqah dar, n.m. A possessor of an estate; a landlord.

تعلم ta'allum (A) n.m. Learning; knowledge; study.

تعلی ta'alli (A) n.f. Exalting oneself; appearing conspicuous; boasting; bragging.

تعلی کی لینا یا تعلی کرنا ta'alli ki lena ya ta'alli karna, v. To boast; to brag.

تعلیل ta'lil (A) n.f. Stating a reason; making an excuse; changing one of the weak letters to another (grammar).

تعلیم ta'līm (A) n.f. Teaching; instruction; tuition.

تعلیم پانا ta'lim pānā, v. To receive instruction.

تعلیم دینا یا تعلیم کرنا ta'līm denā yā ta'līm karnā, v. To teach; to instruct.

تعمق ta'amuq (A) n.m. Deep thinking; probing; getting to the bottom.

تعمیر ta'mir (A) n.f. Building; structure; repairing; construction; making a place habitable.

تعمیر کرنا ta'mir karnā, v. To build; to construct.

تعمیر ہونا ta'mir honā, v. To be built.

تعمیرات خورد ta'mirāt-ĕ-khurd, n.f. Minor works.

تعمیرات کلاں ta'mirāt-ĕ-kalān, n.f. Major works.

تعمیق ta'miq (A) n.f. Deliberation; careful thinking; prudence; foresight.

تعمیل ta'mil (A) n.f. Compliance; service; performance; execution.

تعمیل حکم کرنا ta'mil-ĕ ḥukm karnā, v. To carry out an order.

تعمیل شده ta'mil shudah, adj. Complied with.

تعمیل معاهده ta'mil-ĕ mu'āhidah, n.m. Execution of a contract or agreement or treaty.

تعمیل میں ta'mil men, adv. In compliance with.

تعویذ ta'wiz (A) n.m. An amulet; a charm; having recourse to the deity; asking protection; a kind of a structure of masonry work over a grave.

تعویق ta'wiq (A) n.f. Suspending; averting; delaying; postponing.

تعیش ta'aiyush (A) n.m. Rejoicing; living a pleasant life; procuring a livelihood by toil and labour.

تعین ta'iyun (A) n.m. Appointing; appointment; establishing; fixation; assigning; deputing; allotment.

تعین تنخواه ta'iyun-ĕ tankhah, n.m. Fixation of pay.

تعین دار ta'iyun dār, n. Allottee.

تعین کرنا ta'iyun karna, v. To appoint; to fix; to determine; to allot.

تعینات ta'iyunāt, adj. Appointed; fixed; deputed.

تعیناتی ta'iyunāti, n.f. Posting; appointment; detachment of the police force; the duty.

تعیین ta'yin (A) n.f. Fixation; appointment.

تغار taghār (P) n.m. A tub; a bucket; a trough; a pail; a platter; mason's mud or lime pit.

تغافل taghāful (A) n.m. Negligence; neglect; forgetfulness; indifference; inattention; inadvertance; unmindfulness.

تغافل شعار یا تغافل کیش taghaful shi'ar ya taghāful kesh, adj. Careless; inattentive; unmindful; indifferent.

تغذیه taghẕiyah (A) n.m. Food; nourishment; feeding; nutrition.

تغزل taghazzul (A) n.m, Composing an ode; versification.

تغیر taghaiyyur (A) n.m. Alteration; change; removal.

تغیر و تبدل taghaiyyur-ŏ-tabaddull; n.m. Changes; alterations; revolutionary changes.

تغیر کرنا taghaiyyur karnā, v. To alter; to remove; to dismiss; to discharge (from office).

تغیر ہونا taghaiyyur honā, v. To be altered; to be changed; to be removed.

تغیرات ہرسالہ taghaiyyurāt-ĕ har sālah, n.m. Annual alterations; a register maintained by Teḥṣildārs to note annual changes in possessions.

تف tuf (P) n.m. Spittle; saliva; shame! fie! curse.

تف کرنا tuf karnā, v. To spit out.

تفاخر tafākhur (A) n.m. The act of boasting; glorying; boast; vaunt.

تفاسیر tafāsīr (A) n.f. Commentaries; explanations (plu. of تفسیر tafsir).

تفاصیل tafāṣīl (A) n.f. Details (plu. of تفصیل tafṣil).

تفاوت tafawut (A) n.m. Distance; difference distinction; disparity; interval.

تفتیش taftish (A) n.f. Research; inquiry; investigation; examination; search.

تفتیش جرائم taftish-ĕ jarāim, n.f. Criminal investigation.

تفحص tafahhuṣ (A) n.m. Investigation; inquiry; search; disquisition.

تفرقہ tafriqah (A) n.m. Separation; dispersion; distinction; dissension; division.

تفرقہ انداز tafriqah andāz, n. One who creates dissensions.

تفرقہ ڈالنا tafriqah ḍālnā, v. To separate; to sow discord or dissension.

تفریح tafriḥ (A) n.f. Rejoicing; exhilarating; amusement; gratification; diversion; entertainment.

تفریحاً tafrīḥan, adv. By way of amusement; for the sake of recreation; in fun; in jest.

تفریح طبع tafriḥ-ĕ ṭab', n.f. Hilarity; recreation; cheerfulness; amusement.

تفریحی محاصل tafriḥi maḥāṣil, n.m. Entertainment duty or tax.

تفریط tafriṭ (A) n.f. Decrease; deficiency.

تفریق tafriq (A) n.f. Separation; division; classification; partition; subtraction.

تفریق کرنا tafrīq karnā, v. To subtract; to separate; to classify; to analyse; to divide.

تفسیر tafsīr (A) n.f. Explanation; commentary; paraphrase.

تفصیل tafṣil (A) n.f. Explanation; detail; analysis; separation; division; particulars.

تفصیل کرنا tafṣil karnā, v. To detail; to explain fully.

تفصیل وار tafṣil wār, adv. In detail.

بالتفصیل bit-tafṣīl, adv. In extenso.

بتفصیل ذیل ba-tafṣil-ĕ zail, adv. As given below; as follows.

تفصیلی تخمینے tafṣīlī takhmine, n.m. Detailed estimates.

تفصیلی مد tafṣīlī madd, n.f. Detailed head.

تفصیلات tafṣilāt, (plu) n.f. Details; particulars.

تفضیل tafẓil (A) n.f. Pre-eminence; excellence; preference.

اسم تفضیل ism-ĕ-tafẓil, n.m. An objective in the comparative or superlative degree.

تفضیل بعض tafẓil-ĕ ba'z, n.f. Preference over others; comparative degree of adjectives.

تفضیل کل tafẓil-ĕ kull, n.f. Preference over all things; superlative degree of adjectives.

تفضیل نفسی tafẓīl-ĕ nafsī, n.f. Personal excellence; positive degree of adjectives.

تفقہ tafaqquh (A) n.m. Knowledge of Muslim law; expertness in Islamic jurisprudence; possessing power of discrimination.

تفکر tafakkur (A) n.m. Anxiety; reflection; meditation; considering; cogitation.

تفنگ tafang (P) n.f. Anything through which a thing is blown; a musket; a peashooter.

تفنن tafannun (A) n.m. Amusement; pastime; relaxation.

تفنن طبع tafannun-ĕ taba' n.m. Entertainment; amusement or relaxation.

تفوق tafawwuq (A) n.m. Superiority; preference.

تفویض tafwiz (A) n.f. Committing to another's care; entrusting.

تفویض اختیارات tafwiz-ĕ ikhtiyārāt, n.m. Delegation of powers.

تفویضی حکم tafwizi hukm, n.m. Delegation order.

تفہم tafahhum (A) n.m. Understanding; apprehending; conceiving.

تفہیم tafhim (A) n.f. Making one understand; teaching; instructing; informing.

تقابل taqābul (A) n.m. Encountering; standing face to face; drawn up in opposite camps.

تقاریب taqārib (A) n.f. (plu. of تقریب taqrib); Ceremonies; rites; festivals.

تقاریر taqārir (A) n.f. (plu. of تقریر taqrir); Speeches; discourses.

تقاضا taqāzā (A) n.m. Demanding payment of a debt; pressing settlement of a demand or claim; exigence; urgency; importunity.

تقاضائے سن ۔ عمر یا وقت taqāzā-ĕ sinn, 'umr ya waqt adv. Habits or natural tendencies of different ages (childhood, youth, manhood).

تقاضا کرنا taqāzā karnā, v. To demand payment of; to dun; to urge; to press.

تقاطر taqātur (A) n.m. Dropping continuously; distilling drop by drop.

تقاوی taqāwi (A) n.f. Advances given to cultivators at the time of sowing or for the purchase of implements or digging wells.

تقاویم taqāwim (A) n.m. & f. (plu. of تقویم taqwim). Calendars.

تقدس taqaddus (A) n.m. Purity; sanctity; holiness.

تقدم taqaddum (A) n.m. Priority; precedence; eminence.

تقدیر taqdir (A) n.f. Fate; destiny; divine decree; predestination; lot; luck; evaluation.

تقدیر آزمانا taqdir āzmānā, v. To try one's luck.

تقدیر بگڑنا taqdir bigārnā, v. To face adverse circumstances.

تقدیر پھرنا taqdir phirnā, v. To have a change in circumstances (from bad to good or from good to bad).

تقدیر پھوٹ جانا taqdir phūt jānā, v. To be put in adverse circumstances; to come under an unlucky star; to fall into adversity.

تقدیر جاگنا taqdir jāgnā, v. To have luck; to have a better lot; to be fortunate or prosperous.

تقدیر کا پلٹا کھانا taqdir kā paltā khānā, v. See تقدیر پھرنا taqdir phirnā.

تقدیر کے آگے تدبیر نہیں چلتی taqdir ke āge tadbir nahin chalti, prov There is no cure for bad luck.

تقدیس taqdis (A) n.f. Sanctification; purity; sanctity; magnifying.

تقدیم taqdim (A) n.f. Giving precedence (to); priority; precedence; performance; presentation.

تقرب taqarrub (A) n.m. Striving to draw near; nearness; access; approach; propinquity; proximity.

تقرب حاصل کرنا taqarrub hāsil karnā, v. To obtain access or admittance (to).

تقرر taqarrur (A) n.m. Appointment; nomination; fixation.

پروانۂ تقرر parwānah-ĕ taqarrur, n.m. Letter of appointment.

تقریب taqrib (A) n.f. Bringing near; occasion; ceremony; festival; motive.

تقریباً *taqriban, adv.* About; nearly; approximately.

تقریر *taqrir* (A) *n.f.* Speaking; discoursing; oration; recital; speech; argument;- reasoning; exposition.

تقریر کرنا *taqrir karnā, v.* To speak; to lecture; to discourse.

تقریری *taqrirı, adj.* Addicted to talking much talkative; argumentative; oral; verbal.

تقسیم *taqsim* (A) *n.f.* Division; dividing; distributing; sharing; partition.

تقسیم بحصہ رسدی *taqsim-ba-hissah-ĕ-rasadi, n.f.* Pro-rata distribution; apportionment.

تقسیم ترکہ *taqsim-ĕ tarkah, n.f.* Distribution of a legacy.

تقسیم کار *taqsim-ĕ kaı, n.f.* Distribution of work.

تقسیم کرنا *taqsim karnā, v.* To distribute; to divide; to share; to part; to apportion; to assort.

تقسیم مرکب *taqsim-ĕ-murakkab, n.f.* Compound division.

تقسیم مفرد *taqsim-ĕ-mufrad, n.f.* Simple division.

تقسیم مکمل *taqsim-ĕ mukammal, n.f.* Exact distribution; process of division without remainder.

تقسیم نامہ *taqsım namah, n.m.* Partition deed.

تقسیم ہونا *taqsim honā, v.* To be divided.

محرر تقسیم *muharrir-ĕ taqsim, n.m.* Circulating clerk.

تقصیر *taqṣir* (A) *n.f.* Error; crime; sin; fault; omission; shortcoming; mistake.

تقصیر وار *taqṣir wār, adj.* Blamable; faulty; criminal; guilty; convict; culpable.

تقطیر *taqtīr* (A) *n.f.* Causing to dropping; drop by drop distilling; painful discharge of urine in drops.

تقطیع *taqti'* (A) *n.f.* Dissection; cutting into parts; scanning of verse; the pause in reading poetry.

تقلید *taqlid* (A) *n.f.* Imitation; copy; following in the foot-steps (of); mimicry.

تقلید کرنا *taqlid karnā, v.* To imitate; to ape; to mimic; to copy; to follow.

تقویٰ *taqwā* (A) *n.f.* Fear of God; guarding oneself from sin; abstinence; piety.

اہل تقویٰ *ahl-ĕ taqwā, n.m.* Pious and holy people; God-fearing persons; men of piety; the out.

تقویت *taqwiyat* (A) *n.f.* Strengthening; establishing; confirming; confidence; strength; support.

تقویت کرنا یا دینا *taqwiyat karnā yā denā, v.* To strengthen; to encourage; to back up.

تقویم *taqwim* (A) *n.f.* Making straight; adjusting; regulating; fixing; settling; almanac; calendar.

تقویم پارینہ *taqwim-ĕ-pārinah, n.f.* An old calendar; a useless thing.

تقویم سال *taqwim-ĕ sāl, n.f.* Calendar year.

تقویم مصروفیت *taqwim-ĕ masrūfiat, n.f.* Engagement calendar.

تقی *taqi* (A) *adj.* Pious; devout.

تقیہ *taqiyyah* (A) *n.m.* Fear of God; caution; pious fraud or subterfuge (allowed in certain cases only).

تک *tak* (H) *prep. conj.* Till; to; upto; until; while; towards; near to; as far as; to the extent of. *n.m.* A scale; a balance.

تک *tuk, n.f.* A rhyme.

تک بندی *tuk bandi, n.f.* Making verses; insipid poetry.

تک میں تک ملانا *tuk men tuk milānā, v.* To rhyme; to agree with.

بے تکی *be tuki, adj.* Unconnected; irrelevant; meaningless; without rhyme or reason.

تکا *tikka, n.m.* A small piece of flesh; a steak; a slice; a chop.

تکا بوٹی کرنا *tikkā boti karnā, v.* To tear to bits; to chop into small pieces.

تکا *tukkā* (H) *n.m.* A sort of arrow with blunt point or no point at all; a small hill or mountain; an eminence.

لگا تو تیر نہیں تو تکا *lagā to tīr nahin to tukkā, prov.* No better than straw is the dart that fails its mark.

تکالیف *takālīf* (A) *n.f.* (*plu.* of تکلیف *taklīf*); Distresses; difficulties; hardships; trials.

تکان *takān* (H) *n.m.* Fatigue; motion; agitation; gesture.

تکان چڑھنا *takān charhnā, v.* To be fatigued; to be tired.

تکبر *takbbur* (A) *n.m.* Pride; arrogance; haughtiness; insolence; loftiness.

تکبیر *takbīr* (A) *n.f.* Praises of God; repeating the Muslim creed, saying اللہ اکبر *Allah-ŏ akbar* (God is great).

تکثیر *taksīr* (A) *n.f.* Increasing; multiplying; enlarging; augmenting.

تکثیف *taksīf* (A) *n.f.* Rendering thick or dense; condensation; density; thickness.

تکدر *takaddur* (A) *n.m.* Dregs; turbidness; dulness; moroseness; sullenness; disquietude of mind.

تکذیب *takzīb* (A) *n.f.* Accusing of falsehood; giving one the lie; contradiction.

تکرار *takrār* (A) *n.m.* Repeating often; repetition; tautology; dispute; wrangle; altercation; contention; controversy; the chorus or burden of a song.

تکرار کرنا *takrār karnā, v.* To repeat; to argue; to quarrel; to dispute; to debate; to wrangle.

تکریم *takrīm* (A. *n.f.* Honour; reverence; respect; treating with respect; honouring.

تکڑی *takṛī* (H) *n.f.* Balance; scale.

تکسر *takassur* (A) *n.m.* Breaking; being broken or shattered; being spent or debilitated; carrying figures (Arith.).

تکسیر *taksīr* (A) *n.f.* Breaking to pieces; carrying figures (arith.).

تکفل *takafful* (A) *n.m.* Taking security; becoming security for another; bail; undertaking.

تکفیر *takfīr* (A) *n.f.* Accusing one of impiety and calling him an infidal: calling one an unbeliever.

تکفیل *takfīl* (A) *n.f.* Standing surety for another; furnishing security; giving bail.

تکفین *takfīn* (A) *n.f.* Laying in the coffin; shrouding.

تکفین کرنا *takfīn karnā, v.* To shroud; to coffin.

تکل *tukkal* (H) *n.f.* A kind of paper-kite.

تکلا *taklā* (H) *n.m.* A spindle.

تکلف *takalluf* (A) *n.m.* Ceremony; formality; strict observance of the rules of etiquette; trouble; inconvenience; extravagance.

تکلف برطرف *takalluf bar ṭaraf, adv.* Formality apart; ceremony aside.

تکلف کرنا *takalluf karnā, v.* To take pains; to be ceremonious (in).

تکلف مزاج *takalluf mizāj, adj.* Ceremonious.

بے تکلف *be takalluf, adj.* Plain; unceremonious.

تکلفات *takallufāt, n.m.* (*plu.* of تکلف *takalluf*); formalities; ceremonies.

تکلفات دربار *takallufāt-ĕ darbar, n.m.* Extravagances of a court; spending much; lavish expenditure.

تکلفات رسمی *takallufāt-ĕ rasmi, n.m.* Ceremoious attention; empty or formal compliment.

تکلفات مجلس *takallufāt-ĕ majlis, n.m.* Ceremonies of society; etiquette.

تکلم *takallum* (A) *n.m* Conversation; eloquence; talking; speaking.

تکلی *taklī* (A) *n.f.* A weaver's reed.

تکلیف *taklīf* (A) *n.f.* Imposition of a burden; trouble; difficulty; inconvenience; ailment; affliction; annoyance; hardship; duty; responsibility.

تکلیف آٹھانا *taklīf uṭhānā, v.* To suffer.

تکلیف دینا *taklif denā*, *v.* To cause trouble; to annoy; to inconvenience; to trouble; to vex.

تکلیف کرنا *taklif karnā*, *v.* To take the trouble.

تکملہ *takmilah* (A) *n.m.* Perfection; completion; complementary angle; appendix.

تکمہ *tukmah* (P) *n.m.* A loop; a botton; an eye loop; a button-hole; small rounded projection.

تکمیل *takmil* (A) *n.f.* Finishing; completion; excellence; perfaction; performance; consummation.

تکمیل تمسک *takmil-ĕ tamassuk*, *n.f.* Execution of a bond.

تکمیل رهن *takmil-ĕ rahn*; *n.f.* Termination of a mortgage.

تکمیل کرنا *takmil karnā*, *v.* To execute; to complete; to authenticate.

تکمیل کو پهونچانا *takmil ko pahuṅchānā*, *v.* To complete; to bring to a conclusion or termination.

تکنا *taknā*, *v.* To gaze; to stare at; to watch; to look at; to wait (for); to expect; to have recourse (to); to look out (for).

تکون *tikon*, *n.f.* A triangle; a three-cornered figure.

تکونیا، تکونا *tikoniyā*, *tikonā*, *adj.* Triangular.

تکوین *takvin* (A) *n.f.* Causing to be; creating; causing to be born.

تکیہ *takyah* (P) *n.m.* A pillow; bolster; prop; support; reliance; the abode of a faqir.

تکیہ دینا *takyah denā*, *v.* To receive respectfully; to give support.

تکیہ کرنا *takyah karnā*, *v.* To rely upon; to depend upon.

تکیہ کلام *takyah kalām*, *n.m.* An expletive; a needless word or phrase habitually introduced into speech.

تکیہ لگانا *takyah lagānā*, *v.* To lean; to rely; to bolster.

تگ *tag* (P) *n.f.* Running; flying; rushing.

تگاپو *tagāpū*, *n.f.* Bustle; toil; labour; search.

تگ و دو یا تگ و تاز *tag-ŏ dau yā tag-ŏ-tāz*, *n.f.* Running about; great exertion; fatigue; gallop.

تگنا *tignā* (H) *adj.* Threefold; triple; thrice;

تگنی کا ناچ نچوانا *tigni kā nāch nachvānā*, *id.* To embarrass; to harass.

تل *til* (H) *n.m.* The seed of the sesamum; the oil sead; a mole; the pupil of the eye; a small particle.

تل برابر *til barābar*, *adj.* Very little; scanty.

تل بهگا *til bhuggā*, *n.m.* Sweetmeat made by crushing sesamum seeds with sugar.

تل چاولی *til chāolī*, *n.f.* Mixture of rice and sesamum seeds.

تل چٹا *til chaṭṭā*, *n.m.* A cockroach.

تل دهرنے کی جگہ نہ هونا *til dharne ki jagāh nah honā*, *id.* To be overcrowded; to be overfilled; to be full to capacity.

تل شکری *til shakrī*, *n.f.* A kind of sweetmeat made of sesamum seeds.

تل تل *til til*, *adv.* Little by little.

تلوں میں تیل نہ هونا *tiloṅ meṅ tel nah honā*, *id.* To be intractable; to be unbenefitting.

تل *tul* (H) *adj.* Equal; like; similar.

تل بیٹھنا *tul baiṭhānā*, *v.* To turn out to be equal; to sit straight and erect; to be prepared.

تلا *talā* (H) *n.m*; Sole of a shoe; bottom.

تلا *tillā* (P) *n.m.* Drawn gold; gold lace border (of a turban); golden thread.

تلا کاری یا سازی *tillā kārī yā sāzi*, *n.f.* Gilding.

تلا دان *tulā dān*, (H) *n.m.* Alms equal in weight of the distributor; a gift of gold to Brahmans equal in weight to the person of the donor.

تلا دانی یا تلے دانی *tilādānī yā tile dānī*, *n.f.* A small bag for holding needles, thread, etc.

تلاش *talāsh* (A) *n.f.* Search; investigation; quest; inquiry.

تلاش کرنا talāsh karnā, v. To search; to seek; to look for.

تلاش معاش talāsh-ĕ ma'āsh, n.f. Search for employment.

تلاشی talāshi (A) n.f. Search; seeking; investigation. n.m. one who searches.

تلاشی لینا talāshi lenā, v. To institute a search.

جامه تلاشی jāmah talāshi, n.f. Searching a person.

خانه تلاشی khānah talāshi, n.f. Searching a house (for stolen property).

تلاطم talātum (A) n.m. Dashing of waves; buffeting; a sea-storm.

تلافی talāfi (A) n.f. Compensation; recompense; reparation; making amends; retaliation; revenge.

تلافی مافات talāfi-ĕ māfāt. Making good the loss; compensation.

تلامذه talāmizah (A) n. m.(plu. of تلمیذ talmiz); Students; scholars; pupils.

تلانا tulānā (H) v. To cause to be weighed.

تلاوت tilāwat (A) n.f. Reading (the Quran).

تلبیس talbis (A) n.f. Concealing (truth or faults); covering; knavery; counterfeiting; deception; cheating; fraud; fallacy; imposture; misrepresentation.

تلبیس سکه talbis-ĕ sikkah, n.f. Counterfeiting coins.

تلبیس شخصی talbis-ĕ shakhṣi, n.f. Impersonation.

تلبیس لباس talbis-ĕ libās, n.f. Disguising.

تلبیه talbiyah (A) n.m. The words uttered by pilgrims at the time of Haj proclaiming "I am present to serve Thee, my Lord"; to say لبیک labbaik.

تلچھٹ talchhat (H) n.f. Residue; sediment; leavings.

تلخ talkh (P) adj. Bitter; acrid; acrimonious; acid; pungent; unpalatable.

تلخ رو talkh rū, adj. Morose; stern.

تلخ کام talkh kām, adj. Bitter in palate; distasteful.

تلخ گو talkh go, adj. Harsh; caustic; of bitter speech.

تلخ مزاج talkh mizāj, adj. Ill-tempered.

تلخ و ترش talkh-ŏ tursh, n.m. Vicissi tudes of life; sour and bitter.

تلخی talkhi (P) n.f. Bitterness; acrimony; pungency; acidity.

تلخیص talkhiṣ (A) n.f. Abstraction; abbreviation; purifying; cleaning.

تلذذ talazzuz (A) n.m. Taste; deliciousness; enjoyment; delight; pleasure.

تلسی tulsi (H) n.f. Sweet basil.

تلطف talattuf (A) n.m. Kindness; favour; blandishment; obligations.

تلطف کرنا talattuf karnā, v. To oblige; to show kindness or favour.

تلف talaf, n.m. Ruin; destruction; waste; loss; expense; prodigality; consumption.

تلف کرنا talaf karnā, v. To ruin; to destroy; to consume; to waste,

تلف هونا talaf honā, v. To be destroyed; to be ruined; to be wasted; to be lost.

تلفظ talaffuz (A) n.m. Pronunciation; expression; utterance.

تلقین talqin (A) n.f. Instruction; information; religious instruction; teaching.

تلک tilak (S) n.m. Mark made by Hindus with coloured earth or unguents on the forehead and between the eye-brows on occasion such as installation to office; coronation of a king; a freckle.

تلک دهاری tilak dhāri, n.m. One who is marked with tilak.

تلک لگانا tilak lagānā, v. To mark with a tilak on the forehead.

تلک talak, adv. Until; upto; as far as.

تلمذ talammuz (A) n.m. Becoming a pupil.

تلملانا tilmilānā, talmalānā (H) v. To be agitated or uneasy; to grieve; to be tantalized; to toss about in anguish; to be restless; to be impatient.

تلمیح talmiḥ (A) n.f. Passing reference to an old event or story in one's writing.

تلمیذ talmīẕ (A) n.m. A pupil; a student; a scholar; a disciple.

تلنا talnā (H) v. To fry; to roast.

تلنا tulnā (H) v. To be weighed.

تلوا talwā (H) n.m. The sole of the foot.

تلوا چاٹنا talwā chāṭnā, v. To flatter.

تلوا سہلانا talwā sahlānā, v. To flatter; to coax; to adulate.

تلوا کھجلانا talwā khujlānā, v. Itching of the sole; expecting to go out on a journey.

تلوا نہ لگنا talwā nah lagnā, v. To be restless.

تلووں سے آگ لگنا talwoṅ se āg lagnā, v. To be excessively angery.

تلووں سے ملنا talwoṅ se malnā, v. To trample; to tread on.

تلوے چھلنی ہونا talwe chhalni honā, v. To toil hard; to have a tiring journey.

تلوے سے لگنا talwe se lagnā, v. To follow meekly and humbly.

تلوار talwār (H) n.f. Sword.

تلوار چلانا talwār chalānā, v. To use a sword; to strike with a sword.

تلوار چلنا talwār chalnā, v. To be fighting with swords.

تلوار کا گھاؤ talwār kā ghāo, n.m. A sword cut; a sword-wound.

تلوار کھینچنا talwār khenchnā, v. To draw a sword.

تلوار میان میں کرنا talwār miyān meṅ karnā, v. To sheathe the sword.

تلون talawwun (A) n.m. Changing colours (like a chameleon); fickleness; capriciousness; fidgeting; changeableness.

تلون طبع یا مزاج talawwun ṭaba' yā mizāj, adj. Capricious; whimsical; fretful; fickle-minded.

تلون مزاجی talawwun mizāji, n.f. Caprice; capriciousness; fretfulness.

تلی tali (H) n.f. The bottom of anything; the sole of a shoe.

تلی tilli (A) n.f. Spleen; milt.

تلے tale, adv. Below; down; beneath; under; at the foot of; at the bottom of; on the ground.

تلے اوپر tale ūpar, adv. One upon the other.

تلے اوپر کی اولاد tale ūpar ki aulād, n.f. Children born in succession.

تلیٹی taliṭi (H) n.f. Bottom; foot of the mountain; sub-mountainous region.

تلیر tilyar (H) n.m. Starling.

تم tum (H) pron. You.

تماثل tamāṣul (A) n.m. Resembling; similarity.

تمازت tamāzat, n.f. Intense heat.

تماشا tamāshā (A) n.m. Entertainment; show; exhibition; a spectacle; a sight; amusement; sport; fun; pleasure; anything strange or funny.

تماشا بین یا تماش بین tamāshā bin yā tamāsh bin, n. Spectator; a libertine.

تماشا بینی - تماش بینی tamāshā bini yā tamāsh bīnī, n.f. Luxury; libertinism; spectatorship.

تماشا کرنا tamāshā karnā, v. To exhibit; to act a play; to make sport or fun of; to jeer; to jest.

تماشا کرنیوالا tamāshā karne wālā, n.m. A showman; one who makes sport; an actor.

تماشے کی بات tamāshe ki bāt, n.f. A funny thing; a pretty jest.

تماشاگاہ tamāshūgāh, n.f. A place of show; a theatre.

تماشائی tamāshā'ī, n.f. A spectator; a looker-on; a rake; an epicure.

تمام tamām (A) adj. Entire; whole; complete; perfect; finished; conclusion; end.

تمام تر tamām tar, adv. Wholy; completely; entirely.

تمام شد tamām shud, v. Finished; completed; done.

تمام کرنا tamām karnā, v. To finish; to complete; to conclude.

تمام ہونا tamām honā, v. To be finished; to be completed; to be concluded; to come to an end.

کام تمام ہونا kām tamām honā, v. To be done with· to be dead.

تمام و کمال tamam-ŏ kamāl, adj. Whole and entire; full and complete; thorough.

تمانا tumānā, v. To cause to be carded.

تمباکو tambākū (H) n.m. Tobacco.

تمت tammat (A) v. Finished; completed.

تمتع tamatto' (A) n.m. Utilization; delight; gaining.

تمتمانا tamtamānā (H) v. To glow; to blush; to become red in the face; to flash; to twinkle; to sparkle.

تمتماہٹ tamtamāhat, n.f. Flush; glow; growing red.

تمثال timsāl (A) n.f. Resemblance; picture; figure

تمثیل tamsīl (A) n.f. Similitude; allegory; example; parable; apologue; a counterpart or duplicate; a facsimile; resemblance.

تمثیل لانا tamsīl lānā, v. To allegorize; to adduce examples.

تمثیلاً tamsilan, adv. Allegorically; for example; by way of similitude.

تمجید tamjīd (A) n.f. Glorification of God.

تمدن tamaddun (A) n.m. Social intercourse; living together; civilisation.

تمرد tamarrud (A) n.m. Stubbornness; obstinacy; resistence; disobedience; insolence, rebellion.

تمسخر tamaskhur (A) n.m. Buffoonery; joking; jesting.

تمسک tamassuk (A) n.m. Bond; receipt; a note; a promissory note.

تمسک حاضر ضامنی tamassuk-ĕ hāzir zāmini, n.m. Bond or recognizance as a security for personal appearance.

تمسک مصنوعی tamassuk-ĕ maṣnu'i, n.m. A fabricated bond; a forged bond.

تمسک قرضہ tamassuk-ĕ qarzah, n.m. A debt obtained through a bond.

تمغا tamghā (P) n.m. A medal; a royal grant or charter; a diploma; a stamp on gold, silver, &c.; a brand or mark on an animal; a tax on travellers.

تمکنت tamkanat (A) n.f. Dignity; gravity; majesty; honour; grandeur.

تمکین tamkin (A) n.f. Majesty; dignity; authority; power.

تملق tamalluq (A) n.m. Cajoling; caressing; dalliance; flattery; adulation; ceremony.

تمن tuman (T) n.m. A host; a crowd; troops; squadron; caste; clan; brotherhood.

تمندار tumandār, n.m. Commander of a tuman.

تمنا tamannā (A) n.f. Wish; desire; inclination; request; hope; longing; prayer; supplication; petition.

تمنا کرنا tamanna karnā, v. To wish; to desire; to pray (for).

تمنچہ tamanchah (P) n.m. A pistol.

تموج tamawwuj (A) n.m. Agitation; billowing (of waves); fluctuation (of water).

تمول tamawwul (A) n.m. Being or becoming rich.

تمہارا tumhārā (H) pron. Yours; your; of you.

تمہید tamhid (A) n.f. Preliminary; preamble; preface; introduction; preparation; adjustment; arrangement; settlement; management; confirmation.

تمہید آٹھانا tamhid uthānā, v. To open a subject.

تمہیدیں باندھنا *tamhiden bāndhnā, v.* To lay down promises; to make vain suppositions.

تمہیدی *tamhidi, adj.* Preliminary; introductory.

تمہیں *tumhin* (H) *pron.* You; you alone.

تمہیں *tumhen, pro.* To you.

تمیز *tamiz* (A) *n.f.* Discernment; judgment; discretion; sense; distinction; observance of rules of etiquete.

تمیزدار *tamizdār, adj.* Judicious; discreet; mannerly; well-mannered.

تمیز کرنا *tamiz karnā, v.* To distinguish; to appreciate; to discriminate; to discern; to clean.

بے تمیز *be tamiz, adj.* Indiscreet; unmannerly.

حرف تمیز *ḥarf-ĕ tamiz, n.m.* An adverb.

تن *tan* (P) *n.m.* The body; person.

تن آسان *tan āsān, adj.* Indulgent; indolent.

تن آسانی *tan āsāni, n.f.* Bodily ease; indulgence.

تناور *tanāwar, adj.* Big; stout; corpulent.

تن پرور *tan parwar, adj.* Over-careful about the body; self-indulgent; luxurious; selfish.

تن پروری *tan parwari, n.f.* Self-indulgence; selfishness.

تن تنہا *tan tanhā, adj.* All alone; all by oneself; solitary.

تندرست *tandurust, adj.* Healthy; vigorous.

تندرست کرنا *tandurust karnā, v.* To cure.

تندرست ہونا *tandurust honā, v.* To recover.

تندرستی *tandurusti, n.f.* Bodily health, vigorousness.

تندرستی ہزار نعمت ہے *tandurusti hazār ni'mat hai, prov.* Nothing like health; health is better than wealth.

تن دہی *tan dihi, n.f.* Diligence; great attention; effort; application, exertion.

تن من *tan man, n.m.* Body and soul.

تن من دھن *tan man dhan, n.m.* Body, soul and wealth; every thing one possesses.

تن من مارنا *tan man mārnā, v,* To restrain one's appetite or desires; to suppress feelings or emotions; to concentrate one's attention or faculties (on).

تن من سے *tan man se, adv.* With all one's heart and soul.

تن من وارنا *tan man wārnā, v.* To be prepared to sacrifice one's life; to do one's best.

تن *tun* (H) *n.m,* Name of a tree, the wood of which is used for furniture.

تنّا *tannā* (A) *v.* To stretch; to tight.

تنازع *tanāzu'* (A) *n.m.* Wrangling; strife; contention; dispute; struggle.

تنازع للبقا *tanāzu' lil-baqā, n.m.* Struggle for existence.

تناسب *tanāsub* (A) *n.m.* Resemblance; proportion; relation.

تناسب اعضا *tanāsub-ĕ a'zā, n.m.* Due proportion of the limbs.

تناسب مرکب *tanāsub-ĕ murakkab, n.m.* Compound proportion.

تناسب مفرد *tanāsub-ĕ mufrad, n.m.* Simple proportion.

تناسب منقلب *tanāsub-ĕ munqalib, n.m.* Inverse proportion.

تناسخ *tanāsukh* (A) *n.m.* Transmigration; transformation; the passing of a soul into another body after death (Hindu conception); metempsychosis.

تناسل *tanāsul* (A) *n.m.* Generation; lineage; uninterrupted desent through a series of generations.

آلۂ تناسل *ālah-ĕ tanāsul, n.m.* Generative organ.

تنافر *tanāfur* (A) *n.m.* Repugnance; aversion; putting together words which are difficult to pronounce.

تناقض tanāquẓ (A) n.m. Incompatibility; contradiction; discrepancy; contrast.

تناول tanāwul (A) n.m. Eating; taking meals and drinks.

تناول كرنا يا فرمانا tanāwul karnā yā farmānā, v. To eat.

تنبو tanbū (H) n.m. A tent.

تنبوره tanbūrah (P) n.m. Tambourine; a musical instrument.

تنبول tanbūl (H) n.m. The betel leaf.

تنبولن tanbolan, n.f. A woman betel-leaf seller.

تنبولى tanbolī, n.m. A betel-leaf seller.

تنبيه tambīh (A) n.f. Admonition; correction; beating; punishment; reproof; warning.

تنبيه كرنا tambīh karnā, v. To admonish; to warn; to reprimand.

تنتر tantar (H) n.m. One of the Hindu sacred books teaching mystical formulas of worship.

تنتر منتر tantar mantar (H) n.m. Charm; enchantment.

تن تنى tuntunī (H) n.f. A rough kind of guitar.

تنخواه tankhwāh (P) n.m. Pay; assignment; salary; wages.

تنخواه دار tankhwāh dār, n.m. One who receives pay or salary; a paid servant.

تند tund (P) adj. Quick; rapid; swift; fast; hot; spirited; fierce; furious; sharp; severe; acrid; acrimonious; rough; bold; violent.

تند خو tund khū, adj. Irascible; furious; passionate; fretful.

تند رفتار tund raftār, adj. Fast-going; fleeting.

تند زبان tund zabān, adj. Eloquent; talking rapidiy.

تند مزاج tund mizāj, adj. Hot-headed; passionate.

باد تند bād-ĕ tund, n.f. Furious wind; storm; tempest.

تندور tandūr (H) n.m. An oven; a stove.

تندى tundī (P) n.f. Fierceness; acrimony; sharpness; impetuosity; swiftness; severity; violence; fury.

تنديل tundail (H) n.m. A fat person; pot-bellied; stout.

تنزل tanazzul (A) n.m. Descent; fall; decline; decay; degradation; demotion.

تنزل كرنا tanazzul karnā, v. To demote; to degrade; to descend.

تنزل هونا tanazzul honā, v. To fall off; to decline; to be demoted; to be degraded.

تنزيل tanzīl (A) n.f. Revelation of the Quran; receiving hospitably; causing to alight.

تنزيه tanziyah (A) n.m. Keeing apart from impurities; purity; holiness.

تنسيخ tanṣīkh (A) n.f. Cancellation; quashing; revocation; repeal; abrogation.

تنصيب tanṣīb (A) n.f. Installation.

تنصيف tanṣīf (A) n.f. Dividing into two equal parts; bisection.

تنظيم tanẓīm (A) n.f. Orderlng; arranging; administration; organisation; composing verses; threading pearls.

تنعم tana'um (A) n.m. Living a luxurious life; ease; prosperity.

تنفر tanaffur (A) n.m. Aversion; disgust; shunning.

تنفس tanaffus (A) n.m. Respiration; breathing.

آلات تنفس ālāt-ĕ tanaffus, n.m. Respiratory organs.

نظام تنفس nizām-ĕ tanaffus, n.m. Respiratory system.

تنفسى امراض tanaffusī amrāẓ, n.m. Respiratory diseases.

تنقيح tanqīḥ (A) n.f. Cleaning; polishing; purging; investigation; ascertaining; search; inquiry; issue.

تنقیح طلب tanqiḥ ṭalab, adj. To be determined or decided; requiring decision.

تنقیح کرنا ۔ تنقیح نکالنا ۔ تنقیح قایم کرنا tanqiḥ karnā yā tanqiḥ nikālnā yā tanqiḥ qāim karnā, v. To determine; to settle; to draw up issues; to frame issues.

تنقید tanqid (A) n.f. Criticism; fault finding; review.

تنقیہ tanqiyah (A) n.m. Purging; cleaning (the bowels); winnowing grain; decision; settlement.

تنک tunuk (P) adj. Weak; delicate; thin; brittle; mean; furious.

تنک مزاج tunuk mizāj, adj. Irritable; peevish; whimsical; captious; fretful.

تنکا tinkā (H) n.m. A straw; a blade of grass; grass; a mote; a particle.

تنکا دانتوں میں لینا tinkā dāntoṅ meṅ lenā, v. To make submission; to ask for mercy; to confess inferiority.

تنکا نہ رہنا tinkā nah rahnā, v. To be robbed of everything.

تنکا ہو جانا tinkā ho jānā, v. To become emaciated; to become thin and lean.

تنکے چننا tinke chunnā, v. To be intoxicated; to be insane or mad.

تنکے کا سہارا لینا tinke kā sahārā lenā, v. To catch at a straw.

تنکے کا پہاڑ بنانا tinke kā pahāṛ banānā, v. To make mountains out of mole-hills.

تنکنا tinaknā (H) v. To flutter; to palpitate; to throb; to flare up; to fly into a passion.

تنکیر tankir (A) n.f. Using as a common noun; to ruffle; to molest.

تنگ tang (H) adj. Contracted; tight; narrow; straitened; scanty; poor; distressed; dejected; sad; a horse-belt; a girth; a bag; a sack.

تنگ آنا tang ānā, v. To be dejected; to be utterly sick of; to be utterly weary; to have one's patience exhausted.

تنگ حال tang ḥāl, adj. Poor; distressed; in straitened circumstances.

تنگ دست tang dast, adj. Poor; miserly; stingy; penniless.

تنگ دستی tang dasti, n.f. Poverty; want; destitution.

تنگ دل tang dil, adj. Norrow-minded; illiberal; miser; niggard.

تنگ دهن tang dahan, adj. Small-mouthed; an epithet of a sweetheart.

تنگ ظرف tang ẓarf, adj. Narrow-minded; shallow; mean.

تنگ کرنا tang karnā, v. To tighten; to narrow; to contract; to vex; to tease; to pester.

تنگ وقت tang waqt, n.m. Hour of difficulty; eleventh hour.

تنگ ہاتھ ہونا tang hāth honā, v. To be penniless; to be in straits.

تنگ ہونا tang honā, v. To be badly off; to be without a penny.

تنگنائے tangnāe, n.f. A strait; a narrow place or passage.

تنگی tangi (P) n.f. Straitness; narrowness; hardship; difficulty; poverty; scantiness; want; a bag; a sack.

تنگی ترشی tangi turshi, n.f. Poverty; stringiness; extreme frugality.

تنگی ہونا tangi honā, v. To be in poverty; to lead a hard and miserable life.

تننا ۔ تنّا tannā, v. To stretch; to dull tight; to sit upright or straight.

تنور tanūr (A) n.m. An oven; a stove.

تنوع tanawwo' (A) n.m. Variety; to be of different kinds.

تنومند tanomand (P) adj. Robust; well built; corpulent;

تنویر tanwir (A) n.f. Illuminating; enlightening; illumination.

تنوین tanwin (A) n.f. Nunnation.

تنہ tanah (P) n.m. Trunk of a tree; a stem; a stalk.

تنہا tanhā (P) *adj.* Alone; single; solitary; only; unique.

تنہائی tanhāi (P) *n.f.* Loneliness; privacy; solitude.

تنی tani (H) *n.f.* A string with which garments are tied.

تنی میں گانٹھ دینا *tani men gānth denā, v.* To betroth; to tie a knot in order to remember.

تو to, *adv.* Then; therefore; in that case; at that time; moreover; that; also; for; yes; well.

تو بھی *to bhi, adv.* Even then; nevertheless; yet; still.

تو tū (H) *pron.* Thou; thee.

تو تڑاق کرنا *tū tarāq karnā, v.* To address rudely; to wrangle; to engage in loud vulgar argument.

تو تو میں میں *tū tū main main, n.f.* Wrangling; altercation; loud argument.

توا tawā (H) *n.m.* An iron plate on which bread is baked; a shard placed over the tobacco in a *chilam*; leaden or iron platform put down in a well to cool the water; a gramophone record.

اُلٹا توا *ulṭā tawā, adj.* Black as the bottom of a frying pan; jet black.

تواب tawwāb (A) *n.m.* Acceptor of repentence; God.

تواتر tawātur (A) *n.m.* Following in succession; continuation; succession.

توارد tawārud (A) *n.m.* Occurrence of the same idea to two persons; unintentionally inserting the sense of another's verses in one's own poems.

تواریخ tawārikh (A) *n.f.* (*plu.* of *tārikh* تاریخ) Dates; histories; annals; chronicles.

توازن tawāzun (A) *n.m.* Counterbalance; poise.

تواضع tawāzo' (A) *n.f.* Humility; attention; civility; affected kindness; hospitality; entertainment.

تواضع سمرقندی *tawāzo'-ĕ samarqandi, n.f.* False politeness; empty compliments.

تواضع شیرازی *tawāzo'-ĕ shirāzi, n.f.* Simple fare; homely diet.

تواضع کرنا *tawāzo' karnā, v.* To entertain; to make a present to; to receive with politeness.

توافق tawāfuq (A) *n.m.* Concord; agreement; hormony; coincidence; the relation between two numbers which have a common divisor.

توالد tawālud (A) *n.m.* Being born generation after generation.

توام tau am (A) *n.m.* Twins.

توانا tawānā (P) *adj.* Powerful; able; strong; robust.

توانائی *tawānāi, n.f.* Strength; power; ability.

توانگر tawāngar (P) *adj.* Rich; wealthy; opulent; powerful.

تونگری tawāngari (P), *n.f.* Richness; wealth; opulence.

توبڑا tobṛā (H) *n.m.* The bag out of which horses eat; a horse's nose-bag.

توبہ taubah (P) *n.m.* Promising to sin no more; penitence; repentence; renunciation; conversion.

توبہ توبہ *taubah taubah, intj.* Heaven forbid! fie! good gracious! never again!

توبہ تلا کرنا *taubah tillā karnā, v.* To repent; to appeal to God for forgiveness.

توبہ شکن *taubah shikan, adj.* Faithless; one who violates a vow.

توبہ شکنی *taubah shikni, n.f.* Faithlessness.

توبہ کرانا *taubah karānā, v.* To make one repent.

توبہ کرنا *taubah karnā, v.* To vow not to sin any more; to adjure; to renounce.

توبہ گاہ *taubah gāh, v.* Penitentiary.

توبیخ ***taubīkh*** (A) *n.f.* Threatening; rebuke; speaking harshly; reproach.

توپ ***top*** (T) *n.f.* A cannon; a gun; (*Fig.*) a corpulent person.

توپ انداز ، توپچی ***top andāz, topchi*** (P) *n.m.* A gunner; an artillery man; a cannoneer; a bombardier.

توپ چلانا ، توپ چھوڑنا ، توپ داغنا ، توپ لگانا ، توپ مارنا ***top chalānā, top chhoṛnā, top dāghnā, top lagānā, top mārnā,*** *v.* To fire a gun; to fire a cannon; to cannonade.

توپ خانہ ***top khānah,*** *n.m.* An artillery; an arsenal; a park of artillery; a battery.

توپ سے آڑانا ***top se uṛānā,*** *v.* To blow off with a cannon; to condemn a person to be blown off with a gun.

توت ***tūt*** (A) *n.m.* Mulberry.

توتا ***totā*** (P) *n.m.* A parrot; the cock of a matchlock.

توتا پالنا ***totā pālnā,*** *v.* To nurse a sore; to conceal a foul disease.

توتا چشم ***totā chashm,*** *adj.* Faithless as a parrot; disloyal; treacherous.

توتے کی سی آنکھیں پھیرنا ***tote ki si ānkhen phernā,*** *v.* To become indifferent (to); to withdraw the affections from.

توتے آڑنا ھاتھوں کے ***tote uṛnā hāthon ke,*** *v.* To be confounded; to be non-plussed; to be bewildered; to be taken aback.

توتلا ***totlā*** (H) *n.m.* One who speaks indistinctly as a child; lisper; stammerer; stutterer.

توتی ***tūti*** (P) *n.f.* A small singing bird; a sweet-tongued or eloquent speaker.

توتی بولنا ***tūti bolnā,*** *v.* To acquire power and authority; to be known all over; to have attained perfection in some art or science.

توتی کی آواز نقارخانے میں کون سنتا ھے ***tūti ki āwāz naqqār khāne men kaun suntā hai,*** *prov.* None cares to listen to the woes of a poor man in the assembly of the rich; no one listens to the poor notes of a flute where orchestral music is available.

توتیا ***tūtiyā*** (P) *n.m.* Blue vitriol; sulphate of copper.

توثیق ***tauṣīq*** (A) *n.f.* Confirmation; verification; ratification.

توثیق کرنا ***tauṣīq karnā,*** *v.* To confirm; to verify.

توجہ ***tawajjuh*** (A) *n.m.* Inclination; attention; care; favour; regard; kindness; tendency.

توجہ طلب ***tawajjuh ṭalab,*** *adj.* Requiring attention; calling for consideration.

توجہ مبذول کرنا ***tawajjuh mabẕūl karnā,*** *v.* To direct or draw or invite attention.

توجیہ ***taujīh*** (A) *n.f.* A statement; a descriptive roll; adjustment of accounts; an allowance made to land-holders; explaining; accounting for; assessment.

توجیہ نویس ***taujīh nawīs,*** *n.m.* A keeper of descriptive rolls.

توحید ***tauḥīd*** (A) *n.f.* Declaring God to be one; believing in the unity of God; unitarianism.

تودہ ***tūdah*** (P) *n.m.* A mound; a heap; a mark to shoot at.

تودہ خاک ***tūdah-ĕ khāk,*** *n.m.* A heap of dust.

تورات ***taurāt*** (A) *n.f.* The Old Testament.

تورع ***tawarru'*** (A) *n.f.* Piety; piousness.

توڑ ***toṛ*** (H) *n.m.* Break; rupture; counteraction; remedy; refutation; whey; the distance of a gun shot.

توڑ پھوڑ ***toṛ phoṛ,*** *n.f.* Breaking; damage; destruction; ravage; espionage; subversion.

توڑ دینا ***toṛ denā,*** *v.* To break; to spoil; to disrupt.

توڑ ڈالنا toṛ ḍālnā, v. To pull down; to break and destroy.

توڑ کرنا toṛ karnā, v. To counteract; to give a counterblow.

توڑ لینا toṛ lenā, v. To pluck (flowers, fruit); to win over.

توڑا toṛā (H) n.m. Deficiency; scarcity; want; a purse containing one thousand rupees; the match of a gun; a plough-share; a gold or silver chain; a bank; a piece of rope.

توڑے دار بندوق toṛe dār bandūq, n.f. A matchlock.

توڑنا toṛnā, v. To break; to tear; to rend; to demolish; to violate; to win over; to pluck (fruits); to discontinue; to stop; to plough; to break into; to reduce (in Arith.)

دم توڑنا dam toṛnā, v. To be at the point of death; to die.

روٹی توڑنا roṭī toṛnā, v. To eat the bread of idleness.

توس tos, n.m. (corrp. of English) Toast.

توسط tawassuṭ (A) n.m. Mediation; means; affinity.

توسل tawassul (A) n.m. Conjunction; copulation; means; recommendation.

توسن tausan (P) n.m. A young unbroken horse; a high-blooded noble steed; a war-horse; a plump horse; an unmanageable horse.

توسیع tausī' (A) n.f. Extension; enlargement; prolongation.

توشک toshak (P) n.f. A mattress.

توشہ toshah (P) n.m. Provisions for a journey; provision; supplies.

توشہ‌خانہ toshah k͟hānah, n.m. Place where furniture is kept; a store-room; a wardrobe.

توشدان ، توشہ دان toshdān yā toshah dān, n.m. Tiffin carrier; a cartridge box.

عاقبت کا توشہ a'qibat kā toshah, n.m. Good deeds; provision for the next world; laying up treasure in heaven.

توصیف tauṣīf (A) n.f. Description; commendation; describing; qualifying; eulogizing.

توضیح tauẓīḥ (A) n.f. Making clear or evident; manifestation; account of collections; illustration; explanation.

توغل tawag͟hul (A) n.m. Engrossment; absorption; great practice.

توفیر taufīr (A) n.f. Increase of revenue, increasing; excess; surplus.

توفیق taufīq (A) n.f. Divine guidance; God's graciousness; help; power.

توقع tawaqqo' (A) n.f. Expectation; hope; desire; wish.

توقع رکھنا tawaqqo' rakhnā, v. To hope; to desire; to rely upon; to expect.

توقف tawāqquf (A) n.m. Pause; delay; hesitation; respite; suspension; cessation.

توقف کرنا tawaqquf karnā, v. To pause; to hesitate; to wait; to delay; to halt; to stay.

توقیر tauqīr (A) n.f. Honour; respect; reverence; veneration.

توکل tawakkul (A) n.m. Reliance; trust in God; perfect reliance on God.

توکل پر بیٹھنا tawakkul par baiṭhnā, v. To trust in God; to rest in hope; to sit idle.

علی التوکل a'lat-tawakkul, adv. Relying on God; at random; haphazard.

تول tol (H) n.m. Weighing; weight, standard weight.

تولا tolā (H) n.m. A weight of 12 māshās; a weighman.

تولا tawallā (A) n.m. Attachment; affection; hope.

تولائی tawallāi (A) n.m. One who shows affection or attachment; a sect of Shias, which loves Hazrat Ali but does not curse other Caliphs preceding him.

تولد tawallud (A) n.m. Birth; nativity.

تولنا tolnā (H) v. To weigh; to put in the scales; to estimate.

نظروں میں تولنا **nazroṅ meṅ tolnā**, *v.* To estimate the worth of someone or something by merely looking at the object.

تولیا **tauliyā** (H) *n.m.* A towel.

تولیت **tauliyat** (A) *n.f.* Trustee-ship; superintendence of any business; appointing one as governor or supervisor.

تولید **taulīd** (A) *n.f.* Birth; generation; begetting; production; growth.

تومڑی **tūmṛī** (H) *n.f.* A kind of hollow gourd; a kind of firework, made of a hollow earthen pot filled with powder.

تومنا **tūmnā** (H) *v.* To card cotton or wool with the finger preparatory to combing.

تونبا **tūṅbā** (H) *n.m.* The hollow gourd stringed as a guiter.

توند **tond** (H) *n.f.* A pot-belly; a large belly; corpulence.

توندل **tondal**, *adj.* Pot-bellied; corpulent.

توهم **tawahhum** (A) *n.m.* Imagination; superstition; fancy.

توهین **tauhīn** (A) *n.f.* Disgrace; contempt; defamation; dishonour; insult.

توهین عدالت **tauhin-ĕ a'dālat**, *n.f.* Contempt of court.

توهین کرنا **tauhīn karnā**, *v.* To offer an insult; to dishonour; to insult; to defame.

ته **tah** (P) *n.f.* Surface; foundation; depth; layer; stratum; bottom; ground; fold; plait. *prep.* Beneath; under.

ته آب **tah āb**, *adv.* Under water. *n.f.* Bottom of the river.

ته بازاری **tah bazārī**, *n.f.* Ground rent of a stall in the market.

ته به ته **tah bah tah**, *adv.* Plait by plait; fold on fold; layer by layer.

ته به ته کرنا **tah bah tah karnā**, *v.* To pile one over another; to fold.

ته بچھانا **tah bichhānā**, *v.* To lay; to put a layer.

ته بند - تهمد **tah band yā tahmad**, *n.m.* A cloth worn round the waist.

ته پیچ **tah pech**, *n.m.* A cap or cloth worn under the turban.

ته تیغ کرنا **tah tegh karnā**, *v.* To put to sword; to murder.

ته جمانا **tah jamānā**, *v.* To plait; to place fold on fold.

ته خانه **tah khānā**, *n.m.* A cavern; a cellar; an under-ground chamber; a lower storey; a vault; a subterranean abode.

ته دار **tah dār**, *adj.* Having bottom; having folds; having depth.

ته دیگی **tah degī**, *n.f.* The scrapings of a pot; the burnt part of victuals that sticks to the bottom of a pot.

ته دینا **tah denā**, *v.* To tinge slightly.

ته کرنا **tah karnā**, *v.* To fold up.

ته کو پہنچنا **tah ko pahuṅchanā**, *v.* To get to the bottom of; to discover; to find-out.

ته نشست **tah nishast**, *n.f.* Sediment.

ته نشین هونا **tah nashīn honā**, *v.* To sink at the bottom; to settle down; to sink into the mind.

ته و بالا **tah-ŏ bālā**, *adj.* Upside down; disarranged.

ته و بالا کرنا **tah-o-bālā karnā**, *v.* To turn upside down; to subvert; to overthrow; to disarrange.

تهاپ **thāp** (H) *n.f.* A tap; flap; thump; the sound of a small drum when struck with the palm of the hand.

تهاپا **thāpā** (H) *n.m.* Mark of the paw; mark made with the palm of the hand on the wall of a house.

تهاپنا **thāpnā** (H) *v.* To beat; to make cakes of cow-dung for fuel.

تهاپی **thāpī** (H) *n.f.* The sound of patting; the instrument with which potters beat their clay; a bat; a beater.

تهال **thāl** (H) *n.m.* A larg flat dish made of brass or bronze; a tray.

تھالا thālā (H) n.m. The basin or trench dug round the root of a tree for holding water; the excavation in which a tree is to be planted.

تھالی thāli, n.f. A small flat dish; a platter; a salver.

تھالی کا بینگن thāli kā baiṅgan, n.m. A turncoat; a time-server; one who flatters for gain.

تھامنا thāmnā (H) v. To prop; to support; to maintain; to hold; to retain.

تھان thān (H) n.m. A piece (of cloth); a stall for cattle; a manger; locality; dwelling; place.

تہاں tahāṅ (H) adv. Thither; there.

جہاں تہاں jahāṅ tahāṅ, adv. Everywhere; in each place.

تھانہ thānah (H) n.m. A subordinate police station; the inside of the lines of an army; a heap of bamboos.

تھانہ بٹھانا thānah biṭhānā, v. To station a police picket.

تھانیدار thāne dār, n.m. A police officer; one in charge of a police station.

تھاہ thāh (H) n.f. Bottom (of a river or a sea); end.

تہائی tihāi, adj. The third part; one-third.

تھپڑ thappaṛ (H) n.m. A slap; a blow; cuff.

تھپکنا thapaknā, v. To pat (a child) to sleep; to pacify.

تھپیڑا thapeṛā (H) n.m. A slap; the dashing of the waves; gust; blast of wind; the scalp.

تہتر tihattar (H) adj. & n. Seventy-three.

تہجد tahajjud (A) n.m. A prayer said after mid-night; wakefulness.

تہجی tahajji (A) n.f. Spelling; orthography.

حروف تہجی ḥurūf-ĕ tahajji, n.m. Letters of the alphabet.

تہجی کرنا tahajji karnā, v. To spell; to name the letters that form a word.

تہدید tahdid (A) n.f. Threatening; frightening; threat.

تہذیب tahẕib (A) n.f. Purifying; adorning; refinement; polish; edification; civilization; politeness.

تہذیب اخلاق tahẕib-ĕ akhlāq, n.f. Civilization; good breeding.

تہذیب یافتہ tahzib yāftah, adj. Civilized; polished; educated; polite.

تہرا tihrā (H) adj. Triple; three-fold.

تھرانا tharrānā, v. To tremble; to quiver; to shudder.

تھرتھرانا thartharānā, v. To tremble; to quiver; to shiver; to shake; to quake; to vibrate.

تھرتھری، تھرتھراھٹ tharthari, thartharāhaṭ, n.f. Tremour; shaking; trembling; quivering; shivering; vibration.

تھرکنا thiraknā, v. To dance with expressive action and gesture; to dance joyously.

تہری tehri (H) adj. Triplicate.

تہری tahri (H) n.f. A kind of dish.

تہس نہس tahas nahas, adj. Ruined; destroyed; dispersed; over-thrown.

تھکا thakā (H) adj. Weary; tired; exhausted.

تھکا اونٹ سرائے کو دیکھتا ھے thakā ūnṭ sarāe ko dekhtā hai, prov. A drowning man catches at a straw.

تھکا بیل thakā bail, n.m. A lazy fellow; a shirker; a sluggard.

تھکا ماندہ thakā māndah, adj. Dog-tired; worn out; distracted.

تھکان ۔ تکان ۔ تھکاوٹ ۔ تھکن thakān, takān, thakāwaṭ, thakan (H) n.f. Weariness; exhaustion; fatigue; lassitude.

تھکانا thakānā (H) v. To tire; to harass; to weary; to fag; to fatigue.

تھکنا thaknā (H) v. To be wearied; to be fatigued; to be exhausted; to tire; to fag.

تھگلی thigli (H) n.f. A patch.

تھل thal (H) n.m. Land; dry land; a desert; place; ford; spot; site.

تهل تهل کرنا *thal thal karnā*, *v.* To undulate; to wave; to fluctuate as a thick or glutinous fluid; to shake as the flabby flesh of a fat man.

تہلکہ *tahlukah* (A) *n.m.* (Commonly pronounced as *tahalkah*); Ruin; destruction; perdition; alarm; consternation; agony; panic.

تہلیل *tahlil* (A) *n.f.* Praising God by proclaiming, *Lā-ilah illallah*, there is no God but the one God.

تهم *tham* (H) *n.m.* A pillar; a post; a column.

تہمت *tuhmat* (A) *n.f.* False accusation; calumny; suspicion of guilt; slander; aspersion; imputation; falsely charging one with a crime.

تہمت لگانا *tuhmat lagānā*, *v.* To accuse; to calumniate; to belie; to slander; to asperse; to traduce.

تہمتی *tuhmatī* *n.m./f.* A slanderer; false accuser; calumniator.

تهمنا *thamnā* (H) *v.* To stop; to cease; to be restrained.

تهن *than* (H) *n.m.* Udder; teat.

تہنیت *tahniyat* (A) *n.f.* Congratulation; wishing one joy or prosperity.

تہوار *tihwār* (H) *n.m.* Festival.

تھوپنا *thopnā* (H) *v.* To plaster; to pile; to heap; to assign; to impose (upon).

تھوتھا *thothā* (H) *n.m.* An arrow without a point; name of a medicine. *adj.* Hollow; empty; toothless.

تھوتھا چنا باجے گھنا *thothā chanā bāje ghanā*, *prov.* Empty vessels make much noise.

تھوتھنی *thothnī* (H) *n.f.* The mouth of an animal (as a horse, camel or hog).

تہور *tahawwur* (A) *n.m.* Temerity; rashness; intrepidity.

تھوڑا *thoṛā* (H) *adj.* Little; less, small; scarce; few; scanty; meagre.

تھوڑا بہت *thoṛā bahut*, *adj.* More or less.

تھوڑا تھوڑا *thoṛā thoṛā*, *adj.* A little; very little. *adv.* Little by little.

تھوڑا کرنا *thoṛā karnā*, *v.* To lessen; to reduce.

تھوڑا ھونا *thoṛā honā*, *v.* To be reduced; to be in short supply.

تھوڑے دنوں سے *thoṛe dinoṅ se*, *adv.* Of late; since the last few days.

تھوڑے سے تھوڑا *thoṛe se thoṛā*, *adj.* Very little; as little as little can be.

تھوک *thok* (H) *n.m.* Multitude; mass; heap; wholesale.

تھوک دار *thok dār*, *n.m.* Holder of a principal share in a village who is responsible for the payment of revenue; a wholesale dealer.

تھوک فروش *thok farosh*, *n.m.* A wholesale vendor; whole-saler.

تھوک *thūk* (H) *n.m.* Spittle.

تھوک بلونا *thūk bilonā*, *v.* To talk nonsense.

تھوک دینا *thūk denā*, *v.* To give up; to renounce in disgust.

تھوک کر چاٹنا *thūk kar chāṭnā* *v.* To break one's promise; to back out; to withdraw what one has given of free will.

تھوک لگانا *thūk lagānā*, *v.* To defeat; to harm; to apply spittle (an abuse).

تھوکنا *thūknā*, *v.* To spit.

تھوھر *thohar* (H) *n.m.* Name of a plant, the cactus.

تہی *tihī* (P) *adj.* Empty; vain; void; vacant.

تہی دست *tihi dast*, *adj.* Empty-handed; poor; indigent.

تہی دماغ *tihī dimāgh*, *adj.* Empty-headed; ignorant; foolish.

پہلو تہی کرنا *pahlū tihī karnā*, *v.* To abstain; to refrain from.

تھئی *thai* (H) *n.f.* A heap or pile (of cakes, clothes, &c).

تھیلا *thailā* (H) *n.m.* A large bag; a sack; a haversack.

تھیلی thailī (H) *n.f.* A purse.

تھیوا thewā (H) *n.m.* A stone set in a ring.

تہیہ tahiyyah (H) *n.m.* Preparation; determination; putting in order; arrangement.

تہیہ کرنا tahiyyah karnā, *v.* To make preparation (for); to make a determination.

تیار taiyār (P) *adj.* Ready; prepared; finished; complete; fully developed; plump; in full vigour; fat; ripened (fauit); alert; ripe.

تیار کرنا taiyār karnā, *v.* To make ready; to prepare; to provide; to train; to put in order; to fatten.

تیار ہونا taiyār honā, *v.* To be alert; to be ready or prepared (for).

تیاری taiyārī, *n.f.* Readiness; preparation; good condition; arrangement; pomp; magnificence; plumpness.

تیاگ tiyāg (S) *n.m.* Relinquishment; abdication; renunciation; abandonment.

تیاگنا tiyāgnā, *v.* To give up; to abandon; to resign.

تیاگی tiyāgī, *n.m.* An abandoner; a renouncer; a hermit; a recluse; a religious ascetic.

تیتر tītar (H) *n.m.* A partridge.

بن تیتر ban tītar, *n.m.* Sand grouse; a rock pigeon.

تیتری، تتری titarī, titrī (H) *n.f.* A butterfly; a female partridge.

تیج tej (H) *n.m.* Splendour; glory.

تیج tīj (H) *n.f.* Third day of a lunar fortnight.

تیجا tījā (H) *n.m.* The third day after death on which oblations are offered; the offerings made on this occasion.

تیر tīr (P) *n.m.* An arrow; the 4th Persian month; the planet mercury.

تیر انداز ' تیر زن tīr andāz, tīr zan, *n.m.* Bowman; an archer.

تیر اندازی tīr andāzī, *n.f.* Archery.

تیر بہ ہدف tīr bah hadaf, *adj.* Hitting the mark; very effective.

تیر پھینکنا ـ چلانا tīr phaiṅknā yā chalānā, *v.* To shoot an arrow; to do something wonderfull.

تیر فلک tīr-ĕ falak, *n.m.* The planet mercury.

تیرا terā (H) *pron.* Thy; thine.

تیراک tairāk (H) *n.m./f.* Swimmer.

تیرانا tairānā (H) *v.* To cause to swim; to cause to float.

تیرتھ tīrath (H) *n.f.* A sacred place; a place of pilgrimage.

تیرگی tīragī (P) *n.f.* Darkness; obscurity; gloam; dulness; strain.

تیرنا tairnā (H) *v.* To swim; to float.

تیرہ terah (H) *n. & adj.* Thirteen.

تیرہ tīrah (P) *adj.* Dark; obscure.

تیرہ بخت tīrah bakht, *adj.* Unfortunate.

تیرہ دل tīrah dil, *adj.* Black-hearted; malicious.

تیرھواں terhwān, *adj.* Thirteenth.

تیز tez (P) *adj.* Sharp; keen; pungent; acute; hot; fiery; caustic; acrid; strong; impetuous; violent; swift; pointed; clever.

تیز پرواز tez parwāz, *adj.* Swift in flight.

تیز رو ـ رفتار tez rau yā raftār, *adj.* Fast-going; rapid; swift; fleet foot.

تیز طبع tez taba', *adj.* Quick of apprehension; of an acute intellect.

تیز عقل ـ تیزفہم tez 'aql yā tez fahm, *adj.* Intelligent; acute; apt.

تیز فہمی tez fahmī, *n.f.* Quickness of apprehension; intelligence; acumen; acuteness; aptness.

تیز قدم ـ گام tez qadam yā gām, *adj.* Swift; quick; fast-going.

تیز نگاہ tez nigāh, *adj.* Sharp-sighted.

تیز ہونا tez honā, *v.* To be sharpened; to be whetted; to lose one's temper.

تیزاب tezāb (P) *n.m.* Ar acid; *aqua fortis.*

تیزی tezi (P) n.f. Sharpness; pungency; swiftness; impetuousity; shrewdness; fleetness; acrimony.

تیس tis (H) n. & adj. Thirty.

تیسرا tīsrā (H) adj. Third.

تیسرے tisre (H) adv. Thirdly.

تیسواں tiswāṅ, adj. Thirtieth.

تیشہ teshah (P) n.m. Carpenter's axe; an adze.

تیغ tegh (P) n.f. A scimitar; a dagger; a sword.

تیغ بکف tegh bakaf, adj. Sword in hand.

تیغ زن tegh zan, n.m. A swordsman.

تیغا teghā (P) n.m. A short, broad scimitar; name of a trick in wrestling.

تیقن tayaqqun (A) n.m. Ascertainment; certainty.

تیکھا tikhā (H) adj. Angry; passionate; pungent; sharp; bright; graceful.

تیل tel (H) n.m. Oil.

تیل چڑھانا tel charhānā, v. To anoint the head, shoulders, hands and feet of the bride and bridegroom during the marriage ceremonies.

تیل لگانا tel lagānā, v. To rub oil on; to anoint.

تیل مٹی کا tel mitti kā, n.m. Kerosine oil; mineral oil.

تیلی teli (H) n.m. An oil man.

تیلی تمبولی teli tamboli, n.m. Low caste people.

تیلی کا بیل teli kā bail, n.m. A hard-working man; an overworked wretch.

تیلن telan (H) n.f. The wife of a teli.

تیلیا teliyā (H) adj. Oily; greasy.

تیلیا سرنگ teliyā surung, n.m. A dark brown horse.

تیلیا ککریزی teliyā kakrezi, n.m. A deep purple colour.

تیمار timār (P) n.m. Care; attention; regimen of the sick; infirmity; sickness; indisposition; affliction.

تیمار دار timār dār, n. One who looks after a sick person.

تیمار داری timār dāri, n.f. Nursing; looking after an invalid.

تیمار گاہ timārgāh, n.f. A public dispensary; a relief post.

تیمم tayammum (A) n.m. Purifying before prayers with sand or dust where water is not available.

تین tin (H) n. & adj. Three.

تین پانچ tin pāṅch, id. Contention; dispute; quarrel; knavish.

تین پانچ کرنا tin pāṅch karnā, id. To quarrel; to dispute.

تین تیرہ tin terah, adj. Dispersed; scattered.

تین تیرہ کرنا tin terah karnā, v. To put to rout; to scatter to the winds; to dissipate.

تینتالیس taintālis, n. & adj. Fourty-three.

تینتیس taintīs, n. & adj. Thirty-three.

تیندوا tendūā (H) n.m. A leopard.

تیور tewar (H) n.m. Peculiar expression of the eyes; look; aspect; expression; countenance; the forehead; the brow.

تیور بدلنا tewar badalnā, v. To change countenance; to change one's regard or affection.

تیور بگڑنا tewar bigaṛnā, v. To undergo a change of countenances; to be angry.

تیورانا tevrānā (H) v. To have a swimming in the head; to be giddy; to stagger.

تیوری tevri (H) n.f. A frown; a scowl.

تیوری چڑھانا۔بدلنا tevri charhānā yā badalnā, v. To frown; to knit the brow.

تیوری میں بل ڈالنا tevri meṅ bal ḍālnā, v. To contract the brow; to show displeasure.

تیوہار teohār. See تہوار tehwār.

تیئیس te'is (H) n. & adj. Twenty-three.

ٹ te. It is the fifth letter of the Urdu and eleventh letter of the Hindi alphabet. It does not occur in the Arabic or Persian alphabets. Its sound or pronunciation differs from that of ت in being formed by the forcible application of the tip of the tongue to the palate, instead of the roots of the teeth.

ٹاپ **ṭāp** (H) *n.f.* A stroke with the forefoot of a horse; the sound of a horse's hoof; tramp of a horse.

ٹاپا **ṭāpā** (H) *n.m.* A hen-coop; a bamboo frame for catching fish.

ٹاپنا **ṭāpnā** (H) *v.* To keep looking for; to look about or search in vain; to leap or spring over a wall (low phrase).

ٹاپو **ṭāpū** (H) *n.m.* A small island.

ٹاٹ **ṭāṭ** (H) *n.m.* Canvas; sack cloth; the capsular pod of green gram.

ٹاٹ باف **ṭāṭ bāf**, *n.m.* A weaver of canvas.

ٹاٹ بافی **ṭāṭ bāfī**, *n.f.* Embroidery.

ٹاٹ بافی جوتا **ṭāṭ bāfī jūtā**, *n.m.* An embroidered shoe.

ٹال **ṭāl** (H) *n.f.* A fire wood yard; evasion; putting aside; stalk; deferring; a heap (of grain etc.); a rick; a bell tied to the neck of an animal.

ٹال مٹول **ṭāl maṭol**, *n.f.* Putting off; evasion; stalk; chicanery; prevarication; shuffling.

ٹال مٹول کرنا **ṭal maṭol karnā**, *v.* To put off; to evade; to practise delay.

ٹالا **ṭālā** (H) *n.m.* Putting off; evasion.

ٹالا بالا بتانا **ṭālā bālā batānā**, *v.* To put off; to make excuses.

ٹالنا **ṭālnā**, *v.* To evade; to put off; to postpone; to avoid; to prevaricate; to defer; to ward off; to delay; to turn aside; to pretend.

ٹالی **ṭālī** (H) *n.f.* A small bell.

ٹامک ٹوئیے مارنا **ṭāmak ṭoiye mārnā**, *v.* To guess; to conjecture; to follow conjecture.

ٹانٹ **ṭāṅṭ** (H) *n.f.* The crown of the head; skull.

ٹانٹ کھجلانا **ṭāṅṭ khujlānā**, *v.* To have itch on the skull; to scratch the head; to invite shoe beating.

ٹانٹ گنجی ہونا **ṭāṅṭ ganjī honā**, *v.* To become bald; to be beaten (to the extent of losing head's hair).

ٹانک **ṭāṅk** (H) *n.f.* A weight equal to four *māshahs*; share; valuation.

ٹانکا **ṭāṅkā** (H) *n.m.* A stitch; solder; a stone cistern.

ٹانکا ادھڑنا **ṭāṅkā udhaṛnā**, *v.* Opening of a stitch; to be exposed.

ٹانکا بھرنا **ṭāṅkā bharnā**, *v.* To put a stitch in.

ٹانکا کھلنا **ṭāṅkā khulnā**, *v.* Opening out of a stitch; to have one's secrets exposed.

ٹانکا لگانا **ṭāṅkā lagānā**, *v.* To stitch (a garment); to join; to sew; to solder.

ٹانکنا **ṭaṅknā** (H) *v.* To stitch; to cobble; to solder; to join (to); to enter; to annex.

ٹانکی **ṭāṅkī** (H) *n.f.* A chisel; a small hole; a notch; a dent; a square piece cut out of a water-melon to examine its quality; a kind of ulcer or cancer.

ٹانگ **ṭāṅg** (H) *n.f.* The leg; a share.

ٹانگ یا ٹانگیں اٹھانا **ṭāṅg yā ṭaṅgeṅ uṭhānā**, *v.* To copulate; to raise the leg.

ٹانگ اڑانا **ṭāṅg aṛānā**, *v.* To meddle with other people's affairs; to interfere (in).

ٹانگ برابر **ṭāṅg barābar**, *adj.* Very small in size.

ٹانگ تلے سے نکالنا **ṭāṅg tale se nikālnā**, *v.* To subdue; to make submissive.

ٹانگ تلے سے نکلنا **ṭāṅg tale se nikalnā**, *v.* To yield; to submit.

ٹانگ توڑنا *ṭāṅg toṛnā, v.* To render useless; to dabble in pursuits of which one has very little knowledge.

ٹانگ سے ٹانگ باندھنا *ṭāṅg se tāṅg baṅdhnā, v.* To seat by one's side; not to allow one to stir out.

ٹانگ لینا *tāṅg lenā, v.* To seize or lay hold of the leg(a dog); to pester; to vex.

ٹانگیں رہ جانا *ṭaṅgen rah jānā, v.* To be tired; to be unable to walk further.

ٹانگ دینا *ṭāṅg denā, v.* To hang up; to suspend.

ٹانگنا *ṭaṅgnā, v.* To hang up; to suspend; to dangle; to hang by a string.

ٹائیں ٹائیں فش *ṭāiṅ ṭāiṅ fish, prov.* All talk and no sense.

ٹبا *ṭibbā* (H) *n.m.* A height; a sand drift.

ٹبر *tabbar* (H) *n.m.* Family; household.

ٹپ *ṭup* (H) *n.m.* Sound of a drop of rain or other liquid; the tub of a tonga or a carriage.

ٹپا *tappā* (H) *n.m.* The name of a mode in music; the bound of a ball; a sort of hook; spring; leep; jump; shot; a stage; a long stitch in sewing; a small tract of country comprising one village or more; post office (in Southern India).

ٹپا بھرنا - مارنا *tappā bharnā yā mārnā, v.* To sew with a long stitch; to read in desultory or unmethodical manner.

ٹپا کھانا *tāppā khānā, v.* To bound (a ball).

ٹپس *tippas* (H) *n.f.* Contrivance; access; approach; claim; alliance; foundation.

ٹپس لڑانا - لگانا *tippas larānā yā lagānā, v.* To seek ways and means; to contact; to make out a claim.

ٹپک پڑنا *ṭapak paṛnā, v.* To fall like a drod; to arrive unexpectedly; to drop off (as fruit).

ٹپکا *tapkā, n.m.* Continuous dropping; fruit falling when ripe (particularly mangoes); a windfall.

ٹپکا لگنا *ṭapkā lagnā, v.* To become leaky; to leak; falling down of ripe mangoes.

ٹپکانا *ṭapkānā, v.* To cause to drop or drip; to distil.

ٹپکاؤ *ṭapkāo* (H) *n.m.* Distillation; dripping.

ٹپکنا *tapaknā, v.* To leak; to drop; to drip; to distil; to fall down (fruits).

ٹٹ پونجیا *ṭaṭ pūnjyā* (H) *adj.* A petty merchant; a merchant of small capital.

ٹٹروٹوں *tutrutūṅ* (H) *n.m.* The cooing of a dove. *adj.* Alone; all alone.

ٹٹکارنا *ṭiṭkārnā, v.* To urge an animal on by clacking the tongue.

ٹٹکاری *ṭiṭkārī* (H) *n.f.* The sound made by drawing the tongue from the roof of the mouth and drawing it sharply forward with a view to urge animal to go forward.

ٹٹو *ṭaṭṭū* (H) *n.m.* A pony; an under-sized horse.

بھاڑے کا ٹٹو *bhāṛe kā ṭaṭṭū, adj.* A hired pony; mercenary; hireling.

ٹٹول *ṭaṭol* (H) *n.f.* Touch; feeling; search; groping.

ٹٹولنا *ṭaṭolnā* (H) *v.* To feel; to grope; to search by feeling; to examine by feeling.

ٹٹی *taṭṭī* (H) *n.f.* A frame-work of bamboo; a screen; a matted shutter; a frame for illumination; a privy; a latrine.

ٹٹی جانا *ṭaṭṭī jānā, v.* To perform the office of nature; to go to the privy.

ٹٹی کی اوٹ میں شکار کھیلنا *taṭṭī kī oṭ meṅ shikār khelnā, v.* To do something underhand; to form an ambuscade.

ٹٹی لگانا *taṭṭī lagānā, v.* To screen; to put up an enclosure; to fence.

ٹٹیری *tatirī* (H) *n.f.* A sandpiper; a toy which when revolved gives the sound of a sandpiper.

ٹچا *tuchchā* (H) *n.m.* A mean fellow; a rake; a blackguard.

ٹخنا *takhnā* (H) *n.m.* The ankle joint.

ٹڈا *tiddā* (H) *n.f.* A grasshopper.

ٹڈی ṭiḍḍī (H) *n.f.* A locust.

ٹڈی دل *ṭiḍḍī dal, n.m.* A large swarm of locusts.

ٹر ṭar (H) *n.f.* The croaking of a frog; prate: jabber; chattering; a festival after 'Id.

ٹرٹر *ṭarṭar* (H) *n.f.* Jabber; chattering.

ٹرٹر کرنا *ṭarṭar karnā, v.* To chatter; to croak; to be insolent.

ٹرا *ṭarrā, adj.* Addicted to chattering; talkative;

ٹرانا *ṭarrānā, v.* To chatter; to croak (as, a frog); to murmur; to grumble; to be rude; to be insolent.

ٹرخانا، ٹرکانا *ṭarkhānā, ṭarkānā, v.* To put off; to work carelessly; to make excuses.

ٹسر *ṭasar* (H) *n.f.* A kind of silk cloth; inferior kind of silk.

ٹسر مسر *ṭasar masar, n.f.* Delay; hesitation; putting off.

ٹس سے مس نہ ہونا *ṭas se mas nah honā, v.* Not to be moved; not to be effect; not to feel.

ٹسوے *ṭisve* (H) *n.m.* Tears; false or hypocritical tears.

ٹسوے بہانا *ṭisve bahānā, v.* To weep; to shed corcodile tears.

ٹک *ṭak* (H) *n.f.* Sight; look; temper; disposition; nature.

ٹک باندھنا *ṭak bāṅdhnā, v.* To stare at; to gaze steadfastly.

ٹک لگانا *ṭak lagānā, v.* To expect; to long for; to wait for.

ٹک *ṭuk* (H) *adj.* A little. *adv.* For a while; a little while; for a moment.

ٹکا *ṭakā* (H) *n.m.* A copper coin equal to two pices; money; wealth.

ٹکا بھر *ṭakā bhar, adj.* As much as a *ṭakā*; a little.

ٹکا پاس نہ ہونا *ṭakā pās nah honā, v.* To be very poor; to be absolutely out of pocket.

ٹکا پنسیری لگانا *ṭakā panserī lagānā, v.* To sell very cheap.

ٹکا سا جواب دینا *ṭakā sā jawāb denā, v.* To refuse point-blank; to reject instantly; to give a point-blank refusal.

ٹکانا *ṭikānā* (H) *v.* To cause to lodge; to fix in any place; to station; to put (one) up; to lay on; to give a slap.

ٹکاؤ *ṭikāo* (H) *n.m.* Abode; residence; permanence.

ٹکٹ *ṭikaṭ* (H) *n.m.* (*corr.* of English); A ticket; a postage stamp; a label; a pass; a court-fee stamp; passport.

چسپانی ٹکٹ *chaspānī ṭikaṭ, n.m.* Adhesive stamp.

ٹک ٹک *ṭik ṭik, n.f.* The sound used by a bullock cart driver to urge bullock to move on.

ٹکٹکی *ṭikṭikī* (H) *n.f.* A tripod on which criminals are flogged; fixed look; stare; an anxious look; gaze.

ٹکٹکی باندھنا یا لگانا *ṭikṭikī bāṅdhnā yā lagānā, v.* To regard with a fixed look; to gaze steadfastly (at); to stare (at).

ٹکٹکی سے باندھنا *ṭikṭikī se bāṅdānā, v.* To bind on the tripod and flog.

ٹکر *ṭakkar* (H) *n.f.* Striking or knocking against; collision; butting; knock; encounter; competition; rivalry; comparison; rival; antagonist; match.

ٹکر کھانا *ṭakkar khānā, v.* To strike against; to collide; to bump against; to vie against; to meet with a loss or misfortune; to be dashed (against); to stumble.

ٹکر لڑانا *ṭakkar laṛānā, v.* To butt; to strike against.

ٹکر لگانا *ṭakkar lagānā, v.* To dash against; to enter into rivalry.

ٹکر لگنا *ṭakkar lagnā, v.* To collide; to knock against; to be hit; to be injured.

ٹکر مارنا *ṭakkar mārnā, v.* To knock against; to knock down; to strive.

برابر کی ٹکر کا ***barābar kī ṭakkar kā,*** *adj.* Equally good; good; of equal strength or quality; equally matched.

پہاڑ سے ٹکر لینا ***pahāṛ se ṭakkar lenā,*** *v.* To fight against heavy odds.

ٹکرانا ***ṭakrānā,*** *v.* To knock one body against another; to bring into collision; to dash together; to clash together; to butt.

ٹکر ٹکر دیکھنا ***ṭukar ṭukar dekhnā,*** *v.* To give one a surprised look; to gaze despondently; to look eagerly.

ٹکر ٹکر یا ٹک، ٹک دیدم دم نہ کشیدم ***ṭukar ṭukar yā ṭuk ṭuk dīdam dam nah kashīdam,*** *id.* Gazed at it despondently and kept quiet.

ٹکڑا ***tukṛā*** (H) *n.m.* A piece; a bit; a morsel; a part; a fraction; a clause or paragraph; livelihood.

ٹکر گدا ***ṭukaṛ gadā,*** *n.m.* A beggar; one who begs for a living.

ٹکڑا مانگنا ***ṭukṛā māṅgnā,*** *v.* To beg alms.

چاند کا ٹکڑا ***chāṅd kā ṭukṛā,*** *adj.* A very beautiful person; a charming creature.

ٹکڑوں پر پڑنا ***ṭukṛon par paṛnā,*** *v.* To be dependent (on).

ٹکڑے ٹکڑے ***tukṛe tukṛe,*** *adv.* In pieces; piecemeal.

ٹکڑے کرنا ***ṭukṛe karnā,*** *v.* To break into pieces; to divide; to separate.

ٹکڑی ***ṭukṛī*** (H) *n.f.* A piece; a bit; a slice; a piece of cloth; a flock of birds (pigeons); a band of men, &c.

ٹکسال ***ṭaksāl*** (H) *n.f.* A mint.

ٹکسال باہر ***ṭaksāl bāhar,*** *adj.* Unidiomatic or unchaste words; unpolished; unclassical; a counterfeit coin.

ٹکسال چڑھنا ***ṭaksāl chaṛhnā,*** *v.* To be educated; to bear the stamp of the mint.

ٹکسالی ***ṭaksālī,*** *adj.* Pertaning to a mint; true; genuine; pure; chaste.

ٹکسالی زبان ***ṭaksālī zabān,*** *n.f.* Good idiom; idiomatic language.

ٹکسالیہ ***ṭaksāliyah,*** *n.m.* An officer of the mint; coiner; mint-master.

ٹکلی ***ṭiklī*** (H) *n.f.* An ornament worn by women on the forehead; a small round cake; a wafer.

ٹکنا ***ṭiknā*** (H) *v.* To stay; to lodge; to last; to put up; to remain; to tarry.

ٹکنا ***ṭaknā*** (H) *v.* To be stitched; to be sewn.

ٹکوا ***ṭakvā*** (H) *n.m.* A chopper; an axe-like weapon.

ٹکور ***ṭākor*** (H) *n.m.* Fomentation; cataplasm.

ٹکورنا ***ṭakornā*** (H) *v.* To foment; to apply warmth (to).

ٹکھیائی ***ṭakhyāī*** (H) *n.f.* A harlot; a third-rate prostitute.

ٹکی - ٹکیا ***ṭikkī yā tikkiyā*** (H) *n.f.* A small cake; a wafer; a tablet.

ٹل جانا ***ṭal jānā,*** *v.* To get out of the way; to decamp; to pass by or away; to withdraw; to vanish.

ٹلنا ***ṭalnā*** (H) *v.* To withdraw; to move; to go away; to shrink from; to flinch.

ٹم ٹم ***ṭam-ṭam*** (H) *n.f.* (*corr.* of English); Tandem.

ٹماخ ***ṭimākh,*** *n.m.* Show; pump; make-up.

ٹمٹمانا ***ṭimṭimānā*** (H) *v.* To give a faint light; to twinkle; to flicker; to be at the last gasp.

ٹمٹماہٹ ***ṭimṭimāhaṭ*** (H) *n.f.* Twinking; glimmer; flickering.

ٹن ٹن ***ṭan ṭan,*** *n.f.* Ringing of a bell.

ٹنٹا ***ṭanṭā*** (H) *n.m.* Wrangling; brawl; noisy quarrel.

ٹنٹے باز ***ṭanṭe bāz,*** *n.* A quarrelsome person; a brawler.

ٹنٹا ***ṭunṭā.*** See ٹنڈا ***ṭunḍā.***

ٹنڈ ***ṭunḍ*** (H) *n.m.* A chopped hand or branch; stump of a branch or arm.

ٹنڈا ***ṭunḍā*** (H) *adj. & n.m.* Handless; one whose hands have been cut off or one who is born without hands.

ٹنڈی ṭunḍī (H) *n.f.* The navel. (See also ٹنڈا tunḍā).

ٹنگنا ṭangnā, *v.* To hang up; to be hung.

ٹوپ ṭop (H) *n.m.* A hat; a cap which covers the ears and the back of the head; a kind of hood; a thimble.

ٹوپا ṭopā (H) *n.m.* A cap; a grain measure.

ٹوپی ṭopī (H) *n.f.* A cap; a hat; a gun-cap.

ٹوپی اچھالنا ṭopī uchhālnā, *v.* To jump with joy; to throw up one's cap in token of pleasure.

ٹوپی دار بندوق ṭopidār bandūq, *n.f.* A match-lock.

ٹوٹ ṭūṭ (H) *n.f.* Breaking; fracture; loss; harm; deficiency.

ٹوٹ پھوٹ ṭūṭ phūṭ, *n.f.* Pieces; fragments; damage; fracture; loss.

ٹوٹ جانا ṭūṭ jānā, *v.* To break; to be broken.

ٹوٹ پڑنا ṭūṭ paṛnā, *v.* To rush in; to fall upon; to attack bitterly.

ٹوٹا ṭūṭā (H) *adj.* Broken; demolished; decayed; damaged.

ٹوٹا پھوٹا ṭūṭa phūṭā, *adj.* Broken to pieces; damaged; demolished. *n.m.* Loss; damage.

ٹوٹا ṭoṭā (H) *n.m.* Loss; deficiency; detriment; damage; scarcity; candle's end; a piece of a cloth, wood or bamboo.

ٹوٹا آٹھانا ṭoṭā uṭhānā, *v.* To suffer loss; to make restitution.

ٹوٹا بھرنا toṭā bharnā, *v.* To make good a loss or damage; to indemnify; to refund.

ٹوٹا پڑنا ṭoṭā paṛnā, *v.* To incur or suffer a loss.

ٹوٹرو ṭoṭrū (H) *n.m.* A kind of turtle-dove.

ٹوٹکا ṭoṭkā (H) *n.m.* A charm; an amulet; a superstitious remedy; a spell.

ٹوٹنا ṭūṭnā, *v.* To be broken; to be fractured; to break or burst; to be separated; to disassociate; to rush upon; to pine.

ٹوک ṭok, *n.f.* Hindrance; interruption; prevention; parole; influence of an evil eye.

ٹوکرا ṭokrā (H) *n.m.* A large basket.

ٹوکری ṭokrī (H) *n.f.* A small basket.

ٹوکنا ṭoknā, *v.* To challenge; to prevent; to question; to interrogate; to envy; to accost.

ٹولا ṭolā (H) *n.m.* A particular part of a town inhabited by men of one class or trade; a crowd; a group; a ward; a large pebble.

ٹولی ṭolī (H) *n.f.* A company; a society; a crowd; a group.

ٹونا ṭonā (H) *n.m.* Charm; fascination; enchantment; witch-craft.

ٹونے باز ṭūne bāz, *n.* A charmer; a conjurer; a magician.

ٹونٹی ṭonṭī (H) *n.f.* A spout.

ٹونڈی ṭonḍī (H) *n.f.* The navel.

ٹونگنا ṭungnā, *v.* To peck; to nibble.

ٹوہ ṭoh (H) *n.f.* Search; spying; watching secretly.

ٹوہ لگانا ṭoh lagānā, *v.* To trace; to find out; to investigate secretly.

ٹوہنا ṭohnā (H) *v.* To search; to grope for; to look for.

ٹھاٹ ṭhāṭ (H) *n.m.* A frame of bamboo for thatching; arrangement; adjustment.

ٹھاٹھ ṭhāṭh (H) *n.f.* Dignity; pomp; splendour; state; retinue; plenty; abundance.

ٹھاٹھ بدلنا ṭhāṭh badalnā, *v.* To change one's attitude or posture.

ٹھاٹھ کے ساتھ ṭhaṭh ke sāth, *adv.* With great pomp and show.

ٹھاٹھیں مارنا ṭhāṭheṅ mārnā, *v.* Striking of waves against the shore; to surge.

ٹھاکر ṭhākur (H) *n.m.* An idol; the Supreme God; a master; lord; landholder; a chief (among certain castes of Rajputs); the head of a village; a person of rank or authority.

ٹھاکر دوارہ **ṭhākur duwārah**, *n.m.* An idol temple.

ٹھاننا **ṭhānnā**, *v.* To resolve or fix (in the mind); to intend; to be intent on; to be determined; to set one's heart on.

ٹھپا **ṭhappā** (H) *n.m.* An instrument for stamping with; a stamp; an impression; printing type; fount; a die; a mould; broad silver lace.

ٹھپا لگانا **ṭhappā lagānā**, *v.* To stamp; to put a stamp on.

ٹھٹ **ṭhaṭ** (H) *n.m.* Throng; crowd; multitude.

ٹھٹھا **ṭhaṭhā** (H) *n.m.* Loud laughter; fun; a joke, a jest.

ٹھٹھا کرنا **ṭhaṭhā karnā**, *v.* To joke; to jest; to ridicule; to deride.

ٹھٹھا لگانا ۔ مارنا **ṭhaṭhā lagānā, mārnā**, *v.* To burst with laughters.

ٹھٹھے باز **ṭhaṭhe bāz**, *n.* Jocular; jester; a funny fellow; a humourous person; waggish; comical; facetious.

ٹھٹھے بازی **ṭhaṭhe bāzī**, *n.f.* Joking; jesting; sporting; fun; jocularity.

ٹھٹھے میں اڑانا **ṭhaṭhe meṅ uṛānā**, *v.* To turn off in jest; to make fun of; to ridicule.

ٹھٹھرانا **ṭhiṭhrānā**, *v.* To chill; to benumb.

ٹھٹھرنا **ṭhiṭharnā** (H) *v.* To be chilled with cold; to be frozen; to be benumbed; to shiver.

ٹھٹھک ۔ ٹھٹک **ṭhiṭhak yā ṭhiṭak** (H) *n.f.* The state of stopping suddenly or of standing amazed.

ٹھٹھکنا ۔ ٹھٹکنا **ṭhiṭhaknā yā ṭhiṭaknā** (H) *v.* To shrink; to stop; to stand amazed; to draw back in amazement; to hesitate; to stagger.

ٹھٹھول **ṭhaṭhol** (H) *n.f.* Joking; jesting; humour; fun; derision. *adj* Banterer; humourous; jocose; waggish; jocular; jester; humourist.

ٹھٹھیرا **ṭhaṭherā** (H) *n.m.* One who makes pots of hardware or metal; a brazier; a tinker.

ٹھڈا **ṭhaḍḍā** (H) *n.m.* The back stick of a paper kite; the backbone.

ٹھڈا **ṭhuḍḍā** (H) *n.m.* A kick; kicking with the boot.

ٹھڈی **ṭhuḍḍī**, *n.f.* The chin; hard and non-crisp parched grain.

ٹھرا **ṭharrā** (H) *n.m.* An inferior kind of country wine; a kind of shoe worn by villagers.

ٹھس **ṭhas** (H) *adj.* Crammed; stuffed; hard; solid; not hollow; stupid; dull headed.

ٹھسا **ṭhassā** (H) *n.m.* Pride; pomp and show.

ٹھسلنا ۔ ٹھسوانا **ṭhuslanā yā ṭhuswānā** (H) *v.* To cause to stuff; to cause to fill.

ٹھسنا **ṭhusnā** (H) *v.* To be stuffed; to be filled.

ٹھسوانا **ṭhuswānā** (H) *v.* To cause to stuff; to cause to fill (to capacity).

ٹھک ٹھک **ṭhak ṭhak**, *n.f.* A sound of hammering; troublesome business.

ٹھکانا **ṭhikānā** (H) *n.m.* Fixed abode; precise whereabouts; proper place; certainty; source; origin; goal; destination; limit; boundary.

ٹھکانا ڈھونڈنا **ṭhikānā ḍhūnḍhnā**, *v.* To look for a residence or employment.

ٹھکانا کرنا **ṭhikānā karnā**, *v.* To find a room (for); to arrange; to account (for); to find a husband or wife (for).

ٹھکانے کا آدمی **ṭhikāne kā ādmī**, *n.m.* A clever man; an intelligent person; a gentleman.

ٹھکانے کی بات **ṭhikāne kī bāt**, *n.f.* A reasonable thing.

ٹھکانے لگانا **ṭhikāne lagānā**, *v.* To settle a person's hash; to assassinate; to kill; to dispose off; to marry (of); to spend; to accomplish.

ٹھکانے لگنا **ṭhikāne lagnā**, *v.* To be killed; to be terminated; to be disposed off.

بے ٹھکانے **be ṭhikāne**, *adj.* Out of place; inconsistent; indeterminate; uncertain; meaningless.

ٹھکرانا ṭhukrānā (H) v. To kick against; to kick ; to trample upon.

ٹھکنا ṭhuknā (H) v. To be beaten; to be chastised; to be hammered.

ٹھگ ṭhag (H) n.m. A cheat; a fraudulent; a robber; a plunderer; a cut-throat; a swindler; an assassin.

ٹھگ بازی - ٹھگ بدیا ṭhag bāzī, ṭhag biddiyā, n.f. The art of tricking or swindling.

ٹھگائی ، ٹھگی ṭhagāi, ṭhāgi (H) n.f. Cheating, robbery; swindling; theft.

ٹھگنا ṭhagnā (H) v. To rob; to cheat; to deceive; to beguile; to swindle.

ٹھگنی ṭhagnı (H) n.f. A female robber or cheat.

ٹہل ṭahal (H) n.f. Service; attendance; business; work; drudgery; servitude; housewifery; house-keeping.

ٹہل کرنا ṭahal karnā, v. To serve; to drudge; to attend upon.

ٹہلانا ṭahlānā, v. To cause to walk to and fro; to make one dance attendance; to get one out of the way; to dismiss; to remove.

ٹہلنا ṭahalnā, v. To walk to and fro; to rove; to ramble; to take a walk.

ٹھلیا ṭhilyā n.f. A water pot; a small earthen pitcher.

ٹھمری ṭhumri (H) n.f. A species of metre; a variety of song; a kind of verse.

ٹھمک چال ṭhumak chāl (H) n.f. Graceful carriage; a dignified gait; a stately air.

ٹھمکنا ṭhumaknā (H) v. To walk with grace and stateliness; to dance joyously.

ٹھمکی ṭhumkī, n.f. A jerk; jerking a paper-kite to keep it up when wind is light.

ٹھمکی دینا ṭhumkı denā, v. To give a jerk (to the paper-kite).

ٹھن ٹھن ṭhan ṭhan (H) n.f. Tinkle; jingle.

ٹھن ٹھن گوپال ṭhan ṭhan gopāl, n.m. A fool; a blockhead; nothing; nought.

ٹھنّا- ٹھننا ṭhannā (H) v. To be fixed in the mind; to be ascertained; to be resolved; to be determined.

ٹھنٹھ ṭhunṭh (H) n.m. Leafless branch of a tree; a stump; an amputated hand.

ٹھنڈ ṭhanḍ (H) n.f. Cold; chilliness; chill.

ٹھنڈا، ٹھنڈی ṭhanḍā, ṭhanḍi, adj. Cold; refreshed; calm; cool; cold-blooded; cold-hearted; dull; inactive (market); extinguished; alloyed; dead; pacified; mild; frozen; impotent.

ٹھنڈا کرنا ṭhanḍā karnā, v. To cool; to extinguish; to comfort; to assuage; to soothe; to make cold; to kill.

ٹھنڈا لوھا گرم لوہے کو کاٹتا ھے ṭhanḍā lohā garm lohe ko kāṭṭā hai, prov. A soft answer turneth away wrath.

ٹھنڈا ہونا ṭhanḍā honā, v. To become cold; to be extinguished; to rest; to be soothed; to be dead.

کلیجا ٹھنڈا ہونا kalaijā ṭhanḍā honā, v. To be satisfied; to be pleased; to have one's revenge.

ٹھنڈی سانس ṭhanḍi sāns, n.f. Cold breath.

ٹھنڈے ٹھنڈے ṭhanḍe ṭhanḍe, adv. In the cool of the day; while it is cool; in the morning or evening.

ٹھنڈے سانس بھرنا ṭhanḍe sāns bharnā, v. To sigh in despair; to heave a deep sigh.

ٹھنڈائی ṭhanḍāi (H) n.f. Refrigerant medicine; cooling drink (bhang).

ٹھنڈک ṭhanḍak (H) n.f. Coolness; chilliness; comfort.

ٹھنڈک پڑنا ṭhanḍak paṛnā, v. To be cooled; to have a desire for revenge gratified.

ٹھنکانا ṭhankānā (H) v. To sound; to ring a coin or metal; to chink; to produce a sound; to cause to knock or hammer.

ٹھنکنا ṭhinaknā (H) v. To sob; to whimper; to whine; to jingle; to clink; to shoot (as, headache).

ٹھنگنا، ٹھنگنی ṭhingnā, ṭhingnı (H) adj. Of small stature; dwarfish.

ٹہنی ṭahnī (H) n.f. A branch of a tree; a twig

ٹھور ṭhaur (H) n.m. Place; spot; residence; room.

ٹھورٹھکانا thaur ṭhikānā, n.m. Abode; a residence; a halting place.

ٹھوڑی ṭhoṛi (H) n.f. The chin.

ٹھوڑی پکڑنا ṭhoṛi pakaṛnā, v. To platter; to assuage.

ٹھوڑی تارا ṭhoṛi tārā, n.m. A mole on the chin.

ٹھوس ṭhos (H) adj. Solid; compact; hard; heavy.

ٹھوک بجا کے ṭhok bajā ke, adv. After thorough sifting or testing; after close examination.

ٹھوک دینا ṭhok denā, v. To shove in; to push in.

ٹھوکر ṭhokar (H) n.f. Any projecting thing or stone on a road, which causes stumbling; obstacle; a kick; a stumble; the toe (of a shoe).

ٹھوکر کھانا ṭhokar khānā, v. To trip; to stumble; to suffer a loss.

ٹھوکر لگنا ṭhokar lagnā, v. To come into collision with; to collide with something; to learn a lesson.

ٹھوکر مارنا ، لگانا ṭhokar mārnā, lagānā, v. To strike against; to kick or spurn; to deried; to despise.

ٹھوکریں کھانا ṭhokreṅ khānā, v. To stumble; to suffer misfortune; to be ill-treated.

ٹھوکریں کھاتے پھرنا ṭhokreṅ khāte phirnā, v. To be ill-treated; to be tossed about by misfortune.

ٹھوکنا ṭhoknā (H) v. To drive in; to beat; to hammer; to thump.

ٹھونسنا ṭhūṅsnā (H) v. To thurst in; to stuff; to fill to capacity; to impose (upon).

ٹھونگا ṭhoṅgā (H) n.m. A beak; bill; striking with the beak.

ٹھہرانا ، ٹھیرانا ṭhahrānā ṭhairānā (H) v. To cause to stop; to cause one to stay; to settle; to appoint; to fix on; to conclude.

ٹھہراؤ ، ٹھیراؤ ṭhahrāo, ṭhairāo (H) n.m. Settlement; permanence; agreement; stop; halt; rest; stillness.

ٹھہرنا ، ٹھیرنا ṭhahrnā, ṭhairnā (H) v. To stop; to stand; to remain; to be stationary; to be frozen; to cease; to last; to stay; to wait; to halt.

ٹھیا thiyā (H) n.m. Sitting place; support.

ٹھیٹھ ، ٹھیٹ ṭheth, ṭhet (H) adj. Real; genuine; idiomatic; pure.

ٹھیس ṭhes (H) n.f. A knock; a blow; a push.

ٹھیک ṭhik (H) adj. Firm; strong; exact; correct; fit; right; proper; regular. adv. Exactly; clearly; justly; truly.

ٹھیک ٹھاک ṭhik ṭhāk, adj. All right; quite right; quite correct.

ٹھیک کرنا ṭhik karnā, v. To correct; to adjust; to ascertain; to fit; to beat; to punish; to put to right; to bring one to his senses.

ٹھیکا ṭhekā (H) n.m. Contract; piecework; hire; lease; work done on contract or by job, a resting place; a small tambourine.

ٹھیکا بجانا ṭhekā bajānā, v. To play on accompaniment (ḍholak) with a singer.

ٹھیکا لینا ṭhekā lenā, v. To contract; to monopolise.

ٹھیکا حین حیات ṭhekā ḥin-ĕ ḥayāt, n.m. A lease for the term of one's life.

ٹھیکے پر ṭheke par, adv. On contract basis.

ٹھیکرا ṭhikrā (H) n.m. A broken piece of earthenware; a large potsherd.

روزی کا ٹھیکرا rozi kā ṭhikrā, n.m. Means by which one lives; means of livelihood.

ٹھیکری ṭhikrī (H) n.f. A small piece of broken earthenware; a potsherd.

ٹھیکے دار ṭheke dār (H) n.m. A contractor; a lease holder.

ٹھیلا ṭhelā (H) n.m. A push; a trolly; a trailer; a wheel barrow.

ٹھیلنا *ṭhelnā* (H) *v.* To shove; to push; to move forward; to elbow; to jostle; to propel.

ٹھینگا *ṭhengā* (H) *n.m.* A small club; a thumb.

ٹیپ *ṭīp* (H) *n.f.* A bill; a note of band; a cheque; raising the voice in singing; a high or shrill note; lime or cement painting; a slap; the 5th and 6th lines of a verse consisting of six lines; the third couplet of a sextain.

ٹیپ ٹاپ *ṭīp ṭāp, n.f.* Decoration; equipage; adornment; ostentation; splendour; pomp; show.

ٹیڑھ *ṭeṛh* (H) *n.f.* Crookedness.

ٹیڑھا، ٹیڑھی *ṭeṛhā, ṭeṛhī, adj.* Crooked; bent; awry; angry; hump-backed; uneven; displeased; obstinate.

ٹیڑھا بانکا *ṭeṛhā bāṅkā, adj.* A beau; a fop; a cocomb; a handsome youth.

ٹیڑھا بیڑھا *ṭeṛhā beṛhā, adj.* Crooked; zigzag.

ٹیڑھا پن *ṭeṛhā pan, n.m.* Crookedness.

ٹیڑھا کرنا *ṭeṛhā karnā, v.* To bend; to make crooked; to distort.

ٹیڑھا ہونا *ṭeṛhā honā, v.* To be crooked; to be displeased.

ٹیڑھی آنکھ سے دیکھنا *ṭeṛhī āṅkh se dekhnā, v.* To see with an angry look.

ٹیڑھی کھیر *ṭeṛhī khīr, n.f.* A difficult and somewhat impossible task.

ٹیس *ṭīs* (H) *n.f.* A throb; throbbing; a shooting pain; stitching.

ٹیس اٹھنا ، مارنا *ṭīs uṭhnā, mārnā, v.* To throb; to have shooting pain.

ٹیک *ṭek* (H) *n.f.* A prop; a pillar; a support; reliance; promise; vow; resolve; burden of a song.

ٹیکا *ṭīkā* (H) *n.m.* A mark made on the forehead; an ornament of gold or silver worn on the forehead; stain; blot; vaccination; inoculation; injection; a ceremony connected with betrothal; dowry.

ٹیکا لگانا *ṭīkā lagānā, v.* To inoculate; to vaccinate; to inject.

کلنک کا ٹیکا لگنا *kalank kā ṭīkā lagnā, v.* To get a bad name; to be stigmatized.

ٹیکنا *ṭeknā* (H) *v.* To support; to prop.

ٹینٹوا *ṭenṭūā* (H) *n.m.* The wind pipe; the throat.

ٹینٹوا دبانا *ṭenṭūā dabānā, v.* To throttle; to strangle; to choke.

ٹیں ٹیں *ṭeṅ ṭeṅ* (H) *n.f.* An imitative or inarticulate sound; the screech of a parrot.

ٹیں ٹیں کرنا *ṭeṅ ṭeṅ karnā, v.* To screech, to prate; to murmur.

ٹینی *ṭenī* (H) *adj.* Small in size; a hybrid species of hen; tiny; small.

ٹیوا *ṭewā* (H) *n.m.* Calculation of nativity; habit; custom.

ث *ṣe* is the fourth letter of the Arabic, the fifth of the Persian and the sixth of the Urdu alphabets. According to *abjad* it represents the numerical value of 500.

ثابت *ṣābit* (A) *adj.* Firm; fixed; constant; stable; ascertained; certain; valid confirmed; established; stationary; real; whole; *n.m.* A fixed star.

ثابت قدم *ṣābit qadam, adj.* Immovable; firm; steady; stable; resolute; permanent; constant; persevering; steadfast.

ثابت کرنا *ṣābit karnā, v.* To prove; to verify; to confirm; to establish; to render durable.

ثابت ہونا *ṣābit honā, v.* To be proved or confirmed; to be established.

ثاقب *ṣāqib* (A) *adj.* Shining brightly; glistening; splendid; sublime; high.

ثالث *ṣāliṣ* (A) *n.m.* A third person; an arbitrator; a mediator; a judge.

ثالث بالخیر *ṣāliṣ bil-khair, n.m.* An unprejudiced arbitrator; an impartial mediator.

ثالث حصری ṣāliṣ-ĕ ḥaṣri, *n.m.* A reliable mediator; a mediator acceptable to both parties.

ثالث نامه ṣāliṣ nāmah, *n.m.* A deed of award; an award by arbitration.

ثالثی ṣālṣi, *n.f.* Mediation; arbitration.

ثالثاً saliṣan, *adv.* Thirdly; in the third place.

ثالوث sālūs (A) *n.m.* The trinity.

ثانوی sānawī (A) *adj.* Secondary.

ثانی sāni (A) *adj.* Second. *n.m.* Match; equal; the second.

ثانیاً saniyan, *adv.* Secondly.

ثانیه ṣāniyah (A) *n.m.* A second; sixtieth part of a minute; a moment.

ثبات sabāt (A) *n.m.* Permanence; stability; endurance; firmness; steadiness; resolution; constancy; soundness.

ثبت sabt (A) *n.m.* Firmness; permanence; fixedness; an impression; a seal; writing.

ثبت کرنا ṣabt karnā, *v.* To inscribe; to subscribe; to write; to impress upon; to register; to enter.

ثبت ہونا ṣabt honā, *v.* To be inscribed; to be written.

ثبوت ṣubūt (A) *n.m.* Firmness; stability; constancy; conviction; proof; testimony; demonstration; evidence.

ثبوت بادی‌النظر ṣubūt-ĕ bādi-un-nazar, *n.m.* *Prima facie* proof; the obvious proof.

ثبوت تائیدی ṣubūt-ĕ tā'idi, *n.m.* Corroborative evidence.

ثبوت تحریری ṣubūt-ĕ tahrīrī, *n.m.* Documentary evidence.

ثبوت تردیدی ṣubut-ĕ tardīdi, *n.m.* Rebutting evidence.

ثبوت صریح ṣubūt-ĕ ṣarīḥ, *n.m.* Direct proof.

ثبوت ضمنی ṣubūt-ĕ zimni, *n.m.* Collateral evidence.

ثبوت قرائنی ṣubut-ĕ qarā'inī, *n.m.* Circumstantial evidence.

ثبوت قطعی ṣubūt-ĕ qaṭa'i, *n.m.* Conclusive proof.

ثبوت لسانی ṣubūt-ĕ lisānī, *n.m.* Verbal evidence.

ثبوت وصیت نامه ṣubūt-ĕ waṣiyat nāmah, *n.m.* Probate of a bill.

بار ثبوت bār-ĕ ṣubūt, *n.m.* The burden of proof; the onus of proof.

ثروت ṣārwat (A) *n.f.* Wealth; power; influence; affluence.

ثری ṣarā (A) *n.m.* The earth.

تحت الثری taḥt-uṣ-ṣarā, *n.f.* Under the earth; the nether regions.

ثریا ṣuraiyyā (A) *n.m.* The Pleiades; cluster of seven brilliant stars in Taurus.

ثریا جاه ṣuraiyyā jāh, *adj.* The exalted one.

ثعلب مصری ṣa'lab miṣrī (A) *n.f.* Salep; a medicinal root considered in the East to be a strong restorative.

ثقافت ṣiqāfat (A) *n.f.* Culture.

ثقالت ṣiqālat (A) *n.f.* Heaviness; burden; weight.

ثقاهت ṣiqāhat (A) *n.f.* Being trustworthy or reliable; trustworthiness.

ثقل ṣiql (A) *n.m.* Heavy load; gravity; weight; indigestion.

ثقلین ṣaqalain (A) *n.m.* Human beings and genii; both the worlds.

ثقه ṣiqah (H) *n.m.* A confident person; a trusted friend; worthy of confidence; a reliable companion.

ثقیل ṣaqil (A) *adj.* Heavy; indigestible; slow; sluggish; dull; inactive.

ثلث ṣulṣ (A) *n.m.* The third part; one-third.

ثمار ṣimār (A) *n.m.* (*plu.* of ثمر ṣamar) Fruits.

ثمر، ثمره ṣamar, ṣamrah (A) *n.m.* Fruit; produce; profit; offspring; advantage; result; reward.

ثمر بخش ṣamar bakhsh, *adj.* Yielding fruit.

ثمر دار ṣamar dār, *adj.* Fruit-bearing; fruitful.

ثمن ṣaman (A) n.m. Price; value; estimated cost.

ثنا ṣanā (A) n.f. Praise; applause; eulogy.

ثنا خوان ، ثناگر ṣanā khwān, ṣanā gar, n. A praiser.

ثواب ṣawāb (A) n.m. Requital; reward; the reward of virtue in a future state.

ثوابت ṣawābit (A) (plu. of ثابت ṣābit) The fixed stars.

ثور ṣaur (A) n.m. A bull; Taurus; the sign of Zodiac.

ج

ج jīm is the fifth letter of the Arabic, the sixth of the Persian and the seventh of the Urdu alphabet. In *abjad* it has the numerical value of 3.

جا jā (P) n.f. Place; seat; room; space; occasson.

جابجا jā bajā, adv. Here and there; everywhere.

جا بے جا jā-be-jā, adv. Right or wrong; in place or out of place; at all times.

جا ضرور jā zarūr, n.m. A privy; a lavatory; a latrine.

جانشین jā nashīn; n. A deputy; a vicegerent; a viceroy; a successor.

جانشینی jā nashīnī, n.f. Sitting in the place; lieutenancy; vicegerency.

جانماز jā-namāz n.f. A carpet or mat on which prayers are said; a prayer mat.

جابر jābir (A) adj. Despotic, n.m. A despot; a tyrant.

جاپ jāp (S) n.m. Muttering prayers or counting beads.

جاترا (یاترا) jātrā (yātrā) (H) n.f. Pilgrimage; departure; march; journey; festival; procession of idols.

جاتری (یاتری) jātrī (yātrī), n. A pilgrim.

جاٹ jāṭ (H) n.m. The name of a tribe among Rajputs; an agriculturist.

جاجم jājam (H) n.m. A chequered linen cloth spread over a carpet.

جادو jādū (P) n.m. Magic; enchantment; conjuring; charm; effect of evil spirit.

جادو کرنا jādū karnā, v. To conjure; to charm; to enchant.

جادوگر jādūgar, n.m. A conjurer; a wizard; a magician; a sorcerer.

جادوگرنی jādūgarnī, n.f. A socreress; a witch.

جادوگری jādūgarī, n.f. Magic; necromancy; conjuration; enchantment.

جادہ jādah (A) n.m. A pathway; a road; route; the right road; a highway.

جاذب jāẕib (A) adj. Absorbent; attractive; drawing; alluring. n.m. A blotter.

جاذبہ jāẕibah, n.f. The power of attraction; the power of absorption.

جار jār (A) n.m. A neighbour; giving *kasrah* to the last letter of a word. adj. That which draws or attracts.

حرف جار ḥarf-ĕ jār, n.m. A preposition.

جارجٹ jārjaṭ, n.f. (corr. of English): Georgette; a kind of silk cloth.

جاروب jārūb (P) n.f. A broom; besom.

جاروب کش jārūb kash, n. A sweeper.

جاری jārī (A) adj. Running; flowing; proceeding; current; usual; continuing; in force (law); prevalent.

جاری رکھنا jārī rakhnā, v. To carry on; to continue; to maintain.

جاری رہنا jārī rahnā, v. To continue; to remain in use.

جاری کرنا jārī karnā, v. To begin; to start; to issue; to circulate; to institute; to set on foot.

جاری ہونا jārī honā, v. To flow; to issue from; to pass current; to be in force; to prevail; to proceed.

جاڑا jāṛā (H) *n.m.* Winter; coldness; cold.

جاڑا چڑھنا jāṛā chaṛhnā, *v.* To be attacked by cold or shivering.

جاڑا لگنا jāṛā lagnā, *v.* To feel cold; to be shivering.

جازم jāzim (A) *adj.* Rendering the last letter of a word quiescent.

جاسوس jāsūs (A) *n.* A spy; an emissary.

جاسوسی jāsūsī (A) *n.f.* Spying; espionage.

جاسوسی کرنا jāsūsi karnā, *v.* To act as a spy.

جاکٹ jākat (Corr. of English) Jacket.

جاگنا jāgnā (H) *v.* To wake up; to be awoke; to be vigilant.

جاگیر jāgir (P) *n.f.* Land given by government as reward for services rendered or for other governmental purposes; a fief; a feud.

جاگیر دوام jāgir-ĕ dawām, *n.f.* A rent free estate given as a grant in perpetuity.

جاگیردار jāgir dār, *n.m.* Holder of rent free estate;; a grantee; a feudatory.

جاگیر داری jāgir dāri, *n.f.* Feudalism.

جال jāl (H) *n.m.* A net; a snare; a sash; a grating; a magic; a cobweb; a trap; a lattice; an illusion,

جال بچھانا، پھیلانا jāl bichhānā, phailānā, *v.* To spread a net; to set a trap.

جال پھینکنا jāl phainknā, *v.* To throw a net in the water for catching fish.

جال ڈالنا jāl ḍālnā, *v.* To cast a net; to lay a snare; to set up a trap.

جال میں پھنسنا۔آنا jāl meṅ phaṅsnā, ānā, *v.* To be entrapped; to be entangled.

جال کرچ jāl kirch (H) *n.f.* A sword and sash.

جالا jālā (H) *n.m* A cobweb; spider's web; a pellicle, cataract; a water-weed used in refining sugar.

جالی jālī (H) *n.f.* A network; lattice; trellis-work; the thick coating of a mango-stone; lace; a coil; grate; a caul; the integument in which a foetus is enveloped.

جالی پڑنا jālī paṛnā, *v.* Hardening of the stone of a mango.

جالینوس jālīnūs (U) *n. prop.* The Greek physician, Galen.

جام jām (P) *n.m.* A goblet; a bowl; cup; glass drinking vessel.

جام جم jām-ĕ jam, *n.m.* The mirror of Jamshid, in which he saw whatever he wished to see.

جام جہاں نما jam-ĕ jahāṅ numā, *n.m.* A pharos; a lighthouse; (See also جام جم jām-ĕ jam).

جام چڑھانا jām chaṛhānā, *v.* To drink off cup of wine.

جام صحت پینا jam-ĕ ṣiḥḥat pīnā, *v.* To drink to the health of; to drink a toast in a person's honour.

جامد jāmid (A) *adj.* Styptic; incapable of growth or increase; astringent, that stops bleeding; not derived (Gram.).

اسم جامد ism-ĕ jāmid (A) *n.m.* Primitive or concrete noun (not derived from any root and from which no word is derived).

جامدانی jāmdānī, *n.f.* Cloth in which flowers are woven (generally muslin); a portmanteau; kind of leather basket

جامع jāmi' (A) *adj.* Collective; completing; comprehensive. *n.f.* A great mosque.

جامع الکمالات jāmi'-ul-kamālāt, *adj.* Most learned; skilled in all sciences.

جامع مسجد jāmi' masjid, *n.f.* The principal mosque, where the people assemble for prayers, especially on Fridays.

جامعہ jami'ah (A) *n.m.* University; community; society.

جامن jāman (H) *n.f.* Sour milk used to curdle fresh milk; rennet; coagulator; a ferment; a tree and its fruit.

جامنی *jāmanī* (H) *adj.* Of mauve colour.

جامہ *jāmah* (P) *n.m.* A garment; robe; gown; vest

جامہ‌تلاشی *jāmah talāshi*, *n.f.* Searching the person; searching a persons clothes.

جامہ دانی *jāmah dāni*. See جامدانی *jāmdānī*.

جامے سے باہر ہونا *jāme se bāhir honā*, *v.* To be unable to restrain or control oneself; to be in an ungovernable rage.

جان *jān* (P) *n.f.* Life; soul; spirit; mind; energy; vigour; animation; the essence of a thing; a sweetheart; dear; beloved.

جان آنا *jān ānā*, *v.* To be refreshed; to regain strength; to be animated.

جان آفرین *jān āfrīṅ*, *n.m.* Creator of life; animator; God.

جان باز *jān bāz*, *adj.* Venturesome; spirited; daring; intrepid.

جان بچانا *jān bachānā*, *v.* To save one's skin; to shirk.

جان بحق تسلیم ہونا *jān baḥaqq taslīm honā*, *v.* To surrender one's soul to God; to die, to expire.

جان بخشی *jān bakhshi*, *n.f.* Sparing life; pardon; forgiveness; granting of life.

جانبر ہونا *jānbar honā*, *v.* To survive; to outlive.

جان بلب *jān balab*, *ādj.* Dying; at the point of death.

جان بھاری ہونا *jān bhārī honā*, *v.* To be weary of life.

جان پر بننا *jān par bannā*, *v.* To be in danger of one's life.

جان پر کھیلنا *jān par khelnā*, *v.* To risk one's life; to run the hazard; to endanger one's life.

جان پڑنا *jān paṛnā*, *v.* To revive; to be refreshed.

جان تصدق کرنا *jān taṣadduq karnā*, *v.* To sacrifice one's life.

جان توڑ کر لڑنا *jān toṛ kar laṛnā*, *v.* To fight desperately.

جان جوکھوں *jān jokhoṅ*, *n.f.* Risk of life.

جان چرانا *jān churānā*, *v.* To shirk one's duty; to shrink from.

جان چھڑانا *jān chhuṛānā*, *v.* To get rid of; to escape.

جان چھڑکنا *jān chhiṛaknā*, *v.* To strain every nerve; to go to the extent of endangering one's life for another; to work wholeheartedly.

جان دار *jān dār*, *adj.* & *n.* Having life; active; powerful; spirited; an animal.

جان دینا *jān denā*, *v.* To die; to sacrifice oneself; to die for.

جان سپار *jān sipār*, *adj.* Resigning one's life into the hands of another (an apithet of a lover).

جان ستاں *jān sitāṅ*, *adj.* Destroying life; taking life; killing.

جان سوختہ *jān sokhtah*, *adj.* Having the soul inflamed; in very great trouble.

جان سوز *jān soz*, *adj.* Heart-inflaming; soul-tormenting.

جان سے جانا *jān se jānā*, *v.* To die.

جان سے مارنا *jān se mārnā*, *v.* To kill; to take one's life.

جان سے ہاتھ دھونا *jān se hāth dhonā*, *v.* To despair of life; to have no hope of life; to be tired of life.

جان فزا *jān fazā*, *adj.* Life-increasing; animating.

جان فشاں *jān fishāṅ*, *adj.* Ready to sacrifice one's life for another; zealous; fervent.

جانفشانی *jān fishānī*, *n.f.* Extreme diligence; devotion to duty.

جان کا لاگو ہونا *jān kā lāgū honā*, *v.* To pursue one to death.

جان لیوا *jān levā*, *adj.* Deadly; fatal.

جان کاہ *jān kāh*, *adj.* Soul-exhausting; heart-breaking; pathetic; afflicting.

جان کسی پر دینا *jān kisī par denā*, *v.* To be excessively in love.

جان کندنی ، کنی *jān kandanī, kanī*, *n.f.* Agonies of death; agony; torture.

جان کو رونا *jān ko ronā*, *n.* Wishing to be dead.

جان کھانا ، مارنا *jān khānā, mārnā*, *v.* To annoy; to vex; to exhaust one's patience; to oppress; to perplex; to plague.

جان کی امان *jān kī amān*, *n.f.* Life's safety; pardon; quarter.

جان کے برابر رکھنا *jān ke barābar rakhnā*, *v.* To regard one like dear life.

جان کے لالے پڑنا *jān ke lāle paṛnā*, *v*, To have no hope of life; to be on the point of death.

جانگداز *jān gudāz*, *adj.* Life-consuming; baneful; parnicious.

جان لینا *jān lenā*, *v.* To kill; to deprive one of life.

جان میں جان آنا *jān meṅ jān ānā*, *v.* To be revived; to be comforted; to be satisfied.

جان نثار *jān niṣār*, *adj.* Devoted; sacrificing one's life.

جان نثاری *jān niṣārī*, *n.f.* Devotedness.

بے جان *be jān*, *adj.* Lifeless; extremely weak; dead.

جان *jān* (H) *n.f.* Knowledge; apprehension; awareness.

جان بوجھ کے *jān būjh ke*, *adv.* Wilfully; purposely; knowingly.

جان پہچان *jān pehchān*, *n.f.* Acquaintance.

جان کر انجان بننا *jān kar anjān bannā*, *v.* To pretend ignorance.

جان لینا *jān lenā*, *v.* To apprehend; to perceive.

جانا *jānā* (H) *v.* To go; to depart; to pass; to set out; to disappear; to fall off; to wither.

جانے دو *jāne do*, *imper.* Let it go; never mind.

جانے دینا *jāne denā*, *v.* To let go; to set free; to pardon.

جاناں *jānāṅ* (P) *n.m.* Lives; souls; a beloved one; a sweetheart.

جانب *jānib* (P) *n.f.* Side; direction. *adv.* Towards.

این جانب *iṅ jānib*, *n.m.* This side; this person; the speaker; the writer (of a letter).

جانبدار *jānib dār*, *adj.* Partial; biased. *n.m.* A supporter; a partisan.

جانبداری *jānib dārī*, *n.f.* Supporting; seconding; partiality.

جانبین *jānibain*, *n.m.* Both sides or parties. *adj.* Mutual.

جانبین سے *jānibain se*, *adv.* Mutually; reciprocally; from both sides.

جانچ *jāṅch* (H) *n.m.* Test; trial; examination; assay; proof; verification; appraisement.

جانچنا *jāṅchnā* (H) *v.* To examine; to test; to try; to prove; to enquire into; to assay; to gauge.

جانگلو *jāṅglū* (H) *adj.* Wild; not domesticated.

جانگھیا *jāṅglyā* (H) *n.m.* A kind of short-drawers reaching half-way down the thighs; wrestlers breeches.

جاننا *jānnā* (H) *v.* To know; to understand; to recognise; to become aware of; to apprehend; to judge; to deem; to think; to believe; to conceive; to fancy.

جانور *jānwar* (P) *n.m.* Possessing life; an animal; a bird; a foul; blockhead; stupid.

جانی *jānī* (P) *adj.* Of or relating to life; of the heart or soul; cordial; hearty; *n.m.* A beloved; a friend; a lover.

جانی دشمن *jānī dushman*, *n.m.* A mortal enemy; a sanguine or blood-thirsty foe.

جاوتری *jāwatrī* (H) *n.f.* Mace; the bark of the nutmeg.

جاوداں jāwidān (P) adj. Eternal; everlasting; perpetual.

جاودانی jāwidāni, n.f. Eternity.

جاوید jāwid, adj. Always; eternal; undying.

جاہ jāh (P) n.f. Dignity; grandeur; high rank.

جاہ و جلال jāh-ŏ jalāl, n.m. Rank and grandeur; dignity; splendour; magnificence; pomp.

جاہ و حشم jāh-ŏ ḥasham, n.m. Rank and dignity.

جاہ و منصب jāh-ŏ manṣab, n.m. Rank and position.

جاہل jāhil (A) adj. Ignorant; illiterate; rude; uncivilised; barbarous; brutal; unmannered.

جائداد jā'edād (P) n.f. Property; estate; assets.

جائداد آبائی jā'edād-ĕ ābāi, n.f. Ancestral property or estate.

جائداد اجمالی jā'edād-ĕ ijmāli, n.f. Joint property or estate.

جائداد استمراری jā'edād-ĕ istimrāri, n.f. Assignment of land in perpetuity.

جائداد خاص jā'edād-ĕ khāṣ, n.m. One's personal property.

جائداد ارضی jā'edād-ĕ ārẓi, n.f. Landed property.

جائداد غیر مقبوضہ jā'edād-ĕ ghair maqbūẓah, n.f. Property not in possession.

جائدادغیر منقولہ jā'edād ghair manqūlah, n.f. Immovable property.

جائداد قرق کرنا jā'edād qurq karnā, v. To take possession of property in execution.

جائداد متروکہ jā'edād-ĕ matrūkah, n.f. Abandoned property.

جائداد متنازعہ jā'edād-ĕ mutnāzi'ah, n.f. Property in suit or under litigation; property in dispute; disputed property.

جائدادمرہونہ jā'edād-ĕ morhūnah, n.f. Mortgaged property.

جائداد مشترکہ jā'edād-ĕ mushtarikah, n.f. Joint property; property held jointly.

جائداد معافی jā'edād-ĕ muā'fi, n.f. Rent-free property; rent-free grant.

جائداد معافی دوام jā'edād mu'āfi-ĕ dawām, Permanent land grant.

جائداد مقروقہ jā'edād-ĕ maqrūqah, n.f. Attached or mortgaged property.

جائدادمکسوبہ jā'edād-ĕ maksūbah, n.f. Self-acquired property.

جائدادمکفولہ jā'edād-ĕ makfūlah, n.f. Hypothecated property.

جائداد منقولہ jā'edād-ĕ manqūlah, n.f. Movable property.

جائداد موروثی jā'edād-ĕ mourūṣi, n.f. Ancestral or inherited estate.

جائز jā'iz, (H) adj. Lawful; legal; permitted; right; proper; warrantable; authorised; allowable; admissible; just; granted.

جائز رکھنا jā'iz rakhnā,. v. To receive as right; to allow; to admit; to justify; to tolerate; to legalise.

جائز قرار دینا jā'iz qarār denā, v. To legalise; to uphold.

ناجائز nājā'iz, adj. Unlawful; illegal; inadmissible; wrong; unjust.

ناجائز طور سے nājā'iz ṯaur se, adv. Illegally; unlawfully.

جائزہ jāi'zah (A) n.m. Examination; review; checking; a mark made in checking an account; survey.

جایزہ لینا jā'izah lenā, v. To check an account; to survey; to examine.

جائفل jā'efal (A) See جائے پھل jā'e phal.

جائے jāi'e (P) n.m. Place; room; spot.

جائے اعتراض jā'e e'tirāẓ, n.m. Room for objection; the time or place of opposition.

جائے پناہ jā'e panāh, n.f. An asylum; place of refuge.

جائے ضرور *jā'e zarūr*, See جا ضرور *jā zarūr*.

جائے پھل *jā'e phal* (H) *n.m.* Nutmeg.

جب *jab* (H) *adv.* At the time; when; as soon as; since; in case.

جب تک *jab tak, adv.* By that time; until; as long as; whilst.

جب سے *jab se, adv.* Since.

جب کبھی *jab kabhī, adv.* Whenever.

جبھی *jabhī* (H) *adv.* At that very time; therefore.

جبھی تو *jabhi to, adv.* Hence; on that account; therefore.

جبار *jabbār* (A) *adj.* Omnipotent; mighty; *n.m.* One of the attributive names of God.

جبر *jabr* (A) *n.m.* Compulsion; coercion; force; power; extortion; outrage; imposition; reduction of fractions to integrals.

جبر کرنا *jabr karnā, v.* To oppress; to compel; to use force.

جبر و تعدی *jabr-ŏ-ta'adi, n.m.* Violence and oppression.

جبر و مقابلہ *jarb-ŏ-muqābalah, n.m.* Algebra.

جبراً *jabran̲* (A) *adv.* Forcibly; by force; violently.

جبراً و قہراً *jabran̲-ŏ-qahran̲, adv.* By force and violence; willingly or unwillingly.

جبرائیل یا جبریل *jibrāil yā jibrīl* (A) *n.m.* Archangel; Gabriel.

جبروت *jabrūt* (A) *n.f.* Omnipotence; the world or sphere of omnipotence; heaven.

جبری *jabri, adj.* Forced; compulsory; conscriptional.

جبری بھرتی *jabri bharti, n.f.* Conscription.

جبڑا *jabṛā* (H) *n.m.* The jaw; the part of the face from the corners of the mouth to the jaws.

جبلت *jabillat* (A) *n.f.* Nature; natural disposition; temperament; essence; creation; form.

جبلی *jibillī* (A) *adj.* Inherited; natural; constitutional; innate; essential.

جبہ *jubbah* (A) *n.m.* A robe or gown; a long coat; a coat of mail.

جبہ *jabah* (A) *n.m.* The forehead.

جبہ سا *jabah sā, adj.* Rubbing one's forehead on the ground beseeching and begging earnestly.

جبہ سائی *jubahsāi, n.f.* The act of rubbing the forehead on the ground; beseeching earnestly.

جبیں *jabiṅ* (P) *n.f.* The forehead.

جپ *jap* (S) *n.m.* Muttering of prayers and counting the beads of a rosary.

جپ جی *jap ji, n.f.* A sacred book of Sikhs.

جپنا *japnā* (H) *v.* To count one's beads; to repeat the name of God silently.

جتانا ، جتلانا *jatānā, jatlānā* (H) *v.* To cause to be known; to point out; to warn; to caution; to show; to enjoin to apprize; to admonish; to declare; to instruct.

جتانا ، جتوانا *jitānā, jitwānā* (H) *v.* To cause to win or conquer.

جتاؤ *jutāu* (H) *adj.* Arable; culturable.

جتائی *jutāi* (H) *n.f.* The act of ploughing the field; tillage.

جتن *jatan* (H) *n.m.* Effort; endeavour; striving; exertion; diligence; perseverance.

جتنا *jutnā* (H) *v.* To be ploughed; to labour; to toil.

جتنا ، جتنی *jitnā, jitni, adv.* As much as; so much; as much; as many.

جتنا گڑ ڈالو گے اتنا ہی میٹھا ہوگا *jitnā guṛ ḍāloge utnā hi mīṭhā hogā, prov.* The deeper the well the warmer the water; the more the sweat the greater the reward.

جتنی چادر دیکھو اتنے ہی پاؤں پھیلاؤ *jitnī chādar dekho utne hī pāoṅ phailāo, prov.* Cut your coat according to your cloth; stretch not your feet beyond your sheet.

جتنی دیگ اتنی ہی کھرچن *jitnī deg utnī hī khurchan, prov.* Spend less get less; the more you venture the more you win.

جتنی دولت اتنی مصیبت *jitnī daulat utnī muṣībat, prov.* More the money more the worry.

جتوانا *jutwānā* (H) *v.* To cause to join or yoke; to have a field ploughed or tilled; to cause to plough.

جتھا *jathā* (H) *n.m.* A company; a band; a gang; a party; mob; multitude; flock; strength.

جتیانا *jutīānā* (H) *v.* To beat with a shoe.

جٹ *juṭ* (H) *n.f.* A pair; like; the second; equal.

جٹا *jaṭā* (H) *n.f.* Matted hair.

جٹا دھاری *jaṭā dhārī, n.m.* One who has matted hair; a mendicant wearing matted hair; the cockscomb flower; amaranth.

جٹنا *juṭnā* (H) *v.* To unite closely together; to combine; to congeal; to work; to labour.

جٹھانی *jiṭhānī* (H) *n.f.* Wife of the elder brother of the husband.

جثہ *juṣṣah* (A) *n.m.* Figure of human body; corporeal figure; body.

ججمان *jajmān or jijmān* (H) *n.m.* A person who assists in the performance of sacrifice, employs priests for the purpose and pays the expenses of it; a person who has right to certain services (as those of the *brahmans*, barbers and some others).

جچا *jachā* (H) *adj.* Tested; tried; proved.

جچا تلا *jachā tūla, adj.* Weighed and measured; correct in all respect.

جچنا *jachnā* (H) *v.* To be estimated; to be appraised.

جد *jadd* (A) *n.m.* A grandfather; ancestor; good fortune; happiness; prosperity dignity; glory (of God).

جد *jidd* (A) *n. f.* Labour; toil; exertion; trial; endeavour.

جد وجہد *jidḍ-ŏ jahd jahd or juhd, n.f.* Effort; hard Labour; toil; exertion.

جد و جہد کرنا *jidd-ŏ jahd karnā, v.* To endeavour; to strive; to labour.

جدا *judā* (P) *adj.* Separate; distinct; away; apart; aside; asunder; peculiar; extra-ordinary.

جدا جدا *judā judā, adv.* Separately; one by one; severally; distinctly.

جدا کرنا *judā karnā, v.* To disjoin; to part; to disunite; to detach; to disengage; to distinguish.

جداگانہ *judā gānah, adv.* Separately; apart.

جدا ہونا *judā honā, v.* To be separated.

جدال *jidāl* (A) *n.m.* Altercations; contest; dispute.

جدال و قتال *jidāl-ŏ qitāl, n.m.* Fighting; contention; contest; affray; battle.

جدائی *judāī* (P) *n.f.* Separation; absence.

جدت *jiddaṭ* (A) *n.m.* Innovation; newness; originality.

جدل *jadal* (A) *n.m.* Fighting; battle; encounter; altercation; contention.

جدوار *jadwār* (A) *n.m.* Zedoary; a kind of aromatic ginger-like substance used in medicine.

جدول *jadwal* (A) *n.f.* Marginal lines; a table (of a book); an astronomical table; a rivulet; schedule.

جدول بندی *jadwal bandī, n.f.* Tabulation.

جدولی *jadwalī, adj.* Marked with lines.

جدولی پیمانہ *jadwalī paimānah, n.m.* Scheduled scale.

جده *jaddah* (A) *n.f.* Grand mother; a seaport of Arabia where pilgrims, travelling by sea to Mecca, land.

جدھر *jidhar* (H) *adv.* Where; wherever; whither; there.

جدھر رب اُدھر سب *jidhar rab udhar sab, prov.* He who has God on his side has everything.

جدی *jaddi* (H) *adj.* Ancestral.

جدی *jadi* (A) *n.m.* A sign of the zodiac; a kid; a he-goat; the sign of Capricorn; the polar star.

خط جدی *khatt-ĕ jadi, n.m.* The tropic of Capricorn.

جدید *jadid* (A) *adj.* New; modern; fresh.

جذام *juzām* (A) *n.m.* Leprosy.

جذام خانہ *juzām khānah, n.m.* A lazaretto; a hospital for lepers.

جذامی *juzāmi* (P) *n.m.* Leperous; a leper.

جذامیت *juzāmiyat, n.f.* Leprosity.

جذب *jazb* (A) *n.m.* Absorption; drawing; allurement; attraction;

جذب کرنا *jazb karnā, v.* To attract; to absorb; to imbibe; to draw.

جذب ہونا *jazb honā, v.* To be absorbed; to be soaked.

جذب مقناطیسی *jazb-ĕ miqnātisi, n.m.* Magnetic attraction.

جذبہ *jazbah* (A) *n.m.* Passion; rage; fury; violent desire; feeling.

جذر *jazr* (A) *n.m.* The square root; origin; root.

جذر المال *jazr-ul māl, n.m.* The fourth root.

جر *jarr* (A) *n.m.* Drawing; dragging; base; foundation; foot of a mountain; the vowel *kasrah* at the end of a word.

حرف جر٬ جار *harf-ĕ jarr, yā jār, n.m.* A preposition.

جرثقیل *jarr-ĕ saqil n.m.* Mechanics (the science); a difficult task.

جراب *jurrāb, n.m.* Sock; stocking; leggings; hose.

جرأت *jur'at* (A) *n.f* Courage; boldness; daring; valour; audacity; bravery; temerity.

جرأت کرنا *jur'at karnā, v.* To dare; to have the audacity or courage to presume.

جراثیم *jarāsim* (A) *n.m.* (*plu.* of جرثومہ *jarsūmah*) Bacteria.

جراح *jarrāh* (A) *n.m.* A surgeon.

جراحی ٬ جراحیت *jarrāhi, jarrāhiyat* (A) *n.f.* Surgery.

عمل جراحی *'amal-ĕ jarrāhi, n.m.* Surgical operation.

حلقہ جراحیت *hc ɪah-ĕ jarrāhiyat, n.m.* Surgical ward.

جرار *jarrār* (A) *c. l.* Warlike; brave; mighty; numerous.

جرائد *jarrā'id* (A) *n.m.* (*plu.* of جریدہ *jaridah*); Newspapers; journals.

جرائم *jarā'im* (A) *n.m.* (*plu.* of جریمہ *jarimah*) Faults; crimes; sins.

جرائم خلاف وضع فطری *jarāim khilāf-ĕ waza'-ĕ fitri, n.m.* Unnatural offences.

جرائم خفیفہ *jarā'im-ĕ khafifah, n.m.* Petty offences.

جرائم سنگین *jarā'im-ĕ sangin, n.m.* Serious crimes; felony.

جرائم مقابلۂ سرکار *jarā'im muqābilah-ĕ sarkār, n.m.* Offences against the State.

رجسٹرجرائم *rajister jarā'im, n.m.* Crime register.

جرثومہ *jarsūmah* (A) *n.m.* Bacterium.

جرثومیاتی *jarsumiyāti, adj.* Bacteriological.

جرثومہ دان *jarsumah dan, n.* Bacteriologist.

جرثومیات *jarsūmiyāt* (A) *n.m.* Bacteriology.

جرح *jarah* (A) *n.m.* Wound; Sore; scar; objection; rebutting evidence; cross-examination.

جرح کرنا *jaraḥ karnā*, v. To cross examine (a witness).

جرس *jaras* (A) *n.m.* A bell.

جرعہ *jur'ah* (A) *n.* One draught; a drop; gulp; sip.

جرعہ کش *jur'ah kash*, *n.* A drinker.

جرگہ *jargah* (P) *n.m.* Forming a circle; putting men and animals in a rank or row; a flock or drove of deer &c.; ring of men or beasts; jury; a bench of judges.

جرم *jirm* (A) *n.m.* The body of an A hing, animals or inanimate; a crack.

جرم *jurm* (A) *n.m.* A crime; fault; transgression; offence; a criminal act; guilt.

اثبات جرم *iṣbāt-ĕ jurm*, *n.m* Proved guilt.

ارتکاب جرم *irtikāb-ĕ jurm*, *n.m.* Commitment of an offence.

اقبال جرم *iqbāl-ĕ jurm*, *n.m.* Confession of guilt.

اقدام جرم *iqdām-ĕ jurm*, *n.m.* Attempt to commit an offence.

بے جرم *be-jurm*, *adj.* Innocent; guiltless.

ثبوت جرم *ṣubūt-ĕ jurm*, *n.m.* Proof of guilt.

جرم خفیف *jurm-ĕ khafīf*, *n.m.* Minor or petty offence.

جرم سے منکر ہونا *jurm se munkir honā*, *v.* To plead not guilty.

جرم شدید *jurm-ĕ shadid*, *n.m.* A grievous a offence.

جرم عظیم *jurm-ĕ 'azim*, *n.m.* Capital crime; great offence.

جرم قابل دست اندازی *jurm qābil-ĕ dast andāzi*, *n.m.* Cognisable offence.

جرم قابل ضمانت *jurm qābil-ĕ zamānat*, *n.m.* Bailable offence.

جرم کا مرتکب ہونا *jurm kā murtakib honā*, *v.* To commit an offence.

جرم واجب القتل *jurm wājib-ul-qatl*, *n.m.* Offence punishable with death.

جرمانہ *jurmānah* (P) *n.m.* Fine; penalty.

جرمانہ دینا *jurmānah denā*, *v.* To pay a fine; to pay a penalty.

جرمانہ کرنا *jurmānah karnā*, *v.* To fine.

جرمیات *jurmiyat*, *n.m.* Criminology.

جری *jari* (A) *adj.* Valiant; brave; intrepid; bold.

جری *juri* (H) *n.m.* Rinderpest; a malignant and contagious disease of cattle.

جریان *jaryān* (A) *n.m.* Running; flowing; flux (of blood, urine &c.); circulation; flow; fleet; gonorrhoea; spermatorrhoea.

جریب *jarib* (G) *n.f.* A sort of wooden dart with an iron point; a land measure of 60 yards; a corn measure; a chain; a stick.

جریب کرنا یا ڈالنا *jarib karnā yā ḍālnā*, *v.* To make a measure of land by chain; to measure

جریب کش *jarib kash* *n.m.* A land surveyor; a measurer.

جریب کشی *jarib kashi*, *n.f.* Measurement of land.

جریدہ *jaridah* (A) *adj.* Alone; separate; solitary; unattended (when travelling); unincumbered. *n.m.* Newspaper; gazette.

جڑ *jaṛ* (H) *n.f.* Root; origin; foundation; basis.

جڑ اکھاڑنا *jaṛ ukhāṛnā*, *v.* To root out; to uproot, to exterpate.

جڑ پکڑنا *jaṛ pakaṛnā*, *v.* To take root; to be firmly rooted.

جڑ کاٹنا *jaṛ kāṭnā*, *v.* To lay the axe at the root; to cut the root of; to destroy utterly; to destory root and branch.

جڑانا *jaṛānā* (H) *v.* To cause to be set with jewels; to have jewels studded.

جڑاؤ *jaṛāū* (H) *adj.* Studded; set with stones.

جڑائی *jaṛāi* (H) *n.f.* Price paid for setting jewels; the act of setting jewels.

جڑائی *juṛāi* (H) *n.f.* Mending; the price for mending.

جڑنا jurṇā (H) v. To strike; to lay on (a blow); to stick on; to stud; to fix; to set jewels.

جڑنا jurṇā (H) v. To be joined; to join; to unite; to come to hand; to be had; to be obtained.

جڑواں jurwāṅ (H) n.m. The twins; a pair.

جڑوانا jurwānā (H) v. To cause to join; to cause to unite; to get a thing mended.

جڑوانا jarwānā. See جڑانا jarānā.

جڑی jaṛi (H) n.f. The root of a medicinal herb.

جڑی بوٹی jaṛi būṭi. n.f. Medicinal herbs; drugs.

جڑیا jaryā (H) n.m. A jeweller; setter of jewels.

جز juz (P) adv. Besides; except.

جز ' جزو juz, juzw (A) n.m. Part; ingredient; portion; a full sheet of paper; folder; a part of a book consisting of eight leaves; part of a verse.

جزو بدن ہونا juzw-ĕ badan honā, v. To become part of the body; to be digested or assimilated.

جز بندی juz bandi, n.f. Binding of a book.

جز دان juz dān, n.m. A cloth in which books are wrapped up; a satchel; a portfolio.

جز رس juz ras, adj. Penetrating; sagacious; frugal; economical.

جز رسی juz rasi, n.f. Frugality; economy.

جز ضربی juz-ĕ ẓarbī, n.m. Factors.

جز وقتی ملازمت juz waqtī mulāzimat, n.f. Part time service.

جز و کل juz-ŏ kull, adv. Totally; entirely; from top to bottom. adj. The whole.

جز و لا یتجزیٰ juzw-ĕ lā-yatajazzā, n.m. Individable atom; any thing too small to be divided.

جزولا ینفک juzw-ĕ lā yanfak, n.m. Inseparable part.

جزوی ' جزئی juzwi juz'i, (A) adj. Petty; trivial; in part; a little.

جزویات ' جزیات juzwiyāt, juziāt (A) n.f. Particulars; small parts; details.

جزا jazā (A) n.f. Retaliation; compensation; requital; return; reward; retribution.

جزاک اللہ jazākallah, excl. May God reward thee! God bless you!

جزائر jazā'ir (A) n.m. (plu. of جزیرہ jazirah) Islands.

جزبز jiz biz (P) adj. Offended; displeased; angry.

جزبز ہونا jiz biz honā, v. To be offended; to be displeased.

جزر jazr (A) n.m. The ebb tide; the reflux of the sea.

جزر و مد jazr-ŏ madd, n.m. The ebb and flow of the sea.

جزع jaza' (A) n,f. Impatience; perplexity.

جزع و فزع jaza'-ŏ faza', n.f. Bewailing; crying; weeping bitterly.

جزم jazm (A) n.m. Decision; determination; the orthographical character (jazm) placed over a letter to show that it is quiescent or has no vowel following it.

عزم بالجزم 'azm-bil-jazm, n.m. Firm resolve; settled purpose.

جزیرہ jazirah (A) n.m. An island.

جزیرہ نما jazirah numā, n.m. A peninsula.

جزیہ jiziyah (A) n.m. A tribute; capitation-tax; a poll-tax.

جس jis (H) pron. Whom; what; who; which; that; anyone.

جس پر jis par, adv. Whereupon.

جس پر بھی jis par bhi, adv. Notwithstanding.

جس جس jis jis, adv. Whichever; each of which.

جس جگہ jis jagah, adv. Where; wherever.

جس دم jis dam, adv. While; when; whilst.

جس طرح jis ṭarah, adv. According to; as.

جس طرف jia ṭaraf, adv. Wherever.

جس قدر jis qadr, adv. As much as; to what degree or extent.

جس کا (کی) jis kā (ki), adv. Whose; of whom.

جس کسی کا jis kisi kā, adv. Of whomsoever.

جس کسی کو jis kisi ko, adv. To whomsoever.

جس وقت jis waqt, adv. When; whenever.

جس کا کام اسی کو ساجے jis kā kām usī ko sāje, adv. Everyman to his trade.

جسکا کھائے اسکا گائے jis kā khāe us kā gāe, prov. Everyman piaises the bridge he passes over.

جسکے ھاتھ ڈوئی اسکا سب کوئی jis ke hāth ḍoi us kā sab koī, prov. Everyman is a friend to him who gives generously.

جس کی لاٹھی اس کی بھینس jis ki lāṭhī us ki bhaiṅs, prov. Might is right.

جسے پیا چاھے وھی سھاگن jise piyā chāhe wohī suhāgan, prov. Fancy passes beauty.

جسارت jasārat (A) n.f. Boldness; courage; presumption; Intrepidity; temerity.

جسامت jasāmat (A) n.f. Corpulency; bulkiness; dimensions.

جست jast (P) n.f. A leap; jump; bound; spring; leaping; jumping.

جست بھرنا ' کرنا ' مارنا jast bharnā, karnā, mārnā, v. To jump; to leap; to bound; to spring.

جست jist (H) n.m. Zinc; pewter.

جستجو justjū (P) n.f. Search; investigation; quest; inquiry; seeking; scrutiny; examination.

جستہ جستہ jastah jastah, adv. From here and there, little by little.

جسد jasad (A) n.m. The body.

جسم jism (A) n.m. Body; material substance.

جسم جمادی jism-ĕ jamādi, n.m. A metallic body.

جسم حیوانی jis m-ĕ haiwānī, n.m. Animal body.

جسم نباتی jism-ĕ nabātī, n.m. Vegetable body.

جسمانی ' جسمی jismāni, jismi (A) adj. Carporeal; material; carnal; physical.

جسمانی صحت jismāni sehhat, n.f. Physical fitness.

جسمانی ورزش jismānī warzish, n.f. Physical exercise.

جسمانیت ' جسمیت jismāniyat, jismiyat, n.f. Materiality.

جسیم jasim (A) adj. Corpulent; bulky.

جشن jashn (P) n.m. A jublee; a feast; rejoicings; festivity.

جشن منانا jashn manānā, v. To celebrate a festival.

جعل ja'l (A) n.f. Forgery; counterfeit.

جعل ساز ja'l sāz, n.m. A fabricator; a forgerer.

جعل سازی ja'l sāzī, n.m. Forgery.

جعلی ja'li (A) adj. Counterfeit; forged; not genuine.

جعلی دستاویز ja'li dastāwez, n.f. A forged document.

جعلی سکے ja'li sikke, n.f. Counterfeit coins.

جغرافیہ jughrāfiyah (G) n.m. Geography.

جغرافیائی jughrāfiyāi, adj. Geographical.

جفا jafā (P) n.f. Oppression; violence; injury; injustice.

جفا پیشہ ' جفا جو ' جفا شعار ' جفا کار ' جفا کیش ' جفا گستر jafā peshah, jafā jū, jafā shi'ār, jafā kār, jafā kesh, jafā gustar, adj. Oppressive; unjust; cruel. n.m. Oppressor; tyrant.

جفا کاری jafā kārī, n.f. Oppression; tyranny.

جفا کش jafā kash, adj. Hardworking; energetic.

جفا کفا jafā kafā, n.m. Hardship; trial; calamity.

جفت juft (P) n.m. Evenness; pair; a couple; match; mate.

جفته juftah (P) n.m. Running together (the threads in cloth); a crease; a wrinkle; the buttocks. adj. Bent; wrickled.

جفتی jufti (P) n.f. Pairing (of animals).

جفتی کھانا juftī khānā, v. To capulate; to pair (as animals); to go with; to join.

جفر jafar yā jafr (P) n.m. The art of making amulets or charms; the art of prediction.

جکڑ بند jakaṛ band (H) n.f. Tightness; fast binding. adj. Tight; fast bound; well strung.

جکڑ جانا jakaṛ jānā (H) v. To become stiff or rigid; to be tightly bound; to be closely joined together.

جکڑنا jakaṛnā (H) v. To tighten; to draw tight; to bind; to fasten; to tie; to pinion; to become rigid.

جگ jag (H) n.m. The world; the earth; the universe; a feast; a sacrifice or religious ceremony in which oblations are presented.

جگ بیتی jag biti, n.f. Concerning other people; tales or deeds of other people.

جگ ہنسائی jag hansā'ī, n.f. Public ridicule.

جگ jug (H) n.m. An age of the world; a period; an age; an epoch.

جگ جگ jug jug, adv. Always; for ever; eternally; constantly.

جگادری jugādri (H) n.m. A seasoned and experienced person. adj. Tall; corpulent.

جگالی jugālī (H) n.f. Chewing the cud; the cud.

جگالی کرنا jugālī karnā, v. To chew the cud; to ruminate.

جگانا jagānā (H) v. To waken; to rouse from sleep.

جگت jagat (S) n.m. The world; all created things. n.f. The rim of a well.

جگت استاد یا گرو jagat ustād yā gurū, n.m. A renowned teacher.

جگت سالا jagat sālā, n.m. Brother of a prostitute; a mean-fellow.

جگت jugat (H) n.f. Dexterity; contrivance; punning; counsel; address; wit; a pun; a humour; art; a significant expression.

جگت باز jugat bāz, n. Punster; quibbler; skilful; dexterous.

جگت بازی jugat bāzī, n.f. Quibble; pun; witicism.

جگت بولنا jugat bolnā, v. To pun.

جگتی یا جگتیا jugtī yā jugtiyā (H) adj. Artful; clever; cunning; punning; facetious.

جگر jigar (P) n.m. The liver; vitals; heart; mind; soul; courage.

جگر خراش jigar kharāsh, adj. Heart-rending.

جگر دوز jigar doz, adj. Heart piercing; pathetic.

جگر سوختہ jigar sokhtah, adj. Heart inflamed; in love.

جگر سوز jigar soz, adj. Most troublesome; tormenting.

جگر نگار jigar figār, adj. Heart broken; heart wounded.

جگر کاوی jigar kāwī, n.f. Anxiety; trouble of mind; hard labour.

جگر گوشہ jigar goshah, n.m. Lobe of the liver; one dear or beloved; a son.

جگرا jigrā (H) n.m. Courage; daring; valour.

جگری jigrī (P) adj. Belonging to the liver; hepatic; intimate; dear; beloved; close (friend).

جگمگ جگمگ jagmag jagmag (H) adj. Shining; glittering; radiative.

جگمگانا *jagmagānā* (H) *v.* To shine; to glitter; to dazzle.

جگمگاهٹ *jagmagahat* (H) *n.f.* Glitter; splendour; dazzle.

جگنو *jugnū* (H) *n.f.* A glow-worm; a fire-fly

جگنی *jugnī* (H) *n.f.* An ornament worn round the neck.

جگہ *jagah* (H) *n.f.* Place; quarter; room; vacancy; post; fit; occasion.

جگہ جگہ *jagah jagah, adv.* Everywhere.

جگہ دینا *jagah denā, v.* To make room for.

جل *jul* (H) *n.m.* Deceit; cheating; trick.

جل باز *jul bāz, n.* A knave; a cheat.

جل دینا *jul denā, v.* To cheat.

جل کھیلنا *jul khelnā, v.* To circumvent; to practice deceit or trickery

جل میں آنا *jul meṅ ānā, v.* To be cheated or tricked; to fall into the trick (of).

جل *jull* (A) *n.f.* A housing or covering for an animal; a cloth for covering a horse; a horse cloth.

جل *jal* (H) *n.m.* Water.

جل پان *jal pān, n.m.* Any light repast; a luncheon.

جل پری *jal parī, n.f.* A mermaid.

جل ترنگ *jal tarang, n.m.* Musical glasses or harmonicon; brass cups or china bowls partly filled with water, the edges of which when beaten with stick produce harmonical notes.

جل ترئی *jal tura'i, n.f.* Fish.

جل تھل *jal thal, n.m.* Land and water.

جل تھل ایک ہونا *jal thal ek honā, v.* To rain in great abundance.

جل مانس *jal mānus, n.m.* A merman.

جلّ *jalla* (A) *adj.* Glorious; great, eminent.

جلّ شانہٗ یا جلالہٗ *jalla yā shanohū, jalālohū, phr.* Eminent is God's glory.

جل اٹھنا *jal uṭhanā* (H) *v.* To blaze up; to break out (fire).

جل مرنا *jal marnā* (H) *v.* To be burnt to death; to die out of envy.

جلا - جلی - جلے *jalā, jalī, jale* (H) *adj.* Burnt.

جلا بھنا *jalā bhuṇā, adj.* Scorched; enraged; irascible; wounded.

جلے پر نون چھڑکنا *jale par nūn chhiṛaknā, v.* To apply salt to a wounded part; to add insult to injury; to exult over one in trouble.

جلے تن *jale tan, adj.* Bad tempered; jealous.

جلی کٹی سنانا *jalī katī sunānā, v.* To say things bitter and stinging.

جلا *jilā* (A) *n.f.* Brightness; splendour; polishing; polish; lustre.

جلا دار *jilā dār, adj.* Bright; brilliant; resplendent.

جلا دینا *jilā denā, v.* To polish.

جلا کار *jilā kār, n.m.* A polisher; nickel plater.

جلاب *jullāb* (A) *n.m.* A purgative; purge.

جلاب لگنا *jullāb lagnā, v.* To have motions; to have motions on account of fright.

جلاپا *jalāpā* (H) *n.m.* Envy; jealousy; spite; anger; rage.

جلاد *jallād* (A) *n.m.* An executioner; hard-hearted; cruel.

جلاد فلک *jallād-ĕ falak, n.m.* The planet Mars.

جلا دینا *jilā denā* (H) *v.* See جلانا *jilānā*.

جلال ، جلالت *jalāl ، jalālat* (A) *n.m. & n.f.* Grandeur; eminence; glory; majesty; state; dignity; power.

جلالی *jalāli* (A) *adj.* Glorious; majestic; illustrious; great; terrible; wrathful.

جلالیه *jalāliyah* (A) *n.m.* A person who worships the more terrible attributes of God; a kind of pigeon; a follower of Sayed *Jalāl Bokhārī*, a saint of *Bokhārā*.

جلانا *jalānā* (H) *v.* To burn; to kindle; to inflame; to fire; to light; to make jealous.

جلانا *jilānā* (H) *v.* To give life (to); to vivify; to animate; to recover anything almost dead; to revive.

جلا وطن *jalā waṭan* (A) *adj.* Banished; exiled.

جلا وطن کرنا *jalā waṭan karnā, v.* To banish; to make one to abandon one's country.

جلا وطن ہونا *jalā waṭan honā, v.* To be exiled; to be made to abandon one's country; to emigrate.

جلا وطنی *jalā waṭanī* (A) *adj.* Banishment.

جلاها *jullāhā* (H) *n.m.* A weaver.

جلب *jalb* (A) *n.m* Getting; acquiring; drawing.

جلب منفعت *jalb-ĕ manfi'at, n.m.* Profiteering; deriving profit.

جلد *jald* (P) *adv.* At once; quickly; rashly.

جلد باز *jald bāz, adj.* Expeditious; fleet; hasty; precipitate.

جلد بازی *jald bāzī, n.f.* Haste; agility; expedition.

جلد *jild* (A) *n.f.* The skin; leather; the binding of a book; a volume; a book.

جد باندهنا *jild bāndhnā, v.* To bind a book.

جلد بند، ساز، گر *jild band, sāz, gar, n.m.* A book-binder.

جلد بندی *jild bandī, n.f.* Book-Binding.

جلدی *jildī* (P) *adj.* Pertaining to skin.

جلدی *jaldī* (H) *n.f.* Quickness; hurry; haste; celerity; precipitation; rashness; abruptness; impetuosity.

جلدی سے *jaldī se, adv.* Quickly.

جلدی کرنا *jaldī karnā, v.* To make haste; to hasten; to hurry; to be precipitate; to be rash.

جلسه *jalsah* (A) *n.m.* Meeting; assembly; committee; party; entertainment; a social gathering; feast.

جلق *jalaq* (A) *n.m.* Masturbation; self-defile ment; onanism; self abuse.

جلق لگانا *jalaq lagānā, v.* To commit self-abuse; to masturbate.

جلقی *jalaqi, adj.* Masturbator.

جلن *jalan* (H) *n.f.* Burning; inflammation; heat; passion; jealousy.

جلنا *jalanā* (H) *v.* To burn; to be kindled; to be enraged; to burn with jealousy, envy or love.

جلندر ، جلندھر *jalandar, jalandhar* (H) *n.m.* Dropsy.

جلو *jilow* (T) *n.f.* Splendour; pomp; state; retinue; equipage; train; suit; court; bridle; reins. *adv.* In front; forward; ahead; in company (of).

جلو خانه *jilow khānah, n.m.* Porch; vestibule; ante-chambar.

جلوانا *jalwānā* (H) *v.* To cause to burn; to cause to be burnt; to cause someone to set fire (to).

جلوت *jalwat* (A) *n.f.* Gongregation; crowd; comman place.

جلوس *jalūs* (A) *n.m.* Pomp; splendour; glory; procession; accession to a throne.

جلوه *jalwah* (A) *n.m.* Lustre; splendour; manifestation; effulgence; display; show; displaying a bride to her husband unveiled in the presence of their relatives.

جلوه گه *jalwah gāh, n.f.* Nuptial throne; theatre; place of display; present.

جلوه گر *jalwah gar, adj.* Manifest; conspicuous; splendid; present.

جلوه گری *jalwah garī, n.f.* Manifestation; affectation; conspicuity; splendour.

جلی jali (A) adj. Apparent; evident; conspicuous.

خط جلی khatt-ĕ jali, n.m. Large plain handwriting.

ذکر جلی zikr-ĕ jali, n.m. Praising God in a loud voice.

جلیبا jalebā (H) n.m. Fruit of mulbery tree.

جلیبی jalebī (H) n.f. A kind of sweetmeat.

جلیس jalis (A) n. A companion; chum; a fast friend; comrade.

جلیل jalīl (A) adj. Great; glorious; illustrious.

جلیل القدر jalil-ul-qadr, adj. Glorious; illustrious; august; high in dignity.

جم jamm (A) adj. Much; big; great; huge.

جم غفیر jamm-ĕ ghafir, n.m. A great multitude; a concourse.

جمادات jamādāt (A) n.m. Minerals ; fossils ; stones; things incapable of growth.

جمادی الاخر ، جمادی الثانی jamādi-ul-ākhir, jamādī-us-sāni (A) n.m. Name of the sixth Hijri month.

جمادی الاول ، جمادی الاولیٰ jamādi-ul-awwal, jamādi-ul-ūlā (A) n.m. Name of the fifth Hijri month.

جماع jimā' (A) n.m. Copulation; sexual union; coition; sexual intercourse.

جماعت jamā'at (A) n.f. A Society; a body; a company; an assembly; congregation; a troop; a class; association.

جماعت بندی jamā'at bandi, n.f. Classification.

جماعت وکلا jamā'at-ĕ wokalā, n.f. Bar association.

جماعت وار jamā'at wār, adj. Classified; by classes; by groups.

جماعت سے کرامت ہے jamā'at se karāmat hai, prov. Union is strength.

جمال jamāl (A) n.m. Beauty; elegance; comeliness; prettiness.

جمال گوٹا jamāl goṭā (H) n.m. Name of a purgative nut.

جمالی jamālī (A) adj. Lovable; amiable; display of God's beneficence. n.m. A kind of musk-melon.

جمانا jamānā (H) v. To coagulate; to freeze; to congeal; to consolidate; to implant; to impress; to fix; to lay down; to make adhere (to).

جماؤ jamāo (H) n.m. Cohesion; adhesion; freezing; collection; accumulation; accretion; coagulation; a gathering.

جماہی ، جمائی jamāhī, jāmā'i (H) n.f. Gaping; yawning.

جماہی لینا jamāhi lenā, v. To yawn; to gape.

جمائی Jamā'i (H) n.m. Son-in-law.

جمبو jambū (H) n.m. A metal water pot with a narrow neck; a jackal; the rose-apple tree and its fruit.

جم جم jam jam (H) adv. Always; constantly; perpetually.

جمشید jamshid, jamshed (P) n. prop. Name of an ancient king of Persia.

جمع jama' (A) n.f. A collection; total; sum; capital; stock; assets; collections; revenue; receipts; a congregation; conjunction; accumulation; assembly; amount; sum-total; credit; addition (Arith.); the plural (of a word).

جمع بندی jama' bandi, n.f. Rental; accounts of the revenues; rent roll; assessment; settlement of the revenues.

جمع خرچ jama' kharch, n.m. Debit and credit; receipts and disbursements; cash account; current account.

جمع کرنا jama' karnā, v. To collect; to amass; to add together; to make up an account; to balance an account.

جمع نویس jama' nawis, n.m. An accountant.

جمع ہونا jama' honā, v. To be collected; to be gathered together; to be added.

جمعدار *jama'dār* (A & P) *n.m.* A headman; of a body of men; an officer of the army; head a sweeper.

جمعرات *juma'rāt*, *n.f.* Thursday.

جمعہ *juma'h* (A) *n.m.* Friday.

جمعیت *jam'iyat* (A) *n.f.* Collection; assemblage; organisation; congregation; multitude; tranquillity; rest; content.

جمعیت خاطر *jama'iyat-ĕ khāṭir*. *n.f.* Peace of mind; satisfaction.

جمگھٹ *jamghaṭ* (H) *n.m.* A crowd; a multitude.

جمل *jamal* (A) *n.m.* A camel.

جمل *jumal* (A) *n.m.* The reckoning of the words according to *abjad*; (the *plu.* of جملہ *jumlah*) Sentences.

جملہ *jumlah* (A) *n.m.* The whole; the sum, aggregate; total amount; a sentence; a clause.

جملہ معترضہ *jumlah mu'tarizah*, *n.m.* A parenthetical sentence or clause; a clause or sentence added merely to create effect.

فی الجملہ *-fil-jumlah*, *adv.* On the whole; in substance.

من جملہ *min jumlah*, *adv.* From or out of the whole.

جمنا *jamnā* (H) *n.f.* Name of a river in India, near Delhi.

جمنا *jamnā* (H) *v.* To germinate; to take root; to become fixed; to be coagulated; to be congealed; to be frozen; to be consolidated; to adhere; to stick; to insist on; to be firmly established; to have a firm hold.

جمود *jamūd* (A) *n.m.* Inactivity; inertness; inaction; deadlock; stalemate.

جمہور *jumhur* *n.m.* The populace; the people; a whole people; masses.

جمہوری سلطنت *jumhūrī salṭanat*, *n.f.* A republic; a democracy.

جمیع *jamī'* (A) *adj.* The whole; all; collective.

جمیل ، جمیلہ *jamīl*, *jamīlah* (A) *adj.* Beautiful; elegant; comely; pleasing.

جن *jinn* (A) *n.m.* One of the genii; a spirit; an elf; a demon; a headstrong person; a resoulte person.

جنا *janā* (H) *v.* Brought forth; begotten. *n.m.* A person.

جناب *janāb* (A) *i.n.t.j.* Your highness! your honour ! sir! *n.f.* Vestibule; threshold; side; margin; brink.

جناب عالی *janāb-ĕ 'āli*, *intj.* Exalted sir! your honour! your excellency! &c.

جناب من *janāb-ĕ man*, *intj.* My dear sir!

جنابت *janābat* (A) *n.f.* Pollution; loss of sperma.

جنات *jinnat* (A) *n.m.* (*plu.* of جنی *jinni*) The genii.

جناح *janāḥ* (A) *n.f.* A pinion; a wing; a wing of an army.

جنازہ *janāzah* (A) *n.m.* A bier; a funeral; a corpse.

جنانا *janānā* (H) *v.* To cause to deliver (offspring); assisting an expectant mother in child birth.

جنائی *janāi* (H) *n.f.* A midwife.

جنبان *jumbān* (P) *adj.* Moving; vibrating; trembling, shaking; tremulous.

جنبش *jumbish* (P) *n.f.* Motion; movement; agitation; shake; vibration; gesture.

جنبش دینا *jumbish dena*, *v.* To shake; to move.

جنبہ *jambah* (A) *n.f.* Position; aspect; side.

جنبہ داری *jambahdāri*, *n.f.* Partiality; favour; support.

جنت jannat (A) n.f. A garden; paradise.

جنتا jantā (H) n.m. An instrument for drawing wire; the people; masses; public.

جنتر jantar (H) n.m. A machine; an instrument; a magic square; an amulet; a musical instrument; a dial; an observatory.

جنتر منتر jantar mantar, n.m. Juggling; conjuring; observatory.

جنتری jantri (H) n.m. A perforated steel plate for drawing wire; a calendar; an almanac.

جنتی jannati (A) adj. Of paradise; heavenly; those whose abode is paradise; the deceased person for whom the wish is that he may reside in paradise.

جنجال janjāl (H) n.m. Trouble; difficulty; plague; embarrassment; entanglement; bother; fuss; perplexity; encumbrance.

جنجال میں پھنسنا janlāl meṅ phaṅsnā, v. To get into trouble; to be surrounded by difficulties.

جنجالی janjālī, n.m. A troublesome person; one who causes trouble; a quarrelsome person.

جنس jins (A) n.f. Kind; species; sort; class; crops; products; sex; gender; family; race; articles; wares; merchandise; grain; corn; movables; ornaments.

جنس ادنی jins-ĕ adnā, n.f. An inferior article; inferior grain.

جنس اعلی jins-ĕ a'lā, n.f. Superior-goods or wares.

جنس قوی jins-ĕ qawī, n.f. The sterner sex.

جنس لطیف jins-ĕ latif, n.f. The fair-sex.

جنس وار jins wār, adv. According to kind or species. n.m. A table prepared by the paṭwārī of different kinds of produce of a particular area.

ابنائے جنس abnā'e jins, n.m. Mankind.

بجنسہ ba-jinsihi, adv. In every particular; as it is; in its entirety.

جنسی jinsī (A) adj. Generic; relating to sex.

جنسی بھوک jinsi bhūk, n.f. Sexual appetite

جنسی کشش jinsi kashash, n.f. Sex-appeal.

ہم جنسی ham jinsi, n.f. Similarity of kind; homogeneousness.

جنسیات jinsiyāt (A) n.f. Sexology.

جنسیت jinsiyyat (A) n.f. Sexuality.

لا جنسیت lā jinsiyyat, n.f. Sexlessness.

ہم جنسیت ham jinsiyyat, n.f. Homosexuality.

جنگ jang (P) n.f. Battle; war; combat; fight.

جنگ آزمودہ jang āzmūdah, adj. Tried in war; a veteran; brave; warlike.

جنگ‌جو jang jū, adj. Contentious; litigious, quarrelsome; war-monger.

جنگ دیدہ jang dīdah, adj. Experienced in war.

جنگ زرگری jang-ĕ zargari, n.f. Show-fight; a collusive fight between two parties to defraud a third.

جنگ کرنا jang karnā, v. To make or wage war; to quarrel; to squabble.

جنگ و جدل jang-ŏ-jadal, n.f. Fighting; battle; conflict; brawl; squabble.

بعد از جنگ ba'd az jang, adv Post-war; after the battle.

جنگل jaṅgal (H) n.m. A wood; a forest; a jungle.

جنگل جانا ، پھرنا jaṅgal jānā, phirnā, v. To go to the wood to ease one's self; to perform the offices of nature.

جنگل میں منگل jaṅgal meṅ maṅgal, n.m. A feast in the forest; getting luxuries of a civilised life in a God forsaken land.

جنگل میں مور ناچا کس نے دیکھا *jaṅgal meṅ mor nāchā kis ne dekhā, prov.* Wasting one's sweetness in the desert air.

جنگلا *janglā* (H) *n.m.* A fence; a railing; a woody country; forest; name of a musical mode.

جنگلا لگانا *janglā lagānā, v.* To fence; to rail; to enclose.

جنگلی *jangli* (H) *adj.* Wild; savage; clownish; boor; barbarian.

جنگلی بلی *jangli billi, n.f.* A wild cat.

جنگلی پیاز *jangli piyāz, n.f.* Squills.

جنگلی سرو *jangli sarv, n.m.* Wild cypress.

جنگلی سور *jangli sūar, n.m.* Wild boar.

جنگلی کوا *janglī kawwā, n.m.* A raven.

جنگی *jangi* (H) *adj.* Warlike; relating to war; martial. *n.m.* A combatant; a warrior.

جنگی بیڑا *jangi beṛā, n.m.* An armada; a fleet.

جنگی جہاز *jangī jahāz, n.m.* Man of war.

جنگی لاٹ *jangi lāṭ, n.m.* Commender-in-chief of the navy; admiral.

جنم *janam* (H) *n.m.* Birth; life; existence.

جنم اشٹمی *janam ashṭami, n.f.* The birthday of *Krishnā*; a festival of the *Hindūs*.

جنم بھوم ' جنم استھان *janam bhūm, janam asthān, n.m.* Birth place; fatherland.

جنم پتری *janam pattri, n.f.* Horoscope.

جنم دن *janam din, n.m.* Birthday.

جنم لینا *janam lenā, v.* To be born.

جنم کا ' جنمی *janam kā, janmi, adj.* Inherited; inborn; natural.

جنوانا *janwānā* (H) *v.* See جنانا *janānā*.

جنوائی *janwā'i* (H) *n.f.* A midwife's fee; the act of a midwife.

جنوب *janūb* (A) *n.m.* The south.

جنوبی *janūbi, adj.* Southern.

جنون *junūn* (A) *n.m.* Madness; insanity; lunacy.

جنون ہونا ' جنون چڑھنا *junūn honā, junūn chaṛhnā, v.* To become mad or furious; to become very angry.

جنونی *junūni, adj.* Mad; insane; self-willed; wildly impulsive or foolish person.

جنہیں *jinheṅ* (H) *pro.* Whom; whomsoever.

جنین *janīn*(A) *n.* Foetus; embryo.

جنیو *janeo* (H) *n.m.* Sacred thread worn by *Hindus* especially *Brahmans*.

جو *jo* (H) *pro.* Who; what, which that. *conj.* If.

جو چیز' جو کچھ *jo chīz, jo kuchh, pro.* Whatever; whichever.

جو کوئی *jo koi, pro.* Whoever.

جو ہو سو ہو *jo ho so ho, phr.* Come what may; whatever the consequence.

جو پھل چکھا نہیں وھی میٹھا *jo phal chakkhā nahiṅ wohi miṭhā, prov.* Forbidden fruit tastes sweet.

جو چڑھیگا سو گریگا *jo chaṛhegā so giregā, prov.* Pride goeth before a fall.

جو گرجتا ہے وہ برستا نہیں *jo garajtā hai woh barastā nahiṅ, prov.* Barking dogs seldom bite.

جو مزا چوبارے نہ بلخ نہ بخارے *jo mazā chaubāre nah bal<u>kh</u> nah bu<u>kh</u>āre, prov.* East or west, home is best; home sweet home; no place like home.

جو ہانڈی میں ہوگا وھی نکلیگا *jo hāṅḍi meṅ hogā wohi nikle gā, prov.* Nothing comes out of a sack but what is put in it; what is in the heart the tongue speaketh.

جو *javv* (A) *n.m.* The space between earth and sky; ether.

جو jaw (H) n.m. Barley; a clove of garlic; a kind of stitch in needle work.

جو jū (P) adj. Seeking; Seeker (used in comp. as جنگجو jangjū warrior).

جو ، جوئے ، جوئبار jū, jūe, jūebār (P) n.f. A river; a brook.

جوا jūā (H) n.m. Gambling; gaming; playing with dice; a yoke.

جوا خانه juā khānah, n.m. A gaming house; a gambling den.

جوا کھیلنا jūā khelnā, v. To gamble.

جواب jawāb (A) n.m. Answer; reply; defence; double; equal, parallel; match; dismissal.

جواب با ثواب jawāb bā ṣawāb, n.m A proper answer.

جواب دعویٰ jawāb-ĕ dā'wā, n.m. The answer to a plaint.

جواب ده jawāb deh, adj. Answerable; responsible; amenable; accountable. n.m. Answerer.

جواب دهی jawāb dehī, n.f. Liability; being responsible; responsibility.

جواب دهی کرنا jawāb dehī karnā, v. To respond; to defend a suit; to explain; to answer.

جواب دهی سے بری کرنا jawāb dehī se barī karna. v. To exonerate; to relieve one of a responsibility.

جواب دینا jawāb denā, v. To answer; to reply; to account for; to give an account of; to dismiss; to discharge; to disband.

جواب سوال jawāb sawāl, n.m. Question and answer; altercation; conversation; argument.

جواب طلب کرنا jawāb ṭalab karnā, v. To call for an explanation; to call to account.

جواب قطعی jawāb-ĕ qaṭa'i, n.m. A definite answer.

جواب ملنا jawāb milnā, v. To be dismissed or discharged.

جوابی jawābī (A) n.m. A respondent; counterpart; a bill of exchange which is not paid till notice is received of the bills having been taken up; the chorus, especially in repeating an elegy. adj. Responsive.

جواد jawād (A) adj. Liberal; beneficient; bountiful; very generous.

جوار jiwār (A) n.m. Vicinity; neighbourhood; adjacency.

جوار joār (H) n.f. Indian millet; Indian corn.

جوار jawār (H) n.m. Flood-tide.

جوار بهاٹا jawār bhāṭā (H) n.m. Ebb and flow of the tide.

جوارح jawāriḥ (A) n.m. Limbs of man or of a carnivorous animal.

جوارش jawārish (P) n.f. A stomachic medicine; a digestive medicine.

جواری jūāri (H) n.m. A gambler; a thread stretched over the bridge of a musical instrument such as sitār beneath the strings whereby the sound is improved.

جواز jawāz (A) n.m. Permission; toleration; lawfulness; propriety; permit; licence; pass.

جوالا jūālā (S) n.f. Blaze; flame; fire; heat; passion.

جوالا مکهی jūālā mukhi, n.f. A volcano; a title of the goddess Devī Durgā.

جواله jauvālah (A) adj. Fast revolving; fast spinning.

جوان jawān (P) adj. Young; a youth; lad; young man; adult; young woman.

جوان بخت jawān bakht, adj. Fortunate; one having bright prospects.

جوان سال *jawāṅ sāl, adj.* Youth; in the prime of youth.

جوان مرد *jawāṅ mard, adj.* Brave; bold; manly; generous; couragous. *n.m.* A fine young fellow; a brave man; a hero.

جوان مردی *jawāṅ mardī, n.f.* Manliness; bravery; courage; generosity; magnanimity gallantry.

جوان مرگ *jawāṅ marg, adj.* Dead in the prime of youth.

جوانی *jawānī* (P) *n.f.* Youth; season of youth; adolescence; manhood.

جوانی چڑھنا *jawānī chaṛhnā, v.* To attain puberty; to be adolescent; to be affected by youthfull lust.

جوانی ڈھلنا *jawānī ḍhalnā, v.* To cross the threshold of youth; to become old.

جوانب *jawānib* (A) *n.f. & n.m.* (*plu.* of جانب *jānib*) Parts; sides; environs; quarters.

جواهر ، جواهرات *jawāhir, jawāhirāt* (A) *n.m.* (*plu.* of جوهر *jauhar*) Jewels; gems; essences; substances.

جواهرخانه *jawāhir khānah, n.m.* A jewellery vault.

جواهر نگار *jawāhir nigār, adj.* Studded with jewels; ornamented.

جوبن *joban* (H) *n.m.* Beauty; fineness of figure; youth; bloom; adolescence; prime; properly developed breasts.

جوبن پر آنا *joban par ānā, v.* To bloom; to reach the age of puberty.

جوت *jot* (H) *n.f.* Lustre; brilliance; light; moonlight; flame of a candle or lamp; vision; a glance of the eye; soul; spirit.

جوت *jot* (H) *n.f.* Cultivation; ploughing; the rent paid by the cultivator; cultivated land; the strap or cord that fastens the yoke of a plough to the neck of the ox.

جوتا *jūtā* (H) *n.m.* A shoe; a slipper; a pair of shoes.

جوتا مارنا *jūtā mārnā, v.* To give one a shoe beating; to apply the shoe.

جوتری *jawatrī* (H) *n.f.* Mace; dried outer covering of nutmeg used as spice.

جوتش *jotish* (H) *n.m.* Astrology; astronomy.

جوتشی *jotishī* (H) *n.m.* An astrologer; an astronomer.

جوتنا *jotnā* (H) *v.* To yoke; to plough; to till; to force one to do a thing.

جوتی *jūtī* (H) *n.f.* A shoe; a slipper; a pair of shoes.

جوتی پر مارنا *jūti par mārnā, v.* To despise; to disdain; to condemn; not to care a damn.

جوتی پیزار *jūti paizār, n.f.* A fight with shoes; an open fight.

جوتی پیزارکرنا *jūti paizār karnā, v.* To fight with shoes.

جوتی خور *jūtī khor, adj.* Beaten with slippers; mean; abject.

جوتیاں اٹھانا *jūtiyāṅ uṭhānā, v.* To do menial service

جوتیاں چٹخاتے پھرنا *jūtiyāṅ chaṭkhāte phirnā, v.* To loaf about, to walk about aimlessly.

جوتیاں سیدھی کرنا *jūtiyāṅ sīdhī karnā, v.* To perform menial service; to pay homage to; to cringe.

جوتیوں میں دال بٹنا *jūtioṅ meṅ dāl baṭnā, v.* To have a domestic quarrel, to have discord.

جوٹھا *jūṭhā* (H) *n.m.* Refuse; leavings of food.

جود *jūd* (A) *n.m.* Liberality; munificence; generosity.

جودت *jaudat* (A) *n.f.* Quickness of apprehension; ingenuity; excellence; intelligence; benignity.

جور jaur (A) n.m. Violence; oppression; tyranny.

جورو jorū (H) n.f. A wife.

جورو کا بھائی jorū kā bhāi, n.m. Brother-in-law; wife's brother.

جورو کا غلام jorū kā ghulām, n.m. A hen-pecked husband.

جوڑ joṛ (H) n.m. A connecting link; a joint; a pair; a match; sum; total; junction; a patch; a seam; addition; combination; connection.

جوڑ بٹھانا joṛ biṭhānā, v. To fit in a join; to dovetail.

جوڑ توڑ joṛ toṛ, n.m. Device; craft; intrigue; conspiracy.

جوڑ توڑ کرنا joṛ toṛ karnā, v. To contrive; to conspire; to intrigue.

جوڑ جوڑ joṛ joṛ, n.m. Every joint of the body.

جوڑ دینا joṛ denā, v. To join; to add up; to unite.

جوڑ لگانا joṛ lagānā, v. To patch; to sum up; to add; to fit in a join.

جوڑا joṛā (H) n.m. Counterpart; match; pair; a suit (of clothes); a couple; a pair (of shoes); husband and wife.

جوڑا jūṛā (H) n.m. A top-knot of the hair; the hair done up in a knot behind; the crest or plume of a nightingale; a rope of twisted grass used as a support for a round bottomed jar.

جوڑنا joṛnā (H) v. To join; to unite; to add; to total; to lay by; to harness; to set (a bone); to match; to mate; to pair; to patch; to connect; to calculate; to cement; to mend; to solder; to tie; to annex; to affix.

جوڑی joṛi (H) n.f. A pair; couple; partner; mate; match; equal; counterpart.

جوڑی دار joṛī dār, n.m. A omrade; a friend; a fellow traveller; a companion.

جوز jauz (A) n.m. A nut; a nutmeg.

جوزا jauzā (A) n.m. The sign Gemini; Orion.

جوش josh (P) n.m. Heat; effervescence; excitement; zeal; enthusiasm; passion; lust; emotion.

جوش آنا josh ānā, v. To boil; to flow over; to be excited; to swell with anger.

جوش ترش josh-ĕ tursh, n.m. Tartaric acid.

جوش جوانی josh-ĕ jawāni, n.m. The fire of youth.

جوش خون josh-ĕ khūn, n.m. Boiling of the blood; plethora; maternal or paternal affection.

جوش دینا josh denā, v. To cause to boil; to boil.

جوش زن josh zan, adj. Boiling; in a state of ebullition.

جوش شیریں josh-ĕ shiriṅ, n.m. Sodium bicarbonate.

جوش کھانا josh khānā, v. To boil up; to swell; to overflow; to be excited; to be enraged.

جوش مارنا josh mārnā, v. To boll; to ferment; to chafe; to rage; to be in a frenzy.

جوش و خروش josh-ŏ kharosh, n.m. Excitement; roar; passion; enthusiasm.

جوشاں joshāṅ (P) adj. Boiling; bubbling up; enraged; excited.

جوشاندہ joshāṅdah (P) n.m. A decoction; boiling of certain medicinal herbs to extract essence.

جوشن jaushan (P) n.m. An ornament worn by women on the upper arm; a coat-of-mail; armour; armlet.

جوع jū' (A) n.f. Hunger; appetite.

جوع البقر، جوع الکلب jū'-ul-baqar, jū'-ul-kalb, n.f. Voraciousness; gluttony; canine hunger.

جوف jauf (A) n.m. Cavity; hollow; interior space; belly.

جوق jauq, jūq (A) n.m. A troop or body of men.

جوق در جوق jauq dar jauq, adv. In troops; n large numbers.

جوکھوں - جوکھم jokhoṅ, jokham (H) n.f. Risk; danger; a hazardous undertaking or business.

جوکھوں اٹھانا jokhoṅ uṭhānā, v To risk; to hazard; to venture; to suffer a loss.

جوکھوں کا کام jokhoṅ kā kām, n.m. A hazardous task; a dangerous undertaking.

جوکھوں میں ڈالنا jakhoṅ meṅ ḍālnā, v. To endanger; to place in jeopardy.

جوکھوں میں پڑنا jokhoṅ meṅ paṛnā, n.m. To run a risk; to be endangered.

جوگ jog (H) n.m. Abstract contemplation; meditation; religious devotion; the yogā system of philosophy; a fortunate moment.

جوگ سادھنا jog sādhnā, v. To lead the life of an ascetic.

جوگ لینا jog lenā, v. To retire from the world; to become an ascetic.

جوگن jogan (H) n.f. Female of jogi.

جوگی jogī (H) n.m. An ascetic; a devotee; a hermit.

جوگیا jogyā (H) n.m. [Reddish; yellow colour; the colour worn by jogis; the name of a musical mode, a kind of pigeon.

جولاں jolāṅ (P) n.m. Fetters; irons.

پابجولاں pā-ba-jolāṅ, adj. With the feet in irons; fettered; chained.

جولان jaulān (P) ādj. Moving about; coursing; springing; wandering.

جولانگاہ jaulāngāh, n.f. A place of exercise (for troops or for horses).

جولانی jaulāni (P) n.f. Strength of body or mind; acumen; fleetness; quickness; swiftness.

جولائی jaulāı (E) n.m. The month of July of the Christian calendar.

جوں jūṅ (H) adv. & prep. As; like; such as.

جوں توں jūṅ tūṅ, adv. In the same way; as before; in some way or other; anyhow.

جوں توں کر کے jūṅ tūṅ karke, adv. Somehow; anyhow; by any means; by some means or other; with great difficulty.

جوں جوں jūṅ jūṅ, adv. As long as; as far as.

جوں کا توں jūṅ kā tūṅ, adv. As it was; the very same; precisely the same; unaltered.

جونہیں، جونہی jonhiṅ, juṅhi, adv. As soon as; the very moment, no sooner than.

جوں jūṅ (H) n.f. A louse; a thing as small as a louse.

جوں پڑنا jūṅ paṛnā, v. To become lousy.

جون jūn (H) n.f. Time; period; age; birth; transmigration.

جون بدلنا، جون پلٹنا jūn badalnā, jūn palaṭnā, v. To transform; to metamorphose.

جون jūn (E) n.m. The month of June of the Christian era.

جونا jūnā, n.m. A roop of grass for cleaning vessels or tying bundles.

جونسا jauṅsā, adj. Whichever; anyone.

جونک، جوک jonk, jok (H) n.f. A leech.

جونک لگانا joṅk lagānā, v. To apply leeches.

جوہر jauhar (A) n.m. A gem; a jewel; a pearl; atom; skill; knowledge; secret; nature; matter; substance; essence; acid; virtue; worth; merit.

جوہر دار jauhar dār, adj. Scimitar marked with jauhar.

جوہر دکھانا jauhar dikhānā, v. To show what one is made of; to show one's mettle.

جوہر فرد jauhar-ĕ fard, n.m. An indivisible atom; an unrivalled or unequalled person.

جوہر کھلنا jauhar khulna, v. To expose; to shine; exposure of one's virtues or faults.

اہل جوہر ahl-ĕ jauhar, n.m. Men of merit or worth.

جوہری jauhari (A) n.m. A jewler; an appraiser or setter of precious stones.

جوہڑ jauhar (H) n.m. A pit filled with water during the rainy season; a pond.

جوہی jūhi (H) n.f. Jasmine; a kind of fireworks; an insect destructive to certain crops.

جوئندہ jo'indah (P) n. & adj. A seeker; an inquirer; one who searches for.

جوئندہ یابندہ jo'indah yābindah, prov. One who seeks gets; seek and thou shalt find.

جویا ، جویاں joyā, joyān (P) adj. See جوئندہ jo'indah.

جہات jihāt (A) n.f. (plu. of جہت jihat). Directions.

جہاد jihād (A) n.m. War; a crusade; supreme effort; religious war waged by Muslims.

جھاری jhāri (H) n.f. A pitcher with a long neck and a spout; an ewer.

جھاڑ jhāṛ (H) n.m. A shrub; a bramble; a lustre or chandelier; a kind of firework; bushes; brake; series; succession.

جھاڑ جھنکاڑ jhāṛ jhankāṛ, n.m. Brambles; large dry bushes.

جھاڑا jhāṛā (H) n.m. A purge; a search; an incantation; easing oneself.

جھاڑا دینا jhāṛā denā, v. To submit to a search.

جھاڑا لینا jhāṛā lenā, v. To search a person minutely.

جھاڑ پھونک jhāṛ phūṅk, n.f. Juggling; conjuring; hocus pocus; exorcising; incantation.

جھاڑن jhāṛan (H) n.f. A coarse cloth for wiping furniture; a duster.

جھاڑنا jhāṛnā (H) v. To sweep; to brush; to dust; to clean; to drop; to knock off (by shaking); to strike; to flap; to beat (bushes); to comb; to exorcise; to repeat spells or charms (over); to shake off; to cast (feathers); to scold; to rebuke; to admonish.

جھاڑنا پھونکنا jhāṛnā phūṅknā, v. To exorcise; to repeat spells or charms (over).

جھاڑو jhāṛū (H) n.f. A broom; a whisk.

جھاڑو تارا jhāṛū tārā (H) n.m. A comet.

جھاڑو پھر جانا jhāṛū phir jānā, v. To have a clean sweep of everything; to lose everything.

جھاڑو پھیرنا ، پھیر دینا jhāṛū phernā, pher denā, v. To make away with everything; to leave nothing; to ruin; to undo.

جھاڑو دینا jhāṛū denā, v. To sweep.

جھاڑی jhāṛi (H) n.f. A forest; wood; underwood; brushwood; bush; shrub; a thicket.

جہاز jahāz (A) n.m. A ship; a vessel.

جہاز کا جہاز jahāz kā jahāz, adj. Huge; magnificent; very big; as big as a ship itself.

جہازی jahāzi (A) adj. Naval; nautical. n.m. A sailor; a kind of scimitar.

جہازی کتا jahāzi kuttā, n.m. Greyhound.

جھاگ jhāg (H) n.m. Foam; froth; scum.

جھاگ لانا jhāg lānā, v. To froth and fume; to foam with rage.

جہال juhhāl (A) n.m. (plu. of جاھل jāhil); Fools; simpleton; ignorant people.

جھال jhāl (H) n.f. A hot taste as of a red pepper; sharpness; acrimony; pungency; joining or soldering of metals; a large basket; a cascade; waves; billows; passion.

جھالا ، جھلّا jhala, jhallā (H) n.m. Rain which falls on one spot and not another close to it; local showers.

جہالت jahālat (A) n.f. Ignorance; illiteracy; imperfect knowledge; barbarism; brutality.

جھالر jhālar (H) n.f. Fringe; frill.

جھالر دار jhālar dār, adj. Fringed.

جھالنا jhālnā (H) v. To season pickles; to solder.

جھام jhām (H) n.m. A kind of large hoe for excavating earth in well sinking.

جھاما jhāmā (H) n.m. A pumice stone (used to rub off dirt from hand and feet).

جہان jahān (P) n.m. The world.

جہان آرا jahān āra, adj. World adorning.

جہان آفریں jahāñ āfrin, n.m. Creator of the world; God.

جہاں باں jahāñ bāñ, n. & adj. Protector of world; a sovereign.

جہاں بانی jahāñ bāni, n.f. Ruling or governing the world; exercising autho- the rity, administering the laws.

جہاں بیں jahāñ biñ, n. & adj. World-seeing; the eye; a traveller.

جہاں پناہ jahāñ panāh, n.m. Protector of the world; refuge of the world; His Majesty. intj. Your Majesty!

جہاندار jahāñ dār, n.m. Ruler of the world; a king.

جہانداری jahāñ dāri, n.f. Government; dominion; empire

جہاں دیدہ jahāñ didah, adj. Experienced; seasoned; widely travelled.

جہاں سوز jahāñ soz, adj. World-inflaming.

جہاں گرد jāhāñ gard, adj. Going round the world. n.m. A traveller; a tourist.

جہاں گیر jahāñ gir, adj. World-taking; world-conquering. n.m. A great conqueror; name of the son of emperor Akbar.

جہاں گیری jahāñ giri, n.f. World conquest; world domination; a sort of bracelet invented by Jahāñgir. adj. Of or relating to Jahāñgir.

جہاں نما jahāñ numā, adj. Exhibiting the world.

جہانی jahāni, (P) adj. Relating to the world.

آں جہانی āñjahāni, adj. Of the other world; departed; deceased.

جہاں jahāñ (H) adj. Where; which place; in which place.

جہاں تک jahāñ tak, adv. As far as.

جہاں جہاں ، جہاں کہیں jahāñ jahāñ, jahāñ kahiñ, adj. Wherever; wheresoever.

جہاں سے jahāñ se, adv. Whence; from where.

جہاں کا تہاں jahāñ kā tahāñ, adv. In the same place as before; as one was.

جھانٹ jhāñt (H) n.f. The hair of the private part; pubic hair; pubes.

جھانجن - جھانجھن jhāñjan, jhañjhan (H) n.f. An ornament worn on the akles.

جهانسا *jhāṅsā* (H) *n.m.* Deception; cheating; a trick.

جهانسا بتانا یا دینا *jhaṅsā batānā yā deṇā*, *v.* To deceive; to cheat.

جهانسے میں آنا *jhaṅse meṅ āṇā*, *v.* To be deceived; to be cheated.

جهانک *jhāṅk* (H) *n.f.* Peeping; spying; *n.m.* A herd of deer; a flock of birds; a host of locust.

تاک جهانک *tāk jhāṅk*, *n.f.* Secret looks; peeping; planning.

جهانکنا *jhāṅknā* (H) *v.* To peep; to spy; to pay a short visit (to one).

جهانکی *jhāṅki* (H) *n.f.* A show; a peep show; a scene in a play.

جهانواں *jhāṅwāṅ* (H) *n.m.* See جهاما *jhāmā*.

جهاؤ *jhāū* (H) *n.m.* A plant which abounds along the banks of rivers and is much used for making baskets.

جهائیاں *jhaiyāṅ* (H) *n.f.* Freckles; black spots on the face.

جهپانا *jhipānā* (H) *v.* To humiliate; to put to shame.

جهپٹ *jhapaṭ* (H) *n.f.* A leap; a spring; a bound; an onset; a jerk.

جهپٹ لینا *jhapaṭ lenā*, *v.* To snatch; to spring; to pounce upon; to snap at.

جهپٹ میں آنا *jhapāṭ meṅ ānā*, *v.* To be bewitched; to be run down.

جهپٹا *jhapaṭṭā* (H) *n.m.* Assault; sudden attack; a snatch; a spring; the spring of a tiger; a stoop of a bird of prey.

جهپٹا مارنا *jhapaṭṭā mārnā*, *v.* To snatch; to make a rush; to stoop down; to spring; to pounce upon.

جهپٹنا *jhapaṭnā* (H) *v.* To spring; to pounce; to swoop; to snatch; to run; to fly (at); to make a sudden attack (on); to snap (at).

جهپکنا ، جهپکانا *jhapaknā, jhapkānā* (H) *v.* To wink; to blink; to lower the eyelids (through drowsiness, fear or shame); to nap; to doze off.

جهپکی *jhapki* (H) *n.f.* Drowsiness; a nap.

جهپکی لینا *jhapki lenā*, *v.* To take a nap; to doze off.

جهت *jihat* (A) *n.f.* Direction; side; surface; form; cause; reason; account; sake.

جهٹ ، جهٹ پٹ ، جهٹ سے *jhaṭ, jhaṭ paṭ, jhaṭ se* (H) *adv.* Quickly; instantly; hastily.

جهٹ پٹا *jhuṭ puṭā* (H) *n.m.* Twilight; light darkness before sunrise or after sunset.

جهٹکا *jhaṭkā* (H) *n.m.* A jerk; a violent pull; a shake; twitch; slaughtering an animal by cutting off the head with one stroke; broken asunder; torn by a sudden jerk.

جهٹکنا *jhaṭaknā* (H) *v.* To jerk; to shake; to twitch; to become lean.

جهٹلانا *jhutlānā* (H) *v.* To belie; to falsify.

جهجهر *jhajjar* (H) *n.m.* A goblet; a porous goblet; a large porous water jar.

جهجهک *jhijak* (H) *n.f.* A start (through surprise, astonishment or fear); recoil; shyness; timidity; hesitation.

جهجهکنا *jhijaknā* (H) *v.* To start or boggle; to shrink; to recoil; to startle; to hesitate.

جهد *johd, jahd* (A) *n.f.* Struggle; endeavour; exertion; effort; assiduity; earnestness.

جهر *jahr* (A) *n.m.* Speaking with a loud voice; speaking audibly; a female offering.

جهر *jhar* (A) *n.f.* The sound made in tearing cloth; prattle; jabber.

جهر جهرا *jhir jhirā* (H) *adj.* Very thin cloth; badly woven (cloth).

جهر جهری *jhur jhuri* (H) *n.f.* Shivering that precedes fever; ague; shaking; shivering.

جهرمٹ *jurmut* (H) *n.m.* A multitude; a crowd; assembly; ball; a shawl twisted round the head like a turban.

جهرنا *jharnā* (H) *n.m.* A spring; a cascade; a waterfall; a perforated skimmer.

جهروکا *jharokā* (H) *n.m.* A window; a lattice; a casement; an eye-let hole; an air hole.

جهری *jhurri* (H) *n.f.* A wrinkle.

جهری *jhirī* (H) *n.f.* A slit; a narrow aperture; a chink.

جهڑ *jhaṛ* (H) *n.f.* Heavy rain; a downpour; continued showers of rain; bolt of a lock.

جهڑ بیری *jhaṛ beri* (H) *n.f.* A wild *ber* or plum tree; *jujube.*

جهڑپ *jhaṛap* (H) *n.f.* Skirmish; contention; flame; pungency; fight; cock fight; heat; fieriness; acrimony.

جهڑکنا *jhiṛaknā* (H) *v.* To scold; to rebuke; to chide; to speak snappishly.

جهڑکی *jhirkī* (H) *n.f.* Rebuff; snappishness; scolding; rebuke.

جهڑنا *jhaṛnā* (H) *v.* To drop; to fall off (leaves or fruits or feathers or hair); to shake; to shed; to pour; to be discharged (copulation).

جهڑوس *jharūs* (H) *n.m.* A shameless fellow; a very old and shameless fellow; a pimp.

جهڑی *jhaṛī* (H) *n.f.* Continued rain.

جهڑی لگنا *jhaṛī lagnā*, *v.* To rain continually.

جهک، جهک جهک *jhak, jhak jhak* (H) *n.f.* Folish talk; nonsense; jabber; chatter; dispute.

جهک مارنا *jhak mārnā*, *v.* To act fruitlessly or absurdly; to babble; to prate.

جهکانا *jhukānā* (H) *v.* To cause to stoop; to tilt; to bend downwards; to bow; to incline; to nod; to make a nod.

جهکاؤ *jhukāo* (H) *n.m.* The state of being bent downwards; stoop; inclination; curve; bend; flexibility.

جهکڑ *jhakkaṛ* (H) *n.m.* A storm; a tempest; a squall; a sudden blast; a gale; a hurricane.

جهکنا *jhuknā* (H) *v.* To bend; to bow; to stoop; to be tilted; to incline to dip (as a scale); to submit.

جهکی *jhakkī* (H) *adj.* Passionate; talkative; wrathful; violent.

جهگڑا *jhagṛā* (H) *n.m.* Wrangling; a quarrel; brawl; contention; squabble; strife; dispute.

جهگڑا اٹهانا *jhagṛā uṭhānā*, *v.* To set a-wrangling; to raise a quarrel.

جهگڑا کرنا *jhagṛā karnā*, *v.* To quarrel; to wrangle; to dispute.

جهگڑالو *jhagṛālū* (H) *adj. & n.* Quarrelsome; wrangling; contentious; a brawler; an arguer; a disputer.

جهگڑنا *jhagaṛnā* (H) *v.* To dispute; to quarrel; to argue.

جہل *jahl* (A) *n.m.* Ignorance; stupidity.

جہل مرکب *jahl-ĕ murakkab*, *n.m. & f.* Total ignorance; pretension to knowledge of what one knows very little or nothing.

جہلا *juhalā* (A) *n.m.* (*plu.* of جاهل *jāhil*). The ignorant; the illiterate; fools.

جهلانا *jhallānā* (H) *v.* To be angry; to fly into passion.

جهلانا *jhulānā* (H) *v.* To swing; to rock a cradle; to dangle.

جهلجهلانا *jhaljhalānā* (H) *v.* To glitter; to glare; to throb; to ache; to burn; to beat.

جهلجهلاهٹ *jhaljhalāhaṭ* (H) *n.f.* Glitter; glare; splendour.

جھلسانا ۔ جھلسنا *jhulsānā, jhulasnā* (H) *v.* To singe; to scorch; to brand.

جھلسنا ، جھلس جانا *jhulasnā, jhulas jānā* (H) *v.* To be singed or scorched or burnt.

جھلک *jhalak* (H) *n.f.* Blink; glimpse; brightness; glitter; glare; refulgence; reflection of light; lustre; shine.

جھلکنا *jhalaknā* (H) *v.* To shine; to glare; to glitter; to flash; to glisten.

جھلکی *jhalkī* (H) *n.f.* A glance; a flash; glimpse.

جھلمل *jhilmil* (H) *n.m.* A kind of gauze; a shutter; a venetian blind; the flashing of waves; the twinkling of star or light.

جھلمل کرنا *jhilmil karnā*, *v.* To sparkle; to flash; to twinkle.

جھلملانا *jhilmilānā* (H) *v.* To twinkle; to glimmer; to flicker; to undulate (as the flame of a candle or water).

جھلملی *jhilmilī* (H) *n.f.* A shutter; a venetian blind.

جھلنا *jhalnā* (H) *v.* To fan; to be soldered; to be repaired.

جھلوانا *jhalwānā* (H) *v.* To cause to fan; to cause to solder.

جھلی *jhillī* (H) *n.f.* A thin skin; the omentum; a pellicle; the membrane in which the foetus is enveloped; a cricket.

جھمکا *jhumkā* (H) *n.m.* A bell-shaped pendant (of an ear-ring); a bunch or cluster of flowers or fruits; Ursa Major; the Pleiades.

جھمیلا *jhamelā* (H) *n.m.* Altercation; row; bother; entanglement; complication; dilemma; difficulty.

جھنجھٹ *jhanjhaṭ* (H) *n.f.* Quarrel; contention; argument; difficulty; dilemma.

جھنجھٹیا *jhanjhaṭyā* (H) *adj.* Quarrelsome; contentious. *n.m.* A quarrelsome fellow.

جھنجھلانا *jhunjhlānā* (H) *v.* To be peevish or fretful; to rage; to storm; to be irritable or petulant.

جھنجھلاہٹ *jhunjhlāhaṭ* (H) *n.f.* Peevishness; irritation; anger.

جھنجھنا *jhunjhunā* (H) *n.m.* A child's rattle.

جھنجھنانا *jhanjhanānā* (H) *v.* To rattle; to jingle; to tinkle; to clink; to tingle; to ring.

جھنجھناہٹ *jhanjhanāhaṭ* (H) *n.f.* Jingling; rattling; tinkling; clinking.

جھنجھنی *jhunjhunī* (H) *n.f.* Fetters; irons.

جھنجھوڑنا *jhanjhoṛnā* (H) *v.* To shake; to rouse; to gnash with the teeth; to pull and gnaw flesh with the teeth.

جھنڈ *jhunḍ* (H) *n.m.* Bushes; underwood; thicket; a clump of trees; a multitude; a crowd; a herd; a flock; a swarm.

جھنڈ کے جھنڈ *jhunḍ ke jhunḍ*, *n.m.* Dense crowds; clusters of trees; flocks of birds.

جھنڈا *jhanḍā* (H) *n.m.* A flag; flagstaff; a banner; a standard; an ensign; a streamer.

جھنڈا گاڑنا *jhanḍā gāṛnā*, *v.* To conquer; to overcome or vanquish.

جھنڈا لہرانا *jhanḍā lahrānā*. *v.* To raise a standard; to fly a flag.

جھنڈے پر چڑھانا *jhanḍe par chaṛhānā*, *v.* To make famous; to expose; to render infamous; to defame.

جھنڈی *jhanḍi* (H) *n.f* A little flag.

جھنک *jhanak* (H) *n.f.* The sound of *ghungrū*, an ankle ornament; jingling; rattling.

جھنکار *jhankār* (H) *n.f.* Jingle; rattle; tinkling; clinking; ringing;

جہنم *jahannum* (A) *n.f.* Hell; hell fire.

جہنمی *jahannumī*, *adj.* Infernal; belonging to hell.

جھوٹ *jhūṭ* (H) *n.m.* A lie; a falsehood.

جھوٹ بنانا jhūṭ banānā, v. To frame or invent a lie.

جھوٹ بولنا jhūṭ bolnā, v. To tell a lie; to lie; to utter a falsehood.

جھوٹ جاننا jhūṭ jannā, v. To regard or consider as a falsehood; to disbelieve.

جھوٹ سچ jhūṭ sach, n.m. Fabrication; mixing truth and falsehood.

جھوٹ سچ لگانا jhūṭ sach lagānā, v. To misrepresent; to calumniate.

جھوٹ کا پتلا jhūṭ kā putlā, adj. A perfect liar; an embodiment of falsehood; a very unreliable person.

جھوٹ کے پاؤں نہیں ہوتے jhūṭ ke pāoṅ nahiṅ hote, prov. Falsehood has no legs to stand upon; falsehood is soon found out.

جھوٹ کی پوٹ jhūṭ ki pot, adj. A bundle of lies.

جھوٹ موٹ jhūṭ mūṭ, adv. In jest; for nothing at all; all lies.

جھوٹا jhūṭā (H) n.m. A liar; a false person. adj. Untrue; not genuine; fabricated.

جھوٹا پڑنا jhūṭa parnā, v. To be proved false.

جھوٹی jhūṭi (H) adj. False; untrue. n.f. A liar.

جھوٹی خبر jhūṭi khabar, n.f. A false report; a rumour.

جھوٹی قسم jhūṭi qasam, n.f. A false oath.

جھوٹی گواھی jhūṭi gawāhi, n.f. A false testimony; false evidence.

جھول jhol (H) n.m. Wrinkling or bagginess (as of ill made clothes); brood; farrow; a birth; palsy; soup.

جھول ڈالنا jhol ḍālnā, v. To crease; to puker; to make baggy.

جھول نکالنا jhol nikālnā, v. To remove a rumple or crease (from); to raise a brood.

جھول jhūl (H) n.f. Body clothes of cattle; housings.

جھولا jholā (H) m.n. A knapsack; the palsy.

جھولا jhūlā (H) n.m. A swing; the swinging rope; a cradle.

جھولنا jhūlnā (H) v. To swing; to oscillate; to sway to and fro; to linger over; to dangle. n.m. A kind of poem; a cradle.

جھولی jholi (H) n.f. A wallet; a sack; a pouch; a bag.

جھومر jhūmar (H) n.m. A company; a band; an assembly; an ornament worn by women on the head and which falls on the forehead; a kind of dance in which the dancers join hands.

جھومنا jhūmnā (H) v. To sway to and fro or from side to side; to swing; to rock; to stagger; to droop; to gather or lower (as clouds).

جھونپڑا ' جھونپڑی jhoṅpṛā, jpoṅpṛi (H) n.m./f. A cottage; a hut.

جھونٹا jhoṅṭā (H) n.m. Coil of a woman's hair; the knot of hair at the back part of the head; the motion of the swing.

جھونکا jhoṅkā (H) n.m. A puff or gust of wind; blast; blow; a contact; breeze or current (of wind).

جھونکنا ' جھونک دینا jho ṅknā, jhoṅk denā (H) v. To supply fuel to the furnace; to throw in; to caste; to waste; to squander; to set fire to; to throw dust; to throw away (the lives of men uselessly).

جھیپ ' جھینپ jhep, jheṅp (H) n.f. Shame; shyness.

جھیپنا ' جھینپنا jhepnā, jheṅpnā (H) v. To feel ashamed; to be humiliated; to feel shy.

جہیز johez (A) n.m. Bride's portion; dowry. the paraphernalia of a bride.

جھیکنا jhīknā (H) v. To grieve; to lament; to whine; to think of anything with sorrow.

جھیل jhīl (H) n.f. A lake; a pool; marsh; low ground; swamp; morass.

جھیلنا jhelnā (H) v. To bear; to endure; to undergo.

جھینگا jhingā (H) n.m. A shrimp; a prawn.

جھینگر jhingar (H) n.m. A cricket.

جی jī (H) n.m. Life, soul; self; spirit; mind; conscience; any living thing; disposition; temperament; courage; energy; health; a form of address or answering.

جی آ جانا jī ā jānā, v. To fall in love (with); to have the heart set on.

جی اٹھنا jī uṭhnā, v. To turn away one's affections; to come to life.

جی اچٹنا jī uchaṭnā, v. To be disgusted; to be weary (of); to be sick (of); to be fed up (with).

جی اداس ہونا jī udās honā, v. To be depressed; to be sorrowful; to be gloomy; to be sad.

جی اکتا جانا jī uktā jana, v. See جی اچٹنا jī uchaṭnā.

جی باغ باغ ہونا jī bāgh bāgh honā, v. To be highly pleased.

جی برا کرنا jī burā karnā, v. To give offence (to); to displease; to vomit.

جی بھر آنا jī bhar ānā, v. To be touched with compassion; to be deeply moved; to be sad.

جی بڑھانا jī baṛhānā, v. To encourage; to inspire with courage or confidence.

جی بہلانا jī bahlānā, v. To amuse oneself; to divert the mind (of).

جی بیٹھنا jī baiṭhnā, v. To be disappointed; to be dejected; sinking of heart.

جی پر کھیلنا jī par khelnā, v. To risk one's life; to run the hazard.

جی پگھلنا jī pighalnā, v. To feel pity or compassion (for); to be deeply moved.

جی جان سے قربان jī jān se qurbān, adv. Wholly devoted.

جی جلانا jī jalānā, v, To grieve; to hurt; to plague; to perplex.

جی جلنا jī jalnā, v. To be vexed or troubled in mind; to be hurt.

جی چاہنا jī chāhnā, v. To desire; to long for.

جی چرانا jī churānā, v. To shirk work; to escape from duty.

جی چھوٹنا jī chūṭnā, v. To be disheartened or discouraged; to be exhausted.

جی چھوڑنا jī chhoṛnā, v. To lose courage; to be disheartened.

جی دار jī dār, adj. Brave; courageous.

جی دھڑکنا jī dhaṛaknā, v. To have palpitation of the heart; to shudder.

جی رکھنا jī rakhnā, v. To please; to comfort; to console.

جی سے اتر جانا jī se utar jānā, v. To lose one's good opinion; to be disliked; to be degraded; to lose favour (with).

جی سے جانا jī se jānā, v. To die.

جی کرنا jī karnā, v. To take courage; to dare; to desire; to wish; to long for.

جی کی جی میں رہنا jī kī jī meṅ rahnā, v. Remaining of a charished desire unfulfilled.

جی گھبرانا jī ghabrānā, v. To feel uneasy or agitated.

جی گھٹنا jī ghuṭnā, v. To feel uneasy; to feel suffocated.

جی لگانا jī lagānā, v. To fall in love (with); to place or fix the mind (on).

جی لگنا ji lagnā, v. To contract affection for person or thing; to feel at home (with); to have an interest (in).

جی مارنا ji mārnā, v. To mortify one's desires; to take life.

جی ملانا ji milānā, v. To contract friendship.

جی متلانا ji matlānā, v. To feel nausea.

جی میں آنا ji meṅ ānā, v. To occur (to one).

جی میں بیٹھنا ji meṅ baiṭhnā, v. To be impressed on the mind.

جی میں جی آنا ji meṅ ji ānā, v. To be comforted; to be refreshed.

جی میں رکھنا ji meṅ rakhnā, v. To keep to oneself.

جی میں گھر کرنا ji meṅ ghar karnā, v. To find a place in one's heart; to be pleasant or agreeable.

جی نکلنا ji nikalnā, v. To die; to expire; to desire or love excessively; to fear exceedingly.

جی ہارنا ji hārnā, v. To be discouraged; to be depressed; to be spiritless.

جے jai (H) n.m. Conquest; victory; triumph. excl. Bravo! hurra! all hail!

جیب jaib (A) n.f. The pocket; the breast collar of a garment; the heart; the bosom.

جیب تراش jaib tarāsh, n.m. A pick-pocket.

جیب خاص jaib-ĕ khāṣ, n.m. A privy purse.

جیب خرچ jaib kharch, n.m. Pocket money.

جیب کترا jaib katrā, n.m. A pick pocket.

جیب کترنا jaib katarnā, v. To pick one's pocket.

جیب گھڑی jaib ghari, n.f. A pocket watch.

جیب ، جیبھ jib, jibh (H) n.f. The tongue.

جیبھ پکڑنا jibh pakaṛnā, v. To silence; to interrupt some one talking.

جیبھ چاٹنا jibh chāṭnā, v. To covet; to long for something unattainable.

جیبھ چلانا jibh chalānā, v. To boast beyond one's ability; to talk of being great.

جیبھ کاٹنا jibh kāṭnā, v. To forbid by signs; to bite the tongue in astonishment; to be struck with terror or astonishment.

جیبھ نکالنا jibh nikālnā, v. To be extremely fatigued or thirsty; to pant.

جیت jit (H) n.f. Victory; gain; success.

جیت لینا jit lenā, v. To win; to overcome.

جیت ہونا jit honā, v. To gain a victory; to attain success.

جیتا جاگتا ، جیتی جاگتی jitā jāgtā, jiti jāgti, adj. Alive and well; living and healthy; alive and flourishing.

جیتنا jitnā(H) v. To win; to conquer; to overcome; to beat.

جیتے جی jite ji (H) adv. Whil one is alive; in the life time (of).

جیتے جی مرنا jite ji marnā, v. To lead a miserable life; to endure extreme misery or anguish.

جیٹھ jeṭh (H) n.m. The husband's elder brother; the name of the second Hindū month (May-June).

جیٹھانی jeṭhāni (H) n.f. Wife of the husband's elder brother.

جیجا jijā (H) n.m. Brother-in-law or sister's husband.

جیجی jiji (H) n.f. A sister.

جے جے ونتی jaijaiwanti (H) n.f. Name of a rāgni or musical mode.

جید jaiyyid (A) adj. Good; excellent; strong; bulky.

جیسا ، جیسی ، جیسے jaisā, jaisi, jaise (H) adv./adj. In the manner; which; as; such as; according as.

جیسے چاہو jaise chāho, adv. As you please.

جیسے کا تیسا jaise kā taisā, adv. As before; such as it was; the self-same; unaltered.

جیسے کو تیسا jaise ko taisā, prov. Measure for measure; tit for tat.

جیش jaish (A) n.m. Army.

جیغہ jighah (P) n.m. An ornament of gold worn on the turban; a plume.

جیل خانہ jel khānah, n.m. A jail, a prison; gaol.

جین jain (S) n.m. A sect of Hindūs who worship a number of saints whom they regard as superior to Hindū gods.

جینا jīnā (H) v. To live; to exist. n.m. Living.

جیوٹ jiywat (H) adj. & n.m. Brave; courageous.

جیون jiwan (H) n.m. Life; existence; living.

جیون مرن jiwan maran, n.m. Life and death; transmigration.

چ che—called also jim-ĕ-farsi or jim-ĕ-'ajmi, is the seventh letter of the Persian alphabet and the eighth of that Urdu. It sounds like ch in the English word "check". It does not figure in the Arabic alphabet. The numerical value of چ che according to the abjad, is the same as that of ج jīm i.e. three.

چابک chābuk (P) adj. Active; alert. n.m. A horse-whip; a whip.

چابک دست chābūk dast, adj. Nimble; active; alert; quick; adroit; dextrous.

چابک پھٹکارنا chābuk phaṭkārnā, v. To crack a whip.

چابک سوار chābuk sawār, n.m. A person who breaks or trains a horse; a jockey; a good-rider.

چابکی chābuki (P) n.f. Activity; celerity; agility; alertness.

چابنا chābnā (H) v. To chew; to masticate; to gnaw; to bite; to crunch.

چابی chābi (H) n.f. A key.

چاپ chāp (H) n.f. Sound of footsteps.

چاپلوس chāplūs (P) n. A flatterer; a wheedler; a sycophant.

چاپلوسی chāplūsī (P) n.f. Flattery; sycophancy; fawning.

چاٹ chāt (H) n.f. Licking; taste; relish; longing; craving; a habit; wish; a spicy eatable.

چاٹ پڑنا ، لگنا chāt parnā, lagnā, v. To acquire a taste or longing (for); to crave (for).

چاٹ جانا ، چاٹ لینا chāt jāna, chāṭ lenā, v. To lick up; to lap; to consume; to devour.

چاٹنا chāṭna (H) v. To lick; to lap; to eat; to consume; to devour; to taste.

چاٹی chāti (H) n.f. A churn; an earthen vessel for churning.

چاچا chāchā (H) n.m. A paternal uncle.

چاچی chāchi (H) n.f. A paternal aunt.

چادر chādar (P) n.f. A sheet; a table-cloth; a coverlet; a sheet of iron; a waterfall; a cascade; a veil.

چادر اُتارنا chādar utārnā, v. To insult o disgrace a woman; to tear off woman's veil.

چادر اوڑھنا chādar oṛhnā, v. To put on a veil; to cover oneself with a sheet.

چادر بچھانا *chādar bichhānā, v.* To spread a sheet; to lay the cloth (on).

چادر تان کر سونا *chādar tān kar sonā, v.* To be in ease and comfort; to live a comfortable life; to enjoy a care-free sleep.

چادر چڑھانا *chādar chaṛhānā, v.* To place a cloth as an offering over the tomb of a saint.

چادر سے پاؤں باہر پھیلانا *chādar se pāon bāhar phailānā, v.* To stretch one's feet beyond the sheet; to live above one's means.

چار *chār* (P & H) *adj.* Four.

چار آدمی *chār ādmī, n.m.* A jury of four men.

چار آنکھیں ھونا *chār ānkhen honā, v.* To see one another; to come face to face (with).

چار آئینہ *chār ā'inah, n.m.* A kind of armour having four breast plates.

چار ابرو کا صفایا *chār abrū kā ṣafāyā, n.m.* Shaving of the head, beard, eyebrows and whiskers.

چار اجساد *chār ajsād, n.m.* Four elements (earth, air, fire and water).

چار بالش *chār bālish, n.m.* A kind of large cushion; a sofa; a couch; a throne.

چار بند *chār band, n.m.* The four joints of human bodies; limbs.

چار بیتی *chār baitī, n.f.* A stanza of four lines; a quatrain; a quartet.

چار پائی *chār pāī, n.f.* A bedstead; a bed.

چار پائی پر پڑنا *chār pāī par paṛnā, v.* To become ill; to be confined to bed.

چار پایہ *chār pāyah, n.m. & adj.* A quadruped; four-legged.

چار تال *chār tāl, n.f.* A tune on tombourine.

چار تخم *chār tukhm, n.m.* A medicine for dysentry, composed of four different kinds of seeds.

چار جامہ *chār jāmah, n.m.* A kind of saddle made of cloth and without a tree.

چار چالے *chār chāle, n.m.* The going of the bride and bridegroom to their respective homes four times in the month after their marriage.

چار چاند لگنا *chār chānd lagnā, v.* To have a great abundance of wealth, honour and rank; to get a four-fold increase in one's dignity and glory.

چار چشم *chār chashum, adj.* Faithless; incanstant; untrustworthy.

چار خانہ *chār khānah, n.m.* Check; chequered cloth; cloth ornamented with squares.

چار دانگ *chār dāṅg, n.m.* The four quarters of the globe.

چار دن کی چاندنی *chār din kī chāndnī, n.f.* Temporary enjoyment of life; a transitory enjoyment.

چار دن کی چاندنی اور پھر اندھیری رات ہے *chār din kī chāndnī aur phir andherī rāt hai, prov.* To every spring there is an autumn.

چار دیواری *chār dīwārī, n.f.* Rampart; an enclosure; city-wall; boundary wall.

چار زانو بیٹھنا *chār zānū baiṭhnā, v.* To squat.

چار شنبہ *chār shambah, n.m.* Wednesday.

چار عنصر *chār 'unṣar, n.m.* The four elements (earth, air, fire and water).

چار کھونٹ *chār khūṅṭ, n.m.* See چار دانگ *chār dāṅg.*

چار گوشہ *chār goshah, adj.* Quadrangle.

چار گنا *chār gunā, adj.* Four-fold.

چاروں *chāroṅ, adj.* The four; all the four.

چاروں شانے چت گرنا chāron shāne chit girnā, v. To fall flat on the back sprawling.

چار یار chār yār, n.m. The four successors of the Holy Prophet.

چارا chārā (H) n.m. Herbage; fodder; food for cattle; bait for fish.

چارا ڈالنا chārā ḍalnā, v. To give fodder (to); to bait (a hook).

چارہ chārah (P) n.m. Remedy; cure; expedient; help; aid; resource.

چارہ جوئی chārah joi, n.f. Seeking remedy.

قانونی چارہ جوئی کرنا qānūni chārah joi karnā, v. To seek legal remedy, to file a suit.

چارہ سازی ، چارہ گری chārah sāzi, chārah gari, n.f. Preparing a remedy; remedying; curing.

چار و ناچار chār-ŏ nāchār, adv. Willy-nilly; whether one likes it or not.

چاشت chāsht (P) n.m. The time between sunrise and the meridian; the meal taken at this time; breakfast.

چاشنی chāshni (P) n.f. Flavour; relish; a mixture of sweet and sauce; a syrup; the viscous state of a syrup; toast.

چاشنی دار chāshni dār, adj. Sweet and sour; tasty.

چاق chāq (T) adj. Active; alert; erect; ready; in spirits; hail an hearty

چاق چوبند chāq chauband, adj. Healthy; active; smart; alert; agile; nimble; muscular; vigorous.

چاقو chāqū (P) n.m. A knife; a pen-knife.

چاک chāk (P) adj. Rent; slit; torn; lacerate.

چاک کرنا ahāq karnā, v. To rend to slit; to tear; to split.

چاک گریباں chāk girebāṅ, adj. Having the collar rent; sad; afflicted.

چاک chāk (H) n.m. A potter's wheel; ring of earth or wood; a pulley over which the well-rope passes; a mill-stone.

چاکر chākar (P) n.m. A servant; an under-servant; menial.

چاکری chākri (H) n.f. Service; menial employment.

چاکسو chāksū (P) n.m. A medicine for the diseases of the eye.

چال chāl (H) n.f. Gait; walk; carriage; movement; custom; conduct; trick; stratagem; method; way; pace of a horse; a move in chess.

چال چلن chāl chalan, n.m. Character; conduct.

چال چلنا chāl chalnā, v. To behave deceitfully; to deceive; to practise tricks or deception (on); to play a game.

چال ڈھال chāl ḍhāl, n.f. Gait; motion; manner; method; style; mode.

چال میں آنا chāl men ānā, v. To fall into the trap; to be tricked; to be cheated; to fall into the scheming (of).

چالا chālā (H) n.m. Departure; the ceremony of the departure of a newly married girl from her husband's house to her parents.

چالاک chālāk (P) adj. Active; clever; expert; artful; cunning; astute; alert; fleet; nimble; dextrous.

چالاکی chālāki (P) n.f. Smartness; alertness; nimbleness; dexterity; agility; fleetness; sharpness; artfullness; cleverness; expertness; craftiness.

چالاکی کرنا chālāki karnā, v. To practise cunning; to over-reach.

چالان chālān (H) n.m. An invoice; a remittance; list of goods depatched; a memorandum of money received and invested; forwarding a criminal case to a magistrate for trial.

چالیس chālis (A) adj. Forty.

چالیسا chālisā (H) n.m. A period of forty (days or years); a hero of forty fights.

چالیسواں chāliswāṅ (H) adj. Fortieth. n.m. The fortieth day after the death of a person.

چام chām (H) n.m. Hide; skin; leather.

چام کے دام چلانا chām ke dām chalānā, v. To introduce a leather currency; to make the best use of a wind-fallen authority.

چانپ chāṅp (H) n.f. The back of a gun; the stocks; the rack; (corr. of English) chop (as mutton chop).

چانٹا chāṅṭā (H) n.m. A slap; a cuff.

چاند chāṅd (H) n.m. The moon; a target; a white spot in the forehead of cattle; name of an ornament. n.f. The crown of the head.

چاند چڑھنا khāṅd chaṛhnā. v. Rising of the (new) moon.

چاند رات chāṅd rāt, n.f. The night of the new moon; the first night of a lunar month.

چاند کا ٹکڑا chāṅd kā ṭukṛā, adj. A very beautiful person; a beauty.

چاند گہن chāṅd gahan, n.m. Lunar eclipse.

چاند ماری chāṅd mārī, n.f. Target practice; firing at a target.

خالی کا چاند khālī kā chāṅd, n.m. A month in which no festival falls.

عید کا چاند ہونا 'id kā chāṅd honā, v. To become (like) the 'Id moon; to appear seldom; to be seen very rarely.

چاندنی chāṅdnī (H) n.f. Moonlight; moon beam; a white cloth spread over a carpet; anything white and shining; name of a very white flower.

چاندنی چھٹکنا chāṅdnī chhaṭaknā, v. Spreading of the moon light.

چاندنی رات chāṅdnī rāt, n.f. Moonlit night.

چاندی chāndī (H) n.f. Silver; wealth; profit; gain; advantage.

چاندی کا ورق chāndī kā worq, n.m. A thin silver leaf.

چاندی ہونا chāndī honā, v. To be burnt to ashes; to earn much; to make good money.

چانڈو chāṅḍū. See چنڈو chanḍū.

چاول chāwal (H) n.m. Rice; one-eighth of a rattī.

چاہ chāh (P) n.m. A well; a pit.

چاہ ذقن ، چاہ زنخداں chāh-ĕ zaqan, chāh-ĕ zanakhdān, n.m. The dimple of the chin.

چاہ کن را چاہ در پیش chāh kan rā chāh dar pesh, prov. He who digs a well for others often falls into it.

چاہ chāh (H) n.f. Desire; love; affection; need; wish; liking; choice; appetite.

چاہت chāhat (H) n.f; Desire; wish; longing; will; love; affection; fondness.

چاہنا chāhnā (H) v. To like; to love; to wish; to will; to want; to demand; to approve; to ask for; to crave.

چاہئے chāhiye (H) v. Is necessary; is proper or right; should or ought; must.

چاہیتا chāhītā (H) adj. Beloved; darling; agreeable; desirable. n.m. A sweetheart; a beloved.

چاہیتی chāhitī (H) adj. Darling; desirable. n.f. A beloved; a sweetheart.

چاؤ chāū (H) n.m. Wish; longing; desire; eagerness; zest; pleasure; taste; a kind of bamboo.

چاؤ چوچلا chāū chochlā, n.m. Fondling; caressing; caress; dalliance; toying.

چاؤش chāūsh (P) n.m. An usher; a herald; a door keeper.

چائے chāe (H) n.f. Tea.

چائے دانی chāe dānī, n.f. Tea-pot.

چبا چبا کے بات کرنا *chabā chabā ke bāt karnā* (H) *v.* To speak affectedly; to speak indistinctly; to munch one's word; to mince; to speak haughtily or scornfully.

چبانا *chabānā* (H) *v.* To chew; to gnaw; to masticate; to bit (the lip); to crunch.

چبنی ہڈی *chabnī haḍḍī* (H) *n.f.* Gristle; cartilage.

چبوانا *chabwānā* (H) *v.* To cause to chew; to cause to masticate.

ناک چنے چبوانا *nāk chane chabwānā*, *v.* To torment; to harass; to trouble; to vex.

چبوترا *chabūtrā* (H) *n.m.* A terrace; a platform.

چبھن *chubhan* (H) *n.f.* Pricking; pinching or griping pain; colic.

چبھنا *chubhnā* (H) *v.* To be stuck or thrust (into); to be pricked or pierced; to be goaded; to penetrate; to be disagreeable.

چبھونا *chubhonā* (H) *v.* To thrust or stick (into); to pierce; to goad; to sting; to penetrate.

چبینا *chabinā* (H) *n.m.* Something put in the mouth to be munched or chewed; parched grain used as food.

چپ *chap* (P) *adj.* Left (hand or side).

چپ و راست *chap-ŏ rāst*, *n.m.* The left and the right.

چپ *chup* (H) *n.f.* Silence; stillness; quietness. *inter.* Silence.

چپ چاپ *chup chāp*, *adv.* Silently; quietly; soundlessly. *adj.* Quite; silent.

چپ چپاتے *chup chupāte*, *adv.* Secretly; soundlessy; stealthily.

چپ رہنا'چپ سادھنا *chup rahnā*, *chup sādhnā*, *v.* To remain silent; to keep quiet; to give no answer.

چپ کرانا ' چپانا *chup karānā*, *chupānā*, *v.* To make silent; to pacify.

چپ لگنا *chup lagnā*, *v.* To be struct; dumb; to lose power of speech.

چپ ہونا *chup honā*, *v.* To keep quiet; to be silent; to make no reply.

چپا *chappā* (H) *n.m.* A hand breadth; a measure of four fingers; a span.

چپا چپا *chappā chappā*, *n.m.* Every nook and corner; every inch of ground.

چپاتی *chapāti* (H) *n.f.* A thin cake of unbeavered dough.

چپت *chapat* (H) *n.m.* A slap; a cuff; a box.

چپٹا *chapṭā* (H) *adj.* Flattened; compressed; shallow; flat. *n.m.* A man with a flat nose.

چپٹانا *chipṭānā* (H) *v.* To glue; to attach tightly; to fasten or join; to put on patches; to stick (to); to embrace.

چپٹنا *chipṭnā* (H) *v.* To stick; to adhere; to cling (to).

چپٹی *chapṭī* (H) *adj.* Flat; compressed. *n.f.* A woman with flat nose; homosexuality (between two women)

چپچپا *chipchipā* (H) *adj.* Gluey; sticky; adhesive; glutinous.

چپچپانا *chipchipānā* (H) *v.* To be adhesive; to be sticky; to be glutinous.

چپچپاہٹ *chipchipāhaṭ* (H) *n.f.* Adhesiveness; glutinousness; stickiness.

چپراس'چپڑاس *chaprās*, *chapṛās* (H) *n.f.* A breastplate worn on a belt by *chapṛāsīs*; a badge; a clasp; a buckle; the office of the *chapṛāsī*.

چپراسی ' چپڑاسی *chaprāsī*, *chapṛāsī* (H) *n.m.* One who wears a *chaprās* or badge; a messenger; a peon; an orderly.

چپڑ چپڑ *chapaṛ chapaṛ* (H) *n.f.* The sound of lapping; the sound made in eating.

چپڑا *chipṛā* (H) *n.m.* One who has a constant discharge of matter from the eyes; blear-eyed.

چپڑنا *chuparnā* (H) *v.* To lubricate; to oil; to grease; to anoint; to besmear.

چپڑی *chupṛi* (H) *adj.* Oiled; greasy; oily; unctuous; smooth; plausible.

چپڑی بات *chupṛi bāt, n.f.* Flattery; soft and honeyed words.

چپڑی روٹی *chupṛi roṭi, n.f.* Loaf smeared with butter or *ghee.*

چپقلش *chapqalish* (T) *n.f.* A row; an altercation; crowding; want of room.

چپک *chipak* (H) *n.f.* Adhesiveness; stickiness; name of a bird; goatsucker. *imper.* Stick (to).

چپکانا *chipkānā* (H) *v.* To make adhere; to compress; to paste; to fix.

چپکنا *chipaknā* (H) *v.* To stick; to adhere; to be compressed.

چپکے چپکے *chupke chupke* (H) *adv.* Stealthily; silently; quielty.

چپل ، چپلی *chappal, chapli* (H) *n.f.* A sandle; a slipper.

چپن *chappan* (H) *n.m.* A large lid or cover of a pot.

چپنی *chapni* (H) *n.f.* A small lid of a pot.

چپو *chappū* (H) *n.m.* A paddle; an oar.

چپو مارنا ، چلانا *chappū mārnā, chalānā, v.* To row; to paddle.

چپی *chappi* (H) *n.f.* Kneading (the limbs); massage.

چپیٹ *chapeṭ* (H) *n.f.* A slap; a sudden misfortune; loss; a blow.

چت *chit* (S) *n.f.* The mind; life; soul; heart; attention; memory; thought.

چت چور *chit chor, adj.* Heart stealing; beloved; darling.

چت *chit* (H) *adj.* Prostrate; lying flat on the back.

چت کرنا *chit karnā, v.* To throw one down on one's back (in wrestling); to discomfit; to overcome; to overpower.

چت لیٹنا *chit leṭnā, v.* To lie on one's back.

چتا *chitā* (H) *n.f.* A funeral pile; pyre.

چتر *chatra* (H) *n.m.* An umbrella; a parasol.

چتر، چترا *chitra, chitrā* (S) *n.m.* A drawing; a painting; a picture; a portrait.

چتر کار *chitra kār, n.m.* A painter; an artist.

چتر *chutra* (S) *adj.* Expert; experienced; clever; sharp; wise.

چترائی *chutrāi* (S) *n.f.* Wisdom; cleverness; cunningness; expertness; knowledge.

چتکبرا، چتلا *chitkabrā, chitlā* (H) *adj.* Spotted; speckled.

چتون *chitwan* (H) *n.f.* Sight; look; glance; aspect; appearance.

چتون چڑھانا *chitwan chaṛhānā, v.* To frown; to wrinkle the brow (in anger); to look angry.

چتھڑا، چیتھڑا *chithṛā, chīthṛā* (H) *n.m.* A rag; tatter.

چیتھڑے لگانا *chīthṛe lagānā, v.* To be clothed in rags; to be in rags.

چیتھڑے چیتھڑے کر دینا *chithṛe chīthṛe kar denā, v.* To tear to pieces or bits.

چتی *chitti* (H) *n.f.* A spot; a stain.

چتی دار *chittī dār, adj.* Stained; spotted; speckled.

چتیرا *chaterā* (H) *n.m.* A person who paints flowers (on); a painter; an engraver.

چٹ *chiṭ* (H) *n.f.* A bit; a chip; a rag; a scrap of paper; a slip.

چٹ ، چٹ پٹ *chaṭ, chaṭ paṭ* (H) *adv.* Quickly; instantly; without delay.

چٹ پٹ ہونا chaṭ paṭ honā, v. To die instantaneously; to die in no time.

چٹ چٹ chaṭ chaṭ, (H) n.f. The sound of repeated mopping or cracking; the sound of crackling of a burning body; the sound made in cracking fingers; the sound of quickly repeated strokes.

چٹ کر جانا ، کرنا chaṭ karjānā, karnā (H) v. To eat up; to lick the platter clean; to devour.

چٹا chiṭṭā (H) adj. White.

چٹاخ chaṭākh, n.f. The sound of cracking or beating.

چٹاخ پٹاخ chaṭākh paṭākh, adv. At once; in quick succession; without hesitation.

چٹاخا ، چٹاکا chaṭākhā, chaṭākā (H) n.m. A crash; a smack; an explosion.

چٹان chaṭān (H) n.f. Rock; rocky ground; a large block of stone.

چٹانا chaṭānā (H) v. To cause to lick or lap; to cause to taste.

چٹائی chaṭāi (H) n.f. A mat.

چٹ پٹا ، چٹ پٹی chaṭ paṭā, chaṭ paṭī (H) adj. Tasty; spicy; pungent.

چٹخ جانا chaṭakh jānā, v. To crack; to split.

چٹخارا chiṭkhārā (H) n.m. A cluck made with the tongue to indicate that the thing tasted is excellent.

چٹخارے بھرنا chaṭkhāre bharnā, v. To smack a clucking noise with the tongue in approval of the excellence of the thing tasted.

چٹک ـ مٹک chaṭak maṭak, (H) n.f. Blendishment; coquetry; pomp and show; wanton gait; grandeur; magnificence.

چٹکانا، چٹخانا chaṭkānā, chaṭkhānā (H) v. To crack; to mop (the fingers); to split; to fire off a musket.

چٹکلا chuṭkulā (H) n.m. Pleasantry; facetiae; wit; humour; a pun; joke or trick; a specific cure.

چٹکلا چھوڑنا chuṭkulā chhoṛnā, v. To utter a jest or pleasantry; to let off a squib.

چٹکنا، چٹخنا chaṭaknā, chaṭkhnā (H) v. To crackle (as wood in the fire); to crack (as whip); to split; to open out; to bloom (flower); to speak rudely.

چٹکنی ، چٹخنی chaṭkanī, chaṭkhanī (H) n.f. The bolt of a door.

چٹکی chuṭkī (H) n.f. A pinch; a pinch (of); an ornament worn on the toes; a snap of the fingers; a twist given to lace; the hammer of a gun.

چٹکی بجانا chuṭkī bajānā, v. To snap the fingers.

چٹکی بجاتے میں chuṭkī bajāte meṅ, adv. In a moment; in a trice.

چٹکی بھر chuṭkī bhar, adj. So much as a pinch can hold; as much as can be hold between a finger and the thumb; very little.

چٹکی بھرنا ، چٹکی لینا chuṭkī bharnā, chuṭkī lenā, v. To pinch; to nip; to taunt.

چٹکیوں میں اڑانا chuṭkiyoṅ meṅ uṛānā, v. To turn off in a joke; to turn into ridicule; to put one off with a joke.

چٹکیلا chaṭkīlā (H) adj. Pungent; tasty; splendid; bright; gaudy; gay.

چٹلا chuṭlā (H) n.m. A lock of hair worn on the back of the head.

چٹنی chaṭnī (H) n.f. A kind of pickle or sauce; marmalade.

چٹنی بنانا ، کرنا chaṭnī banānā, karnā, v. To make or prepare a sauce; to grind very fine; to beat black and blue; to punish very severely.

چٹو chaṭṭū (H) n.m. A kind of mortar; a glutton; voracious; epicurion; gourmand.

چٹوانا chatwānā (H) v. To cause to lick or lap up.

چٹورا chatorā (H) n.m. An epicure; a greedy person; one who wastes his money on delicacies.

چٹھا chitthā (H) n.m. A memorandum of the money paid to servants; rent roll; pay-sheet; a balance-sheet.

کچا چٹھا kachchā chitthā, n.m. Full account; unsavoury details.

چٹھی chitthi(H) n.f. A note; a letter; a billet; a chit; a bill; a draft; a certificate.

چٹھی بانٹنا chitthi bāntnā, v. To deliver letters.

چٹھی ڈالنا chitthi ḍālnā v. To post a letter; to make a lottery or raffle.

چٹھی رساں chitthī rasān, n.m. A postman; one who delivers letters.

چٹی chatti (H) n.f. Deficiency; want; penalty; fine; damages.

چٹی chitti (H) adj. White.

چٹیا chutiyā (H) n.m. The plait or tie of hair behind; a lock of hair left on the head unshaved; a pigtail kept by Hindūs.

چٹیل chatyal (H) adj. Bare; bleak; desolate; treeless tract of land.

چچا chachā (H) n.m. Father's brother; paternal uncle.

چچا زاد بھائی chachā zād bhāi, n.m. A cousin; a paternal uncle's son.

چچڑی chichri (H) n.f. A tick or louse (of dogs or sheep).

چچوڑنا chachornā (H) v. To suck; to suckle.

چچی chachi (H) n.f. Aunt; paternal uncle's wife.

چچیرا chacherā (H) adj. Descended from or related through a paternal uncle.

چخ chakh, n.f. Quarrel; strife; contest; tumult; uproar.

چخ چخ chakh chakh, n.f. Foolish altercation; prattle; chatter; babble.

چخے chakhe, intj. Be off! away; begone; avaunt.

چدانا chudānā (H)v. Copulation; prostitution; to have sexual intercourse with men.

چڈھا chaddhā (H) n.m. The groin; a clown; a buffoon.

چڈھی chaddhi (H) n.f. Riding on a man or animal's back.

چر char (H) n.f. Sound made in tearing cloth; a sandbank or island formed by the current of a river; a ford; a shoal.

چراغ charāgh chirāgh (P) n.m. A lamp; a light.

چراغ بڑھانا، بجھانا، ٹھنڈا کرنا، گل کرنا charāgh barhānā, bujhānā, thundā karnā, gull karnā, v. To extinguish a lamp; to put out a light.

چراغ پا ہونا charāgh pā honā, v. To be angry.

چراغ جلنا یا روشن ہونا charāgh jalnā yā raushan honā, v. To be lighted (lamp).

چراغ دان chargh dān, n.m. A lamp-stand; a candlestick.

چراغ دکھانا charāgh dikhānā, v. To show a light.

چراغ میں بتی پڑنا charāgh men batti parnā, v. Approaching of the night.

گھی کے چراغ جلنا ghī ke charāgh jalnā, v. To live in fine style; to make great pomp and show.

بے چراغ be charāgh, adj. Unlit; abandoned; deserted; a home without a male child.

چراغاں chirāghān (P) n.m. Illumination; display of lights; visiting a saint's tomb and depositing a lamp or some money there.

چراغی chirāghi (P) n.f. A present made to the keeper of a tomb of a saint; present made to soothsayers.

چراگاه charāgāh (P) n.f. A pasture; a meadow; grazing ground.

چرانا charānā (H) v. To graze; to pasture; to feed; to lead one by the nose; to make a fool (of).

چرانا churanā (H) v. To steal; to rob; to filch; to absorb; to suck.

آنکھ چرانا āṅkh churānā, v. To turn away the eyes; to take a furtive glance (at); not to look a person in the face.

چراند chirānd (H) n.f. The smell of burning leather, hair, etc.

چرائتا chirāetā (H) n.m. A species of gentian; a medicinal herb.

چرب charb (P) adj. Oily; greasy; glib; sharp; fat.

چرب زبان charb zabān, adj. Smooth-tongued; flattering; conversable; entertaining.

چرب زبانی charb zabāni, n.f. Fairness of speech; fine talk; plausibility; flattery; speciousness of language.

چرب غذا charb ghizā, n.f. Rich food; dainties.

چربه charbah (P) n.m. Tracing paper; tracing; copy.

چربه آتارنا charbah utārnā, v. To make a tracing; to copy.

چربی charbi (P) n.f. Fat; suet; grease; tallow.

چربی دار charbi dār, adj. Fat; greasy.

چرپرا charparā (H) adj. Acrid; biting; pungent; hot; smart.

چرپرانا charparānā (H) v. To smart; to burn; to tingle (as wound).

چرپراهٹ charparāhaṭ (H) n.f. Pungency; sharpness; acridity.

چرتر، چلتر charittar, chalittar (S) n.m. Conduct; behaviour; disposition; manner; carriage; talent; arts; tricks; adventures; deeds; cunning; deceit.

چرچا charchā (H) n.m. Gossip, rumour; talking over past events; recapitulating old incidents; argument; report.

چرچا کرنا charchā karnā, v. To talk about; to spread a report.

چرچا هونا charchā honā, v. To be talked about; to be discussed.

چرچرانا charcharānā, chirchirānā (H) v. To crackle; to smart; to creak (as shoes); to be pungent or sharp.

چرچراهٹ chirchirāhaṭ, charcharāhaṭ (H) n.f. Pain; affliction; a cracking sound; pungency; sharpness.

چرخ charkh (P) n.m. A wheel; potter's wheel; a lathe; the sky; the heavens; the celestial glob; circular motion; rotation; a falcon.

چرخ اخضر charkh-ĕ akhẓar, n.m. The ethereal sphere.

چرخ اطلس charkh-ĕ aṭlas. The crystalline sphere or heaven.

چرخ بریں charkh-ĕ barīn, n.m. The seventh heaven.

چرخ چڑھانا charkh chaṛhānā, v. To turn on a lathe; to rotate; to whirl.

چرخ هنڈولا charkh hanḍolā, n.m. A merry-go-round.

چرخه charkhah (P) n.m. A spinning wheel; a reel; the axis of a pulley. adj. Thin; weak; poor; worn-out.

چرخه کاتنا charkhah kātnā, v. To spin.

چرخه پونی charkhah punī, n.m. Spinning and carding; woman's responsibility.

چرخه هوجانا charkhah hojānā, v. To become worn out; to become old.

چرخی charkhī (P) n.f. A spinning wheel; a pulley; a reel; a kind of fireworks; a kind of toy; catharine-wheels; the instrument with which the seed is separated from cotton; a pulley used in drawing water from a well; a dumb-waiter.

چرخی فانوس charkhi-ĕ fānūs. A revolving lantern made of talc with pictures all round; a magic lantern.

چرس charas (H) n.m. A large leather bag or bucket; an urn; the exudation of the flowers or hemp collected with the dew and prepared for use as an intoxicating drug.

چرسا charsā (H) n.m. Hide of an ox or buffalo; a skin; dressed leather; a large leather bucket.

چرسی charsi (H) n.m. One addicted to smoking charas.

چرک chirk (P) n.m. Dirt; filth; ordure; pus.

چرکا charkā, adj. White spotted (a form of leprosy). n.m. A slight wound; scratch.

چرکٹا charkaṭā (H) n.m. The person who feeds and looks after the elephant; a low fellow.

چرکنا chiraknā (H) v. To have scanty stools.

چرکیں chirkin (P) adj. Filthy; dirty; foul. n.m. The pen name of a well known poet.

چرم charm (P) n.m. Leather; skin; hide.

چرمی charmi (P) adj. Made of leather; leathern.

چرن charan (H) n.m. The foot; foot of a verse.

چرن چھونا یا لینا charan chhūnā yā lenā, v. To touch the feet of (out of respect); to pay respects.

چرنا charnā (H) v. To graze; to eat the grass. n.m. Half trousers.

چرنا chirnā (H) v. To be torn or split; to split.

چرند، چرندہ charind charindah (P) n.m. A quadruped; a beast; an animal that grazes.

چرند و پرند charind-ŏ parind, n.m. Beasts and birds.

چروانا charwānā (H) v. To cause to graze.

چروانا chirwānā (H) v. To cause to tear; to cause to split or cleave.

چرواہا charwāhā (H) n.m. A grazier; a shepherd; a herdsman.

چرواہی charwāhi (H) n.f. The rent or fee paid for pasturage; a female grazier.

چروائی، چرائی chirwāi, chirāi (H) n.f. Wages for sawing or cutting wood.

چری chari (H) n.f. Unripe corn cut for use as fodder; a piece of land held rent free; a kind of bracelet.

چڑ chiṛ (H) n.f. Mocking; vexation antipathy; irritation; aversion.

چڑا chiṛā (H) n.m. A cock-sparrow.

چڑانا chiṛānā (H) v. To vex; to irritate; to provoke; to offend; to mock; to jeer; to make grimaces.

چڑچڑ chiṛ chiṛ (H) n.f. Prattle; jabber; silly talk.

چڑچڑا chiṛchiṛā (H) adj. Cross; peevish; offended.

چڑچڑاپن chiṛchirā pan (H) n.m. Peevishness; fretfulness.

چڑنا chiṛnā (H) v. To be vexed; to be irritated; to fret; to be provoked.

چڑھا جانا charhā jānā (H) v. To gulp down.

چڑھانا charhānā (H) v. To cause to ascend; to raise; to lift; to offer (oblations); to string (a bow); to brace (a drum); to dye (with colour); to fix (a bayonet); to drink; to imbibe; to quaff; to apply; to put; to spread; to pull (up); to cause to mount.

چڑھاؤ charhāo (H) n.m. Ascent, rise; acclivity; swelling; inundation; flood; tide; rise in price or rent.

اُتار چڑھاؤ utār charhāo, n.m. Ascent and discent; rise and fall; ebb and flow.

چڑھاوا charhāwā (H) n.m. An offering; oblation; anything presented as a token of respect.

چڑھائی charhāi (H) n.f. Ascent; rise; acclivity; attack; assault; invasion.

چڑھنا charhnā (H) v. To ascend; to mount; to advance; to rise; to attack; to embark; to climb; to be braced (as a drum); to be strung (as bow); to be offered (as a sacrifice).

چڑی chiri (H) n.f. A hen-sparrow.

چڑی مار chiri mār, n.m. A bird-catcher; a fowler.

چڑیا chiryā (H) n.f. A sparrow; a bird.

چڑیا خانہ یا گھر chiryā khānah, ghar, n.m. An aviary; the zoo.

سونے کی چڑیا sone ki chiriyā, n.f. A very valuable prize.

چڑیل churail (H) n.f. A hog; a slut; the ghost of a woman who died during pregnancy.

چسانا chusānā (H) v. To cause or give to suck.

چسپاں chaspān (P) adj. Viscous; coherent; sticking together; adhesive; pasted; stuck; applicable; suitable; to the point.

چسپاں کرنا chaspān karnā, v. To paste; to affix; to join together.

چسپانی chaspāni (P) adj. Adhesive.

چست chust (P) adj. Active; fleet; clever; quick; brisk; smart; narrow; tight.

چست چالاک chust chālāk, adj. Active; alert; agile.

چستی chusti (P) n.f. Activity; expedition; nimbleness; smartness; skill; dexterity; alertness; activeness.

چسک chasak (H) n.f. Pain; throbbing pain, a stitch.

چسکا chaskā (H) n.m. Ardent desire; relish; taste; habit.

چسکا پڑنا chaskā parnā, v. To acquire or have taste for.

چسکنا chasaknā (H) v. To throb; to have shooting pain.

چسکی chuski (H) n.f. A draught of water or other liquid; a sip.

چسکی لگانا chuski lagānā, v. To sip, to have a draught.

چسنا chusnā (H) v. To be sucked.

چسنی chusni (H) n.f. A sucking bottle; a sucking stick for infants; a nipple.

چشتی chishti (P) n.m. An inhabitant of Chisht; a sect of Muslims.

چشم chashm (P) n.f. The eye; hope; expectation.

چشم بد دور chashm-ĕ baddūr. Int. God preserve you from evil eyes! away malicious glances!

چشم براہ ہونا chashm barāh honā, v. To expect with impatience.

چشم بیمار chashm-ĕ bimār, n.m. A languid eye; an eye that looks half closed from modesty; an epithet of beauty.

چشم پوشی chashm poshī, n.f. Conniving at; pretending not to see; overlooking.

چشم پوشی کرنا chashm poshī karnā, v. To turn one's eyes away; to overlook; to connive (at).

چشم داشت chashm dāsht, n.f. Hope; expectation; desire; trust confidence.

چشم زدن chashm zadan, n.f. Winking.

چشم زدن میں chashm zadan men, adv. In the winks of an eye; in a trice; in a moment; in an instant; instantly.

چشم نمائی chashm numāi, n.f. Reproof; rebuke; reprimand; scold; warning.

چشم نمائی کرنا chashm numāi karnā, v. To rebuke; to reprove; to reprimand.

چشم و چراغ chashm-ŏ chirāgh, n.m. Light of the eye; dearly beloved.

آهو چشم āhū chashm, adj. Soft-eyed; having the eyes of a gazelle or fawn; an epithet of beauty.

چشمک chashmak (P) n.f. Wink; winking; misundestanding; spectacles.

چشمه chashmah (P) n.m. A fountain; a spring; source; spectacles.

چغا chughā, see چوغا chūghah.

چغد chughad (P) n.m. An owl. (Fig.) Foolish person.

چغل chughl (P) n.m. A tell-tale; a tale-bearer; a back biter; a small pebble placed on the hole of the chilam to prevent the tobacco from slipping down the hole.

چغل خور chughal khor, n.m. A tale-bearer; a back-biter.

چغل خوری chughal khori, n.f. Back-biting; tale bearing.

چغلی chughlī (P) n.f. Tale-bearing; back-biting.

چغلی کھانا chughli khānā, v. To back, bite, to slander.

چفتی chafti (P) n.f. A flat ruler.

چق chiq (T) n.f. A hanging screen made of split bamboos.

چقماق chaqmāq (T) n.f. A flint for striking fire.

چقندر chuqandar (P) n.m. Beet; Beet-root.

چک chik (H) n.f. A pain in the loins or back.

چک chak (H) n.m. Landed property; a farm; tenure.

چک بندی chak bandi, n.f. Marking the boundaries of an estate.

چکا chakkā (H) n.m. Circular or round; a wheel; anything round and flat; a heap of material, masonry etc. adj. Condensed; thick.

چکا چوند chakāchaund (H) n.f. The state of being dazed or dazzled; the effect of sudden and strong flash of light on the eyes; radiance.

چکارا chikārā (H) n.m. A kind of antelope found on the banks of the Jamunā; a kind of fiddle.

چکاری chikāri (H) n.f. A mosquito like insect. n.m. A hunting knife.

چکان chakān (P) adj. (used in comp.) Dropping; distilling.

چکانا chukānā (H) v. To finish; to adjust matters; to settle an account or the price of an article; to pay off debt; to liquidate.

چکاور chakāwar (H) n.m. The name of a disease in the feet of horses.

چکائی chukāi (H) n.f. Settlement; adjustment; wages for settlement; omission; an unintentional error.

چکتی chakti (H) n.f. A tablet; a patch of leather; a round plate of metal; the tail of the sheep called Dumbah.

چکٹ chikkat (H) adj. Filthy; covered with grease and dirt.

چکٹنا chikatnā (H) v. The be sticky, dirty, filthy &c.

چکر chakkar (H) n.m. A potter's wheel; a discus; a circle; a whirlwind; an eddy; ring; circumference; circuit; whirligig; merry-go-round; a circular course; giddiness; vertigo; perplexity, misfortune.

چکر آنا chakkar ānā, v. To become giddy; to faint.

چکر دینا chakkar denā, v. To turn round and round; to lounge a horse; to deceive; to delude.

چکر کھانا *chakkar khānā, v.* To whirl; to revolve; to go round; to take a round-about or indirect road; to turn round and round.

چکر میں آنا *chakkar men ānā, v.* To be involved in difficulties; to be in for trouble.

چکر میں ڈالنا *chakkar men ḍālnā, v.* To involve one in difficulty; to perplex; to lead astray.

چکرانا *chakrānā* (H) *v.* To be perplexed; to be taken aback; to become giddy; to be puzzled.

چکرورتی *chakarvartī* (S) *n.m.* A universal monarch; an emperor; the title of one of the great families of *Brahman* in *Bengāl*.

چکلا *chaklā* (H) *n.m.* A round and broad block; a round plate on which bread is rolled; any quarter of a town particularly the one inhabited by prostitutes; a brothel. *adj.* Wide; broad; round; circular.

چکلی *chaklī* (H) *n.f.* The pulley (of a well) on which the well-rope revolves; a small round stone, used for grinding spices.

چکما *chakmā* (H) *n.m.* A game at cards; cheating; trickery.

چکما دینا *chakmā denā, v.* To play a trick (on); to inflict a loss; to cheat.

چکما کھانا *chakmā khānā, v.* To be deceived; to be cheated; to suffer a loss.

چکن *chikan* (P) *n.f.* Embroidery; embroidered cloth.

چکن دوز *chikan doz* (P) *n.m.* An embroiderer.

چکنا ، چکنی *chiknā, chiknī* (H) *adj.* Greasy; oily; glossy; sleek; slippery; polished; smooth; mild; soft; beautiful; showy.

چکنا چپڑا *chiknā chuprā, adj.* Well dressed; dandified.

چکنا گھڑا *chiknā ghaṛā, n.m.* A shameless person.

چکنی جورو *chiknī jorū, n.f.* A slippery wife; an unfaithful wife.

چکنی چپڑی باتیں کرنا *chiknī chupṛī bāten karnā, v.* To wheedle; to flatter; to use oily speech.

چکنی سپاری یا ڈلی *chikni supāri yā dali, n.f.* Beetle-nut prepared by boiling it in milk.

چکنی مٹی *chikni matti, n.f.* Clay; clayey soil.

چکنا *chuknā* (H) *v.* To be finished; to be exhausted; to be settled (price, accounts); to be adjudicated; to be adjusted.

چکنا چور *chaknā chūr* (H) *adj.* Broken to pieces; fatigued to the point of exhaustions; absolutely exhausted.

چکنا چور کرنا *chaknā chūr karnā, v.* To break to pieces; to shatter; to exhaust completely.

چکنا چور ہونا *chakna chūr honā, v.* To be broken to pieces; to be completely exhausted.

چکناھٹ *chiknāhat* (H) *n.f.* Oiliness; smoothness; gloss; polish; beauty.

چکنائی *chiknāi* (H) *n.f.* Grease; oil; fat; butter; fat of meat.

چکوا *chakwā* (H) *n.m.* The ruddy-goose called the *Brahmani* duck.

چکوتا *chakautā* (H) *n.m.* A stipulated hire or wages; agreement; adjustment; settlement; bargain.

چکوترا *chakotrā* (H) *n.m.* A fruit of the lime kind; pompelmoose; shaddock.

چکور *chakor* (H) *n.m.* The Indian red-legged partridge.

چکھانا *chakhānā* (H) *v.* To cause to taste; to make one taste; to cause to suffer or inflict punishment (on)

چکھنا *chakhnā* (H) *v.* To taste; to relish; to suffer.

چکئی *chakai* (H) *n.f.* A top; a small round wooden toy; ruddy-goose.

چکی chakki (H) n.f. A millstone; a mill; a grindstone; the knee pan.

چکی پیسنا chakki pisnā, v. To grind in a mill; to work a mill; to undergo hardship.

چکی راهنا chakki rāhnā, v. To notch millstones.

چکی کا پاٹ chakki kā pāt, n.m. A mill stone.

چگانا chugānā (H) v. To cause fowls to pick up food with the beak; to take fowls out to pick up food; to cause to peck.

چگنا chugnā (H) v. To peck; to pick up food with the beak; to feed.

چگونگی chigūnagi (P) n.f. Circumstances; manner; nature of a thing; quality; howness.

چگونه chigūnah (P) adv. How; of what kind; in what manner.

چل chal (H) int. Go away ! be off ! away! begone !

چل بسنا chal basnā, v. To pass away; to expire; to die.

چل چلاؤ chal chalāo, n.m. Uncertainty of life; the last hours of life.

چل دینا chal denā, v. To march; to leave; to decamp.

چل جانا chal jānā (H) v. Arising of a quarrel.

دماغ چل جانا dimāgh chal jānā, v. To go mad; to become insane.

چل chul (H) n.f. Itch; scratching; sexual passion.

چلا، چله chillā, chillah (P) n.m. The forty days of Lent in which the religious people in the East sometimes retire to their cells or to mosques and engage themselves in fasting and divine worship; the period of forty days after child birth during which a woman remains unclean; the fast of Lent; quarantine.

چلا chillā (H) n.m. The string of a bow; gold threads put in the border of a turban.

چلا باندهنا chillā bāndhnā, v. To make a vow; to tie a thread on a tomb as a vow.

چلا چڑهانا chillā charhānā, v. To string a bow; to bend a bow.

چلا کهینچنا chillā khenchnā, v. To complete forty days of fasting and devotion; to bend a bow; to prepare for battle.

چلانا chillānā (H) v. To scream; to shriek; to roar, to bawl; to cry out; to exclaim; to complain; to rage.

چلانا chalānā (H) v. To impel; to stir; to cause to move; to propel; to drive; to discharge or fire; to originate; to put into circulation; to give currency (to); to issue; to advance money on interest; to transact business; to carry out; to put in execution; to enforce; to help one to walk.

چلاؤ chalāū (H) adj. Shaky; unstable; transitory; a make-shift arrangement; frails; inconstant; fickle.

چلاؤ chulāo (P) n.m. A dish of boiled rice of the kind of *pulāo* but without any meat.

چلبلا chulbulā (H) adj. Restless; fidgety; airy; gay; sportive; coquettish.

چلبلانا chulbulānā (H) v. To be restless; to fidget.

چلبلاهٹ، چلبلا پن chulbulāhaṭ chulbulā pan (H) n.f. Restlessness; sportiveness.

چلت پهرت chalat phirat (H) n.f. Action; activity; agility; gait; gesture; revolution.

چلتا، چلتی chaltā, chalti (H) adj. Going; moving; flowing (stream); current; passable (coin); flourishing; thriving (business); efficient; usual; powerful; potent; fast; in force.

چلتا پرزه chaltā purzah, n.m. A sharper; a cheat; a swindler; a very clever person.

چلتا کرنا chaltā karnā, v. To get going; to send away; to dispose of; to kill.

چلتی دکان chalti dukān, *n.f.* A thriving business.

چلتر chalittar (H) *n.m.* See چرتر *charitar.*

چلچلاتی دھوپ chulchulātī dhūp (H) *n.f.* Blazing sun.

چلغوزہ chilghozah (P) *n.m.* The kernels of the pine; a small nut like pistachio.

چلم chilam (H) *n.f.* The part of *huqqah* which contains tobacco and the fire.

چلمچی chilamchi (P) *n.f.* A wash-hand basin of metal.

چلمن chilman (H) *n.m.* A hanging screen made of reeds or split bamboo for keeping out glare; a venetian blind; a lattice.

چلن chalan (H) *n.m.* Gait; course; conduct; behaviour; custom; way; manner; fashion; ceremony; currency; procedure.

چلنا chalnā (H) *v.* To move; to go; to proceed; to be in demand; to travel; to flow; to run; to walk; to sail; to have influence; to be effective; to be in force.

چلنی chalnī, see چھلنی *chhalnī.*

چلو chullū (H) *n.m.* A handful; the palm of the hand contracted so as to held water.

چلو بھر chullū bhar, *adj.* A handful of (any liquid).

چلو بھر پانی میں ڈوب مرنا chullū bhar pānī meṅ ḍūb marnā, *v.* To be grealty abashed or ashamed.

چلو سے پانی پینا chullū se pānī pīnā, *v.* To drink water out of the palm of the hand.

چلوانا chalwānā (H) *v.* To make one walk; to make one walk a good bit.

چلیپا chalīpā (P) *n.f.* A cross; a crucifix; anything crooked or bent.

چمار chamār (H) *n.m.* A worker in leather; a shoemaker; a cobler; a tanner; a currier.

چماری chamāri (H) *n.f.* The wife of a *chamār*.

چمپا champā (H) *n.m.* A shrub bearing fragrant yellow flowers.

چمپا کلی champā kali, *n.f.* A kind of necklace.

چمپت ہونا champat honā (H) *v.* To disappear; to vanish; to run away; to scamper off; to decamp.

چمپئی champai (H) *adj.* Of the colour of *champā*; yellow; golden.

چمٹا chimṭā (H) *n.m.* Tongs; forceps; pincers.

چمٹانا chimṭānā (H) *v.* To cause to adhere; to fix; to paste; to embrace.

چمٹنا chimaṭnā (H) *v.* To adhere; to stick; to cling (to); to take in close; to follow close at the heels of; to dog; to embrace; to be pasted.

چمٹی chimṭī (H) *n.f.* Pincers; pinch.

چمچہ chamchah (P) *n.m.* A spoon; a ladle.

چمچہ بھر chamchah bhar, *adj.* Spoonful.

چمچہ ہر دیگی chamchah-ĕ har degi, *adj.* A sponger; one who meddles with every body's affairs.

چمچی chamchi (H) *n.f.* A small spoon.

چمرخ chamrakh (H) *n.f.* A piece of leather attached to a spindle. *adj.* Thin; lean; weak.

چمڑا chamṛā (H) *n.m.* Skin; hide; leather.

چمڑا ادھیڑنا ، کھینچنا chamṛā udheṛnā, khenchnā, *n.m.* To skin; to flay; to beat severely.

چمڑی chamṛī (H) *n.f.* Skin.

چمک chamak (H) *n.f.* Glitter; brilliance; splendour; flash; glare; gleam.

چمک دار chamak dār, *adj.* Shining; glittering; brilliant.

چمک دمک chamak damak, *n.f.* Splendour; glitter; brilliance.

چمکارنا chumkārnā (H) *v.* To make a kissing sound with the lips; to coaxe or quiet children; to speak kindly (to); to soothe; to caress.

چمکانا *chamkānā* (H) *v.* To cause to glitter or glow; to brighten; to cause to flourish or prosper; to carry to great prosperity; to display; to polish; to make lively or active.

چمکنا *chamaknā* (H) *v.* To shine; to glitter; to sparkle; to do well; to prosper; to be lively; to be brisk; to thrive; to be startled; to fly into a passion; to become angry.

چمکی *chamki* (H) *n.f.* Glitter, spangle; sparkling object; tinsel.

چمگادڑ *chimgādar* (H) *n.f.* A bat; a flying-fox.

چمن *chaman* (P) *n.m.* A flower garden; a flower-bed; a blooming or flourishing place.

چمن بندی کرنا *chaman bandi karnā, v.* To lay out a garden.

چمن زار *chaman zār, n.m.* A meadow; a garden.

چمنستان *chamnistān* (P) *n.m.* A flower-bed; a garden.

چنا *chanā* (H) *n.m.* Gram; the chickpea; vetches.

لوہے کے چنے *lohe ke chane, n.m.* An extremely difficult task.

چننا *chunnā* (H) *v.* To gather; to select; to arrange; to pick; to choose; to plait (cloth); to crimp (cloth).

چنار *chanār* (P) *n.m.* The poplar tree; a tall tree the leave of which are partly green and partly red resembling a man's hand often emitting sparks of fire.

چناں و چنیں *chunāṅ-ō chuniṅ* (P) *n.f.* Like this and that; evasion; subterfuge; grandiloquence.

چنانچہ *chunāṅcheh* (P) *adv.* Accordingly; therefore; so that; in such a manner; for example.

چناؤ *chunāo* (H) *n.m.* Selection; election.

چنائی *chunāi* (H) *n.f.* Building up a wall; masonry work.

چنبر *chambar* (P) *n.m.* A cover for the *chilam* (of *huqqah*); a circle; a hoop of a tub; a ring; a lid.

چنبیلی *chambali* (H) *n.f.* The jasmine.

چنت *chunnat* (H) *n.f.* Plaiting; crimping; plaits; ruffles.

چنتا *chintā* (H) *n.f.* Thought; consideration; reflection; anxiety; care; doubt; danger.

چنچل *chanchal* (H) *adj.* Moving; restless; unsteady; wanton; playful; fickle.

چنچنا *chinchinā* (H) *adj.* Peevish; fretful; cross; angry.

چنچنانا *chinchinānā* (H) *v.* To be stung; to be nettled; to scream; to squeak; to squall.

چند *chand* (P) *adj.* How many; how much; how often; how long; a little; a few.

چند بار *chand bār, adv.* Many a time; quite often.

چند روزہ *chand rozah, adj.* Temporary; transitory; for a few days; ephemeral.

ہر چند *har chand, adv.* Although; however; nevertheless; notwithstanding; with all that.

چندا ، چندر ، چندر ما *chandā, chandra, chandarmā* (H) *n.m.* The moon.

چندر مکھی *chandra mukhi, adj.* As beautiful as the moon. *n.m.* Moon-flower.

چنداں *chandāṅ* (P) *adj.* So much; much; many; more; *adv.* So great; rather.

چنداں مضائقہ نہیں *chandāṅ muẓāiqah nahiṅ, phr.* Of not much consequence; does not matter.

چندن *chandan* (S) *n.m.* Sandal wood or sandal tree.

چندن هار chandan hār (H) n.m. A necklace composed of moon-shaped pieces of gold, silver, &c.

چنده chandah (H) n.m. Subscription; contribution; donation.

چندها chundhā (H) adj. Dim-sighted; weak-eyed; purblind. n.m. Blinkard; one whose eyes are too weak to bear daylight.

چندهیانا chundhiyānā (H) v. To be purblind; to see dimmly; to be dazzled by excess of light.

چندی chindī (H) n.f. A small piece of rag.

چندی چندی کرنا chindī chindī karnā, v. To break into pieces; to reduce to fragments.

چندے chande (P) adj. A little; a while; a few; some. adv. Sometime; for sometime.

چندیا chandyā (H) n.f. The crown of the head; a small cake.

چنڈال chanḍāl (H) n.m. Low-caste; an outcast; a miser; a wretch; a miscreant.

چنڈال چوکڑی chanḍāl chaukṛī, n.f. A company of four or more miscreants.

چنڈو chandū (H) n.m. An intoxicating drug made of opium.

چنڈو باز chanḍū bāz, n.m. One addicted to smoking chanḍū.

چنڈو خانه chanḍū khānah, n.m. A house in which chanḍū is smoked.

چنڈول chanḍol (H) n.m. A sedan with two poles; a plaything consisting of four little earthen pots joined together; the name of a bird.

چنری chunrī (H) n.f. A coloured dopaṭṭah or scarf of a female; a parti-coloured scarf.

چنگ chang (P) n.m. A kind of harp.

چنگ نواز chang nawāz, n.m. A harper; a harpist.

چنگا changā (H) adj. Healthy; cured; sound; good; pure; true.

چنگاری chingāri (H) n.f. A spark (of fire).

چنگاری ڈالنا chingāri ḍālnā, v. To throw a fire-brand (into); to cause a quarrel; to sow discard.

چنگهاڑ chinghāṛ (H) n.f. Scream; screech; trumpeting of an elephant.

چنگهاڑنا chingharnā, v. To scream; to roar; to trumpet; to screech.

چنگل ، چنگل changal, changul (P) n.m. A claw; a hand; grasp; clutch.

چنگی chungī (H) n.f. A cess; actroi duty; town duties; a tax gathered from grain merchants (being as much grain as a man can grasp in his hand).

چنگیر changer (H) n.f. A flower pot; a tray; a trough; a small basket for keeping loaves (of bread).

چننا chunnā (H) v. To pick, to elect; to select; to choose; to gather; to build (a wall); to crimp (cloth).

چنوانا chunnwānā (H) v. To cause to select or pick or put in order; to cause to build (a wall); to cause to crimp (cloth).

چنور chaṅwar (H) n.m. Handful of peacock feathers used to whisk off flies.

چنی chunni (H) n.f. A small ruby.

چنیا chunyā (H) adj. Very small.

چنیا بطخ chunyā baṭakh, n.f. A small duck.

چنیا بیگم chunyā begam, n.f. Opium.

چنیا گوند chunyā gond, n.m. Gum Arabic.

چنیں chuniṅ (P) adv. Like this; such; thus; in this manner.

چو chau (H) adj. Four.

چوبارا chaubārā, n.m. A room on the house-top with four doors or windows; a summer-house; an assembly room of a village court.

چوبچه chaubachah (H) n.m. A small reservoir of water; cistern.

چوبغلا chaubughlā, n.m. A kind of jacket not open under the arms.

چوبندی chaubandī, n.f. Giving the horse all the four new shoes.

چوبولا chaubolā, n.m. A verse of four-lines.

چو پایه chau pāyah, n.m. A quadruped; an animal; a beast.

چو پہلو chau pahlū, adj. Four-sided.

چو پہیا chau pahiyā, n.f. A four wheeled cart.

چو تارا chau tārā, n.m. A four stringed musical instrument.

چوتالا chau tālā, n.m. A mode in music.

چوتھ chauth, adj. One-fourth of the produce, levied as tax; the fourth part.

چوتھا، چوتھی chauthā, chauthī, adj. Fourth.

چوتھائی chauthāī, adj. Fourth.

چوتھی chauthī (H) n.f. A ceremony on the fourth day of marriage.

چوتہی chautahī (H) n.f. A bed sheet of four folds.

چوراها chau rāhā, n.m. The junction of four roads; crossing of roads.

چورس chauras, adj. Rectangular; all around.

چوکنا chaukannā, adj. (Lit. having four ears.) Circumspect; cautious; alert; watchful.

چوکنا هونا chaukannā honā, v. To be on the alert.

چوکور chaukor, adj. Four sided; quadrilateral.

چوکھونٹا chaukhūntā, adj. Four-cornered; square.

چوگنا chaugunā, adj. Four times; quadruple.

چو گوشه chaugoshah, adj. Four cornered.

چولڑا chaulaṛā, adj. A necklace with four strings or four rows.

چوماسا chaumasa, n.m. The four months of the rainy season.

چو مکها، چومکھی chaumukhā, chaumukhī, adj. Having four faces.

چومکھی لڑنا chaumukhī laṛnā, v. To attack from all sides.

چوهٹا chauhattā, n.m. A market where four streets meet.

چوا chawwā (H) n.m. An aggregate of four; a quadruped.

چوالیس chawālīs (H) adj. Forty-four.

چوب chob (P) n.f. Wood; timber; a post; pole of a tent; a staff; a drumstick; a club; a mace.

چوب چینی chob chīnī, n.f. The name of a medicine; china-root.

چوب دار chob dār, n.m. A mace bearer; an usher; a herald; a servant whose business is to report the arrival of an authority.

چوب کاری chob kārī, n.f. A kind of embroidery; beating with a stick.

چوبا chobā (H) n.m. A peg; nail; wedge; a bolt; sweetened rice.

چوبی chobī (P) adj. Wooden; of wood.

چوبے chobe (H) n.m. A *Brahman* acquainted with the four *Vedās*.

چوبیس chaubīs (H) adj. Twenty-four.

چوپال chaupāl (H) n.f. A kind of summer house or pavilion, generally built jointly by several people as a resting place; a place of public meeting of the village people.

چوپان chaupān (P) n.m. A shepherd; a cowherd.

چوپٹ chaupaṭ (H) adj. Open all round; wide open; ruined; destroyed.

چوپٹ کرنا chaupaṭ karnā, v. To raze to the ground; to destroy; to demolish.

چوپڑ chaupaṛ (H) n.f. A game played with oblong dice; the cloth on which it is played.

چوت chūt (H) n.f. Vulva; private part of a woman.

چوتڑ chūtaṛ (H) n.m. The back-side; the buttocks; bum; hip; rump.

چوتڑ بجانا chūtaṛ bajānā, v. To be overjoyed.

چوتڑ پیٹنا chūtaṛ piṭnā, v. To lament; to grieve.

چوتڑ دکھانا chūtaṛ dikhānā, v. To flee; to run away; to show the clean pair of heels.

چوتیا chūtiyā (H) n.m. A blockhead; dunce; a foolish person.

چونتیس chauntīs (H) adj. Thirty-four.

چوٹ choṭ (H) n.f. A hurt; a blow; bruise; damage; injury; fall; shock; loss (in trade); stroke; spite; rivalry; competition; taunting.

چوٹ کرنا choṭ karnā, v. To hurt; to wound; to attack; to cast a spell; to taunt.

چوٹ کھانا choṭ khānā, v. To be hurt; to suffer loss; to receive a blow.

چوٹ لگنا choṭ lagnā, v. To be wounded; to be hurt.

چوٹا chottā (H) n.m. A petty thief; a pilferer.

چوٹی chotti (H) n.f. A woman pilferer.

چوٹی choṭī (H) n.f. Top; summit; peak; the plait or tie of hair behind; a lock of hair on the top of the head; a top-knot; the crest of a bird.

چوٹی کرنا choṭī karnā, v. To braid the hair.

چوٹی کا ھونا choṭī kā honā, v. To be pre-eminent; to excel; to be unrivalled.

چوچلا، چونچلا chochlā, chonchlā (H) n.m. Playfulness; blendishments; endearing arts and expressions; coquetry; toyishness; fondling; sport; airs; affectation.

چوچی chūchi (H) n.f. Breast; pap; teat; nipple; dug.

چوچی پینا chūchi pinā, v. To suck the breasts.

چودہ chaudah (H) adj. Fourteen.

چودنا chodnā (H) v. To copulate; to have sexual intercourse.

چودھر chaudhar (H) n.f. The office of a chaudhari, headman.

چودھرات، چودھرائی chaudhrāt, chaudhrāi (H) n.f. The business of a chaudharī, headman.

چودھری chaudhari (H) n.m. The headman of a village; the headman of a trade; a tit e of land-holders.

چور chor (H) n.m. A thief; a robber. adj. Treacherous; sly.

چور بازاری chor bāzārī, n.f. Black marketing.

چور بازاریا chor bāzāryā, n.m. Black marketeer.

چور پڑنا chor paṛnā, v. Breaking into a house; thieving; stealing.

چور پہرہ chor pahrā, n.m. The advanced guard of an army.

چور چکار chor chikār, n.m. Thieves; pilferers.

چور خانہ chor khānah, n.m. A secret room; a secret drawer.

چور دروازہ chor darwāzah, n.m. A trap-door; a back door.

چور زمین chor zamin, n.f. A quagmire; bog.

چور محل chor mahal, n.m. The apartments of the concubines of great men. n.f. A mistress; a keep; a concubine.

چور منڈلی chor manḍlī, n.f. Gang of thieves; a game of children.

چور chūr (H) adj. Very tired; bruised, powdered; intoxicated.

چور چور chūr chūr, adj. Broken to fragments; reduced to powder.

چور چور ہونا chūr chūr honā, v. To be broken into small pieces; to be very tired.

نشے میں چور ہونا nashe meṅ chūr honā, v. To be intoxicated; to be steeped in liquor; to be dead drunk.

چورا chūrā (H) n.m. Filings; powder; sawdust; bruised grain.

چورا کرنا chūrā karnā, v. To break to bits; to powder.

چوراسی chaurāsi (H) adj. Eighty-four.

چورانوے chaurānwe (H) adj. Ninety-four.

چورما chūrmā (H) n.m. A kind of sweet-dish made of sugar and crumbled bread.

چورن chūran (H) n.m. A powder made of medicines for promoting digestion; aromatic powder; a digestive powder.

چوری chauri (H) n.f. A fly flapper made of peacock feathers or horses hair.

چوری chori (H) n.f. Theft; robbery; stealth.

چوری چوری chori chori, adv. Stealthily; clandestinely; secretly.

چوری کرنا chori karnā, v. To steal.

چوری لگانا chori lagānā, v. To accuse one of theft.

چوڑا chauṛā (H) adj. Broad; wide.

چوڑا چکلا chauṛā chaklā, adj. Extensive; broad; wide.

چوڑان، چوڑائی chauṛān, chauṛāi (H) n.f. Breadth; width; extension.

چوڑھا chūṛhā (H) n.m. A sweeper.

چوڑی chūṛī (H) n.f. Bangles or rings made of glass or lac; a gather; a pucker.

چوڑی دار chūṛī dār, adj. Drawers or sleeves, made too long to make them crumple into plaits; puckered.

چوڑیاں پہنتا chūṛiyān pahannā, v. To put on bangles; to marry again; to become effeminiate; to behave like women.

چوڑیاں ٹھنڈی کرنا chūṛiyāṅ ṭhanḍi karnā, v. To break one's bangles (as women do on the death of their husbands).

چوزہ chūzah (P) n.m. A chicken; a young bidr; a young boy or girl.

چوزہ باز chūzah bāz, n.f. An old woman who keeps a young lover; an old woman fond of stripling.

چوسٹھ، چونسٹھ chausaṭh, chaunsaṭh (H) adj. Sixty-four.

چوسر chausar (H) n.m. A game.

چوسنا chūsnā (H) v. To suck; to absorb; to drink in; to imbibe.

چوغہ ، چغا chūghah, chughā (T) n.m. A cloak.

چوک chūk (H) n.f. Omission; error; fault; mistake; failing; miss; oversight; blunder; sour; acid; a medicine made of boiled lemon-juice and pomegranates.

چوک chauk (H) n.m. A crossing of roads; a market; a centre; a square.

چوکا chaukā (H) n.m. The place in which *Hindūs* dress or eat their victuals; an aggregate of four; four runs (in cricket), a square slab; the four front teeth; a brick.

چوکر chokar (H) n.m. Husk of wheat, barley, &c.

چوکڑی chaukaṛi (H) n.f. A carriage with four horses; a bound; a spring; a leap.

چوکڑی بھرنا chaukaṛī bharnā, v. To bound; to leap; to bounce.

چوکڑی بھولنا chaukaṛī bhūlnā, v. To forget one's bound; to be fascinated; to have one's senses benumbed; to be bewildered or comfounded; to be perplexed.

چوکس chaukas (H) adj. Cautious; careful; alert; sharp; watchful; accurate; diligent; active; circumspect.

چوکس رہنا chaukas rehnā, v. To be careful or cautious; to be watchful; to be on one's guard (against).

چوکسی chauksi (H) *n.f.* Watching; vigilance; circumspection; alertness; carefulness; activeness.

چوکسی کرنا chauksi karnā, *v.* To keep watch over; to guard; to be on the alert.

چوکنا chūknā (H) *v.* To blunder; to mistake; to err; to fail; to miss; to miscarry.

چوکھٹ chaukhaṭ (H) *n.f.* Frame of a door; a threshold; still and lintel of a door frame.

چوکھٹا chaukhṭā (H) *n.m.* A frame; a frame of a picture or a looking glass.

چوکی chaukī (H) *n.f.* A frame to sit on; a stool; a bench; a chair; a guard's post; a watch; a police station; an outpost; a band of musicians; an ornament worn on the breast.

چوکی دار chauki dār, *n.m.* A watchman; a guard; a sentinel.

چوکی داری chauki dāri, *n.f.* The pay or work of a watchman.

چوکی دینا chauki denā, *v.* To watch; to guard; singing by a group of musicians on the tomb of a saint.

چوگا chogā (H) *n.m.* Food of birds brought up from the crop; foods of birds in general.

چوگان chaugān (P) *n.m.* Polo; a hockey like game but played on horse-back.

چوگان باز chaugān bāz, *n.m.* A polo-player.

چوگان گاہ chaugān gāh, *n.m.* A polo-ground.

چول chūl (H) *n.f.* A tenon; a dovetail; the part of joiner's work which fits into another; a pivot upon which a door turns; an axle-tree arm.

چولیں ڈھیلی ہو جانا chūleṅ ḍhīlī ho jānā, *v.* To be tired; to be exhausted through hard labour; joints becoming dislocated or loose.

چولا cholā (H) *n.m.* The body; a cloak; a garment worn by a bride at her wedding.

چولا بدلنا cholā badalnā, *v.* To transmigrate.

چولا چھوڑنا cholā chhornā, *v.* To die; to expire.

چولائی chaulāi (H) *n.f.* A kind of vegetable.

چولھا chūlhā (H) *n.m.* A fire place; a hearth; an oven.

چولی choli (H) *n.f.* A small jacket; a bodice; a waistcoat; the body of a gown; a jacket; a small betel basket.

چولی دامن کا ساتھ ہونا choli dāman kā sath honā, *v.* To be as closely united as the body and the skirt; to be on very good terms; to be necessaıy adjunct; *sine qua non.*

چوما chūmā (H) *n.m.* Kiss.

چوما چاٹی chūmā chāṭi, *n.f.* Dalliance; billing and cooing.

چومنا chūmnā (H) *v.* To kiss.

چون chūn, (H) *n.m.* Flour; lime.

چوں chūṅ (H) *n.f.* A low noise; squeaking; the sound of breaking wind.

چوں چوں chūṅ chūṅ (H) *n.f.* Squeaking; chirruping; warbling.

چوں نہ کرنا chūṅ nah karnā, *v.* To make not the slightest noise; to remain perfectly quiet or agreeable.

چون chawwan (H) *adj.* Fifty-four.

چونا chonā (H) *v.* To leak; to ooze; to drop; to distil; to be filtered; to drop from the tree when ripe; to menstruate.

چونا chūnā (H) *n.m.* Lime.

چونا لگانا chūnā lagānā, *v.* To defame; to defeat; to deceive.

چونے کی بھٹی chūne kī bhaṭṭī, *n.m.* A lime-kiln.

چونتیس chauṅtīs (H) *adj.* Thirty-four.

چونچ chońch (H) *n.f.* Beak; bill; point.

چونچال chūnchāl (H) *adj.* Clever; active; robust.

چونڈا chūnḍā (H) *n.m.* The head; hair braided on top of a woman's head; top-knot.

چونسٹھ chauńsaṭh (H) *adj.* Sixty-four.

چونک اٹھنا chauńk uṭhnā (H) *v.* To wince; to start up; to be alarmed.

چونک پڑنا chauńk paṛnā (H) *v.* To start up; to bounce.

چونکانا chauńkānā (H) v. To waken; to rouse; to startle.

چونکنا chauńknā (H) *v.* To start; to be ogle; to start up from sleep; to be roused; to be startled.

چونکه chūńkeh (P) *adv.* Since; as; because.

چونگا chońgā (H) *n.m.* A funnel; a tube; a cylindrical tin case; a joint of bamboo.

چون و چرا کرنا chūn-ŏ chirā karnā, *v.* To demand why and wherefore; to wrangle; to dispute.

چونی chawanni, *n.f.* A four-anna piece.

چوھا chūhā (H) *n.m.* A rat; a mouse.

چوھے دان chūhe dān, *n.m.* A rat trap.

چوھان chauhān (H) *n.m.* A clan of *Rājpūts*.

چوھتر chauhattar, chuhattar (H) *adj.* Seventy-four.

چوھڑا chūhṛā (H) *n.m.* See چوڑھا chūṛhā.

چوھیا chūhiyā (H) *n.f.* A little mouse or rat.

چه chah (P) *n.m.* (*contract. of* چاه); A well.

چه chah (P) A particle affixed to various Persian nouns to form diminutives such as, کوچه kūchah, a small street, باغیچه bāghīchah, a small garden.

چھ chhe (H) *adj.* Six.

چھابڑی chhābṛī (H) *n.f.* A flattened basket made of twigs or reeds used by hawkers for selling their wares.

چھاپ chhāp (H) *n.f.* Stamp; print; copy; impression; seal; ring.

چھاپا chhāpā (H) *n.m.* Print; impression; stamp; seal; edition; raid; attack; ambush.

چھاپا مارنا chhāpā mārnā, *v.* To make a night attack; to raid; to surprise.

پتھر کا چھاپا paththar kā chhāpā, *n.m.* Lithography.

چھاپے خانه chhāpe khānah, *n.m.* A printing press.

چھاپنا chhāpnā (H) *v.* To print; to publish; to stamp.

چھاتا chhātā (H) *n.m.* An umbrella; a parasol.

چھاتی chhātī (H) *n.f.* Breast; chest; bosom; bubby; spirit; fortitude; endurance.

چھاتی پر پتھر رکھنا chhātī par paththar rakhnā, *v.* To have patience.

چھاتی پر سانپ لوٹنا chhātī par sāńp loṭnā, *v.* To burn with jealousy.

چھاتی پر مونگ دلنا chhātī par mońg dalnā, *v.* (*Lit.* to grind pulse on the breast); to do something in presence of another merely to vex him.

چھاتی پکڑ کر رہ جانا chhātī pakaṛ kar rah jānā, *v.* To grieve or mourn in silence.

چھاتی پھٹنا chhātī phaṭnā, *v.* Bursting of the heart with grief.

چھاتی پیٹنا chhātī piṭnā, *v.* To lament; to regret; to repent; to beat the breast in sorrow.

چھاتی سے لگانا chhātī se lagānā, *v.* To fondle; to embrace.

چھاتی نکال کر چلنا chhātī nikāl kar chalnā, *v.* To strut; to stalk.

چھاج chhāj (H) *n.m.* A winnowing-fan; a cow catcher.

چھا جانا chhā jānā (H) *v.* To spread; to cover; to swarm; to overcast.

چھاچھ chhāchh (H) *n.f.* Butter-milk; whey.

دودھ کا جلا چھاچھ بھی پھونک پھونک کر پیتا ہے *dūdh kā jalā chhāchh bhī phūṅk phūṅk kar pītā hai, prov.* A burnt child dreads fire; experience is the best teacher.

چہار *chahār* (P) *adj.* Four.

چہار دہ *chahār dah* (P) *adj.* Fourteen.

چہار شنبہ *chahār shambah.* See چار شنبہ *chār shambah.*

چہارم *chaharum, adj.* The fourth.

چھاڑ، چھاڑا *chhāṛ, chhāṛā* (H) *n.f.* A bank of a river; land gained from a river.

چھاڑ چھڑیلا *chhāṛ chhaṛelā* (H) *n.m.* Name of a medicinal herb.

چھاگل *chhāgal* (H) *n.f.* A leathern bottle having a spout; a foot ornament.

چھال *chhāl* (H) *n.f.* Peel; skin; rind; bark.

چھال اُتارنا *chhāl utārnā, v.* To peel; to pare.

چھالا *chhālā* (H) *n.m.* A blister; pimple; pustule.

چھالیا *chhālyā* (H) *n.f.* Betel-nut.

چھان *chhān* (H) *n.f.* Husk; chaff; thatched roof; a roof.

چھان بین *chhān bin* (H) *n.f.* Investigation; examination; sifting; close search.

چھانا *chhānā* (H) *v.* To thatch; to roof; to overspread; to overcast.

چھانٹ *chhāṅṭ* (H) *n.f.* Refuse; cuttings; selection; extraction; siftings. *imper.* Select; sort out or choose.

چھانٹ لینا *chhāṅṭ lenā, v.* To select; to choose.

چھانٹن *chhāṅṭan* (H) *n.f.* Cuttings; chips; scrapings; refuses.

چھانٹنا *chhāṅṭnā* (H) *v.* To pare; to cut; to clip; to prune; to crop; to trim; to dress; to clean; to choose; to select; to sort out; to cut out (clothes); to abridge; to separate the husk from grain by pounding it in a mortar; to husk.

چھان مارنا ۔ ڈالنا *chhān mārnā, ḍālnā* (H) *v.* To search; to explore.

چھاننا *chhānnā* (H) *v.* To strain; to filter; to sift; to search; to investigate; to examine.

چھاؤں *chhāoṅ* (H) *n.f.* Shade; shadow spread; the reflection of any object in a mirror.

چھاؤنی *chhāoni* (H) *n.f.* A cantonment; barracks or huts for soldiers; thatching.

چھاؤنی چھانا *chhāoni chhānā, v.* To thatch a roof; to encamp.

چھب *chhab* (H) *n.f.* Beauty; grace; charm; splendour; brilliancy; shape; farm; figure; decoration.

چھبیس *chhabbis* (H) *adj.* Twenty-six.

چھبیلا، چھبیلی *chhabilā, chhabilī* (H) *adj.* Handsome; graceful; gay; comely; well-dressed.

چھپ، چھپ چھپ *chhap, chhap chhap* (H) *n.f.* The sound caused by something falling in or something striking water.

چھپا *chhipā, chhupā* (H) *adj.* Hidden; concealed.

چھپا رستم *chhūpā rustam, n.m.* A genius unknown.

چھپانا *chhīpānā, chhupānā* (H) *v.* To conceal; to hide; to cover.

چھپاؤ *chhipāo* (H) *n.m.* Concealment; lurking; secrecy.

چھپائی *chhapāi* (H) *n.f.* The cost of printing; the act of printing; edition.

چھپر *chhappar* (H) *n.m.* A thatched roof; a hut.

چھپر چھانا *chhappar chhānā, v.* To thatch a hut.

چھپر پھاڑ کر دینا *chhappar phāṛ kar denā, v.* To give in a miraculous manner; to surprise one with an unexpected gift.

چھپر کھٹ *chhappar khaṭ* (H) *n.f.* A bedstead with canopy and curtains.

چھپکا chhapkā (H) n.m. A splash of water; a small net for catching pigeons; an ornament.

چھپکلی chhupkali (H) n.f. A lizard.

چھپن chhappan (H) adj. Fifty-six.

چھپنا chhupnā, chhipnā (H) v. To be concealed; to hide; to be hidden; to be absent; to disappear; to lurk; setting (of the sun).

چھپنا chhapnā (H) v. To be printed; to be stamped.

چھپوانا chhapwānā (H) v. To cause to print.

چھت chhat (H) n.f. A roof; ceiling.

چھت گیری chhat giri, n.f. A ceiling-cloth.

چھتا chhattā (H) n.m. A honey-comb; a bee-hive; a covered street.

چھتر chhatr, chhattar (H) n.m. A big umbrella; a house set apart for (charitable) entertainment of strangers, guests &c.

چھتری chhattri (H) n.m. A man of the second (military) tribe of Hindūs.

چھتری chhatri (H) n.f. A hood or covering of a bed; a small umbrella; bamboo frame for pigeons to perch on; an ornamental pavilion or dome built over a grave or samādh.

چھتیانا chhatyānā (H) v. To take an aim (at); to raise a gun to the shoulder.

چھتیس chhāttis (H) adj. Thirty-six.

چھتیسا ، چھتیسی chhatisa, chhatisi (H) adj. Cunning; crafty; prude; artful; one who knows thirty-six postures in copulation and yet affects modesty and simplicity.

چھٹ chhut (H) (contr. of چھوٹا chhotā—small); used in comp. as in چھٹ پنا یا چھٹ پن chhut panā yā chhut pan—Infancy, childhood.

چھٹا chhaṭā (H) ādj. Sixth.

چھٹا ہوا chhatā huā (H) adj. Out and out; consummate; picked; sorted; selected.

چھٹانا chhūtānā (H) v. To cause to be separated.

چھٹانک chhatānk (H) n.f. Sixteenth part of a seer.

چھٹائی chhuṭāi (H) n.f. Littleness; smallness.

چھٹکارا chhutkārā (H) n.m. Exemption; release; rescue; liberty; leisure; liberation; disengagement; deliverance; discharge; divorce.

چھٹکارا پانا chhuṭkārā pānā, v. To be released; to be rescued; to be freed.

چھٹکنا chhitaknā (H) v. To be scattered; to be dispursed; shining of the stars or moonlight.

چھٹنا chhatnā (H) v. To be pruned; to be separated; to be sifted; to be reduced; to be picked up; to decay. n.m. A kind of sieve.

چھٹنا chhuṭnā (H) v. To be set free; to be discharged; to be librated; to be acquitted; to be let off; to be left or abandoned; to be separated; to slip (from); to escape; to be let loose; to be fired; to be set in motion (train); to be omitted; to come off (as colour from cloth).

چھٹی chhaṭi (H) adj. Sixth; n.f. Sixth lunar day; a ceremony performed on the sixth day after child birth.

چھٹی chhuṭṭi (H) n.f. Leave; holiday; vacation; leisure; furlough; discharge; release; acquital; intermission; freedom; death.

چھجا chhajjā (H) n.m. Gallery; a portico; a balcony; the expanded branches of a tree.

چہچہا ، چہچہاہٹ chahchahā, chahchahāhaṭ (H) n.m./n.f. The song of a bird; warbling; chirping of birds.

چہچہانا chahchahānā (H) v. To sing (as, a nightingale); to whistle; to warble (as, birds).

چھچھڑا ، چھیچھڑا chhichhṛā, chhichhrā (H) n.m. Slough (of a wound); the unusable part of flesh.

چھچھلتی ہوئی chhachhaltī hoī (H) *adj.* Touching lightly; cursory; skipping.

چھچھورا chhachhorā (H) *adj.* Petty; trifling; puerile; childish; shallow; showy.

چھچھورپن *chhachhorpan*, *n.m.* Childishness; puerility; show; display.

چچھوندر chhachhūndar (H) *n.f.* The musk-rat; a mole; a squib (firework).

چھدا chhuddā (H) *n.m.* Blame; obligation; slander.

چھدنا chhidnā (H) *v.* To be pierced or bored.

چھرا chhurā (H) *n.f.* A large knife; a dagger.

چھرا chharrā (H) *n.m.* A small shot.

چہرہ chehrā (P) *n.m.* Face; countenance; visage; a portrait; a visor; a mask.

چہرہ مہرہ *chehrā mohrā*, *n.m.* Features.

چھری chhurī (H) *n.f.* A knife; a small dagger.

چھری تلے دم لینا *chhuri tale dam lenā*, *v.* To be patient under difficult circumstances.

چھری مارنا *chhurī mārnā*, *v.* To stab.

میٹھی چھری *mīṭhi chhuri*, *n.f.* One who, with a smooth face, brings about the ruin of another; a secret enemy; a treacherous friend.

چھریرا chharerā (H) *adj.* Thin; light weight; thin and tall.

چھڑ chhaṛ (H) *n.f.* A pole or bamboo; a fishing-rod; the pole of a spear; stem; stalk.

چھڑا chhaṛā (H) *adj.* Alone; single; unmarried; solitary; separate. *n.m.* An ornament worm on the legs.

چھڑانا ، چھڑوانا chhuṛānā, chhuṛwānā (H) *v.* To have one released; to get one his liberty; to cause to set free; to cause to liberate; to get delivered; to get discharged.

چھڑکاؤ chhirkāo (H) *n.m.* Sprinkling; watering.

چھڑکنا chhirknā (H) *v.* To sprinkle; to water; to asperse.

چھڑکوانا chhiṛakwānā (H) *v.* To cause another to sprinkle.

چھڑنا chhaṛnā (H) *v.* To beat rice; to separate the husk from grain.

چھڑنا chhiṛnā (H) *v.* To commence; to begin; to be played (on).

چھڑوانا chhaṛwānā (H) *v.* To cause to beat rice.

چھڑی chhaṛi (H) *n.f.* A walking stick; a switch; a cane; a rod, a wand; a procession of the followers of *Shāh Madār*.

چھکا chhakkā (H) *n.m.* The sixth (at cards &c); aggregate of six runs (at cricket); a cage with a net attached to it.

چھکا پنجہ کرنا *chhakkā panjāh karnā*, *v.* To play tricks; to practise deceit; to deceive.

چہکار chahkār (H) *n.f.* Singing or chirping (of birds).

چھکڑا chhakṛā (H) *n.m.* A kind of carriage; a cart; a two-wheeled bullock cart; a cart for carrying goods.

چہکنا chahaknā (H) *v.* To whistle; to warble; to chirrup; to sing (birds).

چھکے چھوٹ جانا chhakke chhuṭ jānā (H) *v.* To be confounded; to be bewildered; to lose all one's wits.

چھل chhal (H) *n.m.* Fraud; trick; deception; knavery; artifice; evasion.

چھل بل *chhal bal*, *n.f.* Trickery; force and fraud; artifice; stratagem; pomp and show; lustre; glory.

چہل chohal (H) *n.f.* Cheer; jollity; mirth; merriment; festivity.

چہل کرنا *chohal karnā*, *v.* To make merry; to carol.

چہل chehal (P) *adj.* Forty.

چہل قدمی *chehal qadmī*, *n.f.* Walk; ramble; stroll.

چھلا chhalla (H) n.m. A ring.

چھلے دار chhalle dār, adj. Ringed; annular; curled.

چھلانگ chhalāṅg (H) n.f. A spring; a leap; a bound.

چھلانگ لگانا ، مارنا chhalāng lagānā, mārnā, v. To spring to jump; to leap.

چھلاوا chhalāwā (H) n.m. Ignis fatuus; will-o'-the-wisp; a light seen on marshy grounds supposed to be due to spontaneous combustion of gas from decaying organic matter, which is believed to mislead travellers.

چہل پہل chahal pahal (H) n.f. Life; stir; bustle; activity; merriment; mirth.

چھلکا chhilkā (H) n.m. Crust; husk; shell; peel; scale; rind; bark; skin.

چھلکا اُتارنا chhilkā utārnā, v. To husk; to blanch; to peel.

چھلکانا chhalkānā (H) v. To spill.

چھلکنا chhalaknā (H) v. To be spilt; to overflow.

چہلم chahlum (P) adj. The fortieth day of mourning.

چھلنا chhalnā (H) v. To deceive; to cheat; to evade; to make excuses; to circumvent.

چھلنا chhalnā (H) n.m. A strainer; a cloth through which anything is strained.

چھلنا chhilnā (H) v. To be scrached; to be peeled; to be scraped.

چھلنی chhalnī (H) n.f. A sieve; a strainer.

چھلنی ہونا chhalni honā, v. To be pierced or perforated; to be full of holes; to be battered.

چھلیا chhalya (H) adj. Treacherous; deceitful; fraudulent; artful; false; perfidious. n.m. A deceiver; a betrayer.

چھم چھم chham chham (H) n.f. The sound of heavy rain; jingle of small bells.

چھن chhun, chhan (H) n.m. The sound made by a drop of water falling on a hot plate; the tinkle of small bells; the clink of rupees.

چھناکا chhanākā (H) n.m. The clink of rupees.

چھنال chhināl (H) n.f. A harlot; a prostitute.

چھنال پن - چھنالا chhināl pan, chhinālā, n.m. Harlotery; prostitution; whoredom; fornication; unlawful sexual intercourse; lewdness.

چھنٹائی chhanṭāi (H) n.f. Cleaning; sifting; sorting; punning; the price paid for cleaning.

چھنگا chhangā (H) n.m. One having six fingers.

چھنگلی، چھنگلیا chhunglī, chhungaliyā (H) n.f. The little finger.

چھننا chhannā (H) v. To be strained; to be sifted; to be cleaned. n.m. A strainer.

چھننا chhinnā (H) v. To be deprived; to be snatched; to be wrested.

چھنوانا chhinwānā (H) v. To cause to snatched; to cause to wrest.

چھنوانا chhanwānā (H) v. To cause to sift; to cause to strained; to cause to search.

چھو chhū (H) n.f. The act of blowing or exorcising or uttering a prayer or incantation; the blowing or breathing sound made by a washerman when beating clothes on a stone.

چھومنتر chhū mantar, n.m. A charm.

اُڑن چھو ہونا uṛan chhū honā, v. To vanish; to disappear suddenly.

چھوارا، چھوہارا chhūārā, chhūhārā (H) n.m. A dried date.

چھوانا chhūānā (H) v. To touch; to cause to touch.

چھوت chhūt (H) n.f. Defilement; infection; contamination; touch.

چھوٹ لگنا chhūt lagnā, v. To be infectious (discease); to be infected by touch.

چھوٹ chhūṭ (H) n.f. Remission of revenue; remission; leaving; separation; divorce; release; disjunction; radiance or splendour of jewels; giving money off-hand or at will to jugglers, dancers &c at entertainments.

چھوٹا ' چھوٹی (H) adj. Little; small; younger; junior; minor; subordinate; trifling; low; mean.

چھوٹا منہ بڑی بات chhoṭā munh baṛi bāt, prov. Big words out of a small mouth; boastful words spoken by a weak stomach.

چھوٹی بات chhoṭi bāt (H) n.f. A trifling matter or affair.

چھوٹائی chhoṭāi (H) n.f. Smallness; littleness.

چھوٹنا chhūṭnā (H) v. To escape; to be set free; to get loose; to be abandoned; to be dismissed.

چھو چھو chhū chhū (H) n.f. A dry nurse.

چھوڑنا chhoṛnā (H) v. To leave; to desert; to spare; to pardon; to abdicate; to abstain from; to let go; to release; to resign; to emit; to discharge; to fire; (a gun); to shoot; to set aside; to quit; to forgive; to forsake.

چھوکرا chhokrā (H) n.m. A boy; a lad; a servant.

چھوکری chhokrī (H) n.f. A girl; a lass; a maid servants; a slave girl.

چھولداری chholdārī (H) n.f. A kind of small tent for servants; a pavilion.

چھونا chhūnā (H) v. To touch; to feel; to meddle with.

چھوئی موئی chhūī mūī (H) n.f. A sensitive plant; touch-me-not; a delicate or frail thing.

چھہتر chhihattar (H) adj. Seventy-six.

چھیاسٹھ chhiyāsaṭh (H) adj. Sixty-six.

چھیاسی chhiyāsī (H) adj. Eighty-six.

چھیالیس chhiyālīs (H) adj. Forty-six.

چھیانوے chhiyānwe (H) adj. Ninety-six.

چھیپ chhīp (H) n.f. Discoloration or spot on the skin; a discease of skin; fishing rod; the act of a buffalo's pushing with its horns; a rod with a rag at one end for flying pigeons.

چھیپی chhipī (H) n.m. A cloth-printer.

چہیتا chahītā. See چاہیتا chāhītā.

چہیتی chahītī. See چاہیتی chāhītī.

چھیج chhij (H) n.f. Decrease; diminution; waste; decay.

چھیجنا chhījnā (H) v. To decrease; to decay; to pine away.

چھیچڑا chhichṛā. See چھچھڑا chhichhṛā.

چھید chhed (H) n.m. A hole; an orifice; an opening.

چھیدنا chhednā (H) v. To pierce; to bore; to perforate; to penetrate.

چھیڑ chheṛ (H) n f. Touch; irritation; vexation, flirtation; molestation; fondling.

چھیڑ چھاڑ' چھیڑ خانی chheṛ chhāṛ, chheṛ khānī, n.f. The act of vexing, provoking or exciting; flirtation; stricture; animadversion; fondling.

چھیڑنا chheṛnā (H) v. To irritate; to vex; to excite; to abuse; to insult; to aggress; to stir up; to make fun of; to commence; to play a musical instrument; to start singing.

چھیلا chhailā (H) n.m. A fop; a handsome fellow; a cox-comb.

چھیلن chhīlan (H) n.f. Parings; peelings; scrapings.

چھیلنا chhīlnā (H) v. To peel; to skin; to pare; to erase; to scrape; to scratch.

چھینٹ chhīnṭ (H) n.m. Chint; spray of water; the odd days of a month.

چھینٹا chhinṭā (H) n.m. Slot; spot; splash; sprinkling; light rain; scattering; a ball of opium; deception; fraud; taunting.

چھینٹا دینا، مارنا chhinṭā denā, mārnā, v. To sprinkle; to bespatter; to tempt; to deceive.

چھینک chhink (H) n.f. Sneezing; sneeze.

چھینکا chhinkā (H) n.m. A network in which pots are hung, as in a swinging tray; a muzzle for cattle.

چھینکنا chhinknā (H) v To sneeze.

چھیننا، چھین لینا chhīnna, chhin lenā (H) v. To snatch; to wrench; to pluck; to rob; to take forcible possession of; to deprive of.

چھینی chheni (H) n.f. A chisel; a piercer; a punch; an instrument for piercing with.

چیپ chep (H) n m. Viscosity; stickiness; glue.

چیپی chepi (H) n.f. A slip pasted on.

چیت chait (H) n.m. The twelfth month of the *Hindū* calendar, corresponding to March-April.

چیتا chitā (H) n.m. A panther; a small hunting leopard.

چیتل chital (H) adj. Spotted; speckled. n.m. A spotted deer; a leopard; a large spotted snake.

چیتھڑا chithṛā (H) n.m. A rag; a frayed or torn piece of cloth.

چیچڑ chichaṛ (H) n.f. Matter or filth in the inner corner of the eye.

چیچڑی chichṛi (H) n.f. The tick.

چیچک chechak (H) n.f. The small-pox.

چیچک رو chechak rū, adj. Pock-marked face; pitted with the small-pox.

چیخ chīkh (H) n.f. A scream; screech; shriek.

چیخ مارنا chikh mārnā, v. To scream; to cry out; to shriek.

چیدہ chidah (P) adj. Gathered; selected; picked; elected; sorted.

چیر chir (H) n.f. Rent; wound; cut; slit; strip; tear; tearing; attire.

چیر پھاڑ chir phāṛ, n.f. Performing a surgical operation; amputation; dissection.

چیرا chirā (H) n.m. A chequed turban; a parti-coloured turban; incision; cut; wound; a slit.

چیرنا chirnā (H) v. To rend; to tear; to cut open; to split; to slit; to cleave; to saw.

چیرہ chirah (P) adj. Powerful; bold; brave.

چیرہ دست chirah dast, adj. Powerful; vigorous; oppressive; disobedient; refractory; rebellious.

چیڑ chiṛ (H) n.m. A fig tree; a pine tree.

چیز chiz (P) n.f. Thing; commodity.

چیز بست chiz bast, n.f. Chattels; baggage; furniture; goods.

چیستان chistān (P) n.f. An enigme; a riddle; a puzzle.

چیکٹ chikat (H) n.f. A mixture of oil and dust. adj. Oily; greasy; dusty.

چیل chil (H) n.f. A kite; a pine tree.

چیل جھپٹا chil jhapaṭṭā, n.f. A game played by children.

چیلا، چیلی chelā, cheli (H) n.m./n.f. A servant or slave brought up in the house; a disciple; a follower; a pupil.

چیلے چانٹے chele chānṭe, n.m. Pupils; disciples.

چین chain (H) n.m. Ease; relief; repose; tranquillity; comfort; rest; peace.

چین کرنا chain karnā, v. To be at ease or comfort; to make oneself comfortable.

چین chin (P) n.f. A wrinkle; a pucker; crease; fold.

چیں بجبیں ہونا chīṅ bajabīṅ honā, v. To frawn; to knit the brow; to scowl.

چیں chīṅ (H) n.f. Cry; squeak; chirp.

چیں بلانا chīṅ bulānā, v. To make one cry out.

چیں بولنا chīṅ bolnā, v. To utter a cry of helplessness; to squeak.

چیں چیں کرنا chīṅ chīṅ karnā, v. To chirp; to grumble; to cry out; to murmur.

چینا chīnā (H) n.m. A kind of corn; a bait; a grain.

چینی chīnī (H) n.f. White sugar; Chinese language. n.m. A Chenese. adj. Of or belonging to China.

چیونٹا cheyūṅṭā (H) n.m. A large black ant.

چیونٹی cheyūṅṭī (H) n.f. A small ant.

چیونٹی کو پر لگنا cheyūṅṭī ko par lagnā, v. To be nearing death; when ants get wings it is generally believed that they have come to the end of their lives.

چیونٹیوں کو موت ہی کا ریلا بس ہے cheyūṅṭioṅ ko mūt hī kā relā bas hai, prov. The dew is a tempest to the ants.

ح

ح ḥe. The sixth letter of the Arabic, the eighth of Persian and the ninth of Urdu alphabets; is commonly called hā'e-i-muhmilah and the ha'e ḥuṭṭī. In the abjad it has the numerical value of eight. It is one of the six guttural letters; its sound being an aspiration much stronger and formed deeper in the throat than that of ہ he.

حاتم ḥatim (A) n.m. Name of an Arab chief of the tribe of طے ṭai, famous for his boundless liberality.

حاتم کی قبر پر لات مارنا ḥātim ki qabr par lāt mārnā, v. To be more generous than Hātim himself; Oul Heroding Herod.

حاجات ḥajāt (A) (plu. of حاجت ḥājit); Wants; needs; necessities.

حاجب ḥājib (A) n.m. A door keeper; a chamberlain.

حاجت ḥājat (A) n.f. Need; want; necessity; poverty; requirement; hope; wish; call of nature.

حاجت براری روائی ḥājat barārī, rawāī, n.f. Producing or supplying what is wanted or desired.

حاجت رفع کرنا ḥājat rafa' karnā, v. To relieve one's necessities; to supply a want; to go to the privy; to ease nature.

حاجت مند ḥājat maṅd, adj. Needy; necessitous; indigent; hoping; depending.

حاجی ḥājī (A) n.m. A person who has performed pilgrimage to Mecca.

حاجی الحرمین ḥājī-ul-ḥaramain, n.m. A pilgrim to both the sacred places Mecca and Madina.

حادث ḥādiṣ (A) adj. New; just appearing; recent; just begun; created (not eternal).

حادثہ ḥādisah (A) n.m. Accident; occurrence; misfortune; incident; event; adventure; calamity.

حادہ ḥāddah (A) adj. Contracted.

زاویۂ حادہ zawiyah-ĕ ḥāddah, n.m. An acute angle.

حاذق ḥāẕiq (A) adj. Skilful; intelligent; eminent; perfect; competent; excelling; adept.

حار ḥār (A) adj. Hot; ardent; difficult; troublesome; severe.

حارج ḥārij (A) n.m. An obstacle; obstruction; hindrance.

حاسد ḥāsid (H) *adj.* Envious. *n.m.* An envious man; an enemy.

حاسه ḥāssah (A) *n.f.* Facluty of perception or feeling.

حاشا ḥāshā (A) *adv.* & *intj.* Besides; excepting; far be it from!

حاشاللہ، حاشا وکلا hāshā lillah, ḥāshā wa-kallā, *intj.* God forbid; by no means; no; never.

حاشیہ ḥāshiyah (A) *n.m.* Margin; hem; border; a marginal note.

حاشیہ بردار ḥāshiyah bardār, *n.m.* A menial; a person of inferior rank.

حاشیہ چڑھانا ḥāshiyā chaṛhānā, *v.* To write marginal notes; to make additions; to make comments; to lengthen or improve a story.

حاشیہ چھوڑنا ḥāshiyah chhoṛnā, *v.* To leave a margin on paper.

حاشیہ دار ḥāshiyah dār, *adj.* Having a border; having marginal comments.

حاشیہ کا گواہ ḥāshiyah ka gawāh, *n.m.* An attesting witness; a marginal witness; a witness to the execution of a deed.

حاشیہ نشین ḥāshiyah nashīn, *n.m.* A servant of a person of high rank; a companion; a favourite.

حاصل ḥāṣil (A) *n.m.* Produce; product; result; inference; acquisition; gain; object; profit; ultimate; consequence; a tax; duty; custom; revenue; crop.

حاصل بازاری ḥāṣil bāzārī, *n.m.* Collections or duties of a market.

حاصل تفریق ḥāṣil tafrīq, *n.m.* Remainder; balance.

حاصل جمع ḥāṣil jama', *n.m.* The total; the sum; the sum-total.

حاصل تقسیم ḥāṣil taqsīm, *n.m.* Quotient.

حاصل ضرب ḥāṣil ẓarb, *n.m.* The product in multiplication.

حاصل کرنا ḥaṣil karnā, *v.* To acquire; to gain; to collect; to learn; to produce; to get; to obtain.

حاصل کلام ḥāṣil kalām, *adv.* In short: briefly.

حاصل ہونا ḥāṣil honā, *v.* To be acquired; to be obtained; to accrue.

حاضر ḥāẓir (A) *adj.* Present; ready at hand; willing; content; in attendance; the second person (Grammar).

حاضر باش ḥāẓar bāsh, *adj.* Constant or regular in attendance.

حاضر باشی ḥāẓir bāshī, *n.f.* Constant or regular attendance.

حاضر جواب ḥāẓar jawāb, *adj.* Ready with an answer; ready witted; pert.

حاضر جوابی ḥāẓar jawābī; *n.f.* Readiness in replying; repartee.

حاضر رهنا ḥāẓir rahnā, *v.* To wait on; to be present.

حاضر ضامن ḥāẓir ẓāmin, *n.m.* A person offering bail or security for the appearance of another in a court; a bondsman.

حاضر ضامنی ḥāẓir ẓāminī, *n.f.* Security for personal appearance; giving bail for another.

حاضر کرنا ḥāẓir karnā, *v.* To present; to produce; to lay before; to propose; to make ready; to summon.

حاضر و ناظر ḥāẓar-ŏ nāẓir, *adj.* Present and seeing; omnipresent and omniscient.

حاضر ہونا ḥāẓir honā, *v.* To be present; to be at hand; to attend; to be at the service of; to be ready.

غیر حاضر ghair ḥāẓir, *adj.* Absent; not present; not forthcoming.

حاضرات ḥāẓirāt (A) *n.f.* Imprisonment or commanding of evil spirits; invocation of spirits; raising the devil.

حاضرات کرنا ḥāẓirāt karnā, *v.* To invoke evil spirits; to exorcise.

حاضراتی ḥāẓrātī (A) *n.m.* A necromancer; a conjuror; an exorciser.

حاضری ḥāẓri (A) n.f. Presence; attendance; appearance; audience; levee; muster-roll; breakfast; desert; an offering made to a saint; roll-call.

حاضری کھانا ḥāẓri khānā, v. To have breakfast.

حاضری لینا ḥāẓri lenā, v. To mark attendance; to call the roll; to call out the names (of).

چھوٹی حاضری chhoṭi ḥāẓri, n.f. Early morning breakfast of tea and toast &c.

حافظ ḥāfiẓ (A) n.m. A guardian; a governor; preserver; protector; the Preserver of all things; God; having a good memory; one who knows the whole Qurān by heart; a blind man; the poetical name of celebrated poet of Persia (Mohammad Shamsuddin Shīrāzī).

حافظ حقیقی ḥāfiẓ-e haqīqī, n.m. The true protector; God.

حافظه ḥāfiẓah (A) n.m. Good memory; the retentive faculty of the mind; a retentive memory.

حاکم ḥākim (A) n.m. A ruler; a governor; a judge; a commander; a master; a chief; an official.

حاکم اعلیٰ، حاکم بالا ḥākim-ĕ ālā, ḥākim-ĕ bālā, n.m. The permanent power; the highest authority.

حاکم دیوانی ḥākim-ĕ dīwāni, n.m. An officer of the civil court.

حاکم زیردست ḥākim-ĕ zerdast, n.m. A subordinate officer.

حاکم ضلع ḥākim-ĕ ẓilā', n.m. Deputy Commissioner; sheriff.

حاکم فوجداری ḥākim-ĕ faujdārī, n.m. A judge of a criminal court.

حاکم وقت ḥākim-ĕ waqt, n.m. The ruler of the day.

حاکمانه ḥākimānah (P) adv. Authoritatively; judicially.

حاکمیت ḥākimiyyat (A) n.f. Sovereignty; jurisdiction.

حال ḥāl (A) n.m. State; condition; the present time; business; statement; case; narrative; spiritual ecstasy; circumstance; situation.

حال آنا ḥāl ānā, v. To be inspired; to be thrown into ecstasy.

حالانکه ḥālānkeh, adv. Though; whereas; however; even.

حال پرسی ḥāl pursī, n.m. Enquiring after health.

حال سے بے حال ہونا ḥāl se be-ḥāl honā, v. To become ill-conditioned; to be in bad circumstances.

بہر حال bahar ḥāl, adv. In any case; at any rate.

خوش حال khūsh ḥāl, adj. In good circumstances; prosperous.

فی الحال filḥāl, adv. At present.

حال و قال ḥāl-ŏ qāl, n.m. State; condition.

حالات ḥālāt (A) n.m. (plu. of حالت ḥālat) Circumstances; facts; particulars; conditions; cases; natures.

حالت ḥālat (A) n.f. State; condition; nature; circumstance; position of one's affairs.

حالت غیر ہونا ḥālat ghair honā, v. To be in the agonies of death; to be in bad condition.

حالت نزع ḥālat-ĕ niza', n.f. Agony; being on the point of death.

بری حالت burī ḥālat, n.f. Bad condition; bad circumstances.

حامد ḥāmid (A) n.f. One who praises.

حامض ḥāmiẓ (A) adj. Sharp; sour; acid; pungent.

حامل ḥāmil (A) n.m. A carrier; a bearer; a porter.

حامله ḥāmilah (A) n.f. Pregnant.

حامله ہونا ḥāmilah honā, v. To be pregnant; to conceive.

حامی ḥāmī (A) n.m. A protector; a patron; helper; supporter; defender.

حامی بهرنا *ḥāmī bharnā, v.* To promise; to consent; to own; to be responsible for; to give assurance; to acknowledge.

حاوی *ḥāwī* (A) *adj.* Comprehending; getting within one's grasp; perfect; skilled.

حائض، حائضه *ḥāiẓ, ḥāiẓah* (A) *n.f.* A woman having menses.

حائل *ḥāil* (A) *adj.* Intervening. *n.m.* Hinderance; obstacle; prevention.

حائل هونا *ḥāil honā, v.* To come in the way; to interrupt; to disturb.

حب *ḥubb* (A) *n.f.* Love; friendship; desire; affection; wish.

حب الوطن *ḥubb-ul-waṭan, adj.* Love of one's country; patriotism.

حب ذات *ḥubb-ĕ-ẕāt, n.m.* Love of one's self; egotism; conceit.

عمل حب *a'mal-ĕ ḥubb, n.m.* A love charm.

حب *ḥab* (A) *n.f.* A grain; a pill; kernel of a fruit; a seed.

حباب *ḥubāb, ḥabāb* (A) *n.m.* A bubble; an ornament.

حباب آٹهنا *ḥubāb uṭhnā, v.* To bubble.

حبذا *habbaẕā* (A) *interj.* Bravo ! well done !

حبس *ḥabs* (A) *n.m.* Confinement; imprisonment; close; retention; a place of confinement; prison.

حبس البول *ḥabs-ul-baul, n.m.* Retention of urine; a strangury.

حبس بیجا *ḥabs-ĕ bejā, n.m.* Wrongful confinement.

حبس دم *ḥabs-ĕ dam, n.m.* Asthma; suffocation; keeping the breath in for a long time.

حبس دوام *ḥabs-ĕ dawām, n.m.* Transportation for life.

حبش یا حبشه *Habash yā Habashah* (A) *n.m.* The country of *Habashīs* or Negroes; Abyssenia.

حبشی *ḥabashī* (A) *n.m.* Abyssenian; negro; a kafir; a black-man.

حبل *ḥabl* (A) *n.f.* Rope; cord.

حبل المتین *ḥabl-ul matīn, n.f.* Strong rope; the Quran.

حبل الورید *ḥabl-ul warīd, n.f.* Jugular vein; one of the large veins on each side of the neck.

حبوب *ḥubūb* (A) *n.m.* (*plu.* of حب *hab*) Pills; grains.

حبه *ḥabbah* (A) *n.m.* One berry; one grain; one seed; a small piece or portion.

حبه بهر *ḥabbah bhar, adv.* A little.

حبیب *ḥabīb* (A) *n.m.* Beloved; sweetheart; a friend; a comrade.

حتیٰ *ḥattā* (A) *conj.* Until; upto; so that; in such a manner and thus; as far as; to the extent of.

حتی الامکان، حتی الوسع، حتی المقدور *ḥattā-al-imkān, ḥattā-al-wasa', ḥattā-al-maqdūr, adv.* To the best of one's ability; as far as lies in one's power.

حتمی *ḥatmī* (A) *adj.* Final; permanent; definite; certain.

حج *ḥajj* (A) *n.m.* The act of moving round or going to a sacred place; visiting a place of pilgrimage; pilgrimage to Mecca.

حج اصغر *ḥajj-ĕ aṣghar, n.f.* The minor pilgrimage to Mecca; the non-seasonal *ḥajj*.

حج اکبر *ḥajj-ĕ akbar, n.m.* The greater pilgrimage to Mecca—generally falls on a Friday.

امیر الحج *amīr-ul-ḥajj, n.m.* The chief of a caravan of pilgrims.

حجاب *ḥijāb* (A) *n.m.* A veil; a curtain; modesty; bashfulness; shame; night.

حجاب آٹهانا *ḥijāb uṭhānā, v.* To remove the veil; to lose sense of shame.

حجاب آٹهنا *ḥijāb uṭhnā, v.* Losing the sense of shame; removal of the veil.

حجاب کھانا ḥijāb khānā, v. To blush; to feel shame.

حجاج ḥujjaj (A) n.m. (plu. of حاج ḥājj—حاجی ḥāji) Pilgrims.

حجام ḥajjām (A) n.m. A barber; a shaver; a hair dresser; a phlebotomist.

حجامت ḥajāmat (A) n.f. Shaving; hair dressing.

حجامت بنانا ḥajāmat banānā, v. To shave; to spoil; to plunder.

حجامی ḥajjāmī (A) n.f. The profession of a barber.

حجت ḥujjat (A) n.f. Argument; proof; reason; discussion; objection; pretext; excuse; altercation; disputation.

حجت کرنا ḥujjat karnā, v. To discuss; to argue; to adduce an argument; to raise an objection; to bring forward an excuse; to dispute.

حجتی ḥujjatī, adj. Argumentative; quarrelsome. n.m. Disputant; a sophist; caviller.

حجر ḥajar (A) n.m. A stone.

حجر اسود ḥajar-ĕ aswad, n.m. The black stone of the Ka'aba (in Mecca).

حجره ḥujrah (A) n.m. A cell; a closet; a small room; a private room.

حجله ḥujlah (A) n.m. An ornamental pavilion or chamber, with curtains, for a bride; the marriage-bed; the female partidge.

حجم ḥujm (A) n.m. Thickness; volume; size.

حد ḥadd (A) n.f. Boundary; limit; extremity; extent; bar; restrictive ordinance of God and the punishment for non-observance thereof. adv. At most; at least; very; utmost point or degree.

از حد az ḥadd, adv. Beyond limit; extremely; excessively.

حد اقل ḥadd-ĕ aqall, n.f. Minimum.

حد اکثر ḥadd-ĕ akṣar, n.f. Maximum.

حد باندھنا ḥadd bāndhnā, v. To fix limits; to bound; to define; to terminate.

حد بست ḥadd bast, n.m. Settlement of boundaries.

حد بندی ḥadd bandī. n.f. Fixing the boundaries.

حد بلوغ ḥadd-ĕ balūgh, n.f. Age of puberty.

حد سے بڑھنا ḥadd se barhna, v. To go beyond limits; to transgress; to encroach upon; to overstep bounds; to exceed one's powers.

حد سے زیاده ḥadd se ziyādah, adv. Very much; beyond bounds; extremely.

حد شکنی ḥadd shikani, n.f. Encroachment.

حد کرنا ḥadd karnā, v. To go beyond bounds; to exceed limits; to push anything to extremity; to reach the utmost limits.

حد متوسط ḥadd-ĕ mutawassaṭ (A) n. Medium.

حد ہونا ḥadd honā, v. To exceed bounds; to be very surprising.

حدت ḥiddat (A) n.f. Sharpness; vehemence; virulence; fury; acrimony; poignancy.

حدث ḥadaṣ yā ḥadṣ (A) n.m. Something happening for the first time; something not known before; a novelty; an innovation; an accidental cause of impurity which forbids recital of prayer without fresh ablution (according to Muslims).

حدوث ḥudūṣ (A) n.m Novelty; invention; the being new or recent.

حدود ḥudūd (A) n.f. & n.m. Boundaries; confines; limits; definitions; penal laws.

حدود اربعه ḥudūd-ĕ arb'ah, n.m. & f. The four boundaries.

حدود ارضی ḥudūd-ĕ arẓi, n.m. & f. Local limits.

حدود شرعیه ḥudūd-ĕ shar'aiyah, n.m. & f. Religious inhibitions and penalties; penal laws.

حدیث ḥadiṣ (A) n.m. History; tradition; narration of a saying or action of the Holy Prophet.

حدید ḥadid (H) *n.m.* Iron; a helmet.

حدیقه ḥadiqah (A) *n.m.* A walled garden.

حذاقت ḥiẕāqat (A) *n.f.* Intelligence; wisdom.

حذر ḥaẕar (A) *n.m.* Caution; prudence; fear.

حذف ḥaẕf (A) *n.m.* Taking away; ejecting; cutting off a letter or syllable of a word; apocope; omission; rejection; dropping.

حذف کرنا ḥaẕf karnā, *v.* To omit; to drop; to cut off.

حر ḥurr (A) *adj.* Free; noble.

حرارت ḥarārat (A) *n.f.* Heat; burning; fever; warmth; ardour; fervour; zeal; anger.

حرارت غریزی ḥarārat-e gharizī, *n.f.* Natural heat of the body.

حراره ḥarārah (A) *n.m.* Emotion; heat; anger; sharpness; rage.

حراست ḥirāsat (A) *n.f.* Watch; guarding; custody; escort; lock up.

حراست میں لینا ḥirāsat men lenā, *v.* To take into custody; to detain.

حراف، حرافه ḥarrāf, ḥarrāfah (A) *adj.* Deceitful; cunning; clever; tricky.

حرام ḥarām (A) *adj.* Unlawful; forbidden; prohibited; sacred; wrong. *n.m.* Unlawful act.

حرام خور ḥarām khor, *n.m.* One who lives on the wages of iniquity or unlawful gains; a corrupt person; a usurer.

حرام زاده ḥarām zādah, *n.m.* Illegitimate; bastard.

حرام زدگی ḥarām zadgī, *n.f.* Illegitimacy; rascality; villainy.

حرام کاری ḥarām kārī, *n.f.* Forbidden acts (particularly, adultery and fornication); violation of divine inhibitions.

حرام کھانا ḥarām khānā, *v.* To receive the wages of iniquity, to get money by unlawful means; to take bribe.

مال حرام، حرام کا مال māl-ĕ ḥarām, ḥarām kā māl, *n.m.* Ill-gotten wealth.

مال حرام بود بجائے حرام رفت māl-ĕ ḥarām būd bajāe ḥarām raft, *porv.* Ill-got, ill-spent.

حرام مغز ḥarām maghz, *n.m.* Spinal marrow.

حرامی ḥarāmi (A) *adj.* & *n.m.* (*Lit.* a thief). Illegitimate; bastard; wicked; villain.

حرب ḥarb (A) *n.f.* War; battle.

حربه ḥarbah (A) *n.m.* Arms and armaments; implements of war.

حربی ḥarbī (A) *adj.* Warlike; relating to war.

حرج ḥarj (A) *n.m.* Confusion; harm; obstacle.

حرج مرج ḥarj marj, *n.m.* Favourable and adverse circumstances; loss and profit; confusion.

حرز ḥirz (A) *n.m.* A fortification; an asylum; a place of refuge; an amulet; a charm.

حرص ḥirṣ (A) *n.f.* Eager; desire greediness; avidity; ambition.

حرصی ḥirṣī See حریص ḥariṣ.

حرف ḥarf (A) *n.m.* A letter of the alphabet; a particle (*Gram.*); changing; turning; border; brink; a margin; the summit of a mountain; blame; censure; the reproach; speech; talk.

حرف آنا ḥarf ānā, *v.* To suffer reproach; to be stigmatised.

حرف بحرف ḥarf baḥarf, *adv.* Literally; word for word.

حرف بٹھانا یا جمانا ḥarf biṭhānā yā jamānā, *v.* To compose (for printing).

حرف تردید ḥarf-ĕ tardid, *n.m.* Disjunctive conjunction.

حرف تشبیه ḥarf-ĕ tāshbih, *n.m.* The adverb of similitude.

حرف تعریف ḥarf-ĕ ta'rif, *n.m.* The definite article.

حرف تنکیر ḥarf-ĕ tankir, *n.m.* The indefinite article.

حرف جار ḥarf-ĕ jār, *n.m.* A preposition.

حرف رکھنا ḥarf rakhnā, v. To stigmatize; to impute a fault to one; to lay blame (upon).

حرف شرط ḥarf-ĕ sharṭ, n.m. Conditional conjunction.

حرف علت ḥarf-ĕ i'llat, n.m. A vowel.

حرف گیری ḥarf giri, n.f. Criticism; cavilling.

حرف لانا ḥarf lanā, v. To defame; to blot; to blame; to brand; to blemish.

حرف ندا ḥarf-ĕ nidā, n.m. Interjection.

حرفاً حرفاً ḥarfan̲ ḥarfan̲ (A) adv. Letter by letter; syllable by syllable; literally.

حرفت، حرفه ḥirfat, ḥirfah (A) n.f./n.m. Trade; art; profession; craft; skill; ingenuity; cleverness; cunning.

اهل حرفه ahl-ĕ ḥirfah, n.m. Workmen; artisans; men of skill.

نشان حرفه nishān-ĕ ḥirfah, n.m. Trade mark.

حرفی ḥarfi (A) adj. Literal; relating to letters.

حرکات ḥarakāt (A) n.f. (plu. of حرکت ḥarakat) Movements; motions; actions; the vowel points.

حرکات و سکنات ḥarakāt-ŏ sakanāt, n.f. Gestures; postures; alternate movements and rests.

حرکت ḥarakat (A) n.f. Motion; gesture; action; misdemeanour; fault; agitation; hinderance; interruption; a short vowel.

حرکت دینا ḥarakat denā, v. To move; to set in motion.

حرکت کرنا ḥarakat karnā, v. To act; to make a move; to mark; to act unproperly; to fornicate; to do an improper thing.

حرم ḥaram (A) adj. Sacred; forbidden. n.m. A sanctuary; the sacred territory of Mecca. n.f. Wife; a concubine; a female slave; women's apartment.

حرم سرا ḥāram sarā, n.m. A seraglio; women's apartments.

حرمین شریفین ḥaramain sharīfain (A) n.m. The two sacred places, Mecca and Medina.

حرمان ḥirmān (A) n.m. Repulse; disappointment; despondence.

حرمان نصیب ḥirmān naṣib, adj. Disappointed; unfortunate.

حرمت ḥurmat (A) n.f. Dignity; honour; reverence; reputation; chastity; esteem.

حرمت والا ḥurmat wālā, adj. Respectable; honourable; sacred.

حرمل ḥarmal (A) n.m. Wild rue.

حروف ḥurūf (A) n.m. (plu. of حرف ḥarf) Letters.

حروف تہجی hurūf-ĕ tahajji (A) n.m. The letters of alphabet.

حریت ḥurriyyat (A) n.f. Emancipation; liberty; freedom.

حریر ḥarir (A) n.m. Silk; silk-cloth.

حریری ḥarirī (A) adj. Silken; thin; lean.

حریص ḥariṣ (A) adj. Covetous; greedy; gluttonous.

حریف ḥarif (A) n.m. A rival; an opponent; an adversary; an enemy. adj. Cunning; clever.

حریم ḥarim (A) n.m. The boundry walls of the Ka'aba; a sacred place; a sanctuary; a house or dwelling.

حزب ḥizb (A) n.m. A party; a band; a company; union; portion.

حزب الاحرار ḥizb-ul-aḥrār, n.m. Liberal party.

حزب العمال ḥizb-ul-'ummal, n.m. Labour party or union.

حزب المستبدین ḥizb-ul-mustabiddin. n.m. Conservative party.

حزب الله ḥizb ullah, n.m. God's party; a party of saintly persons.

حزم ḥazm (A) n.m. Firmness of mind; firm resolution; steadfastness; perseverance; care; foresightedness.

حزن ḥuzn (A) *n.m.* Grief; sadness; affliction; sorrow.

حزیں ḥazīṅ (A) *adj.* Sad; sorrowful; melancholy; grieved; afflicted.

حس ḥiss (A) *n.f.* Feeling; sense; sentiment; imagination.

حس باطنی ḥiss-ĕ bāṭinī, *n.f.* Internal sense; perception.

حس ظاہری ḥiss-ĕ ẓāhiri, *n.f.* External sense; sensation.

حس مشترک ḥiss-ĕ mushtarik, *n.f.* Common sense.

حساب ḥisāb (A) *n.m.* Counting; reckoning; computation; calculation; accounts; arithmetic; rate; sense.

حساب بے باق کرنا ḥisāb be bāq karnā, *v.* To pay off debts; to settle an account.

حساب پاک کرنا ḥisāb pāk karnā, *v.* To clear accounts.

حساب پاک ہونا ḥisāb pāk honā, *v.* Adjustment of accounts.

حساب جوڑنا ḥisāb joṛnā, *v.* To make up an account; to total; to add up; to calculate.

حساب دار ḥisāb dār, *n.m.* Account keeper; an accountant.

حساب داں ḥisāb dān, *n.m.* An arithmetician; an accountant.

حساب دینا ḥisāb denā, *v.* To give or render an account.

حساب رکھنا ḥisāb rakhnā, *v.* To keep accounts; to register in account books.

حساب کتاب ḥisāb kitāb, *n.m.* Accounts.

حساب کرنا ḥisāb karnā, *v.* To calculate; to make up an account; to settle an account.

حساب لگانا ḥisāb lagānā, *v.* To calculate; to estimate.

حساب لینا ḥisāb ienā, *v.* To take an account from.

حساب میں لینا ḥisāb meṅ lenā, *v.* To take into account; to consider.

حساب نویس ḥisāb nawīs, *n.m.* An accountant; a ledger writer.

حسابی ḥisābi, *adj.* Of or relating to accounts; accountable; accurate; correct; just. *n.m.* An accountant.

حساس ḥassās (A) *adj.* Emotional; sensitive; possessed of all the five senses; accute; shrewd.

حسب ḥasab (A) *n.m.* Pedigree; nobility; lineage; numbering; computation; rate; price; measurement; measure; proportion: value; way; mode; manner.

حسب و نسب ḥasab-ŏ nasab, *n.m.* Lineage; pedigree.

حسب ḥasb (A) *adv.* In conformity with; according to.

حسب الارشاد، حسب الحکم، حسب ہدایت ḥasb-ul-irshād, ḥasb-ul-ḥukm, ḥasb-ĕ hidāyat. *adv.* According to the order; as desired; as ordered.

حسب حال ḥasb-ĕ ḥāl, *adv.* As the circumstances demand; as exigency may require.

حسب ذیل ḥasb-ĕ zail, *adv.* As follows; as under.

حسب ضابطہ ۔ قاعدہ ḥasb-ĕ ẓābiṭah, qā'edah, *adv.* According to rule; in accordance with the procedure.

حسب قانون ḥasb-ĕ qānūn, *adv.* Legally.

حسب معمول ḥasb-ĕ ma'mūl, *adv.* Usually; as usual.

حسب موقعہ ḥasb-ĕ mauqa', *adv.* As the circumstances may justify.

حسد ḥasad (A) *n.f.* Envy; jealousy; malice; emulation.

حسد رکھنا، کرنا ḥasad rakhnā, karnā, *v.* To bear malice; to be jealous.

حسرت ḥasrat (A) *n.f.* Regret; grief; intense sorrow; desire; longing.

حسرت آلوده، زده ḥasrat ālūdah, zadah, adj. Full of sorrow; overwhelmed with grief; afflicted with sorrow; grief-stricken.

حسرت بھرا ḥasrat bharā, adj. Desirous; full of desire; grief-stricken.

حسن ḥusn (A) n.f. Beauty; elegance; comeliness; goodness; pleasingness.

حسن اتفاق ḥusn-ĕ ittifāq, n.m. Lucky chance.

حسن اخلاق ḥusn-ĕ akhlāq, n.m. Courtesy; politeness; good manners.

حسن انتظام ḥusn-ĕ intiẓām, n.m. Good discipline; good management.

حسن تدبیر ḥusn-ĕ tadbīr, n.m. Sound policy; sound planning.

حسن ظن ḥusn-ĕ ẓann, n.m. A good opinion; a favourable view.

حسود ḥasūd (A) adj. Envious; malignant; grudging.

حسین ḥasīn (A) adj. Beautiful; handsome; elegant; comely; charming.

حسینی ḥusainī, n.m. Of or relating to Imam Hussain; a species of grape.

حشر ḥashr (A) n.m. Meeting; gathering; congregation; concourse; commotion; tumult; wailing; lamentation; resurrection; doomsday.

حشر برپا کرنا ḥashr barpā karnā, v. To weep and wail aloud; to make a dreadful noise.

یوم الحشر yaum-ul-ḥashr, n.m. The day of resurrection.

حشرات ḥasharāt (A) n.m. (plu. of حشره ḥashrah); reptiles; insects; animalcules.

حشرات الارض ḥasharāt-ul-arẓ, n.m. Insects which live in holes; innumerable insects brought to life during the rains.

حشفه ḥashfah (A) n.m. Glans penis; the head of penis.

حشم ḥasham (A) n.m. Train (of servants); equipage; suite.

حشمت ḥashmat (A) n.f. State; dignity; wealth; riches; pomp; equipage; retinue.

حشو ḥashw (A) n.m. Stuffing (a pillow, a bed, a cushion); rubbish; trash.

حشیش (A) n.m. Hay; dry grass; an intoxicating beverage prepared from the leaves of the hemp.

حصار ḥiṣār (A) n.m. A fort; fortress; castle; bulwark; fortification; enclosure; fence.

حصر ḥaṣr (A) n.m. Besiege; blockade; dependence; reliance; counting; surrounding; reckoning.

حصص ḥiṣaṣ (A) n.m. (plu. of حصه ḥiṣṣah); Parts; portions; shares.

حصن ḥiṣn (A) n.m. A fortress; a fort; fortification.

حصن حصین ḥiṣn-ĕ ḥaṣīn, n.m. An impregnable fortress.

حصول ḥuṣūl (A) n.m. Acquisition; attainment; profit; advantage; produce; achievement.

حصه ḥiṣṣah (A) n.m. Share; part; lot; portion.

حصه دار ḥiṣṣah dār, n.m. A sharer; a share holder; a partner.

حصه داری ḥiṣṣah dārī, n.f. Partnership; sharing.

حصه رسدی ḥiṣṣah rasadī, n.f. A proportional share; an equal share.

حصه کرنا ḥiṣṣah karnā, v. To share; to distribute; to divide; to apportion.

حضرت ḥaẓrat (A) n.m. Dignity; nearenss; a title applied to a great man.

حضرت ظل سبحانی ḥaẓrat ẓil-ĕ subḥānī, n.m. The shadow of God; the king; his Majesty.

بڑے حضرت baṛe ḥaẓrat, n.m. A superior; a consummate knave or rascal.

حضور **ḥuẓūr** (A) *n.m.* Presence; presence of a superior authority; attendance; court; government. *intj.* Your Majesty! You Highness!

حضور پر نور **ḥuẓūr pur nūr**, *n.m.* His Illustratious Majesty.

حضور والا، حضور اقدس **ḥuẓūr-ĕ wālā, ḥuẓūr-ĕ aqdas**, *n.m.* The high or exalted presence.

حضوری **ḥuẓūri** (A) *n.m.* An attendant; courtier. *n.f.* Presence.

حطیم **ḥaṭim** (A) *n.m.* A wall outside the *Ka'aba*; a stone between *Rukn* and *Zamzam*; a year old plant. *adj.* Broken.

حظ **ḥaẓẓ** (A) *n.m.* Pleasure; delight; flavoure; taste.

حظ اٹھانا **ḥaẓẓ uṭhānā**, *v.* To enjoy; to derive pleasure.

حظ نفسانی **ḥaẓẓ-ĕ nafsāni**, *n.m.* Sexsual pleasure.

حفاظت **ḥifāẓat** (A) *n.f.* Guarding; preserving; custody; security; safety.

حفاظت کرنا **ḥifāẓat karnā**, *v.* To preserve; to guard; to be on one's guard; to defend.

حفظ **ḥifẓ** (A) *n.m.* Memory; preservation; guardianship; respect; learning by heart.

حفظ کرنا **ḥifẓ kārnā**, *v.* To commit to memory; to learn hy heart.

حفظ ماتقدم **ḥifẓ-ĕ mātaqaddum** (A) *n.m.* A precautionary measure.

حفظ مراتب **ḥifẓ-ĕ marātib**, *n.m.* Observing etiquette; attention to the degree or ranks of persons.

حفیظ **ḥafiẓ** (A) *n.m.* Guardian; protector; name of God.

حق **ḥaqq** (A) *adj.* Just; right; true. *n.m.* The truth; the deity; God; justice; equity; rectitude; right; due; just claim; lot; portion; duty.

حق ادا کرنا **ḥaqq adā karnā**, *v.* To perform one's duty; to render one his due.

حق آسائش **ḥaqq-ĕ āsāi'sh**, *n.m.* Right of convenience.

حق السعی **ḥaqq-us-sa'i**, *n.m.* The wages of labour; recompense of trouble; commission.

حق العباد **ḥaqq-ul-'ibād**, *n.m.* The rights of human beings.

حق اللہ **ḥaqq-ullah**, *n.m.* The rights of God.

حق الناس **ḥaqq-un-nās**, *n.m.* The rights of the people.

حق ارجاع نالش **ḥaqq-ĕ-irj'a-ĕ-nālish**, *n.m.* Right of appeal.

حق بجانب **ḥaqq bajānib**, *adj.* Deserving; justified.

حق پرست **ḥaqq parast**, *adj.* Worshipper of God; a pious man.

حق تصنیف **ḥaqq-ĕ taṣnif**, *n.m.* Copyright.

حق تعالیٰ **ḥaqq ta'alā**, *n.m.* The Most High God.

حق تلفی کرنا **ḥaqq tālfi karnā**, *v.* To usurp the rights of others; to wrong a person; to encroach upon other person's claims.

حق ثابت کرنا **ḥaqq ṡābit karnā**, *v.* To prove one's claim.

حق جو **haqq jū**, *adj.* Seeker after truth.

حق خود ارادیت **ḥaqq-ĕ khūd irādiyat**, *n.m.* Right of self-determination.

حق دار **ḥaqq dār**, *adj.* Rightful; having right or claim (to).

حق دبانا، مارنا **ḥaqq dabānā, mārnā**, *v.* To usurp a right; to deprive one of his right.

حق رائے دہی **ḥaqq-ĕ ra'e dihi**, *n.m.* Right to vote.

حق رسی **ḥaqq rasi**, *n.f.* Justice; relief.

حق شفعہ **ḥaqq-ĕ shufa'ah**, *n.m.* Right of pre-emption.

حق شناس **ḥaqq shināṡ**, *adj.* Rendering to everyone his due; knowing and performing one's duty; pious; righteous.

حق شناسی ḥaqq shināsı, n.f. Knowledge of what is of God; doing even-handed justice.

حق مالکانه ḥaqq-ĕ-mālikānah, n.m. Proprietory right.

حقا ḥaqqā (A) adv. By God; truly; verily.

حقارت ḥiqārat (A) n.f. Contempt; scorn; disdain; affront disgrace; vileness; baseness; despicableness.

حقارت کرنا ḥiqārat karnā, v. To bate; to despise.

حقارت کی نظر سے دیکھنا ḥiqārat ki nazar se dekhnā, v. To look down upon; to bate.

حقانی ḥaqqāni (A) adj. Divine; of the deity.

حقائق ḥaqā'iq (A) n.f. (plu. of حقیقت ḥaqiqat) Truths; facts.

حقنه ḥuqnah (A) n.m. A syringe; a clyster; aenema.

حقوق ḥuqūq (A) n.m. (plu. of حق haqq). Rights; dues; privileges; just claims; laws; salary.

حقوق زوجیت ḥuqūq-ĕ zaujiyat, n.m. Conjugal rights.

حقوق مدنی ḥuqūq-ĕ madani, n.m. .Civic rights.

علم حقوق ilm-ĕ ḥuqūq, n.m. Science of laws.

حقه ḥuqqah (A) n.m. A casket or little box; a smoking pipe.

حقه باز ḥuqqah bāz, n.m. A smoker of the pipe; a juggler; an impostor.

حقه بردار ḥuqqah bardār, n.m. The servant who prepares the huqqah or smoking pipe.

حقه پانی بند کرنا ḥuqqah pānī band karnā, v. To excommunicate; to bycott some one.

حقیت ḥaqıyyat (A) n.f. Proprietory right; ownership right.

حقیر ḥaqīr (A) adj. Contemptible; despicable; abject; vile; base; mean.

حقیر جاننا ḥaqīr jānnā, v. To despise; to hate; to condemn.

حقیقت ḥaqīqat (A) n.f. Truth; fact; reality; account; narration; state; condition.

حقیقتاً ḥaqiqatan (A) adj. In truth; in reality; truly.

حقیقی ḥaqiqi (A) adj. Real; true; certain; accurate; just; actual; own.

حقیقی بھائی ḥaqiqi bhā'i, n.m. A full brother; own brother; real brother.

حقیقی رشته ḥaqiqī rishtah, n.m. A relative of the full blood.

حکام ḥukkām (A) n.m. (plu. of حاکم ḥākim); Rulers; commanders; officers; authorities.

حکایت ḥikāyat (A) n.f. Story; tale; narrative; history; romance.

حکم ḥukm (A) n.m. Order; command; decree; authority; jurisdiction; precept; permission; article (of faith); decision; rule; control; ordinance; statute; law; sanction.

حکم امتناعی ḥukm-ĕ imtinā'i, n.m. Order of prohibition; injunction.

حکم بجا لانا ḥukm bajā lānā, v. To execute or carry out an order.

حکم بردار ḥukm bardār, adj. Obedient.

حکم جاری کرنا ḥukm jārī karnā, v. To issue an order.

حکم چلانا ḥukm chalānā, v. To exercise authority; to rule; to govern.

حکم دینا ḥukm denā, v. To give or pass an order; to order.

حکم رانی ḥukm rānī, n.f. Rule; sovereignty; sway.

حکم ضبطی ḥukm-ĕ zabatī, n.m. Order of resumption or forfeiture.

حکم ظهری ḥukm-ĕ zahri, n.m. Endorsement on the petition.

حکم عدولی کرنا ḥukm 'udūlī karnā, v. To infringe or violate an order.

حکم قطعی ḥukm-ĕ qaṭa'ī, n.m. A final order.

حکم کرنا ḥukm karnā, v. To order; to command; to award; to sentence; to decree.

حکم لگانا ḥukm lagānā, v. To express a definite opinion; to assert positively; to predict.

حکم ناطق ḥukm-ĕ nāṭiq, n.m. Peremptory order.

حکم نامہ ḥukm nāmah, n.m. Written orders or decree.

حکم ḥakam (A) n.m. An umpire; a mediator; an arbitrator.

حکما ḥukamā (A) n.m. (plu. of حکیم ḥakīm) Philosophers; sages; physicians.

حکمت ḥikmat (A) n.f. Wisdom; knowledge; skill; cleverness; philosophy; mystery; device; the function of a physician.

حکمت عملی ḥikmat-ĕ 'amalī, n.m. Practical skill; judicial management; tactics; politics; policy.

حکمت مدنی ḥikmat-ĕ mudanī, n.f. Political science.

حکمتی ḥikmatī, adj. Ingenious; clever; wise; skilfull; artful; philosophical.

حکمی ḥukmī (A & P) adj. Imperative; infallible; dutiful; obedient.

حکومت ḥukūmat (A) n.f. Dominion; sovereignty; government; jurisdiction; sway; authority; power; rule.

حکومت امراء ḥukūmat-ĕ umarā, n.f. Aristocratic government.

حکومت جتانا ḥukūmat jatānā, v. To show of one's authority.

حکومت جمہوری ḥukūmat-ĕ jamhūrī, n.f. Democracy; republic; people's government.

حکومت شخصی ḥukūmat-ĕ shakhṣī, n.f. One man rule; monarchy; despotic government; dictatorship.

حکومت کرنا ḥukūmat karnā, v. To govern; to rule; to exercise authority.

حکیم ḥakīm (A) n.m. A sage; a philosopher; a physician; a doctor.

حکیم مطلق ḥakim-ĕ muṭlaq, n.m. The supreme sage; God.

نیم حکیم nīm ḥakīm, n.m. An unqualified or inexperienced doctor; a quack.

حکیمانہ ḥakīmānah (A & P) adj. Philoso phical; sage-like; physician-like.

حکیمی ḥakīmī, n.f. The practice of medicine.

حل ḥall (A) n.m. Solving; solution; untying; loosing; analysis.

حل کرنا ḥall karnā, v. To solve; to loosen; to liquify; to dilute.

حل و عقد ḥall-ŏ a'qd, n.m. Management; administration.

حل ہونا ḥall honā, v. To be dissolved; to be diluted; to be solved.

حلال ḥalāl (A) adj. Legal; lawful; right; admissible; legitimate; showing religious sanction; killed as prescribed by Islamic law.

حلال خور ḥalāl khor, n.m. A sweeper; one who eats what is lawful; one whose earnings are lawful.

حلال کرنا ḥalāl karnā, v. To make lawful; to slaughter according to the Muslim way.

حلالہ ḥalālah (A) n.f. A woman who marries her divorcer again after she has been divorced by her second husband.

حلاوت ḥalāwat (A) n.f. Sweetness; taste; relish; deliciousness.

حلت ḥillat (A) n.f. Legality; lawfulness.

حلف ḥalf (A) n.f. An oath.

حلف اٹھانا ḥalf uṭhānā, v. To take an oath.

حلف دروغی ḥalf daroghī, n.f. False swearing; perjury.

حلف دینا ḥalf denā, v. To administer an oath.

حلف نامہ **ḥalf nāmah**, *n.m.* A declaration on oath; affidavit.

حلفاً **ḥalafan̲** (A) *adv.* On oath.

حلق ، حلقوم **ḥalq, ḥalqūm** (A) *n.m.* The windpipe; the throat.

حلقہ **ḥalqah** (A) *n.m.* A ring; a circle; an assembly; fraternity; a loop; a loop of a button hole; a knocker (of a door); circuit of a village; a ward.

حلقہ باندھنا **ḥalqah bāndhnā**, *v.* To form a circle.

حلقہ بگوش **ḥalqah bagosh**, *n.m.* A slave; a servant; a disciple.

حلقہ بگوشی **ḥalqah bagoshi**, *n.f.* Servitude; slavery.

حلم **ḥilm** (A) *n.m.* Gentleness; clemancy; mildness; affability; gravity; calmness; toleration.

حلوا **ḥālwā** (A) *n.m.* A kind of sweet dish made of flour, ghee and sugar.

حلوہ خوردن روئے باید **ḥalwā k̲h̲ūrdan rū'e bāyad**, *prov.* To achieve honour and glory in the world one must possess skill and ability.

حلوا سمجھنا **ḥalwā samajhnā**, *v.* To regard something as very easy; to have something at on's fingers' tips.

حلوائی **ḥalwā'ī** (A) *n.m.* A confectioner; a sweetmeat-seller.

حلوائی کی دکان دادا جی کی فاتحہ **ḥalwā'ī kī dukān dādā ji kī fātiḥah**, *prov.* Cocks make free with horse's corn.

حلول **ḥulūl** (A) *n.m.* Alighting; descending; entering; penetrating; transmigrating.

حلیف **ḥalīf** (A) *n.m.* Ally; comrade; sworn friend.

حلیم **ḥalīm** (A) *adj.* Mild; humane; gentle. *n.f.* A dish prepared with meat and several cereals.

حلیہ **ḥulyah** (A) *n.m.* Appearance; features; distinctive marks; identity.

حمار **ḥimār** (A) *n.m.* A maḷe ass.

حماقت **ḥamāqat** (A) *n.f.* Folly; stupidity.

حمال **ḥammāl** (A) *n.m.* A porter; a carrier of burdens.

حمام **ḥammām** (A) *n.m.* A hot bath; a bagnio; a Turkish bath.

حمام کرنا **hammām karnā**, *v.* To take a hot bath.

ایک حمام میں سب ننگے **ek ḥammām men sab nange**, *prov.* All are naked in the bath room; an evil in which most people indulge.

حمامہ **ḥammāmah** (A) *n.f.* A pigeon.

حمامی **ḥammāmi** (A) *n.m.* A bath keeper; the attendant of a bath.

حمائل **ḥamā'el** (A) *n.f.* A sword belt hung from the shoulders; a necklace of flowers; a small *Qurān* suspended to the neck as an amulet; pocket edition of the *Qurān*.

حمائل کرنا **ḥamā'el karnā**, *v.* To sling across the shoulders.

حمایت **ḥimāyat** (A) *n.f.* Protection; guardianship; patronage; support; defence; countenance.

حمایت کرنا **ḥimāyat karnā**, *v.* To support; to protect; to back; to patronise; to defend; to guard.

حمایتی **ḥimāyati** (A) *n.m.* A protector; a defender; a partisan.

حمد **ḥamd** (A) *n.f.* Praise of God.

حمد کرنا **ḥamd karnā**, *v.* To praise (God).

حمق **ḥumq** (A) *n.m.* Foolishness; folly; stupidity.

حمل **ḥaml** (A) *n.m.* A burden; a load; pregnancy; the fruit of the womb; transportation; conveyance.

حمل اسقاط ہونا **ḥaml isqāṯ honā**, *v.* To miscarry; to abort.

حمل سے ہونا **ḥaml se honā**, *v.* To become pregnant; to conceive.

حمل و نقل ḥaml-ŏ-naql, n.m. Transport.

حملہ ḥamlah (A) n.m. Attack; onset; assault; storm; charge; invasion.

حملہ آور ḥamlah āwar, n.m. An assailant; an invader.

حملہ کرنا ḥamlah karnā, v. To attack; to assault; to storm; to invade; to assail.

حمیت ḥamiyat (A) n.m. Ardour; zeal; care or concern for what is sacred; concern for what one is bound to honour or defend.

حمید، حمیدہ ḥāmīd, ḥamidah (A) adj. Praised; laudable; glorious.

اخلاق حمیدہ ، اوصاف حمیدہ ā<u>kh</u>lāq-ĕ ḥamidah. auṣāf-ĕ ḥamīdah, n.m. Laudable qualifications or manners.

حنا ḥinnā (A) n.f. The Indian privet; a shrub, the leaves of which are used for dyeing the hands, feet and hair.

حنا بندی ḥinnā bandī, n.f. Applying or adorning with ḥinnā.

حنان ḥannān (A) adj. The most merciful. n.m. The name of God.

حنائی ḥinnā'i (P) adj. Of the ḥinnā colour; red.

حنائی کاغذ ḥinnā'i kā<u>kh</u>az, n.m. Cream coloured paper.

حنجرہ ḥanjarah (A) n.m. The throat; gullet.

حنظل ḥanzal (A) n.m. Bitter apple; the wild gourd.

حنوط ḥanūṭ (A) n.m. Aromatics used for embalming (the dead person).

حنیف ḥanīf (A) n.m. A lover of the religion of God; a pious man; a followers of Abraham.

حوا ḥawwā (A) n.f. Eve; the mother of mankind.

حوادث ḥawādiṣ (A) n.m. (plu. of حادثہ ḥādiṣah). Occurrances; accidents; misfortunes.

حواری ḥawārī (A) n.m. A friend; a companion; a disciple; associate; apostles of Jesus Christ.

حواس ḥawās (A) n.m. The senses.

حواس باختہ ḥawās bā<u>kh</u>tah, adj. Out of one's senses; insensible; crazy.

حواس ٹھکانے ہونا ḥawās ṭhikāne honā, v. To have one's senses about.

حواس خمسہ ḥawās-ĕ <u>kh</u>amsah, n.m. The five senses (seeing; hearing; smelling; tasting and touching).

حواشی ḥawāshī (A) n.m. (plu. of حاشیہ ḥāshiyah) Margins; borders; attendants.

حوالات ḥawālāt, n.f. A lock-up; custody; things given in charge.

حوالدار ḥawāldār, n.m. A petty military officer.

حوالہ ḥawālah (A) n.m. Charge; custody; care; possession; reference; quotation.

حوالہ دینا ḥawālah denā, v. To make a reference; to quote an authority.

حوالے کرنا ḥawāle karnā, v. To make over; to surrender; to consign.

حوالی ḥawālī (A) n.f. Environs; suburbs.

حوالی موالی ḥawālī mawālī, n.m. Companions; friends; attendants.

حوائج ḥawā'ij (A) n.m. & f. (plu. of حاجت ḥājat) Needs; necessities; wants.

حور ḥūr (A) n.f. A virgin of Paradise; a black-eyed nymph; a celestial bride promised to all good Muslims in the next world.

حوصلہ ḥauṣalah (A) n.m. Capacity; courage; spirit; resolution; desire.

حوصلہ مند ḥauṣalah mānd, adj. Ambitious; courageous.

حوصلہ نکالنا ḥauṣalah nikālnā, v. To satisfy one's ambition.

عالی حوصلہ ‘ālī ḥauṣalah, adj. High-minded; aspiring.

حوض hauẓ, n.m. A reservoir; a cistern; pond; the basin of a fountain; a tank.

حونق hawannaq (A) n.m. A fool; a stupid person.

حویلی haweli (A) n.f. House; dwelling; a large and spacious building.

حی ḥaiy (A) adj. Alive; living; having life.

حیا ḥayā (A) n.f. Modesty; shame; shyness.

حیا دار ḥayā dār, adj. Modest; bashfully; retiring; shy.

بے حیا be hayā, adj. Immodest; impudent; shame-proof.

بے حیائی be hayā'ī, n.f. Shamelessness.

حیات ḥayāt (A) n.f. Life; existence.

حیات تازہ ḥayāt-ĕ tāzah, n.f. New life; regeneration; recovery from severe illness; the pleasure derived from meeting a friend.

حیات مستعار ḥayāt-ĕ musta'ār, n.f. Frail existence; life depending on the will of God.

حیثیت ḥaisiyat (A) n.f. Rank; capacity; ability; merit; means; status; condition of life; prestige; position.

حیثیت عرفی ḥaisiyat-ĕ 'urf i, n.f. Reputation; character.

حیران ḥairān (A) adj. Confounded; astonished; amazed; perplexed; disturbed; worried.

حیران کرنا ḥairān karnā, v. To confound; to amaze; to astonish; to perplex; to discompose.

حیران و سر گردان ḥairān-ŏ sargardān, adj. Wandering about in a distracted or bewildered state of mind.

حیرت ḥairat (A) n.f. Stupor and perturbation of mind; astonishment; amazement; wonder.

حیرت افزا ḥairat afzā, adj. Astonishing.

حیرت زدہ ḥairat zadah, adj. Wonder-struck; aghast; amazed; struck with astonishment.

حیص بیص ḥaiṣ baiṣ (A) n.f. Confusion; dilemma; perplexity; difficulty; hesitation; suspense.

حیض ḥaiẓ (A) n.f. The menses; menstrual course.

حیضی بچہ ḥaiẓi bachah, n.m. A wicked child; a brat.

حیطہ ḥiṭah (A) n.m. A court; a place; an enclosure.

حیف haif (A) interj. Ah ! alas ! n.m. Inequity; oppression; pity.

حیلہ ḥilah (A) n.m. Stratagem; deceit; artifice; pretence; trick; service; employment.

حیلہ باز - ساز - گر ḥilah bāz, sāz, gar, adj. Artful; wily; fraudulent; deceitful.

حیلہ حوالہ ḥilah ḥawālah, n.m. Chicanery; pretence; evasion; prevarication.

حیلہ کرنا ḥilah karnā, v. To practise deceit; to pretend; to represent falsely.

حیلے رزق ، بہانے موت ḥile rizq, bahāne mot, prov. Livelihood is earned by some means and death occurs by some cause.

حین ḥin (A) n.m. Time; space; interval of time.

حین حیات ḥin-ĕ ḥayāt, n.f. Life time; life long; during the life time.

حیوان ḥaiwān (A) n.m. An animal; living being; beast; brute; a stupid fellow; a blockhead.

حیوان مطلق ḥaiwān-ĕ muṭlaq, n.m. An animal; an absolute fool.

حیوان ناطق ḥaiwān-ĕ nāṭiq, n.m. A rational animal; a man.

حیوانی ḥaiwānī (A) adj. Brutish; beastly; pertaining to animals.

حیوانیت ḥaiwāniyyat (A) n.f. Beastliness; brutality; animal nature.

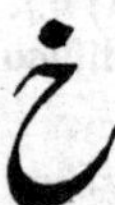

خ khe, called khā-ĕ manquta or khā-ĕ mu'jama is the seventh letter of the Arabic, the ninth of the Persian and tenth of the Urdu alphabet. It is a guttural letter, formed by compression of the top of the throat near the mouth, and contains a mixture of the sounds of k and h. It has no corresponding sound in English language. In abjad it stands for 600.

خاتم khātam (A) n.m. A ring; a seal after which no writing is admissible.

خاتم النبین khātam-un-nabiyyin, n.m. The seal of the prophets; the last of the prophets; the prophet after whom no prophet will be sent.

خاتم khātim (A) n.m. Finishing; ending; one who ends or brings to conclusion; a ring worn on the fingers; a seal.

خاتمہ khātimah (A) n.m. Conclusion; end; finish; epilogue; appendix.

خاتمہ بالخیر khātimah bil-khair n.m. Happy ending; happy conclusion.

خاتمہ ہونا khātimah honā, v. To end; to die.

خاتون khātūn (T) n.f. A lady; a noble woman; a matron.

خادم khādim (A) n.m. A servant; an attendant.

خادمہ khādimah (A) n.f. A female servant.

خار khār (P) n.m. A thorn; spine; thistle; bramble; a cock's spur; grudge; jealousy.

خار پشت khār pusht, n.m. A porcupine; a hedge-hog.

خار دار khār dār, adj. Thorny; barbed; troublesome; arduous.

خار زار khār zār, n.m. A thicket of thorns.

خار کھانا khār khānā, v. To feel jealous or envious.

خار و خس khār-ŏ-khas, n.m. Sweepings, rubbish; anything vile.

خارا khārā (P) n.m. A hard stone; a flint; granite; a kind of marble.

خارا شگاف khārā shigāf, adj. Stone-splitting; very strong and sharp.

خارج khārij (A) adj. Being out of; excluded; extraneous; rejected; outcaste.

خارج از بحث khārij az bahṣ, adj. Out of question; beside the point.

خارج از عقل khārij az 'aql, adj. Senseless; meaningless; foolish.

خارج قسمت khārij qismat, n.m. Quotient.

خارج کرنا khārij karnā, v. To exclude; to expel; to strike off; to cast off.

خارج ہونا khārij honā, v. To be excluded; to be struck off.

خارجہ khārijah (A) n.m. What is excluded or rejected; a catch-word. adj. Foreign; external.

خارجہ حکمت عملی khārijah ḥikmat-ĕ 'amali, n.f. Foreign policy.

امور خارجہ umūr-ĕ khārijah, n.m. External affairs.

محکمہ خارجہ mahkamā-ĕ khārijah, n.m. Forgeign Department.

وزیر خارجہ wazir-ĕ khārijah, n.m. Minister for foreign affairs.

خارجی khāriji (A) n.m. A schismatic; an outcast; a sect of Muslims who do not reckon Hazrat 'Ali among the legal successors of the Holy Prophet. adj. Extraneous; external.

خارش ، خارشت khārish, khārisht (P) n.f. The itch; the mange; scabies.

خارشی khārishi (P) adj. Itchy; mangy; suffering from scabies.

خارق عادات khāriq-ĕ 'ādāt (A) *adj.* Contrary to nature; unnatural; unusual. *n.m.* Mircales.

خازن khāzin (A) *n.m.* Custodian; treasurer.

خاشاک khāshāk (P) *n.m.* Sweepings; shavings; rubbish; trash.

خاص khāṣ (A) *adj.* Particular; peculiar; special; appropriate; specific; personal; private; proper; excellent; noble; fine; unmixed; only.

خاص تحصیل khāṣ taḥṣīl, *n.f.* The *teḥṣīl* at the headquarters of a district.

خاص دان khāṣ dān, *n.m.* A betel dish with cover.

خاص کر khāṣ kar, *adv.* Especially; particularly.

خاص و عام khāṣ-ŏ.'ām, *n.m.* The high and low; the general public.

خاصا khāṣā, *adj.* Good; charming; delightful; pretty; fair; neither good nor bad; of medium quality; tolerable; moderate.

خاصہ khāṣah (A) *n.m.* Dinner; the dainty food of great men; a private or personal attendant; a kind of fine cloth.

خاصہ khāṣṣah (A) *n.m.* Habit; nature; manner; method.

خاصیت khāṣiyyat (A) *n.f.* Peculiarity; peculiar nature; natural disposition.

خاطر khāṭir (A) *n.f.* The heart; mind; whatever occurs to the mind: thought; memory; inclination; propensity; account; sake; behalf; will; choice; regard; respect; favour.

خاطر جمع khāṭir jama, *n.f.* Tranquality; rest; repose; quite; content.

خاطر جمع کرنا , رکھنا khāṭir jama' karnā rakhnā, *v.* To set one's mind at ease; to be calm and collected.

خاطر خواہ khāṭir khawāh, *adv.* According to one's wishes; as one desires; to one's satisfaction.

خاطر داری khāṭir dārī, *n.f.* Consideration; regard; satisfaction; encourgement; comfort; gratification; hospitality; entertainment.

خاطر میں رکھنا khāṭir meṅ rakhnā, *v.* To remember; to bear in mind.

خاطر میں لانا khāṭir meṅ lānā, *v.* To regard; to give a thought to; to care for; to attend to; to think of.

خاقان khāqān (T) *n.m.* A king; an emperor; the title of Chinese and Turkish kings.

خاک khāk (P) *n.f.* Dust; earth; land; ashes; territory.

خاک اڑانا khāk uṛānā, *v.* To defame; to wander. to saunter about.

خاک اڑنا khāk uṛnā, *v.* To be ruined; to be deserted.

خاک پھانکنا khāk phāṅknā, *v.* To wander away; to stray; to wander about.

خاک چھاننا khāk chhānnā, *v.* To go about aimlessly; to labour hard for nothing; to go through fruitless toil.

خاک ڈالنا khāk ḍālnā, *v.* To throw dust on; to conceal an ugly affair; to pay no attention.

خاکروب khāk rob, *n.m.* A sweeper.

خاکسار khāk sār, *n.m.* Humble; low; unimportant; poor.

خاکساری khāk sārī, *n.f.* Humility; humbleness.

خاک کا پتلا khāk kā putlā, *n.m.* Man; one made of earth.

خاک میں ملانا khāk meṅ milānā, *v.* To destory; to demolish.

خاک میں ملنا khāk meṅ milnā, *v.* To be ruined; to die; to perish.

خاک ہو جانا khāk ho jānā, *v.* To be ruined; to molder or perish.

خاکستر khākistar (P) *n.f.* Ashes; calx (of metals).

خاکستر ہونا khākistar honā, *v.* To be reduced to ashes.

خاکستری khākistri (P) adj. Of the colour of ashes; ashy; gray.

خاکشی ، خاکسی khākshi, khāksi (P) n.f. A small weight used by goldsmiths; a red bramble; a small red seed used in medicine.

خاکنائے khāknā'e (P) n.f. An isthmus.

خاکہ khākah (P) n.m. A plan; a sketch; a draft; an outline; a caricature.

خاکہ اتارنا khākah utārnā, v. To trace; to make a tracing of.

خاکہ اڑانا khākah uṛānā, v. To ridicule; to make a jest of; to give a bad name to.

خاکی khāki (P) adj. Of the dust; dusty; earthy; terrestrial; dust-coloured; a kind of arrow.

خاکی انڈا khāki aṅdā, n.m. A wind egg; an unfertilized egg incapable of producing chicken; a bastard.

خاگینہ khāginah (P) n.m. A kind of dish made of eggs, fried eggs; an omelet; a pan-cake.

خال khāl (A) n.m. A mole on the face; an artificial spot made for ornament.

خال خال khāl khāl, adj. Little; very little; rare; here and there; occasional.

خالص khāliṣ (A) adj. Pure; genuine; real; sincere (friend).

خالصہ khāliṣah (A) adj. Pure; a revenue collector's office; crown or Government lands; a name for the Sikhs.

خالق khāliq (A) n.m. The creator; God.

خالو khālū n.m. An uncle (maternal), husband of mother's sister.

خالہ khālah (A) n.f. Maternal aunt; mother's sister.

خالہ جی کا گھر khālah ji kā ghar, n.m. A place of rest and security; an easy matter.

خالی khāli (A) adj. Empty; vacant, void, deserted; blank; not filled up; unoccupied; free; exempt; ineffective.

خالی کرنا khāli karnā, v. To empty; to evacaute; to clear out.

خالی ہاتھ khāli hāth, adj. Empty handed; penniless; poor.

خام khām (P) adj. Raw; unripe; green; crude; inexpert; vain; unbaked; immature; not solid; imperfect.

خام خیالی khām khiyāli, n.f. Vain imaginations; crude ideas.

خام عقل khām 'aql, adj. Fool; of weak understanding.

خام کو کام سکھا لیتا ہے khām ko kām sikhā letā hai, prov. Experience is the best teacher; work makes the raw hand expert.

خاموش khāmosh (P) adj. Silent.

خاموشی khāmoshi (P) n.f. Silence; taciturnity.

خامہ khāmah (P) n.m. A pen; a writing reed.

خامی khāmi (P) n.f. Rawness; immaturity; inexperience; imperfection

خان khān (P) n.m. Lord; prince; a title used by Pathāns

خاندان khāndān (P) n.m. Family; lineage; dynesty; race; house; household.

خاندانی khāndāni (P) adj. Hereditary; ancestral; of good birth.

خانساماں khānsāmāṅ (P) n.m. A butler; a house-steward; a cook.

خانقاہ khānqāh (A) n.m. A convent; abode of holy men; the tomb of a saint.

خانگی khāngi (P) adj. Domestic; private; household. n.f. A prostitute; a harlot.

خانم khānum (P) n.f. A lady; a woman of rank; princess; a wife.

خانماں khānumāṅ (P) n.m. Houshold furniture; house; family; everything belonging to the house.

خانواده khānwādah (P) n.m. A family; a house; a tribe; line of mystics.

خانه khānah (P) n.m. House; dwelling; chamber; room; a drawer; a compartment; a column; a partition.

خانه آبادی khānah ābādi, n.f. Prospertity; marriage.

خانه بدوش khānah badosh, adj Wanderer; nomadic. n.m. A traveller; a pilgrim; a gipsy; a rover; a vagabond.

خانه بدوشی khānah badoshi, n.f. Roving; wandering; travelling.

خانه برانداز khānah barāndāz, n.m. A prodigal; a spendthrift.

خانه بربادی khānah barbādi, n.f. Destruction of a house or family.

خانه پری khānah puri, n.f. Filling in the column.

خانه تلاشی khānah talāshi, n.f. House search.

خانه جنگی khānah jangi, n.f Domestic feuds; civil war; domestic bickering.

خانۂ خدا khānah-ĕ-khudā, n.m. The house of God; the Ka'abah; a mosque; a temple; a church.

خانه خراب khānah kharāb, adj. Ruined; base; abject; a wretch.

خانه خرابی khānah kharābi, n.f. Ruin; destruction.

خانه داری khānah dāri, n.f. House-keeping; house-hold management.

خانه دوست khāna dost, adj. Fond of staying at home; a stay-at home person.

خانه زاد khanah zād, n.m. The child of a slave.

خانه ساز khānah sāz, adj. Home made.

خانه شماری khānah shumāri, n.f. A census.

خانه نشین khānah nashin, adj. Retired; pensioner; idle; unemployed.

صاحب خانه ṣāhib-ĕ khānah, n.m. Master of the house.

کتب خانه kutub khānah, n.m. Library.

خاور khāwar (P) n.m. The east or the west.

خاوند khāwand (P) n.m. Lord; master; husband.

خائف khā'if (A) adj. Afraid; fearful; frightened; timid.

خائن khā'in (A) adj. Unfaithful; treacherous; perfidious; cheat.

خایه khayah (P) n.m. A testicle; an egg.

خایه بردار khāyah bardār (P) n.m. A cringing fellow; a fawner.

خباثت khabaṣat (A) n.f. Wickedness; corruptness; depravity.

خبث khubs (A) n.m. Malice; malignity; impurity; displeasure; evil.

خبر khabar (A) n.f. News; information; intelligence; advice; report; rumour; account; notice; knowledge; announcement; tidings; awareness.

خبر اڑانا khabar uṛānā, v. To spread a rumour; to carry tales.

خبر پہنچانا khabar pahunchānā, v. To give information; to send word.

خبر دار khabar dār, adj. Watchful; careful; cautious; on guard; having knowledge; acquainted.

خبر دار کرنا khabar dār karnā, v. To forewarn; to caution; to warn; to put on one's guard.

خبر داری khabar dāri, n.f. Charge; care; custody; getting information; guarding; guardianship.

خبر دهنده khabar dehindah, n.m. An informer; a reporter.

خبر دینا khabar denā, v. To inform; to report; to acquaint; to give information.

خبر رسان khabar rasān, n.m. A messenger; one who gives information.

خبر رکھنا khabar rakhnā, v. To be well informed; to be wide awake; to be acquainted with; to be informed.

خبر گیری khabar girī, n.f. Looking after; giving due care and attention; managing; management; protection; spying; informing.

خبر گیری کرنا khabar gīrī karnā, v. To look after; to take care.

خبر لگانا khabar lagānā, v. To obtain information; to fish out news; to search for.

خبر لینا khabar lenā, v. To look after; to enquire into; to take care; to support; to trace; to get information.

خبر هونا khabar honā, v. To be informed; to have knowledge of.

بے خبر be khabar, adj. Ignorant; uninformed; insensible.

خبط khabt̤ (A) n.m. Craze; derangement of mind; madness; foolishness.

خبطی khabt̤ī (A&P) adj. Foolish; crazy; insane; mad.

خبیث khabīs̤ (A) adj. Wicked; malignant; impure; bad; corrupt; foul; filthy; miser; wretched.

ختم khatm (A) n.m. Conclusion; end; seal; termination; a recitation of the whole Quran. adj. Done; finished; terminated.

ختم المرسلین khatm-ul-mursalin, n.m. Seal of those sent by God; the last of the prophets; the Holy Prophet, Mohammad (peace be on Him).

ختم کرنا khatm karnā, v. To conclude; to finish; to terminate.

ختم هونا khatm honā, v. To come to an end; to be finished; to die.

ختن khutan (P) n. prop. A district in Turkistan famous for musk.

ختنه khatnah (A) n.m. Circumcision.

ختنه کرنا khatnah karnā, v. To circumcise.

خٹا khuṭṭā (A) n.m. A testicle.

خجالت khajālat (A) n.m. Shame; sense of shame; bashfulness.

خجسته (P) adj. Happy; fortunate; blessed; auspicious.

خجل khajil (A) adj. Modest; bashful; abashed; ashamed.

خجل کرنا khajil karnā, v. To put one to shame.

خچر khachchar (H) n.m. A mule.

خد khadd (A) n.m. Cheek; a furrow; an opening.

خد و خال khadd-ŏ khāl, n.m. Features.

خدا khudā (P) n.m. God; lord; the Supreme Being; master; owner; creator.

خدا پرست khudā parast, adj. God-worshipper; pious; godly; devout.

خدا چاهے، خدا کرے khudā chāhe, khudā kare, adv. If God wills; God willing.

خدا حافظ khudā ḥāfiz̤, adv. God be your protector; good-bye.

خدا خدا کر کے khudā khudā kar ke, adv. With great difficulty; after much prayer.

خدا داد khudā dād, adj. God-given; granted by God; natural.

خدا را khudā rā, adv. For God's sake; for Heaven's sake.

خدا رسیده khudā rasīdah, adj. Pious; virtuous; godly.

خدا سلامت رکھے khudā salāmat rakhe, interj. May God protect you! may you live long !

خدا سمجھے khudā samjhe. interj. May God punish him! may God deal with him!

خدا شکر خورے کو شکر هی دیتا هے khudā shakar khore ko shakar hi detā hai. prov. He that eats good meal shall have a good meal.

خدا گنجے کو ناخن نه دے khudā ganje ko nākhun nah de, prov. A great fortune in the hands of a fool is a great misfortune.

خدا شناس khudā shināṣ, adj. Good knowing; pious; godly.

خدا کی پناہ khudā ki panāh, interj. God preserve us !

خدا کی لاٹھی میں آواز نہیں khudā kī lāṭhi meṅ āwāz nahīṅ, prov. The long arm of the Almighty makes no sound when it strikes.

خدا لگتی کہنا khudā lagti kahnā, v. To speak the truth; to say what is right and just.

خدا نخواستہ khudū nakhwāstah, interj. God forbid.

خدا واسطے کی دشمنی khudā wāsṭe kī dushmanī, n.f. Purposeless enmity.

خدایا khudāyā, interj. O God !

خدام khuddām (A) n.m. (plu. of خادم khādim); servants.

خداوند khudāwand (P) n.m. Master; lord; possessor; husband.

خدا وند نعمت khudāwand-ĕ ni'mat, n.m. (a form of address to superiors) Lord of bounty; beneficent master; rich; apulent.

خداوندی khudāwandī (P) n.f. Sovereignty; lordship; divinity; providence.

خدائی khūda ī (P) n.f. Godhead; divinity; providence; the world; people. adj. Divine.

خدائی خوار khudā'i khār, n.m. A shameless person; a vagabond; a wanderer.

خدائی کرنا khudā'i karnā, v. To perform something miraculous.

خدشہ khadshah (A) n.m. Fear; alarm; danger; doubt; apprehension; solicitude; anxiety.

خدم khudam (A) n.m. (plu. of خادم khādim) Servants.

خدمت khidmat (A) n.f. Service: attendance; employment; office; appointment; duty; use; function.

خدمت گار khidmat gār, n.m. Servant; attendant; a table servant; a butler.

خدمت گاری khidmat gāri, n.f. Service; attendance.

خدمتی khidmati (P) n.m. Servant; attendant.

خدنگ khadang (P) n.m. An arrow; the white poplar (a tree from which arrows are usually made).

خدیو khadeive (P) n.m. A great prince; a sovereign; a king; the title of the Egyptian kings.

خر khar (P) n.m. An ass.

خر دماغ khar dimāgh, adj. Stupid; pigheaded; proud; peevish; perverse.

خر دماغی khar dimāghı, n.f. Stupidity; obstinacy; perverseness.

خروار kharwār, n.m. An ass load.

خراب kharāb (A) adj. Bad; depraved; ruined; depopulated; deserted; abandoned; miserable; spoiled; waste; poor; wretched; defiled; corrupt; obscene.

خراب خستہ kharāb khastah, adj. Ruined; dilapidated; miserable; spoiled.

خراب کرنا kharāb karnā, v. To spoil; to pollute; to rape; to lay waste; to corrupt; to vitiate; to mar; to depopulate; to desolate.

خرابات kharābāt (A) n.f. & m. A tavern; a brothel; a bar.

خراباتی kharābātī (A) n.m. A hunter of taverns and brothels; a rake; a debauchee; a drunkard.

خرابہ kharābah (A) n.m. Devastation; ruin; a bad place; a ruined place.

خرابی kharābī (P) n.f. Badness; depravity; ruin, desolation; destruction; mischief; misery; an ill or evil; defect.

خراٹا kharāṭā (A) n.m. Snoring.

خراٹے لینا kharāte lenā, v. To snore.

خراج kharāj (A) n.m. Tribute; tax; duty; rent; revenue.

خراد kharād (P) n.f. A lathe.

خراد چڑھنا kharād charhnā, v. To be put on the lathe; to be polished; to have intercourse with refined society.

خرادی kharādi, n.m. A turner.

خراس kharās (P) n.m. A flour-mill worked by camels or oxen.

خراش kharāsh (P) n.f. Scratching; scraping; excoriation.

خرافات khurāfāt (A) n.f. Senseless or improper speech; obscene language.

خرافات بکنا khurāfāt baknā, v. To talk nonsense; to use abusive language.

خرام kharām (P) n.f. Pace; stately gait; graceful walking; walk.

خوش خرام khush kharām, adj. Walking elegantly.

خراماں خراماں kharāmāṅ kharāmāṅ (P) adv. With a stately or graceful movement.

خرانٹ khurānṭ (H) adj. Old; experienced; crafty.

خربزہ ' خربوزہ ' خرپزہ kharbūzah, kharbūzah, kharpūzah (P) n.m. The musk-melon.

خرچ kharch (P) n.m. Expenditure; spending; disbursement; expense; outgoing; money; allowance.

خرچ اخراجات kharch akhrājāt, n.m. Expenditure.

خرچ دینا kharch denā, v. To advance money for expenses; to give one allowance.

خرچ متفرقات kharch-ĕ mutfarriqāt, n.m. Contingencies.

خرچ ہونا kharch honā, v. To be spent.

خرچنا، خرچ کرنا kharchnā, kharch karnā, v. To use; to spend.

خرچہ kharchah n.m. Costs of law-suits; costs; expenses.

خرچہ دلانا kharchah dilāna, v. To award costs.

خرچی kharchī (P) n.f. Provisions for a journey; wages of harlotry. adj. prodigal; lavish.

خرخشہ kharkhashah (P) n.m. A tumult; crowd; riot; causeless wrangling; quarrelling; encounter; dispute.

خرد khirad (P) n.m. Wisdom; intelligence; intellect.

خرد مند khirad mand, adj. Wise; intelligent.

خرد مندی khirad mandī, n.f. Wisdom; sagacity; intelligence.

خرد khurd (P) adj. Small; little; young; minute.

خرد بین khurd bīn, n.f. Microscope.

خرد سال khurd sāl, adj. Young; of tender age.

خردہ khurdah (P) n.m. Any thing small; a fragment; pedlar's small wares; small coin; small change.

خردہ فروش khurdah farosh, n.m. A pedler; a retailer of small wares; a hawker.

خردہ گیری khurdah girī, n.f. Seizing on trifling faults; cavilling.

خرفہ khurfah (A) n.m. A kind of vegetable; a herb used in pickles or salads.

خرق عادت kharq-ĕ 'ādat (A) n.m. An event out of the usual course of nature; contrary to nature; a miracle.

خرقہ khirqah (A) n.m. A patched garment; dress of a religious mendicant.

خرقہ پوش khirqah posh, n.m. A mendicant; a devotee.

خرگوش khargosh (A) n.m. A hare; rabbit.

خرم khurram (P) adj. Delightful; cheerful; pleased; merry; glad; happy; fresh.

خرما khurmā (P) n.m. A date; fruit of the date tree; a sweetmeat.

خرمن khirman (P) n.m. Harvest; heap or stock of unthrashed corn; barn; produce.

خرموش kharmūsh (P) n.m. A species of large rat.

خرمہرہ kharmohrah (P) n.m. The small shell used as coin; cowries.

خرمی khurramī (P) n.f. Cheerfulness; pleasure; delight; gladness; mirth; joy.

خروج khuruj (A) n.m. Going out; going forth; attack; assault; rebellion; tumult; riot.

خروش kharosh (P) n.m. Loud noise; cry; tumult; clamour; a crash.

خرید kharīd (P) n.f. Purchase; price; buying. adj. Purchased.

خرید و فروخت kharīd-ŏ-farokht, n.f. Buying and selling; business; transactions; trading; commerce.

قیمت خرید qimat -ĕ kharid, n.f. Cost price.

خریدار kharīdār (P) n.m. Purchaser; buyer.

خریداری kharidāri (P) n.f. Purchasing; buying.

خریدنا kharidnā, v. To buy; to purchase.

خریطہ kharīṭah (A) n.m. A purse; a letter bag; a hold-all; a map; a chart.

خریف kharīf (A) n.m. Autumn; the autumnal crops.

خریفی kharīfi (A) adj. Autumnal.

خزاں khazān (P) n.f. Autumn; the fall of the leaf; decay; old age.

خزاں دیدہ، رسیدہ khazān dīdah, rasīdah, adj. Having seen or experienced autumn; old and experienced.

خزاں نا آشنا khazān nā āshnā, adj. One who has not seen autumn; yet in the prime of youth; inexperienced.

خزانچی khazānchi (P) n.m. A treasurer; a cashier.

خزانہ khizānah (A) n.m. A treasury; magazine; granary; treasure.

خزانہ عامرہ khizānah-ĕ-'āmirah, n.m. The royal treasury; the government treasury.

خزف khazaf (P) n.f. An earthen vessel; pottery; potsherbs; broken shells.

خزینہ khazinah (P) n.m. A treasury; a magazine; a godown.

خس khas (P) n.f. Hay; rubbish; the sweet-scented roots of a grass of which ṭaṭṭīs are made.

خس پوش khas posh, adj. Covered with thorns or dried grass.

خس و خاشاک khas-ŏ-khāshāk, n.m. Sweepings; rubbish; useless sticks and straws.

خسارہ khasārah (A) n.m. Loss; damage; plunder; devastation.

خست khissat (A) n.f. Stinginess; parsimony; averice; meanness; miserliness; niggardliness.

خستگی khastagī (P) n.f. A wound; a sore; sickness; fatigue; exhaustion; crispiness.

خستہ khastah (P) adj. Wounded; broken; sick; sorrowful; crisp.

خستہ حال khastah hāl, adj. Afflicted; distressed.

خسر khusar yā khusur (P) n.m. Father-in-law.

خسران khusrān (A) n.m. Damages; loss; injury.

خسرو khusrau (P) n.m. Great king; a royal surname; name of a celebrated king; name of a famous poet of Delhi.

خسروانہ khusrwānah (P) adj. & adv. Kingly; royal; princely; prince-like.

خسروی khusrawī (P) adj. Belonging to a king; royal; imperial, regal.

خسره khasrah n.m. A list of the fields in a village. n.m. Measles.

خسک khasak (P) n.m. Rubbish; thorn; barbed-wire; caltrop.

خسوف khusūf (A) n.m. An eclipse of the moon.

خسیس khasīs (A) adj. Stingy; parsimonious; miserly; penurious; sordid; avaricious; ignoble.

خشت khisht (P) n.f. A brick or tile.

خشتی khishtī (P) adj. Of bricks or tiles.

خشخاش khashkhāsh (P) n.m. Poppy seed; the unit of weight.

خشک khushk (P) adj. Dry; withered; cynic.

خشک سالی khushk sālī, n.f. Drought; dry season; dearth.

خشکہ khushkaḥ (P) n.m. Boiled rice.

خشکی khushkī (P) n.f. Land; dryness; cynicism. dry flour laid down under and over bread when it is rolled.

خشم khashm (P) n.m. Anger; passion; rage; fury.

خشم آلود khashm ālūd, adj. Tainted or disfigured with rage; burning with rage; extremely angry.

خشم گیں یا خشم ناک khashm giṅ yā khashm nāk, adj. Enraged; angry; passionate; wrathful.

خشوع khushū' (A) n.m. Humiliation.

خشونت khushūnat (A) n.f. Roughness; hardness; severity; rigidness; disdain; fierceness; indignation; austerity; animosity.

خشیت khashiyyat (A) n.f. Fear; terror; dread.

خصلت khaṣlat (A) n.f. Habit; custom; quality; property; mode; talent; virtue; disposition; nature. (plu. of خصال khiṣāl).

خصم khaṣm (A) n.m. An enemy; antagonist; a master; proprietor; husband.

خصوص khuṣūṣ (A) n.m. Doing anything particular; affair; business. adv. Particularly.

خصوصاً khuṣūṣan (A) adv. Especially; particularly.

خصوصیات khuṣūṣiyāt (A) n.f. (plu. of خصوصیت khuṣūṣiyyat). Special features; particular points; peculiarities.

خصوصیت khuṣūṣiyyat (A) n.f. Peculiarity; singularity; attachment; friendship; intimacy.

خصوصی khuṣūṣi (A) adj. Private; personal; special; secret.

خصومت khuṣūmat (A) n.f. Enmity; strife; contention; quarrelling; wrangling.

خصّی khaṣṣī (A) n.m. Castrated; an eunuch.

خصیہ khuṣyah (A) n.m. Testicle.

خضاب khiẓāb (A) n.m. A hair dye; a hair tincture.

خضاب کرنا khiẓāb karnā, v. To dye the hair; to apply hair-dye.

خضر khiẓr yā khiẓar (A) n.m. Name of a prophet, who is said to have discovered the fountain of life and drunk of it; a leader; a guide.

خضوع khuẓū' (A) n.m. Humility; humbling oneself; lowliness.

خط khatt (A) n.m. A letter; epistle; a note; script; a line; a streak; mark; writing; hand-writing; moustaches; beard.

خط استوا khatt-ĕ istiwā, n.m. The equator.

خط بنانا khatt banānā, v. To shave the chin; to dress or trim the beard.

خط جدی khatt-ĕ jaddī, n.m. The Tropic of Capricorn.

خط جلی khatt-ĕ jalī, n.m. Large or bold hand-writing.

خط سرطان khatt-ĕ sartān, n.m. The Tropic of Cancer.

خط شکستہ khatt-ĕ shikastah, n.m. A running hand.

خط عمود khatt-ĕ 'umūd, n.m. A perpendicular line.

خط کھینچنا khatt khĕnchnā, v. To draw a line.

خط متوازی khatt-ĕ mutawāzi, n.m. A parallel line.

خط مستدیر khatt-ĕ mustadir, n.m. A circular line.

خط مستقیم khatt-ĕ mustaqim, n.m. A straight line.

خط منحنی khatt-ĕ munhani, n.m. A curved line.

خط نستعلیق khatt-ĕ nasta'liq, n.m. Plain round Persian writing.

خط نسخ khatt-ĕ naskh, n.m. A kind of Arabic hand-writing.

خط و کتابت khatt-ŏ-kitābat, n.f. Correspondence.

خطا khatā (A) n.f. A mistake; a slip; an oversight; fault; failure; a miss.

خطا کار - وار khatā kār, wār, adj. Guilty; at fault.

خطا کرنا khatā karnā, v. To err; to commit error; to miss.

خطا ہونا khatā honā, v. To fail; to err; to make a mistake.

خطاب khitāb (A) n.m. Title; address; conversation; speech.

خطاب کرنا khitāb karnā, v. To deliver a lecture; to address; to accost.

خطابت khattābat (A) n.f. Preaching; eloquence; rhetoric.

خطاط khattāt (A) n.m. A good writer; a penman.

خطائی khatā'i (P) adj. Of or belonging to خطا khatā northern China.

نان خطائی nān-ĕ khatā'i, n.f. A cake made of flour, sugar and butter according to the one made in خطا khatā (northern China).

خطبہ khutbah (A) n.m. Sermon; oration; introduction; prologue.

خطر khatar (A) n.m. Coming into the mind; thought; remembrance; danger; peril; risk; fortune; hazard; jeopardy.

خطر ناک khatar nāk, adj. Dangerous; hazardous; frightful.

خطرہ khatrah (A) n.m. Danger; fear; risk; venture.

خطرہ مول لینا khatrah mol lenā, v. To run the risk.

خطرے میں ڈالنا khatre meṅ ḍālnā, v. To endanger; to risk; to venture; to hazard.

خطرے میں نہ لانا khatre meṅ nah lānā, v. Not to care a fig for; to attach no value (to).

خطوط khutūt (A) (plu. of خط khatt); Lines; stripes; letters; epistles.

خطمی khatmi (A) n.f. Marsh mallow; medicinal seeds.

خطہ khittah (A) n.m. A region; country; territory; district; a plot of land.

خطی khatti (A) adj. Linear; literal; in writing.

خطیب khatib (A) n.m. A preacher; a public speaker or orator.

خطیر khatir (A) adj. Great; important; honourable; dignified.

خفا khafā yā khifā (A) n.f. Concealment; secrecy.

خفا khafā yā khifā (P) adj. Angry; displeased; enraged.

خفت khiffat (A) *n.f.* Lightness of weight; levity of conduct; want of dignity; affront; indignity; slight; disgrace; humiliation; abasement.

خفت آمیز khiffat āmez, *adj.* Disgraceful.

خفت آٹھانا khiffat uṭhānā, *v.* To suffer disgrace or indignity or slight; to be disgraced.

خفقان khafaqān (A) *n.m.* Palpitation of heart; hysteria.

خفگی khafgi yā khafagi (P) *n.f.* Displeasure; anger; indignation.

خفی khafī (A) *adj.* Fine or small (writing; type); imperceptible; not apparent; hidden; concealed.

خفیف khafīf (A) *adj.* Light; of no weight or consequence; of light character; immoral; undignified; insignificant; small; slight; trivial; petty; frivolous; unimportant.

خفیف ہونا khafīf honā, *v.* To be put to shame; to be regarded lightly; to become ashamed; to be slighted; to be vilified.

ضرر خفیف zarar-ĕ khafīf, *n.m.* A minor hurt.

خفیفہ khafīfah (A) *adj.* Small; minor. *n.f.* A small cause court.

خفیہ khufyah (A) *adj.* Concealed; disguised; hidden.

خفیہ پولیس khufyah polis, *n.f.* Criminal Investigation Department.

خفیہ نویس khufyah nawis, *n.m.* Writer of secret intelligence; a secret informer.

خفیہ نویسی khufyah nawīsi, *n.m.* Secret intelligence writing.

خفیہ کارروائی khufyah kārrwā'i, *n.f.* Secret execution of business or work; investigating secretly; private enquiry.

خلا khalā (A) *n.m.* Space; vacancy; hallowness; vaccum; a vacant place.

خلا ملا khalā malā, *adj.* Empty and full. *n.m.* Sincere friendship; close intimacy; warm attachment; unfringed friendship.

خلاص khalāṣ (A) *n.m.* Deliverance; emancipation; liberation; redemption. *adj.* Free; liberated; redeemed.

خلاصہ khulāṣah (A) *n.m.* Essence; extract; the best part of anything; substance; abstract; abridgement inference; moral; conclusion; epitom; summary; precis. *adj.* Spacious; roomy; open; plain; evident.

خلاصہ کرنا khulāsah karnā, *v.* To abridge; to curtail; to explain; to summarise; to shorter; to condense; to epitomise; to make an abstract.

خلاصی khalāṣi, *n.f.* Deliverance; libration; redemption; discharge; exemption; release; freedom. *n.m.* A sailor; an artillery-man; a worker on a railway-line; a trolly-driver; a tent pitcher.

خلاصی پانا khalāṣi pānā, *v.* To be released; to be set free; to be liberated.

خلاف khilāf (A) *n.m.* Opposition; contrariety; hostility; falsehood. *prep. & adj.* Against; in opposition (to); contrary (to); versus; opposite.

خلاف بیانی khilāf bayāni, *n.f.* Contradiction; misrepresentation.

خلاف حکم khilāf-ĕ hukm, *adj.* Contrary to orders.

خلاف دستور ' ضابطہ ' قاعدہ khilāf-ĕ dastūr, zābiṭah, qā'idah, *adj.* Contrary to custom or rule; irregular.

خلاف سمجھنا khilāf samajhnā, *v.* To think otherwise; to regard one as an opponent.

خلاف شرع khilāf-ĕ shara', *adj.* Against religion; unlawful; illegal.

خلاف طبع khilāf-ĕ taba', adj. Against the will or disposition of.

خلاف عقل khilāf-ĕ 'aql, adj. Contrary to reason.

خلاف قیاس khilāf-ĕ qiyās, adj. Inconceivable; absurd; improbable; anomalous.

خلاف مرضی khilāf-ĕ marzi, adj. Contrary to the will.

خلاف ورزی کرنا khilāf warzi karnā, v. To oppose; to disobey; to misbehave.

خلاف وضع فطری khilāf-ĕ waza'-ĕ fitri, n.m. Against the law of nature; sodomy; sexual connection between two males.

خلاف ہونا khilāf hona, v. To be opposed to; to oppose.

خلافت khilāfat (A) n.f. The office or dignity of a Caliph.

خلاق khallāq (A) n.m. The Creator.

خلال khilāl (A) n.m. Tooth-pick; a prickle; a straw used as picker; defeat (at cards).

خلائق khalā'iq (A) n.f. (plu of خلق khalq); Created things; people; the creation.

خلجان khaljān (A) n.m. Beating; agitation; distraction; anxiety.

خلخال khalkhāl (A) n.m. A ring of gold or silver with bells attached to it, worn round the ankle.

خلد khuld (A) n.m. & f. Eternity; paradise.

خلش khalish (P) n.f. Prick; pain; anxiety; solicitude; suspicion; apprehension.

خلط khilt (A) n.m. One of the four humours of the human body.

خلط khalt (A) n.m. Confusion; mixture; medley; entanglement.

خلط ملط khalt malt, adj. Intermixed; jumbled.

خلع khula' (A) n.m. Pulling off; throwing off; deposing; removing from office; divorce obtained by a wife for a ransom by her or some other person on her behalf.

خلعت khila't yā khala't (A) n.m. & f. A dress; a robe of honour confered by princes as a mark of distinction.

خلعت پہنانا' دینا khila't pahnānā dena, v. To invest one with a robe of honour.

خلف khalaf (A) n.m. A successor; an heir; a favourite son; posterity; descendants. adj. Dutiful.

خلفاء khulafa' (A) n.m. (plu. of خلیفہ khalifah) Caliphs.

خلق khulq (A) n.m. Nature; habit; politeness; civility; quality; good disposition; amiability; good manners.

خلق khalq (A) n.f. The people; mankind; creation.

خلقت khilqat (A) n.f. Creation; nature; people; populace; the world.

عجیب الخلقت 'ajib-ul-khilqat, adj. A strange creature; a monster; a prodigy.

خلقی khilqi (A) adj. Natural; inherent.

خلل khalal (A) n.m. Interruption; breach; confusion; damage; derangement; ruin; break; disturbance; disorder; injury; rupture; hindrance; unsoundness; flaw; defect.

خلل آنا khalal anā, v. Occurence of disorder or disturbance.

خلل انداز ہونا khalal andāz hona, v. To interfere; to disturb; to interrupt.

خلل پذیر khalal pazir, adj. Disordered; troubled.

خلل دماغ khalal-ĕ dimagh, n.m Madness; melancholia; craze.

خلل ڈالنا *khalal ḍālnā, v.* To interrupt; to disturb.

خلو *khilw* (A) *n.m.* Vacuity; emptiness.

خلوت *khalwat* (A) *n.f.* Retirement; solitude; privacy; a closet; private apartment; private conference.

خلوت خانه، گاه *khalwat khānah, gāh, n.m.* A place of retirement; private apartment; closet; cabinet.

خلوت گزین، نشین *khalwat guzīn, nashīn, adj.* Sitting in solitude; a hermit; recluse; retired; sitting in solitude.

خلوص *khulūṣ* (A) *n.m.* Purity; sincerity; friendship; affection; candor.

خلیج *khalīj* (A) *n.f.* A bay; a gulf.

خلیرا *khalerā, adj.* Descended from or related to a maternal aunt.

خلیرا بھائی *khalerā bhā'i, n.m.* The son of a maternal aunt; a cousin.

خلیفه *khalīfah* (A) *n.m.* A Caliph; the successor of the Holy Prophet; a barber; a cook &c.

خلیق *khalīq* (A) *adj.* Of good disposition; kind; affable; benign; civil; polite; obliging; courteous; well-disposed.

خلیل *khalīl* (A) *n.m.* A true and sincere friend.

خلیل الله *khalīl ullah* (A) *n.m.* The friend of God; Abraham.

خلیه *khaliyah* (A) *n.m.* Cell (*Biology*).

خم *kham* (P) *n.m.* A coil; fold; curl; ringlet; bend; curve; bending; crookedness; the part of a noose which encircles the neck.

خم ٹھوکنا *kham thoknā, n.m.* To strike the hands against the arms before wrestling; to challenge.

خم چوگاں *kham-ĕ chaugān, n.m.* The curved stick with which polo is played.

خمدار *khamdār, adj.* Bent; curved; twisted; crooked; curled.

خم دینا *kham denā, v.* To bend; to twist.

خم‌وچم *kham-ŏ cham, n.m.* Graceful motion; coquetry; blandishment of a mistress.

خم *khum* (P) *n.m.* A large jar; a still; an alembic.

خم خانه، کده *khum khānah, kadah, n.m.* A liquor-house; a tavern; an inn.

خم کے خم چڑھانا *khum ke khum charhānā, v.* To drink to excess; to be dead drunk; to be a habitual drinker.

خمار *khumār* (A) *n.m.* Intoxication; the effect of intoxication (pain and headache); sickness caused by an over-dose of drink.

خمار آلوده *khumār ālūdah, adj.* Intoxicated.

خمر *khamr* (A) *n.m.* Wine.

خمرا *khumrā, n.m.* A sect of Muslim *faqīrs*.

خمس *khums* (A) *adj.* Fifth.

خمسه *khamsah* (A) *n.m.* A stanza of five line.

خمیازه *khamyāzah* (P) *n.m.* Stretching; gaping; retribution; pandiculation; return; punishment.

خمیازه کھینچنا *khamyāzah khenchnā, v.* To receive the punishment of one's crimes or faults; to gape or yawn.

خمیدگی *khamīdagī* (P) *n.f.* Crookedness.

خمیده *khamīdah* (P) *adj.* Bent; crooked.

خمیر *khamīr* (A) *n.m.* Leaven; yeast.

خمیر اٹھانا *khamīr uṭhānā, v.* To ferment.

خمیره *khamīrah* (A) *n.m.* A thick syrup; a kind of tobacco.

خمیری *khamīrī* (A) *adj.* Leavened.

خنازیر *khanāzīr* (A) *n.m.* (*plu.* of خنزیر *khinzīr*); Hogs; glandular swellings in the neck; scrofula.

خناس khannās (A) n.m. The devil; a wicked person; calumniator.

خناق khunāq (A) n.m. The quinsy; suffocation; strangulation.

خنثیٰ khunṣā (A) n.m. A hermaphrodite; a eunuch.

خنجر khanjar (A) n.m. A dagger; a double edged large knife.

خنجری khanjari, n.f. A mode of printing or staining-silk; a small tambourine.

خنخنانا khunkhunānā, v. To snuffle; to speak through the nose.

خنداں khandāṅ (P) adj. Laughing; merry; joyous.

خندق khandaq (A) n.m. A ditch; a moat.

خنده khandah (P) adj. Laughing. n.m. laughter; a laugh; a laughing-stock.

خنده آور khandah āwar, adj. Laughable; that which produces laughter.

خنده رو ، خنده پیشانی khandah rū, khandah peshānī, adj. Cheerful; of smiling countenance; having a cheerful appearance.

خنده روئی khandah rū'ī, n.f. Cheerfulness.

خنزیر khinzīr (A) n.m. A hog.

خنک khunuk (P) adj. Cold; cool; temperate; fortunate.

خنکی khunkī (P) n.f. Coldness; chill; coolness; temperateness.

خو khū (P) n.f. Habit; custom; disposition; nature.

خوبو khūbū, n.f. Character; behaviour.

خو پڑنا khū paṛnā, v. To develop a habit.

خو چھوڑنا khū chhoṛnā, v. To give up a habit.

خو ڈالنا khū ḍālnā, v. To habituate; to accustom; to get into a habit; to introduce a custom.

خوگر، پذیر، گرفته khū gar, pazīr, giriftah, adj. habituated; accustomed; addicted.

خواب khwāb (P) n.m. Sleep; dream; vision; nap.

خواب آلوده khwāb ālūdah, adj. Sleepy; drowsy.

خواب آور khwāb āwar, adj. producing sleep; anodyne; soporific; hypnotic.

خواب پریشاں khwāb-ĕ parīshāṅ, n.f. A dreadful dream.

خواب خرگوش khwāb-ĕ khargosh, n.f. Deep sleep.

خواب دیکھنا khwāb dekhnā, v. To dream.

خواب کی باتیں khwāb kī bāteṅ, n.f. Baseless things; useless talk.

خواب گاه khwāb gāh, n.f. Sleeping apartment; bed-room; darmitory.

خواب و خیال khwāb-ŏ khayāl, n.m. A vision; a phantom; delusion.

خوابیده khwābidah (P) adj. Sleepy; drowsy; sleeping; asleep.

خواتین khwātīn (plu. of خاتون khātūn); Women; ladies.

خواجه khwājah (P) n.m. A man of distinction; a rich merchant; a governor; a gentleman; lord; master. (plu. خواجگان khwājgān).

خواجه خضر khwājah khiẓr yā khiẓar. (See خضر khiẓar).

خواجه سرا khwājah serā, n.m. A eunuch; chief of a household; one who has charge of a seraglio.

خوار khwār (P) adj. Wretched; distressed; deserted; friendless; poor; abject.

خوارج khawārij (A) (plu. of خارجی khārji) n.m. Schismatics. (plu. of خارجه khārījah) Externals; the exterior.

خوارق khwāriq (A) n.m. Miracles. (plu. of خارق khāriq).

خواری khwārī (P) n.f. Distress; friendlessness; abjectness; wretchedness.

خواستگار khwāstgār (A) n.m. A petitioner; applicant; a suitor; a candidate; a bidder.

خواستگاری khwāstgārī (P) n.f. Candidateship; desire; solicitation; application.

خواسته khwāstah (P) adj. Desired; wished for; having willed or wished.

خواص khawāṣ (A) n.m. (plu. of خاص khāṣ); Top-ranking persons; gentry; special or favourite attendants. (plu. of خاصیت khāṣṣiyyat). Qualities; peculiarities.

خوان khwan (P) n.m. A tray.

خوان پوش khwān posh, n.m. A tray cover.

خوانچه khwānchah (P) n.m. A small tray.

خواندگی khwāndagi (P) n.f. Reading; reciting; recital.

خوانده khwāndah (P) adj. Able to read and write; educated.

نا خوانده nā khwāndah, adj. Illiterate; ignorant; uneducated.

خوانین khwānin (P) n.m. (plu. of خان khān); Lords; nobles; grandees; big people.

خواه khwāh (P) adj. (used in con.p.); Wishing; desiring; requiring; soliciting. conj. Either or whether.

ترق خواه taraqqi khwāh, adj. Wishing for advancement.

خاطر خواه khātir khwāh, adv. Satisfactorily; to heart's content.

خواه مخواه khwāh makhwāh, adv. Willing or not willing; positively; at all events.

خواهان khwāhān (P) adj. Wishing; desirous; seeker.

خواهر khwāhar (P) n.f. A sister.

خواهش khwāhish (P) n.f. Wish; desire; inclination; will; request; demand.

خواهش مند khwāhish mand, adj. Desirous; suoticilos.

خواهی نخواهی khwāhī nakhwāhī. See خواه نخواه khwāh makhwāh.

خوب khūb (P) adj. Good; excellent; well; beautiful; pleasant; amiable.

خوب رو، صورت khūb rū, ṣūrat, adj. Beautiful; handsome; pretty.

خوب روئی،صورتی khūb rū'i, ṣūrati, n.f. Beauty; handsomeness; comeliness.

خوباں khūbān (P) n.m. Beautiful persons; fair ones; sweethearts.

خوبانی khūbānī (P) n.f. An apricot; a dried apricot.

خوب کلاں khub kalan (P) n.m. A seed of a cooling quality.

خوبی khūbi (P) n.f. Goodness; excellence; virtue; pleasantness; well-being; elegance.

بخوبی bakhūbi, adv. With ease; well.

خوجه khojah, n.m. A eunuch.

خود khod (P) n.m. A helmet.

خود khūd (P) n. & adj. Self; private; personal; own.

خود آرائی khūd ārā'ī, n.f. Self-decoration.

خود بخود khūd bakhūd, adv. Automatically; voluntarily; of one's own accord.

خود بدولت khūd badaulat, intj. Yourself! your worship! your honour! your majesty!

خود بیں khūd bin, adj. Self conceited; proud; arrogant; presumptuous; vain.

خود بینی khūd bīnī, n.f. Pride; self-conceit; vanity.

خود پرست khūd parast, adj. Self-conceited; selfish.

خود پرستی khūd parastī, n.f. Self-conceit; selfishness.

خود پسند khūd pasand, adj. Self-complacent; self-conceited; having superiority complex.

خود دار khūd dār, adj. Self-possessing; self respecting.

خود رائے khūd rā'e, adj. Self-conceited; self-willed; wilful; headstrong; wayward; opinionated.

خود رفتگی khūd raftagi, n.f. Intoxication; senslessness; drunkenness.

خود رفته khūd raftah, adj. Senseless; intoxicated; drunk.

خود ستائی khūd satā'i, n.f. Self-praise.

خود سر khūd sar, adj. Obstinate; stubborn; wilful; arrogant; independent.

خود سری khūd sari, n.f. Obstinacy; arrogance; wilfulness.

خود غرض khūd gharaẓ, adj. Selfish; self-interested; designing.

خود غرضی khūd gharẓi, adj. Self-seeking; selfishness.

خود کار khūd kār, adj. Autamotic; self-propelled; self-working.

خود کاشت khūd kāsht, n.f. Cultivation by the owner; cultivation of one's own field.

خود کرده khūd kardah, adj. One's own doing; made by oneself.

خود کشی khūd kushi, n.f. Suicide.

خودکشی کرنا khūd kushi karnā, v. To commit suicide.

خود مختار khūd mūkhtār, adj. Independent; free.

خود نما khūd numa, adj. Proud; ostentatious; vain; self-conceited.

خود نمائی khūd numā'i, n.f. Self-conceit; vanity; pride; ostentation.

خودی khūdi (P) n.f. Egotism; self; selfishness; vanity; pride; conceit; presence of mind.

بے خودی be khūdi, n.f. Being beside oneself; ecstasy; transport; madness.

خور khor (P) adj. Eating; drinking; devouring (used in comp.) n.m. Little food.

خور و نوش khor-ŏ nosh, n.f. Food and drink.

خوراک khorāk (P) n.f. Food; victuals; diet; daily allowance; a dose of medicine.

خورد برد khūrd burd (P) n.f. Peculation; embezzlement; fraud.

خورد برد کرنا khūrd burd karna, v. To make away with; to misappropriate; to embezzle.

خوردنی khūrdani (P) n.f. Things eatable; provisions.

خورسند khūrsand (P) adj. Contented; pleased; happy.

خورسندی khūrsandi (P) n.f. Happiness; pleasure; contentment; satisfaction.

خورش khūrish. See خوراک khūrāk.

حورشید khūrshid (P) n.m. The sun.

خوش khūsh (P) adj. Pleasing; glad; happy; pleased; gay; merry; well off; willing; sweet; delicious; elegant; acceptable; amiable; cheerful; content; delighted; pleasant; good; healthy; wholesome; beautiful; fair.

خوش آمدید khush āmded, interj. Well come !

خوش آمدید کہنا khūsh āmded kahnā, v. To welcome.

خوش آواز khūsh āwāz, adj. Sweet-voiced; melodious.

خوش آئند khūsh āyand, adj. Pleasing; agreeable; amiable; charming.

خوش اسلوب khūsh aslūb, adj. Well-formed; elegant; pleasing.

خوش اطوار khūsh aṭwār, adj. Well-conducted; well-bred; mannerly.

خوش الحان khūsh ilḥān, adj. Melodious; sweet-voiced.

خوش الحانی khūsh ilḥānī, n.f. Melodiousness.

خوش اندام khūsh andām, adj. Well-built; attractive appearance.

خوش باش khūsh bāsh, adj. One living comfortably or at ease; unrestrained; free to stay or depart; merry; cheerful.

خوش بو khūsh bū, n.f. Perfume; odour; fragrance.

خوش بو دار khūsh bū dār, adj. Aromatic; fragrant; sweet-smelling; odoriferous.

خوش بیان khūsh bayān, adj. Eloquent; perspicuous. n.m. An eloquent speaker; an orator.

خوش پوشاک khūsh poshāk, adj. Well-dressed; well turned out.

خوش حال khūsh ḥāl, adj. In pleasant or easy circumstances; prosperous; happy; fortunate.

خوش خبری khūsh khabarī, n.f. Good or happy news; glad tidings.

خوش خرام khush kharām, adj. Walking elegantly, or with a stately gait; graceful in walking.

خوش خصال khūsh khiṣāl, adj. Well-bred; of good disposition.

خوش خط khūsh khaṭṭ, adj. Having good hand; a good penman.

خوش خطی khūsh khaṭī, adj. Fine hand writing.

خوش خلق khūsh khulq, adj. Of pleasant manners; civil; of good disposition; polite; affable; well-bred.

خوش خوراک khūsh khorāk, adj. Enjoining a good diet.

خوش خیال khūsh khayāl, adj. A good writer or poet; having good ideas.

خوش دامن khūsh dāman, n.f. Mother-in-law.

خوش ذائقه khūsh zā'iqah, adj. Pleasing to the taste; tasteful; high-flavoured; palatable; dainty.

خوش رفتار khūsh raftār, adj. Graceful in walking or in motion.

خوش رنگ khūsh rang, adj. Of bright or pleasant or good colour.

خوش رو khūsh rū, adj. Having a beautiful or charming face.

خوش رهنا khūsh rahnā, v. To be happy.

خوش زبان khūsh zabān, adj. Eloquent; plausible.

خوش سلیقه khūsh salīqah, adj. Of pleasant manners or method; well-bred; polite.

خوش طالع khūsh ṭāli', adj. Fortunate; lucky.

خوش طبع khūsh ṭaba', adj. Of cheerful disposition; joculor.

خوش طینت khūsh ṭīnat, adj. Good-natured.

خوش فعلی khūsh fi'lī, n.f. Pleasantness of action.

خوش فکر khūsh fikr, adj. Of good thoughts or ideas.

خوش فهم khūsh fahm, adj. One who takes the bright side of a thing; sensible; intelligent.

خوش فهمی khūsh fahmī, n.f. Vain imagination.

خوش قسمت khūsh qismat, adj. Of good fortune.

خوش قسمتی khūsh qismatī, n.f. Good fortune.

خوش کرنا khūsh karnā, v. To gratify; to please; to delight; to amuse; to gladden; to rejoice; to satisfy.

خوش گپیاں khūsh gappiyāṅ, n.f. Idle gossip; merry talk; pleasant conversation.

خوش گزران khush guzrān, adj. Living in ease and comfort.

خوش گلو khūsh glū. See خوش الحان khūsh ilḥān.

خوش گو khūsh go. See خوش بیان khūsh bayān.

خوش گوار khūsh gawār, adj. Pleasant; agreeable; wholesome; sweet; easy; delicious.

خوش لباس khūsh libās, adj. Well-dressed.

خوش نصیب khūsh naṣīb. See خوش قسمت khūsh qismat.

خوش نصیبی khūsh naṣībi. See خوش قسمتی khūsh qismati.

خوش نما khūsh numā, adj. Pleasant to the sight; good-looking; beautiful.

خوش نمائی khūsh numā'i, n.f. Beauty; splendour.

خوش نوا khūsh nawā. See خوش الحان khūsh ilhān.

خوش نوائی khush nawā'i. See خوش الحانی khūsh ilhāni.

خوش نویس khūsh nawis, n.m. A fine penman; a calligraphist.

خوش نویسی khūsh nawīsi, n.f. Fine writing; calligraphy.

خوش وقتی khūsh waqtī, n.f. Happiness.

خوش و خرم khush-ŏ khurram, adj. Cheerful; happy; well-to-do: gay.

خوش ہونا khush honā, v. To be glad; to rejoice; to be pleased.

خوشا khūshā (P) intj. Happy ! how fortunate! blessed !

خوشامد khūshāmaa (P) n.ſ. Flattery.

خوشامد کرنا khūshāmad karnā, v. To flatter.

خوشامدی khūshamadī (P) n. & adj. A flatterer.

خوشنود khūshnūd (P) adj. Pleased; delighted; happy.

خوشنودی khūshnūdi, (P) n.f. Pleasure; delight; happiness; joy.

خوشه khoshah (P) n.m. An ear of corn; a spike; a bunch (of grapes &c.).

خوشه چین khoshah chin, n.m. A gleaner; one who picks up droppings.

خوشی khūshī (P) n.f. Delight; pleasure; cheerfulness; gaiety; happiness; gladness; mirth; joy; consent.

خوشی خوشی، خوشی سے khūshī khūshī, khūshī se, adv. Happily; gladly; cheerfully; joyfully; with pleasure; willingly.

خوشی کرنا، منانا khūshi karnā, manānā, v. To rejoice; to enjoy; to please oneself; to be delighted; to make a feast.

خوشی میں آنا khūshī men ānā, v. To be pleased; to get into a state of delight.

خوض khauẓ (A) n.m. Deep thought or meditation; search; attention; consideration.

خوف khauf (A) n.m. Fear; dread; terror.

خوف دلانا khauf dilānā, v. To frighten; to terrify; to threaten.

خوف زده khauf zadah, adj. Frightened; terrified; afraid.

خوف زده ہونا، خوف کرنا، خوف کھانا khauf zadah honā, khauf karnā, khauf khānā, v. To fear; to be afraid.

خوف ناک khauf nāk, adj. Terrifying; frightful, dreadful.

خوک khūk (P) n.m. A hog; a swine; a pig.

خوگر khūgar (P) adj. Accustomed; habituated; inured.

خوگیر khūgir (P) n.m. Stuffing of saddles; a pack-daddle.

خوگیر کی بھرتی khūgir ki bhartī, n.f. Rags; rubbish; stuffing; odds and ends; the stuffing of a saddle.

خول khol, n.m. A case; a sheath; a cover.

خول چڑھانا khol charhānā, v. To sheathe; to cover.

خولنجان kholanjān (P) n.m. Galingale (a kind of medicine)

خون khūn (P) n.m. Blood; murder; killing; slaughter; homicide.

خون آب ـ خوناب ـ خونابه *khūn āb, khūnāb, khūnābah, n.m.* Bloody water; tears of blood.

خون آشام *khūn āshām, adj.* Drinking blood; cruel, ferocious.

خون آلوده *khūn ālūdah, adj.* Stained with blood; bloody; blood-stained.

خون بار *khūn bār, adj.* Raining or shedding blood.

خون بہا *khūn bahā, n.m.* Ransom; a penalty for murder.

خون بہانا *khūn bahānā, v.* To shed blood.

خون پانی ایک کرنا *khūn pānī ek karnā, v.* To work very hard; to leave no stone unturned.

خون پینا *khūn pīnā, v.* To suck blood; to vex.

خون تھوکنا *khūn thūknā, v.* To spit blood; to suffer a shock; to work oneself to death.

خون چکاں *khūn chakāṅ, adj.* Blood dropping; blood oozing out; bleeding.

خون خرابا *khūn kharābā, n.m.* Killing; murdering; murder; bloody fight.

خون خوار *khūn khwār, adj.* Blood-thirsty; murderous; cruel. *n.m.* An animal that preys on others; a murderer.

خون خواری *khūn khwārī, n.f.* Blood-thirstiness; blood-shedding.

خون ریز *khūn rez, adj.* Assassin; murderer; cut-throat; blood-shedder.

خون ریزی *khūn rezī, n.f.* Blood-shed; slaughter; carnage; massacre.

خون سفید ہونا *khūn sufed honā, v.* To be unkind; to be callous.

خون کا پیاسا *khūn kā piyāsā, adj.* Blood-thirsty; bitter enemy.

خون کا دباؤ *khūn kā dabā'o, n.m.* Blood pressure.

خون کا دورہ *khūn kā daurah, n.m.* Circulation of blood.

خون کرنا *khūn karnā, v.* To assassinate; to kill; to murder.

خون ہونا *khūn honā, v.* To be murdered; to be killed.

خونی *khūnī (P) n.m.* Murderer; assassin. *adj.* Sanguinary; bloody; relating to blood.

خونیں *khūnīn (P) adj.* Bloody; of the colour of blood; blood stained.

خویش *khwesh (P) pro.* Self; own. *n.m./f.* A kinsman; a close relative; a family.

خویش و اقربا *khwesh-ŏ aqrabā, n.m.* Kith and kin; kinsmen; relations.

خیابان *khiyābān (P) n.m.* A flower-bed; a flower garden.

خیار *khiyār (A) n.m.* Cucumber.

خیارین *khiyārain (A) n.m.* Cucumber and musk-melon seeds, used in medicine.

خیاط *khayyāṭ (A) n.m.* A tailor; a seamster.

خیال *khayāl (A) n.m.* Thought; idea; imagination; conception; notion; fancy; whim; care; concern; opinion; regard; respect; consideration; vision; a kind of song.

خیال باطل یا فاسد *khayāl-ĕ bāṭil yā fāsid, n.m.* Misconception; false notion; a wrong idea.

خیال باندھنا *khayāl bāndhnā, v.* To form an idea; to imagine; to frame an image in the mind.

خیال بندی *khayāl bandī, n.f.* Train of thoughts; forming an idea.

خیال پڑنا *khayāl parṇā, v.* To occur; to come to mind; to think; to pursue a thing.

خیال چھوڑنا *khayāl chhoṛnā, v.* To give up the idea of; to relinquish all thought of; to be out of conceit with.

خیال رکھنا *khayāl rakhnā, v.* To bear in mind; to remember.

خیال کرنا *khayāl karnā, v.* To imagine; to fancy; to think; to consider; to conceive; to care; to regard.

خیال میں نہ لانا ***kh**ayāl meṅ nah lānā, v.* To pay no attention (to); to show no respect for.

خیال نہ رہنا ***kh**ayāl nah rahnā, v* To forget (about); to loose all recollection of.

خیال نہ کرنا ***kh**ayāl nah karnā, v.* Not to think (of); not to pay any attention (to); to take no notice of.

خیالات ***kh**ayālāt* (P) (*plu.* of خیال ***kh**ayāl*) *n.m.* Imaginations; ideas; thoughts; fancies.

خیالی ***kh**ayālī* (A) *adj.* Ideal; fanciful; imaginary; fantastical; visionary.

خیالی پلاؤ ***kh**ayālī pulā'o, n.m.* Imaginary banquet; vain speculation; castles in the air.

خیالی پلاؤ پکانا ***kh**ayālī pulā'o pakānā, v.* To build castles in the air; to indulge in vain fancies.

خیانت ***kh**iyānat* (A) *n.f.* Unfaithfulness to a trust; breach of trust; perfidy; treachery; treason; embezzlement; defalcation.

خیر ***kh**air* (A) *adj.* Good; best; well; safe. *adv.* Very well. *n.f.* Goodness; welfare; happiness; health.

خیر اندیش، خیر خواہ ***kh**air andesh, **kh**air **kh**wāh, adj.* Well-wisher.

خیر اندیشی ***kh**air andeshi, n.f.* Well-wishing,

خیر باد ***kh**air bād, intj.* May he prosper! farewell ! *n.f.* Well-wishing at parting.

خیر باد کہنا ***kh**air bād kehnā, v.* To bid farewell; to say good bye.

خیر خبر ***kh**air **kh**abar, n.f.* News; good news.

خیر گزرنا ***kh**air guzarnā, v.* To escape an accident.

خیر مانگنا ، خیر منانا ***kh**air mangnā, **kh**air manānā, v.* To pray for safety; to pray for one's welfare.

خیر محض ***kh**air-ĕ maḥaẓ, adj.* Embodiment of virtue; very pious.

خیر مقدم کرنا ***kh**air maqdam karnā, v.* To welcome; to receive cordially; to give a warm reception (to).

خیر و عافیت ***kh**air-ŏ 'āfiyat, n.f.* Well-being; health and prosperity.

خیرات ***kh**airāt* (A) *n.f.* Alms; charity.

خیرات خانہ ***kh**airāt **kh**ānah, n.m.* Alms-house; poor-house.

خیراتی ***kh**airāti* (P) *adj.* Charitable.

خیراتی شفا خانہ ***kh**airāti shafā **kh**ānah, n.m.* A charitable dispensary.

خیرگی ***kh**īrgi* (P) *n.f.* Darkness; dazzle; shamelessness.

خیرہ ***kh**īrah* (P) *adj.* Dark; dazzled; wicked; vain; immodest.

خیریت ***kh**airiyyat* (A) *n.f.* Welfare; safety; happiness.

خیز ***kh**ez* (P) *adj.* (in *comp.*) Rising; leaping; bounding; galloping. *n.m.* Leap; bound; rising.

خیزاں ***kh**ezāṅ* (P) *adj.* Rising; bounding; springing up.

افتاں و خیزاں *uftān-ŏ **kh**ezān, adv.* Now rising now falling, with great difficulty.

خیزش - خیزی ***kh**ezish, **kh**ezi* (P) *n.f.* Rising; erection (of sexual organ); lust; concupiscence.

خیل ***kh**ail* (P) *n.m.* A body of men; a host; a multitude; a tribe.

خیمہ ***kh**aimah* or ***kh**emah* (A) *n.m.* A tent; a pavilion.

خیمہ دوز ***kh**aimah doz, n.m.* A tent-maker

خیمہ زن ***kh**aimah zan, adj.* Pitcher of tent.

خیمہ زن ہونا ***kh**aimah zan honā, v.* To have a tent pitched; to stay in a tent: to camp.

خیمہ گاہ ***kh**aimah gāh, n.m./f.* Encamping ground; a camp.

د

د dāl, is the eighth letter of the Arabic, the tenth of the Persian and the eleventh of the Urdu alphabet. In reckoning by *'abjad'* it stands for four. Its sound is much softer and more dental than that of the English *d*.

داب *dāb* (A) *n.m.* Custom; manner; institution; state; condition.

داب *dāb* (P) *n.m.* Fear; terror; magnificence; pomp; ostentation.

داب *dāb* (H) *n.f.* Pressure; weight; force; control; check; restraint; impression (in printing).

داب بٹھانا *dāb biṭhānā, v.* To exercise authority over; to bring under control; to give full impression (print).

داب بیٹھنا ، لینا *dāb baiṭhnā, lenā, v.* To take possession illegally; to embezzle; to usurp; to grasp; to seize.

داب دینا *dāb denā, v.* To bury; to inter.

داب رکھنا *dāb rakhnā, v.* To withhold; to detain; to conceal; to press; to keep back; to take possession by fraud or force.

دابنا *dābnā* (H) *v.* To press down; to suppress; to restrain; to snub; to squeeze; to hug.

داتا *dātā* (H) *n.m.* One who gives generously; donor; benefactor; patron; alms-giver; God.

داخل *dā<u>kh</u>il* (A) *adj.* Entering; penetrating; arriving; included; inserted; produced; registered; filed; inner.

داخل خارج *dā<u>kh</u>il <u>kh</u>ārij, n.m.* Mutation; registration; proceedings of the transfer of property to the new proprietor.

داخل دفتر *dā<u>kh</u>il daftar, adj.* Placed with records; filed.

داخل کرنا *dā<u>kh</u>il karnā, v.* To admit; to insert; to enter; to place or fix in; to include; to deposit; to enrol; to enlist; to file; to pay.

داخل ہونا *dā<u>kh</u>il honā, v.* To enter; to arrive; to penetrate; to be inserted; to be filed; to be included; to be deposited; to be enrolled; to be registered.

داخلہ *dā<u>kh</u>ilah* (A) *n.m.* Admission; entrance; admission fee; payment of money; a receipt of payment.

داخلی *dā<u>kh</u>ilī* (A) *adj.* Contained; included; interior; internal; inclusive; belonging to; inherent.

داخلی موضع *dā<u>kh</u>ilī mauẓa', n.m.* A newly formed village, attached to or included in the older village.

داد *dād* (H) *n.m.* Ring-warm; herpes.

داد *dād* (P) *n.m.* Gift; law; aquity; justice; complaint; appeal; revenge; praise.

داد پانا *dād pānā, v.* To obtain justice; to deserve praise.

داد چاہنا *dād chāhnā, v.* To demand justice; to seek redress; to wish for praise.

داد خواہ *dād <u>kh</u>wāh, n.m.* A petitioner, a complainant; a plaintiff.

داد خواہی *dād <u>kh</u>wāhī, n.f.* Application for justice; a suit for redress.

داد دہی ۔ گستری *dād dihī, gastrī, n.f.* Administering of justice.

داد دینا *dād denā, v.* To do justice; to redress; to make reparation; to give due appreciation.

داد رس *dād ras, n.m.* A judge.

داد رسی *dād rasī, n.f.* Redress of grievances.; justice.

داد فریاد *dād faryād, n.f.* Application or cry for justice or redress.

داد فریاد کرنا *dād faryād karnā, v.* To cry for justice or redress; to apply for redress.

داد کو پہنچنا dād ko pahuṅchnā, v. To respond to cries for help; to come to the aid of; to dispense justice.

داد گر dād gar, n.m. Administrator of justice; a judge.

داد لینا dād lenā, v. To get a praise for one's doings.

داد ملنا dād milnā, v. To obtain justice or redress; to be appreciated.

داد نہ فریاد dād nah faryād, n.f. Injustice; tyranny; high-handedness.

داد و دہش dād-ŏ dihish, n.f. Liberality; beneficience; bounty; charity.

داد و ستد dād-ŏ sitad, n.f. Money transaction; giving and taking money; buying and selling; settlement of accounts.

دادا dādā (H) n.m. Paternal grand-father; an old man; a fop; a *goonda*.

دادرا dādrā (H) n.m. (from دادر dādar, a frog) A kind of song which resembles the quick tones of a frog.

دادی dādī (H) n.f. A paternal grand-mother.

دار dār (P) n.f. A piece of wood; gibbet; gallows; an impaling stake.

دار پر کھینچنا یا چڑھانا dār par kheṅchnā yā chaṛhānā, v. To impale; to hang (a man); to execute (by hanging)

دار کش dār kash, n.m. A hangman; an executioner.

دار و گیر dār-ŏ gir, n.f. Serging; tumult; entanglement.

دار dār (P) adj. Having; holding; (used at the end of *comps.* as حصہ دار ḥiṣṣah dār shareholder, زمیندار zamindār land-lord).

دار dār (A) n.m. Abode; habitation; place; dwelling; house; country.

دارالآخرت dār-ul-āk͟hirat, n.m. The next world.

دارالاقامہ dār-ul-iqāmha, n.m. Hostel; boarding house; lodge; hotel.

دارالامان یا امن dār-ul-amān yā amn, n.m. The house of peace and safety; a country with which there is peace.

دارالبقا dār-ul-baqā, n.m. The next world; the eternal abode.

دارالجزا dā-ul-jazā, n.m. The place of reward; the next world.

دارالحرب dār-ul-ḥarb, n.m. The country of an enemy; a country of infidel where war can be waged (according to Islamic law).

دارالحکومت dār-ul-ḥukumat, n.m. Capital; head quarter; metropolis.

دارالخلافہ dār-ul-k͟hilāfah, n.m. The seat of a Caliph; capital; metropolis.

دارالسلطنت dār-ul-salṭanat, n.m. The seat of a king; the royal residence; metropolis.

دارالشفا dār-ush-shafā, n.m. A hospital.

دارالضرب dār-uẓ-zarb, n.m. A mint.

دارالعلوم dār-ul-'ulūm, n.m. A college; a university.

دارالعمل dār-ul-'amal, n.m. This world; universe.

دارالفنا dār-ul-fanā, n.m. The abode of mortals; the perishable abode.

دارالمکافات dār-ul-mūkāfāt, n.m. The abode of recompense or retaliation; this world.

دارالنعیم dār-ul-na'īm, n.m. Paradise.

دارا dārā (P) n.m. Darius (the emperor of Persia); holder; possessor; sovereign; king.

دار چینی dār chīnī (P) n.f. Cinnamon.

دارو dārū (H) n.f. Spirituous liquor; wine; gun-powder.

دارو dārū (P) n.f. Medicine; remedy; cure.

دارو درمان dārū darmān n.m. Medical treatment.

داروغا، داروغہ dārog͟hā, dārog͟hah (P) n.m. An overseer; an inspector; a superintendent; the headman of an office; manager; director.

داروغه آبکاری dāroghah-ĕ ābkārı, n.m. Excise inspector.

داروغه پولیس dāroghah-ĕ polis, n.m. Police sub-inspector.

داروغه توپ خانه dāroghah-ĕ top khānah, n.m. An officer in charge of artillery or arsenal.

داروغه جنگلات dāroghah-ĕ janglāt, n.m. A forester or forest ranger.

داروغه جیل dāroghah-ĕ jel, n.m. Superintendent of jail.

داروغه صفائی dāroghah-ĕ ṣafā'ı, n.m. Sanitary inspector.

داروغه فارم dāroghah-ĕ farm, n.m. Farm supervisor.

داروغه محصولات dāroghah-ĕ maḥṣūlat, n.m. Tax inspector.

داروغائی ۔ داروغگی dāroghā'ı, dāroghgi (A) n.f. The office or duty of a dāroghah.

دارین dārain (A) n.m. The two abodes, this world and the next.

داڑھ dāṛh (H) n.f. See ڈاڑھ ḍāṛh.

داڑھی dāṛhi (H) n.f. See ڈاڑھی ḍāṛhi.

داس dās (S) n.m. A slave; a servant; a follower.

داسا dāsā (H) n.m. A piece of wood projecting from a wall to support the thatch; a wall plate.

داستان dāstān (P) n.f. A story; a fable; a tale.

داستان گو dāstān go, n.m. A story-teller.

داسی dāsi (H) n.f. A Hindu maid-servant.

داشت dāsht (P) n.f. Bringing up; taking care of; care; patronage; service.

یاد داشت yād dāsht, n.f. A memorandum; a note book; memory.

داشته dāshtah (P) n.f. A keep; a concubine; an unlawful wife. adj. Kept; taken care of.

داعی dā'ī (A) n.m. One who calls or invites; claimant; plaintiff; instigator; author; cause.

داعی الی الخیر dā'i ilal khair, n.m. One who calls people towards goodness and piety; a well-wisher.

داعیه dā'iyah (A) n.m. Petition; suit; plaint; claim; motive; cause, desire; wish.

داغ dāgh (P) n.m. A mark; a spot; a speck; a blemish; a brand; a stigma; a scar; grief; calamity; misfortune; loss; injury; damage.

داغ اٹھانا dāgh uṭhānā, v. To suffer a misfortune or calamity.

داغ بیل dāgh bel, n.f. Marking out the lines of a road with a spade; demarcation.

داغ بیل ڈالنا dāgh bel ḍālnā, v. To lay the foundation (of); to give a start; to demarcate.

داغ دار dāgh dār, adj. Spotted; branded; stained; marked; scarred, burnt.

داغ دینا dāgh denā, v. To brand; to mark by burning with a hot iron; to scar; to cause grieve (to); to cause depression (to).

داغ لگانا dāgh lagānā, v. To defame; to stain; to sully; to blacken; to wound; to brand.

داغ لگنا dāgh lagnā, v. To be damaged; to get a bad name; to be stigmatised; to be branded.

داغنا dāghnā, v. To mark by burning with hot iron; to stigmatize; to fire (a gun).

داغی dāghi, adj. Spotted; stained; branded; spoiled.

دافع dāfi' (A) adj. Repelling; repellent; repulsing; driving away.

داکھ dākh (H) n.f. Raisin; a grape.

دال dāl (A) adj. Indicative (of); signifying; expressive (of); typical. n.f. A letter, د.

دال فے عین ہونا dāl fe 'ain honā, v. To go away; to disappear.

دال dāl (H) n.f. Pulse; vetches; a crust; a scale; a scab; concentration of rays of light.

دال چپاتی dāl chapati, n.f. Pulse and bread; humble food.

دال دلیا dāl dalya, n.m. Coarse fare; whatever is to be had for a meal.

دال روٹی dāl roṭi, n.f. Poor sustenance; bare existence.

دال گلنا dāl galnā, v. To have an advantage; to avail; to have influence; to be effective.

دال میں کالا ہونا dal men kālā hona, v. To find something wrong or suspicious; to smell a rat.

دال نہ گلنا dāl nah galnā, v. To fail; to have no effect.

دالان dālān (P) n.m. Varandah.

دام dāma (A) intj. May it be perpetuated or may it last for ever!

دام دولتہ' dāma daulatohu, intj. May his fortune or prosperity last for ever!

دام ظلہ' dāma zillohu, intj. May his protection of us continue!

دام ملکہ' dāma mulkohu, intj. May his kingdom be ever-lasting!

دام dām (P) n.m. A net; a snare.

دام میں لانا dām men lana, v. To ensnare; to entrap.

دام dam (H) n.m. Price; value; cost; money.

دام بھرنا dām bharnā, v. To pay the price or value of; to pay penalty.

دام دینا dām dena, v. To pay the price.

داماد dāmad (P) n.m. Son-in-law.

دامان، دامن dāmān, daman (P) n.m. Skirt (of a garment) sheet (of a sail); the foot of a mountain; the part of a river which always remains under water; a lap.

دامن پکڑنا dāman pakarna, v. To cling to the skirt (of); to come under the protection (of); to become a follower (of); to be a plaintiff.

دامن پھیلانا dāman phailana, v. To beg; to supplicate; to petition.

دامن چھڑانا daman chhuṛanā, v. To get rid of; to escape from; to shake off.

دامن گیر daman gir, adj. Holding one's skirt; a claimant; a plaintiff; a dependent; an accuser; an adherent.

دامنی dāmanī (P) n.f. A saddle-cloth; scarf; furniture; housings; an ornament worn on the forehead.

دان dān (P) adj. Knowing; understanding (used in comp. as نکتہ دان nuktah dān, subtle, penetrating). n.m. Pot; vase; case; receptacle (used in comp. as, قلمدان qalamdān, pencase, گل دان gul·dān flower-vase).

دان dān (S) n.m. Gift; present; offering; alms; charity; donation; dowry.

دان پن dān pun, n.m. Charity; alms.

دانا dana (P) adj. Wise; sage; learned.

دانا بینا danā bina; adj Knowing and seeing; learned; wise.

دانائی dana'I (P) n.f. Wisdom; sagacity.

دانت dānt (H) n.m. A tooth; a tusk.

دانت اکھاڑنا dānt ukharna, v. To extract teeth.

دانت تلے انگلی دینا یا دبانا dant tale ungli dena ya dabāna, v. To bite the finger; to be surprised; to be amazed; to wonder.

دانت بنانا dānt banana, v. To set artificial teeth; to make a denture.

دانت بنانے والا dant banane walā, n.m. A dentist.

دانت پیسنا، چبانا، کٹکٹانا، کچکچانا dāṅt pisnā, chabānā, kitkitānā, kichkichānā, v. To gnash one's teeth in anger; to whine; to be angry.

دانت رکھنا، ہونا dāṅt rakhnā, honā, v. To have a very great desire for.

دانت کریدنا dāṅt kurednā, v. To pick teeth.

دانت کھٹے کرنا dāṅt khaṭṭe karnā, v. To set the teeth on edge; to dishearten; to frustrate; to baffle; to defeat.

دانت مارنا dāṅt mārnā, v. To bite.

دانت نکالنا dāṅt nikālnā v. To laugh; to grin; to express or confess inability and helplessness.

دانت نکلنا dāṅt nikalnā, v. To cut teeth.

دانتوں میں آنگلی دینا dāṅtoṅ meṅ uṅgli denā, (See دانت تلے آنگلی دینا dāṅt tale uṅgli denā).

دانتا dāṅtā (H) n.m. The tooth of a comb or saw or other instrument of the kind; a cog of a wheel.

دانتا کلکل dāṅtā kilkil, n.f. Constant quarrels.

داتن dāṅtan (H) n.f. A wooden tooth brush.

دانتی dāṅtī (H) n.f. Row of teeth; a sickle.

دانست dānist (P) n.f. Opinion; view; knowledge.

دانستہ dānistah, adv. Knowingly; wittingly.

دیدہ و دانستہ dīdah-ŏ dānistah, adv. Deliberately; intentionally.

دانش dānish (P) n.f. Knowledge; science; learning.

دانش کدہ dānish kadah, n.m. Faculty; a college.

دانش گاہ dānish gāh, n.f. University.

دانش مند، ور dānish mand, war, adj. Learned; wise; sagacious; intellectual.

دانش مندی dānish mandī, n.f. Learning; wisdom; sagacity; intellectuality.

دانگ dāṅg (P) n.f. The sixth part of dinār; a weight equal to the fourth part of a drachm; side or quarter of a town; side; direction.

دانہ dānah (P) n.m. Grain; corn; food; seed; berry; bread; dice; pustule; small-pox; a pimple.

دانہ بندی dānah bandī, n.f. A rough survey of crops; assessment of the revenue of standing crops.

دانہ پانی dānah pānī, n.m. Food and drink; victuals; subsistence.

دانہ دار dānah dār, adj. Granulated.

دانی dānī (S) adj. Liberal; bountiful; charitable; munificent.

داور dāwar (P) n.m. God, a sovereign; a just prince.

داہنا dāhnā (H) n.m. Right (hand).

دائر dā'ir (A) adj. Encircling; going round; pending; in process; under consideration (law).

دائر کرنا dā'ir karnā, v. To institute or file (a suit); to establish; to set up.

دائرہ dā'irah (A) n.m. A circle; a ring; an orbit; a circumference; a large tambourine.

دائم dā'im (A) adj. Perpetual; permanent; ceaseless; eternal; continual; always.

دائم الحبس dā'im-ul-ḥabs, adj. Imprisoned for life.

دائم المرض dā'im-ul-marẓ, adj. Always sick; ever-sick.

دائمی dā'imī (P) adj. Continual; lasting; durable; permanent.

دائن dā'in (A) n.m. One who borrows; a debtor.

داؤد Dāūd (A) n.m, David (prophet and king of Israel).

داؤد خانی dāūd khānī, n.m. A kind of white wheat.

داؤدی dāūdī (A) adj. Of or relating to David; armour; coat of mail; a shrub that bears a flower, like chrysanthimum; name of firework like that shrub.

داؤں dāoṅ (H) n.m. Turn; strategem; artifice; a trick in wrestling; a move; a throw of dice; time; pounce; clutch; grasp; ambuscade.

داؤں پر چڑھنا dāoṅ par chaṛhnā, v. To be overpowered by the opponent; to be entraped.

داؤں پڑنا dāoṅ paṛnā, v. To have a good throw (of dice).

داؤں پھینکنا dāoṅ phaiṅknā, v. To throw the dice.

داؤں پیچ dāoṅ pech, n.m. Tricks.

داؤں دینا dāoṅ denā, v. To give one his turn; to trick; to take in; to deceive.

داؤں کرنا dāoṅ karnā, v. To employ a trick in westling.

داؤں کھیلنا dāoṅ khelnā, v. To play a trick; to deceive.

داؤں لگانا daoṅ lagānā, v. To throw the dice; to stake; to lie in ambush; to ambuscade.

داؤں لگنا dāoṅ lagnā, v. To get an opportunity; to get a chance.

داؤں گھات dāoṅ ghāt, n.m. Ambuscade; tricks; stratagem.

داؤں میں آنا dāoṅ meṅ ānā, v. To be deceived.

دائی dā'ī (H) n.f. A midwife; a wet nurse.

دائی جنائی dā'ī janā'ī, n.f. A midwife.

دائی سے پیٹ چھپانا dā'ī se peṭ chhupānā, v. To try to conceal what one knows already or has suspected to be the case.

دائی کھلائی dā'ī khilā'ī, n.f. A dry nurse.

دائی گیری dā'ī girī, n.f. Midwifery.

دائیں dā'eṅ (H) adj. On the right hand side.

دائیں بائیں dā'eṅ bā'eṅ, adj. Right and left.

دایہ dāyah (P) n.f. A nurse; a midwife.

دایہ گری dāyah garī, n.f. Midwifery.

دب dubb (A) n.m. Bear.

دب اصغر dubb-ĕ aṣghar, n.m. The little bear; (constellation).

دب اکبر dubb-ĕ akbar, n.m. The great bear (constellation).

دب جانا dab jānā (H) v. To be buried; to be supressed; to withdraw; to be mortified; to be overpowered.

دبا لینا dabā lenā (H) v. To encroach upon; to seize; to keep possession by force; to cover up; to overcome.

دباغ dabbāgh (A) n.m. A tanner; a currier.

دباغت dabāghat (A) n.f. Tanning.

دبانا dabānā (H) v. To press down; to suppress; to squeeze; to sow; to restrain; to keep under; to subdue; to crush; to check; to usurp; to curb; to awe.

دباؤ dabāo (H) n.m. Pressure; constraint; influence; authority; strength; crush; suppression.

دباؤ ڈالنا dabāo ḍālnā, v. To press; to influence; to over-awe.

دبدبہ dabdabah (P) n.m. Pomp and show; dignity; majesty; state; parade.

دبدھا dubdhā (H) n.m. Doubt; suspense; uncertainty; dilemma.

دبدھا کرنا dubdhā karnā, v. To doubt; to mistrust.

دبر dubur (A) n.f. The backside; posterior; podex.

دبستان dabistān (P) n.m. A school.

دبک جانا dubak jānā, v. To fear; to hide.

دبکانا dabkānā (H) v. To snub; to rebuke; to daunt; to threaten.

دبکنا dubaknā (H) v. To shrink from fear; to lie in ambush; to crouch.

دبلا - دبلا پتلا - دبلی - دبلی پتلی dublā, dublā patlā, dubli, dubli patli (H) adj. Thin; lean; meagre; poor; weak.

دبلا پن dublā pan, n.f. Leanness; thinness; emaciation; meagreness; weakness.

دبنا dabnā (H) v. To be suppressed; to be checked; to be restrained; to be squeezed; to be pressed down; to be bowed down; to give way; to be withheld; to be overcome; to be quelled; to be snubbed; to be crouch; to be hidden; to be burried.

دبنگ ḍabang (H) adj. Ill-fashioned; crude; rough; rude; uncouth; bold; forward; courageous; bulky; presumptuous. n.m. A bully; a blusterer.

دبوچ لینا daboch lenā (H) v. To seize; to hold down; to grasp; to clutch.

دبوچنا dabochnā (H) v. To seize; to squeeze; to pounce upon; to seize by the throat.

دبے پاؤں dabe pāoṅ (H) adv. With silent steps; treading softly and gently.

دبیر dabīr (P) n.m. A writer; a secretary; notary.

دبیر فلک dabīr-ĕ falak, n.m. The planet Mercury.

دبیز dabīz (P) adj. Thick; coated; strong.

دبیل dabel (H) adj. & n. Subject; subordinate; person under subjection.

دت dut (H) intj. Away ! begone ! run away !

دتکار dutkār (H) n.m. Reproof; rebuke; reprimand.

دتکارنا dutkārnā (H) v. To reprove; to drive away; to rebuke; to reprimand.

دجال dajjāl (A) n.m. A one-eyed man; a liar; a great deceiver; an imposter; anti-Christ.

دجل dajl (A) n.m. Deception; a lie.

دجلہ Dajlah (A) n.m. The river Tigris; a lake.

دخان duk͟hān (A) n.m. Smoke: steam.

دخانی duk͟hāni (A) adj. Smoky; working with steam.

دخانی جہاز duk͟hāni jahāz, n.m. A steamer.

دخانی کل duk͟hāni kal, n.f. A steam engine.

دخت duk͟ht (P) n.f. (abbrev. of دختر duk͟htar) Daughter.

دخت رز duk͟ht-ĕ raz, n.f. Wine.

دختر duk͟htar (P) n.f. Daughter; a girl; a virgin.

دخل dak͟hl (A) n.m. Entrance; admission; access; reach; possession; occupation; progress; proficiency; knowledge; wisdom; skill; possibility; interference; intrusion; molestation.

دخل بیجا، ناجائز dak͟hl-ĕ bejā, nājā'iz, n.m. Unlawful possession; trespass.

دخل بالجبر dak͟hl bil jabr, n.m. Forcible possession; possession by the use of force.

دخل پانا dak͟hl pānā, v. To get admission; to obtain possession; to have access; to be admitted.

دخل در معقولات dak͟hl dar ma'qūlāt, n.m. Unnecessary interference: uncalled for intrusion.

دخل دینا dak͟hl denā, v. To interpose; to interfere; to give possession.

دخل نامہ dak͟hl nāmah, n.m. A writ of possession of lands; a document giving the right of occupancy.

دخل یابی dak͟hl yābi, n.f. Taking or obtaining possession; permission to enter.

دخول duk͟hūl (A) n.m. Entrance; admission; penetration.

دخیل dakhil (A) adj. Admitted; allowed entrance; adopted (a word); interfering; possessing; occupying.

دخیل کار dakhil kār, n.m. An occupant.

دخیل کاری dakhil kārı, n.f. Hereditory occupancy.

ددھار، ددھیل dudhār, dudhail (H) adj. Giving much milk; milch.

ددھی dudhdhi (H) n.f. A medicinal herb containing milk-like juice; a kind of white and red stone; breast; nipple; a teat.

ددھیال dadhiyāl (H) n.f. Paternal grandfather's family.

در dar (P) n.m. A door; a gate; entrance; threshold. prep. In; into; within; to; about; by.

درآمد darāmad n.f. Income; • return; Imports.

درآمد برآمد darāmad barāmad, n.f. Import and export; receipts and payments; income and expenditure; ingress and egress; incoming and outgoing; arrival and departure; admission and withdrawal; entrance and exit.

درآنا dar ānā, v. To come in; to penetrate; to succeed.

درباب، دِرباره dar bāb, dar bārah, adv. With regard to. prep. For; respecting.

دربان dar bān, n.m. A door-keeper; a porter.

دربدر dar badar, adv. From door to door.

در بدر پھرنا dar badar phirnā, v. To go from door to door; to wander about.

در بندی dar bandı, n.f. Lock-out; bolting of the door.

در پردہ dar pardah, adj. Concealed; hidden; veiled. adv. Privately; secretly.

در پے ہونا dar pae honā, v. To follow; to pursue; to be in pursuit of; to be at hand; to be in search of; to be after.

در پیش dar pesh, adj. Placed before; in front; under consideration; under trial.

در پیش ہونا dar pesh hona, v. To be in front or before; to be in hand; to be on foot; to occur; to be necessary; to happen; to lay before; to be introduced.

در حقیقت dar ḥaqiqat, adv. As a matter of fact; undoubtedly.

درکار darkār, adj. Necessary; wanting.

درکنار dar kinār, adv. Aside; apart; out of the way.

در گزر کرنا dar guzar karnā, v. To pardon; to pass over; to forgive; to neglect; to overlook.

در گور dar gor, intj. May you die ! to your grave !

در و دیوار dar-ŏ diwār, n.m. Every dwelling; every nook and corner.

در dar (H) n.m. Price; rate; value; esteem; tariff; fixed standard; pole; pillar; column.

در dur (H) intj. Stand off ! avaunt !

در durr (A) n.m. A pearl.

در افشان durr afshān, adj. Scattering pearls; eloquent.

در افشانی durr afshāni, n.f. Eloquence.

در بچہ durr bachah, n.m. An earring with only one pearl.

در بہشت durr bahisht, n.f./m. A kind of sweetmeat; a kind of mango.

در شہوار durr-ĕ shahwār, n.m. A big pearl; a pearl worthy of a prince or a king.

در ناسفتہ durr-ĕ nāsuftah, n.m. Unpierced or unbored pearl; a virgin.

در یتیم، در یکتا durr-ĕ yatim, durr-ĕ yaktā, n.m. A pearl found alone in the shell; a very precious pearl.

درا *darā* (P) *n.f.* A bell.

دراڑ *darāṛ* (H) *n.f.* A crack; a fissure; rift; rent.

دراز *darāz* (P) *adj.* Long; tall; extended; stretched out.

دراز دست *darāz dast, adj.* Long handed; oppressive.

دراز دستی *darāz dasti, n.f.* Oppression; tyranny.

دراز قد *darāz qadd, adj.* Tall; of stature.

دراز کرنا *darāz karnā, v.* To lengthen; to prolong, to stretch.

دراز گوش *darāz gosh, adj.* Long-eared. *n.m* A hare.

دراز ہونا *darāz honā, v.* To lie down; to take rest.

دراز *daräz* (H) *n.m.* (*corr.* for English); Drawers (of chest etc.)

درازی *darāzi* (P) *n.f.* Length; extension; tallness.

درانتی *darāṅtī* (H) *n.f.* A kind of sickle; reaping hook.

درانی *durrāni* (P) *n.m.* The name of a tribe of *Pathāns*, living about *Kandhār*; they were so called because they wore pearls in the ear.

دراوڑ *drāwaṛ* (S) *n.m.* Dravidian; belonging to the *Dravidās*; the Dravid people and country from the coast of Madras to Cape Comorin.

درایت *darāyat* (A) *n.f.* Knowledge; sense; temperament; disposition; habit.

دربار *darbār* (P) *n.m.* A house; court; hall of royal audience; the holding of a court; a levee.

دربار خاص *darbār-ē khāṣ, n.m.* Private audience; a meeting of the privy council; cabinet meeting.

دربار عام *darbār-ē ʻām, n.m.* General audience; a public meeting.

دربار کرنا *darbār karnā, v.* To hold a court.

درباری *darbāri* (P) *n.m.* A courtier; courtly; elegant; elegant and polished language; one entitled to a seat in a *darbār*;

درج *durj* (A) *n.m.* A small casket for depositing gems.

درج *darj* (A) *n.m.* A closet; writing; anything written on; a volume.

درج کرنا *darj karnā, v.* To register; to write; to copy; to invest.

درج ہونا *darj honā, v.* To be inserted; to be entered in a book; to be registered.

درجن *darjan* (H) *n.f.* (corr. for English) A dozen.

درجہ *darjah* (A) *n.m.* Grade; class; degree; rank; division; compartment; step; gradation; dignity; plight; degree of a circle.

درجہ بدرجہ *darjah badarjah, adv.* Step by step; degree by degree; gradually; each in its place; according to one's rank.

درخت *darakht* (P) *n.m.* A tree.

درخشاں *darakhshāṅ* (P) *adj.* Shining; brilliant; flashing; resplendent.

درخشانی *darakhshāni* (P) *n.f.* Splendour; brilliance.

درخشندگی *darakhshindagi* (P) *n.f.* Brightness; splendour.

درخشندہ *darakhshindah* (P) *adj.* Shining; glittering; lucid; refulgent.

درخواست *darkhwāst* (P) *n.f.* Application; request; entreaty; proposal; petition; appeal; tender; offer.

درخواست کرنا *darkhwāst karnā, v.* To request; to apply; to beg; to entreat.

درخواست کنند darkhwāst kunindah, n.m. An applicant; a petitioner.

درخور darkhūr (P) adj. Fit; suitable; proper.

درخور اعتنا darkhūr-ĕ iʻtinā, adj. Worthy of attention.

درد dard (P) n.m. Pain; ache; affliction; sympathy; affection; compassion.

درد آلود dard ālūd, adj. Pained; grieved.

درد آمیز dard āmez, adj. Painful; distressing; pathetic; touching piteous; compassionate.

درد انگیز dard angez, adj. Pitiable; exciting compassion; pathetic.

دردزہ dard-ĕ zih, n.m. Pains or throes of labour; travail; pains in childbirth.

درد سر dard-ĕ sar, n.m. Headache; trouble; vexation.

درد شکم dard-ĕ shikam, n.m. Colic pain

درد کرنا dard karnā, v. To feel the pains or compassion (for); to ache; to pain.

درد گردہ dard-ĕ gurdah, n.m. Pains in the kidneys; renal colic.

درد مند dard mand, adj. Compassionate; sympathetic; pitiful.

درد مندی dard mandī, n.f. Compassion; sympathy; affliction.

درد ناک dard nāk, adj. Painful; afflictive; piteous; sorrowful.

درد ہونا dard honā, v. To ache; to pain.

بے درد be dard, adj. Unsympathetic; pitiless; cruel; stone-hearted.

درد durd (P) n.f. Sediment; dregs; lees.

دردرا dardara (H) adj. Half pounded; coarsely ground.

درز darz (P) n.f. A seam; a crack; flaw; fissure; a narrow shred.

درزن darzan (P) n.f. A seamstress; wife of a tailor; a woman tailor.

درزی darzī (P) n.m. A tailor; a seamster.

درس dars (A) n.m. Reading; learning to read; a lecture; a lesson.

درس دینا dars dena, v, To give a lesson; to teach; to instruct.

درس گاہ dars gāh, n.m. School, college; educational institution.

درس لینا dars lenā, v. To read a lesson.

درس dars ya daras (H) n.m. Sight; view; look.

درست durust (P) adj. Right; fit; proper; true; correct; precise; exact; well; safe; sound.

درست کرنا durust karnā, v. To correct; to fit; to arrange; to adjust; to put in order; to repair; to rectify; to mend; to restore.

درستی durusti (P) n.f. Soundness; justness; accuracy; amendment; rectitude; fitness; exactness; reformation; correction.

درسی darsi (A) adj. Relating to study; educational.

درشت durusht (P) adj. Rough; hard; rigid; morose; stiff; stern; oppressive; fierce; harsh; coarse.

درشتی durushti (P) n.f. Roughness; harshness; severity; fierceness; asperity; moroseness.

درشن darshan (H) n.m. Interview; appearance; sight of an image of a god; visiting a sacred shrine.

درشنی darshani (H) adj. Payable at sight; at sight; good looking; beautiful; handsome; sightly.

درشنی ہنڈی darshanı hundị, n.f. A bill of exchange payable at sight.

درک dark (A) n.m. Understanding; perception; knowledge; comprehension.

درگاہ dargāh (P) n.f. A shrine; a royal court; threshold; a palace; door; a mosque; tomb of a reputed saint.

درگت durgat (H) n.f. Bad treatment.

درم · درہم diram, dirham (P) n.m. Money; a weight of 3½ mashas; a coin of the value of two pence.

درمان · درمن darman, darman (P) n.m. Medicine; remedy, cure; drug.

درماندگی darmandagi (P) n.f. Helplessness; misery; misfortune; distress; want; penury.

درماندہ darmāndah (P) adj. Helpless; destitute; distressed.

درمیان darmiyan (P) n.m. Middle; midst; interval. adv. & prep. During; in the course of; in the midst of; between.

درمیانہ darmiyānah (P) adj. Middling; in the middle; between; intermediate.

درمیانہ درجہ darmiyānah darjah, n.m. Medium; middle class; intermediate class.

درمیانی darmiyāni (P) adj. Midmost; intermediate; medium.

درند · درندہ darind, darindah (P) adj. Tearing; rapacious; fierce; ravenous; ferocious. n.m. Beast of orey; ravenous beast.

درنگ dirang (P) n.m. Delay; hesitation; dilemma.

دروازہ darwazah (P) n.m. Door; gate.

دروازہ بند کرنا، بھیڑنا dazwāzah band karna, bherṇā, v. To shut the door.

دروازہ کھولنا dar vazah kholnā, v. To open the door.

درو بست daro bast (F) adj. Whole; entire.

درود darud (A) n.m. Benediction; blessing; prayer; salutation; (esp. of Prophet Muhammad).

درود بھیجنا darud bhejna, v. To send blessings; to praise; to salute.

دروغ darogh (P) n.m. A lie; falsehood.

دروغ حلفی darogh ḥalfi, n.m. Perjury; swearing falsely.

دروغ گو darogh go, n.m. A liar.

دروغ گوئی darogh go'i, n.f. Lying; falsehood.

درون darun (P) prep. In; within. n.m. The heart; bowels.

درویش darwesh (P) n.m. A dervish; a beggar; a mendicant.

درویشانہ darweshanah (P) adj. Dervish-like; beggar-like.

درویشی darweshi (P) n.f. A way of life, doctrine or office of a dervish; poverty; medicancy.

درہ darrā yā darah (P) n.m. A valley (between two hills through which a stream flows); a pass or way (between two mountains); a mountain pass; a glen; a fissure.

درہ durrah (P) n.m. A scourge made of twisted thongs; a sort of a whip to punish offenders with.

درہم darham (P) adj. Confused; confounded; jumbled.

درہم برہم darham barham, adj. Confused; disarranged; confounded.

دری dari (H) n.f. A small carpet.

دری dari (P) n.f. Name of an ancient dialect of Persia (in comp.) Rending; tearing (as عصمت دری 'iṣmat darī, rape).

دریا darya (P) n.m. A large river; the sea; waters.

دریا اترنا darya utarna, v. To recede (river).

دریا برد daryā burd, n.f. Land cut or washed away by the river; diluvium.

دریا برد ہو جانا daryā burd ho jana, v. To be washed away by river (land).

دریا چڑھنا daryā charhnā, v. To be in spate (river); to inundate.

دریا دل daryā dil, adj. Generous; liberal; large-hearted.

دریا دلی daryā dili, n.f. Great liberality; generosity.

دریا کوزے میں بند کرنا darya kūze men band karnā, v. To say much in a few words; to attempt the impossible.

نیکی کر دریا میں ڈال neki kar daryā meṅ ḍāl, prov. Do not expect a return for the good you have done.

دریا میں رهنا اور مگرمچھ سے بیر darya meṅ rahna aur magarmachh se bair, prov. It is hard to reside in Rome and quarrel with the Pope.

دریافت daryāft (P) n.f, Discovery; investigation; understanding; comprehension; ascertaining; detection.

دریافت کرنا daryāft karnā, v. To discover; to enquire; to ascertain; to investigate; to find out; to detect; to discern; to perceive.

دریافت هونا daryaft hono, v. To be ascertained; to be discovered.

دریائی daryā'i (P) adj. Aquatic; marine; riverain. n.m. A kind of silk-cloth.

دریائی گھوڑا daryā'i ghora, n.m. The sea-horse; the hippopotamus.

دریائی نارجیل daryā'i nārjel, n.m. Sea-coconut.

دریبا dareba (H) n.m. A betal stall in a market.

دریچه darichah (P) n.m. A window; casement.

دریده daridah (P) adj. Torn; rent.

دریده دهن daridah dahan, adj. Open-mouthed: plain-spoken; rude; impudent.

دریغ daregh (P) n.m. A sigh; sorrow; grief; repugnance; disinclination; denial; regret.

دریغ کرنا daregh karna, v. To withhold from; to think much of; to be niggard or grudging in respect of.

دریوزه daryūzah (P) n.m. Beggary; begging.

دریوزه گر daryūzah gar, n.m. A beggar; a mendicant.

دڑبا darbā (H) n.m. A pigeon house; a dove-cote.

دزد duzd (P) n.m. A thief; a robber.

دزد حنا duzd-ĕ ḥinā, n.m. The white spot left after applying حنا ḥinā to hands or feet.

دزدیده duzdidah (P) adj. Stolen; pilfered.

دزدیده نظر duzdidah nazar, n.f. Side glance; shy look; looking through the corner of the eye.

دس das (H) adj. Ten.

دساتیر dasātir (A) n.m. (plu. of دستور dastur) Rules; constitutions; customs; manners; modes.

دساور disawar (H) n.m. A foreign country; foreign market.

دساوری disawari (H) adj. Belonging to a foreign country. n.m. A kind of imported betel leaf.

دساوری مال disāwari mal, n.m. Imported goods.

دست dast (P) n.m. Hand; cubit, power; purge; evacuation.

دست آور dast āwar, adj. Purgative; cathartic.

دست اندازی dast andazi, n.f. Interference; encroachment; intrusion; exercise of authority.

دست اندازی کرنا dast andazi karnā, v. To coerce illegally; to interfere; to meddle; to exercise the authority.

دست بدست dast badast, adj. Hand to hand.

دست بدعا هونا dast badu'ā honā, v. To put up the hands in prayer; to pray (for).

دست برد dast burd, n.f. Plunder; power; aggression; encroachment; usurpation; superiority; advantage.

دست بردار ہونا *dast bardār honā*, *v.* To give up; to wash one's hand off; to withdraw from; to leave off; to desert; to resign; to abstain; to cease; to relinquish; to retire.

دست برداری *dast bardārī*, *n.f.* Renunciation; withdrawal.

دست بستہ *dast bastah*, *adj.* With folded hands (in token of respect). *adv.* Humbly; respectfully.

دست بوس ہونا ، دست بوسی کرنا *dast bos honā*, *dast bosī karnā*, *v.* To kiss the hands (of); to salute.

دست پناہ *dast panāh*, *n.m.* Pair of tongs.

دست خط *dast khaṭṭ*, *n.m.* Signature, a manuscript; chirography.

دستخط کرنا *dast khaṭṭ karnā*, *v.* To sign; to endorse.

دست خطی *dast khaṭṭī*, *adj.* Signed; endorsed; written with one's own hand.

دست دراز *dast darāz*, *n.m.* An oppressor; extortionate.

دست درازی *dast darāzī*, *n.m.* Oppression; violence.

دست درازی کرنا *dast darāzī karnā*, *v.* To practice violence; to plunder; to oppress.

دسترس *dastras*, *n.f.* Ability; power; means; facility; dexterity; skill; attainment; acquisition.

دست شفا *dast-ĕ shifā*, *n.m.* A complimentary term for a skilled physician.

دست قدرت *dast-ĕ qudrat*, *n.f.* Power; ability; strength; nature's work.

دست کار *dast kār*, *n.m.* An artisan; a manufacturer; a handicraftsman.

دستکاری *dast kārī*, *n.f.* Handicraft; manufacture.

دست گاہ *dast gāh* (H) *n.f.* Power; ability; strength; intellect; skill.

دست گیر *dast gīr*, *n.m.* One who holds the hand (of); a helper; protector; a saint.

دست گیری *dast gīrī*, *n.f.* Aid; Help; assistance; support; protection; patronage; friendship.

دست مال *dast māl*, *n.m.* A handkerchief; a towel.

دست نگر *dast nigar*, *adj.* Needy; wanting; in need.

دست و گریباں ہونا *dast-ŏ girebān honā*, *v.* To be engaged in combat.

دست یاب *dast yāb*, *adj.* Forthcoming; available.

دست یاب ہونا *dast yāb honā*, *v.* To get; to acquire; to be attained; to be available.

دست یابی *dast yābī*, *n.f.* Availability; procurement.

دستار *dastār* (P) *n.f.* Turban.

دستار فضیلت *dastār-ĕ fazīlat*, *n.f.* A robe or turban of honour; a diploma.

دستانہ *dastānah* (P) *n.m.* A glove; a gauntlet.

دستاویز *dastāwez* (P) *n.f.* A bond; an instrument; a note of hand; title-deed; certificate; document; deed.

دستاویز انتقال *dastāwez-ĕ intiqāl*, *n.f.* A transfer deed; mutation certificate.

دستاویز بیع بالوفا *dastāwez-ĕ bai' bilwafā*, *n.f.* A deed of conditional sale.

دستاویز جعلی *dastāwez-ĕ ja'lī*, *n.f.* A forged document.

دستاویز ضمانت *dastāwez-ĕ zamānat*, *n.f.* A bail-bond.

دستاویز لادعویٰ *dastāwez-ĕ lā d'avā*, *n.f.* A deed of renunciation.

دستاویز مہر *dastāwez-ĕ mahr*, *n.f.* A deed of dower.

دستاویز ہبہ *dastāwez-ĕ hibah*, *n.f.* A deed of gift or bequest.

دسترخوان *dastarkhwān* (P) *n.m.* A table-cloth; a piece of cloth spread on the ground on which meal dishes are placed.

دستک **dastak** (P) *n.m.* Knocking at the door; summons; making a call; commission; passport; citation.

دستک دینا **dastak denā**, *v.* To knock at the door.

دستکی **dastaki** (P) *n.f.* A pocket book; a falconer's glove.

دستور **dastūr** (P) *n.m.* Custom; usage; fashion; manner; mode; a minister; rule; regulation; constitution.

دستورالعمل **dastūr-ul-'amal**, *n.m.* A rule; regulation; model, a manual; a code; rules of practice; procedure; *modus operandi*.

مجلس دستور ساز **majlis-ĕ dastūr sāz**, *n.f.* Constituent assembly.

دستوری **dastūrī** (P) *n.f.* Perquisites; fees; commission of a broker. *adj.* Constitutional; customary.

دستہ **dastah** (P) *n.m.* A handle; a pestle; a quire of paper; a bundle consisting of 24 arrows; a skein of thread; a division of an army; a brigade; squadron; a bundle; a bunch; a group.

دستہ پولیس **dastah polis**, *n.m.* A police force.

دستی **dastī** (P) *n.f.* A torch or link carried in the hands; a vessel with a handle; a vessel that may be carried in the hand; a small pen-case; a handkerchief; a hand-trick in wrestling. *adj.* Of or from the hand; by hand.

دسواں **daswāṅ** (H) *adj.* Tenth.

دسہرہ **dusahrah** (S) *n.m.* A Hindū festival observed on the tenth of اسوج *Asūj* or September-October.

دشت **dasht** (P) *n.m.* A desert; a forest; an arid plain.

دشت پیما ، گرد ، نورد **dasht paimā, gard, naward**, *n.m.* One who travels in deserts; a wanderer.

دشت پیمائی ، گردی ، نوردی **dasht paimā'ī, gardī, nawardī**, *n.f.* Travelling or wandering over deserts.

دشتی **dashtī** (P) *adj.* Of the forest; wild; savage.

دشمن **dushman** (P) *n.m.* An enemy; a foe; an adversary.

دشمن جانی **dushman-ĕ jānī**, *n.m.* A deadly foe; a mortal enemy.

دشمن دلی **dushman-ĕ dilī**, *n.m.* An enemy at heart; a hidden foe.

دشمن سوئے نہ سونے دے **dushman so'e nah sone de**, *prov.* An enemy is a constent spy.

دشمنی **dushmanī** (P) *n.f.* Enmity, hostility; hatred; detestation.

دشمنی ڈالنا **dushmanī ḍālnā**, *v.* To sow enmity.

دشنام **dushnām** (P) *n.f.* Abuse; invective.

دشنہ **dashnah** (P) *n.m.* A dagger.

دشوار **dushwār** (P) *adj.* Difficult; orduous; hard.

دشواری **dushwārī** (P) *n.f.* Difficulty; hardship.

دعا **du'ā** (A) *n.f.* Benediction; blessing; salutation; prayer; wish; invocation; imprecation; supplication.

دعائے خیر **du'ā-ĕ khair**, *n.f.* A prayer for one's well-being.

دعا دینا **du'ā denā**, *v.* To give a blessing; to bless or pray for.

دعا سلام کہنا **du'ā salām kehnā**, *v.* To send one's compliments.

دعا مانگنا **du'ā māṅgnā**, *v.* To invoke blessings; to pray.

دعا گو **du'ā go**, *n.m.* One who blesses or prays for; a well-wisher.

بد دعا **bad du'ā**, *n.f.* A curse; imprecation.

دعاوی **da'āwī** (A) *n.m.* (*plu.* of دعوی *da'wā*). Claims; law-suits; demands.

دعائیہ du'āiyah (A) *adj.* Of or relating to prayer; benedictory.

دعوت da'wat (A) *n.f.* Invitation; convocation; a feast; banquet; entertainment; fare; repast; a treat.

دعوت جنگ da'wat-ĕ jang, *n.f.* Proclamation of war.

دعوت شیراز da'wat-ĕ shiraz, *n.f.* A homely and unceremonious feast.

دعوت کرنا da'wat karnā, *v.* To invite; to give a feast.

دعوت ولیمہ da'wat-ĕ walimah, *n.f.* A marriage feast.

دعویٰ da'wạ (A) *n.m.* Claim; law suit; charge; pretension; demand; accusation.

دعویٰ بے جا da'wā-ĕ bejā, *n.m.* A false and unfounded claim.

دعویٰ بے دخلی da'wạ-ĕ be dakhli, *n.f.* An action for dispossession.

دعویٰ بلا دلیل da'wạ bilā dalil, *n.f.* An unsupported claim.

دعویٰ جمانا da'wạ jamānā, *v.* To establish claim.

دعویٰ خارج کرنا da'wạ khārij karnā, *v.* To dismiss a suit or claim.

دعویٰ دار dā'wạ dār, *n.m.* Plaintiff; claimant; pretender.

دعویٰ زائدالمیعاد da'wạ zā'id-ul-mi'ād, *n.f.* A time-barred claim.

دعویٰ شفعہ da'wạ-ĕ shuf'ah, *n.m.* Claim for pre-emption.

دعویٰ مہر da'wā-ĕ mahr, *n.m.* A claim to dower.

دعویٰ وراثت da'wạ-ĕ wirāṣat, *n.m.* A claim to inheritence.

دغا daghā (P) *n.f.* Deceit; treachery; cheating; fraud; deception; artifice; delusion.

دغا باز daghā bāz, *adj.* Deceitful; fraudulent; cheat; treacherous; imposter; betrayer; traitor; swindler.

دغا بازی daghā bāzi, *n.f.* Cheating; imposture; trickery; villainy; treachery; deceitfulness.

دغا دینا ، کرنا daghā denā, karnā, *v.* To deceive; to cheat; to act deceitfully or treacherously.

دغدغہ daghdaghah (A) *n.m.* Alarm; disturbance; tumult; fear; dread; awe.

دغنا daghnā, *v.* To be marked or branded; to be fired off (as a gun).

دغیلا daghilā (H) *adj.* Spotted; stained; rotten.

دف daf (P) *n.m.* Tambourine.

دفاتر dafātir (A) *n.m.* (*plu.* of دفتر daftar) Offices.

دفائن dafāin (A) *n.f.* (*plu.* of دفینہ dafinah) Hidden treasures.

دفتر daftar (P) *n.m.* An office; department; a book; register; roll; record; a large volume; an account-book.

دفتری daftari (P) *n.m.* An office keeper; one who has charge of office stationery &c. *adj.* Official.

دفتی dafti, *n.m.* The boards of the binding of a book; a paste-board.

دفع dafa' (A) *n.m.* Repulsion; repelling; warding off; preventing.

دفع الوقتی dafa'-ul-waqti, *n.f.* Beguiling the time.

دفع دار dafa' dār, *n.m.* An officer commanding a small body of cavalry.

دفع کرنا dafa' karnā, *v.* To repel; to ward off; to avert; to remove; to give up; to discard; to prevent; to dispel.

دفع ہونا dafa' honā, *v.* To be turned back; to be repelled; to be defeated; to depart.

دفعتاً dafa'tan (A) *adv.* All at once; suddenly.

دفعہ daf'ah (A) *n.f.* Time; moment; turn; clause; section; article; class.

دفیعه daf'iyyah (A) n.m. Repulsion; averting; prevention; cure; remedy; preventive; warding off.

دفن dafn (A) n.m. Burial; concealment; internment.

دفن کرنا dafn karnā, v. To bury; to inter; to hide; to conceal.

دفن ہونا dafn honā, v. To be buried; to be interred.

دفنانا dafnanā, v. To bury; to inter.

دفینه dafinah (A) n.m. Hidden treasure; hoard; treasure-trove.

دق diqq (A) n.f. A hectic fever; consumption; tuberculosis. adj. Thin; slender; minute; vexed; troubled; indisposed; ailing.

دق کا مریض diqq kā mariz, n.m. Tuberculous; tubercular.

دق کرنا diqq karnā, v. To torment; to tease; to annoy; to plague; to irritate; to vex.

دق ہونا diqq honā, v. To be irritated; to be annoyed; to be teased; to be vexed; to be perplexed.

دقائق daqā'iq (plu. of دقیقه daqiqah) n.m. Subtleties; minute points.

دقت diqqat (A) n.f. Difficulty; trouble; uneasiness; intricacy; abstruseness; deligence; perplexity; a nice point; minute point; a delicate affair; close application; industry.

دقت میں پڑنا diqqat meṅ parnā, v. To get into trouble; to be involved in difficulty.

دقیق daqiq (A) adj. Subtle; nice; delicate; slender; minute; fine; obstruse; difficult; deep.

دقیقه daqiqah (A) n.m. A delicate question; a minute; a particle; a trifling matter; a moment of time; anything small.

دقیقه فرو گذاشت نه کرنا daqiqah faroguzāsht nah karnā, v. To leave no stone unturned; to do one's very best.

دقیقه رس daqiqah ras, adj. Intelligent; subtle; able to tackle delicate questions; quick of apprehension.

دکان dukān, dukkān (P) n.f. A shop.

دکان بڑھانا dukān baṛhāna, v. To close the shop.

دکان چلانا dukān chalānā, v. To run a shop.

دکان چلنا dukān chalnā, v. To have a good sale.

دکان دار dukān dār, n.m. A shop-keeper.

دکان داری dukān dāri, n.f. Shopkeeping; buying and selling.

دکان کرنا dukān karnā, v. To keep a shop; to run a shop.

دکان لگانا dukān lagāna, v. To open or set a shop.

دکھ dukh (H) n.m. Suffering; distress; affliction; misery; pain; ache; annoyance; bother.

دکھ اٹھانا dukh uṭhānā, v. To suffer pain; to bear pain; to be afflicted.

دکھ بٹانا dukh baṭānā, v. To share one's sorrows; to sympathise.

دکھ بھرنا ، بھوگنا dukh bharnā, bhognā, v. To labour; to suffer misfortune.

دکھ دینا dukh denā, v. To give trouble or pain; to torment.

دکھ سکھ dukh sukh, n.m. Pain and pleasure; ups and downs of life.

دکھ کا مارا dukh kā mārā, adj. Afflicted; unfortunate.

دکھانا dukhānā (H) v. To inflict pain; to torment; to hurt; to grieve.

دکھانا dikhānā (H) v. To show; to exhibit; to display; to expose.

دکھاوا ، دکھاوٹ dikhāwā, dikhāwaṭ (H) n.m. Show; ostentation; display; exhibition.

دکھائی dikhā'i (H) n.f. Showing; show; display.

دکھائی دینا dikhā'i denā, v. To be seen; to appear; to be sighted.

دکھڑا dukhṛā (H) n.m. Misfortunes; calamities; troubles.

دکھڑا رونا dukhṛā ronā, v. To relate the story of one's sufferings.

دکھلانا dikhlānā, (H) v. (obso.) See دکھانا dikhānā.

دکھن، دکن dakkhan, dakan (H) n.m. South; the Deccan.

دکھنا dukhna (H) v. To ache; to pain; to smart.

دکھنی dakhni (H) adj. Southern; southerly wind.

دکھی، دکھیا، دکھیارا، دکھیاری dukhi, dukhyā, dukhyārā, dukhyāri (H) adj. Afflicted; in distress or pain; sick; poor; sorrowful; sad.

دگانہ dugānah (P) n.m. Two prostrations at prayer.

دگدا dugdā (H) n.f. Hesitation; doubt; uncertainty; commotion; agitation; (see also دبدھا dubdhā).

دگر digar (P) adj. Other; another.

دگر گوں digar gūṅ, adj. Of another complexion or colour; altered; changed.

دگلا daglā (H) n.m. A kind of quilted coat.

دگنا dugnā (H) adj. Double; two-fold.

دل dil (P) n.m. Heart; mind; soul; courage; conscience; generosity; wish; inclination.

دل آرا dil ārā, adj. Beloved; sweetheart.

دل آرام dil ārām, n.m. A sweetheart; a beloved.

دل آزار dil āzār, adj. Vexing; cruel; tormenting.

دل آزاری dil āzāri, n.f. Vexing of the heart; anxiety; trouble.

دل آنا dil ānā, v. To fall in love (with).

دل آور، دلاور dil āwar, dilāwar, adj. Intrepid; brave; valiant; bold; courageous.

دل آوری، دلاوری dil āwari, dilāwari, n.f. Boldness; heroism; valour.

دل آویز، دلاویز dil āwez, dilāwez, adj. Attractive; captivating, pleasing.

دلاویزی dilāwezī, n.f. Attractiveness; attraction; allurement.

دل اچٹنا dil uchaṭnā, v. To be disgusted; to be weary.

دل اچاٹ ہونا dil uchāṭ honā, v. To be tired; to be disgusted; to be weary.

دل باغ باغ ہونا dil bāgh bāgh honā, v. To be highly pleased.

دل بجھنا dil bujhnā, v. To be disappointed; to be dispirited.

دلبر dilbar, adj. Heart-ravisher; lovely; attractive; beloved; sweetheart.

دل بری dil bari, n.f. Loveliness; comfort; pacification.

دل برا کرنا dil burā karnā, v. To take offence; to take ill; to become displeased.

دل برا ہونا dil burā honā, v. To be displeased; to be offended; to be inclined to vomit.

دل برداشتہ ہونا dil bardāshtah honā, v. To be disgusted; to be averse.

دل بڑھانا dil baṛhānā, v. To encourage; to give one heart.

دل بستگی dil bastagi, n.f. Affliction or anguish of mind; attachment; friendship; love.

دل بند dil band, adj. Charming; attractive.

دل بھر آنا dil bhar ānā, v. To be on the verge of weeping; to have a tendency to cry.

دل بھر جانا dil bhar jānā, v. To be satiated; to be satisfied; to be sick of.

دل بہلانا dil bahlānā, v. To amuse; to divert; to entertain.

دل بہلنا dil bahalnā, v. To be amused; to be diverted.

دل بیٹھ جانا dil baiṭh jānā, v. Sinking of the heart; to be dispirited.

دل پسند، دل پذیر *dil pasand, dil pazir, adj.* Pleasant; agreeable.

دل پھٹنا *dil phaṭnā, v.* To break one's heart.

دل پھرنا *dil phirnā, v.* To be disgusted; to be sick of.

دل تڑپنا *dil taṛpnā, v.* To be anxiously eager for; to be dying for.

دل تنگ *dil tang, adj.* Distressed; sorrowful; sad; miserly; close-fisted.

دل توڑنا *dil toṛnā, v.* To dishearten; to disappoint; to mortify.

دل ٹھکنا *dil ṭhuknā, v.* To be inclined (to).

دل جلا *dil jalā, adj.* Daring; bold; courageous; loving.

دل جمعی *dil jama'ī, n.f.* Satisfaction; security; peace; assurance; care of mind; confidence.

دل جمعی کرنا *dil jama'ī karnā, v.* To give satisfaction; to satisfy one.

دل جمنا *dil jamnā, v.* To have satisfaction; to have assurance; to be attentive.

دل جوئی *dil jo'ī, n.f.* Making every effort to please.

دل جوئی کرنا *dil jo'ī karnā, v.* To try to please; to comfort.

دل چرانا *dil churānā, v.* To steal the heart (of); to abstain from an enterprise; to evade; to avoid; to shirk.

دل چسپ *dil chasp, adj.* Interesting; pleasing; alluring; charming; delightful; pleasant; entertaining.

دل چسپی لینا *dil chaspī lenā, v.* To take interest or delight in.

دل چلا *dil chalā, adj.* Brave; enterprising; resolute; generous.

دل خراش *dil kharāsh, adj.* Heart rending; vexacious; grieved to the heart; excruciating.

دل خواہ *dil khwāh, adj.* Beloved; desirable.

دل خوش کرنا *dil khūsh kernā, v.* To please; to gladden the heart (of); to enjoy.

دل دادہ *dil dādah, adj.* Lover; enamoured (of).

دل دار *dil dār, adj.* Possessing or delighting the heart; charming; beloved; sweetheart. *n.m.* A lover; a sweetheart.

دل داری *dil dārī, n.f.* Consolation.

دلداری کرنا *dil dārī karnā, v.* To console; to show kindness; to encourage.

دل دکھانا *dil dukhānā, v.* To hurt one's feelings.

دل دوز *dil doz, adj.* Heart-piercing; heart-rending.

دل دھلنا *dil dihalnā, v.* To fear; to be frighten; to palpitate.

دل دھی *dil dihī, n.f.* Encouragement; consolation; solace; attention.

دل دینا *dil denā, v.* To lose one's heart; to fall in love (with).

دل ربا *dil rubā, adj.* Fascinating; bewitching; alluring; heart-ravishing. *n.m.* A sweetheart.

دل ربائی *dil rubā'ī, n.f.* Allurement; charm.

دل رکھنا *dil rakhnā, v.* To please; to comfort; to console; to conciliate; to encourage.

دل سوختہ *dil sokhtah, adj.* Grieved; afflicted; suffering.

دل سوز *dil soz, adj.* Heart-burning; moving; touching; pathetic; passionate; ardent; ferment.

دل سے آترنا *dil se utarnā, v.* To be banished from one's heart; to be disliked.

دل شاد *dil shād, adj.* Cheerful; glad; happy.

دل شکستہ *dil shikastah, adj.* Broken-hearted; comfortless.

دل فریب *dil fareb, adj.* Heart-alluring; beautiful; charming; lovely; enticing; fascinating.

دل فگار *dil figār, adj.* Melancholy; mournful; pensive.

دل کڑا کرنا *dil kara karnā, v.* To summon up courage, to harden the heart.

دل کش *dil kash, adj.* Attractive; winning; lovely; alluring; fascinating; charming.

دل کشا *dil kushā, adj.* Pleasing; delightful.

دل گداز *dil gudāz, adj.* Heart-dissolving; pitiful.

دل گردہ *dil gurdah, n.m.* Courage; valour.

دل گیر *dil gir, adj.* Melancholy; oppressed in mind; low-spirited; sad; afflicted; occupying or captivating the heart.

دل گیری *dil giri, n.f.* Sadness; sorrow; affliction; concern.

دل لگانا *dil lagana, v.* To be attracted by; to be in love; to be amused.

دل لگنا *dil lagnā, v.* To be enamoured (of); to be charmed; to be in love.

دل لگی *dil lagi, n.f.* Amusement; merriment; jolling; diversion; attachment; inclination.

دل لینا *dil lena, v.* To win the heart (of); to ascertain the wishes (of).

دل مسوس کر رہ جانا *dil masos kar rah jana,* To bear patiently; to suffer in silence.

دل میں رکھنا *dil men rakhna, v.* To keep something secret; to bear a thing in mind.

دل میں گھر کرنا *dil men ghar karna, v.* To take one's heart; to become intimate; to contract intimate friendship.

دل نشیں کرنا *dil nashin karna, v.* To impress upon the mind.

دلنواز *dil nawaz, adj.* Soothing the mind; fascinating; attractive.

دل والا *dil walā, adj.* Generous; brave.

دل و جان سے *dil-ō jān se, adv.* Heartily; willingly.

دل ھی دل میں *dil hi dil men, adv.* In the inmost heart; secretly.

ایک دل ھو کر *ek dil ho kar, adv.* With one heart; unanimously.

دل *dal* (H) *n m.* A large army; crowd; mob; thickness.

دل بادل *dal bādal, n.m.* A mass of clouds; a large army; a large tent; a large pavilion.

دل دار *dal dār, adj.* Thick; fleshy; full of flesh

دلار *dulār* (H) *n.m.* Fondness; love; affection; endearment.

دلارا ، دلاری *dulāra, dulārī, adj.* Dear; darling; sweetheart; beloved; apple of the eye.

دلاسا *dilāsā* (P) *n.m.* Consolation; comfort; encouragement.

دلاسا دینا *dilāsā denā, v.* To console; to soothe; to encourage; to comfort.

دلال *dallāl* (A) *n.m.* A broker; a salesman; an agent.

دلالت *dalālat* (A) *n.f.* Token; indication; sign; proof; guidance; evidevce; argument.

دلالت کرنا *dalālat karnā, v.* To point; to show; to guide; to denote; to argue; to indicate; to prove; to allude (to).

دلالہ *dallalah* (A) *n.f.* Procuress; a go-between.

دلالی *dallāl'i n.f.* Business of a broker; brokerage.

دلانا *dilāna* (H) *v.* To cause to give; to cause to pay; to assign; to cause to yield; to put in possession.

دلائی *dulā'i* (H) *n.f.* A quilt; a double sheet.

دلائل *dalā'il* (A) *n.m.* (*plu.* of دلیل *dalīl*) Reasons; proofs; arguments.

دلتی *dulatti* (H) *n.f.* A kick (with the hind legs of a quadruped).

دلتی مارنا *dulatti mārnā, v.* To kick with the hind legs (quadruped).

دلدر *daliddar* (H) *n.m.* Poverty; pouperism; refuse; bad fate; misfortune.

دلدل ***duldul*** (A) *n.m.* Th name of the mule of *Hazrat 'Ali*, which was given to him by the Holy Prophet.

دلدل ***daldal*** (H) *n.f.* Marsh; quagmire; bog; swamp.

دلدلی ***daldāli*** (H) *adj.* Swampy; boggy.

دلق ***dalq*** (A) *n.f.* A mendicant's habit made of patches and shreds; a patched garment.

دلق پوش ***dalq posh***, *adj.* Clothed in rags or patched garment.

دلکی ***dulki*** (H) *n.f.* Trot (of a horse).

دلنا ***dalnā*** (H) *v.* To grind coarsely; to split pulse.

دلوانا ***dalwānā*** (H) *v.* To cause to be coarsely ground.

دلوانا ***dilwānā*** (H) *v.* To cause to give or to pay.

دلها ***dulhā*** (H) *n.m.* A bridegroom.

دلهن ***dulhan*** (H) *n.f.* A bride; newly wedded women.

دلی ***dili*** (P) *adj.* Hearty; cordial.

دلیا ***dalyā*** (H) *n.m.* Half-ground or coarsely pounded grain; coarse meal; wheat &c cooked after pounding.

دلیر ***daler*** (P) *adj.* Bold; daring; intrepid; courageous; valiant; animated; insolent; presumptuous.

دلیرانه ***dalerānah*** (P) *adv.* Boldly; bravely; intrepidly.

دلیری ***daleri*** (P) *n.f.* Bravery; valour; boldness; courage; intrepidity.

دلیل ***dalīl*** (A) *n.f.* Argument; reason; proof; demonstration.

دلیل پیش کرنا ***dalīl pesh karnā***, *v.* To bring forward proof or argument.

دلیل لانا ***dalīl lānā***, *v.* To adduce proofs; to argue; to plead.

دم ***dam*** (A) *n.m.* Blood.

دم الاخوین ***dam-ul-akhwain*** (A) *n.m.* Dragon's blood; a gum used as a medicine.

دم ***dam*** (P) *n.m.* Breath; life; vitality; energy; spirit; a moment; a pull of *ḥūqqā*; a whift; deceit; wheedling; trick; the edge of a sword; the point of a spear.

دم اُلٹنا ***dam ulatnā***, *v.* To gasp; to be suffocated; to be confused.

دم باز ***dam bāz***, *adj.* Artful; treacherous. *n.m.* A deceiver; a wheedler.

دم بخود ***dam bakhūd***, *adj.* Silent; struck dumb; aghast.

دم بخود هونا ***dam bakhud honā***, *v.* To be confounded; to be pertified.

دم بدم ***dam badam***, *adv.* Every moment; continually; constantly; breath by breath.

دم بند کرنا ***dam band karnā***, *v.* To silence (one).

دم بند هونا ***dam band honā***, *v.* To hold one's breath; to be unable to speak or answer.

دم بھر کو ***dam bhar ko***, *adv.* For a moment.

دم بھر میں ***dam bhar men***, *adv.* In a second; in a moment.

دم بھرنا ***dam bharnā***, *v.* To sing the praises of; to laud; to take the side of; to help undeservedly; to believe; to acknowledge; to confess.

دم پخت ***dam pukht***, *n.m.* A stew; simmering; cooking in steam or slow fire.

دم پھولنا ***dam phūlnā***, *v.* To pant; to gasp; to breathe short; to be exhausted.

دم پھونکنا ***dam phuṅknā***, *v.* To breathe; to inspire.

دم توڑنا ***dam toṛnā***, *v.* To breathe one's last; to die.

دم خم ***dam kham***, *n.m.* Edge or temper (of a blade); strength; vigour; stamina.

دم دلاسا dam dilāsā, n.m. False-hope; flattering words; make-believe; soothing; encouragement; comfort; coaxing.

دم دینا dam denā, v. To temper steel; to give one's life; to die; to deceive; to coax; to wheedle; to inveigle; to allow to simmer or stew.

دم رکنا dam ruknā, v. To be suffocated; to be choked.

دم سادھنا dam sādhnā, v. To hold one's breath (as faqirs do for hours on end).

دم ساز damsāz, n.m. A friend; an intimate friend; a companion; one singing or reciting together. adj. Concordant; harmonious; agreeing in sentiment; assenting; intimate.

دم سوکھنا ، خشک ہونا dam sūkhnā, khushk honā, v. To be terribly afraid (of); to have no courage left.

دم شمشیر dam-ĕ shamshir, n.m. The edge of a sword.

دم قدم dam qadam, n.m. Life and motion; existence; health and strength.

دم کرنا dam karnā, v. To blow; to repeat incantations over.

دم کش dam kash, adj. Drawing in the breathe; breathing; gasping; keeping silent.

دم کھینچنا dam kheṅchnā, v. To remain breathless; to remain silent; to smoke; to suspend breath.

دم لگانا dam lagānā, v. To smoke; to have a pull at the huqqa.

دم لینا dam lenā, v. To rest oneself; to halt; to take breath.

دم مارنا dam mārnā, v. To utter a word or breath; to speak; to boast of.

دم میں آنا dam meṅ ānā, v. To be cheated; to be deceived; to be simmered.

دم میں دم آنا dam meṅ dam ānā, v. To recover from a faint; to return to one's senses; to revive.

دم نہ مارنا dam nah mārnā, v. Not to be able to say a word.

دم dum (P) n.f. Tail; end.

دم چھلا dum chhallā, n.m. Tail of a paper-kite; one who is always at the heels of another; a hanger-on.

دم دبا کر یا نوک دم بھاگنا dum dabā kar yā nok dum bhāgnā, v. To run away; to turn tail; to flee.

دم دبانا dum dabānā, v. To put the tail between the legs; to drop the tail and run (as a dog).

دم ہلانا dum hilānā, v. To wag the tail (as a dog); to be faithful.

دماغ dimāgh (A) n.m. Brain; head; intellect; mind; pride; haughtiness; airs; conceit; intoxication.

دماغ آسمان پر کرنا dimāgh āsmān par karnā, v. To be exceedingly proud or haughty.

دماغ پریشان کرنا dimāgh pareshān karnā, v. To produce a confused state of mind; to bother.

دماغ تازہ کرنا dimāgh tāzah karnā, v. To refresh one's brain; to have mental enjoyment.

دماغ چاٹنا dimāgh chātna, v. To talk foolishly; to prattle; to prate; to jabber.

دماغ چٹ dimāgh chaṭ, adj. Talkative person.

دماغ سوزی کرنا dimāgh sozi karna, v. To cudgel one's brain.

دماغ دار dimāgh dār, adj. Haughty; proud; arrogant; disdainful.

دماغ کرنا dimāgh karnā, v. To be proud or haughty; to be vain; to put on airs; to be insolent.

دماغ میں خلل ہونا dimāgh meṅ khalal honā, v. To suffer from a brain disease; to have the brain deranged.

دماغ ہونا dimāgh honā, v. To be vain; to be proud; to be haughty.

عالی دماغ 'ālī dimāgh, adj. High minded.

دماغی dimāghi (A) adj. Of the brain; mental.

دماغی پریشانی dimāghi pareshāni, n.f. Mental worry.

دمامہ damāmah (P) n.m. A kettle-drum; noise; pomp and glory.

دمچی dumchi (P) n.f. A crupper; the lower part of the back.

دمدمہ damdamah (P) n.m. A mound; a raised battery; an entrenchment; a heap of earth (as a mole makes); a cavalier; report.

دمڑی damṛī (H) n.f. The third part of a paisā; a nominal coin; 25 kachchā bighās.

دمڑی کے تین تین ہونا damṛi ke tin tin honā, v. To sell dirt cheap; to be reduced to abject poverty; to be ruined; to be demolished.

دمڑی کی بڑھیا ٹکا سر منڈائی damṛi kī būṛhyā ṭakā sar munḍā'ī, prov. Paying much attention to a very minor and unimportant matter. It is easier to build a new house then to patch an old one.

دمک damak (H) n.f. Glitter; flush; ordour; flash; bloom.

دمکنا damaknā (H) v. To glow; to shine; to glare; to glitter; to bloom.

دمل dummal (P) n.m. See دنبل dumbal.

دمن daman (P) n.m. A foot of a mountain (contraction of دامن dāman).

دموی damawi (A) adj. Plethoric; of or relating to the blood.

دمہ damah (P) n.m. Asthma; a pair of bellows.

دمی dami (P) n.f. A kind of small tobacco pipe or huqqah.

دمیدہ damidah (P) adj. Blown or blossomed; shot forth; opened out; blossoming; broken forth (the dawn of day); vegetated (a plant).

دن din (H) n.m. Day; day-time; time; circumstances; lot; fate; period of life; age.

دن آنا din ānā, v. To arrive (the time or season for); to be numbered (one's days); to have monthly courses.

دن اندھا din āndhā, adj. Blind in day-time; day-blind.

دن بھاری ہونا din bhāri honā, v. To be in straitened circumstances; to lead a hard life.

دن بھر din bhar, adv. The whole day; all the day long.

دن پورے کرنا din pūre karnā, v. To drag out one's days; to pass one's days as best as one can.

دن پھرنا din phirnā, v. To begin to have better times; to take a favourable turn.

دن چڑھنا din charhnā, v. To dawn (day); to rise (sun).

دن چڑھے din chaṛhe, adv. Late in the day.

دن چھپنا din chhupnā, v. Setting of the sun; approaching of the night.

دن دونی اور رات چوگنی ترقی کرنا din dūnī aur rāt chaugnī taraqqi karnā, v. To prosper by leaps and bounds; to have great luck in life.

دن دھاڑے din dhāṛe, adv. In broad day light; in day-time; in public; openly.

دن ڈھلنا din ḍhalnā, v. Going down (of the sun).

دن ڈھلے din ḍhale, adv. In the evening; in the afternoon.

دن عید رات شب برات din 'id rāt shab-ĕ barāt, v. Rejoicing by day and by night; merry-making all the twenty four hours.

دن عیش کے گھڑیوں میں گزر جاتے ھیں din 'aish ke gharyoṅ meṅ guzar jāte haiṅ, prov. Pleasant hours fly fast.

دن کاٹنا din kāṭnā, v. To pass one's days in hardship or pain; to pass one's days willy-nilly; hardship.

دن کٹنا katnā, v. Passing of the days in difficutlty.

دن کو دن اور رات کو رات نہ سمجھنا din ko din aur rāt ko rāt nah samajhnā, v. To take no notice of time; to be working day and night; to be working very hard.

دن نکلنا din nikalnā, v. To dawn; to rise (sun).

بڑے دن baṛe din, n.m. Christmas time; longer days.

دنایت danāyat (A) n.f. Meanness; baseness.

دنباله dumbālah (P) n.m. A tail; the outer angle or corner of the eye; the stern of a vessel.

دنباله دار dumbālah dār, adj. Tailed; having a tail.

دنبل duṅbal (P) n.m. An abscess; a boil; a bubo.

دنبه dumbah (P) n.m. A kind of sheep with a thick fatty tail.

دندان daṅdān (P) n.m. A tooth.

دندان شکن جواب دینا daṅdān shikan jawāb denā, v. To silence a person; to make a crushing reply.

دندان مصری dandān-ĕ misrī, n.f. Barley-sugar.

دندانه dandānah (P) n.m. The tooth of a saw.

دندنانا daṅdanānā (H) v. To be in high spirits; to sing for joy; to be contented and independent.

دنگ daṅg (P) adj. Astonished; struck; distressed; careless; foolish.

دنگ رہ جانا daṅg rah jānā, v. To be astonished.

دنگا daṅgā (H) n.m. A rcw; a riot; quarrel; disturbance; breach of the peace; wrangling; tumult; confusion.

دنگا کرنا daṅgā karnā, v. To make a disturbance; running riot; to incite to rebellion.

دنگل daṅgal (H) n.m. A tumultous assembly; a crowd; a wrestling arena; an amphic theatre.

دنگل لڑنا daṅgal laṛnā, v. To wrestle; to have a wrestling bout.

دنی danī (A) adj. Mean; low; vile; base; ignoble.

دنیا dunyā (A) n.f. The world; life or people of this world; worldly goods; the good things of this life; wealth.

دنیا دار dunyā dār, adj. Worldly; a person of the world.

دنیا داری dunyā dārī, n.f. Worldly affairs; worldly goods; worldliness; intercourse; a show of politeness; attention to worldly concerns.

دنیا ساز dunyā sāz, adj. Showy; ostentatious; formal; crafty; cunning.

دنیا و مافیها dunyā-ŏ māfihā, n.f. The world and all that is in it.

دنیاوی، دنیوی dunyāwī, dunyawī, adj. Belonging to the world; worldly.

دو do, (H) du (P) adj. Two.

دو آبه do ābah, n.m. A tract of land lying between two rivers.

دو آتشه do ātishah, adj. Double-distilled; a superior quality wine.

دو اسپه do aspah, n.f. A relay of two horses; carriage drawn by two horses.

دو انی do annī, n.f. A two-anna bit; the eighth part of a rupee.

دوباره *dobārah*, *adv*. Twice; doubly; a second time; again.

دو بدو *du bado*, *adv*. Face to face; confronting; in the presence of.

دو بلدا *du baldā*, *n.m*. A cart drawn by two bullocks.

دو پایه *do pāyah*, *adj*. Two-legged; biped; *n.m.* man.

دوپٹا *dopaṭṭā*, *n.m*. A wrapper; a cloth thrown loosely over the head and shoulders by women.

دوپلڑی *dopalṛi*, *n.f*. An Indian cap consisting of two pieces.

دوپہر *dopahar*, *n.f*. Midday; noon.

دو پہر ڈھلے *dopahar ḍhale*, *adj*. Past meridian; P.M.

دو پیازہ *do payāzah*, *n.m*. A kind of dish in which a double quantity of onion is used, and which has little or no gravy.

دو تا *do tā*, *adj*. Doubled; bent.

دو تارا *do tārā*, *n.m*. A kind of shawl; a guitar of two strings.

دو تہی *do tahī*, *n.f*. A cloth having two folds (used for lying upon).

دو ٹوک *do ṭok*, *adj*. Two-pieced; clear; plain; decisive.

دو ٹوک جواب دینا *do ṭok jawāb denā*, *v*. To give a short and decisive answer; to give a flat refusal.

دو چار ہونا *do chār honā*, *v*. To meet; to face; to have an interview.

دو چند *do chand*, *adj*. Two fold; double.

دو دن کا مہمان *do din kā mehmān*, *adj*. Transient; passing away.

دو دھارا *do dhārā*, *adj*. A double-edged sword.

دو راہا *do rāhā*, *n.m*. A bi-secting road; a road dividing into two leading different ways.

دو رخا *do rukẖā*, *adj*. Double faced; facing both sides; the same on both sides.

دو رسا *do rasā*, *n.m*. A mixture of two kinds of tobacco.

دو رنگا *do rangā*, *adj*. Capricious; double-dealer; hypocrite; of two colours; piebald.

دو رنگی *do raṅgī*, *adj*. Having two colours; *n.f*. duplicity; hypocrisy; double-dealing.

دو روزہ *do rozah*, *adj*. (The space of two days) short-lived; transient.

دو رویہ *do royah*, *adj*. Two faced; hypocrite; on both sides, right and left (row of houses; trees &c).

دو زانو بیٹھنا *do zānū baiṭhnā*, *v*. To sit on the hams; to squat.

دو سالہ *do sālah*, *adj*. Of two years; two years old; biennial; lands that have been under cultivation for two years.

دو سوتی *do sūti*, *n.f*. A kind of cloth, the threads of which are double.

دو سیری *do seri*, *n.f*. A weight of two seers.

دو شاخہ *do shākẖah*, *n.m*. The fork of a tree; a pair of legs.

دو شالہ *do shālah*, *n.m*. A pair of shawls.

دو شنبہ *do shambah*, *n.m*. Monday.

دو طرفہ *do ṯarfah*, *adj*. Two-sided; mutual.

دو عملی *do 'amali*, *n.f*. The rule of two masters; dyarchy.

دو غزلہ *do ghazlah*, *n.m*. Two peoms of the same metre and rhyme.

دو فصلی ، دو ساکھی *do faṣli*, *do sākhi*, *n.f*. Land yielding two crops in a year, or a tree bearing fruit twice a year.

دو کرنا *do karnā*, *v*. To cut in two; to bisect.

دو گانہ *do gānah*, *n.m*. See دگانہ *dugānah*.

دو لتی *do lattī*, *n.f*. See دلتی *dulatti*.

دو معنی *do ma'nī*, *adj*. Having two meanings (also ذو معنی *ẕu ma'nī*).

دو منزلہ *do manzilah*, *adj*. Of two storeys (a house); of two decks (a ship).

دو مونہی do mūṅhī, n.f. A serpant having two mouths.

دو نالی do nālī, n.f. A double-barelled gun.

دو نیم do nīm, adj. Two halves; divided in two.

دو ہتڑ do hattar, n.m. Beating with both hands together; giving a slap with both hands.

دو ہتھا ، دو ہتھی do hathā, do hathhī, adj. Having two handles.

دوا duā (H) n.m. The two or deuce at cards; dice.

دوا dawā (A) n.f. Medicine; remedy; a cure.

دوا خانہ dawā k͟hānah, n.m. A dispensary; an apothecary's shop.

دوا دارو dawā dārū, n.f. Medical treatment; remedy; cure.

دوا دارو کرنا dawā dārū karnā, v. To treat a patient.

دوا ساز dawā sāz, n.m. A compounder (of medicines); a dispenser.

دوا فروش dawā farosh, n.m. A druggist.

دوا کرنا dawā karnā, v. To undergo medical treatment; to cure; to heel.

دوات dawāt (A) n.f. An inkpot.

دوار davvār (A) adj. Moving; revolving.

دوارا، دوار dwārā, dwār (H) n.m. A gate; a door; place; way.

دوالا diwālā (H) n.m. See دیوالا dewālā.

دوام dawām (A) n.m. Perpetuity; lasting; perseverance; permanence. adv. Always; eternally; perpetually.

دوامی dawāmī (A) adj. Permanent; lasting; constant; continual; continuous; incessant; perennial.

دواں dawāṅ (P) adj. Running.

دوائر dawā'ir (A) n.m. (plu. of دائرہ dā'irah); Circles.

دوب dūb (H) n.f. A kind of fine, soft, green grass.

دوبھر dūbhar (H) adj. Difficult; burdensome; troublesome.

دوج dūj (H) n.f. The second day of lunar fortnight.

دوجا dūjā (H) adj. Second; secondary.

دود dūd (P) n.m. Smoke; vapour; haze.

دود کش dūd kash, n.m. Chimney.

دود ماں dūd māṅ (P) n.m. A noble family; a great tribe; house; race or generation.

دودھ dūdh (H) n.m. Milk; the juice or milk of certain plants.

دودھ بڑھانا dūdh barhānā, v. To wean (a child).

دودھ بھائی dūdh bhā'ī, n.m. A foster-brother.

دودھ پلانا dūdh pilānā, v. To suckle.

دودھ پلائی dūdh pilā'ī, n.f. A wet nurse.

دودھ پیتا بچہ dūdh pītā bachchah, n.m. An infant; inexperienced person.

دودھ چھڑانا dūdh chhuṛānā, v. See دودھ بڑھانا dūdh baṛhānā.

دودھ دھنا dūdh dohnā, v. To milk.

دودھ کا دودھ پانی کا پانی کرنا dūdh kā dūdh pānī kā pānī karnā, v. To seperate chalk from cheese; to dispense God's justice.

دودھوں نہاؤ اور پوتوں پھلو dūdhoṅ nahāo aur pūtoṅ phalo, intj. May God give you wealth and children.

دودھار، دودھل dūdhār, dūdhl (H) adj. See ددھار dudhār

دودھیا dūdhyā (H) adj. Giving milk; milky; white; raw; unripe; bhang mixed with milk.

دور dūr (P) adj. Distant; remote; far; at a distance.

دور از کار dūr az kār, adj. Unconcerned.

دور آفتادہ dūr uftādah, adj. Remote; far off.

دور اندیش dūr andesh, adj. Far-sighted; prudent; farseeing; provident; penetrating; circumspect; sagacious; wise.

دور اندیشی dūr andeshī, n.f. Farsightedness; circumspection; carerfulness.

دور باش dūr bāsh, intj. Be off ! avaunt !

دور بھاگنا dūr bhāgnā, v. To run away from; to shun; to abstain from; to abhor; to avoid.

دور بین dūr bīn, n.m. A telescope; a spy-glass. adj. Having the quality of seeing distant objects; far-seeing; far-sighted; prudent; provident; ingenious.

دور بینی dūr bīnī, n.f. Fore-sight; prudence.

دور دراز dūr darāz, adj. Very far off; very distant; long.

دور دور dūr dūr, adj. At a great distance.

دور رہنا dūr rahnā, v, To remain at a distance; to keep at arm's length.

دور کرنا dūr karnā, v. To dispel; to remove; to dispossess; to avert; to dismiss; to turn out.

دور کی سوجھنا dūr kī sūjhnā, v. To see a long way off; to hit upon a novel idea.

دور ہونا dūr honā, v. To be removed; to be dispelled.

دور کے ڈھول سہانے dūr ke ḍhol sohāne, prov. Distant drums are gratifying.

دور daur (A) n.m. Revolving; revolution (of a body or of time); passing round (cups of wine); circular motion; a kind of argument (reasoning in a circle); age; period; cycle; tour; turn; time; circuit; vicissitude; course; circumference; orbit; circulation.

دور دورہ daur daurah, n.m. Rule; sway; jurisdiction; dominion; reign.

دوران daurān (A) n.m. Time; age; fortune; vicissitude; a revolution; period; circle; cycle; pendency; duration.

دوران خون daurān-ĕ khūn, n.m. Circulation of blood.

دوران سر daurān-ĕ sar, n.m. A swimming in the head; dizziness; giddiness; vertigo.

دورہ daurah (A) n.m. Circuit; tour; revolution; turn.

دورہ کرنا daurah karnā, v. To go on tour; to tour about; to review.

دوری dūrī (P) n.f. Distance; remoteness; absence; separation; farness.

دوڑ dauṛ (H) n.f. Run; incursion; attack; assault; endeavour; struggle; effort; race; running; course; career; military expedition; raid.

دوڑ دھوپ dauṛ dhūp, n.f. Running about; toil and bustle; very great effort.

دوڑ دھوپ کرنا dauṛ dhūp karnā, v. To toil hard; to bustle; to run hither and thither.

دوڑانا dauṛānā (H) v. To cause to run; to make a horse gallop; to drive; to impel; to actuate; to speed; to send in pursuit; to give wings to thoughts; to soar on the wings of fancy.

دوڑنا dauṛnā (H) v. To run fast; to gallop; to go fast; to attack; to rush at; to circulate; to fall upon; to pervade (as poison in the system).

دوز doz (P) adj. Sewing; piercing (used in comp. as, خیمہ دوز khaimah doz, a tent-maker زر دوز zar doz, an embroiderer).

دوزخ dozakh (P) n.m./f. Hell; the belly.

دوزخی dozakhī (P) adj. Hellish; infernal; damned; a dweller in hell; sinner; glutton; greedy.

دوست dost (P) n.m. A friend; a lover; a sweetheart.

دوست رکھنا dost rakhnā, v. To hold dear; to love; to like a person.

دوست نما دشمن dost numā dushman, n.m. A secret enemy; a snake in the grass; an enemy in disguise.

دوست نواز dost ṇawāz, n.m. A cherisher of friends.

دوستانہ dostānah (P) adv. Friendly; amicably; affectionately; n.m. Friendliness.

دوستی dosti (P) n.f. Friendship; affection; amity; attachment.

دوستی کا دم بھرنا dosti kā dam bharnā, v. To affect friendship; to pretend to be a friend; to make a boast of friendship for.

دوسرا ، دوسری dūsrā, dūsri (H) adj. Second; next; other; equal; match; a duplicate; the following (day).

دوسرے dūsre (H) adv. Secondly; in the second place; again; on the other hand.

دوش dosh (P) n.m. Shoulder; last night.

دوش بدوش dosh badosh, adv. Shoulder to shoulder.

دوش dosh (H) n.m. Fault; blame, defect; columny; offence; wrong; sin.

دوش لگانا dosh lagānā, v. To accuse one of an offence; to blame; to columniate.

دوشمال doshmāl (P) n.m. A towel or duster used by butchers, grooms &c.

دوشیزگی doshizagi (P) n.f. Virginity; maidenhood.

دوشیزہ doshizah (P) n.f. Virgin; spinster.

دوشینہ doshinah (P) adj. Of last night. n.m. A shoulder's load; what is carried on the shoulder.

دوغ dogh (P) n.m./f. Butter-milk; curd; churned milk.

دوغلا ، دوغلی doghlā, doghli adj. Mixed; cross-bred; mongrel.

دول dowel, diwal, duwal (plu. of دولت daulat); Wealth; riches; countries; kingdoms.

دولت daulat (A) n.f. Riches; happiness; felicity; fortune; prosperity; empire; state; country; cause; means.

دولت خانہ daulat khānah, n.m. A mansion; a palace; a house (in a polite sense).

دولت مند daulat mand, n.m. A wealthy person. adj. Wealthy; rich; opulent.

دولت مندی daulat mandi, n.f. Wealth; opulence; prosperity; happiness; riches.

بدولت badolat, adv. By means of; by the favour of; by the good fortune of.

در دولت dar-ĕ daulat, n.m. Threshold of a house.

نو دولت nau daulat, n.m. An upstart; one who has become rich overnight.

دولھا dūlhā (H) n.m. See دلھا dulhā.

دوم dowum (P) adj. Second; inferior.

دون dūn (H) n.f. Boasting; vanity.

دون کی لینا dūn ki lenā, v. To boast; to brag; to be braging habitually.

دون dūn (A) adj. Base; vile; ignoble; mean; inferior; contemptible.

دون ہمت dūn himmat, adj. Maan-spirited; low-minded.

دونا daunā (H) n.m. Leaves folded up in the shape of a cup, for holding sweetmeats etc.

دونا dūnā (H) adj. Double; two-fold; twice as much.

دونوں donoṅ (H) adj. Both; both of them.

دوھا dohā (H) n.m. A Hindi couplet; distich.

دوھائی dohā'i (H) adj. Crying out for justice; a cry for help and mercy; exclamation; plaint.

دوھائی مچانا dohā'i machānā, v. To cry repeatedly for justice or help; to make reiterated complaints.

دوھتا dohtā (H) n.m. A daughter's son.

دوھتی dohtī (H) n.f. A daughter's daughter.

دوھرا dohrā (H) adj. Double; twice; two-folds.

دوھرا ھو جانا dohrā ho jānā, v. To be doubled up or bent.

دوھرانا dohrānā (H) v. To repeat or do something over again; to revise; to reduplicate.

دوھنا dohnā (H) v. To milk.

دوھنی dohni (H) n.f. A milk pail.

دوئی dū'ī (P) n.f. Being two or two-fold; duality; a second; another; disunion; strangeness.

دہ deh (P) n.m. A village.

دہ بندی deh bandi, n.f. A detailed statement of villages, and their assessments.

دہ dah (P) adj. Ten.

دہ چند dah chand, adj. Ten times; ten-fold.

دہ در دنیا صد در آخرت dah dar dunyā sad dar ākhirat, prov. Ten spent in charity in this world will be rewarded with a hundred in the next; charity will be returned ten times more in the next world.

دھات dhāt (H) n.f. Ore; metal; mineral; fossil; semen.

دھار dhār (H) n.f. Edge (of a sword); sharpness; stream; current; line; a strain of milk, oil, etc.

دھار دار dhār dār, adj. Sharp; edged.

دھار نکالنا dhār nikālnā, v. To sharpen; to produce an edge.

دھارا dhārā (H) n.m. A stream; a current; a water-course; a channel.

دھارنا dhārnā (H) v. To hold; to bear; to wear; to disguise; to keep; to place; to sustain; to support; to uphold; to pour (water).

دھاری dhārī (H) n.f. A line; lineament; a stripe; a streak.

دھاری دار dhārī dār, adj. Lined; striped; streaked.

دھاڑ dhāṛ, dahāṛ (H) n.f. A loud cry; thundering; roar.

دھاڑیں مار کر رونا dhāren mār kar ronā, v. To weep bitterly; to cry aloud.

دھاڑنا dahāṛnā (H) v. To roar (as a tiger).

دھاڑی dihāri (H) n.f. Daily wages; remuneration.

دھاک dhāk (H) n.f. Pomp; glory; renown; fame; fear; terror

دھاک باندھنا ، بٹھانا dhāk bāndhnā, biṭhānā, v. To establish the fame of; to be very famous; to be held in awe.

دھاکا dahākā (H) n.m. Tens; the place of tens in arithmetic; fear; shock; terror.

دھاگا dhāgā (H) n.m. Thread.

دھاگا ڈالنا dhāgā ḍālnā, v. To thread a needle.

دھان dahān (P) n.m. The mouth; an orifice.

دھان dhān (H) n.m. The rice plant; paddy; rice in the husk.

دھاندل dhāṅdal (H) n.f. Wrangling; cheating; subterfuge; trick; chicanery.

دھاندل کرنا dhāṅdal karnā, v. To cry aloud; to play false; to deal unfairly.

دھاندلی dhāṅdli (H) n.f. Trickery; cheating; sharp practices.

دھانس dhāṅs (H) n.f. Coughing from taking snuff; coughing caused by irritating or pungent substances.

دھانسنا dhāṅsnā (H) v. To cough (a horse).

دھانہ dahānah (P) n.m. The bit of a bridle; the mouth; the mouth of a water bag, river or water-course; anything which covers the mouth.

دھانی **dhānī** (H) *adj.* Light green *n.m.* A kind of rice.

دھاوا **dhāwā** (H) *n.m.* Running; over-running an enemy's country; attack; assault; a long expedition; march; crowding together; name of a tree.

دھاوا بولنا، کرنا، مارنا **dhāwā bolnā, karnā, mārnā**, *v.* To attack; to surprise; to make a long rapid march; to make a raid; to make a sudden attack; to undertake an expedition.

دھائی **dhā'ī** (H) *n.f.* The figure ten; decimal; the tenth part; the tens.

دھائی **duhā'ī** (H) *n.f.* See دوھائی *dohā'ī*.

دھبا **dhabbā** (H) *n.m.* Spot; stigma; blot; brand; a stain (on cloth, etc.).

دھبا ڈالنا، لگانا **dhabbā ḍālnā, lagānā**, *v.* To blot; to stain.

دھبا لگنا **dhabbā lagnā**, *v.* To be stained; to be branded; to be blamed.

دھپ **dhap** (H) *n.m.* Sound; clock; noise; slap; thud; thump.

دھپا **dhappā** (H) *n.m.* A slap; box; thump; blow; loss; damage; deception.

دھپا لگنا **dhappā lagnā**, *v.* To suffer a loss.

دھپا مارنا **dhappā mārnā**, *v.* To thump; to damage; to cheat; to deceive.

دھت **dhat** (H) *n.f.* Mania; a bad habit; vice.

دھت **dhut** (H) *adj.* Intoxicated. *intj.* Be off !

دھتا **dhattā** (H) *n.m.* Act of driving away; evasion; trick; deception; putting off.

دھتا بتانا **dhattā batānā**, *v.* To put off; to deceive; to turn one away.

دھتکارنا **dhutkārnā** (H) *v.* To drive out; to reprove; to revile.

دھتورا **dhatūrā** (H) *n.m.* A norcotic plant and poison. *Datura fastuosa* (thorny apple).

دھجی **dhajjī** (H) *n.f.* A strip of cloth; a rag; a shred.

دھجیاں آڑانا، بکھیرنا **dhajjiāṅ uṛānā, bakhernā**, *v.* To disgrace; to expose one to infamy; to tear in pieces; to beat black and blue.

دھچکا **dhachkā** (H) *n.m.* See دھکا *dhakkā*.

دھر **dahr** (A) *n.m.* Time; long pericd of time; an age; the world; custom; habit.

دھرا **dhurā** (H) *n.m.* An axle; the wooden portion of an axle; boundary; an axis.

دھرا **duhrā** (H) *adj.* See دوھرا *dohra*.

دھرانا **duhrānā** (H) *v.* See دوھرانا *dohrānā*.

دھرپد **dhurpad** (H) *n.f.* A kind of song; the introductory stanza of a song, which is repeated as a kind of chorus.

دھرتی **dhartī** (H) *n.f.* The earth; land; soil; ground.

دھرتی ماتا **dhartī mātā**, *n.f.* Mother earth.

دھرم **dharam** or **dharm** (S) *n.m.* Faith; religion; duty; caste; justice; virtue; righteousness; religious; obligation; piety; right dealing; good works.

دھرم آتما ، دھرماتما **dharam ātmā dharmātmā**, *adj.* Virtuous; just; pious; holy.

دھرم باپ **dharam bāp**, *n.m.* An adopted father; a godfather.

دھرم بگاڑنا **dharam bigāṛnā**, *v.* To destroy one's caste or religion.

دھرم پتنی **dharam patnī**, *n.f.* A wife who is of the same caste as her husband.

دھرم راج **dharam rāj**, *n.m.* A just ruler; a government where justice is administered.

دھرم سالہ، شالہ **dharam sālah, shālah**, *n.f.* A building used for a pious purpose; a place where alms are distributed; a rest-house for travellers and pilgrims; an alms-house.

دھرم شاستر **dharam shāstar**, *n.m.* The Hindu laws or scriptures; religious code.

دھرنا *dharnā* (H) *n.m.* The act of sitting at the door of the debtor to enforce payment of the debt; dunning.

دھرنا دینا، مارنا *dharnā denā, mārnā, v.* To enforce payment of debt by sitting doggedly at the door of the debtor.

دھرنا *dharnā* (H) *v.* To put down; to put in one's charge; to lay hold of; to keep; to apply (the mind or ear); to grasp; to assume; to have; to possess.

دھروانا *dharwānā* (H) v. To cause to place.

دھری *dhurī* (H) *n.f,* An exle; a pole; an axis.

دھریہ *dahriyah* (A) *n.m.* An atheist; a materialist; an infidel; an unbeliever.

دھڑ *dhaṛ* (H) *n.m.* The body; trunk; a drum played in the arena when a wrestler wins.

دھڑا *dhaṛā* (H) *n.m.* A weight; faction; a party; side.

دھڑا باندھنا، کرنا *dhaṛā bhāṅdhnā, karnā, v.* To balance a scale; to equipoise; to make up a party or side.

دھڑا دھڑ *dhaṛā dhaṛ* (H) *n.f.* A smart or sharp succession of sounds as of falling bodies, of blows or of firing; rattling or banging. *adv.* Successively.

دھڑام *dhaṛām* (H) *n.f.* The sound of the falling of a heavy body.

دھڑکا، دھڑکن *dhaṛkā, dhaṛkan* (H) *n.m./f.* Fear; suspense; doubt; palpitation; throb; thunder; tripidation; beat; alarm.

دھڑکنا *dhaṛaknā* (H) *v.* To palpitate; to beat (heart).

دھڑلا *dhaṛallā* (H) *n.m.* Sound of beating or hammering; a crowd; band; host; swarm; boldness; bravery.

دھڑلے سے *dhaṛalle se, adv.* Openly; fearlessly; forcibly.

دھڑی *dhaṛi* (H) *n.f.* A five-seer weight; five seers.

دھڑیوں *dhaṛyoṅ* (H) *adv.* In abundance.

دھسا *dhussā* (H) *n.m.* A coarse woollen cloth; shawl.

دھسان *dhasān* (H) *n.m.* A swamp; a bog; a slough; a quagmire.

دھسانا *dhasānā* (H) *v.* To cause to sink into.

دھسنا *dhasnā* (H) *v.* To give way; to sink; to enter, to be thrust into.

دھش *dehish* (P) *n.f.* Charity; gift; bounty; alms.

دھشت *dahshat* (A) *n.f.* Fear; terror; awe; dread.

دھشت انگیز *dahshat aṅgez, adj.* Threatening; menacing; horrible; hideous; terrifying; awe-inspiring.

دھشت زدہ *dahshat zadah, adj.* Terrified; scared; frightened; panic-stricken; terror-striken; alarmed.

دھشت کھانا *dahshat khānā, v.* To be terror-striken; to be panicky.

دھشت ناک *dahshat nāk, adj.* Frightening; alarming; dreadful.

دھقان *dahqān* (P) *n.m.* A villager; a husbandman.

دھقانی *dahqānī* (P) *adj.* Rustic; clownish; boorish; rude. *n.m.* A villeger; a peasant; a husbandman.

دھک *dhak* (H) *n.f.* Sudden impression of terror; shock; a louse.

دھک سے رہ جانا *dhak se rah jānā, v.* To become paralysed through fear; to stand aghast; to be struck dumb.

دھک دھک کرنا *dhak dhak karnā, v.* To palpitate.

دھکا *dhakkā* (H) *n.m.* A jolt; push; jostle; shock; calamity; damage; loss; a blow of misfortune or affliction.

دھکا پیل ، دھکم دھکا *dhakkā pel, dhakkam dhakkā, n.f.* Shoving and pushing; jostling.

دھکا دینا *dhakā denā, v.* To shove; to push; to turn out; to shut the door on one; to bring any calamity on one.

دھکے کھانا dhakke khānā, v. To be pushed or knocked; to wander about aimlessly; to suffer misfortune; to be kicked.

دھکا لگنا dhakkā lagnā, v. To suffer a shock; to suffer loss; to turn out ill.

دھکانا dahkānā (H) v. To burn; to kindle; to inflame.

دھکڑ پکڑ dhukar pukar (H) n.f. Palpitation; agitation; suspense.

دھکنا dahaknā (H) v. To burn; to blaze up; to be consumed with grief.

دھکیل دینا dhakel denā (H) v. To push; to shove down; to precipitate.

دھکیلنا dhakelnā (H) v. To shove; to push; to jostle.

دھگڑ ، دھگڑا dhaggar, dhagṛā (H) n.m. Husband; lover; paramour.

دھل duhal (P) n.m. A drum; a tabor.

بیانگ دھل babāng-ĕ duhal, adv. With the beat of drum.

دھل جانا dahal jānā (H) v. To fear; to be frightened; to be scared; to be shocked.

دھلا dahlā (H) n.m. The ten (at cards).

دھلا دینا، دھلانا dahlā denā, dahlānā (H) v. To frighten; to scare; to menace.

دھلائی dhulā'ī (H) n.f. Washing; price paid for washing.

دھلنا dahalnā (H) v. To tremble with fear; to be mightily afraid; to be shocked.

دھلوانا dhulwānā (H) v. To get (something) washed; to cause others to wash.

دھلیز dehlīz (P) n.f. A portico; a threshold.

دھلیز کا کتا dehlīz kā kuttā, n.m. A hanger on; a parasite.

دھم dahum (P) adj. Tenth.

دھم dham (H) n.f. A thud.

دھم سے dham se, adv. Falling heavily; unexpectedly (coming in).

دھما چوکڑی dhamā dhaukṛī (H) n.f. Noise; tumult; riot; bustle.

دھماکا dhamākā (H) n.m. The report of a gun; thud; crash; thump; a firelock; a kind of cannon carried on an elephant.

دھمک dhamak (H) n.f. Noise of footsteps overhead; thumping; throbbing; shooting pain; pulsation; fall on the ground producing a shock.

دھمکانا dhamkānā (H) v. To threaten; to menace; to chide; to over-awe.

دھمکنا dhamaknā (H) v. To throb; to shoot with pain; to make a rush; to palpitate: to thump.

دھمکی dhamkī (H) n.f. Threat; menace; snubbing; threatening.

دھمکی دینا dhamkī denā, v. To threaten; to snub.

دھمکی میں آنا dhamkī men ānā, v. To be frightened; to be over-awed; to be coerced by threats.

دھن dhun (H) n.f. Air; tune; keynote; leading note; ambition; inclination; any absorbing thought; application; diligence; preseverance; assiduity; racking pain in the bones.

دھن dhan (H) n.m. Property, wealth; fortune; riches; treasure; good fortune; prosperity; opulence.

دھن dahan (P) n.m. Mouth.

دھنا dahnā (H) adj. Right; right side; the opposite of left.

دھنا، دھننا dhunnā (H) v. To comb or to card cotton; to beat; to pound; to thrash.

سر دھننا sar dhunnā, v. To rack one's brains; to be greatly vexed; to be under sheer ecstacy.

دھند dhund (H) n.f. Mist; haze; fog; mistiness; haziness; thick cloudy weather; foul weather; dim-sightedness; purblindness.

دھندا **dhandā (H) n.m. Occupation; avocation; work; employment; business.**

دھندلا **dhundlā (H) adj. Dim; misty; foggy; dull.**

دھندلا پن **dhundlā pan, n.m. Dimness; mistiness.**

دھندلکا **dhundalkā, dhundlakā (H) n.m. Mist; light darkness.**

دھنک **dhanak (H) n.f. A rainbow; fine narrow lace: embroidery.**

دھنکنا **dhunaknā (H) v. See دھنا dhunnā.**

دھنکی **dhunki (H) n.f. The bow with which cotton is cleaned or carded.**

دھنی **dhani (H) adj. Rich; wealthy; fortunate; persevering. n.m. Owner; proprietor; a husband.**

دھنیا **dhanyā (H) n.m. Coriander seed.**

دھنیا **dhunyā (H) n.m. A carder; a comber (of cotton).**

دھواں **dhūān (H) n.m. Smoke.**

دھواں دھار **dhūāṅ dhār, adj. Smoky; misty; excessively dark; fuming; angry; fiery.**

دھوبن **dhoban (H) n.f. A washerwoman; a laundry woman; a kind of bird; wagtail.**

دھوبی **dhobī (H) n.m. A washerman; a laundrer.**

دھوبی پاٹ **dhobi pāt, n.m. A washerman's stone or board on which he beats clothes for washing; a trick in wrestling.**

دھوبی گھاٹ **dhobi ghāt, n.f. A place for washing clothes.**

دھوبی کا کتا نہ گھر کا نہ گھاٹ کا **dhobi kā kuttā nah ghar kā nah ghāt kā, prov. A dog who runs after two bones catches neither.**

دھوپ **dhūp (H) n.f. Sunshine; heat of the sun; sunlight.**

دھوپ پڑنا **dhūp parnā, v. To be sunny; to be hot**

دھوپ چڑھنا **dhūp charhnā, v. Rising of the sun; to be broad daylight.**

دھوپ چھاؤں **dhūp chhāoṅ, n.f. A kind of cloth; sunshine and shade (a kind of game played in the moonlight).**

دھوپ کھانا **dhūp khānā, v. To bask in the sun.**

دھوپ گھڑی **dhūp ghaṛi, n.f. Sun dial.**

دھوپ میں بال سفید ہونا **dhūp meṅ bāl safed honā, v. To become old without gaining experience; to pass one's life in ignorance.**

دھوپ نکلنا **dhūp nikalnā, v. To be sunny; rising or shining of the sun.**

دھوتی **dhoti (H) n.f. Loin cloth; a cloth worn round the waist, passing between the legs and fastened behind.**

دھوکا **dhokā (H) n.m. Deceit; deception; delusion; blunder; hesitation; doubt; disappointment; false appearance; a mirage; a scarecrow.**

دھوکا بازی **dhokā bāzi, n.f. Fraud; imposture.**

دھوکا دینا **dhokā denā, v. To deceive; to cheat; to make believe.**

دھوکا کھانا دھوکے میں آنا **dhokā khānā, dhoke meṅ ānā, v. To be deceived; to be taken in; to be missed; to be deceived by appearances; to make a false step.**

دھوکے کی ٹٹی **dhoke ki tatti, n.f. A false screen.**

دھوکے میں رکھنا **dhoke men rakhnā, v. To feed with false hopes or promises.**

دھول **dhūl (H) n.f. Dust.**

دھول اڑانا **dhūl urānā, v. To throw dust; to disgrace; to defame; to wander.**

دھول اڑنا **dhūl urnā, v. To be ruined; to be disgraced.**

دھول جھاڑنا **dhūl jhāṛnā, v. To dust; to beat.**

دھول کی رسی بٹنا dhūl kī rassī baṭnā, v. To attempt an impossibility; to labour in vain (*Lit.* to make ropes with the sand).

دھول dhaul (H) n.m. A thump; a slap.

دھول جڑنا، مارنا، لگانا dhaul jaṛnā, mārnā, lagānā, v. To thump; to slap; to give a slap.

دھول دھپا dhaul dhappā, n.m. A fight with fists; a row; thumping and slapping; a kind of game.

دھولا dhaulā (H) adj. White (hair); any white thing, especially milk or hair.

دھوم dhūm (H) n.f. Fame; pomp; tumult; bustle; report; noise; rumour.

دھوم دھام dhūm dhām, n.f. Pomp; parade; pomp and show; bustle; noise; tumult.

دھوم مچانا dhūm machānā, v. To make a noise; to create an uproar; to cry aloud; to roar.

دھوم مچنا، ہونا dhūm machnā, honā, v. To be noised abroad; to become famous or notorious.

دھونا dhonā (H) v. To wash; to efface.

دھونس dhauṅs (H) n.f. Bullying; threatening; assault; threat; menace.

دھونس جمانا، دینا dhauṅs jamānā, denā, v. To threaten; to bully.

دھونس میں آنا dhauṅs meṅ ānā, v. To be influenced by a threat; to be tricked or cheated.

دھونکنا dhauṅknā (H) v. To blow with a bellows; to puff; to breathe upon.

دھونکنی dhauṅknī (H) n.f. Bellows.

دھونی dhūnī (H) n.f. Persevering; assiduousness; smoke; a fire lighted by a *Hindū Faqīr* over which he sits by way of penance.

دھونی دینا dhūnī denā, v. To smoke; to importune; to expose to odorous fumes; to fumigate.

دھونی رمانا، لگانا dhunī ramānā, lagānā, v. To light a fire after the manner of a *faqir*; to become a *faqir*.

دھونی لینا dhūnī lenā, v. To inhale smoke; to undergo fumigation.

دھی dahī (H) n.m. Thick sour milk; coagulated milk; curd; tyre.

دھیان dhyān (H) n.m. Meditation; reflection; contemplation; thought; consideration; imagination; attention; observation; regard; mental contemplation of the divinity.

دھیان بٹانا dhyān baṭānā, v. To distract attention.

دھیان دینا، لگانا dhyān denā, lagānā, v. To pay attention; to take notice of; to contemplate.

دھیان رکھنا dhyān rakhnā, v. To keep in view; to think about; to bear in mind.

دھیان میں نہ لانا dhyān meṅ nah lānā, v. To disregard; to pay no attention to.

دھیرج dhīraj (H) n.f. Fortitude; patience; composure.

دھیرج رکھنا dhīraj rakhnā, v. To have patience or perseverance; to be firm.

دھیرے دھیرے dhīre dhīre (H) adv. Slowly; gently; softly.

دھیلا dhelā (H) n.m. Half-a-pice.

دھیلی dhelī (H) n.f. Half-a-rupee.

دھیما، دھیمی dhīmā, dhīmī (H) adj. Slow; lazy; gentle; subdued; dim; slight; mild; temperate; lulled; allayed.

دھیما پڑنا dhīmā paṛnā, v. To become calm; to become less severe; to relax.

دھیمے دھیمے dhīme dhīme, adv. Softly; gently.

دھینگا مشتی dhīngā mushti (H) n.f. Violence; wrangling; tumult; hurly-burly; fist-fight.

ڈالنا دے دینا، دے de denā, de ḍālnā (H) v. To give; to bestow; to hand over.

مارنا دے de mārnā (H) v. To throw on the ground; to dash something (against).

دیا diyā (H) n.m. An earthen lamp.

دیا بتی کرنا diyā battī karnā, v. To light a lamp.

دیا بڑھانا diyā baṛhānā, v. To put out a lamp.

دیا سلائی diyā salā'ī, n.f. A match-stick.

دیا dayā (H) n.f. A gift; mercy; kindness; favour; fellow-feeling; clemency; benevolance; affection; tenderness.

دیار diyār (A) n.m. A country; region; province; cedar tree.

دیا قوذہ dayā qūẕah (P) n.m. A medicine prepared from poppy seeds, used in cold and cough.

دیانت diyānat (A) n.f. Honesty; justice; piety; virtue.

دیانت دار diyānat dār, adj. Honest; just; conscientious.

دیانت داری diyānat dāri, n.f. Honesty; probity.

دیبا debā (P) n.m. Silk brocade; gold tissue.

دیباچہ dībāchah, debāchah (P) n.m. Preface; introduction; preamble; exordium.

دیپ dīp (S) n.m. A lamp; a light.

دیپ مالا dīp mālā, n.f. A row of lamps; illumination; decorating profusely with lights as sign of festivity.

دیپک dīpak (S) n.m. A light; a candle; a lamp; a kind of firework; name of a musical mode, sung at noon in the hot-weather. or sung in the evening.

دیت diyat (A) n.f. The law of retaliation; the price of blood; the fine paid for murder, wounding or maiming; blood money; compensation for man-slaughter.

دیجور daijūr (P) n.f. Dark night. adj. Dark; pitch-dark.

دید dīd (P) n.f. Sight; show; spectacle; seeing.

دید نہ شنید dīd nah shunīd, adj. (Lit. Neither seen nor heard); strange; extra-ordinary; unique.

دیدار dīdār (P) n.m. Sight; interview.

دیدارو dīdārū, adj. Good looking; handsome.

دیدنی dīdani (P) adj. Worth seeing; fit to be seen; visible.

دیدہ dīdah (P) adj. Seen (used in comp. as جہاں دیدہ jahāṅ dīdah—one who has seen the world).

دیدہ دانستہ dīdah dānistah, adv. Willingly; knowingly; purposely.

دیدہ dīdah (P) n.m. The eye.

دیدہ پھٹی dīdah phaṭī, adj. Having large staring eyes; impudent; shameless.

دیدہ ریزی dīdah rezi, n.f. Work requiring great effort; work fatiguing to the eye; hard work.

دیدے پھاڑنا dīde phāṛnā, v. To look steadfastly; to gaze; to stare.

دیدے کا پانی ڈھلنا dīde kā pānī ḍhalnā, v. To become shameless.

دیدے مٹکانا dīde maṭkānā, v. To make eyes at; to wanton with the eyes.

دیدے نکالنا dīde nikālnā, v. To get into a passion or rage; to be enraged.

دیر dair (P) n.m. A temple where idols are worshipped; a place of idol worship; a church.

دیر der (P) n.f. Delay; tardiness; slowness.

دیر آید درست آید der āyad durust āyad, prov. The longed for object is welcome indeed when eventually it comes; better late than never.

دیر پا der pā, adj. Durable; lasting.

دیر تک der tak, adv. For a long time.

دیر خوابی der khwābī, n.f. Late sleeping.

دیر لگانا der lagānā, v. To delay; to loiter about.

دیر ہونا der honā, v. To be late.

دیرینہ derinah (P) adj. Old; ancient; experienced.

دیس ، دیش des, desh (H) n.m. Country; territory; region.

دیس بدیس پھرنا des bades phirnā, v. To wander from country to country; to travel about.

دیس نکالا des nikālā, n.m. Exile; banishment; ostracism.

دیسی desi (H) adj. Of the same country; local; native; indigenous; home-made; belonging to the country.

دیکھ بھال ، دیکھا بھالی dekh bhāl, dekhā bhālī (H) n.f. Looking after; care; looking; search; checking.

دیکھا بھالا dekhā bhālā (H) adj. Seen and tried.

دیکھا دیکھی dekhā dekhi (H) adv. In imitation.

دیکھا کرنا dekhā karnā (H) v. To keep looking; to be in the habit of looking; to be waiting.

دیکھا ہوا dekhā hūā, adj. Seen; known; experienced; perceived.

دیکھتے دیکھتے dekhte dekhte (H) adv. Before the eyes; in the presence of.

دیکھتے رہ جانا dekhte rah jānā (H) v. To gaze in vain; to stand gazing in wonder or disappointment.

دیکھتے رہنا dekhte rahnā (H) v. To keep a watch; to look after; to keep an eye on.

دیکھنا dekhnā (H) v. To look at; to see; to observe; to behold; to search; to inspect; to take care; to scan; to weigh well; to feel (pulse); to prove; to bear the sight of; to experience.

دیکھنا بھالنا dekhnā bhālnā, v. To look at; to examine; to inspect; to try.

دیکھنے میں آنا dakhne men ānā, v. To appear; to be visible.

دیگ deg (P) n.f. A cauldron; a big pot; a boiler.

دیگچہ degchah (P) n.m. A kettle.

دیگچی degchī (P) n.f. A small kettle.

دیگر dīgar (P) adj. Other; another; again.

دیمک dimak (P) n.f. White-ant.

دیمک خوردہ dimak khūrdah, adj. Eaten by white-ants.

دیمک لگنا dimak lagnā, v. To be eaten by white-ants.

دین din (A) n.m. Faith; religion.

دین پناہ din panāh, adj. Defender of the faith.

دین دار dīn dār, adj. Religious; pious; virtuous.

دین داری dīn dārī, n.f. Religiousness; religiosity; piety.

دین dain (A) n.m. Debt; liability.

دین den (H) n.m. Gift; giving; bestowing.

لین دین len den, n.m. Traffic; pecuniary transaction on interest; dealings; barter.

دینا denā (H) v. To give; to grant; to confer; to yield; to afford; to produce; to offer; to pay; to allot; to emit; to give forth; to raise (a cry for help); to lay (eggs).

دینار dīnār (A) n.m. A coin; a ducat.

دینی dini (A) adj. Religious; spiritual.

دیو deo (P) n.m. A giant; a spirit; a devil; monster; demon.

دیو زاد deo zād, adj. Demon-born or begotten.

دیو dev (H) n.m. A god; a deity.

دیو مالا dev mālā, n.f. Mythology.

دیو ناگری dev nāgrī, n.f. The nāgrī character; the character on which Sansikrat is usually written.

دیوار dīwār (P) n.f. A wall.

دیوار چین، دیوار قہقہہ dīwār-ĕ chin, diwār-ĕ qahqahah, n.f. The great wall of China—one of the wonders of the world.

دیوار کے بھی کان ھیں diwār ke bhī kān haiṅ, prov. Walls have ears; do not let your secrets be overheard.

دیوار گیری dīwār girī, n.f. Tapestry or cloth to adorn a wall.

دیوالی diwalī (H) n.f A Hindū festival of lamp lighting in honour of Lakhshmī (goddess of wealth).

دیوالہ dewālah (H) n.m. Bankruptcy.

دیوالہ نکالنا dewālah nakālnā, v. To declare bankruptcy; to become insolvent.

دیوالیہ dewāliyah (H) n.m. Bankrupt.

دیوان dīwān (P) n.m. A royal court; a chief officer of state; a tribunal; a secretary; a minister; a financial secretary; a book of poetical pieces in which rhymes of different poems end successively with a particular letter of the alphabet; a dais or cushioned platform.

دیوان خاص dīwān-ĕ khāṣ, n.m. Privy council chamber; the cabinet.

دیوان خانہ diwān khānah, n.m. A hall of audience; a court.

دیوان عام dīwān-ĕ ʻām, n.m. Public hall of audience.

دیوانگی dīwānagī (P) n.f. Madness; lunacy; insanity.

دیوانہ dīwānah (P) n.m. Mad; insane; lunate; frenzied; inspired; lover.

دیوانی dīwānī (P) n.f. A civil court; office or jurisdiction of a diwān. adj. Mad (woman).

دیوتا devatā (S) n.m. A demigod; a divinity; an object of worship; a good man.

دیوٹ diwaṭ (H) n.m. A lamp-stand.

دیوث dayyūṣ (A) n.m. Shameless fellow; one who lives on the prostitution of his wife.

دیودار deodār (H) n.m. The cedar tree.

دیور dewar (H) n.m. Husband's younger brother.

دیورانی dewarānī (H) n.f. Wife of husband's younger brother.

دیوی devī (H) n.f. A goddess; a female deity; a queen; a pious woman.

دیہ deh (P) n.m. A village or town.

دیہی dehī (P) adj. Belonging to a village; rural.

دیہات dehāt (P) n.m. (plu. of دیہ deh) villages.

ڈ

ڈ ḍāl, is the twelfth letter of the Urdu alphabet. It has no corresponding sound or character in the Arabic or Persian, nor in any European language. It is pronounced by applying the tip of the tongue inverted to the palate. In reckoning by abjad it stands for 4.

ڈاب ḍāb (H) n.m. A kind of grass used in making ropes; a sword belt; an unripe cocoanut.

ڈابر ḍābar (H) n.m. A lake; a pond; a water pot; a vessel for washing hands in.

ڈاٹ ḍāṭ (H) n.f. A stopper; a cork; an arch; a keystone.

ڈاٹ لگانا ḍāṭ lagānā, v. To cork; to put a stopper on; to arch.

ڈار ḍār (H) n.f. Line; row; herd; flock; a branch; bough.

ڈاڑھ ḍāṛh (H) n.f. A jaw-tooth; grinder.

ڈاڑھ گرم ھونا ḍāṛh garm honā, v. To eat.

ڈاڑھی ḍāṛhī (H) *n.f.* A beard.

ڈاڑھی پیٹ میں ہونا *ḍāṛhī peṭ meṅ honā, v.* To be wise; prematurely.

ڈاڑھیں مار کر رونا *ḍāṛheṅ mār kar ronā* (H) *v.* To weep bitterly.

ڈاک *ḍāk* (H) *n.f.* The post or mail; a post office; relays of men or horses for the post.

ڈاک بنگلہ *ḍāk banglah, n.f.* A *ḍāk* bunglow; a rest house.

ڈاک چوکی *ḍāk chaukī, n.f.* A stage or station where a relay of horses is posted.

ڈاک خانہ *ḍāk khānah, n.m.* Post office.

ڈاک گاڑی *ḍāk gāṛī, n.f.* The mail train or the mail van.

ڈاک لگانا *ḍāk lagānā, v.* To post relays of horses or runners.

ڈاکا *ḍākā* (H) *n.m.* An attack by a gang of robbers or bandits.

ڈاکا پڑنا *ḍākā paṛnā, v.* To be attacked by dacoits.

ڈاکا ڈالنا *ḍākā ḍālnā, v.* To commit a dacoity; to rob.

ڈاکا زنی *ḍākā zanī, n.f.* Dacoity; highway robbery; burglary; Robbery; felony; brigandage; banditry.

ڈاکو *ḍākū* (H) *n.m.* A robber; a bandit; a pirate; a dacoit; a highwayman; a brigand; a felon.

ڈاکیا *ḍākyā* (H) *n.m.* A postman; a letter carrier.

ڈال *ḍāl* (H) *n.f.* A branch; a bough; a basket used for raising water by artificial means for irrigation purposes.

ڈال کا پکا *ḍāl kā pakkā, adj.* Ripened on the tree.

ڈال کا ٹوٹا *ḍāl kā ṭūṭā, adj.* Plucked from the tree; fresh, in very good condition; fine.

ڈال دینا *ḍāl denā* (H) *v.* To throw away; to cast away; to abandon; to occasion; to lay down.

ڈالر *ḍallar* (E) *n.m.* Unit of the United States gold and silver coinage equivalent to about three Rupees.

ڈالنا *ḍālnā* (H) *v.* To throw down; to fling; to drop; to shed; to pour; to lay; to destroy; to miscarry; to put on; to wear; to sow; to scatter; to vomit; to impose; to take a woman as a concubine.

ڈالی *ḍālī* (H) *n.f.* A branch; a bough; an open basket; a present of fruits, sweetmeats &c spread out on a tray.

ڈامچا *ḍāmchā* (H) *n.m.* A raised platform constructed to watch the fields from.

ڈانٹ ، ڈانٹ ڈپٹ *ḍānṭ, ḍānṭ ḍapaṭ* (H) *n.f.* Threat; menace; rebuke; awe.

ڈانٹنا *ḍānṭnā* (H) *v.* To threaten; to menace; to brow beat.

ڈانڈ *ḍānḍ* (H) *n.m.* A stick; staff; oar; a measure of length; a pole of four to six cubits; a measure of time; highland; barren land.

ڈانڈا *ḍānḍā* (H) *n.m.* Land marks; road; field boundary; boundry line; ridge; a path for cattle.

ڈانڈی *ḍānḍī* (H) *n.m.* A rower; a boatman. *n.f.* A kind of conveyance used in the hills.

ڈانگ *ḍāng* (H) *n.f.* High land; summit of a hill; a stick; a club.

ڈانواں ڈول *ḍāṅwāṅ dol* (H) *adj.* Lost; wandering about; homeless; destitute; ruined; unsteady; errant.

ڈانواں ڈول پھرنا *ḍāṅwāṅ ḍol phirnā, v.* To wander about (like a lost sheep).

ڈاین *ḍāyn* (H) *n.f.* A witch; an ugly old woman.

ڈب *ḍab* (H) *n.f.* Strength; power; authority; a kind of pocket; the leather of which oil-pots are made.

ڈبا ḍabbā (H) *n.m.* A leathern vessel for holding oil.

ڈبا ḍibbā (H) *n.m.* A small box; a children's disease.

ڈباؤ ḍubāu (H) *adj.* Out of man's depth; deep enough to drown in; drowning.

ڈبڈبانا dubḍubānā (H) *v.* To be filled with tears.

ڈبری ḍabrī (H) *n.f.* Division of profits among the village community according to their respective shares.

ڈبکی ḍubkī (H) *n.f.* A dip; plunge; diving.

ڈبونا ḍubonā (H) *v.* To drown; to cause to sink; to dip; to immerse; to flood; to ruin; to destroy; to waste.

ڈبی ḍibbī (H) *n.f.* A small box.

ڈبیا ḍibyā (H) *n.f.* A very small box.

ڈپٹ ḍapaṭ (H) *n.f.* Rebuke; menace; challenge; threat. (used with ڈانٹ ḍānt).

ڈپٹانا ḍapṭānā (H) *v.* To gallop a horse.

ڈپٹنا ḍāpaṭnā (H) *v.* To call out; to shout; to attack; to rebuke; to threaten; to gallop; to run.

ڈٹ جانا ḍaṭ jānā (H) *v.* To oppose face to face; to stand opposite; to put a bold front.

ڈٹنا ḍaṭnā (H) *v.* To stop; to stay; to contend; to cope with.

ڈر ḍar (H) *n.m.* Fear; awe; dread.

ڈرپوک ḍarpok, *adj.* Timid; coward.

ڈرانا ḍarānā (H) *v.* To frighten; to scare; to terrify; to alarm; to daunt.

ڈراؤنا ḍarāonā (H) *adj.* Frightful; terrifying; terrible; horrible; dreadful.

ڈرنا ḍarnā (H) *v.* To fear; to be frightened; to be terrified; to be scarred.

ڈسنا ḍasnā (H) *v.* To bite; to sting (as a venomous anima!).

ڈف ḍaf (H) *n.m.* See دف *daf.*

ڈفالی ، ڈفالچی ḍafālī, ḍafalchī (H) *n.m.* One who plays on the instrument called دف *daf.*

ڈفلی ḍaflī (H) *n.f.* A small tambourine.

ڈکار ḍakār (H) *n.f.* A belch; eructation.

ڈکار جانا ḍakār jānā, *v.* To embazzle; to defalcate; to gulp; to swallow.

ڈکار لینا ḍakār lenā, *v.* To belch; to bellow.

ڈکار نہ لینا ḍakār nah lenā, *v.* Not to belch; not to make the least sign; to defalcate; to eat ferociously.

ڈکارنا ḍakārnā (H) *v.* To swallow; to gulp down; to embazzle.

ڈکرانا ḍakrānā (H) *v.* To low as an ox; to make a loud noise; to cry aloud or bitterly.

ڈکوت ḍakaut (H) *n.m.* A caste of Hindus, descended from a Brahman father and a milk-woman mother. They subsist on alms on Saturday and are skilled in astrology.

ڈکوسنا ḍakosnā (H) *v.* To drink off; to eat up (used sarcastically).

ڈکیت ḍakait (H) *n.m.* A robber; a pirate; a dacoit.

ڈکیتی ḍakaitī (H) *n.f.* Robbery; dacoity.

ڈگ ḍig (H) *n.m.* A pace; one step; a stride; a measure.

ڈگ بھرنا ḍig bharnā, *v.* To step out; to stride.

ڈگڈگی ḍugḍugī (H) *n.f.* A small drum used by jugglers; a small drum used for making proclamations.

ڈگر ḍagar (H) *n.f.* A path; track; road; highway.

ڈگری ḍigrī (E) *n.f.* Decree.

ڈگری آخری یا قطعی ḍigrī ākhrī yā qaṭ'ī, *n f.* Final decree.

ڈگری پانا، حاصل کرنا ḍigrī pānā, ḥāṣil karnā, v. To obtain a decree.

ڈگری جاری کرانا ḍigrī jārī karānā, v. To sue out execution.

ڈگری جاری کرنا ḍigrī jārı karnā, v. To enforce a decree.

ڈگری دار digrī dār, n.m. A decree holder.

ڈگری دینا ḍigri denā, v. To adjudge; to decree.

ڈگری یک طرفہ ḍigri yak tarfah, n.f. Ex-parte decree.

ڈگمگانا dagmagānā (H) v. To totter; to stagger; to shiver.

ڈگی duggi (H) n.f. Proclamation; publicity; announcement.

ڈل dal (H) n.m. A division of an army; a brigade; wealth; a blind well; a lake in the Kashmir valley.

ڈلا dalā (H) n.m. A large lump; a clod.

ڈلوانا dalwānā (H) v. To cause to throw; to cause to put in.

ڈلی dali (H) n.f. A lump (as betel nut); a piece; a bit.

ڈلیا dalya (H) n.f. A basket without a cover; a tray.

ڈمرو ḍamrū (H) n.m. A small drum shaped like an hour-glass, hold in one hand and beaten with the fingers.

ڈنٹھل danthal (H) n.m. The stalk which is left after the grain or fruit is cut away; the knots in stalks as of grain &c; straw; chaff.

ڈنڈ daṅd (H) n.m. The part of the arm between the elbow and the shoulder; a kind of gymnastic exercise; compensation for injury; penalty; tax; punishment.

ڈنڈ بھرنا daṅd bharnā, v. To pay damages; to pay a fine.

ڈنڈ پیلنا daṅd pelnā, v. To make gymnastic exercises.

ڈنڈ ڈالنا ḍaṅḍ dālnā, v. To levy or impose a tax.

ڈنڈا ḍaṅḍā (H) n.m. A staff; a club; a rod; an ensign-staff; a wall enclosing a house; a collector of market duties.

ڈنڈا ڈولی کرنا ḍaṅḍā ḍolī karnā, v. To lift one up by his arms and legs; a game played by children.

ڈنڈے بجاتے پھرنا ḍaṅḍe bajāte phirnā, v. To wander about; to do nothing.

ڈنڈے کھیلنا ḍaṅḍe khelnā, v. To play with sticks.

ڈنڈوت ḍaṅḍot (S) n.f. Prostration before an idol; obeisance; salutation; bowing.

ڈنڈی ḍaṅḍi (H) n.f. The beam (of a pair of scales); a handle; a staff; a stalk; a lever; a yard; a kind of blue dye; an ear-ring; male organ.

ڈنڈی مارنا ḍaṅḍī mārnā, v. To give short weight.

ڈنک daṅk (H) n.m. The sting (of a scorpion or wasp &c).

ڈنک لگانا، مارنا ḍaṅk lagānā, mārnā, v. To sting.

ڈنکا ḍaṅkā (H) n.m. A drum stick; a kettle-drum.

ڈنکا بجانا ḍaṅkā bajāna, v. To beat a drum; to reign; to exercise authority; to make a name for one's self; to rejoice

ڈنکا بجنا daṅkā bajnā, v. To be famous.

ڈنکے کی چوٹ کہنا daṅke kı chot kehnā, v. To proclaim by beat of drum; to announce to the public.

ڈنگر ḍangar (H) n.m. Cattle; animals.

ڈوآ ḍoā (H) n.m. A large wooden spoon.

ڈوب ḍob (H) n.m. A dip; a dive; a plunge; immersion.

ڈوب دینا dob denā, v. To dip; to immerse.

ڈوبا **ḍobā** (H) *n.m.* Dip; dropping the pen in the inkpot to draw ink.

ڈوبتے کو تنکے کا سہارا **ḍūbte ko tinke kā sahārā**, *prov.* A drowning man catches at a straw.

ڈوب مرنا **ḍūb marnā** (H) *v.* To drown oneself; to die by drowning.

ڈوبنا، ڈوب جانا **ḍūbnā, ḍūb jānā** (H) *v.* To sink; to drown; to be immersed or deluged; to be destroyed or wasted; to be absorbed (in business, study, &c.)

ڈوڈا **ḍoḍā** (H) *n.m.* A seed-vessel (especially of the poppy and cotton).

ڈور **ḍor** (H) *n.f.* A rope; a string; a line; cord; thread.

ڈورا **ḍorā** (H) *n.m.* Thread; cord; line; a ladle; edge of a sword &c.

آنکھ کا ڈورا **ānkh kā ḍorā**, *n.m.* A blood-shot eye (from intoxication or other causes).

گردن کا ڈورا **gardan kā ḍorā**, *n.m.* A graceful motion of the neck in dancing.

ڈورے ڈالنا **ḍore ḍālnā**, *v.* To stitch; to braid the hair; to spread a net; to attract; to ensnare; to coax.

ڈوری (H) *n.f.* A string; a cord; thread; rope; a chain or line used in land measurement; braid.

ڈوریا **ḍoryā** (H) *n.m.* Striped muslin; lace; a dog-keeper.

ڈول **ḍol** (H) *n.m.* A bucket for drawing water.

ڈول **ḍaul** (H) *n.m.* Manner; method; mode; shape; fashion; form; figure; pattern; constitution; the raised boundary of a field.

ڈولا **ḍolā** (H) *n.m.* A kind of cradle which is hung from a tree; a kind of sedan in which women are carried.

ڈولا دینا **dolā denā**, *v.* To give a daughter to a superior by way of tribute; to give a daughter in marriage.

ڈولچی **ḍolchī** (H) *n.f.* A small bucket for drawing water.

ڈولنا **ḍolnā** (H) *v.* To move; t shake; to be shaken; to roam; to ramble; to wander; to swing; to move; to tremble; to deviate.

ڈولی **ḍolī** (H) *n.f.* A kind of small sedan.

ڈوم **ḍom** (H) *n.m.* A low caste of Hindus; a class of musicians; persons who make ropes, mats &c and remove dead bodies.

ڈومنی **ḍomnī** (H) *n.f.* The wife of a ڈوم ḍom; a kind of bird.

ڈونڈی **ḍonḍi** (H) *n.f.* Proclamation by beat of drum.

ڈونڈی پیٹنا **ḍonḍi pīṭnā**, *v.* To proclaim by beat of drum; to announce publicly; to proclaim to the public.

ڈونگا **ḍongā** (H) *n.m.* A canoe; a boat; a trough; a dish; a spoon.

ڈونگرے **ḍongre** (H) *n.m.* Heavy showers.

ڈوئی **ḍo'ī** (H) *n.f.* A wooden spoon; a ladle.

ڈھاٹا **ḍhāṭā** (H) *n.m.* A piece of cloth tied under the beard to make the hair incline upward.

ڈھارس **ḍhāras** (H) *n.f.* Firmness of mind; confidence; courage; boldness; fortitude; encouragement; comfort.

ڈھارس بندھنا **ḍhāras bandhnā**, *v.* To have courage; to keep the spirits.

ڈھارس بندھانا، دینا **ḍhāras bandhānā, denā**, *v.* To solace; to comfort; to give courage; to animate.

ڈھاک **dhāk** (H) *n.m.* Name of a tree (*Butia frondesa*).

ڈھاک کے تین پات **ḍhāk ke tin pāt**, *prov.* To be always short of money; to be obstinate and unchanging.

ڈھاکا ḍhākā (H) n.m. The thick wood of ḍhāk trees; the capital of East Pakistan (Dacca).

ڈھال ḍhāl (H) n.f. Slope; declinity; manner; mode; mould; fashion; a shield.

ڈھالنا ḍhālnā (H) v. To cast metal; to mould; to shape; to spill; to compose a sentence.

ڈھالو ḍhālū (H) adj. Sloping; slanting.

ڈھانا ḍhānā (H) v. To break; to batter; to knock down or raze a building; to demolish; to bring calamity upon one.

ڈھانپنا ḍhānpnā (H) v. To cover; to conceal; to hide.

ڈھانچ ، ڈھانچا ḍhānch, ḍhāncha (H) n.m. A frame; a skeleton; a plan; a sketch.

ڈھانکنا ḍhānknā (H) v. See ڈھانپنا ḍhānpnā.

ڈھائی ḍhā'ī (H) adj. Two and a half.

ڈھائی گھڑی کی آنا ḍhā'ī gharī kī ānā, v. To die in two-and-a-half hours; to die very soon (a curse used by women).

ڈھب ḍhab (H) n.m. Shape; form; manner; breeding; behaviour; mode; method; fashion; style; way; address; dexterity; art; position; practice.

ڈھب پر چڑھانا ، لگانا ḍhab par charhānā, lagānā, v. To mould after one's liking.

ڈھب پرچڑھنا ḍhab par charhna, v. To be moulded to one's will; to be brought under the influence or power of.

ڈھبری ḍhibrī (H) n.f. A nut; a screw.

ڈھٹائی ḍhiṭā'ī (H) n.f. Forwardness; audacity; shamelessness; impudence; obstinacy; boldness; presumption; audaciousness; presumptuousness.

ڈھچر ḍhachar (H) n.m. See ڈھانچ ḍhānch. adj. Old and emaciated.

ڈھڈو ḍhaḍḍo (H) n.f. An old woman; a hag; a strumpet.

ڈھرا ḍharrā (H) n.m. An ancient custom; manner; mode; usage.

ڈھکنا ḍhaknā (H) n.m. A Lid; a cover. v. To cover; to conceal; to hide.

ڈھکوسلا ḍhakoslā (H) n.m. Meaningless talk; cheating; deception; delusion; babble.

ڈھلان ḍhalān (H) n.m. Declinity; slope.

ڈھلائی ḍhulā'ī (H) n.f. Act of carrying; price paid for carrying or for transporting.

ڈھلتی پھرتی چھاؤں dhaltī phirtī chhāon (H) adj. Changeableness of worldly things; vicissitudes of life or fortune.

ڈھلکانا ḍhalkānā (H) v. To tilt; to overturn; to spill; to pour; to roll.

ڈھلکنا ḍhalaknā (H) v. To roll; to incline.

ڈھل مل یقین ḍhul mul yaqīn (H) adj. Credulous; indecisive; wavering; undependable.

ڈھلنا ḍhalnā (H) v. To be cast (a metal); to be shaped; to be moulded; to decline; to reced; to become old.

دن ڈھلنا din ḍhalnā, v. Declining of day.

ڈھلواں ḍhalwāṅ (H) adj. See ڈھالو ḍhālū.

ڈھلوانا ḍhalwānā (H) v. To cause to cast (metal); to cause to mould; to cause to shape.

ڈھلوانا ḍhulwānā (H) v. To cause to carry; to cause to transport.

ڈھنڈوانا ḍhunḍwānā (H) v. To cause to seek; to cause to search.

ڈھنڈورا ḍhanḍorā (H) n.m. Publication or proclamation by beat of drum.

ڈھنڈورچی dhanḍorchī (H) n.m. A town crier; one who proclaims by beat of drum.

ڈھنڈیا پڑنا ḍhunḍyā parnā (H) v. To be looked for; to be sought.

ڈھنگ ḍhang (H) n.m. Behaviour; manner; breeding; gracefulness; mode; method.

ڈھوانا *ḍhawānā* (H) *v.* To cause to demolish; to cause to ruin.

ڈھور *ḍhor* (H) *n.m.* Cattle.

ڈھول *ḍhol* (H) *n.m.* A large drum.

ڈھول کا پول *ḍhol kā pol*, *n.m.* Hollowness of the drum; good to look at but hollow within.

ڈھولا *dholā* (H) *n.m.* Name of a famous lover; a *punjabī* folk song; a gay deceiver; a child; a son; a heap; a mound; bank of a river.

ڈھولک، ڈھولکی *ḍholak, ḍholkī* (H) *n.m./f.* A small drum; tomtom.

ڈھولی *ḍholī* (H) *n.f.* A bundle of two hundred betel-leaves.

ڈھونا *ḍhonā* (H) *v.* To carry; to remove; to transport.

ڈھونڈنا *ḍhūṅḍnā* (H) *v.* To seek; to search; to look for.

ڈھونگ *ḍhoṅg* (H) *n.m.* Deceit; artifice; trick; strategem.

ڈھونگیا *ḍhoṅgyā* (H) *adj.* Deceitful; impostor; hypocrite.

ڈھے پڑنا، جانا، ڈھینا *ḍhae paṛnā, jānā, ḍhaenā* (H) *v.* To fall down; to collapse; to be demolished.

ڈھیٹ، ڈھیٹھ *ḍhiṭ, ḍhīṭh* (H) *adj.* Forward; bold; daring; impudent; obstinate; presumptuous; shameless.

ڈھیر *ḍher* (H) *n.m.* A heap; a parcel; accumulation. *adj.* Much; abundant; enough.

ڈھیر کرنا *ḍher karnā*, *v.* To accumulate; to heap up; to kill.

ڈھیر ہو جانا *ḍher ho jānā*, *v.* To become a heap; to fall down; to die; to be killed.

ڈھیرا *ḍherā* (H) *n.m. & adj.* Squinting; squint-eyed.

ڈھیری *ḍherī* (H) *n.f.* A small heap; accumulation; squint-eyed

ڈھیل *ḍhīl* (H) *n.f.* Looseness; slackness; laziness; remissness; inattention; delay.

ڈھیل دینا *ḍhīl denā*, *v.* To let loose; to loosen; to yield; to relax; to let go.

ڈھیلا، ڈھیلی *ḍhīlā, ḍhīlī* (H) *adj.* Loose; slack; lazy; remiss: inattentive; unrestricted; impotent; coward.

ڈھیلا پن *ḍhīlā pan*, *n.m.* Slackness; looseness; clumniness.

ڈھیلا پڑ جانا *ḍhīlā haṛ jānā*, *v.* To become loose; to skulk.

ڈھیلا *ḍhelā* (H) *n.m.* A clod of earth; a lump of clay, chalk &c; eye-ball.

ڈھیلا لینا *ḍhelā lenā*, *v.* To use a clod of earth for purification after passing urine.

ڈھینکلی *ḍhenklī* (H) *n.f.* A contrivance for drawing water, for irrigation purposes.

ڈیرا *ḍerā* (H) *n.m.* A dwelling; a tent.

ڈیرا ڈالنا *ḍerā ḍālnā*, *v.* To encamp; to linger on; to pitch a tent; to loiter.

ڈیڑھ *derh* (H) *adj.* One and a half.

ڈیڑھ اینٹ کی مسجد جدا بنانا *ḍeṛh īṅṭ kī masjid judā banānā*, *v.* To withdraw from majority and form a small party of one's own.

ڈیل *ḍīl* (H) *n.m.* Stature; body; bulk; size.

ڈیل ڈول *ḍīl ḍaul*, *n.m.* Shape; figure; body; bulk.

ڈینگ *ḍīṅg* (H) *n.f.* Boasting; vaunting; pride.

ڈینگ مارنا، ہانکنا *ḍīṅg mārnā, hāṅknā*, *v.* To boast; to brag; to make a boast of.

ڈیوڑھا *ḍeoṛhā* (H) *adj.* One and a half.

ڈیوڑھا درجہ *ḍeoṛhā darjah*, *n.m.* Inter-class.

ڈیوڑھی *ḍeoṛhī* (H) *n.f.* A threshold; a porch; entrance.

ڈیوڑھی دار *ḍeoṛhī dār*, *n.m.* A door-keeper; a watch man.

ذ

ذ zāl, called dāl-ĕ mo'jama, is the ninth letter of the Arabic, eleventh of the Persian and thirteenth of the Urdu alphabet. It is pronounced by the Arabs like th, in the English word then, but in Persian and Urdu it bears the sound of the letter z. In reckoning by abjad it stands for 700.

ذات zāt (A) n.f. Having possessed of; endowed with; division; kind; the essence; nature; soul; self; substance; property; the body; person; caste; race; breed.

ذات‌الجنب zāt-ul-janb, n.m. Pleurisy.

ذات‌الریہ zāt-ul-riyah, n.m. Inflammation of the lungs; pneumonia.

ذات‌الصدر zāt-uṣ-ṣadr, n.m. Inflammation of the chest.

ذات باہر zāt bāhar, adj. An outcaste.

ذات باہر کرنا zāt bāhar karnā, v. To put out of caste; to excommunicate.

ذات پات zāt pāt, n.f. Tribe; caste; lineage; racialism.

ذات شریف zāt-ĕ sharīf, (ironic) A consummate knave.

ذات میں بٹا لگنا zāt men baṭṭā lagnā, v. To lose honour; to get a bad name.

ذاتی zātī (A) adj. Personal; innate; real; essential; constitutional; natural; material; intrinsic; inherent; inborn.

ذاتی تعلق zātī ta'alluq, n.m. Personal relation.

ذاتی حیثیت zātī ḥaiṣiyyat, n.f. Personal status.

ذاتی لیاقت zātī liyāqat, n.f. Real merit; intrinsic value.

ذاتی معاملات zātī mu'āmlāt, n.m. Personal affairs.

ذاکر zākir (A) adj. Remembering; grateful; n.m. A grateful person; one who praises God; one who recites elegies of the martyrs of kerbalā.

ذائقہ zā'iqah (A) n.m. The sense of tasting; relish; taste.

ذائقہ دار zā'iqah dār, adj. Tasty; savoury.

ذبح zabaḥ (A) n.m. Slaughter; sacrifice.

ذبح کرنا zabaḥ karnā, v. To kill; to slaughter; to sacrifice.

ذبح ہونا zabaḥ honā, v. To be killed; to be sacrified.

ذبیح zabīḥ (A) adj. Slaughtered; sacrificed; n.m. An intended victim; a sacrifice.

ذبیح اللہ zabiḥ ullah, n.m. A surname of Prophet Ismael, whom Prophet Abraham offered to sacrifice.

ذبیحہ zabīḥah (A) n.m. An animal lawfully slaughtered and fit for food.

ذخائر zakhā'ir (A) n.m. (plu. of ذخیرہ zakhīrah) Treasure; stores; victuals; provision.

ذخیرہ zakhīrah (A) n.m. Provision; store; treasure; hoard; munitions.

ذخیرہ کرنا zakhīrah karnā, v. To store; to stock.

ذرا zarā, adj. A little; little while. intj. Would you ! please !

ذرا سا zarā sā, adj. A little; trivial; trifling; a little while; short.

ذرا ذرا کرکے zarā zarā karke, adv. Little by little; by degrees.

ذرات zarrāt (A) n.m. (plu. of ذرہ zarrah). Atoms; particles.

ذراع zirā' (A) n.m. A yard; a cubit; the forearm.

ذرائع zarā'i' (A) n.m. (plu. of ذریعہ zarī'ah) Means; mediums; agencies; sources.

ذره zarrah (A) n.m. An atom; a particle; a jot.

ذریت zurriyat (A) n.f. Progeny; generation; desendents; offsprings.

ذریعه zari'yah (A) n.m. Means; agency; medium; influence; intervention; intercession; source.

ذریعه پیدا کرنا zari'yah pedā karnā, v. To find means; to make interest.

بذریعه bazari'yah, adv. By means of; by virtue of; through the intervention of.

ذقن zaqan (A) n.f. The chin.

ذکا zaka (A) n.m. Acumen; sharpness of mind; penetration; sagacity.

ذکاوت zakāwat (A) n.f. Acuteness of mind; acumen; ingenuity; wit; sagacity; shrewdness.

ذکر zikr (A) n.m. Remembrance; memory; mention; commemoration; talk; account; recital; praise; fame; reading of the Quran and recital of the praise and names of God.

ذکر کرنا zikr karna, v. To recite; to mention; to relate; to express; to state; to praise God.

ذکر مذکور zikr mazkur, n.m. Mention; reference; talk; conversation.

ذکر zakar (A) n.m. Male organ of generation; penis.

ذکور zukūr (A) n.m. The male sex; males; men.

ذکی zakī (A) adj. Acute; ingenius; sharp; clever; fiery; flaming.

ذل zill (A) n.m. Gentleness; ease; tractableness; method; mode.

ذلالت - ذلت zalālat, zillat (A) n.f. Insult; disgrace; baseness; indignity; vileness; abjectness; dishonour; abusement; affront; contemptibleness.

ذلت اٹھانا zillat uthānā, v. To suffer dishonour or disgrace (at the hands of).

ذلیل zalīl (A) adj. Abject; base; mean; wretched; contemptible; shameless; submissive.

ذلیل کرنا zalīl karna, v. To abase; to insult; to debase.

ذلیل النفس zalīl-un-nafs, adj. Mean-spirited; abject; submissive.

ذلیل ہونا zalīl hona, v. To be brought low; to be disgraced.

ذم zam (A) n.f. Reproach; accusation; blame; detraction; censure.

ذمه zimmah (A) n.m. Responsibility; trust; obligation; charge; subjection; duty; service; fidelity; lineage; security; burden (of proof).

ذمه دار zimmah dar, adj. Responsible; answerable; trustee; assignee.

ذمه داری zimmah dari, n.f. Charge; trust; engagement; obligation; responsibility; liability.

ذمه لینا zimmah lena, v. To take in charge of; to take responsibility; to be surety for; to take care of.

ذمی zimmi (A) n.m. A non-Muslim who lives in a Muslim country and pays tax (*jazīah*) to Government.

ذنب zunb (A) n.m. A crime; a sin; a fault; misdeed; misdemeanour.

ذو zu (A) n.m. Owner; lord; master. adj. (in comp.) possessed of; endowed with.

ذو اربعة الاضلاع zū arb'a-tul-azlā', adj. A quadrilateral figure.

ذو اضعاف اقل zū azā'af-ē aqall, n.m. Least common multiple. (L.C.M.)

ذوالجلال zul-jalāl, adj. Glorious; splendid.

ذوالفقار zulfaqār, n.m. A celebrated sword which fell into the hands of the Holy Prophet in the battle of Badr and was then given to *Hazrat Ali*.

ذوالقرنین z̤ūlqarnain, n.m. Lord of the two horns (East and West); an epithet of Alexander, the Great.

ذوالمنن z̤ūlminan, adj. & n.m. Possessor of obligation (God).

ذو معنی z̤ū ma'nī, adj. Having two meanings.

ذوق z̤auq (A) n.m. Taste; delight; joy; pleasure.

ذوی z̤awī (A) adj. (plu. of ذو z̤ū); Having; possessing; endowed with.

ذوی‌الارحام z̤awi-l-ārḥām, n.m. Relatives through the mother.

ذوی‌الاقتدار z̤awi-l-iqtidār, n.m. Powerful; holding authority; endowed with power.

ذہانت z̤ihanat (A) n.f. Intelligence; acuteness; acumen; sagacity.

ذہب z̤ahab (A) n.m. Gold; the yolk of an egg.

ذہن z̤ehn (A) n.m. Acuteness (of mind); acumen; sagacity; wit; understanding; mind; memory; ingenuity; ability.

ذہن لڑانا z̤ehn laṛānā, v. To think; to consider; to ponder over.

ذہن نشین کرنا z̤ehn nashīn karnā, v. To impress on the mind; to fix in the mind; to instil.

ذہین z̤ahin (A) adj. Of or relating to intellect; intellectual; acute; ingenius; sagacious.

ذی z̤ī (A) n.m. See ذو z̤u.

ذی اختیار z̤ī ikhtiyār, adj. Authorized; one in authority.

ذی استعداد z̤ī isti'dād, adj. Able; acute; sagacious.

ذی اقتدار z̤ī iqtidār, adj. Having competent powers.

ذی‌الحجہ z̤il hijjah n.m. The last month of the Muslim year, on the 9th of which the pilgrimage of Mecca takes place.

ذی حیات z̤ī ḥayāt, adj. Endowed with life; animal being.

ذی خرد z̤ī khirad, adj. Endowed with sense; wise.

ذی رتبہ z̤ī rutbah, adj. Of rank or distinction.

ذی روح z̤ī rūḥ, adj. Having life; animal beings.

ذی شعور z̤ī sha'ūr, adj. Intelligent.

ذی عزت z̤ī 'izzat, adj. Honourable; respectful.

ذی قعد z̤ī qa'd, n.m. The 11th month of the Muslim year.

ذی ہوش z̤ī hosh, adj. Sensible; wise.

غیر ذی روح ghair z̤ī rūḥ, adj. Inanimate objects.

ذیابیطس z̤ayābitūs, (A) n.m. Diabetes.

ذیل z̤ail (A) n.m. The lower extremity of a garment; the train of a robe; retinue; that which follows; an appendix; a part of a district.

ذیل‌دار z̤aildār, n.m. An officer incharge of a ذیل z̤ail (villages or towns).

ذیل میں z̤ail meṅ, adv. As below; as follows; as under.

حسب ذیل ḥasb-ĕ z̤ail, adv. As below; as follows.

مفصلہ ذیل mufaṣṣalah z̤ail, adv. As detailed below.

ر

ر re, called rae moḥmalā and rae ghair manquta, is the tenth letter of the Arabic, twelfth of the Persian and fourteenth of Urdu alphabet. In reckoning, according to adjad, it stands for 200.

راب rāb (H) n.f. the thick liquid prepared from گڑ guṛ; treacle; syrup; molasses.

رابطہ rābiṭah (A) n.m. Connection; union; alliance; liaison; system; bond; regularity; communication.

رانپی، راپی rāpi, rāṅpi (H) n.f. A shoemaker's knife.

رات rāt (H) n.f. Night.

رات بھاری ہونا rāt bhāri hona, v. To have a long wearisome night.

رات تھوڑی اور سانگ بہت rāt thoṛi aur sāng bahut, prov. The night is short and the play long; life is short as compared with the work we have to do in this world; art is long and time is fleeting.

رات دن rāt din, adv. Day and night.

رات کی رات rāt ki rāt, adv. Just for a night.

راتوں رات rātoṅ rāt, adv. During the night; within one night.

آدھی رات ādhi rāt, n.f. Midnight.

راتب rātib (A) n.m. Daily allowance for food; stipend; a pension; provision; food for dogs, elephants &c.

راج rāj (H) n.m. Government; sovereignty; royalty; reign; kingdom; dominion; administration; a mason; a brick-layer.

راجستان، راج استھان rāj isthān, rājistan, n.m. Royal palace; capital; seat of government; of Rajputs.

راج بھون rāj bhawan, n.m. Royal residence; country palace.

راج بہا rāj bahā, n.f. A small-branch of a canal.

راج بھنڈار rāj bhanḍār, n.m. Royal or government treasury.

راج بھنگ ہونا rāj bhang honā, v. Declining of a ruling dynasty.

راج پاٹ rāj pāṭ, n.m. Dominion; kingdom.

راج پوت rāj pūt, n.m. A martial tribe of the Hindus.

راج پھوڑا rāj phoṛā, n.m. Carbuncle.

راج دربار rāj darbār, n.m. Royal audience; royal court.

راج دلاری rāj dulāri, n.f. A princess.

راج دھانی rāj dhāni, n.f. A palace; capital; metropolis.

راج رانی rāj rāni, n.f. A queen.

راج روگ rāj rog, n.m. A mortal disease; consumption.

راج سبھا rāj sabhā, n.f. King's assembly.

راج کرنا rāj karnā, v. To reign; to rule; to govern.

راج کمار rāj kumār, n.m. A prince.

راج کماری rāj kumāri, n.m. A princess.

راج کوی rāj kavi, n.m. Poet laureate.

راج گدی rāj gaddi, n.f. Throne; enthronement.

راج گری rāj gari, n.f. Masonry; a mason's work.

راج مزدور rāj mazdūr, n.m. Masons and labourers.

راج نیتی rāj niti, n.f. Political science; system of government; jurisprudence.

راج واڑا rāj wāṛā, n.m. See رجواڑا rajwāṛā.

راج ہٹ rāj haṭ, n.f. Royal persistence.

راج ہنس rāj hans, n.m. A goose.

راجا rājā (H) n.m. A ruler; a king; a prince; a monarch; a sovereign; a barber.

راجح rājiḥ (A) adj. Superior; excelling.

راجع rāji' (A) adj. Inclined; bent.

راحت rāḥat (A) n.f. Rest; repose; respite; comfort; ease; tranquility; relief; pleasure.

راحت افزا rāḥat āfzā, adj. Soothing; comforting; promoting to one's comfort.

راحت جاں rāḥat-ĕ jāṅ, adj. Comforting; giving comfort to one's soul; family; children; beloved.

راحم rāḥim (A) adj. Merciful; compassionate; pitying.

راڑ rāṛ (H) n.f. Fray; tumult; dispute; war; battle.

راز rāz (P) n.m. A mystery; a secret.

راز دار rāz dār, adj. Trusty; faithful; confident.

راز داری rāz dārī, n.f. Keeping of secrets; secrecy.

راز دان rāz dān, adj. Acquainted with a secret; a friend; one who knows the secrets of another.

راز سر بستہ، راز نہفتہ rāz-ĕ sar bastah, rāz-ĕ nihuftah, n.m. A close secret.

راز فاش کرنا rāz fāsh karnā, v. To betray a secret.

راز و نیاز rāz-ŏ niyāz, n.m. Secret conversation; loving prattle; tĕtĕ-ā-tĕtĕ.

رازق rāziq (A) n.m. Cherisher; sustainer; affording sustenance; (one of the attributes of God).

راس rās (A) n.m. The head; head of cattle; peak; top; summit; highest point; a cape.

راس الجدی rās-ul-jaddi, n.m. The winter solstice.

راس السرطان rās-us-sarṭān, n.m. The summer solstice; the point from which summer begins.

راس المال rās-ul-māl, n.m. Principle; capital; stock.

راس rās (H) n.f. Adoptability; suitability; noise; a drama; a circular dance; a show; reins.

راس آنا rās ānā, v. To be agreeable.

راسدھاری rās dhāri, n.m. A dancing boy who acts the parts of *Krishnā* or *Gopis* in a religious play.

راست rāst (P) adj. Right; true; good; just; upright; honest; sincere; right; (opposite to left); straight; even; level.

راست باز rāst bāz, adj. Honest; upright; righteous; faithful; candid; sincere; trustworthy.

راست بازی rāst bāzī, n.f. Honesty; integrity; fair play; uprightness; fidelity; plain dealing.

راست گفتاری rāst guftāri, n.f. Veracity; speaking the truth.

راست گو rāst go, adj. Truthful.

راست گوئی rāst go'i, n.f. Speaking the truth; truthfulness.

راستہ rāstah (P) n.m. Road; way; path; lane; manner.

راستہ بتانا rāstah batānā, v. To guide; to show the way (to); to dismiss.

راستہ دیکھنا rāstah dekhnā, v. To wait for; to watch.

راستہ کترانا rāstah katrānā, v. To slink away; to dodge.

راستی rāsti (P) n.f. Uprightness; honesty; veracity; truth; rectitude; fidelity.

راسخ rāsikh (A) adj. Firm; constant; sincere; durable; solid; steady; established; well-versed.

راشد rāshid (A) adj. Pious; orthodox; follower of right path; following the right way.

راشی rāshī (A) n.m. One who gives bribes.

راضی rāẓi (A) adj. Willing; satisfied; contented; agreed; pleased.

راضی برضا ہونا rāẓī barāẓā honā, v. To be resigned to the will of God; to submit to the will of God.

راضی خوشی rāẓī khūshī, adj. Well and happy.

راضی کرنا rāẓi karnā, v. To satisfy; to please; to reconcile; to conciliate.

راضی نامہ rāẓi nāmah, n.m. Compromise; a deed of compromise.

راضی ہونا rāẓi honā, v. To be content; to agree; to assent; to accede to; to consent; to acquiesce; to be satisfied.

راعی rā'i (A) n.m. Shepherd; pastor; a ruler.

راغ **rāgh** (P) *n.m.* A meadow; a desert; a meadow touching a desert; a valley.

راغب **rāghib** (A) *adj.* Willing; wishing; desirous; inclined towards.

راغب کرنا *rāghib karnā, v.* To make one agree to; to incite to; to encourage; to tempt.

رافت **rāfat** (A) *n.f.* Pity; tenderness; kindness; compassion; clemency.

رافضی **rāfzī** (A) *n.m.* A heretic; a schismatic; a dissenter.

راقم **rāqim** (A) *n.m.* A writer; a correspondent.

راکب **rākib** (A) *n.m.* A rider; a person on board.

راکشس **rākshas** (S) *n.m.* A demon; an evil spirit.

راکھ **rākh** (H) *n.m.* Ashes.

راکھ ہونا *rākh honā, v.* To be reduced to ashes.

راکھی **rākhī** (H) *n.f.* A red or yellow string bound round the wrist of a person to act as a preventive on the occasion of Hindu festival of *Salono*.

راگ **rāg** (H) *n.m.* Classical music; melody; song; tune; a musical mode; emotion; love; affection; anger; sorrow; colour; dye.

راگ الاپنا *rāg alāpnā, v.* To beat one's own drum; to blow one's own trumpet; to sing.

راگ رنگ *rāg rang, n.m.* Music and merriment; merry-making; festivities.

راگ گانا *rāg gānā, v.* To sing one's own song; to tell one's own story; to sing.

راگنی **rāgnī** (H) *n.f.* Modification of the musical mode called *rāg*; a mode in music.

راگی **rāgī** (H) *n.m.* A singer, well-versed in classical music; lustful; a lover; a libertine. *adj.* Passionate; sensual.

رال **rāl** (H) *n.f.* Resin; pitch; saliva; spittle.

رال ٹپکنا *rāl ṭapaknā, v.* Running of the mouth; dribbling of saliva; watering of the mouth; showing keen desire to possess.

رام **rām** (P) *adj.* Obedient; tame; submissive; tractable; passified; appeased.

رام کرنا *rām karnā, v.* To tame; to subdue; to bring round.

رام **rām** (S) *n.m.* God; the Hindu god, *Rama Chandrā*. *adj.* Pleasing; lovely; beautiful; charming.

رام رام *rām rām, n.m.* A form of salutation of Hindus.

رام کہانی *rām kahanī, n.f.* The *Ramayan*; a long story.

رام لیلا *rām līlā, n.f.* A Hindu festival; *Dusehrā*.

رامائن **rāmāyan** (H) *n.f.* Name of a great epic poem of the Hindus regarding the exploits of *Rām Chandrā*.

رامش **rāmish** (P) *n.f.* Repose; ease; joy; mirth; harmony; modulation.

ران **rān** (P) *n.f.* The thigh.

ران تلے کرنا *rān tale karnā, v.* To be mounted on; to subdue.

رانا **rānā** (H) *n.m.* The title of a Rajput prince.

رانپی **rānpī** (H) *n.f.* See راپی *rāpī*.

رانده **rāndah** (P) *adj.* Rejected; driven out; expelled.

رانڈ **rānd** (H) *n.f.* A window; a slut.

رانڈ کا سانڈ *rānḍ kā sānḍ, n.m.* Son of a window; a spoilt child; a contemptible worthless fellow.

رانگ **rāng** (H) *n.f.* Pewter; tin.

رانی **rānī** (H) *n.f.* A queen; a princess.

رانی rāni (P) adj. Driving (in *compos.* as جهاز رانی *jahāz rāni*, navigation).

راول rāwal (H) n.m. A chieftain; a soldier; a warrior; a prince; a soothsayer; an astrologer.

راوی rāwi (A) n.m. A historian; a narrator; a reciter; the author of a fable, fiction or romance.

راہ ' رہ rāh, rah (P) n.f. Road; way; passage; path; progress; means of access; custom; fashion; journey; method.

راہ بتانا rāh batānā, v. To guide; to show the way; to dismiss from service; to discharge; to expell; to deceive.

راہ بر ' رہبر rāh bar, rahbar, n.m. A guide; a conductor.

راہ بری ' رہبری rāh bari, rahbari, n.f. Guidance; conducting.

راہ پرآنا rāh par ānā, v. To find one's way; to amend one's manners.

راہ پر لانا rāh par lānā, v. To show one the right path; to reform; to bring round.

راہ پیدا کرنا rāh pedā karnā, v. To establish relations with; to form an acquaintance with.

راہ تکنا rāh taknā, v. See راہ دیکھنا rāh dekhnā.

راہ چلتا rāh chaltā, n.m. Way-farer; traveller.

راہ چھوڑنا rāh chhoṛnā, v. To get out of the way; to leave the road.

راہ دار rāh dār, n.m. A road patrol; a collector of toll duties.

راہ داری rāh dāri, n.f. Toll duties; toll; transit duties.

راہ دکھانا rāh dikhānā, v. To show the way; to make one wait for.

راہ دیکھنا rāh dekhnā, v. To wait for; to expect.

راہ دینا rāh denā, v. To make way for; to admit; to allow to pass.

راہ راست rāh-ĕ rāst, n.f. Straight road; good conduct.

راہ رو rāh rau, n.m. A traveller; a wayfarer.

راہ زن - رہزن rāh zan, rahzan, n.m. A highway man; a robber.

راہ زنی - رہزنی rāh zanī, rahzani, n.f. Highway robbery.

راہ کھوٹی کرنا rāh khoṭi karnā, v. To delay or linger on the road.

راہ گیر rāh gir, n.m. A traveller; a wayfarer.

راہ گزر rāh guzar, n.f. Road; way; a path; a pass.

راہ لگنا rāh lagnā, v. To pursue one's own course; to cease meddling with other people's affairs.

راہ لینا rāh lenā, v. To depart; to go one's way; to set out.

راہ نکالنا rāh nikālnā, v. To find a way out of a difficulty; to devise a new mode of conduct; to open or make a new road.

راہ نما - رہنما rāh numā, rahnumā, n.m. A conductor; a leader; a guide; a pilot.

راہ نمائی ' رہنمائی rāh numā'ī, rahnumāi n.f. Guidance; pilotage.

راہ وار rāh wār, n.m. An ambling horse.

راہ و رسم ' راہ و ربط rāh-ŏ rasm, rāh-ŏ rabṭ, n.f. Intercourse; friendly relations.

راہب rāhib (A) n.m. A monk; a hurmit; a Christian priest.

راہن rāhin (A) n.m. A mortgager; a pawner; a pledger.

راهنا rāhnā (A) v. To roughen a mill-stone.

راہو rāhū (H) n.m. Name of a demon who is supposed to seize the sun and the moon and causes an eclipse.

راہی rāhi (P) n.m. A traveller; a way-farer.

رائتا ra'etā (H) n.m. A salad; pumpkin &c pickled in curd.

رائج rā'ij (A) adj. Customary; current; common; usual; in force; in fashion.

رائج الوقت rā'ij-ul-waqt, adj. Current; in force; fashion of the time.

رائج کرنا rā'ij karnā, v. To make current; to give currency to; to introduce.

رائگاں rā'egān (P) adj. Useless; fruitless; vain; unprofitable.

راؤ rā'o (H) n.m. A prince; chief; warrior.

رائی rā'i (H) n.f. A kind of mustard seed with small grains; a small particle.

رائی بھر rā'i bhar, adj. Very little; as much as a mustard seed.

رائی کا پہاڑ بنانا rā'i kā pahār banānā, v. To make a mountain out of a mole-hill.

رائے rā'e (H) n.m. A Hindu title; a prince; a chief; a lord.

رائے بیل rā'e bel, n f. A species of jasmine.

رائے rā'e (A) n.f. Opinion; judgment; advice; counsel.

رائے زنی کرنا rā'e zani karnā, v. To express one's opinion.

رائے عامہ rā'e 'āmmah, n.f. Public opinion.

رائے قاطع rā'e-qāṭi', n.f. A casting vote.

رب rabb (A) n.m. God; lord; protector; preserver; master; governor.

رب العالمین rabb-ul-'ālamin, n.m. Lord of the universe; God.

رب rubb (A) n.m. Juice; thick syrup; extract; inspissated juice.

ربا rubā (P) adj. Robbing; ravishing (in compos. as دل ربا dilrubā, heart-ravishing).

ربا ribā (A) n.m. Interest; compound interest.

رباب rabāb, rubāb (A) n.m. A kind of violin.

رباعی rubā'i (A) n.f. A stanza of four lines; a quatrain; tetrastich.

ربانی rabbānī (A) adj. Divine; Godly.

ربڑ rabar (E) n.m. Rubber; eraser.

ربڑی rabri (H) n.f. Thickened or condensed milk sweetmeat.

ربط rabt (A) n.m. Connection; relation; bond; consistency; friendship; practice; intercourse.

ربط بڑھانا rabṭ barhanā, v. To become familiar; to improve one's acquaintance.

ربط ضبط rabt zabt, n.m. Intercourse; organization; intimacy.

بے ربط be rabt, adj. Disconnected; incoherent.

ربع ruba' (A) adj. A fourth part; a quarter.

ربع مسکون ruba'-ĕ maskūn, n.m. The inhabited quarter of the earth (the other three-quarters being water).

ربوبیت rabubiyyat (A) adj. Providence; the quality of being a preserver.

ربیع rai' (A) n.f. The spring; the spring harvest.

ربیع الاول rabi'-ul-awal, n.m. The third month of the Muslim year.

ربیع الثانی rabi'-us-sani, n.m. The fourth month of the Muslim year.

رپٹ rapat (H) n.f. (corr. from the English) Report.

رپٹانا raptānā (H) v. To cause to move rapidly; to cause to slip.

رپٹنا rapatnā (H) v. To move rapidly; to slip; to slide.

رپلی rupalli (H) n.f. (Diminutive of روپیہ) rupee.

رت rut (H) n.f. Season; weather.

رت بدلنا rut badalna, v. Changing of weather or season.

رت rat (H) n.f. (contr. of رات rāt) Night.

رت جگا *rat jagā, n.m.* A vigil; a night of social enjoyment (by women), a night of prayer and occupation in religious performances.

رتالو *ratālū* (H) *n m.* A yam; a large tropical esculent root.

رتبہ *rutbah* (A) *n.m.* A rank; stair; honour; dignity; distinction.

رتبہ دار *rutbah dār, adj.* Of high rank noble; eminent; distinguished.

کم رتبہ *kam rutbah, adj.* Of low rank.

رتن *ratan* (H) *n.m.* A precious stone; jewel; gem; the pupil of the eye; anything precious.

رتن جوت *ratan jot, n.f.* A plant; a medicine.

رتن مالا *ratan mālā, n.f.* A necklace of jewels; pearl-necklace; a kind of flower; name of a book on astronomy.

رتنا ولی *ratnā walı* (H) *n.f.* A necklace of gems.

رتوندھا *ratoṅdhā* (H) *n.m.* Blindness at night.

رتوندھیا *ratoṅḍhyā* (H) *n.m.* Night-blind.

رتھ *rath* (H) *n.f.*/*m.* A four-wheeled carriage, used in ancient fighting and racing; an Indian chariot.

رتھ بان *rath bān, n.m.* One who drives a رتھ *rath*; a charioteer.

رتی *ratti* (H) *n.f.* A weight equal to eight barley corns.

رتی بھر *ratti bhar, adj.* Weighing equal to a *ratti*.

رتی رتی *ratti ratti, adv.* To a farthing; to a pie.

رٹ *raṭ* (H) *n.f.* Repetition.

رٹنا *raṭnā* (H) *v.* To repeat; to reiterate; to recite over and over again; to memorize in this way.

رجا *rijāl* (H) *n.m.* (*plu.* of رجل *rajul*); Men.

رجال *rijāl* (H) *n.m.* (*plu.* of رجل *rajul*); Men.

رجائیت *rajā'iyat* (A) *n.f.* Optimism.

رجب *rajab* (A) *n.m.* The seventh month of the Muslim year.

رجحان *rujḥān* (A) *n.m.* Inclination; tendency; preference.

رجز *rajaz* (A) *n.m.* Verses read at the battle-field to arouse the martial spirit of soldiers.

رجز خوانی *rajaz k͟hwāni, n.f.* Recitation of exciting verses.

رجسٹر *rajisṭar* (E) *n.m.* Register.

رجسٹر پیمائش *rajisṭar-ĕ paimā'ish, n.m.* Survey register.

رجسٹر ترسیل *rajisṭar-ĕ tarsil, n.m.* Despatch register.

رجسٹر جائداد *rajistar-ĕ jā'idād, n.m.* Property register.

رجسٹر جرائم *rajistar-ĕ jarā'im, n.m.* Crime register.

رجسٹر رسید *rajistar-ĕ rasid, n.m.* Receipt register.

رجسٹر سامان *rajisṭar-ĕ sāman, n.m.* Stock register.

رجسٹر محصلی *rajisṭar-ĕ muhassali, n.m.* Daily collection register.

رجسٹری *rajstarı, n.f.* (*corr.* from the English) Registration.

رجعت *raj'at* (A) *n.f.* Return; going back; remarrying a divorced wife in accordance with the prescribed way; the resurrection.

رجعت قہقری *raj'at-ĕ qahqari, n.f.* Retracing one's steps.

رجم *rajm* (A) *n.m.* Stoning to death; strewing a grave with tones.

رجواڑا *rajwāṛā* (H) *n.m.* A country under the control of a *rājā*.

رجوع rujū' (A) n.m./f. Return; bent; reference; appeal; inclination.

رجوع کرنا ruju' karnā, v. To turn; to return; to incline; to refer to; to have recourse to; to bring into court; to appeal.

رجولیت rajūliyyat (A) n.f. Manliness; virility.

رجھانا rijhānā (H) v. To please; to enchant; to captivate; to ravish; to charm.

رچانا rachānā (H) v. To decorate; to celebrate; to stain with ḥinā; to make merry.

رچنا rachnā (H) n.f. Make; form; arrangement; fabrication; workmanship; literary production. v. To fabricate; to produce; to be held; to be absorbed.

رحل riḥl (A) n.f. A stand for the Quran; a book stand.

رحلت riḥlat (A) n.f. Marching; departure; removal; death; demise.

رحم riḥm (A) n.m. The womb.

رحم raḥm (A) n.m. Mercy; pity; compassion; kindness; tenderness.

رحم دل raḥm dil, adj. Tender-hearted; kind hearted.

رحم کرنا، کھانا raḥm karnā, khānā, v. To take pity; to feel pity for.

رحمان raḥmān (A) adj. Most merciful; most forgiving (God).

رحمانی raḥmāni (A) adj. Divine.

رحمت raḥmat (A) n.f. Divine mercy; pity; kindness; divine blessing.

رحیم raḥim (A) adj. Merciful; very merciful (God).

رحیمی raḥimi (A) n.f. Mercifulness.

رخ rukh (P) n.m. Face; countenance; cheek; side; point; quarter; the castle at chess

رخ بدلنا یا پھیرنا rukh badalnā yā phernā, v. To become angry; to turn away the face; to turn away from; not to pay attention; to reject.

رخ کرنا rukh karnā, v. To turn the face (towards); to attend to; to accede to; to lean or incline towards.

رخت rakht (P) n.m. Goods and chattels; property; apparatus; furniture; apparel; clothes; baggage.

رخت باندھنا rakht bāndhna, v. To pack up; to depart; to set off.

رخسار rukhsār (P) n.m. The cheek; face; countenance; complexion; aspect

رخش rakhsh (P) n.m. A horse; name of the famous horse of Rustam; brilliance; splendour; the rays or reflection of light.

رخشاں rakhshan (P) adj. Dazzling; resplendent.

رخشندہ rakhshandah (P) adj. Bright; resplendent.

رخصت rukhṣat (A) n.f. Leave; permission; dismissal; discharge; indulgence; licence; facilitation.

رخصت اتفاقی rukhṣat-ĕ ittifāqi, n.f. Casual leave.

رخصت بلا تنخواہ rukhṣat bila tankhwāh, n.f. Leave without pay.

رخصت رعایتی rukhṣat-ĕ ri'āyati, n.f. Privilege leave.

رخصت طبی rukhṣat-ĕ tibbi, n.f. Leave on medical certificate; medical leave.

رخصت غیر معمولی rukhṣat-ĕ ghair ma'muli, n.f. Extraordinary leave.

رخصت دینا rukhṣat denā, v. To give leave; to permit; to dismiss.

رخصت کرنا rukhṣat karnā, v. To give leave; to permit; to bid farewell; to discharge; to dismiss.

رخصت مانگنا rukhṣat māṅgnā, v. To ask leave; to request for indulgence.

رخصت ہونا rukhṣat honā, v. To take leave; to depart.

رخصتانہ rukhṣatānah (P) n.m. A parting present; a present made on dismissing a person.

رخصتی rukhṣati (P) *n.f.* Anything given on parting; departure of bride from her parent's home to the home of her husband. *adj.* On leave.

رخنه rakhnah (P) *n.m.* A gap; a hole; a hitch; obstacle; a fracture; a notch; a slit; a chink; a crack.

رخنه انداز rakhnah andāz, *adj.* Obstructing; hindering.

رخنه ڈالنا rakhnah ḍālnā, *v.* To put obstacles in the way; to obstruct.

رخنه نکالنا rakhnah nikālnā, *v.* To pick holes in; to find fault with.

رد radd (A) *n.m.* Rejection; casting off; opposition; refutation; vomiting; repulsion; resistance; restitution; returning.

رد کرنا radd karnā, *v.* To return; to refuse; to reject; to oppose; to disprove; to abrogate (a law); to confute; to refute; to repel; to vomit.

رد و بدل radd-ŏ badal, *n.m.* Change; alteration; discussion; altercation; agitation; controversy.

رد و قدح، رد و کد radd-ŏ qadaḥ, radd-ŏ kadd, *n.f.* Discussion; refutation; dispute; argument; altercation.

رد هونا radd hona, *v.* To be rejected or returned.

ردا rida (A) *n.f.* A cloak put on when going out; a cloak or mantle worn by dervishes; a sheet.

ردا raddā (A) *n.m.* A layer of bricks on a wall.

ردا رکھنا raddā rakhnā, *v.* To lay down a layer.

ردی radi, raddi (A) *adj.* Rejected; waste; worthless; bad; hurtful; away; refuse; *n.f.* waste paper.

ردی دان radi dān, *n.m.* Waste-paper basket.

ردی کرنا radi karnā, *v.* To waste; to reject.

ردیف radif (A) *n.f.* A man riding behind another on the same horse; the rhyming word of a poem; rare-guard.

ردیف وار radif war, *adv.* Alphabetically; according to the last letter of each stanza.

رذالت razālat (A) *n.f.* Meanness; baseness.

رذیل razil (A) *adj.* & *n.m.* A man of a low caste; a mean fellow; a vagabond; villain.

رڑکنا riṛaknā (H) *v.* To churn.

رز raz (P) *n.f.* A vineyard; a vine; a grape.

رزاق razzāq (A) *n.m.* The giver of sustenance; Providence; God; an attribute of God.

رزاق razzāqi, *n.f.* Providing daily bread; an attribute of God.

رزق rizq (A) *n.m.* Food; support; subsistence; daily bread.

رزم razm (P) *n.m.* War; battle; combat.

رزم گاه razm gāh, *n.f.* A battlefield.

رزمی razmi (P) *adj.* Relating to war.

رزمیه razmiyyah (P) *adj.* An epic poem.

رس ras (H) *n.m.* Juice; spirit; syrup; liquor; broth; essence; pith; potion; poison; taste; relish; enjoyment; quicksilver; mercury; gum.

رس بهرا ras bhara, *adj.* Juicy; tasteful.

رس بهری ras bhari, *adj.* Liquid; luscious; full of juice. *n.f.* Respberry.

رس ٹپکنا ras ṭapakna, *v.* to be very juicy; to be over flowing with juice; to be in full maturity; to be full of sexual desire.

رس ras (P) *adj.* Arriving; reaching. (used in *comp.* as in فریاد رس *faryād ras*, a protector; a dispenser of justice).

رسا rasā (P) *adj.* Quick of apprehension; arriving; (in *compos.* as in ذهن رسا *zahan rasā*. comprehensive mind).

رسا rassā (H) *n.m.* A rope; cable.

رسالت risālat (A) n.f. Divine mission; apostleship; prophethood; divine message.

رساله risālah (A) n.m. A troop of horses; cavalry; a squadron; a treatise; a magazine; pamphlet; tract.

رساله دار - رسالدار risālah dār, risāldār, n.m. An officer of cavalry; the commander of a squadron.

رساول rasāwāl (H) n.m. A dish of rice boiled in the juice of sugar-cane.

رساں rasāṅ (P) adj. Causing to arrive; arriving. (in compos. as in چٹھی رساں chitthi rasāṅ a postman.)

رسائل rasāil (A) n.m. (plu. of رساله rasālah) Magazines; squadrons.

رسائی rasā'i (P) n.f. Access; entrance; approach; reach; quickness of apprehension; acuteness; skill; wisdom; mental penetration; talent.

رساین rasāyan (H) n.m. Alchemy; a mineral or metallic preparation; chemistry.

رسائن بنانا rasāyan banānā, v. To turn base metals with silver or gold.

رساینی rāsāyanī (H) n.m. Alchemist.

رستاخیز - رستخیز rastākhez, rustakhez (P) n.m. The last day; the day of judgement; the day of resurrection; doomsday.

رستگار rastgār (P) adj. Liberated.

رستگاری rastgārī (P) n.f. Liberation; deliverance.

رستم rustam (P) n.m. One of the twelve champions of Persia; a hero; a brave man.

رسته rastah (P) n.m. See راسته rāstah.

رسد rasad (P) n.f. Store of grain laid in for an army; food; grain; provisions; import; rations; allowance of food; supplies.

رسد رسانی rasad rasānī, n.f. Furnishing supplies for an army.

رسدی rasadī (P) adj. Ratable; proportionate.

رس کپور ras kāpūr (H) n.m. Corrasive sublimate; a preparation of mercury.

رسل rasl (A) n.m. Sending news, messages, letters.

رسل و رسائل rasl-ŏ rasā'il, n.m. Communication; correspondence.

رسل rusul (A) n.m. (plu. of رسول rasul) Prophets; messengers.

رسم rasm (A) n.f. Marking; writing; drawing of a line; custom; settled mode; established usage; model; plan; law; canon; precept; a literary game played by children.

رسم پر چلنا rasm par chalnā, v. To act according to custom.

رسم الخط rasm-ul-khatt, n.m. The mode of writing.

رسم ڈالنا rasm dālnā, v. To introduce a practice.

رسم و رواج rasm-ŏ riwāj, n.m. Custom and usage.

رسماً rasman (A) adv. Formally; according to custom; officlally.

رسمی rasmi (A) adj. Formal; ordinary; usual; customary; common; middling; second rate.

رسمیات rasmiyyāt (A) n.f. Formalities; customs; usages.

رسن rasan (P) n.f. Rope; string; cord.

رسنا risnā (H) v. To drop slowly; to drip; to leak; to ooze.

رسوا ruswā (A) adj. Infamous; ignominious; dishonoured; disgraced.

رسوائی ruswā'ī (P) n.f. Disgrace; infamy; dishonour; disrepute; ignominy; opprobrium.

رسوت rasaut (H) n.f. A kind of callyrium, extracted from the root of the Amomum anthorhizum.

رسوخ rasūkh (A) n.m. Friendship; influence: access; firmness; stability.

رسوخ حاصل کرنا **rasū<u>kh</u> hāṣil karnā**, *v.* To have access (to); to acquire influence or favour.

رسول **rasūl** (A) *n.m.* A messenger; a prophet.

رسولی **rasaulī** (H) *n.f.* Tumour; proud flesh; everescence.

رسوم **rusūm** (A) *n.f.* (*plu.* of رسم *rasm*) Customs; usages; fees; duties; taxes; postage.

رسوم عدالت **rusūm-ĕ 'adālat**, *n.f.* Court fees.

رسوئی **raso'ī** (H) *n.f.* Kitchen; victuals; dressed food.

رسی **rassī** (H) *n.f.* String; cord; rope.

رسی جل گئی پر بل نہیں گیا **rassī jal ga'ī par bal nahīṅ gayā**, *prov.* A rope may burn out but wouldn't give up its twist; habits take long to depart.

رسی دراز ہونا **rassī darāz honā**, *v.* To get a long rope; to enjoy liberty of action; to enjoy long life.

رسی ڈھیلی چھوڑنا **rassī ḍhīlī chhoṛnā**, *v.* To let the reins drop; to grant one freedom of action; to give a person rope enough to hang himself.

رسی بٹنا **rassī baṭnā**, *v.* To twine a rope; to twist a rope.

رسیا **rasyā** (H) *n.m.* One who enjoys life; one who makes pleasure his pursuit; an epicure; a rake.

رسید **rasīd** (P) *n.f.* A receipt; an acknowledgement of arriving or receiving.

رسید دینا **rasīd denā**, *v.* To give a receipt; to issue an acknowledgement.

رسید نقدی **rasīd-ĕ naqdī**, *n.f.* Cash memo.

رسیدگی **rasīdagī** (P) *n.f.* Arrival; ripeness; maturity; perfection.

رسیدہ **rasīdah** (P) *adj.* Arrived; received; ripe; mature; overtaken by; at hand (used in *compos.* as in خدا رسیدہ *<u>kh</u>udā rasīdah*, *n.m.* One who has reached God; a saint; a holy and pious man.)

رسیلا **rasīlā** (H) *adj.* Juicy; luxurious; rakish; voluptuous.

رشتہ **rishtah** (P) *n.m.* String; thread; line; series; relationship; connection; kinship; affinity; alliance.

رشتہ دار **rishtah dār**, *n.m.* Relation; kinsman.

رشتہ داری **rishtah dārī**, *n.f.* Relationship.

رشد **rushd** (A) *n.m.* Rectitude; right way; piety; dutifulness; development; adolesence.

رشک **rashk** (P) *n.m.* Jealousy; envy; grudge; malice; spite; emulation.

رشوت **rishwat** (A) *n.f.* Bribe; illegal gratification.

رشوت خور **rishwat <u>kh</u>or**, *n.m.* One who takes bribes.

رشوت ستانی **rishwat sitānī**, *n.f.* Taking bribe; to extort bribe.

رشی **rishī** (S) *n.m.* An inspired poet or sage; a pious person; a saint.

رشید **rashīd** (A) *adj.* Guided in the right way; pious; righteous.

رضا **riẓā** (A) *n.f.* Pleasure; contentment; approval; leave; permission; assent.

رضا جوئی **riẓā jo'ī**, *n.f.* Asking for leave; seeking the good pleasure or approbation of.

رضا کار **riẓā kār**, *n.m.* A volunteer.

رضا مند **riẓā mand**, *adj.* Consulting; agreeing; willing; permitting.

رضا مندی **riẓā mandī**, *n.f.* Consent; willingness.

رضا و رغبت **riẓā-ŏ ra<u>gh</u>bat**, *n.f.* Free consent and pleasure.

رضاعت **raẓā'at** (A) *n.f.* Suckling; fosterage; affinity between persons nursed by the same female.

رضاعی raẓā'ī, (A) adj. Foster; sucking; (used in comp. as in, رضاعی بھائی raẓā'i bhā'ī, Foster brother.)

رضائی raẓā'ī, n.f. Quilt; coverlet.

رضوان riẓwān (A) n.m. Good pleasure; complacency; Paradise; doorkeeper of Paradise.

رضوی riẓwī (A) n.m. A descendent of Imām Mūsā Ali Riẓā.

رطب raṭb (A) adj. Moist; tender; fresh; green; verdant.

رطب اللسان raṭb-ul-lisān, adj. Celebrated; frequently praising a person.

رطب و یابس raṭb-ŏ yābis, n.m. Moist and dry; the good and the bad.

رطوبت ruṭūbat (A) n.f. Moisture; dampness; humidity; saliva; juiceness; sap.

رعایا ri'āyā (A) n.f. Subjects; tenants; peasantry; common people; the public.

رعایت ri'āyat (A) n.f. Partiality; relaxation; remission; indulgence; bias; regard; honour; kindness.

رعایت کرنا ri'āyat karnā, v. To show partiality or favour.

رعایتی ri'āyatī (A) adj. Favoured; complimentary. n.m. A favoured person.

رعب ru'b (A) n.m. Awe; fear; terror; awe-inspiring presence; dignity.

رعب بٹھانا ، جمانا ، ڈالنا ru'b bithānā, jamānā, ḍālnā v. To inspire with awe; to frighten; to terrify; to over-awe.

رعب دار ru'b dār, adj. Awe inspiring; commanding.

رعب میں آنا ru'b meṅ ānā, v. To be overawed by.

رعب و داب ru'b-ŏ dāb, n.m. Awe; great pomp and show; display of rank and dignity.

رعد ra'd (A) n.m. Thunder.

رعشہ ra'shah (A) n.m. Tremor; shaking; the shaking palsy.

رعشہ دار ra'shah dār, adj. Palsied; suffering from the shaking palsy.

رعنا ra'nā (A) adj. Moving gracefully; lovely; beautiful; graceful; delicate; tender.

رعنائی ra'nā'ī (A) n.f. Graceful movements; loveliness; grace; beauty; delicacy; tenderness.

رعونت ra'ūnat (A) n.f. Pride; arrogance; haughtiness.

رعیت ra'iyyat (A) n.f. Subjects; people; tenants; peasants (of a landlord); a dependent.

رعیت پرور، رعیت نواز ra'iyyat parwar, ra'iyyat nawāz, adj. Benevolent; protector of subjects; cherisher of subjects.

رغبت raghbat (A) n.f. Strong desire; inclination; wish; curiosity; esteem; affection; pleasure.

رغم raghm (A) n.m. Contempt; dislikeness; shame; aversion; repugnance; abhorrence.

علی الرغم al-ar-raghm, adv. In spite of opposition; in spite of disagreement.

رفاقت rifāqat (A) n.f. Companionship; friendship; society; adherence; loyalty.

رفاقت کرنا rifāqat karnā, v. To associate with; to accompany; to keep company with; to be friend.

رفاہ rifāh (A) n.m. Comfortable state of life; contentment; enjoyment of life; repose; quiet; tranquillity.

رفاہ عام rifāh-ĕ 'ām, n.f. Public good; public welfare.

رفت و گذشت raft-ō guẓasht (P) adj. Past and gone; dead and forgotten.

رفتار raftār (P) n.f. Speed; pace; walk; going; motion.

رفتار و گفتار raftār-ŏ guftār, n.f. Conduct; demeanour; behaviour.

رفتگاں **raftagān** (P) *n.m. & adj.* Those who are gone; the departed ones.

رفته **raftah** (P) *adj.* Gone; departed; lost; deceased.

رفته رفته **raftah raftah**, *adv.* In course of time; gradually; by degrees; leisurely; step by step.

رفرف **rafraf** (A) *n.m.* Conveyance of the Holy Prophet when he ascended to heaven from Jerusalem.

رفض **rafẓ** (A) *n.m.* Heresy; the creed of a heretic; schism.

رفع **rafa'** (P) *n.m.* Elevation; ascending; exaltation; removal; vowel-point of the Nominative.

رفع دفع **rafa' dafa'** (A) *n.m.* Deciding; settling; finishing.

رفع شر **rafa'-ĕ sharr**, *n.m.* Settling a dispute; stopping a mischief.

رفع کرنا **rafa' karnā**, *v.* To remove; to settle; to set at rest.

رفعت **rifa't** (A) *n.f.* Elevation; dignity; exaltation; eminence; height; altitude; promotion; nobility.

رفقا **rufaqā** (A) *n.m.* (*plu.* of رفیق *rafīq*) Friends; comrades; companions.

رفل **rafal** (H) *n.f.* A kind of fine muslin.

رفو **rafū, rufū** (A) *n.m.* Darning; mending; darn.

رفو چکر هونا **rafū chakkar honā**, *v.* To abscond; to decamp; to slink away.

رفو کرنا **rafū karnā**, *v.* To darn; to mend.

رفو گر **rafū gar**, *n.m.* A darner; one who darns shawls etc.

رفو گری **rafū garī**, *n.f.* Darning.

رفیع **rafī'** (A) *adj.* High; sublime; exalted; elevated.

رفیع الشان ، رفیع القدر **rafī'-ush-shān, rafī-ul-qadr**, *adj.* A person of dignity; a person of high rank.

رفیق **rafīq** (A) *n.m.* A friend; ally; associate; comrade; companion; accomplice; confiderate.

رقابت **raqābat** (A) *n.m.* Rivalry; competition; antagonism.

رقاص **raqqāṣ** (A) *n.m.* A dancer.

رقاصه **raqqāṣah** (A) *n.f.* A female dancer.

رقبه **raqbah** (A) *n.m.* An enclosure; an area; environ's esplanade; superficial contents.

رقبه نکالنا **raqbah nikālnā**, *v.* To find out or calculate the area.

رقت **riqqat** (A) *n.f.* Thinness; liquidity; minuteness; subtleness; flimsiness; affection; tenderness; softness; ecstasy; weeping.

رقص **raqṣ** (A) *n.m.* A dance; dancing.

رقعات **ruq'āt** (A) *n.m.* (*plu.* of رقعه *ruq'ah*); Notes; a collection of letters.

رقعه **ruq'ah** (A) *n.m.* A piece; scrap of paper; a letter; a note; a billet; an invitation.

رقم **raqm** (A) *n.m.* Notation of numerals; arithmetic; figure; number; item; amount; sum; total; manner; method; a royal edict; handwriting; mark; sign.

رقم کرنا **raqm karnā**, *v.* To mark; to note; to write; to commit to writing; to record; to enter.

رقم وار **raqm wār**, *adv.* Item by item; in detail.

رقیب **raqīb** (A) *n.m.* A rival; a competitor; one who watches; one who guards.

رقیق **raqīq** (A) *adj.* Thin; fine; liquid; subtle; delicate; unsubstantial; attenuated; flimsy.

رقیق القلب **raqīq-ul-qalb**, *adj.* A kind-hearted person.

رکاب **rakāb** (A) *n.f.* A stirrup; train.

رکابدار **rakābdār**, *n.m.* An attendant when riding; a companion.

پا برکاب **pā barakāb**, *adj.* Ready to start.

هم رکاب **ham rakāb**, *adj.* In attendance; riding in company with.

رکابی **rakābī** (P) *n.f.* A small dish.

رکابی مذهب **rakābī maẕhab**, *adj.* A parasite; one who joins every feast uninvited.

رکاؤ یا رکاوٹ **rukāo yā rukāwaṭ** (H) *n.f.* Hinderance; prevention; obstacle; blocked; stoppage; delay.

رکعت **raka't** (A) *n.f.* Bending; a part of the prayer which includes standing bending and prostration.

رکن **rukn** (A) *n.m.* A piller; support; prop; foot of a verse; essential part; fundamentals of faith; basic principle; precept; commandment; injunction; rule of action; maxims.

رکنا **ruknā** (H) *v.* To stop; to rest; to refrain from; to desist from; to be prevented; to be hindered; to falter in speech.

رکوع **rukū'** (A) *n.m.* Bowing the head and the body in prayer.

رکھ رکھاؤ **rakh rakhā'o** (H) *n.m.* Looking after; care-taking; manners; behaviour; mode.

رکھ لینا **rakh lenā** (H) *v.* To accept; to employ; to take; to engage.

رکھائی **rukhā'i** (H) *n.f.* Roughness; dryness; insipidity; indifference; carelessness; disinterestedness.

رکھشا **rakhshā** (H) *n.f.* Protection; preservation; care; safety; custody; support; patronage.

رکھنا **rakhnā** (H) *v.* To keep; to put down; to keep back; to reserve; to possess; to hold; to lay by; to employ; to stake; to mortgage.

رکھوالا **rakhwālā** (H) *n.m.* A guard; a keeper; a watchman; a shepherd; a cowherd.

رکھوالی **rakhwālī** (H) *n.f.* Watch; guard; care; custody.

رکھوانا **rakhwānā** (H) *v.* To cause to keep; to cause to put; to give in charge.

رکیک **rakik** (A) *adj.* Thin; shallow; shameless; disgraceful; indecent.

رکین **rakīn** (A) *adj.* Strong; stable; resolute.

رگ **rag** (P) *n.f.* A vein; an artery; fibre; sinew.

رگ زن **rag zan** (P) *n.m.* A surgeon; a bleeder; a phlebotomist.

رگ مرنا **rag marnā**, *v.* To lose virility; to become impotent.

رگ و ریشه **rag-ŏ reshah** *n.m.* Every vein; veins and fibres; nature; constitution.

رگ جاں، شاہ رگ **rag-ĕ jān, shah rag**, *n.m.* An artery; the jugular vein.

رگڑ **ragaṛ** (H) *n.f.* Rubbing against; friction; a scratch; abrasion; attrition.

رگڑ کھانا **ragaṛ khānā**, *v.* To be rubbed; to be grazed; to collide with.

رگڑا **ragṛā** (H) *n.m.* Rubbing; polishing; quarrelling; wrangling; an ointment for the eye

رگڑا جھگڑا **ragṛā jhagṛā**, *n.m.* Discussion; altercation; quarrel; debate; wrangling; argument.

رگڑنا **ragarnā** (H) *v.* To rub; to scour; to grate; to grind; to chafe; to fret.

رگیدنا **ragednā** (H) *v.* To pursue; to chase; to hunt; to drive off; to drag.

رلا ملا **ralā milā** (H) *adj.* Mixed; adultrated; alloyed.

رلانا **rulānā** (H) *v.* To cause to weep; to vex; to displease; to afflict; to tease.

رلنا **rulnā** (H) *v.* To be lost; to be ruined; to be scattered.

رم ram (P) n.m. Terror; scare; flight.

رم rim (E) n.m. Ream; a package of 20 quires of paper.

رم جھم rim jhim (H) n.f. Pattering sound (of rain).

رمال rammāl (A) n.m. A fortune-teller; a soothe-sayer; a practiser of geomancy; a conjurer.

رمان rummān (A) n.m. A pomegranate.

رمانا ramānā (H) v. To entice; to beguile; to take possession of; to cause to wander; to divert.

رمتا ramtā (H) adj. Roaming; wandering.

رمتا جوگی ramtā jogi, adj. A wandering ascetic.

رمز ramz (A) n.f. Sign; hint; wink; enigma; riddle; irony; an insinuation; ambiguous expression; allusion; sarcasm; innendo.

رمز شناس ramz shinās, adj. One who takes a hint.

رمضان ramaẕān (A) n.m. The name of the ninth lunar month of the Muslim calendar, in which Muslims fast and are prohibited from eating, drinking and conjugal duty, between dawn and sunset. On the 27th of this month the *Quran* began to de cend.

رمق ramaq (A) n.f. The last gasp; a little; a spark; the last breath; departing spirit or soul; tincture.

رمل ramal (A) n.m. Foretelling by figures; divination; geomancy.

رمنا ramnā (H) v. To roam; to rove; to wander; to enjoy. n.m. A park; a pasture land; a chase (for game); a hunting preserve; a meadow.

رموز rumūz (A) n.m. (plu. of رمز ramz); Signs; hints; enigmas; riddles.

رمیدگی ramidagi (P) n.f. Flying in terror; running away.

رن ran (H) n.m. Battle; war; combat; conflict; wood; waste; desert.

رن پڑنا ran paṛnā, v. Ensuing of the battle; breaking out a heavy fighting.

رنج ranj (P) n.m. Grief; affliction; pains; toil; anguish of mind; disgust; sorrow; suffering; sadness; distress; inconvenience; trouble.

رنج آٹھانا • سہنا ranj uṭhānā, sahnā, v. To suffer sorrow or pain &c.

رنج دینا ranj denā, v. To give pain; to vex; to wound one's feelings.

رنج کرنا ranj karnā, v. To grieve or lament over; to take offence; to be vexed.

رنج مول لینا ranj mol lenā, v. t. To court trouble; to be in difficulties.

رنجش ranjish (P) n.f. Grief; unpleasantness; coolness; indignation; misunderstanding; affliction; anguish of mind.

رنجور ranjur (P) adj. Sick; afflicted; grieved sad; infirm; ill; distressed.

رنجوری ranjuri (P) n.f. Affliction; anguish; sickness.

رنجیدگی ranjidagi (P) n.f. Affliction; vexation; sadness; displeasure.

رنجیدہ ranjidah (P) adj. Afflicted; offended; grieved; displeased; vexed; chagrined; sad; sorrowful.

رنجیدہ خاطر rajidah khāṯir, adj. Afflicted in mind; grieved; displeased.

رند rind (P) n.m. An irreligious person; a free-thinker; a sceptic; a reprobate; a rake; a libertive; a black-guard; a vagabond; a drunkard.

رندانہ rindānah (P) adj. Dissolute; licentious; rakish; like a debaucher.

رندنا randna (H) v. See رندہ پھیرنا randah pherna.

رنده randah (H) n.m. A carpenter's plane; a rasp; a grater.

رنده پھیرنا randah pherna, v. To plane; to level (wood).

رندی rindī (P) n.f. Trick; pond; debauchery; drunkenness,

رنڈاپا ranḍāpā (H) n.m. Widowhood.

رنڈوا ranḍwā (H) n.m. A widower.

رنڈی ranḍī (H) n.f. A prostitute; a harlot; a whore; a bad character woman.

رنڈی باز ranḍī bāz, n.m. A whoremonger; a rake; a fornicator.

رنڈی بازی ranḍi bāzi, n.f. Whoring; fornication.

رنڈیا ranḍyā (H) n.f. A widow.

رنگ rang (P) n.m. Colour; dye; paint; pigment; fashion; style; character; nature; a suit (cards); dancing and singing; enjoyment; merriment.

رنگ آمیزی rang āmezi, v. Colouring; being of various colours; painting; fickleness; inconstancy; variableness; stratagem.

رنگ آمیزی کرنا rāng āmezi karnā, v. To taint facts; to colour facts.

رنگ آڑنا ، آترنا rang urnā, utarnā, v. To lose colour; to fade; to become pale; to be grieved.

رنگ افشانی rang āfshānī, n.f. Scattering colour.

رنگ اندھا rang āndhā, adj. Colour blind.

رنگ بدلنا rang badalnā, v. To change colour; to change one's manner; to be fickle.

رنگ برنگ - رنگا رنگ rang birang, rangā rang, adj. Of various colours; of various sorts; multi-coloured; variegated.

رنگ بگڑنا rang bigarnā, v. To change colour; changing the state or condition of anything.

رنگ بھرنا rang bharnā, v. To paint; to colour; to apply colour to.

رنگ پھیکا پڑ جانا rang phīkā par jānā, v. To become pale or dull or dim.

رنگ چڑھانا rang charhānā, v. To dye; to paint.

رنگ چڑھنا rang charhnā, v. To be elated with liquor; to be merry; to be painted or dyed; to be exalted.

رنگ دار rang dār, adj. Coloured; showy; fine; painted.

رنگ دیکھنا rang dekhnā, v. To examine the state or condition of; to consider the consequences or result of something.

رنگ ڈھنگ rang ḍhang, n.m. Appearance; aspect; fashion; style.

رنگ رلیاں rang ralyāṅ, n.f. Sport; merriment; pleasure; mirth; pleasant society of lovers, music and dancing; rejoicings; revelry.

رنگ روپ rang rūp, n.m. Colour; complexion; form; character; appearance.

رنگ ریز rang rez, n.m. A dyer.

رنگ ریزی rang rezi, n.f. Dying; painting.

رنگ ساز rang sāz, n.m. Colour-manufacturer; a painter; a dyer.

رنگ فق ہونا rang faq honā, v. To grow pale (from fear or astonishment).

رنگ کرنا rang karnā, v. To paint; to colour; to enjoy oneself; to lead a life of pleasure.

رنگ کھیلنا rang khelnā, v. To sport with colour; to sprinkle red colour (at *holī* or other festive occasions).

رنگ لانا rang lanā, v. To present a fine appearance or form; to bloom; to flesh up; to change; to bring about a change,

رنگ محل rang maḥal, n.m. An apartment for festive enjoyments; a building dedicated to voluptuous enjoyments.

رنگ میں بھنگ ہونا rang meṅ bhang honā, v. Spoiling of a sport.

رنگ نکالنا rang nikalnā, v. To look bright; to show off; to come off with flying colours.

رنگانا ـ رنگوانا rangānā, rangwānā (H) v. To cause to be coloured; to get coloured.

رنگائی ـ رنگوائی rangā'ī, rangwā'ī (H) n.f. Price paid for colouring, dying or painting &c.

رنگت rangat (H) n.f. Colour; dye; hue; design; complexion; form; condition.

رنگترہ rangtarah (H) n.m. An orange.

رنگروٹ rangrūṭ (H) n.m. (cor. from the English) Recruit.

رنگنا rangnā (H) v. To colour; to dye; to paint.

رنگیلا ـ رنگیلی rangīlā, rangīlī (H) adj. Guady; showy; airy; gay; bright; fine; jovial; buxom; addicted to pleasure.

رنگین rangīn (P) adj. Coloured; variegated; gaudy; ornamented; adorned; ornate; flowery (as style, language &c); elegant; gay; lively; addicted to pleasure; embellished; figurative; metaphysical; alligorical.

رنگین ادا rangīn ādā, adj. Of elegant manner.

رنگین مزاج rangīn mizāj, adj. See رنگیلا rangīlā.

رنگینی rangīnī (P) n.m. Bright-colouring; variety; gaudiness; showiness.

رنگینی عبارت rangīnī-ē ʻibārat, n.f. A florid style.

رو rau (P) adj. Going; going before; (used in compos. as in پیش رو pesh rau going before; a leader); n.m. water current; rivulet; stream; tumult; uproar; anger; malice; inclination; ambition; army; crowd.

رو rau (P) adj. Growing; germinating (used in compos. as in خود رو k͟hud rau Growing by itself; wild).

رو rū (P) n.m. Face; countenance; surface; cause; mode; sake; reason.

رو برو rū barū, n.m. Presence. adv. Face to face; before; over against; in front of; in the presence of.

رو بصحت rū baṣiḥḥat, adj. Convalescing; recovering.

رو بکار rū bakār, adj. Ready for business; approaching; intent on; in hand; on foot; transacting business. n.m. A proceeding; an order; a record; a warrant.

رو بکاری rū bakārī, n.f. Proceedings of a case.

رو پوش rū posh, adj. Hiding (the face). concealed; being internally one thing and externally another; absconding.

رو پوش ہونا rū posh honā, adj. To be concealed; to hide one's face; to conceal oneself; to abscond.

رو پوشی rū poshī, n.f. Concealment; absconding.

رو دار rū dār, adj. Good looking; pleasing. n.m. A man of rank and dignity.

رو رعایت rū riʻāyat, n.f. Partiality; favour.

رو سے rū se, adv. According to; in accordance with; by way of.

رو سیاہ rū siyāh, adj. Disgraced; infamous; sinner; criminal; unfortunate.

رو سیاہی rū siyāhī, n.f. Disgrace; dishonour; criminal conduct.

رو شناس rū shināṣ, adj. An acquaintance; one who is known by sight; casual acquaintance; cap-acquaintance.

رو شناسی rū shināsī, n.f. Acquaintance; casual acquaintance.

رو کش rū kash, n.m. A cover of a mirror. adj. Opponent; averse; resembling.

رو گرداں rū gardāṅ (P) adj. Inattentive; disobedient; deserting; abandoning; averse; turning away the face.

رو گردانی rū gardānī, n.f. Disaffection; revolt; disobedience; aversion.

رومال rūmāl (P) n.m. A handkerchief; a towel; a napkin.

رومالی rūmālī, n.f. A handkerchief worn about the head; a triangular piece of cloth wound round the loins by wrestlers.

رو نما rū numā, adj. Appearing.

رو نمائی rū numā'ī, n.f Showing the face; unveiling; appearing before others; a sight of the face.

روا rawā (H) n.m. Gold or silver filings; a grain or particle of sand: gunpowder; a kind of flour; a bit; a piece; a little.

روا rawā (P) adj. Right; allowable; admissible; lawful; current; worthy; proper; suitable; accurate.

روا دار rawā dār, adj. One who approves; one who hold a thing to be right; approving; tolerant; indulgent; enduring.

روا داری rawa darī, n.f. Toleration; approbation; approval; confirmation; consent; endurance.

روا رکھنا rawā rakhnā, v. To uphold; to justify; to consider lawful.

روابط rawābit (A) n.m. (plu. of رابطہ rābiṭah) Relations; connections.

رواج riwāj (A) n.m. Usage; custom; fashion; currency; practice; prevalence.

رواج پانا - پکڑنا riwāj pānā, pakarnā, v. To be in vogue; to be current; to have effect; to become prevalent.

رواج دینا riwāj denā, v. To make current or customary; to introduce.

رواجی rawājī (A) adj. Current; ordinary; customary.

روا روی rawā rawī, n.f. Hurry; hastey confusion; cursoriness.

رواں rawāṅ (P) adj. Going; running; moving; flowing; sharp; active; brisk. n.m. Life; soul.

رواں پڑھنا rawāṅ paṛhnā, v. To read fluently; to read without spelling the words.

رواں حساب rawāṅ ḥisāb, n.m. Current account.

رواں کرنا rawāṅ karnā, v. To get going; to despatch; to send; to make current.

رواں ہونا rawāṅ honā, v. To be current.

سال رواں sāl-ĕ rawāṅ, n.m. The current year.

عمر رواں 'umr-ĕ rawāṅ, n.m. Fleeting life.

رواں roāṅ (H) n.m. The hair of the body; down; wool; fur.

رواں دار - روئیں دار roāṅ dār, roe'ṅ dār, adj. Furred; downy.

روانگی rawāngī (P) n.f. Despatch; departure; passing; travelling; going; setting out.

روانہ rawānah (P) n.m. A pass; a passport. adj. Despatched; departed; proceeding.

روانی rawānī (P) n.f. Going; proceeding; running; fluency.

روایات riwāyāt (A) n.f. (plu. of روایت riwāyat); Histories; narrations; traditions; legends.

روایت riwāyat (A) n.f. A narrative; tale; fiction; fable; a tradition; a legend.

روباہ robāh (P) n.f. A fox.

روباہ بازی robāh bāzī, n.f. Stratagem; wile; trick; cunningness; artfulness; deceit; subterfuge.

روپ rūp (H) n.m. Face; countenance; appearance; feature; beauty; condition; manner; mode; picture; elegance; colour; brilliance; splendour; unit; the known quantity.

روپ بدلنا rūp badalnā, v. To change one's countenance; to change form or appearance.

روپ بگاڑنا rūp bigāṛnā, v. To disfigure; to deface; to spoil the beauty of.

روپ بنانا - دھارنا rūp banānā, dhārnā, v. To personate; to assume a character; to act a part; to beautify or adorn.

روپا rūpā (H) n.m. Silver; base silver.

روپہلا - روپہلی rupahlā, rupehlī (H) adj. Silvered; silvery; made of silver.

روپیا، روپیہ rupiyā, rupiyah (H) n.m. A rupee, so called because it was originally made of silver; coin; money; cash; wealth.

روپیہ بھنانا ، تڑانا rupiyah bhunānā, toṛānā, v. To change a rupee for smaller coins.

روٹ roṭ (H) n.m. A large loaf; a thick bread; a sweet cake offered to a god.

روٹی roṭī (H) n.f. A cake or bread; a loaf; food; sustenance; livelihood.

روٹی پکانا roṭī pakānā, v. To cook bread; to make loaves.

روٹی چپڑنا roṭī chupaṛnā, v. To butter the bread.

روٹی کپڑا roṭī kapṛā, n.m. Bread and clothes; maintenance; allowance.

روٹیاں توڑنا roṭiyāṅ toṛnā, v. To be a hanger on; to eat the bread of idleness.

روٹھنا rūṭhnā (H) v. To be offended or displeased; to be cross; to take offence; to have a misunderstanding with a friend; to be cool; to quarrel; to be angry.

روح rūḥ (A) n.f. Soul; spirit; life; the vital principle; the essence of anything; divine revelation.

روح افزا rūḥ āfzā, adj. Exhilarating; prolonging life.

روح الامین rūḥ-ul-āmiṅ, n.m. The Angel Gabriel.

روح القدس rūḥ-ul-quds, n.m. The Holy Spirit.

روح اللہ rūḥ ullah, n.m. The Spirit of God; the Holy Ghost; Jesus Christ.

روح پرواز کرنا ، نکلنا ruḥ parwāz karnā, nikalnā, v. To die; to give up the ghost; to be frightened to death.

روحانی rūḥāni (A) adj. Spiritual; of or concerning the spirit; having a soul.

روحانیت rūḥāniyyat (A) n.f. Spirituality.

رود rūd (P) n.m. A stream; a river; a torrent; flowing water; the string of a musical instrument.

رود بار rūd bār, n.f. A place abounding in rivers and streams.

روداد - روئداد rūdād rū'edād (P) n.f. Narrative; statement; report; proceedings; account; occurance; incident.

روداد جلسہ rūdad-ĕ jalsah, n.f. Proceedings of a meeting.

روداد مقدمہ rūdād-ĕ muqaddamah, n.f. Proceedings of a case.

روداد نویس rūdād nawīs, n.m. Reporter.

روڑا roṛā (H) n.m. A stone; a small piece of stone or brick; a brick bat; a caste among Hindus.

روڑی roṛī (H) n.f. Piece of broken stone or brick; pebble; metal; shingle; red clay with which the *tilak* is made.

روز rūz, roz (P) n.m. A day; hire for the day. adj. Every day; per diem; daily; per day.

روز افزوں roz afzūṅ, adv. Increasing daily; increasing day by day.

روز بروز roz baroz, adv. Daily; day by day; constantly.

روز داد، روز جزا، روز حساب، روز حشر، روز قیامت roz-ĕ dād, roz-ĕ jazā, roz-ĕ ḥisāb, roz-ĕ ḥashar, roz-ĕ qiyāmat, n.m. Day of judgement; doomsday; the day of resurrection.

روز روز roz roz, adv. Day by day; every day; always.

روز روشن *roz-ĕ raushan*, *n.m.* Broad daylight.

روز مره *roz marrah*, *adj.* & *n.m.* Customary; usual; every day; daily talk.

روز نامچه *roz nāmchah*, *n.m.* A diary; a daily account book.

روز نامه *roz nāmah*, *n.m.* A daily newspaper; calendar; a journal.

روز و شب *roz-ŏ shab*, *adv.* Day and night; constantly.

روز ولادت *roz-ĕ wilādat*, *n.m.* Birthday.

روزانه *rozānah* (P) *adv.* Daily; by day. *n.m.* Daily wages; daily allowance.

روزگار *rozgār* (P) *n.m.* Time; age; the world; season; service; employment; earning.

روز گار چھوٹنا *rozgār chhūṭnā*, *v.* To be unemployed; to be dismissed from service; to be out of work; to be out of employment.

روز گار لگنا *rozgār lagnā*, *v.* To obtain employment; to get an appointment; to get service.

روزن *rauzan*, *rozan* (P) *n.m.* A hole; a window.

روزه *rozah* (P) *n.m.* A fast; lent.

روزه افطار کرنا، کھولنا *rozah ifṭār karnā*, *kholnā*, *v.* To break a fast.

روزه توڑنا *rozah toṛnā*, *v.* To kill a fast; to break a fast before time.

روزه خور *rozah khor*, *n.m.* One who does not fast.

روزه دار *rozah dār*, *n.m.* One who keeps a fast; a fasting person.

روزه رکھنا *rozah rakhnā*, *v.* To keep a fast; to observe a fast.

روزی *rozī* (P) *n.f.* Daily sustenance; daily food or allowance; maintenance; provisions; employment; wages; livelihood.

روزی ده، روزی رسان *rozī dih*, *rozī rasān*, *n.m.* The giver of daily bread; providence; God.

روزینه *rozīnah* (P) *n.m.* Daily wages; daily earnings; daily allowance; stipend.

روزینه دار *rozinah dār*, *n.m.* Stipendiary; one who receives daily wages or allowance.

روستا *rostā* (P) *n.m.* A village; a villager; a peasant; a rustic.

روستائی *rostā'ī*, (P) *n.m.* A peasant; a villager.

روش *ravish* (P) *n.f.* Custom; fashion; law; rule; practice; avenue; walk; passage; way; gait; behaviour; course; mode.

روشن *raushan*, *roshan* (P) *adj.* Light; lighted; illuminated; bright; conspicuous; shining; evident; clear; manifest; splendid; luminous.

روشن دان *raushan dān* (P) *n.m.* A ventilator; a skylight.

روشن دماغ *raushan dimāgh*, *adj.* High minded. *n.f.* A snuff.

روشن ضمیر، روشن طبع *raushan ẓamīr*, *raushan taba'*, *adj.* Enlightened in mind; a genius.

روشنائی *raushanā'ī*, *roshnā'ī* (P) *n.f.* Ink; light; splendour; brightness.

روشنی *raushanī* (P) *n.f.* Light; illumination; splendour; brightness; eyesight.

روشنی طبع *raushanī-ĕ ṭaba'*, *n.f.* Acuteness; sagacity.

روشنی کرنا *raushanī karnā*, *v.* To illuminate; to light a lamp.

روضه *rauẓah* (A) *n.m.* A garden; a mausoleum.

روضهٔ رضوان *rauẓah-ĕ riẓwān*, *n.m.* Paradise.

روغن *raughan* (P) *n.m.* Oil; butter; grease; varnish; polish; colour; glassiness; sleekness.

روغن بلسان *raughan-ĕ balsān*, *n.m.* Balsam.

روغن تلخ، روغن سیاه *raughan-ĕ talkh*, *raughan-ĕ siyāh*, *n.m.* Mustard oil.

روغن زرد *raughan-ĕ zard*, *n.m.* Clarified butter; ghee.

روغن نفت *raughan-ĕ naft*, *n.m.* Kerosene oil.

روغنی raughani (P) *adj.* Greasy; oily; buttered; fried in butter.

روک rok (H) *n.m.* Prevention; prohibition; restraint; stop; hindrance; limitation; bar; restriction; interruption; stay; shelter; obstacle; barrier.

روک تھام rok thām, *n.f.* Prevention, restraint; check; stay; support; a temporary remedy.

روک ٹوک rok tok, *n.f.* Obstacle; resistence; hindrance; prohibition; opposition; obstruction.

بے روک ٹوک be rok tok, *adv.* Without hindrance.

روکڑ rokaṛ (H) *n.m.* Cash; ready; money; stock.

روکڑ بکری rokaṛ bikri, *n.f.* Ready-money sale.

روکڑ بہی rokaṛ bahī, *n.f.* Cash book.

روکڑیا rokaṛyā (H) *n.m.* A treasurer; a cashier.

روکنا roknā (P) *v.* To check; to detain; to withhold; to stop; to restrain; to prohibit; to hinder; to interrupt; to impede; to oppose; to avert; to protect; to screen; to cover; to block.

روکھ rūkh (H) *n.m.* A tree.

روکھا rūkhā (H) *adj.* Dry; plain; insipid; blunt; harsh; unaffecting; cold; unkind; cross; rough; unbuttered; indifferent; unfriendly; simple.

روکھا جواب rūkhā jawāb, *n.m.* A curt answer.

روکھا سوکھا rūkhā sūkhā, *adj.* Dry; plain; blunt; harsh. *n.m.* A poor meal; a plain food.

روکھا پن، روکھائی rūkhā pan, rūkhā'ī, *n.f.* Dryness; plainness; roughness; staleness; insipidity; indifference; coldness; incivility; unfriendliness.

روگ rog (H) *n.m.* Disease; sickness; defect; plague.

روگ پالنا، لگا لینا rog pālnā, lagā lenā, *v.* To bring illness on oneself; to catch a disease.

روگی rogi (H) *n.m.* A sick person; an invalid. *adj.* Sick.

رولا raulā (H) *n.m.* Noise; tumult; alarm; riot; sedition.

رولا مچانا raulā machānā, *v.* To make a noise; to kick up a row; to raise a commotion; to create a disturbance.

رولنا rolnā (H) *v.* To roll; to smoothe; to plane; to polish; to rub; to sift; to winnow; to pick up; to gather up; to make money in abundance.

روم rom (H) *n.m.* Hair; down; the small hair of the body.

روم rūm (A) *n.m.* The Turkish Empire; Asia Minor.

رومان rūmān (E) *n.m.* Romance.

رومی rūmī (A) *n.m.* A Turk; a Grecian.

رونا ronā (H) *v.* To cry; to weep; to mourn; to be sad or sorrowful; to be melancholy. *n.m.* Lamentation; grief; weeping.

رونا پیٹنا، رونا دھونا ronā piṭnā, ronā dhonā, *v.* To mourn; to cry; to weep bitterly.

رونا رونا ronā ronā, *v.* To relate one's tale of woe.

رونا، رونہ rawannā, rawannah *n.m.* A passport; a pass.

رونڈ raund, *n.f.* (corr. from English) Round; patrol; the round guards.

روندنا raundnā (H) *v.* To trample on; to tread down; to ride over.

رونق raunaq (A) *n.f.* Lustre; brightness; elegance; beauty; symmetry; colour; splendour; freshness; flamishing state or condition.

رونق افروز ہونا raunaq āfroz honā, *v.* To arrive; to reach; to grace the occasion.

پر رونق pur raunaq, adj. Busy; full of bustle and activity.

رونگٹا raungṭā, rongṭā (H) n.m. The small hair of the body; down; fine wool.

رونگٹے کھڑے ہونا raungṭe khaṛe honā, v. Standing of the hair on end (from cold or fear &c).

رونی صورت roni ṣūrat, adj. Of a sad countenance; about to weep.

روهو rohū (H) n.f. A kind of fish; the corners of the eyelids.

روئداد rū'edād (P) n.f. See روداد rudād.

روئی ru'ī (H) n.f. Cotton.

روئی دار ru'i dār, adj. Stuffed with cotton.

روئی دهننا ru'i dhunnā, v. To cord cotton.

روئی کا گالا ru'ī kā gālā, n.m. A flake of cotton.

روئے rūe (P) n.m. See رو rū.

روئیدگی ro'idagī (P) n.m. Vegetation; growth.

رویا royā (A) n.m. A vision; a dream.

رویائے صادقہ royā-ĕ ṣādiqah, n.m. True dreams.

تعبیرالرویا ta'bīr-ur-royā, n.f. Interpretation of dreams.

رویت ro'yat, rūyat (A) n.m. Appearance; seeing; sight; regard; consideration; aspect of the planets.

رویت ہلال royat-ĕ hilāl, n.m. Appearance of the new moon.

رویہ rawaiyah (P) n.m. Custom; manner; behaviour; conduct; fashion; rule; law.

رہ rah (P) n.f. (contraction of راہ) See راہ rāh.

رہ جانا rah jānā (H) v. To stay; to remain; to fail; not to be fulfilled; not to be completed; to linger behind.

رہا rihā (P) adj. Released; disengaged; freed; liberated.

رہا کرنا rihā karnā, v. To release; to set at liberty; to discharge; to liberate.

رہا سہا rahā sahā (H) adj. Left out; remnant; remainder.

رہانا rahānā (H) v. To have a millstone roughened.

رہائش rahā'ish (P) n.f. Stay; halt; abode; residence.

رہائش اختیار کرنا rahā'ish ikhtiyār karnā, v. To take up abode; to reside; to stay.

رہائی rihā'i (P) n.f. Liberation; escape; deliverance; relief; acquitted; discharge; release; salvation; exemption.

رہائی پانا rihā'ī pānā, v. To be released; to be discharged; to be set at liberty; to be set free.

رہبان ruhbān (A) n.m. (plu. of راہب rāhib); Monks.

رہبانیت ruhbāniyyat (A) n.f. Monkery; priesthood.

رہٹ rahaṭ (H) n.m. Persian wheel; a wheel to draw water with from a low level; succession; continuation.

رہڑا، رہڑو rehṛā, rahṛū (H) n.m. A cart; a sledge.

رہن rihn, rahn (A) n.m. A mortgage; a pledge.

رہن اراضی rihn-ĕ ārāẓi, n.m. Land mortgage.

رہن انتفاعی rihn-ĕ intifā'i, n.m. A profitable mortgage.

رہن بالقبض rihn bilqabẓ, n.m. Mortgage with possession.

رہن دار rihn dār, n.m. A mortgagee.

رہن رکھنا rihn rakhnā, v. To mortgage; to pledge.

رہن نامہ rihn nāmah, n.m. A mortgage deed.

فکِ رہن fakk-ĕ rihn, n.m. Redemption of a mortgage.

رہن سہن rahn sahn (H) n.m. Mode of living.

رهنا rahnā (H) v. To live; to dwell; to reside; to stay; to stop; to remain; to be; to exist; to last; to continue; to escape; to be left; to be stunted or paralized.

رهنے دینا rahne denā (H) v. To permit to stay; to allow to remain.

رهوار rahwār (P) n.m. An ambling horse.

رهین rahin (A) adj. Mortgaged; under obligation; thankful.

رهین منت rahin-ĕ minnat, adj. Under obligation of; obliged to; indebted to.

رؤسا r'osā (A) n.m. (plu. of رئیس ra'is) Chiefs; princes; heads.

رؤف r'ūf (A) adj. Kind; merciful.

رئی ra'ī (H) n.f. A churning staff; bran.

رئی چلانا ra'ī chalānā, v. To churn.

رئیس ra'īs (A) n.m. A prince; a chief; a head of a department; a noble man.

ری rī (H) intj. (contraction of اری arī) A vocative particle used by way of disrespect or admiration among women; O ! Hallo !

رے re (H) intj. (contraction of ارے āre) A vocative particle used by way of disrespect or admiration. O ! Hallo !

ریا riyā (A) n.m. Hyprocrisy; dissimulation; subterfuge; evasion; affectation; pretence.

ریا کار riyā kār, adj. Deceitful; hypocrite; dissembler; pretender.

ریا کاری riyā kāri, n.f. Hypocricy; pretence; dissimulation.

ریاح riyāh (A) n.m./f. (plu. of ریح riḥ) Air; winds; flatulence.

ریاست riyāsat (A) n.f. Government; dominion; sway; rule; nobility; high mindedness.

ریاض riyāẓ (A) n.m. (plu. of روضه rauẓah); Gardens.

ریاضت riyāẓat (A) n.f. Training; discipline; religious exercise; devotion; abstinence; austerity.

ریاضت کرنا riyāẓat karnā, v. To perform religious exercise; to spend much time in worship; to practice abstinence.

ریاضتی riyāẓati (A) adj. One who devotes much attention to religious exercises; devotee; ascetic.

ریاضی riyāẓi (A) n.m. Mathematics.

ریاضی دان riyāẓi dān, n.m. A mathematician.

ریت ret (H) n.f. Sand; dust; filings.

ریت rīt (H) n.f. Custom; usage; rite; habit; regulation; rule; plan; fashion.

ریت رسم rīt rasm, n.f. Manners and customs.

ریتلا، ریتیلا، ریتلی، ریتیلی retlā, retelā, retli, retelī (H) adj. Sandy.

ریتنا retnā (H) v. To file; to polish; to rasp.

ریتی retī (H) n.f. A file; sandy ground on the shore of a river.

ریٹھا rīṭhā (H) n.m. The soap-wort; soap-nut.

ریجھنا rījhnā (H) v. To be pleased; to be gratified; to be delighted; to incline (to); to fall in love.

ریچھ richh (H) n.m. A bear.

ریح riḥ (A) n.f. Air; wind; flatulence.

ریح کا درد riḥ kā dard, n.m. Rheumation; rhumatic gaut.

ریحان riḥān (A) n.m. An odoriferous plant; sweet basil.

ریحی riḥī (A) adj. Windy; flatulent.

ریختہ rekhtah (P) adj. Poured out; scattered; mixed. n.m. The Urdu language; mortar; plaster.

ریختی rekhtī, n.f. Verse written in the language of women.

ریڑھ rīṛh (H) *n.f.* The back-bone.

ریڑھی reṛhī (H) *n.f.* A cart; a hand cart; a barrow.

ریز rez (P) *adj.* Pouring; scattering; dropping; shedding; (used in *compos.* as in اشک ریز *ashk rez* shedding tears).

ریزش *rezish* (P) *n.f.* Running at the nose; flowing in small quantities; pouring out; scattering; effusion.

ریز گاری *rez gārī n.f.* Small coins; change.

ریزگی *rezgi* (P) *n.f.* A scrap; a bit; a piece.

ریزہ *rezah* (P) *n.m.* A scrap; a piece; a bit; crumb; a minute fragment; an atom; a piece of cloth; a moulding box; a labouring boy (employed in masonry work).

ریزہ چینی *rezah chīnī, n.f.* Picking up of scraps.

ریزہ ریزہ *rezah rezah, adj.* Broken in pieces; in pieces; very small.

ریس *rīs* (H) *n.f.* Equality; emulation; copying.

ریس کرنا *rīs karnā, v.* To be envious of; to vie with; to copy.

ریش *rish* (P) *n.f.* Beard.

ریشم *resham* (P) *n.m.* Silk.

ریشمی *reshmī* (P) *adj.* Silken; made of silk.

ریشہ *reshah* (P) *n.m.* Fibre; filament; string of a mango etc; vein; tissue; roots.

ریشہ دار *reshah dār, adj.* Fibrous; stringy.

ریکھا *rekhā* (H) *n.f.* Line; mark; fate; destiny; stripe; row; a furrow; lines on the palm of the hand.

ریگ *reg* (P) *n.f.* Sand.

ریگ مال *reg māl, n.m.* Sand paper.

ریگ ماھی *reg māhi, n.f.* Skink; sand fish; a lizard-like sandy fish (used in medicine in a dried state).

ریگ زار *reg zār, n.m.* A sandy region or place.

ریگستان *registān* (P) *n.m.* A sandy desert; a sandy place.

ریل *ril* (E.) Reel; a spool; a bobbin.

ریل پیل *rel pel, n.f.* Abundance; plenty; bustle; crowd.

ریل گاڑی *rel gāṛi* (H) *n.f.* Railway train.

ریلا *relā* (H) *n.m.* A flood; a torrent; rushing; rush; push; assault; a line or string of men or animals.

رین *rain* (H) *n.f.* Night.

رین بسیرا *rain baserā, n.m.* A night's halt.

رینٹ *renṭ* (H) *n.f.* Mucus from the nose; snivel; snot.

ریں ریں *reṅ reṅ* (H) *n.f.* Crying or moaning of a child; the discordant note of a stringed instrument.

ریندھنا *riṅdhnā* (H) *v. & n.m.* To cook; to prepare food; cooking (used with پکانا *pakānā*).

رینکنا *reṅknā* (H) *v.* To bray (as an ass).

رینگنا *riṅgnā* (H) *v.* To crawl; to creep.

ریوڑ *rewaṛ* (H) *n.m.* A flock of sheep or goats.

ریوڑی *rewṛi* (H) *n.f.* A kind of sweetmeat.

ریوڑی کے پھیر میں آنا *rewṛi ke pher meṅ ānā, v.* To be involved in difficulties.

ریوند *rewaṅd* (P) *n.m.* Rhubarb.

ریوند چینی *rewaṅd-e chīnī, n.m.* The Chinese rhubarb.

ریہ *riyah* (A) *n.m.* The lungs.

ڑ

ڑ ṛe, Is the fifteenth letter of the Urdu alphabet and is pronounced with the tip of the tongue turned towards the roof of the mouth. It has the sound of hardened *r* and is often interchanged with ڈ *ḍāl*. In reckoning by *abjad* it has the value of 200. This letter does not occur as the first letter of a word and therefore no words are being given under it.

ز

ز ze, is called *zāi mo'jama* or *zai manqūtā*, is the eleventh letter of the Arabic, thirteenth of the Persian and the sixteenth of the Urdu alphabet. Its sound is that of the English z and in reckoning by *abjad* it stands for 7.

زا *zā* (P) *adj*. Born; (used in *compos*. as مرزا *mirzā* born of a noble).

زاج *zāj* (P) *n.m.* Vitriol, copper sulphate,

زاج سفید *zāj-ĕ sufed, n.m.* Alum.

زاد *zād* (A) *n.m.* Food; provisions; increase.

زاد راہ *zād-ĕ rāh, n.m.* Provisions for a journey.

زاد *zād* (P) *n.m.* Offspring; son; born of; birth.

زاد بوم *zād būm, n.m.* Native land; birthplace.

زادہ، زادی *zādah, zādi* (P) *adj*. Born of; (used in *compos*. as شاہ زادہ *shāh zādah* born of a king; a prince شاهزادی *shāhzādī*, a princess).

زار *zār* (P) *n.m.* Groan; lamentation; multitude; place where anything grows in abundance; garden; desire; wish. *adj.* Afflicted; groaning; lean; humble; lamenting.

زار زار *zār zār, adv.* Bitterly.

زار زار یا زار و قطار رونا *zār zār ya zār-ŏ qaṭār ronā, v.* To weep bitterly.

زار و نزار *zār-ŏ nizār, adj.* Emaciated; weak.

حال زار *ḥāl-ĕ zār, n.m* Bad circumstances; poverty; want.

سبزه زار *sabzah zār, n.m.* A meadow; a lawn.

گلزار *gulzār, n.m.* A garden of roses.

لالہزار *lālahzār, n.m.* A bed or garden of tulips.

زاری *zāri* (A) *n.f.* Crying; lamentation; wailing; groaning.

زاغ *zāgh* (P) *n.m.* A crow; vitriol; a mode of song.

زال *zāl* (P) *adj.* Old; grey-haired. *n.m.* The name of the father of *Rustam*.

زانو *zānū* (P) *n.m.* The thigh; the knee; lap.

زانو بدلنا *zānū badalnā, v.* To change the knees; to rest the knees alternately in kneeling.

دو زانو بیٹھنا *do zānū baiṭhnā, v.* To kneel; to sit on the haunches.

زانی *zānī* (A) *n.m.* An adulterer; a whoremonger.

زانیہ *zāniyah* (A) *n.f.* An adultress; a whore; a strumpet.

زاویہ *zawiyah* (A) *n.m.* An angle; a corner; a secluded corner.

زاویہ اندرونی *zāwiyah-ĕ andarūnī, n.m.* An interior angle.

زاویہ بیرونی *zāwiyah-ĕ berūni, n.m.* An exterior angle.

زاویہ حادہ *zāwiyah-ĕ ḥāddah, n.m.* An acute angle.

زاویہ قائمہ zāwiyah-ĕ qā'imah, n.m. A right angle.

زاویہ متبادلہ zāwiyah-ĕ mutabādilah, n.m. Alternate angle.

زاویہ متناظرہ zāwiyah-ĕ mutanāẓirah, n.m. Corresponding angle.

زاویہ منفرجہ zāwiyah-ĕ munfarijah, n.m. An obtuse angle.

زاہد zāhid (A) n.m. A hermit; a devotee; an abstinent; a devout person; a zealot. adj. Religious; devout.

زائچہ zā'ichah (P) n.m. Horoscope; astronomical table; one's natal star; birth certificate.

زائد zā'id (A) adj. Superfluous; surplus; redundant; over and above; exceeding; in excess; more.

زائدالمیعاد zā'id-ul mī'ād, adj. Time-barred.

زائر zā'ir (A) n.m. A pilgrim; a visitant.

زائل zā'il (A) adj. Vanishing; perishing; deficient; failing; waning; declining.

زبان zabān (P) n.f. The tongue; language; dialect; speech; flame (of a candle &c).

زبان آور zabān āwar, adj. Eloquent; fluent; voluble.

زبان آوری zabān āwari, n.f. Eloquence; fluency; volubility of the tongue.

زبان بدلنا zabān badalnā, n.f. To go back from one's word.

زبان بگاڑنا zabān bigāṛnā, v. To spoil one's tongue.

زبان بگڑنا zabān bigaṛnā, v. To use foul language.

زبان بند کرنا zabān band karnā, v. To silence; to hush; to prevent one from speaking.

زبان بند ہونا zabān band honā, v. To be speechless; to be tongue-tied; to be unable to speak.

زبان پر چڑھنا zabān par chaṛhnā, v. Coming frequently to the tongue; to be talked about; to learn by heart.

زبان پر رکھنا zabān par rakhnā, v. To taste.

زبان پر لانا zabān par lānā, v. To mention; to utter; to speak.

زبان پلٹنا zabān palaṭnā, v. To eat one's word; to go back from one's word; to retract; to withhold one's promise.

زبان چلانا zabān chalānā, v. To talk much; to abuse; to give one abuse.

زبان چلنا zabān chalnā, v. To speak fluently; to speak glibly.

زبان حال zabān-ĕ ḥāl, adv. Self-evident state of affairs.

زبان خلق کو نقارۂ خدا سمجھو zabān-ĕ khalq ko naqqārah-ĕ khudā samjho, prov. What all men say is always true.

زبان دان zabān dān, n.m. A linguist; one skilled in language; a poet.

زبان دانی zabān dāni, n.f. Knowledge of languages.

زبان دراز zabān darāz, adj. Loquacious; abusive; impudent; one having a long tongue.

زبان درازی zabān darāzi, n.f. Abuse; impudence.

زبان دینا zabān denā, v. To give one's word; to promise.

زبان سنبھالنا zabān sambhālnā, v. To be careful in talk; to hold one's tongue.

زبان سے نکالنا zabān se nikālnā, v. To utter; to speak; to pronounce.

زبان سے نکلنا zabān se nikalnā, v. To escape one's lips.

زبان سینا zabān sinā, v. To be tongue-tied; to remain silent, to have lost one's speech.

زبان کے چٹخارے لینا zabān ke chaṭkhāre lenā, v. To smack the lips over; to relish,

زبان کاٹنا zabān kāṭnā, v. To interrupt one's speech.

زبان کا چسکا zabān kā chaskā, n.m. Ardent desire to taste.

زبان کا میٹھا zabān kā miṭhā, n.m. Honey-tongued.

زبان کو لگام دینا zabān ko lagām denā, v. To hold one's tongue; to curb.

زبان کھولنا zabān kholnā, v. To speak out; to give tit for tat.

زبان هارنا zabān hārnā, v. To promise; to give one's word.

زبان هلانا zabān hilānā, v. To speak; to say a few words.

زبان هی هاتهی پر چڑهائے زبان هی سر کٹائے zabān hī hāthī par chaṛhā'e, zabān hī sar kaṭā'e, prov. It is his tongue which brings honour or dishonour to a man.

زبان شیریں ملک گیری zabān shiriṅ mulk giri, prov. Sweet tongue conquers the hearts and conquered hearts win a kingdom: soft words cost nothing.

زبانه zabānah (P) n.m. A flame (of a candle); a blaze.

زبانی zabānī (P) adj. Verbal; oral; traditional; viva voce; by word of mouth.

زبانی امتحان zabāni imtiḥān, n.m. Oral examination; oral test.

زبانی جمع خرچ zabani jama' kharch, n.m. All talk and no substance; mere words.

زبانی حساب zabāni hisāb, n.m. Mental arithmetic.

زبده zubdah (A) n.m. The best of anything; the cream.

زبر zabar (P) n.m. Above; superior; greater; heavy; upper part, top. The vowel point (´).

زبر هونا zabar honā, v. To have the upper hand; to have an advantage.

زبردست zabardast, adj. Vigorous; violent; powerful; oppressive; tyrannical; harsh; overbearing; superior.

زبردستی zabardastī, n.f. Violence; oppression; powerfulness.

زبرجد zabarjad (A) n.m. A kind of emerald; a topaz; a chrysolite; a jasper; a beryl.

زبور zabūr (A) n.f. The Psalms of David.

زبون zabūn (P) adj. Bad; Ill; evil; faulty; mean; unlucky; wicked; infirm; helpless; unfortunate.

زبونی zabūni, (P) n.f. Vileness; wickedness; faultiness; infirmity; weakness; helplessness; disgrace; meanness.

زٹل zaṭal (H) n.f. Nonsense; foolish talk; false stories; chattering; tattle.

زٹل باز zatal bāz, adj. One who talks nonsense; a prattler; an idle talker.

زٹل مارنا ، زٹل هانکنا zaṭal mārnā, zaṭal hāṅknā, v. To chatter; to talk nonsense; to quibble; to tell false and idle stories.

زٹلی zaṭallī (H) adj. One who tells false and idle stories; an idle talker.

زجاج zujāj (A) n.m. A glass; a glass flask or bottle.

زجر ، زجر و توبیخ zajar, zajar-ŏ taubikh (A) n.m. Chiding; threatening; forbidding harshly.

زچ zich (H) adj. Vexed teased.

زچ کرنا zich karnā, v. To tease; to vex; to annoy; to defeat; to checkmate; to overcome.

زچ هونا zich honā, v. To be teased or vexed; to be sick; to grow lean and poor.

زچه zachchah (P) n.f. A lying in woman; a woman who has recently given birth to a child.

زچه خانه zachchah khānah, n.m. Nursing home; maternity home; maternity hospital.

زچگی *zachchagi* (P) *n.f.* Maternity.

زحاف *zihāf* (A) *n.m.* Change in the meter of a verse.

زحل *zuhal* (A) *n.m.* The planet Saturn.

زحمت *zahmat* (A) *n.f.* Disquietude; uneasiness of mind; trouble; pain; sickness; hardship; affliction.

زحمت آٹھانا *zahmat uthānā, v.* To undergo hardship; to endure; to do a bit of hard work.

زخار *zakhār* (A) *adj.* Overflowing; full to the brim; raging (the sea.)

زخم *zakhm* (P) *n.m.* A wound; a sore; a gash; a cut; damage; loss; fracture.

زخم بھر جانا *zakhm bhar jānā, v.* Healing up of the wound.

زخم پر نمک چھڑکنا *zakhm par namak chhiṛaknā, v.* To sprinkle salt on a wound; to afflict the afflicted person.

زخم پکنا *zakhm paknā, v.* To suppurate.

زخم کاری *zakhm-ĕ kārī, n.m.* A very grave injury; a mortal wound; a fatal blow.

زخم کرنا *zakhm karnā, v.* To wound; to injure.

زخم کھانا *zakhm khānā, v.* To be wounded; to be injured.

زخمه *zakhmah* (P) *n.m.* Plectrum (of a guitar); an instrument for plucking strings of a guitar.

زخمی *zakhmī* (P) *adj.* Wounded; hurt; injured.

زخمی کرنا *zakhmī karnā, v.* To stab; to attempt to kill; to injure.

زد *zad* (P) *n.f.* Object aimed at; target; range; striking; beating; smitting; loss; blow; damage.

زد پڑنا *zad paṛnā, v.* To get affected; to suffer a loss.

زد میں ھونا *zad men honā, v.* To be within range.

زد و کوب *zad-ŏ kob, n.f.* Assaulting and beating; thrashing.

زده *zadah* (P) *adj.* Struck; stricken; beaten; oppressed. (used in *compos.* as in, مصیبت زده *muṣībat zadah*, afflicted).

زر *zar* (P) *n.m.* Gold; riches; money; wealth; polen; fine substance discharged by male flowers.

زر اصل *zar-ĕ āṣl, n.m.* Principal sum; pure gold.

زر افشاں، زرفشاں *zar-ĕ āfshān, zarfishān, adj.* Charitable; bountiful; lustrous.

زر امانت *zar-ĕ āmānat, n.m.* Deposit money; trust money.

زر باف *zar bāf, n.m.* One who works in gold thread; embroiderer; brocade; gold tissue.

زر بافی *zar bāfī, n.f.* Embroidery; weaving in gold.

زر بفت *zar baft, n.m.* Brocade.

زر بیعانه *zar-ĕ bai'ānah, n.m.* Earnest money.

زر پیشگی *zar-ĕ peshgī, n.m.* Advance money.

زر خرید *zar kharīd, adj.* Purchased (with money).

زرخیز *zarkhez, adj.* Productive; fertile; rich (soil).

زرخیزی *zarkhezī, n.f.* Fertility; productiveness.

زر دار *zar dār, adj.* Wealthy; rich.

زر دوز *zar doz, n.m.* One who embroiders.

زر دوزی *zar dozī, n.f.* Embroidery.

زر کوب *zar kob, n.m.* Gold beater.

زر گر *zar gar, n.f.* A goldsmith.

زر گری *zar garī, n.f.* Business of a goldsmith; a kind of dialect.

زر گل *zar-ĕ gul, n.m.* Pollen; the yellow anther dust.

زر لگان *zar-ĕ lagān, n.m.* Land revenue.

زر مطالبہ zar-ĕ muṭālabah, n.m. Claims; demands; debts.

زر معاوضہ zar-ĕ mu'āwiẓah, n.m. Compensation.

زر منافع zar-ĕ munāfa', n.m. Profits; income; savings.

زر نقد zar-ĕ naqd, n.m. Cash; ready money.

زر نگار zar nigār, adj. Gilt; guilded.

زر نگاری zar nigāri, n.f. Gilding; gold plating.

زر یافتنی zar-ĕ yāftani, n.f. Payable amounts; amount of money to be received; demands; outstandings.

زراعت zarā'at (A) n.m. Agriculture; tillage; tilling; husbandry; crop.

زراعت پیشہ zarā't peshah, n.m. An agriculturist; a cultivator.

زراعتی zarā'ati (A & P) adj. Agricultural.

زرافہ ، زراف zarrāfah, zarrāf (A) n.m. Giraffe.

زرد zard (P) adj. Yellow; pale; wan; livid.

زرد آلو zard ālū, n.m. An apricot.

زرد پڑنا ، ہو جانا zard paṛnā, ho jānā, v. To turn pale; to become weak and feeble.

زرد چوب zard chob, n.f. Turmeric.

زرد رنگ zard rang, n.m. Yellow colour. adj. Bashful.

زرد رو zard rū, adj. Bashful; ashamed.

زردہ zardah, n.m. A sweet dish made of rice; chewing tobacco.

زردی zardi (P) n.m. Yellowness; paleness; yolk of an egg; jaundice.

زرق برق zarq barq (P & A) n.f. Glare; glitter; splendour; show; thunder and lightning. adj. Gaudy; splendid.

زرہ zirah (P) n.f. Chain armour; iron armour made with rings.

زرہ پوش zirah posh, adj. A person in armour.

زری zari (P) n.m. Anything woven with gold threads; gold brocade.

زری باف zari bāf, n.m. A gold-lace worker.

زریں zarrin (P) adj. Golden; made of gold.

زریں مرغ zarrin murgh, adj. The name of a bird; the sun.

زریں موقعہ zarrin mauqa'h, n.m. A golden opportunity.

زرینہ zarīnah (P) adj. Golden; of gold. n.m. Things made of gold.

زشت zisht (P) adj. Ugly; deformed; hideous; inhuman.

زشت خو zisht khū, adj. Of ugly habits or disposition.

زشت رو zisht rū, adj. Ugly; repulsive to sight; unpleasing.

زشتی zishtī (P) n.f. Ugliness, repulsiveness; indecency.

زعفران za'farān (A) n.f. Saffron.

زعفرانی za'farānī (A) adj. Saffron coloured; yellow; of saffron. n.m. Yellow colour.

زعم za'm (A) n.m. Assertion; presumption; opinion; speaking from belief; arrogance; pride; vanity.

زعما zu'amā (A) n.m. (plu. of زعیم za'īm); Leaders; top-ranking men.

زعیم za'īm (A) n.m. A leader.

زغند یا زقند zaghand yā zaqand (P) n.f. A jump; leap; spring.

زفاف zifāf (A) n.m. Taking a bride to her husband's house; consummation of marriage.

زقوم zaqūm (A) n.m. A thorny or prickly plant, having a very bitter taste.

زک zak (H) n.m. Defeat; repulse; insult; check; injury; affront.

زک اٹھانا zak uṭhānā, v. To be defeated; to suffer a loss; to be insulted.

زک دینا zak denā, v. To defeat; to put to shame; to insult.

زکا zakā (A) n.f. Purity; piety.

زکام zukām (A) n.m. Rheum; catarrh; cold.

زکاوت zakāwat (A) n.f. Intelligence; ingenuity; probity; purity.

زکواۃ zakāt (A) n.f. Alms; charity; two and half per cent of annual profits to be given in charity by Muslims to the class of people specified in the Quran.

زکی zaki (A) adj. Pure; pious; virtuous. n.m. One who regularly pays zakāt.

زلال zulāl (A) adj. Pure; wholesome (water); limpid; clear; lucid. n.m. Limpid water.

زلزلہ zalzalah (A) n.m. An earthquake. (plu. of زلازل zalāzil.)

زلزلہ پیما zalzalah paimā, n.m. Seismometer.

زلف zulf (P) n.f. A curling lock (of hair) hanging over the temple or ear; ringlet; tress.

زلف پریشان zulf-ĕ pareshān, n.f. Dishevelled locks.

زلف تابدار zulf-ĕ tābdār, n.f. Lustrous curling locks.

زلف دراز zulf-ĕ darāz, n.f. Long locks.

زلفی zulfi (P) n.m. The chain by which a door is fastened; a sword knot.

زلہ zallah (P) n.m. Victuals carried home by the guests from an entertainment; crumbs; leavings of food.

زلہ ربا zallah rubā, adj. Gleaner; crumb eater.

زمام zamām (A) n.f. Rein; bridle.

زمان zamān (A) n.m. Time.

زمانہ zamānah (P) n.m. Time; age; period; season; the world; tense (Grammar).

زمانہ دیکھنا zamānah dekhnā, v. To see the way of the world; to get experiences of life.

زمانہ ساز zamānah sāz, adj. A time-server; a turn coat.

زمانہ سازی zamānah sāzi, n.f. Time-serving; turning with the tide; sycophancy.

زمرد zumurrud (A) n.m. An emerald.

زمردین zumurrudin (A&P) adj. Of the colour of an emerald.

زمرہ zumrah (A) n.m. A troop; a group; crowd; multitude.

زمزمہ zamzamah (P) n.m. Singing; chanting; modulation; a concert.

زمزمہ پرداز zamzamah pardaz, adj. Singer; songster.

زمستان zamistān (P) n.m. Winter.

زمن zaman (A) n.m. Time.

زمہریر zamharir (A) n.m. Cold; intense cold.

زمین zamin (P) n.f. The earth; ground; soil; land; floor; a region; country.

زمین آسمان کا فرق zamin āsmān kā farq, n.m. A world of difference; a great difference.

زمین آسمان کے قلابے ملانا zamin āsmān ke qulābe milānā, v. To exaggerate to the extreme; to leave no stone unturned.

زمین بوس ہونا zamin bos honā, v. To make a profound bow; to kiss the ground; to show great humility.

زمین پیمائی zamin paimā'i, n.f. Land survey.

زمین دار zamin dār, n.m. A land holder; a landlord; a big cultivator of land.

زمین داری zamin dāri, n.f. Landed property; land held by a zamindār; an estate; landlordship.

زمین دوز zamin doz, n.f. Level with the ground; under-ground; subterranean.

زمین شناس *zamin shinās, n.m.* Geologist.

زمین غیر مزروعہ *zamin-ĕ ghair mazrūa'h, n.f.* Waste and uncultivated land.

زمین کا پیوند ہونا *zamin kā paiwand honā, v.* To mingle with the dust; to die.

زمین کا گز *zamin kā gaz, n.m.* A traveller.

زمین مرہونہ *zamin-ĕ marhūnah, n.f.* Mortgaged land.

زمین مزروعہ *zamin-ĕ mazrua'h, n.f.* Cultivated land.

زمین میں گڑ جانا *zamin men gaṛ jānā, v.* To be greatly ashamed.

زمینی *zaminī (P) adj.* Earthly; terrestrial.

زن *zan (P) n.f.* A woman; a wife. *adj* Beater; striker (used in *compos.* as in خندہ زن *khandah zan,* نغمہ زن *naghmah zan* etc).

زن مدخولہ *zan-e madkhūlah, n.f.* Concubine.

زن مرید *zan murid, adj.* Hen-pecked.

زن منکوحہ *zan-ĕ mankūḥah, n.f.* A married woman; a lawful wife.

زن و فرزند *zan-ŏ farzand, n.m.* Wife and children; family.

زنا *zinā (A) n.m.* Adultery; fornication.

زنا بالجبر *zinā bil-jabr, n.m.* Rape; forcible violation of a woman.

زنا زادہ *zinā zādah, n.m.* A bastard; child born as a result of adultery.

زنا کار *zinā kār, n.m.* An adulterer; a fornicator.

زنا کاری *zinā kāri, n.f.* Adultery; illicit intercourse; fornication; harlotry.

زنار *zunnār (A) n.m.* The sacred thread worn by the Hindus; a Hindu's rosary.

زنار بند، زنار دار *zunnār band, zunnār dār, n.m.* One who wears the sacred thread.

زنا شوئی *zinā sho'ī (P) n.f.* Relationship of wife and husband.

زنانہ *zanānah (P) adj.* Feminine. *n.m.* The female apartment; the seraglio; eunuch.

زنبور *zambūr (P) n.m.* A wasp; a hornet, a bee; pincers.

زنبورہ *zambūrah (P) n.m.* A large bee; a hornet; a small gun.

زنبیل *zambil (P) n.f.* A basket; a wallet; a purse.

زنجبیل *zanjabil (A) n.f.* Dry-ginger.

زنجیر *zanjir (P) n.f.* A chain.

زنخ یا زنخ دان *zanakh yā zanakh dān (P) n.f.* The chin; the pit in the chin.

زنخا *zankhā, n.m.* An effeminate person; impotent; eunuch.

زندان *zindān (P) n.m.* A prison; a jail.

زندانی *zindānī (P) n.m.* A prisoner; a captive.

زندقہ *zandaqah (A) n.m.* Impiety; unbelief; heresy; atheism.

زندگانی *zindagānī (P) n.f.* Life; living; existence; livelihood.

زندگی *zindagī (P) n.f.* Life; living; existence.

زندگی تلخ ہونا *zindagī talkh honā, v.* To be sick of life.

زندگی سے تنگ آنا *zindagī se tang ānā, v.* To be tired of life.

زندہ *zindah (P) adj.* Alive; living.

زندہ دل *zindah dil, adj.* Cheerful; lively; gay; mirthful.

زندہ دلی *zindah dilī, n.f.* Cheerfulness; gaiety.

زندہ در گور *zindah dar gor, adj.* Half dead; as good as dead; leading an unpleasant life.

زندہ کرنا *zindah karnā, v.* To bring to life; to restore to life.

زندیق *zindīq (A) n.m.* An infidal; a fire worshipper; a follower of Zoroaster; an unbeliever.

زنگ zaṅg (P) n.m. Rust; a small bell; canker.

زنگ آلودہ zaṅg ālūdah, adj. Rusty; covered with rust.

زنگ لگنا zaṅg lagnā, v. To become rusty.

زنگار zangār (P) n.m. Verdigris; rust.

زنگاری zangāri (P) adj. Rust-coloured; of the colour of verdigris; green.

زنگی zangī (P) n.m. An Ethiop; an inhabitant of Ethiopia; a negro; a moor.

زنہار zinhār (P) adv. On no account; by no means; never. interj. Take care! beware! mind you!

زوال zawāl (A) n.m. Decline; wane; declination; cessation; misery; wretchedness; setting of the sun; decay; failure; fall.

زوال پذیر zawāl paẕīr, adj. Declining; decaying; fading; transitory.

زوائد zawā'd (A) n.m. (plu. of زائد zā'd) Additions; superfluities; augmentations.

زوج zauj (A) n.m. A couple; a pair; spouse; husband or wife; consort.

زوجہ zaujah (A) n.f. A wife.

زوجیت zaujiyyat (A) n.f. The married state.

حقوق زوجیت ḥuqūq-ĕ zaujiyyat, n.m. Conjugal rights.

زود zūd (P) adv. Quickly; soon; swiftly; suddenly.

زود رنج zūd ranj, adj. Irascible; sensitive; touchy.

زود فہم zūd fahm, adj. Quick of understanding; sharp witted.

زور zor (P) n.m. Force; strength; virtue; power; vigour; violence; effort; weight; influence; stress; coercion.

زور آزمانا zor āzmānā, v, To try one's strength.

زور آور zor āwar, adj. Powerful; strong.

زور آوری zor āwarī, n.f. Power; force.

زور بازو سے zor-ĕ bāzū se, adv. By the strength of arms; by dint of hard work.

زور دار zor dār, adj. Strong; powerful.

زور دینا zor denā, v. To strengthen; to stress; to press; to support.

زور ڈالنا zor ḍālnā, v. To press; to bear upon; to compel.

زور لگانا zor lagānā, v. To do one's best; to use influence.

زور مارنا zor mārnā, v. To try one's hardest; to strive; to toil.

زہ zih (P) n.f. Giving birth; childbirth; a bow-string; a ledge; the border or edge of anything.

زہار zihār (P) n.m. The lower part of the body; pubic hair.

زہاد zuhhād (A) n.m. (plu. of زاہد zāhid) Religious men; pious men; devout persons.

زہد zuhd (A) n.m. Devotion; abstinence; continence.

زہر zahr (P) n.m. Poison; venom; anything injurious or disagreeable.

زہر آلودہ zahr ālūdah (P) n.m. Poisoned.

زہر خند zahr khand, n.m. A forced laugh; a sarcastic laughter.

زہر دار zahr dār, adj. Poisonous.

زہر قاتل یا زہر ہلاہل zahr-ĕ qātil yā zahr-ĕ halāhal, n.m. Deadly poison.

زہر کے گھونٹ پینا zahr ke ghūnṭ pīnā, v. To bear patiently.

زہر لگنا zahr lagnā, v. To regard as poison; to be hateful to.

زہر مار کرنا zahr mār karnā, v. To swallow reluctantly; to be forced to do a thing; to act unwillingly.

زہر مہرہ zahr mohrah, n.m. Bezoar; an antidote to poison.

زهره zahrah (P) n.m. Gall-bladder; bile; boldness; spirit; pluck; plight; courage.

زهره آب هونا zahrah āb honā, v. To be much distressed or terrified; to be struck with fear.

زهره zuhrah (A) n.f. The planet Venus.

زهره جبیں zuhrah jabīṅ, adj. Venus in countenance; beautiful; handsome.

زهریلا' زهریلی zahrīlā, zahrīlī, adj. Poisonous.

زہے zihe (P) interj. How good ! How fine ! Excellent !

زیادتی ziyādatī (P) n.f. Abundance; excess; increase; surplus; augmentation; addition; oppression; violence; tyranny.

زیادتی کرنا ziyādati karnā, v. To use force; to exceed limits.

زیاده ziyādah (P) adj. More; additional; too much; excessive.

زیارت ziyārat (A) n.f. Pilgrimage; visiting (a shrine).

زیارت کرنا ziyārat karnā, v. To go on a pilgrimage; to pay a visit (to a shrine).

زیارت گاه ziyārat gāh, n.m. A shrine; a place of pilgrimage.

زیاں ziyāṅ (P) n.m. Injury; damage; loss; harm; mischief; detriment; deficiency.

زیاں کار ziyāṅ kār, adj. Mischievous; hurtful; evil-doer; injurious; destructive.

زیاں کاری ziyāṅ kārī, n.f. Injury; hurtfulness; doing mischief.

زیب zeb (P) n.f. Ornament; beauty; elegance.

زیب تن کرنا zeb tan karnā, v. To wear; to put on.

زیب دینا zeb denā, v. To behove; to suit; to adorn.

زیب و زینت zeb-ŏ zinat, n.f. Elegance; adorning; ornamentation.

زیبا zebā (P) adj. Adorned; beautiful; becoming; befitting; proper; graceful.

زیبائش zebā'sh (P) n.f. Ornament; beauty; adorning.

زیبائشی zebā'shī (P) adj. Ornamental; elegant; beautiful.

زیتون zaitūn (A) n.m. An olive; the olive tree.

زید zaid (A) n.m. A fictitious name often used with عمر و بکر 'Umar and Bakar (like Tom, Dick and Harry in English).

زیر zer (P) prep. & adj. Under; below, inferior. n.m. The vowel point called کسره kasrah in Arabic.

زیر بار کرنا zer bār karnā, v. To make some one to foot the bill; to burden a person in this manner; to oblige.

زیر بار هونا zer bār honā, v. To be in debt; to be obliged to a person; to be under a debt of gratitude.

زیر باری zer bārī, n.f. Indebtedness; burden.

زیر تجویز zer-ĕ tajwiz, adj. Under consideration; under trial; subjudice.

زیر تحقیقات zer-ĕ tahqīqāt, adj. Under investigation or enquiry.

زیر جامه zer jāmah, n.m. Drawers.

زیر حراست zer-ĕ hirāsat, adj. Under custody.

زیر دست zer dast, n.m. A subject; a vassal; a subordinate. adj. Inferior; powerless; subdued; vanquished.

زیر کرنا zer karnā, v. To subdue; to overpower; to defeat.

زیر لب zer-ĕ lab, adv. In whispers; in an undertone; in an inarticulate manner.

زیر لب کہنا zer-e lab kehnā, v. To speak softly and undertone; to mumble; to mutter.

زیر مشق zer-ĕ mashq, n.m. Leather or card-board pad placed under the paper to facilitate in writing. adj. Under-study; under-practice.

زیر نگیں zer-ĕ nagiṅ, adj. Subjugated; submissive.

زیر و زبر zer-ŏ zabar, adj. Topsy-turvy; inverted; overturned; mixed; upside down.

زیر و زبر کرنا zer-ŏ zabar karnā, v. To ransack; to disintegrate.

زیر zir (P) n.f. A fine, soft sound; the smallest string of a lute &c; the treble (in music).

زیر و بم zer-ŏ bam, n.m. Treble and bass; low and high tune.

زیرک zīrak (P) adj. Intelligent; wise; acute.

زیرکی zīrakī (P) n.f. Intelligence; wisdom; sagacity.

زیرہ zīrah (P) n.m. Cummin-seed; pollen.

زیرہ سیاہ zirah siyāh, n.m. Carraway-seed.

زیرہ سفید zīrah sufaid, n.m. White cummin.

زیریں zeriṅ (P) adj. Lower.

زیست zist (P) n.f. Life; existence.

زین zīn (P) n.f. A saddle.

زین پوش zin posh, n.m. Saddle-cloth; housing.

زین ساز ziṅ sāz, n.m. A saddler.

زین zain (A) n.m. Ornament; beauty; grace; honour.

زینت zīnat (A) n.f. Beauty; elegance; decoration.

زینہ zīnah (P) n.m. A ladder; steps; stairs.

زینہار zīnhār (P) See زنہار zinhār.

زیور zewar (P) n.m. Jewel; ornament (plu. زیورات zewrāt).

ژ zhe, called zāi fārsī or zāi 'ajmī, is the fourteenth letter of the Persian and the seventeenth of the Urdu alphabet. It sounds like s in the English word 'pleasure', and that sound is expressed here by 'zh'. It has no corresponding letter in Arabic. In reckoning, according to abjad, it stands for seven.

ژاژ zhāzh (P) n.m. A kind of camel's thistle; a trifling or indecent speech.

ژاژ خا zhāzh khā, adj. A trifler; an idle-talker.

ژاژ خائی zhāzh khā'i, n.f. Trifling or obscene talk.

ژالہ zhālah (P) n.m. Hail; dew; frost.

ژالہ باری zhālah bārı, n.f. Hail-storm.

ژرف zharf (P) adj. Deep (water or pit); penetrating; acute of mind.

ژرف نگاہی zharf nigāhi, n.f. Keen intellect; deep insight.

ژند zhaṅd (P) n.f. Old Persian; sacred book of the fire-worshipers; an old patched garment.

ژولیدگی zholidagī (P) n.f. Distress; perplexity; entanglement.

ژولیدہ zholidah (P) adj. Entangled; intricate; dishevelled.

ژولیدہ حال zholīdah hāl, adj. Distressed; perplexed; in a bad way.

ژولیدہ مو zholidah mū, adj. Entangled hair; uncombed head.

ژیان zhiyān (P) adj. Terrible; rapacious; furious; angry.

شیر ژیان sher-ĕ zhiyān, n.m. A fierce lion.

س sin, is the twelfth letter of the Arabic fifteenth of the Persian and eighteenth of the Urdu alphabet. It is usually named as *sīn-ĕ mohimilah*. In *abjad* it stands for 60.

سا *sā* (H) *adj.* Like; resembling; so; (used in *comp.* as چھوٹا سا *chhotā sā* a little one; a small one کالا سا *kālā sā*, blackish. *adv.* used as suffix, meaning which, any etc. as کوئی سا *ko'i sā*, anyone; whatever کون سا *kaun sā*, which particular one).

سابر *sābar* (H) *n.m.* An elk; a species of large stag; imitation chamois leather; an instrument used by burglars for breaking into a house.

سابق *sābiq* (A) *adj.* Former; prior; preceding; foregoing; outstripping; passing over.

سابق الذکر *sābiq-uz-zikr*, *adj.* Aforementioned; above-mentioned.

سابق میں *sābiq meṅ*, *adv.* Previously; heretofore; in the past.

سابقاً *sābiqan* (A) *adv.* Formerly; previously; before.

سابقہ *sābiqah* (A) *adj.* Previous; past; ancient; preceding. *n.m.* Friendship; intimacy; acquaintance; correspondence; contact.

سابقہ پڑنا *sābiqah parnā*, *v.* To come in contact with; to have to deal with; to become acquainted with.

سابقین *sābiqīn* (A) *n.m.* (*plu.* of سابق *sābiq*) The formerly great; eminent people in the past; virtuous or superior people in ages gone by.

سات *sāt* (H) *adj.* Seven.

سات پانچ *sāt pāṅch*, *n.f.* Cheat; tricks; hesitation.

سات پانچ کرنا *sāt pāṅch karnā*, *v.* To practise tricks on; to hesitate; to be in doubt; to be unable to make a decision in an emergency.

سات پردوں میں رکھنا *sāt pardoṅ meṅ rakhnā*, *v.* To preserve; to keep with good care.

سات پشت *sāt pusht*, *n.f.* Seven generations; over a long period.

سات سمندر *sāt samundar*, *n.m.* Seven seas; the whole world; a kind of game.

سات سمندر پار *sāt samundar pār*, *adj.* Over the seven seas; far off.

سات سہیلیوں کا جھمکا *sāt saheliyoṅ kā jhumkā*, *n.m.* The Pleiades.

ساتگیں *sātgīṅ* (P) *n.m.* A goblet· a wine cup.

ساتوں *sātoṅ* (H) *adj.* All seven.

ساتواں *sātwāṅ* (H) *adj.* Seventh.

ساتھ *sāth* (H) *adv.* With; together; along with; towards. *n.m.* Society; company; troop; herd; flock.

ساتھ چھوٹنا *sāth chhūṭnā*, *v.* To be separated from.

ساتھ دینا *sāth denā*, *v.* To join; to help; to take the part of; to associate with; to co-operate with.

ساتھ رہنا *sāth rahnā*, *v.* To live together; to cohabit with.

ساتھ ساتھ چلنا *sāth sāth chalnā*, *v.* To walk side by side; to go together in life.

ساتھ کا کھیلا *sāth kā khelā*, *n.m.* A playmate; a play-fellow.

ساتھ لگے پھرنا *sāth lage phirnā*, *v.* To follow (one) about.

ساتھ والا *sāth wālā*, *n.m.* Companion; comrade.

ساتھ ہو لینا *sāth ho lenā*, *v.* To join; to join the company of.

ساتھ ہی *sāth hī*, *adv.* Immediately; along with.

ساتھن *sāthan* (H) *n.f.* A female companion.

ساتھی sāthi (H) n.m. Companion; comrade; supporter.

ساٹھ sāṭh (H) adj. Sixty.

ساٹھا sāṭhā (H) n.m. Sixty years old.

ساٹھا پاٹھا sāṭhā pāṭhā, n.m. A sixty year old man behaving like a young person.

ساٹھی، سٹھی sāṭhi, saṭṭhi (H) n.f. A kind of rice which ripens in sixty days from the time of sowing.

ساج sāj (P) n.m. The teak tree; a grind stone.

ساجد sājid (A) adj. Prostrating in prayer; prostrating in adoration; an adorer.

ساجن sājan (H) n.m. A lover; a husband; lord; sweetheart.

ساجھا sājhā (H) n.m. Partnership; association; share.

ساجھے میں sajhe meṅ, adv. Jointly; in partnership; together.

ساجھی sājhī (H) n.m, A partner; a shareholder; a cooperator; an associate.

ساجھی ہونا sājhī honā, v. To enter into partnership; to become a partner.

ساحر sāhir (A) n.m. An enchanter; a magician; a necromancer; a conjurer.

ساحرہ sāḥirah (A) n.f. Female magician; enchantress.

ساحری saḥirī (A & P) n.f. Magic; necromancy; sorcery; enchantment; conjuration.

ساحل sāḥil (A) n.m. The sea shore; beach; coast; sea-board.

ساخت sāk͟ht (P) n.f. Make manufacture; construction; fashion; formation; structure; form; figure; mould; pretence; fabrication.

ساختہ sāk͟htah (P) adj. Made; formed; artificial; not natural; counterfeited; frigned; surreptitious.

ساختہ پرداختہ sāk͟htah pardāk͟htah, n.m. Done and effected; anything done; act; deed.

بے ساختہ be sāk͟htah, adv. Spontaneously; extempore; impromptu; unpremeditated; at the spur of the moment.

سادات sādāt (A) n.m. (plu. of سادت sādat) Masters; descendents of the Holy Prophet.

سادگی sādagi (P) n.f. Plainness; want of ornament; artlessness; simplicity; openness; sincerity; frankness.

سادہ sādah (P) adj. Simple; plain; sincere, open; artless; blank; candid; guileless; unadorned; beardless.

سادہ پن sādah pan, n.m. See سادگی sādagī.

سادہ دل sādah dil, adj. Artless; simple; stupid.

سادہ کار sādah kār, n.m. A goldsmith.

سادہ لوح sādah lauḥ, adj. Artless; simple; simpleton; stupid.

سادہ لوحی sādah lauḥī, n.f. Simplicity; stupidity.

سادھنا sādhnā (H) v. To perform; to practise; to exercise; to train; to habituate; to regulate; to maintain; to teach; to learn to use; to correct; to rectify.

سادھو sādhū (H) adj. Pious; honest; virtuous; holy; simple; innocent. n.m. A religious person; a kind of mendicant; an ascetic.

سادی sādi, adj. Plain; simple; artless; simpleton; white.

سار sār (H) n.f. Juice; pith; value; worth; vigour; strength; excellence; chess; manure; iron; a cow house.

سارا sārā (H) adj. All; the whole; entire.

ساراً sārā (P) adj. Pure; excellent; undefiled; sweet-smelling.

ساربان sārbān (P) n.m. A camel driver.

سارس sāras (H) *n.m.* A species of heron; a crane.

سارق sāriq (A) *n.m.* A thief; a plunderer.

سارنگ sārang (S) *n.m.* A musical mode or *rāg* sung at midday; a peacock; the cry of a peacock; a snake; elephant; lion; a cloud; a spotted deer; a woman; water; a lamp; a frog; a species of bee.

سارنگی sārangi (H) *n.f.* A musical instrument like a fiddle.

سارنگیا sārangyā (H) *n.m.* A fiddler; one who plays on a *sarangi*.

ساری sāri (H) *n.f.* A dress consisting of one piece of cloth worn by woman round the body and passing over the head. *adj.* The whole; entire.

ساری sāri (H) *adj.* Passing; penetrating; flowing; pervading; infecting; contagious; infectious.

ساڑھی sārhi (H) *n.f.* The same as ساری *sari*. *n.f.* The spring harvest.

ساڑھے sāṛhe (H) *adj.* With one half more in excess of the stated number.

ساز sāz (P) *adj.* (used in *comp.*) Making; feigning; preparing; counterfeiting. *n.m.* Apparatus; accountrements; harness; furniture; equipment; a musical instrument; concord; disposition.

ساز باز sāz bāz, *n.f.* Conspiracy; intrigue; ornament apparatus; accountrement.

ساز باز کرنا sāz bāz karnā, *v.* To plot; to conspire; to make designs against.

ساز گار sāz gār, *adj.* In accordance with; harmonizing; favourable; agreeing.

ساز و سامان sāz-ŏ sāmān, *n.m.* Property; materials; furniture.

سازش sāzish (P) *n.f.* Conspiracy; confideracy; intrigue; combination; collusion.

سازش کرنا sāzish karnā, *v.* To conspire; to plot together; to enter into a conspiracy; to intrigue.

سازشی sāzishi (P) *adj.* Conspirator; collusive; fraudulent; intriguer.

سازندہ sāzindah (P) *n.m.* One who makes or arranges; musician; musical performer.

ساس sās (H) *n.f.* Mother-in-law.

ساعت sā'at (A) *n.m.* A moment; minute; hour; watch; clock; time-piece; time.

ساعد sā'id (A) *n.f.* The fore-arm.

ساعی sā'i (A) *n.m.* An attempter; an endeavourer.

ساغر sāghar (P) *n.m.* A cup; a wine-cup; a bowl; a goblet.

ساغری sāghari (P) *n.f.* The space between the tail and anus of a horse. *adj.* Pertaining to *sāghar*; a goblet.

سافل sāfil (A) *n.m.* The lower part of the body; a mean fellow.

ساق sāq (A) *n.f.* The shank; leg from the knee to the ankle; the trunk or stem of a tree.

ساقط sāqiṭ (A) *adj.* Dropped; fallen; lost; out of use.

ساقط کرنا sāqiṭ karnā, *v.* To eliminate; to fell; to degrade; to render null and void; to cause to lose value.

ساقط ہونا sāqiṭ honā, *v.* To be fallen; to be lost; to lapse; to be degraded; to be eliminated; to drop down; a lose value.

ساقی sāqī (A) *n.m.* A cup bearer; a page; a sweetheart; the beloved one.

ساکت sākit (A) *adj.* Silent; quiet; mute; at rest.

ساکت ہونا sākit honā, *v.* To remain quiet; to remain immobile.

ساکن sākin (A) *n.m.* An inhabitant; a consonent not followed by a vowel. *adj.* Quiescent (letter); quiet; tranquil.

ساکھ sākh (H) n.f. Reputation; credit; trust; testimony; evidence of a witness; season.

ساگ sāg (H) n.m. Vegetables; greens; pot-herbs; culinary herbs; edible plants.

ساگ پات sāg pāt, n.m. Greens; pot-herbs.

ساگر sāgar (S) n.m. The sea; the ocean.

ساگوان sāgwān (H) n.f./m. Teak-wood or tree.

ساگو دانہ sāgū dānah (P) n.m. Sago.

سال sāl (H) n.m. Common timber tree; inferior timber; a hole made by driving a pin into the ground; perforation; boring.

سال sāl (P) n.m. A year.

سال آیندہ sāl-ĕ āyndah, n.m. Next year.

سال بسال sāl basāl, adv. Year by year.

سال حسابی ، سال مالی sāl-ĕ ḥisābi sāl-ĕ māli, n.m. Financial year.

سال خوردہ sāl khūrdah, adj. Old; experienced; aged.

سال رواں sāl-ĕ rawāṅ, n.m. Current year.

سال شمسی sāl-ĕ shamsi, n.m. Solar year; calendar year.

سال قمری ، سال ہجری sāl-ĕ qamarī, sāl-ĕ hijrī, n.m. Lunar year; the Muslim year.

سال عیسوی sāl-ĕ ʻisvi, n.m. The Christian year; Anno Domini.

سال کبیسہ sāl-ĕ kabīsah, n.m. The leap year having 13 months which comes round every three years.

سالگرہ sāl girah, n.f. Birthday; anniversary of one's birth.

سال مہاجنی sāl-ĕ mahājanī, n.m. Commercial or mercantile year.

سال نامہ sāl nāmah, n.m. Calendar; a year book; annual issue of a paper.

سال وار sāl wār, n.m. Annually; year by year.

سالہا سال sālhā sāl, n.m. Many years; a long time; series of years; several years.

سالا sālā (H) n.m. A wife's brother; a brother-in-law.

سالار sālār (P) n.m. A chief; prince; leader; head; captain; commander of an army; a general.

سالار جنگ sālār-ĕ jang, n.m. One who leads an army in battle; commander-in-chief.

سالانہ sālānah (P) adj. Yearly; annual.

سالانہ نقشہ‌جات sālānah naqshahjāt, n.m. Annual returns; annual statistics.

سالک sālik (A) n.m. A traveller; a devotee.

سالم sālim (A) adj. Safe; sound; perfect; whole.

سالمہ sālimah (A) n.m. An atom, a molecule.

سالن sālan (H) n.m. Meat, fish or vegetable curry.

سالو sālū (H) n.m. A kind of red cloth.

سالوتری sālotari (H) n.m. A horse doctor; a veterinary surgeon; farrier.

سالوس sālūs (P) n.f. Hypocrisy; trick; fraud; deceit; subterfuge.

سالی sāli (H) n.f. Wife's sister; sister-in-law.

سامان sāmān (P) n.m. Furniture; apparatus; necessaries; instruments; tools; necessary preparations; arrangements; mode; custom; habit; understanding; probity; opulence; power.

سامان جنگ sāmān-ĕ jang, n.m. War material; ammunition; armaments.

سامان کرنا sāmān karnā, v. To make preparation for; to provide.

سامراج sāmrāj (S) n.m. Imperialism.

سامری sāmrī (A) n.m. A magician who made a golden calf for the Israelites.

سامع sām'i (A) *n.m.* One who hears; a listener; audience

سامعہ sām'iah (A) *n.m.* The sense of hearing; audition.

سامنا sāmnā (H) *n.f.* The front part; opposition; facing; confronting.

سامنا کرنا sāmnā karnā, *v.* To encounter; to confront; to answer boldly; to oppose; to be insolent.

سامنا ہونا sāmnā honā, *v.* To brave; to come face to face (with).

سامنے sāmne (H) *adv.* In front; before; opposite; in presence of.

سامنے آنا sāmne ānā, *v.* To confront; to come in front of; to oppose.

سامنے ہونا sāmne honā, *v.* To face; to challenge; to stand face to face.

سامی sāmi (A) *adj.* Sublime; exalted; high.

سان sān (H) *n.f.* A whetstone; a grindstone; sign; clue; indication.

سان چڑھنا sān chaṛhnā, *v.* To be sharpened; to be whetted.

سان دھرنا sān dharnā, *v.* To sharpen; to whet.

سان گمان sān gumān, *n.m.* Understanding and imagination; sign; trace; notion.

سان نہ گمان sān nah gumān, *adv.* Unawares; without any sign or notion; all of a sudden.

سانپ sāṅp (P) *n.m.* A serpent; a snake.

سانپ سونگھ جانا sāṅp sūngh jānā, *v.* To be bitten by a snake; to be dead silent.

سانپ کا کاٹا رسی سے ڈرتا ہے sāṅp kā kāṭā rassī se ḍartā hai, *prov.* A burnt child dreads the fire.

سانپ مرے نہ لاٹھی ٹوٹے sāṅp mare nah lāṭhī ṭūṭe, *maxim.* To proceed in a very cautious and intelligent manner.

سانپ نکل گیا اب لکیر پیٹا کرو sāṅp nikal gayā ab lakīr pīṭā kar, *maxim.* There is no use crying over spilt milk.

سانپن sāṅpan (H) *n.f.* A female snake.

سانٹ ، سانٹھ sāṅṭ, sāṅṭh (H) *n.f.* Confederacy; joining; sticking; contact; union; cohesion.

سانجھ sāṅjh (H) *n.f.* Evening; dusk; nightfall.

سانچ sāṅch (H) *n.f.* Truth; reality.

سانچ کو آنچ نہیں sāṅch ko āṅch nahiṅ, *prov.* Truth is always victorious; a clever conscience bears no trouble.

سانچا sāṅchā (H) *n.m.* A mould; a matrice.

سانچے میں ڈھالنا sāṅche meṅ ḍhālnā, *v.* To mould.

سانحہ sāniḥah (P) *n.m.* An occurance; an event; an incident.

ساندا sāṅdā (H) *n.m.* A rope by which a cow's legs are tied at the time of milking it.

سانڈ sāṅḍ (H) *n.m.* A bull; a stallion; an independent or extravagant fellow.

سانڈا sāṅḍā (H) *n.m.* A species of sand lizard.

سانڈنی sāṅḍnī (H) *n.f.* A female camel; a dromedary.

سانڈنی سوار sāṅḍni sawār, *m.n.* A camel rider or driver; a messenger who comes on a camel.

سانڈیا sāṅḍyā (H) *n.m.* A young male camel; a wheel used in lace-making.

سانس sāṅs (H) *n.m./f.* Breath; sigh; a fissure.

سانس بھرنا sāṅs bharnā, *v.* To take a deep sigh.

سانس پھولنا sāṅs phūlnā, *v.* To pant.

سانس رکنا sāṅs ruknā, *v.* To be suffocated.

سانس روکنا sāṅs roknā, *v.* To suffocate; to stifle.

سانس لینا sāṅs lenā, *v.* To breathe.

سانسی sāṅsī (H) *n.m.* A criminal tribe; nomade.

سانگ sāṅg (H) n.m. Acting; impersonation; mockery; farce; a play; a representation; a drama.

سانگ بھرنا sāṅg bharnā, v. To act the part of; to play the fool; to mock; to represent a character.

سانگی sāṅgi (H) n.m. Actor; player; a support on which the pole of a cart is propped.

سانتا sānnā (H) v. To knead; to mix up; to stain; to implicate; to smear.

سانولا sāṅwlā (A) adj. Of a dark or sallow colour; of handsome countenance; of nut brown colour.

سانی sānī (H) n.f. Chaff or straw mixed with grain used as food for cattle; forage.

ساون sāwan (H) n.m. The fourth month of the Bikrami Calendar, corresponding to July—August.

ساون هرے نه بھادوں سوکھے sāwan hare nah bhadoṅ sūkhe, prov. Neither sprouting in spring nor fading in autumn; remaining ever thesame.

ساون کی جھڑی sāwan kī jhaṛī, n.f. Persistent rain; incessant down pour.

ساون کے اندھے کو هرا هی هرا سوجھتا هے sāwan ke aṅdhe ko harā hī harā sūjhtā hai, prov. To a jaundiced eye everything is yellow.

ساونت sāwant (H) n.m. A hero; a warrior.

ساونی sāwnī (H) n.f. The autumn harvest.

ساهو sāhū (H) n.m. A well-wisher; a patron; a benefactor.

ساهوکار sāhūkār (H) n.m. A banker; a money-lender.

ساهوکارا sāhūkārā (H) n.m. Money-market; exchange of money; money lending.

ساهوکاری sāhūkārı (H) n.f. Trade; commerce; banking business; exchange of money.

ساهی، سیه sāhī, sih (H) n.f. A porcupine.

سائبان sā'ebān (P) n.m. A canopy; a sunshade; a thatched roof; the roof of a tent.

سائر sā'ir (A) n.m. The whole; the rest; walking; wandering; travelling; current; contingent; tax; duty; octroi.

سائر خرچ sā'ir kharch, n.m. Contigent expenses.

سائس، سائیس sā'is, sā'is (P) n.m. A groom; a horse-keeper.

سائسی sā'isı, n.f. The business of a groom.

سائل sā'il (A) n.m. An applicant; a petitioner; a beggar; a mendicant.

سائی sā'ī (H) n.f. Earnest money. (P) n.f. rubbing (in comps.)

سائی دینا sa'ī denā, v. To give earnest money.

سائیں sā'in (H) n.m. Master; lord; husband; the Supreme Being; God; religious mendicant.

سائیں سائیں sā'eṅ sā'eṅ (H) n.f. A rustle; whistle; whiz.

سایه sāyah (P) n.m. Shadow; shade; shelter; protection; a spectre; an apparition.

سایه پڑنا sāyah paṛnā, v. To came under one's influence; to imitate the manners of another.

سایه دار sāyah dār, adj. Shady.

سایه ڈالنا sāyah ḍālnā, v. To cast a shadow; to afford shelter or protection; to show favour to.

سایه هونا sāyah honā, v. To be possessed by an evil spirit.

سب sab (H) adj. All; entire; whole; every; total; undivided.

سب ایک هی تھیلی کے چٹے بٹے هیں sab ek hi thailī ke chaṭṭe baṭṭe haiṅ, prov. All are chips of the same block.

سب سے بھلی چپ sab se bhalī chup, prov. Silence is best; silence is gold.

سب کا سب sab kā sab, *adv.* All together; the whole; completely.

سب sabb (A) *n.f.* Abuse; reproach; slander; disgrace; injury.

سب و شتم sabb-ŏ shatm, *n.f.* Abusive language; reproach.

سبابه sabbābah (A) *n.f.* The fore-finger.

سبب sabab (A) *n.m.* Cause; reason; ground; means; instrument; motive; affinity; relation;hip.

به سبب bah sabab, *adv.* On account of; by means of.

سبت sabt (A) *n.m.* The day of rest (Friday for Muslims, Saturday for Jews and Sunday for Christians); the sabbath day; the Lord's day.

سبحان subḥān (A) *adj.* Holy; glorifying or praising (God).

سبحان الله subhān allah, *interj.* God be praised ! Holy God ! Good God !

سبد sabad (P) *n.m./f.* A basket.

سبد گل sabad-ĕ gul, *n.m./f.* Bunch of flowers.

سبز sabz (P) *adj.* Green; unripe; verdant; flourishing; fresh.

سبز باغ دکھانا sabz bāgh dikhānā, *v.* To excite desire and hope by deceitful promises; to practise deception.

سبز قدم sabz qadam, *adj.* Unfortunate; unlucky; ill-omened.

سبز ہونا sabz honā, *v.* To flourish; to grow.

سر سبز sar sabz, *adj.* Fertile; productive; fruitful; rich (soil).

سبزه sabzah (P) *n.m.* Verdure; green; herbage; sweet basil; green stone for an earring; an insipient beard; bloom; an iron-grey horse; hemp.

سبزه زار sabzah zar, *n.m.* A place abounding in verdure; a meadow; a lawn.

سبزی sabzī (P) *n.f.* Greenness; verdure; greens; potherbs; a goblet or flask for wine; an intoxicating liquor made of *bhang* (hemp).

سبزی فروش sabzī farosh, *n.m.* A greengrocer.

سبزی منڈی sabzī mandī, *n.f.* Vegetable market.

سبط sibṭ (A) *n.m.* A grand-child; the Jews.

سبطین sibṭain (A) *n.m.* Imam Hassan and Hussain, the grandsons of the Holy Prophet.

سبع saba' (A) *adj.* Seven.

سبق sabaq (A) *n.m.* Lesson; lecture; going forward; advancing.

سبق دینا sabaq denā, *v.* To instruct; to teach a lesson; to admonish;

سبقت sabqat (A) *n.f.* Going before; outstripping; surpassing; preceding; excellence; aggression; taking the lead; superiority; precedence.

سبقت کرنا sabqat karnā, *v.* To precede; to advance; to surpass.

سبقت لے جانا sabqat le jānā, *v.* To excel; to surpass; to outstrip; to take the lead; to bear away the palm from.

سبک subuk, sabuk (P) *adj.* Light; delicate; trifling; debased; unsteady; trivial; frivolous; futile.

سبک بار subuk bār, *adj.* Lightly burdened; unencumbered.

سبک پا subuk pā, *adj.* Swift-footed; nimble.

سبک پائی subuk pā'ī, *n.f.* Nimbleness of foot.

سبک پرواز subuk parwāz, *adj.* Swift in flight.

سبک خیز subuk khez, *adj.* Quickly or swiftly rising; swift; vigilant; alert; nimble.

سبک دوش *subuk dosh, adj.* Relieved of responsibility; lightly laden.

سبک رو *subuk raw, adj.* Light paced; easy-going.

سبک سر *subuk sar, adj.* Light headed; unsteady; contemptible; mean.

سبک گام *subuk gam, adj.* Light-footed; active; brisk.

سبک مزاج *subuk mizāj, adj.* Fickle minded; irresolute.

سبکی *subki* (P) *n.f.* Lightness; delicacy; levity; frivolousness; indignity; dishonour; disgrace; contempt.

سبکی *subki* (H) *n.f.* Sob.

سبکیاں لینا *subkiyān lenā, v.* To sob.

سبو *sabū, subū* (P) *n.m.* An ewer; a jar; a pitcher; a cup; a glass; tumbler.

سبو بدوش *sabū badosh, n.m.* A carrier or bearer of the pitcher.

سبوس *sabūs* (P) *n.m.* Bran; chaff; pollard.

سبھا *sabhā* (H) *n.f.* An assembly; meeting; company; convention; council; a court.

سبھا پتی *sabhā pati, n.m.* A president; a chairman.

سبھاؤ *subhāo* (H) *n.m.* Good disposition; nature; behaviour; treatment. *adj.* Well-disposed; of good quality.

سبیل *sabīl* (A) *n.f.* Road; way; path; mode; manner; course; instrument; means; water or refreshing drinks given to thirsty travellers during the first ten days of *Muharram*.

سبیل پلانا *sabīl pilānā, v.* To offer water or refreshing drinks during *Muḥarram*.

سبیل لگانا *sabīl lagānā, v.* To keep a stall for supplying water to thirsty travellers.

فی سبیل اللہ *fī sibīl illah, adv.* In the way of God; for the sake of God.

ابن السبیل *ibn-us-sabīl, n.m.* A traveller.

سپاٹ *sapāṭ* (H) *adj.* Flat; smooth; even.

سپاٹا *sapāṭā* (H) *n.m.* A long run; a quick march; a leap; a bound; a spring.

سپاٹا بھرنا *sapāṭā bharnā, v.* To take a long jump.

سپارہ، سیپارہ *sipārah, sīpārah* (P) *n.m.* One of the 30 chapters of the *Qurān*.

سپاری *supārī* (H) *n.f.* Betel-nut; *glans penis*.

سپاس *sipās* (P) *n.m.* Praise; thanks.

سپاس گزاری *sipās guzārī, n f.* Thanksgiving.

سپاس نامہ *sipās nāmah, n.m.* Laudatory address; address of welcome.

سپاہ *sipāh* (P) *n.m.* Army; soldiery; troops; force.

سپاہ سالار *sipāh sālār, n.m.* A general; a commander; commander-in-chief.

سپاہ گری *sipāh gari, n.f.* The military profession; military tactics; soldiering.

سپاہی *sipāhī* (P) *n.m.* A soldier; a messenger of a court.

سپاہیانہ *sipāhiyānah* (P) *adj.* Soldier-like; soldierly.

سپر *sipar* (P) *n.f.* A shield.

سپر اندازی *sipar āndāzī, n.f.* Throwing away the shield; surrendering.

سینہ سپر ہونا *sīnah sipar honā, v.* To be ready to fight; to show a bold front.

سپرد *supurd, sipurd* (P) *n.f.* Charge; care; keeping; giving over; trust; commitment delivery; submission; resignation.

سپرد کرنا *supurd karnā, v.* To give in-charge; to consign; to entrust.

سپردائی *sapardā'ī* (H) *n.m.* Musician attendant on dancing girls.

سپردگی *supurdagi* (P) *n.f.* Delivery; commitment by a magistrate; charging; surrender; consigning; entrusting.

سپستان sapistān (P) n.m. A glutinous fruit used as a medicine.

سپنا supna (H) n.m. A dream.

سپند sipand (P) n.m. Wild rue.

سپوت sapūt (H) n.m. A dutiful son.

سپورن sapūran (H) n.m. Full moon.

سپولیا sapoliyā (H) n.m. Young snake, just hatched.

سپہ sipah (P) (contr. of سپاہ sípāh) See سپاہ sipāh.

سپہر sipahr (P) n.m. The sphere; the celestial globe; the sky; fortune; time; the world.

سپھل suphal (H) adj. Bearing good fruit; fruitful; profitable; useful; successful.

سپید suped (P) See سفید sufed.

سپیدہ supedah (P) n.m. Dawn of the day; the eucalyptus tree; white paint.

سپیدی supedī (P) See سفیدی sufedī.

سپیرا saperā (H) n.m. A snake-catcher; a snake-charmer.

ست sat (H) adj. True; right; actual; real; seven. n.m, Power; strength; essence; courage; truth; goodness; virtue; juice.

ست بچن sat bachan, n.m. A true statement.

ست پوتی sat potī, n.f. Mother of seven sons.

ست خصمی sat k͟haṣmī, n.f. A woman who has had seven husbands; a woman who has insatiable sexual desire.

ست کونا sat konā, adj. Seven cornered; heptagonal.

ست لڑا sat laṛā, n.m. A necklace of seven strings.

ست ماسا sat māsā, n.m. A child born in the seventh month of pregnancy.

ست منزلہ sat manzilah, adj. A seven-storied house.

ست ناجا sat nājā, n.m. A mixture of seven different grains; medley; hotch-potch.

ستار sitār (P) n.m. A kind of guitar with three strings.

ستار نواز sitār nawāz, n.m. One who plays on the guitar.

ستار sattār (A) n.m. One who covers the failings (of); an attribute of God. adj. Covering; concealing.

ستار العیوب sattār-ul-'uyūb, n.m. One who covers the sins of (with the veil of His mercy); God.

ستارہ sitārah (P) n.m. A star; a kind of firework; name of a musical instrument with three strings; an ornament.

ستارہ اچھا ہونا sitārah achchhā honā, v. To have lucky stars.

ستارہ بلند ہونا sitarah buland honā, v. To be very fortunate.

ستارہ چمکنا sitārah chamaknā, v. To be in good luck; to have the star in the ascendant.

ستارہ دمدار sitārah-ĕ dumdār, n.m. A comet.

ستارہ شناس sitārah shinās, n.m. An astrologer; an astronomer.

ستارہ شناسی sitārah shināsī, n.f. Astrology; astronomy.

ستارہ صبح sitārah-ĕ subḥ, n.m. The morning star.

ستارہ قطبی sitārah-ĕ quṭabī, n.f. A polar star.

ستاروں بھرا siṭāroṅ bharā, adj. Starry; full of stars.

ستاروں بھری رات sitāroṅ bharī rāt, n.f. Star-spangled night.

ستاروں کا جھرمٹ sitāroṅ kā jhurmuṭ, n.m. Galaxy of stars.

ستارہ گردش میں ہونا sitārah gardish meṅ honā, v. To be in bad luck; to be out of luck's way.

ٹوٹنے والا ستارہ ṭūṭne wālā sitārah, n.m. A shooting star.

ستاسی sattāsi (H) adj. Eighty-seven.

ستان sitān (P) adj. Taking; seizing; captivating (used in compos. as جاں ستان jān sitāṅ—taking life; killing).

ستان sitān (P) n.m. Place; station; (used as affix as گلستان gulistān—a flower garden).

ستانا satānā (H) v. To tease; to vex; to trouble; to harm; to interrupt; to annoy; to grieve; to harass.

ستانوے sattānwe (H) adj. Ninety-seven.

ستاون sattāwan (H) adj. Fifty-seven.

ستائش sitā'ish, satā'ish (P) n.f. Praise; encomium; returning thanks.

ستائیس sattā'is (P) adj. Twenty-seven.

ستتر satattar (H) adj. Seventy-seven.

ستر satr (A) n.m. Concealing; covering; veiling; the privities.

ستر عورت satr-ĕ 'aurat, n.m. Hiding of nakedness. (Nakedness in men consists of parts of the body from the navel of the calf and in women the whole body excepting face, hands and feet).

ستر sattar (H) adj. Seventy.

سترا بہترا sattrā bahattarā (H) adj. Old; dating; decrepit.

ستروان sattarwāṅ (H) adj. Seventieth.

سترہ sattarah (H) adj. Seventeen.

سترھواں sattarahwāṅ, adj. Seventeenth.

ستلی sutlī (H) n.f. Coarsy twine; string.

ستم sitam (P) n.m. To tyranny; oppression; injury; violence; outrage; vexation; injustice.

ستم دیدہ، رسیدہ، زدہ sitam didah, rasidah, zadah, adj. Oppressed.

ستم ظریفی sitam zarīfī, n.f. Elegance or ingeniousness in tyranny.

ستم کرنا sitam karnā, v. To tyrannise over; to oppress.

ستم گر، شعار sitam gar, shi'ār, adj. Tyrant; oppresser.

ستمبر sitamber (E) n.m. September, the ninth month of the Christian calendar.

ستو sattū (H) n.m. Barley parched and ground and made into a paste drunk.

ستو باندھ کے پیچھے پڑنا sattū bāndh ke pichhe paṛnā, v. To pursue or persecute a person continuously.

ستوان sutwāṅ (H) adj. Delicate; fine; thin.

ستوان ناک sutwān nāk, adj. Delicate nose; fine elongated nose.

ستوانا sutwānā (H) v. To cause to clean; to cause to wring; to cause to squeeze; to cause to skin.

ستودہ sitūdah (P) adj. Praised; laudable; celebrated; glorious.

ستودہ صفات sitūdah ṣifāt, adj. Of laudable qualities.

ستون sutūn, satūn, sitūn (P) n.m. A pillar; a column; a prop.

ستھرا suthrā (H) adj. Neat; elegant; adorned; excellent; well; tidy; clean; clean-shaved.

ستھرائی suthrā'ī (H) n.f. Neatness; beauty; elegance; goodness.

ستی satī (H) n.f. A woman who burns herself on the funeral pile of her husband; a faithful wife. adj. Chaste; virtuous; constant.

ستیا sattyā (S) n.m. Power; strength.

ستیاناس sattyānās (H) n.m. Destruction; devastation; ruin.

ستیاناس کرنا sattiyanas karnā, v. To spoil: to destroy.

ستیاناس ہونا sattiyanas hona, v. To be destroyed or ruined.

ستیز، ستیزہ satez, satezah (P) n.m. Conflict; contention; battle; strife; combat; fight.

ستیہ گرہ sattiyah garah (S) n.m. Solemn promise; passive resistance.

سٹ sat (H) n.f. A league; union; close attachment.

سٹ لڑانا sat laṛāna, v. To conspire; to intrigue; to make friend.

سٹا sitta (H) n.m. An ear of Indian corn.

سٹا satta (H) n.m. An engagement to supply grain &c for which advances have been made; a mercantile transaction; speculation; a market; a bond; a bank.

سٹے باز satte baz, n.m. A speculator.

سٹپٹانا satpatana (H) v. To be confounded; to be surprised; to be restless.

سٹکنا، سٹک جانا satakna, satak jāna (H) v. To run away; to disappear; to flee; to sheer off; to slink away.

سٹھیانا sathiyanā (H) v. To be sixty years of age; to lose one's mental balance as a result of age; to be decrepit.

سٹی sittı (H) n.f. The senses; wisdom.

سٹی گم ہونا sittı gum honā, v. To lose one's senses; to be confounded.

سج saj (H) n.f. Good appearance; decoration; preparation; dress.

سج دھج saj dhaj, n f. Beautiful form; elegance; decoration; bedecking; ornamentation.

سجاد sajjād (A) adj. Adoring; bowing the body in adoration; prostrating much in prayer.

سجادہ sajjādah (A) n.m. Prayer carpet of Muslims; a mosque.

سجادہ نشین sajjādah nashin, n.m. A saint; a spiritual superior attached to a mosque or religious endowment; a Muslim ascetic.

سجانا sajana (H) v. To adorn; to decorate; to assort; to bedeck; to arrange in order; to mend.

سجانا sujana (H) v To cause to swell.

سجاوٹ sajāwat (H) n.m. Preparation; ornament; arrangement; decoration; adoring.

سجدہ sajdah, sijdah (A) n.m. Prostration; bowing in prayer so as to touch the ground with the forehead; adoration to God.

سجدہ کرنا sajdah karna, v. To adore.

سجدہ گاہ sajdah gah, n.m. Mosque; temple; a carpet for prayer; the place of performing the prayer.

سجع saja' (A) n m. Rhyme; poetry; metre; poesy; prose cadence.

سجع گو saja' go, n.m. A rhymer; an eloquent speaker.

سجل sijil (H) n.m. The recording angel. adj. right; proper; good; well-arranged.

سجن sijn (A) n.m. A prison.

سجن sajan (H) n.m. A friend; a respectable person; a sweetheart; a lover; a husband.

سجنا sajnā (H) v. To fit well; to be made ready; to be decorated; to be adorned.

سجنی sajni (H) n.f. A female friend; a mistress.

سجوانا sajwānā (H) v. To cause one to adorn or decorate.

سجھانا sujhānā (H) v. To show; to make understand; to point out.

سجی sajjı (H) n.f. A kind of mineral; impure carbonate of soda.

سجیلا sajilā (H) *adj.* Well-shaped; handsome; beautiful, graceful; decorated.

سچ sach (H) *n.m.* Truth; veracity; accuracy. *adj.* True; veritable; genuine, *adv.* Indeed; in earnest; actually; truly.

سچ ماننا sach mānnā, *v.* To trust in the accuracy of; to believe to be true.

سچ مچ sach much, *adj./adv.* True; truly.

سچا ، سچی sachchā, sachchī (H) *adj.* True; sincere; genuine; real, honest; faithful; loyal; sure; pure; unalloyed; full (weight); bonafide (transaction).

سچائی sachchā'ī (H) *n.f.* Truth; honesty; purity; genuineness.

سحاب saḥāb (A) *n.m.* A cloud.

سحر seḥr (A) *n.m.* Magic; enchantment; sorcery; fascination.

سحر saḥar (A) *n.m.* Dawn; morning.

سحری، سحرگاھی saḥarī, saḥar gāhi (A & P) *n.f.* Food taken by Muslims a little before dawn during the fasting month of *Ramazān*. *adj.* Of or relating to dawn.

سخا، سخاوت sak͟hā, sak͟hāwat (A) *n.f.* Liberality; generosity; munificence; charity.

سخت sak͟ht (P) *adj.* Hard; stiff; strong; obstinate; violent; excessive; cruel; very difficult; hard hearted; harsh; severe; stingy; troublesome; vehement; painful; austere; rigid. *adv.* Very; intensely; violently; extremely; severely.

سخت جان sak͟ht jān, *adj.* Tough; die-hard.

سخت دل sak͟ht dil, *adj.* Hard-hearted; stern; austere; severe.

سخت سست کہنا sak͟ht sust kehnā, *v.* To reproach; to scold; to chide; to abuse.

سخت گیر sak͟ht gir, *adj.* Holding fast; rigid; cruel.

سخت گیری sak͟ht gīrī, *n.f.* Taking by force; extortion; cruelty.

سختی sak͟hti (P) *n.f.* Hardness; obstinacy; cruelty; vehemence; hardship; adversity; firmness; rigidity; hard heartedness; hardness; severity; strictness; poverty; distress.

سختی کرنا sak͟htī karna, *v.* To use force or violence; to treat with harshness or severity.

سخن sak͟hun sukhan, suk͟hun (P) *n.m.* Speech; language; words; things; business; affair.

سخن پرداز sak͟hun pardāz, *adj.* Eloquent; talking.

سخن پرور sak͟hun parwar, *adj.* One who adheres to one's word; one who fulfills his promise; a bigoted person.

سخن چیں sak͟hun chin, *n.m.* A critic; an informer; a spy; a tale bearer.

سخن دان sak͟hun dān, *adj.* Skilled in language; eloquent; intelligent. *n.m.* A poet.

سخن دانی sak͟hun dāni, *n.f.* Knowledge of speech; eloquence.

سخن دینا sak͟hun denā, *v.* To make a promise; to pledge one's word.

سخن رانی sak͟hun rāni, *n.f.* Oratory; rhetoric; speech.

سخن رس sak͟hun ras, *adj.* Intelligent; eloquent; comprehending what is said.

سخن ساز sak͟hun sāz, *n.m.* An orator; a poet; a deceiver; a speaker.

سخن سازی sak͟hun sāzī, *n.f.* Oratory; eloquence; fabrication; elocution; address.

سخن سنج sak͟hun sanj, *n.m.* A wise and prudent man; intelligent; a poet; an orator.

سخن شناس sak͟hun shinās, *adj.* Having the ability to judge words; knowing or conversant in language.

سخن طرازی sak͟hun ṯirāzī, *n.f.* Eloquence.

سخن فہم *sakhun fahm, adj.* Intelligent; quick of apprehension.

سخن فہمی *sakhun fahmi, n.f.* Intelligence; understanding; apprehension.

سخن گو *sakhun go, n.m.* A poet; eloquent; a spokesman; a representative. *adj.* Eloquent.

سخن گوئی *sakhun go'i, n.f.* The art of poetry.

سخن نشنو *sakhun na-shanau, adj.* Not attending to advice; heedless.

سخن *sakhun war, adj.* Eloquent.

سخن وری *sakhun wari, n.f.* Eloquence.

کم سخن *kam sakhun, adj.* A reserved person.

سخی *sakhi* (A) *adj.* Liberal; generous; bountiful. *n.m.* A liberal person.

سد *sadd* (A) *n.m.* A wall; a barrier; an obstacle, impediment; ditch; rampart; an obstruction of any kind; fence; dam.

سد راہ *sadd-ĕ rāh, n.m.* Obstruction of the road; an obstacle; a stumbling-block.

سد سکندر *sadd-ĕ sikandar, n.m.* Alexander's wall.

سدا *sadā* (H) *adv.* Always; perpetually; ever.

سدا برت *sadā bart, a.m.* Daily distribution of alms.

سدا پھل *sadā phal, adj. & n.m.* Constantly bearing fruit; a perenninal fruit bearing tree.

سدا سہاگن *sadā suhāgan, n.f.* Name of a bird; a kind of flower; a prostitute; a woman's benediction, meaning "may your husband live for ever."

سدا سکھی *sadā sakhi, n.m.* A class of *faqirs* who dress themselves like women.

سدرشن *sudarshan* (S) *adj.* Handsome; good-looking.

سدرہ *sidrah* (A) *n.m.* Plum tree; name of a tree in Paradise; one of a species of lote tree.

سدرۃ المنتہی *sidra-tul-muntahā, n.f.* A stop in the seventh heaven; a tree of knowledge in Paradise.

سدہ *suddah* (A) *n.m.* Obstruction in the nose; any obstruction in the body.

سدھ *sudh* (H) *n.m.* Consciousness; memory; remembrance; intelligence.

سدھ بدھ *sudh budh, n.f.* Consciousness; presence of mind; care; perception; correct knowledge or understanding.

سدھ لینا *sudh lenā, v.* To take care of; to look after.

بے سدھ *be sudh, adj.* Senseless; careless.

سدھارنا *sidhārnā* (H) *v.* To set out; to go; to depart; to leave this world; to die.

سدھارنا *sudhārnā* (H) *v.* To mend; to improve; to adjust; to arrange; to adorn; to polish.

سدھانا *sadhānā* (H) *v.* To tame or train animals to perform.

سدھرنا *sudharnā* (H) *v.* To be corrected; to be mended.

سدھنا *sadhnā* (H) *v.* To be fully disciplined or instructed or trained; to be tamed.

سدھوانا *sadhwānā* (H) *v.* To cause to train; to cause to tame.

سدیشی *sudeshī* (H) *adj.* See سودیشی *sūdeshi.*

سڈول *suḍaul* (H) *adj.* Well-shaped; graceful; pretty; elegant.

سر *sar* (P) *n.m.* Head; top; pinnacle; origin; end; point; beginning; front; face; commencement; chief; principal; inclination; desire; intention.

سر اجلاس *sar-ĕ ijlās, adv.* In court.

سر افراز *sar afrāz, adj.* Exalted; promoted.

سر افگندہ *sar afgandah, adj.* Head cast down; in low spirits.

سر انجام *sar anjām*, *n.m.* Preparation; arrangement; result; end.

سر انجام دینا، کرنا *sar anjām denā, karna*, *v.* To manage; to provide; to arrange; to accomplish.

سر انگشت *sar-ĕ angusht*, *n.m.* Tip of the finger; finger's end.

سر باز *sar bāz*, *adj.* Intrepid; risking one's life or head; reckless. *n.m.* A soldier.

سر بازار *sar-ĕ bāzār*, *adv.* In public; openly.

سر بام *sar-ĕ bām*, *adv.* On top of the house.

سر براہ، سر براہ‌کار *sar barāh*, *sar barāhkār*, *n.m.* A manager; an agent.

سر براہی کرنا *sar barāhī karnā*, *v.* To manage.

سر بستہ *sar bastah*, *adj.* Hidden; shut; closed; secret; inextricable; wearing a turban.

سر بسر *sar basar*, *adv.* All; wholly; entirely; from end to end.

سر بلند *sar buland*, *adj.* Eminent; glorious; exalted.

سر بلندی *sar bulandī*, *n.f.* Exaltation; eminence.

سر بمہر *sar bamuhr*, *adj.* Sealed; closed and sealed.

سر پرست *sar parast*, *n.m.* A guardian; a patron.

سر پرستی *sar parasti*, *n.f.* Patronage.

سر پنچ *sar panch*, *n.m.* President; chairman; umpire.

سر پوش *sar posh*, *n.m.* A cover; a lid.

سر پیچ، پیش *sar pech, pesh*, *n.m.* An ornament worn in the turban.

سر تابی *sar tābī*, *n.f.* Rebellion; refraction.

سر تا پا *sar tā pā*, *adv.* From head to foot; totally; entirely; entirely.

سرتاج *sar tāj*, *n.m.* A chief; a leader.

سر تسلیم خم کرنا *sar-ĕ taslīm kham karnā*, *v.* to submit; to obey instructions.

سر چشمہ *sar chashmah*, *n.f.* Fountain head; spring.

سرحد *sarḥadd*, *n.m.* Boundary; border; frontier.

سر خط *sar khaṭ*, *n.m.* An agreement to hire service; bill of sale; a lease (of a house); a receipt given to an *asāmī*.

سر خوش *sar khūsh*, *adj.* Cheerful; gay; merry; tipsy.

سر خیل *sar khail*, *n.m.* Head of a family or troop.

سردار *sardār*, *n.m.* A chief; a commander; a leader.

سرداری *sardārī*, *n.f.* Headship; supremacy; rule.

سر دست *sar-ĕ dast*, *adv.* At present; immediately; at hand.

سر دفتر *sar daftar*, *n.m.* A superintendent; a chief accountant.

سر راہ *sar-ĕ rāh*, *adv.* On the road.

سر رشتہ *sar rishtah*, *n.m.* Department; regulation; business.

سر زد ہونا *sar zad honā*, *v.* To happen; to occur; to appear; to come to light; to be accomplished.

سر زمین *sar zamīn*, *n.f.* Country; limits; region; territory; confines.

سر زنش *sar zanish*, *n.f.* Reproof; reprimand; chiding; rebuke.

سر زوری *sar zori*, *n.f.* Rebellion; insubordination; violence.

سر سبز *sar sabz*, *adj.* Verdant; flourishing; fertile; victorious; successful.

سر سبزی *sar sabzī*, *n.f.* Verdure; freshness; prosperity; flourishing state.

سر شام *sar-ĕ shām*, *n.f.* About evening time; evening.

سر قلم کرنا *sar qalam karnā*, *v.* To behead; to slay.

سر کرنا *sar karnā*, *v.* To conquer; to accomplish; to obtai victory.

سرکش *sar kash, adj.* Refractory; rebellious.

سرکشی *sar kashi, n.f.* Rebellion; insurrection; refraction.

سرکشی کرنا *sar kashi karna, v.* To rebel.

سرکوبی *sar kobi, n.f.* Punishment; reproot; reproach; beating the head.

سر گران *sar garān, adj.* Tipsy; proud, arrogant; drunk.

سرگرانی *sar garāni, n.f.* Heaviness of head; pride.

سرگردان *sar gardān, adj.* Wandering; confounded; distressed; humbled; stupified; straying.

سرگردانی *sar gardānı, n.f.* Distress; confusion; amazement; stupifaction; perplexity.

سرگرم *sar garm, adj.* Zealous; ardent; active; earnest; eager; attentive; diligent; inflamed with love.

سرگرمی *sar garmı, n.f.* Activity; diligence; eagerness; zeal; earnestness; love.

سرگروہ *sar garoh, n.m.* Ring-leader; commander.

سرگذشت *sar guzasht, n.f.* History; story; account of circumstances; narrative; event; accident; adventure.

سرگوشی *sar goshi, n.f.* Whispering.

سرمست *sar mast, adj.* Intoxicated (with wine or power); in a state of dead drunkenness; overcome with liquor.

سرمستی *sar masti, n.f.* Intoxication.

سرمو *sar-ĕ mū, n.m.* The point of a hair; a hair's breadth.

سرنامہ *sar nāmah, n.m.* Title at the beginning of a letter; address; superscription.

سرنگوں *sarnigūn, adj* Down cast; with head hanging down; ashamed; upset;

سرنوشت *sar nawisht, n.f.* Destiny; fate; fortune.

سروسامان *sar-ŏ sāmān, n.m.* Necessaries; apparatus: furniture; luggage.

سرو کار *sar-ŏ kār, n.m.* Concern; relation; object.

سر ہونا *sar hona, v.* To be conquered; to be subdued.

سر *sir (H) n.m.* Head; skull; highest part; top; crown; beginning; commencement; pinnacle.

سر آنکھوں پر *sir ānkhon par, adv.* By all means; with great pleasure.

سر آنکھوں پر بٹھانا *sir ānkhon par bithānā, v.* To show great respect; to receive most cordially or cheerfully.

سر اٹھا کے چلنا *sir uthā ke chalnā, v.* To walk with the head on high; to walk conceitedly.

سر اٹھانا *sir uthānā, v.* To rebel; to rise up against one.

سر اڑانا *sir uṛanā, v.* To cut the head; to kill.

سر بھاری ہونا *sir bhāri honā, v.* To be giddy; to have a headache.

سر پر *sir par, adv.* Close at hand; very near.

سر پر اٹھا لینا *sir par uthā lenā, v.* To make a great noise; to cause a tumult.

سر پر پڑنا *sir par paṛnā, v.* To fall to one's lot

سر پر چڑھانا *sir par charhānā, v.* To spoil (a child) to make much of an undeserving inferior.

سر پر چڑھنا *sir par charhnā, v.* To be spoilt by kindness; to behave with great rudeness; to insult.

سر پر خاک ڈالنا *sir par khāk ḍālnā, v.* To lament; to mourn.

سر پر رکھ *sir par rakhna, v.* To treat

سر پر ھاتھ رکھنا **sir par hāth rakhnā**, *v.* To foster; to patronise; to take under one's protection.

سر پھٹنا، پھوٹنا **sir phaṭnā, phūṭnā**, *v.* To have a splitting headache; breaking of head.

سر پھوڑنا **sir phoṛnā**, *v.* To break one's head; to strike one's head against.

سر پھٹول **sir phuṭawwal**, *n.f.* Head-breaking; wrangling; fighting.

سر پیٹنا **sir piṭnā**, *v.* To mourn; to lament.

سر توڑنا **sir toṛnā**, *v.* To subdue; to crush; to do one's best.

سر تھوپنا **sir thopnā**, *v.* To transfer one's responsibility to another; to hold someone else responsible.

سر جھکانا **sir jhukānā**, *v.* To bow; to submit.

سر چڑھا **sir chaṛhā**, *adj.* Spoiled by over indulgence; proud; haughty; rude.

سر دھننا **sir dhunnā**, *v.* To lament; to grieve over one's troubles; to shake one's head from affliction or surprise.

سر دے دے مارنا **sir de de mārnā**, *v.* To be desperate.

سر دینا **sir denā**, *v.* To pledge one's head.

سر سفید ھونا **sir safaid honā**, *v.* To become grey or old.

سر سے پاؤں تک **sir se pāon tak**, *adv.* From head to foot; entirely.

سر سے کفن باندھنا **sir se kafan bāndhnā**, *v.* To engage in a desperate undertaking; to be prepared to die in a venture.

سر سے کھیلنا **sir se khelnā**, *v.* To shake the head under the influence of an evil spirit; to be prepared to sacrifice one's life.

سر سہرا ھونا **sir sehrā honā**, *v.* To be responsible for success; to have the bedge of honour.

سر کٹا **sir kaṭā**, *adj.* Beheaded.

سر کھانا **sir khānā**, *v.* To worry; to tease; to bother.

سر کھپانا **sir khapānā**, *v.* To be bothering one's head; to rake one's brain.

سر کھجانا **sir khujānā**, *v.* To court punishment.

سر کے بل **sir ke bal**, *adv.* Headlong; with head foremost; at full speed; willingly.

سر گنجا کرنا **sir ganjā karnā**, *v.* To beat severely.

سر گھومنا **sir ghūmnā**, *v.* To suffer from vertigo; to be of unsound mind.

سر مارنا **sir mārnā**, *v.* To do one's best; to search diligently; to take great pains; to make a strenuous efforts.

سر منڈاتے ھی اولے پڑے **sir munḍāte hi ole paṛe**, *prov.* Misfortune greeted his first venture.

سر منڈانا **sir munḍānā**, *v.* To adopt a life of mendicity.

سر مونڈنا **sir mūnḍnā**, *v.* To shave another's head; to cheat a person.

سر نہ پیر **sir nah pair**, *adj.* Groundless; baseless.

سر نہوڑانا **sir nahoṛānā**, *v.* To hang down the head; to be down-cast; to be gloomy; to meditate; to be ashamed.

سر نیچا کرنا **sir nichā karnā**, *v.* To be ashamed; to lower one's head in shame.

سر ھونا **sir honā**, *v.* To insist upon; to quarrel; to worry.

سر **sur** (H) *n.m.* Tone; note; tune; accent; music; melody; song; air breathed through the nostrils; a vowel.

سر ملانا **sur milānā**, *v.* To sing in tune; to tune an instrument in harmony with another.

اونچا سر **unchā sur**, *n.m.* Major key; alto.

بے سر **be sur**, *adj.* Out of tune; inharmonious.

دھیما سر dhimā sur, n.m. The tenor; contralto.

نیچا سر nichā sur, n.m. A low tone; the bass.

سر sirr (A) n.m. A secret; a mystery.

سرا sirā (H) n.m. Beginning; end; extremity; top; point; tip.

سرے سے sire se, adv. From the beginning; from the very start; ab initio.

سراب sarāb (A) n.m. The mirage; illusion.

سراپا sarāpā (P) n.m. Appearance; features; identity. adv. From head to foot; totally.

سراج sirāj (A) n.m. A lamp; the sun; a candle.

سرادھ sarādh (H) n.m. Funeral obsequies.

سراسر sarāsar (P) adv. Wholly; entirely; from beginning to end; from one end to the other.

سراسیمگی sarāsimagī (P) n.f. Perplexity; amazement; confusion of the mind.

سراسیمه sarāsimah (P) adj. Confounded; distracted; distressed; confused; amazed.

سراغ surāgh (P) n.m. Search; sign; footsteps; tracks.

سراغ رساں surāgh rasāṅ, n.m. A detective; a spy.

سراغ رسانی surāgh rasāni, n.f. Searching; tracking;

سراغ لگانا surāgh lagānā, v. To trace out; to search out; to discover; to seek; to detect.

سراغ ملنا surāgh milnā, v. To be on the track of; to obtain a clue; to get an inkling of.

سرا گائے surā gā'e (H) n.f. The bushy-tailed cow of Tibet.

سراهنا sarahnā (H) v. To praise; to applaud; to approve; to commend.

سرائی sarā'i (P) n.f. Singing; modulation; (used in comp. as مدح سرائی madah sarā'i Singing praises of).

سرا، سرائے sarā, sarā'i (P) n.f. An inn; a caravan serai; a temporary lodging for travellers.

سرایت sirāyat (A) n.f. Contagion; penetration; infection; conduction.

سرپٹ sarpat (H) n.f. Gallop.

سرپٹ دوڑنا sarpat dorna, v. To gallop; to run at full speed.

سرجن surjan (S) n.m. A respectable person.

سرخ surkh (P) adj. Red. n.m. One ratti ⅛ of a māshā.

سرخ باد surkh bād, n.m. A disease in which part of the body becomes red.

سرخ بید surkh bed, n.f. A kind of cane; a medicinal plant.

سرخ رو surkh rū, adj. Successful: exonerated; unabashed.

سرخ روئی surkh rū'i, n.f. Honour; fame; success.

سرخ و سفید surkh-ŏ sufaid, adj. Red and white; fair; plump.

سرخ ہونا surkh honā, v. To be red; to be ripe; to be flushed; to become red with anger.

سرخاب surkhāb (P) n.m. The ruddy goose; a species of lark.

سرخاب کا پر لگنا surkhāb kā par lagnā, v. To be exalted; to be advanced in dignity; to receive greater honours or titles; to be a great or wonderful man; to do anything exceptional.

سرخه surkhah (P) n.m. A pigeon of red colour; a roan horse; white or grey or cream coloured horse.

سرخی surkhi (P) n.f. Redness; blood; brick dust.

سرخی مائل surkhi mā'il, adj. Reddish; slightly red.

سرد sard (P) adj. Cold; damp; dull; lifeless; dead.

سرد بازاری sard bāzāri, adj. Dullness of market; slump.

سرد خانہ sard khānah, n.m. Cold storage; refrigeratory; a cool room for summer.

سرد کرنا sard karnā, v. To cool; to refrigerate.

سرد مزاج sard mizāj, adj. Cool tempered; cold; apathetic.

سرد مہر sard mehr, adj. Cold or lukewarm (friend).

سرد مہری sard mehri, n.f. Coldness; lukewarmness; indifference; coolness.

سرد ہونا sard hona, v. To become cold; to become chilled; to become lukewarm or indifferent; to die.

سردہ sardah (P) n.m. A kind of melon exported from Kabul.

سردی sardi (P) n.f. Cold; coldness; dampness; catarrh.

سردی پڑنا sardi paṛnā, v. To be chilly or cold.

سردی لگنا sardi lagnā, v. To feel cold; to shiver with cold; to suffer from cold.

سرسام sarsām (P) n.m. Delirium; frenzy; inflation of the brain.

سرسرانا sarsarānā (H) v. To rustle; to creep along as a snake.

سرسرانا sursurānā (H) v. To shiver with cold.

سرسراہٹ sarsarāhat (H) n.f. Hissing sound.

سرسری sarsari (P) adj. Easy; facile; careless; without attention or consideration; trivial; trifling; by the way; cursory.

سرسری sursuri (H) n.f. An insect bred in grain; a weevil; titillation.

سرسوں sarson (H) n.f. A species of mustard; sesame.

سرشار sarshār (P) adj Brimful; intoxicated; overflowing; redundant; glutted.

سرشاری sarshari (P) n.f. Intoxication; fullness; overflowing.

سرشت sarisht (P) n.f. Nature; temperament; disposition; complexion; intellect.

سرشک sarashk (P) n.m. A tear.

سرطان sarṭān (A) n.m. A crab; the sign Cancer; a cancer; a disease in the feet of a cattle.

سرعت sur'at (A) n.f. Haste; speed; velocity quickness; rapidity.

سرغنہ sarghanah (P) n.m. A chief; a leader; one unequalled; a ring-leader.

سرف sarf (A) n.m. Extravagance; prodigality.

سرفہ surfah (P) n.m. Cough.

سرقہ sarqah (A) n.m. Robbery; theft; larceny; plagiarism.

سرکار sarkār (P) n.f. Lord; master; the king's court; government; estate; property; a superintendent; a title of respect given to a superior.

سرکاری sarkāri (P) adj. Belonging to the state or the government or to the king's court.

سرکاری اہلکار یا ملازم sarkāri ahlkār yā mulāzim, n.m. Government servant.

سرکانا sarkānā (H) v. To remove from its place; to push aside; to move out of the way; to shift.

سرکنا sarakna (H) v. To move aside; to get out of the way; to draw back; to glide; to slide.

سرکنڈا sarkanḍā (H) n.m. A reed.

سرکہ sirkah (P) n.m. Vinegar.

سرکی **sirki** (H) *n.f.* A screen made of reeds or bamboo sticks.

سرگ **surg** (S) *n.m.* Heaven; paradise; the sky.

سرگ باشی **surg bāshī**, *adj.* Dead; late.

سرگشتگی **sargashtagı** (P) *n.f.* Wondering; affliction; astonishment.

سرگم **sargam** (H) *n.f.* The gamut; the descending scale (music).

سرگین **sargin** (P) *n.m.* Cow-dung.

سرما **sarmā** (P) *n.m.* Winter.

سرمائی **sarmā'ı** (P) *adj.* Wintery; pertaining to winter; winter clothing.

سرمایہ **sarmāyah** (P) *n.m.* Capital; stock in trade; funds; means; materials.

سرمایہ لگانا **sarmāyah lagānā**, *v.* To invest a capital.

سرمد **sarmad** (A) *adj.* Eternal; perpetual; everlasting.

سرمہ **surmah** (P) *n.m.* Collyrium; antimony reduced to fine powder for applying to the eyes.

سرمہ آلودہ یا سرمگیں **surmah āludah yā surmagīn**, *adj.* Eyes stained with collyrium.

سرمہ دانی **surmah dānī**, *n.f.* A small box for holding collyrium.

سرمہ لگانا **surmah lagānā**, *v.* To apply collyrium to the eyelids.

سرمہ ہونا **surmah honā**, *v.* To be reduced to very fine powder.

سرمئی **surma'ī** (P) *adj.* Of the colour of collyrium; grayish.

سرنگ **surang** (H) *n.f.* A mine; an underground passage. *n.m.* Red colour.

سرنگ اڑانا **surang uṛānā**, *v.* To explode a mine.

سرنگ لگانا **surang lagānā**, *v.* To mine; to break into a house.

سرنگیا **surangyā** (H) *n.m.* A miner; one who lays down mines.

سرو **sarv, saro** (P) *n.m.* The cypress tree.

سرو اندام **saro andām**, *adj.* Having a body as graceful as the cypress.

سرو رواں **saro-ĕ rawāṅ**, *adj.* A moving cypress; a person moving about gracefully.

سرو سہی **saro-ĕ sahi**, *n.m.* A cypress with two branches going up straight; a tall and graceful sweetheart.

سرو قامت، سرو قد **saro qāmat, saro qadd**, *adj.* As tall and straight as a crypress tree; tall and graceful.

سروپ **sarūp, surūp** (H) *n.m.* A handsome face; beauty; appearance; form; identity; shape. *adj.* Handsome; well-formed; beautiful.

سروتا **sarotā** (H) *n.m.* A kind of scissors for cutting betel-nut.

سرود **sarod** (P) *n.m.* A song; a melody; a lyre; modulation.

سرور **surūr** (A) *n.m.* Pleasure; joy; cheerfulness; exhilaration; slight intoxication.

سرور **sarwar** (P) *n.m.* A chief; a leader; lord; master.

سرور کائنات **sarwar-ĕ kā'nāt**, *n.m.* Chief of created being (The Holy Prophet).

سروری **sarwarī** (P) *n.f.* Chiefship; sovereignty; rule; sway.

سروش **sarosh** (P) *n.m.* An angel; a voice from heaven; the 17th day of the solar month.

سرھانا **sirhānā, sarhānā** (H) *n.m.* The head of a bedstead or tomb; the head part or side of anything; the place where the head rests or reclines; a pillow.

سری **sirī** (S) *n.f.* The head.

سری srı (S) *n.f.* Goddess of plenty and prosperity; prosperity; beauty; an auspicious word prefixed to the proper names of persons.

سریانی *suryāni* (P) *adj.* & *n.f.* Syriac; the syriac language.

سریر *sarir* (A) *n.m.* A throne; a raised couch; a couch frame.

سریر *sarir* (S) *n.m* Body; body of any animate being.

سریش *saresh yā sirish* (P) *n.m.* Glue; starch.

سریع *sarī'* (H) *adj.* Quick; nimble; ready; swift; making haste.

سریع التاثیر *sarī'-ut-tāṣir*, *adj.* Penetrating; quick in taking effect.

سریع الفہم *sarī'-ul-fahm*, *adj.* Quick of understanding.

سریلا، سریلی *surīlā, surīlī* (H) *adj.* Melodious; harmonious; musical.

سرین *surīn* (P) *n.f.* Buttocks; thighs; hips.

سڑ *sir* (H) *n.f.* Madness; lunacy.

سڑا، سڑی *sarā, sarī* (H) *adj.* Rotten; putrid; stinking; ulcerating; musty.

سڑانا *saṛānā* (H) *v.* To cause to rot; to ferment.

سڑاند *saṛānd* (H) *n.f.* A disagreeable smell; smell of putrid meat; rottenness; putrefaction; stink; stinch.

سڑک *saṛak* (H) *n.f.* A road; a street.

سڑک کاٹنا *saṛak kātnā*, *v.* To make a road.

سڑکنا *suṛuknā* (H) *v.* To gulp down; to swallow by gulps.

سڑکی *suṛki* (H) *n.f.* The sudden slackening of the string of a paper kite; a sip.

سڑن *siṛan* (H) *n.f./adj.* A mad or crazy woman.

سڑنا *saṛnā* (H) *v.* To rot; to decompose; to decay

سڑی *siṛī* (H) *adj.* Mad; insane; crazy; lunatic. *n.m.* A mad man.

سڑیل *saṛyal* (H) *adj.* Rotten; worthless; crazy; peevish; having a bad temper.

سزا *sazā* (P) *n.f.* Correction; punishment; penalty; retribution; chastisement; requital.

سزا پانا *sazā pānā*, *v.* To be punished.

سزا دینا *sazā denā*, *v.* To punish; to chastise.

سزا وار *sazā wār*, *adj.* Liable; suitable; deserving; befitting; worthy.

سزا وار ہونا *sazā wār honā*, *v.* To deserve; to merit.

سزا یاب *sazā yāb*, *adj.* Punished; liable to punishment.

سزا یافتہ *sazā yāftah*, *adj.* One who has been punished for an offence.

سزاول *sazāwal* (T) *n.m.* A tax-gatherer; a rent collector; a supervisor; a superintendent; a bailiff.

سست *sust* (P) *adj.* Loose; frail, lazy; negligent; slothful; slow; tardy; inactive; indolent; dull; downcast; sluggish.

سست اعتقاد *sust e'tiqād*, *adj.* Incredulous; sceptical; lose in confidence; slow to believe; fickle.

سست پیماں *sust paimān*, *adj.* Slow in fulfilling engagements; unsteady; fickle.

سست رفتار *sust raftār*, *adj.* Slow; slow to move; easy-going.

سست کرنا *sust karnā*, *v.* To relax; to diminish the speed of; to throw cold water on.

سست ہونا *sust honā*, *v.* To be lazy; to be sad; to be dejected.

سستا، سستی *sastā, sastī* (H) *adj.* Cheap.

سستانا *sastānā* (H) *v.* To rest; to lie down for a while; to repose a little.

سستائی *sastā'ī* (H) *n.f.* Cheapness.

سستی *susti* (P) *n.f.* Relaxation; languor; laziness; slothfulness; inaction; idleness; slowness; negligence; tardiness.

سستی کرنا *susti karnā*, *v.* To delay; to procrastinate; to be lazy; to be sluggish.

سسر *susar* (H) *n.m.* A father-in-law.

سسرا *susrā* (H) *n.m.* A father-in-law (an abuse).

سسرال *susrāl* (H) *n.f.* Father-in-law's house or family.

سسرال کا کتا *susrāl kā kuttā*, *n.m.* A son-in-law who sponges on his father-in-law.

سسری *susrī* (H) *n.f.* Mother-in-law; a term of abuse.

سسکارنا *suskārnā* (H) *v.* To hiss (as snake); to sibilate.

سسکنا *sisaknā* (H) *v.* To sob; to sigh; to gasp; to quiver through fear.

سسکی *siski* (H) *n.f.* Sobbing; sighing.

سسکیاں بھرنا *siskiyāṅ bharnā*, *v.* To sob; to sigh; to breathe convulsively.

سطح *saṭaḥ* (A) *n.f.* Surface; superficies (in *Geom.*) a plane; a platform; a terrace; a flat roof.

سطحی *saṭḥī* (A) *adj.* Flat; superficial.

سطر *saṭar* (A) *n.f.* A line; row; rank; series; lineament; delineating; describing; ruling (lines).

سطر بندی *saṭar bandī*, *n.f.* Ruling; lines for writing on.

سطوت *saṭwat* (A) *n.f.* Power; authority; dominion; awe; majesty.

سطور *suṭūr* (A) *n.f.* (*plu.* of سطر *saṭar*) Lines.

سعادت *sa'ādat* (A) *n.f.* Prosperity; happiness; good fortune; auspiciousness.

سعادت مند *sa'ādat mand*, *adj.* Fortunate; prosperous; happy; dutiful; obedient.

سعادت مندی *sa'ādat mandī*, *n.f.* Prosperity; dutifulness.

سعد *sa'd* (A) *n.m.* Felicity; prosperity. *adj.* Fortunate; auspicious.

سعد اکبر *sa'd-ĕ akbar*, *n.m.* The planet Jupiter.

سعدین *sa'dain* (A) *n.m.* The planets Jupiter and Venus.

قران السعدین *qirān-us-sa'dain*, *n.m.* The conjunction of two auspicious planets, Jupiter and Venus.

سعی *sa'i* (A) *n.f.* Attempt; endeavour; effort; enterprise; essay; purpose.

سعی سفارش *sa'ī sifārish*, *n.f.* Recommendation; hard struggle.

سعی لا حاصل *sa'ī-ĕ lā ḥāṣil*, *n.f.* A futile effort; a vain attempt.

سعی کرنا *sa'i karnā*, *v.* To make an endeavour; to attempt; to strive; to try; to exert oneself.

سعید *sa'īd* (A) *adj.* Fortunate; happy; august; auspicious.

سعیر *sa'īr* (A) *n.f.* Fire; hell-fire; name of a part of hell reserved for idolators.

سفارت *sifārat* (A) *n.m.* Embassy; acting as a messenger of peace; mediation; making peace.

سفارش *sifārish* (P) *n.f.* Recommendation; intercession; influence.

سفارش کرنا *sifārish karnā*, *v.* To recommend; to support claim of.

سفارش نامه ، سفارشی چٹھی *sifārish nāmah*, *sifārshī chiṭṭhī*, *n.m.* A recommendatory letter.

سفارشی ٹٹو *sifārshī ṭaṭṭū*, *n.m.* One appointed merely on recommendation.

سفاک *saffāk* (A) *adj.* Shedder of blood; cruel; butcher.

سفال *sifāl* (P) *n.m.* Earthenware; potsherd; a tile; a shard.

سفالی sifālī (P) *adj.* Earthen; of earth.

سفاهت sifāhat (P) *n.f.* Folly; foolishness; stupidity; ignorance; insolence.

سفته suftah (P) *adj.* Bored; pierced (a pearl); perforated.

سفر safar (A) *n.m.* Journey; voyage; travel.

سفر خرچ *safar kharch, n.m.* Travelling expenses; travelling allowance.

سفر کرنا *safar karnā, v.* To travel; to go on a journey; to depart; to retire; to die.

سفر مینا *safar mainā,* (*corr.* from the Eng.) Sappers and miners.

سفر نامه *safar nāmah, n.m.* An account of a journey.

سفرجل safarjal (A) *n.m.* A quince.

سفری safarī (P) *adj.* & *n.m.* Concerning a journey; provisions for a journey; a traveller.

سفله siflah (A) *adj.* Ignoble; mean: contemptible; miserly; low; base; stingy; envious.

سفله پن *siflah pan, n.m.* Meanness; baseness.

سفله خو *siflah khū, adj.* Mean-spirited; of a base or ignoble disposition.

سفلی siflī (A) *adj.* Lower; inferior; infernal.

سفلی عمل *siflī a'mal, n.m.* Magic wrought through evil spirits.

سفوف safūf (A) *n.m.* A powder.

سفید sufaid, safaid, safed (P) *adj.* White; blank.

سفید پوش *sufaid posh, adj.* A man dressed in clean clothes; a well-dressed man.

سفیده sufaidah (P) *n.m.* Chalk; flour; white lead; white poplar; ceruse.

سفیدی sufaidī (P) *n.f.* Whiteness; white-washing; white of an egg; leprosy; morning; light.

سفیدی پھیرنا *sufaidī phernā, v.* To white-wash.

سفیر safīr (A) *n.m.* An ambassador; an envoy; a messenger.

سفینه safīnah (A) *n.m.* A ship; a vessel; a boat; a blank book; a notice; summons.

سفیه safīah (A) *adj.* Foolish; stupid; ignorant.

سقا saqqā (A) *n.m.* A water-carrier; a cup-bearer.

سقاوه saqāwah, *n.m.* A bath-room; a public bath.

سقر saqar (A) *n.m.* Hell; hell fire.

سقف saqf (A) *n.f.* Roof; ceiling; canopy; the sky; a platform.

سقم suqm (A) *n.m.* Flaw; defect; fault; disease.

سقم نکالنا *suqm nikālnā, v.* To find fault with.

سقمونیا saqmūniyā (G) *n.f.* Scammony; dried juice exuding from the root of *convolvulus skammonia.*

سقنقور saqanqūr (A) *n.m.* The skink; a small limbed lizard.

سقوط suqūṭ (A) *n.m.* Falling off; miscarriage; elimination.

سقیم saqīm (A) *adj.* Sick; ailing; infirm; disordered; faulty.

سکارنا sakārnā (H) *v.* To accept (a bill of exchange).

سکت sakat (H) *n.f.* Power; strength; ability.

سکتر sikattar, *n.m.* (*corr.* from the English) Secretary.

سکته saktah (P) *n.m.* Trance; swoon; apoplexy; a pause; vacancy; hiatus.

سکته هونا *saktah honā, v.* To fall into a swoon.

سکر sukr (A) *n.m.* Intoxication; an intoxicating drink; wine.

سکرات sakrāt (A) n.f. Fainting; subject to fits; insensibility; agony of death.

سکڑا ہوا سکڑی ہوئی sukṛā howā sukṛī hoī (H) adj. Shrunk; contracted; narrow; strait; small; tight.

سکڑنا sukaṛnā (H) v. To be shrunk or contracted; to shrink; to draw in; to dwindle; to shrivel.

سکنا saknā (H) v. To be able; can; to be able to do.

سکنا siknā (H) v. To be roasted; to be parched.

سکنجبین sikanjbīn (P) n.f. (Lit. vinegar and honey) Lime juice or other acid mixed with sugar; a refreshing drink.

سکندر sikandar (P) n.m. Alexander.

سکندری sikandarī (P) adj. Of or relating to Alexander; stumbling; tripping up.

سکندری کھانا sikandarī khānā, v. To stumble; to trip up.

سکنہ sakanah (A) n.m. (plu. of ساکن sākin) Inhabitants.

سکوت sukūt (A) n.f. Silence; quietness; peace.

سکورہ sakorah (P) n.m. A small earthen vessel.

سکوڑنا sakoṛna (H) v. See سکیڑنا sukeṛnā.

سکون sukūn (A) n.m. Quietude; peace; rest; tranquillity.

سکونت sukūnat (A) n.f. Residence; habitation; dwelling.

سکونت پذیر ہونا sukūnat pazīr honā, v. To reside.

سکہ sikkah (A) n.m. A coining die; an impression on money; stamped coin; sterling; current coin; a seal.

سکہ بٹھانا sikkah biṭhānā, v. To introduce one's coin; to establish one's rule or authority.

سکہ بنانا sikkah banānā, v. To coin money.

سکۂ جعلی sikkah-ĕ ja'lī, n.m. Counterfeit coin; spurious coin.

سکہ رائج الوقت sikkah rā'ij-ul-waqt, n.m. The current coin.

سکہ زن sikkah zan, n.m. A coiner; one who stamps coins.

سکھ Sikh (H) n.m. A follower of Guru Nanak; a Sikh; disciple; scholar.

سکھ sukh (H) n.m. Ease; comfort; easy circumstances; happiness; pleasure; relief; solace; content; tranquillity; gratification.

سکھ پال sukh pāl, n.f. Easy chair; a palanquin.

سکھ پانا sukh pānā, v. To get relief; to get leisure.

سکھ چین sukh chain, n.m. Rest; tranquillity; ease; leisure.

سکھ درشن sukh darshan, n.m. A shrub, the juice of which is used for earache.

سکھ کی نیند sukh kī nīnd, n.f. Sound sleep.

سکھانا sukhānā (H) v. To dry up; to cause to wither; to emaciate; to evaporate.

سکھانا sikhānā (H) v. To teach; to instruct; to admonish; to advise; to discipline.

سکھائی sikhā'ī (H) n.f. Teaching; instruction.

سکھی sakhī (H) n.f. A woman's female friend; a companion; a handmaid.

سکھی sukhī (H) adj. Happy; contented; at ease; tranquil; comfortable; glad.

سکیڑنا sukeṛnā (H) v. To shrivel; to shrink; to tighten; to contract; to gather up.

سگ sag (P) n.m. A dog.

سگ بازاری sag-ĕ bāzārī, n.m. A country dog.

سگ شکاری sag-ĕ shikārī, n.m. A hound.

سگا، سگی sagā, sagī (H) adj. Own; full; born of the same parents; uterine; real friend; intimate.

سگائی sagā'ī (H) n.f. Betrothal; a second marriage among the lower classes; relationship; friendship.

سگائی کرنا sagā'ī karnā v. To betroth; to contract a marriage; to affiance.

سگرئی sugra'ī (H) n.f. A musical mode or rāgnī sung in the forenoon.

سگند sugand (H) n.f. Good smell; odour; perfume. adj. Fragrant; sweet-smelling.

سگھڑ sughaṛ (H) adj. Accomplished; expert; elegant; beautiful; virtuous.

سگھڑ پن sughaṛ pan, n.m. Elegance; accomplishment; expertness; beauty.

سل sil (H) n.f. A stone; a rock; a flat stone on which candiments &c are ground with a muller; threshold; door frame.

سل sill (A) n.f. Consumption; hectic fever; ulceration of the lungs.

سلاجیت salājit (H) n.f. Storax; red chalk; bituman.

سلاح silāḥ (A) n.f. Arms; weapons; implements of war; armour.

سلاح بند silāh band, adj. Armed.

سلاح خانہ silāḥ khānah, n.m. Arsenal; armoury.

سلاخ salākh, n.m. An iron bar; a stake; a spit; a probe.

سلاست salāsat (A) n.f. Clearness; plainness; facility; simplicity; gentleness; easiness; perspicuity.

سلاسل salāsil (A) n.f. (plu. of سلسلہ silsilah) Chains.

سلاطین salāṭīn (A) n.m. (plu. of سلطان sulṭān) Kings; monarchs; emperors.

سلام salām (A) n.m. Salutation; peace; safety; compliment; good-bye.

سلام پھیرنا salām phernā, v. To finish the prayer.

سلام پیام salām payām, n.m. Discourse; talk; conversation.

سلام دینا، کہنا salām denā, kehnā, v. To send one's compliments; to express or desire to call on a person.

سلام علیکم salām 'alaikum, interj. Peace be with you!

سلام کرنا salām karnā, v. To salute.

سلام لینا salām lenā, v. To accept and return salutation (of).

سلامت salāmat (A) adj. Safe; well; sound.

سلامت رو salāmat rau, adj. An economist.

سلامت روی salāmat rawī, n.f. Good management; economy.

سلامتی salāmatī (A) n f. Safety; peace; health; security; well-being.

سلامتی کا جام پینا salāmatī kā jām pinā, v. To drink to the health of; to quaff a cup to the health (of).

سلامی salāmī, n.f. Salutation; reception; welcome; a salute of guns; presentation of arms; a present to a superior or a bridegroom; pavement of stones across the bed of a water-course; a present given to the landlord for granting lease.

سلانا silānā (H) v. To cause to sew or stitch.

سلانا sulānā (H) v. To put to sleep; to quieten; to lull; to calm; to murder; to kill.

سلائی silā'ī (H) n.f. Seam; sewing; needlework; the price for sewing.

سلائی salā'ī (H) n.f. A large needle used for applying collyrium to eyes; knobby needles used for knitting or crochet work.

سلب salb (A) n.m. Seizing by force; plunder; negation; denial; spoil; booty; a negative argument in logic.

سلجھانا suljhānā (H) v. To unravel; to disentangle; to solve a problem; to analyse; to settle a case; to untie a knot.

سلجهاؤ suljhāo (H) n.m. Disentanglement; unravelling.

سلجهنا sulajhnā (H) v. To be disentangled; to be unravelled; to be settled (a case).

سلح silaḥ (A) n.m. Arms.

سلح پوش silaḥ posh, adj. Wearing armour.

سلسبیل salsabīl (A) n.f. Name of a fountain in paradise; wine; limpid water.

سلسل البول salsal-ul-baul (A) n.m. Diabetes; a morbid copiousness of urine.

سلسلانا salsalānā (A) v. To creep; to crawl; to feel a creeping or tickling sensation; to itch; to rankle; to cause to simmer or boil.

سلسلاهٹ salsalāhaṭ (H) n.f. A creeping or itching sensation; titillation; rankling.

سلسله silsilah (A) n.m. A chain; series; succession; pedigree; genealogy; arrangement; mode; descent of a family.

سلسله وار silsilah wār, adj. Linked together; arranged; classified; unbroken; consecutive.

سلطان sulṭān (A) n.m. A king; a sovereign; an emperor; an absolute monarch.

سلطانه sulṭānah (A) n.f. A queen; an empress.

سلطانی sulṭānī (A) adj. Regal; royal; princely; belonging to a sovereign. n.f. Sovereignty; empire; dominion; dignity or office of a king.

سلطانی گواه sulṭānī gawāh, n.m. Crown witness.

سلطنت salṭanat (A) n.f. Empire; kingdom; region; dominion; realm.

سلف salaf (A) adj. & n.m. Past; preceding; former (times); ancestors; predecessors.

سلفه sulfah (H) n.m. Little ball of tobacco smoked in a ḥuqqā without the intervention of a tile.

سلفه هونا sulfah honā, v. To be consumed; to be utterly destroyed or ruined.

سلک silk (A) n.f. A thread; cause; road; wire.

سلگانا sulgānā (H) v. To light; to inflame; to kindle; to ignite; to stir a fire; to incite; to stir up.

سلگنا sulagnā, silagnā (H) v. To light; to be kindled; to be inflamed; to burn without flame.

سلمه salmah (H) n.m. A band of embroidery.

سلمه ستاره salmah sitārah, n.m. A kind of embroidery consisting of small stars between embroidered bands.

سلنا silnā (H) v. To be sewn; to be stitched.

سلو sallū (A) n.m. Narrow strips of leather with which shoes are stitched.

سلوانا silwānā (H) v. To cause to sew or stitch.

سلوائی silwā'ī (H) n.f. The price of sewing.

سلوتری selotrī (H) n.m. A veterinary doctor.

سلوٹ silwaṭ, salwaṭ (H) n.f. Crease; line; wrinkle.

سلوک sulūk (A) n.m. Road; way; journey; manner; mode; conduct; behaviour; intercourse; usage; treatment; civility; kindness; attention.

سلوک سے رهنا sulūk se rahna, v. To be on good terms.

سلوک کرنا sulūk karnā, v. To treat kindly; to entertain; to be at peace with; to befriend.

سلونا، سلونی salonā yā salaunā, salonī (H) adj. Salted; seasoned; tasteful; dark-complexioned; brunette; beautiful; expressive; handsome.

سلونو salūno (H) *n.f.* A Hindu festival, held on the full moon in *Sāwan*.

سلوىٰ salwā (A) *n. m.* Quail.

سلی sillī (H) *n.f.* A whetstone; a block of stone; a bone; a small kiln.

سلیس salīs (A) *adj.* Easy; simple; plain.

سلیقہ salīqah (A) *n.m.* Good disposition; good taste; method; mode; knowledge; dexterity; address; skill; careful observance of rules of etiquette.

سلیقہ دار salīqah dār, *adj.* Discriminate; possessing genius; well-mannered; discrete.

سلیقہ شعار salīqah shi'ār, *adj.* Of good disposition.

صاحب سلیقہ ṣāḥib-ĕ salīqah, *n.m.* A man of taste.

سلیم salīm (A) *adj.* Pacific; mild; weak; affable; perfect; healthy.

سلیم الطبع salim-uṭ-ṭaba', *adj.* Mild; gentle; right-minded; affable.

سم samm (A) *n.m.* Poison; venom.

سم الفار samm-ul-fār, *n.m.* Arsenic; ratsbane.

سم sum (P) *n.m.* A hoof.

سم لینا sum lenā, *v.* To pare the hoofs (of); to trip; to stumble (a horse).

سما، سماں، سمے samā, samān, same (H) *n.m.* Time; season; plenty; abundance; state; condition; concord; harmoy; unison.

سماں باندھنا samān bāndhnā, *v.* To make a picture of; to depict; to represent; to be in concord or harmony.

سما جانا samā jānā (H) *v* To be absorbed; to be included; to be entered.

سماج samāj (S) *n.m.* Society; congress; assembly; association; meeting; club; multitude; concert.

سماجت samājat (A) *n.f.* Entreaty; solicitation; flattery; adulation.

سماجت کرنا samājat karnā, *v.* To entreat; to solicit.

سماجی samājī (H) *adj.* Of or relating to the society. *n.m.* Musicians who attend dances.

سماچار samāchār (H) *n.m.* News; tidings; intelligence; advice; account of circumstances or health &c; practice; conduct; behaviour; condition; state.

سمادھ samādh (H) *n.f.* The tomb of a *jogī*, who has been buried alive to acquire self immolation.

سمادھی samādhī (S) *adj.* Absorbed in contemplation. *n.m.* Promise; agreement; religious vow; tomb; grave.

سماع samā' (A) *n.m.* Hearing; listening; sense of hearing; music; a song; ecstacy caused by music.

سماعت samā'at (A) *n.f.* Hearing.

سماعت کرنا samā'at karnā, *v.* To hear a case or try a suit; to entertain or take cognizance of a complaint.

سماعی samā'ī (A) *adj.* What has been heard of or received by hearsay; traditional; (in grammar) irregular.

سماق samāq (A) *n.m.* The hardest species of marble; porphyry.

سمانا samānā (H) *v.* To be contained in; to be accommodated in; to occupy the whole space.

سماوار samāwār (P) *n.m.* A small and handy filter used for making tea and keeping it hot.

سماوی samāvī (A) *adj.* Heavenly; celestial.

سماء samā' (A) *n.m.* The heavens; the firmament; the sky; a canopy; altitude.

سمائی samā'ī (H) *n.f.* The act of accommodating too many in a small place; the act of containing anything in; room; space.

سمبندھ **sambandh** (H) *n.m.* Connection; relation; affinity; intercourse; union, association; communication.

سمپورن **sampūran** (H) *adj.* Perfect; full; complete.

سمت **simt yā samt** (A) *n.f.* Way; path; a part; quarter; side; direction.

سمت الراس **simt-ur-rās**, *n.f.* The vertical point in the heavens; the Zenith.

سمٹ جانا **simaṭ jānā** (H) *v.* To shrink; to contract; to shrivel.

سمٹنا **simaṭnā** (H) *v.* To shrink; to be contracted; to be concentrated; to be drawn together; to shrivel.

سمجھ **samajh** (H) *n.f.* Understanding; comprehension; knowledge; opinion; conception; thought; mind; discernment.

سمجھ آنا **samajh ānā**, *v.* To understand; to believe; to think; to recover one's senses; to grow to years of discretion.

سمجھ بوجھ **samajh būjh**, *n.f.* Comprehension; understanding; intelligence.

سمجھ دار **samajh dār**, *adj.* Prudent; wise; intelligent.

سمجھ کے کرنا **samajh ke karnā**, *v.* To act intelligently; to exercise discretion.

سمجھ میں آنا **ṣamajh meṅ ānā**, *v.* To be comprehended; to understand.

سمجھانا **samjhānā** (H) *v.* To make clear; to describe; to instruct; to correct; to advise; to remonstrate with; to explain; to account for; to warn; to convince; to satisfy.

سمجھانا بجھانا **samjhānā bujhānā**, *v.* To advise; to admonish.

سمجھنا **samajhnā** (H) *v.* To think; to consider; to understand; to learn; to comprehend; to suppose; to deem; to fancy; to come to an understanding.

سمجھوتا **samjhautā** (H) *n.m.* Mutual understanding; giving confidence; convincing; compromise.

سمدھن **samdhan** (H) *n.f.* A son or daughter's mother-in-law.

سمدھی **samdhī** (H) *n.m.* A son or daughter's father-in-law.

سمدھیانہ **samdhiyānah** (H) *n.m.* The family of a son or daughter's parents-in-law.

سمرتی **samriti** (H) *n.f.* Holy books of Hindus; contemplation.

سمع **sama'** (A) *n.m.* Hearing; the ear.

سمع خراشی **sama' kharāshī**, *n.f.* Jarring on the ear; dazing the brains.

سمک **samak** (A) *n.f.* A fish, the sign Pisces of the Zodiac; a fish on which the earth is supposed to rest.

سمن **samman** (E) *n.m.* Summons.

سمن **saman** (P) *n.f.* Jasmine.

سمند **samand** (P) *n.m.* A high-bred horse; a steed; courser; bay or chestnut colour of a horse.

سمندر **samundur** (P) *n.m.* The salamander; a kind of lizard supposed to live in fire; spirit living in fire.

سمندر **samundar** (H) *n.m.* Ocean; sea.

سمندر پھل **samundar phal**, *n.m.* A medicine.

سمندر جھاگ یا پھین **samandar jhāg yā phen**, *n.m.* The foam of the sea; the dorsal scale or bone of the cuttle-fish.

سمندر سوکھ **samundar sokh**, *n.m.* A medicinal plant.

سمندر کھار **samundar khār**, *n.m.* Arsenic.

سمور **samūr** (A) *n.m.* A weasel; a marten; a sable; sable-skin.

سموسا samosā (A) n.m. A triangular puff containing mixture of boiled potatoes; peas and minced meat; a sort of a pie.

سموم samūm (A) n.f. A hot pestilential wind.

سمونا samonā (H) v. To make lukewarm; to mix cold water with hot water.

سميت samet (H) adj. Together with; alongwith; connected; united together.

سميت samiyyat (A) n.f. Poisonousness; poisonous properties.

سمیٹنا sameṭnā (H) v. To accomplish; to roll together; to wrap up; to collect; to condense.

سن san (H) n.m. A kind of flax; hemp.

سن سے san se (H) adv. With a whiz; rapidly; all at once.

سن سے نکل جانا san se nikal jānā, v. To pass quickly.

سن sinn (A) n.m. An age; period of life; years; a tooth; nib of a pen.

سن بلوغ، سن بلوغت sinn-ĕ balūgh, sinn-ĕ balūghat, n.m. Age of puberty; mature age; state of being a major.

سن تمیز یا شعور sinn-ĕ tamīz yā sha'ūr, n.m. Years of discretion; maturity of age.

سن رسیده sinn rasīdah, adj. Old; of advanced age.

کم سن kam sinn, adj. Young; juvenile.

سن sun (H) adj. Without sensation; insensible; numb; paralyzed; palsied; struck dumb; still as death.

سن سان sun sān, adj. Dismal; lonely; dreary; desolate; silent; void.

سن ہونا sun honā, v. To be benumbed.

سن لینا sun lenā (H) v. To hear; to know.

سناه سننا sunnā (H) v. To listen; to hear; to attend (to).

سنا sana (A) n.m. The common senna of medicine (cassia senna); a medicinal herb.

سناتن sanātan (H) adj. Eternal; perpetual; firm; permanent.

سناٹا sannāṭa (H) n.m. Roaring (of the waves); howling (of the wind); violent blast or gust; the rumbling noise made by wind and rain; bluster; noise; vehemence; listlessness; stillness; a howling wilderness; a stunning blow or shock.

سناٹے سے برسنا sannāṭe se barasnā, v. To rain cats and dogs.

سناٹے میں رہ جانا sannāṭe men rah jānā, v. To be struck motionless with terror or astonishment.

سنار sunār (H) n.m. Goldsmith.

سنارن sunāran (H) n.f. The wife of a goldsmith.

سناری sunārī (H) n.f. The business of a goldsmith.

سنان sinān (P) n.f. Spear-head.

سنانا sunānā (H) v. To speak at; to tell; to proclaim; to announce; to inform; to advise; to bid; to warn; to say or repeat a lesson.

سنبل sumbul (A) n.m. A plant having sweet odour to which the Persians compare the locks of their sweethearts; spikenard; the hyacinth.

سنبل خطائی sumbul-ĕ khaṭā'ī, n.m. Angelica; aromatic plant used in cooking and medicine.

سنبل هندی sumbul-ĕ hindī, n.m. Spikenard; hyacinth.

سنبوسه sambosah (P) See سموسا samosā.

سنبھالنا sambhālnā (H) v. To support; to sustain; to hold up; to check.

سنبھلنا sambhalnā (H) v. To be supported; to recover from a fall; to stand; to be firm.

سنت sant (H) n.m. A devotee; a saint. adj. Pious; virtuous; venerable.

سنت sunnat (A) *n.f.* Traditions of the Holy Prophet; ordinance of religion; a religious ceremony; circumcision; cutting off the fore-skin.

سنت کرنا sunnat karnā, *v.* To circumcise; cutting off the fore-skin.

سنتره santarah (H) *n.m.* Orange.

سنتری santrī (H) *n.m.* Sentinel; watchman.

سنجاب sanjāb (P) *n.f.* Ermine; fur; the grey squirrel; the fur of the squirrel.

سنجاف sanjāf (P) *n.f.* Border; hem; fringe; frill; edge; flounce.

سنجاف لگانا sanjāf lagānā, *v.* To tack fringe on to the outer part of a garment.

سنجوگ sanjog (H) *n.m.* Connection; cohesion; union; contact; living together; association; combination; accident; event; chance.

سنجوگ کرنا sanjog karnā, *v.* To join or unite (with); to associate (with).

سنجوگی sanjogī (H) *n.m.* An asectic who does not observe the vow of continence, but has a family.

سنجھلا sanjhlā (H) *n.m.* & *adj.* The third of four brothers; of the third rank or degree.

سنجیدگی sanjīdagī (P) *n.f.* Solemnity; gravity; seriousness; considerateness.

سنجیده sanjīdah (P) *adj.* Grave; weighty; considerate; composed; serious; approved.

سنچائی sinchā'ī (H) *n.f.* Price for watering or irrigating; the act of irrigating.

سند sanad (A) *n.f.* A certificate; a diploma; a testimonial; a credential; a proof; a warrant; a charter; a document; a grant.

سند کارگزاری sanad-ĕ kārguzārī, *n.f.* A certificate of services rendered.

سند معاف sanad-ĕ mu'āfī, *n.f.* Rent free grant.

سند یافته sanad yāftah, *adj.* Certified; chartered; accredited.

سندان sandān (P) *n.f.* An anvil.

سندر sundar (H) *adj.* Beautiful; handsome; comely; seemly; pretty; good; virtuous.

سندرتا sundartā (H) *n.f.* Beauty; handsomeness; elegance; gracefulness.

سندری sundarī (H) *n.f.* Beauty; comeliness; a handsome woman.

سندس sundus (A) *n.m.* Fine silk brocade or satin.

سندور sandūr. See سیندور sendūr.

سنده sindh, sindhu (H) *n.m.* Sea; ocean; the river Indus; the country along the Indus; name of a former province of West Pakistan; name of a musical mode.

سندھی sindhī (H) *adj.* Belonging to *Sindh*. *n.m./f.* A resident of *Sindh*; the language of the people of *Sindh*.

سندیس، سندیسا sandes, sandesā (H) *n.m.* A message; information.

سنڈا sanḍā (H) *adj.* Fat; stout; sturdy; strong. *n.m.* A big or fat ox; hardened excrement; *Scybala*.

سنڈا مشٹنڈا sanḍā mushṭanḍā, *adj.* Well-developed; fat; plump; stout.

سنڈاس sanḍās (H) *n.m.* A latrine; a water-closet; a sink.

سنسار sansār (H) *n.m.* The world; the universe; mankind.

سنسکرت sanskrit (S) *adj.* Perfect; embelished; decorated; ornamented; language formed by accurate grammatical rules. *n.f.* The sacred and classical language of the Hindus.

سنسنانا sansnānā (H) *v.* To jingle; to ring; to whistle; to feel a tingling sensation; to rustle; to whiz; to hiss; to simmer; to faint.

سنسناهٹ **sansanāhaṭ** (H) *n.f.* Whiz; hiss; simmering; twinkling; ringing; jingling; fainting.

سنسنی **sansanī** (H) *n.f.* Tingling sensation; a dreary or desolate state.

سنک **sanak** (H) *n.f.* Madness; insanity; lunacy.

سنکنا **sinaknā** (H) *v.* To blow the nose.

سنکھ **sankh** (H) *n.m.* A conch-shell; a trumpet; a kind of ornament. *adj.* Simple; artless; ten billions.

سنکھ بجانا **sankh bajānā**, *v.* To blow a shell.

سنکھنی **sankhnī** (H) *n.f.* One of the four kinds of women; a tall and beautiful woman with long eyes and hair, neither stout nor thin, having irritable disposition and strong passions.

سنکھیا **sankhiyā** (H) *n.f.* Arsenic; a kind of poison.

سنگ **sang** (P) *n.m.* A stone; weight.

سنگ آستان **saṅg-ĕ āstān**, *n.m.* The door-sill.

سنگ اسود **saṅg-ĕ aswad**, *n.m.* The black stone in the Ka'aba.

سنگ باری **saṅg bārī**, *n.f.* Showering stones; pelting with stones.

سنگ پارس **saṅg-ĕ pāras**, *n.m.* Touch-stone; philosopher's stone.

سنگ پشت **saṅg pusht** (P) *n.m.* A tortoise; turtle.

سنگ تراش **saṅg tarāsh**, *n.m.* A stone-cutter; lapidary; sculptor.

سنگ تراشی **saṅg tarāshī**, *n.f.* Sculpture; stone cutting.

سنگ جراحت **saṅg-ĕ jarāḥat**, *n.m.* A species of stalactite or steatite; soap-stone.

سنگ خارا **saṅg-ĕ khārā**, *n.m.* A hard stone; flint.

سنگ دانہ **saṅg dānah**, *n.f.* The gizzard; bird's second stomach.

سنگ دل **saṅg dil**, *adj.* Hard-hearted: merciless.

سنگ دلی **saṅg dilī**, *n.f.* Hard-heartedness; cruelty.

سنگ راہ **saṅg-ĕ rāh**, *n.f.* An obstacle; a hindrance.

سنگ ریزہ **saṅg rezāh**, *n.m.* Gravel; pebble.

سنگ سار **saṅg sār**, *adj.* Stoned; stoned to death.

سنگ سار کرنا **sang sār karnā**, *v.* To stone to death; to lapidate.

سنگ ساز **saṅg sāz**, *n.m.* One who makes correction on the lithographic stone.

سنگ سرخ **saṅg-ĕ surkh**, *n.m.* Red stone; granite.

سنگ سرما **saṅg-ĕ surmā**, *n.m.* Antimony.

سنگ سماق **saṅg-ĕ samāq**, *n.m.* Porphyry, a hard rock stone of Egypt.

سنگ لاخ **saṅg lākh**, *adj.* Stony; rocky; abounding in rocks.

سنگ گردہ **saṅg-ĕ gurdah**, *n.m.* Kidney stone.

سنگ مثانہ **saṅg-ĕ māṣānah**, *n.m.* Gravel stone; stone in the bladder; calculus.

سنگ مرمر **saṅg-ĕ marmar**, *n.m.* Marble.

سنگ مقناطیس **saṅg-ĕ miqnātıs**, *n.m.* The loadstone.

سنگ موسیٰ **saṅg-ĕ mūsā**, *n.m.* Black-stone; black slate.

سنگ یشب **saṅg-ĕ yashab**, *n.m.* A kind of jasper or agate.

سنگ **saṅg** (H) *adv.* Along with; with; in company of; together; side by side; conjointly. *n.m.* Association; company; union.

سنگار، سنگھار **siṅgār, siṅghār** (H) *n.m.* Decoration; ornament; embellishment; toilet; dress.

سنگار دان **siṅgār dān**, *n.m.* Dressing table.

سنگار کرنا **siṅgār karnā**, *v.* To adorn; to decorate; to embellish.

سنگار میز singār mez, n.f. Toilet table.

سولہ سنگار solah singār, n.m. Sixteen appliance of a woman's toilette.

سنگت saṅgat (H) n.f. Coition; intercourse; friendship; congregation; company; society; a place of worship; party.

سنگترہ saṅgtarah (P) n.m. Orange.

سنگتی sangati (H) n.m. Associate; companion; comrade.

سنگرھنی saṅgrahanī (H) n.f. Diarrhoea; irregular state of the bowels.

سنگم sangam (H) n.m. Meeting; union; confluence of rivers; junction of planets; sexual intercourse; company; mixture.

سنگھ singh (H) n.m. A lion; sign Leo of the Zodiac; a title used by Hindus and Sikhs.

سنگھاڑا singhāṛā (H) n.m. Water chestnut; water caltrops; root of the excelent water lily; a handkerchief folded diagonally; anything trianguler.

سنگھاسن siṅghāsan (H) n.m. A throne.

سنگھانا sunghānā (H) v. To cause to smell; to make one smell.

سنگی saṅgī (H) n.m. A companion; a comrade; an accomplice; a kind of silk cloth.

سنگیت saṅgit (S) n.m. A concert; the art of singing with music and dancing; the exhibition of song, dancing and music as a public entertainment.

سنگین saṅgīn (P) adj. Made of stone; stony; hard; strong; heavy; weighty; solid; severe; close-woven. n.f. A bayonet.

سنگین جرم saṅgin jurm, n.m. A capital offence; murder.

سنگین سزا saṅgin sazā, n.f. Severe punishment.

سنگینی saṅgīnī (P) n.f. Hardness; heaviness; solidity; intensity.

سنن sunan (A) n.f. (plu. of سنت sunnat) Traditions; rules; traditions of the Holy Prophet.

سنوار saṅwār (H) n.f. Preparation; arrangement; correction, amendment; rectification; curse.

خدا کی سنوار khudā kī saṅwār, intj. May God correct you !

سنوارنا saṅwārnā (H) v. To prepare; to adjust; to arrange; to accomplish; to dress; to decorate; to adorn; to correct; to mend.

سنورنا saṅwarnā (H) v. To be prepared; to make a toilet; to be adorned; to be decorated; to be amended: to come right again; to prosper.

سنہ sanh (A) n.m. Year; era.

سنہ بکرمی sanh-ĕ bikramī, n.m. Bikramajit's era which is 52 years ahead of the Christian era.

سنہ جلوس sanh-ĕ julūs, n.m. The year of accession to the throne.

سنہ عیسوی san-ĕ ʻīswī, n.m. The Christian era.

سنہ ھجری sanh-ĕ hijrī, n.m. The Muslim era.

سنہرا، سنہری sunahrā, sunahrī (H) adj. Golden; gilded; gold-coloured.

سنی ان سنی کرنا sunī an sunī karnā (H) v. To turn a deaf ear (to).

سنی سنائی suni sunā'ī (H) adj. Hearsay; what one has heard.

سنی sunnī (A) n.m. An orthodox Muslim; follower of sunnat-wal-jumā'at sect.

سنیاس sannyās (S) n.m. Relinquishment; abandonment; abandonment of the world.

سنیاسی sannyāsī (S) n.m. A religious mendicant; an ascetic; a Brahman of the fourth order.

سنیچر sanīchar (S) n.m. Saturn (the planet); Saturday; misfortune; poverty; penury; a miser; a glutton.

سنین sanin (A) n.m. (plu. of سنہ sanh); Eras; years; ages.

سو sū (P) n.f. Side; direction.

سو بسو sū basū, adv. On every side; all round; side by side.

سو sau (H) adj. A hundred.

سو جان سے sau jān se, adv. With all one's heart.

سو علاج ایک پرھیز sau 'ilāj ek perhez, prov. Prevention is better than cure.

سو کے سوائے sau ke sawae, adj. Twenty five per cent; hundred twenty five for a hundred.

سو so (H) adv. & conj. So; so that; therefore; hence; because of; thereupon; accordingly.

سوا sawā (H) adj. One and a quarter.

سوا suā (H) n.m. A packing needle; a large needle; an ear of corn.

سوا soā (H) n.m. Fennel; an aromatic plant with yellow flowers.

سوا siwā (P) adv. Except; save; but; over and above; other than; besides; more; additional.

سواد sawād, swād (H) n.m. Relish; taste; flavour; pleasure; sweetness.

سواد sawād (A) n.m. Blackness; soot; smoke; environs of a city; country houses; territory belonging to a town; neighbourhood; vicinity; ability.

سواد اعظم sawād-ĕ āẓam, n.m. Greater part of a country; majority.

سوار sawār (P) n.m. A rider; a traveller on horse back; a horse man; a cavalry-man; a trooper. adj. Mounted; tipsy.

سوار ھونا sawār honā, v. To ride; to mount.

سواری sawārī (P) n.f. Riding; conveyance; cavalcade; horsemanship.

سوال sūāl, sawāl (A) n.m. Question; petition; application; request; proposition; problem; query; demand.

سوال‌جرح sawāl-ĕ jirah, n.m. Cross-examination.

سوال جواب sawāl jawāb, n.m. Questionnaire; question and answer.

سوال جواب کرنا sawāl jawāb karnā, v. To argue; to plead; to discuss.

سوال حل کرنا sawāl hal karnā, v. To solve a question or a problem.

سوال کرنا sawāl karnā, v. To question; to ask; to beg; to request.

سوال دیگر جواب دیگر sawāl digar jawāb digar, prov. Cross purposes and crooked answers.

سوالی sawālī (A & P) n.m. A beggar; a petitioner.

سوامی sawāmī (S) n.m. Master; owner; husband; lord; the head of a religious order.

سوانح sawāniḥ (A) n.m. (plu. of سانح sāneḥ) Occurrences; events; incidents; accidents; historical events.

سوانح نگار sawāniḥ nigār, n.m. A biographer; a reporter; a historian.

سوانح عمری sawāniḥ 'umrī, n.f. Biography; narration of life history.

سوانگ swāṅg (H) n.m. See سانگ sāṅg.

سوانگی swāṅgī (H) n.m. See سانگی sāṅgī.

سوایا، سوائی sawāyā sawā'ī (H) adj. A quarter more; one and a quarter.

سوبھاؤ' سبھاؤ sūbhāw, subhāo (S) n.m. Natural disposition; quality; nature; natural state.

سوت sūt (H) n.m. Thread; wire; a tendril; a line; yarn; cord; filament; a row; one-sixteenth of a tassū.

سوت و سوتا sot, sotā (H) n.m. A spring; a fountain; a rivulet; a stream; current; source of a river.

سوت' سوتن saut, sautan (H) n.f. A co-wife; a second wife; a rival.

سوتک sūtak (H) n.m. Uncleanliness contracted by members of a Hindu family on the birth of a child or on the death of a relative.

سوتی sūtī (H) adj. Made of cotton thread; cotton cloth.

سوتیلا' سوتیلی sautelā, sautelī (H) adj. Child from a different wife; belonging to a co-wife.

سوتیلا باپ sautelā bāp, n.f. Step-father.

سوتیلا بھائی sautelā bhā'ī, n.m. Step-brother.

سوتیلی بہن sautelī bahn, n.m. Step-sister.

سوتیلی ماں sautelī māṅ, n.f. Step-mother.

سوجن sūjan (H) n.f. Swelling; inflammation.

سوجنا sūjnā (H) v. To swell; to rise; to be puffed up; to look sulky.

سوجھ sūjh (H) n.f. Foresight; vision; perception; understanding.

سوجھ بوجھ sūjh būjh, n.f. Understanding; knowledge; intelligence; prudence.

سوجھنا sujhnā (H) v. To perceive; to come to mind; to seem; to appear.

سوجی sūjī (H) n.f. Flour in fine granules; coarsely ground flour.

سوچ soch (H) n.f. Thought; reflection; attention; regard; anxiety; consideration; meditation; reverie; imagination; idea; notice.

سوچ بچار soch bichār, n.m. Consideration; caution; discretion.

سوچ میں رہنا soch meṅ rahnā, v. To be absorbed in thought; to muse.

سوچنا sochnā (H) v. To think; to reflect; to consider; to meditate; to regard; to imagine; to conceive; to ponder; to observe; to mind.

سوختگی sokhtagī (P) n.f. Burning; combustion; heart-burning; vexation.

سوختنی sokhtanī (P) adj. Fit for burning; deserving to be burnt.

سوختہ sokhtah (P) adj. Burnt; scarched.

سوختہ جاں یا دل sokhtah jāṅ yā dil, adj. Burnt or consumed with love or grief; grieved; love-sick.

سوختی sokhti, n.f. Grief; Sorrow; suffering.

سود sūd (P) n.m. Profit; gain; interest; usury.

سود بٹا sūd baṭṭā, n.m. Profit and loss.

سود پر دینا sūd par denā, v. To lend money on interest.

سود پر لینا sud par lenā, v. To borrow money at interest.

سود خور sūd khor, n.m. A usurer.

سود خوری sūd khorī, n.f. Usury

سود در سود sūd dar sūd, n.m. Compound interest.

سود کھانا sūd khānā, v. To take interest; to lend money on interest.

سود لگانا sūd lagānā, v. To charge interest; to calculate interest.

سود مرکب sūd-ē murakkab, n.m. Compound interest.

سود مفرد sūd-ē mufrad, n.m. Simple interest.

سود مند sūd mand, adj. Profitable; beneficial; advantageous; useful.

سود مندی sūd mandi, n.f. Profitableness; advantage.

سود مساوی‌الاصل sūd mussāwi-ul-aṣl, n.m. Interest equal to principal.

بے سود be sūd, adj. Useless; fruitless.

سودا saudā (A) n.m. The black-bile; frenzy; madness; fixed desire; ambition; melancholy; monomania; hyperchandria. adj. Black.

سودا ہونا saudā honā, v. To persist keenly in the fulfilment of a desire; to have a fit of madness.

سودا saudā (P) n.m. Trade; traffic; marketing; bargaining; goods; wares; fruits.

سودا پٹانا، کرنا saudā paṭānā, karnā, v. To strike a bargain.

سودا پٹنا، ہونا saudā paṭnā, honā, v. Striking of a bargain.

سودا خریدنا، لینا saudā kharīdnā, lenā, v. To make purchases.

سودا سلف saudā sulf, n.m. Traffic; barter; goods; wares.

سوداگر saudāgar (P) n.m. A merchant.

سوداگری saudāgarī (P) n.f. Commerce; trade.

سوداگری مال saudāgarī māl, n.m. Merchandise.

سوداوی saudāwī (A) adj. Melancholic; atrobilious.

سوداوی مزاج saudāwī mizāj, adj. Melancholic temperament.

سودائی saudā'ī (A) adj. Melancholic; insane; mad.

سودی sūdī (P) adj. On interest; borrowed at interest.

سودیشی swadeshī (S) adj. Of one's own country; indigenous.

سور sūr (S) n.m. A hero; a warrior; a wise man, a learned man.

سور sūar (H) n.m. A hog; a swine.

سور کا بچہ sūar kā bachchah, n.m. A pig; the young one of a pig.

سور کا گوشت sūar kā gosht, n.m. Swine-flesh; pork; ham; bacon.

سوراج sūrāj (S) n.m. Self-government; home-rule.

سوراخ sūrākh (P) n.m. A hole; a passage; orifice; inlet.

سوراخ دار sūrākh dār, adj. Perforated; porous; having holes.

سورت sūrat (A) n.f. A chapter or division of the Quran; a sign; a vestige.

سورج sūraj (H) n.m. The sun.

سورج بنسی sūraj bansī, n.m. The solar race.

سورج گرہن گہن sūraj girahn, gahan, n.m. The solar eclipse.

سورج مکھی sūraj mukhi, n.m. The sun-flower; a kind of fan or parasol.

سور داس sūrdās (H) n.m. Name of a Hindu poet and singer, who was blind, hence a blind man.

سورگ swarg (S) n.m. See سرگ surg.

سورما sūrmā (H) adj. Brave; valiant; bold.

سورنجان sūranjān (P) n.m. Name of a medicine; meadow-safforn; dog's bane.

سوز soz (P) n.m. Burning; heat; passion; inflammation; vexation; heart-burning; a stanza of an elegiac poem. adj. Inflaming; burning; exciting.

سوز خوان soz khwān, n.m Reciter of an elegy; one who chants a dirge.

سوز و گداز soz-o gudāz, n.m. Burning and melting; an impassioned style in poetry.

سوزاک suzāk (P) n.m. Gonorrhoea.

سوزاں sozāṅ (P) adj. Burning; flaming.

سوزش sozish (P) n.f. Burning; inflammation; pain; vexation; ardour; solicitude.

سوزن sozan (P) n.f. A needle; pricker of a gun.

سوزنی sozni (P) n.f. A kind of small embroidered carpet; quilted linen; tambour-work, a kind of coverlet.

سوزی sozi (P) n.f. Conflagration; burning (used in comp.)

سوسمار sūsmār (P) n.m. The porpoise.

سوسن sosan (P) n.f. A lily; the iris.

سوسنی sosnī (P) n.m. A bluish colour. adj. Iris-coloured; purple.

سوسی sūsī (H) n.f. A kind of coarse cloth made of silk and cotton.

سوغات saughāt (P) n.f. A rich present; a rarity; a curiosity.

سوغاتی saughāti (P) adj. Fit to be given as a present; rare; choice.

سوق sūq (A) n.m. Bazaar; market; street.

سوقیانه sūqiyānah (A) adj. Of the market; common; low or vulgar (language).

سوکن saukan (H) n.f. A co-wife; the second wife of a husband.

سوکھا sūkhā (H) adj. Dry; parched; withered; without profit; shrivelled; juiceless; thin. n.m. Dry-land; draught; a dry-year; dry tobacco eaten with betel-leaf; consumption; a disease of children.

سوکھا پڑنا sūkhā paṛnā, v. Occuring of a draught.

سوکھا ٹالنا، ٹرخانا sūkhā tālnā, ṭarkhānā v. To send away someone without doing anything for him.

سوکھنا sūkhnā (H) v. To dry; to wither; to pine away; to become emaciated; to evaporate; to fall away; to shrivel; to dwindle; to dry up.

سوگ sog (P/S) n.m. Affliction; grief; sorrow; lamentation; anguish; mourning.

سوگ کرنا، منانا sog karnā, manānā, v. To grieve; to mourn.

سوگ وار sog wār, adj. Sorrowful; grieved; afflicted; mourning.

سوگ واری sog wārī, n.f. Affliction; mourning; sorrow; grief.

سوگن sogan (H) adj. Afflicted (woman).

سوگند saugand (P) n.m. An oath.

سوگند دینا saugand denā, v. To administer an oath.

سوگند کھانا saugand khānā, v. To swear; to take an oath.

سوگی sogī (H) adj. Sorrowful; sad; afflicted; mournful.

سول sūl (H) n.m. A thorn; a spike; a dart; trident; colic; the point of a spear; stomachache; a sharp and acute pain.

سوله solah (H) adj. Sixteen.

سولھواں solahwāṅ, adj. Sixteenth.

سولی sūlī (H) n.f. Gibbet; gallows; an impaling stake.

سولی دینا sūlī denā, v. To hang; to impale; to execute.

سولی پر جان ہونا sūlī par jān honā, v. To suffer severe torture or agony; to be in constant fear of one's life.

سوم sūm (H) n.m. A miser; a niggard.

سوم sowim , som (P) adj. Third.

سوموار somwār (H) n.m. Monday.

سونا، سونی sūnā, sūni (H) adj. Void; empty; desolate; deserted; unoccupied; lonely.

سونا کر جانا sūnā kar jānā, v. To leave void or desolate; to leave; to depart.

سونا sonā (H) v. To sleep; to die; to repose; to depart; to cohabit.

سونا sonā (H) n.m. Gold; riches.

سونے پر سہاگا sone par suhāgah, adj. Adding to beauty or elegance.

سونے کا پانی sone kā pānī, n.m. Gilding.

سونے کا پترا sone kā patrā, n.m. Gold plate.

سونے کی چڑیا sone ki chiṛyā, n.f. A golden bird; a wealthy person.

سونے کا نوالہ sone kā niwālah, n.m. An expensive banquet; a delicious morsel.

سونے کا ورق sone kā warq, n.m. Gold leaf.

سونپنا sauṅpnā (H) v. To hand over; to deliver; to commit to the charge of; to consign; to entrust; to deposite; to give custody of.

سونتنا sūṅtnā (H) v. To strip leaves off vegetables; to draw (a sword); to rub down.

سونٹا soṅṭā (H) n.m. A club; a mace; a pestle; a cudget.

سونٹھ soṅṭh (H) n.f. Dry ginger; something precious; cheap article.

سوندھا ، سوندھی soṅdhā, soṅdhī (H) adj. Sweet smelling; smelling like new earth; fragrant.

سونڈ sūṅḍ (H) n.m. An elephant's trunk.

سونڈی sūṅḍī (H) n.f. A small, brown insect in corn; a weevil; an insect destructive to grain.

سونف sauṅf (P) n.f. Anise seed; seed of sweet fennel.

سونف کا عرق sauṅf kā 'araq, n.m. Anise water.

سونگھا sūṅghā (H) n.m. A person who can discover hidden things by smelling them; a hound.

سونگھنا sūṅghnā (H) v. To smell.

سونگھنی sūṅghnī (H) n.f. Snuff.

سوھا sūhā (H) adj. Deep red; crimson. n.m. Name of a rāg or musical mode.

سوھاگا، سہاگا sohāgā, suhāgā (H) n.m. Borax; a wooden plank used as harrow.

سوھان sohān (P) n.m. A file; whetstone; rasp.

سوھان روح sohān-ĕ rūḥ, adj. Troublesome; vexatious; torturing; annoying.

سوھن sohan (H) adj. Beautiful; handsome; pleasing; charming. n.m. A friend; a lover; a file; a kind of sweetmeat.

سوھنا sohnā (H) v. To shine; to look beautiful or graceful; to suit; to fit. adj. Beautiful; handsome.

سوھنی sohanī (H) n.f. A musical tune or rāgnī; a beautiful woman; a broom; a brush. adj. Charming; pleasing.

سوء sū (A) adj. Evil; bad; vicious.

سوء اتفاق sū-ĕ ittefāq, n.m. Mishap; as ill luck would have it.

سوء ادب sū-ĕ adab, n.m. Insolence; rudeness; bad manners.

سوء ظن sū-ĕ ẓann, n.m. Suspicion; doubt.

سوء ھضمی sū-ĕ hazmī, n.f. Indigestion.

سوئی sū'ī (H) n.f. A needle; hands of a watch or clock; the pointer of a compass; tongue of a balance; a pin.

سوئی پرونا sū'ī pironā, v. To thread a needle.

سوئی کا کام sū'ī kā kām, n.m. Needle-work; embroidery.

سوئی کا ناکا sū'ī kā nākā, n.m. The eye of a needle.

سوئی کے ناکے سے اونٹ گذارنا sū'ī ke nāke se ūnṭ guzārnā, v. To make a camel pass through the eye of a needle; to perform a miracle; to achieve the impossible.

سویاں siwayyān (H) n.f. Paste turned into slender threads; macaroni; vermicelli.

سویداالقلب، سویدا suwaidā-ul-qalb, suwaidā (A) n.m. The black part or grain of the heart; the heart's core.

سویرا sawerā (H) n.m. Early morning; dawn; day break.

سویمبر **suember** (S) *n.m.* Public selection of a husband by a lady of high rank from among a number of assembled suitors.

سویمبر رچانا **suember rachānā**, *v.* To assemble suitors for the selection of a husband.

سہ **seh** (P) *adj.* Three.

سہ حرفی **seh ḥarfī**, *adj.* Triliteral; of three letters.

سہ درہ **seh darah**, *adj.* Three-doored (room).

سہ سالہ **seh sālah**, *adj.* Triannual.

سہ شنبہ **seh shambah**, *n.m.* Tuesday.

سہ فصلہ **seh faṣlah**, *adj.* Having three harvests.

سہ کرر **seh karrar**, *adj.* Three times as much.

سہ ماہی **seh māhī**, *adj.* Quarterly.

سہ منزلہ **seh manzilah**, *adj.* Three-storeyed; having three floors.

سہا **suhā** (A) *n.m.* An obscure star in the constellation of the Greater Bear.

سہار **sahār** (H) *n.f.* Patience; tolerance; endurance.

سہارا **sahārā** (H) *n.m.* Assistance; aid; help; support; prop; reliance; association; dependence.

سہارا دینا **sahārā denā**, *v.* To support; to help; to assist.

سہارا ڈھونڈھنا **sahārā ḍhūṅḍhnā**, *v.* To seek help or support.

سہارا لینا **sahārā lenā**, *v.* To depend on; to seek help.

سہارنا **sahārnā** (H) *v.* To tolerate; to bear; to endure; to be patient.

سہاگ **suhāg** (H) *n.m.* Auspiciousness; good fortune; a red mark on the head of a woman whose husband is alive; the happy and auspicious state of wifehood; the conjugal state; a marriage song.

سہاگ اترنا، لٹنا **suhāg utarnā, luṭnā**, *v.* To become a widow.

سہاگ بھری **suhāg bharī**, *adj.* Happy and beloved wife.

سہاگ پڑا **suhāg puṛā**, *n.m.* A casket of jewels presented by the bridegroom to his wife; a basket containing cosmetics, comb, bangles &c presented by the bridegroom to the bride.

سہاگ رات **suhāg rāt**, *n.m.* The nuptial night.

سہاگ سیج **suhāg sej**, *n.f.* The nuptial bed.

سہاگا **suhāgā** (H) *n.m.* See سوھاگا **sohāgā**.

سہاگن **suhāgan** (H) *n.f.* A woman whose husband is alive; a favourite wife; a woman loved by her husband.

سہانا **suhānā** (H) *adj.* Agreeable; pleasant; charming. *v.* To be agreeable; to be pleasing; to be approved of.

سہج **sahaj** (H) *adj.* Easy; not difficult; facile; simple; slow.

سہج سبھاؤ **sahaj subhāo**, *n.m.* Natural disposition; natural ease.

سہج سے **sahaj se**, *adv.* Slowly; by degrees; gradually, in a low tone; in due course.

سہرا **sehrā** (H) *n.m.* A garland worn on the fore-head by the bride and the bridegroom at the marriage ceremony.

سہل **sahl** (A) *adj.* Easy; simple; not difficult.

سہل انگاری **sahl aṅgārī**, *n.f.* Indifference; carelessness.

سہلانا **sahlānā** (H) *v.* To rub gently; to tickle; to titillate.

سہم **sahm** (A) *n.m.* An arrow; a share; a portion; (*plu.* سہام **sihām**).

سہم جانا، سہمنا **sahm jānā, sahmnā** (H) *v.* To be afraid; to fear; to be alarmed.

سہنا **sahnā** (H) *v.* To bear; to suffer; to endure.

سہو sahv (A) n.f. Error; mistake; omission; negligence.

سہو قلم sahv-ĕ qalam, n.m. A slip of pen; oversight.

سہو کتابت sahv-ĕ kitābat, n.m. A clerical error.

سہواً sahwan (A) adv. Erroneously; by mistake; inadvertently; by oversight.

سہولت suhūlat (A) n.f. Ease; facility; gentleness; mildness; smoothness; softness; plainness.

سہی sahi (H) adv. Let it be so; very well.

سہیل suhail (A) n.m. The star Canopus; the dog star.

سہیلی saheli (H) n.f. A woman's female companion; a handmaid; damsel; a female friend.

سی سی sī si (H) n.f. A hissing sound.

سے se (H) prep. With; by; from; of; at; since; out of; to; through; than.

سیاپا siyāpā (H) n.m. Mourning over the dead; beating the breast over the dead body.

سیاح sayyāḥ (H) n.m. A traveller; a pilgrim; an itinerant. adj. Travelling; itinerant.

سیاحت، سیاحی siyāḥat, sayyāḥī (A) n.f. Voyaging; journeying; voyage; pilgrimage.

سیادت siyādat (A) n.f. Dominion; sovereignty; rule; governing; leadership.

سیار sayyār (A) n.m. A wanderer; a person taking the air or wandering or travelling for amusement; a traveller.

سیارہ sayyārah (A) n.m. A planet.

سیاست siyāsat (A) n.f. Politics; right ordering; rule; government; administration; management; chastisement; punishment.

سیاست دان siyāsat dān, n.m. A politician.

سیاست مدن siyāsat-ĕ mudun, n.m. Political science; civic economy; the art of government.

سیاست منزل siyāsat-ĕ manzil, n.m. Domestic economy.

سیاق siyāq (A) n.m. Accounts; arithmetic; enumeration.

سیاق و سباق siyāq-ŏ sabāq, n.m. Accounts; connection; coherence.

سیال sayyāl (A) adj. Flowing rapidly like a torrent; rapid; fluid; liquid.

سیانا syānā (H) adj. Wise; clever; cunning; artful; shrewd; sly; knowing; sagacious; prudent; mature (in understanding); grown up. n.m. Conjurer; miser; sorcerer.

سیان پن، سیانا پن syān pan, syānā pan, n.m. Sagacity; cleverness; cunningness; niggardliness.

سیاہ siyāh (P) adj. Black; dark; unfortunate; bad; sombre.

سیاہ باطن siyāh bāṭin, adj. Evil-minded; hypocrite.

سیاہ بخت siyāh bakht, adj. Unlucky; unfortunate.

سیاہ بختی siyāh bakhti, n.f. Misfortune.

سیاہ پوش siyāh posh, adj. Clad in black dressed in mourning.

سیاہ چشم siyāh chashm, adj. Black-eyed; unkind; cruel.

سیاہ فام siyāh fām, adj. Black; of black complexion.

سیاہ کار siyāh kār, adj. Wicked; lewd; sinful; cheat; tyrannical; sinner.

سیاہ کاری siyāh kāri, n.f. Lewdness.

سیاہ گوش siyāh gosh, n.m. A lynx; a kin of wild cat.

سیاہی siyāhī (P) n.f. Ink; blackness; darkness; lamp black.

سیب seb (P) n.m. An apple.

سیپ، سیپی sip, sīpi (H) n.f. A shell; an oyster shell; a kind of mango.

سیتا پھل sītā phal (H) *n.m.* The custard apple; the sweet pumpkin.

سیتلا sītlā (H) *n.f.* Small-pox.

سیٹھ seṭh (H) *n.m.* A rich banker; a millionaire; a capitalist; a merchant.

سیٹھا sīṭhā (H) *adj.* Tasteless; insipid.

سیٹھا پن sīṭhā pan (H) *n.m.* Tastelessness.

سیٹی sīṭī (H) *n.m.* Whistle.

سیج sej (H) *n.f.* A bed; a couch.

سیج بچھانا، لگانا sej bichhānā, lagānā, *v.* To prepare or arrange a bed.

سیچنا، سینچنا sīchnā, sīṅchnā (H) *v.* To water; to irrigate; to lave.

سیچائی ، سینچائی sīchā'ī, sīṅchā'ī (H) *n.f.* Irrigation; the cost of irrigation.

سیخ sīkh (P) *n.f.* A spit; a skewer; any long and thin piece of metal.

سیخ پا ہونا sīkh pā honā, *v.* To rear; to be extremely upset.

سیخ پر لگانا sīkh par lagānā, *v.* To roast; to put on a spit.

سید saiyyid (A) *n.m.* Lord; master; a prince; the head; a chief; a descendant of the Holy Prophet.

سید زادہ saiyyid zādah, *n.m.* Born of a *saiyyid*; a descendant of the Holy Prophet.

سیدانی saidānī, *n.f.* The wife of a *saiyyid*.

سیدھ sīdh (H) *adj n.f.* Straightness; directness; aim; direction.

سیدھ باندھنا sīdh bāndhnā, *v.* To take aim; to gain a direct line.

سیدھ میں sīdh meṅ, *adv.* Straightforth.

سیدھا، سیدھی sīdhā, sīdhī (H) *adj.* Straight; erect· correct; honest; direct; upright; straight forward; right; fair.

سیدھا پن sīdhā pan, *n.m*, Straightness; simplicity; honesty.

سیدھا سادہ sīdhā sādhā, *adj.* Simple.

سیدھا کرنا sīdhā karnā, *v.* To straighten; to make smooth; to correct; to chestise; to take aim.

سیدھا ہاتھ sīdhā hāth, *n.m.* Right hand.

سیدھا ہونا sīdhā honā, *n.m.* To be set righ; to be tamed.

سیدھی راہ چلنا sīdhī rāh chalnā, *v.* To take the right path.

سیدھی طرح sīdhī ṭaraḥ, *adv.* In right way; rightly.

سیدھے منہ بات نہ کرنا sīdhe muṅh bāt nah karnā, *v.* To be proud; to be elated; to over-estimate oneself.

سیر sair (A) *n.f.* Walk; excursion; taking the air; perambulation; moving about; strolling; recreation; amusement.

سیر سپاٹا sair sapāṭā, *n.m.* Walking about for amusement.

سیر کرنا sair karnā, *v.* To take a walk; to take the air; to stroll; to perambulate.

سیر گاہ sair gāh, *n.f.* A walk; a place for walking; passage; a place of recreation.

سیر و شکار sair-ŏ shikār, *n.m.* Shooting and hunting.

سیر siyar (A) (*plu.* of سیرت sīrat) Qualities; virtues; morals; manners; ways of life.

سیر ser (P) *adj.* Full; satiated; satisfied; tired.

سیر چشم ser chashm, *adj.* Satisfied; contented; generous. *n.m.* A contented person; a generous person.

سیر حاصل ser ḥāṣil, *adj.* Very productive (land); detailed (review).

سیر ser (H) *n.m.* A weight of sixteen *chhaṭāks*.

سیراب serāb (P) *adj.* Full of water; saturated; well-watered; satisfied; fresh; blooming; moist.

سیرابی serābī (P) *n.f.* Moistness; juiciness; freshness; succulence; humidity.

سیرت sīrat (A) n.f. Quality; nature; disposition; character; conduct.

سیروا serwā (H) n.m. The head and foot pieces of a bed-frame.

سیری serī (P) n.f. Satiety; repletion; fulness.

سیڑھی sīṛhī (H) n.f. A ladder; stair case; step; degree.

سیڑھی سیڑھی چڑھنا sīṛhī sīṛhī chaṛhnā, v. To climb step by step.

سیزده sezdah (P) adj. Thirteen.

سیز دهم sez dahum (P) adj. Thirteenth.

سیس sīs (H) n.m. The head; the fore-head.

سیس پهول sīs phūl, n.m. An ornament for the head; husband.

سیس ناگ sīs nāg, n.m. The king of the serpent race.

سیس نوانا sīs niwānā, v. To bow; to give respect.

سیسا sīsā (H) n.m. Lead.

سیف saif (A) n.f. A sword.

سیف زبان saif zabān, adj. One whose curses prevail; having a tongue like a sword; sharp-tongued.

سیفه saifah (A) n.m. A book-binder's knife.

سیفه کرنا saifah karnā, v. To cut the edges of the pages of a book smooth and even.

سیفی saifī (A) adj. & n.f. Sword-shaped; cursing; a rosary; imprecation curse; an evil charm.

سیکڑه، سینکڑه saikṛah, sainkṛah (H) n.m. A hundred. adv. Per cent.

سیکھ sīkh (H) n.f. Instruction; study; advice; incitement; admonition; lesson; learning.

سیکھ دینا sīkh denā, v. To advise.

سیکھ لینا sīkh lenā, v. To take advise; to learn from; to consult.

سیکھنا sīkhnā (H) v. To acquire knowledge; to learn.

سیل sīl (H) n.f. Dampness; moisture.

سیل sail (A) n.m. A flowing; a flow of water; a current; a torrent; flood.

سیلا، سیلی sīlā, sīlī (H) adj. Damp; cool; moist.

سیلا selā (H) n.m. A kind of mantle; a silk turban; a loin; a kind of rice.

سیلاب sailāb (A/P) n.m. A flood; a torrent; a deluge; inundation.

سیلابی sailābī (P) adj. Relating to or depending on inundation.

سیلابی نهریں sailabī nahreṅ, n.f. Inundation canals.

سیلان sailān (A) n.m. Flow.

سیلان رحم sailān-ĕ raḥim, n.f. Leucarrhoea.

سیلانی sailānī (H) adj. Walking or going about for amusement; wanderer.

سیلنا sīlnā (H) v. To become damp.

سیلی sailī (P) n.f. A blow with the edge of the open hand on the neck; a slap; a cuff.

سیم sīm (P) n.f. Silver; a wire; a string.

سیم تن sīm tan, adj. Silver-bodied; fair; beautiful.

سیم sem (H) n.f. The flat or broad bean; water-logging.

سیم زده sem zadah, adj. Water-logged (land).

سیما sīmā (P) n.m. Face; forehead; similitude; countenance; aspect.

سیماب sīmāb (P) n.m. Quicksilver; mercury.

سیماب مزاج، طبع sīmāb mizāj, ṭabaʻ, adj. Mercurial; liable to changes; lively; gay; readywitted.

سیمابی sīmābī (P) adj. Of the colour of mercury; mercurial; short-tempered.

سیمرغ sīmurgh (P) n.m. A bird of the size of thirty birds; a fabulous bird; a griffin; an eagle.

سیمیں sīmīṅ (P) adj. Of silver; silvery; white.

سینا **sīnā**, *sainā* (A) *n.m.* The Taurus mountains.

سینا **senā** (H) *n.f.* An army; forces.

سینا پتی **senā pati**, *n.m.* The commander of an army.

سینا **sīnā** (H) *v.* To sew; to stitch; to darn.

سینا **sainā** (H) *v.* To hatch; to foster; to adore.

سینتالیس **saintālīs** (H) *adj.* Forty-seven.

سینتنا **saintnā** (H) *v.* To keep carefully; to put aside; to arrange; to set in order.

سینتیس **saintīs** (H) *adj.* Thirty-seven.

سیندور **sendūr** (H) *n.m.* Red lead; vermillion; minium.

سیندوریا **sendūriyā** (H) *adj.* Of red colour. *n.m.* A kind of mango.

سیندھ **sendh** (H) *n.f.* Home-breaking; a hole made in the wall by thieves.

سیندھ لگانا **sendh lagānā**, *v.* To break into a house.

سینک **sīnk** (H) *n.f.* The clump of the grass of which brooms are made; a tooth pick; a stripe.

سینکنا **senknā** (H) *v.* To foment; to warm; to heat.

سینگ **sīng** (H) *n.m.* A horn.

سینگ مار **sīng mārnā**, *v.* To butt; to gore.

سینگ نکلنا **sīng nikalnā**, *v.* To get horns; to get maturity; to become mad or foolish.

سینہ **sīnah** (P) *n.m.* Breast; bosom; chest.

سینہ افگار, چاک **sīnah afgār, chāk**, *n.m.* Afflicted; troubled.

سینہ بند **sīnah band**, *n.m.* A bodice; stays.

سینہ بہ سینہ **sīnah bah sīnah**, *adv.* Breast to breast; descending from father to son.

سینہ زنی کوبی **sīnah zanī, kobī**, *n.f.* Beating the breast.

سینہ زور **sīnah zor**, *adj.* Headstrong; obstinate; proud of one's strength.

سینہ زوری **sinan zorī**, *n.f.* Obstinacy; oppression; strength; force.

سینہ سوزی **sīnah sozī**, *n.f.* Anguish; torment.

سینی **sīnī** (P) *n.f.* A tray; a trough; a salver.

سیو **sewā** (H) *n.f.* Service; worship; attendance on.

سیوا کرنا **sewā karnā** *v.* To serve; to attend on.

سیوتی **sewtī** (H) *n.f.* A white rose; the dog-rose.

سیوک **sewak** (H) *n.m.* A servant; an attendant; a worshipper; a votary; a disciple.

سیون **sīwan** (H) *n.f.* Sewing; seam; darning.

سیہ، سیہی **seh, sehī** (H) *n.f.* See ساہی **sāhī**.

سیئہ **saiyi'ah** (A) *n.f.* Evil deeds (*plu.* سیئات *saiyi'āt*).

ش **shīn**, is the nineteenth letter of the Urdu, sixteenth of the Persian and thirteenth of the Arabic alphabet, and has the sound of *sh* in the word "shoe". According to *abjad* it stands for 300.

شاب **shābb** (A) *n.m.* A youth; a young man; one in the prime of manhood.

شاباش **shābāsh** (P) *intj.* Bravo! well done! excellent! (*contraction of* شادباش *shādbāsh*).

شاباشی **shābāshī**, *n.f.* Praise; applause.

شاباش دینا، شاباشی دینا **shābāsh denā, shābāshī denā**, *v.* To praise; to applaud.

شاخ shākh (P) n.f. A bough, a branch (of a tree); a twig; a cutting; a horn; difficulty; dilemma; objection; obstacle; extremity; fragment.

شاخدار shākhdār, adj. Branchy; horned.

شاخ در شاخ shākh dar shākh, adj. Branched out or diffused; entangled.

شاخ زعفران shākh-ĕ za'frān, n.m. (Lit. a twig of saffron). A person who thinks too highly of his merit; a self-conceited person.

برات عاشقاں بر شاخ آہو barāt-ĕ a'āshiqāṅ bar shākh-ĕ āhū, prov. False promises; promises made to by the beloved which are generally not kept.

شاخسار shākhsār (P) n.f. Full of branches; a place abounding in trees; a garden; a bower.

شاخسانہ shākhsānah, n.m. Noise; rumpus; row; columny; difficulty; dilemma.

شاخہ shākhah (P) n.m. The pillory; a yoke; a branch; a bough; a tree.

شاد shād (P) adj. Happy; glad; cheerful; pleased; delighted; joyful; exulting.

شاد کام shād kām, adj. Happy; contented; joyous.

شاد کرنا shād karnā, v. To gladen; to rejoice; to exhilarate; to delight.

شاداب shādāb (P) adj. Full of water; fresh; pleasant; agreeable; verdant; succulent; green. n.m. Fresh herbage.

شادابی shādābi (P) n.f. Freshness; greenness; verdure; moisture; succulence.

شاداں shādāṅ (P) adj. Cheerful.

شادمان shādmān (P) adj. Happy; joyous; pleased; delighted; joyful; gay; merry; glad.

شادمانی shādmānī (P) n.f. Merriment; rejoicing; pleasure; delight; gaiety; gladness.

شادی shādi (P) n.f. Pleasure; delight; joy; wedding; festivity; marriage; rejoicing.

شادی کرنا ، رچانا shādi karnā, rachānā, v. To celebrate a marriage; to marry; to feast; to rejoice.

شادی مرگ shādī marg, n.f. Death from joy; death in the midst of celebration and rejoicing.

شادی ہونا shādi honā, v. To be married.

شادیانہ shādyānah (P) n.m. Festive music at marriage or other joyous occasions. adj. Relating to marriage or rejoicings.

شادیانے بجانا shādyāne bajānā, v. To rejoice; to play festive music.

شاذ، شاذ و نادر shāẕ, shāẕ-ŏ nādir (A) adj. Uncommon; extraordinary; abnormal; anomalous; miraculous. adv. Rarely; seldom.

شارح shāriḥ (A) n.m. A commentator; annotator; expositor; interpreter.

شارع shāri' (A) n.m. A law-giver; a legislator; a highway; a road.

شارع عام shāri' 'ām, n.m. A thoroughfare.

شارک shārak (P) n.f. A species of nightingale, which learns to talk; a مینا mainā; a starling.

شاستر shāstr (S) n.m. An order or command; rule; a code of law; Hindu holy writ; a philosophy; literature; science.

شاستری shāstrī (S) adj. Skilled in holy science; skilled in Hindu law or holy books; master of Sanskrit language.

شاطر shāṭir (A) adj. Clever; sly; wanton; cunning; vicious. n.m. A chess-player; a messenger; a courier.

شاعر shā'ir (A) n.m. A poet.

شاعرانہ shā'irānah (A/P) adj. Poet-like; exaggerated view.

شاعره *shā'irah* (A) *n.f.* A poetess.

شاعری *shā'irī* (A) *n.f.* The art of poetry; poetic composition; hyperbole; exaggeration.

شاغل *shāghil* (A) *adj.* Occupied; busy; employed; attentive.

شافع *shāfi'* (A) *n.m.* One who deprecates; one who intercedes; advocate; patron; a mediator.

شافعی *shāfi'ī* (A) *n.m.* A follower of Imam Shafei; follower of Imam Abu Abdullah Muhammad bin Idris, one of the chiefs of the four principal sects of the Muslim religion.

شافی *shāfī* (A) *adj.* Healing; health-giving; sanative; salutary (answer); categorical; decisive; final. *n.m.* A healer; a restorer of health.

شاق، شاقه *shāqq, shāqqah* (A) *adj.* Difficult; hard; perplexing; troublesome; severe; burdensome; grievous; afflicting.

شاکر *shākir* (A) *adj.* Grateful (for); thankful; content; praising.

شاکی *shākī* (A) *adj.* Complaining; querulous. *n.m.* A complainant; a back-biter; murmerer; a blamer.

شاگرد *shāgird* (P) *n.m.* A pupil; a disciple; a scholar; a servant; apprentice.

شاگرد پیشه *shāgird peshah, n.m.* Disciples; apprentices; pupils; servants.

شاگردی *shāgirdī* (P) *n.f.* Pupilage; apprenticeship; learning; studying.

شال *shāl* (P) *n.f.* A shawl.

شال باف *shāl bāf, n.m.* A weaver of shawls; one who makes shawls.

شال دوز *shāl doz, n.m.* One who embroiders shawls.

شام *shām* (P) *n.f.* Evening.

شام و سحر *shām-ŏ saḥar, n.m.* Morning and evening.

شام *shām* (A) *n.f.* The iron head or ring of a wooden pestle; the ferule of a stick or umbrella.

شام *shām* (A) *n.m.* Name of a country; Syria.

شام *shām* (H) *n.m.* A name of Krishna. *adj.* Black.

شام کلیان *shām kaliyān* (H) *n.m.* A musical mode sung at even-tide.

شاما *shāmā* (H) *n.f.* A beautiful Indian song bird.

شامت *shāmat* (A) *n.f.* Bad luck; mischance; misfortune; disaster; punishment.

شامت اعمال *shāmat-ĕ a'māl, n.f.* Punishment of bad deeds; evil days; misfortune.

شامت آنا *shāmat ānā, v.* To face bad-luck; to meet with disaster.

شامت کا مارا *shāmat kā mārā, adj.* Unfortunate.

شامل *shāmil* (A) *adj.* Comprising; including; surrounding from all sides; included (in); blended (with); annexed; connected; mingled; common; universal.

شامل حال *shāmil-ĕ ḥāl, adj.* Connected with circumstances; accompanied by; if (a certain) circumstance favoured; comprising circumstances; similarly circumstanced.

شاملات *shāmilāt, n.m. & n.f.* Things included; the concerns that comprise (all parts); an undivided property; partnership; a coparcenary estate; land held in common or in partnership by a village.

شامه *shāmmah* (A) *n.f.* The sense of smell.

شامی *shāmī* (A) *adj.* Belonging to Syria. *n.m.* A Syrian.

شامی کباب *shāmī kabāb, n.m.* A kind of *kabāb*, made of flat rounded cakes of mince-meat.

شامیانہ shāmiyānah (P) n.m. A canopy; an awning; a pavilion.

شان shān (A) n.f. Business; affair; condition; state; dignity; quality; nature; disposition; importance pomp; lustre; eminance; glory; grandeur.

شان دار shān dār, adj. Splendid; grand; pompous; stately. n.m. A person of state and dignity; a man of rank.

شان دکھانا shān dikhānā, v. To make a display.

شان گھٹنا shān ghaṭnā, v. To be derogatory.

شان و شوکت shān-ŏ shaukat, n.f. Splendour; pomp and show; glory.

شانت shānt (S) adj. Calm; appeased; tranquil; humbled; dead; deceased.

شانتی shāntī (S) n.f. Quitness; rest; comfort; repose; tranquillity.

شانہ shānah (P) n.m. A comb; the shoulder

شاہ shāh (P) n.m. A king; a prince; a monarch; the king at chess or cards; a title assumed by faqīrs and saiyyids. adj. Excellent; great; principal.

شاہباز، شہباز shāhbāz, shahbāz (P) adj. Royal; noble; generous. n.m. A royal falcon.

شاہ بلوط shāh ballūt, n.m. Chestnut; the oak.

شاہ تیر، شہتیر shāh tīr, shahtīr, n.m. A beam; a large beam supporting the roof.

شاہ خاور shāh-ĕ k͟hāwar, n.m. The sun.

شاہ پر shāh par, n.m. The strongest feather in a bird's wing.

شاہ ترہ،شہترہ shāh tarah, shahtarah, n.m. A herb formerly used in medicine; fumitory.

شاہ توت، شہتوت shāh tūt, shahtūt, n.m. Mulberry tree or its fruit.

شاہ راہ shāh rāh, n.f. The highway; a public road.

شاہ رگ shāh rag, n.f. The jugulor vein.

شاہ زادہ، شہزادہ shāh zādah, shahzādah, n.m. A prince.

شاہ زادی، شہزادی shāh zādī, shahzādī, n.f. A princess.

شاہ سوار shāh sawār, n.m. A good rider.

شاہ کار shāh kār, n.m. A master piece.

شاہ نشین، شہہ نشین shāh nashīn, shahnashīn, n.m. The royal seat; a principal seat in an assembly; a president seat; a balcony.

شاہنشاہ، شہنشاہ shāhinshāh, shahinshāh (P) n.m. King of kings; an emperor.

شاہانہ shāhānah (P) adj. Royal; princely; regal. n.m. Wedding dress.

شاہد shāhid (A) n.m. One who bears witness; a deponent.

شاہد shāhid (P) n.m. A sweetheart; a beloved object; a female friend.

شاہی shāhi (P) n.f. Reign; soveriegnty; royalty; dominion. n.m. A follower of the sect of Hazrat Ali. adj. Royal; imperial; kingly; regal.

شاہین shāhīn (P) n.m. A royal white falcon.

شائبہ shā'ibah (A) n.m. Doubt; suspicion, uncleanliness; foulness; pollution; stain.

شائستگی shā'istagī (P) n.f. Politeness; good manners; affability; fitness; aptitude; propriety; expediency; consistency.

شائستہ shā'istah (P) adj Well-bred; polite; decent; courteous; gentle; docile; worthy; honourable; suitable; proper.

شائع shā'i (A) adj. Published; revealed; broadcaste, apparent; divulged; diffused; notorious; distressed.

شائع کرنا shā'i karnā, v. To publish; to reveal; to propagate; to spread about.

شائق shā'iq (A) *adj.* Full of desire; desirous; fond; zealous; ardent; longing for; lascivious.

شایان shāyān (P) *adj.* Suitable; fit; worthy; deserving; legal.

شاید shāyad (P) *adv.* Perhaps; perchance; possibly; probably.

شب shab (P) *n.f.* Night.

شب باش shab bāsh, *adj. & n.m.* A night lodger.

شب باشی shab bāshi, *n.f.* Staying for the night.

شب بخیر shab bakhair, *interj.* Good-night! may the night pass well!

شب برات shab barāt, *n.f.* The fifteenth night of Sha'bān.

شب بیدار shab bedār, *adj.* Waking all night; one who spends his night in prayer.

شب بیداری shab bedārī, *n.f.* A vigil; a night of prayer and worship.

شب تاب shab tāb, *n.f.* A firefly; a glow-worm.

شب تار shab-ĕ tār, *n.f.* A dark night.

شب چراغ shab chirāgh, *n.m.* A carbuncle; a gem of the ruby kind.

شب خوابی shab khwābī, *n.f.* Night clothes; sleeping at night.

شب خون shab khūn, *n.m.* A night attack.

شب خیزی shab khezī, *n.f.* Rising at night (for prayer).

شبدیگ shabdeg (P) *n.f.* A dish of meat and turnips cooked all night.

شب رنگ shab rang, *adj.* Dark-coloured.

شب زفاف shab-ĕ zifāf, *n.f.* The first night after marriage on which the bride and bridegroom meet.

شب زندہ دار shab zindah dār, *adj.* Waking all night (for prayer or for study); vigilant.

شب قدر shab qadr, *n.f.* The 27th night of the month of *Ramazān* (on which date the Quran began to be revealed).

شب کور shab kor, *adj.* Night blind.

شب کوری shab korī, *n.f.* Nigh blindness.

شب گوں shab gūn, *adj.* Dark as night.

شب ماہ ، شب مہتاب shab-ĕ māh, shab-ĕ mahtāb, *n.f.* Moonlit night.

شب نم، شبنم shabnam, *n.f.* Dew; a kind of fine linen.

شب و روز shab-ŏ roz, *adv.* Night and day; always; all the time.

شباب shabāb (A) *n.m.* Youth; prime of life.

شبان shubān (P) *n.m.* A shepherd; a pastor.

شباهت shabāhat (A) *n.f.* Resemblance; likeness; similarity.

شبد shabd (S) *n.m.* Sound; voice; a song; a hymn.

شبستان shabistān (P) *n.m.* A bed chamber.

شبه shibh (A) *n.m.* An image; resemblance; similitude; likeness.

شبه shubah (A) *n.m.* Doubt; suspicion; uncertainty; scruple; hesitation.

شبه کرنا،هونا shubah karnā, honā, *v.* To suspect; to doubt; to distrust.

شبینه shabīnah (P) *adj.* Nocturnal; nightly.

شبیه shabīh (A) *n.f.* Picture; portrait; likeness; image; resemblance; similarity.

شپر shappar (P) *n.f.* A bat; a night-flier.

شتا shitā (A) *n.m.* Witty.

شتاب shitāb (P) *adj.* Quick; speedy; hasty. *adv.* Quickly; soon; expeditiously. *n.f.* Haste; quickness.

شتابی shitābī (P) *n.f.* Quickness; haste; despatch. *adv.* Quickly; hastily.

شتر shutur (P) *n.m.* A camel.

شتر بان shutur bān, *n.m.* A camel driver; a camel-keeper.

شتر بے مہار shutur-ĕ be muhār, *adj.* Uncontrolled; refractory; incorrigible.

شتر خانه *shutur khānah*, *n.m.* A camel shed.

شتر غمزه *shutur ghamzah*, *n.m.* Undesirable coquetry; undue-blandishment.

شتر کینه *shutur kinah*, *adj.* Bearing malice (like a camel); remarkably malicious person.

شتر مرغ *shutur murgh*, *n.m.* An ostrich.

شتری *shutri* (P) *n.f.* A kind of kettle-drum carried on a camel; a drum covered with camel's skin; camel colour; a carpet or blanket made of camel hair.

شتم *shatm* (A) *n.f.* Villifying; upbraiding; reproach; contempt; outrage; injury; villainy.

شجاع *shujā'* (A) *adj.* Brave; bold; courageous.

شجاعت *shajā'at* (A) *n.f.* Bravery; valour.

شجر *shajar* (A) *n.m.* A tree; a plant.

شجر نامه، شجره *shajar namah*, *shajarah* (P & A) *n.m.* A genealogical tree; a field map; a list of saints or holy predecessors (in the form of a genealogical tree) given to disciplse.

شحیم *shaḥim* (A) *adj.* Bulky; very fleshy.

شخص *shakhṣ* (A) *n.m.* A person; an individual; being; body.

شخصی *shakhṣi* (A) *adj.* personal.

شخصی حکومت *shakhṣi ḥukūmat*, *n.f.* Absolute monarchy.

شخصیت *shakhṣiyyat* (A) *n.f.* Personality; individuality; nobility; rank; dignity; honour.

شد *shadd* (A) *n.m.* Rendering hard or strong; intensifying; emphasizing.

شد و مد *shadd-ŏ madd*, *n.f.* Emphasis; intensity; stress; force; severity.

شدائد *shadā'id* (A) *n.m.* (*plu.* of شدت *shiddat*) Difficult things; difficulties; hardships; tribulations.

شد بد *shud bud* (A) *n.f.* Slight knowledge; knowing very little about a matter.

شدت *shiddat* (A) *n.f.* Violence; force; vehemence; severity; affliction; difficulty.

شدنی *shudani* (P) *n.f.* What is destined to be; what must happen; an occurrence; a happening.

شدھ *shuddh* (S) *adj.* Pure; clean; unpolluted; bright; white; innocent; true; genuine; unmixed.

شدھی *shuddhi* (S) *n.f.* Purity; cleanness; freedom from impurity; purification.

شدید *shadid* (A) *adj.* Violent; strong; acute; intrepid; vehement; intense; severe; rigorous; difficult; afflicting; heinous; atrocious.

شر *sharr* (A) *n.m.* Wickedness; depravity; evil; wrong doing.

شر اٹھانا *sharr uṭhānā*, *v.* To raise a quarrel; to cause a breach of the peace.

شراب *sharāb* (A) *n.f.* Wine; spirit; spirituous liquor.

شراب خانه *sharāb khānah*, *n.m.* A tavern; a distillery.

شرابور *sharābor* *adj.* Wet through; dripping; drenched; soused.

شرابی *sharābi* (P) *adj.* Intoxicated. *n.m.* A drunkard.

شرار *sharār* (A) *n.m.* A spark or sparks of fire.

شرارت *shararat* (A) *n.f.* Wickedness; vice; mischief; depravity; villainy.

شراره *sharārah* (A) *n.m.* A spark of fire; a flash; a gleam.

شرافت *sharāfat* (A) *n.f.* Nobility; civility; good manners; politeness.

شرائط *sharā'iṭ* (A) *n.m.* (*plu* of شرط *sharṭ*); Stipulations; conditions; terms; signs; marks; requirements.

شرائین sharā'in (A) n.f. (plu. of شریان sharyān) Arteries.

شرب shurb (A) n.m. Drinking; drink; beverage.

شربت sharbat (A) n.m. Beverage; drink; syrup.

شربتی sharbati, n.m. A kind of lime or lemon; light orange colour. adj. Of the colour of syrup; reddish.

شرح sharḥ, sharaḥ (A) n.f. Explanation; commentary; annotation; description; rate; proportion; charge.

شرح بندی sharaḥ bandi, n.f. Table of rates.

شرح کرنا sharaḥ karnā, v. To define; to explain; to comment; to detail; to fix the rate of.

شرر sharar (A) n.m. Sparks of fire; malice.

شرر بار، شرر فشاں sharar bār, sharar fishāṅ, adj. Raining sparks of fire; blowing sparks of fire.

شرط sharṯ (A) n.f. Condition; stipulation; agreement; term; provision; a wager; mark; a bet.

شرط بدنا یا لگانا sharṯ badnā, lagānā, v. To lay a wager; to bet; to bargain; to stipulate.

بشرطیکہ ba sharṯekeh, adv. On condition that; provided that.

بلا شرط bilā sharṯ , adv. Unconditional.

شرطیہ sharṯiyyah (A) adv. Surely; certainly; undoubtedly. adj. Conditional.

شرع shara' (A) n.m. Law; equity; the divine code of life; a dogma; a high road.

شرعاً shara'n̲ (A) adv. According to the law; legally.

شرعاً و عرفاً ṣhara'n̲-ŏ ;urfan̲, adv. According to religious and social law.

شرعی shara'ī (A) adj. Lawful; religious; conformable to the Shara'; dogmatic.

شرف sharaf (A) n.m. Dignity; honour; excellence; eminence; rank; glory; exaltation; nobility.

شرف ہونا sharaf honā, v. To be honoured; to be exalted; entering of a planet in its sign.

شرف یاب sharaf yāb, adj. Exalted; honoured; ennobled; attaining nobility.

شرفاء shurafā (A) n.m. (plu. of شریف sharīf) Nobles; grandees; persons of high rank; persons of good family.

شرق sharq (A) n.m. Rising; the east.

شرق سے غرب تک، شرقاً غرباً sharq se gharb tak, sharqan̲ gharban̲, adv. From East to West.

شرقی sharqī (A) adj. Eastern; oriental.

شرک shirk (A) n.m. Infidality; polytheism; belief in the plurality of God; paganism; company; society; partnership.

شرک جلی shirk-ĕ jalī, n.m. Conspicuous paganism; idolatry.

شرک خفی shirk-ĕ k̲hafī, n.m. Imperceptible unbelief; infidality.

شرکاء shurakā (A) n.m. (plu. of شریک sharīk) Partners; participants.

شرکت shirkat (A) n.f. Partnership; society; company.

شرم sharm (P) n.f. Shame; modesty; bashfulness.

شرم رکھنا sharm rakhnā, v. To protect one from being shamed or subjected to indignity.

شرم سار sharm sār, adj. Abashed; ashamed.

شرم ساری sharm sārī, n.f. Shame; bashfulness; disgrace.

شرم گاہ sharm gāh, n.f. Private parts of the body.

شرم گین sharm gin, adj. Ashamed; bashful; immodest.

شرم ناک sharm nāk, adj. Shameful; disgraceful.

بے شرم be sharm, adj. Shameless; devoid of sense of shame.

شرما شرمی sharmā sharmi, adv. Through shame; modestly.

شرمانا sharmānā, v. To feel shame; to be bashful; to put one to shame.

شرمندگی sharmindagi (P) n.f. Bashfulness; shame; disgrace.

شرمندگی اٹھانا sharmindagi uṭhānā, v. To suffer shame or disgrace.

شرمندہ sharmindah (P) adj. Ashamed; blushing; bashful.

شرمندہ احسان sharmindah-ĕ iḥsān, adj. Under obligation.

شرمندہ ہونا sharmindah honā, v. To feel ashamed; to be ashamed; to blush.

شرمیلا ، شرمیلی sharmīlā, sharmīli, adj. Bashful; modest.

شروع shurū' (A) n.m. Beginning; commencement.

شروع سے آخر تک shurū' se ākhir tak, adj. From beginning to end.

شروع کرنا shurū' karnā, v. To commence; to begin; to institute; to take the lead; to set up; to inaugurate.

شریان shiryān (A) n.f. An artery.

شریر sharīr (A) adj. Vicious; wicked; corrupt; bad; evil; naughty.

شریر sharir (S) n.m. See سریر sarir.

شریعت shari'at (A) n.f. Revealed law; law; statute; ordinance; justice; equity.

شریف sharif (A) adj. Noble; eminent; honourable; high-born; legitimate; gentle, n.m. A chief of a tribe or caste.

شریف النفس sharif un-nafs, adj. Of noble soul; having a noble heart.

شریف زادہ sharif zādah, adj. Of high birth; of a good family; of legitimate birth.

شریفہ sharifah, n.m. A custard apple.

شریک sharik (A) n.m. A partner; a participant; an associate; an accomplice; a comrade; an ally; a confederater; a colleague; a friend. adj. Joint; united; included.

شریک کرنا sharik karnā, v. To make a partner; to include; to join.

شریک ہونا sharik honā, v. To be a partner; to partake; to join; to participate.

شست shast (P) n.f. Aim; thumb; finger; front.

شست باندھنا ، لگانا shast bāndhnā, lagānā, v. To take aim at; to present a gun.

شست shist (P) n.f. A fishing rod; a large fishing hook.

شستگی shustagi (P) n.f. Cleanliness; purity.

شستہ shustāh (P) adj. Washed; cleaned; dressed; prepared; pure.

شش shash (P) adj. Six.

شش پہلو shash pahlu, adj. Hexagonal; having six sides.

شش در shash dar, n.m. A cube; a die. adj. Confounded; perplexed; astonished.

شش ماہی shash māhi, adj. Half-yearly; six-monthly.

شش و پنج shash-ŏ panj, n.m. Confusion; perplexity; hesitation.

ششم shashum (P) adj. Sixth.

شط shaṭ (A) n.m. Bank of a river.

شطرنج shaṭranj (A) n.f. Chess.

شطرنج باز shaṭranj bāz, n.m. A chess player.

شطرنجی shaṭranji (P) n.m. A kind of chequered carpet.

شعار shi'ār (A) n.m. Habit; custom; method; manner; an under garment; mark; signal; sign: (also used in comps. as in, كفايت شعار kafāyat shi'ār, frugal or وفا شعار wafā sḥi'ār, Faithful).

شعارى shi'ārī (A) adj. Customary; habitual; relating to custom.

شعاع shu'ā' (A) n.f. The rays of the sun; sunshine; light; lustre; splendour.

شعاع زنى shu'ā' zani, n.f. Radio-activity.

شعاعى thu'a'i (A) adj. Radiant; full of rays; radial.

شعاعى علاج shu'ā'i 'ilāj, n.m. Radio-therapy.

شعائر sha'ā'ir (A) (plu. of شعيره sha'īrah) Signs; customs; rites; ceremonies.

شعبان sha'bān (A) n.m. The eighth month of the Hijri year.

شعبده shu'badah (P) n.m. Sleight of hand; juggling; conjuration.

شعبده باز shu'badah bāz, n.m. A juggler; a conjurer.

شعبه shu'bah (A) n.m. A channel in which water flows; a crack in a mountain; a water-course; a branch; a department; ramification.

شعر sha'r (A) n.m. Hair.

شعر shi'r (A) n.m. Poetry; verse; a couplet.

شعرا shu'arā (A) n.m. (plu. of شاعر shā'ir) Poets; bards.

شعريت shi'riyat (A) n.f. Poetical beauty.

شعله shu'lah (A) n.m. Flame; blaze; flash; light.

شعله بار shu'lah bār, adj. Raining fire or flame.

شعله بهبوكا shu'lah bhabūkā, adj. Beautiful; bright, enraged; furious.

شعله بهبوكا هونا shu'lah bhabūkā honā, v. To turn red with rage.

شعله جوالا shu'lah-ĕ jawwālā, n.m. An encircling flame; a beloved.

شعله خو shu'lah khū, adj. Fiery in disposition; having a fiery temper.

شعله رخ يا رو shu'lah rukh yā rū, adj. Flame faced; having a bright countenance; blazing beauty.

شعله زن shu'lah zan. adj. Blazing; flashing; brilliant.

شعله فشان shu'lah fishān, adj. Scattering flames.

شعور shu'ūr (A) n.m. Wisdom; intellect; good management; shrewdness; sense.

شغال shaghāl (P) n.m. A jackal.

شغب shaghab (A) n.m. Noise; tumult.

شغف shaghaf (A) n.m. Ardour; zeal; enthusiasm; inclination.

شغل shaghl, shughl (A) n.m. Occupation; employment.

شفا shifā (A) n.f. Cure; healing; recovery; convalescence.

شفا خانه shifā khānah, n.m. A hospital.

شفاعت shafā't (A) n.f. Recommendation; intercession; entreaty; deprication.

شفاف shaffāf (A) adj. Transparent; clear; pellucid; very thin.

شفتالو shaftālū (P) n.m. A peach.

شفعه shuf'ah (A) n.m. Pre-emption.

شفق shafaq (A) n.f. Evening twilight.

شفق پهولنا shafaq phūlnā, v. Appearance of the twilight.

شفقت shafaqat (A) n.f. Kindness; affection; favour; mercy; clemency; compassion; condolence.

شفیع shafi' (A) n.m. Advocate; patron; intercessor; possessing a right of pre-emption founded on contiguity.

شفیق shafiq (A) adj. Affectionate; compassionate; merciful. n.m. A kind friend.

شق shaqq (A) n.m. Cleaving; splitting; a rent; a crack; a fissure; dawn of day.

شق القمر shaqq-ul-qamar, n.m. Splitting of the moon (a miracle of the Holy Prophet).

شق ہونا shaqq honā, v. To be torn; to be rent.

شق shiqq (A) n.f. One half of a thing; a part; a clause; side; direction; division; kind.

شقاوت shaqāwat (A) n.f. Misery; disgrace; poverty; villainy.

شقائق shaqā'iq (A) n.m. A tulip.

شقہ shuqqah (A) n.m. A letter from a superior; a royal order.

شقی shaqi (A) adj. Wretched; miserable; villianous; vicious.

شقیقہ shaqiqah (A) n.m. Temple of the head.

شک shakk (A) n.m. Doubt; suspense; hesitation; uncertainty; incredulity.

شک پڑنا shakk parnā, v. To have a doubt.

شک ڈالنا shakk ḍālnā, v. To create a doubt; to cast a doubt upon.

شک کرنا shakk karnā, v. To suspect; to doubt.

شکار shikār (P) n.m. Hunting; the chase; prey; game; animal food; plunder; booty.

شکار بند shikār band, n.m. Cords or bag for tying game in.

شکار کرنا shikār karnā, v. To hunt; to prey upon; to ensnare; to catch.

شکار کھیلنا shikār khelnā, v. To go a hunting.

شکار گاہ shikār gāh, n.f. A hunting ground.

شکار ہونا shikār honā, v. To be hunted; to become a victim of; to fall a prey to.

شکاری shikāri (P) n.m. A sportsman; a hunter; a fowler; an angler; a fighter. adj. Relating to hunting; of the chase.

شکاری کتا shikāri kuttā, n.m. A hunting dog; a hound.

شکایت shikāyat (A) n.f. A complaint; illness; lamentation; accusation.

شکایت رفع کرنا shikāyat rafa' karnā, v. To remove the cause of a complaint.

شکتی shakti (S) n.f. Ability; strength; capacity; the energy or active power of a god.

شکر shukkar (S) n.m. The planet Venus; Friday.

شکر shukr (A) n.m. Thanks; gratefulness; gratitude.

شکر کرنا shukr karnā, v. To thank; to return thanks.

شکر گزار shukr guzār, adj. Grateful, thankful.

شکر گزاری shukr guzāri, n.f. Thanksgiving; gratitude; thankfulness.

شکرانہ shukrānah n.m. Gratitude; acknowledgement of gratitude; thanksgiving.

شکر shakar, shakkar (P) n.f. Sugar.

شکر پارہ shakar pārah, n.m. A kind of sweetmeat, made from rice flour, butter and sugar.

شکر خورہ shakar khorah, n.m. One who is fond of sweets; a bird which is very fond of sweets.

شکر ریز shakar rez, adj. Scattering sugar; mellifluous.

شکر قندی shakar qandi, n.f. Sweet potato.

شکر لب shakar lab, adj. Sugar-lipped; having sweet speech.

شکره *shikrah* (P) *n.m.* A hawk; falcon.

شکرین *shakarin* (P) *adj.* Sugary; of sugar. *n.f.* Saccharin.

شکست *shikast* (P) *n.f.* Defeat; rout; failure; loss; deficiency; fracture; a breach; breakage

شکست خورده *shikast khurdah, adj.* Defeated; routed; broken off; interrupted.

شکست و ریخت *shikast-ō rekht, n.f.* Dilapidation; damage.

شکستگی *shikastagi* (P) *n.f.* Breaking; brokenness; breakage; fracture; infirmity; sadness; dejection; sickness; affliction; violation.

شکسته *shikastah* (P) *adj.* Broken; sick; wounded; weak; infirm; impaired; bankrupt. *n.m.* A running hand; a kind of writing (in persian or Urdu).

شکسته بال' شکسته پر *shikastah bāl, shikastah par, adj.* Broken down; distressed; afflicted; wretched.

شکسته پا *shikastah pā, adj.* Infirm; broken down; unable to move about; unable to do anything; unable to perform a duty; helpless.

شکسته حال *shikastah hāl, adj.* Distressed; wretched; broken down; ruined; reduced to straits; in straitened circumstances.

شکسته خاطر *shikastah khāṭir, adj.* Distressed in mind; afflicted; offended; grieved.

شکسته دل *shikastah dil, adj.* Broken hearted; distressed; afflicted.

شکل *shakl* (A) *n.f.* Shape; form; figure; effigy; likeness; appearance; resemblance; model; pattern; diagram; image; formation; map; proposition.

شکل بگاڑنا *shakl bigārnā, v.* To disfigure; to disgrace.

شکل بنانا *shakl banānā, v.* To make a likeness of; to make a face; to make face at; to give a shape to; to assume a character.

شکل نکالنا *shakl nikālnā, v.* To find a way out; to think; to get over a difficulty; to give something a form.

شکل و شمائل *shakl-ō shamā'il, n.f.* Appearance and character.

هم شکل *ham shakl, adj.* Similar; of the same form or figure.

شکم *shikam* (P) *n.m.* The belly; stomach.

شکم پرور *shikam parwar, n.m.* A glutton; an epicure; a pamperer of his belly.

شکمی *shikamī* (P) *adj.* Of or relating to the belly; secret; private; subordinate; big-bellied; dependent; subtenanted.

شکن *shikan* (P) *n.f.* A fold; a wrinkle; curl; plait; crease. *adj.* Breaking (used in *compos.* as, بت شکن *but shikan*, an idol breaker).

شکن پڑنا *shikan paṛnā, v.* To be creased; to be wrinkled.

شکن ڈالنا *spikan ḍālnā, v.* To crease; to fold.

شکنجه *shikanjah* (P) *n.m.* Stocks for the legs; boards in which binders press books; book binder's press; clamp; rock; torture; torment; pain.

شکنجے میں کھینچنا *shikanje meṅ kheṅchnā, v.* To put in a press; to torture; to punish; to torment.

شکوک *shukūk* (A) *n.m.* (*plu.* of شک *shakk*) Doubts; suspicions.

شکوه *shikwah* (A & P) *n.m.* Complaint; reproach; chiding; upbraiding.

شکوه *shikoh* (P) *n.m.* State; dignity; grandeur; pomp; majesty; manificence.

شکی *shakkī, adj.* Suspicious; sceptical; doubtful; perplexing.

شکی مزاج *shakkī mizāj, adj.* Undetermined; wavering; hesitating; incredulous; of a sceptical turn of mind.

شکیب، شکیبائی **shikeb, shikebā'ī** (P) *n.f.* Patience; long-suffering; toleration.

شکیل **shakil** (A) *adj.* Well-shaped; handsome; comely; well-formed.

شگاف **shigāf** (P) *n.m.* Slit; crack; rent; fissure; the split in a pen; indentation; cleft; chasm; flaw; crevice; splitting; rending; breaking; cracking.

شگفتگی **shiguftagī** (P) *n.f.* Pleasure; delight; beauty; astonishment; blooming; expansion; expanding of a flower; flourishing state.

شگفته **shiguftah** (P) *n.m.* Expanded; blown; blooming; flourishing.

شگفته خاطر **shiguftah khāṯir**, *adj.* Cheerful; happy; delightful.

شگن **shugun** (P) *n.m.* *Contraction of* شگون *shagūn.*

شگوفه **shigūfah** (P) *n.m.* A bud; a blossom; a squib.

شگوفه چھوڑنا **shigūfah chhoṛnā**, *v.* To let off a squib; to fib.

شگوفه لانا **shigūfah lānā**, *v.* To produce something new and wonderful; to bud; to bring forth young shoots.

شگون **shagūn, shugūn** (P) *n.m.* An omen; an augury; a gift of money.

شگون کرنا **shagūn karnā**, *v.* To begin a work at an auspicious time.

شگون لینا **shagūn lenā**, *v.* To practise augury.

شل **shall** (A) *adj.* Paralytic; having the hands withered; fatigued; tired; palsied; crippled.

شلجم، شلغم **shaljam, shalgham** (P) *n.m.* A turnip.

شلوار **shalwār** (P) *n.f.* Trousers; breeches; pantaloon.

شلوک **shlok** (S) *n.m.* A hymn of praise; a verse; a stanza; a distich.

شلوکا **shalukā** (H) *n.m.* A waistcoat; a child's bib.

شلیته **shalītah** (H) *n.m.* A canvas bag; baggage stuffed in before loading on cattle.

شماتت **shamātat** (A) *n.f.* Rejoicing at the misfortune or affliction of another.

شمار **shumār** (P) *n.m.* Counting: numbering; number; account; estimation; calculation.

شمار کرنا **shumār karnā**, *v.* To count; to number; to reckon; to compute.

شماره **shumārah** (P) *n.m.* Number; issue of a paper.

شماری **shumārī** (P) *n.f.* Counting; enumeration; a rosary used in *compos.* as in مردم شماری *mardum shumārī*, Census (of population).

شمال **shimāl** (A) *n.m.* The north; the north wind.

شمال مشرق **shimāl mashriq**, *n.m.* The north-east.

شمال مغرب **shimāl maghrib**, *n.m.* The north-west.

شمالی **shimālī** (A) *adj.* Northern.

شمالی ھوا **shimālī hawā**, *n.f.* The north wind.

شمائل **shamā'il** (A) *n.m.* (*plu. of* شمیله *shamīlah*). Good qualities; virtues; excellences; talents; dispositions; customs; northerly winds or regions.

شمر **shimar** (A) *n.m.* Name of one of *Yazīd's* generals who killed *Imām Hussain* in the plains of *Karbalā* (hence) merciless; infamous; ignoble.

شمس **shams** (A) *n.m.* The sun.

شمس العلما **shams-ul-'ulamā**, *n.m.* The sun of the learned (a title confined on very learned people).

شمسه shamsah (P) n.m. Picture wrought in silk; tassels affixed to a rosary.

شمسی shamsi (P) adj. Solar.

شمشاد shamshad (P) n.m. The box tree; a tall and upright tree; the graceful figure of a beloved.

شمشیر shamsher, shamshir (P) n.f. A sword.

شمشیر باز shamsher bāz, adj. A sword player; a gladiator.

شمشیر بازی shamsher bazi, n.f. Sword-play.

شمشیر زن shamsher zan, n.m. A swordsman.

شمشیر زنی shamsher zani, n.f. Swordsmanship; use of the sword.

شمع shama' (A) n.f. A lamp; a candle.

شمع دان shama' dān, n.m. A candle-stick; a candle-holder.

شمله shamlah (P) n.m. The end of a turban or *kamarband* tucked in the folds; a narrow kind of shawl for tying round the waist or the head.

شمول shumūl (A) n.m. The whole; contents; inclusion. adj. Comprehending; containing; surrounding on all sides; including.

شمه shammah (A) n.m. Smell; odour; a particle; a little; an atom; habit; custom.

شمه بهر shammah bhar, adj. A little; very little.

شمیم shamīm (A) n.f. Odour; smelling; scent.

شناخت shinākht (P) n.f. Recognition; identification; understanding; knowledge.

شناخت کرنا shinākht karnā, v. To recognise; to identify; to know; to become acquainted with.

شناس shinās (P) adj. Knowing; acquainted with; intelligent; (used in *compos.* as, دست شناس dast shinās, a palmist).

شناسا shināsā (P) adj. Intelligent; knowing. n.m. One who knows.

شناسائی shināsa'i (P) n.f. Acquaintance; knowledge.

شناسی shinasi (P) n.f. Knowing (used in *compos*).

شناور shinawar (P) n.m. A swimmer.

شناوری shinawari (P) n.f. Swimming.

شنبه shambah (P) n.m. Saturday.

شنجرف ' شنگرف shanjraf, shangaraf (P) n.m. Red sulphuret of mercury; cinnabar; vermilion.

شنگ shang (P) adj. Amorously playful; pretty; jocular; jolly; elegant and sweet in manners; beautiful; handsome. n.m. A thief; a robber; a knave.

شنگرفی shangrafi (P) adj. Of vermilion colour.

شنوائی shinawā'i (P) n.f. Hearing; attending; paying attention to; giving a hearing.

شنوائی ہونا shinawā'i honā, v. To obtain a hearing; to be attended to; to be considered.

شنید shanid (P) n.f. Act of hearing.

شنیدنی shanidani (P) adj. Fit for or worthy of hearing.

شنیده shanidah (P) adj. Heard. n.m. That which is heard; a rumour.

شنیده کے بود مانند دیده shanidah kai bawad manind-ĕ didah, prov. Seeing is believing; believe your eyes more than your ears.

شنیع ' شنیعه shanī', shanī'ah (A) adj. Disgraceful; shocking; abominable; base; evil; bad.

شو shau, shū (P) n.m. (contr. of شوہر shauhar) Husband.

شوال shawwāl (H) n.m. The tenth month of the Hijri year on the first day of which 'Id-ul-Fitr is celebrated.

شواله *shivālah* (H) *n.m.* A temple or shrine dedicated to *Shivā*.

شواهد *shawāhid* (A) *n.m.* (*plu.* of شاهد *shāhid*) Witnesses; instances; proofs.

شوبها *shobhā* (S) *n.f.* Radiance; lustre; elegance; beauty; comeliness; dress; decoration.

شوخ *shokh* (P) *adj.* Bright; fast (colour); sprightly; brisk; mischievous; bold; insolent; shameless; wanton; saucy; buxom; sly; humorous; presumptuous; daring.

شوخ چشم *shokh chashm*, *adj.* Impudent; mischievous; bold; wanton-eyed; unceremonious.

شوخ چشمی *shokh chashmi*, *n.f.* Wantonness; impudence.

شوخ مزاج *shokh mizāj*, *adj.* Of gay disposition.

شوخ و شنگ *shokh-ŏ shang*, *adj.* Gay and playful; pert; saucy; wanton; *l'allegro*.

شوخی *shokhi* (P) *n.f.* Playfulness; mischief; coquetry; boldness; sauciness; forwardness; wantonness; humour; fun.

شودر *shūdar* (S) *n.m.* The fourth and servile caste among the Hindus; a low caste; untouchables.

شور *shor* (P) *n.m.* Noise; outcry; disturbance; tumult; uproar; renown; clamour; zeal; ordour; fervour; agitation; anxiety. *adj.* Salty; brackish; very bitter.

شور زمین *shor zamin*, *n.f.* Saline soil; barren and uncultivable land.

شور شرابا *shor sharābā*, *n.m.* Noise; tumult; disturbance.

شور کرنا یا مچانا *shor karnā yā machānā*, *v.* To make a noise; to hoot; to kick up a row.

شوروشر٬شوروشغب *skor-ŏ sharr*, *shor-ŏ shaghab*; *n.m.* Disturbance; tumult; buslte; clamour; uproar.

شوریٰ *shūrā* (A) *n.f.* Consultation; convention; deliberation; agrument; mixture.

شوربا *shorbā* (P) *n.m.* Broth; soup.

شور بور *shor bor*, *adj.* Very wet; drenched.

شورش *shorish* (P) *n.f.* Confusion; Commotion; tumult; insurrection; brackishness; saltiness.

شوره *shorah* (P) *n.m.* Nitre; saltpetre.

شوره پشت *shorah pusht*, *adj.* Unruly; refractory; disturbing.

شورِیت *shoriyyat* (P) *n.f.* Saltiness; brackishness.

شوریدگی *shoridagi* (P) *n.f.* Madness; love; passion.

شوریده *shoridah* (P) *adj.* Disturbed; dejected; mad; desperately in love.

شوریده سر *shoridah sar*, *adj.* Mad; rebellious.

شوشه *shoshah* (P) *n.m.* A particle; part piece; rubbish; filth; an ingot; a chip.

شوشه اٹھانا یا چھوڑنا *shoshah uṭhānā yā chhoṛnā*, *v.* To start mischief; to create trouble.

شوق *shauq* (A) *n.m.* Taste; ardour; zeal; eagerness; fondness; desire; longing; love; pleasure; interest; curiosity; avidity.

شوق سے *shauq se*, *adv.* With pleasure.

شوقین *shauqin*, *adj.* Fond of; desirous; eager; enthused; lascivious; devoted to.

شوقیه *shauqiyah* (A) *adv.* Lovingly; eagerly.

شوکت *shaukat* (A) *n.f.* Dignity; magnificence; grandeur; state; pomp; power; might.

شوم *shūm* (A) *adj.* Unlucky; unfortunate; black; miser.

شومی *shūmi*, *n.f.* N dliness; avaric stinginess.

شوہر *shauhar* (P) *n.m.* A husband.

شہ *shah* (P) *n.m.* (*contr.* of شاہ *shāh*) A king; check at chess. *adj.* Royal; great; large; (in *compos* as شہ زور *shah zor*, gallant; powerful).

شہ *shah*, *n.f.* Ecouragement; incitement.

شہہ دینا *shah denā*, *v.* To encourage; to incite.

شہاب *shahāb* (A) *n.m.* A red colour.

شہاب ثاقب *shihāb-ĕ-ṣāqib* (A) *n.m.* A brightly shining star; a shooting star; a meteor.

شہادت *shahādat* (A) *n.f.* Evidence; witness; testimony; martyrdom.

شہادت کی انگلی *shahādat kī uṅglī*, *n.f.* The fore-finger.

شہامت *shahamat* (A) *n.f.* Bravery; generosity; ingenuity; stoutness of heart; heroism; prowess; agility; swiftness, courage, greatness, power.

شہد *shahd* (P) *n.m.* Honey; anything very sweet.

شہد کی مکھی *shahd kī makhkhī*, *n.f.* A bee.

شہد لگا کر چاٹنا *shahd lagā kar chāṭnā*, *v.* To take great care in the preservation of something quite unimportant.

شہدا *shuhdā* (H) *n.m.* A rake; prodigal; debauchee; a blackguard; a scoundrel; a vagabond.

شہداپن ، شہدپن *shuhdā pan*, *shuhdpan*, *n.m.* Dissoluteness; debauchery.

شہداء *shuhadā* (A) *n.m.* (*plu.* of شہید *shahīd*) The martyrs.

شہر *shahr* (A) *n.m.* Month.

شہر *shahr* (P) *n.m.* A city.

شہر آشوب *shahr āshob*, *n.m.* One who disturbs the peace of a city; a poem describing a ruined city.

شہر بسانا *shahr basānā*, *v.* To found a city; to set up a town.

شہر بدر *shahr badar*, *adj.* Banishment; expulsion from one's country or town *adj.* Banished.

شہر پناہ *shahr panāh*, *n.f.* Walls of a city; fortifications of a town; ramparts.

شہرخموشاں *shahr-ĕ-khamoshān*, *n.m.* A cemetery.

شہر گرد ، شہر گشت ، شہر پیما *shahr gurd*, *shahr gasht*, *shahr paimā*, *n.m.* A city patrol; a city perambulator; a wanderer; omnibus.

شہر یار *shahryār* *n.m.* A prince; a king; a despotic ruler.

شہر یاری *shahryārī*, *n.f.* Royalty; soverieg-nty. *adj.* Royal; imperial.

شہرت *shuhrat* (A) *n.f.* Renown; fame celebrity report; rumour.

شہرت پیدا کرنا *shuhrat paidā karnā*, *v.* To become famous; to build up a reputation.

شہرہ *shuhrah* (A) *n.m.* Fame; renown; reputation; divulging; publishing; report; rumour.

شہرہ آفاق *shuhrah-ĕ āfāq*, *adj.* Known the world over; renowned; of world fame.

شہری *shahrī* (P) *n.m.* A citizen; a townsman. *adj.* Belonging to a city.

شہریت *shahriyyat* (P) *n.f.* Civics; peopling; polished manners; good manners of city people; civility; citizenship.

شہلا *shahlā* (A) *adj.* Having dark grey eyes with a shade of red.

شہنائی *shahnā'ī* (P) *n.f.* A kind of musical pipe; a flute; a clarion; flageolet.

شہوار *shahwār* (P) *adj.* Worthy of a king; princely.

شہوانی *shahwānī* (A) *adj.* Sexual; carnal.

شہوت *shahwat* (A) *n.f.* Sexsuality; lust, desire; lechery.

شہوت انگیز *shahwat angez, adj.* Lust; enciting; provocative of desires; lascivious.

شہوت پرست *shahwat parast, adj.* Sexsualist; desirous of satisfying lust; a rake; a lascivious person.

شہوت پرستی *shahwat parastī, n.f.* Sexsuality; lustfulness.

شہود *shuhūd* (A) *n.m.* The being present; witnesses; evidences. *adj.* Present.

شہید *shahīd* (A) *n.m.* A martyr.

شئی *sha'ī* (A) *n.f.* A thing; an object; an article; a matter.

شیاطین *shayāṭīn* (A) *n.m.* (plu. of شیطان *shaiṭān*) Devils; demons.

شیام *shyām* (S) *adj* Black; dark blue.

شیب *shaib* (A) *n.m.* Greyness; Senility; old age.

شیخ *shaik͟h* (A) *n.m.* A venerable old man; a chief of a tribe or of a village; a new convert to Islam; a caste.

شیخ چلی *shaik͟h chillī, n.m.* A traditionary jester; a fool; a rogue.

شیخانی *shaik͟hānī, n.f.* A woman belonging to a *shaik͟h* family; the wife of a *shaik͟h*.

شیخوخیت *shaik͟hūk͟hiyyat* (A) *n.f.* Old age.

شیخی *shek͟hī, n.f.* Boasting; bragging.

شیخی باز، شیخی خورا *shek͟hī bāz, shek͟hī k͟horā, n.m.* A boaster; braggart.

شیخی بگھارنا، مارنا *shek͟hī bagharnā, marnā, v.* To boast; to brag.

شیخی نکالنا *shek͟hī nikālnā, v.* To have one's pride humbled.

شیدا *shaidā* (P) *adj.* Maddened with love; deeply in love. *n.m.* A lover; a madman.

شیر *sher* (P) *n.m.* A tiger; a lion; a brave man.

شیر ببر *sher babar, n.m.* A lion.

شیر قالین *shur-ĕ qālīn, n.m.* A carpet lion; a figure head; a braggart.

شیر کی خالہ *sher kī k͟hālā, n.f.* A cat.

شیر مرد *sher mard, n.m.* A brave man. *adj.* Brave; overpowering; valorous.

شیر ہونا *sher honā, v.* To overcome; to be powerful; to be encouraged.

شیر *shīr* (P) *n.m.* Milk.

شیر پیما *shīr paimā, n.m.* Lactometer.

شیر خوار *shīr k͟hwār, n.m.* A suckling; an infant; a babe.

شیروشکر *shīr-ŏ shakar, n.m.* Affection; close intimacy; intimate friendship; a kind of silk cloth. *adj.* Mixed; intimate.

شیر و شکر ہونا *shīr-ŏ shakar honā, v.* To be intimate friends.

شیر گرم *shīr garm, adj.* Lukewarm; milk warm.

شیر مال *shīr māl, n.m.* A bread made with milk or kneaded with milk.

شیرازہ *shīrāzah* (P) *n.m.* Stitching the back of a book; organisation.

شیرازہ بکھرنا *shīrāzah bikharnā, v.* To be disorganised; to be mismanaged

شیرازہ بندی *shīrāzah bandī, n.f.* Binding a book; management; administration; organisation.

شیرنی *shernī, n.f.* A lioness; a tigress.

شیرہ *shīrah* (P) *n.m.* Syrup; juice; new wine; must; essence; sap; treacle; molasses.

شیریں *shīrīṅ* (P) *adj.* Sweet; pleasant; gentle.

شیرینی *shīrīnī* (P) *n.f.* Sweetness; sweetmeat.

شیشم shīsham (H) n.f. A kind of tree and its wood.

شیش محل shīsh maḥal, n.m. A glass house; a house adorned with glass; an apartment fitted with mirrors.

شیشه shīhah (P) n.m. Glass; bottle; a looking glass; a glass pane; a flask.

شیشه دکھانا shīshah dikhānā, v. To show a looking glass.

شیشی shīshi, n.f. A small glass; a small bottle.

شیطان shaiṭān (A) n.m. A satan; the devil; the demon.

شیطان کی آنت shaiṭān kī ānt, adj. & n.f. Anything very long and tedious.

شیطان کی خاله shaiṭān kī khālah, n.f. A wicked woman.

شیطانی shaitānī, adj. Devilish; diabolical; n.f. Wickedness; mischief.

شیطانی حرکت shaiṭānī ḥarkat, n.f. A diabolical act; wickedness.

شیطانی وسوسه shaiṭānī waswasah, n.m. Atheistic doubts.

شیطنت shaiṭanat (A) n.f Mischief; malice; wickedness; devil's tricks.

شیعه shī'ah (A) n.m. A follower of Haẓrat. 'Ali; a supporter; a company.

شیفتگی sheftagi (P) n.f. Amour; madness; love.

شیفته sheftah (P) adj. Distracted with love; mad; enamoured.

شیون shewan (P) n.m. Grief; lamentation; mourning.

شیوه shewah (P) n. Manner; habit; way; trade; business; peculiar way; method.

ص ṣād yā suād called sad-ĕ muhmilah, is the twentieth letter of the Urdu, seventeenth of the Persian and fourteenth of the Arabic alphabet and it has the sound of s. But in Arabic it has a rather prolonged sound which might be expressed by a ss. In abjad it has a value of 90.

ص-ص ṣuād, n.m. As an abbreviation it is used for the word صحیح which is written on documents or accounts as ص to indicate that they have been and are in order.

صابر ṣabir (A) adj. Patient; enduring.

صابن یا صابون ṣāban yā ṣābūn (A) n.m. Soap.

صابونی ṣābūni, adj. Of or relating to soap; mixed with soap. n.f. A kind of sweetmeat.

صاحب ṣāḥib (A) n.m. Master; lord; ruler; a gentleman; companion; a title of courtesy. adj. Possessing; possessed of; endowed with.

صاحب اختیار ṣāḥib-ĕ ikhtiyār, adj. (One) vested with authority or power.

صاحب اخلاق ṣāḥib-ĕ akhlāq, adj. Well behaved; of good manners; polite.

صاحب اقبال ṣāḥib-ĕ iqbāl, adj. Fortunate; lucky; prosperous.

صاحب تاج و تخت ṣāḥib-ĕ tāj-ŏ takht, n.m. A king; possesser of the crown and throne.

صاحب تدبیر ṣāḥib-ĕ tadbir, n.m. A tactful and prudent person; a diplomatist; a politician. adj. Wise; clever; well-experienced.

صاحب تمیز ṣāḥib-ĕ tamiz, adj. Intelligent.

صاحب جائداد ṣāḥib-ĕ jā'idād, n.m. A landlord; one who owns property.

صاحب جمال ṣāḥib-ĕ jamāl, n.m. A handsome young man; a beautiful young thing.

صاحب حال و قال ṣāḥib-ĕ ḥāl-ŏ qāl, *adj.* Intelligent; polite; (a) well-informed (person).

صاحب خانہ ṣāḥib-ĕ *khānah*, *n.m.* Master of the house; host.

صاحب دل ṣāḥib-ĕ *dil*, *adj & n.m.* Pious; a pious man; a good fellow.

صاحب ذوق ṣāḥib-ĕ *zauq*, *adj.* Endowed with taste; (a man) of tastes; an enthusiast.

صاحب زادہ ṣāḥib *zādah*, *n.m.* A young gentleman· son of a .good family; a young master.

صاحب زبان ṣāḥib-ĕ *zabān*, *n.m.* Linguist.

صاحب سلامت ṣāhib *salāmat*, *n.f.* Intimacy; acquaintance; compliments.

صاحب عدالت ṣaḥib-ĕ *'adālat*, *n.m.* A magistrate.

صاحب عقل ṣāḥib-ĕ *'aql*, *adj.* Intelligent; wise.

صاحب فراش ṣāḥib-ĕ *farāsh*, *adj.* Bed ridder.

صاحب قران ṣāḥib-ĕ *qirān*, *saḥibqirān*, *adj.* Of auspicious birth; born at a time when the Venus and the Mercury are in one sign.

صاحب قلم ṣāḥib-ĕ *qalam*, *n.m.* A writer; a poet.

صاحب کتاب ṣāḥib-ĕ *kitāb*, *n.m.* One to whom God reveals a Book; a prophet.

صاحب کمال ṣāḥib-ĕ *kamāl*, *adj.* Perfect; excellent; proficient; one endowed with consumate ability and skill; thoroughly accomplished.

صاحب نظر ṣāḥib-ĕ *nazar*, *adj.* Discerning; intelligent; pious.

صاحبان ṣāḥibān (A & P) *n.m.* (*plu.* of صاحب ṣāḥib) Nobles; masters; gentlemen.

صاحبہ ṣāḥibah (A) *n.f.* A lady; a woman of rank. *adj.* Possessing; endowed with.

صادر ṣādir (A) *adj.* Emanating from; proceeding; going forth; issued; passed; produced; happened; arrived.

صادر کرنا ṣādir *karnā*, *v.* To issue or to pass an order.

صادر ہونا ṣādir *honā*, *v.* To be issued; to be enacted; to be derived; to happen; to proceed; to be produced; to be emerged; to emanate from.

صادق ṣādiq (A) *adj.* True; sincere; faithful; veracious; (a) man) of his word; just.

صادق آنا sādiq *ānā*, *v.* To come true; to suit; to fit; to apply.

صادق‌القول ṣadiq-ul-qaul, *adj.* True to one's word.

صاد کرنا ṣād *karnā*, *v.* To approve; to sanction; to grant.

صاعقہ sā'iqah (A) *n.f.* Lightning; thunderbolt.

صاف ṣāf (A) *adj.* Clean; pure; innocent; clear; bright (sky); smooth; legible; apparent; frank; indisputable; precise (account); plain; simple; distinct. *adv.* Clearly; cleanly; entirely.

صاف باطن ṣāf *bāṭin*, *adj.* Having a clear conscience.

صاف چھوٹنا ṣāf *chhūṭnā*, *v.* To get clean off; to escape unpunished.

صاف دل ṣāf *dil*, *adj.* Open hearted; candid; frank; guileless; pure-hearted.

صاف شفاف ṣāf *shaffāf*, *adj.* Transparent; brilliant.

صاف صاف ṣāf ṣāf, *adv.* Plainly; openly; flately.

صاف صاف سنانا ṣāf ṣāf *sunānā*, *v.* To admonish without reserve; to abuse.

صاف صاف کہنا ṣāf ṣāf *kahnā*, *v.* To say frankly; to be straightforward.

صاف کرنا *ṣāf karnā*, *v.* To clean; to cleanse; to purify; to wash; to make a fair copy; to make clear.

صاف کر جانا *ṣāf kar jāna*, *v.* To make a clean sweep(of); to ransack; to finish; to eat everything up.

صاف نکل جانا *ṣāf nikal jānā*, *v.* To get clean away; to get off scot-free; to make off with all speed.

صافہ *ṣāfah*, *n.m.* A cloth worn round the head; a turban.

صافی *ṣāfi* (A) *n.f.* A cloth for straining liquid; a filter; a rag for wiping slates; a dish-clout; a cloth with which kettle is lifted off the fire; a duster. *adj.* Clear; pure.

صالح ، صالحہ *ṣāliḥ, ṣāliḥah* (A) *adj.* Virtuous; chaste; good; righteous; (a) sedate or steady (person.)

صامت *ṣāmit* (A) *adj.* Silent; mute; irrational; inanimate.

صانع *ṣāni'* (A) *n.m.* A maker; an artificer; a craftsman; the Creator.

صانعِ قدرت *ṣāni'-ĕ qudrat, n.m.* The author of Nature; God.

صائب *ṣā'ib* (A) *adj.* Right; going straight to the point; well aimed.

صائب الرائے *ṣāib-ur-ra'e, adj.* Right thinking; having sound judgement.

صائم *ṣā'im* (A) *n.m.* One who abstains from food; one who fasts; fasting.

صبا *ṣabā* (A) *n.f.* A gentle breeze; an easterly breeze; a morning breeze; zephyr.

صباح *ṣabāḥ* (A) *n.f.* Morning; day-break; dawn.

علی الصباح *'al-aṣ-ṣabāḥ, adv.* Early in the morning; at dawn.

صباحت *ṣabāḥat* (A) *n.f.* Beauty; gracefulness; comeliness.

صبح *ṣubḥ* (A) *n.f.* Morning; dawn; day-break.

صبح خیز *ṣubḥ khez, adj.* Rising early in the morning. *n.m.* An early riser; an early morning thief.

صبح دم *ṣubḥ dam, adv.* Early in the morning; at dawn.

صبح شام کرنا *ṣubḥ shām karnā, v.* To put off from time to time; to evade; to dilly-dally.

صبح صادق *ṣubḥ ṣādiq, n.f.* Dawn of day.

صبح صبح *ṣubḥ ṣubḥ, adv.* Early in the morning.

صبح کا تارا *ṣubḥ kā tārā, n.m.* The morning star; the Venus.

صبح کاذب *subḥ kāẕib, n.f.* The time just before day-break; the light before day-break.

صبح و مسا *ṣubḥ-ŏ masā, n.f.* Morning and evening.

صبر *ṣabr* (A) *n.m.* Patience; endurance; self-restraint; resignation; submission; suffering.

صبر آنا *ṣabr ānā, v.* To get over one's grief; to endure.

صبر بٹورنا یا لینا *ṣabr baṭornā yā lena, v.* To store up calamity or evil; to reap the reward of misdeeds.

صبر پڑنا *ṣabr paṛnā, v.* To be under a curse.

صبر کرنا *ṣabr karnā, v.* To keep patience; to wait; to endure; to exercise self-restraint.

صبوح *ṣabūḥ* (A) *n.f.* Wine drunk in the morning; wine left over for use in the morning; morning draught.

صبوحی *ṣabūḥī* (A) *n.f.* A bottle for holding wine; the morning draught of wine.

صبوری *ṣabūrī* (P) *n.f.* Patience; forbearance.

نا صبوری *nā ṣabūri, n.f.* Impatience; restlessness.

صبی ṣabī (A) n.m. An infant; a youth (plu. صبیان ṣibyān).

صبیح ، صبیحہ ṣabīḥ, ṣabiah (A) adj. Beautiful; handsome.

صبیہ ṣabiyyah (A) n.f. A damsel; a girl; a daughter.

صحابہ ṣaḥābah (A) n.m. (plu. of صاحب ṣāḥib) Companions of the Holy Prophet.

صحابی ṣaḥābi (A) n.m. One of the companions of the Holy Prophet.

صحائف ṣāḥā'if (A) n.m. (plu. of صحیفہ ṣaḥīfah) Books; volumes; leaves; pages.

صحبت ṣuḥbat (A) n.f. Companionship; society; company; an assembly; association; conversation; intercourse; carnal intercourse; cohabitation.

صحبت آٹھانا ṣuḥbat uṭhānā, v. To be in one's company.

صحبت داری ṣuḥbat dārī, n.f. Keeping company with; associating; copulation.

صحبت کرنا ṣuḥbat karnā, v. To keep company with; to cohabit; to copulate.

صحبت یافتہ ṣuḥbat yāftah, adj. Trained in good society; well-bred.

صحت ṣiḥḥat (A) n.f. Health; soundness of body; sound health; perfection; integrity; accuracy; validity; correction; confirmation.

صحت بخش ṣiḥḥat bakhsh, adj. Health giving; healthy; sanatory.

صحت بخش مقام ṣiḥḥat bakhsh maqām, n.m. A sanatorium; a health resort.

صحت نامہ ṣiḥḥat nāmah, n.m. A certificate of health; a corrigendum.

صحرا ṣaḥrā (A) n.m. A desert; a wilderness; a forest; a plain.

صحرائے اعظم saḥrā'e a'ẓam, n.m. The great desert.

صحرائے لق و دق ṣaḥrā-ĕ laq-ŏ daq, n.m. A lonely wilderness.

صحرا نشیں ṣaḥrā nashīṅ, n.m. A hermit living in a desert; an inhabitant of desert; a bedouin of Arabia.

صحرا نورد ṣaḥrā naward, n.m. A wanderer of the desert.

صحرائی ṣaḥrā'i (A) adj. Of the desert; wild; uncivilized.

صحن ṣaḥn (A) n.m. A courtyard; an area; compound; open space.

صحن چمن ṣaḥn-ĕ chaman, n.m. A lawn.

صحیح ṣaḥiḥ (A) adj. Right; correct; accurate; perfect; entire; genuine; sound; healthy; certain; just; pure; authentic; true; proper.

صحیح البدن ṣaḥiḥ-ul-badn, adj. Having a sound body.

صحیح العقل ṣaḥiḥ-ul-'aql, adj. Of sound mind; of good intellect.

صحیح النسب ṣaḥiḥ-un-nasb, adj. Legitimate.

صحیح سالم ، سلامت ṣaḥiḥ sālim, salāmat, adj. Safe and sound.

صحیفہ ṣaḥīfah (A) n.m. A book; a volume; a leaf; a page; a letter.

صد ṣad (P) adj. Hundred; cent.

صد آفریں ṣad āfarīṅ, intj. Well done!

صد برگ ṣad barg, n.m. Marigold.

صدھا ṣad hā adj. A great many; hundreds.

صدا ṣadā (A) n.f. Sound; echo; voice; noise.

صدابصحرا ṣadā baṣaḥrā, n.m. A cry in the wilderness.

صدا دینا ṣadā denā, v. To call; to answer a call.

صدا کرنا یا لگانا ṣadā karnā yā lagānā, v. To call out; to wail; to beg.

صدارت ṣadārat (A) n.f. Presidentship; chairmanship; chancellorship; premiership.

صداقت ṣadaqat (A) n.f. Truth; sincerity; candour; fidelity; friendship.

صدر ṣadr (A) n.m. The breast, chest; bosom; the highest part; the highest person; chief; the first place or seat; headquarter; the seat of Government; a military cantonment.

صدر اعظم sadr-ĕ 'a'zam, n.m. The premier.

صدرالصدور ṣadr-us-ṣudur, n.m. The chief judge; chancellor.

صدربازار ṣadr bāzār, n.m. The main street (of a cantonment); Urdu bazaar.

صدر مجلس ، صدر نشین sadr-ĕ-majlis, ṣadr nashin, n.m. President; chairman.

صدرمدرس ṣadr madarris, n.m. Headmaster.

صدر مقام ṣadr maqām, n.m. A capital; metropolis.

صدری ṣadri (P) n.f. A waistcoat; a jacket; adj. relating to chest.

صدف ṣadaf (A) n.f. A shell; a mother of pearl.

صدق ṣidq (A) n.m. Truth; sincerity; verocity.

صدق دل سے یا نیت سے ṣidq dil se yā niyyat se, adv. Sincerely; honestly.

صدقہ ṣadqah (A) n.m. Alms; sacrifice; gifts to the poor; favour; grace; propitiatory offerings.

صدقے جانا ṣadqe jānā, v. To become a sacrifice for the welfare of another.

صدقے کرنا ṣadqe karnā, v. To sacrifice for the welfare of another.

صدمہ ṣadmah (A) n.m. A shock; a blow; accident; calamity; colision; injury; confusion; adversity; a stroke of bad luck; an adventure; suffering.

صدمہ آٹھانا ṣadmah uṭhānā, v. To suffer a blow; to meet with misfortune; to experience a shock.

صدمہ پہنچانا ṣadmah punhchānā, v. To give one a blow; to bring injury on one; to hurt; to give one a shock.

صدمہ جانکاہ ṣadmah-ĕ jānkāh, n.m. Grievous injury; a terrible blow.

صدور ṣudūr (A) n.m. Proceeding; issuing; emanating; (plu. of صدر ṣadr) presidents chairmen.

صدی ṣadi, (A) n.f. A century; a centenary.

صدیق ṣiddiq (A) adj. Just; true; sincere. n.m. A faithful witness of the truth; a sincere friend.

صدیق ṣadiq (A) n.m. A friend.

صراحت ṣarahat (A) n.f. Clarity; clearness; pureness; specification; palpableness.

صراحت کرنا ṣarahat karnā, v. To make clear; to elucidate; to specify.

صراحتاً ṣarāhatan (A) adv. Clearly; plainly; expressly; evidently; openly; explicitly.

صراحی ṣurāhi (A) n.f. A goblet; a long-necked flask.

صراحی دار ṣurāhi dār, adj. Goblet-shaped.

صراط ṣirāṭ (A) n.f. Road; way.

صراط مستقیم ṣirāt-ĕ mustaqim, n.f. A direct road; the right way.

صراف ṣarrāf (A) n.m. A banker; a money changer.

صرافہ ṣarrāfah n.m. A bank; the exchange; a money-market; the place where bankers transact business.

صرافی ṣarrāfi n.f. Banking; money-changing; discount.

صرافی کرنا ṣarrāfi karnā, v. To carry on the business of a banking.

صرصر ṣarṣar (A) n.m. A cold violent wind.

صرع ṣura' (A) n.f. Epilepsy; the falling sickness. adj. Pure; genuine; unadulterated; clear; evident.

صرف ṣarf (A) n.m. Change; expenditure; cost; etymology; conjugation (grammar); changing; turning; converting; volubility; vicissitudes of fortune.

صرف کرنا ṣarf karnā, v. To spend; to disburse; to pass; to employ; to consume.

صرف و نحو ṣarf-ŏ naḥv, n.f. Grammar.

صرف هونا ṣarf honā, v. To be consumed; to be spent; to be disbursed.

صرفه ṣarfah (A) n.m. Expense; economy; advantage; profusion; profit; utility; surplus; prodigality; the twelfth mansion of the moon.

صرفه کرنا ṣarfah karnā, v. To economise; to be thrifty.

صرفی ṣarfī (A) adj. Etymological; relating to grammar; n.m. A grammarian; an etymologist.

صرف ṣirf (A) adj./adv. Only; mere; sheer; unmixed; purely; exclusively.

صریح ṣarīḥ (A) adj. Apparent; evident; clear; palpable; great; manifest.

صریح انکار کرنا ṣarīḥ inkār karnā, v. To refuse point blank.

صریحاً ṣarīhan (A) adv. Clearly; evidently; explicitly; openly; plainly.

صریر ṣarīr (A) n.f. The scratching sound made by a pen; the grating of a door.

صعب ṣa'b (A) adj. Hard; difficult; rough; arduous; troublesome; perverse.

صعوبت ṣa'ūbat (A) n.f. Difficulty; hardship; trouble; distress.

صعود ṣu'ūd (A) n.m. Ascent; accession; mounting; climbing; ascending; involution (Alg.).

صغار ṣighār (A) adj. (plu. of صغیر ṣaghīr) Unimportant people; the young ones.

صغار و کبار ṣighār-ŏ kibār, n.m. The small and the great; the poor and the rich; the important and the unimportant people.

صغر sighar (A) n.m. Smallness; minuteness.

صغر سنی ṣighar sinī, n.f. Tender age: minority.

صغریٰ ṣughrā (A) adj. Less; least; smallest. n.f. The minor term of a syllogism.

صغیر ṣaghīr (A) adj. Small; slender; inferior; tender; minor.

صف ṣaff (A) n.f. Series; order; line; rank; file; row; a mat.

صف آرا ṣaff ārā, adj. Arrayed; marshalled; drawn in a line.

صف آرائی یا صف بندی ṣaff ārā'ī yā ṣaff bandī, n.f. Array; battle-array; parade; tactics.

صف باندھنا ṣaff bāndhnā, v. To draw up in ranks.

صف بسته ṣaff bastah, adj. Drawn up in a line or row.

صف جنگ ṣaff-ĕ jung, n.f. The ranks of war; the field of battle.

صف در، صفدر ṣaff dar, adj. & n.m. Rank-breaking; a violent warrior; one who breaks the enemy ranks.

صف در صف ṣaff dar ṣaff, adj. In rank and file.

صف ماتم ṣaff-ĕ mātam, n.f. A mat for the mourners; a carpet spread for mourners or condolers to sit on in mourning.

صفا ṣafā (A) adj. Pure; clean; clear; brilliant; bright; polished; free from care; serene. n.f. A hill near Mecca.

صفاچٹ کرنا ṣafā chaṭ karnā, v. To shave clean; to lick a plate perfectly clean; to eat everything up.

صفات șifāt (A) *n.f.* (*plu.* of صفت șifat) Qualities; attributes.

صفاتی șifāti (A) *adj.* Acquired qualities; extrinsic attributes.

صفائی șafā'i (P) *n.f.* Purity; cleanliness; clearness; conservancy; clearance; settlement; destruction; perspicuity.

صفائی کرنا șafā'i karnā, *v.* To purify; to cleanse; to make short work of; to settle matters; to effect a compromise; to destroy.

صفت șifat (A) *n.f.* Praise; quality; attribute; manner; like; resembling an adjective.

صفت موصوف șifat mauṣūf, *n.m.* An adjective with its substantive.

صفحه șafḥah (A) *n.m.* A page; a leaf (of a book); face; surface; disc; plate.

صفحه هستی șafḥah-ĕ hasti, *n.m.* The leaf of existence; the face of the earth.

صفر șafar (A) *n.m.* The second month of the Hijri year.

صفر șifar (A) *n.m.* A cypher; a zero; naught.

صفرا șafrā (A) *n.m.* Bile; gall, yellow; pale; livid.

صفراوی șafrāvi (A) *adj.* Billious.

صفوف șufūf (A) *n.f.* (*plu.* of صف șaff) Lines; ranks; rows; mats.

صفی șafī (A) *adj.* Pure; just; righteous.

صفیر șafīr (A) *n.f.* Sound; whistling; hissing noise; blowing; singing (of a bird); a sapphire.

صل șall (A) *v.* To praise; to bless.

صل علی șall-ĕ 'alā, *intg* Blessed be! very fine!

صلا șalā (A) *n.f.* Call; invitation; proclamation; challenge of a foe; cry of a salesman.

صلائے عام șalā'e ām, *n.f.* An open challenge or invitation.

صلابت șalabat (A) *n.f.* Firmness; hardness; rigour; severity; majesty; awe; dignity.

صلاح șalaḥ (A) *n.f.* Peace; concord; treaty; rectitude; integrity; goodness of state or condition; prosperity; advice; counsel, choice.

صلاح دینا salāḥ dena, *v.* To advise; to counsel.

صلاح کار șalāḥ kar, *n.m.* A counsellor; an adviser.

صلاح کرنا șalāḥ karna, *v.* To consult; to take advice.

صلاح لینا șalāḥ lenā, *v.* To take advice; to consult.

صلاح مشوره șalāh mashwarah, *n.m.* Mutual consultation.

صلاحیت șalaḥiyyat (A) *n.f.* Virtue; integrity; goodness; probity; sanctity; capacity; fitness; competence.

صلب șalb (A) *n.f.* Crusification; burning; teasing; fretting; vexing.

صلب șulb (A) *n.m.* The loins; spine; the back-bone; offspring.

صلبی șulbī (A) *adj.* Descended or sprung from; legitimate.

صلح șulḥ (A) *n.f.* Peace; reconciliation; treaty; truce; concord; friendship.

صلح شکنی șulḥ shikani, *n.f.* Breach of the peace.

صلح کرنا șulḥ karna, *v.* To be reconciled; to make a truce.

صلح کل șulḥ kul, *adj.* Desirous of making friends with all; a peace loving person.

صلح نامه șulḥ nāmah, *n.m.* A treaty of peace; a compromise deed.

صلعم șal'am (A) (Shortening of the words (صلی الله علیه و سلم), may the blessing and mercy of God be upon him.

صلوات ṣalawāt (A) *n.f.* (*plu.* of صلواة *salāt*); Prayers; blessings; benedictions.

صلواتیں سنانا ṣalawāteṅ sunānā, *v.* (ironic and colloq.) To curse; to abuse roundly.

صلواة ṣalāt (A) *n.f.* Prayer; supplication; benediction; one of the five prayers enjoined on Muslims in the course of a day; the فاتحه *Fātiḥah* or the opening chapter of the *Qurān*.

صله ṣilah (A) *n.m.* Conjunction; connection; a present; a gift; renumeration; recompense; a reward; poetic license; the relative particle.

صلۂ رحم یا رحمی ṣilah-ĕ raḥm yā raḥmī, *n.m.* Loving or treating one's own relatives well.

صلیب ṣalīb (A) *n.f.* A cross; a crucifix. *adj.* Hard; three cornered.

صم ṣumm (A) *adj.* Deaf.

صم', بکم' ṣummun bukmun, *adj.* Deaf and dumb; mute; speechless.

صمد ṣamad (A) *n.m.* Lord; master; the eternal; God. *adj.* Eternal; high; perpetual.

صمدانی ṣamadānī (A) *adj.* Divine; eternal.

صمصام ṣamṣām (A) *n.f.* A sharp sword.

صمغ ṣamagh (A) *n.m.* Gum.

صمغ عربی ṣamagh-ĕ ʻarabī, *n.m.* Gum Arabic (used as a medicine).

صمیم ṣamīm (A) *adj.* Pure; unmixed; sincere. *n.m.* Core; bottom.

صنادید ṣanādīd (A) *n.m.* (*plu.* of صندید *ṣandīd*) Princes; chiefs; noblemen; misfortunes; dangers; formidable events.

صناع ṣannāʻ (A) *adj.* Very skilful or expert in workmanship. *n.m.* A skilful artist.

صنائع ṣanā'eʻ (A) (*plu.* of صناعت *ṣanāʻat*) Arts; artifices; miracles.

صنائع بدائع ṣanā'eʻ badā'eʻ, *n.m.* Rhetoric; figures of speech; rare and wonderful works of arts.

صندل ṣandal (A) *n.m.* Sandal wood; sanders.

صندلی ṣandalī (A&P) *adj.* Made of sandal wood; *n.m.* An eunuch; *n.f.* A bench; a seat; a chair.

صندوق ṣundūq yā ṣandūq (A) *n.m.* A box; a trunk; cabinet; case; chest; coffer; coffin.

صندوقچه ، صندوقچی ṣandūqchah, ṣandūqchī, *n.m.* A small box; a casket.

صنعت ṣanʻat (A) *n.f.* Art; trade; skill; industry; manufacturing; work of art; miracle; handicraft; fabrication; machine; mystery; a figure of speech.

صنعت گر ṣanʻat gar, *n.m.* An artist; a mechanic; a craftsman; an artisan.

صنعت گری ṣanʻat garī, *n.f.* Manufacture; mechanism; art; producing great works of art; skill.

صنعتی ṣanʻatī, *adj.* Artistic; industrial.

صنف ṣinf (A) *n.f.* Species; kind; sort.

صنف نازک ṣinf-ĕ nāzik, *n.f.* Fair sex; woman-kind.

صنم ṣanam (A) *n.m.* An idol; a mistress; a lover; a sweetheart; a game among children.

صنم خانه یا کده ṣanam khānah yā kadah, *n.m.* An idol temple; a pagoda.

صنوبر ṣanobar (A) *n.m.* A cone-bearing tree; fir; pine-tree.

صواب ṣawāb (A) *n.m.* Rectitude; right saying or doing; right course; a virtuous action; success.

صواب دید ṣawāb dīd, *n.f.* Approval; good opinion; advisability; expediency.

صوبجات ṣūbajāt (P) *n.m.* (*plu.* of صوبہ ṣūbah) Provinces.

صوبہ ṣūbah (A) *n.m.* A province.

صوبہ دار ṣubah dār, *n.m.* The governor of a province; a military commissioned officer.

صوبہ داری ṣubah dāri, *n.f.* Governorship of a province.

صوت ṣaut (A) *n.f.* Sound; voice; clamour; noise; calling for help; shout; shriek of distress.

صور ṣūr (A) *n.m.* A horn; a trumpet.

صور ṣuwar (A) *n.f.* (*plu.* of صورت ṣūrat) Forms; figures; shapes.

صورت ṣūrat (A) *n.f.* Form; figure; shape; face; countenance; appearance; probability; aspect; manner; means; condition; state; circumstance; plight; mood (*Gram.*)

صورت آشنا ṣūrat āshnā, *adj.* Known by sight; slight acquaintance; a cap acquaintance.

صورت آشنائی sūrat āshnā'i, *n.f.* Acquaintance.

صورت بدلنا ṣūrat badalnā, *v.* To change; to transform; to metamorphose.

صورت بگاڑنا ṣūrat bigaṛnā, *v.* To disfigure; to deform.

صورت بنانا ṣūrat banānā, *v.* To give shape to; to form; to personate; to disguise; to feign; to make faces at one.

صورت پذیر ہونا ṣūrat pazīr honā, *v.* To come to pass; to come into existence; to assume or receive form.

صورت حال sūrat-ĕ ḥāl, *n.f.* A statement of facts or circumstances of a case; a written declaration; the present condition; state of affair.

صورت دکھانا ṣūrat dikhānā, *v.* To appear; to present oneself.

صورت کرنا ṣurat karna, *v.* To plan.

صورت گر ṣūrat gar, *n.m.* A painter; a sculptor.

صورتاً ṣūratan (A) *adv.* Apparently; as it appears.

صوری ṣūri (A) *adj.* Exterior; apparent; external.

صوف ṣūf (A) *n.m.* A kind of mixed cotton and silk cloth; a kind of woollen cloth; a piece of cloth dropped in the inkpot to help proper inking of the pen.

صوفی ṣūfi (A) *n.m.* A sect of Muslim devotees; an abstemious person; one clothed in woollen clothes. *adj.* Wise; woollen.

صولت ṣaulat (A) *n.f.* Fury; violence; impetuosity.

صوم ṣaum (A) *n.m.* Fasting.

صومعہ ṣauma'h (A) *n.m.* A monastery; the cell of a recluse; hermitage.

صہبا ṣahbā (A) *n.f.* Wine; especially red wine.

صیاد ṣaiyyād (A) *n.m.* A hunter; a fowler; a fisherman.

صیام ṣiyyām (A) *n.m.* (*plu.* of صوم saum) Fast; (*plu* of صائم sā'im) Fasting person.

صیانت ṣiyānat (A) *n.f.* Preserving; guarding; keeping; preservation; support; defence.

صید ṣaiḍ (A) *n.m.* Game; prey; chase; quarry.

صید افگن ṣaid afgan, *n.m.* A hunter; one who kills game.

صید گاہ said gāh, *n.f.* Hunting ground.

صیغہ ṣighah (A) *n.m.* A mould (for casting metal); trade; profession; section; department; tense; case; person; gender and number (*Gram.*); a form of words used at a Muslim marriage.

صیغہ گردانا ṣighah gardānnā, *v.* To conjugate.

صیقل ṣaiqal (A) *n.f.* Polishing; cleaning.

صیقل گر ṣaiqal gar, *n.m.* A polisher; a burnisher.

صیہونیت saihūniyat (A) *n.f.* Zionism.

ض zād yā zuād, called ẓād-i-mu'jamah is the twenty-first letter of the Urdu, the eighteenth of the Persian and the fifteenth of the Arabic alphabet. Its pronunciation, in Arabic, has the mixed sound of *dw*, but in Urdu it is pronounced like ẓ. In *abjad* it stands for 800.

ضابط ẓābiṭ (A) *n.m.* A governor; a master; a possessor. *adj.* Strict; punctual; patient; disciplinarian; restrainer; tolerating.

ضابطگی ẓābiṭagi (P) *n.f.* Conformity to rule or law.

بے ضابطگی be ẓābiṭagi, *n.f.* Irregularity; contravention of rules and regulations.

ضابطہ ẓābiṭah (A) *n.m.* Ordinance; rule; regulation; custom; law; code; canon; legal procedure.

ضابطہ برتنا ẓābiṭah baratnā, *v.* To act according to law.

ضابطہ تعزیری ẓābiṭah-ĕ ta'zīri, *n.m.* Penal code.

ضابطہ تعلیم ẓabiṭah-ĕ ta'līm, *n.m.* Educational code.

ضابطہ دیوانی ẓābiṭah-ĕ dīwāni, *n.m.* Civil procedure code.

ضابطہ فوجداری ẓābiṭah-ĕ faujdāri, *n.m.* Criminal procedure code.

با ضابطہ bā ẓābiṭah, *adj.* Regular; formal; according to law.

بے ضابطہ be ẓābiṭah, *adj.* Irregular; unusual; illegal.

خلاف ضابطہ khilāf-ĕ ẓābiṭah, *adj.* Contrary to law and procedure; irregu ar.

ضامن ẓāmin (A) *n.m.* A surety; sponsor; bondsman; security.

ضامن در ضامن zamin dar zamin, *n.m.* A collateral security.

ضامن دینا ẓāmin denā, *v.* To give security.

ضامن لینا ẓāmin lenā, *v.* To ask for security.

ضامنی ẓāminī (A) *n.f.* Security; surety; bail; pledge; guarantee.

فعل ضامنی fe'l · ẓāminı, *n.f.* Security for good conduct.

ضائع ẓa'i' (A) *adj.* Lost; destroyed; perished; wasted; fruitless; abortive.

ضائع کرنا ẓā'i' karnā, *v.* To destroy; to lose; to consume; to waste; to misapply.

ضائع ہونا ẓa'i' hona, *v.* To be wasted; to be lost; to prove fruitless.

ضبط ẓabṭ (A) *n.m.* Guarding; watching over; regulation; taking possession of; confiscation; check; control; government; direction; discipline.

ضبط کرنا ẓabṭ karnā, *v.* To take possession of; to seize; to forfeit; to confiscate; to preserve; to restrain; to control; to check.

ضبط ہونا ẓabṭ honā, *v.* To be seized; to be confiscated; to be forfeited.

ضبطی ẓabṭi, *n.f.* Confiscation; forfeiture; seizure.

ضبطی کا حکم ẓabṭi ka hukm, *n.m.* Confiscation order.

ضخامت ẓakhāmat (A) *n.f.* Thickness; bigness; bulkiness; volume; corpulence; bulk.

ضخیم ẓakhīm (A) *adj.* Voluminous; thick; bulky.

ضد ẓidd (A) *n.f.* The contrary; opposite (of); opposition; contrariety; persistence; stubbornness.

ضد کرنا ẓidd *karnā, v.* To persist; to persevere; to spite; to contradict; to baffle; to importune.

ضد ہونا ẓidd *honā, v.* To be possessed of a spirit of opposition; to be opposed to; to be antagonistic to.

ضدی ẓiddi *adj.* Perverse; naughty; stubborn; wilful; wayward and unmanageable (as a child); obdurate.

ضدین ẓiddain (A) *n.f.* Two things that are opposed to each other; two opposites.

اجتماع ضدین *ijtimā'-ĕ ẓiddain, n.m.* A combination of the two opposites.

ضراب ẓarrāb (A) *n.m.* A coiner; a mint-master; one who stamps or coins.

ضرار ẓirār (A) *n.m.* Reciprocal injury.

ضرب ẓarb (A) *n.f.* A blow; beating; striking; violence; injury; emphasis; impression; stamping; coining; multiplication (*Arith.*); recital.

ضرب اٹھانا ẓarb *uṭhānā, v.* To suffer a loss.

ضرب المثل ẓarb-ul-*maṣal, n.f.* A saying; a proverb.

ضرب دینا ẓarb *denā, v.* To multiply.

ضرب شدید ẓarb-ĕ *shadīd, n.f.* Grievous hurt.

ضرب لگانا ẓarb *lagānā, v.* To give a blow; to strike; to stamp.

ضرب مرکب ẓarb-ĕ *murakkab, n.f.* Compound multiplication; compound injury.

ضرب مفرد ẓarb-ĕ *mufrad, v.* Simple multiplication; simple injury.

ضرب مہلک ẓarb-ĕ *muhlik, v.* Fatal injury.

حاصل ضرب *ḥāṣil* ẓarb, *n.m.* The product (of multiplication).

دارالضرب *dār-uẓ-ẓarb n.f.* A mint.

ضربات ẓarbāt (A) *n.f.* (*plu.* of ضرب ẓarb) Blows; injuries.

ضرر ẓarar (A) *n.m.* Injury; damage; detriment; loss; ruin; defeat; affliction; anguish; poverty; mischief; harm; disadvantage; deficiency.

ضرر آٹھانا ẓarar *uṭhānā, v.* To bear a loss; to incur a loss.

ضرر رساں ẓarar *rasāṅ, adj.* Harmful; injurious.

ضرر رسانی ẓarar *rasāni, n.f.* Causing injury; injuring; hurting; damaging.

ضرور ẓarūr (A) *adj.* Necessary; expedient; unavoidable; needful; requisite; urgent; essential; indispensable; obligatory. *adv.* Of course; absolutely; urgently; certainly; without fail; peremptorily.

ضرورت ẓarūrat (A) *n.f.* Need; compulsion; force; violence; constraint; want; necessity; exigency.

ضرورت پڑتا ẓarūrat *paṛnā, v.* To have the need of; to have occasion for.

ضرورت مند ẓarūrat *mand, adj.* Needy; indigent; necessitous.

ضرورت ایجاد کی ماں ہے ẓarūrat *ijād kī māṅ hai, prov.* Necessity is the mother of invention.

ضرورت کے وقت گدھے کو بھی باپ بنا لیتے ھیں ẓarūrat *ke waqt gadhe ko bhī bāp banā lete haiṅ, prov.* Many kiss the child for nurse's sake.

ضرورتاً ẓarūrata*n̲* (A) *adv.* By necessity; out of necessity; necessarily.

ضروری ẓarūrī, *adj.* Necessary; indispensable; unavoidable.

ضروریات ẓarūriyāt (A) *n.f.* necessaries; necessities; requisites.

ضروریات زندگی ẓarūriyāt-ĕ ẓindagi, *n.f.* Necessities of life.

ضریح zarih (A) n.f. A grave; a tomb; a model of the tomb of Imam Hasan and Husain.

ضعف zu'f (A) n.m. Weakness; feebleness; infirmity.

ضعف آنا zu'f ānā, v. To swoon; to faint.

ضعف باہ zu'f-ĕ bāh, n.m. Weakness of virility; sexual weakness.

ضعف بصارت zu'f-ĕ basārat, n.m. Weakness of eyesight.

ضعف جگر zu'f-ĕ jigar, n.m. Weakness of the liver.

ضعف دماغ zu'f-ĕ dimāgh, n.m. Weakness of brain; imbecility of mind.

ضعف مثانہ zu'f-ĕ masānah, n.m. Irritability of the bladder.

ضعف معدہ zu'f-ĕ mi'dā n.m. Weak digestion; dyspepsia.

ضعفاء zu'afā' (A) n.m. (plu. of ضعیف za'īf), Weak people.

ضعیف za'īf (A) adj. Weak; infirm; feeble; old; poor; impotent; emaciated; faint; frail.

ضعیف‌الاعتقاد za'īf-ul-'itiqād, adj. Of weak faith or belief; credulous.

ضعیف البنیان za'īf-ul-bunyān, adj. Of frail foundation.

ضعیف الجثہ za'īf-ul-jussah, adj. Weak or emaciated in body; insignificant in size or body.

ضعیف‌العقل za'īf-ul-a'ql, adj. Weak-minded.

ضعیف ہونا za'if honā, v. To be weak; to become old.

ضعیفی za'īfī, n.f. Old age; infirmity; weakness; exhaustion.

ضل zall (A) n.m. An error; fault; vice.

ضلالت ، ضلال zalāl, zalālat (A) n.m./f. Error; fault; vice: ruin; perdition; deviation from the right path.

ضلع zila' (A) n.m. A part; a district; a division; a column (in the page of a book); the art of speaking with double meaning; a kind of punning.

ضلعدار zila'dār, n.m. An officer of the canal department; a district superintendent; a revenue officer.

ضم zamm (A) n.m. Merger; conjunction; incorporation; the vowel point (ُ) pesh.

ضماد zimād (A) n.m. A plaster; liniment; embrocation; ointment; bandage; fillet; poultice.

ضمانت zamānat (A) n.f. Surety; security.

ضمانت دینا یا داخل کرنا zamānat denā yā dākhil karnā, v. To furnish security; to give bail.

ضمانت کے قابل zamānat ke qābil, adj. Bailable

ضمانت نامہ zamānat nāmah, n.m. A security bond: a deed of suretiship.

ضمانتی zamāntī. See ضامن zāmin.

ضمائر zamā'ir (A) n.f. (plu. of ضمیر zamır) Personal pronouns.

ضمن zimn (A) n.m. Clause; section; circumstances; the contents; anything contained or inserted; anything comprehended; subject; idea; conception; suretiship; an obligation.

ضمن میں zimn men, adv. Enclosed; in the fold of; in the course of; by the way.

ضمناً zimnan (A) adv. By the way; by the by: incidentally; by implication; tacitly.

ضمنی zimni (A&P) adj. Implicative; collateral; corroborative.

ضمیر zamīr (A) n.f. The mind; heart; thought; reflection; sense; conscience; conception; idea; comprehension; a personal pronoun.

ضمیمہ ẓamimah (A) *n.m.* An addition; an appendix; a supplement.

ضمیمہ کرنا ẓamimah karna, *v.* To enclose; to annex: to append.

ضمیمہ ہونا ẓamimah hona, *v.* To be enclosed; to be appended.

ضو ẓau (A) *n.f.* Light; sunlight.

ضو فشاں ẓau fishān, *adj.* Shedding light.

ضوابط ẓawabiṭ (A) *n.m.* (*plu.* of ضابطہ ẓābiṭah) Laws; canons; rules; regulations.

قواعد و ضوابط qawā'id-ŏ ẓawābiṭ, *n.m.* Rules and regulations.

ضیا ẓiyā (A) *n.f.* Light; splendour; brilliancy; resplendence.

ضیافت ẓiyāfat (A) *n.f* Feast; a bonquet; convivial entertainment; hospitality; invitation.

ضیافت کرنا ẓiyāfat karnā, *v.* To entertain; to feast; to treat.

ضیغم ẓaigham (A) *n.m.* A lion.

ضیف ẓaif (A) *n.m.* A guest.

ضیق ẓiq (A) *n.f.* Anguish; vexation; melancholy; affliction; anxiety; doubt; oppression of spirit; anything that tortures the mind.

ضیق النفس ẓiq-un-nafs, *n.m.* The asthma; shortness of breath.

ضیق میں آنا یا ہونا ẓiq men ānā yā honā, *v.* To be anxious; to be vexed; to be in straitened circumstances.

ط

ط ṭoe, is the twenty-second letter of the Urdu, the nineteenth of the Persian and the sixteenth of the Arabic alphabet. In Urdu it has the sound of ت but in Arabic it has a stronger and harsher sound than that of ت. In *abjad* it stands for 9.

طاب ṭāb (A) *adj.* Sweet; agreeable; good; pure; exellent.

طابع ṭābi' (A) *n.m.* Printer; seal.

طارق ṭāriq (A) *n.m.* The morning star; a night traveller; name of a great Muslim general who conquered Spain.

طاری ṭāri (A) *adj.* Happening; occurring; intervening.

طاری ہونا ṭāri honā, *v.* To overcome; to overshadow.

طاس ṭās (A) *n.m.* A drinking cup; goblet; bowl; the vessel in which water is cooled; basin of a river; the part of a country through which a river flows; brocade.

طاسہ ṭāsah (A) *n.m.* A kettle-drum; a sort of tambourine.

طاعات ṭā'āt (A) *n.f.* (*plu.* of طاعت ṭā'at) Acts of devotion.

طاعت ṭā'at (A) *n.f.* Obedience; devotion; submission.

طاعون ṭā'ūn (A) *n.m.* Plague; pestilence;

طاغوت ṭāghūt (A) *n.m.* The name of a idol, formerly worshiped by the Arabs; devil; satan.

طاغی ṭāghi (A) *adj.* Violent; rebellious; refractory; insubordinate.

طاق ṭāq (A) *n.m.* An arched building; arch; cupola; a recess in a wall; a shelf; a niche; a window; odd number; *adj.* Unique; singular; rare, old; unrivalled.

طاق ابرو ṭāq-ĕ abrū, *n.m.* The arch of the brow.

طاق بھرنا ṭāq bharnā, *v.* To place a lighted lamp in a mosque as a votive offering.

طاق جفت ṭāq juft, *n.m.* The game of guessing odd or even.

طاق کرنا ṭāq karnā, *v.* To accomplish; to give one a very good training.

طاق هونا ṭāq honā, v. To be accomplished; to be most efficient.

طاق‌نسیاں پر رکھنا ṭāq-ĕ nisyān par rakhnā, v. To forget about a thing; to put in cold storage.

طاقت ṭāqat (A) n.f. Strength; power; might; capacity; ability; energy; power of endurance; force; patience.

طاقت آزمائی ṭāqat āzmā'i, n.f. Trial of strength.

طاقتور ṭāqat war, adj. Powerful; strong.

طاقچہ ṭāqchah (P) n.m. A small recess; a small shelf.

طاقی ṭāqī (P) adj. Wall-eyed (a horse); squint-eyed (a man); arched.

طالب ṭālib (A) n.m. A seeker; an enquirer; a lover; a candidate.

طالب خدا ṭālib-ĕ khudā, n.m. One who seeks God.

طالب دنیا ṭālib-ĕ dunyā, n.m. Worldly minded; a man of the world.

طالب دیدار ṭālib-ĕ dīdār, n.m. One who longs for the sight (of his beloved); a lover; a suitor.

طالب زر ṭālib-ĕ zar, n.m. A lover of wealth.

طالب علم ṭālib-ĕ i'lm, n.m. A seeker after knowledge; a student.

طالب علمی ṭālib-e i'lmi, n.f. Studentship.

طالب‌ومطلوب ṭālib-ŏ maṭlūb, n.m. The lover and the beloved.

طالع ṭāli' (A) adj. Rising (as the sun); arising; appearing. n.m. Fortune; prosperity; destiny; lot.

طالع آزما ṭāli' āzmā, adj. Adventurist.

طالع آزمائی ṭāli' āzmā'i, n.f. Trying one's luck.

طالع شناس ṭāli' shinās, n.m. A fortune-teller; a soothsayer; an asrologer.

طالع‌مند ، طالع‌ور ṭāli' mand, ṭāli' war, adj. Fortunate; wealthy.

طالوت ṭālūt (A) n.m. Saul (the king).

طامع ṭāmi' (A) adj. Covetous; greedy; desirous.

طاؤس ṭāūs (A) n.m. A peacock.

طاهر ṭāhir (A) adj. Pure; chaste.

طائر ṭā'ir (A) n.m. A bird.

طائر روح ṭā'ir-ĕ rūḥ, n.m. The soul; the life.

طائر قبلہ نما ṭā'ir-ĕ qiblah numā, n.m. The magnetic needle of a conpass.

طائر قدس ṭā'ir-ĕ quds, n.m. The heavenly bird; Gabrial.

طائفہ ṭā'ifah (A) n.m. A gang a band of dancing girls and musicians; a band; a troop; suit; equipage; a carwan.

طب ṭibb (A) n.f. A science of medicine; medical treatment.

طبابت ṭabābat yā ṭibābat, n.f. The practice of medicine; the medical ar.

طباخ ṭabbākh (A) n.m. A cook

طباشیر ṭabāshīr (A) n.f. The sugar of the bamboo.

طباع ṭabbā' (A) adj. Intelligent; quick witted.

طباعت ṭabā'at (A) n.f. Printing.

طباعی ṭabbā'i (A) n.f. Inteligence; quick comprehension.

طباق ṭabāq (A) n.m. A large dish or tray; a plate; a basin; a bowl; a vessel for kneading dough (in).

طبائع ṭabāi' (A) n.f. (plu. of طبیعت ṭabi'at) Natures; dispositions; temperaments.

طبع ṭaba' (A) *n.f.* Natural temper; disposition; temperament; quality; edition (of a book); print; impression.

طبع آزمائی ṭaba' āzmā'ī, *n.f.* Trial of skill or genius.

طبع زاد ṭaba' zād, *adj.* An original invention; invention made without the aid of a model. *n.m* Production of genius.

طبع کرنا ṭaba' karnā, *v.* To print; to publish.

طبعی ṭaba'ī (A) *adj.* Natural; innate; physical; constitutional.

طبق ṭabaq (A) *n.m.* Cover; tray; leaf; disc; a layer or stratum.

طبقه ṭabaqah (A) *n.m.* Storey; floor; stage; rank; (*plu.* طبقات ṭabaqāt).

طبقه بندی ṭabaqah bandī, *n.f.* Classification.

طبل ṭabl yā ṭabal, (A) *n.m.* A drum.

طبله ṭablah, *n.m.* A small tambourine.

طبی ṭibbī (A) *adj.* Medical.

طبیب ṭabīb (A) *n.m.* A native physician.

طبیعت ṭabī'at (A) *n.f.* Nature; temperament; mind; disposition; intrinsic quality; property; constitution.

طبیعت آنا ṭabī'at ānā, *v.* To be fond (of); to fall in love (with); to get attached (to).

طبیعت الجهنا ṭabī'at ulajhnā, *v.* To be entangled; to be puzzled.

طبیعت بحال هونا ṭabī'at bahāl honā, *v.* To recover from illness.

طبیعت بگڑنا ṭabī'at bigaṛnā, *v.* To feel sick; to be excited; to feel nausea.

طبیعت بهرجانا ṭabī'at bhar jānā, *v.* The mind to be satisfied; to be satiated.

طبیعت بهلنا ṭabī'at behalnā, *v.* To be amused or diverted.

طبیعت پر زور ڈالنا ṭabī'at par zor ḍālnā, *v.* To exert; to press one's mind.

طبیعت ثانیه ṭabī'at-ĕ ṣāniyah, *n.f.* Second nature.

طبیعت علیل هونا ṭabī'at aliil honā, To be indisposed; to fall sick.

طبیعت لگنا ṭabī'at lagnā, *v.* To take interest in; to be attached to.

طبیعت نه لگنا ṭabī't nah lagnā, *v.* To be disinclined towards; to feel uncomfortable.

طبیعی ṭabī'ī (A) *adj.* Natural; innate; physical; intrinsic. *n.m.* Naturalist; physicist.

طپاں ṭapāṅ (P) *adj.* Palpitating; throbbing.

طپیده ṭapīdah (P) *adj.* Agitated; distressed; heated; palpitating.

طحال ṭiḥāl (A) *n.* Spleen; milt.

طرار ṭarrār (A) *adj.* Eloquent; sharp tongued.

طراره ṭarrārah *n.m.* Sharpness; quickness; speed; expedition.

طرارے بهرنا ṭarrare bharnā, *v.* To run at full speed; to stretch out.

طراری ṭarrarī, *n.f.* Quickness; sharpness.

طراز ṭarāz yā ṭirāz (A & P) *n.m.* Embroidery; ornamental border; lace; fringe.

طرازی ṭarāzī (P) *n.f.* Adorning; ornamenting.

طراوت ṭarāwat (A) *n.f.* Freshness; greenness; verdure; dampness; moisture; humidity.

طرب ṭarab (A) *n.f.* Joy; mirth; cheerfulness; hilarity; merriment.

طرب انگیز ṭarab angez, *adj.* Exciting mirth or joys.

طرح ṭarḥ (A) *n.f.* Manner; mode; form; design; position; description; plan; air; laying foundation; condition; ejection; throwing; a line or verse set.

طرح اڑانا ṭarḥ urānā, *v.* To copy; to imitate; to sketch.

طرح بطرح ṭarḥ baṭarḥ; *adj.* Varied.

طرح دار ṭarḥ dār, *adj.* Beautiful; graceful; well-shaped; handsome; elegant; stylish.

طرح دینا ṭarḥ denā, *v.* To disregard; to turn a deaf ear to; to pass over; to overlook; to set a verse.

طرح دکھانا ṭarḥ dikhānā, *v.* To assume airs; to affect.

طرح ڈالنا ṭarḥ ḍālnā, *v.* To lay the foundation of; to plan out.

طرز ṭarz (A) *n.f./m.* Fashion; manner; form; way.

طرز اڑانا ṭarz uṛānā, *v.* To copy a fashion.

طرزتحریر ṭarz-ĕ taḥrir, *n.f.* Style or mode of writing.

طرز کلام ṭarz-ĕ kalām, *n.m.* Manner of talking; learned discourse; diction; phraseology; idiom.

طرف ṭaraf (A) *n.f.* Side; margin; corner; quarter; extremity; direction; end; limit. *prep.* Towards; in the direction of; in lieu of.

طرف دار ṭaraf dār, *n.m.* A partisan; an assistant; follower; prejudiced; supporter. *adj.* Partial.

طرفداری ṭaraf dāri, *n.f.* Partiality; partisanship; attachment to a party; assistance.

طرفداری کرنا ṭaraf dāri karnā, *v.* To side with; to be partial.

ایک طرف ek ṭaraf, *adj.* Apart; separate.

برطرف bar ṭaraf, *adv.* Aside; out of the question. *adj.* Dismissed (from office).

برطرف کرنا bar ṭaraf karnā, *v.* To put aside; to dismiss.

طرفگی ṭurfagī (P) *n.f.* Rareness; wonderfulness.

طرفه ṭurfah (A) *adj.* Strange; agreeable; wonderful; extraordinary; rare.

طرفه ماجرا ṭurfah mājrā, *n.m.* A wonderful fact; something rare.

طرفه معجون ṭurfah ma'jūn, *n.f.* A mixture of the opposites.

طرفة ṭarfat (A) *n,f.* Winking of the eye.

طرفة العين میں ṭurfah-tul-a'in meṅ, *adj.* In the twinkling of an eye; immediately.

طرفین ṭarafain (A) *n.m.* Both parties; parties concerned.

طرق ṭuruq (A) *n.m.* (*plu.* of طریق ṭarīq) Ways; methods; manners; roads; fashions; customs.

طره ṭurrah (P) *n.m.* An ornamental tassel worn in the turban; a crest; a tuft; forelock; curl; border; ringlet; nosegay.

طره دار ṭurrah dār, *adj.* Crested.

طره لگانا ṭurrah lagānā, *v.* To be vain.

طریق ṭariq (A) *n.m.* Way; path, manner; fashion; road; rite; observance; custom; religion.

طریق الشمس ṭariq ush-shams, *n.m.* The sun's course; the ecliptic.

طریقت ṭarīqat (A) *n.f.* Way; path; mode; rule; rite, fashion; religion; custom, observances.

اهل طریقت ahl-ĕ ṭarīqat, *n.m.* Religious persons; devotees; a sect of صوفی Sufi.

طریقه ṭarīqah (A) *n.m.* Manner; custom; rite; method; way.

طریقه بتانا ṭarīqah batānā, *v.* To show the way; to direct; to point out the proper course.

طریقه برتنا ṭarīqah baratnā, *v.* To work a system.

طشت ṭasht (P) *n.m.* A large basin; ewer or cup; a bowl.

طشت ازبام هونا ṭasht az bām honā, *v.* Leakage of a secret; to come to be known; to be known all over.

طشتری tashtari, *n.f.* A small plate; a saucer.

طعام ṭa'ām (A) n.m. Victuals; food; eating.

طعمہ ṭu'mah (A) n.m. Food; bait; a lure; prey.

طعن ṭa'n (A) n.m. Blame; reproach; chiding; censure; disapprobation; taunt; reviling.

طعن و تشنیع ṭa'n-ŏ tashni', n.f. Reproach; taunt.

طعنہ ṭa'nah (A) n.m. See طعن ṭa'n.

طعنہ تشنہ ṭa'nah tishnah, n.m. See طعن و تشنیع ṭa'n-o-tashnī'.

طعنہ دینا ṭa'nah denā, v. To taunt; to ridicule; to deride.

طعنہ زنی ṭa'nah zani, n.f. Reproaching; taunting; jeering.

طعنہ مارنا ṭa'nah marnā, v. To jeer; to reproach; to ridicule; to taunt.

طغرا ṭughrā (A) n.m. A sort of hand-writing; a monogram; letters; diplomas on which royal titles are written in large thick characters; the imperial signature.

طغیان ṭughyān (A) n.m. Rebellion; sedition; insolence; perverseness; disobedience.

طغیانی ṭughyānī (A) n.f. Over-flowing; deluge; inundation; excess; flood; spate.

طغیانی پرھونا ṭughyānī per honā, v. To be in spate; to be flooded.

طغیانی کی نہریں ṭughyānī kī nahreṅ n.f. Inundated canals.

طفل ṭifl (A) n.m. An infant; a child; a young of an animal.

طفل شیر خوار ṭifl-ĕ shīr khwār, n.m. A suckling child; a baby.

طفل مکتب ṭifl-ĕ maktab, n.m. A school boy; raw and unexperienced person.

طفلانہ ṭiflānah (A) adj. Childlike; childish.

طفلی' طفولیت ṭiflī, ṭafuliyat (A) n.f. Infancy; childhood.

طفیل ṭufail (A) n.m. Intervention; mediation; means. adj. By the means of; through the agency of.

طفیلی ṭufailī (P) n.m. A companion; a glutton; a loafer; a parasite; a sponger; a hanger on.

طلا ṭilā (A) n.m. Gold; gold fringe; liniment; ointment; plaster.

طلا ساز یا طلا کار ṭilā sāz yā ṭila kār, n.m. A gilder.

طلاق ṭalāq (A) n.f. Divorce; repudiation.

طلاق دینا ṭalāq denā, v. To divorce; to repudiate, to cast away.

طلاق نامہ ṭalāq nāmah, n.m. A deed of divorce.

طلاقت ṭalāqat (A) n.m. Eloquence; fluence.

طلائی ṭilā'ī (A) adj. Golden.

طلب ṭalab (A) n.f. Search; enquiry; demand; desire; wish; application; request; solicitation, pay; wages; salary; sending for; summons.

طلب بجھانا ṭalab bujhānā, v. To satisfy one's desire or appetite for drinking or smoking.

طلب کرنا ṭalab karnā, v. To seek; to ask for; to summon; to demand; to require.

طلب گار ṭalab gār, n.m. A seeker; a claimant; a creditor. adj. Desiring; seeking; desirous.

طلب نامہ ṭalab nāmah, n.m. Summons; citation.

طلبانہ ṭalabānah, n.m. Fees paid to peons for serving a process; process serving fees.

طلبہ' طلاب ṭalabah, ṭullāb (A) n.m. (plu. of ṭālib طالب) Students; pupils; seekers.

طلبی ṭalabī, n.f. Summons; request; demand.

طلسم ṭilism (A) n.m. An Enchantment; a magic; a spell; talisman.

طلسم باندھنا ṭilism bāndhnā, v. To perform a wonder.

طلسمی ، طلسماتی ṭilismī, ṭilismātī, *adj.* Talismanic; magical; mystical.

طلعت ṭal'at (A) *n.f.* Appearance; countenance; face; aspect.

طلوع ṭulū' (A) *n.m.* Rising (as of the sun, moon or stars).

طلوع ہونا ṭulū' honā, *v.* To rise (see &c.)

طماع ṭammā' (A) *adj.* Covetous; avaricious; wishful; greedy.

طمانچہ ṭamāṅchah (P) *n.m.* A slap; a buffet; a blow; a box; thump.

طمانچہ مارنا، جڑنا ṭamāṅchah mārnā, jaṛnā, *v.* To give a slap or blow.

طمانیت ṭamaniyat (A) *n.f.* Rest; repose; tranquillity; calmness; composure; happiness; joy; satisfaction.

طمطراق ṭamṭarāq (P) *n.m.* Pomp; show, magnificence; granduer.

طمع ṭama' (A) *n.f.* Coveting; greed; ambition; avarice; covetousness; greediness; allurement; temptation; avidity.

طمع خام ṭama'-ĕ khām, *n.f.* Desire for the impossible.

طمع دینا ṭama' denā, *v.* To allure; to tempt; to bribe; to covet.

طمع کرنا ṭama' karnā, *v.* To covet; to get tempted.

طمنچہ ṭamanchah, *n.m.* A pistol.

طمنچہ چھوڑنا ṭamanchah chhornā, *v.* To fire a pistol

طناب ṭanāb (A) *n.f.* Rope of a tent.

طناز ṭannāz (A) *adj.* Playful; mirthful; facetious; satirist; jocund; jocose; sportive; coquettish.

طنازی ṭannāzi, *n.f.* Playfulness; facetiousness; jocoseness.

طنب ṭunub (A) *n.f.* Cord or rope of a tent or curtain.

طنبور ṭaṅbūr(A) *n.m.* A Turkish guitar with six wires or strings; a drum; a tambour.

طنبورہ ṭaṅbūrah (A) *n.m.* A guitar; a small kind of tambour.

طنز ṭanz (A) *n.m.* Mocking, ridiculing; sneer; taunt; sarcasm; satire; pleasantry.

طنز کرنا ṭanz karnā, *v.* To taunt; to mock.

طنزاً ṭanzan (A) *adj.* In joke; jeeringly; tauntingly; ironically; sneeringly; sarcastically.

طنطنہ ṭanṭanah (A) *n.m.* Sound; noise; pomp; dignity; state; pride; vanity; rumour; show of authority; clamour, hubbub.

طواف ṭawāf (A) *n.m.* Turning round and round; circumambulating; making a circuit of holy Ka'aba or other holy place; encompassing; pilgrimage.

طوالت ṭawālat (A) *n.f.* Protractedness; prolonging.

طوائف ṭawā'if (A) *n.m.* (*plu.* of طائفہ ṭā'ifah) Bands; groups; hordes. *n.f.* A dancing girl; a female singer; a prostitute.

طوائف الملوکی ṭawā'if-ul-mulūki, *n.f.* Anarchy; disorder.

طوبیٰ ṭūbā (A) *adj.* Very delicious; fragrant; sweet smelling. *n.m.* The name of a tree in Paradise whose fruit is said to be most delicious.

طور ṭaur (A) *n.m.* Manner; condition; state; mode; conduct; fashion.

طور طریقہ ṭaur tarīqah, *n.m.* Ways; manners; practices.

طور بے طور ہونا ṭaur be ṭaur honā, *v.* To be in a critical condition; to be at the point of death; to be topsy turvy.

بطور ba ṭaur, *adv.* In the way of.

طور ṭur (A) *n.m.* Mount Sanai.

طوس ṭūs (P) *n.m.* Name of a city in خراسان *khurāsān*; a sort of woollen cloth.

طوسی ṭūsī (P) *adj.* A resident of طوس ṭūs as Firdausi. *n.m.* Brown or purple colour.

طوطا ṭoṭā (P) *n.m.* See توتا *toṭā*.

طوطی ṭūṭī (P) *n.f.* See توتی *tūṭī*.

طوطیا ṭūṭiyā (P) *n.* Blue vitriol; sulphate of copper.

طوع ṭau' (A) *n.m.* Obedience; obeying.

طوعاً و کرھاً ṭau'an wa karhan (A) *adv.* Willingly or unwillingly; willy-nilly.

طوفان ṭūfān (A) *n.m.* A storm of wind and rain; a hurricane; tempest, inundation; deluge; flood; riot; commotion; calumny; a great affliction.

طوفان آٹھانا ṭūfān uṭhānā, *v.* To raise a commotion; to calumniate; to make a great noise.

طوفان برپا کرنا ṭūfān barpā karnā, *v.* To kick up a row; to agitate furiously.

طوفان لگانا ṭūfān lagānā, *v.* To calumniate; to defame.

طوفان ھونا ṭūfān honā, *v.* To be a very quarrelsome person.

طوفانی ṭūfānī, *adj.* Stormy; tempestuous; quarrelsome; violent; boisterous; slanderous.

طوق ṭauq (A) *n.m.* A collar; a yoke; a necklace; a chain.

طول ṭūl (A) *n.m.* Length; longitude; diffusiveness; prolixity.

طول البلد ṭul-ūl-balad, *n.m.* Longitude.

طول پکڑنا ṭūl pakaṛnā, *v.* To be drawn out; to keep a matter prolonged; to take long; to last.

طول دینا ṭūl denā, *v.* To lengthen; to elongate; to spin a long yarn.

طول طویل ṭūl ṭawīl, *adj.* Very long; diffuse.

طول کلام ، طول سخن ṭūl-ĕ kalām, ṭūl-ĕ sakhun, *n.m.* Prolixity; verbosity; length of discourse; circumlocution.

طولاً ṭūlan, *adv.* Lengthwise; by length.

طولانی ṭūlānī (A) *adj.* Lengthy; very long.

طومار ṭūmār (A) *n.m.* A heap; a volume; a long story; a book; a roll of papers; an account book.

طومار باندھنا ṭūmār bāndhnā, *v.* To concoct a story; to fabricate falsehood; to go to a great length; to make a long story of.

طویل ṭawīl (A) *adj.* Long; tall.

طویله ṭawelah (A) *n.m.* A stable; a stall; a long rope with which cattle are tied; a tether.

طهارت ṭahārat (A) *n.f.* Cleanliness; ablution; purity; sanctity.

طهر ṭuhr (A) *n.m.* Purification (after menses).

طهور ṭahūr (A) *adj.* Pure; purifying.

طے ṭai (A) *n.m.* Rolling up; folding; travelling; passing or crossing over; plait; a fold; crease.

طے شده ṭai shudah, *adj.* Settled; decided.

طے کرنا ṭai karnā, *v.* To fold; to roll up; to pass over; to settle; to dispose of; to bring to a conclusion; to constrain; to abridge.

طیار ṭaiyyār (A) *adj.* Flying; running swiftly; fleet; a winged animal. *adj.* Ready.

طیاره ṭaiyyārah (A) *n.m.* Airplane.

طیاری ṭaiyyārī (P) *n.f.* Readiness; preparation; flying.

طیب ، طیبه ṭaiyyib, ṭaiyyibah (A) *adj.* Good; sweet; agreeable; pure; chaste.

طیب ṭīb (A) *n.f.* Perfume; odour, essence; willingness.

به طیب خاطر ba ṭib-ĕ khāṭir, adv. Gladly; willingly.

طیبات ṭaiyyibāt (A) n.f. (plu. of طیبه taiyyibah) Pious women; joys.

طیر ṭair (A) n.m. A bird.

طیش ṭaish (A) n.m. Levity; folly; anger; passion; rage; indignation.

طیش دلانا ṭaish dilānā, v. To enrage.

طینت ṭīnat (A) n.f. Nature; disposition; temperament; genius; a piece of clay.

طیور ṭuyūr (A) n.m. (plu. of طیر ṭair) Birds.

ظ

ظ zoe (in Arabic zā) is the seventeenth letter of the Arabic, twentieth of the Persian and twenty-third of the Urdu alphabet. In Urdu it has the sound of ز z and according to abjad has the numeral value of 900.

ظالم zālim (A) n.m A tyrant; an oppressor. adj. Tyrannical; unjust; cruel.

ظالمانه zālimānah (A & P) adj. Cruel. adv. Cruelly.

ظاهر zahir (A) adj. Apparent; evident; open; manifest; plain; visible; conspicuous. n.m. Outward condition; the outside.

ظاهر بین، پرست zāhir bin, parast, n.m. A superficial observer; one who takes things for what they seem. adj. Minding the outside or external; influenced by outward show.

ظاهر دار zāhir dār, adj. Showy; formal; ostentatious; pretentious; hypocrite; plausible.

ظاهر داری zāhir dārı, n.f. Show; formality; ceremony.

ظاهر داری برتنا zāhir dārī baratnā, v. To make a show of; to pretend; to pass off (for).

ظاهرکرنا zāhir karnā, v. To show; to disclose; to reveal; to exhibit; to pretend; to make a show of; to expose; to announce.

ظاهر میں zahir men, adv. Openly; apparently; plainly; evidently; seemingly; prima facie.

ظاهر و باطن zāhir-ŏ bātin, n.m. Outward appearance and inward qualities; the inside and outside of a person.

ظاهر هونا zāhir honā, v. To become public; to be revealed; to be disclosed; to appear; to become manifest.

ظاهرا zāhirā, adv. Outwardly; manifestly; plainly..

ظاهری zāhiri, (P) adj. External; outward; as it appears from outside.

ظرافت zarāfat (A) n.f. Wit; humour; jocularity; pleasantry; elegance; beauty; politeness.

ظرافتاً zarāfatan (A) adv. In jest; by way of jest; facetiously.

ظرف zarf (A) n.m. Ingenuity; elegance of manners; politeness; beauty; a vase; a vessel.

ظرف زمان zarf-ĕ zamān, n.m. Adverb (of time).

ظرف مکان zarf-ĕ makān, n.m. Adverb (of place)

تنگ ظرف taṅg zarf, adj. Narrow-minded.

عالی ظرف 'ālī zarf, adj. Broad-minded; magnanimous.

ظروف zurūf (A) n.m. (plu. of ظرف zarf) Vessels; utensils.

ظریف zarıf (A) adj. Polite; witty; jocose; comical; ingenius; good; clever.

ظفر zafar (A) n.m. Victory; triumph; gain; success.

ظفر موج zafar mauj, adj. Victorious.

ظفر یاب zafar yāb, adj. Victorious; conquerer.

ظل zill (A) n.m. Shadow; shade; protection; (Geom.) Projection.

ظل اللہ zill lullah, n.m. Shadow of God; King.

ظلم zulm (A) n.m. Oppression; injustice; injury: tyranny; outrage; hardship; violence; wrong; extortion.

ظلم توڑنا، ڈھانا، کرنا zulm torṇā, ḍhanā, karnā, v. To oppress; to tyrannise; to do wrong.

ظلمات zulmāt (A) n.f. (plu. of zulmat ظلمت) Darknesses: regions of darkness; a dark place where the water of immortality is said to be.

ظلمت zulmat (A) n.f. Darkness.

ظلوم zulūm (A) adj. Cruel; most oppressive; tyrannical.

ظن zann (A) n.m. Suspicion; jealousy; evil opinion; wrong impression; presumption.

ظن غالب zunn-ĕ ghālib, n.m. Strong presumption;

ظن کرنا zann karnā, v. To suspect; to surmise.

ظنی zanni (A) adj. Supposed; suspected; believed.

ظہار zihār (A) n.m. Uttering something which has the effect of a divorce; saying to wife "you are like a mother to me."

ظہر zuhr (A) n.m. Midday· the time immediately after the declining of the sun noon.

ظہر zahr (A) n.f. The back.

ظہری zahri, (A) adj. Written on the back of a document.

ظہور zahūr (A) n.m. Appearing; arising; visibility; manifestation; coming to pass; becoming visible.

ظہور میں آنا zuhūr men ānā, v. To appear; to occur; to arise.

ظہیر zahir (A) n.m. An assistant; an ally; an associate.

ع 'ain, called, 'ain-i-mohmilah, is the eighteenth letter of the Arabic, the twenty-first of the Persian and twenty-fourth of the Urdu alphabet. It is peculiarly semitic and occurs in such Urdu words as are borrowed from the Arabic. Its numerical value according to abjad is 70.

عابد 'ābid (A) n.m. An adorer (of God); a worshipper; votary; devotee. adj. Devout; pious; godly; (Fem. عابدہ).

عاج 'āj (A) n.m. Ivory.

عاجز 'ājiz (A) adj. Powerless; weak; humble; dejected; helpless; incompetent; impotent; frustrated; meek; hopeless.

عاجز آنا یا ہونا 'ājiz ānā yā honā, v. To be rendered helpless; to fall short (of).

عاجزانہ 'ājizānah, adv. Humbly; meekly; helplessly; in a weak manner.

عاجزی 'ājizi, n.f. Powerlessness; humility; helplessness; submissiveness; supplication; inability; entreaty.

عاجزی کرنا 'ājizi karnā, v. To implore; to supplicate; to make humble entreaty to; to beseech.

عاجل 'ājil (A) adj. Hastening; speedy; quick; agile; quickly passing away; hasty.

عاد 'ād (A) n.m. A factor (Arith.); an ancient race.

عاداعظم 'ād-ĕ 'āzam, n.m. Highest common factor (Arith).

عاد مشترک 'ād-ĕ mushtarak, n.m. Common factor (Arith.).

عادات 'ādāt (A) n.f. (plu. of عادت 'ādat) Customs; habits.

عادت 'ādat (A) n.f. Habit; custom; practice; manner; usage,

عادت پڑنا 'ādat paṛnā, v. To become a habit; to habituate; to be accustomed; to get the habit of; to be addicted to.

عادت ڈالنا 'ādat ḍālnā, v. To adopt a habit; to get accustomed to; to familiarize.

عادتاً 'ādatan̲ (A) Adv. Habitually; from habit.

عادل 'ādil (A) adj. Just; equitable; upright; sincere; righteous.

عادلانہ 'ādilānah, adv. In a just manner; giving a fair deal.

عادی 'ādī (A) adj. Addicted to; accustomed; habitual; passing; superseding; unjust; wicked.

عادی کرنا 'ādī karnā, v. To accustom (to); to habituate.

عادی مجرم 'ādī mujrim, n.m. Habitual criminal or offender.

عادی ہونا 'ādī honā, v. To form a habit; to be addicted (to).

عار 'ār (A) n.f. Disgrace; shame; reproach; ignominy; bashfulness; modesty.

عارہونا 'ār honā, v. To feel ashamed; to have a feeling of shame.

عارض 'āriẓ (A) n.m. The cheek; the sides of the face; an incident; happening; befalling; an accident; an obstacle; an occurrence.

عارض سیمیں 'āriẓ-ĕ sīmīn, n.m. Silvery cheeks; bright face.

عارض ہونا 'āriẓ honā, v. To happen; to befall; to prove an obstacle; to debar; to complain; to lodge a complaint.

عارضہ 'āriẓah (A) n.m. Disease; trouble; infirmity; sickness; disorder; impediment; obstacle; want; an accident; an event; anything necessary to be done.

عارضہ لاحق ہونا 'āriẓah lāḥiq honā, v. To become a victim of; to have an obstacle.

عارضی 'āriẓī (A) adj. Accidental; casual; not real; temporary.

عارف 'ārif (A) n.m. A holy man; devotee; a mystic; a learned person. adj. Wise; sagacious; pious; devout; possessing knowledge of God and of His kingdom.

عارفانہ 'ārifānah (A & P) adv. Piously; wisely; acutely; devoulty.

عاری 'ārī (A) adj. Void of; tired; weary of; incompetent; incapable of; naked; free from.

عاریت 'āriyyat (A) n.f. Borrowed article; anything on loan which is to be returned.

عاریتاً 'āriyatan̲ (A) adv. On loan.

عاریتاً لینا 'āriyatan̲ lenā, v. To borrow for use.

عاریتی 'āriyyati, adj. Borrowed; lent.

عازم 'āzim (A) adj. Bound for a place; intending; determining; being resolved on; applying the mind to an undertaking.

عاشق 'āshiq (A) n.m. A lover; a paramour; a suitor.

عاشق مزاج 'āshiq mizāj, adj. Having the disposition of a lover; Sportive; merry; amorous.

عاشق ہونا 'āshiq honā, v. To be in love; to fall in love (with).

عاشقانہ 'āshiqānah (A & P) adj. Amorous; lover-like.

عاشقی 'āshiqi, n.f. Making love; amour; love; courtship; gallantry; the state of being in love.

عاشورہ 'āshūrah (A) n.m. The first ten days of Muḥarram.

عاصم 'āṣim (A) adj. Virtuous; chaste, protected; safe.

عاصی 'āṣi (A) adj. Sinner; rebellious; disobedient. n.m. A sinner; a criminal; a rebel.

عاطفت 'āṭifat (A) *n.f.* Kindness; benevolence; sympathy; affection.

عافیت 'āfiyat (A) *n.m.* Health; safety; welfare; happiness; prosperity.

عاق 'āqq (A) *adj.* Cutting off (from); severing; undutiful; disobedient; rebellious; refractory.

عاق کرنا 'aqq karnā, *v.* To sever; to disown; to disinherit

عاقبت 'āqibat (A) *n.f.* The end; termination; conclusion; futurity; future life. *adv.* Finally; at the end; at last; after all.

عاقبت اندیش 'āqibat andesh, *adj.* Provident; considerate; discreet; looking into futurity; far seeing; prudent.

عاقبت اندیشی 'āqibat andeshī, *n.f.* Foresight; prudence; regard to the future or consequences.

عاقبت بگاڑنا 'āqibat bigāṛna, *v.* To mar one's future state of bliss; to spoil one's career.

عاقرقرحا 'āqarqarḥā (A) *n.m.* Pellitory; a medicine.

عاقل 'āqil (A) *adj.* Wise; sensible; intelligent.

عاقلانہ 'āqilānah, *adv.* Prudently; wisely.

عالم 'ālam (A) *n.m.* The world; universe; regions; state; beauty; the public; scene; period; condition; peoples; creatures; age; concourse.

عالم آرا 'ālam ārā, *adj.* World adorning or beautifying.

عالم افروز 'ālam afroz, *adj.* World-illuminating.

عالم بالا 'ālam-ĕ bālā, *n.m.* The world above the heavens; the people of the heavens.

عالم پناہ 'ālam panāh, *n.m.* Asylum of the world; a king.

عالم تاب 'ālam tab, *adj.* World-inflaming; world-warming; world-illuminating.

عالم خیال 'alam-ĕ khayal, *adj.* Regions of thought; imaginary world.

عالم سفلی 'alam-ĕ siflī, *n.m.* The lower region; the earth.

عالم علوی 'alam-ĕ 'ulwī, *n.m.* The upper region; heavens.

عالم غیب 'alam-ĕ ghaib, *n.m.* The unknown region; the invisible world; the next world.

عالم فانی 'alam-ĕ fānī, *n.m.* The perishable world; this world.

عالم گیر 'alam gīr, *adj.* World-conquering; world-wide; universal.

عالم مستی 'ālam-ĕ mastī, *n.m.* Intoxication; lasciviousness; lustfulness; heat period.

عالم 'ālim (A) *n.m.* A learned man; one versed in science and literature. *adj.* Learned; knowing; wise; intelligent; sage.

عالم الغیب 'ālim-ul-ghaib, *n.m.* The Omniscient; knowing the visible and the invisible.

عالمانہ 'ālimānah, *adv.* Like a learned man; wisely.

عالمی 'ālamī (A) *adj.* World-wide; universal; global.

عالی 'ālī (A) *adj.* High; sublime; elevated; eminent; exalted; grand.

عالی تبار 'ālī tabar, *adj.* Of high descent; of noble lineage.

عالی جاہ 'ālī jāh, *adj. intej.* Of high rank; your highness! your excellency! magnificent.

عالی جناب 'ālī janab, *adj./intej.* Of high rank; your highness!

عالی خاندان 'ālī khāndān, *adj.* Of noble birth; of a high family.

عالی دماغ *'āli dimāgh, adj.* Sharp-witted; intelligent; wise.

عالی رتبہ یا قدر *'āli rutbah yā qadr, adj.* Of high dignity or position; greatly esteemed.

عالی شان *'āli shan, adj.* Magnificent; splendid; of high rank.

عالی ظرف *'āli zarf, adj.* Magnanimous.

عالی فطرت یا ہمت *'āli fitrat yā himmat, adj.* High-minded; ambitious.

عام *'ām* (A) *adj.* Common; public; general; ordinary.

عام فہم *'ām fahm, adj.* Intelligible to all; simple and easy.

عامرہ *'āmirah* (A) *adj.* Royal; imperial; abundant; full; rich; inhabited; cultivated; fertile.

عامل *'āmil* (A) *n.m.* A worker; a doer; an agent; an operator; an administrator; a ruler; a governor; collector of revenue; a conjurer; a magician.

عامہ *'āmmah* (A) *adj.* Relating to the masses; common; whole; entire.

عامی *'āmi* (A) *adj.* Common. *n.m.* Commoner.

عامیانہ *'āmiyānah* (A) *adj.* Vulgar; popular.

عائد *'ā'id* (A) *adj.* Turning towards; happening; befalling; referring to; coming back; reverting; being restored; returning; subject to; liable; exposed to.

عائد ہونا *'ā'id honā, v.* To alight; to rest upon; to be liable to; to come upon; to be subject to.

عبا *'abā* (A) *n.f.* A cloak; a garment made of goat's hair and generally black in colour.

عباد *'ibād* (A) *n.m.* (*plu.* of عبد *'abd*); Servants; slaves.

عبادات *'ibādāt* (A) *n.f.* (*plu.* of عبادت *'ibādat*) Adoration; prayers.

عبادت *'ibādat* (A) *n.f.* Divine worship; adoration; obedience; service; prayer.

عبادت کرنا *'ibādat karnā, v.* To worship.

عبادت گاہ *'ibādat gāh, n.f.* A place of worship; a mosque; a church; a temple.

عبارت *'ibārat* (A) *n.f.* Composition; style; mode of expression; phraseology; diction; passage of a book.

عبارت آرائی *'ibārat ārā'i, n.f.* Word painting; vigour of style; beautiful expression; ornamenting of style; phraseology.

عبث *'abas* (A) *adj.* Of no avail; vain; profitless; bootless; trifling; idle; absurd. *adv.* In vain; to no purpose; idly; absurdly; uselessly. *n.m.* Vanity; absurdity.

عبد *'abd* (A) *n.m.* A servant of God; a devotee; a slave.

عبرانی، عبری *'ibrānī, 'ibri* (A) *adj.* Hebrew.

عبرت *'ibrat* (A) *n.f.* Warning; admonition; an example.

عبرت انگیز *'ibrat angez, adj.* Serving as a warning; admonitory; exemplary.

عبرت پذیر *'ibrat pazir, adj.* Taking warning.

عبرت پکڑنا *'ibrat pakaṛnā, v.* To take warning (from); to be warned; to take a lesson.

عبرت دلانا *'ibrat dilānā, v.* To make an example of; to teach a lesson.

عبرت‌نما *'ibrat numā, adj.* Exemplary.

عبرت ہونا *'ibrat honā, v.* To be warned; to prove a warning.

عبودیت *'ubūdiyyat* (A) *n.f.* Servitude; devotion; adoration; subjection; reverence; service (of God).

عبور *'ubūr* (A) *n.m.* Passing; crossing (a river); passing over.

عبور دریائے شور *'ubūr daryāe shor, n.m.* Transportation beyond the seas.

عبور کرنا *'ubūr karnā, v.* To pass; to cross (a river).

عبیر *'abir* (A) *n.m.* Saffron; ambergris.

عتاب *'itāb* (A) *n.m.* Reproof; reprimand; reproach; rebuke; anger; displeasure.

عتاب کرنا *'itāb karnā*, *v.* To reprimand; to rebuke.

عتیق *'atiq* (A) *adj.* Ancient; antiquated.

عجائب *'ajā'ib* (A) *n.m.* (*plu.* of عجیبہ *'ajībah*) Wonders; curiosities; miracles; wonderful things.

عجائب خانہ *'ajā'ib khānah*, *n.m.* A museum.

عجائب و غرائب *'ajā'ib-ŏ gharā'ib*, *n.m.* Wonders; curiosities; wonderful and strange things.

عجائبات *'ajā'ibāt* (A) *n.m.* (*plu.* of عجائب *'ajā'ib*) Curiosities; wonders.

عجب *'ajab* (A) *n.m.* Wonder; astonishment. *adj.* Wonderful; astonishing; strange; rare; amazing; miraculous.

عجب *'ujb* (A) *n.m.* Hautiness; arrogance; self-conceit; self-admiration; vanity; pride.

عجز *'ajz* (A) *n.m.* Powerlessness; weakness; impotence; wretchedness.

عجلت *'ijlat* (in Urdu *'ujlat*) (A) *n.m.* Haste; speed; velocity.

عجم *'ajam* (A) *n.m.* Persia; foreigners; barbarians; dumb people; all people except the Arabs.

عجمی *'ajamī* (A) *adj.* Persian; dumb; mute.

عجوبہ *'ajūbah* (*correct* اعجوبہ *u'jūbah*) (A) *n.m.* A wonderful thing; a miracle.

عجوزہ *'ajūzah* (A) *n.f.* An aged woman; a hag.

عجیب *'ajib* (A) *adj.* Wonderful; surprising; rare; astonishing; admirable; unique.

عدالت *'adālat* (A) *n.f.* A court of justice or law; assize; tribunal; a bench; justice; law; equity.

عدالتی *'adālatī*, *adj.* Judicial.

عدالتی کارروائی *'adālatī kār rawā'ī*, *n.f.* Judicial proceedings.

عداوت *'adāwat* (A) *n.f.* Enmity; hostility; hatred; strife; animosity; hate; malice.

عداوت رکھنا *'adāwat rakhnā*, *v.* To bear malice.

عداوتی *'adāwatī*, *adj.* Malicious; hostile; inimical.

عدت *'iddat* (A) *n.f.* Waiting period of a widow or a divorced woman.

عدد *'adad* (A) *n.m.* Number; a figure, one of anything.

عددی *'adadī* (A) *adj.* Numeral; numerical.

صفت عددی *ṣifat-ĕ 'adadi*. Numeral adjective.

عدل *'adl* (A) *n.m.* Justice; equity; rectitude.

عدل کرنا *'adl karnā*, *v.* To do justic; to decide.

عدل گستری *'adl gustarī*, *n.f.* Administration of justice.

عدم *'adam* (A) *n.m.* Non-existence; non-entity; nothing; privation; annihilation; want; default.

عدم ادائیگی *'adam adā'igī*, *n.f.* Non-payment.

عدم استطاعت *'adam istiṭā'at*, *n.f.* Insolvency; want of power or strength; inability to perform.

عدم پیروی *'adam pairawī*, *n.f.* Default of prosecution; non-appearance.

عدم تعمیل *'adam t'amil*, *n.f.* Non-compliance; non-execution; non-service.

عدم ثبوت *'adam ṣubūt*, *n.m.* Absence of proof; want of proof.

عدم جواز *'adam jawāz*, *n.m.* Illegality; absence of authority.

عدم حاضری 'adam ḥāẓiri, n.f. Non-attendance.

عدم فرصتی 'adam furṣatī, n.f. Want of leisure; busyness.

عدم مداخلت 'adam mudākhalat, n.f. Non-intervention.

عدم واقفیت 'adam wāqifiyyat, n.f. Want of information or knowledge; unconsciousness.

کالعدم kāl 'adam, adj. Non-existent; null and void.

کالعدم کرنا kāl 'adam karnā, v. To rescind; to quash; to make void.

کالعدم ہونا kal 'adam honā, v. To become extinct; to come to naught.

ملک عدم mulk-ĕ 'adam, n.m. Next world.

عدن 'adn (A) n.f. Eden; Paradise.

عدو 'adū (A) n.m. Enemy; foe.

عدول 'adūl (A) n.m. Declining; refusing; receding; deserting; returning.

عدول حکمی کرنا 'adūl ḥukmī karnā, v. To disobey orders; to refuse to obey; to be refractory.

عدیل 'adīl (A) n.m. One who dispenses justice. adj. Equitable; just; equal; alike; equivalent.

عدیم 'adīm (A) adj. Not to be found; destitute (of); deprived (of); lacking; being without.

عدیم الفرصت 'adīm-ul-furṣat, adj. Very busy; having no leisure.

عدیم المثال 'adīm-ul-miṣāl, adj. Without a like or parallel; unparalleled; incomparable.

عذاب 'aẕāb (A) n.m. Pain; torment; misfortune; punishment; anguish.

عذاب دینا 'aẕāb denā, v. To torture; to torment.

عذاب مول لینا 'aẕāb mol lenā, v. To bring difficulties to oneself; to invite trouble.

عذاب میں پھنسنا 'aẕāb men phansnā, v. To be involved in difficulties; to suffer pain or punishment.

عذار 'aẕār (A) n.m. Cheek; face.

عذب البیان 'azbul bayān (A) adj. Sweat-tongued; aloquent.

عذر 'uẕr (A) n.m. Excuse; apology; objection; plea.

عذر بے جا 'uẕr-ĕ be jā, n.m. Improper plea.

عذر خواہ 'uẕr khwāh, adj. Apologising; an apologist.

عذر خواہ ہونا 'uẕr khwāh honā, v. To raise an objection.

عذر خواہی 'uẕr khwāhi, q.f. Apology.

عذر دار 'uzr dār, n.m. An objector; a claimant.

عذر داری 'uẕr dārī, n.f. Statement of objections; a cross demand.

عذر قانونی 'uẕr-ĕ qānūnī, n.m. A legal objection.

عذر کے قابل 'uẕr ke qābil, adj. Excusable; objectionable.

عذرلنگ 'uẕr-ĕ lang, n.m. A lame excuse.

عذرا 'aẕrā (A) n.f. A virgin; the sign virgo.

عرائض 'arā'iẓ (A) n.f. (plu. of عریضہ 'ariẓah) Petitions; representations.

عرب 'arab (A) n.m. Arabia; an Arabian.

عربدہ 'arbadah (A) n.m. Conflict; dispute.

عربی 'arabī (A) n.f. The Arabic language; adj. Arabian.

عرس 'urs (A) n.m. Anniversary of a saint.

عرش 'arsh (A) n.m. A roof; a throne; a canopy; the highest sphere (where the throne of God is).

عرش بریں ' عرش معلیٰ 'arsh-ĕ barīn, 'arsh-ĕ mu'allā, n.m. Empyrean; the highest heaven.

عرش پر جھولنا arsh par jhūlnā, v. To rise high up in rank.

عرش پر چڑھانا 'arsh par charhānā, v. To give one a high rank; to exalt; to praise one to the skies.

عرش پر دماغ ہونا 'arsh par dimāgh honā, v. To be very self-conceited; to be proud or haughty.

عرش کے تارے توڑنا 'arsh ke tāre torna, v. To work wonders; to achieve something unachievable.

عرشہ 'arshah (A) n.m. A ship board; a deck.

عرصہ 'arṣah (A) n.m. Time; duration; period; interval; space of time; scope; space; area; a field; a court; a plain; courtyard; chess-board.

عرصہ تنگ ہونا 'arṣah tang honā, n. To have the scope limited.

عرصہ حیات 'arṣah-ĕ ḥayāt, n.m. Span of life.

عرصہ محشر 'arṣah-ĕ maḥshar, n.m. The plain where people will assemble on the day of resurrection.

عرض 'arẓ (A) n.f. A petition; request; solicitation; representation; exposition; breadth; latitude; width; a military muster; a review.

عرض بیگی 'arẓ begi, n.m. An officer who presents letters and representations; an usher.

عرض حال 'ārz-ĕ ḥāl, n.m. A statement of facts; a brief narrative.

عرض داشت 'arz dāsht, n.f. A written petition; a memorial.

عرض کنندہ 'arẓ kunindah, n.m. A petitioner; a solicitor.

عرض معروض 'ārẓ ma'ruz, n.f. The purport or matter of a petition.

عرضاً 'arẓan (A) adj. Breadthwise; as a request; by chance.

عرضی 'ārẓi, n.f. A petition; application; representation; memorial.

عرضی دعویٰ 'ārẓi da'wā, n.m. The first pleading in a suit; a petition of plaint.

عرضی نویس 'ārẓi nawis, n.m. A petition-writer; scrivener; a notary.

عرف 'urf (A) adj. Known (by the name of); commonly called. n.m. Alias.

عرفاً 'urfan (A) adv. According to common law; commonly; arbitrarily.

عرفات 'arafāt (A) n.m. Name of a place about twelve miles from Mecca, where the pilgrims halt and perform Hajj.

عرفان 'irfān (A) n.m. Knowledge; discernment; science; wisdom.

عرفہ 'arfah (A) n.m. The day before the Id or other festival; a vigil.

عرفی 'urfi (A) adj. Well known; notorious; public.

عرق 'araq (A) n.m. Juice; essence; spirit; sop; perspiration.

عرق آجانا 'araq ājānā, v. To sweat; to perspire.

عرق آلودہ 'araq ālūdah, adj. Sweaty; perspiring.

عرق ریزی کرنا 'araq rezi karnā, v. To work hard

عرق عرق ہو جانا 'araq 'araq ho jānā, v. To be drenched in perspiration; to prespire through shame.

عرق کھینچنا 'araq khainchnā, v. To distil.

عرق گیر 'araq gir, n.m. Sweat-cloth (for horses); a pad; a saddle cloth.

عرق 'irq (A) n.f. Vein; soot; nerve; a blood vessel.

عرق النسا 'irq-un-nisā, n.m. Sciatica; a nervous disease.

عروج 'urūj (A) n.m. Ascension; rising; exaltation; height.

عروس 'urus (A) n.f. A bride.

عروسی 'urusi, adj. Bridal; nuptial; a marriage feast.

عروض 'uruz (A) n.m. Versification; prosody.

عروق 'uruq (A) n.f. (plu of عرق 'irq) Veins; nerves.

عریان 'uryan (A) adj. Nacked; bare; nude; devoid (of).

عریانی 'uryāni (A) n.f. Nakedness; nudity.

عریض 'ariz (A) adj. Broad; wide.

عریضہ 'arīzah (A) n.m. A humble petition; a petition; an application.

عز 'izz (A) n.m. Glory; dignity; grandeur; power; excellence; might.

عزا 'aza (A) n.f. Mourning; condolence.

عزاخانہ 'azā khānah, n.m. House in mourning; house of condolence.

عزا دار 'azā dār, adj. In mourning. n.m. One who mourns; a lamenter.

عزا زیل 'āzāzīl (A) n.m. A devil; satan; the fallen angel.

عزائم 'azā'im (A) n.m. (plu of عزم 'azm) Resolutions; undertakings.

عزت 'izzat (A) n.f. Grandeur; glory; dignity; honour; respect; esteem; reputation; fame.

عزت اُتارنا یا بگاڑنا 'izzat utārnā yā bigārnā, v. To disgrace; to insult; to dishonour: to defame; to violate the chastity of.

عزت دار، والا 'izzat dār, wālā adj. Honourable; respectfull; respected; esteemed; powerful.

عزت دینا 'izzat dena, v. To exalt; to dignify; to do honour; to confer honour or dignity upon.

عزت رکھنا 'izzat rakhnā, v. To preserve one's honour or good name.

عزت رہنا 'izzat rahna, v. To be held in esteem; to preserve honour or dignity or good name.

عزت کا لاگو ہونا ، عزت کے پیچھے پڑنا 'izzat ka lāgū honā, 'izzat ke pichhe parna, v. To be bent on ruining the honour or reputation of.

عزت کرنا 'izzat karna, v. To pay respect; to honour; to dignify.

عزت لینا 'izzat lenā, v. To dishonour; to disgrace; to insult; to abuse; to put to shame; to destroy the reputation of.

عزت مآب 'izzat maab, adj. Honourable; master of all honour.

عزت میں بٹا لگنا یا فرق آنا 'izzat men batta lagna ya farq ānā, v. To have one s reputation or character sullied.

بے عزت be 'izzat, adj. Disgraced; dishonoured.

عزرائیل 'izrā'il (A) n.m. The angel of death.

عزل 'azl (A) n.m. Removal from office; dismissal.

عزلت 'uzlat (A) n.f. Retirement; retiring.

عزلت گزیں 'uzlat guzīn, n.m. A recluse; a hermit.

عزم 'azm (A) n.m. Design; resolution; intention; purpose; undertaking; determination; aim.

عزیز 'azīz (A) adj. Lear; beloved; darling; worthy; respected; honoured; esteemed; excellent; precious; friend; powerful; superior. n.m. A dear friend; a relative; a titte of the king of Egypt; an attribute of God, meaning "Omnipotent."

عزیز جاننا یا رکھنا 'azīz jannā yā rakhna, v. To love; to hold dear; to esteem or value highly.

عزیمت 'azimat (A) n.f. Resolution; determination; charm; spell; power of compelling spirits to attend on one; an obligatory ordinance of God.

عساکر 'asakir (A) n.m. (plu. of عسکر 'askar) Armies; troops.

عسر ' عسرت 'usr, 'usrat (A) *n.m.* & *n.f.* Difficulty; distress; hardship; poverty.

عسکر 'askar (A) *n.m.* An army; force; troop.

عسکری 'askari (A) *n.m.* A soldier. *adj* Relating to the army; military.

عسل 'asal (A) *n.m.* Honey.

عسیر 'asīr (A) *adj.* Difficult; hard.

عشاق 'ushshāq (A) *n.m.* (*plu.* of عاشق 'ashiq) Lovers.

عشاء 'ishā' (A) *n.f.* The first watch of the night.

عشاء کی نماز 'ishā' ki namāz, *n.f.* The prayer of the first watch of the night.

عشاء 'ashā' (A) *n.m.* The evening meal; supper.

عشاء ربانی āshā'-ĕ rabbāni, *n.m.* The sacrament of the Lord's supper.

عشائیہ 'ashā'iyah (A) *n.m.* Supper: dinner.

عشبہ 'ushbah (A) *n.m.* Sarsaparilla.

عشر 'ashar (A) *adj.* Ten.

عشر 'ushr (A) *n.m.* A tenth part; a tithe.

عشر عشیر 'ushr-ĕ 'ashīr, *adj.* The tenth of a tenth; a hundredth part; very little.

عشرت 'ishrat (A) *n.f.* Pleasure; enjoyment; delight; mirth; society; pleasant and familiar conversation.

عشرت خانہ یا کدہ 'ishrat khānah yā kadah, *n.m.* A pleasure house; a place of entertainment.

عشرہ 'ashrah (A) *n.m.* The first ten days of *Muharram*; ten days; a decade.

عشرہ کاملہ 'ashrah-ĕ kāmilah, *n.m.* Ten days of fasting before and after the pilgrimage if sacrifice is not offered at *Ka'abah.*

عشرہ مبشرہ 'ashrah-ĕ mubasharah, *n.m.* The most pious ten companions of the Holy Prophet.

عش عش کرنا 'ash 'ash karnā, *v.* To be greatly pleased with; to admire greatly; to praise; to rejoice.

عشق 'ishq (A) *n.m.* Over great love; excessive passion.

عشق باز 'ishq baz, *n.m.* A lover; a gallant; amorous.

عشق بازی 'ishq bāzi, *n.f.* Gallantry; amour; love-making.

عشق پیچہ ' پیچاں 'ishq pechah, pechaṅ, *n.m.* American jasmine.

عشقی 'ishqi (P) *adj.* Amatory; erotic; relating to love.

عشوہ 'ishwah (A) *n.m.* Coquetry; blandishment; ogling; amorous; playfulness; a beacon; a fire seen from a distance; a confused and dubious affair; a dangerous affair; the beginning of darkness at night.

عشوہ ساز ' گر 'ishwah sāz, gar, Coquette; amorously playful.

عشوہ گری 'ishwah gari, *n.f.* Coquetry; ogling.

عشیر 'ashir (A) *n.m.* A tenth part; one-tenth.

عصا 'aṣā (A) *n.m.* A club; a staff; a sceptre; a stick.

عصا بردار 'aṣā bardār, *n.m.* A mace-bearer.

عصا پیری 'aṣā-ĕ piri, *n.m.* An old man's son; an old man's staff.

عصب 'aṣab (A) *n.m.* A tendon; a nerve; a ligament; muscle; sinew.

عصبانی 'aṣabānī (A) *adj.* Nervous; mad; angry; restless; frenzied.

عصبیت 'aṣabiyyat (A) *n.m.* Bigotry; prejudice

عصر 'aṣr (A) *n.m.* Time; age; extract; essence; pith; gist.

عصر کی نماز 'aṣr ki namāz, *n.f.* Afternoon prayer.

هم عصر ham 'aṣr, *n.m.* A contemporary.

عصرانه *'aṣrānah* (A) *n.m.* Afternoon tea; a tea party.

عصفور *'uṣfūr* (A) *n.f.* A sparrow.

عصمت *'iṣmat, 'aṣmat* (A) *n.f.* Defence; protection (from sin); chastity; honour.

عصیان *'iṣyān* (A) *n.m.* Sin; transgression; violence; rebellion.

عضله *'uẓlah* (A) *n.m.* Muscle; tissue; part of the body (*plu.* عضلات *'uẓlāt*).

عضو *'uẓv* (A) *n.m.* Member; limb; joint.

عضو تناسل *'uẓv-ĕ tanāsul, n.m.* Generative organ.

عضو معطل *'uẓv-ĕ mu'aṭṭal, n.m.* A useless limb; a good-for-nothing fellow.

عطا *'aṭā* (A) *n.f.* A gift; present; favour; bounty; endowment.

عطا کرنا *'aṭā karnā, v.* To confer; to bestow; to grant; to accord.

عطار *'aṭṭār* (A) *n.m.* A druggist; an apothecary; a perfumer.

عطارد *'aṭṭārad* (A) *n.m.* The planet Mercury.

عطاری *'aṭṭāri* (A) *n.f.* The business of a perfumer or druggist.

عطائی *'aṭā'i* (A) *n.m.* A self-taught or self-made man; one who possesses natural gifts; an amateur; a quack.

عطر *'iṭr, 'aṭr* (A) *n.m.* Perfume; essence; extract; fragrance.

عطر دان *'iṭr dān, n.m.* Perfume box; scent-case.

عطر کھینچنا *'iṭr khenchnā, v.* To extract the essence.

عطر لگانا *'iṭr lagānā, v.* To apply perfume; to rub scent.

عطش *'aṭash* (A) *n.f.* Thirst.

عطف *'aṭf* (A) *n.m.* Kindness; favour; bounty; affection; a present; inclination; a connective.

عطیه *'aṭiyyah* (A) *n.m.* A grant; assignment.

عظام *'uẓām* (A) *adj.* (*plu.* of عظیم *'aẓim*) Great (persons).

عظمت *'aẓmat* (A) *n.f.* Greatness; magnitude; magnificence; pomp; haughtiness.

عظمی *'uẓmā* (A) *adj.* Greatest.

عظیم *'aẓim* (A) *adj.* Great; high in dignity; large.

عظیم الشان *'aẓim-ush-shān, adj.* Of high station or dignity; magnificent.

عفت *'iffat* (A) *n.f.* Purity; chastity; modesty; decency; virtue; abstinence; continence.

عفریت *'ifrit* (A) *n.m.* Anything frightful or horrible; a demon; spectre; an ogre.

عفو *'afū* (A) *n.m.* Absolution; forgiveness; pardon; remission of sins; excess; surplus.

عفونت *'afūnat* (A) *n.f.* Stinking; stink; corruption; infection.

عفیف *'afif* (A) *adj.* Chaste; virtuous; modest; decorous.

عفیفه *'afifah* (A) *n.f.* A chaste woman; a modest woman.

عقاب *'iqāb* (A) *n.m.* Chastisement; punishment; torture.

عقاب *'uqāb* (A) *n.m.* An eagle.

عقائد *'aqā'id* (A) *n.m.* (*plu.* of عقیده *'aqidah*) Articles of faith; religious tenets.

عقب *'aqab* (A) *adj.* Behind; after; slow. *n.m.* The rear; the heel.

عقبی *'uqbā* (A) *n.f.* End; conclusion; accomplishment; futurity; future state; the next world.

عقد *'aqd* (A) *n.m.* A knot; the marriage knot; marriage; agreement; a covenant; a collar; a necklace; a string.

عقد کرنا *'aqd karnā, v.* To wed; to marry.

عقد نامہ *'aqd nāmah, n.m.* Marriage contract.

عقد ہونا *'aqd honā, v.* To be married.

عقدہ *'uqdah* (A) *n.m.* A knot; a problem; an excrescence at the joints; a mystery; an enigma; an entanglement; an impediment in speech; perplexed affairs; confused words.

عقدہ کشا *'uqdah kushā, adj.* Resolvent of perplexities or difficulties.

عقدہ کشائی *'uqdah kushā'ī, n.f.* The untying or opening of knots or removing of difficulties.

عقرب *'aqrab* (A) *n.m.* A scorpion; the sign Scorpio; a quarrelsome person.

عقرقرحا *'aqar qarḥā.* See عاقر قرحا *'āqar qarḥā.*

عقل *'aql* (A) *n.m.* Opinion; wisdom; sense; understanding; intellect; reason; knowledge; intelligence.

عقل انسانی *'aql-ē insānī, n.f.* Reason; Intellect.

عقل پر پردہ پڑ جانا *'aql par pardah paṛ jānā, v.* To be out of one's wits; to be confused and not to know right from wrong.

عقل چکرانا *'aql chakrānā, v.* To wonder at; to be astonished; to be confused and distracted.

عقل حیوانی *'aql-ē ḥaiwānī, n.f.* Animal instinct.

عقل دنگ ہونا *'aql dang honā, v.* To be astonished.

عقل دوڑانا *'aql dauṛānā, v.* To use one's head; to exercise one's intelligence; to think; to guess.

عقل سے باہر *'aql se bāhar, adj.* Inconceivable; unreasonable; non-sensical; beyond comprehension.

عقل کا دشمن *'aql kā dushman, n.m.* A fool; a blockhead.

عقل کل *'aql-ē kul, n.m.* The sole counsellor; the angel Gabrial.

عقل کے گھوڑے دوڑانا *'aql kē ghoṛe dauṛānā, v.* To exercise one's intellect; to use one's sense.

عقل کے ناخن لو *'aql ke nākhun lo, intj.* Sharpen your wits! be wise!

عقل ماری جانا *'aql mārī jānā, v.* To lose one's wits.

عقل مند *'aql mand, adj.* Wise; intelligent; sensible.

عقل مندی *'aql mandī, n.f.* Intelligence; sagacity; ingenuity; wisdom.

عقل میں آنا *'aql men ānā, v.* To understand.

عقل میں فتور آنا *'aql men futūr ānā, v.* To lose one's intelligence; to be out of wit.

عقلا *'uqalā* (A) *adj.* (*plu.* of عاقل *'āqil*) The wise; the prudent.

عقلاً *'aqlan* (A) *adv.* Reasonably; prudently; by inference; by guess.

عقلی *'aqlī, adj.* Rational; mental, intellectual; judicious.

عقوبت *'uqūbat* (A) *n.f.* Punishment; torture; torment; chastisement.

عقیدت *'aqīdat* (A) *n.f.* Faith; firm belief; a creed.

عقیدہ *'aqīdah* (A) *n.m.* A creed; a doctrine; tenet, a fundamental article of faith.

عقیق *'aqīq* (A) *n.m.* A cornelian.

عقیقہ *'aqīqah* (A) *n.m.* The Muslim ceremony of shaving the head of a newly born child on the sixth day after birth and a sacrifice made on that day; a feast given on that day.

عقیل *'aqīl* (A) *n.m.* A wise and intelligent man; a sensible man.

عقیله 'aqilah (A) n.f. A wise woman.

عقیم 'aqīm (A) adj. Barren; having no children; childless.

عکاس 'akkās (A) n.m. A photographer.

عکاسی 'akkasī, n.f. Photography.

عکس 'aks (A) n.m. Reflection; inversion; photograph; a shadow or reflected image; counterpart; reverse; converse of a proposition in Geometry; spite; opposition.

بر عکس bar 'aks, adv. On the reverse of; contrary to; contrarily; in opposition to; on the contrary.

عکسی 'aksī, adj. Reflective; photographic; illustrated.

عکسی تصویر 'aksī taṣvīr, n.f. A photograph.

علا 'alā (A) n.m. Glory; exaltation; sublimity; superiority.

علا 'ulā (A) adj. High.

علاتی 'allātī (A) adj. Step-brother or sister from the mother's side.

علاج 'ilāj (A) n.m. Medical treatment; medicine; cure; antidote; relief.

علاج بالضد 'ilāj-biẓ-ẓidd, n.m. Allopathy.

علاج بالمثل 'ilāj-bil-miṣl, Homoeopathy.

علاج کرنا 'ilāj karnā, v. To treat medically; to cure; to remedy; to apply a remedy; to find out ways and means of doing a thing.

لا علاج lā 'ilāj, adj. Incurable; irremediable.

علاقه 'ilāqah (A) n.m. Jurisdiction; an estate; region; division; area; circle; tenure; intercourse; connection; affinity; dependency; interest; relation; concern; friendship; business, tape; lace.

علالت 'alālat (A) n.f. Ailment; malady; infirmity.

علام 'allām (A) adj. Most-knowing; all-knowing; omniscient (God); very scientific; very learned.

علام الغیوب 'allām-ul-ghayyūb, adj. Knowing all mysteries; an epithet of God.

علامات 'alāmāt (A) n.f. (plu. of علامت 'alāmat) Signs; marks; symptoms; flags; standards; ensigns.

علامت 'alāmat (A) n.f. A mark; a sign; a symptom; a symbol; an index; a badge; a device; a standard; a flag; coat of arms; ensign; emblem; a signal.

علامت استفهام 'alāmat-ĕ istifhām, n.f. Sign of interrogation.

علامت بلوغت 'alāmat-ĕ bulūghat, n.f. Sign of maturity.

علامه 'allāmah (A) adj. Very learned person.

علانیه 'alāniyah (A) adv. Openly; publicly; aloud.

علاوه 'ilāwah (A) adv. Besides; moreover.

علاوه ازیں 'ilāwah aziṅ, adv. In addition to this; notwithstanding this; moreover.

علائق 'alā'iq (A) n.m. (plu. of علاقه 'ilāqah) Relations; connections; disputes; quarrels; intricacies of life.

علت 'illat (A) n.f. Fault; defect; bad habit; disease; sickness; malady; infirmity; cause; pretence; pretent; excuse; basis; the ground of a charge or accusation.

علت صوری 'illat-ĕ ṣūrī, n.f. Formal cause; apparent cause.

علت غائی 'illat-ĕ ghā'ī, n.f. Final cause; the real reason.

علت مادی 'illat-ĕ māddī, n.f. Material cause.

علت و معلول 'illat-ŏ ma'lūl, n.m. Cause and effect.

علت لگا لینا 'illat lagā lenā, v. To become an addict; to get used to a vice or a bad habit.

علتی 'illatī, adj. Having a fault or vice; of bad habits.

علل 'ilal (A) n.f. (plu. of علت 'illat) Causes.

علم 'ilm (A) n.m. Knowledge; science; literature; learning; doctrine.

علم آب 'ilm-ĕ āb, n.m. Hydrostatics.

علم آواز 'ilm-ĕ āwāz, n.m. Acoustics.

علم اخلاق 'ilm-ĕ akhlāq, n.m. Moral philosophy.

علم ادب 'ilm-ĕ adab, n.m. Ethics; moral science; literature.

علم الارض 'ilm-ul-arẓ, n.m. Geography.

علم الہی 'ilm-ĕ ilahī, n.m. Theology.

علم بلاغت ، بیان ، کلام ، معانی 'ilm-ĕ balāghat, bayān, kalām, ma'ānī, n.m. Rhetoric; oratory; eloquence.

علم جان یا اجسام حیوانات 'ilm-ĕ-jān yā ajsām-ĕ ḥaiwānāt, n.m. Physiology.

علم جمادات 'ilm-ĕ-jamādāt, n.m. Mineralogy.

علم حفظ صحت 'ilm-ĕ ḥifẓ-ĕ ṣiḥḥat, n.m. Hygiene.

علم حیوانات 'ilm-ĕ ḥaiwānāt, n.m. Zoology.

علم دین 'ilm-ĕ dīn, n.m. The science of religion.

علم رمل 'ilm-ĕ ramal, n.m. Geomancy; cleromancy.

علم روشنی 'ilm-ĕ raushani, n.m. Photology.

علم ریاضی 'ilm-ĕ riyāẓī, n.m. Mathematics.

علم شعاع 'ilm-ĕ shu'ā', n.m. Optics; photography; radiology.

علم طبعیات 'ilm-ĕ ṭabiy'āt, n.m. Natural philosophy.

علم طبقات الارض 'ilm-ĕ ṭabqāt-ul-arẓ, n.m. Geology.

علم عروض 'ilm-ĕ 'urūẓ, n.m. Prosody; versification.

علم غیب 'ilm-ĕ ghaib, n.m. The occult sciences; divination; fore-knowledge.

علم قیافه 'ilm-ĕ qayāfah, n.m. Physiognomy.

علم کیمیا 'ilm-ĕ kimiyā, n.m. Chemistry.

علم لدنی 'ilm-ĕ ladunni, n.m. Inspired knowledge.

علم مساحت 'ilm-ĕ masāḥat, n.m. Mensuration.

علم مقناطیس 'ilm-ĕ miqnāṭis, n.m. Magnetism.

علم موجودات 'ilm-ĕ maujūdāt, n.m. Natural science.

علم موسیقی 'ilm-ĕ mausīqī, n.m. Science of music.

علم نباتات 'ilm-ĕ nabātāt, n.m. Botany.

علم نجوم یا ہیئت 'ilm-ĕ nujūm yā hai'at, n.m. Astronomy.

علم و فضل 'ilm-ŏ faẓl, n.m. Knowledge and virtue.

علم ہندسه 'ilm-ĕ hindsah, n.m. Geometry.

علم ہوا 'ilm-ĕ hawā, n.m. Aerology.

علم 'alam (A) n.m. A standard; a banner; a spear; a proper noun (Gram.).

علم بردار 'alam bardār, n.m. Standard bearer.

علما 'ulamā (A) n.m. (plu. of عالم 'ālim) The learned; doctors of law and religion.

علمی 'ilmī (A) adj. Scientific; literary.

علمیت 'ilmiyyat, n.f. Learning; scholarship.

علو 'uluw (A) n.m. Eminence; height; sublimity.

علوم 'ulūm (A) n.m. (plu. of علم 'ilm) Sciences.

علوم جدید یا مروجه 'ulūm-ĕ jadīd yā murawwajah, n.m. Modern sciences.

علوم قدیم 'ulūm-ĕ qadīm, n.m. Ancient sciences.

علوم متعارفه 'ulūm-ĕ-muta'ārifah, n.m. axioms.

علوم مشرق 'ulūm-ĕ mashriqī, n.m. Oriental sciences.

علوم مغربی 'ulūm-ĕ maghribī, n.m. Western or Europeon sciences.

علوم و فنون 'ulūm-ŏ-funūn, n.m. Arts and sciences.

علوی 'alawī (A) n.m. A descendent or follower of Hazrat Alī.

علحدگی 'alāhidagī (P) n.f. Separation.

علحده 'alāhidah (A) adj. Separate; apart. adv. Separately; apiece; distinct; disconnected; asunder; being apart.

علحده رکھنا 'alāhidah rakhnā, v. To set apart.

علی 'alī (A) adj. High in rank; eminent; noble. n.m. Son-in-law of the Holy Prophet, and the fourth Caliph.

علیک سلیک 'alaik salaik, n.f. Acquaintance; familiarity; cap acquaintance.

علیه 'alaihi (A) adv. On him.

علیه الرحمة 'alaih-ir-rahmat, intj. On him (be) the mercy (of God).

علیه السلام 'alaih-is-salām, intj. Peace be upon him; God's blessings be on him.

علیهم 'alaihim (A) adv. On them.

علیل 'alīl (A) adj. Indisposed; sick; weak; out of sorts.

علیم 'alīm (A) adj. Wise; learned. n.m. One who knows everything; an epithet applied to God.

عم 'amm (A) n.m. An uncle; father's brother.

عماد 'imād (A) n.m. A lofty pillar; confidence; reliance; trust; support.

عمارات 'imārāt (A) n.m. (plu. of عمارت 'imārat) Buildings; structures; edifices.

عمارت 'imārat (A) n.f. A building; a structure; an edifice; a fortification; habitation.

عماری 'amārī (A) n.f. A litter or rider's seat with a canopy on an elephant or camel.

عمال 'ummāl (A) n.m. (plu. of عامل 'āmil) Agents; rulers; governors; collectors of revenue.

عمامه 'imāmah (A) n.m. A turban; a tiara.

عمائد 'amā'id (A) n.m. (plu. of عمدة 'umdat) Pillars; supports.

عمائد سلطنت 'amā'id-ĕ saltanat, n.m. Pillars of the state; ministers.

عمد 'amd yā 'amad (A) n.m. Intention; resolution.

عمداً 'amdan yā 'amadan (A) adv. Deliberately; designedly; intentionally; purposely; wilfully; in cold blood.

عمدة 'umdat (P) n.f. A prop; a stay; a support; trust; a pillar; a grandee; confidence; reliance; a title bestowed on people of high rank.

عمدةالملک 'umdat-ul-mulk, n.m. A minister; an officer of high rank.

عمدگی 'umdagī (P) n.f. Greatness; excellence; worth; dignity.

عمده 'umdah (A) adj. Great; fine; nice; noble; major; grand; sumptuous; excellent; important.

عمر 'umr (A) n.f. Age; life-time; period of life; the span of life.

عمر پٹه 'umr pattah, n.m. A lease for life.

عر دراز هو 'umr darāz ho, intj. May (you) live long! may (your) life be long!

عمر رسیده 'umr rasidah, adj. One advanced in years.

عمر طبعی 'umr-ĕ taba'ī, n.f. Natural or normal age.

عمر نوح 'umr-ĕ nūh, n.f. Long life.

عمره 'umrah (A) n.m. Pilgrimage to Mecca on days other than the Hajj days.

عمق 'umuq (A) n.m. Depth; profoundity; intensity.

عمل 'amal (A) n.m. Action; effect; practice; administration; government; jurisdiction; rule; operation; deed; charm; spell; process; time (of day); an enema; an intoxicating drink; habit of taking intoxicants.

عمل پڑھنا 'amal paṛhnā, v. To mutter a spell or charm; to practice a spell.

عمل جراحی 'amal-ĕ jarrāḥi, n.m. Surgery; surgical operation.

عمل داری 'amal dārī, n.f. Government; reign; collectorship.

عمل دخل 'amal dakhl, n.m. Rule; possession; sway.

عمل در آمد کرنا 'amal dar āmad karnā, v. To act upon; to enforce.

عمل در آمد ہونا 'amal dar āmad honā, v. To be acted upon.

عملاً 'amalan̲ (A) adv. Practically; in fact; truly; indeed.

عمله 'amalah (A) n.m. Operators; staff; establishment; administrators; governors; collectors of revenue.

عمله فعله 'amalah f'ilah, n.m. Office staff; office establishment.

عملی 'amali (A) adj. Practical; artificial; addicted to drugs.

عمود 'amūd yā 'umūd (A) n.m. A perpendicular; pole; a pillar; a cudgel; a mace.

عموم 'umūm (A) adj. Common; general; universal.

بالعموم یا عموماً bil-'umūm yā 'umūman̲, adv. Generally; commonly.

عمومیت 'umūmiyyat (A) n.f. Generalisation.

عمیق 'amiq (A) adj. Deep; profound; intense; thorough; intellectually deep; deeply felt.

عمیم 'amīm (A) adj. Full; perfect; reaching everything; all comprehensive; universal.

عناب 'unnāb (A) n.m. The jujube tree and its fruit.

عنابی 'unnābī adj. Of the colour of the jujube; of red colour.

عناد 'inād (A) n.m. Enmity; obstinacy; perverseness; resistance; stubbornness.

عنادل 'anādil (A) n.f. (plu. of عندليب 'andalib) Nightingales.

عناصر 'anāṣir (A) n.m. (plu. of عنصر ('unṣur) Elements.

عنان 'inān (A) n.f. A bridle; a rein.

عنایت 'ināyat (A) n.f. Favour; bounty; kindness; support; gift; present.

عنب 'inab (A) n.m. The grapes.

عنبر 'ambar (A) n.m. Ambergris.

عنبر اشهب 'ambar-ĕ ashhab, n.m. Black ambergris.

عند 'ind (A) adv. Near; before; with; about; at; on; according to.

عندالاستفسار 'ind-al-istifsār, adv. On or during interrogation; upon enquiry or investigation.

عندالضرورت 'ind-aẓ-ẓurūrat, adv. In time of need; when required.

عندالطلب 'ind-aṭ-ṭalab, adv. On demand.

عندالله 'ind-allah, adv. With or before God.

عندالملاقات 'ind-al-mulāqāt, adv. During the interview.

عندالوصول 'ind-al-waṣūl, adv. On receipt; on arrival.

عندالوقوع 'ind-al-wuqū', adv. At the occurrence of the event; in such an event.

عندليب 'andalib (A) n.f. A nightingale; a thrush.

عندیہ **'indiyah** (A) *n.m.* (One's own) opinion; intention.

عندیہ پانا ، لینا ، معلوم کرنا **'indiyah pānā, lenā, m'alūm karnā**, *v.* To ascertain the opinion of; to gauge the view (of).

عنصر **'unṣar, 'unṣur** (A) *n.m.* Element; origin.

عنصری **'unṣuri** (A) *adj.* Elementary; original.

عنفوان **'unfuwān** (A) *n.m.* The beginning (of) vigour; a flower of youth.

عنفوانِ شباب **'unfuwān-ĕ shabāb**, *n.m.* The prime or bloom of youth.

عنقا **'anqā** (A) *n.m.* A fabulous bird; the phoenix. *adj.* Rare; wonderful; curious; hard to find.

عنقا ہونا **'anqā honā**, *v.* To be rare.

عنکبوت **'ankabūt** (A) *n.f.* A spider.

عنوان **'unwān** (A) *n.m.* Heading; title; title of a book; preface; something whereby another thing is known; a pointer; mode; manner.

عوارض **'awāriẓ** (A) *n.m.* (*plu.* of عارضہ *'ārizah*) Diseases; troubles; obstacles; charges; tones.

عواقب **'awāqib** (A) *n.m.* (*plu.* of عاقبت *'āqibat*) Consequences; results.

عوام **'awāmm** (A) *n.m.* (*plu* of عام *'ām*) The vulgar; the common people; populace; the public.

عوام‌الناس **'awāmm-un-nās**, *n.m.* The public; the populace at large; mankind.

عوامل **'awāmil** (A) *n.m.* (*plu.* of عاملہ *'amilah*) Governing words in grammar; rulers; governors; collectors of revenue.

عود **'ūd** (A) *n.m.* Timber; wood; aloes wood; a staff; a stick; a lute or harp.

عود سوز **'ūd soz**, *n.m.* A vessel in which عود 'ūd is burnt.

عود **'aud** (A) *n.m.* Returning; relapsing; a man of abilities, experience and prudence.

عود کرنا **aud karnā**, *v.* To return; to relapse.

عورت **'aurat** (A) *n.f.* Nakedness; nudity; a woman; a wife; a female (*plu.* عورات *'aurāt*).

عورت ذات **'aurat ẕāt**, *n.f.* Woman-kind; the female sex.

عوض **'iwaẓ** (A) *n.m.* Reward; retribution; retaliation; substitution of onething for another; exchange; recompense; compensation. *adv.* Instead; for.

عوض‌معاوضہ **'iwaẓ mu'āwiẓah**, *n.m.* Bartering; tit for tat.

عوضانہ **'iwaẓānah** *n.m.* Exchange; compensation.

عوضی **'iwazi** (A) *n.m.* A substitute; a person acting for another; *locum tenens*. *adj.* Officiating.

عوضی دینا **'iwaẓi denā**, *v.* To supply substitute.

عوضی کرنا **'iwazī karnā**, *v.* To officiate.

عہد **'ahd** (A) *n.m.* Time; season; reign; contract; obligation; promise; treaty; vow; oath; mandate; injunction; engagement; stipulation; covenant; agreement; will; testament.

عہد باندھنا **'ahd bāndhnā**, *v.* To make a vow; to take an oath, to make a promise.

عہد توڑنا **'ahd toṛnā**, *v.* To break one's promise; to back out.

عہد شکن **'ahd shikan**, *adj.* Faithless to one's word or engagement.

عہد شکنی **'ahd shikani**, *n.f.* Breach of faith, contract or engagement.

عہد کرنا **'ahd karnā**, *v.* To make a promise; to give one's word: to promise; to make a vow.

عہد نامہ 'ahd nāmah, n.m. A covenant; a charter; a treaty; articles of peace.

عہد و پیمان 'ahd-ŏ paimān, n.m. Agreement; treaty; articles of agreement.

عہد و پیمان کرنا 'ahd-ŏ paimān karnā, v. To covenant; to bargain.

عہدہ 'uhdah (A) n.m. A commission; an obligation; office; post; appointment; employment; duty.

عہدہ برا 'uhdah barā, adj. Performing an engagement; being able to accomplish an undertaking; being successful.

عہدہ برا ہونا 'uhdah barā honā, v. To come out successful; to achieve the object.

عہدہ برآئی 'uhdah barā'ī, n.f. Discharge of a duty; completion of an engagement; performance; success.

عہدہ دار 'uhdah dār, n.m. An officer; one employed ; an office holder; an official; a civil or military authority.

عیادت 'iyādat (A) n.f. Visiting of the sick; enquiring after a sick person.

عیاذاً باللہ 'iyāẕ-an-billah (A) intj. May God avert! God protect!

عیار 'ayār yā 'iyār (A) n.m. A mark; proof; test; standard; touch.

عیار 'aiyyār (A) adj. Cunning; sly; shrewd; artful; crafty. n.m. A knave; an impostor.

عیاری 'aiyyāri (A) n.f. Cunningness; deception; imposture; craftiness; knavery; slyness.

عیاش 'aiyyāsh (A) adj. Luxurious; voluptuous; rakish; addicted to pleasure.

عیاشی 'aiyyāshi, n.f. Luxury; joviality.

عیال 'ayāl yā 'iyāl (A) n.m. Family; children; household; domestics.

عیال دار 'ayāl dār, adj. Having a family. n.m. A family man.

عیال داری 'ayāl dārī, n.f. Family or worldly affairs.

عیاں 'ayāṅ (A) adj. Clear; manifest; conspicuous; visible; apparent; evident.

عیاں کرنا 'ayāṅ karnā, v. To make clear or manifest; to lay bare or open.

عیب 'aib (A) n.m. Fault; defect; vice; blemish; sin; infirmity; disgrace, infamy; imperfaction; faultiness; unsoundness.

عیب بیں 'aib bīṅ, adj. Fault-finder; severely cirtical; a caviller.

عیب پوش 'aib posh, adj. A screener of faults or defects; one who connives at the faults of others.

عیب جو 'aib jū, adj. A fault-finder; censorious; malicious; a carper; one who seeks faults of others, a critic; malignant; caviller.

عیب جوئی 'aib jū'ī, n.f. Fault finding; criticism; cavil.

عیب چیں 'aib chiṅ, adj. Fault-finder; a critic; a caviller.

عیب چینی 'aib chīnī, n.f. Picking out faults; culling errors.

عیب دار 'aib dār, adj. Defective; faulty.

عیب لگانا 'aib lagānā, v. To defame; to speak ill off; to accuse; to stigmatize; to asperse.

عیب نکالنا 'aib nikālnā, v. To pick holes; to find fault with.

عیبی 'aibī, adj. Defective; faulty; vicious; squint-eyed.

عید 'īd (A) n.f. A festival; a holy day; a feast day; the Muslim festival of Id.

عیدالفطر 'id-ul-fiṭr, n.f. A Muslim festival, observed on the first of Shawwāl.

عید قربان ' عیداضحیٰ ' عیدالضحیٰ 'id-ĕ-qurbān 'īd-ĕ-aẓhā,' īd-uẓ-ẓuḥā, n.f. A Muslim festival, observed on the tenth of Zulhijjah just after the performance of pilgrimage in commemoration of Abraham's offering his son Ismail for sacrifice.

عید گاه 'id gāh, n.f. A place or a mosque where Muslims assemble for prayers on Id day.

عیدی 'idi, n.f. A present which is usually made on 'Id day.

عیسائی 'isā'i, adj. Christian.

عیسیٰ، عیسا 'Isā (A) n.m. Jesus.

عیسیٰ مسیح 'isā masih, n.m. Jesus Christ.

عیسوی 'isawi (A) adj. Belonging to or concerning Jesus; Christian.

عیش 'aish (A) n.m. Pleasure; delight; luxury; a life of pleasure and enjoyment.

عیش کرنا 'aish karnā, v. To enjoy oneself.

عیش و عشرت 'aish-ō 'ishrat, n.m. Pleasantness of life; luxurious enjoyment.

عین 'ain (A) n.f. The eye; sight; fountain; spring; the sun; the very essence; the original thing. adj. Very; exact; intrinsic; real; just.

عین بعین 'ain-ba-'ain, adj. Exact copy.

عین الیقین 'ain-ul-yaqin, n.m. Believing at sight only; certainty; positive knowledge.

بعینه ba'ainihi, adv. In his very presence; exactly; truly.

عینک 'ainak (A) n.f. Spectacles; glasses to aid the eye.

عینی 'aini (A) adj. Of or relating to the eye.

عینی گواه 'aini gawāh, n.m. An eye-witness.

عیوب 'uyūb (A) n.m. (plu. of عیب 'aib) Vices; defects; faults.

عیون 'uyūn (A) n.m. (plu of عین 'ain) Springs; fountains; eyes.

غ ghain, called ghain-ĕ mu'jamah, is the nineteenth letter of the Arabic, twenty-second of the Persian and twenty-fifth of the Urdu alphabet. Its numerical value, according to abjad, is 1000.

غار ghār (A) n.m. A cavern; a pit; a den or lair (of a wild beast); a deep gush or wound.

غارت ghārat (A) n.f. Plunder; ravage; devastation; pillage; calamity; raid.

غارت کرنا ghārat karnā, v. To plunder; to ravage; to spoil; to lay waste.

غارت گر ghārat gar, n.m. A raider; a plunderer; an oppressor.

غارت گری ghārat gari, n.f. Pillage; destruction; plundering.

غارت ہونا ghārat honā, v. To be ruined; to be destroyed.

غازه ghāzah (P) n.m. Red coloured powder with which women paint their faces; rouge; a face-powder; perfumed powder for the hair and skin.

غازه کاری ghāzah kari, n.f. Painting the face with red colour.

غازی ghāzi (A) n.m. A conqueror; a hero; one who fights against infidels.

غاصب ghāṣib (A) n.m. A plunderer; a usurper.

غافل ghāfil (A) adj. Negligent; neglectful; remiss; inattentive; indolent; imprudent; thoughtless; unmindful; unconscious.

غالب ghālib (A) adj. Overcoming; overpowering; victorious; predominant; excelling; superior; triumphant. adv. Often; very often; likely; most probable; most likely.

غالب آنا یا ہونا ghālib ānā yā honā, v. To overcome; to surmount; to conquer; to excel; to surpass; to subdue.

غالباً ghālibā̱n (A) adv. Probably; most probably; apparently; certainly; most likely; chiefly.

غالی ghāli (A) adj. Dear; high priced; precious; passing prescribed limits.

غالیچه ghālichah (P) n.m. A small carpet.

غائب ghā'ib (A) adj. Absent; Concealed; invisible; unapparent. n.m. The invisible; the future; the third person (Gram.).

غائب کرنا ghā'ib karnā, v. To remove stealthily; to make away with; to secrete.

غائب ہونا ghā'ib honā, v. To vanish; to disappear.

غائبانہ ghā'ibānah (A & P) adv. In the absence of; invisibly; secretly.

غائر ghā'ir (A) adj. Descending; deep.

غائی ghā'i (A) adj. Final.

غایت ghāyat (A) adj. & adv. Superlative; excessive: extreme; uttermost: excessively; extremely; chiefly.

غبار ghubār (A) n.m. Clouds of dust; dust; a dust storm; impurity; foulness; vapour; fog; mist; vexation; affliction; perplexity; the smallest Arabic or Persian handwriting.

غبار آلودہ ghubār ālūdah, adj. Covered or polluted with dust; dusty.

غبار خاطر ghubār-ĕ khāṭir, n.m. Affliction; trouble of mind; vexation; displeasure.

غبار نکالنا ghubār nikālnā, v. To give vent to ill-feeling; to be in a temper; to take revenge.

غبارا ghubārā, n.m. A balloon; a fire-balloon; a mortar for throwing shells.

غبغب ghabghab (A) n.m. A dewlap; a double chin.

غبن ghabn (A) n.m. Cheating; defrauding; fraud; deceit; loss (of mony &c); misappropriation; defalcation; embezzlement; unlawful abstraction.

غبن کرنا ghabn karnā, v. To misappropriate; to embezzle.

غبی ghabi (A) adj. Weak in mind; having little intelligence; imprudent; dull; forgetful; negligent.

غت ربود ghat rabūd, adj. Confused; jumbled.

غٹاغٹ ghṭāghaṭ, n.f. Sound made in drinking quickly; gulping down.

غٹر غوں ghuṭar ghūṅ, n.f. Cooing.

غچا ghachchā, n.m. Deceit; fraud.

غچا دینا ghachchā denā, v. To deceive; to defraud.

غدار ghaddār (A) adj. Treacherous; perfidious; disloyal; fraudulent; sly. n.m. A traitor; a cheat.

غدر ghadar (A) n.m. Mutiny; disorder; sedition; disturbance; riot; confusion; perfidy; disloyalty; villainy.

غدود ghudūd (A) n.m. (plu. of غدہ ghaddah) Glands; granulous swelling; hard lumps formed in the flesh; tumor.

غدیر ghadīr (A) n.f. A lake or pool; the festival of the succession of Hazrat Ali, as the Prophet's successor, celebrated by the Shī'ah.

غذا ghizā (A) n.f. Food; diet; victuals; provisions; aliment; nutriment; sustenance; support; fare; nourishment.

غذائے ثقیل ghizā-ĕ saqil, n.f. Heavy food; rich food; oily, greasy food; food hard to digest.

غذائے لطیف ghizā-ĕ laṭif, n.f. Light food; easily digestible food.

غذائی ghizā'ī (A) adj. Nutritious; nourishing; alimental.

غذائیت ghiẕā'iyat (A) n.f. Aliment; nutrition.

غرا gharrā (A) adj. Splendid; shining; conspicuous; noble; illustrious; resplendent.

غرابت gharābat (A) n.f. Strangeness; newness; foreignness; remoteness.

غرارہ gharārah (A) n.m. A large sack; gargle; a parted skirt worn by Pakistani women.

غراں gharrāṅ, ghurrāṅ (P) adj. Rapacious; fierce; roaring.

غرانا ghurrānā, v. To growl; to roar; to frown.

غرائب gharā'ib (A) n.m. (plu. of غریبہ gharībah) Wonderful things; strange things; curiosities.

غرب ghurb (A) n.m. The setting of the sun; the west; a bucket.

غربال ghirbāl (A) n.f. A sieve; a riddle.

غرباء ghurabā (A) n.m. (plu. of غریب gharīb) The poor; strangers; paupers.

غربت ghurbat (A) n.f. Poverty; humility; lowliness; wretchedness; foreign travel; travelling; emigration; being far from one's country and friends.

غربت زدہ ghurbat zadah, adj. Oppressed; wretched; impoverished.

غربی gharbī (A) adj. Western; occidental.

غرض gharaẓ (A) n.f. Intention; object; aim; purpose; end; business; meaning; design; wish; view; occasion, use; want; interest; selfishness; motive; concern; necessity.

غرض آشنا gharaz āshnā, adj. Selfish; interested.

غرض آلودہ gharaẓ ālūdah, adj. Interested; selfish.

غرض کا دیوانہ gharaz kā diwānah, n.m. A slave to one's desires or passions.

غرض کا یار gharẓ kā yār, n.m. A self-seeking person.

غرض مند gharaẓ maṅd, adj. Needy; interested; desirous of; wishing for selfish; designing.

غرض نکالنا gharaẓ nikālnā, v. T. ıav one's end served.

الغرض al-gharaẓ, adv. In short; in a word; briefly.

بے غرض be gharaẓ, adj. Disinterested.

غرغرہ ghargharah (A) n.m. Gargling.

غرق gharq (A) n.m. Drowning; immersion; sinking. adj. Drowned; immersed; sunk.

غرقاب gharqāb (P) adj. Drowned. n.m. Very deep water; a whirlpool.

غروب ghurūb (A) n.m. Setting (of the sun, moon etc.); sunset.

غرور ghurūr (A) n.m. Pride; haughtiness; vanity; vain glory.

غرور کا سر نیچا ghurūr kā sar nichā, prov. Pride goeth before a fall.

غرور کرنا ghurūr karnā, v. To be proud; to boast.

غرہ gharrah (A) adj. Haughty; proud; cross; deluded. n.m. Pride; vanity; haughtiness.

غریب gharīb (A) n.m. A foreigner; a stranger; a traveller. adj. Poor; destitute; mild; humble; needy; strange; foreign; wonderful; innocent; indigent.

غریب پرور gharīb parwar, adj. Cherisher of the poor.

غریب خانہ gharīb khānah, n.m. A humble dwelling; my house.

غریب الوطن ' غریب الدیار gharīb-ul-watan, gharīb-ud-diyār, n.m. A foreigner; a stranger in a foreign land.

غریب غرباء **gharib ghurabā**, *n.m.* Poor people; paupers.

غریب مار **gharib mār**, *n.f.* Oppression of the poor; troubling the poor.

غریب نواز **gharib nawāz**, *adj.* Kind to the poor; hospitable; courteous to strangers.

غریب نوازی **gharib nawāzi**, *n.f.* Hospitality; kindness to the poor; courtesy or attention to strangers.

غریبانہ **gharibānah** (A & P) *adj.* Fit for the poor; in a humble way. *adv.* Like a poor man; humbly; like a stranger.

غریبی **gharibi** (A & P) *n.f.* Poverty; indigence; humility; mildness; meekness; the state of being a foreigner; foreignness.

غریبی آنا **gharibi ānā**, *v.* To be reduced to poverty.

غریق **ghariq** (A) *n.m.* A drowning person. *adj.* Immersed; drowned.

غریق رحمت **ghariq-ĕ rahmat**, *adj.* Overwhelmed with mercy; submerged in the grace of God; dead.

غڑاپ **gharāp** *n.f.* The sound of something falling into the water.

غڑاپ سے **gharāp se**, *adv.* In a crack; suddenly.

غزال، غزالہ **ghazāl, ghazālah** (A) *n.m. f.* A young deer; a fawn; a gazelle; the sun; a delicate young person.

غزل **ghazal** (A) *n.f.* An ode: an amatory poem.

غزل کہنا **ghazal kehnā**, *v.* To compose an ode.

غزوہ **ghazwah** (A) *n.m.* A war against infidels, in which the Holy Prophet himself took part (*plu.* غزوات **ghazwāt**).

غسال **ghassāl** (A) *n.m.* One whose business is to wash dead bodies before burial; a washer of the dead.

غسالہ **ghusālah** (A) *n.f.* A female washer of the dead.

غسل **ghusl** (A) *n.m.* Bathing; ablution.

غسل آفتابی **ghusl-ĕ āftābi**, *n.m.* A sun bath.

غسل خانہ **ghusl khānah**, *n.m.* A bath; bath room; bagnio.

غسل صحت **ghusl-ĕ ṣiḥḥat**, *n.m.* Bathing after recovery from illness.

غسل میت **ghusl-ĕ maiyyat**, *n.m.* Washing the dead body.

غش **ghash**, (A) *n.m.* Stupor; fainting; a faint; swoon.

غش آنا، پڑنا، کھانا **ghash ānā, parnā, khānā**, *v.* To faint; to swoon.

غشی **ghashi** *n.f.* Fainting; swooning.

غصب **ghaṣb** (A) *n.m.* Violence; force; oppression; ravishing; plunder; usurpation; embezzlement.

غصب کرنا **ghaṣb karnā**, *v.* To usurp; to take by force.

غصہ **ghuṣṣah** (A) *n.m.* Anger; passion; rage; anxiety; grief; suffocation (with grief or anger).

غصہ اتارنا، نکالنا **ghuṣṣah utārnā, nikālnā**, *v.* To retaliate; to be angry or in a passion (with).

غصہ پی جانا یا مارنا **ghuṣṣah pi jānā yā mārnā**, *v.* To suppress one's anger; to grieve; to worry.

غصہ دلانا **ghuṣṣah dilānā**, *v.* To enrage; to offend; to irritate; to put out of temper.

غصہ کرنا **ghussah karnā**, *v.* To be angry; to be enraged; to be in a passion.

غصہ ناک پر ہونا **ghuṣṣah nāk par honā**, *v.* To get angry for nothing; to be easily offended; to be very irritable.

غصے میں بھر جانا **ghusse meṅ bhar jānā**, *v.* To become enraged.

غصیل، غصیلا **ghussail, ghuṣīlā**, *adj.* Wrathful; passionate; choleric; furious.

غضب ghaẓab (A) n.m. Violence; oppression; compulsion; passion; rage; fury; wrath; anger; calamity; outrage.

غضب آلوده ghaẓab ālūdah, adj. Wrathful; indignant.

غضب توڑنا ghaẓab toṛnā, v. To wreak one's vengeance on.

غضب ٹوٹنا ghaẓab ṭūṭnā, v. To meet with misfortune; to be overtaken by a calamity; to be visited by wrath of God.

غضب ڈھانا ghaẓab ḍhānā, v. To tyrannise (over); to practise cruel oppression (on); to commit an impropriety.

غضب کرنا ghaẓab karnā, v. To be enraged or indignant; to tyrannise (over); to oppress.

غضب ناک ghaẓab nāk, adj. Full of rage; indignant; enraged; furious; wrathful.

غضنفر ghaẓanfar (A) n.m. A lion; a hero; a brave man; a powerful man; big-bodied man.

غفار ghaffār (A) adj. Very forgiving; merciful; an epithet applied to God.

غفران ghufrān (A) n.m. Forgiveness; pardon; remission of sins; absolution.

غفلت ghaflat (A) n.f. Carelessness; negligence; remissness; unmindfulness; unconsciousness; drowsiness; stupor; insensibility; swoon.

غفور ghafūr (A) adj. Forgiving; clement; merciful; the forgiving one; God.

غفیر ghafīr (A) adj. Great; large; numerous; many; huge.

غل ghul (P) n.m. Noise; din; outcry; tumult.

غل غپاڑا ghul ghapāṛā, n.m. Clamour; disturbance; brawl; shouts; roar.

غل کرنا ، مچانا ghul karnā, machānā, v. To make a noise; to hoot; to bawl; to shout; to raise a tumult.

غلاظت ghilāẓat (A) n.f. Filth; dirt; night-soil; offal; thickness; coarseness; hardness; roughness; bulkiness; rudeness; churlishness; roughness of language or manners.

غلاف ghilāf (A) n.m. A case; a cover; a sheath; a pillow case; an envelope; a scabbard; the foreskin.

غلام ghulām (A) n.m. A boy or youth; a young man who has attained maturity; a slave; a bondsman; a servant; the knave at cards.

غلام گردش ghulām gardish, n.m. A shed for servants to sit under; an enclosed varandah of tent or house to keep the air cool.

غلامی ghulāmī (A & P) n.f. Servitude; slavery; vassalage.

غلبہ ghalabah (A) n.m. Victory; conquest; overcoming; superiority; advantage; invasion; tyranny; assault; strength; influence; mastery; excess.

غلبہ پانا ghalabah pānā, v. To get the upper hand; to obtain mastery over; to get the better (of).

غلبہ کرنا ghalabah karnā, v. To overpower; to overcome; to conquer; to get the upper hand; to come out victorious.

غلبۂ رائے ghalabah-ĕ rā'e, n.m. Majority of votes.

غلط ghalaṭ (A) adj. Wrong; untrue; erroneous; inaccurate; incorrect. n.m. Error; mistake.

غلط العام ghalaṭ-ul-'āmm, n.m. A common mistake (in language); a fallacy.

غلط العوام ghalaṭ-ul-'awām, n.m. A vulgor error.

غلط ٹهہرانا ghalaṭ thahrānā, v. To hold to be wrong or erroneous; to show the fallacy of; to expose.

غلط فہمی ghalaṯ fahmī, n.f. Misunderstanding; misapprehension; misconception.

غلط کار ghalaṯ kār, adj. Delusive.

غلط کاری ghalaṯ kārī, n.f. Delusion; deception.

غلط گو ghalaṯ go, adj. One who spreads falsehood; a narrator of falsehoods.

غلط نامہ ghalaṯ nāmah, n.m. Errata.

غلطاں ghalṯān (P) adj. Rolling; wallowing.

غلطاں پیچاں ghalṯāṅ pechāṅ, adj. Wallowing; rolling; involved; confounded; absorbed in thought.

غلطی ghalaṯī (A) n.f. A mistake; an error; fallacy; inaccuracy; an oversight; a slip (of the pen &c); miscalculation.

غلغلہ ghulghulah (P) n.m. Noise; tumult; a kind of dish.

غلمان ghilmān (A) n.m. (plu. of غلام ghulām) Handsome boys who will attend on the virtuous in Paradise.

غلو ghulū (A) n.f. Excess; transgression; exaggeration; commotion.

غلہ ghallah (A) n.m. The produce of the earth; grain; corn; the sale proceeds of the day and the box in which they are kept.

غلہ بھرنا ghallah bharnā, v. To store up grain.

غلہ فروش ghallah farosh, n.m. A grain merchant.

غلہ ، غلیلہ ghullah, ghulela, n.m. A pellet; a bullet; a marble.

غلیظ ghalīz (A) adj. Dirty; filthy; thick; gross; rude; coarse; obscene.

غلیل ghulel, n.f. A catapult; a pellet bow.

غم gham yā ghamm (A) n.m. Grief; sorrow; woe; mourning; lamentation; sadness; concern; care.

غم خوار gham khwār, adj. Condoling; pitying; sympathising; comforter; an intimate friend; afflicted; sad.

غم خواری gham khwārī, n.f. Sympathy; condolence; affliction; commiseration.

غم دیدہ ، رسیدہ ، زدہ gham dīdah, rasīdah, zadah, adj. Afflicted; grieved.

غم غلط کرنا gham ghalaṯ karnā, v. To forget one's grief or sorrow; to solace; to divert one's mind.

غم کدہ gham kadah, n.m. House of sorrow or trouble.

غم کرنا gham karnā, v. To grieve; to lament.

غم کھانا gham khānā, v. To suffer grief; to feel or show sympathy for another; to have patience.

غم گسار gham gusār, adj. One who consoles; a comforter; an intimate friend.

غم گین gham gīn, adj. Sorrowful; depressed; grieved; sad; woeful.

غم گینی gham gīnī, n.f. Sadness; sorrowfulness.

غم ناک gham nāk, adj. Sorrowful; sad; woeful.

غماز ghammāz (A) n.m. A back-biter; a tale-bearer; an informer.

غمازی ghammāzī (A) n.f. Back-biting; tale-bearing.

غمزہ ghamzah (A) n.m. A wink; an amorous glance; coquetry; ogling.

غمی ghamī, n.f. Grief; sorrow; mourning; death.

غناء ghinā (A) n.m. Singing; vocal music; a song; a tune.

غناء ghanā' (A) n.m. Riches; wealth; sufficiency; content.

غنائم ghanā'im (A) n.m./f. (plu. of غنیمت ghanīmat) Plunder; booty.

غنچه ghunchah (P) n.m. A bud; a rose-bud.

غنچه دهن ghunchah dahan, adj. Having a mouth like a rose-bud; a beloved; a sweetheart.

غنڈہ ghunḍah, n.m. A bully; a rascal; a vagabond.

غنغنانا ghunghunānā, v. To mutter; to grumble; to speak through the nose; to sing through the nose; to buzz; to hum.

غنودگی ghanūdgi (P) n.f. Drowsiness.

غنہ ghunnah (A) n.m. A sound through the nose; buzzing of flies. adj. Quiescent; nasal (the letter ں).

غنی ghani (A) adj. Rich; wealthy; opulent; independent. n.m. A rich person.

غنیم ghanīm (A) n.m. An enemy; an adversory; a foe; a plunderer.

غنیمت ghanīmat (A) n.f. Plunder; a prize; abundance; good fortune; a blessing; a boon; a God-send.

غواص ghawwāṣ (A) n.m. A diver; one who dives into the sea in search of pearls.

غواصی ghawwāṣi (A) n.f. Sea diving for pearls; the art or business of a diver.

غوامض ghawāmiẓ (A) n.m. (plu. of غامض ghāmiẓ) Obscure matters; abstruse questions.

غوث ghuaṣ (A) n.m. A title of Muslim saints who spend most of their time in God-worship and it is commonly believed that they are so engrossed in worship that their heads and limbs fall asunder.

غور ghaur (A) n.m. Deep thought; reflection; meditation; deliberation; close attention; consideration.

غور کامل ghaur-ĕ kāmil, n.m. Full consideration.

غور کرنا ghaur karnā, v. To consider; to reflect; to investigate; to fathom by consideration or investigation; to think; to consider thoughtfully; to regard with attention.

غور و پرداخت ghaur-ŏ pardākht, n.f. Attendance on; attention to; maintenance of.

غوری ghauri (P) n.f. A plate; a kind of porcelain. adj. Relating or belonging to غور ghaur, a province in Afghanistan.

غوطہ ghoṭah (A) n.m. A dip; a dive; plunge; (into water); dipping; diving; immersion.

غوطہ باز، غوطہ خور ghoṭah bāz, ghoṭah khor, n.m. A diver; one who plunges into water.

غوطہ دینا ghoṭah denā, v. To dip; to plunge under water; to duck under water.

غوطہ کھانا ghoṭah khānā, v. To be dipped; to dive; to be deceived; to be cheated.

غوطہ مارنا ghoṭah mārnā, v. To plunge; to dive; to dip.

غوغا ghaughā (P) n.m. Noise; disturbance; uproar; clamour; alarm; brawl; hubbub.

غوغائی ghaughā'i (P) adj. Noisy; clamorous; false; nonsensical. n.m. A noisy or turbulent fellow; a disturber.

غوک ghūk (P) n.m. A frog; a toad; a butt for archers.

غول ghool (A) n.m. A company; band; herd; crowd; throng; mob; gang.

غول بیابانی ghool-ĕ bayābāni, n.m. A demon that haunts woods or deserts.

غول کے غول ghool ke ghool, n.m. Crowds; whole crowds.

غیاث ghiyās (A) n.f. Deliverance from difficulty; redress; aid; assistance; succour.

غیب ghaib (A) adj. Concealed; invisible; hidden; absent; latent; mysterious. n.m. Invisibility; mystery; absence.

غیب دان ghaib dān, n.m. Having knowledge of hidden things; a prophet; a seer; diviner; the omniscient Being.

غیب دانی ghaib dānī, n.f. Knowledge of hidden things or mysteries.

غیبت ghībat (A) n.f. Speaking ill of someone behind his back; slander; backbiting.

غیبت ghaibat (A) n.f. Absence.

غیبی ghaibī (A) adj. Absent; invisible; of the invisible world; heavenly; divine.

غیر ghair (A) n.m. A stranger; a foreigner; an outsider; another person. adj. Other; different; strange; foreign; bad. adv. Besides; different from. prep./adv. & negative prefix. Without; beside; except, save; but; other than; different from; contrary to; the reverse of; not; un; in; ir; &c.

غیر اختیاری ghair ikhtiyārī, adv. Done without exercise of the will; unintentionally; involuntary.

غیر سمجھنا ghair samajhnā, v. To regard one as a stranger.

غیر متاثر ghair mutāssir, adj. Ineffective; ineffectual.

غیر مترقبہ ghair mutarraqbah, adj. Unexpected.

غیر متناسب ghair mutanāsib, adj. Unproportional.

غیر متناہی ghair mutanāhī, adj. Unending; limitless.

غیر محدود ghair maḥdūd, adj. Unlimited; boundless.

غیر مشروط ghair mashrūṭ, adj. Unconditional.

غیر مطلوب ghair maṭlūb, adj. Unwanted; undesirable.

غیر معتبر ghair mu'tabar, adj. Incredible; unreliable; deceitful; dubious; not trustworthy

غیر معمولی ghair ma'mūlī, adj. Unusual; extraordinary.

غیر معین ghair mu'aiyan, adj. Undetermined; fluctuating; undefined; uncertain; unstable; vague; unsettled; indefinite; unfixed.

غیر مکمل ghair mukammal, adj. Imperfect; incomplete.

غیر ملکی ghair mulkī, adj. Exotic; foreign.

غیر مناسب ghair munāsib, adj. Unsuitable; unbecoming.

غیر منقولہ ghair manqūlah, adj. Immovable; fixed.

غیر منکوحہ ghair mankūḥah, adj. Unmarried; illegitimate.

غیرت ghairat (A) n.f. Care of what is sacred and invoilable; sense of honour; honour; courage; modesty; bashfulness; shame; envy; indignation; enmity.

غیرت کھانا ghairat khānā, v. To experience shame.

غیرت مند ghairat mand, adj. Modest; bashful; jealous; emulous; envious.

بے غیرت be ghairat, adj. Shameless.

بے غیرتی be ghairatī, n.f. Shamelessness.

بے غیرتی پر کمر باندھنا be ghairatī par kamar bāndhnā, v. To be lost to all sense of shame.

غیریت ghairiyyat, n.f. Strangeness;

غیظ ghaiẓ (A) n.m. Rage; fury; anger.

غیظ و غضب ghaiẓ-ŏ ghaẓab, n.m. Rage and fury.

غین ہونا ghain honā, v. To be dead drunk.

غیور ghayyūr (A) adj. Very jealous in point of honour; high-minded. n.m. An epithet of God.

ف

ف fe, is the twentieth letter of the Arabic, the twenty-third of the Persian and the twenty-sixth of the Urdu alphabet. Numerically it stands for 80.

فاتح fātiḥ (A) adj./n.m. Opening; conquering; one who opens; a conqueror.

فاتحه fātiḥah (A) n f. Commencement; opening chapter; introduction; the opening سورة sūrah or chapter of the Qurān; prayers for the dead or the saints.

فاتحه پڑھنا fātiḥah paṛhnā, v. To pray for the dead; to give up a thing as lost.

فاتحه دينا fātiḥah denā, v. To make offerings to saints with prayers.

فاتر fātir (A) adj. Weak; sluggish; idle; infirm; unsound; disturbed.

فاتر العقل fātir-ul-'aql, adj. Having unsound mind; an unintelligent person.

فاجر fājir (A) n.m. A fornicator; an adulterer; a sinner; a whore-monger. adj. sinful; unchaste; libertine.

فاجره fājirah (A) n.f. Adultress; unchaste woman.

فاجعه fāji'ah (A) n.f. Tragedy. adj. Tragic.

فاحش fāḥish (A) adj. Obscene; indecent; impudent; shameless; immodest; foul; evil; nefarious; enormous; excessive.

فاحشه fāḥishah (A) n.f. A harlot; a prostitute; anything abominable.

فاختہ fākhtah (A) n.f. A dove; a ringed turtle-dove.

فاختہ آڑانا fākhtah uṛānā, v. To be prosperous; to be free from care and anxiety.

وہ دن گئے جب خلیل خاں فاختہ آڑایا کرتے تھے wuh din ga'e jab khalil khān fākhtah urāyā karte the, prov. Gone is the goose that lay the golden eggs.

فاختئی fākhta'ī, n.f. Dove-colour; fawn colour.

فاخر fākhir (A) n.m. A boaster; one who takes delight in boasting. adj. Excellent; precious; honourable.

فاخره fākhirah (A) adj. Elegant; splendid; showy.

فارس fāris (A) n.m. A horseman; a cavalier.

فارس fārs (P) n.m. Persia.

فارسی fārsi (P) n.f. The Persian language.

فارسی بگھارنا fārsi baghārnā, v. To speak a Persian of one's own; to speak high Dutch.

فارغ fārigh (A) adj. Disengaged; unoccupied; free; at leisure; absolved; contented; at ease; discharged.

فارغ البال fārigh-ul-bāl, adj. Independent; in easy circumstances; free from care; unrestrained; unchecked.

فارغ البالی fārigh-ul-bālī, n.f. Easy circumstances; freedom from care and anxiety.

فارغ خطی fārigh khaṭṭī, n.f. A dead of release or discharge; a deed of dissolution of partnership; written acquittance.

فاروق fārūq (A) adj. & n.m. One who distinguishes between right and wrong; the title of Hazrat 'Umar, the second Caliph of Islam.

فاسخ fāsikh (A) adj. Breaker; violetor.

فاسد، فاسده fāsid' fāsidah (A) adj. Corrupt; vicious; depraved; perverse; wicked; wrong; malignent; guilty; culpable.

فاسق fāsiq (A) n.m. Transgressor; sinner; a fornicator; an adulterer; a worthless fellow. adj. Impious.

فاسقه fāsiqah (A) n.f. An adultress; a wanton woman. adj. Lewd; wanton; immoral.

فاش fāsh (P) adj. Apparent; manifest; known; notorious; gross; serious.

فاش غلطی کرنا fāsh ghalaṭi karnā, v. To commit a gross or serious mistake.

فاش کرنا fāsh karnā, v. To disclose; to lay bare; to lay open; to let out; to divulge; to reveal; to discover; to betray.

راز فاش کرنا rāz fāsh karnā, v. To disclose or betray a secret.

فاصل fāṣil (A) adj. Separator; divider.

فاصله fāṣilah (A) n.m. Distance; space; intermediate space; interval; break; discontinuity; separation; duration; gap.

فاضل fāẓil (A) adj. Superfluous; over and above; more than enough; accomplished person; proficient; abundant; in excess; remainder; virtuous. n.m. Surplus; excess revenue; residue; an accomplished person; a scholar.

فاضل اجل fāẓil-ĕ ajall, n.m. A highly talented man; an ocean of learning.

فاضل باقی fāẓil bāqi, n.f. Balance in favour; surplus.

فاضل باقی نکالنا fāẓil bāqi nikālnā, v. To strike the balance.

فاطمی fāṭimī (A) adj. Descendants of Hazrat Fatimah, the daughter of the Holy Prophet; the Fāṭemite dynasty.

فاعل fā'il (A) adj & n.m. Doing; operating; making; doer; maker; performer; operator; agent; a sodomite; (Gram.) subject; nominative.

فاعل حقیقی fā'il-ĕ ḥaqiqi, n.m. The actual performer; God.

فاعل مختار fā'il-ĕ mukhtār, n.m. Free to do as one pleases; a free agent.

فاعل و مفعول fā'il-ŏ maf'ūl, n.m. The subject and the object.

فاعلی fā'ili (A) adj. Active; operative; efficient; effective.

حالت فاعلی hālat-ĕ fā'ili, n.f. Nominative case.

فاقه fāqah (A) n.m. Starvation; fasting; want; poverty.

فاقه کرنا fāqah karnā, v. To go without food; to fast.

فاقه کش fāqah kash, adj. A famished person; one who fasts from want of food.

فاقه کشی fāqah kashi, n.f. Fasting from necessity.

فاقه مست fāqah mast, adj. One who starves, but conceals his distress; one who is cheerful in poverty.

فاقه مستی fāqah masti, n.f. Cheerfulness in adversity.

فاقوں مرنا fāqon marnā, v. To starve; to die of hunger.

فاقوں کا مارا fāqoṅ kā mārā, n.m. A famished person; one perishing of hunger; a starveling.

فال fāl (A) n.f. Augury; omen; presage; spell; enchantment.

فال کھلوانا fāl khulwānā, v. To cause events to be foretold.

فال کھولنا fāl kholnā, v. To foretell by reference to magical or holy books.

فال گو fāl go, n.m. One who foretells events; an augur; a soothsayer.

فال نامہ *fāl nāmah, n.m.* A book of omens.

فالتو *fāltū, adj.* Spare; surplus; extra; over and above.

فالج *fālij* (A) *n.m.* Paralysis; the palsy; hemiplegia.

فالج گرنا *fālij girnā, v.* To be stricken with palsy; to be palsied or paralysed.

فالسہ *fālsah* (P) *n.m.* A sub-acid fruit.

فالسئی *fālsa'i, adj.* Purple.

فالودہ *fālūdah* (P) *n.m.* A kind of flummery Pressed through a sieve and mixed with sugar and milk. *adj.* Smooth; clear.

فالیز *fālez* (P) *n.f.* A field of melons.

فام *fām* (P) *n.m.* Colour; complexion.

فانوس *fānūs* (P) *n.f.* A glass shade of a candlestick; a lantern; a chandelier.

فانوس خیال *fānūs-ĕ khayāl, n.m.* A magic lantern.

فانہ *fānah* (A) *n.m.* A wedge.

فانی *fānī* (A) *adj.* Mortal; perishable; frail; transitory; inconsistent.

فائدہ *fā'idah* (A) *n.m.* Gain; profit; advantage; outturn; yield; benefit; interest; use; importance; result; ūtility.

فائدہ آٹھانا *fā'idah uṭhānā, v.* To reap benefit; to utilise; to gain; to make a profit.

فائدہ مند *fā'idah mand, adj.* Profitable; advantageous; useful; efficacious; favourable to.

فائز *fā'iz* (A) *adj.* Attaining; acquiring; reaching; obtaining.

فائزالمرام *fā'iz-ul-marām, adj.* Successful; prosperous.

فائض *fā'iẓ* (A) *adj.* Liberal; beneficent.

فائق *fā'iq* (A) *adj.* Superior; excelling; excellent; surpassing.

فبہا *fabihā* (A) *interj.* Very well! excellent! bravo!

فتاح *fattāḥ* (A) *n.m. & adj.* One who opens; one who resolves difficulties; one who awards victory; an epithet of God.

فتاوی *fatāwā* (A) *n.m.* (*plu.* of فتوی *fatwā*) Written verdicts of a Muslim law officer; Muslim case law.

فتح *fatḥ* (A) *n.f.* Victory; success; conquest; an aperture; opening.

فتح پانا *fatḥ pānā, v.* To obtain a victory; to be victorious.

فتح کا نقارہ یا ڈنکا *fatḥ kā naqqārah yā dankā, n.m.* The beat or flourish of drums after vistory has been won.

فتح مند یا یاب *fatḥ mand yā yāb, adj.* Victorious; triumphant; successful.

فتح مندی *fatḥ mandi, n.f.* Victory; triumph.

فتحہ *fatḥah* (A) *n.m.* The vowel point (زبر *zabar*); the beard.

فتراک *fitrāk* (P) *n.m.* Saddle-straps.

فتق *fatq* (A) *n.m.* A rupture; hernia.

فتن *fitan* (A) *n.m.* (*plu.* of فتنہ *fitnah*) Seditions; revolts; evils; factions.

فتنہ *fitnah* (A) *n.m.* Sedition; revolt; mutiny; pest; mischief; perfidy; temptation. *adj.* Naughty; wicked.

فتنہ آٹھانا یا برپا کرنا *fitnah uṭhānā yā barpā karnā, v.* To create disturbance; to raise a tumult; to revolt.

فتنه انگیز یا پرداز fitnah angez yā pardāz, *adj.* Mischievous; seditious; turbulent. *n.m.* A mischief maker; an incendiary; seditious person.

فتنه جو fitnah jū, *adj.* Quarrelsome; seditious.

فتوح futūḥ (A) *n.m.* (*plu.* of فتح fath) Victories; conquests; abundance; easy circumstances.

فتوحات futūḥāt (A) *n.f.* (*plu.* of فتوح futūḥ) Victories; conquests.

فتوحی fatūḥi yā fatoḥi (A) *n.f.* A jacket without sleeves.

فتور futūr (A) *n.m.* Defect; unsoundness; riot; disorder; weakness; infirmity; quarrelling; discord.

فتور برپا کرنا futūr barpā karnā, *v.* To cause disturbance; to sow discord between; to create dissention.

فتور عقل futūr-ĕ 'aql, *n.m.* Unsoundness of mind.

فتور هضم futur-ĕ hazm, *n.m.* Indigestion; dyspepsia.

فتوری ، فتوریا futūrī, fatoriyā, *adj.* Factious; riotous; contentious; deceitful; treacherous. *n.m.* A rebel; a mutineer.

فتوی fatwā (A) *n.m.* Sentence delivered by a قاضی Qāzi; a judicial decree; judgment; sentence; decision; award.

فتوی دینا fatwā denā, *v.* To give a verdict; to pass judgment.

فتیله fatīlah (A) *n.m.* A match; a wick.

فتیله سوز fatīlah soz, A candlestick; a brass or tin lamp.

فجار fujjar (A) *n.m.* (*plu.* of فاجر fājir) Wicked persons; unchaste and adulterous persons.

فجر fajr (A) *n.f.* Early morning; day break; dawn of day.

فجور fujūr (A) *n.m.* Wickedness; adultery; debauchery.

فحش fuḥsh (A) *n.m.* Obscenity; grossness; bawdy. *adj.* Obscene; indecent; bawdy.

فحش بکنا fuḥsh baknā, *v.* To use foul language; to vilify; to revile.

فحوی fahwā (A) *n.m.* Style; contents; signification; sense; drift; meaning; intendent sense.

فحوی کلام fahwā-ĕ kalām, *n.m.* Signification; scope; spirit; tenor of the speech or discourse; sense; meaning; contents.

فخر fakhr (A) *n.m.* Glory; ostentation; pride; a thing to be proud of; boasting; egotism.

فخر سمجھنا fakhr samajhnā, *v.* To take pride in.

فخر کرنا fakhr karnā, *v.* To be proud of; to glory (in); to boast (of).

فخریه fakhriyyah (A) *adv.* With just pride; boastfully. *n.m.* Ostentation; boasting.

فدا fida (A) *n.m.* Sacrifice; devotion; consecration; redemption; devoting one's self to save another; ransom; exchange. *adj.* Devoted to; dying for.

فدا کرنا fidā karnā, *v.* To sacrifice; to devote oneself or a thing (for or to).

فدا هونا fidā honā, *v.* To be sacrificed; to be devoted (to); to love.

فدائی fidā'i (A&P) *n.m.* A lover; one who willingly hazards his life for any one or in an act.

فدوی fidwi (A & P) *adj.* Devoted. *n.m.* Subject or vassal.

فدیه fidyah (A) *n.m.* Ransom.

فر **far, farr (P) n.m.** Pomp; dignity; splendour; glory; lustre; beauty; grace; magnificence.

کرو فر **karr-ŏ farr, n.m.** Pomp and show; pomp and pride; splendour.

فرات **furāt (A) n.m.** The river Euphrates.

فراٹا **farrāṭā n.m.** A rush; rustling; a puff; running over a page; fluttering in the air.

فراٹے بھرنا **farrāṭe bharnā, v.** To run fast; to read fast; to run a race; to fly.

فراخ **farākh (A) adj.** Ample; spacious; wide; large; plentiful; extensive.

فراخ چشم **farākh chashm, adj.** Satisfied; contented.

فراخ حوصلہ **farākh ḥausalah, adj.** Large-minded; high-minded.

فراخ دل **farākh dil, adj.** Open-hearted: large-hearted.

فراخی **farākhī (P) n.f.** Abundance, cheapness; largeness; wideness; amplitude; roominess; prosperity; happiness; girth.

فرار **firār (A) n.m.** Flight; running away.

فرار ہونا **firār honā, v.** To run away; to flee; to abscond.

فراری **firārī yā farrārī (A & P) adj.** Absconded; escaped; fugitive; runaway; fled.

فراری مجرم **firārī mujrim, n.m.** An escaped convict; an absconder.

فراز **farāz (P) n.m.** Ascent; acclivity; height; elevation. *adj.* High; aloft; exalted; lofty; exalting; elevating; ascending.

فرازی **farāzī (P) n.f.** Highness; exaltation.

فراست **firāsat (A) n.f.** Physiognomy; perception; discernment; penetration; sagacity; understanding; insight; acuteness; going deep (with); sounding.

فراش **farrāsh (A) n.m.** A chamberlain; a bed-maker; a servant whose business is to spread the carpets, and prepare the lamps etc.; a tent-pitcher.

فراش خانہ **farrāsh khānah, n.m.** The room where carpets &c are kept.

فراشی **farrāshi (A) n.f.** The business of a فراش farrāsh; spreading carpets.

فراغ **farāgh (A) n.m.** Ceasation; disengagement; competency; completion; leisure; repose; ease; freedom from care or from business.

فراغت **farāghat (A) n.f.** Cessation from labour; respite; breathing time; interval of rest; ease; comfort; convenience; competency; sufficiency; disengagement; leisure; repose; call of nature; abundance; affluence; happiness; easy circumstances.

فراغت پانا **farāghat pānā, v.** To obtain freedom from; to have leisure.

فراغت سے بیٹھنا **farāghat se baiṭhnā, v.** To sit at ease; to sit easy.

فراق **firāq (A) n.m.** Separation; anxiety; grief; absence; departing; distance; distinction.

فراق زدہ **firāq zadah, adj.** Afflicted by separation; separated; distressed.

فراموش **farāmosh (P) adj.** Forgotten; neglected.

فراموشی **farāmoshī (P) n.f.** Forgetfulness.

فرامین **farāmin (P) n.m.** (plu. of فرمان farmān) Orders; commands; mandates; precepts.

فرانسیسی **frānsisī, adj.** French; n.m. A Frenchman.

فراواں **firāwān (P) adj.** Abundant; copious; sufficient; opulent; plenty.

فراوانی **firāwānī (P) n.f.** Abundance; plentifulness.

فراهم farāham (P) adj. Collected; gathered; brought together; accumulated; amassed.

فراهمی farāhamī (P) n.f. Collecting or assembling together.

فرائض farā'iẓ (A) n.m. (plu. of فریضه farīẓah) Divine precepts; obligations; duties; the knowledge of dividing inheritances agreeable to law.

فرائض منصبی farā'iẓ-ĕ mansabī, n.m. Official duties.

فربه farbah (P) adj. Fat; plump; stout and strong; corpulent; fleshy.

فربه اندام farbah andām, adj. Fleshy; plumpy.

فربہی farbahi (P) n.f. Fatness; corpulence; flesh.

فرتوت fartūt (P) adj. Old and descrepit; good for nothing.

فرج farj, furj (A) n.f. Vulva; the orifice of the external organs of generation of the female; vagina; a fissure.

فرجام farjām (P) n.m. End; conclusion; issue; happiness; prosperity; utility; profit.

فرح faraḥ (A) n.f. Joy; gladness; cheerfulness.

فرحاں farḥāṅ (P) adj. Glad; joyful.

فرحت farḥat (A) n.m. Delight; pleasure; joy; cheerfulness; amusement; recreation; diversion.

فرحت افزا farḥat afzā, adj. Increasing delight; entertaining.

فرحت انجام farḥat anjām, adj. Of happy end; successful.

فرحت بخش farḥat bakhsh, adj. Refreshing; pleasant; pleasure-giving; entertaining.

فرخ farrukh (P) adj. Happy; fortunate; auspicious; beautiful.

فرخنده farkhandah (P) adj. Happy; fortunate.

فرخنده طالع ، فرخنده بخت ، فرخنده فال farkhandah tāli', farkhandah bakht, farkhandah fāl, adj. Lucky; fortunate; of happy augury; auspicious; prosperous.

فرد fard (A) n.m. A sheet of paper; list; roll; piece; fragment; verse; a couplet; an individual; one; single; unique; incomparable; the outer fold of a quilt; register; record; statement; account; catalogue.

فرد بشر fard-ĕ bashar, n.m. Human being.

فرد باقیات fard-ĕ bāqiyāt, n.m. Balance sheet.

فرد جرم fard-ĕ jurm, n.m. Calendar of crimes; charge sheet.

فردا fardā (P) adj. Tomorrow; the day of resurrection.

فرداً فرداً fardan fardan (H) adv. Individually; singly; severally; one by one.

فردوس firdaus (A) n.m. A garden; paradise.

فرزانگی farzānagi (P) n.f. Wisdom; science; excellence; learning.

فرزانه farzānah (P) adj. Wise; intelligent; excellent.

فرزند farzand (P) n. A child (son or daughter).

فرزند ناخلف farzand-ĕ nākhalaf, n.m. An undutiful son.

فرزند رشید farzand-ĕ rashid, n.m. A good child.

فرزندی farzandi (P) n.f. The state or condition of a child; childhood; the relation of a son to a parent.

فرزیں farzīṅ (P) n.f. The queen at chess. adj. Wise; learned.

فرس faras (A) n.m. A horse; the knight at chess.

فرسا farsā (P) adj. (used in compos.) Wearing; rubbing; obliterating.

فرستاده firistādah (P) adj. Sent; one who is sent. n.m. A messenger; an ambassador; an envoy.

فرسنگ farsang (P) n.m. A league.

فرسودگی farsudagi (P) n.f. Decay; wear and tear.

فرسوده farsūdah (P) adj. Worn; torn; spoiled by age; obliterated; rubbed; effaced; decayed.

فرش farsh (A) n.m. Floor; pavement; carpet; mattress; a floor-cloth; a cushion; mat.

فرش بچھانا، کرنا farsh bichhānā, karnā, v. To spread; to cover with a carpet; to pave; to fell; to knock down.

فرش فروش farsh furūsh, n.m. Beds and carpets.

فرشتہ farishtah (P) n.m. An angel; an apostle; prophet; messenger (plu. فرشتگان farishtagān).

فرشتہ صفت farishtah sifat, adj. Angelic; angel tempered; heavenly.

فرشی farshi (P) adj. Belonging to a floor or carpet; flat bottomed.

فرصت furṣat (A) n.f. Leisure; freedom; opportunity; rest; leave; recovery; relief.

فرصت پانا، ملنا furṣat pānā, milnā, v. To have time or leisure for; to be at leisure; to find an opportunity; to obtain leave; to be discharged; to be dismissed.

فرصت دینا furṣat denā, v. To allow time, occasion or opportunity for; to give leave.

فرصت ہونا furṣat honā, v. To be at leisure; to recover from illness.

فرض farẓ (A) n.m. Divine command; duty; responsibility; moral obligation; a statute; an ordinance; supposition.

فرض ادا کرنا farẓ adā karnā, v. To discharge one's duty.

فرض کرنا farẓ karnā, v. To impose a duty or obligation; to suppose; to assume; to take for granted; to admit.

فرض کرو farẓ karo, imper. Suppose it was so; take it for granted; assume as a hypothesis.

فرض محال farẓ-ĕ muḥāl, n.m. An impossible or absurd hypothesis; (though it is not possible but even if it were so).

فرض کفایہ farẓ-ĕ kifāyah, n.m. A duty enjoined on all Muslims but if it is performed by one member of a family it is regarded to have been performed by all the family members (as نماز جنازہ namāz-ĕ janāzah, prayer for a deceased).

بالفرض bil-farẓ, adv. On the supposition (that); on the hypothesis (that); granted.

فرضاً farẓan (A) adv. For instance; granting; on the supposition that; hypothetically.

فرضی farẓī (A) adj. Incumbent; obligatory; indispensable; imperative; supposed; fictitious; not real or essential; nominal; assumed, hypothetical.

فرضی نام farẓī nām, n.m. A fictitious or assumed name; pseudonym.

فرط farṭ (A) n.f. Excess; abundance; mastery; superfluity; predominance; a guide post; the top of a hill.

فرط شوق farṭ-ĕ shauq, n.f. Excess of eagerness or desire; deep longing.

فرط محبت farṭ-ĕ maḥabbat, n.f. Excess of love; great affection.

فرع fara' (A) n.f. A branch; a bough; a side issue; a sub-division; a sub-head; a doctrine when put to practice.

فرعون fir'aun (A) n.m. The Pharoah (king of Egypt); a despot; a proud and arrogant person.

فرعون بے سامان fir'aun-ĕ be sāmān, adj. One who is proud despite poverty.

فرعونی، فرعونیت fir'auni, fir'auniyat, n.f. Pride; arogance; despotism.

فرغل farghul (P) n.f. A wrapper; a great coat; cloak; a quilted cloak; a mantle.

فرفر farfar (P) adv. Fast; fluently; quickly.

فرفر پڑھنا farfar parhnā, v. To read fluently.

فرق farq (A) n.m. Difference; distance; distinction; separation; interruption; dispersion; partition; intervening space; interval; defect; deficiency; the head; the top of anything; summit. adj. Distant; separate; distinct. intj. Away! aside!

فرق آ جانا farq ājānā, v. To deteriorate; to degenerate.

فرق پڑنا farq paṛnā, v. Arising of a misunderstanding; to be discordent; to have a misunderstanding.

فرق دلوں میں آنا farq dilon men ānā, v. To have a misunderstanding.

فرقان furqān (A) n.m. Distinguishing truth from falsehood; the Qurān.

فرقت furqat (A) n.f. Separation; distinction; absence (of lovers); disunion.

فرقدان، فرقدین farqdān, farqdain (A) n.m. Two bright stars near the pole.

فرقه firqah (A) n.m. A tribe; a sect; a class; society; kind; company; troop.

فرقه بندی firqah bandi, n.f. Classification; caste system.

فرقه پرست firqah parast, adj. Sectarian.

فرما farmā, n.m. (corr. from the English) The pages of type or stereotype plates arranged and fastened in an iron frame for printing purposes; a forme; a form; a mould.

فرمان farmān (P) n.m. A mandate; order; command; edict; a royal patent; grant; charter.

فرمان بردار farmān bardār, adj. Obedient; complying; subject to orders; charged with orders; compliant. n.m. An employee; an attendant; retainer; vassal; a subject.

فرمان برداری farmān bardārı, n.f. Obedience; execution of orders; featly subjection.

فرمان پذیر farmān pazzir, adj. Obedient; compliant.

فرمان روا farmān rawā, n.m. One entitled to command; a commander; a sovereign.

فرمان روائی farmān rawā'i, n.f. Sovereignty; authority; lordship; sway; rule.

فرمانا farmānā, v. To command; to order; to say; to declare; to affirm; to grant; to vouchsafe; to make or do; to deign.

فرمائش farmā'ish (P) n.f. Order or commission for goods; a requisition; command; will; pleasure.

فرمائش کرنا farmā'ish karnā, v. To give an order; to place an order with.

فرمائشی farmā'ishī (P) adj. As ordered; as desired; made to order; strong; good; excellent.

فرمائشی پڑنا یا کھانا farmā'ishī paṛnā yā khānā, v. To get a sound shoe-beating; to get the deserved punishment.

فرمائشی قہقہہ farmā'ishi qahqahah, n.m. A loud laugh; a horse laugh; homeric laughter.

فرمودہ farmūdah (P) n.m. Order; command; precept. adj. Ordered; uttered; said.

فرنگ farang (P) n.m. Europe.

فرنگستان farangistān (P) n.m. Europe.

فرنگی farangi (P) Eurpean. n.m. An European.

فرنی firnī (P) n.f. A sort of a pudding of ground rice and milk; a dish resembling hasty pudding.

فرنی اور فالودہ ایک بھاؤ نہیں ہوتے firnī aur fālūdah ek bhāo nahin hote, prov. All things in this world have a value of their own.

فرو faro yā firo (P) adj. Down; below, under.

فروتن faro tan, adj Humble; lowly; submissive; depressed.

فروتنی faro tani, n.f. Humility; submission; lowliness.

فرو کرنا faro karnā, v. To quell; to suppress; to curb.

فروکش ہونا faro kash honā, v. To alight; to lodge; to stay; to put up (at).

فرو گذاشت faro guzāsht, n.f. Omission; overlooking; remissness; connivance.

فرو گذاشت کرنا faro guzāsht karnā, v. To omit; to leave out; to pass over; to overlook; to neglect; to fail to take notice (of).

فروماندگی faro māndagi, n.f. Fatigue; helplessness; weakness.

فرومانده faro māndah, adj. Dejected; tired, depressed; fatigued; weary; weak; helpless.

فرو مایگی faro māyagi, n.f. Poverty meanness.

فرومایہ faro māyah, adj. Worthless; poor; ignoble; abject; low; sordid; mean.

فرو ہونا faro honā, v. To subside; to be extinguished; to be put out.

فروخت farokht (P) n.f. Sale; disposal.

فروخت کرنا farokht karnā, v. To sell.

فروخت شده farokht shudah, adj. Sold; disposed off.

فرود farod (P) n.m. Descending; alighting; stopping; halting; arrival and deposit of goods within prescribed limits. prep/. adv. Down; beneath.

فرود گاہ farod gāh, n.f. A halting or landing place; a camping or landing ground; a rest house; a circuit house.

فروزاں furozān (P) adj. Shin ng; luminous: inflaming; resplendent.

فروش farosh (P) adj. Selling; seller (used in compos as حلوا فروش ḥalwā farosh, Sweetmeat seller; a confectioner).

فروشنده faroshindah (P) adj. A seller; a vendor.

فروشی faroshi (P) n.f. (in compos.) Selling.

فروع furū' (A) n.m. (plu. of فرع fara') Branches; summits; tops; heads or chiefs of a family, off-shoots; practical parts of religious doctrine; distant relatives.

فروعی furu'ī (A) adj. Indirect; additional. n.f. Revenue from other sources; additional income.

فروغ farogh (P) n.m. Brightness; light; illumination; splendour; glory; fame; honour.

فروغ پانا farogh pānā, v. To get a name; to rise; to become accomplished; to shine.

فرهنگ farhang (P) n.f. A dictionary; a glossary; wisdom; science; learning; excellence; good breeding.

فریاد faryād (P) n.f. Complaint; charge and suit; crying out for help.

فریاد رس faryād ras, adj. &n.m. A redresser of grievances; a helper, a defender; one who administers unadulterated justice.

فریاد رسی faryād rasi, n.f. Redress; succour; help.

فریاد کرنا faryād karnā, v. To complain; to file a suit against one; to sue; to cry out for help.

فریاد لانا faryād lānā, v. To lodge a complaint.

فریادی faryādi (P) n.m. A complainant; a plaintiff.

فریب fareb (P) n.m. Deceit; trick; deception; fraud; allurement. adj. Deceiving; cheating; alluring; captivating (used in comp. as دل فریب dil fareb, heart captivating.)

فریب آمیز fareb āmez, adj. Deceitful; cunning.

فریب دهی fareb dihī, n.f. Cheating; swindling.

فریب دینا، کرنا fareb denā, karnā, v. To cheat; to deceive; to defraud; to allure; to beguile.

فریب کھانا، فریب میں آنا fareb khānā, fareb men ānā, v. To be deceived; to be cheated; to be deluded by; to be misled.

فریبی farebi, adj. Dishonest; deceitful; delusive; cunning. n.m. A fraud; a cheat; an impostor.

فرید farid (A) adj. Singular; precious; having no equal; incomparable.

فریضه farizah (A) n.m. Divine command; duty.

فریضه ادا کرنا farizah adā karnā, v. To act up to commandments; to perform one's duty; to offer prayers.

فریفته fareftah (P) adj. Enamoured; fascinated; charmed; deluded; seduced, infatuated.

فریفته کرنا fareftah karnā, v. To fascinate; to charm; to delude.

فریفته هونا fareftah honā, v. To be fascinated; to fall in love (with).

فریق fariq (A) n.m. Division; department; section; troop; company; squadron; corps; a party to a suit.

فریقین fariqain (A) n.m. The two parties concerned in a suit; both parties.

فزوں fazūn, fuzūn (P) adj. Increasing; many; much.

فزع faza' (A) n.f. Lamentation; wailing.

فساد fasād (A) n.m. Brawl; outbreak; dissension; intrigue; mischief; disturbance; discord; quarelling; sedition; inequity; wickedness; violence; war; horror; rebellion.

فساد برپا کرنا یا آٹھانا یا مچانا یا کرنا fasād barpā karnā yā uṭhānā yā machānā yā karnā, v. To create or excite a disturbance; to raise a tumult; to riot.

فساد کی جڑ fasād ki jaṛ, n.f. Cause of all troubles; a mischief maker; a fermentor of trouble; a bone of contention.

فسادی fasādi (A & P) adj. Mischievous; seditious; rebellious; quarrelsome; factious.

فسانه fasānah (P) n.m. A romance; a tale; a fable; a fiction.

فسخ faskh (A) n.m. Breach; violation; infraction; infringement; dislocation; dissolving; cancellation.

فسخ کرنا faskh karnā, v. To break off; to cancel; to undo; to annul; to break a contract.

فسردگی fasurdagi (P) n.f. See افسردگی afsurdagī.

فسردہ fasurdah (P) adj. See افسردہ afsurdah.

فسطائی fisṭā'i (A) n.m. Fascist.

فسطائیت fisṭā'iyyat (A) n.f. Fascism.

فسق fisq (A) n.m. Adultery; obscenity; impudence; inequity; sin; impiety; falsehood; insubordination.

فسق و فجور fisq-ŏ fujūr, n.m. Adultery; wickedness; impiety.

فسوں fusūṅ (P) n.m. Enchantment, incantation; a spell; fascination; sorcery.

فسوں ساز ، گر fusūṅ sāz, gar, n.m. An enchanter; sorcerer; magician.

فسوں سازی fusūṅ sāzī, n.f. Enchantment, fascination.

فسوں کرنا fusūṅ karnā, v. To enchant; to use spells or incantations.

فشاں fishāṅ (P) adj. Strewing; scattering; shedding; spreading; diffusing (used in comp. as آتش فشاں ātash fisāṅ, Scattering fire; a volcano).

فشانی fishāni (P) n.f. Spreading; scattering; strewing; shedding (used in comp.)

فشردہ fushurdah (P) adj. Squeezed; pressed.

فصاحت faṣāḥat (A) n.f. Eloquence; fluency of speech; pure or good language.

فصاد faṣṣād (A) n.m. A surgeon; a phlebotomist.

فصادی faṣṣādī (A) n.f. Phlebotomy; surgery.

فصحاء fusahā (A) adj. (plu. of فصیح faṣiḥ) The eloquent.

فصد faṣd (A) n.f. Opening of a vein; bleeding; phlebotomy.

فصد کھولنا faṣd kholnā, v. To bleed; to open a vein.

فصل faṣl (A) n.f. Separation; division; a section; article; clause; chapter; time; season; reaping season; crops; harvest.

فصل استادہ faṣl-ĕ istādah, n.m. A standing crop.

فصل بہار faṣl-ĕ bahār, n.f. Spring season; spring-time.

فصل تخم ریزی faṣl-ĕ tukhm rezī, n.f. Sowing season; seed-time.

فصل خریف faṣl-ĕ kharīf, n.f. The autumnal harvest.

فصل ربیع faṣl-ĕ rabī', n.f. The spring harvest.

فصل کاٹنا faṣl kāṭnā, v. To cut a crop; to harvest.

فصلی faṣli (A & P) adj. Belonging to the harvest or season.

فصلی بٹیرا faṣlī baṭerā (A) n. m. A quail (which visits plains during the harvesting season); a time server; a selfish friend. adj. Slefish; time-serving.

فصلی بخار faṣlī bukhār, n.m. The fever caused by change of season; malaria.

فصلی سال faṣli sāl, n.m. Revenue or harvest year.

فصول fuṣūl (A) n.f. (plu. of فصل faṣl). Seasons; harvests; chapters.

فصیح faṣiḥ (A) adj. Eloquent.

فصیل faṣīl (A) n.f. A city-wall; a rampart; a wall of defence; breast-work; entrenchment.

فضا faẓā (A) n.f. Openness and extensiveness of place; area; a plane; bloom.

فضائل **faẓā'il** (A) *n.m.* (*plu.* of فضیلت *faẓīlat*) ; Virtues; merits; literary attainments; excellences ; learning.

فضل **faẓl** (A) *n.m.* Excellence; virtue; superiority; increase; excess; reward; grace; bounty; learning; wisdom.

فضل کرنا **faẓl karnā**, *v.* To show mercy; to be bountiful; to be gracious.

فضلاء **fuẓalā** (A) *n.m.* (*plu.* of فاضل *fāẓil*) The learned; virtuous or good men.

فضله **fuẓlah** (A) *n.m.* Remainder ; redundance; leaving; refuse; offal; residue; excrement; filth; (*plu.* فضلات *fuẓlāt*).

فضول **fuẓūl** (A) *adj.* Needless ; useless ; redundant; extravagant; superfluous; exuberant.

فضول خرچ **fuẓūl <u>kh</u>arch**, *adj.* Extravagant; prodigal ; profuse. *n.m.* An extravagant person; spendthrift.

فضول خرچی **fuẓūl <u>kh</u>archi**, *n.f.* Extravagance; prodigality; dissipation.

فضول گو **fuẓūl go**, *adj.* A talkative person; one who talks much ; an egotist ; a prolix speaker.

فضه **fiẓẓah** (A) *n.f.* Silver.

فضیتا **faẓītā**, *n.m.* See فضیحت *faẓiḥat*.

فضیحت **faẓiḥat** (A) *n.f.* Disgrace; ignominy; infamy; shame; stain; quarrel: brawl; wrangle.

فضیحت کرنا **faẓiḥat karnā**, *v.* To disgrace; to defame; to expose the faults or vices (of); to quarrel.

فضیحت ہونا **faẓiḥat honā**, *v.* To be disgraced; to be infamous; to be the town talk; to be in every body's mouth.

فضیحتی **faẓiḥati**, *adj.* disgraceful; infamous. *n.f.* Disgrace; ignominy.

فضیلت **faẓīlat** (A) *n.f.* Excellence; perfection; virtue; knowledge; learning; preference; proficiency; superiority.

فضیلت کی پگڑی **faẓīlat ki pagri**, *n.f.* Robe of honour; a diploma.

فضیلت رکھنا **faẓīlat rakhnā**, *v.* To be preferable (to); to be superior (to); to excel; to surpass.

فطانت **fiṭānat, faṭānat** (A) *n.f.* Intelligence; wisdom; perception; shrewdness; skill.

فطر **fiṭr** (A) *n.f.* Breaking a fast.

فطرت **fiṭrat** (A) *n.f.* Nature; creation; form; deceit; intrigue; mechanism; wisdom.

فطرتی **fiṭrati** (A&P) *adj.* Sagacious; wise; cunning; crafty; designing; natural.

فطره، فطرانه **fiṭrah, fiṭrānah** (A) *n.m.* Alms given on *'Id-ul-Fiṭr* day.

فطیری **faṭīrī**, *adj.* Unleavened dough. *n.m.* Unleavened bread.

فعال **fa'āl** (A) *adj.* A great doer; dynamic; an attribute used for God.

فعل **fi'l** (A) *n.m.* Action; work; deed; operation; doing; feigning; pretence; pretext; carnal intercourse; adultery; an unnatural act; (*Gram.*) the verb.

فعل کرانا **fi'l karānā**, *v.* To submit to improper sexual intercourse.

فعل کرنا **fi'l karnā**, *v.* To have sexual intercourse with; to do; to perform; to pretend.

فعل لازم **fi'l-ĕ lāzim**, *n.m.* Intransitive verb; a neuter verb.

فعل متعدی **fi'l-ĕ muta'addi**, *n.m.* Transitive verb.

فعل مجهول **fi'l-ĕ majhūl**, *n.m.* A verb in the passive voice.

فعل معروف fi'l-ĕ ma'rūf, n.m. A verb in the active voice.

فعل ناقص fi'l-ĕ nāqiṣ, n.m. A defective verb.

فعلاً fi'lan̲ (A) adv. In fact; practically; indeed; at present; for the time being.

فعلاً و قولاً fi'lan̲-ŏ qaulān, adv. In word and deed.

فعلی fi'li (A) adj. Practical; actual; present.

فغاں fug̲hāṅ (P) n.m. Clamour; lamentation; complaint; cry of pain or distress.

فِفرو ہونا fafirrū honā, v. To run away; to slink away; to disappear.

فق faqq (A) adj. Lost; gone; faded; dismayed; pale; palled; astonished.

فق پڑ جانا یا ہو جانا faqq paṛ jānā yā ho jānā, v. To turn pale; to look blank.

فقدان fuqdān, fiqdān (A) n.m. Loss; want; scarcity; scantiness; meagerness; shortage.

فقر faqr (A) n.m. Poverty; the practice or vocation of a fakir or dervish; acceptance of life of poverty with resignation and content.

فقر و فاقہ faqr-ŏ fāqah, n.m. Poverty and hunger.

فقراء fuqarā (A) n.m. (plu. of فقیر faqīr) The poor; the destitute; religious mendicants; dervishes; beggars.

فقرہ fiqrah (A) n.m. Sentence; part of a sentence; a phrase; a period; a line; a back-bone; vertebra; one of the segments composing the spinal column.

فقرہ باز fiqrah bāz, adj. Eloquent; artful; glib-tongued.

فقرہ بازی fiqrah bāzī, n. f. Deception.

فقط faqaṭ (A) adv. Merely; simply; only; solely. n.m. End; finis.

فقہ fiqah, fiqh (A) n.f. Knowledge; understanding the science of Islamic law; Islamic jurisprudence; knowledge of religion and law.

فقہا fuqahā (A) n.m. (plu. of فقیہ faqih). Theologians.

فقید faqīd (A) adj. Lost; absent.

فقیدالمثال faqīd-ul-mis̤āl, adj. Incomparable; unique.

فقیر faqīr (A) n.m. A beggar; a mendicant; a dervish; one who leads a holy life. adj. Poor; indigent, penniless; needy.

فقیرانہ faqīrānah (A&P) adv. Like a beggar; beggarly; in the manner of a fakir.

فقیری faqīrī (A&P) n.f. Poverty; beggary; life of a dervish; humility; indigence. adj. Pauper-like.

فقیہ faqih (A) n.m. One well versed in religious laws; a theologian.

فک fakk (A) n.m. The lower and upper jaw; separating two things joined together.

فک اضافت fakk-ĕ iẓāfat, n.m. Omission or dropping of vowel point; deliverance from slavery.

فک الرہن fakk-ur-rehn, n.m. Redemption of a mortgage; liquidation of a debt for which property has been pledged.

فکاہات fukāhāt (A) n.f. (plu. of فکاہہ). Wits and humours.

فکر fikr (A) n.m./f. Opinion; notion; imagination; idea; care; concern; anxiety; counsel, advice; thought; reflection; consideration.

فکر کرنا fikr karnā, v. To consider; to reflect; to care; to ponder; to contrive; to plot against; to be anxious about; to be thoughtful about; to pine; to grieve for.

فکرمند *fikr mand, adj.* Thoughtful; anxious; sad; sorrowful.

فکر مندی *fikr mandi, n.f.* Anxiety; thoughtfulness; sorrow.

فکر معاش *fikr-ĕ ma'āsh, n.f.* To be concerned for food or livelihood.

فگار *figār* (P) *adj.* Wounded; sore; galled; afflicted; confused; distracted.

فلاح *falāḥ* (A) *n.f.* Betterment; prosperity; happiness; profit; safety; refuge.

فلاح *fallāh* (A) *n.m.* An agriculturist; a tiller of the soil.

فلاخن *falākhun* (P) *n.f./m.* A sling for throwing stones; a catapult.

فلاسفه *falāsifah* (A) *n.m.* (*plu.* of فلسفی *falsafi*) Philosophers.

فلاکت *falākat* (A) *n.f.* Misfortune; disgrace; adversity; misery; being out of luck.

فلاکت زده *falākat zadah, adj.* Unfortunate; unlucky; miserable.

فلالین *falālain,* (*corr.* from English) *n.f.* Flannel.

فلاں *fulāṅ* (A) *n.m.* Such a person or thing; so and so; a certain person or thing.

فلزات *filizzāt* (A) *n.f.* Mines; ores; metals.

فلس *fals* (A) *n.m.* A pice; a copper coin; scales of a fish.

فلسفه *falsafah* (A) *n.m.* Philosophy; science.

فلسفی *falsafi* (P) *n.m.* A philosopher.

فلسفیانه *fālsafiyānah* (P) *adj.* Philosophical.

فلفل *filfil* (A) *n.f.* Pepper.

فلک *falak* (A) *n.m.* Sky; heaven; firmament; fortune; fate.

فلک سیر *falak sair, n.f.* Hemp.

فلک الافلاک *falak-ul-aflāk, n.m.* The highest heaven; the empyrean.

فلکی *falaki* (A&P) *adj.* Celestial; heavenly; astronomical.

فلیته *falītah, n.m.* A wick; fuse; torch; a magic wick.

فلیته دینا *falītah denā, v.* To apply a match (to); to set light to.

فم *famm* (A) *n.m.* Mouth; opening.

فن *fann* (A) *n.m.* Art; skill; craft; artifice; technique.

فن کار *fann kar, n.m.* Artist.

فنا *fanā* (A) *n.f.* Mortality; perdition; death; destruction.

فنا پذیر *fanā pizir, adj.* Perishable; transitory; frail.

فنا فی الله *fanā fillah, adj.* Lost in the contemplation of God; a Godly man.

فنا کرنا *fanā karnā, v.* To annihilate.

فنا هو جانا *fanā ho jānā, v.* To perish; to die; to expire.

فنجان *finjān* (A&P) *n.f.* A porcelain dish; a cup.

فندک ،فندق *funduk, finduq* (A) *n.f.* A hazel nut; the filbert nut.

فنون *funūn* (A) *n.m.* (*plu. of* فن *fann*) Arts; ways; modes; tricks; wiles.

فنون لطیفه *fanūn-ĕ laṭifah, n.m.* Fine arts.

فنی *fanni, adj.* Technical.

فواحش *fawāhish* (A) *n.m./f.* (*plu. of* فاحشه *faḥishah*) Harlots; evil deeds; lewdness.

فواد *fuwād* (A) *n.m.* The heart.

فواره *fawwārah* (A) *n.m.* A fountain; a jet; a drain; a spring.

فواکه *fawākih* (A) *n.m.* (*plu. of* فاکه *fākihah*) Fruits.

فوائد fawā'id (A) n.m. (plu. of فائدہ fā'idah) Profits; gains; benefits.

فوت faut (A) n.f. Death; failure; omission.

فوت ہونا faut honā, v. To die; to be lost; to be interred.

فوتی fautī (A&P) adj. Deseased; dead.

فوتی فراری fauti farāri, adj. Dead or absconded; killed and missing; n.m. A list of cultivators who have deserted their cultivation s or home-steads.

فوتی نامہ fauti nāmah, n.m. A list of persons killed; a certificate of death; an obituary.

فوج fauj (A) n.f. An army; a host; a multitude; a crowd.

فوج بحری fauj-ĕ baḥrī, n.f. A fleet; navy.

فوج بھرتی کرنا fauj bhartī karnā, v. To enlist recruits; to recruit for the army.

فوج دار fauj dār, n.m. Commandant of the military force in a district; an office of the police; a magistrate.

فوج داری fauj dārī, n.f. A criminal court; a criminal case.

فوج کشی fauj kashi, n.f. The collecting or mobilising of an army; levying of an army; inroad.

فوج کشی کرنا fauj kashi karnā, v. To invade; to attack; to march an army against.

فوجی faujī (A&P) adj. Military.

فور faur (A) n.m. Haste; Eccelerity.

فی الفور fil faur, adv. Immediately; instantly.

فوراً fauran̲ (A) adv. At once; forthwith; quickly; straight way; directly.

فوز fauz (A) n.f. Victory; advantage; gain; success; salvation.

فوطہ foṭah (P) n.m. Purse; a bag; tax; revenue; testicles; the scrotum.

فوطہ خانہ fotah k̲h̲ānah, n.m. A treassure.

فوطہ دار fatah dār, n.m. Treasurer; cashier; banker.

فوطہ داری foṭah dārī, n.f. Office of revenue collector; bankership.

فوق fauq (A) n.m. loftiness; summit, zenith; superiority; excellence; highest point; altitude. prep. Above.

فوق العادت fauq-ul'-ādat, adj. Extraordinary; unusual.

فوقانی fauqānī (A)adj. Superior; upper; (Gram.) a letter dotted above as (ت).

فوقیت fauqiyyat (A) n.f. Superiority; pre-eminence; preference; excellence; supremacy.

فوقیت چاھنا fauqiyyat chāhnā, v To strive for excellence or superiority; to be ambitious or emulous.

فوقیت پانا fauqiyyat pānā, v. To bear the palm.

فولاد fa ulād or fulād (P) n.m. Steel.

فولادی faulādi (P) adj Made of steel; a pike-stuff.

فہرست fihrist (P) n.f. An inventory; list; index; table of contents; a catalogue; table.

فہرست مضامین fihrist-e-maẓāmin, n.f. Table of contents.

فہم fahm (A) n.m. Understanding; intellect; comprehension; perception.

فہمائش fahmā'ish (P) n. f. Causing one to understand ; warning ; giving instructions or directions ; an order ; explanation.

فہمائش کرنا fahmā'ish karnā, v. To warn; to direct; to caution; to admonish.

فہمیدہ fahmidah (P) adj. Understood; intelligent; wise.

فہوالمراد fahowal-murād (A) phra. That is what I say; this is what I want.

فہیم fahim (A) adj. Intelligent; learned; knowing.

فی fī (A) prep. In; into; among; of; to; with; for; by; n.f. (in Urdū) Defect; fault.

فی نکالنا fi nikālnā, v. To find fault (with).

فیاض faiyyāẓ (A) adj. Liberal; generous; beneficent; munificent; most bountiful.

فیاضی faiyyāẓī (A) n.f. Generosity; benevolence; munificence; liberality.

فیاضی کرنا faiyyāẓi karnā, v. To be liberal.

فیتہ fitah (Port.) n.m. Ribbon; tape.

فیروز firoz (P) adj. Victorious; happy; fortunate.

فیروز بخت fīroz bakht, adj. Victorious; having good fortune.

فیروز مند fīroz mand, adj. Victorious; prosperous.

فیروز مندی fīroz mandī, n.f. Victory; prosperity.

فیروزہ fīrozah (P) n. m. Turquoise.

فیروزی fīrozī (P) adj. Turquoise blue; victory; success; prosperity; fortune.

فیصل faiṣal (A) adj. Decided; settled. n.m. decision; division; separation; decree; determination.

فیصل کرنا faiṣal karnā, v. To decide; to adjust; to settle.

فیصل نامہ faiṣal nāmah n m. A decree; an award.

فیصل ہونا faiṣal hona, v. To be decided or settled; to be adjusted.

فیصلہ faiṣlah (A) n.m. A decree; settlement; decision; adjustment; arbitration.

فیصلہ عدالت faiṣlah-ĕ'adālat, n.m. Judicial decision; decree.

فیصلہ کرنا faiṣlah karnā, v. To decide; to settle.

فیض faiẓ (A) n.m. Liberality; grace; favour; bounty; abundance.

فیض پہنچانا faiẓ puhṅchānā, v. To confer favours (on); to give alms.

فیض رساں faiẓ rasāṅ, adj. Bountiful; generous; beneficent.

فیض عام faiẓ-ĕ'ām n.m. Public good; general munificence.

فیض یاب faiẓ yāb, adj. Benefitted; blessed.

فیضان faiẓān (A) n.m. Beneficence; munificence; generosity; abundance; overflow; benefit.

فیل fīl (A) n.m. An elephant.

فیل بان fīl bān n.m. An elephant driver.

فیل خانہ fīl khānah n.m. Elephant house.

فیل مرغ fīl murgh n.m. Elephant bird; a turkey.

فیل پا، ذات الفیل fīl pā, ẕātulfīl n.m. A disease; elephantiasis.

فیلسوف failsūf (G) n.m. A philosopher; a cunning person; an impostor; adj Intelligent; knowing; cunning; artful; crafty.

فیلسوفی failsūfi n.f. Cunningness; artfulness; Sophistry.

فیوض fuyūẓ (A) n.m. (plu. of فیض faiẓ) Favours; bounties.

ق qāf, is the twenty-first letter of the Arabic, twenty-fourth of the Persian and twenty-seventh of the Urdu alphabet. In *abjad* it stands for 100.

قاب *qāb* (P) *n.f.* A vessel; a case; a frame; a large dish used for serving rice or kneading dough; a large plate.

قاب *qāb* (A) *n.m.* Space; interval; linear; measure; the distance between the middle and extremity of a bow.

قاب قوسين *qāb-a qausain, n.m.* The distance of two bows length; two cubits length.

قابض *qābiẓ* (A) *adj.* Seizing ; possessing ; holding ; grasping; astingent ; constipating. *n.m.* A receiver; a possesser; occupant; occupier; holder.

قابل *qābil* (A) *adj.* Worthy; deserving ; competent; qualified; able; capable; fit; skilful; clever; practicable.

قابل ادا *qābil-ĕ adā, adj.* Payable.

قابل اعتبار *qābil-ĕ i'tibār adj.* Credible; believable ; trustworthy.

قابل اعتراض *qābil-ĕ i'tirāẓ, adj.* Objectionable.

قابل انتقال *qābil-ĕ intiqāl, adj.* Transferable; changeable; mutable.

قابل انعام *qābil-ĕ in'ām, adj.* Deserving a prize.

قابل تعریف *qābil-ĕ ta'rīf, adj.* Praiseworthy.

قابل سزا *qābil-ĕ sazā, adj.* Culpable; punishable.

قابل سماعت *qābil-ĕ samā'at, adj.* Cognizable.

قابل غور *qābil-ĕ ghaur, adj.* Worthy of consideration.

قابل معافی *qābil-ĕ mu'āfī, adj.* Pardonable.

قابل مواخذہ *qābil-ĕ muākhazah, adj.* Capable of falling under judicial notice.

قابلہ *qābilah* (A) *n.f.* A mid-wife; bolt.

قابلیت *qābiliyyat* (A) *n.f.* Capability; accomplishment; ability; fitness; skill; capacity.

قابو *qābū* (P) *n.m.* Power; command; authority; opportunity; possession; hold.

قابو پانا *qābū pānā, v.* To get advantage or power over; to get an opportunity; to get the upper hand; to get hold of.

قابو میں رکھنا *qābū meṅ rakhnā, v.* To keep under control; to restrain.

قابو میں کرنا *qābū meṅ karnā, v.* To subdue; to bring one under control.

قابو میں لانا *qābū meṅ lānā, v.* To get a hold on; to bring one under control.

قابوچی *qābūchī* (T) *n.m.* A door-keeper; a good-for-nothing man; a selfish person.

قاتل *qātil* (A) *n.m.* A murderer; an assassin; homicide; killer. *adj.* Deadly; fatal.

قادر *qādir* (A) *adj.* Potent; powerful; mighty; capable; skilful; competent.

قادر انداز *qādir andāz, adj.* Sure shot.

قادر مطلق *qādir-ĕ muṭlaq, n.m.* The omnipotent.

قارورہ *qārūrah* (A) *n.m.* A broad bottomed bottle for urine; a urinal for a physician in a flask.

قارورہ ملنا *qārūrah milnā, v.* To be in harmony with.

قاری *qārī* (A) *n.m.* A reader (especially of the Quran).

قاز *qāz* (T) *n.f.* A goose or duck.

قاسم *qāsim* (A) *n.m.* A distributor; one who allots.

قاش **qāsh** (T) *n.f.* The eyebrow; a slice; a piece; a steak.

قاشیں کرنا **qāshen karnā**, *v.* To slice,; to cut in pieces; to cut into slices.

قاصد **qāṣid** (A) *n.m.* A messenger; a courier; envoy.

قاصر **qāṣir** (A) *adj.* Unable; impotent; deficient; failing.

قاصر ہونا **qāṣir honā**, *v.* To be deficient; to be unable (to perform).

قاضی **qāẓī** (A) *n.m.* A judge; magistrate.

قاضی الحاجات **qāẓī-ul-ḥājāt**, *n.m.* Supplier of all needs; God; money.

قاضی القضات **qāẓī-ul-quẓẓāt**, *n.m.* A judge of judges; a chief judge.

قاطع **qāṭi'** (A) *adj.* Cutting; rescinding; decisive; definite; conclusive; sharp; incontestible; peremptory; explicit.

قاعدہ **qā'idah** (A) *n.m.* Basis; custom; rule; system; manners; habit; established order; uniformity; institution (Law); maxim; formula; foundation; the rules of grammar; the base of a triangle; a primer.

قاعدہ باندھنا **qā'idah bāndhnā**, *v.* To establish a rule.

قاف **qāf** (A) *n.m.* A fabulous mountain; the mount Caucasus.

قافلہ **qāfilah** (A) *n.m.* A caravan; a body of travellers or traders.

قافلہ سالار **qāfilah sālār**, *n.m.* The leader of a caravan.

قافیہ **qāfiyah** (A) *n.m.* Rhyme; metre; the last word in a verse to which all the other distiches rhyme; cadence; (in poems which terminate in double rhyme the penult syallable is called قافیہ *qāfiyah* and the last one ردیف *radīf*).

قافیہ بندی **qāfiyah bandī**, *n.f.* Rhyming.

قافیہ تنگ کرنا **qāfiyah tang karnā**, *v.* To confuse; to perplex; to reduce one to great straits.

قافیہ تنگ ہونا **qāfiyah tang honā**, *v.* To be in straitened circumstances; to be in difficulties; to be hard pressed.

قاقلہ **qāqulah, qāqilah** (P) *n.m.* Large-sized cardamoms.

قالب **qālib , qālab** (A) *n.m.* A mould; model; form; frame; bust; figure; lifeless form; the body; the centring; shoemaker's last.

قالب بدلنا **qālib badalnā**, *v.* To be transformed; to change one's body.

قالب خالی کرنا **qālib k͟hālī karnā**, *v.* To die.

قالین **qālīn** (T) *n.f.* A woollen carpet; tapestry.

قامت **qāmat** (A) *n.f.* Stature; height; a man's hieght shape ; figure.

قاموس **qāmūs** (A) *n.m.* The ocean; dictionary; the name of an Arabic dictionary.

قانت **qānit** (A) *adj.* Obedient to God; devout ; silent.

قانع **qāne'** (A) *adj.* Satisfied ; contented.

قانون **qānūn** (A) *n.m.* Rule; regulation; law statute; institute; system; custom; state; ordinance.

قانون بنانا **qānūn banānā**, *v.* To frame laws; to legislate ; to make rules.

قانون جنگی **qānūn-ĕ jangī**, *n.m.* Martial law.

قانونچہ **qānūnchah**, *n.m.* A book on medicine ; a musical instrument.

قانون چھانٹنا **qānūn chhāṅṭnā** *v.* To discuss; to argue; to play the lawyer.

قانون دان **qanūn dān**, *n.m.* A lawyer ; a jurist; one versed in law.

قانون دانی **qānūn dānī**, *n.f.* Knowledge of law ; legal acumen.

قانون دیوانی qānūn-ĕ dīwāni, n.m. Civil law.

قانون فوجداری qānūn-ĕ faujdāri n.m. Criminal law.

قانون گو qānūn go, n.m. One who superintends village accounts or پٹواری paṭwāris.

قانون مال qānūn-ĕ māl, n.m. A revenue law.

قانوناً qānūnan, (A) adv. By law; according to law ; under the rules.

قانونی qānūni (A) adj. Legal ; constitutional ; legislative; having the sanction or authority of law.

قانونیا qānūniyā, n.m. A controversialist ; a litigious person; one well versed in the law.

قاہر qāhir (A) adj. Victorious; subduing ; triumphing ; violent; forcible; conquering.

قاہرہ qāhirah (A) n.m. Cairo, capital of Egypt.

قائد qā'id (A) n.m. A leader ; a general; a star in the tail of the Lesser Bear.

قائل qā'il (A) adj. Confessing ; agreeing ; consenting ; acknowledging ; conceding a point ; owning ; subdued ; confuted ; convinced ; confessor ; speaker.

قائل کرنا ، قائل معقول کرنا qā'il karnā, qā'il ma'qūl karnā, v. To convince ; to confute.

قائل ہونا qā'il honā, v. To be convinced ; to yield ; to acknowledge ; to confess ; to consent ; to assent ; to own ; to acquisce.

قائم qā'im (A) adj. Erect ; right ; standing ; stagnant ; firm ; stationary ; constant ; durable ; lasting ; perpendicular; fixed ; stable.

قائم انداز qā'im andāz, n.m. Sure shot.

قائم بالذات qā'im bizzāt, adj. Constant by itself ; an atom ; molecule ; essence.

قائم بالغیر qā'im bil ghair, adj. Depending on others for its existence.

قائم رہنا qā'im rahnā, v. To stand firm; to stick; to keep one's footing.

قائم مزاج qā'im mizāj, adj. Constant or settled temper ; resolute ; of settled mind.

قائم مقام qā'im muqām, adj. Officiating. n.m Representative ; successor ; locum tenens ; viceroy.

قائم مقام ہونا qa'im muqām honā, v. To officiate ; to act for another; to represent.

قائم مقامی qā'im muqāmī, n.f. Deputation representation ; vicegerency ; assigneeship.

قائم ہونا qā'im honā, v. To arise ; to take place; to be set up; to be firm (in).

قائمہ qā'emah (A) n.m. A right angle; a perpendicular.

قائمی qā'emi n.f. Firmness; durability.

قبا qabā (A) n.f. A long gown ; a quilted garment ; a tunic ; a jacket.

قباحت qabāhat (A) n.f. Defect ; Imperfection ; deformity ; deficiency ; baseness ; perversion ; abuse; harm detriment.

قباله qabālah (A) n.m. A title deed ; a bill of sale.

قباله لکھوانا qabālah likhwānā, v. To get a title deed written ; to possess a property ; to become owner of a property.

قباله نویس qabālah nawīs n.m. A deed writer.

قباله نیلام qabālah-ĕ nilām, n.m. A certificate of auction sale.

قبائل qabā'il (A) n.m. (plu. of قبیلہ qabīlah) Tribes; clans; family; wife and children.

قبح qubḥ (A) n.m. Baseness ; deformity.

قبر qabr (A) n.f. A grave ; a tomb.

قبر میں پاؤں لٹکانا qabr meṅ pāoṅ laṭkānā, v. To be one leg in the grave ; to be on the verge of death.

قبر کن qabr kan, n.m. A grave digger.

قبرستان qabristān (A&P) n.m. A burial ground; a cemetery.

قبض qabẓ (A) n.m. Contraction ; astingency ; seizure ; confiscation ; possession; capture; constipation; costiveness; a receipt; voucher.

قبض الوصول qabẓ-ul-wuṣūl, n.m. A receipt; an acknowledgement; an acquittance roll, a discharge.

قبض کرنا qabẓ karnā, v. To seize; to take possession of; to confiscate; to contract; to constipate.

قبضہ qabẓah (A) n.m. Grip; clutch; grasp; power; possession; occupancy; holding; tenure; handle; hilt of a sword; a hinge; the upper arm.

قبضہ مخالفانہ qabẓah-ĕ mukhālifānah, n.m. Adverse possession.

قبضیت qabẓiyyat (A) n.f. Seizure; costiveness; astringency.

قبل qubl (A) n.m. Front; anterior part. adj. First; previous; preliminary; preparatory. adv. Before; beforehand.

قبل ازیں qabl azīṅ, adv. Before this; heretofore.

قبلہ qiblah (A) n.m. The holy Ka'bah in Mecca to which Muslims turn in prayer; an object of veneration and reverence; a form of address for a respectable person; anything opposite.

قبلہ حاجات qiblah-ĕ ḥājāt, n.m. One who supplies another's needs.

قبلہ گاہ qiblah gāh, n.m. A superior; father.

قبلہ نما qiblah numā, n.m. A mariner's compass.

قبور qubūr (A) n.m. (plu. of قبر qabr) Tombs; graves; holsters for pistols.

قبول qabūl yā qubūl (A) n.m. Consent; favourable reception; approbation; assent; admission; acknowledgement; avowal; acceptance; concurrence; recognition.

قبول‌صورت qabūl ṣūrat, adj. Good looking; comely.

قبولنا qabūlnā, v. To accept; to assent; to approve; to make a confession.

قبولی qabūlī (A) n.f. A kind of dish of boiled rice and pulse; a dish made of rice and gram or gram pulse.

قبولیت qabūliyyat, n.f. Acceptance; assent; consent; approbation; a lease; a written agreement; the counterpart of lease.

قبہ qubbah (A) n.m. Dome; vault; cupola; an arch; an alcove.

قبیح qabīḥ (A) adj. Base; vile; bad; shameful; deformed; ugly; detestable; disgraceful.

قبیل qabīl (A) n.m. Race; tribe; family; progeny; category; kindred; species; class; kind; sort.

قبیلہ qabīlah (A) n.m. A family; a tribe; a clan; wife and children.

قبیلہ پروری qabīlah parwarī, n.f. Supporting a family; nepotism.

قبیلہ داری qabīlah dārī, n.f. Taking of a wife; having a large family.

قتال qitāl (A) n.m. Battle; fighting; slaughter.

قتالہ qattālah (A) n.f. A great slayer; a killer; a very beautiful woman.

قتل qatl (A) n.m. Slaughter; killing; homicide; murder, assassination; massacre; execution; bloodshed.

قتل انسان qatl-ĕ insān, n.m. Homicide; murder.

قتل برادر qatl-ĕ barādar, n.m. Fratricide.

قتل پدر qatl-ĕ pidar, n.m. Patricide.

قتل سلطان qatl-ĕ sulṭān, n.m. Regicide.

قتل عام qatl-ĕ ʻāmm, n.m. General massacre.

قتل عمد qatl-ĕ ʻamd, n.m. Wilful murder; homicide.

قتل‌گاہ qatl gāh, n.m. A place of slaughter.

قتل‌مادر qatl-ĕ mādar, n.m. Matricide.

قتلا qatlā, n.m. A piece; a slice; a cutlet.

قتیل qatīl (A) adj. Killed; murdered.

قحبہ qaḥbah (A) n.f. A whore; a prostitute.

قحط qaḥṭ (A) n.m. Famine; dearth; scantiness; scarcity; failure of the harvest; want; lack; drought.

قحط پڑنا qaḥṭ paṛnā, v. Appearance of famine.

قحط زدہ qaḥṭ zadah, adj. Famine-stricken; famished; starving; overwhelmed with dearth.

قحط سالی qaḥṭ sālī, n.f. Famine; drought; dearth.

قد qadd (A) n.m. Stature; size; height; figure.

قدآدم qadd-ĕ ādam, adj. Of the height of man.

قدآور qadd āwar, adj. Tall, commanding stature.

قد و قامت qadd-ŏ qāmat, n.m. Stature; figure (of a person); build; personal appearance; posture.

قدامت qadāmat (A) n.f. Antiquity; priority ancientness; seniority; excellence.

قدامت پسند qadāmat pasand, adj. Conservative; averse to change and progress.

قدح qadaḥ (A) n.m. A goblet; glass; bowl cup.

قدح کش، خوار، نوش qadaḥ kash, khwār, nosh, n.m. A debauchee; a libertine; a drunkard.

قدح qadḥ (A) n.f. Refutation; reproach; satire; lampoon.

قدح کرنا qadḥ karnā, v. To refute; to cross question.

قدر qadr (A) n.f. Dignity honour; rank; merit; position; fate; destiny; price; value; importance; quantity; size; measure; worth; portion; appreciation: estimation; bulk; degree.

قدر دان qadr dān, adj. One who gives due appreciation; an apprec ato · one who knows the worth of

قدر دانی qadr dānī, n.f. Appre iation of merit; due regard to the worth (of); patronage.

قدر شناس qadr shinās, adj. Knowing the worth of.

قدر مشترک qadr-ĕ mushtarak, n. Common value.

قدر و منزلت qadr-ŏ-manzilat, n.f. Rank; dignity; honour.

قدرت qudrat (A) n.f. Power; vigour; ability; potency; force; authority; divine power; omnipotence; the creation; the universe; nature.

قدرت رکھنا qudrat rakhnā, v. To have the power (of or over); to be able (to).

قدرتی qudratī (A&P) adj. Natural; divine; not made or produced by man; inhabited.

قدرتی اسباب qudratī asbāb, n.m. Natural causes.

قدرتی علامات **qudratī 'alāmāti**, *n.f.* Natural features ; phenomena.

قدرے **qadre** (A) *adv.* Somewhat ; a little ; in some measure; to some extent; partially.

قدس **quds, qudus** (A) *n.m.* Holiness; sanctity; Jerusalem; the angel Gabriel. *adj.* Holy; pure.

قدسی **qudsī** (A) *adj.* Holy. *n.m.* The angel Gabriel.

قدسیہ **qudsiyāh** (A) *adj.* Holy ; celestial.

قدغن **qadghan** (P) *n. f.* Prohibition ; injunction.

قدغن کرنا ' لگانا **qadghān karnā, lagānā**, *v.* To prohibit ; to enjoin ; to forbid.

قدم **qadam** (A) *n.m.* A pace ; a step ; a footstep ; a foot ; sole of the foot.

قدم اکھڑنا **qadam ukharnā**, *v.* To be unable to walk properly; not to be able to bear the strains; to retreat.

قدم بقدم **qadam baqadam**, *adv.* Step by step ; by degrees ; slowly.

قدم بوس **qadam bos**, *adj.* Showing respect; prostrating.

قدم بوسی **qadam bosi**, *n.f.* Kissing the feet; obeisance; homage.

قدم چھونا **qadam chhūnā**, *v.* To show respect by touching the feet.

قدم رنجہ فرمانا **qadam ranjah farmānā**, *v.* To take the trouble of coming.

قدم قدم پر **qadam qadam par**, *adv.* At every step.

قدم لینا **qadam lenā**, *v.* To acknowledge the superiority (of); to show respect (to) ; to keep pace.

قدم **qidam** (A) *n.m.* Antiquity ; oldness ; eternity.

قدماء **qudamā.** (A) *n.m.* (Plu. of قدیم **qadīm**) The ancients.

قدمچہ **qadamchah** (A&P) *n.m.* A footboard.

قدوس **quddūs** (A) *adj.* Holy; pure; an epithet of God.

قدوم **qudūm** (A) *n.m.* Arrival ; approach ; accession; advent.

قدوم میمنت لزوم **qudūm-ĕ-maimanat luzūm**, *adj.* Auspicious arrival (of).

قدیر **qadīr** (A) *adj.* Powerful ; an epithet of God.

قدیم **qadīm** (A) *adj.* Old; ancient; entiquated.

قدیمی **qadimī**, *adj.* Old ; ancient ; former ; bygone.

قرابا دین **qarābā dīn** (A) *n.f.* Meteria medica ; pharmacopoeia; compounded medicines; antedote.

قرابت **qarābat** (A) *n.f.* Relationship ; nearness; kin; vicinity; connections; affinity; kindred.

قرابت دار **qarābat dār**, *n.m.* A kinsman; a relative.

قرابت داری **qarābat dāri**, *n.f.* Relationship; affinity.

قرابتی **qarābatī**, *adj.* Related to ; akin ; relative. *n.m.* A relative; a relation.

قرابہ **qarābah** (A) *n.m.* A large glass; a jar, a bottle ; a flagon.

قرابین **qarābīn** (T) *n.f.* A carbine ; a short light musket.

قرأت **qirat** (A) *n.f.* Pronunciation ; reading.

قرار **qarār** (A) *n.m.* Residence; settling; resting; permanence; rest; repose; patience; tranquillity; firmness; stability; steadiness; consistency; quietness; satisfaction; waiting; fixedness.

قرار آنا qarār ānā, v. To be at rest or ease; to become still or quiet.

قرار پانا qarār pānā, v. To be tranquil; to receive satisfaction; to grow calm; to be agreed upon; to be decided.

قرار داد qarār dād, n.f. Resolution; engagement; agreement; contract; settlement; confirmation; convention.

قرارداد مقاصد qarār dād-ĕ maqāṣid, n.f. Objectives resolution; containing objects to be achieved; statement of objects and reasons.

قرار دینا qarār denā, v. To establish; to settle; to decide; to admit; to determine; to adjudge; to resolve.

قرار واقعی qarār wāqa'i, adv. Positively; definitely; rightly; accurately; effectionately; effectually; truly.

قراقر qarāqur (A) n.m. Grumbling (of the bowels); colic pain; griping.

قران qirān (A) n.m. Conjunction of the planets; contiguity; nearness in time; neighbourhood; kindred.

قران السعدین qirān-us-sa'dain, n.m. Conjunction of two auspicious planets, Jupiter and Venus; meeting of two big personalities.

قران qurān (A) n.m. Revealed book of the Muslims.

قران اٹھانا qurān uṭhānā, v. To swear by the Quran; to take an oath on the Quran.

قراول qarāwal (T) n.m. Advanced guard of an army; a sentinel; a picket; a gunner; a hunter; a game-keeper.

قرائن qarā'in (A) n.m. (plu. of قرینہ qarīnah) Conditions; circumstances; conjectures; presumptions.

قرب qurb (A) n.m. Vicinity; proximity; nearness; relationship; kindred; neighbourhood; approach.

قرب وجوار qurb-ō jawār, n.m. Environs; suburbs; vicinity.

قربان qurban (A) n.m. A sacrifice; victim; an offering; the sling of a quiver.

قربان گاہ qurbān gāh, n.f. An altar; a place for offering sacrifice.

قربانی qurbāni (A) n.f. A sacrifice.

قربانی کا بکرا qurbānī kā bakrā, n.m. Scapegoat.

قربت qurbat (A) n.f. Nearness; relationship.

قربیٰ qurbā (A) n.f. Affinity; relationship; near relation.

قرحہ qarhah (A) n.m. A wound; a sore; an ulcer.

قرشی qarashī, qarshī (A) adj. See قریشی quareshī.

قرص qurṣ (A) n.m. The disc of the sun or moon; an orb· a round loaf of bread; a tablet; a pallet; a ball of paste; a wafer; a small silver coin worth about two annas.

قرض qarz (A) n.m. A debt; a loan; money borrowed at interest; credit.

قرض اٹھانا، لینا qarẓ uṭhānā, lenā, v. To borrow; to take a loan.

قرض چکانا qarẓ chukānā, v. To pay off a debt; to discharge a debt.

قرض حسنہ qarẓ-ĕ ḥasanah, n.m. The better kind of loan; loan without interest and repayable when the debtor is in a position to repay.

قرض خواہ qarẓ khwāh, n.m. A creditoı; one who gives a loan.

قرض دار qarẓ dār, n.m. A debtor; one in debt.

قرض دہندہ qarẓ dihindah, n.m. A lender; one who lends money.

قرضه qarẓah (A) n.m. A loan; a debt.

قرطاس qirṭās (A) n.m. Paper.

قرطاس ابیض qirṭās-ĕ abyaẓ, n.m. White paper; blank paper.

قرعه qur'ah (A) n.m. Die; a cast or throw of dice; a wager; drawing lots; a raffle; a ballot; a petty lottery.

قرعہ اندازی qur'ah andāzi, n.f. Division by lots.

قرعه ڈالنا qur'ah ḍālnā, v. To draw lots; to divide by lots.

قرق qurq (A) adj. Attached; forfeited; confiscated; distrained. n.m. An embargo; confiscation; seizure; attaching; enclosure; hinderance; prevention of access.

قرق امین qurq amin, n.m. A bailiff.

قرقی qurqī, n.f. Attachment; seizure; confiscation.

قرقی نامه qurqī nāmah, n.m. A warrant of attachment.

قرمز qirmiz (A) n.m. Crimson; cochineal.

قرمزی qirmizī (A) adj. Crimson coloured; scarlet; red.

قرن qarn (A) n.m. An age; a period of 10 to 120 years; conjunction of the planets; horn (of an animal).

قرنا، قرنائی qarnā, qarnā'i (A&P) n.f. A trumpet; a horn (musical); a bugle; a clarion; a cornet; clarronet.

قرنبیق qaranbiq (A) n.m. An elembic; a still; a retort.

قرنفل qaranfal (G) n.m. A clove.

قرولی qaraulī (P) n.f. A hunting knite; a picquet; grand guard; a hunt; a chase.

قریب qarīb (A) adj. Near; adjacent; relative; akin; neighbouring; approaching; drawing near. adv. Almost; about; near.

قریب الاختتام qarīb-ul-ikhtitām, adj. Near the end; on the point of completion.

قریب الفهم qarīb-ul-fahm, adj. Within the reach of understanding; comprehensive; conceivable; comprehensible.

قریب مرگ qarīb marg, adj. On the point of death.

عن قریب، عنقریب 'an qarīb, adv. Very soon; shortly; nearly; in the near future; imminent.

قریباً qarīban, adv. Shortly; in a short while; nearly; approximately; close upon; about.

قریش quraish (A) n.m. A famous tribe of Arabia to which the Holy Prophet belonged.

قریشی Quareshī (A) adj. Belonging to the tribe of قریش Quraish.

قرین qarīn (A) adj. Connected; adjoining; akin; next; contiguous; allied. n.m. Associate; friend.

قرین قیاس qarīn-ĕ qayās, adj. Conceivable; believable; within the range of possibility.

قرین مصلحت qarīn-ĕ maṣlahat, adj. Advisable; proper; expedient.

قرینه qarīnah (A) n.m. Context; symmetry; conjecture; similarity; analogy; connection; regularity; order; arrangement; manner; cause; way, mode; system.

قرینه سے لگانا، کرنا qarīnah se lagānā, karnā, v. To put in order; to arrange; to do things in a systematical way.

قریه qaryah (A) n.m. A village; a town.

قزاق qazzāq (T) n.m. A robber; a free-booter.

قزاق اجل qazzāq-ĕ ajal, n.m. The angel of death.

قزاقی qazzāqī (T) n.f. The profession of a robber; robbery; free-booting; brigandage.

قزلباش qizlbāsh (T) n.m. An Irani soldier, so-called because they wore red cap, as a distinctive mark.

قسام qassām (A) n.m. A divider; a distributor; an apportioner.

قسام ازل qassām-ĕ azal, n.m. God.

قساوت qasāwat (P) n.f. Cruelty; grief; anguish; pain; chagrin; hardness; anxiety; melancholy; stinginess.

قساوت قلبی qasāwat-ĕ qalbi, n.f. Hardness of heart; hard-heartedness.

قسط qisṭ (A) n.f. Instalment; portion; partition; tax; dividend; justice.

قسط باندھنا qisṭ bāndhnā, v. To pay instalment.

قسط بندی qisṭ bandī, n.f. Settling payment by instalment.

قسط کرنا qisṭ karnā, v. To agree to pay by instalments.

قسم qasam (A) n.m. An oath.

قسم توڑنا qasam toṛnā, v. To violate an oath: to perjure oneself; to abjure.

قسم دینا qasam denā, v. To adjure; to put one under an oath; to administer an oath.

قسم دلانا qasam dilānā, v. To make one swear.

قسم کھانا qasam khāna, v. To swear; to take an oath.

قسم لینا qasam lenā, v. To administer an oath.

قسما قسمی qasmā qasmi, n.f. Swearing on both sides; swearing both parties.

قسم qism (A) n.f. Division; part; portion; kind; sort; species; description; nature.

قسم وار qism wār, adj. Classified; according to the description or quality of.

قسمت qismat (A) n.f. Fate; fortune; lot; destiny; share; portion; district; division; section; head; category; part; distribution.

قسمت آزمائی qismat āzma'i, n.f. Trying one's luck.

قسمت اُلٹ جانا ، پلٹ جانا ، پھر جانا qismat ulat jānā, palat jānā, phir jānā, v. To come under an unlucky star; to fall into adversity.

قسمت پھرنا، جاگنا ، چمکنا qismat phirnā, jāgnā, chamaknā, v. To be fortunate or prosperous; to be in luck.

قسمت سے qismat se, adv. Fortunately; luckily; by chance.

قسمت کا دھنی qismat kā dhani, adj. Fortunate; a lucky person.

قسمت کا لکھا qismat kā likhā, n.m. Apportioned by destiny; as destined.

قسمت کا ھیٹا qismat kā heṭā, adj. An unfortunate person.

قسمت لڑنا qismat laṛnā, v. To have favourable chances; to have a run of luck.

قسمت والا qismat wālā, adj. Fortunate; lucky; prosperous.

قسمت پزیر qismat paẕīr, adj. Divisible; that which can be divided.

قسمیه qasmiyyah (A) adv. On an oath; under an oath.

قسیس qissis (A) n.m. A Christian priest; a bishop; a presbyter.

قسیم qasim (A) n.m. One who distributes; one who divides.

قشر qishr, qashr (A) n.m. Peel; skin; bark; husk; rind; shell; crust.

قشقه qashqah (P) n.m. A mark made by Hindus on their forehead indicating the sect to which they belong.

قصاب qaṣṣāb (A) n.m. A butcher.

قصابہ qaṣābah (A) n.m. A handkerchief tied round the head by women.

قصابہ qaṣṣābah (A) n.f. A female butcher.

قصاص qiṣāṣ (A) n.m. The law of retaliation; punishment for murder.

قصاص لینا qiṣāṣ lenā, v. To retaliate; to punish appropriately; to punish with life-taking.

قصائد qaṣā'id (A) n.m. (plu. of قصیدہ qaṣīdah) Laudatory poems; odes.

قصائی qaṣā'ī, n.m. A butcher; a merciless person.

قصباتی qaṣbātī, adj. Belonging to a قصبہ qaṣbah; urban.

قصبہ qaṣbah (A) n.m. A small town; (plu. قصبات qaṣbāt).

قصد qaṣd (A) n.m. Intention, design; aim; object; resolve; inclination; purpose; project: attempt.

قصد کرنا qaṣd karnā, v. To intend; to resolve; to strive; to pursue; to design; to proceed; to make an attempt; to make one's object or aim; to undertake a journey; to form a design against.

قصداً qaṣdan (A) adv. Intentionally; deliberately; voluntarily; purposely; expressly; willingly.

قصر qaṣr (A) n.m. Diminution; a defect; evening twilight; an edifice; a palace; a citadel; a mansion; a building; an elegant villa.

قصص qiṣaṣ (A) n.m. (plu. of قصہ qiṣṣah) Stories; tales; fables.

قصور quṣūr (A) n.m. Defect; fault; deficiency; omission; want; failure; blame; sin; incorrectness.

قصور کرنا qūṣur karnā, v. To commit a fault; to fail; to be deficient.

قصور وار quṣūr wār, adj. Blame-worthy; at fault.

قصور quṣūr (A) n.m. (plu. of قصر qaṣr) Palaces; palatial houses.

قصہ qiṣṣah (A) n.m. A tale; a story; a fable; a romance; a quarrel; a dispute.

قصہ پاک کرنا qiṣṣah pāk karnā, v. To settle a dispute; to put to death; to kill; to murder; to wipe out of existence.

قصہ پاک ہونا qiṣṣah pāk honā, v. To be wiped out of existence.

قصہ خوان qiṣṣah khwān, n.m. A story teller; a reciter of tales.

قصہ خوانی qiṣṣah khwānī, n.f. Story-telling.

قصہ کوتاہ qiṣṣah kotāh, adv. In short; briefly.

قصہ کوتاہ کرنا qiṣṣah kotāh karnā, v. To cut the long matter short.

قصہ کہانی qiṣṣah kahānī, n.m. Myths and legends.

قصیدہ qaṣīdah (A) n.m. Laudatory poem; an ode; enlogium; encomium.

قضا qaẓā (A) n.f. Fate ; destiny ; decree; chance; death ; fatality ; administration of justice ; judicature ; jurisdiction; mandate ; judgment ; saying a prayer after due time.

قضائے الہی سے مرنا qaẓa ĕ-ilahī se marnā, v. To die a natural death.

قضائے حاجت qaẓā ĕ-ḥājat, n.f. Going to the necessary call of nature.

قضارا یا قضا کار qaẓā rā yā qaẓā kar, adv. By chance.

قضائے عمری qaẓā-ĕ 'umrī, n.f. Saying prayers missed in life ; saying extra prayers.

قضا کرنا qaẓā karnā, v. To die ; to omit saying prayer.

قضائے مبرم qaẓā-ĕ mubram, n.f. Inevitable fate; death for which a time is fixed.

قضائے ناگہانی qaẓā-ĕ nāgahānī, n.f. Sudden death.

قضا و قدر qaẓā-ŏ qadr, n.m. Fate, predestination ; destiny.

قضات quzzāt (A) n.m. (plu. of قاضی qāẓī) Judges ; justices.

قضایا qaẓāyā (A) n.m. (plu. of قضیه qaẓiyah) Quarrels ; disputes ; cases.

قضیب qaẓīb (A) n.m. A long and slender branch ; a rod ; a small sword; penis.

قضیه qaẓiyah (A) n.m. A case; a proposition ; a dispute ; debate ; quarrel; broil, litigation ; law suit ; history ; narrative ; declaration ; determination ; a syllogism ; death.

قضیه مول لینا qaẓiyah mol lenā, v. To interfere without cause in the disputes of another.

قط qaṭṭ (A) n.m. Cutting transversely ; cutting the nib of a pen ; making a pen ; mending a pen.

قط زن، گیر qaṭṭ zan, gīr, n.m. A piece of wood or bone on which the nib of a pen is cut ; a stamp.

قطار qiṭār, qaṭār (A) n.f. A line ; a row ; rank ; order ; series; range; file ; train ; queue.

قطار باندھنا qaṭār bāndhnā, v. To stand in a line ; to form a queue ; to set in a row ; to arrange in a series.

قطامه qaṭṭāmah (A) n.f. A strumpet ; an adultress.

قطب quṭb (A) n.m. The iron spindle or axis on which a millstone turns ; the polar star ; a title or degree of rank among religious mendicants ; a pivot ; a lord ; a chief.

قطب جنوبی quṭb-ĕ junūbī, n.m. The south pole.

قطب شمالی quṭb-ĕ shimālī, n.m. The north pole.

قطب نما quṭb numā, n.m. The mariner's compass.

قطب الاقطاب quṭb ul-aqṭāb, n.m. The lord of lords (among religious mendicants).

قطبی quṭbī (A&P) adj. Polar.

قطر quṭr (A) n.m. A diameter.

قطر دائره quṭr -ĕ-dā'erah, n.m. Diameter of a circle.

قطره qaṭrah (A) n.m. Drop ; a minim; (plu. قطرات qaṭrāt).

قطره قطره qaṭrah qaṭrah, adv. Drop by drop; by drops.

قطع qaṭa' (A) n.m. Cutting (off) ; crossing; intersection; segment; a portion; fashion; model; section; division; style; breaking off ; intercepting; passing; crossing.

قطع تعلق qaṭa'-ĕ ta'alluq, n.m. Separation; abandonment.

قطع تعلق کرنا qaṭa ta'alluq karnā, v. To abandon; to desert; to break off all connections (with).

قطع دائره qaṭa'-ĕ dā'erah, n.m. Segment of a circle.

قطع کرنا qaṭa' karnā, v. To cut ; to cut short ; to perform (a journey) ; to form ; to fashion; to cross ; to pass.

قطع کره qaṭa'-ĕ-kurrah, n.m. Segment of a sphere.

قطع کلام کرنا qaṭa'-ĕ kalām karnā, v. To interrupt the speech of; to put in a word ; to cut in.

قطع نظر qaṭa'-ĕ naẓar, adv. Irrespective of ; independent of; exclusive ; besides; except; save ; in disregard of; at all events.

قطع و برید qaṭa'-ŏ burīd, n.m. Cutting and clipping.

قطع ہونا qaṭa' honā, v. To be cut short ; to be cut ; to be deducted ; to be traversed ; to be passed over.

قطعاً qaṭ'an (A) adv. Positively ; definitely.

قطعه qiṭ'ah yā qaṭ'ah (A) n.m. A piece ; a part; a fragment; a section ; a cutting ; a kind of verse, a stanza ; a piot of land.

قطعه بند qiṭ'ah band, n.m. A kind of verse in which the meaning of the first verse of each stanza is completed in the last.

قطعی qaṭa'i, adj. Final ; imperative; decisive; conclusive. adv. Altogether; entirely ; absolutely ; finally ; conclusively.

قطعی گز qaṭa'i gaz, n.m. A tailor's measure.

قطمیر qiṭmir (A) n.m. The thin pellicle on a date-stone ; name of the dog which accompanied the Seven Sleepers in the Cave.

قعده qa'dah (A) n.m. Sitting; sitting on knees in the prayer ; kneeling.

قعر qa'r (A) n.m. A gulf ; an abyss ; the bottom; depth; a hollow cavity.

قعر دریا qa'r-ĕ daryā, n.m. The deepest place in a river; middle of the river; the depth of a river.

قعود qu'ūd (A) n.m. The act of sitting ; sitting down ; remaining in one place.

قفس qafas (A) n.m. A cage; a lattice ; a net work ; the body.

قفل qufl (A) n.m. A lock ; a bolt.

قفل توڑنا qufl toṛnā, v. To break open a lock.

قفل لگانا qufl lagānā, v. To lock up.

قفلی qufli (A) n.f. A mould (for ice jelly) ; a small saucer-shaped earthen vessel ; a حقه hookah snake.

قل qul (A)n.m. Reading of the سوره sūrah of the Quran at religious feasts held in commemoration of deceased persons, hence conclusion.

قل اعوذیه qul a'ūziah, n.m. A beggar ; a sycophant ; one who lives on alms.

قل هو جانا qul ho jānā, v. To come to an end ; to be all over ; to be dead.

قلا بازی qalābāzi, n.f. A somersault.

قلابازی کهانا qalābāzi khānā, v. To take a somersault.

قلابه qulābah (A) n.m. A hook ; a buckle ; hinge ; link ; hasp ; a staple; a handle.

قلاده qilādah (A) n.m. A collar ; a necklace.

قلاش، قلاچ qallāsh, qallāch (T) adj. Shrewd ; cunning; malicious; wretched; friendless; poor ; addicted to drinking; drunkard. n.m. A rogue ; a knave ; a clown ; a cheat.

قلاقند qallāqand, n.f./m. A kind of sweetmeat.

قلانچ qullānch, n.f. A jump; a spring.

قلب qalb (A) n.m. The heart ; mind ; soul ; understanding ; the intellect ; kernel ; marrow ; pith ; turning ; inversion ; inverse ; counterfeit coin ; the centre or main body of an army. adj. Inverted ; adulterated body ; strongly fortified ; impregnable ; counterfeit.

قلب ساز qalb sāz, n.m. The maker of counterfeit coins.

قلبه qulbah (A) n.m. A plough.

قلبه رانی qublah rāni, n.f. Ploughing ; driving the plough.

قلبی qalbi (A) adj. Cordial ; hearty ; adulterated ; counterfeit.

قلت qillat (A) n.f. Shortage ; want ; deficiency ; scarcity ; difficulty ; dearness ; littleness; paucity ; indigence ; penury ; scantiness; insufficiency.

قلزم qulzum (A) n.m. Clysma, from which this word springs is a town in Egypt near Mount Sinai ; a sea.

بحیره قلزم buḥerah-ĕ-qulzum, n.m. The Red Sea.

قلع قمع qala' qama' (A) n.m. Destruction ; extirpation ; ruination; annihilation.

قلعه qil'ah yā qal'ah (A) n.m. A fort.

قلعه دار qīlah dār, n.m. Commandant of a garrison in a fort ; the governor of fort.

قلعی qala'i (A) *n.f.* Tin.

قلعی کرنا *qala'ī karnā, v.* To tin ; to give a coating of tin to pots; to electro-plate ; to white wash.

قلعی کا کشته *qala'ī kā kushtah, n.m.* Calx of tin ; putty.

قلعی کهلنا *qala'ī khulnā, v.* To be found out; to be discovered or betrayed ; exposure of a man in his true colours.

قلعی کهولنا *qala'ī kholnā, v.* To expose a person.

قلعی گر *qala'i gar, n.m.* A tinner of pots ; a tin-man.

قلعی گری *qala'ī garī, n.f.* The business of tinning pots.

قلفی *qulfi.* See قفلی *quflī.*

قلق *qalaq* (A) *n.m.* Anxiety ; regret ; discomfort ; disquietude ; commotion; perturbation ; trouble.

قلق رهنا *qalaq rahnā, v.* To rankle in the mind; a regret of a thing to remain in mind.

قلق گزرنا *qalaq guzarnā, v.* To feel anxiety or pain; to regret.

قلق هونا *qalaq honā, v.* To feel sorrow; to feel pain; to pine after.

قلقل *qulqul* (A) *n.f.* Gurgling ; the noise made by water in the neck of a bottle when pouring out.

قلم *qalam* (A) *n.m.* A reed ; a pen ; hand-writing ; a mode of writing characters. *n.f.* Cuttings of trees for planting; a slip ; graft; a kind of firework; the upper part of the beard; authority.

قلم بنانا *qalam banānā, v.* To mend a pen; to set the upper part of the beard near the temples.

قلم بند *qalam band, adj.* Hand-written.

قلم بند کرنا *qalam band karnā, v.* To write; to take down ; to take a note of ; to commit to writing.

قلم پاک *qalam pāk, n.m.* A pen-wiper.

قلم تراش *qalam tarāsh, n.m.* Pen-knife.

قلم دان *qalam dān, n.m.* A pen-case ; ink-stand ; writing case.

قلم رو *qalam rau, n.f.* Empire ; dominion; kingdom ; jurisdiction.

قلم زدگی *qalam zadagi, n.f.* Cancellation.

قلم زن کرنا *qalam zan karnā, v.* To draw the pen across ; to cancel; to write off ; to delete.

قلم کار *qalam kār, n.m.* A painter ; engraver ; figured calico.

قلم کاری *qalam kāri, n.f.* Engraving; workmanship ; painting; writing.

قلم کرنا *qalam karnā, v.* To cut off ; to prune.

قلم کشی *qalam kashī, n.f.* Writing.

قلم لگانا *qalam lagānā, v.* To graft ; to plant cuttings.

قلم مو *qalam-ĕ mū, n.m.* A paint brush.

یک‌قلم *yak qalam, adv.* At once; immediately; forthwith; totally; entirely; altogether.

قلماقنی *qilmāqanı* (T) *n.f.* A female armed attendant on a lady.

قلمی *qalamī, adj.* Hand-written; grafted; crystallised; a sheet with long straight lines.

قلمی نسخه *qalamī nuskhah, n.m.* A manuscript; a hand-written book.

قلمی آم *qalamī 'ām, n.m.* Grafted mangoes.

قلمی شوره *qalamī shorah, n.m.* Crystallised saltpetre.

قلندر *qalandar* (P) *n.m.* A Muslim sect of fakirs who shave off the head and the beard and abandon worldly possessions, friends and relatives and travel from place to place worshipping the one God; a bear-dancer; a monkey-dancer.

قلوب *qulūb* (A) *n.m.* (*plu. of* قلب *qalb*) Hearts; minds.

قله qullah (A) n.m. The top; the summit; the peak; a sort of a cap round which turban is tied.

قلی quli (T) n.m. A porter; a coolie; a labourer.

قلیان qalyān (A) n.m. A small and simple tobacco pipe.

قلیل qalil (A) adj. Small; little; few; deficient; scanty; moderate; rare.

قلیه qalyah (A) n.m. Boiled meat dressed with anything; curry; potash from which soda is made.

قمار qimār (A) n.m. Dice ; any game of chance.

قمارباز qimār bāz, n.m. A gambler.

قمارخانه qimār k͟hānah, n.m. A gambling den.

قماش qumāsh (A) n.m. Piecegoods; trifles; things of no value; breeding; manners.

قمچی qamchi (T) n.f. A twig; a horse-whip; a cane; a switch; a bamboo stick.

قمر qamar (A) n.m. The moon.

قمری qamari (A) adj. Lunar.

قمری qumri (A) n.f. A ring-dove; turtledove.

قمقمه qumqumah (P) n.m. A jug; a pitcher; a globe; a round shade or lantern; electric bulb.

قمیص qamīṣ (A) A shirt; chemise.

قنات qanāt (A) n.f. The side of a tent; an external screen of canvas surrounding a tent; a screen.

قنادیل qanādil (A) n.f. (plu. of قندیل qindīl) Candles; lamps; chandeliers; lanterns.

قناعت qanā'at (A) n.f. Contentment; tranquillity; abstinence.

قند qand (A) n.m. Sugar; loaf sugar; white crystallised sugar; sugar candy

قندیل qindīl (A) n.f. A candle; a lamp; a lantern; a chandelier; a shade.

قنوت qunūt (A) n.f. Obedience to God; devotion; piety.

قنوط qunūṭ (A) n.f. Despair.

قنوطیت qunūṭiyyat (A) n.f. Defeatism; frustration; passiveism.

قنصل qànṣal (P) See قونصل qaunṣal.

قوی quwā (A) n.m. (plu. of قوت quwwat) Powers, forces; virtues.

قواعد qawā'id (A) n.m. (plu. of قاعده qā'idah) Rules; regulations; principles; the rules of grammar; drill; military exercise; parade.

قواعددان qawā'id dān, n.m. Well versed in rules and regulations; a drill master; a grammarian.

قوال qawwāl (A) n.m. Professional singer on saints' tombs; a musician; one who speaks well or fluently.

قوالی qawwāli (A) n.f. Singing and playing.

قوام qiwām (A) n.m. Materials; ingredients; syrup; essence; substance; that on which anything rests; straightness.

قوانین qawānīn (A) n.m. (plu. of قانون qānūn) Laws; ordinances; statutes; rules; regulations.

قوت qūt (A) n.f. Food; aliment; livelihood; subsistence; victuals.

قوت quwwat (A) n.f. Power; virtue; authority; faculty; strength; vigour; energy; support.

قوت باصره quwwat-ĕ bāṣirah, n.f. Sight; power of vision.

قوت باه quwwat-ĕ bāh, n.f. Virility; lust.

قوت جاذبه quwwat-ĕ jāẕibah, n.f. Power of absorption; power of attraction.

قوت حافظه quwwat-ĕ ḥāfiẓah, n.f. Faculty of memory.

قوت دافعه quwwat-ĕ dāfe'ah, n.f. Power of expulsion or resistance.

قوت‌ذائقه quwwat-ĕ ẕā'iqah, n.f. Sense of taste.

قوت‌سامعه quwwat-ĕ sāme'ah, n.f. The faculty of hearing.

قوت‌شامه quwwat-ĕ shāmmah, n.f. The sense of smelling.

قوت‌لامسه quwwat-ĕ lamisah, n.f. Sense of touch.

قوت‌ماسکه quwwat-ĕ māsikah, n.f. Power of retention.

قوت‌متخیله quwwat-ĕ mutakhaiyyilah n.f. The power of imagination; the thinking faculty.

قوت‌مدرکه quwwat-ĕ mudrikah, n.f. The power of apprehension; faculty of intellect or conception.

قوت‌ممیزه quwwat-ĕ mumaiyyzah, n.f. Distributive power; discrimination.

قورمه qormah (T) n.m. A highly spiced and tasty curry without turmeric with very little gravy

قوس qaus (A) n.f. A bow; the arc of a circle; the sign Sagittarious.

قوس‌اندرونی qaus-ĕ andarūnī, n.f. The concave side.

قوس‌بیرونی qaus-ĕ bairūnī, n.f. The convex side.

قوس‌قزح qaus-ĕ quzaḥ, n.f. The rainbow.

قوسی qausī (A) adj. Bow-shaped; curved.

قول qaul (A) n.m. Word; saying; speech; assertion; promise; consent; vow; agreement; contract; affirmation.

قول توڑنا qaul toṛnā, v. To break one's word.

قول دینا qaul denā, v. To give word; to promise.

قول صالح qaul-ĕ ṣāliḥ, n.m. A solemn promise; solemn declaration.

قول فیصل qaul-ĕ faiṣal, n.m. Final consent or decision; last word.

قول و قرار qaul-ŏ qarār, n.m. Mutual agreement; treaty; convention.

قول و قرار کرنا qaul-ŏ qarār karnā, v. To covenant; to bind by contract; to back one's word; to stipulate; to make terms.

قول کا پورا qaul kā pūrā, adj. True to one's word; a man of words.

قول و فعل qaul-ŏ fi'l, n.m. Word and deed.

قول هارنا qaul hārnā, v. To give one's word; to promise; to agree; to make terms.

بقول ba-qaul, adv. According to the saying or dictum of.

قولنج qūlanj yā qūlinj (A) n.m. Colic; gripes; griping pain in the bowels.

قوم qaum (A) n.m. Nation; a people; a race; a tribe; a sect.

قومه qaumah (A) n.m. Standing erect after bending in prayer.

قومی qaumī (A) adj. Tribal; racial; national.

قومی حکومت qaumī ḥukūmat, n.m. National government.

قومی مجلس qaumi majlis, n.f. National assembly.

قومیانه qaumiyānā, v. To nationalize.

قومیت qaumiyyat (A) n.f. Nationality.

قونصل qaunṣal (A) n.m. Consul; ambassador.

قوی qawī (A) adj. Strong, powerful; vigorous; firm; mighty.

قوی‌الجثه qawī-ul-juṣṣah, adj. Of mighty frame; gigantic; robust.

قوی هیکل qawī haikal, adj. Of huge or mighty form or size; robust; strong bodied.

قہار qahhār (A) adj. Powerful; imperious; avenging; conqueror; an attribute of God.

قہر qahr (A) n.m. Severity; chastisement; rage; fury; indignation; vengeance; judgment; calamity; punishment. adj. Excessive; great; vehement; very great. Fig. firebrand; incendiary.

قہر الٰہی qahr-ĕ ilāhi, n.m. Divine wrath; divine punishment.

قہر توڑنا qahr toṛnā, v. To rage; to be furious; to frown and fret.

قہر درویش برجان درویش qahr-ĕ darvesh bar jan-ĕ darvesh, prov. A poor man's rage hurts none but himself.

قہراً qahran (A) adv. By force.

قہقری، قہقرا qahqarī, qahqarā (A) n.f. Retrograde motion; retreat; moving or walking backwards.

قہقہہ qahqahah (A) n.m. A loud laugh; a horse laugh.

قہقہہ مارنا qahqahah marnā, v. To laugh loud and long; to laugh out aloud.

قہوہ qahwah (A) n.m. Coffee.

قہوہ خانہ qahwah khānah, n.m. A coffee house.

قے qae (A) n.f. Vomiting; vomit.

قے آنا qae ānā, v. To feel nausea; to be disgusted; to be sick of.

قے آور qae āwar, adj. An emitic; that which causes vomiting.

قے کرنا qae karnā, v. To vomit.

قیادت qiyādat (A) n.f. Leadership; guidance.

قیاس qiyās (A) n.m. Measuring; comparing analogy; rule; judgment; opinion; supposition; thought; guess; theory; syllogism; presumption; conjecture.

قیاس سے باہر qiyās se bāhar, adj. Inconceivable; beyond presumption or conception.

قیاس کرنا، لگانا qiyās karnā, lagānā, v. To think; to suppose; to guess; to estimate; to conceive.

قیاساً qiyāsan (A) adv. By analogy; by conjecture.

قیاسی qiyāsī (A) adj. Imaginary; theoretical; conjectural; analogous; presumptive.

قیافہ qiyāfah (A) n.m. Guess; conjecture; countenance; semblance; imitation; likeness; manners; mode; look; physiognomy.

قیافہ شناس qiyāfah shinās, n.m. A physiognomist.

قیام qiyām (A) n.m. Standing erection; stay; resurrection; stability; permanence; durability; residence; settlement; existence.

قیام پذیر qiyām pazir, adj. Stationary; at rest.

قیام کرنا qiyām karnā, v. To lodge; to rest; to halt; to reside; to rise; to stand.

قیامت qiyāmat (A) n.f. The general resurrection; the Last Day; commotion; the scene of trouble or distress; confusion; tumult; calamity; excess; oppression. adj. Excessively great; extremely; excessive.

قیامت برپا کرنا qiyāmat barpā karnā, v. To raise a tumult; to practise oppression.

قید qaid (A) n.f. Imprisonment; confinement; restraint; obstacle; control; bondage; a bond; an obligation.

قید با مشقت qaid -ĕ bā mushaqqat, n.f. Rigorous imprisonment.

قید بھرنا، کاٹنا qaid bharnā, kāṭnā, v. To undergo the full term of imprisonment.

قید تنہائی qaid-ĕ tanhā'i, n.f. Solitary confinement.

قید خانہ qaid khānah, n.m. Prison; jail.

قید لگانا qaid lagānā, v. To apply restrictions (to); to limit; to attach conditions.

قید محض qaid-ĕ mahz, n.f. Simple imprisonment.

قیدی qaidī (A&P) n.m. A prisoner; a captive; a convict.

قیر qīr (A) n.m. Pitch; tar; besmear with tar.

قیراط qirāṭ (A) n.m. A carot; the twenty-fourth part of an ounce; weight of four barley seeds.

قیف qīf (T) n.f. A funnel.

قیل و قال qil-ŏ qāl (A) n.f. Conversation; altercation; chit chat; dialogue; controversy.

قیلولہ qailūlah (A) n.m. Sleeping at midday; a midday nap.

قیم qaiyyim (A) adj. True; standing erect n.m. Nature; convener; president.

قیمت qīmat (A) n.m. Price; value; cost; worth.

قیمت پانا qīmat pānā, v. To be sold at a good price; to fetch a high price.

قیمت چکانا qīmat chukānā, v. To settle a price.

قیمتاً qīmatan (A) adv. On payment.

قیمتی qīmatī (A&P) adj. Valuable; precious; costly; high priced.

قیمہ qīmah (A) n.m. Minced meat.

قیمہ کرنا qīmah karnā, v. To make mince-meat (of).

قینچی qaiṅchi, n.m. A pair of scissors; a truss.

قینچی سی زبان چلانا qaiṅchī si zabān chalānā, v. To talk very fast.

قیود quyūd (A) n.f. (plu. of قید qaid); Restrictions; limitations; conditions; obligations.

قیوم qaiyūm (A) adj. Everlasting; permanent; lasting; stately; fixed; an epithet of God.

ک kāf, is the twenty-second letter of the Arabic, twenty-fifth of the Persian and the twenty-eighth of the Urdu alphabet. In abjad it stands for 20.

کا kā (H) prep. Of; belonging (to); concerning; adjectival termination.

کابک kābuk (P) n.f. A pigeon-house; a dove-cat.

کابلہ kāblah (H) n.m A bolt.

کابلی kābulī (P) adj. Belonging to Kabul; a native of Kabul; a paṭhān.

کابلی چنے kābulī chane, n.m. Big white gram, the seed of which is said to have been imported from Kabul.

کابوس kābūs (A) n.m. The nightmare.

کابین kābīn (A) n.m. Dowry; a marriage portion or settlement on a wife; a dower.

کابین نامہ kābīn nāmah, n.m. A deed of dowry.

کابینہ kābīnah, n.f. (corr. from English) Cabinet; the council of ministers.

کاتب kātib (A) n.m. A writer; a copyist; a clerk; a scribe.

کاتک kātak (H) n.m. Name of the seventh Hindu month, corresponding to October-November.

کاتنا kātnā (H) v. To spin; to twist.

کاٹ kāṭ (H) n.f. Cutting; a cut; incision; wound; a clip; separation; deduction; amendment; slack; bite; dissection; a chip; part.

کاٹ چھانٹ کرنا kāṭ chhāṅṭ karnā, v. To cut and clip; to deduct; to correct; to prune; to make deductions from.

کاٹ ڈالنا kāṭ ḍālnā, v. To cut off; to ampulate; to hew; to strike off; to mow.

کاٹ کرنا kāṭ karnā, v. To wound; to cut; to cut a passage for; to corrode; to contradict.

کاٹ کھانا kāṭ khānā, v. To bite.

کاٹ کھانے کو دوڑنا **kāṭ khāne ko dauṛnā**, *v.* To fly alone; to be in attacking position; to look daggers at one.

کاٹنا **kāṭnā** (H) *v.* To cut; to saw; to clip; to bite; to sever; to cleave; to mow; to reap; to clear; to dissect; to mutilate; to strike out; to corrode; to exclude; to interrupt; to disjoin; to extract; to pass (days, time).

کاٹنے کو دوڑنا **kāṭne ko dauṛnā**. See کاٹ کھانے کو دوڑنا **kāṭ khāne ko dauṛnā**.

کاٹھ **kāṭh** (H) *n.m.* Wood; timber; stock; block; a pair of stocks; scabbard.

کاٹھ پتلی ، کٹھ پتلی **kāṭh putlī, kaṭh putlī**, *n.f.* A puppet; a toy; a wooden doll.

کاٹھ کا آلو **kāṭh kā ullū**, *n.m.* A great blockhead; a very stupid person. *adj.* Impenetrable; blockhead.

کاٹھ کا گھوڑا **kāṭh kā ghoṛā**, *n.m.* A wooden horse; a lame-man's crutches.

کاٹھ کباڑ **kaṭh kabāṛ**, *n.m.* Wooden articles; a heap of broken furniture.

کاٹھ کی گھوڑی **kāṭh kī ghoṛī**, *n.f.* A bier; a coffin.

کاٹھ کے گھوڑے دوڑانا **kāṭh ke ghoṛe daurānā**, *v.* To spin yarns; to talk nonsense; to make false promises.

کاٹھ کی ھنڈیا بار بار نہیں چڑھتی **kāṭh kī hanḍyā bār bār nahīn chaṛhtī**, *prov.* Once a traitor always a traitor.

کاٹھی **kāṭhī** (H) *n.f.* Wood; timber; a saddle; structure; frame; body; shape.

کاج **kāj** (H) *n.m.* Business; affair; work; action; occupation; a feast (given on the death of an old person); a button hole.

کاجل **kājal** (H) *n.m.* Lamp black; soot.

کاجل لگانا **kājal lagānā**, *v.* To apply lamp-black to the eye.

کاجو **kājū** (H) *n.m.* The cashew nut.

کاجی **kājī** (H) *adj.* Active; assiduous; industrious; busy; employed.

کاچ **kāch** (H) See کانچ **kānch**.

کاچھا **kāchhā** (H) *n.m.* A waist cloth; a pair of very short drawers; the upper part of the thigh.

کاچھی **kāchhī** (H) *n.m.* A gardener or cultivator who cultivates and sells pot-herbs and vegetables.

کاخ **kākh** (P) *n.m.* An upper storey; balcony; turret; a palace; a tower: a villa; battlements.

کاذب **kāẕib** (A) *adj.* False; liar.

کار **kār** (P) *n.m.* Affair; work; labour; action; operation; profession; business; function; duty.

کار آزمودہ **kār āzmūdah**, *adj.* Experienced; practical; expert; veteran.

کار آمد **kār āmad**, *adj.* Useful; serviceable; conducive.

کار براری **kār barārī**, *n.m.* Accomplishment of one's desires; performance.

کار بند **kār band**, *adj.* Obedient; dutiful; acting.

کار بند ھونا **kār band honā**, *v.* To act up to; to comply with.

کار پرداز **kār pardāz**, *n.m.* Manager; agent.

کار پردازی **kār pardāzī**, *n.f.* Management; agency.

کارثواب **kār-ĕ ṣawāb**, *n.m.* A good deed; a good turn.

کار چوب **kār chob**, *n.m.* Embroiderer.

کار چوبی **kār chobī**, *n.f.* Embroidery.

کار خانہ **kār khānah**, *n.m.* Factory; workshop; laboratory; a great work.

کارخانہ الہی **kār khānah-ĕ ilāhī**, *n.m.* God's work; nature.

کار خانہ‌دار **kār khānah dār**, *n.m.* A factory owner; a steward; a butler.

کارخیر **kār-ĕ khair**, *n.m.* A good deed.

کار دار **kār dār**, *n.m.* A manager.

کار روائی kār rawā'ī, n.f. Working; proceeding; conduct, process; action; management.

کار روائی سرسری kār rawā'ī sarsarī, n.f. Summary procedure or trial.

کار روائی کرنا kār rawā'ī karnā, v. To deal with; to discharge a duty; to hold proceedings; to carry on a business.

کار زار kār zār, n.m. Battle; engagement; war; conflict.

کار ساز kār sāz, adj. Adroit, dexterous. n.m. Doer; maker.

کار ساز حقیقی kār sāz-ĕ ḥaqiqī, n.m. The real doer; God.

کار سازی kār sāzī, n.f. Cleverness; dexterity; artifice; trick.

کارستانی kārastānī, n.f. Artifice; trick; policy.

کار سنج kār sang, adj. Appraiser of good work; estimator of worth.

کار فرما kār farmā, n.m. An administrator; a supervisor; any one vested with power.

کار کردگی kār kardagī, n.f. Work; labour; good work; remuneration; labour charges.

کار کردہ kār kardah, adj. Experienced in business.

کار کن kār kun, n.m. Director; manager; attorny. adj. Worker.

کار گہ kār gāh, n.f. A workshop; place where one's work lies.

کار گر kār gar, adj. Efficacious; effective; operative; active (medicine); moving; stirring (action).

کار گر ہونا kār gar honā, v. To be effective; to be productive.

کار گزاری kār guzārī, n.f. Despatch of business; performance of work; good service; agency; urgent business or affairs.

کارمند kār mand, n.m. An employee; a worker in an office.

کارنامہ kār nāmah, n.m. A record of good deeds; a great work; a record or a book of war; a history.

کارنمایاں kār-ĕ numāyāṅ, n.m. A prominent action; a bold action.

کارو بار kāro bār, n.m. Business; trade; employment.

کارتوس kārtūs, n.m. A cartridge.

کارن kāran (H) n.m. Cause; behalf; motive; reason; account; occasion.

کارندہ kāriṅdah (P) n.m. A manager; an agent; an officer; a representative; a worker.

کاروان kārwān (P) n.m. A caravan; a large company of travellers or merchants or pilgrims united for mutual protection on a journey.

کاروان سرائے kārwān sarā'e, n.f. A caravanserai; an inn.

کاری kārī (P) adj. Effective; penetrating; working; fatal.

کاری زخم kārī zakhm, n.m. A deep wound; a mortal wound.

کاریز kārez, n.f. (P) A water course; a conduit; a subterranean or underground canale; a sewer.

کاریگر kārīgar (P) n.m. A workman; an artist; an artisan; a labourer.

کاریگری kārī garī (P) n.f. Skill; workmanship; artistic work.

کاڑھنا kāṛhnā (H) v. To draw; to draw off; to take out; to delineate; to point; to embroider; to find; to detect; to break in; to work figures; to work flowers on cloth; to borrow; to bring out; to scratch out.

کاست kāst (P) n.f. Diminution; loss; damage.

کاسر kāsir (A) adj. Breaker.

کاسنی kāsnī (P) n.f. A plant called endive. adj. Lilac; of light purple colour.

کاسہ *kāsah* (P) *n.m.* A cup; a goblet; a bowl; a plate.

کاسہ پشت *kāsah pusht n.m.* A tortoise.

کاسہ زانو *kāsah-ĕ zānū, n.m.* The knee-cap.

کاسہ سر *kāsah-ĕ sar, n.m.* The skull.

کاسہ گدائی *kāsah-ĕ gadā'ī, n.m.* A beggar's bowl.

کاسہ لیس *kāsah les, adj.* A pot-licker; a parasite; a flatterer.

کاسہ لیسی *kāsah lesī, n.f.* Pot-licking; flattering; boot-licking.

کاش *kāsh* (P) *intj.* Would that! God grant!

کاشکہ *kāshkeh, intj.* May it so happen! God send!

کاشانہ *kāshānah* (P) *n.m.* A house; a dwelling.

کاشت *kāsht* (P) *n.f.* Cultivation; tillage; cultivated land or tract; field; farm; holding; tenure.

کاشت کار *kāsht kār, n.m.* A cultivator; an agriculturist; a farmer.

کاشت کاری *kāsht kārī, n.f.* Agriculture; cultivation; tillage; farming; husbandry.

بے کاشت *be kāsht, adj.* Uncultivated; fallow.

کاشتہ *kāshtah* (P) *adj.* Tilled; cultivated.

کاشف *kāshif* (A) *adj.* Discoverer; detective; revealer; explorer; explainer.

کاشی *kāshī* (H) *n.f.* A glazed tile; a glazed vessel.

کاظم *kāzim* (A) *adj.* Restraining anger; controlling rage.

کاغذ *kāghaz* (P) *n.m.* Paper; a letter; document (*plu.* کاغذات *kāghazāt*).

کاغذ سیاہ کرنا *kāghaz siyāh karnā, v.* To scribble; to write on paper.

کاغذ لفاف *kāghaz-ĕ laffāf, n.m.* A wrapping paper.

کاغذ کی ناؤ *kāghaz kī nāo, n.f.* A paper boat; a frail thing.

کاغذ کے گھوڑے دوڑانا *kāghaz ke ghoṛe dauṛānā, v.* To keep up an active or brisk correspondence.

کاغذی *kāghazī* (P) *adj.* Delicate; soft; thin; made of paper; relating to paper; brittle.

کاغذی بادام *kāghazī bādām, n.m.* An almond having thin or brittle crust.

کاغذی کار روائی *kāghazī kār rawā'ī, n.f.* Red-tapism; official correspondence.

کافر *kāfir* (A) *n.m.* An infidel; an impious person; a sweetheart; a mistress. *adj.* Impious; ungrateful.

کافرانہ *kāfirānah* (A) *adv.* Like an infidel; impiously.

کافری *kāfirī* (A) *n.f.* Infidality; unbelief.

کافور *kāfūr* (A) *n.m.* Camphor.

کافور ہو جانا *kāfūr ho jānā, v.* To run away; to disappear; to scamper off; to vanish; to evaporate.

کافوری *kāfūrī* (A&P) *adj.* Camphorate; white; pure; transparent.

کافہ *kāffah*(A)*adj.& n.m.* The whole; universal; all; a tribe; a multitude.

کافۃ الناس، کافہ انام *kāffah-tun-nās, kāffah anām* (A) *n.m.* All mankind; all people.

کافی *kāfī* (P&A) *adj.* Sufficient; adequate; enough.

کافی و وافی *kāfī-ŏ wāfī, adj.* Enough and too spare.

کاکا *kākā* (P) *n.m.* Elder brother; a slave.

کاکا *kākā* (H) *n.m.* A paternal uncle; a small boy.

کاکڑا *kākṛā* (H) *n.m.* A kind of leather; a kind of measles.

کاکڑا سنگی *kākṛā singī, n.f.* Name of a medicine.

کاکل *kākul* (P) *n.f.* A curl; a lock; a ringlet; a tuft of hair.

کاکی kāki (H) n.f. Aunt; a small girl.

کاگ kāg (H) n.m. A crow; a raven; the uvula.

کال kāl (H) n.m. Death; angel of death; time; season; age; famine; dearth; calamity; a snake.

کال پڑنا kāl parnā, v. Coming of a Famine.

کال کامارا kāl kā mārā, adj. Famine-stricken; a victim of famine; starveling.

کال کوٹھڑی kāl kothri, n.f. A black-hole; a dungeon.

کالا kālā (P) n.m. Goods; commodity; stuff; merchandise; chattels; household furniture; effects; things; a silk cloth.

کالا kālā (H) adj. Black; dark; large; great; terrible. n.m. A black snake.

کالابھجنگ kālā bhujang, adj. Black as snake; very black; jet black.

کالاپانی kālā pānī, n.m. Beyond the sea; transportation across the sea.

کالاپن kālā pan, n.m. Blackness.

کالاپہاڑ kālā pahāṛ, n.m. Black mountain or hill; an elephant.

کالاچور kālā chor, n.m. A great thief; an unknown condemned person; a dark horse; name of a snake.

کالادانہ kālā dānah, n.m. Name of a purgative seed; indigo seed.

کالادیو kālā dev, n.m. A black demon; a great devil; a very black man.

کالازیرہ kālā zirah, n.m. Seeds of nigella indica.

کالاکرنا kālā karnā, v. To blacken; to blot; to scribble; to deface by scribbling.

کالاکلوٹا kālā kalotā, adj. Very black; coal black; jet black.

کالا کوا kālā kawwā, n.m. A black crow; a raven; a very black man.

کالا کوئلا kālā ko'elā, adj. Very black; coal-black.

کالا منہ کرنا kālā muṅh karnā, v. To blacken the face; to disgrace; to bring disgrace (on); to copulate.

کالا منہ ھونا kālā muṅh honā, v. To be disgraced; to do a shameful act.

کالا ناگ kālā nāg, n.m. A black cobra.

کالے کوس kāle kos, n.m. Long distances; unending journey.

کالانعام kālan'ām (A) adv. Like beasts; animal-like.

کالبد kālbud (P) n.m. The body of a man or animal; the human body; the frame; form; model.

کالبدخاکی kālbud-ĕ-dkhāki, n.m. A clay model; the human body.

کالبوت kālbūt (P) n.m. A shoemaker's last; a shoe-last; a boot-tree.

کالک kālak, kālik (H) n.f. Blackness; soot; ink; lamp-black; cloudiness; a female crow; disgrace; black part of the eye; a kind of grain; black spot.

کالک کا ٹیکا kālik kā ṭikā, n.m. A black spot; a stain; a stigma; disgrace.

کالی kālī (A) adj. Black. n.f. Black colour; ink; black spot; a Hindu goddess; name of a snake with a hundred and ten hoods.

کالی آندھی kālī āndhī, n.f. Black storm; hurricane.

کالی بلا kālī balā, n.f. A great evil; a plague; an old hog.

کالی پیلی آنکھیں کرنا kāli pīlī ānkheṅ karnā, v. To turn red with rage; to look very angry and threatening.

کالی تلسی kālī tulsi, n.f. Basil (ocymum sanctum).

کالی زبان kālī zabān, adj. Black-tongue; inauspicious.

کالی زیری kālī zīrī, n.f. Verus-nico, a medicine; black cummin seed.

کالی سیم kālī sem, n.f. A bean.

کالی کلوٹی kālī kaloṭī, adj. Very black (woman).

کالی کھانسی kāli khānsi, *n.f.* Whooping cough.

کالی گھٹا kāli ghaṭā, *n.f.* Black clouds.

کالی مرچ kāli mirch, *n.f.* Black pepper.

کالی هڑ kāli haṛ, *n.f.* Black myrobalan.

کام kām (H) *n.m.* Work ; task ; feat ; tactics; workmanship ; embroidery ; service; office duty ; affair ; business; occupation; action; deed; labour ; employment ; function ; matter; thing ; interest ; a hard task ; a difficult matter ; object ; end ; purport ; needle-work ; desire ; wish ; inclination; the god of love; cupid; lust; pocket; mail; post-bag.

کام آنا kām ānā, *v.* To be of use ; to be used ; to be slain (in battle &c) ; to be wanted ; to be consumed.

کام بگاڑنا kām bigāṛnā, *v.* To spoil or mar the work of ; to baffle ; to foil ; to make a mess of; to put a spoke in one's wheel; to ruin one's reputation or credit.

کام بگڑنا kām bigaṛnā, *v.* To fail in one's business ; to be bankrupt ; to be spoiled.

کام بنانا kām banānā, *v.* To succeed ; to be successful ; to do a job.

کام بن جانا kām ban jānā, *v.* To succeed; to gain one's end.

کام بھگتانا kām bhugtānā, *v.* To execute a job ; to do one's work well.

کام پر لگانا kām par lagānā, *v.* To put to work ; to engage.

کام پڑنا kām paṛnā, *v.* To have business with ; to have occasion for; to come to use ; to be of use ; to prove of service.

کام تمام کرنا kām tamām karnā, *v.* To finish a job; to accomplish; to kill.

کام تمام هونا kām tamām honā, *v.* To be killed; to be put an end to; coming of a task to an end.

کام چلانا kām chalānā, *v.* To carry on business ; to manage ; to keep work going ; to advance work or business.

کام چلاؤ kām chalā'ū, *adj.* serviceable ; sufficient to go on with ; answering as a make-shift; enough for the purpose.

کام چلنا kām chalnā, *v.* To have the work going on ; to have the business established.

کام چمکنا kām chamaknā, *v.* To have a flourishing business.

کام چوپٹ هو جانا kām chaupaṭ ho jānā, *v.* Collapsing of a business; business being ruined.

کام چور kām chor, *adj.* A shirker; an idler; a skulker; work-sly.

کام دار kām dār, *n.m.* A man having business ; manager ; agent. *adj.* Embroidered.

کام دینا kām denā, *v.* To give one work to do; to make over charge; to render good service ; to be serviceable.

کام سے کام هونا kām se kām honā, *v.* To mind one's own business.

کام کاج kām kāj, *n.m.* Labour ; industry ; activity.

کام لینا kām lenā, *v.* To get work; to undertake a job; to take over charge of an office; to make one work; to enact work; to make use of; to use.

کام میں لانا kām men lānā, *v.* To make use of; to use; to bring into use; to employ; to expend.

کام نکالنا kām nikālnā, *v.* To get one's purpose served; to accomplish one's desire; to effect one's purpose; to get one's work done.

کام kām (P) *n.m.* Palate; desire; object; end; purport; design; intention.

کامران kāmrān, adj. Successful in every attempt; fortunate; happy; blessed.

کامرانی kāmrānī, n.f. Success; happiness; good fortune; prosperity; felicity; complete attainment of all one's wishes.

کام گار kām gār, adj. Obtaining whatever is desired; absolute; powerful; fortunate; successful.

کام گاری kām gārī, n.f. Prosperity; success; happiness.

کام یاب kām yāb, adj. Prosperous; happy; successful; satisfied; obtaining one's object or all that one desires.

کامیابی kāmyābī, n.f. Success; happiness; prosperity; attainment of one's wishes.

کام kām (S) n.m. Desire; affection; love; wish; passion; inclination; lust.

کام دیو kām dev, n.m. The god of love; cupid.

کامل، کاملہ kāmil, kāmilah (A) adj. Perfect; complete; accomplished; learned; entire; decisive.

کامنی kāmnī (S) n.f. A loving or affectionate woman.

کامود kāmūd (H) n.m. Name of a musical mode sung at night.

کامی kāmī (H) adj. Lustful; loving; busy.

کان kan (P) n.f. A mine or quarry.

کان کن kān kan, n.m. A miner; a quarryman.

کان کنی kān kanī, n.f. Mining; excavation.

کان نمک kān-ĕ namak, n.m. A salt mine.

کان ملاحت kān-ĕ malāḥat, adj. Rich brown complexion; beautiful; elegant.

کان kān (H) n.m. The ear; the organ of hearing; the handle of a vessel; helm or rudder of a ship; twist; defect; hypothenuse (of a triangle); heed; regard.

کان آشنا ھونا kān āshnā honā, v. To be aware of; to be in the know of; to have heard (of) previously.

کان آڑے یا پھٹے جانا kan uṛe yā phaṭe jānā, v. To be deafened by noise.

کان اینٹھنا یا اٹھنا kān ainṭhnā yā aiṭhnā, v. To pull or wring the ears; to twist the ears; to reprove; to chastise.

کان بجنا kān bajnā, v. To have a ringing in the ear; to fancy that one hears a sound.

کان بچیانا یا دبانا kān bāchiyānā yā dabānā, v. To turn back the ears as horse does when preparing to bite.

کان بندھوانا kān bindhwānā, v. To have ears bored.

کان بہرا کرنا kān bahrā karnā, v. To turn a deaf ear (to); to shut one's ears (to).

کان بھرنا kān bharnā, v. To back-bite; to poison the ears of; to encite a quarrel by tale bearing.

کان بہنا kān bahnā, v. Oozing of puss from the ear.

کان پر جوں نہ چلنا یا رینگنا kān par jūṅ nah chalnā yā riṅgnā, v. To be utterly heedless; to pay no attention at all.

کان پر ھاتھ دھرنا kān par hāth dharnā, v. To deny; to refuse; to disclaim.

کان پڑنا kān paṛnā, v. To be heard; to be audible; to catch the ear.

کان پڑی آواز سنائی نہ دینا kān paṛī āwāz sunā'ī nah denā, v. To be in the midst of a deafening noise.

کان پکڑنا kān pakaṛnā, v. To vow never to do the same thing again; to lay hold of the ear by way of contrition.

کان پھاڑنا kān phāṛnā, v. To make a deafening noise.

کان پھوٹنا kān phūṭnā, v. To be deaf.

کان پھوڑنا *kān phoṛnā, v.* To make a great noise.

کان چھیدنا *kān chhednā, v.* To bore the ears.

کان دھرنا *kān dharnā, v.* To hear; to listen; to attend; to be attentive.

کان کا آلہ *kān kā ālah, n.m.* Ear-trumpet.

کان کا بالا *kān kā bālā, n.m.* Ear-ring.

کان کا پردہ *kān kā pardah, n.m.* The drum of the ear; the tympanum.

کان کاٹنا *kān kāṭnā, v.* To get the better of; to surpass; to overcome; to out wit.

کان کا کچا *kān kā kachchā, adj.* A credulous person; readily believing hearsay.

کان کا میل *kān kā mail, n.m.* Ear-wax; cerumen.

کان کھانا *kān khānā, v.* To worry by constant chattering.

کان کھڑے کرنا *kān khaṛe karnā, v.* To be alarmed; to be on the alert; to prick up one's ears.

کان کھڑے ہونا *kān khaṛe honā, v.* To be alarmed.

کان کھولنا *kān kholnā, v.* To open one's ears; to warn; to caution; to make one understand the implications; to send away with a flea in one's ears.

کان لگانا *kān lagānā, v.* To listen; to over hear.

کان لگنا *kān lagnā, v.* To get into one's confidence (of); to have a sore ear; to be attentive.

کان ملنا *kān malnā, v.* To twist the ear; to punish; to admonish.

کان میں آواز پڑنا *kān men āwāz paṛnā, v.* To happen to hear; to catch the sound of.

کان میں آنگلی دے رکھنا *kān men ungli de rakhnā, v.* To be deaf to what is said; to turn a deaf ear (to).

کان میں بات کہنا *kān men bāt kahnā, v.* To whisper; to utter softly in the ear.

کان میں پارہ بھرنا *kān men pārah bharnā, v.* To pretend not to listen.

کان میں تیل ڈال کے سو رهنا *kān meṅ tel ḍāl ke so rahnā, v.* To pay no heed at all.

کان میں ڈالنا *kān meṅ ḍālnā, v.* To inform; to warn.

کان میں روئی دینا *kān men rū'i denā, v.* To pay no attention; to disregard.

کان نہ هلانا *kān nah hilānā, v.* To remain silent; to be tamed or docile; not to raise one's little finger; to assent quietly.

کان هونا *kān honā, v.* To understand; to comprehend; to be warned; to take a lesson (from).

کانا *kānā, (H) adj.* Blind of one-eye; one-eyed; fruit which has no kernel or has a rotten kernel.

کانا پھوسی *kānā phūsī, n.f.* Whispering.

کانا پھوسی کرنا *kānā phūsi karnā, v.* To whisper; to speak ill of; to backbite.

کانپ *kāṅp (H) n.m.* The curved stick in a paper-kite; rod of the umbrella.

کانپ اٹھنا *kāṅp uṭhnā, v.* To tremble with fear; to shake.

کانپنا *kāṅpnā (H) v.* To shiver; to tremble; to quake; to shake.

کانٹا *kāṅṭā (H) n.m.* A thorn; spine; fork; a spur; the tongue of a balance; fishing-hook; a fishing-bone; a quill; proof; a hooked instrument; a pricker; a thorn in the side; a hateful person.

کانٹا چبھونا *kāṅṭā chubhonā, v.* To prick a thorn

کانٹا سا کھٹکنا *kāṅṭā sā khaṭaknā, v.* To prick as a thorn; to rankle (in); to be regarded as troublesome.

کانٹا سا نکل جانا *kāntā sā nikal jānā*, *v.* To be freed from distress or pain.

کانٹا لگنا *kāntā lagnā*, *v.* To be pricked by a thorn.

کانٹا مارنا *kāntā mārnā*, *v.* To strike with the fins (fish); to underweigh.

کانٹا ہونا *kāṅtā hona*, *v.* To be a thorn in the side or flesh; to become lean and thin.

کانٹوں پر لوٹنا *kānton par lotnā*, *v.* To lie on a bed of thorns; to be in great pain or distress.

کانٹوں میں گھسیٹنا *kānṭon men ghasiṭnā*, *v.* To drag one on thorns; to torment; to punish severely.

کانٹے بونا *kānte bonā*, *v.* To sow thorns; to prepare distress or misfortune for oneself.

کانٹے میں تلنا *kānte men tulnā*, *v.* To be very valuable; to be precious.

کانجی *kāṅji* (H) *n.f.* A kind of sour gruel or vinegar.

کانجی ہوس *kānji haus*, *n.m.* A cattle pound; a lock-up for the cattle.

کانچ *kāṅch* (H) *n.f.* Glass; a disease.

کانچ نکالنا *kāṅch nikālnā*, *v.* To beat severely; to give a severe threshing.

کاندھا *kāṅdhā* (H) *n.m.* The shoulder.

کاندھا بدلنا *kāṅdhā badalnā*, *v.* To change shoulder (in carrying a dead body to the grave-yard).

کاندھا دینا *kāṅdhā denā*, *v.* To lend a shoulder to; to help to carry a dead body to the grave-yard.

کاندھا ہلانا *kāṅdhā hilānā*, *v.* To shrug the shoulder.

کانس *kāns* (H) *n.f.* A kind of grass.

کانگڑی *kāṅgri* (H) *n.f.* A portable stove; a chafingdish.

کانی *kāni* (P) *adj.* Of or relating to a mine.

کانی *kāni* (H) *adj.* Blind of one eye (woman).

کاو *kāw* (P). Digging; excavating; examining; investigating.

کاوکاو *kāw kāw*, *n.f.* Strict investigation; diligent search; trouble; labour.

کاواک *kāwāk* (P) *adj.* Hallow; empty within; tending to decay; cracked; useless; awkward.

کاوش *kawish* (P) *n.f* Digging; searching; research; enquiry; investigation; menacing; disputing; fighting; enmity;scratching one's head when puzzled.

کاہ *kāh* (P) *n.m.* Grass; straw. *adj.* Diminishing; consuming; (used in *comps.*)

کاہ ربا *kāh rubā*, *n.m.* Yellow amber.

کاہ گل ۔ کہگل *kah gil*, *kāhgil*, *n.f.* Straw and mud mixed together for plastering wall with.

کاہ کشاں ۔ کہکشاں *kah kāshān*, *kahkashan*, *n.f.* The milky way; galaxy.

کاہش *kāhish* (P) *n.f.* Anxiety; pining; wear and tear; decline; decay.

کاہل *kāhil* (A) *adj.* Lazy; slow; indolant; languid; relaxed; sick; tardy; indisposed; ailing.

کاہل وجود *kāhil wujud*, *n.m.* A lazy fellow a lazy lezard.

کاہلی *kāhili* (A&P) *n.f.* Indolence; indisposition; remissness; langoure; sloth; apathy; tardiness; neglect; relaxation; idleness; laziness; negligence; sickness.

کاہلی کرنا *kāhili karnā*, *v.* To practise indolence; to be slothful.

کاہن *kāhin* (A) *n.m.* A soothsayer; a magician; a wizard; astrologer; priest.

کاہو *kāhū* (P) *n.m.* The name of a vegetable seed; a lettuce.

کاہی *kāhī* (P) *adj.* Grass-colour; grass-green; moss-green; relating to straw. *n.f.* Greenness.

کاہے کو kāhe ko (H) adv. For what; why; wherefore.

کائنات kā'inat (A) n.f. The world; universe; created things; creatures; worth; value; capital; property; possession.

کائیاں kā'iyān (H) adj. Cunning; crafty; miser.

کائی kā'i (H) n.f. Green scum on stagnant pool; the green mould that sticks to walls and pavements; rust; moss.

کایا kāyā (H) n.f. Body; appearance; person.

کایاپلٹ kāyā palaṭ, n.m. The recovering of freshness and health after sickness; transmigration.

کایاکلپ kaya kālap, n.f. Rejuvinating; an aphrodisiac for making old men young.

کایستھ kāyasth (H) n.m. A caste of Hindus who are usually clerks and accountants.

کب kub (H) n.m. A hump; a poet.

کب kab (H) adv. When; at what time;

کب تک kab tak, adv. Till what time; for how long.

کب سے kab se, adv. Since when.

کباب kabāb (A) n.m. Roasted meat; a roast. adj. Roasted.

کباب کرنا kabāb karnā, v. To burst; to roast.

کباب ہونا kabāb honā, v. To be roasted; to burn; to be enraged; to be desperately in love.

کباب چینی kabāb chīnī, n.f. Cubebs (piper cubeba); causia buds; jungle cloves.

کبابی kabābī (P) adj. Fit to be roasted; used to eating a roast. n.m. One who roasts; the seller of roasted meat; a vandor of کباب kabāb.

کبار kibār (A) adj. (plu. of kabīr کبیر) The great; grandees; nobles.

کباڑ kabāṛ (H) n.m. A heap; rubbish; broken things; broken furniture.

کباڑی یا کباڑیا kabāṛi yā kabāṛiyā, n.m. A dealer in old and broken furniture.

کبائر kabā'ir (A) n.m. (plu. of کبیرہ kabīrah) Major offences; great sins.

کبت kabit (H) n.m. A kind of Hindi verse; poetry.

کبد kabid (A) n.m. The liver; the heart.

کبڈی kabaḍḍī (H) n.f. A youngsters game resembling prisoner's base.

کبر kibr (A) n.m. Grandeur; pride, greatness; dignity; haughtiness.

کبر kibar (A) n.f. Old age.

کبرا kabrā (H) adj. Dirty; grey; variegated; spotted; speckled.

چت کبرا chit kabrā, adj. Piebald.

کبرا kubarā (A) n.m. (plu. of کبیر kabīr) The great; grandees; nobles.

کبریٰ kubrā (A) n.m. The major proposition of a syllogism; (faminine gender of کبیر kabīr); great; senior.

کبریا kibriyā (A) n.m. Grandeur; magnificence; pride; an attribute of God.

کبریت kibrīt (A) n.m. Sulphur; brimstone.

کبریت احمر kibrīt-ĕ aḥmar, n.f. Red sulphur; a philosopher's stone.

کبڑا ، کبڑی kubṛā, kubṛī (H) adj. Crooked; hunch-backed; hump-backed.

کبک kabk (P) n.m. A partridge.

کبک دری kabk-ĕ dari, n.m. A beautiful species of partridge found in hills.

کبک رفتار kabk raftār, adj. Graceful in motion; moving gracefully.

کبوتر kabūtar (P) n.m. A pigeon.

کبوتر باز kabūtar bāz, n.m. One who rears pigeons.

کبوتربازی kabūtar bāzī, n.f. Pigeon-flying; indulging in rearing and flying pigeons.

کبوتری kabūtari, n.f. A female pigeon; a village dancing girl. adj. Blue colour.

کبود kabūd (P) n.m. Azure blue; a kind of azure-coloured leather; a kind of willow; a heron. adj. Dark blue.

کبودچشم kabūd chashm, adj. Blue-eyed.

کبودی kabūdi (P) adj. Blue; azure.

کبھی kabhi (H) adv. Sometimes; rarely; seldom; ever; sometime or other.

کبھی کا kabhī kā, adv. Sometimes ago; long ago.

کبھی کبھی kabhī kabhī, adv. Sometimes; occasionally; at times; now and then.

کبھی نہ کبھی kabhī nah kabhī, adv. Sometimes or other; first or last; rarely; seldom.

کبھی تولا کبھی ماشہ kabhī tolā kabhī māshah, adj. Fickle minded; inconstant.

کبیدگی kabidagı (P) n.f. Grief; affliction.

کبیدہ kabīdah (P) adj. Afflicted; vexed; grieved; moved.

کبیر kabīr (A) adj. Large; immense; great; senior; full-grown.

کبیرپنتھی kabir panthī, n.m. A follower of کبیر kabīr, a famous Hindu fakīr.

کبیرہ kabīrah (A) adj. Big; major; great.

کبیسہ kabīsah (A) adj. Intercalary; (addition of day or month in calendar to harmonize it with solar year).

کپ kup (H) n.m. Barn; stock.

کپا kuppā (H) n.m. A large leathern vessel for holding oil, &c.

کپاھونا kuppā honā, v. To become very fat.

کپاس kapās (H) n.f. Undressed cotton; the cotton plant.

کپٹ kapaṭ (H) n.m. Fraud; trick; adulteration; dissimulation, deceit; subterfuge.

کپٹ رکھنا kapaṭ rakhnā, v. To cherish ill-will.

کپٹی kapaṭi (H) adj. Insincere; deceitful; false; hypocritical; adulterated. n.m. A deceitful person.

کپڑ kopaṛ (H) n.m. Cloth; clothing.

کپڑ چھن کرنا kapaṛ chhan karnā, v. To strain through a cloth; to sift thoroughly.

کپڑا kapṛā (H) n.m. Cloth; clothes; dress; habit.

کپڑا پہننا kapṛā pahennā, v. To put on clothes.

کپڑوں سے ہونا kapṛoṅ se honā, v. To have the menses.

کپکپانا kapkapānā (H) v. To tremble; to shiver.

کپکپاھٹ ، کپکپی kapkapāhat, kapkapi (H) n.f. Shivering; trembling; quacking; shuddering.

کپکپی چڑھنا kapkapi chaṛhnā, v. To shiver with cold; to tremble with fear; to have a fit of ague.

کپلا kaplā (H) n.f. A brown-coloured cow.

کپوت kapūt (H) n.m. A disobedient son; a bad or wicked son; a villainous son.

کپور kapūr (H) n.m. Camphor; name of a flower.

کپور کچری kapūr kachri, n.f. Name of a medicine.

کپورا kapūrā (H) n.m. Testicle.

کپوری kapūrī (H) adj. White like camphor; fragrant. n.m. A kind of betel-leaf.

کپی kuppī (H) n.f. A leathern bottle, a vial.

کتا kutta (H) n.m. A dog; a slave; the spring of a gun lock; trigger; a trade work; the ear of a kind of grass.

کتے خانہ kutte khānah, n.m. A kennel for dogs.

کتے کی موت مرنا kutte ki maut marnā, v. To die the death of a dog; to die an ignoble death.

کتے کا کاٹا kutte kā kātā, adj. Bitten by dog; dog-bite.

کتاب kitāb (A) n.m. A book; a writing; a letter; a despatch.

کتاب آسمانی kitāb-ĕ āsmāni, n.f. A holy book; holy writ; scripture.

کتاب کا کیڑا kitāb kā kirā, n.m. A book-worm.

کتابت kitābat (P) n.f. Writing; calligraphy; copying; profession of a copyist.

کتابہ kitābah (A) n.m. An inscription; an epitaph; a motto; a title page.

کتابی kitābi (A&P) adj. Like a book; oblong.

کتابی تسویہ kitābi taswiah, n.m. Book adjustment.

کتابی چہرہ kitābi chehrah, n.m. An oval face.

کتابی علم kitābi 'ilm. n.m. Book knowledge; no worldly experience; theoretical; not practical.

کتان katān yā kattān (P) n.f. A kind of cloth; fine linen.

کتانا katānā (H) v. To get cotton spun; to cause to spin.

کتائی katā'ī (H) n.f. Spinning; the price paid for spinning.

کتب kutub (A) n.f. (plu. of کتاب kitāb) Books.

کتب خانہ kutub khānah, n.m. Library.

کتب فروش kutub farosh, n.m. A book-seller.

کتبہ katbah (A) n.m. Inscription; epitaph.

کتخدا katkhudā See کد خدا kad khudā.

کتخدائی katkhudā'i (P) n.f. See کد خدائی kad khudā'i.

کترا کر چلنا katrā kar chalnā (H) v. To desert one's companion; to cut the society (of).

کترانا katrānā (H) v. To leave the high road and take to by-paths; to go roundabout; to shrink; to slink away (from).

کتر بیونت katar bewant (H) n.f. Cutting out (clothes); deductions; meditation; consultation; anxiety.

کترن katran (H) n.f. Parings; clippings; cuttings.

کترن kutran (H) n.f. That which is gnawed; bitten off with the teeth.

کترنا katarnā (H) v. To cut; to clip; to pare; to prune; to cut out; to hew; to cut up.

کترنا kutarnā (H) v. To cut with the teeth.

کترنی katarni (H) n.f. Pair of scissors.

کتم ، کتمان katm, kitmān (A) n.m. Concealing; concealment.

کتنا kitnā (H) adv. How much; how many; some; several.

کتوانا katwānā (H) v. To cause to spin.

کتھا katthā (H) n.m. An astingent vegetable extract eaten with betel-leaf; catechu; *terra japonica*.

کتھا kathā (H) n.f. A story; a tale; a fable; relation; narrative; religious recital; sermon.

کتیا kutyā (H) n.f. A bitch; an abuse for a woman.

کتیرا katirā (H) n.m. A gum resembling tragacanth; a clipper.

کٹ kuṭ (H) *n.m.* Name of a medicine; a metal; pulverised paper.

کٹ kaṭ (H) *n.m.* Black colour to make chintz with; cutting.

کٹ جانا kaṭ jānā, *v.* To be cut to pieces; to be wounded; to be killed; to be separated; to be ashamed.

کٹ کھنا kat khanā, *adj.* Addicted to biting.

کٹ مرنا kat marnā, *v.* To fight to the bitter end.

کٹار katār (H) *n.m.* A dagger; a sword; a polecat.

کٹارا katārā (H) *n.m.* A medicinal plant called *globe thislte*; a large dagger; a kind of sugarcane; tamarind.

کٹاری katārī (H) *n.f.* A small dagger.

کٹانا، کٹوانا kaṭānā, kaṭwānā (H) *v.* To cause to cut; to cause to bite.

کٹاؤ kaṭāo (H) *n.m.* A kind of flowering on cloths; cutting.

کٹائی kaṭā'ī (H) *n.f.* Harvest time; reaping season; cutting of crops; reaping; wages for reaping.

کٹر kaṭṭar (H) *adj.* Cruel; merciless; pitiless; bigoted.

کٹڑا katṛā (H) *n.m.* A young male buffalo; market; a mart; suburbs; a part of a city.

کٹڑی katṛī (H) *n.f.* A young female buffalo; a compound; a collection of a few houses; land along the bank of a river.

کٹکٹانا kiṭkiṭānā (H) *v.* To grind one's teeth; to be very uneasy; to suffer distress.

کٹلس kaṭlas *n.m.* A cutlet.

کٹ ملا kaṭ mullā, *n.m.* A great bigot; a hedge-school-master.

کٹنا kaṭnā (H) *v.* To be cut; to be clipped or cut off; to be spent or passed; to be remitted; to be abashed; to be interrupted; to die of wounds; to be killed; to be jealous.

کٹنا kuṭnā (H) *n.m.* A pimp.

کٹناپا kuṭnāpā (H) *n.m.* Pimping.

کٹنائی kuṭnā'ī (H) *n.f.* The wages of a pimp.

کٹنی kuṭnī (H) *n.f.* A bawd; a procuress.

کٹوتی kaṭautī (H) *n.f.* A deduction; discount.

کٹورا kaṭorā (H) *n.m.* A cup or goblet of any metal; a brass bowl.

کٹوری kaṭorī (H) *n.f.* A small brass cup.

کٹھ kaṭh (H) *n.m.* (*dimin. of* کاٹھ *kāth*) Wood; labour.

کٹھ پتلی kaṭh putlī, *n.f.* A puppet; a young delicate girl.

کٹھ پھوڑا kaṭh phoṛā, *n.m.* A wood-pecker.

کٹھ گلاب kaṭh gulāb, *n.m.* A kind of rose; the china rose.

کٹھالی kuṭhālī (H) *n.f.* A small earthen dish; a crucible; a melting pot.

کٹہرا kaṭahrā (H) *n.m.* A railing; a wooden cage; the block on which fodder is cut; a palisade.

کٹھلا kuṭhlā (H) *n.m.* A small store house for grain, a bin; a lime-kiln.

کٹھن kaṭhin, kaṭhan (H) *adj.* Difficult; hard; painful; troublesome; acute; critical.

کٹھور kaṭhor (H) *adj.* Cruel; relentless; hard; solid; severe; callous.

کٹی، کٹیا kuṭī, kuṭyā (H) *n.f.* A cottage; a hut; hermitage.

کٹی kuṭṭī (H) *n.f.* Chopped fodder; pulverised paper used for binding books; pickles; breaking off friendship.

کٹی کرنا kuṭṭī karnā, *v.* To cut into small pieces; to break off (friendship).

کٹیا katyā (H) n.f. A fishing hook; an earthen milk can; a young female buffalo; an ear-ring.

کٹیلا katīlā (H) adj. Thorny; prickly; active; charming. n.m. A species of thistle.

کثافت kaṣāfat (A) n.f. Density; thickness; impurity; repletion; grossness; dirt; filth.

کثرت kaṣrat (A) n.f. Abundance; excess; multitude; the major part; bulk; plurality; multiplicity.

کثرت رائے kaṣrat-ĕ rā'e, n.f. Majority of votes.

کثرت سے kaṣrat se, adv. Abundantly; plentifully.

کثرت سے ہونا kaṣrat se honā, v. To abound; to be found in abundance.

کثیر kaṣīr (P) adj. Many; much; abundant; copious; fruitful.

کثیر الاضلاع kaṣīr-ul azlā', n.f. A polygon.

کثیرترین kāṣir tarīn, adj. Very; many; too many.

کثیرالعیال kaṣīr-ul-'ayāl, adj. One having a large family.

کثیر المعنی kaṣīr-ul-ma'ni, adj. Having many meanings.

کثیرالوقوع kaṣīr-ul wuqū', adj. Frequently happening.

کثیف kaṣīf (A) adj. Dense; impure; opaque; unclean; thick; gross; dirty; dusty.

کثیف الطبع ، کثیف المزاج kaṣīf-uṭ-ṭaba', kaṣīf-ul-mizāj, adj. A man of dirty habits; a peevish person.

کج kaj (P) adj. Crooked; perverse; curved; awry; cross.

کج ادائی kaj adāī' n.f. Perverseness; perversity; crossness in manners.

کج بحث kaj bahs, adj. Reasoning absurdly; one who uses crooked arguments.

کج بحثی kaj baḥṣī, n.f. Absurd reasoning.

کج خلق kaj khulq, adj. Ill-tempered; rude; rough.

کج دلا kaj dilā, adj. A crooked mind; illnatured; perverse.

کج دم kaj dum. See کژ دم kazhdum.

کج رائے kaj rāe, adj. Wrong-headed; pig-headed.

کج رفتار یا رو kaj raftār yā rau, adj. Walking crookedly or obliquely; perverse; unprincipled; irregular.

کج روی kaj rawi, n.f. Perverseness.

کج فہم kaj fahm, adj. A wrong-headed person; stupid.

کج کلاہ kaj kulāh. adj & n.m. One who wears his hat acock; a fop; a bean.

کج کلاہی kaj kulāhi, n.f. Foppery; dandyism; vanity; pride.

کج مج زبان، بیان kaj maj zabān, bayān, adj. Distorted speech or language; the imperfect language of a child; babbling.

کج نظر kaj nazar, adj. Envious; malignant; casting malignant looks.

کج نکالنا kaj nikālnā, v. To straighten; to make straight; to remove the curvature.

کجا kujā (P) adv. Whither; where; whence.

کجات kujāt (H) adj. Of low caste; base; outcast.

کجاوہ kajāwā (P) n.m. A camel's saddle; a pair of dorsers (for camel).

کجکول kajkol (P). See کشکول kashkol.

کجل ، کجلا kajjal kajlā (H) n.m. Lamp-black; soot; collyrium prepared from soot.

کجلانا kajlānā (H) v. To smoulder; to become mildewed.

کجلوٹی kajlauṭi (P) n.f. A pot for keeping کاجل kājal; snuffers used to prepare lamp black.

کجی kajī (P) n.f. Crookedness; crossness; curvature.

کچ kach (H) adj. (contraction of کچا kachchā) Unripe.

کچا، کچی kachchā kachchī, (H) adj. Unripe; crude; immature; uncooked; unbaked, green; raw; built of unbaked earth; clay-built; brittle; not permanent; unfinished; imperfect; silly; inexperienced; simple; weak; not genuine; below a fixed standard; uncertain; incomplete; half-done; not fast colour.

کچاپکا kachchā pakkā, adj. Half-cooked; half-baked; vague; partly of bricks and partly of mud.

کچاپکا کرنا kachchā pakkā karnā, v. To dress, cook or fry partially; to make a bargain but not a firm one.

کچاپن kachchā pan, n.m. Unripeness; rawness; inexperience; simplicity.

کچاتخمینہ kachchā takhmīnah, n.m. Rough estimate.

کچا چٹھا kachchā chiṭṭhā, n.m. Rough accounts; the dark side; evil designs.

کچارنگ kachchā rang, n.m. A colour that fades; temporary colour.

کچاساتھ kachchā sāth, n.m. A family of young children.

کچا سیر kachchā ser, n.m. A weight below the standard of pakkā ser.

کچا کرنا kachchā karnā, v. To make angry; to irritate; to put to the blush; to put to shame; to restrain; to discourse; to make long stitches; to baste.

کچی اینٹ kachchī īnṭ, n.f. Unbaked brick.

کچی پیشی kachchī peshī. Preliminary hearing.

کچی سڑک kachchī saṛak, n.f. An unmettled road.

کچی سلائی kachchī silā'ī, n.f. Basting clothes.

کچی عمر kachchī 'umr, n.f. Immature age: childhood; infancy.

کچی کلی kachchī kali, n.f. A new bud; a budding young girl.

کچی گولیاں کھیلنا kachchī golyān khelnā, v. To play with clay marbles; to be inexperienced.

کچے پکے دن kachche pakke din, n.m. The first four or five months of pregnancy.

کچے تاگے، (دھاگے) میں بندھنا kachche tāge (dhāge) men bandhnā, v. To be submissive.

کچے گھڑے میں پانی بھروانا kachche ghaṛe men pānī bharwānā, v. To make one to undertake a difficult or impossible job.

کچالو kachālū (H) n.m. Name of an esculent root.

کچرا kachrā (H) n.m. The raw musk-melon; a pod; clay; a pot-belly.

کچر کچر kachar kachar, n.f. The sound made in chewing raw food.

کچری kacharī (H) n.f. Name of a fruit.

کچ کچ kich kich, kach kach (H) n.f. Noise; useless talk; altercation; debate; chit chat.

کچ کچانا kich kichānā, v. To grind the teeth; to chatter.

کچلا kuchlā (H) n.m. Vomic nut; nux vomica.

کچلنا kuchalnā (H) v. To crush; to trample, to beat severely.

کچلون kachlūn (H) n.m. A kind of salt, said to promote digestion.

کچلوها kachlohā (H) n.m. Untempered iron.

کچلهو kachlahū (H) n.m. Bloody ichor discharged along with puss.

کچلی kuchli (H) n.f. The canine teeth; an eye tooth; a grinder; fang.

کچنال ، کچنار kachnāl, kachnār (H n.f. A tree, the buds of which form a delicious vegetable.

کچور kachūr (H) n.m The name of a medicinal plant; a drug.

کچوری kachauri (H) n.f. A cake made of flour and bruised pulse fried in ghee or oil.

کچوکا kachokā (H) n.m. Goading; pricking; taunt; censure.

کچومر kachūmar (H) n.m. A kind of pickle made from sliced mango or other fruit.

کچومر کر ڈالنا ، نکالنا kachūmar kar ḍālnā, nikālnā v. To cut to pieces; to beat black and blue.

کچھ kuchh (H) adj. Any; anything; ought; some; something; somewhat; a little; whatever.

کچھ تو kuchh to, adv. A little; ever so little.

کچھ سے کچھ ہونا، کچھ کا کچھ ہونا kuchh se kuchh honā, kuchh kā kuchh honā, v. To be entirely changed; to become quite different.

کچھ کچھ kuchh kuchh, adv. Nearly; somewhat.

کچھ نہ پوچھو kuchh nah pūchho, adv. Do'nt ask me; use your own imagination.

کچھ ہو kuchh ho, adv. Come what may; whatever may happen.

جو کچھ jo kuchh, adv. Whatsoever.

سب کچھ sab kuchh, adv. Every thing; the whole.

کچھار kachhār (H) n.m. Moist low land; marshy land; alluvial soil.

کچہری kachahri (H) n.f. A court of justice; court; office, cutchery; a public office.

کچہری چڑھانا kachahri chaṛhānā, v. To go to the court; to bring an action against one.

کچہری چڑھنا kachahri bharhnā, v. To put a case with court.

کچہری کرنا kachahri karnā, v. To hold a court; to try cases in court.

کچھنا kachhnā (H) n.m. A kind of short breeches which cover very little of the thigh.

کچھوا kachhvā (H) n.m. A tortoise; a turtle.

کچیانا kachiyānā (H) v. To shrink; to be frightened.

کحل kuḥl (A) n.m. Antimony; collyrium.

کحل الجواہر kuḥl-ul-jawāhir, n.m. Collyrium prepared with pearls.

کد kad (P) n.f. A house; a retreat; a den.

کد بانو kad bāno, n.f. The mistress of a family; the bride.

کد خدا kad khudā, n.m. Father of afamily; a married man; a bridegroom.

کد خدائی kād khuda'i, n.f. Marriage; establishing a family.

کد kadd (A) n.f. Examination; search; enquiry; worry; annoyance; exertion; trouble; labour; endeavour; persistence.

کد کرنا kadd karnā, v. To persist; to urge, to importune; to insist upon.

کدو کاوش kadd-ŏ-kāwish, n.f. Search; enquiry; examination; application; diligent search.

کدال kudāl (H) n.m. A kind of hoe or spade; a pickaxe; a mattock.

کدالی kudāli (H) n.f. A small mattock; dibble; spade; hoe.

کدانا kudānā (H) v. To dandle; to cause to leap; to provoke.

کدکنا kudaknā (H) v. To leap; to frisk; to caper; to gambol; to jump.

کدو kaddū (P) n.m. A pumpkin; a gourd.

کدو دانہ kaddū dānah, n.m. A disease in which worms are peased, having the appearance of pumpkin-seeds; intestinal worms.

کدو کش kaddū kash, n.m. A grater; an instrument for cutting up pumpkins etc. into thin shreds.

کدورت kudūrat (A) n.f. Foulness; muddiness; turbidness; impurity; depression of spirits; vexation; affliction; resentment; perturbation; dust; scum.

کدہ kadah (P) n.m. (in comps.) A place; a house; a habitation.

کدھر kidhar (H) adv. Whither; where.

کڈھب kuḍhab (H) n.m. Ill-shaped; ill-mannered; ugly; enormous; difficult; dangerous; shocking; violent; reckless.

کذاب kazzāb (A) n.m. A great liar.

کذب kizb (A) n.m. Lying; a lie.

کر بیٹھنا kar baithnā (H) v. To do a thing; to marry; to perform ; to make.

کر دکھانا kar dikhānā (H) v To perform a difficult task; to accomplish.

کر گزرنا kar guzarnā (H) v. To be forced to do a thing; to accomplish something rather unwillingly or with difficulty.

کر karr (P) n.m. Power; strength; grandeur; pomp. adj. Deaf.

کروفر karr-ŏ-farr, n.f. Pomp and pride; splendour; magnificence; pomp and show.

کرار karrār (A) adj. Attacking violently again and again; impetuous.

کرارا karārā (H) adj. Rigid; stiff; well-baked fresh; unflinching; resolute; crisp.

کرارا پن karārā pan, n.m. Hardness; muscular strength; crispness.

کراڑ karār (H) n.m. A shopkeeper.

کراکل karākul (H) n.m. The name of a bird; heron; curlew.

کرام kirām (A) adj. (plu. of کریم karīm) The noble; the generous; the eminent; the great.

کراماً کاتبین kirāman kātibīn (A) n.m. Recording angels.

کرامات karāmāt (A) n.f. (plu. of کرامت). Miracles; noble and excellent deeds.

کرامت karāmat (A) n.f. Generosity; magnificence; nobleness; excellence; supernatural power; miracle.

کران karān (P) n.m. A shore; boundary; side, coast; margin; bank.

کرانا karānā (H) v To cause to be done, to effect; to make; to assist; to actuate.

کرانی kirānī (H) n.m. A clerk; a nickname for a Christian.

کراہت karāhat (A) n.f. Dislike; disgust; aversion; detestation; abomination; disagreeableness; abhorrence.

کراہت سے دیکھنا karāhat se dekhnā, v. To look down upon; to scorn.

کراہتاً karāhatan (A) adv. Unwillingly; scornfully.

کراہنا karāhnā (H) v. To sigh; to groan; to moan.

کرایہ kirāyah (A) n.m. Fare; rent; hire.

کرایہ اگھانا kirāyah ughānā, v. To realize rents.

کرائے پر چلانا یا دینا kirāe par chalānā yā denā, v. To let; to lease; to hire out.

کرایہ دار kirāyah dār, n.m. A hirer; a tenant; lessee.

کرایہ نامہ kirāyah nāmah, n.m. A lease; a deed of rent.

کرب karb (A) n.m. Anguish; vexation; affliction.

کربلا karbalā (A) n.f. A place in Iraq where Imam Husain, the second son of Hazrat Ali was killed and buried; the burial place of تعزیہ ta'ziyab or martyrs; a place where water is scarce.

کرپا kripā (H) n.f. Grace; kindness; affection; pity; bounty; favour; compassion; mercy.

کرتا kurtā (H) n.m. A shirt; a tunic; waist-coat; jacket.

کرتا دھرتا kartā dhartā (H) n.m. The active or the managing member of a family.

کرتار kartār (H) n.m. The Creator; God.

کرتب kartab (H) n.m. Deed; action; business; exploit; skill; jugglery; experiment.

کرتب کی بدیا ھے - کرنے کی بدیا ھے kartab kī biddiyā hae, karte kī biddiyā hae, prov. Experience is the best teacher.

کرتوت kartūt (H) n.f./m. Action; behaviour; conduct; deed; trick.

کرتی kurti (H) n.f. A bodice; blouse; jumper; a loose outer garment of woman; the informal uniform coat of the army.

کرتی karti (H) n.f. A stuffed dead calf placed near a cow to make her yield milk.

کرچ kirich (H) n.f. A splinter; a sword.

کرچھا karchhā (H) n.m. A large spoon; a ladle; a frying pan.

کرچھی karchhī (H) n.f. A spoon; a ladle; a skein.

کرخت karakht (P) adj. Rigid; hard; solid; dry; austere.

کرختگی karakhtgi (P) n.f. Austerity; hardness; dryness.

کردار kirdār (P) n.m. Action; deed; manner; conduct; behaviour; character.

کردگار kirdgār (P) n.m. God; the Creator; Providence.

کردنی kardanī (P) adj. Fit or necessary to do; practicable; feasable.

کردنی خویش آمدنی پیش kardanī khwesh āmadanī pesh, prov. As you sow so shall you reap.

کردہ kardah (P) adj. (used in comp.) Done; made; executed; effected.

کرسی kursi (A) n.f. A chair; a stool; a throne; a seat; the authority of God; foundation; genealogy; the base of a pillar.

کرسی دینا kursi denā, v. To offer one a chair; to show respect or regard for; to make (one) the president of a meeting.

کرسی نشین kursī nashin, adj. A grandee; a nobleman; enthroned; established in office. n.m. One entitled to the honour of a seat in a دربار darbār.

کرشمہ kirishmah yā karashmah (P) n.m. A wonder; miracle; a phenomenon; a charm; an amorous gesture; coquetry; blandishment; amorous look; ogling.

کرشمہ دکھلانا kirishmah dikhlānā, v. To work wonders; to perform a miracle; to coquet.

کرشن krishn (S) adj. Black; dark blue; blue black; playful. n.m. A Hindu deity; an incarnation of Vishnū, the Apollo of the Hindus.

کرک kirak (H) n.m. Grit; small stone; sand.

کرکٹ karkaṭ (H) n.f. Sweepings; rubbish; trash.

کرکرا، کرکری kirkirā, kirkirī (H) adj. Gritty; sandy.

کرکرا ، کرکری kurkurā, kurkuri (H) adj. Brittle; crispy.

کرکرانا kirkirānā (H) v. To sound like grit; to grate.

کرکری kirkiri (H) n.f. Grittiness; disgrace.

کرکری کرنا kirkirī karnā, v. To disgrace one.

کرکری ہونا kirkirī honā, v. To be disgraced.

کرگس kargas (P) n.m. A vulture; a kind of arrow.

کرگہ kargah (P) n.m. A weaver's shop; loom; a pit in the ground in which the weaver's feet work.

کرم karam (A) n.m. Kindness; generosity; bounty; favour; grace; graciousness; excellence; liberality; benignity; clemency.

کرم کرنا karam karnā, v. To be kind; to show favours; to be generous.

کرم karm (S) n.m. Action; act; deed; devotion; religious acts or duties; fortune; fate; destiny; the accusative case (*Gram.*).

کرم بھوگ karm bhog, n.m. Fulfilling of destiny; suffering pain or enjoying pleasure as a result of one's past deeds.

کرم پھوٹنا karm phūṭnā, v. To have bad luck; to suffer loss.

کرم کو رونا karm ko ronā, v. To repent; to mourn over one's misfortune.

کرم kirm (P) n.m. A worm.

کرم پیلہ kirm pīlah, n.m. Silkworm.

کرم خوردہ kirm khūrdah, adj. Worm-eaten.

کرم کلا karm kallā (P) n.m. Cabbage; cauliflower.

کرمک kirmak (P) n.m. A small worm.

کرمک شب تاب kirmak-ě shab tāb, n.m. Glow-worm.

کرن kiran (H) n.f. Ray; beam; sun beam; moon beam; gold or silver tossels.

کرنا karnā (H) n.m. Name of a kind of citron; citron buds.

کرنا karnā (P) n.m. A kind of trumpet; clarion; a bugle.

کرنا karnā (H) v. To do; to make; to form; to perform; to execute; to effect; to act; to administer; to set; to thrust; to use; to finish.

کرنجوا karanjvā (H) n.m. A medicinal herb; a brown colour; a mixture of *jawar*, *bājrā* and *moth*. (جوار، باجرا، موٹھ)

کرنڈ kuranḍ (H) n.m. Corundum stone used for hoves.

کرنڈی karanḍi (H) n.m. A cloth made of untwisted silk.

کرنی karnī (H) n.f. Actions; deeds; doings; a mason's trowel.

جیسی کرنی ویسی بھرنی jaisī karnī waisī bharnī. prov. As you sow so shall you reap.

کروانا karwānā (H) v. To cause to make or perform.

کروٹ karwaṭ (H) n.f. Sideways; side; sleeping on a side.

کروٹ لینا، بدلنا karwat lenā, badalnā, v. To turn from side to side (in bed).

کرودھ krodh (H) n.m. Anger; passion; resentment; rage; wrath.

کروڑ karoṛ (H) adj. Ten millions.

کروڑپتی karor patī, adj. A millionaire; a very rich person.

کروندا karaundā (H) n.m. Name of a sour fruit; corinda.

کروی kuravī (A) adj. Spherical; globular.

کرہ kurrah (A) n.m. A globe; a sphere; an orb; a spheroid; the region.

کرہ آب kurrah-ě āb, n.m. The region of water.

کرہ آتش kurrah-ě ātash, n.m. The region of fire; the sun.

کرہ ارض kurrah-ě arẓ, n.m. Terrestrial globe; the earth.

کرہ باد kurrah-ě bād, n.m. The region of wind; the atmosphere.

کرہ خاک *kurrah-ĕ khāk, n.m.* The terrestrial globe; the earth.

کرہ فلک *kurrah-ĕ falak, n.m.* The celestial globe.

کرہ نار *kurrah-ĕ nār, n.m.* The region of fire; empyrean.

کریا *kriyā* (H) *n.f.* Deed; obsequies, an oath; action; a verb (*Gram.*).

کریا کرم *kriyā karm, n.m.* Performance of funeral ceremonies; obsequies; religious duties.

کریانہ *kiryānah, n.m.* Grocery; spices.

کریپ *karep* (E) *n.m.* Crape; a silk or imitation silk cloth.

کرید *kured* (H) *n.f.* Investigation; search.

کریدنا *kurednā* (H) *v.* To scratch; to scrape.

کریر *karir* (H) *n.m.* A prickly, leafless plant.

کریز *kuriz* (P) *n.f.* Moulting (of birds).

کریز کرنا *kurīz karnā, v.* To moult.

کریلا *karelā* (H) *n.m.* A kind of bitter vegetable.

کریم *karim* (A) *adj.* Bountiful; magnificent; gracious; liberal; merciful; generous; an epithet of God.

کریہ *karih* (A) *adj.* Disgusting; abominable; detestable; dirty; execrable.

کریہ منظر *karih manzar, adj.* Ugly; hateful; odious; offensive; disgusting.

کڑا *kaṛā* (H) *n.m.* A bracelet; a large ring; an anklet; the handle of a door, or anything in the form of a ring. *adj.* Hard; stiff; strong; unbending; harsh; scarce; cruel; sharp; sly; rude; penetrating.

کڑاڑا *kaṛāṛā* (H) *n.m.* The perpendicular bank of a river; a high and steep river bank.

کڑاکا *kaṛāka* (H) *n.m.* A crash; a loud cracking sound; a rigid fast.

کڑاکا گزرنا *kaṛākā guzarnā, v.* To starve; to go without food; to pass days in extreme poverty.

کڑاکے کا جاڑا *kaṛāke kā jāṛā, n.m.* Severe winter.

کڑاہ *kaṛāh* (H) *n.m.* A big shallow iron boiler; a cauldron.

کڑاهی *kaṛāhi* (H) *n.f.* A frying pan.

کڑاهی چاٹنا *kaṛāhi chāṭnā, v.* To lick the pot.

کڑاهی چڑھنا *kaṛāhi charhnā, v.* To be placed on the fire in a frying pan; to make preparations for a feast.

کڑک *kaṛak* (H) *n.f.* A crash; a crack; thunder; a matchlock; agility.

کڑک *kuṛak* (H) *n.f.* Clucking (of a hen); a clucking hen; a blank; nothing.

کڑک بیٹھنا *kuṛak baiṭhnā, v.* To cluck (a hen).

کڑکڑانا *kaṛkaṛānā* (H) *v.* To gnash the teeth from rage; to give such a sound as oil or butter when boiling hard.

کڑکڑانا *kuṛkuṛānā* (H) *v.* To cluck; to grumble; to tear; to grudge; to cackle.

کڑکنا *kaṛaknā* (H) *v.* To roar; to thunder; to crackle; to be beaten loudly (drum).

کڑوا *karwā* (H) *adj.* Bitter; acrid; brackish; sharp; strong; virulent; harsh; hard hearted; brave; myrrh.

کڑوا بول *kaṛwā bol, n.m.* Harsh words; abuse.

کڑوا تیل *kaṛwā tel, n.m.* Bitter oil; musterd-seed oil.

کڑوا کرنا *kaṛwā karnā, v.* To give or spend unwillingly.

کڑوے کسیلے دن *kaṛwe kasele din, n.m.* Hard and cruel times.

کڑوا لگنا *kaṛwā lagnā, v.* To taste bitter or acrid or pungent; to be displeasing.

کڑوا ہونا karwā honā, v. To be bitter; to be enraged; to be harsh.

کڑواہٹ karwāhat (H) n.f. Bitterness; acrid taste.

کڑھانا kurhāna (H) v. To vex; to trouble; to displease; to afflict; to grieve; to anger; to disgust.

کڑھن kuṛhan (H) n.f. Grief; sorrow; lamentation; mortification; envy.

کڑھنا kaṛhnā (H) v. To be drawn; to be pulled out or extracted; to be boiled; to be delineated; to be drawn or pointed; to escape; to issue; to slip; to spring; to appear.

کڑھنا kuṛhna (H) v. To grieve; to be afflicted; to envy; to pine; to pity; to sympathise.

کڑھی kaṛhi (H) n.f. Curry; a dish made by boiling the ground gram with spices in whey.

کڑی kaṛi (A) n.f A rafter; a beam; a handcuff; hardship; a verse. adj. Hard; stiff; strict.

کڑیل kaṛyal (H) adj. Bony; strong; muscular.

کثر دم kuzhdum (P) n.m. A scorpion.

کس kas (P) n.m. A man; person; any person.

کس و نا کس kas-ŏ-nā kas, n.m. Everybody; the rich and the poor; great or small.

بے کس be kas, adj. Helpless.

فی کس fi kas, adj. Per head; per capita; for each person.

کس kis (H) pron. interrog. What; which; whom; who.

کس طرح kis ṯarah, adv. How.

کس قدر kis qadar, adv. How much; how many.

کس لئے kis liye, adv. Why; wherefore.

کس وقت kis waqt, adv. At what time; when.

کس kus (P) n.f. Vulva.

کساد kasad (A) n.f. Slump.

کساد بازاری kasad bāzari, n.f. Market slump.

کسا کسایا kasa kasaya (H) adj. Ready tied; ready packed; ready harnessed.

کسالت kasālat, n.f. Indisposition; slight illness; laziness.

کسان kisān (H) n.m. A farmer; a husbandman; agriculturist.

کسانا kasānā (H) v. To cause to test; to cause to tighten; to be spoiled (curd) by allowing to remain in a metallic vessel.

کساؤ kasā'o (H) n.m. Astingency; tightening.

کسب kasab (A) n.m. Profession; trade; business; employment; equisition by labour; earning skill; gain.

کسب کرنا kasab karnā, v. To acquire; to gain; to earn.

کسب معاش kasab-ĕ ma'ash, n.m. Earning of livelihood.

کسبت kisbat. See کسوت kiswat.

کسبی kasbī (A&P) n.m. An artisan; an artificer. n.f. A prostitute; a harlot.

کستورا kastūrā (H) n.m. An oyster; a musk-deer; black-bird; thrush.

کستوری kasturi (H) n.f. Musk; the musk-bag.

کسر kasr (A) n.f. Breach; loss; affliction; a fraction (Arith.); root; putting to flight; the vowel (-) bounded like the English i in bill or pin.

کسر اعشاریہ kasr-ĕ 'ashāryah, n.f. Decimal fraction.

کسر اعشاریہ متوالی kasr-ĕ 'ashāryah mutawāli, n.f. Recurring decimal fraction.

کسر بھرنا kasr bhranā, v. To make up a deficiency.

کسرپڑنا kasr paṛnā, v. To suffer a loss; to fail.

کسر دینا kasr denā, v. To cause a loss.

کسر رکھنا kasr rakhnā, v. To leave unfinished; to cherish ill-will.

کسر رهنا kasr rahnā, v. To be incomplete; to be deficient.

کسر شان kasr-ĕ shān, n.f. Loss of dignity; derogation; loss of honour.

کسرعام kasr-ĕ ʻām, n.f. Vulgar fraction.

کسرغیرواجب kasr-ĕ ghair wājib, n.f. An improper fraction.

کسرکرنا kasr karnā, v. To deduct; to decrease; to omit; to subtract.

کسر کھانا kasr khānā, v. To suffer a loss or damage.

کسرمدور kasr-ĕ mudawwer, n.f. Recurring fraction.

کسر مرکب kasr-ĕ murakkab, n.f. A mixed number.

کسرمضاف kasr-ĕ muẓāf, n.f. Compound fraction.

کسرملتف kasr-ĕ multaf, n.f. Complex fraction.

کسرمفرد kasr-ĕ mufrad, n.f. Simple fraction.

کسرنکالنا kasr nikālnā, v. To make up the loss; to make good a deficiency; to take revenge.

کسرت kasrat, n.f. Exercise; physical exercise; training of the body; practice; habit; usage.

کسرتی kasratī, adj. Athletic; developed by exercise. n.m. An athlete.

کسرتی بدن kasratī badan, n.m. A well-trained body.

کسره kasrah (A) n.m. A breaking; the vowel (-).

کسک kasak (H) n.f. Pain; affliction; stitch.

کسل kasal (A) n.m. Laxity; slowness; indolence; weariness; cowardice; depression of spirits; sickness; indisposition; relaxation.

کسل مند kasal mand, adj. Sick; ailing; indisposed; relaxed; weary.

کسم kusum (H) n.m. Safflower; bastard saffron; the red dye of safflower; ophthalmia; the menstrual discharge.

کسمسانا kasmasānā (H) v. To bestir oneself; to move; to shake; to fidget; to become restless.

کسمساهٹ kasmasāhat (H) n.f. Restlessness.

کسنا kasnā (H) v. To tighten; to brace; to tie; to bind; to press; to assay; to prove; to examine; to raise the price; to fry in butter.

کسوانا kaswānā (H) v. See کسانا kasānā

کسوانا kuswānā (H) v. To cause to curse.

کسوت kiswat (A) n.f. Dress; appearance; robe; habit; figure; form; manner; a barber's or surgeon's case; a water bag.

کسوٹی kasauṭī (H) n.f. Touchstone; test; proof.

کسوٹی پر چڑھانا یا لگانا kasauṭī par chaṛhānā yā lagānā, v. To test; to examine; to prove.

کسور kusūr (A) n.f. (plu. of کسر kasr), Fractions; portions.

کسوف kusūf (A) n.m. Solar eclipse.

کسی kassī (H) n.f. A spade; a hoe; a land measure of two steps or two paces.

کسی kisī (H) pron. Anyone; someone.

کسی ایک kisī ek, adv. Anyone; certain.

کسی قدر kisī qadr, adv. A little; to some extent; certain quantity.

کسی نہ کسی kisī nah kisī, adv. Someone or other.

کسے kise (H) *pron.* Whom; to which; to what.

کسے kase (P) *adj.* Someone; somebody; anybody.

کسیانا kasyānā (H) *v.* To become astringent; to be spoiled (curd etc.) by allowing it to remain in a bell-metal vessel.

کسیرا kaserā (H) *n.m.* A brazier; a pewterer; a grey cattle.

کسیرھٹا kaser haṭṭā (H) *n.m.* A market where metallic vessels are sold.

کسیس kasīs (H) *n.m.* Green vitriol; sulphate of iron.

کسیلا kaselā (H) *adj.* Astringent; bitter; pungent.

کسیلا kasīlā (H) *adj.* Strong; vigorous.

کش kash (P) *adj.* (used in *compos.*) Drawing; pulling; enduring; carrying; bearing; suffering. *n.m.* A pull of حقہ ḥukkah.

کش مکش kash makash, *n.f.* Pulling backwards and forwards; bringing and taking away; struggle; wrangle; difficulty.

کش kush (P) *adj.* (used in *compos.*) Killing; destroying; killer; destroyer.

کشا kushā (P) *adj.* (used in *compos.*) Opening; displaying; expanding; solving; loosening; conquering; revealing.

کشاد kushād (P) *n.f.* Opening; loosening; revealing.

کشادگی kushādagī (P) *n.f.* An aperture; expansion; extension; entensiveness; openness; spaciousness; looseness; openness of heart; exhilaration; latitude.

کشادہ kushādah (P) *adj.* Open; uncovered; expanded; spacious; wide; ample; extensive; loose; capacious; displayed; revealed; free; cheerful; frank; drawn forth.

کشادہ ابرو kushādah abrū, *adj.* Open or wide between the eye-brows; cheerful; humorous.

کشادہ جبیں ، کشادہ پیشانی ، کشادہ رو kushādah jabīṅ, kushādah peshānī, kushādah rū, *adj.* Of an open countenance; gay; cheerful; blithe.

کشادہ دل kushādah dil, *adj.* Open-hearted; frank; generous.

کشادہ روئی kushādah rū'i, *n.f.* Openness of countenance; cheerfulness.

کشا کش kashākash (P) *n.f.* Struggle; repeated pulling backwards and forwards; distraction; dilemma; purplexity; difficulty; contention; stretching and straining; great unpleasantness; grief and pain.

کشاں kashān (P) *adj.* (used in *comp.*) Drawing; bearing; suffering; withdrawing.

کشائش kushā'ish (P) *n.f.* Opening; loosening; solving; expansion; enlargement; cheerfulness; hilarity.

کشت و خون kusht-ŏ khūn (P) *n.m.* Carnage; massacre.

کشت kisht (P) *n.f.* A sown-field; a check (at chess).

کشت زار kisht zār, *n.f.* A sown-field.

کشتنی kushtani (P) *adj.* Fit to be killed; worthy of death.

کشتہ kushtah (P) *adj.* Killed; slain. *n.m.* A lover; killed mercury; a preparation of mercury or any other metal; calx.

کشتۂ ناز kushtah-ĕ nāz, *adj.* Killed by blandishments; a lover.

کشتی kishti yā kashti (P) *n.f.* A boat; a bark; a vessel; a ship, a tray; a beggar's bowl; a wallet.

کشتی بان kishtī bān, *n.m.* A boatman; a seaman; a sailor; master of a vessle; navigator; marinar.

کشتی چلانا ، کھینا kishtī chalānā, khenā. *v.* To row a boat.

کشتی *kushti* (P) *n.f.* Wrestling

کشتی باز *kushti bāz*, *n.m.* A wrestler.

کشتی لڑنا *kushti laṛnā*, *v.* To wrestle; to struggle hard.

کشتم کشتا *kushtam kushtā*, *n.f.* Contest; fight; fighting and slaying.

کشٹ *kashṭ* (H) *n.m.* Affliction; pain; distress; hardship; trouble; difficulty.

کشٹا *kishṭā* (H) *n.m.* Dry apricots used in polishing silver articles.

کشش *kashish* (P) *n.f.* Drawing; attraction; pull; allurement.

کشش ثقل *kashish-ĕ s̤iql*, *n.f.* Gravity.

کشش کہربائی *kashish-ĕ kahurbā'ı*, *n.f.* Frictional electricity.

کشش مقناطیسی *kashish-ĕ miqnatısı*, *n.f.* Magnetism; electric attraction.

کشف *kashf* (A) *n.m.* An opening; a manifestation; revelation; solution; explanation; a divine inspiration.

کشفی *kashfi* (A) *adj.* Revealed; manifest.

کشکول *kashkol* (P) *n.m.* A begger's bowl; an album.

کشمش *kishmish* (P) *n.f.* Raisins; currants; dried small grapes (without stones).

کشمشی *kishmishi* (P) *adj.* Of the colour of raisins; reddish brown.

کشمیری *kashmīri* (P) *n.m.* A native of Kashmir. *adj.* Pertaining or belonging to Kashmir.

کشنیز *kishnīz* (P) *n.m.* Coriander; a plant whose seeds are strongly aromatic, stomachic and carminative.

کشود *kushūd* (P) *n.m.* Opening; openness; expansion; solution.

کشور *kishor* (H) *n.m.* A youth; a son; a minor.

کشور *kishwar* (P) *n.f.* A country; a territory; climate; region.

کشور ستانی *kishwar sitāni*, *n.f.* Conquest; subjugation of countries.

کشیدگی *kashidagi* (P) *n.f.* Displeasure; tension; ill-feeling; misunderstanding.

کشیدنی *kashıdani* (P) *adj.* Fit to be drawn.

کشیدہ *kashidah* (P) *n.m.* A kind of needlework. *adj.* Drawn; extended; contracted; sullen; stretched; pulled in; endured; supercilious.

کشیدہ خاطر *kashidah khātir*, *adj.* Displeased; annoyed.

کشیدہ قامت *kashidah qāmat*, *adj.* Tall of stature.

کشیدہ کاڑھنا *kashidah kāṛhnā*, *v.* To embroider; to trace figures in needlework on cloth.

کعب *ka'b* (A) *n.m.* A cube; the ankle; a dice; chessman; draughts.

کعبتین *ka'batain* (A) *n.m.* The two sacred temples of Mecca and Jeruslem; two dice; game with two dice.

کعبہ *ka'bah* (A) *n.m.* The House of Allah at Mecca.

کف *kaf* (P) *n.m.* Froth; spittle; scum; foam; phlegm; hand; sole (of the foot); a handful.

کف افسوس ملنا *kaf-ĕ afsos malnā*, *v.* To wring one's hands with regret; to be sorry for.

کف آور *kaf āwar*, *adj.* Expectorant; medicine which helps discharge of phlegm from the throat.

کف پا *kaf-ĕ pā*, *n.m.* The sole of the foot.

کف دست *kaf-ĕ dast*, *n.m.* The palm of the hand.

کف دست میدان *kaf-ĕ dast maidān*, *n.m.* A level and desert plain; barren land; bleak land.

کف گیر kaf gir, n.m. A skimmer; a sort of a ladle.

کف لانا kaf lana, v. To spit froth; to foam; to fret and frown.

کفار kuffār (A) n.m. (plu. of کافر kāfir) Infidels; idolators.

کفارہ kafārah (A) n.m. Atonement; penitence; penance; expiation for sins.

کفارہ دینا kafārah denā, v. To atone for; to expiate for sins.

کفاف kafāf (A) n.m. Pittance; daily bread; sufficiency; livelihood; enough to keep one from begging. adj. Adequate; on a par; just; sufficient.

کفالت kafālat (A) n.f. Pledge; pawn, security; responsibility, bail; surety; guarantee.

کفالت المال kafālat-ul-māl, n.f. Pecuniary bail.

کفالت نامہ kafālat nāmah, n.m. A bail-bond.

کفایت kifāyat (A) n.f. Enough; abundance; profit; ability; prudence; plenty; surplus; economy; thrift; sufficiency.

کفایت شعار kifāyat shi'ār, adj. Economical; thrifty; sparing; frugal.

کفایت شعاری kifāyat shi'ārī, n.f. Economy; thrift; frugality.

کفایت کرنا kifāyat karna, v. To economise; to suffice; to save; to answer; to serve; to do.

کفایتی kifāyati (A) n.f. Abundance; plenty; sufficiency. adj. Economical; cheap; thrifty; frugal.

کفایہ kifāyah (A) adj. Sufficient; reasonable.

کفچہ kafchah (P) n.m. A spoon; a ladle; skimmer; the hood of a snake.

کفر kufr (A) n.m. Paganism; infidelity; incredulity; ingratitude; heathenism; profanity; blasphemy; unbelief.

کفر بکنا kufr bakna, v. To utter blasphemous language; to talk nonsense.

کفر توڑنا kufr torna, v. To distroy paganism; to overcome one's abstinacy of; to convert one to Islam.

کفر کا فتویٰ دینا kufr ka fatwa dena, v. To condemn one as an infidel.

کفر کچہری kufr kachahri, n.f. Evil company; company where blasphemy is heard.

کفران kufrān (A) n.m. Infidelity; ingratitude.

کفران نعمت kufrān-e ni'mat, n.m. Ingratitude; thanklessness; unbelief.

کفرستان kufristān (P) n.m. The country of the infidels.

کفش kafsh (P) n.f. A shoe; a slipper.

کفش بردار kafsh bardār, n.m. An attendent; a servant.

کفش دوز kafsh doz, n.m. A shoe-maker; a cobbler.

کفن kafan (A) n.m. Grave clotnes; a shroud; a winding sheet.

کفن پھاڑ کے بولنا kafan phar ke bolna, v. To exclaim; to shriek; to make a terrible noise.

کفن چورر kafan chor, n.m. A shroud-thief, caitiff; miscreant; a ruffian.

کفن دفن kafan dafan, n.m. Burial; funeral.

کفن سر سے باندھنا kafan sar se bandhnā, v. To engage in a perilous adventure or undertaking.

کفن کھسوٹ kafan khasot, n.m. A person who snatches even the coffin of a dead man; a plunderer.

کفنانا kafnana, v. To dress for the grave; to shroud; to lay out a corpse.

کفنی kafni, n.f. A dress worn by fakirs.

کفو kufū (A) n.m. Alike; equal; of the same tribe; caste; brotherhood; kin.

کفور kafūr (A) adj. Ungrateful. n.m. A infidel; renegade; disbeliever; idolator.

کفیل kafil (A) n.m. A surety; a security; pledgee; guarantee; hostage; bail.

کفیل ہونا kafil honā, v. To stand surety; to give bail for.

ککا kakkā (H) adj. White; brown; albino.

ککرالی kakrali (H) n.f. A tumour in the armpit.

ککرمتا kukurmuttā (H) n.m. A mushroom; a toadstool.

ککروندا kakronda (H) n.m. Name of a plant and its fruit; celsia.

ککڑ kukkaṛ (H) n.m. A cock; an old man.

ککڑوں کوں kukkṛun kun (H) n.f. The crow of a cock.

ککڑوں کوں کرنا kukkṛūn kūn karnā, v. To crow.

ککڑی kakṛi (H) n.f. A kind of cucumber.

ککڑی kukṛi (H) n.f. A hen; maize.

کل kal (H) n.f. Tomorrow; yesterday; the snear future; the near past; dooms-day.

کل کا لڑکا kal kā laṛkā, n.m. A raw youth; an inexperienced person.

کل کلاں کو kal kalāṅ ko, adv. In future; any time in the future; tomorrow or the next.

کل کل کرنا kal kal karna, v. To dilly dally; to employ delaying tactics; to put off; to postpone.

کل کی بات kal kī bāt, n.f. Quite a recent occurence; late news; news of yesterday.

kal (H) n.f. Ease; comfort; relief; tranquillity; peace; repose.

کل آنا kal ana, v. To have ease of mind; to be comforted; to be at ease.

کل kal pana, v. To have peace of mind.

kal paṛna, v. To be at ease; to be atisfied.

کل نہ پڑنا kāl nah paṛnā, v. To be disturbed in mind; to have no peace of mind; to feel uneasy.

کل kal (H) adj. (contraction of کالا kālā) Black.

کل جیبھا kal jibhā, adj. Black-tongued; malignant; whose curses prevail.

کل سرا kal ṣirā, adj. Black-headed.

کلمونہا kal mūṅhā, muṅha, adj. Black-faced. n.m. A black-faced person or animal; a foreboding or ill-omened countenance.

کلمونہی kal mūṅhi, n.f. An ill-omened woman. adj. Unfortunate; mean.

کل kal (H) n.f. A machine; a lock; a trigger.

کل دار kal dār, n.m. A rupee with a milled rim, formed by a machine; a gun having a trigger.

کل داربندوق kal dār banduq, n.f. A gun having a trigger; a matchlock.

کل کا آدمی kal ka adamī, n.m. A puppet; a mechanical person; a robot.

کل کا گھوڑا kal kā ghoṛā, n.m A mechanical horse; a small well-trained and obedient horse; a bicycle.

کل kal (H) n.m. The worst thing; a wrangle; a quarrel.

کل جگ kal jug, n.m. The fourth age; the worst age.

کل kul (A) adj. All; whole; entire; universe; aggregate.

بالکل bil kul, adv. Wholly; entirely.

کلا kalā (S) n.m. A digit or sixteenth part of the moon's diameter; a trick; art; fine art; somersault.

کلا بازی kalā bazi, n.f. A somersault; tumbling; turning over head and heels; (see also قلا بازی qalā bāzi)

کلا بازی کھانا kalā bāzi khana, v. To take a somersault.

کلا جنگ kalā jang, n.m. A trick in wrestling; an acrobatic feat.

کلاکار kala kar, n.m. An artist. adj. Cunning; artful; crafty.

کلا kallā (H) n.m. The head; the jaws; the cheeks; a bud; a sprout.

کلا به کلا لڑنا kallā bah kallā larna, v. To fight face to face; to fight on equal footing.

کلا توڑ جواب kallā tor jawāb, n.m. A crushing reply.

کلا ٹھلا kallā thallā, n.m. Noise and bustle; pomp and splendour.

کلا دراز kallā darāz, adj. Imprudent; rude; noisy or clamorous; abusive.

کلابتون kalābattun (H) n.m. Gold or silver thread.

کلال kalāl (H) n.m. A distiller; tavern-keeper; an inn-keeper; a seller of spirituous liquors.

کلال خانه kalāl khanah, n.m. A tavern, a liquor-shop.

کلام kalam (A) n.m. A word; speech; discourse; talk; conversation; a writing; a work; an objection; a complete sentence; composition.

کلاماللہ kalām ullah, n.m. The word of God; a holy book, the Quran.

کلام اللہ اٹھانا kalam ullah uthanā, v. To swear by the Quran.

کلام کرنا kalam karna, v. To talk; to speak; to relate; to affirm; to discuss; to reason; to argue; to dispute.

کلام ہونا kalam hona, v. To take objection to; to have a word; to say against.

کلاں kalān (P) adj. Large; great; big; elder; bulky; grand.

کلانچ kulānch (H) n.f. See قلانچ qulanch.

کلاونت kulawant (H) n.m. A kind of singer or musician.

کلاوہ kalāvah (P) n.m. A ball of thread; yarn; skein

کلاہ kulāh (P) n.m. A cap; a hat; a bonnet; a crown.

کلاہ پوش kulāh posh, adj. Wearing a cap.

کلائی kalā'i (H) n.f. The forearm; the wrist; pulse; legunimous seeds.

کلائی کرنا، لڑنا kalā'i karna, larna, v. To contend at twisting wrists.

کلب kalb (A) n.m. A dog.

کل بل kil bil (H) n.f. Crawling of insects; creeping; children; a confused voice of the children.

کلبلانا kulbulānā (H) v. To itch; to fidget; to writhe; to grumble; to toss about in pain; to wriggle as a worm; rumbling of the bowels; to be restless.

کلبلاہٹ kulbulāhat (H) n.f. The act of writhing; vermicular motion; itch; restlessnes

کلبہ kulbah (P) n.m. A hut; a cell.

کلپ kalp (S) n.m. A kind of hair-dye; a day and night of Brahma; scarcity; lack; want; sorrow; grief, lamentation; wailing.

کلپانا kalpanā (H) v. To oppress; to give pain; to afflict

کلپنا kalapna (H) v. To be grieved; to grieve; to be vexed; to be in distress or pain; to repine; to fret; to lament.

کلچہ kulchah (P) n.m. A small loaf; a cake of bread; biscuit; the circular piece of wood at the top of a tent pole. (H) n.m. Capital; principal; stock in trade.

کلر kallar (H) adj. Barren; sterile; unproductive. n.m. Nitre; salt.

کلر لگنا kallar lagnā, v. To be impregnated with nitre; to become barren.

کلڑہ kullarh (H) n.m. A small earthen cup; a cracker.

کلس kalas (H) n.m. Dome; spire; a pinnacle; a peak; a crest.

کلسا kalsā (H) n.m. A brass or copper vessel with a narrow neck.

کلغا kalghā (P) n.m. A flower of red colour; cock's comb.

کلغی kalghi, n.f. An ornament on the turban; a spire on the top of a dome; a pinnacle; a crest, a plume.

کلف kalaf (A) n.m. Starch; stiffness; pimple on the face; a blackish red colour; application; attention.

کلفت kulfat (A) n.f. Trouble; vexation; distress; affliction. (P) n.f. A maid-servant.

کلفت دور ہونا kulfat dūr hona, v. To be relieved; to get rid of the trouble.

کلک kilk (P) n.f. A reed; a pen.

کلکاری kilkāri (H) n f Shout; shriek; scream; a sound expressive of joy; chattering; snorting joyfully

کلکاری مارنا kilkāri mārnā, v. To shout; to cry; to shriek; to express pleasure by a cry.

کلکل kalkal (H) n.m. Wrangling; quarrelling; wordy duel; nonsense talk.

کلکل کرنا kalkal karna, v. To wrangle; to bawdy words with.

کلمات kalımāt (A) n.m. (plu. of کلمہ kalimah) Words; sayings.

کلمہ kalimah (A) n.m. A speech; a word; saying; part of speech; the Muslim confession of faith.

کلمۃالحق kalimah-tul-ḥaqq, n.m. The word of God; truth.

کلمہ پڑھانا kalimah paṛhānā, v. To teach the کلمہ kalimah; to convert one to the Muslim religion.

کلمہ پڑھنا kalimah parhnā, v. To be converted to the Muslim faith: to become a Muslim.

کلمہ تکبیر kalimah-ĕ takbir, n.m. God is great, the slogan of Muslims.

کلمہ شہادت پڑھنا kalimah-ĕ shahādat paṛhnā, v. To say, I declare that there is no god but Allah and I declare that Muhammad is His servant and His Prophet.

کلمہ کفر kalimah-ĕ kufr, n.m. Profane words; blasphemy.

کلمہ گو kalimah go, n.m. A Muslim.

کلنک kalank (H) n.m. Stigma; accusation; scandal; blemish; calumny; suspicion; spot; brand; defamation; aspersion; stain; reproach; disgrace.

کلنک کا ٹیکا لگانا kalank kā tikā lagānā, v. To calumniate; to stigmatize; to defame; to accuse.

کلنک کا ٹیکا لگنا kalank kā tikā lagnā, v. To receive the mark or brand of disgrace; to be branded; to get a bad name; to be stigmatized.

کلنکی kalanki (H) adj. Liable to reproach; blemished; calumniated; soiled; stained. n.m. One who has a stain on his character; a disreputable person.

کلنگ kulang (P) n.m. A fowl of a large breed; a crane; a very tall person.

کلوٹا ، کلوٹی kalotā, kaloti (H) adj. Black; jet black.

کلوخ kulūkh (P) n.m. A clod of earth; an unbaked brick.

کلوخ اندازی kulukh andāzi, n.f. Brick-batting.

کلول kalol yā kllol (H) n.f. Wantonness; play; frolic; merry-making; sport: diversion; gambol; friskiness; enjoyment.

کلول کرنا kalol karnā, v. To sport; to gambol; to frolic; to revel; to frisk.

کلونتا kulwanta (H) adj. Pure; of noble descent; well-born; a nobleman; a gentleman.

کلونجی kalaunji (H) n.f. The black aromatic seed of nigella-indica, used medicinally.

کلہ kallah (P) n.m. See کلا kallā.

کلہاڑا - کلہاڑی kulhara, kulhāri (H) n.m/f. A hatchet; an axe.

کلھیا kulhyā (H) n.f. A small earthen bowl; a cupping glass; a kind of firework.

کلھیا میں گڑ پھوڑنا kulhyā meṅ guṛ phoṛnā, v. To break a lump of sugar in a small cup; to endeavour to do with few hands a work which requires many; to do something impossible.

کلی kulli (H) n.f. Gargling; rinsing the mouth; washing the mouth.

کلی kulli (A) adj. Universal; entire; whole; general; common; all; complete.

کلی kali (H) n.f. A bud; unblown flower; a pipe for smoking; the iron ore.

کلیات kulliyāt (A) n.m. (plu. of کلی kulli). All the works of a poet; formulae.

کلیان kalyān (H) n.m. Welfare; happiness; prosperity; name of a rāg sung at night.

کلیانا kalyānā, v. To blossom; to bloom; to bud.

کلیتاً kulliyatan (A) adv. Totally; universally.

کلیجا kalejā (H) n.m. The liver (of a human being); the vitals; the heart; stomach; mind; courage; spirit; magnanimity; pluck.

کلیجا اُچھلنا kalejā uchhalnā, v. To leap with joy (heart); to be overjoyed; to palpitate.

کلیجا اُلٹنا kalejā ulaṭnā, v. To be exhausted with excessive vomiting.

کلیجا بڑھ جانا kaleja baṛh jānā, v. Enlargement of the liver; to take courage, to be overjoyed.

کلیجا بیٹھا جانا kalejā baiṭhā jānā, v. To be depressed in spirits.

کلیجا پاش پاش ہونا kalejā pāsh pāsh honā, v. To be afflicted; to be heart broken; to be in great distress.

کلیجا پک جانا kalejā pak jānā, v. To be deeply wounded or cut to the quick.

کلیجا پھٹنا kalejā phaṭnā, v. To feel pity; to be disturbed with grief; to burst with envy or jeolausy

کلیجا تر ہونا kalejā tar honā, v. To be at ease; to be well off.

کلیجا تھام کے رہ جانا، مسوسنا kaleja tham ke rah jana ya masosna, v. To suppress one's feelings; to repress one's grief; to choke one's emotions.

کلیجا تھام تھام کے رونا kaleja tham thām ke ronā, v. To weep bitterly and long.

کلیجا ٹھنڈا کرنا kalejā ṭhanḍa karna, v. To satisfy the heart's longings; to obtain one's wish; to get satisfaction.

کلیجا جلنا kaleja jalnā, v. To suffer sorrow; to burn with envy; to mourn; to be heart-sore.

کلیجا چھلنی ہونا kalejā chhalni hona, v. To be pricked through the heart; to suffer heavy shocks.

کلیجا دھک دھک ہونا kalejā dhak dhak honā, v. To be greatly frightened; to be terror-stricken.

کلیجا دھک سے ہونا kalejā dhak se honā, v To be surprised completely.

کلیجا کانپنا kalejā kaṅpna, v. To be afraid; to tremble through fear.

کلیجا منہ کو آنا kalejā muṅh ko ānā, v. To feel sick; to loathe; to be fatigued with excessive vomiting.

کلیجے سے لگا رکھنا kaleje se lagā rakhnā, v. To caress; to embrace; to love exceedingly; to take great care of; to cherish in the heart; to keep next to the heart; to hold very dear

کلیجے میں آگ لگنا kaleje meṅ āg lagnā, v. To feel a burning sensation; to be extremely thirsty.

کلیجی kaleji (H) n.f. The liver of animals.

کلید kalid (P) n.f. Key.

کلیسا kalisā (Gr.) n.m A church; a cathedral.

کلیل kulel (H) n.f. Sport; recreation; friskiness; restiveness of a horse.

کلیل کرنا *kulel karna*, *v.* To frisk about.

کلیم *kalim* (A) *n.m.* A speaker; an interlocutor.

کلیم اللہ *kalim ullah*, *n.m.* A speaker with God; Moses.

کلیمی *kalimi* (A) *n.m* A jew.

کلیہ *kulliyah* (A) *n.m.* Formula; common; generic.

کم *kam* (P) *adj.* Deficient; little; scanty; rare; seldom; few; less.

کم اصل *kam aṣl*, *adj* Low-bred; base-born; mean.

کم بخت *kam bakht*, *adj.* Unfortunate; unlucky; cursed; wretched; villain

کم بختی *kam bakhti*, *n.f.* Ill-luck; misfortune; mishap; adversity, calamity.

کم بختی کے دن *kam bakhti ke din*, *n m.* Hard times; evil days

کم بختی کا مارا *kam bakhti ka mara*, *adj.* Accused; wretched, afflicted; as ill-luck would have it.

کم پایہ *kam payah*, *adj* Of low standard.

کم تر *kam tar*, *adj.* Smaller; less; seldom.

کم ترین *kam tarin*, *adj.* Least; very humble.

کم حوصلگی *kam hauslagi*, *n.f.* Narrow mindedness; illiberality, poor-spiritedness; meanness

کم حوصلہ *kam hauslah*, *adj.* Poor-spirited, unambitious; unaspiring; coward.

کم حیثیت *kam haisiyyat*, *adj.* Of small means; of low condition; of low status; mean; beggarly

کم خرچ *kam kharch*, *adj.* Frugal; niggardlyt thrifty, economical close-fisted.

کم خرچ بالا نشین *kam kharch bāla nashin*, *prov* Things of good quality purchased cheep; living in good style at little expense.

کم خرچی *kam kharchi*, *n.f.* Parsimony, economy.

کم خواب، (کمخاب) *kam khwāb* (*kam khab*) (P) *n.m.* Silk or satin worked with gold or silver. *adj.* Sleepless.

کم خوابی *kam khwabi*, *n.f.* Want of sleep; sleeplessness; brocade; embroidery.

کم خور *kam khor*, *adj.* Abstemious; sparing in diet; eating little.

کم ذات *kam zat*, *adj.* Low bred; vile; base.

کم ذاتی *kam zāti*, *n.f.* Low birth; low extraction; baseness.

کم زور *kam zor*, *adj.* Weak; feeble; frail; powerless.

کم زوری *kam zori*, *n.f.* Weakness; debility.

کم سخن *kam sukhn* *adj* Speaking very little; taciturn.

کم سن، عمر *kam sin*, *umr*, *adj.* Young; minor; of tender years.

کم سننا *kam sunna* *v* To be hard of hearing; to be deaf.

کم سنی *kam sini*, *n.f* Youth; nonage; minority.

کم سے کم *kam se kam*, *adv* At least; the very least.

کم ظرف *kam zarf* *adj.* Low born; mean; ignoble; vile; stupid; silly; witless.

کم عقل *kam 'aql*, *adj.* Stupid; gnorant; foolish.

کم عقلی *kam aqli*, *n.f.* Stupidity, want of understanding; folly.

کم فرصتی *kam fursati*, *n.f.* Want of leisure or ease.

کم فہم *kam fahm*, *adj.* Stupid; silly.

کم قیمت *kam qimat*, *adj* Low priced; cheap.

کم کم *kam kam*, *adv.* Little by little; gradually

کم گو kam go, adj. Taciturn; reserved; habitually silent.

کم مایگی kam māyagi, n.f. Scarcity; smallness of means; poverty; indigence.

کم مایہ kam māyah, adj. Deficient in quantity, wealth or capital; poor; indigent.

کم نصیب kam naṣib, adj. Unfortunate.

کم نصیبی kam naṣibi, n.f. Misfortune; bad luck.

کم نظر kam naẓar, adj. Dim-sighted; short-sighted.

کم و بیش kam-ŏ besh, adj. More or less.

کم و کاست kam-ŏ kāst, n.m. Loss; deficiency.

کم ہمت kam himmat, adj. Spiritless; daunted; mean-spirited; cowardly; illiberal.

کم یاب kam yāb, adj. Scarce; rare; uncommon.

کم یابی kam yābi, n.f. Scarcity; rarity.

کما حقہ، kamā ḥaqqo-hū (A) adv. As it should be; justly; properly; duly.

کماد kamād (H) n.m. Sugarcane.

کمار kumar (S) n.m. A son; a lad; an unmarried young prince; a prince.

کماری kumārī (S) n.f. A daughter; a maiden; a virgin; a princess.

کمال kamāl (A) n.m. Perfection; completion; conclusion; excellence; something wonderful; miracle; art; punctuality. adj. Complete; excellent; entire; very great; the greatest exceeding; excessive; extreme.

کمال حاصل کرنا kamal ḥāṣil karnā, v. To attain perfection; to reach the utmost height.

کمالِ درجے کا kamāl darje kā, adj. Of the highest degree; to the utmost; extreme; utmost.

کمال دکھلانا kamāl dikhānā, v. To show consummate skill or power; to work wonders; to perform a miracle; to show ones dexterity.

کمال کرنا kamāl karnā, v. To do something wonderful.

کمال کو پہنچانا kamāl ko pahunchānā, v. To bring to perfection.

کمال کو پہنچنا kamāl ko pahunchnā, v. To attain perfection.

کمالات kamālāt (A) n.m. plu. of کمال kamāl.

کمان kamān (corr. from the English). Command.

کمان افسر kamān afsar, n.m. Commander.

کمان kamān (P) n.f. A bow; an arch; a spring; a fiddle-stick; the sign Sagittarius. adj. Bent; elastic; curved; flexible.

کمانِ ابرو kamān abrū, adj Having arched eye brows.

کمان آتارنا kamān utārnā, v. To unbend a bow; to loosen or unstring a bow.

کمان تاننا یا چڑھانا kamān tannā yā charhānā, To bend a bow; to string a bow.

کمان چڑھنا kamān charhnā, v To be victorious; to overcome.

کمان دار kamān dār, n.m. An archer; one armed with a bow; a bowman.

کمان گر kamān gar, n.m. A bow-maker; a bone-setter

کمانِ گردوں kamān-ē gardūn, n.f The sign Sagittarius.

کمانا kamānā (H) v. To earn; to acquire; to get; to accumulate; to save; to work; to labour; to perform; to clean or curry leather; to clean a privy; to dress or prepare land; to lessen; to diminish; to abate; to do (good); to commit (crime); to fertilize; to exercise.

کمانچہ kamānchah (P) n.m. A small bow; an arched roof, a private room; a steel spring; the bow of a fiddle.

کمانی **kamāni**, *adj.* *n.m.* Spring of watch or carriage etc.

کماؤ **kamā'ū** (H) *adj.* Laborious; bread-winning. *n.m.* Earner; labourer; husband; son.

کمائی **kamā'i** (H) *n.f.* Earnings; gain; work; performance; profits; acquiring.

کمبل **kambal** (H) *n.m.* A blanket.

کمبل پوش **kambal posh**, *n.m.*. A mendicant whose only garment is a blanket.

کمبوہ **kamboh** (H) *n.m.* A tribe.

کمپا **kampā** (H) *n.m.* A stick with bird-lime attached, used by fowlers to catch birds.

کمپانا **kampāna** (H) *v.* To shake; to cause to tremble.

کمپنی **kampani** (E) *n.f.* Company; the East India Company; a banking or trading company.

کمتائی **kamtā'i** (H) *n.f.* Abatement; dificiency; scarcity; diminution.

کمتی **kamti** (H) *adj.* Scanty; little; less.

کمتی بڑھتی **kamti barhti**, *adj.* More or less.

کمر **kamar** (P) *n.f.* The loins; the waist; girdle; zone; belt; the middle of a mountain; the flank of an army; an arch.

کمر باندھنا **kamar bāndhnā**, *v.* To begird; to get ready; to resolve; to be intent on; to arm; to prepare; to gird up the loins.

کمر بستہ **kamar bastah**, *adj.* Ready; having the loins girded; on the alert. in a state of readiness; ready for battle, prepared; armed.

کمر بند **kamar band**, *n.m.* A girdle; a zone; waist-band; belt; a long piece of cloth folded round the waist; the string with which drawers are fastened.

کمر بندی **kamar bandi**, *n.f.* Preparation for battle etc; arming; alertness; getting ready.

کمر پکڑ کے اٹھنا **kamar pakar ke uthnā**, *v.* To become weak.

کمر توڑنا **kamar torna**, *v.* To break the back of; to alienate one's friends and sympathisers; to discourage.

کمر ٹوٹا **kamar tūtā**, *adj.* Hump-backed. impotent

کمر ٹوٹ جانا **kamar tūt jānā**, *v* To be helpless; to be deserted by one's friends; to have the spine broken; to become hump-backed; to suffer a heavy loss; to lose spirit.

کمر ٹھوکنا **kamar thokna**, *v.* To encourage; to support; to pat on the back.

کمر جھکنا **kamar jhukna**, *v.* To be hump-backed; To be paralyzed; to bend.

کمر رہ جانا **kamar reh jānā**, *v.* To have a pain in the loins.

کمر سیدھی کرنا **kamar sidhi karnā**, *v.* To lie down; to rest a while.

کمر کس کے باندھنا **kamar kas ke bāndhnā**, *v.* To be determined on an undertaking.

کمر کسنا **kamar kasnā**, *v.* To get ready; to resolve.

کمر کمر **kamar kamar**, *adj* Upto the waist, waist deep,

کمر کھول کر بیٹھنا **kamar khol kar baithna**, *v.* To sit at ease; to take off the belt; to take rest

کمر لگنا **kamar lagnā**, *v.* To get a back-ache; to have a sore back (horse).

کمر مارنا **Kamar mārnā**, *v.* To strike sideways; to attack an army in flank.

کمر مضبوط کرنا **kamar mazbut karna**, *v.* To take courage in both sides; to offer a strong support; to be helpful.

کمر ہلانا **kamar hilana**, *v.* To endeavour; to copulate.

کمر همت باندھنا kamar-ĕ himmat bāṅdhnā, v. To gird up one's loins.

کمرکھ kamrakh (H) n.m. The name of a sour fruit.

کمره kamrah, n.m. An apartment; a room; a chamber.

کمری kamrī, n.f. A short jacket; a waist-coat.

کمک kumak (P) n.f. Aid; assistance; reinforcement; help.

کملا kamlā (H) n.m. A kind of worm; n.f. Name of a Hindu goddes, Lakshmi.

کملانا kumlānā (H) v. To wither; to fade; to droop; to be blighted.

کملی kamlī (H) n.f. A small blanket.

کمند kamand (P) n.f. A kind of scaling ladder made of cord and chiefly used by thieves; a halter; a noose; a slip-knot; a lasso; the ringlets.

کمند پھینکنا یا ڈالنا kamand phenknā yā ḍālnā, v. To throw up a rope-ladder for scaling.

کمنگر kamangar. See کمان گر kamāngar.

کمہار kumhār (H) n.m. A potter.

کمہاری kumhārī (H) n.f. A potter's wife; a kind of wasp which builds its house of clay.

کمی kamī (P) n.f. Deficiency; loss; abatement; reduction; diminution; decrease; deficit; paucity; littleness; scantiness; scarcity; dearth; fall of price.

کمی بیشی kamī beshī, n.f. Decrease and increase; fluctuation; profit and loss.

کمی نہ کرنا kamī nah karnā, v. To leave no stone unturned.

کمیت kummait (H) n.m. A bay horse.

کمیت kammiyyat (A) n.f. Quantity; number.

کمیدان kumidān (T) n.m. Commander.

کمیرا kamerā (H) n.m. A workman; an assistant; a labourer; a hired worker.

کمیله kamelah (H) n.m. A drug; a slaughter house.

کمین kamīn (P) n.m. Mean; low-bred; wicked. (A) n.f. An ambush.

کمین گاه kamīn gāh, n.f. An ambuscade; a lurking place; a place of ambush.

کمین میں بیٹھنا kamīn men baiṭhnā, v. To lie in ambush.

کمینه kamīnah (P) adj. Mean; ignoble; vulgar; wicked; the least; defective; low; base.

کمینه پن یا کمینگی kamīnah pan ya kamīnagī. n.m. f. Meanness; wickedness.

کن kan (P) adj. Digging; digger; (used in compos. as, چاه کن chhāh kan, well-digger).

کن kan (H) n.m. Side; corner. (contraction of کان kān) Ear.

کن انکھی kan aṅkhī, n.f. A side-glance. (plu. کن انکھیاں kan aṅkhyān).

کن پٹی kan paṭī, n.f. Temple; flat part of head between forehead & either ear.

کن ٹوپ kan ṭop, n.m. A large cap, covering the ears also.

کن سلائی kan salā'ī, n.f. A longish insect of the type of centipede which is supposed to get into the brain through ear.

کن سوئیاں لینا kan sū'yān lenā, v. To overhear.

کن کھجورا kan khajūrā, n.m. A centipede.

کن کٹا kan kaṭā, adj. Earless; lap-eared.

کن kin (H) pron. (plu. of کس kis). Who; whom; which; what.

کن kun (P) adj. Making; doing; (used in compos. as کار کن kār kun. worker)

کنا kannā (H) n.m. The notches o nthe two sides of the upper leather of a shoe; the part of a paper-kite to which the string is tied; side; corner.

کنار kinār (P) n.f. Bosom; embrace; side; margin; edge; aside

بوس و کنار bos-ŏ kinār, n.f. Kissing and hugging; embracing.

در کنار dar kinār, adv. Putting aside; excluding.

کنارا، کنارہ kinārā, kinārah (P) n.m. Side; margin; shore; bank (of a river); beach; border; coast; part; limit; boundary; edge; end; brink; hem.

کنارہ کرنا kinārah karnā, v. To keep aloof; to abstain; to retire; to refrain.

کنارہ کش kinārah kash, adj. Withdrawing.

کنارہ کش ہونا kinārah kash honā, v. To retire; to keep aloof; to withdraw (from).

کنارہ کشی kinārah kashi, n.f. Withdrawal; withdrawing.

کنارے کنارے kināre kināre, adv. By the side of; along the shore; along the bank-side.

کنارے لگانا kināre lagānā, v. To beach a boat; to bring to shore.

کنارے لگنا kināre lagnā, v. To put to shore; to come to an end.

کنارے ہو جانا kināre ho jānā, v. To retire; to withdraw (from); to keep aloof.

کناری kināri (H) n.f. Lace; hem.

کنایہ kināyah (A) n.m. A hint; an allusion; a metaphor; sarcasm; a nod; a sign; nickname.

کنایتاً kināyatan (A) adv. Allusively; metaphorically; indirectly.

کنبہ kumbah, kunbah (H) n.m. Family; tribe; brotherhood.

کنبہ پرور kunbah parwar, adj. The supporter of a family.

کنٹر kontar (E) n.m. Decanter; a large glass bottle

کنٹھ kanth (H) n.m. The throat; wind-pipe; Adam's apple. adj. By heart; committed to memory.

کنٹھ مالا kanth mālā, n.f. A kind of necklace; scrofula; branchocele.

کنٹھ نکلنا kanth nikalnā, v. To attain the age of puberty.

کنٹھا kanthā (H) n.m. A necklace of large beads made of gold or silver; a pearl necklace; a string of beads of wood or seeds worn by faqirs.

کنٹھی kanthi (H) n.f. A small necklace, worn by faqīrs.

کنج kunj (P) n.m. A corner; a confined place; a grave; a bower.

کنج تنہائی kunj-ĕ tanhā'i, n.m. A secluded corner.

کنجا، کنجی kunjā, kunji (H) adj. Blue-eyed.

کنجر kanjar (H) n.m. A class of gipsies who sell strings, eat snakes and carcases and lead a low life. (In the Punjab a class of people who live on prostitution of their women, are known as کنجر kanjar).

کنجری kanjari (H) n.f. A kanjar's wife; a dancing girl.

کنجڑا kunjṛā (A) n.m. A grocer; a vegetable or fruit-seller; a green-grocer.

کنجشک kunjashk, kunjishk (P) n.m. A sparrow.

کنجوس kanjūs (H) n.m. A miser; a niggard.

کنجوس مکھی چوس kanjūs makkhi chūs, n.m. A skin-flint; a miser.

کنجوسی kanjūsi (H) n.f. Stinginess; miserliness.

کنجی kunji (H) n.f. A key; a solution.

کنچن kanchan (H) n.m. Gold; the gipsy class whose females are generally dancers.

کنچنی kānchani (H) n.f. A dancing girl; a prostitute.

کند kund (P) adj. Blunt; slow, obtuse; dull.

کند ذہن **kund zihn**, *adj.* Dull headed: stupid.

کندا **kunda**, *n.m.* The wood to which the barrel and lock of a fire-arm are secured; the stock; the arm of a paper-kite; a staple; condensed milk.

کندن **kundan** (H) *n.m.* Pure gold. *adj.* Bright; fine.

کندہ **kundah** (P) *n.m.* A block; a butcher's block; a gun-stock.

کندہ ناتراش **kundan-ĕ natarash**, *n.m.* A dull, stupid fellow; a dolt; a block-head.

کندہ **kandah** (P) *adj.* Carved; engraved.

کندہ کار **kandah kar**, *n.m.* An engraver; a carver.

کندہ کرنا **kandah karna**, *v.* To engrave; to carve.

کندھا **kandha** (H) *n.m.* The shoulder.

کندھا پکڑ کے چلنا **kandhā pakar ke chalna**, *v.* To walk by leaning on one's shoulder; to walk with another's help.

کندھا دینا **kandhā dena**, *v.* To carry a dead body; to help.

کندہ ڈالنا **kandhā ḍalna**, *v.* To throw off the yoke; to lose spirit; to be discouraged.

کندی **kundi** (H) *n.f.* Calendering cloth.

کندی کرنا **kundi karna**, *v.* To calender; to heat.

کندی گر **kundi gar**, *n.m.* A calenderer.

کنڈ **kunḍ** (H) *n.m.* A pool; a spring; a reservior; a fire-altar.

کنڈا **kunḍa** (H) *n.m.* The iron-ring to which a chain is fastened.

کنڈل **kunḍal** (H) *n.m.* A large ear-ring (worn by جوگی jogi); a circle; a coil; a halo round the sun or moon.

کنڈل مارنا **kunḍal marnā**, *v.* To coil; to form a coil; coiling up of a snake; formation of a halo round the moon.

کنڈلی **kunḍli** (H) *n.f.* A ringlet; a coil; a halo; nativity; haroscope; coiling of a snake.

کنڈلی بنانا **kunḍli banana**, *v.* To curl; to make a haroscope.

کنڈی **kunḍi** (H) *n.f.* An iron catch to fasten a door; a staple; a door chain.

کنڈی بند کر دینا ، دینا ، لگانا **kunḍi band kar dena, dena, lagana**, *v.* To fasten the chain of a door.

کنڈی کھٹکھٹانا **kunḍi khatkhatana**, *v.* To knock at a door; to rattle the chain of a door; to strike for admittance.

کنز **kanz** (A) *n.m.* A treasure.

کنستر **kanaster** (E) *n.m.* Canister.

کنک **kanak** (H) *n.m.* Gold; thorn apple; wheat.

کنکر **kankar** (H) *n.m.* Coarse limestone; gravel.

کنکری **kankari** (H) *n.f.* A small round stone or marble; gravel; pebble; a small piece.

کنکریلا **kankarilā** (H) *adj.* Abounding in gravel; stony; gritty; gravelly.

کنکوا **kankavvā** (H) *n.m.* A large paper-kite.

کنکی **kanki** (H) *n.f.* Broken rice.

کنگال **kangāl** (H) *adj.* Poor; friendless; miserly; miserable; bankrupt; vagrant.

کنگال کر دینا **kangal kar dena**, *v.* To impoverish; to make poor.

کنگال ہو جانا **kangāl ho jana**, *v.* To be reduced to poverty.

کنگرہ، کنگورہ **kungarah, kangurah** (P) *n.m.* A pinnacle; a turret; a parapet; a wall; a niched battlement of a castle; a plume on a helmet; a jewel in a crown; a porthole; vidette.

کنگرہ دار **kungarah dar**, *adj.* Spired; having a turret.

کنگری **kingri, kungri** (H) *n.f.* A sort of a fidale; a kind of lace.

کنگلا kangla. See کنگال kangāl.

کنگن kangan (H) n.m. A bracelet; an ornament for the wrist.

کنگنا kangnā (H) n.m. A string tied round the right hand of the bridegroom or the left of the bride.

کنگنی kangni (H) n.f. A small bracelet; a cornice; millet.

کنگھا kanghā (H) n.m. A comb (used by man, and having teeth on one side only).

کنگھی kanghı (H) n.f. A woman's comb, having teeth on both sides.

کنگھی چوٹی کرنا kanghı choti karnā, v. To braid or to plait the hair; to dress the hair.

کنگھی کرنا kanghi karna, v. To comb.

کنوارا kunwārā (H) n.m. A bachelor; an unmarried man.

کنوارا پن ، کنوار پن kunwārāpan, kunwār pan n.m. Maidenhood; virginhood; bachelorship.

کنواری kunwārı (H) n.f. A maiden; a virgin.

کنواں kunwāṅ (H) n.m. A well.

کنواں جھکانا kunwaṅ jhakānā, v. To make (one) look into (seven) wells as a cure for hydrophobia; to make a person do what one pleases.

کنواں چلانا kunwan chalana, v. To irrigate; to water fields from a well.

کنواں کھودنا kunwān khodnā, v. To dig a well; to dig a pit for any person.

کنویں میں بانس ڈالنا kunweṅ meṅ bāṅs ḍalna, v. To make a thorough search.

کھاری کنواں khāri kunwāṅ, n.m. A well having brackish water.

میٹھا کنواں miṭha kunwaṅ, n.m. A well having sweet water.

کنوتی kanauti (H) n.f. Side hair; side-lock; ear-ring; ears of a horse.

کنور kunwar (H) n.m. A boy; a son; a prince.

کنول kanwal (H) n.m. The lotus; the heart.

کنول روپی kanwal rupi, adj. Like a lotus; beautiful.

کنول نین kanwal nain, adj. Lotus-eyed.

کنہ kunah (A) n.f. Substance; essence; quantity; mode or reason (of a thing); end; the extreme; face; aspect.

کنی kanı (H) n.f.. Spark of a gem; small particle; broken bits of rice; bran.

کنی kanni (H) n.f. Edging; border; a make-weight attached to the lighter end of the paper-kite; powdered tobacco leaves.

کنی باندھنا kanni bāndhna, v. To fillet the lighter end of the paper-kite.

کنی کترانا kannī katrānā, v. To shun; to avoid.

کنی کھانا kanni khānā, v. To fall to one side; to incline to one side (kite).

کنیا kannyā (H) n.f. An unmarried girl under sixteen; a virgin; a maiden; a daughter; the sign Virgo.

کنیانا kaniyānā (H) v. To incline to one side (paper-kite); to shun; to avoid; to dodge.

کنیت kuniyyat (A) n f. A family name; a patronymic appellation.

کنیر kaner (H) n.f. Name of a flower; the oleander.

کنیز kaniz (P) n.f. A slave girl.

کنیسہ kanisah (P) n.m. A church; a chapel.

کو ko (H) prep. To; at; for, on; about.

کو kū (P) n.f. A street; a lane; a market place

کو بکو kū baku, adv. From street to street, from place to place; every where

کوا kavva (H) n.m. A crow; the uvula

کوا اُٹھانا kavva uthana, v. To raise the uvula of a child.

کواڑ kiwāṛ (H) n.m. The shutter or fold of a door; a door; a gate; an entrance.

کواڑ بند کرنا، بھیڑنا، دینا، لگانا kiwāṛ band karna, bheṛnā, denā, lagana, v. To shut a door.

کواکب kavakib (A) n.m. (plu. of کوکب kaukab) Stars; constellations.

کوائف kawa'if (A) n.m. (plu. of کیفیت kaifiyyat) Particulars; conditions.

کوب kob (P) adj. Beating: pounding (in compos).

کوبڑ kūbaṛ (H) n.m. A hump.

کوبہ kobah (P) n.m. A wooden mallet; a cloth breaker; a rammer.

کوبہ کاری kobah kārı, n.f. Beating; thumping; castigating.

کوتاہ kotāh (P) adj. Short; little; small; brief; mean; settled.

کوتاہ اندیش kotāh andesh, adj. Improvident; indiscreet.

کوتاہ بین kotāh bin, adj. Dim-sighted; short-sighted; imprudent; indiscreet.

کوتاہ بینی kotāh bini, n.f. Short-sightedness; imprudence.

کوتاہ دست kotāh dast, adj. Short-handed; weak.

کوتاہ عمر kotah 'umr, adj. Short-lived.

کوتاہ قد kotah qadd, adj. Short of stature; dwarfish.

کوتاہ نظر kotah nazar, adj. Short-sighted; dim-sighted.

کوتاہی kotāhı (P) n.f. Shortness; smallness; deficiency; want; littleness; narrowness; brevity; meanness.

کوتاہی کرنا kotāhī karna, v. To fall short; to fail; to be lacking (in).

کوتل kotal (P) n.m. A led-horse; a horse kept only for show.

کوتوال kotwal (P) n.m. The chief police officer of a town.

کوتوالی kotwali (P) n.f. The chief police station.

کوٹ koṭ (H) n.m. A castle; a fort; a stronghold; a rampart; a magic circle traced with sand or ashes.

کوٹلا koṭla (H) n.m. A fortress.

کوٹنا kuṭna (H) v. To beat; to pound; to thrash; to cudgel; to chastise to hammer.

کوٹھا koṭhā (H) n.m. A house; a warehouse; a barn; a chamber; an upper storey.

کوٹھے پر بیٹھنا koṭhe par baiṭhna, v. To sit on the upper storey; to become a prostitute.

کوٹھڑی koṭhṛi (H) n.f. A small room; a cabin; closet; a store-room; an inner apartment.

کوٹھی koṭhi (H) n.f. A masonry house; a bungalow; a warehouse; a granary; chamber (of a gun); a bank; chest; bin; storehouse.

کوٹھی وال koṭhi wal, n.m. A banker; a wholesale merchant; a warehouse keeper.

کوثر kausar (A) n.m. The name of a fountain or river in Paradise.

کوچ kūch (P) n.m. Departure; decampment; march.

کوچ کرنا kuch karna, v. To depart; to march; to decamp; to die.

کوچ kūch (H) n.m. Weaver's brush.

کوچ kūch (H) n.f. Haunches.

کوچ koch (E) n.m. Coach.

کوچبان koch ban, n.m. A coach-driver.

کوچک kochak (P) adj. Small; little; diminutive; younger.

کوچکی kochaki (P) n.f. Smallness; name of a colour (purple).

کوچہ **kuchah** (P) *n.m.* A narrow street; a lane.

کوچہ بکوچہ **kuchah bakuchah**, *adv.* From lane to lane; everywhere; here and there.

کوچہ بندی کرنا **kuchah bandi karna**, *v.* To mark off the limits of a lane.

کوچہ گردی **kuchah gardi**, *n.f.* Strolling; wandering.

کوچی **kuchi** (H) *n.f.* A brush for painting or plastering or whitewashing; a weaver's brush; a pointed or forked beard.

کود **kud** (H) *n.f.* A spring; a jump; a leap; a bound.

کود پڑنا **kud parna**, *v.* To jump in.

کود پھاند **kud phand**, *n.f.* Leaping and jumping; skipping and dancing about; gambols; capers; wandering; strolling.

کود مارنا **kud marna**, *v.* To jump.

کودک **kodak** (P) *n.m.* A boy; youth; youngster; stripling.

کودن **kodan**, **kaudan** (P) *n.m.* A pack-horse; a stupid person; a simpleton. *adj.* Dull; stupid; slow; thick-headed.

کودنا **kudna** (H) *v.* To jump; to rejoice; to boast; to leap; to bound; to bray; to presume upon.

کودو، کودوں **kodo**, **kodon** (H) *n.m.* A small grain (like millet).

کودوں دے کے پڑھنا **kodoṅ de ke paṛhna**, *v.* To get education at little or no cost; to receive cheap and inferior education; to fail to pay the extra two pence for manners.

کور **kor** (H) *n.f.* Margin; edge; border; side; tip; point; thorn; trifling thing; ten millions; a bud; the womb.

کور دبنا **kor dabna**, *v.* To be helpless; to be over-powered.

کور **kor** (P) *adj.* Blind; sightless.

کور باطن **kor batin**, *adj.* Benighted; stupid; silly; inwardly blind or dark; ignorant.

کور بخت **kor bakht**, *adj.* Unlucky; wretched; unfortunate.

کور بختی **kor bakhti**, *n.f.* Misfortune; calamity.

کور چشم **kor chashm**, *adj.* Blind.

کور نمک **kor namak**, *adj.* Ungrateful; disloyal; unthankful. *n.m.* An ungrateful person.

کورا، کوری **kora**, **kori** (H) *adj.* Unused; new; unhandled; fresh; unbleached; unwashed; blank (paper); undressed; unpractised; untutored; unuttered; stupid; plain; poor; simple.

کورا بچنا **kora bachna**, *v.* To escape unhurt; to go scotfree; to escape unscotched.

کورا برتن **kora bartan**, *n.m.* A new utensil; a bachelor; a virgin.

کورا پن **kora pan**, *n.m.* Newness; inexperience; virginity.

کورنش **kornish** (P) *n.f.* Salutation; adoration; obeisance; homage.

کورنش بجا لانا **kornish baja lana**, *v.* To salute; to pay respect.

کورنشات **kornishāt** (P) *n.f.* (*plu.* of کورنش **kornish**) Salutations.

کوری **kori** (P) *n.f.* Blindness.

کوڑ **koṛ** (H) *adj.* A block-head; simpleton; foolish; stupid.

کوڑ مغز **koṛ maghz**, *adj.* Brain-sick; thick-headed; stupid; empty headed.

کوڑا **koṛa** (H) *n.m.* A whip; a lash; a scourge.

کوڑا لگانا، مارنا **koṛā lagānā**, **marna**, *v.* To whip; to lash.

کوڑا **kauṛa** (H) *n.m.* A shell; a large shell or cowrie.

کوڑا **kūṛā** (H) *n.m.* Sweepings; dirt; rubbish; share; lot.

کوڑا کرکٹ *kūṛā karkaṭ, n.m.* Refuse; rubbish; dung; waste paper; heaps of refuse for manure.

کوڑھ **koṛh** (H) *n.m.* The leprosy.

کوڑھ ٹپکنا یا چونا *koṛh ṭapakna yā chona, v.* To be afflicted with leprosy; oozing out of leprous matter.

کوڑھ میں کھاج نکلنا *koṛh men khaj nikalna, v.* To catch the itch in leprosy; to have one misfortune added to another; one calamity after another.

کوڑھی **koṛhī** (H) *n.m.* A leper. *adj.* Leprous.

کوڑی **koṛī** (H) *n.f.* A score; twenty.

کوڑی **kauṛī** (H) *n.f.* A small shell; a cowrie; the breast bone.

کوڑی بھر *kauṛī bhar, adj.* Very little.

کوڑی پاس نہ ہونا *kauṛī pās nah honā, v.* To be hard up; to be indigent.

کوڑی پھیرا کرنا *kauṛī phera karna, v.* To be running to the market and back unnecessarily; to be coming and going constantly without purpose.

کوڑی کا آدمی *kauṛī ka adamī, n.m.* A worthless fellow.

کوڑی کا ہو جانا *kauṛī ka ho jana, v.* To become worthless; to be of no good.

کوڑی کفن کو نہ ہونا *kauṛī kafan ko nah honā, v.* To be penniless; to be entirely out of pocket.

کوڑی کوڑی *kauṛī kauṛī, adv.* Every pie.

کوڑی کوڑی ادا کرنا *kauṛī kauṛī adā karnā, v.* To pay every farthing; to pay in full.

کوڑی کوڑی جوڑنا *kauṛī kauṛī jorna, v.* To save every bit; to save up every pie.

کوڑی کوڑی کو تنگ ہونا *kauṛī kauṛī ko tang honā, v.* To be reduced to abject poverty.

کوڑی کو نہ پوچھنا *kauṛī ko nah puchhnā, v.* To regard as of no value and unworthy of notice.

کوڑی کے تین تین بکنا *kauṛī ke tin tin bikna, v* To sell very cheap.

کوڑی کے کام کا نہ ہونا *kauṛī ke kam ka nah honā, v.* To be good for nothing; to be worthless.

کوڑی کے مول بکنا *kauṛī ke mol bikna, v.* To sell very cheap.

پھوٹی کوڑی *phuṭī kauṛī, n.f.* Of the value of a broken or blind cowrie; money of the lowest value.

کوڑیالا **kauṛyala** (H) *n.m.* A kind of snake; a rich person; the kingfisher.

کوز **kūz** (P) *n.m.* A hump.

کوز پشت *kūz pusht, adj.* Hump-backed; *n.m.* A hunch-back.

کوزہ **kuzah** (P) *n.m.* An earthen pot for water; a jug; a goblet; a kind of rose; a lump of crystallised sugar.

کوزے میں دریا بند کرنا *kuze men darya band karnā, v.* To give a thing in a nutshell; to explain the whole thing briefly and tersely; *multum in parvo*

کوس **kos** (P) *n.m.* A kettle-drum; a drum.

کوس **kos** (H) *n.m.* A measure of length about two English miles.

کوسوں دور *koson dūr, adj.* At a great distance; far-away.

کوسا **kosā** (H) *n.m.* Curse; malediction; a kind of silk.

کوسنا **kosna** (H) *v.* To curse; to imprecate.

کوش **kosh** (P) *adj.* (in *compos.*) Endeavouring; attempting; labouring.

کوشاں **koshān** (P) *adj.* Struggling; attempting.

کوشش **koshish** (P) *n.f.* Effort, attempt; labour; endeavour; exertion.

کوشک *kushk, kūshak* (P) *n.m.* A palace; a castle; a mansion; a citadel.

کوفت *koft* (P) *n.f.* Beating; great fatigue; pain; vexation; grief; anguish; gold beating; gilding.

کوفته *koftah* (P) *adj.* Pounded; bruised distressed. *n.m.* Pounded meat; small balls of pounded meat.

کوفته و بیخته *koftah-ŏ bekhtāh, adj.* Pounded and sifted.

کوکا *kokā* (T) *n.m.* A foster brother; a nurse's child.

کوکا *kokā* (H) *n.m.* A small nail.

کوکب *kaukab* (A) *n.m.* A star; constellation.

کوکبه *kaukabah* (A) *n.m.* Stars made of gold etc. (worn as an insignia of rank).

کوکنا *kūknā* (H) *v.* To wind up (a clock, a watch, etc.); to cry; to shriek.

کوکنار *koknar* (P) *n.m.* Poppy; poppy-head.

کوکو *kuku* (H) *n.m.* Cooing of a dove.

کوکھ *kokh* (H) *n.f.* The belly; abdomen; the womb; hypochondrium.

کوکھ اجڑ جانا *kokh ujaṛ jana, v.* To miscarry; to lose a child.

کوکھ جلی *kokh jali, adj.* Barren: sterile; barren woman.

کوکھ کی آنچ *kokh kī ānch, n.f.* Maternal love.

کوکھ ماری جانا *kokh marī jānā, v.* To become barren (a woman).

کوکین *kukin* (E) *n.f.* Cocaine.

کول *kaul* (H) *n.m.* A mouthful; a morsel; a handful of grain put in the mill at one time.

کولا *kaulā* (H) *n.m.* Side; corner; side wall; a kind of orange.

کولا، کولھا *kūlā, kūlhā* (H) *n.m.* The hip; buttock; haunch.

کولھو *kolhū* (H) *n.m.* An silman's press; oil-expeller.

کولھو چلانا *kolhū chalānā, v.* To set up an oil press or sugar mill; to run an oil-press.

کولھو کا بیل *kolhū kā bail, n.m.* The ox driving an oil press; a very hardworking person.

کولھو میں پلوا دینا *kolhū meṅ pilwā denā, v.* To torture to death; to crush in an oil mill.

کولی *koli* (H) *n.m.* A weaver.

کولی *kauli* (H) *n.f.* Embrace; grasp of the arms; armful.

کولی بھرنا *kauli bharnā, v.* To embrace; to take or fold one in the arms; to be avaricious or greedy.

کومل *komal* (H) *adj.* Soft; tender; downy; placid; mild; sweet.

کومل *kūmal* (H) *n.f.* Burglary; house breaking.

کون *kaun* (A) *n.m.* That which exists; the universe; the world; existence; nature; essence.

کون و مکاں *kaun-ŏ makān, n.m.* The whole creation; the world; the universe.

کون *kaun* (H) *pron.* Who; which; what; whether.

کون سا *kaun sā, adv.* Which; what; what sort of; what manner of.

کون *kūn* (P) *n.f.* Poleax; the backside; the anus.

کونا *konā* (H) *n.m.* Corner; side; angle.

کونپل *konpal* (H) *n.f.* A young shoot; a bud; a new leaf.

کونپل پھوٹنا *konpal phūtnā, v.* Sprouting of buds or new leaves.

کونج *kūnj* (H) *n.m.* Heron.

کونچ *kūnch* (H) *n.f.* Cow-itch, a weaver's brush.

کونچا kauṅchā (H) n.m. A grain-parcher's iron hook; an iron pan with a handle; a broom.

کونچلی koṅchlī (H) n.f. A new tooth; a lank tooth.

کونچی kūṅchī (H) n.f. A mason's brush.

کونچی پھیرنا یا مارنا kūṅchī phernā yā marnā, v. To whitewash; to paint.

کوند ، کوندا kauṅd, kauṅdā (H) n.f./m. Flash (of lighting); splendour; brightness; dazzling light.

کوندنا kauṅdnā (H) v. To glare; to flash; to glitter; to lighten.

کونڈا kūṅḍā (H) n.m. An earthen jar; a pletter.

کونڈی kūṅḍī (H) n.f. A stone trough; a stone mortar; a bucket.

کونی kūnī (P) n.m. A catamite.

کونین konīn (E) n.f. Quinine.

کونین kaunain (A) n.m. The two worlds, the physical and the spiritual; both kinds of beings, the corporeal and the spiritual; men and angels.

کوہ koh (P) n.m. A mountain; a hill.

کوہ آتش فشاں koh-ĕ ātash fishāṅ, n.m. A volcano.

کوہ پیکر koh paikar, adj. Mountain-like; huge; bulky.

کوہسار koh sār, n.m. A mountainous country; a range of mountains.

کوہ کن koh kan, n.m. A mountain-digger; an epithet of Farhad.

کوہ نور koh-ĕ nūr, n.m. A large diamond.

کوہان kohān (P) n.m. Hump of a bullock or camel.

کوہستان kohistān (P) n.m. A mountainous country; a hilly tract; a high land.

کوہستانی kohistānī (P) adj. Hilly; mountainous. n.m. A hillman; a high lander; a mountaineer.

کوئلا ko'elā (H) n.m. Coal; charcoal.

کوئلے کی کان ko'ele kī kān, n.f. A coal mine.

کوئی ko'ī (H) pron. Any; some; anybody.

کوئی دم میں ko'ī dam meṅ, adv. In a moment; shortly; soon; in an instant; immediately.

کوئی کوئی ko'ī kā'ī, adj. A few; hardly any; rare.

کوئی نہ کوئی ko'ī nah ka i, adj. Some one or the other; somebody.

کویہ، کویا koyah, koyā (P) n.m. Corner of the eye; a slice of the jack fruit; cocoon of the silk worm.

کویل koyal (H) n.f. The Indian cuckoo.

کہ kih (P) pron. Who; what; that; which. conj. That; as; because; for; if; whether.

کہ kih (P) adj. Small; little; slender; mean.

کہتر kih tar, adj. Smaller; less; junior; inferior; low.

کہ و مہ kia-ŏ mih, adj. Small and big; high and low.

کہ kah (P) n.m. (contraction of کاہ kāh) Straw.

کہ ربا kah rubā, n.m. Yellow amber.

کہکشاں kahkashāṅ, n.m. The milkyway; galaxy.

کہگل kahgil, n.f. Straw and mud mixed together for plastering.

کہا kahā (H) n.m. Saying; order; word, confession; affirmation; advice; spoken word; discourse; bidding; command; said; spoken; speech.

کہا سنا kahā sunā, n.m. Speech; advice; pleadings; improper speech; harsh language.

کہا کرنا kahā karnā, v. To do the bidding of; carry out the instructions of.

کہا ماننا kahā mānnā, v. To take one's advice; to mind or heed the bidding of; to obey.

کھاتا khatā (H) *n.m.* Daily account; a day-book; a ledger; a waste-book; account current; an account book; a pit.

کھاتا کھولنا khātā kholnā, *v.* To open an account with.

کھاتے پڑنا khāte paṛnā, *v.* To be entered in an account.

کھاتا پیتا khātā pitā (H) *adj.* A well-off person; well to do.

کھاٹ khāṭ (H) *n.f.* A bedstead; a couch; a bier.

کھاٹ سے آتار لینا khāṭ se utār lenā, *v.* Removing a dying person from his cot and putting him down on the ground (a custom among Hindus).

کھاٹ سے لگ جانا khāṭ se lag jānā, *v.* To be confined to bed; to be bed-ridden.

کھاٹ کھٹولا khāṭ khatolā, *n.m.* Household furniture; goods and chattels; bag and baggage.

کھاٹ نکالنا khāṭ nikālnā, *v.* To die; to give up the ghost.

کھاج khāj (H) *n.f.* The itch; cutaneous eruption.

کھاجا khājā (H) *n.m.* A kind of sweetmeat like pie-crust; a kind of dry fruit; food.

کھاد khād (H) *n.f.* Dung; manure.

کھادی khādi (H) *n.f.* A kind of coarse cotton cloth; کھدر khaddar.

کھار khār (H) *n.m.* Alkali; potash; carbonate of potash or soda; rough or rugged ground. *adj.* Impure.

کھار لگنا khār lagnā, *v.* To be impregnated with alkaline salts.

کہار kahār (H) *n.m.* A palanquin-bearer; a ḍoli-bearer; a scullion; one that supplies water or draws water; a Hindu water-carrier.

کھارا ، کھاری khārā, khāri (H) *adj.* Alkaline; brackish; saltish; saline.

کہاری kahārī (H) *n.f.* The wages of a water-carrier; a female water-carrier.

کھاڑی khāṛi (H) *n.f.* A creek; a bay; a gulf.

کھال khāl (H) *n.f.* Skin; hide; bellows; a rivulet, river; canal; creek; inlet.

کھال آتارنا khāl utārnā, *v.* To skin; to beat blue and black.

کھال کھینچنا khāl khenchnā, *v.* To take the skin off; to flay; to skin.

کھال میں مست ہونا khal meṅ mast honā, *v.* To be satisfied with one's lot.

کھالا khālā (H) *n.m.* A canal; an inlet.

کھان khān (H) *n.f.* A mine; a quarry; (same as کان kān); abundance; a heap; a receptacle; a nest.

کہاں kahāṅ (H) *adv.* Where; whither.

کہاں پر kahāṅ par, *adv.* Where; at what place; to what degree; how long.

کہاں تک kahāṅ tak, *adv.* How long; how far; to what degree.

کہاں سے kahāṅ se, *adv.* Whence; where from.

کہاں کا kahāṅ kā, *adv.* Of what place.

کہانا kahānā (H) *v.* To be called; to cause to be spoken or named.

کھانا khānā (H) *v.* To eat; to consume; to swallow; to drink; to inhale; to embezzle; to get; to suffer; to endure; to corrode; to destroy. *n.m.* Food; feast; dinner; eating; allowance.

کھانا پینا khānā pinā, *v.* To eat and drink. *n.m.* Food; board fare; feast; entertainment.

کھانا کرنا یا دینا khānā karnā yā denā, *v.* To give a feast.

کھانا کھانا khānā khānā, *v.* To take food.

کھانا کھلانا khānā khilānā, *v.* To give a feast or dinner; to entertain; to feed.

کھانے کا کمرہ khāne kā kamrah, *n.m.* A dining room.

کھانے کو دوڑنا khāne ko dauṛnā, *v.* To pounce upon; to threaten; to be pevish.

کھانپ khāṅp (H) *n.f.* A slice.

کہانت kahānat (A) *n.f.* A tale; a story; a prophecy:- divination; soothsaying; priesthood.

کھانچا khāṅchā (H) *n.m.* A basket; a hen-coop; a cage; a tray; a pannier; a pit; a hole; cavity; notch.

کھانچی khāṅchī (H) *n.f.* A small basket.

کھانڈ khāṅḍ (H) *n.f.* Coarse sugar; sugar.

کھانڈا khāṅḍā (H) *n.m.* A double-edged sword; a cutlass; a butcher's cleaver.

کھانڈا بجنا khāṅḍā bajnā, *v.* To fight with a sword.

کھانسنا khāṅsnā (H) *v.* To cough.

کھانسی khāṅsī (H) *n.f.* A cough.

کہانی kahānī (H) *n.f.* A story; a tale; a fable.

کہانی جوڑنا kahānī joṛnā, *v.* To make up a story; to concoct a story.

کہاوت kahāwat (H) *n.f.* A proverb; a saying; an adage.

کھاؤ khā'ū (H) *adj.* Voracious; glutton. *n.m.* A glutton; one who takes bribes.

کھاؤ اڑاؤ khā'ū uṛā'ū, *adj.* Extravagant; prodigal. *n.m.* A spendthrift; an extravagant person.

کھائی khā'ī (H) *n.f.* A trench; a ditch; a moat; a drain.

کھبا khabbā (H) *adj.* A left-hander.

کھب جانا ، کھبنا khub jānā, khubnā (H) *v.* To penetrate; to stick in; to fascinate.

کھپاچ khappāch (H) *n.f.* A piece of wood or bamboo; a splinter; a very lean person.

کھپانا khapānā (H) *v.* To destroy; to make an end of; to absorb; to swallow; to waste; to ruin; to despatch; to use; to spend; to end; to finish; to cause to enter.

کھپت khapat (H) *n.f.* Sale; vent; consumption; expenditure; outlay.

کھپرا khaprā (H) *n.m.* A tile for roofing; a slice; scale; bark; skin; a small insect which destroys wheat grain; an arrow with a broad point.

کھپریل khaprail (H) *n.f.* A tiled house; tiling.

کھپریل چھانا khaprail chhanā, *v.* To tile (a roof).

کھپنا khapnā (H) *v.* To be used up; to be disposed of; to be consumed.

کھتا khattā (H) *n.m.* A cavity in which grain is kept; a subterraneous granary; a treasure; a heap; a stock; store; an ice pit.

کھتونی khataunī (H) *n.f.* A ledger; an account book.

کھتی khatti (H) *n.f.* A small subterrenean granary; an underground granary; a store; a heap; wealth; a purse; a small bag.

کھتیانا khatyānā (H) *v.* To enter in the ledger; to post in an account book.

کھٹ khaṭ (H) *n.f.* The sound of knocking; (*contraction of* کھاٹ khāṭ) bedstead; bed.

کھٹ بنا khaṭ bunā, *n.m.* A bed-weaver.

کھٹ پٹ khaṭ paṭ, *n.f.* Rattle; noise; clatter of horse's hoofs; clashing of weapons; wrangling; contention; quarrel.

کھٹ راگ khaṭ rāg, *n.m.* A troublesome act; discordant wrangling.

کھٹ کھٹ khaṭ khaṭ, *n.f.* Repeated or continuous knocking.

کھٹ khaṭ (H) *adj.* (*contraction of* کھٹا khaṭṭā) Sour.

کھٹ مٹھا *khaṭ miṭhā* *n.m.* A fruit which has a sour-sweet taste. *adj.* Sour and sweet.

کھٹا *khaṭṭā* (H) *adj.* Sour; acid; tart. *n.m.* a citron.

کھٹا پٹی *khaṭā paṭī* (H) *n.f.* Wrangling; clash of weapons; dissension; quarrel; disunity.

کھٹا پٹی ہونا *khaṭā paṭī honā*, *v.* To quarrel; to wrangle.

کھٹاس *khaṭās* (H) *n.f.* Acidity; sourness.

کھٹائی *khaṭā'ī* (H) *n.f.* Sourness; acidity; tartness.

کھٹائی میں پڑنا *khaṭā'ī men paṛnā*, *v.* To be put into the acid; to be put or laid aside; to be postponed for a time; to be put in cold storage.

کھٹائی میں ڈال رکھنا *khaṭā'ī men ḍāl rakhnā*, *v.* To keep in a state of suspense; to put in cold storage.

کھٹک *khaṭak* (H) *n.f.* Pain.

کھٹکا *khaṭkā* (H) *n.m.* Knocking; rattling sound; sound of footsteps; a hitch in the mind; scruple; suspicion; perturbation; anxiety; fear; dread; apprehension; doubt; presentiment; suspense; abatement.

کھٹکا لگنا *khaṭkā lagnā*, *v.* To fear; to doubt; to have a hitch in the mind; to be apprehensive of.

کھٹکنا *khaṭaknā* (H) *v.* To rankle; to rattle; to waver; to clash; to be struck with; to prick; to prove an eye-sore to; to pain like a thorn in the side.

کھٹکھٹانا *khaṭkhaṭānā* (H) *v.* To knock at the door; to shake.

کھٹمل *khaṭmal* (H) *n.m.* A bug.

کھٹولا *khaṭolā* (H) *n.m.* A small bedstead.

کھٹیا *khaṭyā* (H) *n.f.* A small bedstead; a bier.

کھٹیا نکالنا *khaṭyā nikalnā*, *v.* Wishing one to die; to die.

کھٹیک *khaṭik* (H) *n.m.* A tanner; a hunter; a fowler.

کھج *khij* (H) *n.f.* Vexation; irritation; teasing; fretfulness; nickname.

کھجانا یا کھجلانا *khujānā yā khujlānā* (H) *v.* To scratch; to rub gently with the nails; to have the itch; to itch; to tickle.

کھجلی *khujlī* (H) *n.f.* The itch; the mange (in dogs).

کھجلی اٹھنا *khujlī uṭhnā*, *v.* To itch; to feel itchy.

کھجور *khajūr* (H) *n.f.* A date (fruit); a date tree; a sweetmeat.

کھچا کھچ *khachā khach*, *adj.* Crowded; closely packed; crammed.

کھچا کھچ بھرنا *khachā khach bharnā*, *v.* To cram; to stuff together; to be crowded out.

کھچا رہنا *khichā rahnā* (H) *v.* To keep aloof; to shun.

کھچاؤ *khichāo* (H) *n.m.* Pull; drag; attraction; tightness; tension.

کھچائی *khichā'ī* (H) *n.f.* Dragging; pulling; price paid for drawing.

کھچڑا *khichṛā* (H) *n.m.* Name of dish prepared from meat, rice, wheat and various pulses.

کھچڑی *khichṛī* (H) *n.f.* A dish made of split pulse and rice boiled together; a mixture; hodge podge; mixture of black and grey hair; mixture of two or more languages; the flower of the بیر *ber* tree.

کھچڑی پکانا *khichṛī pakānā*, *v.* To concoct schemes; to plot; to conspire.

کھچڑی کرنا *khichṛī karnā*, *v.* To jumble; to make a mess of.

کھچنا *khichnā* (H) *v.* To be drawn; to be pulled away; to be extended; to be estranged.

کھچوانا *khichwānā* (H) *v.* To cause to draw; to cause to be pulled.

کھدانا ، کھدوانا khudānā, khudwānā (H) v. To cause to dig or engrave.

کھدائی ، کھدوائی khudā'i, khudwā'i (H) n.f. Digging; sinking (a well); engraving; cost of engraving or digging; excavating; carving.

کھد بدانا khadbadānā (H) v. To simmer; to bubble; to make a boiling noise; to boil.

کھدر khaddar (H) n.m. Coarse cotton cloth.

کھدنا khudnā (H) v. To be dug; to be engraved; to be carved.

کھڈ khaḍ (H) n.m. A pit; an abyss; a chasm; an opening; a crack in the ground.

کھڈا khaḍḍā (H) n.m. A cavity; a pit.

کھڈی khuddi (H) n.f. Brick compartments in a privy used for calls of nature; the space from which a tooth has fallen out; an oblong patch of the head from which the hair has been shaven.

کھر ، کھرا kuhr, kuhrā (H) n.m./f. Fog; mist.

کھر khur (H) n.m. Hoof; a cloven hoof.

کھر بندی khur bandi, n.f. Renewing a horse's shoes.

کھرا kharrā (H) n.m. A schedule; rough account; memorandum of transaction; the rough draft of a letter or any writing; a sketch; an iron instrument to rub horses with; a curry comb.

کھرا khurrā (H) adj. Rough; ill-tempered; harsh.

کھرا ، کھری kharā, knari (H) adj. Pure; unalloyed; genuine; impartial; honest; good; frank; strict; straightforward; true; sincere; right; valld; excellent.

کھراپن kharā pan, n.m. Honesty.

کھرا کھوٹا kharā khoṭā, adj. Good or bad.

کھری اسامی khari asāmi, n.f. A good paymaster; a trustworthy person.

کہرام kuhrām (H) n.m. Lamentation; weeping; crying aloud.

کہرام مچانا kuhrām machānā, v. to weep and cry aloud.

کہرام مچنا kuhrām machnā, v. To be cried over; to be wept over.

کھراند kharānd (H) n.f. A saltish taste; a burnt taste; stench; offensive smell.

کھرب kharab (H) adj. A billion.

کھرپا khurpā (H) n.m. Hoe; a weeding knife; the knee pan; patella.

کھرپی khurpi (H) n.f. A scraper; a weeding knife, a shovel for cleaning out a bird-cage.

کھرج kharj (H) n.f. The bass (in music).

کھرچن khurchan (H) n.f. Pot scrapings; milk scrapings; a sweetmeat.

کھرچنا khurachnā (H) v. To scrape; to scratch.

کھردرا khurdarā (H) adj. Rough; uneven; unpolished; harsh; shaggy; wrinkled; rugged.

کھرل kharal (H) n.f. A mortar.

کھرل کرنا kharal karnā, v. To powder; to pound; to pulverise.

کھرلی khurli (H) n.f. A manger.

کھرنجا kharanjā (H) n.m. Pavement; causeway; over-burnt bricks.

کھرنڈ khuranḍ (H) n.m. A scab; a scale; the crust which forms on a healing wound or sore.

کھرنڈ بندھنا khuranḍ bandhnā, v. To form a scab.

کہروا kaharwā (H) n.m. A lascivious dance and also a class of songs sung in the morning.

کھریا kharyā (H) n.f. Chalk; a piece of chalk; a chalk-mark.

کھریرا kharairā (H) n.m. A curry comb

کھریرا کرنا kharairā karnā, v. To curry comb (a horse).

کھڑا ، کھڑی khaṛā, khaṛi (H) *adj.* Standing; erect; perpendicular; upright; ready; half-cooked; ripe; vertical; steep.

کھڑا داؤں *khaṛā dāoṅ, n.m.* The last stake.

کھڑا رہنا *khaṛā rahnā, v.* To remain standing; to wait; to stand; to stay.

کھڑا کرنا *khaṛā karnā, v.* To cause to stand; to raise; to set on foot; to stir up; to pitch (a tent); to stop; to place erect; to build; to institute; to bring to a stand; to procure a fictitious person for some purpose.

کھڑا کھیت ، کھڑی فصل *khaṛā khet, khaṛī faṣl, n.m./f.* A standing crop.

کھڑے کھڑے *khaṛe khaṛe, adj.* Standing all the while; for a short while; a split second; just now.

کھڑاؤں *khaṛāoṅ* (H) *n.m.* Sandals; pattens.

کھڑ بڑاہٹ *khaṛbaṛāhaṭ* (H) *n.f.* A clatter of horse's hoofs; tumult; disorder.

کھڑک *khaṛak* (H) *n.f.* An imitative sound.

کھڑکا *khaṛkā* (H) *n.m.* Doubt; apprehension.

کھڑکنا *khaṛaknā* (H) *v.* T^ rattle; to clung; to rustle; to quarrel.

کھڑکھڑانا *khaṛkhaṛānā* (H) *v.* To rattle; to knock; to rap.

کھڑکھڑاہٹ *khaṛkhaṛāhaṭ* (H) *n.f.* Rattle; clatter; jingling.

کھڑکی *khiṛki* (H) *n.f.* A window; back door; wicket gate; shutter; casement.

کھڑنجا *khaṛaṅjā*, See کھرنجا *kharaṅjā*.

کھسرا *khasrā* (H) *n.f.* The measles; a kind of eruptive disease.

کھسر پھسر *khusar phusar* (H) *n.f.* Whispering.

کھسر پھسر کرنا *khusar phusar karnā, v.* To whisper; to talk in a whisper.

کھسکانا *khiskānā* (H) *v.* To move away; to put out of place; to shove out of the way; to make one back out of a bargain; to draw back; to slip into the hands of; to make off with; to steal.

کھسک جانا *khisak jānā* (H) *v.* To slink away; to slip away; to decamp; to abscond.

کھسکنا *khisaknā* (H) *v.* To stir out; to slip away; to slink away.

کھسوٹنا *khasoṭnā* (H) *v.* To pluck; to pull; to tear; to scratch.

کھسیانا، کھسیانی *khisyānā, khisyānī* (H) *adj.* Peevish; mortified; abashed; bashful; humiliated; ready to cry.

کھسیانا پن ، کھسیان پن *khisyānā pan, khisyān pan* (H) *n.m.* Humiliation; mortification fretfulness; vexation.

کھسیانا ہو جانا *khisyānā ho jānā, v.* To look blank; to be ready to cry; to fret.

کھسیانا *khisyanā* (H) *v.* To be abashed; to grin; to gnash the teeth; to look foolish or blank.

کہف *kahaf* (A) *n.m.* A cave; a den.

کھکھوڑنا *khakhoṛnā* (H) *v.* To scoop; to scrape; to scoop out ; to search out.

کھکیڑ *khakeṛ* (H) *n.f.* Labour; worry; vexation.

کھگ *khag* (H) *n.f.* A kind of a turban.

کھل *khal* (H) *n.f.* Oil cake.

کھل پڑنا *khul paṛnā* (H) *v.* To be free; to talk openly.

کھل جانا *khul jānā* (H) *v.* To open; to open out; to have fair weather; to be free; to be out-spoken; to be lost (cattle etc.).

کھل کے *khul ke* (H) *adv.* Comfortably; openly; clearly; freely.

کھل کھیلنا *khul khelnā* (H) *v.* To act without fear; to do openly, what is regarded as an objectionable or indecent action; to indulge openly in vices, which were formerly practised in secret.

کھل جانا *khil jānā* (H) *v.* To open; to blosom; to blow; to bloom.

کھلا ، کھلی khula, khulī (H) adj. Open; unclouded; fair (sky); unrestrained; loose; expanded; exposed; unfolded; unlocked; manifest; unfastened; bare; naked.

کھلا کھلا khula khulā, adj. Open; fair; clear; having more space; unobstractед.

کھلے بندوں، خزانے khule bandon, khazāne adv. Openly; publicly; freely.

کھلاڑ khilāṛ (H) adj. Playsome; frolicsome. n. f. An adultress.

کھلاڑ پن khilāṛ pan, n.m. Playfulness.

کھلاڑی khilāṛī (H) adj. Playful; sportive; frolicsome; player (of a game); fond of play; funny; full of tricks; addicted to gambling. n.m. A juggler; a gamester; an expert of a game.

کھلانا khilānā (H) v. To give to eat; to cause to feed; to cause to take an oath; to cause to play, to allow to play; to amuse to play with; to sport with; to make to blossom; to cause one to show the influence of evil spirits.

کہلانا kahlānā (H) v. To cause to say; to be called; to cause to recommend; to cause to reprove.

کھلائی khilā'ī (H) n.f. Feeding; supporting; payment for nursing; a dry-nurse.

کھلائی پلائی khilā'ī pilā'ī, n.f. Maintenance; charges of maintenance.

کھلبلی khalbalī (H) n. f. Hurry; bustle; agitation; commotion; alarm; tumult; hurly burly; disorder.

کھلبلی پڑنا khalbalī paṛnā, v. To be agitated; to be in a commotion; to be greatly perturbed.

کھلبلی ڈالنا khalbalī ḍālnā, v. To create panic; to throw into confusion; to be greatly agitated.

کھل کھل khil khil (H) n.f. A burst of laughter; tittle; giggle.

کھل کھلا کے ھنسنا khil khilā ke hansnā, v. To burst into laughter; to have a hearty laugh; to have bursts of laughter.

کھلنا khilnā (H) v. To blow; to flower; to bloom; to crack (as paster or parched grain); to be kept separate; to swell; to be delighted; to laugh.

کھلنا khulnā (H) v. To open; to expand: to be exposed; to be set at liberty; to be cleared; to be laid bare; to make known; to become clear; to be set free from restraint; to become loose (as the tongue); to be dispersed (as clouds); to clear up (as the sky); to come back (as appetite); to be opened out (as stitches); to be cut open (as head); to be manifest.

کھلنڈرا ، کھلنڈری khilanḍrā, khilanḍrī (H) adj. Playsome; playful; frolicsome; sportive.

کھلو khillū (H) adj. Humorous; facetious; funny; playsome.

کہلوانا kahalwānā (H) v. To cause to say; to give a message.

کھلوانا khulwānā (H) v. To cause to open; to cause to be opened.

کھلوانا. khilwānā (H) v. To cause to play; to 'cause to eat.

کھلونا khilaunā yā khilonā (H) n.m. A toy; a plaything: a gewgaw; a jester.

کھلی khalī (H) n.m. Oil cake.

کھلی khillī (H) n.f. Jest; joke; humour; wit.

کھلی باز khillī baz, adj. Witty; humorous; funny; playsome.

کھلی بازی khillī bāzi, n.f. Humour; fun; play; jacularity; flirtation.

کھلیان khalyān (H) n.m. A threshing floor; a granary; barn.

کھم ، کھمب ، کھمبا kham, khamb, khamba (H) n.m. A pillar; a post; a column.

کھمبی khumbī (H) n.f. A mushroom.

کھماچ khammāch (H) n.f. Name of a rāgnī.

کہن kuhan (P) adj. Old; ancient.

کہن سال kuhan sāl, adj. Aged; old; ancient; advanced in years.

کہن سالی kuhan sāli, n.f. Old age.

کہن kahan (H) n.f. Say; saying; proverb.

کہنا kahnā (H) v. To tell; to say; to recount; to relate; to affirm; to assert; to avow; to declare; to acquaint: to advice; to speak; to recommend; to utter.

کہنا کرنا، ماننا kahnā karna, mānnā, v. To do the bidding; to carry out instructions; to obey orders.

کھنچاؤ khinchāo. See کھچاؤ khichāo.

کھنچنا khinchna. See کھچنا khichna.

کھنچوانا khinchwana. See کھچوانا khichwanā.

کھنچوائی khinchwā'i. See کھچوائی khichwa'ı.

کھندلنا khundalnā (H) v. To trample; to tread; to beat or work with the feet.

کھنڈ khanḍ n.f. (Contraction of کھانڈ khanḍ) Sugar

کھنڈسار، سال khanḍ sār, sal, n.f. Sugar factory

کھنڈا khanḍā (H) n.m. Bruised rice; a sword; cutlass.

کھنڈت khanḍat (H) n.f. Breaking; tearing; cutting; interruption.

کھنڈت کرنا khanḍat karnā, v. To break; to spoil; to destroy; to interrupt; to refute.

کھنڈر khanḍar (H) n.m. Ruins of a town or house; a broken down building. adj. Distroyed; ruined; dilapidated.

کھنڈرات khanḍarat, n.m. (plu. of کھنڈر khanḍar) The ruins of a town.

کھنڈن khunḍan (H) n.m. Breaking; cutting; refutation.

کھنکھار khankhār (A) n.m. Phlegm; spittle; expectoration.

کھنکھارنا khankharnā (H). v. To hem; to clear the throat; to cough; to expectorate; to hawk.

کھنگالنا khangālnā (H) v. To wash; to rinse; to make clean; to purify.

کھنگر khangar (H) n.m. Over-burnt brick; anything dry and hard.

کہنگی kuhnagi (P) n.f. Oldness; ancientness.

کہنہ kuhnah (P) adj. Old; ancient.

کہنی kuhni (H) n.f. The elbow.

کہنی مارنا kuhnı mārnā, v. To jostle; to push with the elbow.

کھو kho (H) n.f. A cave; a den; a cavern.

کھو بیٹھنا kho baiṭhnā (H) v. To lose; to be deprived of; to fail to retain.

کھو جانا kho jānā (H) v. To be lost.

کھو دینا kho denā (H) v. To waste; to lose; to part with; to be deprived of.

کھوا khawwā (H) n.m. The shoulder.

کھوے سے کھوا چھلنا khawwe se khawwā chhilnā, v. Rubbing of shoulders in an overcrowded place.

کھوپرا khoprā (H) n.m. A cocoanut; the kernel of a cocoanut.

کھوپری khoprī (H) n.f. The skull; brain; pate; head; cranium.

کھوپری کھاجانا khoprī khā janā, v. To eat one's brains; to pester; to torment; to worry.

کھوپری گنجی کرنا khopri ganji karnā, v. To beat severely.

کھوپری میں سوراخ کرنا khoprī men sūrakh karnā, v. To torment; to pester; to bore a hole in the skull (of).

کھوٹ khoṭ (H) n.f. Adulteration; alloy; defect; fault; injury; fraud; insincerity; falsehood; deceit; vice; evil; blunder; mistake; blemish.

کھوٹ ملانا khoṭ milānā, v. To alloy.

کھوٹ نکالنا khot nikālnā, v. To remove impurity of; to find fault with.

کھوٹا، کھوٹی khoṭā, khoṭī (H) adj. Adulterated; false; impure; spurious; perfidious; defective; counterfeit; alloyed; debased. spiteful; fraudulent.

کھوٹا کھرا دیکھنا khoṭa kharā dekhnā, v. To distinguish between good and bad.

کھوٹی بات khoṭi bāt, n.f. Foul language; deception.

کھوج khoj (H) n.f. Search; enquiry; quest; trace; mark.

کھوج کھاج khoj khāj, n.f. Enquiry, investigation; strict search.

کھوج لگانا khoj lagānā, v. To trace; to search; to investigate; to pursue a clue.

کھوج میں رھنا khoj men rahnā, v. To endeavour to pick a hole in another's coat; to be in search for.

کھوج نکالنا khoj nikālnā, v. To discover the track of.

کھوجنا khojnā (H) v. To seek; to search; to enquire; to explore.

کھوجی، کھوجیا khojī , khojyā (H) n.m. A seacher; an investigator; a detective; an inquisitive person.

کھودنا khodnā (H) v. To dig; to delve; to hallow; to engrave; to carve; to undermine; to investigate.

کھورو khaurū (H) n.m. Digging the earth with the hoofs; pawing the ground and ballowing.

کھورو کرنا khaurū karnā, v. To scrape the ground with the hoof.

کھوسا khosā (H) adj. Having little or no beard.

کھوسٹ khūsaṭ (H) adj. Weak; decripit; worthless. n.m. A decrepit old man; a worthless fellow.

کھوکھا khokhā (H) n.m. A paid bill of exchange kept as a voucher; a boy; an empty wooden box used for packing things. adj. Hallow; decayed.

کھوکھلا، کھوکھلی khokhlā, khokhli (H) adj. Hallow; excavated.

کھولانا khaulānā (H) v. To cause to boil.

کھولاؤ khaulā'o(H)n.m. Boiling; boiling point.

کھولنا khaulnā (H) v. To boil.

کھولنا kholnā (H) v. To open; to untie; to unfold; to lay bare; to uncover; to solve; to expose; to losen; to unravel; to disclose; to reveal; to display; to explain; to disengage.

کھونا khonā (H) v. To lose; to get rid of; to make away with; to part with; to waste; to squander.

کھونٹ khūṅt (H) n.m. A corner; an angle side; direction; pivot; central point, ear-wax.

کھونٹا khūṅtā (H) n.m. Stump; a stake (as of wood); a tent-peg; a wooden handle of a hand mill; a pin; a peg; a nail; support; protection.

کھونٹے پر مارنا khūṅṭe par mārnā, v. To spurn; to scorn.

کھونٹے کے بل کودنا khūṅṭe ke bal kūdnā, v. To become insolent; relying on some one's protection; to presume on another's protection.

کھونٹی khūṅṭī (H) n.f. A pin; a peg; root of the hair.

کھونچ khoṅch (H) n.f. Rent; rent in cloth.

کھونچ khūṅch (H) n.f. Hamstring.

کھونچا khauṅchā (H) n.m. The multiplication table of six and half.

کھوندنا khūndnā (H) v. To trample upon; to work with feet; to tread; to dig up (as the earth).

کھوہ khoh (H) n.f. See کھو kho.

کھوئی kho'i (H) n.f. The dry part of sugar-cane after extracting the juice.

کھویا khoyā (H) n.m. Condensed milk; refuse.

کھویا khivaiyyā (H) n.m. A boatsman; one who rows.

کھویا khavaiyā (H) n.m. A great eater.

کھیپ khep (H) n.f. Load; cargo; a periodical supply of grain; a trip with some load; a journey to and fro; voyage; a turn, a piece of base metal inserted in coin; a cracked coin.

کھیپ بھرنا khep bharnā, v. To load.

کھیت khet (H) n.m. A field; a field of battle; land, crop; breed; ground; soil.

کھیت پڑنا khet paṛnā, v. Occuring of the general slaughter.

کھیت رہنا khet rahnā, v. To be killed.

کھیت کاٹنا khet kāṭnā, v. To reap a field.

کھیت کرنا khet karnā, v. To cultivate a field; to sow a field.

کھیت کمانا khet kamānā, v. To manure a field.

کھیت وار جمع بندی khet wār jāmā' bandi, n.f. Amount of the revenue assessed upon each field.

کھیتی kheti (H) n.f. Husbandry; agriculture; farming.

کھیتی باڑی khetī bāṛi, n.f. Husbandry; tillage.

کھیتی باڑی کرنا kheti bāṛi karnā, v. To cultivate; to till.

کھیتی خصم سیتی kheti k͟hasm seti, prov. He who ploughs himself reaps a good harvest.

کھیدا khedā (H) n.m. A trap or enclosure for catching elephants; a strong bird or animal which beats and drives among other birds or animals.

کھیر khir (H) n.f. Rice cooked in milk and pulverized; rice pudding.

کھیر چٹائی khir chatā'ı, n.f. Weaning; the first feeding of a child with khir.

کھیر کا دلیا ہوجانا khir kā dalyā ho jānā, v. To suffer a reverse of fortune; to be ruined or marred; to suffer a loss.

کھیرا khira (H) n.m. A cucumber.

کھیرا khaira (H) n.m. A pigeon. adj. Brown.

کھیری khiri (H) n.f. The udder; breast; pap.

کھیری kheri (H) n.f. The afterbirth; the membrane in which the foetus is enveloped.

کھیس khis (H) n.f. Grinning; showing the teeth; the first milk drawn from a cow after calving.

کھیسیں نکالنا khiseṅ nikālnā, v. To grin; to simper.

کھیس khes (H) n.m. A kind of cloth; damask; a sheet or wrapper of a kind of figured cloth.

کھیسا khisā (H) n.m. (corrup. of کیسہ kisah) A purse; a pocket; a rough glove or rubber (used in bath).

کھیل khil (H) n.f. Inflated parched grain of rice; a particle.

کھیل اڑ کر منہ میں نہ جانا khil uṛ kar muṅh meṅ nah jānā, v. Not to get anything to eat; to be starving.

کھیل کھیل ہوجانا khil khil ho jānā, v. To be split up in particles.

کھیل khel (H) n.m. Play; game; sport; fun; pastime; frolic; coition; tricks; a water trough for cattle.

کھیل بگاڑنا khel bigāṛnā, v. To spoil one's business or game.

کھیل جانا khel jānā, v. To play out one's part; to die.

کھیل سمجھنا khel samajhnā, v. To consider very easy; to regard as child's play; to take the matter as a trifle.

کھیل کرنا *khel karnā*, *v.* To play; to regard as mere play.

کھیل کود *khel kūd*, *n.m.* Skipping and jumping; play and sport.

کھیل کھیلنا *khel khelnā*, *v.* To play a game.

کھیلا کھایا *khelā khāyā* (H) *adj.* Experienced; tried.

کھیلنا *khelnā* (H) *v.* To play; to sport; to gambol; to frolic; to act; to frisk; to be moving the head under the influence of evil spirit.

کہیں *kahin̊* (H) *adv.* Some where; anywhere; wherever.

کہیں سے *kahin̊ se*, *adv.* From anywhere.

کہیں کہیں *kahin̊ kahīn̊*, *adv.* At some places; here and there; in a few places.

کہیں نہ کہیں *kahin̊ nah kahin̊*, *adv.* Somewhere or other.

کھینا *khenā* (H) *v.* To row; to poddle.

کھینچ *khen̊ch* (H) *n.f.* Pull; attraction; drawing; holding (from); aversion; scarcity.

کھینچ تان کے *khen̊ch tān ke*, *adv.* With difficulty; with great effort.

کھینچ دینا *khen̊ch denā*, *v.* To pull.

کھینچ لانا *khen̊ch lānā*, *v.* To pull; to draw.

کھینچ لینا *khen̊ch lenā*, *v.* To pull or draw out; to extract; to extort.

کھینچا تانی *khen̊chā tānī* (H) *n.f.* Struggle; contention; difficulties; scuffle; stretching and straining.

کھینچنا *khen̊chnā* (H) *v.* To pull; to draw; to tighten; to strip off; to delineate; to sketch; to paint (a picture); to endure; to suffer; to drag; to hang; to hold back; to suck up; to distil; to extract.

کھیوا *khewā* (H) *n.m.* Ferry money; fare; a boat; a ferry.

کھیوٹ *khewaṭ* (H) *n.m.* A boatman; a rower; a waterman; a fisherman. *n.f.* Assigned share of revenue; a record of shares; administration paper; a record of mutation.

کھیوٹ دار *khewaṭ dār*, *n.m.* Holder of a share in a village

کھیوٹ کھتونی *khewaṭ khatauni*. *n.f.* A register of village management; a record showing the distribution of lands and the rights of the occupants.

کھیون ہار *khewan hār* (H) *n.m.* See کھویا *khivaiyyā*.

کئی *ka'ī* (H) *adv.* Some; several; many.

کئی ایک *ka'ī ek*, *adj.* A few; some.

کئی بار *ka'ī bār*, *adv.* Many a time; several times; repeatedly; again and again; often.

کی، کے *kī ke*, (H). *prep.* Of.

کے *kae* (H) *pron.* How many; what number.

کیا *kyā* (H) *pron.* What; how; why; whether.

کیا بات ہے *kyā bāt hai*, *adv.* & *intrj.* Not a doubt of it; it goes without saying; excellent! well-done!

کیا پدڑی کیا پدڑی کا شوربا *kyā pidṛī kyā pidṛī kā shorbā*, *prov.* The thing is so trifling; the matter is not worth taking notice of.

کیا خوب *kyā khūb*, *intrj.* Beautiful! wonderful! welldone!

کیا کہنا ہے *kyā kahnā hai*, *intrj.* Wonderful! excellent!

کیاری *kyārı* (H) *n.f.* A bed of flowers; a portion of planted garden; a frame; a border; a bed of salt; a field under cultivation.

کیت *kait* (H) *n.m.* A kind of a tree and its fruit.

کیتلی ketlī (E) n.f. A kettle.

کیٹ kīt (H) n.f. The dregs of oil in lamp; the dregs collected from a huqqa; an insect.

کیچ ، کیچڑ kīch, kīchaṛ (H) n.f. Dirt; mire; mud; slime; mattery discharge which collects in the corner of the eye.

کیچڑ اچھالنا kīchaṛ uchhālnā, v. To throw mud (on).

کید kaid (A) n.m. Deceit; fraud; treachery; tactics; stratagem.

کیر ker (P) n.m. penis.

کیرا kairā (H) adj. Having cat's eyes; squint-eyed.

کیڑا kīṛā (H) n.m. An insect; a worm; a snake; a reptile; a maggot; a vermin.

کیڑا لگنا kīṛā lagnā, v. To be worm-eaten.

کیڑی kīṛī (H) n.f. An ant; a small worm or insect; a leech.

کیس kes (H) n.m. The hair of the head; a cock's comb.

کیسا kaisā (H) pron. adj. How; in what manner; what sort of; on what account; why.

کیسر kesar (H) n.m. Saffron.

کیسری kesrī (H) adj. Yellow dyed with saffron; deep orange colour. n.m. A lion.

کیسہ kīsah (P) n.m. A bag; pocket.

کیش kesh (P) n.m. Faith; religion; sect; manner; quality.

کیف kaif (A) n.m. Intoxication; exhilaration.

کیفر kaifar (P) n.m. Punishment; retribution.

کیفر کردار kaifar-ĕ kirdār, n.m. Recompence for evil done.

کیفر کردار کو پہنچنا kaifar-ĕ kirdār ko pahuṅchnā, v. To suffer for one's evil deeds.

کیفی kaifī (A) adj. Drunk; intoxicated; exhilarated, tipsy; merry. n.m. A drunkard; a sot.

کیفیت kaifiyyat (A) n.f. Narrative; story; state; circumstances; explanation; quality; mode; remarks; condition; account; relation; nature; news; situation.

کیکر kikar (H) n.m. The acacia tree.

کیکر کا گوند kikar kā goṅd, n.m. Gum of acacia.

کیکڑا kekṛā (H) n.m. A crab; a cancer.

کیل kīl (H) n.f. A nail; a tack; a peg; a wedge; a pin; the core of a boil; a gold pin worn in the nose; a pimple.

کیل کانٹا kīl kāṅṭā, n.m. Tools; apparatus; accoutrements.

کیل کانٹے سے درست kīl kāṅṭe se durust, adj. Fully armed; well-equipped.

کیلا kīlā (H) n.m. A warden peg; a nail; a large nail; a bolt; a pin; a fang; tooth.

کیلا kelā (H) n.m. Banana.

کیلنا kīlnā (H) v. To fasten; to pin; to charm a snake; to charm a house; to exorcise; to destroy by magic; to stop by playing the بین bīn; to nail.

کیلوس kailūs (G) n.m. The first stage of digesting food.

کیلی kīlī (H) n.f. A key; a peg; a screw; a pivot; a nail; an axis of rotation.

کیموس kaimūs (G) n.m. Chyme; food converted by gastric secretion into acid pulp; the second stage of digesting food.

کیمیا kīmiyā (A) n.f. Alchemy; chemistry; a specific; panacea.

کیمیا بنانا kīmiyā banānā, v. To transmute the baser metals into gold; to earn money easily; to alchemise.

کیمیا گر kīmiyā gar, n.m. An alchemist; deceiver.

کیمیا گری *kimiyā garī*, *n.f.* Practical chemistry; alchemy.

کینچل، کینچلی *keṅchal, keṅchali* (H) *n.f.* The slough or skin of a snake.

کینچلی بدلنا *keṅchalī badalnā*, *v.* To slough; to put on a new slough; to change clothes.

کینچلی چھوڑنا *keṅchali chhoṛnā*, *v.* To cast off the old slough or skin.

کینچوا *keṅchwā* (H) *n.m.* Man-worm; earthworm; a worm bred in the body.

کینڈا *kaiṅḍā* (H) *n.m.* Mould; a rough plan; sample; gauge.

کینہ *kinah* (P) *n.m.* Malice; rancour, grudge; enmity; spite; hatred; animosity.

کینہ توز، ور *kinah toz, war*, *adj.* Insincere; deceitful; grudging; malicious; spiteful.

کینہ رکھنا *kinah rakhnā*, *v.* To bear enmity.

کیوان *kaiwān* (P) *n.m.* The planet Saturn; the seventh heaven.

کیوٹی *keoṭi* (H) *n.f.* A mixture of different kinds of pulses.

کیوڑا *kewṛā* (H) A kind of tree and its fragrant flower.

کیوں *kyūṅ* (H) *adv.* Why; wherefore; how; what then.

کیوں کر *kyūṅ kar*, *adv.* How; why; what for.

کیوں کہ *kyūṅ keh*, *adv. conj.* Because; in as much as; because that; since; for.

گ *gāf*, called *kāf-i-'ajami*, is the twenty-sixth letter of the Persian and the twenty-ninth of the Urdu alphabet. It does not occur in Arabic. Its numerical value, according to the *abjad*, is the same as that of ک *i.e.* 20.

گا *gā* (H) The sign of the future tense (will, shall).

گابا، گابھا *gābā, gābha* (H) *n.m.* A new leaf springing from the centre of a plantain tree; the inner portion of wood pulp; a fork of a tree; unripe crop; old cotton taken out of a quilt; a leaf in the bud.

گابھ *kābh* (H) *n.m.* Pregnancy of animals.

گابھ ڈالنا *gābh ḍālnā*, *v.* To miscarry (cattle).

گابھن *gābhan* (H) *adj.* Pregnant (animals).

گاجر *gājar* (H) *n.f.* A carrot.

گاجر مولی *gājar mūli*, *n.f.* A worthless stuff; rubbish.

گاد *gād* (H) *n.f.* Sediment; dirt; lees.

گاد بیٹھنا *gād baiṭhnā*, *v.* Settling of the sediment at the bottom.

گارا *gārā* (H) *n.m.* Mud; kneaded clay; mortar; name of a musical mode.

گارا بنانا، کرنا *gārā banānā, karnā*, *v.* To knead clay; to prepare mud for building or plastering.

گارد *gārad*(*corr.* of English) *n.m.* A guard; ward; a guard-room.

گاڑنا *gārnā* (H) *v.* To bury; to hide; to plant; to drive a nail or peg; to drive in; to fix; to pitch; to sink.

گاڑھا *gāṛhā* (H) *n.m.* Coarse cloth.

گاڑھا، گاڑھی gāṛhā, gāṛhī (H) *adj.* Thick; dense; coarse; strong; close.

گاڑھی چھننا gāṛhī chhannā, *v.* To be close friends.

گاڑی gāṛī (H) *n.f.* A cart; a carriage; a coach; a railway carriage; a railway train; a car.

گاڑی بان gāṛī bān, *n.m.* A coachman; a carter.

گاڑی جوتنا gāṛī jotnā, *v.* To yoke bullocks; to harness horses to a conveyance.

گاڑی چلانا gāṛī chalānā, *v.* To drive a cart; to hire or let out carriages.

گاڑی خانہ gāṛī khānah, *n.m.* A carriage house; a garage.

گاڑی ہانکنا gāṛī hānknā, *v.* To drive a cart; to yoke bullocks or horses to a conveyance.

چلتی گاڑی میں روڑا اٹکانا chaltī gāṛī men roṛā aṭkānā, *v.* To obstruct; to put obstacles in the way; to put a poke in the wheel.

گاگر gāgar (H) *n.f.* A water vessel (of metal); a pitcher.

گال gāl (H) *n.m.* The cheek.

گال پچکنا gāl pichaknā, *v.* Sinking of the cheeks; to become emaciated.

گال پر گال چڑھنا gāl par gāl charhnā, *v.* To become very fat.

گال پھلانا gāl phulānā, *v.* To be displeased; to sulk; to resent; to puff out the cheeks.

گالا gālā (H) *n.m.* A pad of cotton; a ball of corded cotton; a wide-mouthed sack.

گالی gālī (H) *n.f.* Abuse; abusive language.

گالی بکنا، دینا gālī baknā, denā, *v.* To abuse; to call names; to revile; to scold.

گالی کھانا gālī khānā, *v.* To get abuse; to be abused.

گالی گفتار ، گالی گلوچ gālī guftār, gālī galoch, *n.f.* Mutual abuse; brawl.

گام gām (P) *n.m.* A foot; a step; pace (of a horse).

گام زن gām zan, *adj.* Stepping out; treading; going forward.

گام زن ہونا gām zan honā, *v.* To start; to commence (journey); to step out.

گانا gānā (H) *v.* To sing; to chant; to make known; to relate; to celebrate; to sing the praises of. *n.m.* Music; song.

گانا بجانا gānā bajānā, *n.m.* Singing and playing; music and song.

گانٹھ gānṭh (H) *n.f.* A knot; a joint; a hardened gland; the navel; a purse; parcel; a bundle; a piece of ginger; a difficulty; a misunderstanding; dissimulation; an obstacle; guile.

گانٹھ باندھنا، دینا، لگانا gānṭh bāndhnā, denā, lagānā, *v.* To tie a knot; to bear in mind; to make a contract.

گانٹھ پڑنا gānṭh parnā, *v.* To be knotted; to be entangled; to arouse ill-feeling.

گانٹھ سے جانا gānṭh se jānā, *v.* To lose money; to suffer a loss.

گانٹھ کا پورا gānṭh kā pūrā, *adj.* Careful in money matters; not allowing a penny to slip out of one's hands; rich; wealthy.

گانٹھ کاٹنا ، کترنا gānṭh kāṭnā, katarnā, *v.* To pick one's pocket; to rob; to plunder.

گانٹھ کھولنا gānṭh kholnā, *v.* To untie a knot; to open a purse; to remove ill-feelings; to be prodigal.

گانٹھ میں رکھنا gānṭh men rakhnā, *v.* To pocket.

گانٹھ لینا gānṭh lenā (H) *v.* To bring over to one's side; to make friend.

گانٹھنا gānṭhnā (H) *v.* To fasten; to thread; to bring over to one's side; to cobble; to clasp; to conceal; to string together; to join; to tie; to stitch together; to interlock.

گانجا gāṅjā (H) n.m. The hump plant and its young leaves and buds prepared as *bhang*.

گاندھی gāndhī (H) n.m. A perfume-seller.

گانڈ، گانڑ gāṅḍ, gāṅṛ (H) n.f. The anus; the privities.

گانڑ پھاڑنا gāṅṛ phāṛna, v. To frighten; to put in a funk; to punish severely.

گانڑ پھٹنا gāṅṛ phaṭnā, v. To be in a great fright.

گانڑ چلنا gāṅṛ chalna, v. To be loose (the bowels); to suffer from diarrhoea.

گانڑ دھونا gaṅṛ dhoṅā, v. To wash after evacuation; to do menial offices.

گانڑ رگڑنا gāṅṛ ragaṛnā, v. To labour or try hard.

گانڑ غلامی کرنا gāṅṛ ghulāmī karna, v. To be highly submissive; to execute all commands.

گانڑ گردن ایک ھوجانا gāṅṛ gardan ek hojānā, v. To be dog tired; to be very much exhausted.

گانڑ میں گھسا جانا gāṅṛ meṅ ghusā jānā, v. To flatter; to wheedle.

گانڈو gāṅdū (H) n.m. A catamite; a sodomite; an impotent man; a coward.

گاہ gāh (P) adv. Sometimes; frequently. n.f. Time; place. (used in *comp.* as in درگاہ *dargāh*, a royal court; a saint's tomb or mausoleum).

گاہ بہ گاہ gāh bah gāh. See گاہے گاہے gāhe gāhe.

گاھک gāhak (H) n.m. A purchaser, a buyer; a customer.

گاھکی gāhakī (H) n.f. Sale; transactions.

گاھن gāhan (H) n.m. A harrow with teeth for removing grass from ploughed land.

گاھنا gāhnā (H) v. To thrash; to scorch; to seek; to tread out corn.

گاہے gāhe (P) adv. Once; sometimes.

گاہے گاہے، گاہے ماہے gahe gahe, gahe mahe, adv. At times; occasionally; some times; seldom.

گاؤ gao (P) n.m. A bull; an ox; a cow.

گاؤ تکیہ gāo takyah, n.m. A large pillow or bolster.

گاؤ خانہ gāo khānah, n.m. A cow-shed or pen.

گاؤ خورد gāe khūrd, adj. Ruined or destroyed; defrauded.

گاؤ دم gāo dum, adj. Tapering; stooping; conical.

گاؤ زبان gāo zabān, n.f. A medicinal herb.

گاؤ شیر gāo shir, n.m. Gum-resin; the medicinal gum of the opoponax tree.

گاؤ شماری gāo shumāri, n.f. Cattle census; a tax upon cattle.

گاؤ فلک gāo-ĕ falak, n.m. The constellation; Taurus.

گاؤ کشی gao kushī, n.f. Cow slaughter.

گاؤ میش gāo mesh, n.m. A buffalo

گاؤدی gāodi (P) n.m. A fool; a simpleton.

گاؤں gāoṅ (H) n.m. A village.

گاؤں بانٹ gāoṅ bāṅt, n.f. Division of villages.

گائے gāe (H) n.f. A cow.

گایتری gāyatri (S) n.f. A sacred verse from the Rig Veda sung at morning and evening devotions.

گایک gāyak (S) n.m. A singer; a songster.

گبر gabr (P) n.m. A fire-worshipper; an infidel, a follower of Zoroaster.

گبرو، گبھرو gabrū, gabhrū (H) n.m. A young man; a youth; a clown.

گبرون gabrūn (A) n.m. A kind of coarse cloth.

گبریلا gubrilā (H) n.m. A species of black beetle found in dunghills or old cowdung.

گبھا gabbha (H) n.m. A bedding; a matress.

گپ gap (H) n.f. Gossip; chat; tattle; a false report.

گپ شپ gap shap, n.f. Prattle; chit chat; false report; idle talk.

گپ مارنا ، ہانکنا gap mārna, hankā, v. To tattle; to gossip.

گپ چپ gup chup (H) adj. Quiet; silent. n.f. Silence; name of a boy's game; a sweetmeat.

گپت gupt (S) adj. Concealed; hidden; invisible; implied. adv. Secretly; privately.

گپت دان gupt dan, n.m. A gift made secretly.

گپت مار gupt mār, n.f. Hurting in such a way as to leave no mark; taunt; gibes; sneer.

گپت مال gupt māl, n.m. Hidden wealth or treasure.

گپتی gupti (H) n.f. A sword stick.

گپڑ gapaṛ (H) n.f. A gossip.

گپڑ چوتھ gapaṛ chauth, n.f. Confusion; under-hand dealings.

گپڑ شپڑ gapaṛ shapaṛ, n.f. Nonsense.

گپھا guphā (H) n.f. A cave; a den; a thicket.

گپھا میں بیٹھنا guphā men baithna, v. Retirement from the world to lead a hermit's life.

گپھا gupphā (H) n.m. A tassel; a bunch of flowers; a wreath.

گپیا ، گپی gapyā, gappī, adj. & n.m. A liar; a prater; an idle talker.

گت gat (H) n.f. Plight; condition; a tune; mode of dancing; funeral rites; cremation; solvation; state; predicament; pace; gait; end; fortune; destiny; a dance procedure.

گت بجانا gat bajana, v. To play a tune; to play an air.

گت بنانا gat banānā, v. Te beat soundly or severely; to beat to a jelly; to beat black and blue.

گت بھرنا یا ناچنا gat bharnā yā nachnā, v. To dance to music.

گت کا gat kā, adj. Good, fine; useful; serviceable.

گتا gattā, n.m. Cardboard.

گتکا gatkā (H) n.m. A cudgel; a club; a foil or blunt wooden sword (used in fencing).

گتھنا guthnā (H) v. To be plaited; to be threaded; to contend.

گتھواں guthwān (H) adj. Plaited; strung together.

گتھی gutthi (H) n.f. A knot; a riddle; a puzzle; complication.

گٹا giṭṭā (H) n.m. The part of the pipe fixed into the top of the metal part of a حقہ ḥuqqah; a corn; a sweatmeat; an ankle-bone; a knee-bone; a stopper.

گٹکا gutkā (H) n.m. A smal ball or block of wood; a manual; a hand book; a magic ball prepared by devotees, the use of which is supposed to make them invisible.

گٹکنا guṭaknā (H) v. To coo (as a dove).

گٹھ gaṭh (H) n.f. (Contraction of گانٹھ gānṭh) A knot; a tie.

گٹھ جوڑ gaṭh jor, n.m. Tying the knot; the nuptial tie; alliance; unity.

گٹھا gatṭhā (H) n.m. A bundle; a package; a clove of onion, garlic etc.; the twentieth part of a جریب jarib.

گٹھانا · گٹھوانا gaṭhānā, gaṭhwānā (H) v. To cause to mend; to cause to join.

گٹھڑ gaṭṭhar (H) n.m. A large bundle; a bale.

گٹھڑی gaṭhr'i (H) n.f. A small bundle; a bag; a packet.

گٹھلی guṭhlī (H) n.f. A stone (of a fruit); a kernel; a seed.

گھٹنا gaṭhnā (H) To be mended; to join.

گٹھوائی gaṭhwāī (H) n.f. The charge for mending (shoes).

گٹھیا gaṭhyā (H) n.f. Rheumatism; pains; a bag; a sack in the joints.

گٹھیلا gaṭhila (H) adj. Knotty; well-set; strong; robust.

گٹی giṭṭī (H) n.f. A reel.

گج gaj (S) n.m. An elephant.

گجر gajar (H) n.m. The strokes of a gong after every four hours; the hourly strokes of a gong; an alarm (clock); a mixture of red and white wheat.

گجر دم gajar dam, adv. Early in the morning; at early dawn; immediately.

گجرا (H) n.m. A garland; the leaf of the carrot; an ornament for the wrist; a bracelet; bracelet of flowers.

گجری gujrī (H) n.f. (Femine of گوجر gujar, milk-man); a milk-maid.

گج گاہ gaj gāh (H) n.m. A string made of several tassels, used as an ornament for an elephant or for a horse.

گج گجا gij gijā (H) adj. Wet; moist; half-ripe.

گج گجانا gij gijānā (H) v. To rattle; to become flabby; to be full of worms.

گچ gach (H) n.m. Mortar; a floor plastered with lime; cement; old mortar knocked off walls.

گچ کاری gach kārī, n.f. Mortar work.

گچھا guchchhā (H) n.m. A bunch; a cluster.

گچھا تارا guchchhā tārā, n.m. The Pleiades.

گچھی guchchhī (H) n.f. A small bunch.

گدا gadā (P) n.m. A beggar; a mendicant.

گدا gaddā (H) n.m. A soft quilted bedding.

گدا gudda (H) n.m. A thick bough or branch of a tree.

گدا ختہ gudakhtah (P) adj. Melted; dissolved.

گداز gudaz (P) adj. Melted; dissolved; thick; plump; melting; dissolving; exterminating. (used in comps. as, دل گداز dil gudāz heart-melting).

گدا گر gadāgar (P) n.m. A beggar; a mendicant.

گدا گری gadāgarī (P) n.f. Begging; living on charity.

گدائی gadāī (P) n.f. Beggary; poverty; want; begging; living on charity.

گدایانہ gadāyanah (P) adv. Beggar-like.

گدر · گدرا gaddar, gadra (H) adj. Half-ripe; thick; plump; well-developed.

گدرانا gadrānā (H) v. To be half-ripe; to attain puberty; to bloom.

گدراہٹ gadrāhaṭ (H) n.f. The state of being half-ripe.

گدڑی gudṛi (H) n.f. Rags; tattered and torn clothes or quilts.

گدڑی میں لعل gudṛi men la'l, adj. A jewel in rags.

گدگدا gudgudā (H) adj. Plump and soft.

گدگدانا gudgudānā (H) v. To tickle; to titillate.

گدگداہٹ · گدگدی gudgudāhaṭ, gudgudī (H) n.f. Titillation; tickling.

گدلا ، گدلی gadlā, gadlī (H) adj. Muddy; foul; dirty; turbid.

گدلاپن gadlā pan, n.m. Muddiness; turbidness.

گدنا gudnā (H) v. To be tatooed.

گدوانا gudwānā (H) v. To cause to tatoo.

گدھ gidh (H) n.m. A vulture.

گدھا gadhā (H) n.m. An ass; a donkey; a fool; a simpleton.

گدھا پن gadhā pan, n.m. Stupidity; folly; foolishness.

گدھا گدھی gadhā gadhī, n.m. A boy's game.

گدھا پیٹنے سے گھوڑا نہیں ہوتا gadhā pīṭne se ghoṛā nahiṅ hotā, prov. Nothing can make a born fool wise.

گدھے پر سوار کرنا gadhe par sawār karnā, v. To put on an ass; to disgrace; to defame.

گدھے کے ہل چلوانا gadhe ke hal chalwānā, v. To ruin; to destroy.

گدھی gadhī (H) n.f. A she-ass.

گدی gaddī (H) n.f. A cushion; a seat; a pack-saddle; a throne; sheet; mat; pillow.

گدی پر بٹھانا gaddī par biṭhānā, v. To instal a king.

گدی پر بیٹھنا gaddī par baiṭhnā, v. To ascend the throne; to be enthroned.

گدی سے اُتارنا gaddī se utārnā, v. To dethrone.

گدی نشین gaddī nashīn, n.m. A prince; a king; a keeper of a saint's tomb.

گدی نشینی gaddī nashīnī, n.f. Accession to the throne.

گدی guddī (H) n.f. Nape of the neck.

گدی بھاننا ، ناپنا guddī bhānnā, nāpnā, v. To slap one on the neck.

گدی سے زبان کھینچنا guddī se zabān kheṅchnā, v. To pull the tongue from the nape; to award death sentence.

گدیلا gadelā (H) n.m. A thick bedding; a cushion.

گڈا gaḍḍā (H) n.m. A bullock-cart; a lump of clay.

گڈا guḍḍā (H) n.m. A doll; puppet; effigy.

گڈا بنانا guḍḍā banānā, v. To make an effigy.

گڈا بنا کے جوتے مارنا guḍḍā banā ke jūte mārnā, v. To make an effigy and beat it with shoes; to raise a person to a position of honour and then disgrace him.

گڈریا gaḍaryā (H) n.m. A shepherd.

گڈ مڈ gaḍ maḍ (H) adj. Disordered; mixed up; muddled; adulterated.

گڈ مڈ کرنا gaḍ maḍ karnā, v. To mix up; to confuse.

گڈ مڈ ہونا gaḍ maḍ honā, v. To be mixed up.

گڈھ gaḍh (H) n.m. See گڑھ gaṛh.

گڈھی gaḍhī (H) n.f. See گڑھی gaṛhī.

گڈی gaḍḍī (H) n.f. A little bundle of vegetables; a bundle of anything; half a ream.

گڈی guḍḍī (H) n.f. A paper-kite; a pinion; joints of bones.

گذارش guzārish (P) n.f. See گزارش guzārish.

گذشت guzasht (P) n.f. See گزشت guzasht.

گذشتنی guzashtanī (P) adj. See گزشتنی guzashtnī.

گذشته guzashtah (P) adj. See گزشته guzashtah.

گر gar (P) (used for اگر agar) If; in the event of. adj. A maker; worker; (used in comps. as, آهن گر āhan gar, a black smith). n.f. Scab; mange. n.m. Desire; strength.

گر **gur** (H) *n.m.* A formula; a short method. (*cont.* of گرو *gurū*), A spiritual guide; a teacher.

گر بھائی **gur bhā'i**, *n.m.* A fellow disciple.

گردوارہ **gurdūārah**, *n.m.* A monastery.

گر ماتا **gurmātā**, *n.f.* Wife of one's religious guide.

گرمکھی **gur mukhi**, *n.f.* The language of the *gurūs*; Punjabi written in Hindi-like characters.

گرادینا **girā denā** (H) *v.* To throw down; to cast; to break down; to demolish.

گراری **garāri** (H) *n.f.* An instrument for twisting thread or string; the block over which the well-rope passes; a pulley.

گرام **girām** (S) *n.m.* A village; a musical scale.

گرامی **girāmī** (P) *adj.* Dear; precious; revered; great; excellent; respectable.

گراں **girāṅ** (P) *adj.* Precious; costly; dear; momentous; important; heavy; grievous.

گراں بار **girāṅ bār**, *adj.* Heavily burdened; heavily laden; fruit bearing; pregnant.

گراں بہا **girāṅ bahā**, *adj.* Costly.

گراں خاطر **girāṅ khāṭir**, *adj.* Unpleasing; dejected; sad.

گراں سر **girāṅ sar**, *adj.* Proud; haughty.

گراں فروش **girāṅ farosh**, *adj.* One who sells dear; one who sells at higher rates.

گراں گذرنا **girāṅ guzarnā**, *v.* To be heavy upon one.

گراں مایہ **girāṅ māyah**, *adj.* Of great value; valuable.

گراں ہونا **girāṅ honā**, *v.* To rise in price; to become more costly.

گرانا **girānā** (H) *v.* To fell; to drop; to shed.

گرانی **girānī** (P) *n.f.* Dearness; dearth; scarcity; rise in price; heaviness; indigestion; weight; importance; draught.

گراؤ **girāū** (H) *adj.* Ready to fall.

گربہ **gurbah** (P) *n.f.* A cat.

گربۂ مسکین **gurbah-ĕ miskīn**, *adj.* A meek but a wicked person; outwardly meek; inwardly wicked.

گر پڑنا **gir paṛnā** (H) *v.* To fall down; to collapse; to drop.

گرتا پڑتا ، گرتے پڑتے **girtā paṛtā, girte paṛte** (H) *adv.* With difficulty.

گرج **garaj** (H) *n.f.* Thundering; roaring; bellowing.

گرجا **girjā** (Portg.) *n.m.* A church; a chapel.

گر جانا **gir jānā** (H) *v.* See گر پڑنا *gir paṛnā*.

گرجنا **garajnā** (H) *v.* To thunder; to roar; to bellow.

گرد **gard** (P) *n.f.* Dust; trifle.

گرد اڑانا **gard uṛānā**, *v.* To raise a dust.

گرد اڑنا **gard uṛnā**, *v.* To be desolate; to fly about (as dust).

گرد آلودہ **gard ālūdah** *adj.* Covered with dust; dusty; dirty.

گرد باد **gard bād**, *n.m.* A whirlwind.

گرد پوش **gard posh**, *n.m.* Dust cover.

گرد **gird** (P) *n.m.* Round; circumference; environs. *adv.* About; near; behind.

گردآور **gird āwar**, *n.m.* An inspector of customs; an officer who supervises the work of a پٹواری *paṭwāri* (a village accountant).

گردآوری **gird āwari**, *n.f.* The functions of a گردآور *gird āwar*.

گرد و پیش **gird-ĕ pesh**, *adv.* On all sides; all round.

گرد و نواح gird-ŏ nawāḥ, n.m. Vicinity; suburbs.

گرد ہونا gird honā, v. To follow; to hang upon; to surround; to gether or collect round.

گردا gardā (H) n.m. Dust.

گرداب girdāb (P) n.m. A whirlpool; an abyss; gulf; vortex.

گرداگرد girda gird (P) adv. On all sides; all round; round about; around.

گردان gardān (P) n.f. Turning; revolving; revolution; winding; conjugation; declension (*in grammar*); revision; inflection; causing to revolve or go round.

گرداننا gardannā v. To conjugate; to inflect; to revise or repeat; to have regard for; to esteem.

گردش gardish (P) n.f. Revolution; vicissitude; misfortune; circulation; reversion; change of fortune; wandering about; vagrancy; hard times; adverse fortune.

گردش آسمان gardish-ĕ āsmān, n.f. Revolution of the spheres.

گردش ایام gardish-ĕ ayyām, n.f. Vicissitudes of fortune.

گردش کرنا gardish karnā, v. To turn round; to revolve; to circulate.

گردش میں آنا gardish men ānā, v. To be unlucky; to be having hard times; to fall into adversity; to be unfortunate.

گردگان girdgān (P) n.m. A walnut: a pellet.

گردن gardan (P) n.f. The neck.

گردن اُڑانا، کاٹنا gardan uṛānā, kāṭnā, v. To behead; to slay; to kill.

گردن پر خون ہونا gardan par khūn honā, v. To be guilty of murder.

گردن پر سوار ہونا gardan par sawār honā, v. To sit on one's head; to compel; to extort.

گردن پھنسانا gardan phansānā, v. To put one's head in a noose; to incur responsibility.

گردن جھکانا gardan jhukānā, v. To bow the head; to submit; to obey; to yield.

گردن زدنی gardan zadani, adj. Deserving to be beheaded.

گردن کٹنا gardan kaṭnā, v. To be beheaded; to be ruined.

گردن مارنا gardan mārna, v. To kill; to put to death.

گردن مروڑنا gardan maroṛnā, v. To strangle; to throttle.

گردن ہلانا gardan hilānā, v. To nod; to shake the head.

گردن ہلنے لگنا gardan hilne lagnā, v. To become old.

گردنا gardnā, n.m. The neck; the cornice.

گردنی gardani (P) n.f. A horse-cloth; a blow on the neck; a ring of silver worn on the neck; a trick in wrestling.

گردنی دینا gardani denā, v. To drive a man by the neck; to turn one out by the scuff of the neck.

گردوں gardūn (P) n.m. The heavens; the firmament; fortune; an engine for pulling up trees by the roots.

گردہ gurdah (P) n.m. Kidney; courage; valour.

گِردہ girdah (P) n.m. Circumference; a round pillow; a round tray; a barrel of a drum.

گردہ gardah (P) n.m. Powder; sketch; powder used by the painters.

گرز gurz (P) n.m. A battle-axe; club; a mace.

گرز بردار gurz bardār, n.m. A mace-bearer.

گرسنگی gursanagi (P) n.f. Hunger.

گرسنہ gursanah (P) adj. Hungry.

گرفت **girift** (P) *n.f.* Grasp; criticism; blame; seizure; capture; clutch; objection; a handle; catch; hold.

گرفت کرنا **girift karnā**, *v.* To find fault with; to criticise; to take exception (to).

گرفتار **giriftār** (P) *adj.* Seized; arrested; involved; captivated; smitten; captive; prisoner; enchained; entangled.

گرفتار کرنا **giriftār karnā**, *v.* To seize; to capture; to captivate; to apprehend; to arrest.

گرفتار ھونا **giriftār honā**, *v.* To become a prisoner; to be involved in; to fall in love with.

گرفتاری **giriftārī** (P) *n.f.* Seizure; captivity; bondage; entanglement. imprisonment; arrest; difficulty.

گرفتگی **giriftagī** (P) *n.f.* Capture; detention; impediment.

گرفته **giriftah** (P) *adj.* Captured; captivated; seized.

گرفته دل ، خاطر **giriftah dil, khāṭir.** *adj.* Afflicted in mind.

گرگ **gurg** (P) *n.m.* A wolf.

گرگ باراں دیده **gurg-ĕ bārāṅ didah**, *adj.* An experienced person; a veteran.

گرگ زاده **gurg zādah**, *n.m.* A wolf's cub; a young wolf.

گرگ کهن **gurg-ĕ kuhan**, *n.m.* An old wolf; an experienced cheat; a tyrant.

گرگا **gurgā** (H) *n.m.* A servant boy; a scullion; a low fellow; a vagabond.

گرگابی **gurgābī** (H) *n.f.* A kind of shoe or slipper; a kind of a pomp shoe.

گرگٹ **girgaṭ** (H) *n.m.* A chameleon.

گرگٹ کے سے رنگ بدلنا **girgaṭ ke se raṅg badalnā**, *v.* To change colours like a chameleon; to turn red or pale with rage.

گرم **garm** (P) *adj.* Hot, warm; burning; ordent; active; zealous; eager; intent on; fiery; choleric; virolent; brisk; lively; thronged or crowded.

گرم اختلاطی **garm ikhtilāṭī**, *n.f.* Warmth of friendship; strong attachment: warm affection.

گرم بازاری **garm bāzārī**, *n.f.* Throng in market; rapid sale; great demand; high value or cost.

گرم بولنا **garm bolnā**, *v.* To speak angrily; to speak readily and to the purpose.

گرم جوشی **garm joshī**, *n.f.* Warmth of affection; cordiality; zeal; friendship.

گرم خبر **garm khabar**, *n.f.* The latest news; the current rumour.

گرم سرد **garm sard**, *adj.* Lukewarm; *n.m.* ups and downs of life.

گرم سرد چشیده **garm sard chashīdah**, *adj.* Well-experienced; seasoned.

گرم کرنا **garm karnā**, *v.* To warm; to heat; to incite; to make angry; to incense.

گرم مزاج **garm mizāj**, *adj.* Hot tempered; passionate.

گرم مسالا **garm masālā**, *n.m.* Spices; ingredients.

گرم ھونا **garm honā**, *v.* To became hot; to be brisk; to be thronged; to get angry.

گرما **garmā** (P) *n.m.* Summer; the hot season; heat.

گرما گرم **garmā garm**, *adj.* Hot and hot; piping hot; fresh; extempore.

گرما گرمی **garmā garmī**, *n.f.* Exchange of hot words; rebuking; reviling.

گرمابه **garmābah** (P) *n.m.* A hot bath; a bathing place; a bath house.

گرمانا **garmānā**, *v.* To heat; to be hot or angry; to enliven; to become enlivened.

گرمائی garmā'ī, n.f. A stimulant; heat; excitement.

گرمی garmī (P) n.f. Heat; warmth; summer; fervour; passion; love; anger; venereal disease; syphilis.

گرمی پڑنا garmī paṛnā, v. To become hot; coming of the summer.

گرمی‌دانہ garmī dānah, n.m. Prickly heat.

گرمی کرنا garmī karnā, v. To produce heat or warmth; to effect fondness; to make a show of affection.

گرمی نکالنا garmī nikālnā, v. To give vent to one's anger; to indulge in carnal intercourse.

گرمی ہونا garmī honā, v. To have syphilis; to become hot (season).

گرنا girnā (H) v. To fall; to drop; to sink; to tumble down; to come down; to befall; to lull (the wind); to attack; to be reduced or degraded; to miscarry; to fall; to fall in price; to fall in one's esteem; to fall in battle; to be beaten.

گرنتھ granth (S) n.f. A literary book; a code; the sacred book of the Sikhs.

گرنتھی granthī (S) n.m. One who reads granth to the public.

گرنڈ garanḍ (H) n.m. An exclosure of mud round a hand mill to collect flour therein.

گرو gurū (S) n.m. A spiritual guide; a religious teacher; a wise man; a tutor. adj. Respectable; honourable.

گرو گھنٹال gurū ghanṭāl, n.m. A thorough knave; a consummate knave; a perfect knave.

گرو girau (P) n.m. Pledge; pawn.

گرو رکھنا girau rakhnā, v. To pledge.

گرو نامہ girau nāmah, n.m. A mortgage deed.

گروانا girwānā (H) v. To cause to fall down; to cause to miscarry; to get demolished.

گروہ guroh (P) n.m. A band; troops; crowd; mob; company; crew; sect; class; group; gang.

گروی girvī, adj. Pledged; pawned; mortgaged. n.m. An insect destructive to standing corn.

گروی رکھنا girvī rakhnā, v. To pledge; to pawn.

گرویدگی girwīdagī (P) n.f. Admiring; following; adoring; adherence; attachment; gratefulness.

گرویدہ girwīdah (P) adj. Attracted; attached to; captivated; enamoured; admiring; believing.

گرہ girah (P) n.f. A knot; a joint; a knuckle; one-sixteenth of a گز gaz (yard).

گرہ پڑنا girah paṛnā, v. Dissention arising between two persons.

گرہ دار girah dār, adj. Jointed; knotted.

گرہ کھلنا girah khulnā, v. Clearing up of a misunderstanding; restoration of friendship; untying of a knot.

گرہ گیر girah gīr, adj. Inclining to be knotty or difficult; defying solution.

گرہ لگانا girah lagānā, v. To tie a knot.

گرہ میں باندھنا girah meṅ bāndhnā, v. To tie a knot (in one's handkerchief) in order to remember (a certain thing); to bear in mind.

گرہ میں رکھنا girah meṅ rakhnā, v. To keep in one's pocket.

گرہست girhast (H) n.f. Household goods; house-keeping; domestic matters; worldly affairs; husbandry.

گرہستن girhastan (H) n.f. A wife, well versed in house-keeping.

گرہستی girhastī, girhistī (H) n.m. One who leads a married life; a householder; a peasant; a husband man . adj. Relating to household affairs.

گرہن **grahn** (S) *n.m.* Eclipse of the sun or moon; a spot.

گرہن پڑنا ، لگنا **grahn parnā, lagnā,** *v.* To be eclipsed; (an eclipse) to take place.

گری **girī** (H) *n.f.* The kernel of any fruit seed.

گریاں **giriyāṅ** (P) *adj.* Weeping; crying.

گریبان **girebān, grebān** (P) *n.m.* The collar; the opening or breast of a garment; pocket; neck.

گریبان پکڑنا **girebān pakarnā,** *v.* To seize by the collar.

گریبان چاک کرنا **girebān chāk karnā,** *v.* To tear one's garment to pieces.

گریبان گیر **girebān gīr,** *adj.* An accuser; a plaintiff; a prosecutor; one who seizes by the collar.

گریبان میں منہ ڈالنا **girebān meṅ muṅh ḍālnā,** *v.* To search one's own heart; to do a little heart-searching before criticising others; to confess and be ashamed of one's own misdeeds.

گریز **gurez** (P) *n.f.* Flight; escape; deviation; aversion; abhorrence; digression; dislike; abstinence; fasting; regression.

گریز پا **gurez pā,** *adj.* Fugitive; runaway; fleeing.

گریز کرنا **gurez karnā,** *v.* To avoid; to evade; to fly.

گریزاں **gurezāṅ** (P) *adj.* Fugitive; fleeing.

گریہ **giryah** (P) *n.m.* Weeping; lamentation; crying; plaint.

گریہ کناں **giryah kunāṅ,** *adj.* Weeping; crying.

گریہ و زاری **giryah-ŏ zārī** (P) *n.f.* Bewailing; lamentation; crying.

گڑ **gur** (H) *n.m.* Molasses; treacle; raw sugar.

گڑ انبا **gur ambā,** *n.m.* Mangoes boiled with molasses.

گڑ دئے مرے تو زہر کیوں دے **gūr diye mare to zehr kiyūṅ de,** *prov.* When sweet words succeed why resort to harsh ones.

گڑ کھائیں ، گلگلوں سے پرہیز **gur khāeṅ, gulgloṅ se parhez,** *prov.* Lumps of sugar he devours but refrains from eating sweet cakes.

گڑ کہنے سے منہ میٹھا نہیں ہوتا **gur kahne se muṅh mīṭhā nahīṅ hotā,** *maxim.* Fine words butter no parsnips.

گڑ کی بھیلی **gur kī bhelī,** *n.f.* A lump of raw sugar.

گڑ بڑ ، گڑ بڑاہٹ ، گڑ بڑی **garbar, garbarāhat, garbarī** (H) *n.f.* Bustle; confusion; disorder; chaos; mismanagement; anarchy; fight.

گڑ بڑ ہونا **gurbar honā,** *v.* To be confused; to be mixed up; to be mismanaged.

گڑ بڑانا **garbarānā** (H) *v.* To be confused; to rumble (the stomach).

گڑجانا **gar jānā** (H) *v.* See گڑنا **garnā.**

گڑ گڑ **gurgur** (H) *n.f.* The rumbling sound produced by water in a حقہ **huqqah;** rumbling in stomach.

گڑ گڑانا **gargarānā** (H) *v.* To thunder; to gurgle.

گڑ گڑانا **girgirānā** (H) *v.* To beseach; to implore humbly and earnestly.

گڑ گڑانا **gurgurānā** (H) *v.* To rumble.

گڑ گڑاہٹ **gargarāhat** (H) *n.f.* Rumbling noise; thundering sound.

گڑ گڑی **gurgurī** (H) *n.f.* A small حقہ **huqqah;** a smoking pipe.

گڑنا **garnā** (H) *v.* To penetrate; to be driven into; to be fixed; to be buried; to sink; to enter; to be ashamed.

گڑوا **garwā** (H) *n.m.* A kind of water-pot.

گڑوانا **garwānā** (H) *v.* To cause to be buried; to cause to be driven into.

گڑونا garoṇā (H) v. To pierce; to drive in; to bore; to perforate; to stick into; to fix at (eyes).

گڑھ gaṛh (H) n.m. A castle; a fort.

گڑھا gaṛhā (H) n.m. A cavity; a hole; a pit; an abyss; a valley.

گڑھی gaṛhī (H) n.f. A small fort; a castle.

گڑیا guṛyā (H) n.f. A doll.

گڑیا کا کھیل guṛyā kā khel, n.m. Playing with dolls; a very easy matter.

گڑے مردے اکھاڑنا gaṛe murde ukhāṛnā (H) v. To renew old grievances; to stir up hot embers.

گز gaz (P) n.m. A yard measure; a ramrod; an iron bar.

گزارش guzārish (P) n.f. A petition; request; representation; explanation; statement; payment.

گزارش کرنا guzārish karnā, v. To represent; to submit; to request.

گزارنا guzārnā, v. To pass (life); to bring to pass; to lay before; to state.

گزاره guzārah, n.m. Living; subsisting; a ferry; a toll; a passage; stay; abode.

گزاره کرنا guzārah karnā, v. To pass one's days; to subsist with difficulty.

گزاف gazāf (P) n.f. A vain or rash speech; a falsehood; a lie.

گزر guzar (P) n.f. Ingress and egress; a pass; a living; a passage; a road.

گزر جانا guzar jānā, v. To pass; to die; to expire.

گزرگاه guzar gāh, n.f. A passage; a ferry.

گزر گه عام guzar gāh-ĕ 'ām, n.f. A thoroughfare; a high-way.

گزران guzrān, n.f. Course of life; livelihood; living.

گزرنا guzarnā, v. To pass by; to go by; to die.

گزرانا guzrānnā, v. To submit; to put up.

گزشت guzasht (P) adj. Past; gone by.

گزشتنی guzashtani (P) adj. Passing; mortal.

گزشته guzashtah (P) adj. Past; elapsed; left.

گزشته را صلوة آینده را احتیاط guzashtah rā ṣalāt āyindah rā iḥtiyāṭ, maxim. Let by gones be by gones; the past is gone think of the future.

گزک gazak (P) n.f. A relish; a sweetmeat made of sesamum and sugar.

گزند gazand (P) n.m. Injury; loss; harm; misfortune; calamity; mischief.

گزیده gazidah (P) adj. Stung; bitten.

گزیده guzidah (P) adj. Selected; chosen.

گزیر guzir (P) n.m. Escape; remedy; help.

گزین guzin (P) adj. Choosing; selecting; preferring; adopting (used in *comps.* as in خلوت گزین <u>kh</u>alwat guzin, preferring seclusion).

گسار gusār (P) adj. Taking away; dissipating; removing (used in *comps.* as in, غم گسار gam gusār, taking away grief; a sympathiser).

گسائیں gusā'in (H) n.m. A saint, a holy man; caste of Brahman; a title of respect.

گستاخ gustā<u>kh</u> (P) adj. Arrogant; insolent; saucy; uncivil; cruel; rude; presumptuous; abrupt; impudent; audacious.

گستاخانه gustā<u>kh</u>ānah (P) adv. Rudely; arrogantly; insolently; impudently.

گستاخی gustā<u>kh</u>i (P) n.f. Rudeness; arrogance; insolence; sauciness; presumption.

گستاخی سے پیش آنا gustā<u>kh</u>i se pesh ānā, v. To be rude; to treat rudely.

گستاخی کرنا gustā<u>kh</u>i karnā, v. To presume; to be arrogant; to behave impudently.

گستاخی معاف gustākhi mu'āf, intj. Pardon me! pardon my rudeness.

گستر gustar (P) adj. Spreading; strewing; scattering; dispensing (used in comps. as in عدالت گستر a'dālat gustar, one who dispenses justice).

گستری gustari (P) n.f. Spreading.

گسستگی gusistagi (P) n.f. Breaking; fracture; interruption.

گسل gusil (P) adj. Destroyer; killer (used in comps. as in, جاں گسل jān gusil).

گشت gasht (P) n.f. The beat or round of a watchman or a postman; touring; going round; a stroll; a walk.

گشت پھرنا ، کرنا ، لگانا ، مارنا gasht phirnā, karnā, lagānā, mārnā, v. To go round; to patrol; to keep watch.

گشت ناچنا gasht nāchnā, v. To dance before the marriage procession.

گشتی gashtī (P) adj. Turning round; circulating.

گشتی چٹھی، مراسلہ gashti chiṭṭhi, murāsalah, n.f./m. A circular letter.

گشتی ملازم gashti mulāzim, n.m. Itinerating official.

گف gaf, adj. Closely woven; of close texture; stout.

گفتار guftār (P) n.f. Speech; discourse; saying; speaking.

گفتگو guftgū (P) n.f. Conversation; discourse; dialogue; chit-chat.

گفت و شنید guft-ŏ shunīd (P) n.f. Conversation; discourse; mutual talk; debate; controversy; contention.

گل gul (P) n.m. A rose; a flower; an issue; ornament; the snuff of a candle or lamp; brand; a mark made by burning; the burnt tobacco left on the tile of a ḥuqqah after smoking.

گل اشرفی gul-ĕ ashrafī, n.m. The marigold.

گل افشاں gul afshān, adj. Scattering rose: strewed with flowers.

گل اندام gul andam, adj. Slender; delicate; beautiful.

گل اورنگ gul-ĕ aurang, n.m. A kind of marigold.

گل بانگ gul bang, n.f. The notes of a nightingale; fame; rumour; good news; the war-cry; loud shouts.

گل بدن gul badan, adj. Delicate; graceful; having rose-like soft body. n.m. A kind of silk cloth.

گل برگ gul barg, n.m. A rose leaf.

گل بکاؤلی gul bakāoli, n.m. A sweet-scented white flower.

گل بوٹا gul būṭā, n.m. Flowers and plants.

گل پوش gul posh, adj. Covered with flowers.

گل پیادہ gul piyādah, n.m. A species of rose without smell; a wild rose.

گل پیرہن gul pairahan, adj. A delicate person.

گل تراش gul tarāsh, n.m. Snuffers; a gardener's scissors for cutting roses.

گل تراشنا gul tarāshnā, v. To snuff a candle.

گل جعفری gul-e ja'farī, n.m. Tagetes patula.

گل جھاڑنا gul jhāṛnā, v. To flick the ash (of a cigarette etc.)

گل چاندنی gul chāndnī, n.m. The moon flower.

گل چشم gul chashm, adj. Afflicted with albugo; albugineous.

گل چہرہ gul chihrā, adj. Rosy faced.

گل چھرے اڑانا gul chhaṛre uṛānā, v. To live expensively; to be enjoying life.

گل چیں gul chīn, n.m. A flower-gatherer; a gardener; a florist.

گل خطمی gul-ĕ khaṭmi, n.m. Marsh-mallow flower.

گل خیرا gul khairā, n.m. Chinese and Persian hollyhick; the gilly flower.

گل دان gul dān, n.m. A flower pot; a flower vase.

گل داؤدی gul-ĕ dāūdi, n.m. Chrysanthemum indicum.

گلدستہ gul dastah, n.m. A nosegay; a bouquet.

گل دوپہر gul-e dopahar, n.m. The marvel of Peru.

گل دم gul dum, n.f. Nightingale.

گل رخ gul rukh, adj. Rosy-cheeked.

گل رعنا gul-ĕ ra'nā, n.m. A beautiful delicate-scented rose.

گل رنگ gul rang, adj. Red; rosy.

گل‌رو gul rū, adj. Rosy cheeked.

گل ریز gul rez, adj. Shedding flowers. n.f. A kind of firework.

گل زار gul zār, n.m. A bed of roses; a garden; a well-populated town.

گل ستاں ، گلستاں gul sitān, gulistān, n.m. A rose garden.

گل سرسبد gul-ĕ sarsabad, n.m. The best flower.

گل سورنجاں gul-ĕ suranjān, n.m. The flower of the hermodactyl plant.

گل سوسن gul-ĕ sosan, n.m. A lily.

گل شبو gul-ĕ shabbū, n.m. A tube rose; a flower budding at night.

گلشن gulshan, n.m. A rose or flower garden.

گل صد برگ gul-ĕ ṣad barg, n.m. The hundred leaved rose; the sun.

گل عباسی gul-ĕ 'abbāsi, n.m. Mitabilis jalopa

گل عذار gul 'azār, adj. Rosy-cheeked.

گل فام gul fām, adj. Red coloured; rosy-faced.

گل فرنگ gul-ĕ farang, n.m. vinca rosea.

گل فروش gul farosh, n.m. Flower-seller; a florist.

گل قند gul qand, n.m. Conserve of roses; candied roses.

گل کاٹنا gul kāṭnā, v. To snuff a candle.

گل کاری gul kāri, n.f. Flowering; figured work; painting of flowers; embroidery.

گل کرنا gul karnā, v. To put out (lamp); to extinguish.

گل کھانا gul khānā, v. To be cauterised or to cauterise oneself; to burn oneself with heated piece of coin as a proof of love (a custom among lovers).

گل کھلانا gul khilānā, v. To sow dissention; to cause a disturbance.

گل کھلنا gul khilnā, v. To open (a bud); to be betrayed; happening of an unexpected thing.

گل کیش gul kesh, n.m. The coxcomb.

گل گشت gul gasht, n.m. Walking in a gardan.

گل گون gul gūn, adj. Rosy; roseate; rose coloured.

گل گونہ gul gūnah, n.m. A cosmetic; face powder.

گل گیر gul gir, n.m. Pickwick; snuffers.

گل لالہ gul-ĕ lālah, n.m. The poppy flower; a tulip.

گل مخمل gul-ĕ makhmal, n.m. Globe amaranth.

گل مہندی gul mehndi, n.m. The balsan.

گل میخ gul mekh, n.f. A stud, a nail.

گل نار، گلنار *gul nār*, *n.m.* The pomegranate flower; scarlet (colour).

گل ھزارہ *gul-ĕ hazārah*, *n.m.* The double poppy.

گل ھونا *gul honā*, *v.* To be extinguished; to go out (a lamp).

گل **gil** (P) *n.f.* Earth; clay; mud.

گل ارمنی *gil-ĕ armanī*. *n.f.* Armenian bole.

گل حکمت *gil ḥikmat*, *n.f.* Closing with mud the mouth of a vessel containing a metal or stone for killing before placing it in the fire.

گل در گل کرنا *gil dar gil karnā*, *v.* To throw earth on the graves of the dead.

گل **gal** (H) *n.m.* (Contraction of گال *gāl* and گلا *galā*) Throat; neck; fishing hook; cheek.

گل بیاں ڈالنا *gal baiyāṅ ḍālnā*, *v.* To throw the arms round the neck of a person; to embrace.

گل بھڑا *gal phaṛā*, *n.m.* The jaw; gill (of a fish).

گل پھولا *gal phūlā*, *adj.* Chubby cheeked.

گل پھیڑ *gal pheṛ*, *n.m.* Swelling of the glands of the neck.

گل تکیہ *gal takyah*, *n.m.* A small pillow to be kept under the cheeks.

گل تنی *gal tanī*, *n.f.* The rope connected with the yoke on the bullocks necks.

گل جندڑا *gal jandṛā*, *n.m.* A sling; a handkerchief used as a sling for the arm.

گل جوٹ کرنا *gal joṭ karnā*, *v.* To yoke the bullocks together.

گل خپ *gal khap*, *n.m.* Boxing; struggling together.

گل خور *gal khor*, *n.f.* A horse's halter.

گل مالا *gal mālā*, *n.f.* A garland.

گل مچھے *gal muchchhe*, *n.m.* Long curled whiskers.

گلا **galā** (H) *n.m.* Throat; neck; voice; collar.

گلا آنا *galā ānā*, *v.* To have sore throat; to have inflamed tonsils.

گلا اٹھانا *gala uṭhana*, *v.* To apply acrid substances to the uvula of a child for cold or cough.

گلا بند ھونا *galā band hona*, *v.* To be choked.

گلا بیٹھنا *galā baithnā*, *v.* To be hoarse.

گلا پکڑنا *galā pakaṛnā*, *v.* To seize one by the throat; to feel a burning in the throat.

گلا پھاڑنا *galā phāṛnā*, *v.* To scream; to shriek.

گلا پھیرنا *galā phernā*, *v.* To modulate the voice in singing.

گلا پھولنا *galā phūlnā*, *v.* To have a swelling of the throat.

گلا دبانا *galā dabānā*, *v.* To strangle; to suffocate; to seize by the neck.

گلا کاٹنا *gala kāṭnā*, *v.* To cut the throat; to defraud; to oppress.

گلا گھوٹنا ، مسلنا *galā ghoṭnā*, *masalnā*, *v.* To choke; to throttle; to squeeze; to hold by the throat.

گلے باندھنا *gale bandhnā*, *v.* To accuse one falsely; to fix an accusation wrongly on.

گلے پڑنا *gale paṛnā*, *v.* To seek the friendship of one who is averse from it; to hang upon one; to importune; to be obligatory or incombent on; to be an incumberance on.

گلے سے اتارنا *gale se utārnā*, *v.* To shake off; to swallow.

گلے کا ڈھولنا *gale kā ḍholnā*, *n.m.* An amulet; a burden.

گلے کا ھار ھونا *gale kā hār honā*, *v.* To pursue one persistently; to plague;

to importune; to seek and persist in a quarrel or dispute.

گلے لگانا gale lagānā, v. To embrace.

گلے لگنا ، ملنا gale lagnā, milnā, v. To hang upon the neck of; to embrace.

گلے میں اٹکنا gale meṅ aṭaknā, v. To be choked.

گلا gallā (H) n.m. A pocket; cash box.

گلاب gulāb (P) n.m. The rose; the rose water.

گلاب پاش gulāb pāsh, n.m. A bottle from which the rose water is sprinkled.

گلاب پاشی gulāb pāshi, n.f. Sprinkling the rose water.

گلاب جامن gulāb jāman, n.f. A kind of sweetmeat.

گلابی gulābi (P) adj. Rosy; rose-scented. n.m. Bottle; flagon.

گلابی آنکھیں gulābi ānkheṅ, n.f. The eyes red with the effect of drinking.

گلابی جاڑا gulābi jāṛā, n.m. The spring season; mild weather.

گلابی رنگ gulābi rang, n.m. Rose-colour; pink colour.

گلاس gilās (E) n.m. A glass; a tumbler; a mug.

گلا سڑا gala saṛā (H) adj. Rotten.

گلال gulāl (H) n.m. A red powder thrown over one another at ہولی Holi.

گلال اڑانا gulāl uṛānā, v. To throw red powder at one.

گلالی gulāli (H) adj. Of red colour; dyed with گلال gulāl.

گلانا galānā (H) v. To dissolve; to waste away; to squander; to soften; to cause to roti to reduce or subdue the body by mortification or austerities.

گلاؤ ، گلاوٹ galuo, galāwat (H) n.f m. Solution: dissolving.

گلاؤ galā'ū (H) adj. Soluble; septical; melter; dissolver.

گلٹی gilṭi (H) n.f. A hard grandular swelling; a tumour; a gland.

گلک gullak (H) n.f. A small cash box; a treasure pot.

گلگل galgal (H) n.m. A citron; name of a bird; a mixture of lime and linseed oil forming gurgling sound; a kind of mortar impenetrable to water.

گلگلا gulgulā (H) n.m. Sweet cakes fried in butter.

گلگلانا gulgulānā (H) v. To soften; to mollify.

گلگلاہٹ gulgulāhaṭ (H) n.f. Softness.

گلنا galnā (H) v. To melt; to dissolve; to waste; to be dissolved; to be wasted away.

گلو gulu (P) n.m. The throat; the windpipe; the gullet; neck.

گلوبند gulū band, n.m. A neck cloth; a muffler.

گلو گیر gulū gīr (P) adj. Seizing by the throat; any acrid food or drink that affects the throat and causes hoarseness.

گلو gilao (H) n.f. A medicinal creeping herb: menropermum glabrum.

گلوری gilauri (H) n.f. Betel leaf prepared and folded up.

گلہ gilah (P) n.m. Complaint; lamentation; blame; reproach.

گلہ کرنا gilah karnā, v. To complain.

گلہ gallah (P) n.m. A flock; a herd; a drove.

گلہ بان gallah ban, n.m. A shepherd; herdsman; pastor.

گلہ بانی gallah bāni, n.f. Flock-keeping.

گلہری gulahrī, gilahrī (H) n.f. A squirrel.

گلی gali (H) n.f. A lane; an alley.

گلی کوچہ gali kūchah, n.m. A narrow lane; lanes and alleys.

گلی گلی gali gali, adv. From street to street; from lane to lane.

گلیاں چھاننا galyāṅ chhānnā, v. To wander about from lane to lane.

گلی gulli, gilli (H) n.f. A span; a cob of Indian corn; a wooden plaything, played with a stick.

گلی ڈنڈا gulli ḍaṅḍā, n.m. Kit-cat; the game of tip-cat.

گلی ڈنڈا کھیلنا gulli ḍaṅḍā khelnā, v. To play at tip-cat; to idle away one's time.

گلیم gilim (P) n.f. A blanket; a woollen cloth.

گم gum (P) adj. Lost; missing; wanting; distracted.

گم راہ gum rāh, adj. Astray; lost; abandoned; erring; wandering; wicked; depraved.

گم راہ کرنا gum rāh karnā, v. To lead astray; to ruin; to mislead; to seduce; to bewilder; to lose.

گم راہ ہونا gum rāh honā, v. To lose one's way; to go astray; to apostatise.

گم راہی gum rāhi, n.f. Erring; deviation; seduction.

گم سم gum sum, adj. Still; silent.

گم شدہ gum shudah, adj. Lost; missing.

گم کرنا gum karnā, v. To lose; to hide.

گم کردہ راہ gum kardah rāh, adj. One who has lost his way; one who is led astray.

گم گشتہ gum gashtah, adj. Lost; wandering.

گم نام gum nām, adj. Obscure; anonymous; nameless; wanting name; unknown; ignoble; inglorious.

گم ہونا gum honā, v. To get lost.

گماشتہ gumāshtah (P) n.m. An agent, a factor; a manager; a representative.

گمان gumān (P) n.m. Doubt; supposition; conjecture; pride; opinion; fancy; notion; imagination; suspicion; distrust.

گمان کرنا gumān karnā, v. To suppose; to doubt; to suspect; to imagine; to fancy; to show pride; to be conceited.

گمبھیر gambhīr (S) adj. Deep; unfathomed; prudent; thoughtful; serious; sedate; grave. n.m. A kind of ulcer.

گملا gamlā (H) n.m. A flower pot; a sort of a large deep pan.

گن gun (H) n.m. Quality; attribute; merit; skill; understanding; virtue.

گن گانا gun gānā, v. To praise; to applaud; to sing the virtues or excellent qualities (of).

گن ماننا gun mānnā, v. To be grateful (for); to acknowledge a favour or benefit.

گن وان gun wān, adj. Skilful; accomplished.

گنا gunā (H) adj. Times; fold (used in comps. as, سو گنا sau gunā, a hundred fold).

گنا gannā (H) n.m. Sugar-cane.

گنے کی پھاندی ganne ki phāndi, n.f. A bundle of sugar-cane.

گنانا ginānā (H) v. See گنوانا ginwānā.

گناہ gunāh (P) n.m. A Fault; crime; sin; guilt.

گناہ بخشنا gunāh bakhshnā, v. To forgive sins; to pardon.

گناہ بے لذت gunāh-ĕ be lazzat, n.m. A sin from which no pleasure is drawn.

گناہ صغیرہ gunāh-ĕ saghirah, n.m. A small sin; a pardonable sin.

گناہ کبیرہ gunāh-ĕ kabīrah, n.m. A grievous sin or offence.

گناہ کرنا gunāh karnā, v. To commit a sin; to sin; to offend.

گناہ گار gunāh gār, n.m. A sinner; a criminal; a culprit.

گناہ گار ٹھہرانا gunāh gār ṭhahrānā, v. To condemn; to hold guilty.

گناہ گاری gunāh gārī, n.f. Sinfulness; guiltiness; loss; mulct; fine; penalty.

گنبد gumbad (P) n.m. A dome; an arch; a vault; a cupola; a tower.

گنبد دار gumbad dār, adj. Domed; vaulted; arched.

گنبد کی آواز gumbad ki āwāz, n.f. Echo of a dome; requittal; redounding of one's evil deeds on himself.

گنت gint (S) n.f. The science of arithmetic; counting.

گنتی gintī (H) n.f. Numbering; reckoning; counting; computing; muster; muster-roll; the first or the last day of a month.

گنتی کے gintī ke, adj. That can be counted; few.

گنتی گنوانا gintī ginwānā, v. To make a false return.

گنتی میں لانا gintī meṅ lānā, v. To count; to reckon; to take into account; to care for.

گٹھیا ، گنٹھیا gaṅṭhiyā, gaṭhiyā (H) n.f. Rheumitism.

گنج gaṅj (P) n.m. A granary; heap; mart; market; treasure; treasury.

گنج بخش gaṅj bakhsh, adj. Wealth-bestowing; very generous; liberal; profuse; extravagant.

گنج شائگاں gaṅj-ĕ shā'igāṅ, n.m. A big treasury; a thing worthy of presentation to kings.

گنج شہیداں gaṅj-ĕ shahīdāṅ, n.m. The burial place of martyrs.

گنج قارون gaṅj-ĕ qārūn, n.m. The wealth of Croesus; countless riches.

گنج gaṅj (H) n.m. Baldness; bald-headedness.

گنجا gaṅjā (H) n.m. A bald man.

گنجان guṅjān, adj. Thick; compact; dense.

گنجانی guṅjānī, n.f. Thickness; denseness.

گنجائش guṅjā'ish (P) n.f. Capacity; room; gain; profit; revenue capacity of a village.

گنجفہ gaṅjifah (P) n.m. A pack of cards; a game of cards.

گنجفہ باز gaṅjifah bāz, n.m. A card player; a trickster; a cheat.

گنجلک guṅjulak (H) n.f. A crease; a knot; complication.

گنجور gaṅjūr, gaṅj-war (P) n.m. Treasurer; the owner of a treasure.

گنجی gaṅjī (H) n.f. A bald woman.

گنجینہ gaṅjīnah (P) n.m. A treasure; a magazine.

گند gaṅd (H) n.f. Stink; filth; odour; smell.

گند اُچھالنا gaṅd uchhālnā, v. To abuse; to use bad language.

گند کٹنا gaṅd kaṭnā, v. To get rid of trouble; to get relief.

گندک ، گندھک gaṅdak, gandhak (H) n.f. Sulphur; brimstone.

گندک کا تیل gandak kā tel, n.m. Sulphuric acid.

گندگی gaṅdagī (P) n.f. Stink; odour; rottenness; putrifaction.

گندگی پھیلانا gaṅdagī phailānā, v. To scatter filth; to use bad language; to make a place dirty.

گندم gaṅdum (P) n.m. Wheat.

گندم از گندم بروید جو زجو gaṅdum az gaṅdum baroyad, jau zi jau, prov. As you sow so shall you reap; the son takes after the father.

گندم گوں **gandum gūn**, *adj.* Wheat coloured; brown; dark brown; tanny.

گندم نما جو فروش **gandum numā jau farosh**, *adj.* A cheat; a hypocrite.

گندمی **gandumī** (P) *adj.* Brownish; of wheat colour.

گندنا **gandnā** (H) *n.m.* A leek; *allium porrum*; a shrub of wild growth resembling garlic;

گنده **gandah** (P) *adj.* Fetid; stinking; rotting; putrid; filthy; dirty.

گنده بروزه **gandah birozah**, *n.m.* A gum obtained from the pine tree; rosin or resin; a kind of ointment.

گنده دهن **gandah dahan**, *adj.* Having a stinking breath.

گندھار **gandhār** (S) *n.m.* The name of a musical mode.

گندھرب **gandharb** (S) *n.m.* A celestial musician; a singer; a kind of bird; a beautiful lady; a sweet melody.

گندھرب بیاه **gandharb biyāh**, *n.m.* A marriage performed without the usual ceremonies.

گندھنا **gundhnā** (H) *v.* To be kneaded; to be plaited.

گندھوانا **gundhwānā** (H) *v.* To cause to knead; to cause to plait; to cause to bread.

گندھی **gandhı** (H) *n.m.* A perfumer; a green bug.

گندی **gandi**, *adj.* Dirty (woman), stinking;- filthy.

گنڈا **gunḍā** (H) *n.m.* A rogue; a rascal; a scoundrel; a black-guard.

گنڈا **ganḍā** (H) *n.m.* Knotted string tied round the neck as a charm; a ring; a circle; a kind of horse-collar; the number four; four کوڑی *kauṛī*; four pices.

گنڈاسا **ganḍāsā** (H) *n.m.* A sort of an axe; a pole axe; a chopper; a battle-axe.

گنڈی **ganḍī** (H) See گانڈو *gāndū*.

گنڈیری **ganḍerī** (H) *n.f.* Sugar-cane cut into small pieces; cut sugar-cane or its knots.

گنگ **gung** (P) *adj.* Dumb; mute; silent. *n.f.* Muteness; dumbness.

گنگ ، گنگا **gang, gangā** (H) *n.f.* A river; a stream; name of a river in India; the Ganges.

گنگا اشنان **gangā ashnān**, *n.m.* Bathing in the Ganges.

گنگا جل **gangā jal**, *n.m.* Water of the Ganges; holy water.

گنگا جلی **gangā jalī**, *n.m.* A vessel in which the Ganges water is kept.

گنگا جلی اٹھانا **gangā jali uṭhānā**, *v.* To swear by the holy water of the Ganges.

گنگا جمنی **gangā jamni**, *adj.* Mixed; made of gold and silver; made of brass and copper.

گنگا جمنی دال **gangā jamnī dāl**, *n.f.* A dish of two pulses mixed together.

گنگا ماتا **gangā mātā**, *n.f.* Holy mother Ganges.

گنگا نہانا **gangā nahānā**, *v.* To be freed from sin or liability.

گنگا شلغم **gangā shalgham**, *n.m.* Large turnips grown on the Ganges.

گنگنا **gungunā** (H) *adj.* Mılk warm; tepid.

گنگنانا **gungunānā** (H) *v.* To hum; to sing softly; to mumble; to murmur; to snuffle.

گنگناہٹ **gungunāhaṭ** (H) *n.f.* A nasal sound; a hum.

گن گن کر **gin gin kar** (H) *adv.* Counting one by one; with difficulty.

گن گن کر دن کاٹنا **gin gin kar din kāṭnā**, *v.* To pass one's days with great difficulty; to live a hard life.

گن گن کر قدم رکھنا **gin gin kar qadam rakhnā**, *v.* To move very cautiously and slowly.

گنا ginnā (H) v. To count; to calculate; to reckon; to compute; to multiply.

گنا gunna (H) v. To put in practice.

گنوار ganwār (H) n.m. A countryman; a villager; boor; clown; churl; rustic; peasant; low-bred;ignorant.

گنوار پن ganwār pan, n.m. Rudeness; rusticity; stupidity.

گنوار کا لٹھ ganwār kā lath, n.m. A fool; an arrant fool.

گنوارو ganwārū (H) adj. Rude; rustic.

گنواری ganwāri (H) n.f. A country woman.

گنوانا ganwānā(H) v. To lose; to throw away. to get ride of; to discharge; to spend in vain; to waste; to squander; to trifle.

گنوانا ginwānā (H) v. To cause to count; to cause to reckon.

گنہ gunah (P) n.m. (contraction of گناہ gunāh) sin; crime; guilt.

گنی guni (H) adj. Virtuous; meritorious; accomplished; skilful; talented.

گنیا gunya (H) n.m. A mason's or carpenter's square; a tri-square; the multiplicand.

گو gū (H) n.m. Excrement; filth; ordure.

گو اچھالنا gū uchhalna, v. To bring disgrace upon oneself.

گو کرنا gū karnā, v. To dirty; to spoils.

گو کھانا gū khānā, v. To eat filth; to do a bad or shameful act; to tell a lie; to be addicted to bribery.

گو موت کرنا gū mūt karnā, v. To nurse a child.

گو go (P) adj. Saying; telling; relating; (used in comps. as قصہ گو qissah go, a tale-teller). conj. In spite of; notwithstanding that.

گو کہ go keh, adv. Although; as if; however.

گو مگو go mago, n.m. Hesitation; reluctance; unwillingness.

گوار gawar (P) adj. Pleasing; agreeable, (in cōmps. as خوشگوار khushgawar, agreeable; ناگوار nā gawar, disagreeable; unpleasant).

گوار gawār (H) n.m. A kind of Indian corn.

گوارا gawara (P) adj. Palatable: digestible; agreeable; pleasant; acceptable; tasty; nice.

گوارا کرنا gāwara karnā, v. To bear; to toleratei to endure, to digest.

گوالا gwāla (H) n.m. A cowherd; a milkman.

گوالن gwiān (H) n.f. A female cowherd; a milkmaid.

گوانا gawana (H) v. To cause to sing.

گواہ gawah (P) n.m. A witness.

گواہ بنانا gawāh banānā, v. To name a person as a witness; to forge evidence.

گواہ تعلیمی gawāh-ĕ ta'limi, n.m. A tutored witness.

گواہ چشم دید gawah-ĕ chashm did, n.m. An eye-witness.

گواہ حاشیہ gawāh-ĕ hāshiyah, n.m. An attesting witness.

گواہ سماعی gawāh-ĕ samā'i, n.m. A hearsay witness.

گواہ کرنا gawāh karnā, v. To make one a witness.

گواہ مدعی gawāh-ĕ mudda'i, n.m. Witness for the prosecution.

گواہ مدعیٰ علیہ gawāh-ĕ mudd'ā-'alaih, n.m. Witness for the defence.

گواہی gawāhi (P) n.f. Evidence; testimony.

گواہی دینا gawāhi dena, v. To bear testimony; to give evidence; to depose; to witness.

گوبر gobar (H) n.m. Cow-dung.

گوبری **gobrī** (H) *n.f.* Plaster made with cow-dung.

گوبری کرنا **gobrī harnā**, *v.* To plaster a wall or floor.

گوبھی **gobhī** (H) *n.f.* A cauliflower; a cabbage.

گوپال **gopāl** (H) *n.m.* H cowherd; a dairy-man.

گوپیا ، گوپھن **gopiyā, gophan** (H) *n.f.* A sling used for throwing stones to drive away the birds; a catapult.

گوپی **gopī**, (H) *n.f.* A milkmaid.

گوت ، گوتر **got, gotar** (H) *n.m.* Parentage; linage; race; pedigree; stock of a family; subdivision of a tribe or caste; tribe; population.

گوتھنا **gūthnā** (H) *v.* To plait; to thread; to string; to stitch; to spit or put on a spit.

گوتی **goti** (H) *adj.* One of the same stock or family; a relative.

گوٹ **guṭ** (H) *n.f.* The hem of a garment; a counter; piece or man at chess, etc. feast; entertainment; a company; a village.

گوٹا **goṭā** (H) *n.m.* Gold or silver lace; a narrow fillet or brocade.

گوجر **gūjar** (H) *n.m.* A cowherd; a dairyman.

گوجرا **gojrā** (H) *n.m.* A mixture of wheat and barley.

گجری ، گوجری **gujrī, gūjri** (H) *n.f.* The wife of a گوجر *gūjar.*

گوچنی **gochnī** (H) *n.f.* A field of wheat and gram sown together; a mixture of wheat and gram.

گود **god** (H) *n.f.* The lap; embrace; adoption; a present made to the bride at different ceremonies.

گود بھری **god bharī**, *adj.* Blessed with a child in arms.

گود بھرنا **god bharnā**, *v.* To give presents to a bride.

گود دینا **god denā**, *v.* To give one's child to another to adopt.

گود کھلانا **god khilānā**, *v.* To carry in one's arms a child; to be the mother of a child; to nurse or bring up a child.

گود لینا **god lenā**, *v.* To adopt (a child).

گود میں بیٹھنا **god men baiṭhnā**, *v.* To leap into one's arms.

گودا **gūdā** (H) *n.m.* Brain; kernel; marrow; pith; crumb (of a loof); gist; substance; pop; pulp.

گودے کی ھڈی **gūde ki haddi**, *n.f.* Marrow bone.

گودام **gudām**, (*corr.* from the English) *n.m.* Godown; storehouse; warehouse; a heap.

گودڑ **gūdaṛ** (H) *n.m.* Old tottered clothes; rags; rubbish; old cotton; a kind of patched covering.

گودڑی **godaṛī** (H) See گدڑی *gudṛi.*

گودی **godī** (H) *n.f.* Lap; bosom; embrace; pier; wharf.

گور **gŏr** (P) *n.f.* A tomb; grave.

گور غریباں **gor-ĕ gharibān**, *n.f.* Burial ground for strangers and the poor.

گور کا منہ جھانک کر آنا **gor kā munh jhānk kar ānā**, *v.* To recover from a very serious illness; to escape from the jaws of death.

گور کن **gor kan**, *n.m.* A grave digger.

گور و کفن **gor-ŏ kafon**, *n.m.* Funeral ceremonies; obsequies.

بے گور **be gor**, *adj.* Unintered; unburied; graveless.

در گور کرنا **dar gor karnā**, *v.* To inter one; to entomb; to bury a person.

گورخر **gor khar** (P) *n.m.* A wild ass; a zebra.

گورستاں **gorristān** (P) *n.m.* Graveyard.

گورا **gorā** (H) *adj.* Fair; white complexioned; beautiful. *n.m.* A European soldier; a European.

گورا چٹا **gorā chittā**, *adj.* Handsome; beautlful; red and white.

گوراده **gorādih**, *n.m.* Land surrounding a village.

گورکھ دھندا **gorakhdhandā** (H) *n.m.* A puzzle-lock; distraction; alarm; disquietude.

گورو **gorū**, *n.m.* See گرو **gurū**.

گوری **gaurī** (H) *n.f.* A musical mode.

گوری **gorī** (H) *adj.* & *n.f.* White; a beautiful woman; a beauty.

گوریا **goryā, gorayyā** (H) *n.f.* A kind of bird.

گوڑنا **goṛnā** (H) *v.* To dig; to scrape; to excavate.

گوز **goz** (P) *n.m.* A fert; flatus; breaking of wind.

گوز شتر سمجھنا **goz-ĕ shutr samajhnā**, *v.* To disregard; to treat lightly; to set at naught.

گوز مارنا **goz mārnā**, *v.* To fert; to break wind.

گوسالا **gausālā** (H) *n.f.* A cowshed.

گوساله **gosālah** (P) *n.m.* A calf.

گوسائیں **gosā'īn** (H) A holy person; a devotee; a cowherd.

گوسفند ، گوسپند **gosfand, gospand** (P) *n.m.* A sheep; a goat.

گوش **gosh** (P) *n.m.* The ear.

گوش بر آواز ہونا **gosh bar āwāz honā**, *v.* To be in a state of expectency; to be expecting some news.

گوش گزار کرنا **gosh guzar karnā**, *v.* To inform; to report; to bring to notice.

گوش گزار ہونا **gosh guzār honā**, *v.* To be informed, to be heard.

گوش مالی **gosh mālī**, *n.f.* Pulling or twisting the ears; chestizement; rebuke.

گوشت **gosht** (P) *n.m.* Meat; flesh.

گوشت خور **gosht khor**, *adj.* Carnivorous; flesh-eating.

گوشت سے ناخن جدا ہونا **gosbt se nākhūn judā honā**, *v.* To give up near relatives; to disown relatives.

گوشت کا لوتھڑا **gosht kā lothṛā**, *n.m.* A lump of flesh; a fat man.

گوشت ناخن ہونا **gosht nākhun honā**, *v.* To be intimate friends; to be on very good terms,

گوش واره **gosh wārah** (P) *u.m.* An earing an embroidered cloth worn in the turban; an abstract of an account; heading of a register or table.

گوشه **goshah** (P) *n.m.* A corner; an angle; a closet; ceil; retirement; privacy; side; the end; horn (of a bow).

گوشه دار **goshah dār**, *adj.* Angular; having corners.

گوشۂ چشم **goshah-ĕ chashm**, *n.m.* The corner of the eye.

گوشۂ عافیت **goshah-ĕ 'āfiyyat**, *n.m.* A secluded corner, a corner of comfort; a refuge.

گوشۂ کمان **goshah-ĕ kamān**, *n.m.* The horn of the bow.

گوشه گزین **goshah guzin**, *adj.* Fond of retirement; seculsion minded.

گوشه گیر **goshah gīr**, *adj.* Retired; secluded; a hermit; recluse.

گوشه گیری **goshah girī**, *n.f.* Retirement; life ef a hermit.

گوشه نشین **gothah nashın**, *adj.* Retired; solitary; recluse.

گوشه نشینی **goshah nashīnī**, *n.f.* A life of seclusion and retirement.

گوکھرو **gokhrū** (H) *n.m.* A prickly shrub; a thorn; corn; narrow twisted silver or gold lace; fretted lace; a pendant; an earring; bells tied round the ankle; an ornament for the wrist; a joint; an iron crow's feet thrown on the ground to check advance of cavalry.

گوگرد **gūgird** (P) *n.m.* Sulphur; brimstone.

گوگرد احمر **gūgird-ĕ aḥmar**, *n.m.* Red sulphur, philosopher's stone.

گوگل **gūgal** (H) *n.m.* Name of a gum; a fragrant gum-resin.

گول **gol** (H) *adj.* Round; circular; ring-shaped; globular; vague; indefinite.

گول بات **gal bāt**, *n.f.* A vague or ambiguous expression; an entangled or doubtful matter; a vague speech.

گول سا **gol sa**, *adj.* Roundish.

گول گول ، گول مول **gol gol, gol mol**, *adj.* Dubious vague; round; roudish.

گول مول کہنا **gol mol kahnā**, *v.* To be vague in speech; double-meaning talk.

گول مال **gol māl**, *n.m.* Embezzlement; confusion; mess.

گول مال کرنا **gol māl karnā**, *v.* To mince matters; to make a mess (of); to embezzle.

گولا **golā** (H) *n.m.* A large ball; a cannon ball; a bomb; a cocoanut; the curb of a well; a round beam; colic; a swelling; a large jar of earth for grain, a pier.

گولا انداز **golā andāz**, *n.m.* A bombardier; a cannonader; a gunner.

گولا چلانا **golā chalānā**, *v.* To cannonade; to bombard.

گولا مارنا **golā marnā**, *v.* To cannonade.

گولائی **golā'ī** (H) *n.f.* Roundness.

گولر **gūlar** (H) *n.m.* A wild fig; a pad (of cotton).

گولک **golak** (H) *n.f.* See گلک **gullak**.

گولی **goli** (H) *n.f.* A bullet; a ball; a marble; a pill; a globule; a gun shot.

گولی چلانا **goli chalanā**, *v.* To charge a gun; to fire a gun.

گولی لگنا **goli lagnā**, *v.* To be shot; to be struck by a bullet.

گولی مارنا **gali mārnā**, *v.* To shoot one down.

گولیں کیھلنا **goliyāṅ khelnā**, *v.* To play marble.

گومڑا **gomṛā** (H) *n.m.* A boil; a swelling; a hump.

گومڑا پڑنا **gomṛā paṛnā**, *v.* To have a swelling.

گوں **gūṅ** (P) *n.m.* Colour; tint; kind; species; mode (used in *comps.* as in دگر گوں **digar gūṅ**, of another colour; or گلگوں **gulgūn**, rose-colour).

گوں **gauṅ** (P) *n.f.* Want; need; advantage; occasion; opportunity; benefit.

گوں کا یار **gauṅ kā yār**, *n.m.* A self-interested or selfish person; a time-server.

گوں نکالنا **gauṅ nikālnā**, *v.* To attain one's end; to serve one's purpose.

گونا **gaunā** (H) *n.m.* Bringing home a bride; consummation of the marriage; happiness.

گونا گوں **gūnā gūn** (P) *adj.* Of various colours; varied.

گونتھنا **gūnthnā** (H) *v.* See گوتھنا **gūthnā**.

گونج **gūnj** (H) *n.f.* Echo; resoundlng; hollow sound; roar; clasp; buzzing.

گونجنا **gūnjnā** (H) *v.* To echo; to roar; to resound; to clasp.

گوند **gonḍ** (H) *n.m.* Gum; gum arabic; a kind of sweetmeat.

گوند دانی **gond dāni**, *n.f.* Gum pot.

گوندھنا **gūndhnā** (H) *v.* To ! nead; to braid; to weave; to plait.

گوندی گوندنی gondi , gondni (H) *n.f.* The name of a tree and of its fruit resembling small gummy berry

گونگا ، گونگی gūngā, gūngi (H) *adj.* Dumb; mute.

گونہ gūnah (P) *n.m.* Colour; species; form; kind; sort.

گوہ goh (H) *n.f.* A lizard; an iguana; the Ganietic alligator.

گوہر gauhar (P) *n.m.* A pearl; a gem; a jawel; lustre of a gem or sword; essence; hidden virtue; nature; substance; descent.

گوہر افشاں gohar afshān, *adj.* Scattering pearls; eloquent.

گوہر بار gauhar bār, *adj.* Raining pearls or gems.

دوہر سنج ، شناس gauhar sanj , shanās, *adj.* Weighing or examining pearls.

گوئندہ go'indah (P) *n.m.* A speaker; an informer; a spy; an approver.

گوئی go'i (P) *n.f.* Speaking; telling; (in comp. as عیب دوئی 'āib go'i, fault-finding).

گوئے goe (P) *n.f.* A ball.

گوئے چوگان goe chaugān, *n.m.* A game of polo; the ball and the stick.

گوئے سبقت لے جانا goe shbqat le jānā, *v.* To excel; to surpass.

گوئیاں gūiyyāṅ (H) *n.f.* A partner at a game; a woman's female friend; a playmate.

گویا goyā, *adv.* As if; through; as it were.

گویا goyā (P) *adj.* Speaking; eloquent; conversible.

گویا gawayyā (H) *n.m.* A singer; a minstrel.

گویائی goyā'i (P) *n.f.* Eloquence; power of speech; command of a language.

گہ gah (P) *n.m.* (Contraction of گاہ gāh). Time; one time; place.

گھات ghāt (H) *n.f.* Aim; design; snare; ambuscade; ambush; opportune moment; opportunity; enmity; treachery; slaughter.

گھات تاکنا ghāt tāknā, *v.* To watch an opportunity (for); to look for an opportune moment.

گھات چلانا ghāt chalānā, *v.* To play a trick; to attack; to take unawares.

گھات میں بیٹھنا ghāt men baithnā, *v.* To waylay; to lurk; to lie in ambush.

گھاتک ghatak (H) *adj.* Murderous; cruel; evil; mischievous; injurious.

ںھاتی ، گھاتیا ghāti , ghātiyā (H) *adj.* Intent on taking one's life; deceitful treacherous; lurking.

گھاٹ ghāṭ (H) *n.m.* A landing place; a quay; wharf; ferry; ford; bathing place on a river side; a place for washing clothes on the bank of a river; the curve in the blade of a sword; a bride's skirt; loss; want.

گھاٹ گھاٹ کا پانی پینا ghāṭ ghāṭ kā pāni pinā, *v.* To see the world; to acquire wide experience; to be very much experienced.

گھاٹ مارنا ghāṭ mārnā, *v.* To smuggle dutiable goods.

گھاٹ مانجھی ghāṭ mānjhī, *n.m.* A ferry man.

گھاٹا ghāṭā (H) *n.m.* Loss; deficiency; scarcity; reduction; damages; abatement acclivity; ascent.

گھاٹا آٹھانا ، پڑنا ghāṭā uthānā , paṛnā, *v.* To suffer a loss; to fall in a venture.

گھاٹی ghāṭi (H) *n.f.* A mountain pass; a valley; a strait; a ravine. a custom-house holding vocal cords.

گھاس ghās (H) *n.f.* Grass; straw; foader; hay.

گھاس پات ghās pāt, *n.f.* Greens; sweepings.

گھاس پھوس ghās phūs, *n.m.* Straw; weeds.

گھاس کاٹنا ghās kāṭnā, v. To cut grass; to do a thing haphazardly or hurriedly.

گھاس کھانا ghās khānā, v. To graze; to eat hemp; to become mad; to lose one's wits or senses.

گھاس کھودنا ghās khodnā, v. To cut grass.

گھاگ ghāg (H) adj. Old; aged; experienced; sly; wily; shrewd; knowing.

گھاگھرا gaāghrā (H) n.m. A petticoat; a gown; a pigeon; the name of a river.

گھاگھرا پلٹن ghāghrā palṭan, n.f. Kilted soldiers; Highland regiment.

گھاگھس ghāghas (H) n.m. A kind of large fowl.

گھامڑ ghāmaṛ (H) adj. Simple; foolish dull; artless; blockhead.

گھان ghān (H) n.m. A batch; as much as is thrown at one time into a mill or frying pan.

گھان آتارنا ghān utārnā, v. To take out of a frying pan; to make ready.

گھان ڈالنا ghān ḍālnā, v. To throw into a frying pan; to begin to fry or grind.

گھانی ghāni (H) n.f. An oil press, a sugar mill, a sugarcane press; quantity to be ground or pressed at one time.

گھاؤ ghā'o (H) n.m. Wound; sore; cut.

گھاؤ بھرنا ghā'o bharnā, v. To heal (a sore or a wound).

گھاؤ کرنا gbā'o karnā, v. To inflict a wound; to wound one's feelings; to give a cut.

گھاؤ کھانا ghā'o khānā, v. To be wounded.

گھاؤ گھپ ghāo ghap, adj. Addicted to swallowing; living from hand to mouth; a spendthrift.

گھائی gha'ī (H) n.f. Cudgelling stratagem; fraud; a show fight with a sword; the angle between the branch and trunk of a tree; space of the root of the branch; the space at the angle or enclosed space at the junction of two fingers or toes; a hole of an oven; a blow with a cudgel; a set of five.

گھایل ghā'yal (H) adj. Wounded; hurt; smitten with love.

گھایل کرنا ghā'yal karnā, v. To inflict a wound; to smite with love.

گھبرانا ghabrānā (H) v. To be confounded; to be confused; to agitate; to be embarrased; to perplex; to confound,

گھبراہٹ ghabrāhaṭ (H) n.f. Perplexity; agitation; consternation; bewilderment; confusion; alarm; perturbation.

گھپ ghup (H) adj. Dark; hidden.

گھپ اندھیرا ghup andhdrā, n.m. Pitch dark

گھپلا ghaplā (H) n.m. Confusion; mess; disorder; jumble; error; complication; entanglement; duplicity; discrepancy (in accounts) unlawful attachment.

گھپلا پڑنا ghaplā paṛnā, v. To be thrown into confusion or disorder; occurrence of a mistake in accounts.

گھپلا ڈالنا ghaplā ḍālnā, v. To make a mess of; to confuse matters.

گھپنا ghupnā (H) v. To be pierced.

گھٹا ghaṭā (H) n.f. Cloudiness; gathering of clouds; dense black clouds; crowds; multitude; troops.

گھٹا آنا ، اٹھنا ، اُمنڈنا ، ہونا ghaṭā anā, uṭhnā, umaṅḍnā, honā, v. Gathering of black clouds in the horizon; to be overcast with black clouds; to be cloudy.

گھٹا چھانا ghaṭā chhānā, v. Lowering of clouds; over-spreading of the black clouds.

گھٹا ٹوپ ghatā ṭop, n.m. Covering of a پالکی pālkī or carriage adj. pitch dark.

گھٹانا ghaṭānā (H) v. To decrease; to subtract; to lessen; to diminish; to reduce; to alloy; to lower; to degrade; to abate.

گھٹاؤ *ghaṭā'o* (H) *n.m.* Deficiency; reduction; depreciation; falling; lowering.

گھٹاؤ بڑھاؤ *ghaṭā'o baṛhā'o, n.m.* Decrease and increase; rise and fall; excess and deficiency; fluctuation; involution and evolution (in *m/g.*)

گھٹنا *ghuṭnā* (H) *v.* To be powdered; to be well-rubbed; to be polished; to be suffocated; to be engaged in talking; to be close friends; to be clean shaved.

گھٹنا *ghuṭnā* (H) *n.m.* The knee,

گھٹنوں میں سر دے لینا *ghuṭnoṅ meṅ sir de lena, v.* To hang down one's head with shame or grief.

گھٹنوں چلنا *ghuṭnoṅ chalnā, v.* To crawl on one's knees.

گھٹنے سے لگے بیٹھے رہنا *ghuṭne se lage baithe rahnā, v.* To be tied to another's apronstrings.

گھٹنا *ghaṭna* (H) *v.* To abate; to decrease; to lessen; to dwindle; to subside; to become depressed; to be compressed; to decline.

گھٹوانا *ghuṭwāna* (H) *v.* To shave clean; to cause to polish.

گھٹی *ghuṭṭi* (H) *n.f.* A kind of medicine given to the newly-born infants just after their birth to clear the *maconium*.

گھٹی میں پڑنا *ghuṭṭi meṅ paṛnā, v.* To be a thing to which one is used from infancy; to become one's second nature.

گھٹیا ' گھٹیل *ghaṭyā, ghaṭyāl* (H) *adj.* Inferior; cheap; low priced.

گھچ پچ *ghich pich* (H) *adj.* Thick; confused; crowdy.

گھر *ghar* (H) *n.m.* House dwelling; home; apartment; drawer; compartment; groove; habitation; a den; family; spring; height; abode; cave; source; origin; socket; place of production; mansin; native place or land.

گھر آباد کرنا *ghar ābād karnā, v.* To make a house; to marry; to take a wife; to beget children.

گھر اجڑنا ' برباد ہونا ' ویران ہونا *ghar ujaṛnā, barbād honā, wirān honā, v.* To have a house broken; to be ruined.

گھر بار *ghar bār, n.m.* Family; household goods; household premises.

گھر بسنا *ghar basnā, v.* To have a wife; to be married.

گھر بگاڑنا *ghar bigāṛnā, v.* To bring ruin to a house; to put a family in difficulties.

گھر بگڑنا *ghar bigaṛnā, v.* To lose a husband or wife (by death or through other causes).

گھر بنانا *ghar banānā, v.* To build a house; to make oneself comfortable.

گھر بھائیں بھائیں کرنا *ghar bhā'eṅ bha'eṅ karnā, v.* The house looking desolate and deserted.

گھر بھر *ghar bhar*, n.m. The whole family.

گھر بیٹھنا *ghar baiṭhnā, v.* Collapsing of a house, to be ruined; to become the wife or mistress of some man.

گھر بیٹھے *ghar baithe, adv.* Seated at home; without moving or exertion.

گھر پڑنا *ghar paṛnā, v.* To marry someone; to become the wife of someone.

گھر پھونک تماشا دیکھنا *ghar phūṅk tamāshā dekhnā, v.* To waste one's substance in idle pleasure; to burn one's house merely for fun.

گھر تک پہنچانا *ghar tak pahuṅchānā, v.* To reach one's home; to accompany one to his house; to convince one throughly.

گھر تک پہنچنا *ghar tak pahuṅchnā, v.* To pursue one to the end; to abuse the members of one's family.

گھر جنوائی *ghar jaṅwā'i, n.m.* A son-in-law who lives in his father-in-law's house.

گھر چڑھ کر لڑنے آنا *ghar chaṛ kar laṛne ānā*, *v.* To go to another's house in order to pick up a quarrel.

گھر چلانا *ghar chalānā*, *v.* To run a house; to provide the expenses for one's household.

گھر دار *ghar dār*, *adj.* Householder; housekeeper.

گھر داری *ghar dārī*, *n.f.* Housekeeping; householding.

گھر دیکھ لینا *ghar dekh lenā*, *v.* To visit a house frequently; to begin paying frequent visits to a house; to spot a house for visitation (by evil spirit).

گھر ڈبونا *ghar ḍobonā*, *v.* To ruin one's a family.

گھر سر پر اٹھانا *ghar sir par uṭhānā*, *v.* To, make a great hue and cry; to manage the affairs of a family.

گھر سے *ghar se*, *adv.* From one's own pocket.

گھر سے دینا *ghar se denā*, *v.* To pay out of one's pocket.

گھر کا ، گھر کی *ghār kā*, *ghar kī*, *adj.* Of the house; belonging to the house; own.

گھر کا آدمی *ghar kā ādamī*, *n.m.* A member of one's family a confidential friend; a familiar person.

گھر کا اجالا گھر کا چراغ *ghar kā ujālā*, *ghar kā charāgh*, *n.m.* The light of the house; a son; a successor,

گھر کا بوجھ اٹھانا *ghar kā bojh uṭhānā*, *v.* To bear the burden of one's family; to be responsible for the upkeep of the house.

گھر کا بھیدی *ghar kā bhedī*, *n.m.* One who knows the secrets of a house; a confident.

گھر کا راستہ لینا *ghar kā rāstah lenā*, *v.* To be off.

گھر کا گھر *ghar kā ghar*, *n.m.* The whole family

گھر کا مال *ghar kā māl*, *n.m.* One's own property.

گھر کا نام ڈبونا *ghar kā nām ḍabonā*, *v.* To bring disgrace on one's family.

گھر کرنا *ghar karnā*, *v.* To build a house; to make a house; to win a place for oneself; to find. favour with; to marry.

گھر کی طرح رہنا *ghar kī ṭarah rahnā*, *v.* live as a member of a family; to be at ease in a house.

گھر کی کھیتی *ghar kī khetī*, *n.f.* Home-produce; one's own cultivation or property; obtainable without spending anything.

گھر کی لونڈی *ghar kī launḍī*, *n.f.* A faithful and loyal maid-servant.

گھر کی مرغی دال برابر *ghar kī murghī dal barābar*, *prov.* No one is hero to his own valet; a prophet is not valued in his own country.

گھر کے لوگ *ghar ke log*, *n.m.* The family people.

گھر گھر مانگتے پھرنا *ghar ghar māngte-phirnā*, *v.* To beg from door to door.

گھر گھسنا *ghar ghusnā*, *n.m. adj.* One who, always keeps at home.

گھر لٹانا *ghaṛ luṭānā*, *v.* To squander one's wealth; to ruin one's family.

گھر لینا *ghar lenā*, *v.* To buy a house; to take a house on rent.

گھر موسنا *ghar mūsnā*, *v.* To break into a house.

گھر میں پڑنا *ghar men paṛnā*, *v.* To be-lodged in a man's house; to become his wife or mistress.

گھر میں چوہے دوڑنا یا گھر میں خاک اُڑنا *ghar meṅ chuhe doṛnā yā ghar meṅ k͟hāk uṛnā, v.* To have nothing in the house to eat.

گھر میں ڈالنا *ghar meṅ ḍālnā, v.* To keep a woman as a mistress.

گھر والا *ghar wālā, n.m.* Husband; master of the house.

گھر والی *ghar wālī, n.f.* Housewife; lady of the house.

گھہر *guhar* (P) *n.m.* See گوھر *gauhar.*

گھرا *gharrā* (H) *n.m.* A rattling noise in the throat; death-rattle; agony; pang.

گہرا ، گہری *gahrā, gahrī* (H) *adj.* Profound deep; weighty; grave; difficult; sound (sleep); close; intimate (friend); strong (liquor).

گہرا خیال *gahrā k͟hayāl, n.m.* A weighty remark; a deep thought.

گہرا رنگ *gahrā raṅg, n.m.* Deep colour.

گہری چھاننا *gahrī chhānnā, v.* To be intoxicated with بھنگ *bhaṅg.*

گہری چھننا *gahrī chhannā, v.* To be close friends; to have a great fight.

گہری نیند *gahrī nīṅd, n.f.* Sound sleep.

گھر آنا *ghir ānā* (H) *v.* To hover (as clouds); to gather together.

گھرانا *gharānā* (H) *n.m.* Family; house; dynasty.

گہراؤ ، گہرائی *gahrāo, gahrā'ī* (H) *n.m.f.* Depth; deepness.

گھرکنا *ghuraknā* (H) *v.* To browbeat; to frown at; to chide; threaten; to scowl.

گھرکی *ghurkī* (H) *n.f.* Rebuke; frown; browbeating; threat.

گھرنا *ghirnā* (H) *v.* To gather (as clouds); to be besieged; to be surrounded; to be enclosed; to be occupied or filled; to be collected around.

گھرنی *ghirnī* (H) *n.f.* A pulley; a wheel for twisting ropes; vertigo.

گھرنی کھانا *ghirnī khānā, v.* To go round; to have a swimming in the head; to roll.

گھروندا *gharauṅdā* (H) *n.m.* A baby-house; a toy-house.

گھریلو *gharelū* (H) *adj.* Tame; domestic; homely.

گھریلو زندگی *gharelū ziṅdagī, n.f.* Private life.

گھڑ *ghuṛ* (H) *n.m.* (Contraction of گھوڑا *ghoṛā*). A horse.

گھڑ سوار ، گھڑ چڑھا *ghuṛ sawār, ghuṛ chaṛhā, n.m.* A horseman; a cavalryman; a bodyguard.

گھڑ دوڑ *ghuṛ dauṛ, n.f.* A horse-race.

گھڑ سال *ghuṛ sāl, n.f.* A stable.

گھڑ منہا *ghuṛ muṅhā, adj.* Horse-faced.

گھڑا *ghaṛā* (H) *n.m.* A water-pot; an earthen water-pot; a pitcher; a jar.

گھڑوں پانی پڑ جانا *ghaṛoṅ pānī paṛ jānā, v.* To be thoroughly ashamed.

گھڑانا ، گھڑوانا *ghaṛanā, ghaṛwānā* (H) *v.* To cause to make (ornaments); to cause to forge.

گھڑائی *ghaṛā'ī* (H) *n.f.* Workmanship; the price paid for making a thing.

گھڑت ، گھڑنت *ghaṛat, ghaṛaṅt* (H) *n.f.* Workmanship; make; invention; make-believe.

گھڑنا *ghaṛnā* (H) *v.* To make; to form; to forge, to fabricate; to coin; to figure; to beat; to invent.

گھڑونچی *ghaṛoṅchī* (H) *n.f.* A stand for water pots.

گھڑی *ghaṛī* (H) *n.f.* The space of 24 minutes; an instrument for measuring time; a clock; a watch a chronometer; time; hour; moment; a sub-division of a village.

گھڑی بنانا ghaṛī banānā, v. To mend a watch; to repair a watch.

گھڑی بھاری ہونا ghaṛī bhārī honā, v. To hang heavy (time).

گھڑی بھر میں ghari bhar meṅ, adv. In a moment; in a trice.

گھڑی ساز ghaṛī sāz, n.m. A watch maker.

گھڑی کوکنا (میں کوک دینا) ghaṛī kuknā, meṅ kūk denā, v. To wind a watch.

گھڑی گھڑی ghari ghari, adv. Many times; again and again; repeatedly; often.

گھڑی میں تولا گھڑی میں ماشہ ghari men tola gharī meṅ māshah, adj. Of a changeable or a fickle disposition.

گھڑیا gharyā (H) n.f. A crucible; earthen melting-pot; a honey-comb; a small water-pot.

گھڑیا ghuṛyā (H) n.f. A small pony; a small sized horse for children to ride on.

گھڑیال gharyāl (H) n.m. A crocodile; a bell; a gong.

گھڑیالی gharyāli, (H) n.m. One who strikes the hours at a gong; time-keeper.

گھس آنا ghus ānā (H) v. To rush in; to enter by force.

گھسانا ghusānā (H) v. To thrust in; to stuff in; to crame; to penetrate; to force in.

گھساوٹ ghisāwāṭ (H) n.f. Friction; wear; abrasion.

گھس پڑنا ، گھس جانا ghus paṛnā, ghus jānā (H) v. To rush in head long or rashly; to enter by force.

گھسٹنا ghisatnā (H) v. To be dragged; to trail.

گھس جانا ghis jānā (H) v. To be rubbed; to wear out.

گھسڑ پھسڑ ghusaṛ phusaṛ (H) n.f. Whispering; stuffing.

گھسنا ghisnā (H) v. To rub; to whet; to be rubbed; to wear out; to be worn.

گھسنا ghusna (H) v. To rush in; to penetrate; to interfere; to meddle.

گھسن پٹی ghissan pitti (H) n.f. Fight; wrangling; quarrel.

گھسوانا ghiswānā (H) v. To cause to rub; to cause to be worn out.

گھسوانا ghuswānā (H) v. To cause to penetrate; to cause to thrust (into).

گھسیارہ ghasyārah (H) n.m. Grass-cutter.

گھسیٹنا ghasiṭnā (H) v. To drag along; to pull; to trail; to scribble.

گھسیڑنا ghuseṛnā (H) v. To thrust (into); to cram; to penetrate; to stiff; to foist.

گھسیلا ghasilā (H) adj. Grassy; yeilding grass; abounding in grass.

گھگرا ghagrā (H) n.m. See گھاگرا ghāgrā.

گھگری ghagri (H) n.f. A small petticoat.

گھگی ghiggī (H) n.f. Hiccup; inability of speech from fear or emotion.

گھگی بندھ جانا ghiggı bandh jānā, v. To lose power of speech; to be dumb founded.

گھگیانا ghigyānā (H) v. To falter in speaking; to be unable to speak (from fear); to beseech; to coax; to fown; to implore.

گھل جانا ، گھلنا ghul jānā, ghulnā (H) v. To melt; to dissolve; to be dissolved; to be mixed with; to be mellowed; to rot (as fruit); to become lean; to waste away.

گھلانا ghulānā (H) v. To melt; to dissolve; to soften; to allure; to entice; to deceive.

گھلاوٹ ghulāwat (H) n.f. Softness; plumpness; dissolvedness; ripeness.

گہما گہمی gahmā gahmī (H) n.f. Hustle and bustle; mirth; cheer; jollity.

گھمانا ghumānā (H) v. To turn round; to brandish; to roll; to circulate; to beguile; to whirl round; to wheel.

گھمری، گھمیر، گھمیری ghumri, ghumer, ghumerī (H) n.f. Vertigo; giddiness; swimming in the head.

گھمسان ghamsān (H) n.m. A tumultuous crowd; a heavy engagement; fight; battle.

گھمسان کا رن ghamsān kā ran, n.m. A heavy fight; a furious fight.

گھمنڈ ghamaṅḍ (H) n.m. Pride; haughtiness; conceit; arrogance; boast.

گھمنڈ کرنا ghamaṅḍ karnā, v. To be proud (of); to show one's assumed greatness; to be puffed up.

گھمنڈی ghamaṅḍi (H) adj. Proud; arrogant.

گھمنی ghumnī (H) n.f. See گھمری ghumrī.

گہن gahan (H) n.m. See گرھن grahan.

گھن ghan (H) n.m. Gathering of the clouds; clouds; sky; anvil; sledge-hammer.

گھن کی چوٹ ghan kī choṭ, n.f. A heavy blow.

گھن چکر ghan chakkar, n.m. A top; a catherine-wheel; a revolving body; a fool.

گھن گھور گھٹا ghan ghor ghaṭā, n.f. Heavy cloud; thundering clouds.

گھن ghin (H) n.f. Disgust; nausea; hatred; abhorrence; shame.

گھن آنا ghin ānā, v. To feel nausea; to be disgusted.

گھن کھانا ghin khānā, v. To abhor; to have an aversion to; to be disgusted.

گھن ghun (H) n.m. A weevil; a wood-louse; rancour; grief.

گھن لگنا ghun lagnā, v. To be eaten by weevil; to be destroyed; to be the victim of a wasting disease.

گہنا gahnā (H) n.m. Jewels; ornaments; pledge; pawn; mortgage; a kind of harrow without teeth.

گہنے رکھنا gahne rakhnā, v. To pawn; to pledge; to mortgage.

گھنا ، گھنی ghanā, ghanī (H) adj. Thick; close; confused; numerous; much; many.

گھنا ، گھنی ghunnā, ghunnī (H) adj. Designedly silent; cunning; malicious; spiteful; revengeful; bearing malice; rancorous.

گہنانا gahnānā (H) v. To be eclipsed (the sun or the moon); to be deformed (as a result of the eclipse).

گھناؤنا ghināonā (H) adj. Disgusting; causing aversion.

گھنٹا ghanṭā (H) n.m. A bell; clock; hour; period.

گھنٹا گھر ghanṭā ghar, n.m. A clock-tower.

گھنٹی ghanṭī (H) n.f. A small metal bell; a gong.

گھنڈی ghunḍī (H) n.f. A cloth button; a tag; a knot; a kind of herb.

گھنڈی لگانا ghunḍi lagānā, v. To button; to insert a cloth button.

گھنڈی کھولنا ghunḍī kholnā, v. To unbutton; to solve a riddle.

گھنگچی ghuṅgchī (H) n.f. A small red and black seed, used as the primary unit of (Indian) weights (رتی ratti).

گھنگر ghuṅgar (H) n.m. Curls.

گھنگر والے ، گھنگریالے ghuṅgar wāle, ghuṅgriyāle adj. Curly (hair).

گھنگرو ghuṅgrū (H) n.m. Small bells; the death rattle.

گھنگرو باندھنا ghuṅgrū bāndhnā, v. To prepare for dancing.

گھنگرو بولنا ghuṅgrū bolnā, v. Rattling of the throat at the time of death.

گھنگنی ghuṅgnī (H) n.f. Boiled corn.

گھنگولنا ghaṅgolnā (H) v. To make (the water) muddy; to shake; to rinse; to stir up; to make turbid.

گھننا ghunnā (H) v. To be eaten by weevils.

گہوارہ gahwārah (P) n.m. A cradle; a swing.

گھوٹا ghoṭā (H) n.m. A wooden pestle for pulverizing (of medicines etc.); a bruiser; a polishing stone.

گھوٹنا ghoṭnā (H) v. To rub; to pound; to grind; to pulverize; to shave; to polish; to glaze; to read over and over again; to commit to memory.

گھور ghor (H) adj. Awful; horrible; deep (colour).

گھورا ghūrā (H) n.m. Sweepings; rubbish; manure; a dust heap; a dung-hill.

گھورا گھاری ghūrā ghārī (H) n.f. Amorous glances.

گھورنا ghūrnā (H) v. To stare at; to ogle; to look at angrily; to gaze intently on; to look about; to fix the eyes on.

گھوڑا ghoṛā (H) n.m. A horse; the knight in chess; the cock (of a gun).

گھوڑا پلاننا ghoṛā palānnā, v. To saddle a horse.

گھوڑا چڑھانا ghoṛā charhānā, v. To cock a gun.

گھوڑا دبانا ghoṛā dabānā, v. To pull the trigger of a gun.

گھوڑا دوڑانا ghoṛā dauṛānā, v. To gallop a horse.

گھوڑا ڈالنا ، پھینکنا ghoṛā ḍālnā, phenknā, v. To race a horse at full speed.

گھوڑی ghoṛī (H) n.f. A mare; a machine for making maccaroni; the bridge of the nose; wooden pincers used in circumcision; a marriage song; a weavers' stand.

گھوڑی ٹپا ghoṛī ṭappā, n.m. A boy's game like 'leap frog'.

گھوڑی چڑھانا ghoṛī charhānā, v. To mount a boy on horse back; to form a marriage or circumcision procession.

گھوسن ghosan (H) n.f. A milkmaid; the wife of a milkman.

گھوسی ghosī (H) n.m. A milkman, a cowherd.

گھولنا gholnā (H) v. To dissolve; to melt.

گھوم ghūm (H) n.m. Rotation; turning round; girth; circumference.

گھومنا ghūmnā (H) v. To rotate; to revolve; to whirl; to stroll; to turn round; to swim (as the head); to become giddy.

گھونٹ ghūṅṭ (H) n.m. A draught; a gulp; a pull at a pipe.

گھونٹ پینا، لینا ghūṅṭ pīnā, lenā, v. To take a draught; to swallow; to have a pull at a pipe.

گھونٹنا ghoṅṭnā (H) v. To press; to squeeze; to throttle; to choke.

گھونسا ghūṅsā (H) n.m. A blow with the fist; a shock.

گھونسا جڑنا ، رسید کرنا ، سہی کرنا ، لگانا، مارنا ghūṅsā jaṛnā, rasid karnā, sahi karnā, lagānā, mārnā, v. To give a blow.

گھونسلا ghoṅslā (H) n.m. A bird's nest; a small cosy house.

گھونسلا بنانا ghoṅslā banānā, v. To make a nest.

گھونسم گھونسا ghūṅsam ghūṅsā (H) n.m. Boxing; fisticuffs.

گھونگٹ ghūṅgaṭ (H) n.m. A veil; a covering over the face.

گھونگٹ کرنا ghūṅgaṭ karnā, v. To veil; to draw a mantle over the face.

گھونگٹ والی ghūṅgaṭ wālī, n.f. A veiled woman.

گھونگر ghūṅgar (H) n.m. See گھنگر ghuṅgar.

گھی ghī (H) *n.m.* Butter; butter-oil; clarified butter; ghee.

گھی چپڑنا *ghī chupaṛnā, v.* To rub with butter.

گھی کھچڑی *ghī khichṛi, n.f.* Close friendship.

گھی کے چراغ جلنا *ghī ke charāgh jalnā, v.* To rejoice over one's success; to be well-off; to prosper.

گھی کے کپے سے جا لگنا *ghī ke kuppe se jā lagnā, v.* To find a hidden treasure; to come in the way of fortune.

گھیا *ghiyā* (H) *n.m.* Pumpkin; gourd.

گھیپنا *ghepnā* (H) *v.* To mingle; to mix; to stir and make into a paste.

گھیر *gher* (H) *n.m.* Circuit; surrounding; enclosing area; boundary; circle; compound; width; fulness (of a robe); skirt.

گھیردار *gher dār, adj.* Ample; loose; extensive.

گھیر گھار کے لانا *gher ghār ke lānā, v.* To surround; to bring with great difficulty.

گھیرا *gherā* (H) *n.m.* Circumference; circle; fence; siege; maze; blockade.

گھیرا ڈالنا *gherā ḍālnā, v.* To lay a siege; to encompass; to blockade.

گھیرنا *ghernā* (H) *v.* To surround; to encompass; to hem in; to hedge; to encircle; to enclose; to blockade; to occupy; to include.

گھیکوار ، گھیگوار *ghīkawār, ghigwār* (H) *n.m.* A medicinal plant.

گیا گزرا *gayā guzrā* (H) *adj.* Worthless; useless; dead and gone.

گیارہ *giyārah* (H) *adj.* Eleven.

گیارھواں *giyārhawān* (H) *adj.* Eleventh.

گیان *giyān* (H) *n.m.* Knowledge; understanding; intelligence; intellect; knowing; wisdom; religious knowledge.

گیان گدڑی *giyān gudṛī, n.f.* Ragged covering of wisdom; friar's rags.

گیان ہونا *giyān honā, v.* To acquire spiritual knowledge.

گیانی *giyānī* (H) *n.m.* A sage; philosopher; a wiseman.

گیاہ *giyāh* (P) *n.f.* Grass; straw.

گیپا *gīpā* (P) *n.m.* A kind of پلاؤ *pulāo.*

گیت *gīt* (H) *n.m.* A song; a hymn.

گیتا *gītā* (H) *n.f.* A mode of music; psalm; a religious book of the Hindus.

گیتی *getī* (P) *n.f.* The world; universe.

گیدڑ *gīdaṛ* (H) *n.m.* A jackal; a coward.

گیدڑ بھبکی *gidaṛ bhabkī, n.f.* Bravado; bullying; blustering.

گیدی *gidī* (P) *adj.* Timid; cowardly; stupid; dolt.

گیدی‌خر *gīdi khar, n.m.* An arrant fool.

گیر *gīr* (P) *adj.* Taking; holding; conquering; covering (used in *comps.* as in عالم گیر *'ālam gīr*, conqueror of the world; universal; global).

گیرو *gerū* (H) *n.m.* Red earth; red chalk; brick dust.

گیروا *gerūā* (H) *adj.* Reddish; like red ochre.

گیسو *gesū* (P) *n.m.* Side-lock; long hair on both sides of the head.

گیسو بریدہ *gesū burīdah, n.f.* A shameless woman.

گیگلا *geglā* (H) *adj.* Simple; silly; soft.

گیل *gail* (H) *n.f.* A road; path; lane; a street; a bunch (of bananas). *adv.* With.

گیل جانا *gail jānā* (H) *v.* To accompany (with).

گیل لگے پھرنا *gail lage phirnā, v.* To follow one about; to be a hanger on.

گیلا ، گیلی *gīlā, gili* (H) *adj.* Wet; moist; damp.

گیلا پن gīlā pan, n.m. Moisture; dampness; wetness humidity.

گیلڑ gailaṛ (H) n.m. A child by a former husband.

گیں gīn (P). An affix to nouns signifying effected with or full of as اندوہ گیں andoh gīn, full of grief; sorrowful.

گینتی genti (H) n.f. A pickaxe.

گیند gend (H) n.f. A ball; a woman's breasts.

گیند بلا gend ballā, n.m. Ball and bat; cricket.

گیند دینا gend denā, v. To bowl.

گیندا gendā (H) n.m. A marigold.

گینڈا geṇḍā (H) n.m. A rhinoceros.

گیہاں gaihān (P) n.m. The world; the universe.

گیہواں gehwān (H) adj. Wheaten.

گیہوں gehūn (H) n.m. Wheat.

ل lām, is the twenty-third letter of the Arabic, the twenty-seventh of the Persian and the thirtieth of the Urdu alphabet. In reckoning by abjad it stands for 30.

لا lā (A) adv. No; not; by no means; without; there is not; has the meaning of the English prefixes un, in, ir, im.

لا آبالی lā ubālī (A) adj. (Lit. I care not) careless; insolent; reckless; licentious; petulant.

لا آبالی پن lā ubālī pan, n.m. Carelessness; recklessness.

لابد lā budd, adv. Necessarily; infallibly. adj. Unavoidable; involuntary; positive; inevitable.

لابدی lā budi, adj. Inevitable; necessary; essential.

لاتعداد lā ta'dād, adj. Numberless; countless.

لاثانی lā ṣānī, adj. Incomparable; unmatched; unequalled.

لاجرم lā jaram, adv. Necessarily; undoubtedly; indispensably; essentially.

لاجواب lā jawāb, adj. Silenced; rendered speechless; disconcerted; confuted; having no reply to give.

لاجواب کردینا lā jawāb kar denā, v. To silence; to render speechless; to cause to have no answer to give.

لاچار lā chār, adj. (A defective compound, should be ناچار nā chār); Having no remedy; helpless; destitute; forlorn; poor; compelled; disabled; pressed; disarmed.

لاچار کرنا lā chār karnā, v. To render helpless; to compel; to press; to disarm.

لاچار ہونا lā chār honā, v. To become helpless; to be incurable; to be disabled; to be compelled.

لاچارگی یا لاچاری lā chāragi, lā chāri, n.f. Helplessness; poverty; inability; destitution; want of means.

لا حاصل lā ḥāṣil, adj. Unprofitable; unavailing; unproductive; abortive; barren; useless; fruitless; not carried forward (Arith.).

لا حل lā ḥall, adj. Insoluble; difficult; abstruse.

لاحول بھیجنا lā ḥaul bhejnā, v. To say لا حول ولا قوۃ الا باللہ (lā haula wa lā quwwatā illā billah) which means there is no power to hold a man from sinning nor any to make him do good deeds except the Grace of Allah; to say "God forbid"; to shun; to imprecate; to drive away evil spirits.

لاخراج lā kharāj, n.f. Rent free (land).

لا دعوی lā da'wā, adj. & n.m. Without claim or demand; a deed or act of relinquishment; a withdrawal of a claim.

لا دوا *lā dawā*, *adj.* Incurable; irremediable.

لاریب *lā raib*, *adv.* Without doubt; undoubtedly; unquestionably.

لازوال *lā zawāl*, *adj.* Imperishable; everlasting; eternal.

لاطائل *lā ṯā'il*, *adj.* Useless; vain; absurd; unprofitable.

لاعلاج *lā i'lāj*, *adj.* Incurable; without remedy.

لاعلم *lā 'ilm*, *adj.* Ignorant; unknowing; unaware.

لاکلام *lā kalām*, *adv.* Undoubtedly; unquestionably; assuredly; positively. *adj.* Taciturn; speechless; indisputable.

لامحاله *lā muḥālah*, *adv.* Assuredly; positively; surely.

لامذهب *lā mazhab*, *adj.* Irreligious; having no religion.

لامکان *lā makān*, *adj.* Homeless; having no dwelling place; omnipresent; God.

لاوارث *lā wāriṣ*, *adj.* Leaving no heir; heirless.

لاولد *lā walad*, *adj.* Without children; childless; without an offspring.

لاهوت *lā hūt*, *n.m.* Divine presence; divine being.

لایزال *lā yazāl*, *adj.* Eternal; ceaseless.

لایعنی *lā ya'ni*, *adj.* Absurd; insignificant; obscene; meaningless; abusive.

لایموت *lā yamūt*, *adj.* Undying; deathless; immortal.

لاینحل *lā yanḥal*, *adj.* Insoluble; difficult; abstruse.

لاینفک *lā yanfak*, *adj.* Inseparable; indivisible.

لابھ *lābh* (S) *n.m.* Profit; gain; requisition; picking; interest; produce; advantage; welfare.

لابھ اٹھانا ، کرنا *lābh uṭhānā, karnā*, *v.* To gain; to make a profit; to win; to acquire; to turn a penny; to earn; to attain.

لات *lāt* (H) *n.f.* A leg; a kick.

لات مارنا *lāt mārnā*, *v.* To kick; to spurn.

لاٹ *lāṭ* (H) *n.f.* A pillar; minaret; steeple; worn-out clothes; shabby garments; a lord; a governor; a commander-in-chief; master; a flame.

لاٹھ *lāṭh* (H) *n.f.* A staff; a minaret; a pillar, frestle; the vertical column of an oil mill.

لاٹھی *lāṭhī* (H) *n.f.* A stick; a club; a crutch.

لاٹھی ٹیک کے چلنا *lāṭhi ṭek ke chalnā*, *v.* To walk with the aid of a stick.

لاٹھی چلانا *lāṭhī chalānā*, *v.* To cudgel.

لاج *lāj* (H) *n.f.* Bashfulness; modesty; sense of decency; reputation; honour; good name.

لاج آنا ، لگنا *lāj ānā, lagnā*, *v.* To feel ashamed; to be abashed.

لاج رکھنا *lāj rakhnā*, *v.* To protect the honour of; to hsve a sense of shame.

لاج سے مرنا ، لاجوں مرنا *lāj se marnā, lājoṅ marnā*, *v.* To feel extremely ashamed; to die of shame.

لاج کرنا *lāj karnā*, *v.* To be ashamed; to be bashful.

لاج کھونا ، گنوانا *lāj khonā, gaṅwānā*, *v.* To lose sense of shame; to be shameless.

لاجورد *lājward* (P) *n.m.* Azure; lapis-lazuli; armenian stone.

لاجوردی *lājwardī* (P) *adj.* Azure; sky-blue.

لاجونتی *lājwantī* (H) *n.f.* A sensitive plant; *mimosa pudica.*

لاحق *lāḥiq* (A) *adj.* Adjoining; contiguous; touching; reaching; overtaking; adhering. *n.m.* An appendage; supplement; connection; a dependent.

لاحقه lāḥiqah (A) *n.m.* (Gram.) An affix; a suffix.

لاد lād (H) *n.f.* Load; burden; freight.

لاد چلنا lād chalnā, *v.* To pack up; to die.

لادنا lādnā (H) *v.* To load; to burden with; to heap upon; to freight.

لادی lādī (H) *n.f.* A small load; washerman's load of clothes.

لادیا lādiyā (H) *n.m.* One who loads; a loader.

لاڈ lāḍ (H) *n.m.* Affection; tenderness; caressing; fondling; endearment; coaxing; love; sport.

لاڈ کرنا lāḍ karnā, *v.* To fondle.

لاڈلا ، لاڈلی lāḍlā, lāḍlī (H) *adj.* Darling; dear; spoilt child; a darling; a pet.

لاڈو lāḍo (H) *n.f.* Darling; favourite (bride or daughter).

لازم lāzim (A) *adj.* Necessary; indispensable; bound; important; constant; urgent; compulsory; needed; required.

لازم آنا lāzim ānā, *v.* To become necessary; to follow out of necessity; to be incumbent on; to become a duty.

لازم جاننا lāzim jānnā, *v.* To consider right or essential; to regard as indispensable.

لازم کرنا lazim karnā, *v.* To make obligatory; to render incumbent.

لازم ملزوم lāzim malzūm, *adj.* Reciprocal; concerning one another; connected with one another; correlative; inseparable; obligatory.

لازمه lāzimah, *n.m.* A necessary corollary; exigency; necessity; an obligation.

لازمی lāzimī, *adj.* Necessary; what must be; inevitable.

لاسا lāsā (H) *n.m.* Anything clammy or glutinous; gum; bird-lime; a bait; glue; the viscous milk of plants.

لاسا لگانا lāsā lagānā, *v.* To catch with bird-lime; to sow dissension; to foment a quarrel.

لاسا ہونا lāsā honā, *v.* To be clammy.

لاش ، لاشه lāsh, lāshah (T) *n.f./m.* A dead body; a carcass; corpse.

لاش پڑنا lāsh parnā, *v.* To fall down dead; to be killed.

لاش ڈالنا lāsh ḍālnā, *v.* To kill a person; to beat severely.

لاغر lāghar (P) *adj.* Lean; meagre; thin; slender.

لاغری lāgharī (P) *n.f.* Leanness; thinness.

لاف lāf (P) *n.f.* Boasting; bragging; vanity; self-praise; conceitedness; falsehood.

لاف زن lāf zan, *adj.* A boaster; a blusterer; a bragger.

لاف زنی lāf zanī, *n.f.* Bragging; boasting.

لاف زنی کرنا ، لاف مارنا lāf zanī karnā, lāf mārnā, *v.* To boast; to brag; to bluster.

لاف و گزاف lāf-ŏ gazāf, *n.f.* Boasting; blustering; bragging.

لاکھ lākh (H) *adj.* A hundred thousand; heaps; a great many. *n.f.* Lac; sealing-wax.

لاکھ پر بھاری lākh par bhārī, *adj.* Very brave; unequalled; matchless.

لاکھ جی سے lākh ji se, *adv.* With all one's heart.

لاکھ کا گھر خاک کر دینا lākh kā ghar khāk kar denā, *v.* To ruin one's name and family; to be reduced to abject poverty.

لاکھ کی بتی lākh kī battī, *n.f.* A stick of sealing-wax.

لاکھ لگانا lākh lagānā, *v.* To shut up; to conceal; to seal.

لاکھ میں ، لاکھوں میں lākh meṅ, lākhoṅ meṅ, *adv. & adj.* Publicly; openly; one in a lakh.

لاکھا lākhā (H) *n.m.* A red dye; lac.

لاکھی lākhī (H) n.f. A red colour procured from lac.

لاگ lāg (H) n.f. Enmity; rancour; spite; grudge; ill-feeling; cost; expenditure; a secret; spell; ratio; approach; competition; attention; affection; love; attachment; affinity; connection; relevancy; correlation.

لاگ ڈانٹ lāg ḍānṭ, n.f. Enmity; ill-feeling.

لاگ رکھنا lāg rakhnā, v. To harbour ill-will; to have a grudge against; to be bent on harming.

لاگ لپیٹ lāg lapeṭ, n.f. Treachery; prejudice; partiality; one sidedness

لاگ لگنا lāg lagnā, v. To fall in love; to take a fancy to; to be anamoured of.

لاگت lāgat (H) n.f. Cost; outlay; expenditure.

لاگت آنا lāgat ānā, v. To cost.

لاگت لگانا lāgat lagānā, v. To spend money on.

لاگو lāgū (H) n.m. Adherent; friend; a supporter; a protector. adj. Attached; desirous; adhering to; applicable to.

لاگو ہونا lāgū honā, v. To pursue a person; to follow persistently; to persecute; to adhere: to be attached; to be intent on; to cling to.

لال lāl (H) n.m. Darling; dear; an infant boy; a son; a ruby; name of a very small bird; red colour. adj. Red; inflamed; florid; red hot; enraged; angry.

لال انگارہ lāl angārah, adj. Red hot; fiery; flushed with rage.

لال بجھکڑ lāl bujhakkaṛ, n.m. A wiseacre; a fool.

لال بیگ lāl beg, n.m. A priest of a class of sweepers; a kind of worm.

لال بیگی ، بیگیا lāl begī, begiyā, n.m. A sweeper; follower of lāl beg.

لال پری lāl pari, n.f. Wine.

لال پلکا lāl palkā, n.m. A kind of pigeon.

لال پیلی آنکھیں نکالنا lāl pīlī āṅkheṅ nikālnā, v. To fly into a passion; to be enraged.

لال چندن lāl chandan, n.m. Red cedar.

لال ڈورا lāl ḍorā, n.m. Red-tape; red streak in the eye.

لال سوداگر lāl saudāgar, n.m. A middleman; a petty merchant.

لال کتاب lāl kitāb, n.f. Land settlement book.

لال کرتی lāl kurtī, n.f. Red-shirts; a British infantry.

لال مرچ lāl mirch, n.f. Chilly.

لال ہونا lāl honā, v. To become red; to be very angry; to fly into a passion; to be ripe (fruit).

لالا lālā (P) adj: Resplendent; brilliant. n.m. A slave; a servant; a herb brought about from Mecca, the smell of which keeps off piles.

لا لا lālā (H) n.m. Master; grandee; Sir; Mr.

لالٹین lāltain, n.f. (corr. from English) Lantern.

لالچ lālach (H) n.m. Greed; ambition; covetousness; avarice; selfishness; longing; temptation.

لالچ دینا lālach denā, v. To tempt; to allure; to entice.

لالچ کرنا lālach karnā, v. To desire; to covet; to long for.

لالچ میں آنا lālach men ānā, v. To be moved by covetousness.

لالچی lālchī (H) adj. Greedy; avaricious; covetous; desirous; interested; selfish.

لاله lālah (P) n.m. A tulip; poppyflower.

لاله رخ lālah rukh, adj. Rosy-cheeked.

لاله زار lālah zār, n.m. A bed or garden of roses.

لاله فام lālah fām, adj. Of bright red colour.

لاله lālah (H) n.m. See لا لا la lā.

لالی la·āli (A) n.m. (plu. of لوء لوء lo'lo') Pearls.

لالی lāli (H) n.f. Redness; blood; bleak-eyes; reputation; honour.

لالی رہ جانا lāli rah jānā, v. Saving honour or good name.

لام lām (Fr. larme) n.m. A line of troops; a brigade; a battle field; a ringlet; rank; row.

لام باندھنا lām bāṅdhnā, v. To line up in ranks; to form a brigade; to array; to mobilize.

لام بندی lām bańdi n.f. Mobilization; recruitment.

لام کاف بکنا lām kāf baknā, v. To abuse; to revile.

لامسه lāmisah (A) adj. Touching; feeling. n.f. The sense of touch or feeling.

لامع lāmi' (A) adj. Shining; bright; splendid.

لانا lānā (H) v. To bring; to induce; to introduce; to persuade; to apply; to carry over; to include; to yield; to buy; to win over, to import; to breed; to produce; to make.

لائحه lā'iḥah (A) n.m. A shining thing; a self-evident matter; splendour; clause; index; programme.

لائحه عمل lā'iḥah-ĕ 'amal, n.m. Programme; rules of practice ; procedure; constitution; modus operandi.

لائق lā'iq (A) adj. Worthy; deserving; adapted; proper; suitable; becoming; expedient; able; capable; qualified; competent; decent.

لائق ہونا lā'iq honā, v. To deserve; to merit; to suit; to be capable.

لاؤ لشکر lā'o lashkar (H) n.m. Army; a large army with its baggage and camp followers.

لب lubb (A) n.m. The essence of anything; the heart; the soul; a kernel.

لب لباب lubb-ĕ lubāb, n.m. The pith; gist; the crux of the question.

لب lab (P) n.m. The lip; the moustache; saliva; brim; edge; verge; margin; shore; bank; brow (of a hill); coast.

لب بند ہونا lab band honā, v. To be silent; closing of the lips with sweet.

لب بسته lab bastah, adj. With lips sealed; quiet.

لب دریا lab-ĕ daryā, n.m. Bank of a river; sea-shore. adv. Near the bank of a river.

لب ریز lab rez, adj. Brimful; overflowing.

لب کھولنا lab kholna, v. To open the mouth; to speak.

لب گور lab-ĕ gor, adj. Nearing death; with one foot in the grave.

لب لگانا lab lagānā, v. To apply saliva; to flatter.

لب و لہجه lab-ŏ lahjah, n.m. Tone; pronunciation; modulation; conversation; voice.

لبوں په جان ہونا laboṅ peh jān honā, v. To be dying.

لبیں لینا labeṅ lenā, v. To shave or clip the moustache.

لباده libādah (P) n.m. A cloak; a wrapper; an outer garment; a gown; a waterproof cloak.

لباڑ ، لباڑی labāṛ, labāṛī (H) n.m. A lier; a foolish talker; a babbler. adj. False; unreal; rascal.

لباڑیا labāṛyā (H) n.m. A great talker; a rascal.

لباس libās (A) n.m. Apparel; clothes; dress; attire; habit; a veil; costume; forgery.

لبالب labālab (P) adj. Brimful.

لبڑ سبڑ labaṛ sabaṛ (H) n.m. Nonsensical talk; gossip.

لبلبی lablabi (H) *n.f.* The sere (sear) spring of a gun-lock.

لبن labn (A) *n.m.* Milk.

لبوب lubūb (A) *n.m.* (*plu.*of لب lubb) Essences; piths; a kind of confection.

لبھانا lubhānā (H) *v.* To entice; to attract; to allure; to charm; to seduce; to draw or win over; to tantalise; to fascinate; to excite desire.

لبیب labib (A) *adj.* Wise; intelligent; judicious.

لبیک labbaik (A) *intej.* 'Here I am to do Thy bidding, my Lord'! is the declaration made by pilgrims during the Haj.

لپ lap (H) *n.m.* A handful; as much as can be held in both palms joined together.

لپ بھر lap bhar, *adj.* A handful.

لپ لپ کرنا lap lap karnā, *v.* To lap like a dog; to beat or throb with fear.

لپ لپ کھانا lap lap khānā, *v.* To eat quickly.

لپاٹی ، لپاٹیا lapāti, lapātiyā (H) *n.m.* A liar; a boaster.

لپائی lipā'i(H) *n.f.* Plastering; close writing.

لپٹ lapaṭ (H) *n.f.* Flame; glow; warmth; sweet smell; scent.

لپٹا lapṭā (H) *n.m.* A kind of molasses; treacle; a kind of pudding; a grass; connection; relation.

لپٹانا lipṭānā (H) *v.* To embrace; to absorb; to intertwine; to fold; to wrap.

لپٹنا lipaṭnā (H) *v.* To cling; to adhere; to embrace; to stick; to persecute; to be folded; to coil round; to be smeared; to wrestle; to fight; to be rolled up; to be encased.

لپڑ lappaṛ (H) *n.m.* A slap; a blow.

لپڑ شپڑ lapaṛ shapuṛ (H) *n.f.* Jumble; prevarication; confused or involved speech; equivocation; perversion of the truth.

لپڑی lupṛī (H) *n.f.* Pap; poultice; a plaster.

لپک lapak (H) *n.f.* Spring; flash; bounce; match; dart; beat; throb; nimbleness; swiftness; elasticity; a bad habit.

لپک جھپک lapak jhapak, *adv.* With a leap or bound; swiftly; nimbly; briskly.

لپک کر lapak kar, *adv.* Hurriedly; quickly; at once.

لپکا lapkā (H) *n.m.* A bad habit; vitiated taste.

لپکا پڑنا lapkā parnā, *v.* To be addicted to a bad habit.

لپکنا lapaknā (H) *v.* To flash; to spring; to bound; to rush forth (upon); to attack; to beat; to hurry; to catch; to attack; to bark; to snap at; to make haste; to step up.

لپکی lapki (H) *n.f.* A stitch; a long stitch.

لپکی بھرنا lapki bharnā, *v.* To baste; to stitch.

لپنا lipnā (H) *v.* To be plastered or whitewashed; to be smeared; to bend (cane); to fit one like a cap.

لپوانا lipwānā (H) *v.* To cause to be plastered, smeared or washed over; to cause to be whitewashed.

لپیٹ lapeṭ (H) *n.f.* Fold; circumference; envelope; cover; complication; ambiguity; loss; evil influence; an attack (as, of an epidemic); a coil; entanglement; hardship; deception; damage.

لپیٹ لینا lapeṭ lenā, *v.* To roll; to envolve; to include in.

لپیٹن lapeṭan (H) *n.f.* A roller on which cloth is wound.

لپیٹنا lapeṭnā (H) *v.* To roll; to furl; to make into a ball; to enclose; to pack; to smear.

لپیٹواں lapeṭwāṅ (H) *adj.* Twistable; wrapped up; ornamented with gold or silver thread; hidden roundabout; indirect (speech); involved or ambiguous (speech).

لت lat (H) n.f. Bad habits; whim; vice.

لت پڑنا lat paṛnā, v. To have a bad habit.

لتا lattā (H) n.m. A rag; scrap of cloth; clothes.

لتے لینا latte lenā, v. To scold; to threaten; to admonish.

لتاڑ latāṛ (H) n.f. Labour; fatigue; insult; misfortune; calamity; over-work; exhaustion; abusive treatment; reviling; rebuke.

لتاڑنا latāṛna (H) v. To treat contemptuously; to revile; to over-work a person; to cause to toil; to rail at; to wear out; to insult; to affront; to bring down; to irritate.

لت پت lat pat (H) adj. Wet; soaked through.

لترا lutrā (H) n.m. A flatterer; a mischief-maker; a back-bitter; a babbler; a tell-tale; a sycophant.

لتراپن lutrā pan, n.m. Flattery; back-biting; deceit; mischief making.

لتھڑنا litharna (H) v. To be draggled; to be besmeared.

لتھیڑنا latheṛnā(H) v. To draggle; to besmear with dirt; to mix together.

لتی latti (H) n.f. The string of a child's tap; a rag; a cloth tied to the ends of a pole to direct the flight of pigeons; to kick when swimming.

لتیا latyā (H) adj. A person of bad habit.

لتیانا latyānā (H) v. To kick.

لٹ laṭ (H) n.f. Tangled hair; a clothed lock; tangled thread.

لٹ دھاری laṭ dhāri, n.m. A faqir with matted hair.

لٹا پٹا luṭā piṭā (H) adj. Robbed and beaten; ruined.

لٹاؤ luṭā'ū (H) adj. A spendthrift; a prodigal.

لٹانا liṭānā (H) v. To lay.

لٹانا luṭānā (H) v. To squander away; tc spend lavishly.

لٹائی loṭā'i (H) n.f. A roller on which the string of a kite is wound.

لٹ جانا luṭ jānā (H) v. See لٹنا luṭnā.

لٹس luṭṭas (H) n.f. Plundering; devastation; ruin.

لٹس مچانا luṭṭas machānā, v. To plunder; to rob.

لٹک laṭak (H) n.f. Fashion; manner of talking, speaking or singing; dangling; an affected gait; a sudden fit; the influence of an evil spirit; hanging; an affected motion in blandishment and coquetry.

لٹکا laṭkā (H) n.m. Incantation; a magic wand; a trick; a simple remedy; a kind of charm.

لٹکانا laṭkānā (H) v. To hang; to suspend.

لٹکن laṭkan (H) n.m. Anything hanging; ear-drops; ringlet; a nose-ring; a pendant; pendulum; plummet; a stand for water pots.

لٹکنا laṭakna (H) v. To hang; to dangle; to delay; to be kept waiting; to be post-poned; to swing.

لٹنا luṭnā (H) v. To be plundered; to be squandered; to be undone; to be defrauded; to be robbed (of); to be ruined.

لٹو laṭṭū (H) n.m. A top; a plummet; a governor (of a steam engine).

لٹو ہو جانا laṭṭū ho jānā, v. To fall in love with; to be enamoured.

لٹوانا luṭwānā (H) v. To cause to be plundered; to cause to be robbed.

لٹھ laṭh (H) n.m. A club; a stick; a measuring rod; a cudgel; a stupid fellow; an illiterate man.

لٹھ بازی laṭh bāzi, n.f. Cudgelling.

لٹھ مارنا laṭh mārnā, v. To strike with club; to speak harshly.

لٹھا **latthā** (H) *n.m.* A beam; a rafter; railway sleepers.

لٹھا **latthā**, *n.m.* A kind of cotton cloth.

لٹھم لٹھا **lattham latthā** (H) *n.f.* Club-fighting; mutual cudgelling; beating with clubs.

لٹھیا **lathyā** (H) *n.f.* A small club; a stick; a cudgel.

لٹھیت **lathait** (H) *adj.* Skilled in club-fighting; obstinate. *n.m.* A clubman.

لٹیا **lutyā** (H) *n.f.* A small brass pot with a spout.

لٹیا ڈبونا **lutyā ḍabonā**, *v.* To bring disgrace upon oneself ; to be ruined.

لٹیا ڈوبنا **lutyā ḍūbnā**, *v.* To be utterly wrecked; to be entirely ruined.

لٹیرا **luterā** (H) *n.m.* A plunderer; a robber; a highway-man; a swindler; a gangster.

لجا **lajjā** (H) *n.f.* Shame; modesty; bashfulness.

لجاجت **lajājat**, *n.f.* Importunity; entreaty; adulation.

لجالو **lajālū** (H) *adj.* Bashful; ignominious; modest, *n.m.* A species of Touch-me-not plant.

لجانا **lajānā** (H) *v.* To be abashed; to be ashamed

لجلجا **lujlujā**, **lajlajā**, (H) *adj.* Viscous; soft; clammy, glutinous; flabby.

لچ **luch** (H) *adj.* Bare; stark-naked; out and out; unmitigated.

لچ بہادر **luch bahādur**, *n.m.* A thorough vagabond.

لچا **luchchā** (H) *n.m.* A vagabond; rake; profligate; liberative; a mean fellow; a wicked man. *adj.* Low; mean; shameless; wicked; lewd; corrupt; given to gambling.

لچا پن **luchchā pan**, *n.m.* Profligacy; wantonness; lasciviousness; rakishness; rascality; immorality; knavery.

لچر **lachar** (H) *adj.* Meaningless; foolish; weak: loose; wanting force or vigour.

لچک **lachak** (H) *n.f.* Elasticity; bending; softness; flexibility; a sprain.

لچک دار **lachak dār**, *adj.* Elastic; soft; flexible.

لچکانا **lachkānā** (H) *v.* To bend; to strain; to bow.

لچکنا **lachaknā** (H) *v.* To bend; to be sprained.

لچھا **lachchhā** (H) *n.m.* A skein; a ball; a tassel; thin shreds of anything.

لچھے دار **lachchhe dār**, *adj.* Shred-like; entangled; confused; involved; serial; consecutive.

لچھمی **lachhmī** (H) *n.f.* The goddes of richness; prosperity; wealth; beauty; splendour.

لچھمی گھر میں آنا **lachhmi ghar men ānā**, *v.* To enjoy good fortune or prosperity.

لچھن **lachchhan** (H) *n.m.* Sign; mark; fashion; manner; system; condition.

لچھن پکڑنا، سیکھنا **lachchhan pakaṛnā, sikhna**, *v.* To learn bad or awkward manners.

لچھن جھڑنا **lachchan jhaṛnā**, *v.* To degenerate; to lose one's beauty; to be corrupted; to be deprived of manners or beauty.

لچئی **lucha'ī** (H) *n.f.* A kind of soft thin fine flour loaf fried in ghee.

لچی **luchchī** (H) *n.f.* A horlet; a pross; a bad character woman.

لحاظ **lihāẓ** (A) *n.m.* A glance; respect; regard; attention; observation; consideration; honour; reference; relation; shame; modesty; deference.

لحاظ اٹھا دینا **lihāẓ uṭhā denā**, *v.* To throw modesty aside; to abandon shame.

لحاظ کرنا **lihāẓ karnā**, *v.* To behold; to regard; to consider; to pay attention to; to pay respect to; to defer.

لحاظ نه کرنا liḥāẕ nah karnā, v To become shameless; to disregard; to pay no attention; to lose the sense of shame.

لحاف liḥāf (A) n.m. A coverlet; a quilt; a counterpane.

لحد laḥad (A) n.f. Grave; tomb; a hollow in which the dead bodies are put.

لحد بهرنا laḥad bharnā, v. To fill the tomb.

لحد کهودنا laḥad khodnā, v. To dig a grave.

لحظه laḥẕah (A) n.m. The twinkling of an eye; a look; a glance; a moment; a minute.

لحظه به لحظه laḥẕah ba laḥẕah, adv. Every moment; minute by minute.

لحظه بهر laḥẕah bhar, adv. For a moment.

لحم laḥm (A) n.m. Flesh; meat.

لحيم laḥīm (A) adj. Fleshy; corpulent; fat.

لحن laḥn (A) n.m. Sound; voice; note; modulation; melody.

لخت lak͟ht (P) n.m. A piece; a bit; a portion; a part; somewhat.

لخت جگر lak͟ht-ĕ jigar, n.m. A piece of one's heart; a darling child; a darling; a son or daughter.

لخ لخ lak͟h lak͟h (P) adj. Weak; lean; feeble.

لخ لخانا lak͟h lak͟hānā, v. To pant from thirst or hunger; to be reduced to extreme feebleness through hunger; to be starved.

لخلخه lak͟hlak͟hah (P) n.m. A strong perfume; a censer.

لدا پهندا ، لدی پهندی ladā phandā, ladī phandī (H) adj. Packed and loaded.

لدانا ladānā (H) v. See لدوانا ladwānā.

لداوا ، لداؤ ladāwā, ladā'o (H) n.m. A load; a cargo, a burden.

لدنا ladnā (H) v. To load; to be ladden; to be carried to one's grave.

لدنی ladunnī (A) adj. Inspired; God given.

لدو laddū (H) n.m. A beast of burden. adj. Fit to carry a load.

لدوانا ladwānā (H) v. To cause to load.

لدهڑ laddhaṛ (H) adj. Thick; heavy; unseemly; dull.

لڈو laḍḍū (H) n.m. A kind of sweetmeat, rolled into balls; benefit, gain; stock.

لڈو کهلانا laḍḍū khilānā, v. To feast one with لڈو laḍḍūs; to bribe a person.

لڈو ملنا laḍḍū milnā, v. To profit; to gain something; to make a profit.

لذت lazzat (A) n.f. Taste; flavour; joy; pleasure; deliciousness; enjoyment; (plu. لذات lazzāt).

لذت اٹهانا lazzat uṭhāna, v. To taste; to enjoy oneself.

لذت نفسانی lazzat-ĕ nafsānī, n.f. Sexsual pleasure.

لذت یاب lazzat yāb, adj. Finding pleasure; getting enjoyment.

لذيذ lazīz (A) adj. Sweet; delicious; tasteful; savoury; nice; delightful; piquant.

لر lar (H) n.m. A measuring rod varying from 4½ to 6½ cubits.

لر lur (P) adj. Stupid; silly.

لرزاں larzāṅ (P) adj. Trembling; tremulous; fearing.

لرزانا larzānā, v. To cause to shake; to quiver.

لرزجانا ، لرزنا laraz jānā, larazna, v. To shake; to tremble; to shiver; to quake; to beat; to throb.

لرزش larzish (P) n.f. Trembling; quivering; quaking.

لرزه larzah (P) n.m. Shaking; an earthquake; tremor; quake.

لڑ laṛ (H) n.f. A string; a row; a strand of a rope; a party; a chain; series; line; company.

لڑاک ، لڑاکا ، لڑاکو laṛāk, laṛākā, laṛākū (H) *adj.* Quarrelsome; contentious.

لڑانا laṛānā (H) *v.* To cause to fight; to bait; to lead an army to battle; to play.

لڑائی laṛā'i (H) *n.f.* Battle; war; fight; quarrel; fighting; wrestling; contest; enmity; hostility.

لڑائی باندھنا laṛā'i bāndhnā, *v.* To make a quarrel.

لڑائی بڑھانا laṛā'i baṛhanā, *n.f.* To foment a quarrel; to fan a fire; to put a stop to fighting.

لڑائی بھڑائی laṛā'i bhiṛā'i, *n.f.* Quarrel; dissension; trouble.

لڑائی بھڑائی پلے باندھنا laṛa'i bhiṛā'i palle bāndhnā, *v.* To involve oneself in a quarrel; to quarrel habitually.

لڑائی ٹھاننا laṛā'i ṭhānnā, *v.* To decide to fight out; to declare war.

لڑائی کا سامان laṛa'i kā sāmān, *n.m.* Ammunition.

لڑائی کا گھر laṛā'i kā ghar, *n.m.* A firebrand; cause of a quarrel.

لڑائی کا گیت laṛā'i kā gīt, *n.m.* Slogans of war; war-song.

لڑائی کا نعرہ laṛā'i kā na'rah, *n.m.* Warcry.

لڑائی کرنا laṛā'i karnā, *v.* To fight; to quarrel; to contend; to wrangle.

لڑائی لڑنا laṛā'i laṛnā, *v.* To wage or carry on a war.

لڑائی لینا laṛā'i lenā, *v.* To invite war; to provoke quarrel.

لڑائی مارنا laṛā'i mārnā, *v.* To win a battle.

لڑائی مول لینا laṛā'i mol lenā, *v.* To pick up a quarrel; to involve oneself in trouble.

لڑائی ہونا laṛā'i honā, *v.* To have a quarrel; to be at war.

لڑ بڑانا laṛ baṛānā (H) *v.* To stutter; to stammer; to stagger; to reel.

لڑ پڑنا laṛ paṭnā (H) *v.* To fall out with; to give up friendship or connection.

لڑکا laṛkā (H) *n.m.* A boy; child; a babe; a son; a youngster. *adj.* Simple; inexperienced.

لڑکا بالا laṛkā bālā, *n.m.* Child; children.

لڑکے بالے laṛke bāle, *n.m.* Family; household.

لڑکے والا laṛke wālā, *n.m.* Father of the bridegroom.

لڑکپن laṛakpan (H) *n.m.* Childhood; boyhood; childishness.

لڑکھڑانا laṛkhaṛānā (H) *v.* To stagger; to stammer; to reel; to trip; to stutter.

لڑکی laṛki (H) *n.f.* A girl, a lass; a daughter.

لڑکی والا laṛki wala, *n.m.* Father of the bride.

لڑمرنا laṛ marna (H) *v.* To fight to death; to cope with.

لڑنا laṛna (H) *v.* To fight; to struggle; to wrangle; to clash with; to cope with; to collide with; to contend; to quarrel; to go to war; to give battle.

لڑنا بھڑنا ، لڑنا جھگڑنا laṛna bhiṛna, laṛna jhagaṛnā, *v.* To fight; to wrangle; to quarrel.

لڑھکنا luṛahknā (H) *v.* To roll; to fall off; to slip; to slide; to roll down; to lie down; to die.

لڑھکنی lurhkani (H) *n.f.* Somersault.

لڑی laṛi (H) *n.f.* A string; a link.

لزوم luzūm (A) *n.m.* Necessity; compulsion; expediency; requisiteness; behaving.

لس las (H) *n.m.* Tenacity; viscosity; clamminess; glutinousness; stickiness.

لس دار las dār, *adj.* Viscous; sticky; clammy; glutinous.

لس لسا las lasā, *adj.* Viscous; adhesive.

لسان **lisān** (A) *n.f.* The tongue; language; dialect; speech; idiom.

لسان العصر *lisān-ul-'aṣr*, The voice of the times; man of the moment.

لسان الغیب *lisān-ul-ghaib, n.f.* A revelation; an oracle.

لسان **lassān** (A) *adj.* Eloquent; fluent; garrulous. *n.m.* An eloquent person; a talkative person.

لسانیت **lassāniyat** (A) *n.f.* Eloquence.

لس لسانا **las lasānā**, *v.* To be clammy; to be viscous.

لسن **lassan** (H) *n.m.* See لہسن *lahsan.*

لسوڑا **lasūrā** (H) *n.m.* A glutinous fruit.

لسی **lassī** (H) *n.f.* Milk and water; diluted milk; whey.

لشتم پشتم **lashtam pashtam** (H) *adv.* Topsy-turvy; with difficulty; with much ado; somehow or other.

لشکارنا **lashkārnā** (H) *v.* To tallyho.

لشکر **lashkar** (P) *n.m.* An army; an encampment; a camp; crowd.

لشکر کشی *lashkar kashī, n.f.* Levying of forces; conduct of an army; leading forth an army; invasion a levy; an army.

لشکر گاہ *lashkar gāh, n.m.* A camp; cantonment; a camping ground.

لشکری **lashkarī** (P) *adj.* Military; of an army. *n.m.* A soldier; a military officer; a general.

لطافت **laṭāfat** (P) *n.f.* Deliciousness; pleasantness; purity; fineness; elegance; delicateness; subtility; exquisiteness.

لطائف **laṭā'if** (A) *n.m.* (*plu.* of لطیفہ *laṭifah*) Wits; humours; jokes.

لطف **luṭf** (A) *n.m.* Kindness; courtesy; grace; benignity; favour; taste; elegance; grace; beauty; delicacy; pleasantness; pleasure; gratification; enjoyment.

لطمہ **laṭmah** (A) *n.m.* A slap on the cheek; a box on the ear; a blow.

لطمۂ موج *laṭmah-ĕ mauj, n.m.* The buffeting waves; blast of wind.

لطیف **laṭif** (A) *adj.* Delicious; agreeable; subtile; light; witty; fine; delicate; courteous; elegant; kind; benevolent; minute; exquisite; savoury.

لطیف طبع *laṭīf ṭaba' adj.* Of gentle disposition; merry-hearted; of cheerful spirit; fine; rose.

لطیف غذا *laṭif ghiẕā, n.f.* Light food; delicious food; spoon diet.

لطیفہ **laṭifah** (A) *n.m.* Pleasantry; jest; joke; raillery; elegance; witticism.

لطیفہ چھوڑنا *laṭifah chhoṛnā, v.* To tell a new tale; to take humorously.

لطیفہ گو *laṭīfah go, n.m.* A witty person; a facetious person; a jester; a wit; *bon-mot.*

لعاب **lu'āb** (A) *n.m.* Viscosity; sliminess; spittle; mucus; saliva.

لعاب دار *lu'āb dār, adj.* Slimy; viscous.

لعب **la'b** (A) *n.m.* Play; sport; game; playing.

لعبت **la'bat, lu'bat** (P) *n.f.* A doll; a puppet; a plaything; a toy.

لعبت بازی *lu'bat bazī, n.f.* Puppet-playing; theaterical representation; playing with dolls or toys.

لعل **la'l** (P) *n.m.* A ruby; the lips of a mistress.

لعل آگلنا *la'l ugalnā, v.* To cast up rubies.

لعن **la'n** (A) *n.f.* Cursing; imprecating; abuse; rebuke.

لعن طعن *la'n ṭa'n, n.f.* Taunts and curses; abuses.

لعن طعن کرنا *la'n ṭa'n karnā, v.* To curse and to taunt; to abuse.

لعنت *la'nat* (A) *n.f.* Abuse; curse; imprecation; anathema; execration; reproach; reproof.

لعنت بھیجنا ، کرنا *la'nat bhejnā, karnā, v.* To imprecate; to curse; to forswear; to shun.

لعنت کا مارا *la'nat kā mārā, adj.* Accused; the accursed one.

لعنت ملامت کرنا *la'nat malāmat karnā, v.* To curse; to reproach.

لعنتی *la'nati, adj.* Accused; the cursed one; execrable.

لعوق *la'ūq* (A) *n.m.* A medicine for licking or sucking.

لعین *la'in* (A) *adj.* Accursed; execrable; abominable; detested.

لغات *lughāt* (A) *n.m.* (*plu.* of لغت *lughat*) Dictionary; lexicon; languages; dialects; words.

لغایت *laghāyat* (A) *adv. & adj.* To the end of; upto; inclusive.

لغت *lughat* (A) *n.m.* Tongue; speech; dialect; word; language; dictionary; glossary; vocabulary; lexicon.

لغت تراشنا *lughat tarāshnā, v.* To coin big words; to use big words.

لغت شناس *lughat shinās, n.m.* Philologist.

لغزش *laghzish* (P) *n.f.* Slipping; shaking; a slip; equivocation; ambiguity; tottering.

لغزش آنا *laghzish ānā, v.* To tremble; to slip.

لغزش کرنا ، کھانا *laghzish karnā, khānā, v.* To slip; to equivocate.

لغو *laghv* (A) *adj.* Absurd; false; foolish; nonsense.

لغوی *lughwi* (A) *adj.* Literal or verbal.

لغوی معنی *lughwi ma'ni, n.m.* The literal or verbal meaning.

لغویت *laghwiyat* (A) *n.f.* Absurdity; foolishness.

لف *laff* (A) *adj.* Folded; wrapped; included; involved; mixed; joined.

لف و نشر *laff-ŏ nashr, n.m.* Folding and spreading; involution and evolution.

لفاظ *laffāz* (A) *adj.* Eloquent; verbose; talkative; prolix; garrulous; wordy.

لفاظی *laffāzi* (A) *n.f.* Eloquence; verbosity; pedantry; volubility.

لفافہ *lifāfah* (A) *n.m.* A cover; envelope; enclosure; a wrapper; an outward case; a secret; whitewash; outward show; anything frail.

لفافہ بنانا *lifāfah banānā, v.* To make an envelope; to make a show or display.

لفافہ کھل جانا *lifāfah khul jānā, v.* To be exposed; to be unmasked; to be laid bare; the disclosure of a secret.

لفظ *lafz* (A) *n.m.* A word; a saying; a term.

لفظ بہ لفظ *lafz bah lafz, adv.* Word by word.

لفظاً *lafzan* (A) *adv.* Literally; distinctly; verbally; expressly.

لفظی *lafzi* (A) *adj.* Verbal; literal.

لفظی بحث *lafzi bahs n.f.* A wordy discussion.

لفظی ترجمہ *lafzi tarjumah, n.m.* A literal translation.

لفظی معنی *lafzi ma'ni, n.m.* Literal meaning.

لفنگا *lafangā* (H) *n.m.* A vain-glorious fellow; a braggert; a loose character.

لقا *liqā* (A) *n.f.* Act of meeting; seeing some one; encountering some one; the face; form; visage; countenance; death.

لقا *laqqā, n.m.* The fan-tail pigeon.

لقب *laqab* (A) *n.m.* A title; a sur-name; by-name; application of honour.

لقلق *laqlaq* (A) *n.m.* A stork.

لقلقہ *laqlaqah, n.m.* The cry of a stork; eloquence; pronunciation; a continual motion of the jaw or of the tongue (in serpents); many sweet smells mixed in one.

لقمان *luqmān* (A) *n.m.* A famous eastern fabulist (supposed to be the same as Aesop); a wise man.

لقمہ *luqmah* (A) *n.m.* A morsel; a mouthful; a bit.

لقمۂ اجل ہونا *luqmah-ĕ ajal honā, v.* To go into the jaws of death; to die.

لقمہ دینا *luqmah denā, v.* To put words in one's mouth; to prime.

لقمہ کرنا *luqmāh karnā, v.* To make a mouthful of; to swallow.

لقندرا *luqaṅdrā, n.m.* A vagabond; rake; a mean fellow; wicked one.

لق و دق *laqq-ŏ daqq* (A) *adj.* Desolate; bleak and barren; dreary; a howling wilderness.

لقوہ *laqwah* (A) *n.m.* Facial paralysis; a spasmodic distortion of the face.

لقوہ مار جانا *laqwah mār jānā, v.* To have paralytic stroke.

لقہ *luqqah, n.m.* See لقندرا *luqaṅdrā.*

لک *luk* (P) *n.m.* Varnish, tarcoal; bitumen.

لکڑ *lakkaṛ* (H) *n.m.* Wood; cudgel; beam; box; log; raft; club.

لکڑ ہارا *lakkaṛ hārā, n.m.* A wood-cutter; a wood-seller.

لکڑی *lakṛi* (H) *n.f.* Wood; timber; a staff; stick; fuel.

لکڑی پھینکنا *lakṛi pheṅknā, v.* Club playing; fencing; to play with cudgels.

لکڑیاں دینا *lakkṛiyān denā, v.* To perform one's obsequies (among Hindus); to place wood on the funeral pyre.

لکشمی *lakshmī* (S) *n.f.* See لچھمی *lachhmi.*

لکنت *luknat* (A) *n.f.* Stammering; stuttering; impediment in speech.

لکہ *lakkah* (P) *n.m.* Spot; stain; blot; speck; part.

لکہ ابر *lakkah-ĕ abr, n.m.* A speck of a cloud.

لکھ *lakh* (H) *adj.* One hundred thousand.

لکھ پتی *lakh pati, adj.* Rich; possessing *lākhs* of rupees; a millioniare.

لکھا *likhā* (H) *adj.* Written. *n.m.* Fate; destiny.

لکھا پڑھا *likhā parhā, adj.* Educated person.

لکھا پورا کرنا *likhā pūrā karnā, v.* To lead a life as one is destined to live; to pass one's days in hardship; to suffer what fate has ordained.

لکھانا *likhānā* (H) *v.* To have something recorded; to dictate; to cause to write; to teach to write.

لکھائی *likhā'i* (H) *n.f.* Act of writing; the wages of writing; the art of writing.

لکھت *likhat* (H) *n.f.* Anything written; penmanship; inscription; writing; a letter; a deed; missive; scripture; a letter; document.

لکھت پڑھت ہونا *likhat paṛhat honā, v.* To be reduced to writing.

لکھنا *likhnā* (H) *v.* To write; to copy; to register; to delineate; to make a draught; to paint; to compose.

لکھنا پڑھنا *likhnā paṛhnā, n.m.* Education. *v.* To read and to write; to receive education.

لکھوانا *likhwānā* (H) *v.* See لکھانا *likhāna.*

لکیر *lakir* (H) *n.f.* A line; lineament; streak; stripe.

لکیر پیٹنا *lakir pitnā, v.* To follow the beaten path; to follow the footprints of one's ancestors; to be a slave to old customs and rites.

لکیر کھینچنا *lakir kheṅchnā, v.* To draw a line; to fix a boundary; to rule; to strike out (with a pen &c).

لگا laggā (H) *n.m.* A long bamboo; a pole used to impel a boat; friendship; similarity; affection, attachment.

لگا کھانا laggā khānā, *v.* To be consistent with; to compete (with); to be equal (of).

لگا لگانا laggā lagānā, *v.* To commence; to form an attachment or intimacy; to begin; to start.

لگا نہ کھانا laggā nah khānā, *v.* To be incompatible; to be inconsistent with.

لگا بندھا lagā bandhā (H) *adj.* Fixed. *n.m.* A friend; a companion.

لگا تار lagā tār (H) *adv.* Constantly; continually; successively; uninterruptedly; *ad seriatim. adj.* Successive; incessant.

لگا دینا lagā denā (H) *v.* To apply; to put to work; to fix; to hoard up.

لگا رہنا lagā rehnā (H) *v.* To persevere; to continue in close contact with; to stick to; to lie in wait; to continue; to be engaged.

لگا لگایا lagā lagāyā (H) *adj.* Fixed; settled.

لگام lagām (H) *n.f.* A bridle; rein.

لگام دینا lagām denā, *v.* To bridle; to curb; to control; to check.

لگان lagān (H) *n.m.* Land revenue; assessment on land; rent.

لگانا lagānā (H) *v.* To apply; to attach; to join; to ascribe; to impose; to plant; to set; to inflict; to plaster; to put to work; to employ; to engage; to impute; to report anything in the way of scandal or malice.

لگانا بجھانا lagānā bujhānā, *v.* To sow dissension; to excite quarrels.

لگاوٹ lagāwaṭ (H) *n.f.* Connection; relation; attachment; application; adherence; affection; sexual intercourse.

لگاؤ lagā'o (H) *n.m.* Relation; connection; intercourse; inclination; affection; adherence; application; contact; attachment.

لگائی lugā'i (H) *n.f.* A woman; wife.

لگائی بجھائی lagā'i bujhā'i (H) *n.f.* Back-biting; creating differences between two persons and then making peace between them

لگ بھگ lag bhag (H) *adv.* About; approximately; almost by; thereabout; near.

لگدی lugdi (H) *n.f.* A lump of something powdered and moistened.

لگڑ بگڑ، لگڑ بھگا lagaṛ bagaṛ, lagaṛ bhaggā (H) *n.m.* A beast of prey; hyena.

لگن lagan (P) *n.m.* A copper trough; a candle-stand; a basin.

لگن lagan (H) *n.f.* Affection; friendship; attachment; love; desire; longing. *n.m.* Appointing the day of marriage; the rising of a sign of the zodiac; a moment.

لگن لگنا lagan lagnā, *v.* To be attached to; to be in love with; to fall in love; to be fond of.

لگنا lagnā (H) *v.* To be attached (to); to be applied; to be connected (with); to come to anchor; to break out (fire); to be planted or set (trees); to be added or appended; to take root or become rooted; to have effect; to lie in wait; to be invested (money); to be expended or consumed (on); to be employed; to be close or contiguous (to); to come into contact (with); to have sexual intercourse (with); to close or shut (doors etc.); to hurt or wound; to be caught or overtaken by (disease); to bear (fruit).

لگوانا lagwānā (H) *v.* To cause to be applied; to get fixed; to cause to be put in; to cause to apply.

لگی lagi (H) *n.f.* Desire; love; passion; hunger.

لگی کو بجھانا lagī ko bujhānā, v. To satisfy one's longing.

لگی لپٹی lagī lipṭī, adj. Obscure; indistinct; partial; prejudiced.

لگی لپٹی کہنا lagī lipṭī kahnā, v. To show partiality; to speak ambiguously; to take sides.

للت lalit (H) n.f. A musical mode; adj. beautiful; charming; pleasant; agreeable.

للچانا lalchānā (H) v. To covet; to excite desire; to be tantalized; to long for.

للکار lalkār (H) n.f. Calling; shouting; cry; challenge; threat.

للکارنا lalkārnā (H) v. To call out; to bawl; to challenge; to threaten.

للو پتو lallo patto (H) n.f. Coaxing; adulation.

للو پتو کرنا lallo patto karna, v. To flatter; to coax.

لله lillah (A) adv. For God's sake; in the name of God.

لله الحمد lilla hil ḥamd, intj. To God be the praise.

لم lam (H) adj. (contraction of لمبا lambā) Long; tall.

لم ٹنگو lam ṭingū, adj. Long legged. n.m. A crane.

لم چھڑ lam chhaṛ, n.m. Long thin stick. adj. Tall.

لم کنا lam kannā, adj. Having long-ears. n.m. A hare.

لم lim (A) n.f. Cause; knack; trick; false accusation.

لمبا lamba (H) adj. Long; tall; great; expanded.

لمبا چوڑا lambā chauṛa, adj. Spacious; long and wide; extensive; of commanding stature.

لمبا دفتر lambā daftar, n.m. A long tale.

لمبان ، لمبائی lambān, lambā'i (H) n.f. Length; tallness.

لمبائی چوڑائی lambā'i chauṛā'i, n.f. Length and breadth; size; surface.

لمبر lambar, n.m. (corr. from English); Number; marks; position; rank; turn.

لمبردار lambar dār, n.m. The headman of a village.

لمبو lambū (H) adj. Long; long-legged; tall.

لمبوترا lambotrā (H) adj. Very long; very tall.

لمبی lambi (H) n.f. A long stride in a horse. adj. Long.

لمبی تاننا lambi tānnā, v. To be down; to die; to sleep at ease; to stretch oneself full length in sleeping.

لمبی چوڑی هانکنا lambī chauṛī hāṅknā, v. To boast; to brag; to tell a tall story.

لمبی سانس بھرنا lambi sāṅs bharna, v. To heave a deep sigh; to lament; to repent; to regret.

لمحہ lamḥah (A) n.m. A minute; moment; twinkling of an eye.

لمحہ بھر lamḥah bhar, adv. For a minute; for a while.

لمس lams (A) n.m. The sense of touch; touch.

لمعہ lama'h (A) n.m. Brightness; glow; light; glimpse. (plu. of لمعات lama'āt).

لن ترانی lan tarānī (A) "Thou shalt never see me." This was the answer given by God when Moses made the request "Lord show thyself to me that I may behold thee". n.f. Boasting; bragging; conceitedness.

لنجا ، لنجی lunja, lunjı (H) adj. Without hands and feet; crippled.

لنڈ lanḍ (H) n.m. Penis; the male organ.

لنڈا lunḍā (H) adj. Tail-cropped; stripped of leaves; without friends; tailless.

لنڈ منڈ *luṅḍ muṅḍ* (H) *adj.* Tailless and bald: without leaves (tree).

لنڈورا *laṅḍorā* (H) *adj.* Tailless; farlorn.

لنڈھانا *luṅḍhānā* (H) *v.* To spill; to overturn.

لنگ *laṅg* (P) *n.m.* Lameness; limp. *adj.* Lame.

لنگ کرنا *laṅg karnā*, *v.* To go lame; to limp (generally animals).

لنگ *liṅg* (S) *n.m.* Male organ of generation; Shiva's genital organ worshipped by Hindus; the sign of gender or sex; (in *Gram.*) gender; a distinguishing mark; a religious mark.

لنگ *luṅg* (P) *n.m.* A cloth worn round the loins; a cloth worn between the legs like a دھوتی *dhotī*.

لنگر *laṅgar* (P) *n.m.* Anchor; a cable; a thick rope; a thick rope for supporting a tent; alms; alms-house; victuals distributed to the poor; a public kitchen; a long strip of cloth worn by wrestlers round the loins.

لنگر اٹھانا *laṅgar uṭhānā*, *v.* To weigh anchor.

لنگر جاری کرنا *laṅgar jāri karnā*, *v.* To set up an alms-house.

لنگر خانہ *laṅgar khānah*, *n.m.* An alms-house.

لنگر ڈالنا *laṅgar ḍālnā*, *v.* To let go the anchor; to cast anchor.

لنگر لنگوٹا *laṅgar laṅgoṭā*, *n.m.* A cloth worn by wrestlers round the loins.

لنگڑا *laṅgṛā*, *n.m.* A kind of mango.

لنگڑا ، لنگڑی *laṅgṛā*, *laṅgṛi* (H) *adj.* Lame; crippled; limping.

لنگڑانا *laṅgṛānā* (H) *v.* To limp; to become lame.

لنگوٹ ، لنگوٹا *laṅgoṭ*, *laṅgoṭā* (H) *n.m.* A cloth generally worn by wrestlers between the legs to conceal nakedness.

لنگوٹ باندھنا *laṅgoṭ bāndhnā*, *v.* To gird up one's loins; to be ready to fight.

لنگوٹ بند *laṅgoṭ baṅd*, *adj.* One devoted to celibacy; a confirmed bachelor; bachelor; one who is faithful to the marriage tie.

لنگوٹ کا سچا *laṅgoṭ kā sachchā*, *adj.* An ascetic; a confirmed bachelor.

لنگوٹی *laṅgoṭī*, *n.f.* See لنگوٹ *laṅgoṭ*.

لنگوٹیا *laṅgoṭiyā*, *n.m.* An old friend; a friend from childhood; a playmate; a crony.

لنگور *laṅgūr* (H) *n.m.* A baboon; a long tailed, black-faced monkey.

لنگی *luṅgī* (H) *n.f.* See لنگ *luṅg*; a turban.

لو *lo* (H) *interj.* Lo! look! take! there! now.

لو *lū* (H) *n.f.* A hot wind.

لو لگنا *lū lagnā*, *v.* To be struck down by hot wind.

لو *lau* (H) *n.f.* The flame of a candle; any pointed flame; the lobe of the ear; attachment; bent of mind; ardent desire; deep meditation; love.

لو لگانا *lau lagānā*, *v.* To have a constant desire (for); to fix the attention (on); to be constant in devotion.

لو لگنا *lau lagnā*, *v.* To be bent on; to be devoted to; to be constant in devotion (to).

لوا *lavā* (A) *n.m.* A kind of bird; clove.

لوا *livā* (A) *n.m.* A standard; a banner.

لواحق *lawāḥiq* (A) *n.m.* (*plu.* of لاحق *lāḥiq*) Relations; dependants; family; appurtenances; kindred; followers; domestic servants.

لوازم ، لوازمات *lawazim*, *lawāzimat* (A) *n.m.* (*plu.* of لازمہ *lāzimah*). Necessaries; baggage: ingredients; requisites; essentials.

لواطت *liwāṭat* (A) *n.f.* Sodomy.

لوبان *lobān* (A) *n.m.* A kind of incense; frankincense; bedzoin; a kind of gum or resin.

لوبان جلانا *lobān jalānā, v.* To burn incense.

لوبان دانی *lobān dānī, n.f.* A censer; a receptacle for incense.

لوبھ *lobh* (S) *n.m.* Avarice; ambition; greediness; covetousness; temptation.

لوبھی *lobhī* (H) *adj.* Covetous.

لوبیا *lobiyā* (H) *n.m.* A kind of bean.

لوتھڑا *lothṛā* (H) *n.m.* A lump of flesh.

لوٹ آنا *lauṭ ānā* (H) *v.* To return; to come back.

لوٹانا *lauṭānā* (H) *v.* To invert; to return; to send back; to turn over.

لوٹ جانا *lauṭ jānā* (H) *v.* To turn back; to go back.

لوٹ پوٹ *loṭ poṭ* (H) *adj.* Tumble and toss; rolling and tossing about; restless.

لوٹ پوٹ ھونا *loṭ poṭ hona, v.* To roll and toss restlessly; to be taken with; to die suddenly; to be in love.

لوٹ *lūṭ* (H) *n.f.* Plunder; booty; spoil; robbery; prize; rapine; unfair dealing.

لوٹ پڑنا *lūṭ paṛnā, v.* To be plundered; to be robbed; to be pillaged.

لوٹ کا مال *lūṭ kā māl, n.m.* Booty; plunder; prize; gain.

لوٹ کھسوٹ *lūṭ khasoṭ, n.f.* Plundering and looting.

لوٹ مار *lūṭ mār, n.f.* Pillage; havoc; devastation.

لوٹ مچانا *lūṭ machana, v.* To plunder; to rob; to sack.

لوٹن *loṭan* (H) *adj.* Tumbling; rolling. *n.m.* The ground tumbler pigeon.

لوٹنا *lauṭnā* (H) *v.* To turn back or over; to return; to retreat.

لوٹنا *lūṭnā* (H) *v.* To plunder; to ruin; to rob; to riot; to charge a high price.

لوٹنا *loṭnā* (H) *v.* To roll; to toss about; to sprawl; to wallow; to lie in bed; to be charmed; to be agitated.

لوث *lauṣ* (A) *n.m.* Contamination; pollution; defilement; impurity.

لوچ *loch* (H) *n.m.* Starch; stickiness; sweetness; delicacy; viscosity; softness; elasticity; beauty.

لوچ دار *loch dār, adj.* Starshy; soft; elastic; agreeable; delicate.

لوچن *lochan* (S) *n.m.* The eye; eye-disease.

لوح *lauḥ* (A) *n.f.* A plank; a table; a board; a tablet; a title page.

لوح تربت *lauḥ-ĕ turbat, n.f.* Gravestone.

لوح طلسم *lauḥ-ĕ ṭalism, n.f.* Talismanic tablet.

لوح محفوظ *lauḥ-ĕ maḥfūẓ, n.f.* The guarded table on which according to Muslim belief, the doings of mankind have been recorded from eternity; the knowledge of the Unseen.

لوح مشق *lauḥ-ĕ mashq, n.f.* Practising tablet (used by school boys).

لوح وقلم *lauḥ-ŏ qalam, n.m.* The tablet and the pen (especially those with which the decrees of God are written).

لودی ، لودھی *lodī, lodhi* (H) *n.m.* Name of a caste of the Pathans.

لوری *lori* (H) *n.f.* A kind of song; a lullaby.

لوری دینا *lori denā, v.* To lull a child to sleep; to sing a lullaby.

لوز *lauz* (A) *n.m.* An almond; a kind of sweetmeat.

لوطی *lūṭi* (A) *n.m.* An inhabitant of Sodom; a sodomite.

لوک *lok* (S) *n.m.* People; world; region; country.

لوک سبھا *lok sabha, n.f.* People's House; the House of the People (Indian Parliament).

لوکا lūkā (H) n.m. Flame; fire; spark; pieces of burning matter thrown out from a conflagration.

لوکا لگانا ، دینا lūkā lagānā, dena, v. To set fire to; to inflame or excite quarrels.

لوکاٹ lokāṭ (H) n.m. A kind of fruit; 'loquat'.

لوکی lauki (H) n.f. A pumpkin; a bottle gourd.

لوگ log (H) n.m. People; folk; caste; husband; man; mankind; family, household.

لوگ باگ log bāg, n.m. People, great and small.

لولا ، لولی lūla, lūlī (H) adj. Having no hands; crippled.

لولا لنگڑا ، لولی لنگڑی lūla langṛā, lūlī langṛī, adj. Lame and crippled.

لولاک laulāk (A) (Had it not been thee) The beginning of a sentence which means, "If I had not intended to create thee (the Holy Prophet) I would not have created the world".

لؤ لؤ lo'l'o (A) n.m. A pearl.

لولی loli (P) n.f. A prostitute; a people in Persia, called also *gurji*.

لولی فلک loli-ĕ falak, n.f. The planet Venus.

لومڑی lomṛi (H) n.f. A fox.

لون lun (H) n.m. Salt; common salt.

لوند laund (H) n.m. An intercalary month; an extra month.

لونڈا launḍa (H) n.m. A boy; a slave boy; a lad; a brat.

لونڈے بازی launḍe bazi, n.f. Sodomy.

لونڈی launḍi (H) n.f. A slave-girl; a bond-maid; a servant girl.

لونڈیا launḍya (H) n.f. A girl; a lass; a daughter.

لونگ laung (H) n.f. Cloves; a nose pin.

لونگ چڑے laung chaṛe, n.m. A kind of dish prepared from peasemeal.

لوہ loh (H) n.m. (contraction of لوہا lohā) Iron.

لوہ چون loh chūn, n.m. Iron filings.

لوہا lohā (H) n.m. Iron.

لوہا بجانا lohā bajānā, v. To fight with sword.

لوہا برسنا lohā barasnā, v. To have a free use of swords; to have a general massacre.

لوہا دینا ، کرنا lohā denā, karna, v. To iron (a cloth).

لوہا لاٹھ lohā lāṭh, n.m. An iron bound club. adj. Hard; strong; difficult; rigid.

لوہا مان جانا loha man jana, v. To acknowledge the superiority of.

لوہے کی چھاتی کر لینا lohe ki chhāti kar lenā, v. To be adamant; to have a heart to suffer a misfortune; to put up a bold front.

لوہے کے چنے چبانا lohe ke chane chabānā, v. To inflict severe punishment.

لوہار lohar (H) n.m. A blacksmith; a worker in iron.

لوہار خانہ lohar khanah, n.m. Smithy; iron factory; a black-smith's workshop.

لوہار کی بھٹی lohār ki bhaṭṭi, n.f. A furnace; a blacksmith's forge.

لوہیا lohiyā (H) n.m. An iron seller. adj. Of iron.

لوئی lo'ī (H) n.f. A blanket; flannel; splendour of the countenance; honour.

لہارن luharan (H) n.f. A female blacksmith; wife of a blacksmith.

لہان luhan (H) adj. Bloody; blood stained.

لہجہ lahjah (A) n.m. The tongue; tone; voice; sound; accent; accentuation; cadence; speech; talk.

لہذا *lihazā* (A) *adv.* Therefore; consequently; for this reason; because.

لہر *lahar* (H) *n.f.* A wave; endulation; whim; fancy; vision; a waving pattern in embroidery; a waving line in cloth; emotion; rapture; excitement; frenzy; fit; the effect of the poison of a snake.

لہر آنا *lahar ānā, v.* To undulate; to wave to and fro; to fluctuate; to play loosely; to put off; to raise delusive hopes in one's mind.

لہر بہر *lahar bahar, n.f.* Prosperity; prime and vigour; glow and glory.

لہرا *lahrā* (H) *n.m.* A quacker; a lively tune; a trill in music.

لہرانا *lahrānā* (H) *v.* To wave; to fluctuate; to bloom.

لہری *lahri* (H) *adj.* Odd; merry; emotional; capricious; fantastic; inconstant; whimsical; fanciful.

لہریا *lahriyā* (H) *n.m.* Wave-like embroidery; watered silk; striped cloth. *adj.* Serpentine; striped; wavy; waved; a mode of dyeing or painting.

لہسن *lahsan* (H) *n.m.* Garlic; a freckle; a blotch; a prickle.

لہک *lahak* (H) *n.f.* Glitter; flash; blaze.

لہک لہک کے بولنا *lahak lahak ke bolnā, v.* To speak aloud.

لہکارنا *lahkārnā* (H) *v.* To fondle; to pat and encourage a horse etc.

لہکانا *lahkānā* (H) *v.* To warble; to quaver; to cause to shine or glitter; to blow up a fire; to make a flame.

لہکنا *lahaknā* (H) *v.* To be kindled or lighted; to rise up into a flame; to glitter; to flash; to shine; to wave; to speak aloud; to warble; to chirrup; to sing

لہلوٹ *lahloṭ* (H) *adj.* Borrowing and never paying; a bad paymaster.

لہلہانا *lahlahānā* (H) *v.* To bloom; to be verdant; to flourish; to wave.

لہلہاہٹ *lahlahāhat* (H) *n.f* Waving; blooming; waving of corn etc. before the wind.

لہنگا *lahṅgā* (H) *n.m.* A petticoat; a skirt.

لہو *lahū* (H) *n.m.* Blood.

لہو آنا *lahū ānā. v.* To pass blood (by stool).

لہو آترنا *lahū utarnā, v.* To be blood shot.

لہو پانی ایک کرنا *lahū pāni ek karnā, v.* To work very hard.

لہو پینا *lahū pinā, v.* To drink one's own blood; to worry a great deal.

لہو تھوکنا ، ڈالنا *lahū thūknā, ḍālnā, v.* To spit blood; to be suffering from consumption.

لہو کا پیاسا *lahū kā piyāsā, adj.* Bloodthirsty; bitter enemy.

لہو کے گھونٹ پینا *lahū ke ghunt pinā, v.* To suffer patiently.

لہو لہان *lahū luhān, adj.* Blood stained; covered with blood.

لہو *lahw* (A) *n.m.* Play; anything ludicrous or jocular; sport.

لہو و لعب *lahw-ŏ l'ab, n.m.* Play; sport; mirth; amusement; game; fun; pastime.

لئیم *la'im* (A) *adj.* Sordid; miserly; reprehensible.

لے *lae* (H) *n.f.* A tune; air; desire; modulation; affection; taste; equal time in music and dancing; melody; symphony; ardent affection or desire; immersion; absorption.

لے *le* (H) *interj.* Take! come! well.

لے آنا *le ānā, v.* To bring; to produce; to fetch; to import.

لیا دیا *liyā diyā, n.m.* Reward of good deeds; a good deed done.

لے آڑنا *le uṛnā, v.* To set off; to run away with; to carry tales.

لیاقت liyāqat (A) n.f. Worth; ability; fitness; capability; capacity; aptitude; adherence; connection; merit; skill; knack; proficiency; suitability.

لے بھاگنا le bhāgnā. v. To run away with; to abduct.

لیپ lep (H) n.m. Ointment; plaster.

لیپ کرنا ، لگانا lep karnā, lagānā, v. To apply a plaster or ointment; to plaster.

لیپا پوتا lepā potā (H) adj. Fully plastered and whitewashed; completed; scrabbled; clean.

لے پالک le pālak, adj. Adopted (child).

لیپنا lepnā (H) v. To plaster; to gloss over; to besmear.

لیت و لعل lait-ŏ la'll (A) n.f. Subterfuge; evasion; procrastination; prevarication.

لیٹنا letnā (H) v. To lie down; to rest; to submit; to melt; to repose; to lie prostrate.

لے جانا le jānā, v. To take away with; to run away with; to convey; to win; to submit.

لیچڑ lichaṛ (H) adj. Stingy; niggardly; miser; a bad paymaster. n.m. A stingy fellow; a bad paymaster.

لیچڑ پن lichar pan, n.m. Stinginess; niggardliness.

لیچی lichi (H) n.f. A friut, scytalia litchi.

لید lid (H) n.f. The dung of horses, donkeys, elephants &c.

لے دے کرنا le de karnā, v. To rebuke; to reprove; to try hard.

لے دے کے le de ke, adv. With great difficulty; after making all efforts; altogether.

لے ڈوبنا le ḍūbnā, v. To ruin another person along with oneself.

لیر lir (H) n.f. A strip or slip of cloth; a rag.

لیر لیر کرنا lir lir karnā, v. To tear to shreds or pieces.

لیر لیر ہونا lir lir honā, v. To be in rags.

لیس lais (H) adj. Ready; dressed; finished; n.m. A spring; an arrow; a kind of vinegar. n.f. Lace.

لیس ہونا lais honā, v. To be ready.

لیس les (H) n.f. Stickiness; viscosity; smallness; littleness; plaster; mark.

لیسدار les dār, adj. Glutinous.

لیس les (P) adj. Licking (used in comps. as in کاسہ لیس kāsā les; a plate-licker)

لیسنا lesnā (H) v. To plaster.

لیک lik (H) n.f. Marks; path; rut; traces of carriage wheels left on roads.

لیک پر چلنا ، لیک لیک چلنا lik ṛar chalnā, lik lik chalnā,, v. To follow the beaten path; to adhere to old established customs.

لیک ، لیکن lek, lekin (P) conj. But; yet; however; still; nevertheless.

لیکھ likh (H) n.f. The egg of a louse; a small louse.

لیل ، لیلة lail, lailat (A) n.f. Night.

لیل و نہار lail-ŏ nahār, n.m. Night and day; circumstances; position.

لیلة الاسریٰ laila-tul-asrạ, n.f. The night on which the Holy Prophet ascended from Jerusalem to Heaven.

لیلة البدر laila-tul-badr, n.f. The night of the full moon.

لیلة القدر laila-tul-qadr, n.f. The night of power; the twenty seventh night of the month of رمضان Ramaẓān when the Quran began to be revealed.

لیلا lelā (H) n.m. A lamb.

لیلا līlā (H) n.f. Sport; play; diversion; theatre performance; amorous sport; phenomenon; wonders.

لیلا وتی lilāwati, n.f. A playful woman.

لیلیٰ ، لیلی lailā, laili (A) adj. Black. n.f. Name of the celebrated beloved of مجنوں Majnūn; a sweetheart; a mistress.

لے لینا le lenā, v. To receive; to accept; to take; to take by force; to extort; to bereave; to take back.

لے مرنا le marnā, v. To try hard and succeed in getting something; to involve one falsely; to calumniate.

لیمو limū (P) n.m. A lemon; lime.

لین len (H) n.m. Taking; receiving.

لین دین len den, n.m. Traffic; trade; money dealings; business; banking; friendly intercourse; buying and selling; borrowing and lending.

لینا lenā (H) v. To receive; to take; to accept; to assume; to buy; to borrow; to win; to conquer; to usurp; to take hold of; to catch.

لینا ایک نہ دینا دو lenā ek nah denā do, id. To have nothing to do (with); to have no connection whatever (with).

لینے کے دینے پڑنا lene ke dene paṛnā, v. To have tables turned on one.

لینے میں نہ دینے میں lene meṅ nah dene meṅ, id. Unconcerned; having nothing to do (with).

لینڈ leṅḍ (H) n.m. Filth; excrement.

لینڈی leṅḍi (H) n.f. Filth. adj. Coward.

لینڈی تر ہونا leṅḍi tar honā, v. To be very proud; to be puffed up.

لینڈی کتا leṅḍi kuttā, n.m. A country dog.

لیوا lewā (H) adj. One who receives or takes.

لئے liye (H) adv. For; on account of; instead of.

لئی la'i (H) n.f. Paste; cement; starch.

م mim, is the twenty-fourth letter of the Arabic, twenty-eighth of the Persian and thirty-first letter of the Urdu alphabet. In abjad it stands for 40.

مآب maāb (A) n.f. The centre or point to which a thing or person returns; fixed abode or seat(of); a repository; receptacle; (also used in comp. as, عزت مآب 'izzat maāb, honourable; the seat of grandeur and glory).

مآثر maāṣir (A) n.m. (plu. of مآثرت māṣarat) Generous qualities handed down by tradition or from ancestors; worthy actions; glories; excellencies; memorable deeds.

مآل maāl (A) n.m. End; aim; consequence; termination; result.

مآل اندیش maāl aṅdesh, adj. Prudent; circumspect.

مآل اندیشی maāl aṅdeshi, n.f. Prudence; minding the consequences.

ما mā (A) adv. Which; what; that which; whatsoever; something; as far as; as long as; whilst; during; as much as; why; wherefore: what; how; no; not.

ما بعد mā ba'd, adj. That which follows after; following.

مابقا، مابقیٰ mā baqā, adj. n.m. The rest, remainder; remnant; balance; arrears.

مابہ الاحتیاج mā bihil-iḥtiyāj, n.m. Whatever is necessary; necessary articles; required things.

مابہ الامتیاز mā bihil-imtiyāz, n.m. Distinctive characteristic or feature.

ما بہ النزاع mā hibin- nizāa', n.m. Bone of contention; reasons of the quarrel.

مابین mā bain, adj. & adv. Internal; interim; space between two bodies; intermediate; intervening; between; among; during; mean-time.

ماتحت mā taḥat, adj. Subordinate; inferior; dependent; subject.

ماتقدم mā taqqadum, adj. What has gone before or what has afore-said; stated above; passed.

ماجرا mā jarā, n.m. Happening; occurrence; state; condition; circumstance; event; incident; accident; adventure.

ماحصل mā ḥaṣal, n.m. Inference; result; profit; produce; the harvest; conclusion; the sum and substance; abstract.

ماحضر mā ḥazar, n.m. Whatever (of the victuals) is ready or prepared or present; pot-luck.

ماحول mā ḥaul, n.m. Surroundings; environments; prevalent conditions.

ماسبق mā sabaq, adj. What precedes or has preceded something; above-mentioned; preceding.

ماسلف mā salaf, adj. What is past; what has gone before; before mentioned or done.

ماسوا mā siwā, adv. Besides; moreover; over and above.

ماشاءالله mā shā' allah, intj. (Lit. what God wills); may God preserve him or it from the evil eye! may God preserve it!

مافات mā fāt, adj. What is past or dead.

مافوق mā fauq, adj. What is superior or excelling; what is excellent.

ما فی الضمیر mā fiz ẓamir, n.m. Intention; motive; design; secret.

مافیها mā fihā, n.m. What it contains.

ماقبل mā qabl, adj. What is before; preceding; before.

ما قبل الذکر mā qabl uz-zikr, adj. Above-mentioned.

ما لا کلام mā lā kalām, adj. What cannot be told; inexpressible; undescribable; unutterable.

ما لا یطاق mā lā yuṭāq, adj. Intolerable; unbearable.

ما لا ینحل mā lā yanḥal, adj. What cannot be solved; insoluble; inextricable.

ما له و ما علیه mā lahū wā mā 'alaih, n.m. The pros and cons of a matter.

ما مضیٰ mā maẓā adj. What is past.

ماورا mā warā, adj. What is behind or beyond. adv. Besides; over and above.

مایحتاج mā yuḥtāj, adj. What is necessary.

ما mā (P) pron. We; us; our.

ما و شما mā-ŏ shumā, n.m. Every body; every one of us.

ما و من mā-ŏ man, n.f. Self-praise; pride; egotism. n.m. All and sundry.

ما mā (H) n.f. See ماں māṅ

ماپ māp (H) n.f. See ناپ nāp.

ماپنا māpnā (H) v. See ناپنا nāpnā.

مات māt (A) n.f. Defeat.

مات دینا، کرنا māt denā, karnā, v. To checkmate; to confound; to outdo; to win.

مات کھانا ، ہونا māt khānā, honā, v. To be defeated; to be beaten.

شہ مات shah māt, n.m. Checkmate.

ماتا mātā (H) n.f. Mother; small-pox.

ماتا پتا mātā pitā, n.m. Parents.

ماتا نکلنا mātā nikalnā, v. To get small-pox.

ماترا mātrā (H) n.f. A vowel or diacritical mark; a measure; a dose; an ingredient; wealth.

ماتم **mātam** (A) *n.m.* Mourning; grief.

ماتم پرسی *mātam pursi, n.f.* Condolence; oblations; funeral obsequies.

ماتم پرسی کرنا *mātam pursi karnā, v.* To condole.

ماتم خانہ ، سرائے ، کدہ *mātam khānah, sarāe, kadah, n.m.* A house of mourning.

ماتم دار *mātam dār, adj.* A mourner; mourning.

ماتم داری *mātam dāri, n.f.* Mourning.

ماتم زدہ *mātam zadah, adj.* Bereaved; afflicted; mourning.

ماتم کرنا *mātam karnā, v.* To lament; to mourn.

ماتمی **mātami** *adj.* Of or concerning mourning; mournful.

ماتمی لباس *mātami libās, n.m.* Mourning dress.

ماتھا **māthā** (H) *n.m.* The forehead; the head; the ridge of the thatch; the prow of a boat; the front of a house; top; summit.

ماتھا پیٹنا *māthā piṭnā, v.* To beat forehead; to make strenuous efforts; to grieve over one's inability or bad luck.

ماتھا ٹھنکنا *māthā ṭhanaknā, v.* Throbbing of the forehead; to have a presentiment of the coming evil.

ماتھا رگڑنا *māthā ragaṛnā v.* To rub the forehead on the ground; to prostrate; to supplicate; to implore humbly; to beseach.

ماتھے مارنا ، متھے مارنا *māthe mārnā, matthe mārnā, v.* To return (with bad grace); to throw back (at); to reject.

ماٹ **māṭ** (H) *n.m.* An earthen jar; an indigo vat; an article of food.

ماٹ کا ماٹ ھی بگڑا ہے *māṭ kā māṭ hi bigṛā hai (H) prov.* The entire vat is spoiled; the whole family is spoiled.

ماجد ، ماجدہ **mājid, mājidah** (A) *adj.* Glorious; honourable.

ماجو پھل **māju phal** (H) *n.m.* A gall-nut; oak-apple.

ماجور **mājūr** (A) *adj.* Rewarded; blessed; compensated.

ماچا **māchā** (H) *n.m.* See مچان *machān.*

ماچس **māchis** (*corr.* from English) *n.f.* A match-stick; a match-box.

ماخذ **mākhaz** (A) *n.m.* Source; origin; derivation; the place from which something is taken; basis.

ماخوذ **makhūz** (A) *adj.* Seized; derived; involved; accused; called to account; punished; adopted; received.

مادر **mādar** (P) *n.f.* Mother.

مادر بخطا *mādar bakhaṭā, adj.* Illegitimate; bastard; mischievous.

مادر زاد *mādar zād, adj.* Born of the same mother; innate; inborn; natural.

مادر زاد برہنہ *mādar zād barahnah, adj.* Stark naked; nude.

مادر زاد نابینا *mādar zād nābinā, adj.* Born blind.

مادری **mādari** (P) *adj.* Motherly; maternal.

مادری زبان *mādari zabān, n.f.* Mother tongue.

مادہ **mādah** (P) *n.f.* A female.

مادہ **māddah** (A) *n.m.* Matter; substance; subject; essence; faculty; power; root; etymology; article; clause.

مادہ پرست *māddah parast, n.m.* A materialist; a naturalist.

مادہ پرستی *māddah parasti, adj.* Materialism; naturalism.

مادی **māddi** (A) *adj.* Material; natural.

مادیان **mādiyān** (P) *n.f.* Mare; a she-ass.

مادیت **māddiyyat** (A) *n.f.* Materiality; substantialness.

مادین mādin, n.f. A female.

مار mār (P) n.m. A snake; a serpent.

مار آستین mār-ĕ āstin, n.m. An enemy in the guise of a friend.

مار گزیدہ mār gazidah, adj. Snake bitten.

مار گیسو mār-ĕ gesū, n.m. Ringlets; tresses; locks.

مارمہرہ mār mohrah, n.m. A ball taken out of the head of a serpent; an antidote for snake poison.

مار mār (H) n.f. Beating; striking; a blow; stroke; punishment; affilcation; bombardment; rushing upon ; curse ; abundance; severity; remedy; lure; a black loamy soil; a rich black loam.

مار بھگانا mār bhagānā, v. To drive away; to put to flight; to put to rout.

مار بیٹھنا mār baiṭhnā, v. to beat; to strike; to embezzle.

مار پڑنا mār paṛnā, v. To be beaten.

مارپیٹ ، دھاڑ ، کٹائی mār piṭ, dhāṛ, kuṭā'i, n.f. Fight; affray; struggle; beating and bruising; assault and battery; drubbing; fighting; thumping and beating severely.

ماردینا mār denā, v. To smite; to beat; to kill.

مار ڈالنا mār ḍālnā, v. To kill; to slay; to murder.

مار رکھنا mār rakhnā, v. To slay; to kill; to withhold payments wrongfully ; to usurp.

مار کھانا mār khānā, v. To be beaten.

مار گرانا mār girānā, v. To knock down; to kill; to complete the destruction of.

مار لانا mār lānā, v. To obtain by plunder; to rob.

مارا mārā (H) adj. Beaten; smitten; struck down; killed; slain; destroyed; recived; spoilt; foundered; overturned; cut off; lost. n.m. One who is beaten or stricken; a victim.

ماراجانا mārā jānā, v. To be slain or killed; to be destroyed or ruined; to be lost.

مارا مار mārā mār, n.f. Varied and toilsome efforts; hurrying; bustle; tumult; rush.

مارا مارا پھرنا mārā mārā phirnā, v. To wander about; to knock about aimlessly.

مارا مار کرنا mārā mār karnā, v. To bustle about; to make all haste; to toil hard; to try one's best; to push on; to hurry up.

مارتول mārtol (Portug. martello) n.m. A hammer; a turn-screw.

مارکا mārkā (corr. from English) n.m. Mark; trade mark; brand.

مارنا mārnā (H) v. To beat; to strike; to hit; to punish; to kill; to slaughter; to destroy; to ruin; to deaden or blunt the edge (of); to embezzle; to withhold wrongfully; to quench; to suppress; to smother; to counteract poison etc.; to threw; to shoot; to discharge a gun; to dart or hurl a missile; to make a sudden assault; to raise or set up a cry; to mortify; to mar; to stamp; to sting; to win; to conquer; to copulate.

مارو mārū (H) n.m. A smiter; slayer; killer; a kettledrum; a warlike musical instrument. n.f. Name of a musical mode or راگنی rāgni.

مارے māre (H)adv. By reasons of; on account of; for the sake of; for.

ماڑی māṛi (H) n.f. Starch; gruel; congee water; upper room; balcony; a shrine sacred to an inferior deity.

ماس māss (S) n.m. A month; moon.

ماس mās (H) n.m. Flesh; meat.

ماس نوچنا mās nochnā, v. To claw; to bite off the flesh; to mangle.

ماسکہ māsikah (A) n.f. Power of retention; focus.

ماش māsh (H) n.m. A kind of vetch; a pulse.

ماشہ māshah (P) n.m. A weight consisting of 8 rattis رتی; a pin.

ماشہ تولا ہونا māshah tolā honā, v. To be fickle; to change; to be undecisive.

ماضی māẓi (A) n.f. Past (time); past (tense).

ماضی احتمالی ، شکیہ māẓi iḥtimāli, shakkiyah, n.f. The past conditional.

ماضی استمراری māẓi istimrāri, n.f. The past imperfect; past progressive.

ماضی بعید māẓi ba'īd, n.f. The past perfect.

ماضی تمنائی māẓi tamannā'i, n.f. The past optative.

ماضی قریب māẓi qarib, n.f. The present perfect.

ماضی مطلق māẓi mutlaq, n.f. The past indefinite.

ماکول mākūl (A) n.m. Edibles; victual, eatable.

ماکولات mākūlāt, (A) n.m. Victuals; eatable things.

ماکولات‌ومشروبات mākūlat-ŏ mashrūbāt, n.m. Eatable and drinkable things.

ماگھ māgh (H) n.m. The tenth month of Bikrimi calender, (January-February).

ماگھ ننگی بیساکھ بھوکی māgh nangi baisākh bhūki, prov. Unclothed in winter and hungry at harvest time; always poor.

مال māl (H) n.f. The distaff string; belting; wreath; a garland.

مال māl (P) adj. Rubbing (used in comps. as, پائمال pā'e-māl, trodden under foot).

مال māl (A) n.m. Riches; wealth; property; possession; merchandise; stock; goods; effects; rent or revenue; any great thing; a dainty; finance; dainties; a granulated rudiment in an indigo vat.

مال اڑانا māl uṛānā, v. To squander wealth; to feed on dainties.

مال اموات māl-ĕ amwāt, n.m. Property left by a deceased person; unclaimed property.

مال برآمد māl-ĕ barāmad, n.m. Export; recovered property.

مال برآمد و درآمد māl-ĕ barāmad-ŏ darāmad, n.m. Exports and imports.

مال حرام māl-ĕ ḥarām, n.m. Illegal property.

مال حصہ داری māl-ĕ ḥiṣṣah dāri, n.m. Joint stock.

مال خانہ māl khānah, n.m. A store-house; a ware-house.

مال دار māl dār, adj. Wealthy; rich; moneyed. n.m. A wealthy man; a proprietor.

مال داری māl dāri, n.f. Wealth; wealthiness.

مال زادی māl zādi, n.f. A whore; a bawd.

مال سائر mal-ĕ sā'ir, n.m. Miscellaneous revenue.

مال شراکت māl-ĕ sharākat, n.m. Joint stock.

مال ضامن māl ẓāmin, n.m. A surety.

مال ضامنی māl ẓāmini, n.f. Security for rent or debt.

مال ضبطی māl-ĕ ẓabṭi, n.m. Attached property; escheat.

مال طیب ، حلال māl-ĕ ṭayyib, ḥalāl, n.m. Legitimate earnings.

مال غنیمت māl-ĕ ghanimat, n.m. Prize; booty; plunder; spoil.

مال غیر منقولہ māl-ĕ ghair manqūlah, n.m. Unmovable property.

مال فرود māl farod, n.m. Landing place of goods; market.

مال کا بندوبست māl kā bandobast, n.m. Settlement of revenue.

مال گاڑی māl gāṛī, n.f. Goods train.

مال گزار mal guzār, n.m. A tenant; a subject; a landlord; a landholder; one who pays revenue.

مال گزاری māl guzārī, n.f. Land revenue; revenue assessment; rent paid in money; payment of rents and taxes.

مال لاوارث māl-ĕ lāwāriṣ, n.m. Unclaimed property; escheat.

مال مارنا māl mārnā, v. To rob; to swindle; to embezzle.

مال متروکہ māl-ĕ matrūkah, n.m. Bequest; legacy.

مال محمولہ māl-ĕ maḥmūlah, n.m. A burden; a load; goods on board; cargo.

مال مست māl mast, adj. One who is proud of his wealth.

مال مسروقہ māl-ĕ masrūqah, n.m. Stolen property.

مال مفت māl-ĕ muft, n.m. Property acquired without labour or trouble.

مال مقروقہ māl-ĕ maqrūqah, n.m. Attached or distrained property.

مال منقولہ māl-ĕ manqūlah, n.m. Movable property.

مال وقف māl-ĕ waqf, n.m. Property endowed for religious purposes; an endowment.

مال و متاع māl-ŏ matā', n.m. Money and effects.

مالا mālā (H) n.f. A rosary; a chaplet; a garland; a necklace; a string of beads; a vocabulary; a dictionary.

مالا پھیرنا mālā pherna, v. To recite a prayer on beads; to pray; to count the beads.

مالا مال mālā māl (P) adj. Replete; rich; wealthy; brimful; abundant.

مالا مال کرنا mālā māl karnā, v. To enrich; to fill to the brim; to heap up.

مالش mālish (P) n.f. Rubbing; polish; burnishing; shampooing; kneading; friction; massage; nausea.

مالش کرنا mālish karnā, v. To rub; to polish; to feel nausea.

مالک mālik (A) n.m. Master; lord; possessor; proprietor; owner; husband; occupier; the Supreme Being; God.

مالک کرنا mālik karnā, v. To make one the owner of; to entitle; to empower.

مالک الملک mālik-ul-mulk, n.m. The lord of the territory or kingdom.

مالکانہ mālikānah (A & P) adj. & adv. Proprietory; like an owner; in the manner of an owner. n.m. An annual or monthly allowance paid to the زمیندار zamīndār by the tenant; an allowance to a zamīndār, ousted from his estate.

مالکانہ رسوم mālikānah rusūm, n.f. Proprietory dues.

مالکوس mālkos (S) n.m. Name of a راگ rāg.

مالن mālan (H) n.f. A gardener's wife; a female gardener.

مالوف māluf (P) adj. Familiar; customary; beloved; habituated.

مالی mālī (P) adj. Pecuniary; financial.

مالی پیش کار mālī peshkār, n.m. Revenue accountant.

مالی سال mālī sāl, n.m. Financial year.

مالی māli (H) n.m. A gardener; a horticulturist.

مالیت māliyat (A) n.f. Value; cost.

مالیدہ malidah (P) n.m. Sweetmeat or cakes made with wheat flour; a fine woollen cloth.

ماما māmā (P) n.f. Mother; maid-servant; a woman servant.

ماما گری māmā garī, n.f. The work of a maid-servant.

ماممتا māmtā (H) n.f. Love; affection; a mother's love; maternal love.

مامن māman (A) n.m. A place of safety or security; place of freedom from fear.

مامور māmūr (A) adj. Ordered; commanded; determined; established.

مامور من اللہ māmūr min allah, adj & n.m. Commissioned by God; commanded by God; an apostle; a prophet.

مامور māmūr honā, v. To be appointed; to be entrusted with a duty.

مامون māmūn (A) adj. Rendered secure; safe; preserved; exempted; firm; constant.

ماموں māmūn (H) n m. Maternal uncle.

مامی māmī (H) n.f. Maternal aunt.

ماں māṅ (H) n.f. Mother.

ماں بہن کرنا māṅ bahan karnā, v. To abuse one's mother and sister.

ماں جایا māṅ jāyā, n.m. Born of the same mother; own brother.

ماں کا دودھ سمجھنا māṅ kā dūdh samajhnā, v. To regard a thing as lawful.

مان mān (S & H) n.m. Respect; regard; hypothesis; good opinion; concept; pride; arrogance; standard; rank; value. adj. Like; resembling.

مان رکھنا mān rakhnā, v. To respect; to honour; to pay heed; to mind; to obey; to protect one's honour.

مان کرنا mān karnā, v. To be vain or proud; to put on airs; to over respect oneself.

مان جانا mān jāna (H) v. To heed; to mind; to acknowledge the superiority (of); to submit; to yield; to confess; to own; to come to terms with; to comply with.

مانجنا māṅjnā (H) v. To cleanse; to scour; to scrub.

مانجھ māṅjh (H) n.f. The middle; a kind of verse.

مانجھا māṅjhā (H) n.m. A paste mixed with ground glass and applied to the string of a kite; a feast given by a bridegroom before his wedding; the trunk of a tree; girth; a bed.

مانجھی māṅjhi (H) n.m. A boatman; a steerman; master of a vessel; sailor; helmsman.

ماند māṅd (H) adj. Dim; faded; dull; faint; eclipsed; tarnished. n.f. A heap of a dung; den; lair's haunt; hole; the den of a wild beast.

ماند پڑ جانا māṅd paṛ jānā, v. To fade; to become eclipsed.

ماندگی māṅdagi (P) n.f. Fatigue; weariness; illness; indisposition.

ماندہ māṅdah (P) adj. Left; weary; remaining; tired.

مانڈ māṅḍ (H) n.m. Rice-water; starch; paste; a class of songs.

مانڈا māṅḍā (H) n.m. Film; speck (on the eye); a cataract of the eye; a thin cake; a kind of bread; a sort of sweetmeat made into small balls.

مانس mānas (H) n.m. A human being; a man.

مانع māni' (A) n.m. Impediment; obstacle; hinderance; prohibition; objection; stopper; preventer; hinderer.

مانع ھونا māni' honā, v. To prevent; to hinder; to prohibit; to stop; to stand in one's way; to object (to); to be a bar or obstacle in the way (of).

مانگ **māṅg** (H) *n.f.* The parting of the hair; a line on the head where the hair is parted; division; want; demand; betrothal; a betrothed girl; a husband.

مانگ اجڑنا **māṅg ujaṛnā**, *v.* To become a widow.

مانگ بنانا ، نکالنا **māṅg banānā, nikālnā**, *v.* To part the hair in the middle.

مانگ بھرنا **māṅg bharnā**, *v.* To give in marriage; to apply red-lead to the مانگ *māṅg*.

مانگ بھری **māṅg bharī**, *n.f.* A married woman; a beloved wife.

مانگ پٹی **māṅg paṭṭī**, *n.f.* Braiding the hair; dividing the hair in the middle.

مانگ پٹی میں لگا رہنا **māṅg paṭṭī meṅ lagā rahnā**, *v.* To take a long time in make-up.

مانگ جلی **māṅg jalī**, *n.f.* A widow.

مانگ سنوارنا **māṅg sanwārnā**, *v.* To braid the hair.

مانگ تانگ کر کام چلانا **māṅg tāṅg kar kām chalānā**, *v.* To beg, borrow or steal; to tide over a difficult period somehow.

مانگ تانگ کر کھانا **māṅg tāṅg kar khānā**, *v.* To live by begging.

مانگ لینا **māṅg lenā**, *v.* To borrow; to ask for something on loan.

مانگ ہونا **māṅg honā**, *v.* To be in demand.

مانگے کا ، کی **māṅgne kā, kī**, *adj.* Borrowed; taken on loan; procured.

مانگنا **māṅgnā** (H) *v.* To require; to demand; to beg; to pray; to crave; to solicit; to desire; to borrow; to send for; to call for; to procure; to request; to entreat.

ماننا **mānnā** (H) *v.* To agree (to); to accept; to heed· to believe; to admit; to acknowledge; to confess; to own; to acknowledge the superiority (of); to assent (to); to consent; to assume; to suppose; to grant; to hold to be true or right; to consider as important; to approve.

مانند **mānind** (P) *adj.* Like; resembling.

مانو **māno** (H) *adv.* Suppose; assume; grant; let it be granted that; as if; as; as though; let. *n.f.* A cat.

مانوس **mānūs** (A) *adj.* Associated; familiar; intimate; cheering; gladdening; attached; friendly; solacing.

ماوا **māwā** (H) *n.m.* Substance; leaven; congee; condensed milk; curd; essence; starch; yolk of an egg.

ماوا **māwā** (A) *n.m.* Habitation; abode; dwelling; place of resort or shelter.

ماہ **māh** (P) *n.m.* The moon; a month.

ماہ بماہ **māh ba māh**, *adv.* From month to month; monthly.

ماہپارہ **māh pārā**, *adj.* Handsome (person); beloved; sweetheart.

ماہ تاب **māh tāb**, *n.m.* Moonlight; moonshine; the moon.

ماہ تابی **māh tābī**, *n.f.* A kind of firework; firework; blue-light; a kind of musk melon; shadock; cloth on which devices of the heavenly bodies in gold or silver are pasted,

ماہ جبیں ، ماہ رو ، ماہ لقا ، ماہ وش **māh jabīn, māh rū, māh laqā, māh wash**, *adj.* Having a face as beautiful as the moon; a beautiful person.

ماہ رواں **māh-ĕ rawāṅ**, *n.m.* Current month.

ماہ شمسی **māh-ĕ shamsī**, *n.m.* A solar month.

ماہ قمری **māh-ĕ qamarī**, *n.m.* A lunar month.

ماہ کنعان **māh-ĕ kin'ān**, *n.m.* The moon of Cannan; Joseph.

ماه وار māh wār, adv. Monthly.

ماه واری māh wāri, adv. Per mensem, n.f. Menses; period of menstruation.

ماهانه māhānah, adv. Monthly. n.m. Monthly pay, wages or salary.

ماهر māhir (A) adj. Skilled (in); expert; well-acquainted; a master (of); an adept.

ماهر ہونا māhir honā, v. To be an expert (in); to be a master (of); to excel (in).

ماہرارضیات māhir-ĕ arẓiyāt, n.m. Geologist.

ماہرالسنہ ، لسانیات māhir-ĕ alsinah, lisāniyāt, n.m. Linguist; philologist.

ماہر تعلیمات māhir-ĕ ta'līmāt, n.m. Educationist.

ماہر حشریات māhir-ĕ ḥashriyāt, n.m. Entomologist.

ماہر ریاضیات māhir-ĕ riyāẓiyāt, n.m. Mathematician.

ماہر طبعیات māhir-ĕ ṭabi'yāt, n.m. Physicist.

ماہر علاج اشعاعی māhir -ĕ 'ilāj-ĕ ish'ā'i, n.m. Radiologist.

ماہر علم الابدان māhir-ĕ 'ilm-ul-abdān, n.m. Physiologist.

ماہر علم تاریخ māhir-ĕ 'ilm-ĕ tārikh, n.m. Historian.

ماہرعلم جغرافیہ māhir-ĕ 'ilm-ĕ jughrāfiah, n.m. Geographer.

ماہر علم حیوانات māhir-ĕ 'ilm-ĕ ḥaiwānāt, n.m. Zoologist.

ماہر علم کیمیا māhir-ĕ 'ilm-ĕ kimiyā, n.m. Chemist.

ماہر علم نباتات mahir-ĕ 'ilm-ĕ nabātāt, n.m. Botanist.

ماہر نفسیات māhir-ĕ nafsiyāt, n.m. Psychologist.

ماہی māhi (P) n.f. A fish.

ماہی بے آب māhi-ĕ be ab. (Lit. A fish out of water). adj. Restless; uneasy,

ماہی پشت māhi pusht, adj. Fish-backed; hog-backed; convex.

ماہی خوار māhi khwār, n.m. Fish-eater; a heron; a cormorant.

ماہی گیر māhi gir, n.m. A fisherman.

ماہی گیری māhi giri, n.f. Fishing.

ماہی مراتب māhi marātab, n.m. Insignia; certain honours conferred on prince and great nobles only.

ماہیت māhiyat (A) n.f. Essence; nature, state; intrinsic value or worth; matter of fact.

ماء mā' (A) n.m. Water; liquid; juice; lustre; splendour; semen.

ماءالجبن mā'ul-jubn, n.m. Whey (particularly of goat's milk).

ماءالحیات mā'-ul-ḥayāt, n m. The water of life; the elixer of life.

ماء اللحم mā'-ul-laḥm, n.m. The juice of flesh; strong soup.

ماء الورد mā'-ul-ward, n.m. Rose-water.

مائع mā'i' (A) adj. That flows; unsolidified; n.m. Fluid; liquid.

مائل mā'il (A) adj. Inclined; bent; inclined towards; fond; desirous; having a propensity or inclination or partiality (for).

مائل کرنا mā'il karnā, v. To persuade; to bend.

ماؤف mā'ūf (A) adj. Afflicted.

مائی mā'i (H) n.f. Mother; mamma; maidservant.

مایا māyā (H) n.f. Prosperity; riches; wealth; apulence; kindness; pity; mercy; compassion; affection; illusion; delusion; mirage; mutual phenomena; show; idealism

مایوس māyūs (A) adj. Without hope; having lost all hope; disappointed.

مایوس کرنا *māyūs karnā*, *v.* To disappoint; to balk; to mar one's hopes.

مایوس ہونا *māyūs honā*, *v.* To be disappointed; to give up all hopes.

مایوسی *māyūsi*, *n.f.* Hopelessness; disappointment; despair.

مایہ *māyah* (P) *n.m.* Stock; capital; wealth; fund; means; leaven; ferment.

مایہ‌دار *māyah dār*, *n.m.* Capitalist; stockist.

مایۂ ناز *māyah-ĕ nāz*, *adj.* Cause of pride.

مباح *mubāḥ* (A) *adj.* Lawful; just; proper; permissible; allowed.

مباح رکھنا ٬ سمجھنا *mubāḥ rakhnā, samajhnā*, *v.* To allow; to hold legal; to regard as valid.

مباح کرنا *mubāḥ karnā*, *v.* To make lawful; to legalise; to make admissible.

مباحث *mabāḥiṣ* (A) *n.m.* (*plu.* of مبحث *mubḥaṣ*) Discussions; debates.

مباحثہ *mubāḥaṣah* (A) *n.m.* Contest; debate; investigation; argumentation; reasoning; discussion; a verbal dispute.

مباحثہ کرنا *mubāḥaṣah karnā*, *v.* To dispute; to debate; to discuss; to argue.

مبادا *mubādā* (P) *adv.* Be it not so; God forbid; perhaps; by no means; lest.

مبادرت *mubadarat* (A) *n.f.* Making haste; haste; vieing with; expedition; precocity.

مبادلہ *mubādalah* (A) *n.m.* Exchange; barter; retaliation; recompense.

مبادی *mabādi, mubādi* (A) *n.m.* (*plu.* of مبدأ *mabdā'*) Beginnings; origins; elements; principles.

مبادی الحساب *mabādi-ul-ḥisāb*, *n.m.* Elements of arithmetic.

مبادی‌العلوم *mabādi-ul-'ulūm*, *n.m.* Elements of knowledge or sciences.

مبارزت *mubārazat* (A) *n.f.* A fight; war.

مبارک *mubārak* (A) *adj.* Auspicious; blessed; august; sacred; holy; happy; fortunate; blessing; congratulation; felicitation. *intj.* Welcome! all hail!

مبارک باد *mubārak bād*, *n.f.* Congratulation; good wishes; wishing success; *intj.* May it be fortunate! hail!

مبارک بادی *mubārak bādi*, *n.f.* Congrantulation; welcome; blessing; felicity.

مبارکی *mubāraki*, *n.f.* See مبارک بادی *mubārak bādī*.

مباشرت *mubāsharat* (A) *n.f.* Copulation; commencement or undertaking of an affair; supervision.

مباشرت کرنا *mubāsharat karnā*, *v.* To supervise; to conduct; to copulate; to have sexual intercourse.

مبالغہ *mubālaghah* (A) *n.m.* Exaggeration; hyperbole; bombast; utmost effort; deligence; care; amplification; dwelling on a subject.

مبالغہ کرنا *mubālaghah karnā*, *v.* To exaggerate; to use hyperboles.

مبانی *mabānī* (A) *n.m.* (*plu* of مبنیٰ *mabnạ*) Buildings; foundations.

مباہات *mubāhāt* (A) *n.f.* Contending for beauty or glory; glorying; boasting; arrogance.

مباہلہ *mubāhalah* (A) *n.m.* A meeting of contending parties where persons or parties invoke curses of God on those who deny God's religion; cursing one another.

مبتدا *mubtada* (A) *n.m.* Commencement; principle; subject of a proposition (of a predicate); substantive noun in the nominative case.

مبتدا و خبر *mubtadā-ō khabar*, *n.m.* The subject and the predicate.

مبتدی *mubtadi* (A) *n.m.* A beginner; a novice; a disciple just commencing to learn; a young scholar.

مبتذل *mubtazal* (A) *adj*. Contemptible; base; degenerate; mean; treated as of little value; common.

مبتلا *mubtalā* (A) *adj*. Involved; fallen into; entangled; overtaken by; affected; afflicted; distressed; distracted; unfortunate; captivated; fascinated; enamoured.

مبحث *mabḥas̤* (A) *n.m.* Disputation; investigation; time or place for disputation.

مبدا *mabdā'* (A) *n.m.* Beginning; source; origin, cause; principle.

مبدل *mubaddal* (A) *adj*. Changed; exchanged; altered. *n.m.* Case in opposition.

مبذول *mabz̤ūl* (A) *adj*. Bestowed; conferred; expended; spent.

مبرا *mubarrā* (A) *adj*. Free; exempted; innocent; guiltless; fur removed from; exonerated.

مبرد *mubarrad* (A) *adj*. Cooled.

مبرم *mubram* (A) *adj*. Made firm by twisting; pressing together; firm; urgent; tight; inevitable.

مبروص *mabrūṣ* (A) *adj*. Leper.

مبسوط *mabsūṭ* (A) *adj*. Dilated; spread out; stretched; expanded.

مبشر *mubashshir* (A) *n.m.* A bearer of glad tidings or good news; an evangelist; an announcer (of good news).

مبصر *mubaṣṣ r* (A) *adj*. Provident; penetrating; far-sighted. *n.m.* An observer.

مبعوث *mab'ūṣ* (A) *adj*. Created; sent.

مبغوض *mabghūẓ* (A) *adj*. Detested; hated; odious.

مبلغ *mablagh* (A) *n.m.* The place of arrival; a sum; ready money; quantity.

مبنی *mabni* (A) *adj* Based on; founded on.

مبہم *mubham* (A) *adj*. Hidden indistinct; equivocal; occult; keeping concealed; ambiguous.

مبہوت *mabhūt* (A) *adj*. Stupefied; astonished; confounded; amazed; struck dumb with astonishment; dumb-founded.

مبہی *mubahhi* (A) *adj*. Provocature: what excites venery.

مبین *mubin* (A) *adj*. Manifest; clear.

مبین *mubaiyyan* (A) *adj*. Declared; made distinct or clear.

مت *mat* (H) *adv*. Do not; don't.

مت *mat* (H) *n.f.* Manner; method; way; mode; system; belief; creed; religion; faith; sect; intelligence; wisdom; judgment; wit; sense; counsel; advice; respect; reverence.

مت پھرنا *mat phirnā*. *v*. To change one's mind; to lose one's senses.

مت دینا *mat denā*, *v*. To give advice; to counsel.

مت ماری جانا *mat mārī jānā*, *v*. To be out of one's wits; to lose one's senses; to act as a fool.

مت میں آنا *mat meṅ ānā*, *v*. To come to one's senses; to be brought round to another man's point of view.

متا *matā* (S) *n.m.* Thought; opinion; advice; mind; consultation; counsel; belief.

متابعت *mutāba'at* (A) *n.f.* Obedience; submission; understanding; following one another; doing something in the same manner after another.

متاثر *mutāas̤s̤ir* (A) *adj*. Impressed; susceptible; affected; moved by.

متاخر *mutaakhkhir* (A) *adj*. Following; coming after.

متاخرین *mutaakhkhirin* (A) *adj*. Those coming after; modern; late. *n.m.* The moderns.

متاسف *mutaassif* (A) *adj*. Sorrowful; regretful; repentant; oppressed with grief; grieving.

متاسفانہ **mutaassifanah** (A) *adv.* Regretfully; Impressively.

متاع **mata'** (A) *n.f.* Goods; valuables; effects; chattels; furniture; merchandise.

متاعی **mutā'i**, *n.f.* A temporary wife.

متامل **mutaammil** (A) *adj.* Contemplative; meditative; reflecting.

متانا **mutāna** (H) *v.* To cause to make water.

متانت **matānat** (A) *n.f.* Firmness; constancy; depth of thought; vigour; solidity.

متاہل **mataahhil** (A) *adj.* Married; family-man.

متبادر **mutabādir** (A) *adj.* Making haste; going ahead hastily; comprehencible.

متبادل **mutabādil** (A) *adj.* Functioning alternately; interchanging; alternate.

متبادلہ **mutabādilah** (A) *adj.* Making an exchange with; mutual; reciprocal.

متبادلہ زاویے **mutabādilah zawiye**, *n.m.* Alternate angles.

متبحر **mutabaḥḥir** (A) *adj.* Very learned; deeply read; ocean of learning.

متبدل **mutabaddil** (A) *adj.* Changing alternately; changed; altered; inverting.

متبرک **mutabarrak** (A) *adj.* Fortunate; august; blessed; holy; heavenly; vener-ble; sanctified; happy.

متبسم **mutabassim** (A) *adj.* Smiling; laughing; risible.

متبع **muttabi'** (A) *n.m.* Follower; disciple; immitator.

متبنیٰ **mutabannā** (A) *n.m.* An adopted son.

متبنیٰ کرنا **mutabannā karna**, *v.* To adopt a son.

متبوع **matbū'** (A) *adj.* Followed; obeyed.

متجاوز **mutajawiz** (A) Exceeding limits; aggressor.

متجسس **mutajassis** (A) *adj.* Seeker; investigator; discerner; finder.

متحد **muttaḥid** (A) *adj.* United.

متحرک **mutaḥarrik** (A) *adj.* Moved; movable; accented with short vowels.

متحرک تصاویر **mutaḥarrik taṣāwir**, *n.f.* Movies; cinema films.

غیر متحرک **ghair mutaḥarrik**. *adj.* Inmovable; not hav ng a vowel; quiescent.

متحمل **mutaḥammil** (A) *adj.* Affable; considerate; enduring; patient; bearing a burden; passive; tolerant.

متحیر **mutaḥaiyyir** (A) *adj.* Astonished; wondering; confounded; amazed; surprised.

متخاصم **mutakhāṣim** (A) *adj.* Hostile; contending.

متخاصمین **mutakhāṣimain** (A) *n.m.* The two contending parties in a suit; plaintiff and defendant.

متخلص **mutakhalliṣ** (A) *adj.* Pure; free (from); surnamed; having a literary title.

متخیل **mutakhaiyyil** (A) *adj.* Imagining; suspecting; fancying.

متخیلہ **mutakhaiyalah** (A) *n.f.* The faculty of thinking.

متداول **mutadawal** (A) *adj.* Current; in use; passing from hand to hand.

متدین **mutadaiyyin** (A) *adj.* Religious; orthodox; honest.

متذبذب **mutaẕabẕib** (A) *adj.* Agitated; anxious; hesitating.

متذکرہ **mutaẕakkirah** (A) *adj.* Stated; referred to.

متذکرہ بالا **mutaẕakkirah balā**, *adj.* Mentioned above; afore-mentioned; referred to above.

متر **mittar, mitra** (S) *n.m.* A friend; a well-wisher; a companion.

مترادف **mutarādif** (A) *adj.* Continued; successive; consecutive; synonymous.

مترتب mutarattab (A) adj. Arranged; compiled.

مترجم mutarjim (A) n.m. Translator; interpreter.

مترجم mutarjam (A) adj. Translated.

متردد mutaraddid (A) adj. Irresolute; hesitating; perplexed; thoughtful; anxious; wandering; wavering; grieved; advesre; ambitious.

مترشح mutarashshih (A) adj. Evident; conspicuous; apparent; dripping; drizzling.

مترقب mutaraqqib (A) adj. Expecting; watching; observing; desiring.

مترقبه mutaraqqabah (A) adj. Expected.

مترکب mutarakkab (A) adj Composed; compounded.

مترنم mutarannim (A) adj. Singer.

متروک matrūk (A) adj. Abolished; obsolete; rejected; relinquished; given up; unused; forsaken; abandoned.

متروک الاستعمال matrūk-ul-isti'mal, adj. Not in use; obsolete; unused; not practised; unusual.

متزلزل mutazalzal (A) adj. Shaken; made to quake; convulsed; shaky; tottering.

متساوی mutasāwī(A) adj. Equal; parallel; right; straight.

متساوی الاضلاع mutasāwi-ul-azla', adj. Equilateral.

متساوی الزوایا mutasawi-uz-zavaya, adj. Equiangular.

متسلط mutasallit (A) adj. Absolute; despotic; grasping.

متشابہ mutashabih (A) adj. Resembling; similar; like. n.m. A simile; suspicion; a metaphor; an allegory.

متشدد mutashaddid (A) adj. Hard task master; violent.

متشرع mutasharri' (A) adj. Orthodox; religious; skilled in law; observing the divine laws.

متشکل mutashakkil (A) adj. Alike; resembling. similar; formed; transformed.

متشنج mutashannij (A) adj. Convulsive.

متصادم mutaṣadim (A) adj. Colliding; clashing.

متصدی mutaṣaddi (A) n.m. An accountant; a clerk. adj. Turning away the face; opposing; daring; attempting; intent on.

متصرف mutasorrif (A) adj. Possessing; extravagant; profuse.

متصف muttaṣaf (A) adj. Defined; qualified by.

متصل ، متصله muttasil, muttaṣilah (A) adj. Adjoining; touching; near; contiguous; continual; successive; uninterrupted.

متصور mutaṣawwar (A) adj. Conceived; considerated; imagined.

متصور ہونا mutaṣawwar honā, v. To be deemed; to be considered.

متضاد mutazād (A) adj. Opposite; contrary; antonym.

متعارف muta'araf (A) adj. Mutually known; known to each other

متعارفه muta'ārafah (A) adj. Evident.

اصول متعارفه uṣūl-ĕ muta'ārafah, n.m. Self-evident truths; axioms.

متعاقب muta'āqib (A) adj. Following; successive; subsequent; pursuing.

متعاقد muta'āqid (A) adj. Making a treaty of alliance; entering with an agreement.

متعاقدین muta'aqidin (A) n.m. Parties entering into a treaty; allies.

متعال muta'al (A) adj. High; sublime; lofty; great; exalted.

متعجب muta'ajjib (A) adj. Astonished; amazed; surprised; wondering; admiring; full of admiration.

متعدد muta'addad (A) adj. Many; various; numerous; numbered; a few.

متعدد بار muta'addad bar, adj. Many a time.

متعدی muta'addi (A) adj. Transgressive; infectious; wicked casual; transitive; active (verb).

متعدی امراض muta'addi amrāẓ. n.m. Infectious diseases; epidemics.

متعرض muta'arriz (A) adj. Opposing; resisting; giving pain or trouble.

متعصب muta'aṣṣib (A) adj. Prejudiced; bigotted; partial; superstitious.

متعفن muta'affin (A) adj. Putrid; corrupted; rotten; stinking; fetid; unpleasant.

متعلق muta'alliq (A) adj. Hanging; suspended; depending on; belonging (to); appendant; concerning; relative to; relevant; appropriate; connected with; attached (to).

متعلق فعل muta'alliq-ē fi'l, n.m. Adverb.

متعلق کرنا muta'alliq karnā, v. To annex; to enclose; to attach; to impute; to ascribe; to refer to; to allot; to entrust; to lay out; to extend; to invest.

متعلقات ' متعلقین muta'alliqāt, muta'alliqin (A) n.m. Domestics; children; family; possession.

متعلقات فعل muta'alliqāt-ē fi'l, n.m. Adverbial adjuncts.

متعلم muta'allim (A) n.m. A scholar; a student; a pupil.

متعه muta'h (A) n.m. Taking a wife for a short time; a temporary marriage (allowed by the شیعہ Shiās).

متعهد muta'ahid (A) n.m. One who enters into an engagement: a contractor; undertaker. adj. Responsible.

متعین ' متعینه muta'aiyyan muta'aiyyanh (P) adj. Fixed; appointed; determined; deputed; constituted; assigned.

متعین کرنا muta'aiyyan karnā, v. To appoint; to depute; to determine.

متعین هونا muta'aiyyan honā, v. To fill an office; to be appointed; to be determined; to be fixed.

متغزل mutaghazzil (A) n.m. A lyricist; a reciter of odes.

متغیر ' متغیره mutaghaiyyar, mutaghaiyyarah (A) adj. Changed altered; disturbed; perplexed; stupified; inconsistant; offended; angry.

متفاوت mutafāwit (A) adj. Mutually differing; contrary; opposite.

متفحص mutafaḥḥiṣ (A) adj. Seeking; investigating.

متفرعات mutafarri'āt (A) n.. Branches; byproducts.

متفرق mutafarraq (A) adj. Separated; miscellaneous; dispersed; scattered; distinct.

متفرق هونا mutafarraq honā. To be dispersed; to be scattered.

متفرقات mutafaraqāt (A) n.f. Various and scattered things; miscellaneous articles; sundries; different items of an account.

متفق muttafiq (A) adj. Agreeing; consenting; united, conspiring.

متفق الرائے muttafiq-ur-rā'e, adj. Unanimous; consenting; agreeing in opinions.

متفق هونا ' هو جانا muttafiq honā, ho jānā, v. To agree together; to agree; to accord; to conspire; to conceive; to confederate; to co-operate.

متفكر mutafakkir (A) adj. Anxious; considering; serious; thoughtful; concerned; pensive; uneasy or disturbed in mind; perplexed.

متفنی mutafanni (A) adj. Cunning; wity; crafty; vicious; artful.

متقابل mutaqābil (A) n.m. A contester; a competitor; per contra.

متقارب mutaqārib (A) adj. Convergent; close. n.m. A meter in prosody.

متقاضی **mutaqāẓi** (A) *adj.* Exacting payment; demanding; haggling.

متقدم **mutaqaddim** (A) *adj.* Ancient; preceding; antique; anterior.

متقدمین **mutaqaddimin** (A) (*plu.* of متقدم *mutaqaddim*) *n.m.* The ancients; predecessors.

متقی **muttaqi** (A) *adj.* Abstemious; God-fearing; pious; sober; temperate.

متکبر **mutakabbir** (A) *adj.* Proud; arrogant; haughty; disdainful; fastidious.

متکبرانہ **mutakabbirānah** (A) *adv.* Proudly; haughtily.

متکفل **mutakaffil** (A) *adj.* Becoming surety for; undertaking.

متکلف **mutakallif** (A) *adj.* Troubling; putting to trouble.

متکلم **mutakallim** (A) *adj.* Speaking; declaiming. *n.m.* The first person (grammar).

متلاشی **mutalāshi** *adj.* seeking; searching; enquiring.

متلاطم **mutalāṭim** (A) *adj.* Dashing together (waves); agitated; buffeting one another.

متلانا **matlānā** (H) *v.* To feel nausea; to be sick at the stomach.

متلذذ **mutalaẓiẓ** (A) *adj.* Relishing; getting delighted; receiving pleasure from.

متلون **mutalawwin** (A) *adj.* Changeable; variable; capricious; alterable; fickle.

متلون مزاج **mutalawwin mizāj**, *adj.* Of fickle disposition.

متلی **matli** (H) *n.f.* Nausea; vomiting.

متماثل **mutamāṣil** (A) *adj.* Identical.

متمتع **mutamatti'** (A) *adj.* Enjoying; relishing deriving benefit from.

متمتع ہونا **mutamatti' honā**, *v.* To enjoy.

متمدن **mutamaddan** (A) *adj.* Civilised; enlightened.

متمرد **mutamarrid** (A) *adj.* Stubborn; refractory; rebellious; disobedient; vicious.

متمکن **mutamakkin** (A) *adj.* Strong; prevalent; dwelling; residing.

متملق **mutamalliq** (A) *adj.* Flattering.

متمنی **mutamanni** (A) *adj.* Desiring; wishing; optative; hoping.

متموج **mutamawwij** (A) *adj.* Billowing; waving; surging.

متمول **mutamawwil** (A) *adj.* Rich; wealthy; affluent.

متمیز **mutamayyaz** (A) *adj.* Distinguished; distinct.

متن **matn** (A) *n.m.* The text of a book; the middle (of a road).

متنازع ، متنازعہ **mutanāza'**, **mutanāza'ah** (A) *adj.* Disputed; contested; the subject of litigation.

متنازعہ فیہ **mutanāza'ah fih**, *adj.* The thing disputed about; subject of litigation or controversy.

متناسب **mutanāsib** (A) *adj.* Similar; proportionate to one another.

متناقض **mutanāqiẓ** (A) *adj.* Opposite; contrary; contradictory.

متناہی **mutanāhi** (A) *adj.* Terminated; determined; arrived at the utmost extreme; finished.

متنبہ **mutanabbah** (A) *adj.* Circumspect; wakeful; vigilant; warned; cautious.

متنبہ کرنا **mutanabbah karnā**, *v.* To warn; to caution.

متنجن **mutanjan** (P) *n.m.* A kind of sweet dish prepared from rice, sugar and meat in equal proportion.

متنفر **mutanaffir** (A) *adj.* Repugnant; offensive

متنفس **mutanaffis** (A) *n.m.* An individual; a living being; a person breathing; an animal.

متواتر mutawātir (A) adv. Successively; repeatedly; continually.

متوارد mutawārid (A) adj. Successive; repeated.

متوازی mutawāzi (A) adj. Parallel.

متواضع mutawāẓi' (A) adj. Entertaining; complimenting; humbling; complaisant.

متوالا ، متوالی matwāla, matwāli (A) adj. Intoxicated; drunk; inebriated.

متوالا ہونا matwālā honā, v. To be intoxicated; to be drunk.

متوالی mutwāli (A) adj. Consecutive; successive; recurring.

متوجہ mutawajjih (A) adj. Attentive; intent; favouring; favourable; turning towards; bound to profitious; having regard towards; procceding towards.

متوجہ کرانا mutawajjih karānā, v. To draw attention of towards.

متوجہ ہونا mutawajjih honā, v. To attend to; to turn the attention to; to address a person; to turn one's face towards; to proceed towards.

متوحش mutawaḥḥish (A) adj. Terrified; scared away; aghast; desolate; frightened.

متورع mutawari' (A) adj. Pious; God-fearing.

متورم mutawarram (A) adj. Swelled; inflated.

متوسط mutawassiṭ (A) adj. Middling; medium; mean; average; moderate; mediocre; intermediate.

متوسل mutawassil (A) adj. Adjoining; conjoined; trusting in God.

متوطن mutawaṭṭin (A) adj. Inhabiting; residing. n.m. Inhabitant; native; immigrant.

متوفی mutawaffi (A) adj. Dead; deceased; the late; defunct.

متوقع mutawaqqi' (A) adj. Expecting; expectant; hopeful.

متوقع ہونا mutawaqqi' honā, v. To expect; to be hopeful.

متوقف mutawaqqif (A) adj. Slow; tardy; delaying.

متوکل mutawakkil (A) adj. Resigned; trusting; resigned to the will of God.

متولد mutawallid (A) adj. Born; generated.

متولی mutawalli (A) n.m. A trustee; a kinsman; a superintendent; a treasurer of a mosque.

متوہم mutawahhim (A) adj. Doubtful; distracting; apprehensive; scrupulous.

متھا matthā (H) n.m. See ماتھا māthā.

متھانی mathānī, (H) n.f. A milkpan; a milk pail; a churner.

متہم muttaham (A) adj. Suspected; accused, arraigned.

متھنا mathnā (H) v. To churn; to knead; to work; to ponder over; to mediate.

متی miti (H) n.f. Date; day; interest.

متی پگنا miti pugnā, v. To be at maturity; to fall due.

متی کاٹا miti kāṭā, n.m. Present worth and discount.

متیقن mutayaqqin (A) adj. Believing; ascertaining.

متین matin (A) adj. Strong; solid; vigorous; important; obstinate; sententious.

حبل متین habl-ē matin, n.f. A strong rope; the true faith.

مٹاپا muṭāpā (H) n.m. Fatness; corpulence; plumpness; bulkiness; bigness.

مٹاپا چڑھنا muṭāpā charhnā, v. To grow fat; to be proud.

مٹانا miṭānā (H) v. To blot out; to erase; to rub off; to efface; to destroy; to abolish; to obliterate, to abrogate.

مٹائی muṭā'i (H) n.f. Fatness; thickness; coarseness; grossness.

مٹ بھیڑ muṭ bheṛ (H) n.f. See مٹھ بھیڑ muṭh bheṛ.

مٹر **matar** (H) *n.f.* Pea; peas.

مٹر گشت **maṭar gasht**, *n.f.* An idle and leisurely walk; ramble; stroll.

مٹک **maṭak** (H) *n.f.* Mincing gait; coquetry; flirtation; ogling.

مٹکا **maṭkā** (H) *n.m* A large earthen pot or jar.

مٹکانا **maṭkāna** (H) *v.* To wink; to cast amatory glances; to make a show; to ogle: to twinkle.

مٹکنا **maṭaknā** (H) *v.* To coquet; to ogle; to flirt.

مٹکی **maṭki** (H) *n.f.* A small earthen pot or jar; a child's coral; a wink; a twinkle; closing the eyes.

مٹنا **miṭnā** (H) *v.* To be effaced; to be erased; to become extinct; to be abolished; to be cancelled; to expire; to come to an end; to cease to exist; to die.

مٹھ **maṭh** (S) *n.m.* A hut; a pagan temple; an abode of a devotee or an ascetic; a Hindu college or convent.

مٹھ **muṭh** (H) *n.m.* Fist; a blow; clutch; grasp.

مٹھ بھیڑ **muṭh bheṛ**, *n.f.* Encounter; conflict; clash; scuffle.

مٹھ بھیڑ ہونا **muṭh bheṛ honā**, *v.* To face one another; to encounter; to confront.

مٹھا **maṭṭhā** (H) *n.m.* Butter milk. *adj.* Slow; slack; heavy; abstinate; sluggish; dull.

مٹھا **muṭṭhā** (H) *n.m.* A handful; a large bundle.

مٹھاس **miṭhās** (H) *n.f* Sweetness; pleasantness.

مٹھائی **miṭhā'i** (H) *n.f.* Sweetmeat; confectionery; sugar.

مٹھو **miṭṭhū** (H) *n.m.* A term of endearment for parrots and children; a parrot.

مٹھولا **maṭholā** (H) *n m.* Masturbation.

مٹھی **miṭṭhi** (H) *n.f.* A kiss.

مٹھی لینا **miṭṭhi lena**, *v.* To kiss.

مٹھی **muṭṭhi** (H) *n.f.* Fist; clutch; grip; handful.

مٹھی بھر **muṭṭhi bhar**, *adj.* A handful.

مٹھی گرم کرنا **muṭṭhi garm karna**, *v.* To give a bribe; to grease the palm of.

مٹھی میں ہونا **muṭṭhi meṅ honā**, *v.* To be in the palm of one's hand; to be under one's power or influence.

مٹھیا **muṭhyā** (H) *n.f.* A small handle; a hilt a corder's stick; a lump of sugar; the thick end of a stick.

مٹی **miṭṭi, maṭṭī** (H) *n.f.* Earth; clay; soil; earth refuse; dirt; filth; sweepings; a corpse; a carcass.

مٹی اٹھنا **miṭṭī uṭhna**, *v.* To die.

مٹی اڑانا **miṭṭi uṛāna**, *v.* To raise dust; to wander; to defame.

مٹی برباد کرنا **miṭṭi barbād karnā**, *v.* To defame the dead; to throw dust (on); to dishonour.

مٹی پلید ہونا **miṭṭi palid honā**, *v.* To be dishonoured; to be beaten severely.

مٹی ٹھکانے لگانا **miṭṭi ṭhikāne lagānā** *v.* Taking the dead body to its last resting place; to bury or inter the dead body; to perform the funeral obsequies.

مٹی خراب کرنا **miṭṭi k͟harāb karna**, *v.* To disgrace; to dishonour; to torment; to make a fool of; to spoil; to destroy; to ruin.

مٹی خراب ہونا ، خوارهونا **miṭṭi k͟harāb honā, k͟hwār honā**, *v.* To be ruined; to be wrecked; to be destroyed; to be disgraced.

مٹی دینا **miṭṭī denā**, *v.* To inter; to bury.

مٹی ڈالنا **miṭṭī ḍālnā**, *v.* To conceal a crime or fault; to hush up a matter.

مٹی سے مٹی مل جانا **mitti se mitti mil jana,** *v.* To be laid in the grave; to be buried; return of the dust to dust.

مٹی کا پتلا ، پنجر **mitti ka putlā, pinjar,** *n.m.* The human frame; the human body.

مٹی کا تیل **mitti kā tel,** *n.m.* Kerosine oil; petroleum; patrol.

مٹی کا عطر **mitti ka 'itr,** *n.m.* The essence of clay.

مٹی کا مادھو **mitti kā mādhū,** *n.m.* A fool; a dunce; a good-for-nothing fellow; a dummy.

مٹی کرنا **mitti karnā,** *v.* To dirty; to spoil; to ruin; to destroy; to fool away (one's money).

مٹی کی مورت **mitti ki mūrat,** *n.f.* A figure of clay; the mortal frame.

مٹی کے مول **mitti ke mol,** *adj.* Dirt cheap; very cheap.

مٹی میں لوٹنا **mitti men loṭnā,** *v.* To roll in mud.

مٹی میں ملانا **mitti men milānā,** *v.* To raze to the ground; to mar; to spoil; to ruin; to destroy.

مٹی میں ملنا **mitti men milnā,** *v.* To be marred, spoiled or ruined; to be disgraced; to die.

مٹیا **maṭyā** (H) *n.f.* A small pitcher.

مٹیا **maṭiyā** (H) *adj.* Of or belonging to earth or clay.

مٹیا پھونس **maṭiyā phūns,** *adj.* Infirm; weak; old.

مٹیا ٹھس **maṭiyā ṭhas,** *adj.* Idle; lazy.

مٹیامحل **maṭiyā mahal,** *n.m.* A habitation.

مٹیالا **maṭyālā** (H) *adj.* Dusty; clayey; earth coloured.

مثاب **muṣāb** (A) *adj.* Fit for a reward.

مثال **miṣāl** (A) *n.f.* Simile; likeness; similitude; parable; instance; example; specimen; model; metaphor.

مثال دینا **miṣāl dena,** *v.* To illustrate; to give an example; to cite an identical incident; to relate a parable.

مثالی **miṣāli** (A) *adj.* Ideal; similar; having a resemblance.

مثانہ **maṣānah** (A) *n.m.* The bladder.

مثبت **muṣbat** (A) *adj.* Affirmative; positive; established; proved; demonstrated.

مثبّت **muṣabbat** (A) *adj.* Fixed; proved; certified; endorsed; marked.

مثقال **misqāl** (A) *n.m.* Weight equal to four and half ماشہ **mashāh.**

مثل **miṣl** (A) *adv.* Like; as; resembling.

مثل **maṣal** (A) *n.f.* Proverb; example; fable; allegory; apologue.

مثلاً **maṣalan** (A) *adv.* For example (e.g.); for instance; as; viz; namely.

مثلث **muṣallas** (A) *n.f.* Triangle; a sort of verse of three lines. *adj.* Three cornered; triple; triangular; trilateral.

مثلث حادالزاویہ **muṣallas hād-uz-zāwiyah,** *n.f.* An acute-angled triangle.

مثلث قائم الزاویہ **muṣallas qāim-uz-zāwiyāh,** *n.f.* A right-angled triangle.

مثلث متساوی الاضلاع **muṣallas mutasāwi-ul-azlā'** *n.f.* An equilateral triangle.

مثلث متساوی الساقین **muṣallas mutasāwi-us-sāqain,** *n.f.* An isoscelles triangle.

مثلث مختلف الاضلاع **muṣallas mukhtalif-ul-azlā'** *n.f.* A scalene triangle.

مثلث منفرج الزاویہ **muṣallas munfarij-uz-zawiyah,** *n.f.* An abtuse-angled triangle.

مثلثی **muṣallaṣi,** *adj.* Triangular.

مثمر **muṣmir** (A) *adj.* Fruit bearing; fruitful; fructuous; productive.

مثمن **muṣamman** (A) *adj.* Octagonal; octangular; eight fold. *n.m.* An octagon; a stanza of eight lines.

مثنوی masnawī (A) n.f. A kind of verse in which the couplets rhyme regularly; a poem in which the second line of each distich rhymes with the same letter.

مثنٰی musannā (A) adj. Duplicate; double; dual; binary. n.m. A copy; the second; counterfoil.

مثنٰی بہ musannā behi, n.m. The original of a copy.

مجادل mujādil (A) adj. Contentious; disputant; quarrelsome.

مجادلہ mujādalah (A) n.m. Contention; disputation; dispute; altercation; conflict; fight; struggle.

مجاز majāz (A) adj. Lawful; legally authorised; admissible; competent; superficial; permitted; licensed; metaphor.

مجاز سماعت majāz-ĕ-samā'at, adj. Competent to hear a case.

مجاز مرسل majāz-ĕ-mursal, n.m. Metonymy; taking part for whole or effect for cause.

مجاز ہونا majāz honā, v. To be empowered; to be competent; to be legally authorised.

مجازاً majāzan (A) adv. Metaphorically; allegorically.

مجازی majāzī (A) adj. Metaphoric; figurative; allusive; hyperbolical; not real; illusive mundane.

مجال majāl (A) n.f. Strength; ability; authority; power; place; room; opportunity; leisure, capacity.

مجال رکھنا ، ہونا majāl rakhnā, honā, v. To have the power; to have the ability (to).

مجالس majālis (A) n.f. (plu. of مجلس majlis) Conferences; assemblies; convivial conversations.

مجالست mujālasat (A) n.f. Assembling; sitting together.

مجامعت mujama'at (A) n.f. Carnal intercourse; concubitus; coition; copulation.

مجاور mujāwir (A) n.m. An attendant of a mosque or a shrine; one attached to a shrine; adjacent; a neighbour.

مجاوری mujāwarī, n f. Constant attendance at a temple or shrine or mosque.

مجاہد mujāhid (A) n.m. A warrior in the defence of true faith; a crusader. adj. Striving.

مجاہدہ mujāhidah, (A) n.m. Making effort; trying hard; great endeavour or struggle.

مجبور majbūr (A) adj. Compelled; helpless; oppressed; forced; constrained; necessitated.

مجبور کرنا majbūr karnā, v. To compel; to force; to render helpless.

مجبور ہونا majbūr honā, v. To be compelled; to be oppressed.

مجبوراً majbūran, adv. By force of circumstances; under compulsion; compulsorily.

مجبوری majburī, n.f. Helplessness; powerlessness; compulsion; constraint; subjection.

مجتبیٰ mujtabā (A) adj. Elected; chosen; elect.

مجتمع mujtama' (A) adj. Convened; assembled; congregated; agreed (in opinion); accumulated together in one place; arriving at full strength.

مجتنب mujtanib (A) adj. Shirker; shunning the society; keeping oneself aloof.

مجتہد mujtahid (A) n.m. A religious director; a superviser or superintendent in religious matters; a prelate adj. Striving; contending; waging war against infidels.

مجد majd (A) n.m. Glory; grandeur; honour derived from ancestor; greatness.

مجدد mujaddid (A) adj. A revivalist; a renewer; modernist; a saint.

مجذوب majzūb (A) adj. Attracted; drawn; abstracted; absorbed in; lost in; fanatic. n.m. One who is absorbed in divine meditation; a man who is not in full possession of his sense; a Godly person.

مجذوب کی بڑ majzūb ki baṛ, n.f. A mad man's boast.

مجذور majzūr (A) n.m. The square of a number.

مجذوم majzūm (A) adj. Leprous; a leper; affected with leprosy.

مجرا mujrā (A) n.m. Allowance; premium; deduction. (H) n.m. Obeisance; respects; visit; audiance; salutation; an elegy; a trial of professional singing.

مجرا پانا mujrā pānā, v. To receive credit (for); to have an interview.

مجرادینا mujrā denā, v. To give credit; to allow an abatement.

مجرا طلبی mujrā ṭalabi, n.f. A counter-claim; counter-charge.

مجرا کرنا mujrā karnā, v. To give credit for; to deduct; to make obeisance.

مجرا ہونا mujrā honā, v. To be carried to account; to be deducted.

مجرائی mujrā'i, n.m. One who pays his respects; a servant; one who recites a dirge; a minister; a visitant. n.f. Allowance; deduction; a reduction in the assessment.

مجرب mujarrab (A) adj. Tried; proved; expert; skilful; experienced; tested; examined; assayed.

مجربات mujarrabāt (A) n.m. Tested prescriptions; specifics.

مجرد mujarrad (A) adj. Solitary; alone; only; unmarried; celibate; single; naked; bare abstract. n.m. A bachelor.

مجردات mujarradāt(A) n.f. Incorporeal beings.

مجردی mujarradi, n.f. Solitude; celibacy; bachelorship; unmarried state; nakedness; solitariness.

مجرم mujrim (A) adj Criminal; culpable; faulty; blamable; censurable. n.m. A criminal; an offender; a sinner; a felon; a culprit.

مجرم اشتہاری mujrim-ě ishtihāri, n.m. A notified criminal.

مجرم ٹھہرانا ، قرار دینا mujrim ṭhahrānā, qarār denā, v. To find one guilty; to convict an offender.

مجرم عادی mujrim-ě 'ādi n.m. Habitual offender.

مجرم فراری mujrim-ě firāri, n.m. An absconding offender.

مجرمانہ mujrimānā, adj. Criminal; culpable.

مجروح majrūḥ (A) adj. Wounded; hurt; smitten.

مجروح کرنا mujrūh karnā, v. To hurt; to wound.

مجروح ہونا ، ہو جانا majrūḥ hona, ho jana. v. To be hurt; to become wounded.

مجسم mujassam (A) adj. Having a body; embodied; corporeal; corpulent; incorporated; incarnate.

مجسم کرنا mujassam karnā, v. To give a corporeal form; to personify.

مجسمہ mujassamah (A) n.m. A statue; an image in marble or bronze.

مجلا mujalla (A) adj. Bright; polished; furnished; illustrated; manifested.

مجلد mujallid (A) n.m. A book binder.

مجلد mujallad (A) adj. Bound (a volume).

مجلس majlis (A) n.f. An assembly; a company; a party; a congregation; convention; association; board; committee.

مجلس دستور ساز majlis-ě dastūr sāz, n.f. Constituent assembly.

مجلس رقص و سرود majlis-ě raqṣ-ŏ-sarod, n.f. A concert; a ball; a dancing party.

مجلس شوریٰ majlis-ě shūrạ, n.f. Consultative committee; advisory committee.

مجلس علمی majlis-ĕ ʻilmī, n.f. A literary institute.

مجلس قانون ساز majlis-ĕ qānun saz, n.f. Legislative assembly.

مجلس قائمه majlis-ĕ qā'imah, n.f. Standing committee.

مجلس کرنا majlis karnā, v. To hold a meeting; to convene a meeting in commemoration of the martyrdom of Imam Hussain.

مجلس وکلا majlis-ĕ wukalā, n.f. Bar association.

مجلسی majlisī (A) adj. Social; civil; concerning a gathering. n.m. A person invited to an assembly.

مجله mujallah (A) n.m. Periodical review.

مجمع majmaʻ (A) n.m. Congregation; gathering; assemblage; crowd; heap; pile; a book of miscellanies; collection.

مجمع البحرین majmaʻ-ul-baḥrain, n.m. Place where two seas or rivers meet; a confluence; concourse.

مجمع الجزائر majmaʻ-ul-jazā'ir, n.m. An archipelago.

مجمع خلاف قانون majmaʻ-ĕ khilaf-ĕ qanun, n.m. An unlawful assembly.

مجمع عام majma-ĕ ʻām, n.m. A public meeting.

مجمل mujmal (A) adj. Abridged; brief; brought together; contracted; an abstract; summary; compendium; abridgment.

مجمل حساب mujmal ḥisāb, n.m. An abstract account.

مجملاً mujmalan (A) adj. In short; in brief; summarily.

مجموعه majmuaʻ (A) n.m. A collective mass (of); a crowd; an assembly; a compendium; an aggregate; a compound perfume; a collection; a form; the whole; the sum; the sum-total. adj. Collected; assembled; contained; all; the whole.

مجموعه تعزیرات majmuaʻ-ĕ taʻzirat, n.m. The Penal code.

مجموعه قانون دیوانی majmuaʻ-ĕ qanun-ĕ diwāni, n.m. The civil procedure code.

مجموعه قوانین majmuaʻ-ĕ qawanin, n.m. Code; Statute Book.

مجموعی majmūʻī (A) adj. Collected; aggregate; total.

مجموعی قیمت majmūʻī qīmat, n.f. Total value.

مجنون majnun (A) adj. Possessed of an evil spirit; insane; madly or desperately in love; a very thin and weak person. n.m. Name of the celebrated lover of Laila.

مجوز mujawwiz (A) adj. Permitting; allowing to pass; proposing; planning.

مجوز mujawwaz (A) adj. Lawful; permitted; proposed.

مجوزه mujawwazah (A) adj Prepared; laid down; prescribed.

مجوس ، مجوسی majūs, majūsī (A) n.m A guebre; a follower of Zoroaster; the magi; a fire-worshipper.

مجوف mujawwaf (A) adj. Hollow; concave; vaulted; empty; vacant.

مجھ mujh (H) pron. Me.

مجھ کو mujh ko, adv. To me; me.

مجهول majhūl (A) adj. Unknown; little known; useless; passive voice; indolent; lazy; idle; slow; slothful; short, (as و and ی) when the former has the sound of o as in bone and the latter that of a as in name.

مجهول النسب majhūl-un-nasab, adj. Of unknown lineage or parentage.

مجهول متعلق majhūl-ĕ mutʻlaq adj. Very indolent or useless person.

مجهولا ، مجهولی majholā, majholī (H) adj. Middling.

مجھے mujhe (H) *pron.* To me; me.

مجیب mujib (A) *adj.* Listening to; granting; consenting; responding; accepting.

مجیب الدعوات *mujib-ud-da'wat, adj.* Granting prayers; listening to requests; God.

مجیٹھ *majīṭh* (H) *n.f.* Name of a drug used for dyeing red.

مجید *majīd* (A) *adj.* Glorious; noble; exalted; high; honourable.

مجیرا *majīrā* (H) *n.m.* Small cymbals; a tinckling ornament for the feet or toes.

مچان *machān* (H) *n.m.* A platform; a dias; a stage; a raised seat; a scaffold; a raised platform or stage from which the farmers watch the fields and drive away birds etc.

مچانا *machānā* (H) *v.* To raise up; to stir up; to excite; to commit; to make; to cause; to perpetuate.

مچکانا *michkānā* (H) *v.* To wink; to blink; to shut and open eyes repeatedly and quickly.

مچکانا *machkānā* (H) *v.* To sprain; to twist.

مچکنا *machaknā* (H) *v.* To have pains in the joints; to creak; to tremble.

مچلانا *machlānā* (H) *v.* To nauseate; to pretend ignorance; to be wayward.

مچلکہ ، مچلکا *muchalka, mubhalkah* (T) *n.m.* A bond; a note of bond; an agreement; a written obligation; recognizance of criminals.

مچلکہ حفظ امن *muchalkah ḥifẓ-ĕ amn, n.m.* A bond to keep the peace.

مچلکہ نیک چلنی *muchalkah nek chalani, n.m.* A bond for good behaviour.

مچلنا *machalnā* (H) *v.* To be refractory; to persist in; to be peevish; to cry; to be obstinate; to sulk; to roll on the ground (as a wayward child); to be disobedient; to cross.

مچنا *machna* (H) *v.* To happen; to be raised up; to be excited; to be noised abroad; to be perpetrated; to be produced.

مچنا *michnā* (H) *v.* To shut; to close.

مچوانا *machwanā* (H) *v.* To cause to be made (a noise); to cause to be raised.

مچوانا *michwanā* (H) *v.* To cause to be closed or shut.

مچھ *machh* (H) *n.m.* A fish; an incarnation of Hindu Diety Vishnū, as a fish.

مچھر *machchhar* (H) *n.m.* A mosquito; a gnat.

مچھر دانی *machchhar dāni, n.f.* A mosquito net.

مچھلی *machhlī* (H) *n.f.* A fish; the flesh of arm or foreleg of an animal; an eardrop made in the form of a fish; the sign Pisces; the 12th sign of the Zodiac.

مچھلی پکڑنا ، مچھلی کا شکار کرنا *machhlī pakarnā, machhli kā shikār karnā, v.* To fish; to angle.

مچھلی کا پر *machhlī ka par, n.m.* Fin; fishbone.

مچھلی کا تیل *machhlī kā tel, n.m.* Fish oil; cod liver oil.

مچھلی کا سریش *machhli kā saresh, n.m.* Fish glue.

مچھلی کا کانٹا *machhlī kā kantā, n.m.* Fish hook; fish-bone.

مچھلی کی طرح تڑپنا *machhli kī ṭaraḥ taṛapnā, v.* To be like fish out of water; to writhe with agony; to flounder.

مچھلی والا *machhli wālā, n.m.* A fishseller; a fish monger; fisherman.

اڑن مچھلی *uṛan machhlī, n.f.* Flying fish; skip-jack fish.

تارا مچھلی *tārā machhli, n.f.* Star fish.

مچھندر *machhandar* (H) *n.m.* A monkey; a dolt; a buffoon; a clown; a merry-andrew.

مچھوا *machhwā* (A) *n.m.* fisherman; a small boat; a skiff; a yacht.

مچھی machhi. See مچھلی machhli.

محابا muḥābā (A) n.m. Respect; regard; friendship; affection; partiality lenient or gentle treatment.

محاذ muḥāz (A) n.m. Front; face.

محاذ جنگ muḥāz-ĕ jang, n.m. War front.

محارب muḥārib (A) n.m. A warrior; a fighter; a soldier; a combatant.

محاربہ muḥārabah (A) n.m. Fight; war; combat; battle.

محاسب muḥāsib (A) n.m. An accountant; an auditor; an examiner; a calculator (of accounts); one who keeps accounts; an arithmetician.

محاسب اعلیٰ muḥāsib-ĕ 'alā, n.m. Auditor general; accountant general.

محاسبہ muḥāsabah (A) n.m. Computation; audit; calculation; account; settlement of accounts.

محاسبہ دار muḥāsabah dār, n.m. An accountant.

محاسبہ کرنا muḥāsabah karna, v. To audit; to check accounts.

محاسبی muḥāsabi, adj. Concerning audit.

محاسبی اشارہ muḥāsabi ishārah, n.m. Audit note.

محاسبی اعتراض muḥāsabi i'tirāẓ, n.m. Audit objection.

محاسبی ضابطہ muḥāsabi ẓābiṭah, n.m. Audit code.

محاسبی ہدایات muḥāsabi hidāyāt, n.f. Audit rules or instructions.

محاسن maḥāsin (A) n.m. (plu. of حسن ḥasan) Virtues; beauties; laudable actions; qualities; the beard and moustaches or whiskers.

محاصر muḥāṣir (A) adj. Besieging; besieger.

محاصرہ muḥāṣarah (A) n.m. A siege; a blockade.

محاصرہ اٹھانا muḥāṣarah uthānā, v. To raise or give up a siege.

محاصرہ کرنا muḥāṣarah karna, v. To besiege; to blockade; to surround; to lay a siege.

محاصرے میں آجانا muḥāṣare men ā jana, v. To be besieged; to be surrounded.

محاصل maḥāṣil (A) n.m. (plu. of محصول maḥṣūl) Profits; produce; gains; receipts; revenue; duties; taxess; rates.

محافظ muḥāfiẓ (A) n.m. A protector; a guardian; a guard; keeper.

محافظ حقیقی muḥāfiẓ-ĕ ḥaqīqi, n.m. The protector; God.

محافظ خانہ muḥāfiẓ khānah, n.m. A record room.

محافظ دفتر muḥāfiẓ-ĕ daftar, n.m. Record keeper.

محافظ ذاتی muḥāfiẓ-ĕ ẓāti, n.m. A bodyguard.

محافظ ذخیرہ muḥāfiẓ-ĕ ẕak͟hirah, n.m. A store-keeper.

محافظ محبس muḥāfiẓ-ĕ maḥbas, n.m. A jailor; a superintendent of jail

محافظت muḥāfaẓat (A) n.f. Preservation; protection; guardianship; custody; care.

محافل maḥāfil (A) n.f. (plu. of محفل maḥfil) Conventions; societies; clubs; meetings.

محافل رسمی maḥāfil-ĕ rasmi, n.f. Social conventions; conventional meetings; official circles.

محاق muḥāq (A) n.m. Waning of the moon; declining of the moon in size and lustre after the 15th; the last three days of the lunar month when the moon does not appear.

محاکات muḥākāt (A) n.f. Talking mutually; telling stories; resembling one another; copying or imitating a thing or action; reproduction.

محاکمہ moḥākamah (A) n.m. Referring a dispute to a judge or referee; settling a case.

محال mahāl (A) n.m. (plu. of محل mahal) Districts; estates; departments; streets; palaces; courts; places; houses.

محال آبکاری mahal-ĕ ābkāri, n.m. Excise department.

محال muhāl (A) adj. Impossible; absurd.

محال مطلق muhal-ĕ mutlaq, adj. Very difficult; absolutely impossible; out of the question.

محالات muhalat (A) n.f. Absurdities; impossibilities; impracticable things.

محامد mahāmid (A) n.m. (plu. of محمده mahmadah) Virtues; laudable deeds.

محاوره muhāwarah (P) n.m. Idiom; usage; current speech; phraseology; colloqiualism; figure of speech; dialogue; phrases used in ordinary conversation; conference; practice (plu. محاورات muhāwarat).

محب muhibb (A) n.m. A friend; a lover.

محب الوطن muhib-ul-waṭan, n.m. Patriot.

محبانه muhibbānah, adv. Friendly.

محبت mahabbat (A) n.f. Friendship; love affection.

محبت آمیز mahabbat āmez, adj. Loving; friendly; affectionate.

محبت رکھنا mahabbat rakhnā, v. To love; to show affection; to feel affection for.

محبت قلبی mahabbat-ĕ qalbi, n.f. Sincere affection; true love.

محبت کا دم بهرنا mahabbat kā dam bharnā, v. To profess love; to talk of love.

محبت کل mahabbat-ĕ kull, n.f. Philanthropy; benevolence.

محبس mahbas (A) n.m. A prison; a jail.

محبوب mahbūb (A) n.m. A friend; a beloved; a sweetheart. adj. Beloved; lovely; liked; loved.

محبوبانه mahbūbānah (A & P) adv. Like a beloved; in the manner of a sweetheart.

محبوبه mahbūbah (A) n.f. A sweeheart; a mistress; a darling. adj. Beloved.

محبوبی ، محبوبیت mahbubi, mahbubiyat (P & A) n.f. Loveliness; amiability; love; affection; possessing the quality of being loved.

محبوس mahbus (A) adj. Confined; shut up; arrested; imprisoned. n.m. A captive; a prisoner.

محتاج muhtaj (A) adj. Needy; poor; indigent; wanting; necessitous; defective; in want. n.m. A poor man; a pauper; a begger; a cripple.

محتاج خانه muhtāj khānah, n.m. A poor house.

محتاج هونا muhtāj honā, v. To be needy and poor.

محتاجی muhtāji, n.f. Poverty; indigence; want; need.

محتاط muhtāṭ (A) adj. Guarded; careful; circumspect; discreet; prudent.

محتجب muhtajib (A) adj. Hidden; concealed; veiled.

محترز muhtariz (A) adj. Careful; aware; cautious; wary; refraining from; keeping aloof.

محترم muhtarim (A) adj. Showing respect; honouring.

محترم muhtaram (A) adj. Honoured; revered; sacred; respectable; venerable; estimable.

محتسب muhtasib (A) n.m. A censor; superintendent of weights, measures and provision ; a police inspector.

محتشم muhtashim (A) adj. Great; powerful; attended by many followers or dependants; having many followers.

محجوب mahjūb (A) n.m. Ashamed; modest; bashful; veiled; secluded; excluded.

محدب muhaddab (A) adj. Convex; bulging.

محدب عدسه muhaddab 'adsah, n.m. Convex lens.

محدث muhaddis̤ (A) n.m. A narrator; a relater; a believer in traditions; having the knowledge of traditions or sayings of the Holy Prophet.

محدث muhdis̤ (A) n.m. An inventor; an Innovator.

محدود mahdūd (A) adj. Limited; bounded; definite; finite.

محدود کرنا mahdūd karnā, v. To limit; to define.

محذوف mahẕūf (A) adj. Omitted; cut off; rejected; implied; understood; elided (as a syllable from a word); taken away.

محراب mihrāb (A) n.f. Arch; shelf; niche; the royal closet or private chamber; the principal place in the mosque, where the priest prays.

محراب دار mihrāb dār, adj. rc hed.

محرابی mihrābi, adj. Arched.

محرر muharrir (A) n.m. A clerk; a scribe; a writer; an amanuensis.

محرر ترسیل muharrir-ĕ tarsil, n.m. Despatcher.

محرر تقسیم muharrir-ĕ taqsim, n.m. A circulating clerk.

محرر حسابات muharrir-ĕ hisābāt, n.m. Accounts clerk.

محرر صغیر muharrir-ĕ ṣaghir, n.m. Junior clerk.

محرر کبیر muharrir-ĕ kabir, n.m. Senior clerk.

محرر متعلقه muharrir-ĕ muta'aliqah, n.m. Dealing clerk.

محرر نقول muharrir-ĕ nuqūl, n.m. Copying clerk.

محرره muharrarah (A) adj. Written; inscribed.

محرری muharrirī, n.f. Clerkship.

محرف muharraf (A) adj. Transposed; perverted; inverted.

محرق، محرقه muhriq, muhriqah (A) adj. Burning; inflammatory; ardent.

محرک muharrik (A) adj. Moving; putting in motion; marking a consonant with a vowel; stimultant; incentive. n.m. A proposer; a mover; an exciter; a stimulant.

محرم muharram (A) n.m. The first month of the Hijra year. adj. Sacred; venerable; forbidden; excluded.

محرم mahram (A) n.m. A spouse; a confident; an intimate friend; anyone who is admitted into the women's apartments or into a sacred place. n.f. A bodice; gussets; brassiere.

محرم راز mahram-ĕ rāz, n.m. A bosom friend; a confident.

محرمات muharramāt (A) n.f. Things forbidden or unlawful.

محرمانه mahramānah (A & P) adv. In private; in a familiar way.

محروسه mahrūsah (A) adj. Fortified (place); garrisoned (place).

محروم mahrūm (A) adj. Deprived of; debarred; excluded; damned or refused (a gift, or good or prosperity); unlucky; prohibited; unfortunate; wretched; plundered; disappointed.

محروم الارث mahrūm-ul-irs̤, adj. Deprived of heredity.

محروم رکھنا mahrūm rakhnā, v. To disappoint; to exclude; to keep one deprived from.

محروم کرنا mahrūm karnā, v. To deprive of; to balk; to frustrate; to exclude; to prohibit; to disappoint; to debar; to defeat.

محرومی ، محرومیت mahrūmi, mahrūmiyat (P&A) n.f. Exclusion; disappointment; deprival; loss; deprivation.

محزون mohzūn (A) adj. Grieved; vexed; afflicted; sad.

محسن muḥsin (A) *n.m.* A benefactor; a patron. *adj.* Beneficent; generous; obliging; benefiting.

محسن کش muḥsin kush, *adj.* Ungrateful.

محسنات muḥsināt (A) *n.f.* Advantages; virtues.

محسوب maḥsūb (A) *adj.* Computed; numbered; carried to account; calculated.

محسوب کرنا mahsūb karnā, *v.* To take into account; to compute.

محسوب ہونا maḥsūb honā, *v.* To be included in the account.

محسود maḥsūd (A) *adj.* Envied; hated.

محسوس mahsūs (A) *adj.* Felt; perceived; sensible; perceptible.

محسوس کرنا mahsūs karna, *v.* To perceive; to feel.

محسوسات mahsusat (A) *n.f.* Perceivable things; sensation; objects of sense; things felt or perceived.

محشر maḥshar (A) *n.m.* Day of resurrection; the Last Day; a place of rising and assembling; a tumultuous and noisy place.

محشر خرام maḥshar khirām, *adj.* Exciting a commotion (like that of the Day of Judgement) by the elegance of a sweetheart's gait.

محشی muḥashshi (A) *adj.* Annotator; writer of marginal notes.

محشیٰ muḥashshā (A) *adj.* Annotated; having notes in the margin; commented on in the margin.

محصل muḥaṣṣil (A) *n.m.* A collector of revenue; a tax gatherer; a bailiff; a dun.

محصن muḥṣan (A) *adj.* Chaste; continent; guarded; preserved.

محصنہ muḥṣanah (A) *n.f.* Chaste woman (*plu.* محصنات muḥṣanāt).

محصور maḥṣūr (A) *adj.* Besieged; beleaguered; surrounded; detained; restrained (*plu.* محصورین mahsūrīn).

محصور کرنا maḥṣūr karna, *v.* To besiege; to encompass; to surround.

محصور ہونا maḥṣur honā, *v.* To be besieged; to be surrounded.

محصول maḥṣūl (A) *n.m.* Tax; duty; excise; custom; postage; produce of anything; income; revenue.

محصول آبکاری maḥṣūl-ĕ ābkārī, *n.m.* Excise duty; taxes on intoxicants.

محصول پرمٹ muḥṣūl parmit, *n.m.* Custom duty.

محصول چکانا maḥṣūl chukānā, *v.* To pay duty or postage.

محصول چور maḥṣūl chor, *n.m.* A smuggler.

محصول ڈاک maḥṣūl ḍāk, *n.m.* Postage.

محصول سائر maḥṣul-ĕ sa'ir, *n.m.* Miscellaneous duties.

محصول سڑک maḥṣūl saṛak, *n.m.* Road-cess; toll.

محصول فروخت maḥṣul-ĕ farokht, *n.m.* Sales tax.

محصول برآمد maḥṣūl-ĕ baramad, *n.m.* Export duties.

محصول درآمد maḥṣūl-ĕ darāmad, *n.m.* Import duties.

بے محصول be maḥṣul, *adj.* Free of tax or duty; tax free.

فرد محصول fard-ĕ maḥṣul, *n.f.* A tariff.

محصولی maḥṣūlī (A) *adj.* Paying revenue or tax or duty; dutiable; taxable; bearing; unpaid. *n.f.* Land paying revenue.

محض maḥẓ (A) *adj.* Pure; mere; absolute; simple; unmixed; unalloyed. *adv.* Merely; purely; altogether; utterly; absolutely; entirely; wholly; solely.

محضر maḥẓar (A) *n.m.* Royal presence; appearance; a general application or petition; a representation; a public attestation; statement of a case or suit laid before a judge.

محضر نامه mahẓar nāmah, n.m. A muster-roll; a public attestation; a list of the persons present at an assembly.

محظوظ mahẓūẓ (A) adj. Delighted; pleased; happy; glad; cheerful; contented; fortunate; blest; rich; wealthy.

محفل mahfil (A) n.f. Place or time of meeting; assembly; congregation; congress.

محفل کرنا mahfil karnā, v. To hold a meeting; to assemble; to have a dance.

محفوظ mahfūẓ (A) adj. Kept safe; preserved; guarded; exempted; committed to memory; protected; sheltered; secure.

محقر muhaqqar (A) adj. Despised; contemptible; poor; low.

محقق muhaqqiq (A) n.m. A verifier; an investigator; a philosopher; a research scholar; inquisitive; investigating the truth of; proving to be true.

محقق muhaqqaq (A) adj. Verified; well-established; authenticated; positive; certain; certified; confirmed; known for truth.

محققانه muhaqqiqānah (A) adv. In a well established manner; truly; certainly; from a philosopher's point of view.

محک mahakk (A) n.m. Touchstone; test.

محکم muhkam (A) adj. Strengthened; strong; firm; fortified.

محکمه mahkamah (A) n.m. A tribunal; court of justice; assize; an office; a department; a bureau.

محکمه آبادکاری ، محکمه بحالیات mahkamah-ĕ ābādkārī, bahāliyāt, n.m. Rehabilitation department.

محکمه آبادی mahkamah-ĕ ābādi, n.m. Colonization department.

محکمه آبکاری mahkamah-ĕ ābkāri, n.m. Excise department.

محکمه انهار mahkamah-ĕ anhār, n.m. Irrigation department.

محکمه بحالی اراضی mahkamah-ĕ bahālī-ĕ arāẓī, n.m. Land reclamation department.

محکمه بندوبست mahkamah-ĕ bandobast, n.m. Settlement department.

محکمه بهرتی mahkamah bhartī, n.m. Recruiting department.

محکمه پولیس mahkamah polis, n.m. Police Department.

محکمه پیمائش زمین mahkamah-ĕ paimā'ish-ĕ zamīn, n.m. Survey department.

محکمه تار mahkamah tār, n.m. Telegraph department.

محکمه تعلقات عامه mahkamah-ĕ ta'lluqqāt-ĕ-'āmmah, n.m. Public relations department.

محکمه تعلیم mahkamah-ĕ t'alim, n.m. Education department.

محکمه جنگلات mahkamah janglāt, n.m. Forest or conservation department.

محکمه چنگی mahkamah chungī, n.m. Octroi department.

محکمه خوراک mahkamah-ĕ khūrāk, n.m. Food department.

محکمه ڈاک mahkamah ḍāk, n.m. Postal department.

محکمه ریل mahkamah rel, n.m. Railway department.

محکمه طبابت mahkamah-ĕ ṭabābat, n.m. Medical department.

محکمه نشر و اشاعت mahkamah-ĕ nashr-ŏ-ishā-'at, n.m. Publicity department.

محکمه مواصلات mahkamah-ĕ mawāṣilāt, n.m. Communication department.

محکوم mahkūm (A) adj. Controlled; subdued subjugated; brought under control; rule governed; condemned. n.m. A subordinate; a subject.

محکومیت mahkūmiyat (A) n.f. Defeat; subjugation; condemnation.

محل mahall (A) n.m. A place; a palatial building; palace; house; mansion; seraglio; quarter; abode; station; location; time; opportunity; occasion. n.f. Wife; queen.

محل خاص maḥall-ĕ k͟hāṣ, n.f. The chief queen.

محل سرا maḥall sarā, n.f. Seraglio; female apartment; harem.

بر محل bar maḥall, adj. Fitting the occasion; appropriate.

بے محل be maḥall, adj. Out of place; inappropriate; inopportune.

محلات maḥqllāt (A) n.m. (plu. of محل maḥall) Palaces (plu. of محله muḥallah) quarters or parts of a town.

محلول maḥlūl (A) adj. Dissolved.

محله muḥallah (A) n.m. A quarter or part of a town; a review or muster (of troops); a street; a ward.

محله دار muḥallah dār, n.m. Headman of a district or علاقه 'ilāqah; a resident of the same quarter.

محمد Muḥammad (A) adj. Highly praised; the praised one. n.m. The Holy Prophet Muhammad.

محمدی Muḥammadī (A) n.m. A follower of Muhammad; a Muslim.

محمل maḥmil (A) n.m. A litter carried on a camel; a support; that in (or on) which anything is borne.

محمود، محموده maḥmūd, maḥmūdah (A) adj. Praised; praiseworthy; laudable; worthy.

محمول، محموله maḥmūl, maḥmūlah (A) adj. Bearing (a meaning); applicable; loaded.

محن miḥan (A) (plu. of محنت miḥnat) Labours; troubles; afflictions; sufferings; trials.

محنت miḥnat (A) n.f. Labour; toil; industry; deligence; application; trouble; difficulty; affliction; trial; perplexity.

محنت اٹھانا miḥnat uṭhānā, v. To undergo trouble; to take pains.

محنت ٹھکانے لگنا miḥnat ṭhikāne lagnā, v. To succeed; to get a reward of one's labour; to be paid adequately for hard work.

محنت شاقه miḥnat-ĕ shāqqah, n.f. Hard labour; continuous hard work.

محنت کرنا miḥnat karnā, v. To labour; to toil; to work hard.

محنت کش miḥnat kash, adj. Consistantly doing hard work; laborious; enduring great labour; afflicted; distressed.

محنت مزدوری miḥnat mazdūrī, n.f. Hand work; earning bread by toil and labour.

محنتانه miḥnatānah (A&P) n.m. Wages; fees; remuneration; hire.

محنتی miḥnatī, adj. Laborious; industrious; hard worker; hardy. n.m. A labourer.

محو maḥv (A) adj. Absorbed; fascinated; charmed; captivated; erased; obliterated; abolished; effaced; forgotten.

محو کرنا maḥv karnā, v. To erase; to efface; to charm; to fascinate.

محو ہونا maḥv honā, v. To be absorbed; to be fascinated; to be effaced or erased.

محور miḥwar (A) n.m. An axis.

محوری miḥwarī, adj. Axial; axile.

محوله moḥawwalah (A) adj. Stated; quoted; referred to.

محوله بالا moḥawwalah bālā, adj. Cited above; referred to above; quoted above.

محویت maḥwiyyat (A) n.f. Obliteration; state of being effaced; state of being absorbed or charmed; fascination; engrossment.

محیی muḥyī (A) adj. Giving life; keeping alive; (an attribute of God).

محیر muḥaiyyir (A) adj. Astonishing; bewildering.

محیط muḥīṭ (A) adj. Encircling; surrounding; comprehending; circumambient; containing; guarding; knowing. n.m. Circumference; the ocean.

محیط ہونا muḥīṭ honā, v. To circumscribe; to surround; to encircle.

مخارج makhārij (A) n.m. (plu. of مخرج makhraj) Expenses; disbursement; expenditure; outlets; sources; roots; organs of speech.

مخاصمت mukhāṣamat (A) n.f. Enmity; hostility; contention; quarrelling; altercation.

مخاطب mukhāṭib (A) n.m. One who addresses another; the speaker.

مخاطب mukhāṭab (A) n.m. One spoken to by another; person addressed; the second person (in grammar).

مخالف mukhālif (A) adj. Opposite; adverse; unfavourable; dissentient; repugnant. n.m. An enemy; an opponent; foe; adversary.

مخالفت mukhālafat (A) n.f. Opposition; dissidence; disobedience; rebellion; disagreement; discord; enmity.

مخالفت کرنا mukhālafat karnā, v. To oppose; to contradict; to resist; to go against; to dissent.

مخبر mukhbir (A) n.m. One who gives news; announcer of news; informer; reporter; spy.

مخبر صادق mukhbīr-ĕ sādiq, adj. Bringer of true intelligence; a title of the Holly Prophet.

مخبری mukhbirī, n.f. The act or office of a reporter or spy; report; information.

مخبری کرنا mukhbirī karnā, v. To inform; to act the spy.

مخبوط makhbūṭ (A) adj. Mad; insane; rendered foolish.

مخبوط‌الحواس makhbūṭ-ul-ḥawās, adj. Senseless; insane; one who has lost his head.

مختار mukhtār (A) adj. Selected; independent; invested with authority; having legal power; authorised; empowered. n.m. Agent; attorney; manager; a delegate.

مختار خاص mukhtār-ĕ khāṣ, n.m. Special agent or representative.

مختار عام mukhtār-ĕ ʻām, n.m. General agent; general manager.

مختار کار mukhtār-ĕ kār, n.m. A director; manager having authority in business.

مختارکاری mukhtār kārī, n.f. Attorneyship.

مختار نامہ mukhtār nāmah, n.m. Power of attorney.

مختار ہونا mukhtāṛ honā, v. To represent; to present one as attorney.

مختاری mukhtārī (A & P) n.f. Independence; power; authority; free will; absoluteness; attorneyship.

مخترع mukhtariʻ (A) n.m. Inventor.

مخترعات mukhtāraʻāt (A) n.f. Inventions.

مختص mukhtaṣṣ (A) adj. Appropriated; peculiar; specific; chosen; elected; special; private; domestic.

مختصر mukhtaṣar (A) adj. Abbreviated; abridged; concise; short; succinct; compendious.

مختصر کرنا mukhtaṣar karnā, v. To abridge; to curtail; to epitomize.

مختصر نویس mukhtaṣar nawīs, n.m. Stenographer; short hand writer.

مختصر نویسی mukhtaṣār nawīsī, n.f. Stenography.

مختصراً mukhtaṣaran (A) adv. Briefly; in short.

مختل mukhtall (A) adj. Confused; confounded; disturbed; corrupted; emaciated.

مختلف mukhtalif (A) adj. Diverse; different; various; discordant; unlike; dissimilar.

مختلف الاضلاع mukhtalif-ul-azlā', adj. Of unequal sides; scalene.

مختلف النوع mukhtalif-un-nau', adj. Of different or various kinds.

مختوم makhtūm (A) adj. Sealed; signed; concluded; finished.

مختون makhtūn (A) adj. Circumcised.

مخدر mukhaddar (A) adj. Concealed; kept behind.

مخدرات mukhaddarāt (A) n.f. Chaste women; veiled women; ladies.

مخدوش makhdūsh (A) adj. Doubtful; alarming; fearful; dangerous.

مخدوم ، مخدومه makhdūm, makhdūmah (A) adj. Served; waited on.

مخرب mukharrib (A) adj. Destroying; spoiling.

مخرج makhraj (A) n.m. Outlet; root; source; issue; place of egress; organ of speech; utterance; pronunciation; articulation; denominator.

مخروطی makhrūṭī (A) adj. Conical; tapering.

مخزن makhzan (A) n.m. A magazine; storehouse; granary; treasury.

مخزن الا دویه makhzan-ul-adwiyah, n.m. Materia medica.

مخزن العلوم makhzan-ul-'ulūm, n.m. Encyclopedia.

مخصوص makhṣūṣ (A) adj. Specified; special; peculiar; private; appropriated; particular.

مخطط mukhaṭṭaṭ (A) adj. Marked with lines; lined; ruled; having an incipient beard.

مخطوب ، مخطوبه makhṭūb, makhṭūbah (A) adj. Betrothed; affianced.

مخطی mukhṭī (A) adj. Committing a sin unintentionally.

مخفف mukhaffaf (A) adj. Abated; alleviated; abridged; light; contemptible; a consonant having a short vowel for a long one.

مخفی makhfī (A) adj. Hidden; secret; occult; private; concealed.

مخل mukhill (A) adj. Disturbing; spoiling; ruining; intruding. n.m. Intruder; intermeddler.

مخل ہونا mukhill honā, v. To meddle; to disturb; to interfere.

مخلا mukhallā, (A) adj. Empty; dismissed; set at liberty; set free; repudiated.

مخلا بالطبع mukhallā biṭ-ṭaba', adj. Unceremonious.

مخلص mukhliṣ (A) adj. Sincere; true; real; loyal. n.m. A sincere friend.

مخلصانه mukhliṣānah (A) adv. Friendly; sincerely.

مخلصی mukhlisī, makhlasī, n.f. Deliverance; liberation; liberty; release.

مخلوط makhlūṭ (A) adj. Mixed; blended; crossbreed; confused; heterogeneous.

مخلوط النسل makhlūṭ-un-nasl, n.m. A crossbreed, a hybrid; mongrel.

مخلوق makhlūq (A) adj. Created; formed. n.f. Creature; creation.

مخلوقات makhlūqāt (A) n.f. Things created; creatures.

مخمر mukhammir (A) adj. Leavening.

مخمس mukhammas (A) n.m. A kind of verse containing five lines; a pentagon. adj. Pentagular; quintupled.

مخمصه makhmaṣah, n.m. Dilemma; perplexity; difficulty.

مخمصه میں پڑنا makhmaṣah meṅ parnā, v. To get into a difficulty; to find oneself in hot water.

مخمل makhmal (A) n.m. Velvet.

مخملی makhmalī, adj. Velvety; soft; of velvet.

مخمور makhmūr (A) adj. Intoxicated; inebriated; drunk.

مخنث mukhannas (A) adj. Effeminate. n.m. An eunuch.

مخنث کرنا mukhannaṣ karnā, v. To emasculate.

مخوف mukhawwif (A) adj. Terrifying; frightful.

مخیر mukhaiyyir (A) adj. Bountiful; charitable; liberal; left to free choice; indifferent; giving an option of two things.

مد madd (A) n.m. Extension; lengthening; prolongation; the flux of the ocean; flood-tide; the mark (-) placed over alif to prolong its sound; office; department. n.f. Column; head of accounts.

مد امانت madd-ĕ amānat, n.f. The head of deposits.

مد بندی madd bandī, n.f. Appropriation (of accounts).

مد حساب madd-ĕ ḥisāb, n.f. Head of account.

مد ظله madda ẓillu-hū, intej. May his shadow or power be extended!

مد مقابل madd-ĕ muqābil, n.m. Opponent; per contra.

مد نظر ، نگاہ madd-ĕ naẓar, nigāh, n.m. Extension or stretch of sight. adv. Before the eyes; in view; in sight.

مد نظر رکھنا madd-ĕ naẓar rakhnā, v. To keep in view.

مد و جزر madd-ŏ jazr, n.m. Tide; the flux and reflux of the sea.

مد mad (S) n.f. Wine; honey; intoxication; spirits; pride; madness; arrogance; passion; happiness; prime of youth; semen.

مد ماتا ، ماتی mad mata, mati, adj. Full of intoxication; showing intoxication; dead-drunk; arrogant.

مداح maddaḥ (A) n.m. A panegyrist; a praiser; eulogist; an encomiast.

مداخل madākhil (A) n.f. (plu. of مدخل madkhal) Income; revenue; rent; gussets; entrance.

مداخل و مخارج madākhil-ŏ makhārij, n.f. Income and expenditure; additions and deductions.

مداخلت mudākhalat (A) n.f. Access; admisions; ingress; entering into; occupancy; intermeddling; intrusion; interference.

مداخلت بیجا mudākhalat-ĕ bejā, n.f. Trespass; illegal entry.

مداخلت کرنا mudākhalat karna, v. To intrude; to trespass; to interfere.

مداد midād (A) n.f. Ink.

مدار madār (A) n.m. Circumference; orbit; centre; seat, a station; a place of turning or returning; a place where one stops or stands; dependence.

مدار ارضی madār-ĕ arẓī, n.m. The earth's orbit.

مدار دعوی madār-ĕ da'wạ, n.m. Grounds of the claim.

مدار کار madār-ĕ kār, n.m. Chief manager of a business.

مدارالمہام madār-ul-mahāmm, n.m. The prime minister; a manager.

دولت مدار daulat madār, n.m. The seat of wealth or government; a ruler.

مدار madār (H) n.m. Name of a plant; swallow-wort.

مدارا ، مدارات mudārā, mudārāt (A) n.f. Politeness; courtesy; hospitality; toleration; humanity; affability.

مدارات کرنا mudārāt karnā, v. To treat; to receive with politeness.

مدارج madārij (A) n.m. (plu. of مدرجہ madrajah) Steps; degrees; ascents; ranks; posts; ways; stages.

مدارس madāris (A) n.m. (plu. of مدرسہ madrasah) Schools; colleges.

مداری madari (H) n.m. A juggler; a bear or monkey dancer; a show-man; a follower of Shah Madar; a conjurer.

مدافع mudāfi' (A) adj. Repeller.

مدافعت mudāfa'at (A) n.f. Repulsion; striving to repel an assailant; self-defence; turning away.

مدام mudām (A) adv. Eternally; permanently; always; continually.

مداومت mudāwamat (A) n.f. Eternity; continuance; continual use; perpetuity.

مداوا ، مداوات mudāwā, mudāwat (A) n.m. n.f. Curing; healing; remedying; applying medicine; medical treatment.

مداهنت mudāhanat (A) n.f. Flattering; over-praising; greasing; hypocrisy.

مدائن madā'in (A) n.m. (plu. of مدینه madinah) Cities; towns.

مدبر mudabbir (A) adj. Skilled in devising; prudent; ingenious; governing. n.m. A counsellor; a statesman; a minister.

مدبران سلطنت mudabbirān-ĕ salṭanat, n.m. Ministers of states.

مدبری mudabbirī, n.f. Statesmanship; ministership.

مدت muddat (A) n.f. Time; interval of time; length of time; duration; a long time; space of time; antiquity.

مدت العمر muddat-ul-'umr, n.f. Space of a life; life-time. adv. During life.

مدت مدید muddat-ĕ madīd, n.f. A long time.

مدت مقرره muddat-ĕ muqarrarah, n.f. A specified time; fixed time; a specified term or period.

ایک مدت ek muddat, n.f. An age; long period.

مدح ، مدحت madḥ, midḥat (A) n.f. Praise; eulogy; encomium.

مدح خوان madḥ khwāṅ, n.m. A pavegryist; a eulogist; a bard; encomiast.

مدخل madkhal (A) n.f. Place of entrance; entrance; income; revenue; rent.

مدخول madkhūl (A) adj. Entered; inserted; put in.

مدخوله madkhūlah (A) n.f. A kept mistress; a concubine.

مدد madad (A) n.f. Help; assistance; reinforcement; succour; aid; labourers; masons; wages.

مدد بانٹنا madad banṭnā, v. To distribute wages.

مدد پہنچانا ، کرنا madad pahuṅchānā, karnā, v. To assist; to help; to reinforce.

مددگار madad gār, n.m. A protector; an ally; an assistant; an auxiliary; a helper.

مدد مانگنا madad māṅgnā, v. To seek assistance or help.

مدر mudirr (A) adj. Causing to flow; uretic; diuretic; exciting discharge of urine.

مدرس mudarris (A) n.m. Teacher; schoolmaster; professor of a college; lecturer.

مدرسه madrasah (A) n.m. School; college; a university; academy; seminary.

مدرسهٔ ابتدائی ، مدرسهٔ تحتانی madrasah-ĕ ibtidā'ī, madrasah-ĕ taḥtānī, n.m. A primary school.

مدرسهٔ اطفال madrasah-ĕ aṭfāl, n.m. A boys school.

مدرسهٔ بالغان madrasah-ĕ bālighān, n.m. An adult school.

مدرسهٔ ثانوی madrasah-ĕ ṣānwī, n.m. A secondary school.

مدرسهٔ جامعه madrasah-ĕ jāmi'ah, n.m. A university.

مدرسهٔ شبینه madrasah-ĕ shabīnah, n.m. A night school.

مدرسة العلوم madrasah-tul-'ulūm, n.m. A college.

مدرسهٔ فوقانی madrasah-ĕ fauqānī, n.m. A high school.

مدرسة العلمین madrasah-tul-mu'alemīn, n.m. A normal school; a training college.

حرفتی مدرسه hirfatī madrasah, n.m. A technical school.

خانگی مدرسه khānagī madrasah, n.m. A private school.

خیراتی مدرسہ khairātī madrasah, n.m. A free school.

زنانہ مدرسہ zanānah madrasah, n.m. A girls school.

سرکاری مدرسہ sarkārī madrasah, n.m. A government school.

صنعتی مدرسہ ṣan'atī madrasah, n.m. An industrial school.

ہم مدرسہ ham madrasah, n.m. School-fellow; school-mate.

مدرسی mudarrisi (A & P) n.f. Teachership; lecturership; professorship.

مدرک mudrik (A) adj Comprehending; understanding; conscious; perceptive.

مدرکہ mudrikah (A) n f. The perceptive faculty of the mind; comprehension; intellectual powers; understanding.

مدعا mudda'ā (A) n.m. Desire; wish; meaning; object; view; stolen property; aim; scope; suit.

مدعا علیہ mudda'ā 'alaih, n.m. A defendant; an accused; the respondent (in a law suit).

مدعا حاصل کرنا mudda'ā ḥāṣil karnā, v. To obtain the object in view.

مدعو mad'ū (A) adj. Invited.

مدعی mudda'i (A) n.m. A claimant; a plaintiff; a complainant; an accuser.

مدعیہ mudda'iyah (A) n.f. A female claimant.

مدغم mudgham (A) adj. Concealed; doubled by تشدید Tashdid; merged; inserted.

مدفن madfan (A) n.m. A tomb; a burial place.

مدفون madfūn (A) adj. Buried; interred; concealed; hidden underground (as treasure).

مدقق mudaqqiq (A) adj Keenly investigating; minutely examining.

مدقوق madqūq (A) adj. Hectic; consumptive.

مدک madak (H) n.f. A mixture of chopped betel-leaves and opium used for smoking.

مدلل mudallal (A) adj Argumentative; supported by evidence; well reasoned; reasonable.

مدمغ mudammigh, adj. Proud; fastidious; foolish; conceited; vain; arrogant; haughty.

مدن madan (G) n.m. The Indian Cupid; love; lust; a medicinal plant (دھتورہ dhatūrah).

مدن mudun (A) n.m. (plu. of مدینہ madinah) Cities; towns.

مدنی madani (A) adj. Civil; concerning cities or towns.

مدنی الطبع madani-uṭ-taba' (A) adj. Gregarious; social; sociable.

مدنیت madaniyyat (A) n.f. Civilization; civics.

مدور mudawwar (A) adj. Circular; globular; spherical; round; going round.

مدہ madh (S) See مد mad.

مدھم maddham (H) adj. Middling; temperate; middle; medium; slow; dull; low: moderate.

مدھم بیچنا maddham bechna, v. To sell at a low price; to sell at a moderate price; to under-sell.

مدھم روشنی maddham raushani, n.f. Dim-light.

مدھم سر maddham sur, n.m. The middle note of the gamut.

مدھم کرنا maddham karna, v. To mitigate; to modify; to moderate; to reduce; to abate.

مدہوش madhosh (A) adj. Astonished; confounded; besotted; intoxicated; drunk; senseless; unconscious.

مدہوشی madhoshi (A&P) n.f. Intoxication; senselessness; astonishment.

مدید **madid** (A) *adj.* Long; extensive; lengthened out; tall.

مدیر **mudir** (A) *n.m.* Editor; director; manager; administrator; headmaster.

مدینہ **madinah** (A) *n.m.* A city; a state; the city of Medina (in Arabia).

مدینۃ الحکما *madina-tul-ḥukamā*, *n.m.* The city of philosophers; Athenes (in Greece).

مدینۃ السلام *madina-tus-salām*, *n.m.* The city of peace; Baghdad.

مدینۃ العلم *madina-tul-'ilm*, *n.m.* The city of knowledge; the Holy Prophet.

مدیون **madyūn** (A) *adj.* Debtor.

مڈ بھیڑ **mud bheṛ**. See مٹ بھیڑ *muṭ bheṛ*.

مذاق **mazāq** (A) *n.m.* Taste; relish; nice; perception; joke; wit; pleasantry; the palate.

مذاقاً **mazāqan** (A) *adv.* Humorously; wittily; in jest.

مذاقیہ **mazāqiyah**, *adj.* Humorous; witty.

مذاکرہ **muzākarah** (A) *n.m.* Things worthy to be remembered; conference; conversation; discussion; negotiation; (*plu.* مذاکرات *muzākarāt*).

مذاہب **mazāhib** (A) *n.m.* (*plu.* of مذہب *mazhab*) Religions; creeds; sects.

مذبح **mazbaḥ** (A) *n.m.* A place of sacrifice; an altar; a slaughter house; shambles; a place for killing cattle or sheep.

مذبذب **muzabzib** (A) *adj.* Wavering; hesitating; fluctuating; ambiguous; doubtful; uncertain; suspended.

مذبوح **mazbūḥ** (A) *adj.* Sacrificed; killed; immolated.

مذبوحی **mazbūḥi**, *adj.* Killing.

مذبوحی حرکات *mazbūḥi ḥarakāt*, *n.f.* Paining activities.

مذکر **muzakkar** (A) *adj.* Masculine (in gender); male.

مذکور **mazkūr** (A) *adj.* Mentioned; recorded; related. *n.m.* Mention; discourse; statement.

مذکورہ **mazkūrah** (A) *adj.* Related; mentioned.

مذکورہ بالا ، مذکورۂ صدر *mazkūrah bālā*, *mazkūrah-ĕ ṣadr*. *adj.* Above-mentioned; aforesaid.

مذلت **mazallat** (A) *n.f.* Baseness; contemptibility; ignominy; contempt; abjectness.

مذمت **mazammat** (A) *n.f.* Blame; satire; abuse; scorn; contempt; censure; a blamable quality or action; evil-speaking.

مذموم ، مذمومہ **mazmūm**, **mazmūmah** (A) *adj.* Blamed; found fault with; censured; despised; scorned; base; mean; contemptible.

مذنب **muznib** (A) *n.m.* A sinner; a criminal. *adj.* Sinful; criminal.

مذہب **muzahhab** (A) *adj.* Gilded; gold-plated.

مذہب **mazhab** (A) *n.m.* Religion; sect; mode; way; path; creed; faith; doctrine; mode of life; line of action; way of living.

مذہبی **mazhabi** (A) *adj.* Religious; godly; concerning religion.

مذہبی سکھ *mazhabi sikh*, *n.m.* A sweeper converted to Sikhism.

مذہبیت **mazhabiyyat** (A) *n.f.* Religiosity.

مذی **mazi** (A) *n.f.* Involuntary seminal discharge.

مرأت **mirā'at** (A) *n.m.* A mirror.

مراتب **marātib** (A) *n.m.* (*plu.* of مرتبہ *martabah*) Degrees; dignities; ranks; places; stages.

مراثی **marāsi** (A) *n.m.* (*plu.* of مرثیہ *marsiyah*) Elegies; funeral notes.

مراجعت **murāja'at** (A) *n.f.* Return; recourse; coming back; repeating; doing over and over again.

مراحل marāḥil (A) n.m. (plu. of مرحله marḥalah) Stages; journeys.

مراحم marāḥim (A) n.m. (plu. of مرحمت marḥamat) Compassions; favours; gifts; kindness.

مراحم خسروانه marāḥim-ĕ khusrwānah, n.m. Royal favours.

مراد murād (A) n.f. Desire; will; intention; purport; inclination; vow; tenor; object; meaning.

مراد برآنا ، مراد پانا murād bar ānā, murād pānā, v. To gain one's wish; to attain one's object.

مراد پوری کرنا murād pūri karnā, v. To grant or gratify the desire.

مراد لینا murād lenā, v. To Infer; to understand (by or from); to mean (by).

مراد مانگنا murād māngnā, v. To pray for a boon; to ask for a favour.

مراد ماننا murād mānnā, v. To make a vow.

مراد مند mūrad mand, adj. Desirous; needy.

مرادوں کے دن murādon ke din, n.m. The bloom or prime of life; the longed for happiness.

مرادف murādif (A) adj. Synonymous. n.m. A hind rider.

مرادی murādī, adj. Understood; implied; secondary meaning; metaphorical; agreeable to one's wishes.

مراری murārī (S) n.m. An enemy of devils; epithet of Lord Krishna.

مراسلت murāsalat (A) n.f. Corresponding; interchange of letters; communication.

مراسله murāsalah (A) n.m. Letter; correspondence (plu. مراسلات murāsalat).

مراسم marāsim (A) n.m. (plu. of رسم rasm) Laws; usages; marks; signs; rules; customs; duties; agreements.

مراعات mura'āt (A) n.m. Looking back upon; privileges; considering; viewing attentively through half-shut eyes; meditating; taking care of; preserving; guarding.

مرافعه murāfa'ah (A) n.m. Appeal in a law suit; an action; statement of a case; litigation; dispute; citing before the judge.

مرافعه آخر murāfa'ah-ĕ ākhir, n.m. Final appeal.

مرافعه اول murāfa'ah-ĕ awwal, n.m. Court of first instance.

مرافعه ثانی murāfa'ah-ĕ ṣānī, n.m. Court of second instance.

مرافعه کرنا murāfa'ah karnā, v. To litigate; to appeal.

مراق mirāqq (A) n.m. Hysteria; hystermania; melancholia.

مراقبه murāqabah (A) n.m. Observation; contemplation; meditation.

مراقبه کرنا murāqabah karnā, v. To watch; to supervise; to meditate.

مراقبے میں جانا murāqabe men jānā, v. To be lost in contemplation; to fall into meditation (on); to be absorbed in meditation.

مراقی mirāqı, adj. Melancholic: crazy.

مرام marām (A) n.m. Aim; object; purpose.

مربا ، مربی murabbā, (A) n.m. A preserve; confection; preserved fruit; jam.

مربع murabba' (A) adj. Four in number; square; quadrangular; four sided; quatrain or stanza of four lines; having quartan ague.

مربوط marbūṭ (A) adj. Bound; fastened; construed; arranged; attached; well put together; consistent (as a book); concordant (in grammar).

مربی murabbı (A) n.m. A guardian; patron; protector; supporter; head; fosterer.

مربی بننا *murabbi bannā.* To become a patron.

مربیانہ *murabbiyānah, adv.* Tutor-like; patronisingly; in the manner of protector or guardian.

مرتاض *murtāẓ* (A) *adj.* Disciplined; asectic; instructed; trained.

مرتا کیا نہ کرتا *martā kiyā nah kartā* (H) *prov.* A drowning man catches at a straw.

مرتب *murattib* (A) *adj.* Putting in order. *n.m.* An editor; a compiler.

مرتب ، مرتبہ *murattab, murattabah* (A) *adj.* Set in order; edited; compiled; arranged; regulated; prepared; classified.

مرتب کرنا *murattab karna, v.* To put in order; to compile; to arrange; to draw up.

مرتبان *martabān* (P) *n.m.* A jar for keeping preserves in; a glazed earthen jar; a vessel of the finest china or parcelain.

مرتبت ، مرتبہ *martabat, martabah* (A) *n.f./n.m.* Degree; dignity; office; charge; rank of honour; class; order.

مرتد *murtadd* (A) *n.m.* An apostate; a renegade; a convert.

مرتد ہونا *murtadd honā, v.* To apostatize.

مرتسم *murtasam* (A) *adj.* Marked; sealed; graphed; drawn.

مرتضیٰ *murtaẓā* (A) *adj.* Chosen; selected; agreeable; a title of Hazrat Ali.

مرتعش *murtaʻish* (A) *adj.* Shivering; quaking; shaking; tumbling; palsied.

مرتفع *murtafaʻ* (A) *adj.* Elevated; exalted; high; sublime; aggrandised; eminent; lofty.

مرتکب *murtakib* (A) *adj.* Venturing upon; attempting; guilty of; committing; perpetreting (crime).

مرتکب جرم *murtakib-ĕ jurm, adj.* Guilty of a crime

مرتکب ہونا *murtakib honā, v.* To commit; to perpetrate.

مرتہن *murtahin* (A) *n.m.* A mortgagee; a pawn broker.

مرتہن قابض *murtahin-ĕ qābiẓ, n.m.* A mortgagee in possession.

مرثیہ *marṣiyah* (A) *n.m.* An elegy; a dirge; lamentation for one dead; funeral notes; an epicedium, especially the one sung during the Muharram in commemoration of Imam Husain.

مرثیہ خواں *marṣiyah k͟hwāṅ, n.m.* A reciter or chanter of مرثیہ *marṣiyah.*

مرجان *marjān* (A) *n.m.* Coral; a small pearl.

مرجانا *marjānā* (H) *v.* To die; to suffer hardship; to be out of a game; to fade; to love.

مرجح *murajjaḥ* (A) *adj.* Preferred; superior; predominant.

مرجع *marjaʻ* (A) *n.m.* Asylum; place of refuge; rendezvous; antecedent (grammar).

مرجع خلائق ، مرجع عام *marjāʻ-ĕ k͟halāʼiq, marjāʻ-ĕ ām, n.m.* An asylum for all.

مرجھانا *murjhānā* (H) *v.* To wither; to fade; to pine; to droop; to be dejected; to be dispirited.

مرچ *mirch* (H) *n.f.* Pepper. *adj.* Hot; pungent; sharp.

دکنی مرچ *dakkni mirch, n.f.* Deccan pepper; white pepper.

کالی مرچ *kāli mirch, n.f.* Black pepper.

لال مرچ *lāl mirch, n.f.* Red pepper; chillies; capcicum.

مرچیں لگنا *mircheṅ lagnā, v.* To smart; to take amiss; to take ill; to be annoyed; to be offended.

مرحبا *marḥabā* (A) *interj.* Hail! Welcome! bravo! God bless you!

مرحلہ *marḥalah* (A) *n.m.* A stage; an inn; a battery; a day's journey; a halting place or station; the bastion of a fort; a difficulty.

مرحلہ طے کرنا *marhalah ṯae karnā, v.* To traverse a long distance; to remove a difficulty.

مرحمت *marhamat* (A) *n.f.* Pity; compassion; mercy; favour; clemency; pardon; a present.

مرحمت کرنا *marhamat karnā, v.* To grant; to confer; to bestow.

مرحوم، مرحومہ *marhūm, marhūmah* (A) *adj.* Dead; deceased; the late; one who has found mercy.

مرخص *murakhkhaṣ* (A) *adj.* Permitted (to leave); licensed; lawful; allowed to depart; dismissed.

مرد *mard* (P) *n.m.* A male; a man; a hero; a fellow; husband.

مرد آدمی *mard ādami, n.m.* A gentleman; a tall strong man; a brave or valiant man; a form of address; my good sir!

مرد باز *mard bāz, adj.* Lascivious (woman); lustful (woman), adultress.

مرد بچہ *mard bachchah, n.m.* The son of a brave man; a brave child.

مرد بننا *mard bannā, v.* To show courage; to be a hero.

مرد خدا *mard-ĕ khudā, n.m.* A pious man; a holy person.

مردمعقول *mard-ĕ ma'qūl, n.m.* A reasonable man; a wise man.

مرد میدان *mard-ĕ maidān, n.m.* A brave man; a man of action.

مردار *murdār* (P) *n.m.* A corpse; carrion. *adj.* Impure; wretch; polluted; profane; ugly. *intj.* Wretch! hussy!

مردارخور *murdār khor, n.m.* A vulture; a carrion-eater; a carrion-crow.

مردارسنگ *murdār sang, n.m.* Litharge; red lead.

مردار مال *murdār māl, n.m.* Ill-gotten wealth; property acquired unlawfully.

مردانگی *mardānagi* (P) *n.f.* Manliness; bravery.

مردانگی کے کام *mardānagi ke kām, n.m.* Brave deeds; feats.

مردانہ *mardānah, adj.* Manly; brave; masculine; male or relating to males. *n.m.* A drawing room for men only.

مردانہ وار *mardānah wār, adv.* Manly; bravely; courageously.

مردانی *mardāni, n.f.* A masculine (woman); *adj.* Relating to males.

مردک *mardak* (P) *n.m.* A manikin; a low fellow; a puppy; a rascal; a little man.

مردم *mardum* (P) *n.m.* A man; a gentleman; a polite man; the pupil of the eye *adj* Civil; humane.

مردم آزار *mardum āzār, adj.* An oppressor; man-oppressing; a tyrant.

مردم آزاری *mardum āzāri, n.f.* Oppression; robbery and murder.

مردم خور *mardum khor, adj.* Man-eater; a cannibal.

مردم خیز *mardum khez, adj.* Producing good men.

مردم دوست *mardum dost, n.m.* A philanthropist.

مردم شماری *mardum shumāri, n.f.* Census.

مردم‌شناسی *mardum shināsi, n.f.* Knowledge of mankind; anthropology.

مردم کشی *mardum kushi, n.f.* Murder; homicide.

مردمک *mardumak* (P) *n.f.* The pupil of the eye.

مردمی *mardumi* (P) *n.f.* Manliness; bravery; civility; humanity.

مردنگ *mirdang* (H) *n.f.* A kind of drum; a tabor.

مردنگی *mirdangi* (H) *n.m.* One who plays on مردنگ *mirdang.*

مردنی *murdani, n.f.* Melancholy; gloominess; dismalness; death; obsequies; death-like stillness; a funeral. (P) *adj.* Fit to die; deserving death; death-like.

مردنی چھانا murdanī chhānā, v. To become deadly pale.

مردوا mardwā, n.m. (by way of contempt) a man; a fellow; a manikin; a wretch.

مردود mardūd (A) adj. Rejected; excluded; reprobated; repulsed; confuted; abandoned; outcast.

مردہ murdah (P) adj. Dead; weak; decrepit. n.m. A corpse; a dead body.

مردہ اٹھانا murdah uṭhānā, v. To perform the funeral rites or obsequies of a dead person.

مردہ خور murdah khor, adj. Corpse-eater; back-biter.

مردہ دل murdah dil, adj. Down hearted; hopeless; lifeless; dispirited; sad; dejected.

مردہ دلی murdah dilī, n.f. Dispiritedness.

مردہ شو murdah shū, n.m. A washer of the dead.

مردی mardī (P) n.f. Manliness; virility; manhood; valour.

مرزبان marzbān (P) n.m. Governor of frontier; a priest of fire-worshipers.

مرزبوم marzbūm (P) n.m. Region; territory; district; empire.

مرزا mirzā (P) n.m. A prince; a grandee; son of a nobleman.

مرزا پھویا mirzā phoiyyā, n.m. A very delicate and simple person.

مرزا منش mirzā manish, adj. Of princely nature or disposition; genteel.

مرزائی mirza'ı (P) n.f. Princedom; gentility; arrogance; pride. n.m. A follower of the Ahmadiya sect.

مرزئی mirz'i, n.f. A native jacket with long, loose sleeve; a native quilted coat.

مرسل mursal (A) n.m. A messenger; a prophet; an apostle; an ambassador. adj. Sent to another with a message.

مرسل الیہ mursal ilaih, n.m. One to whom something is sent.

مرسل mursil (A) n.m. Sender; despatcher.

مرسلہ mursalah (A) adj. Sent; despatched.

مرسلین mursalīn (A) n.m. (plu. of مرسل mursal) Apostles and prophets.

مرشد murshid (A) n.m. An instructor; a guide; a spiritual teacher; a monitor; the head of a religious order; a cunning fellow; a director.

مرصع muraṣṣa' (A) adj. Studded with precious stones; covered with gold; set with jewels. n.m. Texture set with jewels.

مرصع ساز ، کار muraṣṣa' sāz, kār, n.m. A stone-setter; a lapidary.

مرصع کاری muraṣṣa' kārī, n.f. Stone-setting.

مرصوص ، مرصوصہ marṣūṣ, marṣūṣah (A) adj. Very strong; firm; solid.

مرض maraẓ (A) n.m. Sickness; infirmity; disease.

مرض شناس maraẓ shinās, n.m. A pathologist.

مرض‌شناسی maraẓ shināsī, n.f. Pathology; diagnosis.

مرض متعدی maraẓ-ĕ muta'addī, n.m. Infectious disease; epidemic.

مرض‌الموت maraẓ-ul-maut, n.m. Mortal disease; incurable disease.

مرض مہلک maraẓ-ĕ muhlik, n.m. Fatal disease; a dangerous illness; a mortal disease.

مرضی marẓī (A) n.f. Pleasure; assent; consent; volition; choice.

مرضی کے موافق marẓī ke muwāfiq, adv. According to the will or pleasure of; to the satisfaction of; satisfactorily.

مرضی میں آنا marẓī meṅ ānā, v. To like; to please; to meet the wishes of; to prove agreeable to.

مرطوب marṭūb (A) adj. Wet; damp; moist; humid.

مرعوب mar'ūb (A) adj. Terrified; frightened; awe-inspired; browbeaten.

مرغ murgh (P) n.m. A bird; a fowl; a cock.

مرغ باد نما murgh-ĕ bād numā, n.m. A weather-cock.

مرغ باز murgh bāz, n.m. A cock-fighter.

مرغ بازی murgh bāzi, n.f. Cock-fighting; a cock-fight.

مرغ بان murgh ban, n.m. A poultry keeper.

مرغ بانی murgh bani, n.f. Poultry keeping.

مرغ چمن murgh-ĕ chaman, n.m. A fowl of the garden; a nightingale.

مرغ سحر murgh-ĕ saḥar, n.m. The morning bird; the cock; the nightingale.

مرغ شناسی murgh shināsi, n.f. Orinthology.

مرغ margh (P) n.m. A kind of grass.

مرغزار marghzār n.m. A greenland; a pasture; a meadow.

مرغا murghā, n.m. A cock.

مرغابی murghābi (P) n.f. A water fowl; a wild duck.

مرغوب marghūb (A) adj. Desired; desirable; amiable; beautiful; lovely; pleasant; excellent; agreeable; estimable.

مرغول ، مرغوله marghūl, marghūlah (P) n.m. Locks, twisted or plaited; curly hair; a crenated arch.

مرغی murghi, n.f. A hen; poultry.

مرغی انڈے یا انڈے مرغی کی بحث murkhi ande yā ande murghi ki baḥṣ, n.f. The discussion about being the first to be created, the egg or the hen; reasoning in a circle; vicious circle.

مرغی خانه murghi khānah, n.m. Poultry farm.

مرغی میجر murghi majar, n.m. (sarcastically) A poulterer.

مرفوع marfū' (A) adj. Exalted; moved with the vowel ضمه ẓammah.

مرفه muraffah (A) adj. Pleasant; happy; comfortable; prosperous; well-off; contented; quiet; affluent.

مرفه الحال muraffah-ul-ḥāl, adj. In a prosperous condition; in easy circumstances.

مرقد marqad (A) n.m. A bed; a place of sleep; a grave; a tomb; sepulchre.

مرقع muraqqa' (A) adj. Clothed in rags; patched; mended. n.m. A book of drawings; a book of specimens of fine penmanship; an album; a portfolio.

مرقع بن جانا muraqqa' ban jana, v. To be perplexed.

مرقع تصاویر muraqqa'-ĕ taṣawir, n.m. A picture-book.

مرقوم ، مرقومه marqūm, marqūmah (A) adj. Written; described; inscribed.

مرقومه بالا marqūmah bālā, adj. Above-mentioned; above-cited; aforesaid.

مرکانا murkānā (H) v. To twist; to writhe; to snap; to break slightly.

مرکب markab (A) n.m. Ship; horse; camel; a vehicle; anything upon which one rides; anything in which one is borne or carried.

مرکب murakkab (A) adj. Compounded; combined. n.m. A compound; ink.

مرکبات murakkabāt (A) n.m. Compounds (medicine); things compounded (not simple).

مرکز markaz (A) n.m. The centre; the centre of a circle; the upper stroke (as of letters ک kāf and گ gāf).

مرکز ثقل markaz-ĕ ṣiql, n.m. The centre of gravity.

مرکز اندرونی، داخلی markaz-ĕ andrūnī, dākhili, n.m. Incentre.

مرکز بنیادی markaz-ĕ bunyādi, n.m. Radical centre.

مرکز حائط دائره markaz-ĕ ḥā'iṯ-ĕ dā'irah, n.m. Circumcentre.

مرکز خارجی markaz-ĕ khāriji, n.m. Ex-centre.

مرکز عمودی markaz-ĕ 'umūdi, n.m. Ortho-centre.

مرکز گریز طاقت markaz gurez ṭaqat, n.f. Centrifugal force.

مرکز وسطی markaz-ĕ wasṭi, n.m. Mid-centre.

هم مرکز ham markaz, adj. Concentric.

مرکزی markazi (A) adj. Central.

مرکزی حکومت markazi ḥukumat, n.f. Central government.

مرکنا murakna (H) v. To be twisted; to be slightly broken or snapped.

مرکوز marḳūz (A) adj. Fixed; hidden; concealed; comprehended; concentred; Impressed.

مرکوزخاطر markūz-ĕ khāṭir, adj. Impressed upon the mind.

مرکھنا ، مرکھنی markhanā, markhani (H) adj. Addicted to striking or bitting (animal).

مرکی murkī (H) n.f. A kind of ear-ring; the tragus of the ear.

مرگ mirg (H) n.m. A deer.

مرگ نینا mirg nainā, adj. Gazelle-eyed.

مرگ marg (P) n.f. Death.

مرگ اتفاق ، مرگ مفاجات marg-ĕ ittifāqi, marg-ĕ mufājāt, n.f. Sudden death.

مرگ طبعی marg-ĕ ṭab'i, n.f. Natural death.

مرگل margal (H) n.m. Roasted fish; slices of roasted fish; fried fish.

مرگھٹ marghaṭ (H) n.m. The place where Hindus burn their dead.

مرگی mirgī (H) n.f. Epilepsy.

مرگی آنا mirgi ānā, v. To have epileptic fits.

مرگیا mirgiyā (H) adj. Epileptic.

مرلی murlī (H) n.f. A pipe; flute; pipe.

مرمت marrammat (A) n.f. Mending; repairs; rectifying; reparation; amendment; amends; supply of what is wanted.

مرمت طلب marrammat ṭalab, adj. Out of order; broken; repairable; needing repairs.

مرمت کرنا marrammat karna, v. To get repaired; to repair; to mend; to rectify; to set or put right; to punish; to beat.

مرمر marmar (G) n.m. Marble.

مرمرا murmurā (H) n.m. Swollen parched rice; rice pressed flatand and eaten raw.

مرمرین marmarin (P) adj. Made of marble; as white as marble; resembling marble; marbly.

مرمم ، مرممه murammam, murammamah (A) adj. Repaired; rectified; amended

مرن maran (H) n.m. Death; ruin; destruction.

مرنا marnā (H) v. To die; to expire; to cease; to fade; to desire vehemently; to set one's heart upon anything; to dote to wither; to become bankrupt; to be desperately in love with; to long for; to labour or toil hard; to suffer hardship.

مرناجینا marnā jinā, n.m. Life and death pleasure and pain.

مرنے جوگا marne jogā, adj. Fit or deserving to die.

مرنے کی فرصت نہ ھونا marne ki furṣat nah honā, v. To be overwhelmed with work; to be too much pressed with work; not having a moment's leisure.

مرنڈا muranḍā (H) n.m. A kind of sweetmeat.

مروا marvā (H) n.m. Name of a strong scented plant.

مروارید marvārid (P) n.m. Pearl.

مروارید نا سفته marvārid-ĕ nāsuftah, n.m. Unbored pearl.

مروانا marwānā (H) v. To cause to be beaten; to cause to be killed.

مروت **murawwat** (A) *n.f.* Affection; humanity; generosity; urbanity; affability; benevolence; politeness; kindness; human nature; manhood.

مروت توڑنا **murawwat toṛnā**, *v.* To cease to be generous or benevolent; to cease behaving affectionately; to withdraw one's regard (from).

مروت کرنا **murawwat karnā**, *v.* To show regard for; to deal kindly with; to show kindness for.

مروج ' مروجہ **murawwaj, murawwajah** (A) *adj.* Customary; in vogue; prevalent; current; saleable; usual; in force; in general use.

مرور **murūr** (A) *n.m.* Passing; elapsing; a passage; pass; transition.

مروڑ **maroṛ** (H) *n.f.* Twist; gripes; turn; writhe; contortion; obstinacy; vanity; affectation.

مروڑ اٹھنا **maroṛ uṭhnā** *v.* To have gripes or colic.

مروڑپھلی **maroṛ phalī**, *n.f.* A plant, the fruit of which is used as a cure for gripes.

مروڑا **maroṛā** (H) *n.m.* A twisting of the bowels; pain in the bowels; flux; gripes; strain.

مروڑنا **maroṛnā** (H) *v.* To twist; to writhe; to distort; to gripe; to contort; to crunch up.

مروڑی **maroṛī** (H) *n.f.* Twisting; contortion; a screw; a knot.

مروڑی دینا **maroṛī denā**, *v.* To twist.

مروڑی کھانا **maroṛī khānā**, *v.* To be twisted.

مروی **marwī** (A) *adj.* Related; told; alleged.

مرھٹی **marahaṭī** (H) *n.f.* The language of Maharattas; rule of Maharattas; maladministration under the Maharattas; misrule.

مرهم **marham** (A) *n.m.* Ointment; plaster; salve; cure; unguent.

مرهم پٹی کرنا **marham paṭṭī karnā**, *v.* To dress a wound; to apply salve to; to repair; to put in order.

مرھن **murhan** (H) *n.m.* Dried and powdered tobacco.

مرھون **marhūn** (A) *adj.* Pawned; pledged; mortgaged; hypothecated.

مرھون منت **marhūn-ĕ minnat**, *adj.* Bound in gratitude; indebted; under obligation (to).

مرئی **mara'ī** (A) *adj.* Visible.

مری **marī** (H) *n.f.* Plague; pestilence; epidemic; mortality,

مری پڑنا **marī paṛnā**, *v.* Breaking out of plague or pestilence.

مریخ **mirrikh** (A) *n.m.* The planet Mars.

مرید **murīd** (A) *adj.* Desirous. *n.m.* A disciple; a scholar; a follower; a student; a pupil.

مرید کرنا **murīd karnā**, *v.* To make a disciple of; to admit into a religious order.

مریدی **murīdī**, *n.f.* Discipleship; scholarship; tuition; instruction.

مریض **marīẓ** (A) *n.m.* A sick person; a patient.

مریضہ **marīẓah** (A) *n.f.* A female patient.

مریل **maryal** (H) *adj.* Lean; emaciated; weak; feeble; lethargic; indolent; lazy; slow; very much reduced by sickness; very near to death.

مریل ٹٹو **maryal ṭaṭṭū**, *n.m.* A slow moving pony.

مریم **maryam** (A) *n.f.* Mary; virgin.

مریم کا پنجہ **maryam kā panjah**, *n.m.* A sweet scented grass.

مرینہ **marīnah**, *n.m.* A kind of cloth made from wool of a Spanish goat called *marino*.

مڑ جانا muṛ jānā (H) v. To turn back; to turn; to return,

مڑ کر نہ دیکھنا muṛ kar nah dekhnā (H) v. Not to look back; to have no regard (for).

مڑکنا maṛaknā (H) v. To crack; to break; to sprain.

مڑ مڑ کر دیکھنا muṛ muṛ kar dekhnā (H) v. To turn round and look again and again.

مڑنا muṛnā (H) v. To be turned back; to become twisted; to bend; to twine; to turn.

مڑھنا maṛhnā (H) v. To cover; to gild; to case; to cover with leather.

مڑھی maṛhi (H) n.f. A cottage; a temple; a hut; a hermit's cell.

مزا māzā. See مزہ mazah.

مزاج mizāj (A) n.m. A mixture; nature; constitution; complexion; habit of body; temperament; temper; disposition; humour; pride.

مزاج بگاڑنا mizāj bigāṛnā, v. To spoil one's temper.

مزاج بگڑنا mizāj bigaṛnā, v. To be angry; to get out of temper.

مزاج پانا mizāj pānā, v. To know a person's temperament; to feel the temperamental pulse of; to find one in good humour.

مزاج پوچھنا mizāj pūchhna, v. To enquire after one's health.

مزاج دار mizāj dār, adj. Proud; haughty; conceited.

مزاج دان ، شناس mizāj dān, shinās, adj. A confident; knowing the temperament (of); acquainted with the habits and disposition (of).

مزاج شریف، عالی، مبارک mizāj-ĕ sharif, ʻāli, mubārik, adv. How do you do? how are you?

مزاج کرنا mizāj karnā, v. To be proud; to show temper; to give oneself airs.

مزاج نہ ملنا mizāj nah milnā, v. To be proud; to disagree; to be unable to understand one.

مزاج والا ، والی mizāj wālā, wāli, adj. Proud; haughty; conceited.

مزاجاً mizājan (A) adv. Temperamentally; by virtue of properties.

مزاجی mizāji (A) adj. Proud; haughty; temperamental; constitutional; habitual.

مزاح mizāḥ (A) n.m. Jest; joke; fun; frivolity.

مزاحم muzahim (A) adj. Forbidding; hindering; obstructing; inconvenient.

مزاحم ہونا muzāḥim honā, v. To obstruct; to hinder; to impede; to prevent.

مزاحمت muzāḥamat (A) n.f. Prevention; hindrance; impediment; obstacle; opposition; molestation; difficulty; inconvenience; interruption; disturbance.

مزاحمت کرنا muzāḥamat karnā, v. To hinder; to oppose; to put obstacles in the way.

بلا مزاحمت bilā muzāḥamat, adj. Unhindered; undisturbed; uninterrupted; unmolested; unopposed.

مزاحیہ mizāḥiyyah (A) adj. Humourous; jocular; hilarious.

مزار mazār (A) n.m. A place of visitation; a shrine; a tomb; a grave; sepulchre.

مزارع muzāreʻ (A) n.m. A husbandman; an agriculturist; a cultivator.

مزامیر mazāmir (A) n.m. (plu. of مزمار mizmār) Musical instruments.

مزاولت muzāwalat (A) n.f. Routine; daily practice.

مزخرفات muzakhrafāt (P) n.f. idle talks; foolish words; lies.

مزد **muzd** (P) *n.f.* A reward; premium; salary; wages; compensation.

مزدور **muzdūr**, *n.m.* A labourer; a porter; a carrier.

مزدوری **muzdūrī**, *n.f.* Wages; pay; hire; fare; labour; work.

مزرع **mazra'** (A) *n.m.* A field; a corn-field; a farm; a field sown or prepared for sowing.

مزروعه **mazrū'ah** (A) *adj.* Tilled; cultivated; sown.

مزعفر **muz'afar** (A) *n.m.* A sweet dish of rice, prepared with saffron. *adj.* Saffron-coloured; yellow; coloured with saffron.

مزکیٰ **muzakkā** (A) *adj.* Purified; paid زکواة zakāt.

مزکی **muzakkī** (A) *adj.* Purifier; payer of زکواة zakāt.

مزمار **mizmār** (A) *n.f.* A musical reed; a pipe; a flute; a psaltery.

مزمن **muzmin** (A) *adj.* Chronic; of long duration; obstinate (disease).

مزه **mazah** (P) *n.m.* Taste; flavour; relish; pleasure; deliciousness; enjoyment; fun; delicacy.

مزه آنا **mazah ānā**, *v.* To relish; to enjoy.

مزه اٹھانا ، آڑانا ، پانا ، لوٹنا **mazah uṭhānā, uṛānā, pānā, lūṭnā**, *v.* To enjoy; to revel; to carouse.

مزه پڑنا **mazah paṛnā**, *v.* To fall into the habit of; to acquire a taste or longing for.

مزه چکھانا **mazah chakhānā**, *v.* To teach a good lesson; to give one his deserts.

مزا کر کرا هونا **mazah kirkirā honā**, *v.* The game to get spoiled.

مزا کرنا **mazah karnā**, *v.* To enjoy oneself.

مزے کا ، مزیدار **maze kā, mazedār**, *adj.* Delicious; tasteful; palatable.

مزیداری **maze dārī**, *n.f.* Taste; flavour.

مزید **mazīd** (A) *adj.* Increased; augmented. *n.m.* Increase; advantage.

مزین **muzāyyan** (A) *adj.* Adorned; decorated; embellished.

مژده **muzhdah** (P) *n.m.* Good news; good tidings.

مژده سنانا **muzhdah sunānā**, *v.* To announce good news.

مژه **mizhah** (P) *n.f.* The eyelash (*plu.* مژگان *mizhgān*).

مس **mis** (P) *n.m.* Copper.

مس **mas** (A) *n.m.* Touch; sense of touch.

مس کرنا **mas karnā**, *v.* To touch; to feel.

مسا **masā** (A) *n.f.* Evening.

مسا **massā** (H) *n.m.* A wart; a fleshy excrescence.

مسا **missā** (H) *n.m.* Wheat, barley, millet etc. mixed with wheat, grams, peas etc.

مسابقت **musābaqat** (A) *n.f.* A match; a competition.

مساجد **masājid** (A) *n.m.* (*plu.* of مسجد *masjid*) Mosques; temples.

مساحت **misāhat** (A) *n.f.* Measurement; dimension; mensuration; survey; geometry.

مساحت کرنا **misāhat karnā**, *v.* To survey; to measure land.

مساس **misās** (A) *n.m.* Massaging gently; rubbing.

مساعد **musā'id** (A) *adj.* Assisting; aiding; favourable; helping.

مساعدت **musā'adat** (A) *n.f.* Assistance; help; aid.

مساعی **masā'ī** (A) *n.f.* (*plu.* of مسعت *mis'at*) Efforts; trials.

مسافت **masāfat** (A) *n.f.* Distance; space; interval; (*plu.* مسافات *masāfāt*)

مسافت طے کرنا **masāfat ṭai karnā**, *v.* To cover a distance.

مسافر musāfir (A) n.m. Traveller; passenger; stranger.

مسافر پروری ، نوازی musāfir parwari, nawāzi, n.f. Hospitality; protection of travellers.

مسافر خانہ musāfir khānah, n.m. An inn; a sarai; a rest house; a refreshment room.

مسافرانہ musāfirānah, adv. Traveller-like; like passengers; as a stranger.

مسافرت musāfarat (A) n.f. Travelling; travel; journey.

مسافری musāfiri (P) n.f. Travelling; moving about from place to place.

مساکن masākin (A) n.m. (plu. of مسکن maskan) Habitations; mansions; residential quarters.

مساکین masākin (A) n.m. (plu. of مسکین miskin) Poors; indigent.

مسالا masalā (H) n.m. Ingredients; spices; condiments; materials.

مسالا بنانا masālā bānānā, v. To mix spices.

مسالا ٹانکنا masālā tānknā, v. To lace; to stitch a cloth.

مسالا ڈالنا masālā ḍalnā, v. To season.

مسالے دار māsāle dār, adj. Seasoned with spices.

مسالک masālik (A) n.m. (plu. of مسلک maslak) Ways; paths.

مسام masām (A) n.m. Pore (plu. مسامات masamāt).

مسام دار masām dār, adj. Porous; poral; pory.

مسان masān (H) n.m. A place where the dead are burnt or buried; crematorium; a cemetery; a spirit; a disease.

مسانیا masāniyā (H) n.m. One who removes the remains of a burnt corpse; one who removes the influence of an evil spirit.

مساوات musāwāt (A) n.f. Equation; evenness; equality; parallelism; parallel; heedlessness.

مساوات درجہ اول musāwāt-ĕ darjah-ĕ awwal. n.f. Simple equation.

مساوات درجہ دوم musāwāt-ĕ darjah-ĕ dowum, n.f. Quadratic or simultaneous equation.

مساوات ذاتی musāwāt-ĕ ẕāti, n.f. Identities.

مساوی musāwi (A) adj. Equal; parallel; equivalent; neutral; impartial; suitable; convenient.

مساوی الاضلاع musāwi-ul-aẓlā' (A) n.f. An equilateral figure.

مساوی الحجم musāwi-ul-ḥujm, adj. Of equal capacity; of equal volume.

مسائل masā'il (A) n.m. (plu. of مسئلہ masa'lah) Questions; problems; propositions; demands; precepts of the Holy Prophet.

مسبب musabbib (A) n.m. One who causes (things to be done); the first cause.

مسبب الاسباب musabbib-ul-asbāb, n.m. The causer of causes; one who causes things to be done; God.

مسبب حقیقی musabbib-ĕ ḥaqiqi, n.m. The real doer of things; God.

مست mast (P) adj. Drunk; intoxicated; lustful; lascivious; wanton; proud; amarous; careless; drunk with the love of God; one devoid of senses.

مستاجر mustājir (A) n.m. A tenant; a contractor; a farmer; a lessee

مستاجری mustājirī (A & P) n.f. A lease of land; a contract; the act or office of a مستاجر mustājir.

مستانہ mastānah (P) adj. Intoxicated; drunken.

مستتر mustatar (A) adj. Concealed; veiled; hidden.

مستثنی mustaṣnā (A) adj. Excepted; excellent; praised; extraordinary; selected; laudable; excepted from any common rule.

مستثنیٰ کرنا mustaṣnā karnā, v. To except; to exempt; to make an exception.

مستجاب mustajāb (A) adj. Heard; granted; given ear to; acceptable; agreeable.

مستجاب الدعوات mustajāb-ud-da'wāt, adj. One whose prayers are accepted by God.

مستحب mustaḥabb (A) adj. Desirable; preferable.

مستحسن mustaḥsan (A) adj. Virtuous; laudable; commendable; beautiful.

مستحق mustaḥiqq, mustaḥaqq (A) adj. Worthy; having a right to; deserving; rightful; entitled.

مستحق ٹھہرانا mustaḥiqq ṭhahrānā, v. To consider deserving.

مستحق ہونا mustaḥiqq honā, v. To deserve; to be entitled.

مستحکم mustaḥkam (A) adj. Firm; established; strong; fast.

مستدعی mustad'ī (A) adj. Applicant; desiring; wishing.

مستدیر mustadīr (A) adj. Spherical; globular; round.

مسترد mustaradd (A) ajd. Returned; restored; rejected; over-ruled; revoked; recalled; refuted.

مسترد کرنا mustaradd karnā, v. To refund; to restore; to return; to refute; to reject.

مستری mistarī, n.m. A mason; a carpenter; a blacksmith; a master; a head artificer; an artisan.

مستزاد mustazād (A) adj. Increased; additional; extra. n.f. A verse in which every line has an increased short line annexed to it.

مستشرق mustashriq (A) n.m. Orientalist.

مستطیع mustaṭī' (A) adj. Having power; having means.

مستطیل mustaṭīl (A) n.f. A rectangle.

مستعار musta'ār (A)adj. Borrowed; sought; obtained as a loan or trust.

مستعد musta'idd (A) adj. Ready; prepared; capable; fit; proper; worthy; prompt.

مستعدی musta'iddī, n.f. Readiness; promptitude; aptness; worthiness.

مستعفی musta'fī (A) adj. Resigned; seeking to be relieved from.

مستعمره musta'marah (A) n.f. A colony; (plu. مستعمرات musta'marāt).

مستعمل musta'mal (A) adj. In use; employed; applied; established; used; second hand; accustomed; practised; usual.

مستغرق mustaghraq (A) adj. Drowned; immersed; occupied; hypothicated; engrossed in; absorbed.

مستغفر mustaghfir (A) adj. Asking pardon; penitent; repentant.

مستغنی mustaghnī (A) adj. Rich; independent; satisfied; contented; purseproud; disdainful; lofty.

مستغیث mustaghīṣ (A) n.m. A complainant; a plaintiff.

مستفاد mustafād (A) adj. Benefitted; gained; acquired; made use of.

مستفتی mustaftī (A) adj. Desirous of having a verdict according to شریعت sharī'at.

مستفسر mustafsir (A) adj. Asking for explanation or interpretation; inquisitive; questioning; investigating; interrogating.

مستفید ' مستفیض mustafīd, mustafīẓ (A) adj. Profiting; gaining; acquiring.

مستقبل mustaqbil (A) n.m. Future; the future tense.

مستقر mustaqarr (A) n.m. Fixed abode; resting place

مستقل mustaqil (A) adj. Firm; stable; fixed; durable; permanent; independent; absolute; despotic, resolute; steady; unshaken; determined.

مستقل ارادہ mustaqil irādah, n.m. Determination; fixed resolve.

مستقل اسامی mustaqil asāmī, n.f. A permanent post.

مستقل مزاج mustaqil mizāj, adj. Of resolute mind.

مستقلی mustaqilī, n.f. Confirmation.

مستقیم mustaqim (A) adj. Right; straight; erect; direct; faithful.

مستک mastak (S) n.m. Head; the forehead (of elephant); summit of a mountain.

مستلزم mustalzam (A) adj. Acquired; necessitated.

مستند mustanad (A) ajd. Supported; certificated; authenticated; genuine; possessing a degree.

مستنبط mustambaṭ (A) adj. Extracted; selected; drawn out.

مستوجب mustaujib (A) adj. Worthy; deserving; liable; fitting; meriting.

مستور mastūr (A) adj. Covered; veiled; hidden.

مستورات mastūrāt (A) n.f. Veiled women; ladies.

مستوری mastūrī, n.f. Concealment; chastity; retirement; modesty.

مستول mastūl (H) n.m. Mast of a ship.

اگلا مستول aglā mastūl, n.m. Foremast.

پچھلا مستول pichhlā mustūl, n.m. Main mast.

مستولی mustaulī (A) adj. Overcoming; taking possession of; comprehending; subduing; surmounting.

مستوی mustawī (A) adj. Straight; equal; direct; even; level; plane.

مستی mastī (P) n.f. Drunkenness; intoxication; lust; wantonness; pride.

مستی چڑھنا mastī charhnā, v. To be dead drunk; to be elated; to be arrogant; to be defiant; to be disobedient.

مسٹنڈا musṭanḍā. See مشٹنڈا mushṭanḍā.

مسجد masjid (A) n.f. A mosque; a place of worship.

مسجد اقصیٰ masjid-ĕ-aqṣā, n.f. The distant mosque; Bait-ul-Muqaddas, in Jerusalem.

مسجدالحرام masjid-ul-ḥaram, n.f. Inviolable place of worship; the Ka'aba in Mecca.

مسجد جامع masjid-ĕ jāmi', n.f. The mosque in which Friday prayers are offered; the principal mosque of a place; a great mosque.

مسجع musajja' (A). adj. Rythmical (speech); harmonious or measured (periods); rythmical (prose).

مسجود masjūd (A) adj. Worshipped; adored.

مسح masḥ (A) n.m. Drawing the hand over; wiping; washing; anointing; an operation of purifying before prayer; cutting off, perambulating.

مسحور masḥūr (A) adj. Bewitched; enchanted; fascinated.

مسخ maskh (A) n.m. Metamorphosing from a superior to an inferior shape; plagiarism; mutilation.

مسخ شدہ maskh shudah, adj. Mutilated.

مسخر musakhkhar (A) adj. Subdued; overcome; conquered; taken; subjected.

مسخرہ maskharah (A) n.m. A buffoon; a jester; a droll; a laughing stock; a fool.

مسخرہ پن maskharah pan, n.m. Buffoonery; jesting; drollery; derision.

مسدس musaddas (A) adj. Composed of six; hexagonal; hexangular; sexangular. n.m. Hexagon; hexahedron; hexameter; hexastich; sextain; sexangle.

مسدود masdūd (A) adj. Closed; shut; obstructed; stopped.

مسرت masarrat (A) n.f. Happiness; gladness; joy; pleasure; cheerfulness; rapture; delight.

مسرف musrif (A) adj. Prodigal; extravagant; turned from; self-willed; perverse.

مسرور masrūr (A) adj. Glad; pleased; gay; cheerful; delighted; exalting.

مسروق ، مسروقه masrūq, masrūqah (A) adj. Stolen; robbed; illegally possessed.

مسطح musaṭṭaḥ (A) adj. Plane; level; even.

زاويه مسطح zāwiyah-ĕ musaṭṭaḥ, n.m. A plane angle.

سطح مسطح saṭaḥ-ĕ musaṭṭaḥ, n.f. A plane surface.

مسطر misṭar (A) n.m. A ruler; a lined or ruled paper, used as a ruler for unruled sheets of paper.

مسطور masṭūr (A) adj. Written; mentioned; above-mentioned; aforesaid; expressed; above-cited; delineated; ruled (sheets of paper).

مسعود mas'ūd (A) adj. Happy; fortunate; blessed; august.

مسقف musaqqaf (A) adj. Roofed.

مسک misk (A) n.f. see مشک mushk

مسک جانا masak jānā (H) v. To tear; to rend.

مسکا musikkā (H) n.m. A muzzle to prevent oxen from eating.

مسکانا muskānā (H) v. To smile; to grin; to smirk.

مسکت muskit (A) adj. Silencing; making quiet.

مسکرات muskirāt (A) n.f. Intoxicating liquors or drugs; intoxicants.

مسکرانا muskurānā (H) v. To smile; to grin; to smirk; to simper.

مسکراهٹ muskurāhaṭ (H) n.f. A smile; simper; smirk.

مسکن maskan (A) n.m. An abode; a dewling; habitation; residence

مسکن musakkin (A) adj. Anodyne; soothing; opiate; sedative; norcatic.

مسکنا masaknā (H) v. To be torn; to be split; to be rent.

مسکنت maskanat (A) n.f. Humility; lowness; indigence; wretchedness; poverty; misery.

مسکون maskūn (A) adj. Inhabited; habitable.

مسکه maskah (P) n.m. Butter.

مسکین miskīn (A) adj. Poor; miserable; humble; wretched; indigent; meek; needy.

مسکینی miskīnī n.f. Poverty; indigence; meekness.

مسل misl (H) n.f. A file (of papers); record (of a case).

مسل خوان misl khwāṅ, n.m. Reader.

مسل مرتب کرنا misl murattab karnā, v. To prepare the proceedings of case; to prepare or arrange the records of a case.

مسلح musallaḥ (A) adj. Armed; in armour; equipped; clad in mail.

مسلسل musalsal (A) adj. Linked; connected; successive; chained; coherent; placed in order.

مسلط musallaṭ (A) adj. Conquered; subdued; appointed; set over; conquering; ruling.

مسلک maslak (A) n.m. A way; a track; a passage; an institution; regulation; a rule of conduct.

مسلم muslim (A) n.m. One who is obedient (to God); one who professes Islam; a Muslim.

مسلم musallam (A) adj. Preserved; entire; whole; complete; free; admitted; accepted; kept; sound; committed.

مسلمان musalmān (P) n.m. A Muslim; a follower of Islam.

مسلمانی musalmānī (P) n.f. The Muslim faith; circumcision. adj. Concerning Islam.

مسلمه musallamah (A) adj. Admitted on hands; accepted universally.

مسلنا masalnā (A) v. To bruise; to crush; to break with the hand; to press; to rub; to squeeze.

مسلوب maslūb (A) adj. Seized; snatched away; stripped; spoiled; deprived of.

مسلوب الحواس ، مسلوب العقل maslūb-ul-ḥawās, maslūb-ul-'aql, adj. Deprived of senses; one having his senses affected by age.

مسلول maslūl (A) adj. Consumptive; drawn; led; unsheathed.

مسلی mislī, n.m. A criminal who has been brought to book; a notorious criminal.

مسمات ، مسماة musammāt (A) n.f. A title prefixed to the names of females; a lady; feminine of مسمیٰ musammā. adj. Called; named.

مسمار mismār (A) n.m. A nail; a peg; a pin. (P) adj. Demolished; razed; ruined.

مسماع mismā' (A) n.m. Audiophone.

مسمسی musmusī (H) adj. Designedly silent; cunning.

مسمسی صورت musmusī ṣūrat, adj. Outwardly humble, but inwardly cunning.

مسمسانا masmasānā (H) v. To suppress one's feelings or sentiments from fear or awe.

مسموع masmū' (A) adj. Heard; audible; listened to; plausible; valid.

مسموم masmūm (A) adj. Poisoned; venomous.

مسمیٰ musammā (A) adj. Named; called; entitled; appointed; fixed; predetermined; a title prefixed to the names of males.

مسن musinn (A) adj. Aged; advanced in years; old; stricken in years.

مسند masnad (A) n.f. A throne; a large cushion; a prop; a chair; a seat; a couch; a support.

مسند آرا masnad ārā, adj. Adorning a throne.

مسند نشین masnad nashīn, n.m. A reigning prince; a rich man. adj. Enthroned; sitting on the throne.

مسند نشینی masnad nashīnī, n.f. Accesion to the throne.

مسند musnad (A) n.m. Predicate.

مسندالیه musnad ilaih, n.m. Subject.

مسنون masnūn (A) adj. Legalized; lawful; accepted; adopted; sharpened; polished; made smooth; circumcised.

مسواک miswāk (A) n.f. A tooth-brush; a softened stick used for cleaning the teeth.

مسوده masawwadah (A) n.m. A sketch or rough draft (of); the foul or first copy (of); a plan; a scheme.

مسوده گانٹھنا musawwadah gānthnā, v. To draw out a plan; to prapare a scheme.

مسور masūr (H) n.f. A kind of pulse; black pulse; a grain.

مسوڑا masūṛā (H) n.m. The gums (of the teeth).

مسوسنا masosnā (H) v. To twist; to squeeze; to grieve; to regret.

مسہری masahrī (H n.f. A bed curtain for protection against mosquitoes; a bedstead.

مسہل mushil (A) adj. Purgative; laxative; cathartic. n.m. A purgative; an aperient.

مسئله mas'alah (A) n.m. Question; proposition; a maxim; a theorem; a precept of the Holy Prophet; an aphorism.

مسئول mas'ūl (A) adj. Responsible; one liable to be questioned.

مسی misī (P) *adj.* Made of copper.

مسی missi (H) *n.f.* A tooth-powder.

مسی کاجل کرنا missi kājal karnā, *v.* To adorn oneself; to beautify oneself.

مسیح masīḥ (A) *n.m.* Christ.

مسیحائی masīḥā'i (P) *n.f.* The miraculous powers of Christ.

مسیحائی کرنا masīḥā'i karnā, *v.* To cure incurable diseases; to bring to life.

مسیں maseṅ (H) *n.m.* Hair on the face which appears in early youth; down on the lips of a youth.

مسیں بھیگنا maseṅ bhīgnā, *v.* Beginning of the growth of hair on the face.

مشابہ mushābih (A) *adj.* Like; analogous; resembling.

مشابہت mushābahat (A) *n.f.* Similitude; similarity; resemblance; agreement; conformity; analogy; probability.

مشار mushār (A) *adj.* Signified; pointed out; indicated.

مشارالیہ mushār-un ilaih, *n.m.* Abovementioned; said; aforesaid; related above; touched upon before.

مشارب mashārib (A) *n.m.* (*plu.* of مشرب mashrab) Places of drinking; religions; sects.

مشارکت mushārakat (A) *n.f.* Community; society; association; fellowship; copartnership.

مشاطہ mashshāṭah (A) *n.f.* A waiting maid; a bride-maid; a go-between.

مشاعرہ mushā'arah (A) *n.m.* Contending or excelling in poetry; lying or sleeping together under one coverlet; a meeting of poets.

مشاغل mashāghil (A) *n.m.* (*plu.* of مشغلہ mashghalah). Engagements; occupations; pastimes; hobbies.

مشافہہ mushāfahah (A) *n.m.* From lip to lip communication; mouth to mouth conversation; speaking to one's face.

مشاق mashshāq (A) *adj.* Well-practised; proficient.

مشاقی mashshāqi, *n.f.* Practice; exercise.

مشام mashām (A) *n.f.* The smell; sense of smelling.

مشاورت mushāwarat (A) *n.f.* Consultation; conference; counsel.

مشاهد mushāhid (A) *n.m.* Observer.

مشاهده mushāhadah (A) *n.m.* Sight; observation; demonstration; vision; witnessing; beholding.

مشاهده کرنا mushāhadah karnā, *v.* To contemplate; to look at; to view.

مشاهره mushāharah (A) *n.m.* Monthly salary; pay; wages; allowance.

مشاهیر mashāhīr (A) *n.m.* (*plu.* of مشہور mashhūr) Renowned persons; famous people.

مشائخ mashā'ikh (A) *n.m.* (*plu.* of شیخ shaikh) Elders; doctors; patriarchs; old men; holy persons; dervishes.

مشایعت mushāya'at (A) *n.f.* Keeping company; going along.

مشبہ mushabbah (A) *adj.* Likened to; assimilated. *n.m.* A simile.

مشبہ بہ mushabbah bi-hi, *n.m.* That to which anything is likened, or from which a simile is drawn.

مشت musht (P) *n.f.* The fist; blow; handful.

مشت‌استخوان musht-ĕ ustukhwān, *n.f.* A mere skeleton.

مشت خاک musht-ĕ khak, *n.f.* Human being; man.

مشت زن musht zan, *n.m.* A boxer; a masturbator.

مشت زنی musht zani, *n.f.* Boxing; masturbation; self-abuse; self-defilement; onanism.

مشت مالی کرنا musht māli karnā, *v.* To massage.

مشتے نمونہ ازخروارے mushte namūnah az khaīwāre. A handful out of a heap; a pecimen.

مشتاق mushtaq (A) adj. Desirous; longing; ardent; fond; wishful; wishing.

مشتاق ہونا mushtaq hona, v. To long for.

مشتاقانہ mushtāqānah, adv. In a fond way; like one who is desirous of or is longing for.

مشتبہ mushtabah (A) adj. Ambiguous; obscure; suspect; suspectable; dubious.

مشترک ، مشترکہ mushtarak, mushtarakah (A) adj. Common; joint; coparcenary; joint; inheritance; held in partnership; incorporated; shared.

مشتری mushtari (A) n.m. A purchaser; a buyer; the planet Jupiter.

مشتعل mushta'il (A) adj. Flaming; blazing; inflamed; kindled; lighted up; irritated; set on fire.

مشتعل ہونا mushta'il honā, v. To be kindled; to be lighted; to be irritated.

مشتق mushtaqq (A) adj. Derived from; obtained from. n.m. Derivative.

مشتمل mushtamil (A) adj. Comprising; containing; including; extending over; comprehending; inclusive of; common.

مشتمل ہونا mushtamil honā, v. To comprise; to comprehend; to contain.

مشتہر mushtahar (A) adj. Proclaimed; announced; advertised.

مشتہر کرنا mushtahar karnā, v. To advertise; to proclaim; to celebrate; to promulgate; to make public.

مشتہر mushtahir (A) adj. Proclaiming; announcing. n.m. An announcer; an advertiser.

مشتہی mushtahi (A) adj. Creating or whetting appetite; longing; desiring; wishing.

مشٹنڈا ، مشٹنڈی mushtandā, mushtandī (H) adj. Strong-bodied; fat; gigantic; robust.

مشجر mushajjar (A) adj. Figured with the forms of trees and leaves; abounding in trees. n.m. A kind of silk cloth; figured silk; brocade; tapestry.

مشخص mushakhkhaṣ (A) adj. Specified; estimated; ascertained; defined; distinguished; stipulated.

مشخص کرنا mushakhkhaṣ karnā, v. To specify; to ascertain; to distinguish; to individuate.

مشدد mushaddad (A) adj. Doubled, n.m. A letter marked with (ّ) the sign of duplication.

مشرب mashrab (A) n.m. Place of drinking; a reservoir of water, sect; religion; nature; temper.

مشرح musharraḥ (A) adj. Explained; annorated; detailed.

مشرف musharraf (A) adj Exalted; ennobled; honoured; ornamented

مشرق mashtiq (A) n.f. The east; the place of the rising (of the sun).

مشرقی mashriqī (A) adj. Eastern; orientalist; oriental.

مشرک mushrik (A) n.m. A polytheist; an idolator; an infidel; one who denies the unity of God.

مشروب mashrūb (A) adj. Drinkable; that which is drunk; imbibed. n.m. Drink; (plu. مشروبات mashrūbāt).

مشروط mashrūt (A) adj. Agreed upon; stipulated; conditional; pledged; limited; defined.

مشروطاً mashrūtan (A) adv. Conditionally.

مشروع mashrū' (A) adj. Legal; conformable to or prescribed by law; legitimate; just; initiated; commenced; begun.

مشعل mash'al (A) n.f. Torch; a burner; a flam bear; lantern.

مشعلچی mash'alchi (P) n.m. A torch-bearer; a scullion.

مشغلہ mashghalah (A) n.m. Employment; engagement; pastime; amusement; hobby.

مشغول mashghul (A) adj. Employed; occupied; busy; diligent; engaged; anxious.

مشغولی ، مشغولیت masghūli, mashghūliyat (A&P) n.f. Engagement; employment.

مشفق mushfiq (A) adj. Kind; dear; affectionate; showing favour; condoling. n.m. A friend.

مشفقانہ mushfiqānah (A) adv. Kindly; affectionately; friendly.

مشق mashq (A) n.f. Exercise; practice; drawing the letters; combining; a model; an example; usage; use.

مشق کرنا mashq karnā, v. To practise; to exercise; to copy; to imitate.

مشقت mashaqqat (A) n.f. Trouble; labour; pains; toil; assiduity; Inconvenience; distress; affliction; misfortune.

مشقت شدید mashaqqat-ē shadid, n.f. Hard labour.

بامشقت bā mashaqqat, adj. With labour; rigorous.

بلا مشقت bilā mashaqqat, adj. Without labour; simple.

مشقی mashqi (A) adj. Acquired by practice; copied on; practical; relating to copy or exercise. n.f. A slip exercise book.

مشقی اسباق mashqi asbāq, n.m. Practical lessons.

مشک mashk (P) n.f. A leather bag for carrying water; a water bag.

مشک mushk (P) n.m. Musk.

مشک بار mushk bār, adj. Diffusing musk; scented like musk; musky.

مشک بو mushk bū, adj. Fragrant; scented with musk.

مشک فام mushk fām, adj. Musk-coloured; deep-black.

مشک نافہ mushk nāfah, n.m. The musk bag.

مشکل mushkil (A) adj. Difficult; intricate; hard; painful. n.f. Difficulty; hardship; intricacy; complicacy. (plu. مشکلات mushkilāt).

مشکل آسان کرنا mushkil āsān karna, v. To remove a difficulty; to relieve one of a hardship.

مشکل پسند mushkil pasand, adj. Delighting in difficulties; in the habit of writing difficult language.

مشکل سے mushkil se, adv. With difficulty.

مشکل کشا mushkil kushā, adj. One who removes or solves difficulties.

مشکل گزار mushkil guzār, adj. Difficult to pass.

مشکل میں پڑنا mushkil meṅ paṛnā, v. To fall into difficulty; to get into a trouble; to be involved in an intricacy.

مشکوۃ mishkāt (A) n.f. Lamp-stand; a lantern; a glass-shade of a lamp; a glass-chimney; a book on traditions of the Holy Prophet.

مشکور mashkūr (A) adj. Praised; thanked; laudable; agreeable.

مشکوک mashkūk (A) adj. Doubtful; uncertain; ambiguous; tampered with; doubted; problematical.

مشکی mushki (P) adj. Dark; bay; approaching to black colour (of a horse). n.m. A black horse.

مشکی رنگ mushki raṅg, n.m. Black colour.

مشکیزہ mashkizah (P) n.m. A small water bag of leather.

مشکیں mushkiṅ (P) adj. Musky; of musk.

مشکیں mushkeṅ (H) n.f. Both the arms or shoulders.

مشکیں باندھنا ، کسنا mushkeṅ bāndhnā, kasnā, v. To pinion; to tie the hands behind the back.

مشمول ، مشموله mashmūl, mashmūlah (A) adj. comprehended; contained; incorporated with; incorporating; included; contained.

مشورت ، مشوره mashwarat mashwarah (A) n.f./m. Counsel; consultation; advice; conspiracy; plot.

مشوره کرنا mashwarah karnā, v. To consult; to take advice; to deliberate.

مشوش mushawwash (A) adj. Disturbed; confused; intricate; distressed; uneasy; perplexed.

مشوش mushawwish (A) adj. Disturber; that which causes perplexity or uneasiness.

مشهد mashhad (A) n.m. A place of martyrdom; a place of assembly; a tomb.

مشهود mashhūd (A) adj. Attested; proved; evinced; beheld; clear; manifes; present.

مشهور mashhūr (A) adj. Well-known; noted; notorious; famous; celebrated; published; conspicuous; apparent; proclaimed; reported.

مشهور و معروف mashhūr-ŏ ma'rūf, adj. Well-known; reputed.

مشهوری mashhūri, n.f. Reputation; notoriety.

مشی mashi (A) n.f. Walking; going.

مشی فی النوم mashi-fin-naum, n.f. Somnambulism; sleep-walking.

مشیت mashiyyat (A) n.f. Will; pleasure; wish.

مشیت ایزدی mashiyyat-ĕ ezadi, n.f. The will of God; fate.

مشیخت mashikhat (A) n.f. Vanity; pride; seniority.

مشیخت مآب mashikhat maab (A) adj. Full of pride; showy; conceited; vainglorious.

مشیر mushir (A) n.m. A counsellor; a senator; an adviser; secretary.

مشیر خاص mushir-ĕ khāṣ, n.m. Private secretary.

مشیرالدوله mushir-ud-daulah, n.m. An adviser of the state.

مشیر مال mushir-ĕ māl, n.m. Financial adviser.

مشین mashin (E) n.f. Machine.

مشینی mashini, adj. Mechanical.

مصابیح maṣābiḥ (A) n.m. (plu. of مصباح miṣbāḥ) Lamps.

مصاحب maṣāḥib (A) n.m. A companion; a comrade; favourite; an associate; a friend.

مصاحبت muṣāḥabat (A) n.f. Companionship; society; company; familiarity; communion.

مصاحف maṣāḥif (A) n.m. (plu. of مصحف muṣḥaf). Books; volumes.

مصادر maṣādir (A) n.m. (plu. of مصدر maṣdar). The infinitive or nouns of action; sources.

مصارف maṣārif (A) n.m. (plu. of مصرف maṣraf) Expenses; disbursements.

مصارف بے جا maṣārif-ĕ be jā, n.m. Improper or unnecessary expenses.

مصافحه musāfaḥah (A) n.m. Shaking hands (with).

مصافحه کرنا muṣāfaḥah karnā, v. To shake hands; to join hands.

مصالح maṣāliḥ (A) n.m. (plu. of مصلحت maṣlaḥat) Affairs; policies; advices; causes; counsels.

مصالحت muṣālaḥat (A) n.f. Reconciliation; pacification; composition; compromise.

مصالحت کرنا muṣālaḥat karnā, v. To adjust; to compromise; to compound; to make peace with; to become reconciled (to).

مصائب maṣā'ib (A) n.m. (plu. of مصیبت muṣibat) Misfortunes; calamities; miseries.

مصباح miṣbāḥ (A) n.m. A lamp; a lamp light; lantern; a morning wine cup.

مصحح muṣaḥḥiḥ (A) n.m. One who revises or corrects; a moderator; an amendator; a proof-reader.

مصحف muṣḥaf (A) n.m. A book; a page; the Quran.

مصحف اٹھانا muṣḥaf uṭhānā, v. To swear by the Quran.

مصداق miṣdāq (A) n.m. Proof; evidence; whatever verifies or proves a thing to be true.

مصدر maṣdar (A) n.m. Source; origin; a place; spring; theme; the infinitive or noun of action.

مصدر لازم maṣdar-ĕ lāzim, n.m. Intransitive verb.

مصدر متعدی maṣdar-ĕ muta'addi, n.m. Transitive verb.

مصدق muṣaddiq (A) adj. Verifier; affirmer; one who believes another.

مصدق ، مصدقہ muṣaddaq, muṣaddaqah (A) adj. Attested; authenticated; verified; proved to be true; confirmed.

مصر miṣr (A) n.m. A large city; Egypt.

مصر muṣirr (A) adj. Persisting; persevering; obstinate.

مصرع ، مصرعہ miṣra', miṣra'ah (A) n.m. A line of a verse; a hemistitch; throwing down; an arena, where one is thrown down; the shutter of adoor; a leaf of a folding door.

مصرع لگانا miṣra' lagānā, v. To add a line to a hemistitch; to complete a verse; to make a couplet.

مصرف muṣrif (A) adj. Prodigal; wasteful; spending without necessity.

مصرف maṣraf (A) n.m. Expenditure; expense; disbursement; cost; charge; use; consumption; disposal.

مصروع maṣrū' (A) adj. Epileptic; afflicted with or suffering from epilepsy.

مصروف maṣrūf (A) adj. Engaged; employed; busy; occupied, expended; spent; turned; changed; used; declinable.

مصری miṣrī (A) n.f. Sugar-candy; a kind of sword. adj. Egyptian; of Egypt.

مصری کا کوزہ miṣrī kā kūzah, n.m. A cup of sugar-candy; a sweet melon

مصری کھلانا misrī khilānā, v. To perform the betrothal ceremony; to betroth.

مصری کی ڈلی miṣrī kī ḍali, n.f. A lump of sugar; very sweet sugar-cake.

مصطفیٰ muṣṭafā (A) adj. Chosen; selected. n.m. A title of the Holy Prophet.

مصطکی maṣṭakī (G) n.f. Mastic; gum-mastic.

مصطلح muṣṭalaḥ (A) adj. Idiomatic; phraseological; metaphoric.

مصطلحات muṣṭalaḥāt (A) n.f. (plu. of مصطلح muṣṭalaḥ) Phrases; technical terms; idioms.

مصفا muṣaffā (A) adj. Clean; clarified; pure.

مصفی maṣaffi (A) adj. Purifying; refining; cleaning; clarifying; purifier; cleaner; clearer.

مصفی خون muṣaffi-ĕ k͟hūn, adj. Blood purifier.

مصلا ، مصلی muṣallā (A) n.m. A carpet for saying prayers on; a place of prayer; an oratory; a mosque.

مصلح muṣliḥ (A) n.m. An adviser; a reformer; a corrective; an antidote; a mediator; pacifier.

مصلحت maṣlaḥat (H) n.f Expedience; convenience; fitness; welfare; a prudent measure; counsel; advisability; advice; policy; cause; a good thing.

مصلحت بیں maṣlaḥat bin, adj. Prudent; wise; far-seeing.

مصلحت ملکی maṣlaḥat-ĕ mulkī, n.f. Politics; political considerations.

مصلحت وقت maṣlaḥat-ĕ waqt, n.f. Opportune; timeliness; convenient; seasonable; good and proper for the time being.

مصلحتاً maṣlaḥatan (A) adv. For the good (of); for the welfare (of); expediently; advisedly.

مصلوب maṣlūb (A) adj. Crucified; suspended.

مصلی muṣallī (A) adj. & n.m. One who offers a prayer; righteous; a sweeper, convert to Islam.

مصمم muṣammam (A) adj. Determined; fixed; firm.

مصمم اراده muṣammam irādah, n.m. Determination; resolution; decision.

مصنف muṣannif (A) n.m. An author; a composer; a writer.

مصنف ، مصنفه muṣannaf, muṣannafah (A) adj. Composed; written.

مصنفه muṣannifah (A) n.f. An authoress.

مصنوع ، مصنوعه maṣnū', maṣnū'ah (A) adj. Formed; created; artificial; constructed; invented; made; prepared; contrived; false; counterfeit.

مصنوعات maṣnū'āt (A) n.f. (plu. of مصنوعه maṣnū'ah) Manufactures; inventions; works of art; things artificially made.

مصنوعی maṣnū'ī (A) adj. Artificial; fabricated; false; counterfeit.

مصور muṣawwir (A) adj. Forming pictures; painting; drawing. n.m. A painter; a drawer; a photographer; a sculptor.

مصور muṣawwar (A) adj. Printed; illustrated.

مصوری muṣawwiri (A) n.f. Painting; drawing; photography.

مصئون maṣ'ūn (A) adj. Protected; guarded; preserved; safe.

مصیبت muṣibat (A) n.f. Misfortune; calamity; disaster; affliction; adversity; evil; misery; ill.

مصیبت آٹھانا ، بھرنا ، بھگتنا ، جھیلنا muṣibat uṭhānā, bharnā, bhugatnā, jhelnā, v. To wade through misery and trouble.

مصیبت زده muṣibat zadah, adj. Unfortunate; msierable.

مصیبت میں پڑنا muṣibat meṅ paṛnā, v. To be overtaken by misery.

مصیبت ناگہانی muṣibat-ĕ nagahanı, n.f. An unexpected trouble; a bolt from the blue.

مضارع muẓāri' (A) adj Resembling. n.m. (in Grammar) the aorist.

مضاعف muẓā'af (A) adj. Doubled; increased; multiplied.

مضاف muẓāf (A) adj. Added; annexed; related. n.m. A noun or pronoun in the possessive case.

مضاف الیه muẓāf ilaih, n.m. The noun possessed; the noun governed.

مضافات muẓāfāt (A) n.f. Appendages; annexations; additions.

مضافات شہر muẓāfāt-ĕ shahr, n.f. Suburbs.

مضامین maẓāmīn (A) n.m. (plu. of مضمون maẓmūn) Subjects; compositions; contents.

مضایقه muẓāyaqah (A) n.m. Penury; distress; significance; consequence; necessity; poverty; difficulty; moment.

مضبوط maẓbūṭ (A) adj. Strong; firm; fixed; fast; durable; solid; immovable; possessed; occupied; restrained; resolute; cogent; valid.

مضبوطی maẓbūṭi, n.f. Durability; strength; firmness; solidity; cogency.

مضحک muẓḥik (A) adj. Ridiculous; droll.

مضحکه maẓḥakah (A) n.m. Humour; fun; drollery; a pun; laughing stock.

مضحکه آڑانا maẓḥakah uṛānā, v. To ridicule; to droll.

مضحکه خیز **maẓhakah khez**, *adj.* Ridiculous; causing laughter.

مضر **muẓir** (A) *adj.* Pernicious; hurtful; noxious; injurious; mischievous; hateful; deleterious; detrimental.

مضراب **mizrāb** (A) *n.f.* An instrument of striking; the hooked ring with which a guitar is struck; a musical plectrum or bow.

مضرت **maẓarrat** (A) *n.f.* Detriment; damage; injury; harm.

مضرت رساں **maẓarrat rasāṅ**, *adj.* Injurious; troubblesome; hurtful; harmful.

مضروب **maẓrūb** (A) *adj.* Hurt; wounded; injured. *n.m.* Multiplicant.

مضطر **muẓṭarr** (A) *adj.* Distressed; afflicted; in necessity; agitated; scattered; embarrassed; restless; rendered desperate.

مضطرب **muẓṭarib** (A) *adj.* Agitated; afflicted; chagrined; distracted; uneasy; confused.

مضطرب الحال **muẓṭarib-ul-ḥāl**, *adj.* In a state of commotion; troubled; agitated.

مضطرب ہونا **muẓṭarib honā**, *v.* To be agitated; to be uneasy.

مضطربانه **muẓṭaribānah**, *adv.* Confusedly; in an agitated state.

مضمحل **muẓmaḥill** (A) *adj.* Fatigued; exhausted; infirm; loosened; vanishing; idle.

مضمر **muẓmar** (A) *adj.* Concealed; conceived; imagined; the antecedent (in grammar).

مضموم **maẓmūm** (A) *adj.* Added; joined; accumulated; pronounced with the vowel point *zammā* (ʼ); having *zammā* on it.

مضمون **maẓmūn** (A) *n.m.* Contents; sense; meaning; subject; composition; essay; article; subject-matter.

مضمون نگار **maẓmūn nigār**, *n.m.* An essay or article writer; a contributor to a paper.

مضی ما مضی **maẓā mā maẓa** (A) Let bygones be bygones.

مطابع **maṭābi'** (A) *n.m.* (*plu.* of مطبع *maṭba'*) Printing presses.

مطابق **muṭābiq** (A) *adj.* Conformable; suitable; like; identical; answering; agreeable to; equal; corresponding; in accordance with.

مطابق کرنا **muṭābiq karnā**, *v.* To compare with; to make like.

مطابق ہونا **muṭābiq honā**, *v.* To conform (to); to suit; to coincide; to agree with.

مطابقت **muṭābaqat** (A) *n.f.* Conformity; equality; identity; analogy; corresponding to; coincidence; similarity; accordance.

مطاع **muṭa'** (A) *adj.* Superior; patron; obeyed.

مطالب **maṭālib** (A) *n.m.* (*plu.* of مطلب *maṭlab*). Demands: requisitions; researches; wishes; desires; objects; purposes.

مطالبه **muṭālabah** (A) *n.m.* Asking for; requiring; exaction; a demand; claim; amount; requisition.

مطالعه **muṭāla'ah** (A) *n.m.* Contemplation; consideration; reading; study; perusal; turning attention to.

مطالعه کرنا **muṭāla'ah karnā**, *v.* To study; to read; to consider; to peruse.

مطایبه **muṭāyabah** (A) *n.m.* Jesting; joking; pleasantry (*plu.* مطایبات *muṭāyabāt*).

مطب **maṭabb** (A) *n.m.* Practising place or consulting room of a physician.

مطبخ **maṭbakh** (A) *n.m.* A kitchen; a mess.

مطبع **maṭba'** (A) *n.m.* A press; a printing house; a printing press.

مطبوع **maṭbū'** (A) *adj.* Printed; pressed; agreeable; acceptable; worthy; laudable; pleasant; natural; innate; creating with a disposition (to a thing or quality).

مطبوعه **maṭbū'ah** (A) *adj.* Printed; published; pressed.

مطبوعات maṭbū'āt (A) n.f. (plu. of مطبوعه maṭbū'ah) Publications.

مطر maṭar (A) n.m. Rain.

مطرب muṭrib (A) n.m. A musician; a singer; a minstrel.

مطربه muṭribah (A) n.f. A female singer.

مطعون maṭ'ūn (A) adj. Reproached; blamed; chidden.

مطلا muṭallā (A) adj. Gilded; gilt.

مطلب maṭlab (A) n.m. Object; aim; purpose; purport; meaning; demand; motive; proposition; request; a question; petition; intention; wish; desire.

مطلب برآری maṭlab barārī, n.f. Attaining one's object.

مطلب رکھنا maṭlab rakhnā, v. To have an interest; to have some purpose; to be motivated by something.

مطلب کا یار maṭlab kā yār, n.m. A self-interested friend; a friend of one's own interest; a time-serving or selfish friend.

مطلب کی گھات چلنا maṭlab kī ghāt chalnā, v. To pursue after one's own object or interest.

مطلب نکالنا maṭlab nikālnā, v. To be successful in gaining one's object; to serve the purpose.

مطلب نکلنا maṭlab nikalnā, v. To have one's object served.

مطلب ہونا maṭlab honā, v. To have a concern.

مطلبی maṭlabī, adj. Self-seeking; selfish.

مطلع maṭla' (A) n.m. The place of rising; the east; the beginning or exordium of a poem.

مطلع صاف ہونا maṭla' ṣāf honā, v. To be clear (weather); to be clear of obstacles.

مطلع muṭṭala' (A) adj. Informed; aware.

مطلع کرنا muṭṭala' karnā, v. To inform; to give intimation.

مطلق muṭlaq (A) adj. Absolute; altogether; universal; principal; supreme; independent; entire; total. adv. Wholly; of all; not in the least; entirely; altogether.

مطلق العنان muṭlaq-ul-'inān, adj. Free; unchecked; independent; unconcerned.

مطلقاً muṭlaqan (A) adv. Absolutely; (not) at all; entirely; altogether.

مطلقه muṭallaqah (A) n.f. A divorced woman.

مطلوب ، مطلوبه maṭlūb, maṭlūbah (A) adj. Desired; longed for; demanded; necessary; required; wanted.

مطمح نظر maṭmaḥ-ĕ naẓar (A) n.m. Goal; aim; object; end.

مطمئن muṭma'in (A) adj. Enjoying repose; quiet; secure; tranquil; safe; satisfied.

مطول muṭawwal (A) adj. Prolonged; drawn out; long; lengthy.

مطہر muṭahhir (A) adj. Cleansing; purifying; purifier.

مطہر muṭahhar (A) adj. Purified; holy; cleansed.

مطیر maṭīr (A) adj. Raining; dropping.

مطیع muṭī' (A) adj. Obedient; submissive; amenable; subject (to); obsequious.

مظالم maẓālim (A) n.m. (plu. of مظلمه maẓlamah) Tyrannies; injuries; wrongs; places where tyrants are punished; courts of justice.

مظاہر maẓāhir (A) n.m. (plu. of مظہر maẓhar) Sceneries; spectacles; phenomena.

مظاہر قدرت maẓāhir-ĕ qudrat, n.m. Natural phenomena.

مظاہره muẓāharah (A) n.m. Demonstration.

مظفر muẓaffar (A) adj. Victorious; successful; august.

مظفر ومنصور muzaffar-ŏ mansur, adj. Rendered victorious and aided by heaven.

مظلوم mazlūm (A) adj. Injured; oppressed; wronged; treated tyrannically. n.m. One who is treated wrongfully or unjustly.

مظلومی mazlūmi (A&P) n.f. Oppression; tyranny; state of the person oppressed.

مظهر mazhar (A) n.m. A place of spectacle; theatre; stage; object; view.

مظهر muzhir (A) adj. Exhibiting; displaying; manifesting. n.m. Exhibitor; an informer; a witness; a spy.

مع ma' (A) prep. With; together; along with.

مع الخیر ma' al-khair, adv. Safely; in good condition.

مع هذا ma' hazā, adv. Along with this; in addition; besides.

معاً ma'an (A) adv. Together; at the same time; all at once; instantly.

معابد ma'ābid (A) n.m. (plu. of معبد ma'bad) Places of worship.

معاد ma'ād (A) n.f. Place of return; the life to come; the next world; the resurrection; paradise.

معادن ma'ādin (A) n.f. (plu of معدن ma'dan) Mines.

معاذ ma'āz (A) n.f. A place of shelter; refuge.

معاذ الله ma'āz allah, intj. God be the refuge! God forbid!

معارف ma'ārif (A) n.m. (plu. of معرف ma'raf) Knowledges; sciences; acquirements.

معاش ma'ash (A) n.f. Livelihood; subsistence; life; living; means or place of living; landed property; food.

معاشرت mu'āsharat (A) n.f. Living and eating together; mixing with; conversing with; social intercourse; association; intimacy; citizenship.

معاشرتی mu'āsharati (A) adj. Social.

معاشره mu'āsharah (A) n.m. Society.

معاشی ma'ashi (A) adj. Economical.

معاشیات ma'āshiyyat (A) n.f. Political economy.

معاصر mu'āsir (A) adj. Contemporary; (pl. معاصرین mu'āsirin).

معاصی ma'āsi (A) n.m. (plu. of معصیت ma'siyat) Sins; offences; crimes.

معاف mu'af (A) adj. Absolved; exempted; dispensed with; forgiven; pardoned; excused; free.

معاف کرنا mu'āf karnā, v. To pardon; to forgive; to excuse; to dispense with; to remit punishment.

معاف کیجئے mu'āf kijie, intj. Pardon me! pardon.

معافی mu'āfi (A) n.f. Exemption; immunity; pardon; absolution; remission (of punishment, revenue etc.); a rent free grant.

معافی چاهنا ، مانگنا mu'āfi chāhnā, mangnā, v. To ask for pardon; to apologize.

معافی حین حیات mu'āfi hin-ĕ hayat, n.f. Remission for life; a life-long remission of land-revenue; a free grant for life.

معافی دار mu'āfi dar, n.m. A holder of rent free land.

معافی دائمی ، استمراری mu'āfi-ĕ dā'imi، istimrāri, n.f. A grant of land in perpetuity.

معافی نامه mu'āfi nāmah, n.m. A deed of amnesty; an order of exemption from taxes.

معالج mu'ālij (A) n.m. A physician; a doctor.

معالجه mu'ālajah (A) n.m. Curing; healing; treatment; a remedy.

معالجه کرنا mu'ālajah karnā, v. To heal; to cure; to attend (as a physician); to apply a remedy.

معامله mu'āmalah (A) n.m. Affair; business; negotiation; transaction; behaviour; procedure; concern; cause or suit in law; contract; sexual intercourse; dealing; commerce; correspondence; (plu. معاملات mu'āmalāt).

معاملہ پڑنا *mu'āmalah parnā, v.* To have a dealing with; to deal with; to have business transaction.

معاملہ رس ، شناس ، فہم *mu'āmalah ras, shinās, fahm, adj.* One who fully understands a matter; one who dips deep into a matter.

معاملہ سنگین *mu'āmalah-ĕ sangin, n.m.* A serious matter.

معاملہ کرنا *mu'āmalah karnā, v.* To carry on business transactions (with); to buy and sell; to deal with; to negotiate; to contract.

معاملہ ہونا *mu'āmalah honā, v.* To be settled (a business); to bargain.

معاملے کا سچا *mu'āmale kā sachchā, adj.* Honest in dealings.

معاملے کا کھوٹا *muam'ale kā khoṭā, adj.* Dishonest in dealings.

معاند *mu'ānid* (A) *adj.* Perverse; refractory; obstinate; stubborn; disobedient; rebellious.

معاندت *mu'ānadat* (A) *n.f.* Enmity; conflict; wrangle.

معانقہ *mu'ānaqah* (A) *n.m.* Embracing; joining together; throwing the arms round another's neck.

معانی *ma'āni* (A) *n.m.* (*plu. of* معنی *ma'nī*) Meanings; intrinsic qualities.

معاودت *mu'āwadat* (A) *n.f* Returning; coming back; coming or going.

معاوضہ *mu'āwaẓah* (A) *n.m.* Returning; like for like; retaliation; exchange; remuneration; compensation; consideration; barter; revenge.

معاون *mu'āwin* (A) *adj.* Assisting; helping; auxiliary. *n.m.* A helper; an assistant.

معاون جرم *mu'āwin-ĕ jurm, n.m.* An abetter (of an offence); an accessory; an accomplice.

معاون دریا *mu'āwin-ĕ daryā, n.m.* A tributary.

معاونت *mu'āwanat* (A) *n.f.* Help; aid; assistance; succour.

معاہد *mu'āhid* (A) *n.m.* A contractor; a confederate; an ally (*plu.* معاہدین *mu'āhidīn*).

معاہدہ *mu'āhadah* (A) *n.m.* A contract; agreement; confederation; confederacy; alliance; a treaty; a league.

معائب ، معایب *ma'ā'ib, ma'āyib* (A) *n.m.* (*plu. of* معیب *ma'yab*) Vices; faults; blemishes.

معاینہ *mu'āyanah* (A) *n.m.* Inspection; sight; view; beholding; seeing clearly or face to face.

معاینہ کرنا *mu'āyanah karnā, v.* To inspect; to examine.

معبد *m'abad* (A) *n.m.* A place of worship; mosque; temple; church; a place of pilgrimage.

معبر *mu'abbir* (A) *n.m.* An interpreter of dreams.

معبود *ma'būd* (A) *adj.* & *n.m.* Worshipped; adored; a god, a diety; God.

معتاد *mu'tād* (A) *adj.* Accustomed; habituated; customary. *n.f.* A fixed allowance; a due quantity; a dose; custom; habit; use; weight.

معتبر *mu'tabar* (A) *adj.* Confidential; respectable; worthy of confidence; creditable; credible; relied on; reputable; trustworthy; true.

معتبری *mu'tabari, n.f.* Confidence; reliance; credit; respectability; trustworthiness.

معتد *mu'tadd* (A) *adj.* Numbered; computed.

معتدبہ *mu'tadd bi-hi, adj.* Trustworthy; sufficient; enough.

معتدل *mu'tadil* (A) *adj.* Temperate; tolerable; calm; moderate; mild; of a middling sort.

معتدل آب و ہوا *mu'tadil-āb-ŏ hawa, n.f.* Temperate climate.

معترض mu'tariẓ (A) *adj.* Opposing; objecting; hindering; interposing; withstanding; resisting. *n.m.* An objector.

معترض ہونا mu'tariẓ hono, *v.* To object; to obstruct; to impede; to come across.

معترف mu'tarif (A) *adj.* & *n.m.* One who acknowledges; a confessor; affirmer; avower.

معتزلہ mu'tazilah (A) *n.m.* A sect among Muslims who believe in all good from God and all bad from man.

معتصم mu'taṣim (A) *adj.* Preserved; relying on; attendant on.

معتقد mu'taqid (A) *adj.* Confident; believing; an adhering. *n.m.* A believer; an adherent; a faithful servant or friend; a follower of a creed or faith.

معتکف mu'takif (A) *adj.* Constant in devotion; constant in prayer at the temple. *n.m.* One who secludes himself for religious service.

معتمد mu'tamad (A) *adj.* Trustworthy; relied upon; reliable. *n.m.* Secretary.

معتمد علیہ mu'tamad 'alaih, *n.m.* A trustworthy person; a reliable person; a confidant.

معتوب ma'tūb (A) *adj.* Oppressed; persecuted; cursed.

معجزہ mu'jizah (A) *n.m.* A miracle.

معجل mu'ajjal (A) *adj.* Prompt; done without delay.

معجل mu'ajjil (A) *adj.* Hasty; expedient; agile.

معجم ، معجمہ mu'jam, mu'jamah (A) *adj.* Dotted (letter).

معجون ma'jūn (A) *n.f.* An electuary; a compounded medicine; an intoxicating drug prepared from the extract of hemp and sugar; confection.

معدلت ma'dalat (A) *n.f.* Justice; equity; rectitude.

معدن ma'dan, ma'din (A) *n.f.* A mine; a quarry.

معدنی ma'danī (A) *adj.* Mineral.

معدنیات ma'daniyat (A) *n.f.* Minerai substances.

معدود ma'dud (A) *adj.* Numbered; counted; computed; limited.

معدودے چند ma'dud-ĕ chand, *adj.* Very few.

معدوم ma'dum (A) *adj.* Not existent; annihilated; extinct.

معدوم کرنا ma'dum karna *v.* To annihilate.

معدوم ہونا ma'dum hona *v.* To be extinct.

معدہ mi'dah (A) *n.m.* The stomach.

معذرت ma'zirat (A) *n.f.* An excuse; a plea; apology.

معذور ma'zūr (A) *adj.* Excused; excusable; unserviceable; disappointed.

معرا mu'arrā (A) *adj.* Naked; bare; bald; without marginal notes; without translation; plain (text).

معراج mi'raj (A) *n.f.* A ladder; anything by which one ascends; ascension; ascent; ascension of the Holy Prophet to Heaven.

معرب mu'arrab (A) *adj.* A word of a foreign language changed into Arabic.

معرض ma'riẓ (A) *n.m.* Place of meeting or happening; an occurrence; an occasion; a contingency.

معرفت ma'rifat (A) *n.f.* Knowledge; cognizance; science; skill; revelation; education; good breeding; wisdom. *adv.* Through; the medium of; by the hand of.

معرفہ ma'rifah (A) *n.m.* Proper noun.

معرکہ ma'rikah (A) *n.m.* Fight; field of battle; stripe.

معرکہ آرائی ma'rikah ara'i, *n.f.* Marshalling of troops.

معرکے کا ma'rike kā, *adj.* Important; momentous.

معروض ma'ruẓ (A) *n.f.* Representation; petition.

معروضه ma'ruẓah (A) *n.m.* A petition; an application; representation.

معروف ma'ruf (A) *adj.* Known; notorious; noted; celebrated; active (voice of a verb); the letters و and ی when the former has the sound of *u* as in نور *nur* and the latter of *i* in تیر *tir*.

معزز mu'azzaz (A) *adj.* Honoured; esteemed; exalted; revered; dignified; honourable.

معزول ma'zūl (A) *adj.* Deposed; dismissed; degraded.

معزول کرنا ma'zūl karnā, *v.* To dismiss; to discharge; to disgrace; to dethrone.

معزولی ma'zūlī (A) *n.f.* Dismissal; deposition; dethronement.

معشر mu'ashshar (A) *adj.* Composed of or relating to ten; a decagon.

معشوق ma'shūq (A) *n.m.* A beloved, a sweetheart.

معشوقانه ma'shūqānah (A & P) *adj.* Like a beloved; lovely; fascinating.

معشوقه ma'shūqah (A) *n.f.* A beloved; a mistress.

معشوقی ma'shūqi (A & P) *n.f.* Loveliness; the state of being beloved.

معصوم ma'ṣūm (A) *adj.* Defended; preserved; innocent; simple· guileless; infant.

معصومیت ma'ṣūmiyat (A) *n.f.* Innocence; simplicity; infancy.

معصیت ma'ṣiyat (A) *n.f.* Disobedience; sin; defection.

معطر mu'aṭṭar (A) *adj.* Perfumed; fragrant.

معطل mu'aṭṭal (A) *adj.* Vacant; unemployed; disengaged; destitute; out of use; obsolete; idle; suspended; in abeyance; abandoned; unfrequented.

معطل کرنا mu'aṭṭal karnā, *v.* To detain; to keep waiting; to delay; to linger; to suspend.

معطلی mu'aṭṭalī (A) *n.f.* Suspension from office; being out of employment; delay.

معطوف ma'ṭūf (A) *adj.* Inclined; turned; appended; connected. *n.m.* The first of the two words or clauses connected by a conjunction.

معطوف علیه ma'ṭuf 'alaih, *n.m.* The second word or clause joined by a conjunction.

معطی mū'ṭī (A) *adj.* Donor.

معظم ، معظمه mu'aẓẓam, mu'aẓẓamah (A) *adj.* Honoured; respected; exalted; great; revered.

معقول ma'qūl (A) *adj.* Reasonable; probable; understandable; just; pertinent; proper; fair; decent; appropriate; liberal.

معقولات ma'qulāt (A) *n.m.* (*plu.* of معقول *ma'qūl*) Understandable things; fair and appropriate words or things; works of philosophy and logic.

معقولیت ma'qūliyat (A) *n.f.* Reasonableness; probability.

معکوس ma'kus (A) *adj.* Inverted; reversed; reflex; transposed.

معلق mu'allaq (A) *adj.* Suspended; pending; hanging; pendulous.

معلق هونا mu'allaq honā, *v.* To be suspended.

معلم mu'allim (A) *n.m.* An instructor; teacher; preceptor; a pilot.

معلم اول mu'allim-ĕ awwal *n.m.* Aristotle; the first philosopher.

معلم ثانی mu'allim-ĕ sāṇi *n.m.* Abu Nasr Farabi, the teacher of Aristotle's philosophy in Arabic.

معلم ثالث mu'allim-ĕ ṣalis, *n.m.* Avecinna who wrote a number of books on philosophy.

معلم الملکوت mu'allim-ul-malakut, n.m. The instructor of the angels; Satan.

معلمہ mu'allimah (A) n.f. Mistress; lady teacher.

معلمی mu'allimi (A) n.f. Teaching profession; teachership; instruction; pilotage.

معلن mu'lin (A) n.m. Announcer.

معلوم ma'lum (A) adj. Known; evident; apparent; distinguished; obvious; clear.

معلوم کرنا ma'lum karna, v. To know; to find out; to behold; to recognize; to suppose; to deem; to discover; to feel; to perceive.

معلوم ھوتا ہے ma'lum hota hai, adv. It appears; it seems.

معلوم ھونا ma'lūm hona, v. To seem; to appear; to be known; to become known (to); to be discovered.

معلوم نہیں ma'lūm nahin, adv. It is not known. God knows.

معلومات ma'lūmāt (A) n.f. (plu. of معلوم ma'lum) Things known; sciences; informations.

معلی mu'allā (A) adj. Exalted; elevated; high; sublime.

معلی القاب mu'alla alqāb, adj. Of exalted rank or dignity.

معما mu'ammā (A) n.m. A riddle; a puzzle; an enigma; a crossword; a complicated matter; an innuendo; anyth ng obscure; an acrostic.

معما حل کرنا mu'ammā hal karna, v. To solve a puzzle; to untie a knot.

معمار mi'mār (A) n.m. A mason; an architect; a builder.

معماری mi'mārī (A) n.f. Masonry; building; architecture.

معمر mu'ammar (A) adj. Aged; blessed with long-life.

معمور ma'mūr (A) adj. Inhabited; populated; full; replete; abundant; colonized; ample; happy; delightful; prosperous; flourishing; in good condition.

معمورہ ma'mūrah (A) n.m. An inhabited place; a cultivated spot; a delightful spot.

معموری ma'mūrī, n.f. Cultivation; population; fulness; a flourishing condition; happiness.

معمول ma'mul (A) adj. Governed; established; made; prepared; customary. n.m. Habit; custom; practice; fixed allowance; gratuity; object (hypnot.)

معمول باندھنا ma'mul bandhna, v. To practise; to do a thing regularly; to form a habit; to make a habit of.

معمول کے دن ma'mul ke din, n.m. Monthly course; menses.

معمول کے دن ٹل جانا ma'mūl ke din tal jānā, v. To be pregnant.

معمولی ma'mūli (A) adj. Customary; common; ordinary; practised; usual; current; practical.

معنبر mu'ambar (A) adj. Perfumed with ambergris.

معنون mu'anwan (A) adj. Dedicated; prefaced.

معنوی ma'nawi (A) adj. Real; essential; significant; expressive of; ideal; intellectual; implied; intrinsic.

معنی ma'ni, ma'na (A) n.m. Meaning; intended sense; intent; signification; impart; intrinsic quality; spirituality; substance; essence; reality; hidden or interrior part of anything.

معنی بیان کرنا ma'ni bayān karnā, v. To explain the meaning; to interpret; to explain.

معنی دینا ma'nī denā, v. To impart meaning (to); to give an interpretation; to explain the meaning of.

معنی رکھنا ma'nī rakhnā, v. To imply; to have the meaning or sense of.

معونت ma'ūnat (A) n.f. Assistance; aid; favour.

معہود ma'hud (A) *adj.* Agreed on; stipulated; promised; established; resolved; certain; appointed; fixed; determined.

معیار mi'yar (A) *n.m.* A touchstone; a standard; a measure.

معیت ma'iyyat (A) *n.f.* Company (of); association.

معیشت ma'ishat (A) *n.f.* Subsistence; livelihood; living; way of life; daily food.

معین ، معینہ mu'aiyyan, mu'aiyyanah (A) *adj.* Established; fixed; ascertained; appointed; certified.

معین کرنا mu'aiyyan karna, *v.* To fix; to appoint; to establish.

معین mu'in (A) *n.m.* An assistant; a helper; an aider.

معیوب ma'yub (A) *adj.* Defective, infamous; blamable; opprobrious; bad; improper.

مغ mugh (P) *n.m.* A tavern-keeper; a fire-worshipper; (*plu.* مغاں mughān).

مغ بچہ mugh bachah, *n.m.* The son of tavern-keeper or fire-worshipper.

مغالطہ mughālatah (A) *n.m.* Leading into error; delusion; ambiguity; deception; mutual misunderstanding.

مغالطہ دینا mughalatah dena, *v.* To mislead; to delude; to practise deception (on); to lead into error.

مغالطہ ڈالنا mughālatah ḍālnā, *v.* To delude; to lead into error.

مغایر mughāyar (A) *adj.* Contrary; reverse; repugnant.

مغایرت mughāyarat (A) *n.f.* Disagreement; repugnance; contrariety; estrangement.

مغتنم ، مغتنمہ mughtanam, mughtanamah (A) *adj.* Regarded as a prize or blessing; (*plu* مغتنمات mughtanamāt).

مغرب maghrib (A) *n.m.* The west; sunset; the western quarter.

مغرب کی نماز maghrib ki namāz, *n.f.* Evening prayer.

مغرب زدہ maghrib zadah, *adj.* Westernized; having adopted the western mode of living.

مغربی maghribi (A) *adj.* Western; occidental.

مغربیت maghribiyyat (A) *n.f.* Westernization; adoptation of European culture.

مغرق mugharraq (A) *adj.* Immersed; sunken; dipped; gilt; ornamented with gold or silver.

مغرور maghrur (A) *adj.* Proud; arrogant; haughty.

مغروری maghruri, *n.f.* Pride; arrogance; haughtiness.

مغز maghz (P) *n.m.* The brain; marrow; kernel; pith; the chief substance or essence of anything; intellect; pride.

مغز پچی کرنا maghz pichchi karnā, *v.* To rack the brains (of).

مغز چاٹنا maghz chātnā, *v.* To suck the brains (of); to bother one a great deal.

مغز چٹ maghz chaṭ, *adj.* Talkative; idle talker.

مغز کو چڑھ جانا maghz ko charh jana, *v.* To affect the head (of); to be proud; to be self-conceited.

مغز کھانا maghz khānā, *v.* To tease; to worry; to tax the brain

مغز کے کیڑے اڑانا maghz ke kiṛe uṛānā, *v.* To chatter; to brag; to bother a great deal

مغز کے کیڑے جھڑنا ، مغز کی کیل نکلنا maghz ke kiṛe jharnā, maghz ki kil nikalnā, *v.* To be punished; to be chastised; to be humbled.

بے مغز be maghz, *adj.* Brainless; empty headed; dullard.

پر مغز pur maghz, *adj.* Brainy; pithy; clever.

مغزی maghzi, *n.f.* Edging; border; hem.

مغفرت maghfirat (A) n.f. Absolution; remission; pardon; forgiveness.

مغفور maghfūr (A) adj. Pardoned; forgiven; deceased; dead.

مغل mughal (P) n.m. Moghal; an important Muslim tribe inhabiting the Indo-Pakistan sub-continent.

مغلانی mughlānī, n.f. A Moghal woman; an attendant in a woman's apartment; a needle-woman.

مغلائی ، مغلئی mughlā'ī, mughla'ī. See مغلیه mughliyyah.

مغلظ mughallaz̤ (A) adj. Hard; vigorous; severe; very foul; impure.

مغلظات mughallaz̤āt (A) n.f. (plu. of مغلظ mughallaz) Offensive or abusive language; abuses.

مغلظات سنانا mughallaz̤āt sunānā, v. To use abusive language.

مغلق mughlaq (A) adj. Obstruse; knotty; obscure; intricate.

مغلم mughlim (A) adj. Sodomite; lewd; lascivious.

مغلوب maghlūb (A) adj. Conquered; overcome; discomfited; subdued.

مغلوب الغضب maghlūb-ul-ghaẓab, adj. Easily irritable; short tempered.

مغلوبیت maghlūbiyat (A) n.f. Humility; pressure; obedience.

مغلیه mughliyyah (P) adj. Of the Moghals.

مغموم maghmum (A) adj. Sad; grieved; mournful; sorrowful; afflicted; affected.

مغنی mughanni (A) n.m. A singer; a musician.

مغنی mughnī (A) adj. Rendering competent; making free from want; making rich.

مغنیه mughanniyah (A) n.f. A female singer.

مغیلان mughilān (P) n.m. A species of mimasa or acacia tree.

مفاتیح mafatih (A) n.f. (plu. of مفتاح miftāḥ) Keys.

مفاجات mufājāt (A) adj. Sudden; unexpected; happening suddenly or unexpectedly.

مفاخرت mufākharat (A) n.f. Contending for glory (with); boasting; arrogance.

مفاد mafād (A) n.m. Gain; benefit; purport; interest.

مفارقت mufāraqat (A) n.f. Separation; alienation; forsaking; absence.

مفاسد mafāsid (A) n.m. (plu. of مفسده mafsadah) Evils; pernicious things.

مفاصل mafāṣil (A) n.m. (plu. of مفصل mafṣal) Joints of the body.

مفت muft (P) adj. Gratis; free; acquired without cost or labour; given away without return or benefit. adv. Without payment; gratuitously.

مفت خور muft khor, n.m. A parasite; a hanger on; a loafer; a sponger.

مفت را چه گفت muft rā chih guft, prov. Do not look a gift horse in the mouth; a gift however small should always be welcome.

مفت میں muft men, adv. Gratis; for nothing.

مفت هاته لگنا muft hath lagnā, v. To acquire without cost or labour.

مفتاح miftāḥ (A) n.f. A key.

مفتخر muftakhar (A) adj. Honoured; glorified.

مفتری muftarī (A) adj. Knavish; tricky; liar. n.m. A slanderer; calumniator; false accuser; a rogue; a knave.

مفتوح maftūḥ (A) adj. Captured; conquered; subdued; taken; pronounced with the vowel فتح fataḥ (-).

مفتون maftūn (A) adj. Tempted; fascinated; enamoured; captivated; deprived of reason; mad (with love); charmed; demented.

مفتون ہونا maftun hona, v. To be enamoured; to be captivated; to be fascinated.

مفتی mufti (A) n.m. A Muslim jurist or law officer; an expounder of Muslim law.

مفخر mufakhkhar (A) adj. Honoured; esteemed; dignified.

مفر mafarr (A) n.m. A place of refuge; an asylum.

مفرح mufarriḥ (A) adj. Exhilarating; refreshing; stimulating; reviving; recreating; amusing.

مفرحات mufarrihat (A) n.f. Stimulating medicines.

مفرد mūfrad (A) adj. Solitary; single; simple; sole; alone.

مفردات mufradāt (A) n.f. Uncompounded medicines.

مفرس mufarras (A) adj. Transferred to Persian from some other language.

مفرط mufriṭ (A) adj. Excessive; vast; transcendent.

مفرور mafrūr, adj. Fugitive; escaped. n.m. A run away.

مفروش mafrush (A) adj. Spread: carpetted.

مفروض mafrūẓ (A) adj. Supposed; granted; given; requisite as a sacred duty.

مفروضہ mafrūẓah (A) n.m. Hypothesis.

مفسد mufsid (A) adj. Mischievous; factious; incendiary; noxious; mischief-maker; author of evil; seditious.

مفسدانہ mufsidānah (A&P) adv. Seditiously; mischievously; tumultously

مفسدہ mafsadah (A) n.m. A riot; disturbance; tumult; uproar; wanton or unrestrained behaviour.

مفسدہ پرداز mafsadah pardāz, adj. & n.m. One engaged in creating mischief; a noisy raveller; a mischief-maker; rowdy; a rioter.

مفسر mufassir (A) n.m. A commentator; an interpreter.

مفصل mafṣal (A) n.m. Joint of the body.

مفصل mufaṣṣal (A) adj. Detailed; full; distinct; ample; analysed; explained; clear; plain; lengthy. adv. Particularly; distinctly; in detail; fully.

مفصلات mufaṣṣalāt (A) n.m. Rural areas; country-side; suburbs.

مفعول maf'ūl (A) n.m. Accusative or objective case; the participle passive; a catamite; gonymede; pot-boy.

مفعول بہ maf'ūl bihi, n.m. Direct object.

مفعول ثانی maf'ūl-ĕ ṣānī, n.m. Indirect object.

مفعول فیہ maf'ūl fīh, n.m. The locative case.

مفعول لہ' maf'ul lahū, n.m. The oblative case.

مفعول معہ' maf'ūl ma'hū, n.m. Case in opposition with the direct object.

مفقود mafqūd (A) adj. MIssed; not to be found; missing; not traceable; lost; extinct; wanting; looking.

مفقود الخبر mafqūd-ul-khabar adj. One whose whereabout are not known; of whom no information or news is forthcoming.

مفکر mufakkir (A) adj. & n.m. Meditator; considerate; a thinker.

مفلس muflis (A) adj. Poor; wretched; pauper; penniless indigent; beggarly; insolvent; bankrupt. n.m. An insolvent person; a pauper; a penniless.

مفلسی muflisi (A&P) n.f. Poverty; Indigence; bankruptcy; pauperism.

مفلوج maflūj (A) adj. Paralytic.

مفلوک mafluk (A) adj. Indigent; distressed; beggarly; unfortunate; destitute.

مفلوک الحال maflūk-ul-ḥal, adj. In straitened circumstance; indigent; poor.

مفوضہ *mufawwaẓah* (A) *adj.* Ceded; entrusted; delivered; consigned; resigned.

مفہوم *mafhūm* (A) *n.m.* Meaning; sense; tenor; acceptation (of a word or expression). *adj.* Understood; comprehended.

مفید *mufid* (A) *adj.* Profitable; useful; of use; beneficial; solutary; advantageous.

مقابر *maqābir* (A) *n.m.* (*plu.* of مقبرہ *maqbarah*) Tombs; sepulchres; mausoleums; graves; burial places; graveyards.

مقابل *muqābil* (A) *adj.* Opposite; converse; confronting; against; matching; comparing; opposing.

مقابلہ *muqābalah* (A) *n.m.* Comprison; collision; competition; opposition; confronting; contest; contending; presence; facing; meeting face to face; putting side by side.

مقاتلہ *muqātalah* (A) *n.m.* Slaughter; carnage; battle; conflict.

مقادیر *maqādir* (A) *n.f.* (*plu.* of مقدار *miqdār*) Quantities; expressions.

مقادیر غیر متماثلہ *maqādir-ĕ ghair mutamāṣilah, n.f.* Heterogeneous expressions.

مقادیر متماثلہ *maqādir-ĕ mutamāṣilah, n.f.* homogeneous expressions.

مقادیر مجہولہ *maqādir-ĕ majhūlah, n.f.* Unknown quantities.

مقادیر معلومہ *maqādir-ĕ ma'lumah, n.f.* Known quantities.

مقاربت *muqārabat* (A) *n.m.* Approximation; showing affinity; drawing near (to); having sexual intercourse (with).

مقارنت *muqāranat* (A) *n.f.* Connection; conjunction; familiarity; companionship.

مقاصد *maqāṣid* (A) *n.m.* (*plu.* of مقصد *maqṣad*) Objects; aims; purposes; attempts; enterprises; designs; wishes.

مقاطعہ *muqāṭa'ah* (A) *n.m.* Disconnection; separation; cutting off; detachment; strike; boycott.

مقال *maqāl* (A) *n.m.* A word; speech; discourse; a sentence; a saying; an adage; a proverb.

مقالہ *maqālah* (A) *n.m.* A book; an article; a treatise; a discourse.

مقام *maqām* (A) *n.m.* Dwelling; station; place; abode; a place of residence or encamping; a residence; mansion; site; situation; position; halt; occasion; opportunity; basis; dignity; a musical tune; halting of an army.

مقام کرنا *maqām karnā, v.* To halt ; to stay; to put up; to stop; to abide; to settle.

مقامی *maqāmī* (A) *adj.* Local; stationary; residing. *n.m.* A native; resident; local.

مقاومت *muqāwamat* (A) *n.f.* Resistance; opposition; competition.

مقبرہ *maqbarah* (A) *n.m.* A tomb; a mausoleum; sepulchre.

مقبوضہ *maqbūẓah* (A) *adj.* Seized; captured; possessed; occupied.

مقبول *maqbūl* (A) *adj.* Accepted; chosen; received; admitted; pleasing; grateful; taken in good part.

مقبولیت *maqbūliyat* (A) *n.f.* Acceptance; admission; agreeableness; agreement; popularity.

مقتدا *muqtadā* (A) *adj.* Followed; initiated; imitable. *n.m.* Leader.

مقتدر *muqtadir* (A) *adj.* Powerful; strong; able.

مقتدی *muqtadi* (A) *n.m.* A follower; an imitator.

مقتضا *muqtaẓā* (A) *n.m.* Demand; necessity; expediency; requisition; inclination, *adj.* Exacted; required; demanded.

مقتضی *muqtaẓi* (A) *adj.* Requiring; demanding; exacting; advisable; proper; necessary.

مقتل *maqtal* (A) *n.m.* A place of slaughter or of execution.

مقتول maqtūl (A) adj. Killed; slain, n.m. One who is slain.

مقدار miqdār (A) n.f. Quantity; magnitude; measure; size; dimension; space; number; amount; rate; term (of life).

مقدار متغیرہ miqdār-ĕ mutaghaiyyirah, n.f. A variable quantity.

مقدار مجہول miqdār-ĕ majhūl, n.f. An unknown quantity.

مقدار مرکب miqdār-ĕ murakkab, n.f. A compound quantity.

مقدار معروف miqdār-ĕ ma'rūf, n.f. A known quantity.

مقدار مقررہ miqdār-ĕ muqarrarah, n.f. A fixed amount or quantity; a constant quantity.

مقدار منفیہ miqdār-ĕ manfiyyah, n.f. A negative quantity.

مقدر muqaddar (A) n.m. Fate; destiny. adj. Predestined; ordained; destined by God.

مقدر آزمانا muqaddar āzmānā, v. To try one's luck.

مقدر برگشتہ ہونا muqaddar bargashtah honā, v. To be ill-starred; to be unlucky.

مقدر چمکنا muqaddar chamaknā, v. To be well-off; to be thriving; to be prosperous.

مقدرت maqdirat (A) n.f. Power; ability; capacity.

مقدس muqaddas (A) adj. Holy; consecrated; sanctified; hallowed.

مقدم muqaddam (A) adj. Antecedent; prior; preceding; first; superior; more important; chief; placed before. n.m. The advanced guard of an army; a chief; a leader: a village headman; an official of agriculture department; major premise of a syllogism.

مقدم جاننا ، سمجھنا muqaddam jānnā, samajhnā, v. To consider more important; to consider superior; to regard as preferable; to prefer.

مقدم رکھنا muqaddam rakhnā, v. To place first on the list; to give priority; to give preference.

مقدم ہونا muqaddam honā, v. To precede; to top the list; to be first; to be most binding; to stand before.

مقدم maqdam (A) n.m. Arrival; reception; a place to step in.

مقدمہ muqaddamah (A) n.m. The first part; preamble; preface; preliminary; introduction; proceedings; a law suit; a case; litigation; business; subject; affair; matter; thesis; (plu. مقدمات muqaddamāt).

مقدمۃالجیش muqaddamah-tul-jaish, n.m. Advanced guard of an army.

مقدمہ باز muqaddamah bāz, n.m. A litigant; a person engaged in law suits; contending at law; litigator.

مقدمہ بازی muqaddamah bāzī, n.f. Litigation.

مقدمہ قابل دست اندازی پولیس muqaddamah qābil-ĕ dast andāzī-ĕ polis, n.m. A cognizable case; a case capable of falling under judicial notice.

مقدور maqdūr (A) n.m. Power; means; resources; capacity; possibility; ability.

مقدور بھر ، تابہ مقدور، حتی المقدور maqdūr bhar, tā-bah maqdūr, hattal-maqdūr, adv. To the best of one's power or ability.

مقدور چلنا maqdūr chalnā, v. To exercise power or authority.

مقدور نہ رکھنا maqdūr nah rakhnā, v. To be unable to (do a thing).

مقدور ہونا maqdūr honā, v. To have power or ability.

مقر maqarr (A) n.m. Abode; residence; station; place of rest.

مقر muqir (A) adj. Confessing; professing; admitting; affirming; acknowledging. n.m. A confessor; a professor; an affirmer; one who fixes or establishes.

مقر ہونا muqir honā, v. To admit; to confess; to avow; to plead guilty.

مقراض miqrāẓ (A) n.f. Scissors; shears.

مقراضه miqrāzah (A) n.m. Snuffers; a kind of sweetmeat

مقرب muqarrab (A) adj. Admitted; approximate. n.m. A relative; an intimate friend; a favourite.

مقرب‌الخدمت، مقرب بارگه muqarrab-ul-khidmat, muqarrab-ĕ bārgāh, n.m. A personal and private servant.

مقرر muqarrar (A) adj. Established; fixed; ascertained; certain; infallible; unquestionable; appointed; employed; confirmed; determined; imposed; agreed upon; customary; permanent. adv. Assuredly; positively; certainly.

مقرر muqarrir (A) n.m. One who speaks; a speaker; a lecturer.

مقرره muqarrarah (A) adj. Fixed; prescribed; defined; usual; permanent; established.

مقروض maqrūẓ (A) adj. Cut; lent; burdened with debt; indebted. n.m. Debtor.

مقروق، مقروقه maqrūq, maqrūqah (A) adj. Seized; attached; mortgaged; confiscated.

مقرون maqrūn (A) adj. Near; connected; joined; contiguous; amounting to; related.

مقسوم maqsūm (A) adj. Divided; distributed; apportioned; allotted. n.m. A portion; fate; destiny; allotment; the dividend.

مقسوم علیه maqsūm 'alaih, n.m. The divisor.

مقسوم علیه اعظم maqsūm 'alaih a'ẕam, n.m. Greatest common measure.

مقسم muqassim (A) adj. Dividing; distributing; dispersing.

مقشر muqashshar (A) adj. Barked; skinned; peeled.

مقصد maqṣad (A) n.m. Intention; design; meaning; purpose; purport; object; aim; scope; desire; wish.

مقصد بر آنا maqṣad bar ānā, v. To attain one's object; to gain one's wish; to be successful in one's design.

مقصر muqaṣṣar (A) adj. Deficient; defective; falling (of).

مقصود maqṣūd (A) adj. Intended; proposed. n.m. Intent; design; object; aim; view.

مقصوره maqṣūrah (A) adj. Abridged; abbreviated; restricted; diminished; closely-guarded. n.m. The place where the imam stands when leading prayers.

مقطر muqaṯṯar (A) adj. Distilled; exuded in drops.

مقطر muqaṯṯir (A) adj. Distilling; dropping.

مقطع maqṯa' (A) n.m. The last verse of a poem (generally with nom de plume of the poet); abrupt breaking off; a place of separation; a pause; amputating.

مقطع muqaṯṯa' (A) adj. Cut; well-dressed; properly trimmed (as beard); serious; solemn; well-shaped.

مقطعات muqaṯṯa'āt (A) n.m. (plu. of مقطعه) Small forms of verse or small cuts of cloth.

مقعد maq'ad (A) n.m. A place to sit on; the hips; the anus.

مقفیٰ muqaffā (A) adj. Measured; rhythmical.

مقفل muqaffal (A) adj. Locked; bolted.

مقلب muqallib (A) adj. Turning; converting; changing.

مقلب‌القلوب muqallib-ul-qulūb, adj. Changer of intentions or hearts; God.

مقلب muqallab (A) adj. Counterfeited; imitated.

مقلد muqallid (A) n.m. A disciple; a follower.

غیر مقلد ghair muqallid, adj. Not following anybody; one of liberal and independent views.

مقلوب maqlūb (A) adj. Turned; inverted; converted; reversed; changed; reciprocal.

مقلوب مستوی maqlub-ĕ mustawi, n.m. A word or sentence which may be read forward or backward, as درد or داداد in Persian, madam in English; a palindrome, as Adam's first words to Eve "madam, I'm Adam."

مقناطیس maqnātis (GA) n.m. The magnet; a leadstone.

مقنن muqannin (A) n.m. A law-maker; a legislator.

مقوا ، مقوی muqawwa (A) n.m. Card board; paste-board.

مقولہ maqūlah (A) n.m. A maxim; a saying; an adage; a quotation; proverb; aphorism.

مقوی muqawwi (A) adj. Strengthening; invigorating.

مقوی باہ muqawwi-ĕ bāh, adj. An aphrodisiac.

مقوی دل muqawwi-ĕ dil, adj. Cardiac; cordial.

مقوی دماغ muqawwi-ĕ dimagh, adj. Cephalic; a cephalic medicine.

مقوی معدہ muqawwi-ĕ mi'dah, adj. A stomachic.

مقہور maqhūr (A) adj. Oppressed; vexed; disturbed; conquered; overcome.

مقیاس miqyās (A) n.m. A meter; a measuring instrument; the style of a dial; the hand of a watch; the nilometer (in Egypt); a gauge.

مقیاس الحرارت miqyās-ul-hararat, n.m. A thermometer.

مقیاس اللبن miqyās-ul-laban, n.m. A lectometer.

مقیاس الماء miyās-ul-mā'. n.m. Water-gauge; a hydrometer.

مقیاس الموسم miqyās-ul-mausim, n.m. Meteorograph.

مقیاس الہوا miqyās-ul-hawā, n.m. A barometer.

مقید muqaiyyad (A) adj. Fettered; confined; in chains; imprisoned; bound; shackled; strict; dedicated to; addicted; registered.

مقیش muqqaish, n.f. Brocade (gold or silver thread).

مقیشی muqqaishi, adj. Brocaded; embroidered.

مقیم muqim (A) adj. Residing; stationed; fixed.

مکا makka (H) n.f. See مکئی maka'i.

مکا mukka (H) n.m. A thump; a blow with the fist; buffet.

مکا (مکے) باز mukkā (mukke) bāz, n.m. A boxer.

مکا بازی mukkā bāzi, n.f. Boxing.

مکاتب makātib (A) n.m. (plu. of مکتب maktab) Schools; educational institutions.

مکاتیب makatib (A) n.m. (plu. of مکتوب maktub) Letters; epistles; written notes.

مکار makkar (A) adj. Cunning; artful; crafty; deceitful, a pretender.

مکارم makarim (A) n.m. (plu. of مکرمت makromat). Noble actions.

مکاری makkari (A) n.f. Fraud; deceitfulness; cheating; knavery; roguery; imposture; artifice.

مکاشفہ mukdshafah (A) n.m. Displaying; acting openly; disclosure; revelation.

مکافات mukāfat (A) n.f. Retribution; requital; recompense; retaliation; reparation.

مکافات کو پہنچنا mukāfat ko pahunchnā, v. To receive the deserved punishment; to suffer for one's misdeed.

مکالمہ mukālamah (A) n.m. Dialogue; colloquy; conversation between two or more persons; discourse.

مکان makān (A) n.m. A house; a dwelling; a lodging; home; abode; a place; a habitation.

مکت mukt (H) n.m. See مکتی mukti.

مکتب maktab (A) n.m. A school; an academy.

مکتبہ maktabah (A) n.m. A book depot; a book stall; library.

مکتفی muktafī (A) adj. Having enough; satisfied; content.

مکتوب maktūb (A) adj. Written. n.m. A letter; an epistle.

مکتوب الیہ maktūb ilaih, n.m. Addressee.

مکتوم maktūm (A) adj. Concealed; hidden.

مکتی muktī (H) n.f. Release; salvation; remission; pardon; absolution from sin; deliverance of the soul from body and exemption from further transmigration; liberation; acquittal.

مکٹ mukaṭ (H) n.m. A crown; a tiara; a crest.

مکدر mukaddar (A) adj. Turbid; muddy; sullen; gloomy; vexed; displeased; disturbed; troubled; afflicted; anxious.

مکر makr (A) n.m. Cheating; cunning; fraud; wile; artifice; pretence; imposture; disguise; design; plot; device; stratagem; skill in (military) movements; trick; dodge; deceit; evasion.

مکر کرنا makr karnā, v. To cheat; to pretend; to plot; to devise; to design; to deceive; to evade; to guard against a plot; to feign.

مکر makar (S) n.m. The sign Capricorn.

مکرر mukarrar (A) adv. Repeatedly; again; a second time.

مکرر آنکہ mukarrar āṅkih, adv. Post scriptum.

مکرم mukarram (A) adj. Venerable; noble; respected; revered; august; illustrious.

مکرمت makromat (A) n.f. Honour; glory; nobleness; respectability; generosity; grace; beneficence.

مکرمی mukarrami (A) (My dear sir); a mode of address in letters.

مکرنا mukarnā (H) v. To deny; to belie; to refuse to admit.

مکروہ makrūh (A) adj. Hated; odious; abhorred; abominable; detestable; disgusting; obscene; loathsome; unpleasant; unbecoming.

مکروہات makrūhāt (A) n.f. (plu. of مکروہ makrūh) Abominable things; things to be avoided; unpleasant things.

مکری ، مکرنی mukrī, mukarnī (H) n.f. A kind of riddle in short verse, so called from مکرنا mukarnā, to deny; (plu. مکرنیاں mukarniāṅ).

مکڑ ، مکڑا makkaṛ, makṛā (H) n.m. A large spider.

مکڑی makṛī (H) n.f. A spider.

مکڑی کا جالا makṛī kā jālā, n.m. A spider's web; a cob-web; anything very fine and slender.

مکسر mukassar (A) adj. Cubic; broken.

مکسور ، مکسورہ maksūr, maksūrah (A) adj. & n.m. A letter marked with the vowel زیر zer or کسرہ kasrah (-); a fraction (Arith.) adj. Broken; cut.

مکسوراعشاریہ maksūr-ĕ a'shāriyah n.m. A decimal fraction.

مکسورعام maksūr-ĕ 'ām, n.m. Vulgar fraction.

مکشوف makshūf (A) adj. Revealed; disclosed; discovered; open; detected.

مکعب muka'ab (A) adj. & n.m. Cubical; cube.

مکعب نما muka'ab numā, adj. & n.m. Cuboid; of a square or cubic form.

مکلاوہ muklāwah (H) n.m. Departure of the bride for the second time from her parent's home to the home of the bridegroom after marriage.

مکلف mukallaf (A) adj. Done with great pains and care; elaborate; elegant; exquisitely wrought; carefully executed.

مکلف *mukallif* (A) *adj.* Putting to inconvenience or trouble.

مکمل *mukammal* (A) *adj.* Perfect; complete; accomplished; fitted with every requisite.

مکنون *maknūn* (A) *adj.* Hidden; concealed.

مکو *mako* (H) *n.f.* The Cape gooseberry or Brazil cherry; a medicinal plant.

مکوڑا *makoṛā* (H) *n.m.* A large ant.

مکھ *mukh* (H) *n.m.* The mouth; the face.

مکھانا *makhānā* (H) *n.m.* The dried seed of water-lily.

مکھڑا *mukhṛā* (H) *n.m.* The face; the mouth.

مکھن *makhkhan* (H) *n.m.* Butter.

مکھنا *makhnā* (H) *n.m.* A kind of elephant having no tusks; a cock without spurs.

مکھی *makhkhī* (H) *n.f.* A fly; the sight of a gun.

مکھی آڑانا *makhkhi uṛānā*, *v.* To perform servile offices; to flatter; to have ulcers on the body; to be a good marksman.

مکھی پر مکھی مارنا *makhkhi par makhkhi mārnā*, *v.* To produce an exact copy; to copy blindly.

مکھی چوس *makhkhi chūs*, *n.m.* A miser; a niggard; a skin-flint.

مکھیاں بھنکنا *makhkhian bhinakna*, *v.* To be disgusting or dirty.

مکھیاں مارنا *makhkhian marna*, *v.* To sit idle; to be unemployed.

مکھیا *mukhyā* (A) *n.m.* A headman of the village.

مکئی ، مکی *maka'ī*, *makki* (H) *n.f.* Indian corn; maize.

مکی *mukkī* (H) *n.f.* A blow with the fist; a buffet.

مکیانا *mukyānā* (H) *v.* To give a blow; to beat a person with fists.

مکین *makīn* (A) *n.m.* Master of the house; resident; inhabitant.

مگدر *mugdar* (H) *n.m.* A mallet; a club to exercise with in the manner of dumb-bells.

مگر *magar* (P) *conj.* Unless; perhaps; except; if not; only; but; however; moreover.

مگر *magar* (H) *n.m.* An alligator; a crocodile.

مگرا ، مگری *magra magrī* (H) *adj.* Proud; haughty; cunning; crafty; insolent; cross; stubborn.

مگراپن *magra pan*, *n.m.* Obstinacy; stubborness; artifice.

مگس *magas* (P) *n.f.* A fly; a freckle.

مگس ران *magas ran*, *n.m.* A fly-flap.

مگس رانی *magas rānī*, *n.f.* Driving away flies; idleness; inactivity.

مگن *magan* (H) *adj.* Immersed; delighted; pleased; glad; happy; cheerful; joyful; overjoyed; plunged; dipped.

مگن ہونا *magan honā*, *v.* To be transported with joy.

مل *mul* (P) *n.f.* Wine; spirituous liquor.

مل *mall* (H) *n.m.* A wrestler; a boxer; a hero; a warrior.

ملا *mulla* (A) *n.m.* A doctor; a school master; a parish; priest; a judge; a jurist; a decoy bird. *adj.* Learned (in Persian and Arabic).

ملاء اعلی *mala-ē a'lā* (A) *n.m.* The band of angels or residents of the upper regions.

ملاپ *milāp* (H) *n.m.* Agreement; union; concord; peace; reconciliation; adjustment; meeting; pacification; mixing; combination; unity; interview; harmony.

ملا جلا *milā julā* (H) *adj.* United; in harmony.

ملاح *mallāḥ* (A) *n.m.* A boatman; a sailor; a mariner; a seaman; a manufacturer of salt.

ملاح کا لنگوٹا هی بهیگتا هے *mallāḥ kā langoṭā hī bhīgtā hai, prov.* A boatman wets nothing but his loin cloth; a poor man loses comparatively little.

ملاحت *malāḥat* (A) *n.f.* Saltiness; goodness; elegance; beauty; excellence; fineness; delicacy; a rich brown complexion; piquant look or appearance.

ملاحد ، ملاحده *malāḥid, malāḥadah* (A) *n.m.* (*plu.* of ملحد *mulḥid*) Infidels; atheists; heretics.

ملاحظه *mulāḥaẓah* (A) *n.m.* Looking into; contemplating; consideration; view; notice; regard; inspection.

ملاحظه کرنا *mulāḥaẓah karnā, v.* To inspect; to examine; to regard with favour; to look closely or attentively; to view; to heed.

ملاحی *mallāḥi* (A&P) *n.f.* Seamanship; navigation; boat fare; passage money; the profession of a boatman; rebuke; abuse; curse.

ملاحی سنانا *mallāḥī sunānā, v.* To curse; to abuse; to chide; to rebuke; to admonish.

ملار *malār* (H) *n.f.* A musical mode (sung during the rains).

ملار گانا *malār gānā, v.* To be merry.

ملازم *mulāzim* (A) *n.m.* A servant; an attendant.

ملازمت *mulāzamat*(A) *n.f.* Assiduity; diligence; service; duty; attendance; waiting on a superior; paying respects to a superior; employment.

ملازمت اختیار کرنا *mulāzamat ikhtiyār karnā, v.* To take service with; to enter the service of.

ملازمت پیشه *mulāzamat peshah, adj.* A servant by occupation or profession.

ملاطفت، ملاطفه *mulāṭafat, mulāṭafah* (A) *n.f./m.* Courtesy; politeness; favour; kindness.

ملاعین ، ملاعنه *malā'in, malā'inah* (A) *n.m.* (*plu.* of ملعون *mal'ūn*) Cursed persons; excommunicated; detestable persons.

ملاقات *mulāqāt* (A) *n.f.* Interview; meeting; visit; conversation; encountering.

ملاقات بازدید *mulāqāt-ĕ bāz dīd, n.f.* Return visit.

ملاقات رکهنا *mulāqāt rakhnā, v.* To be on visiting terms (with); to be friend (with).

ملاقات کرنا *mulāqāt karnā, v.* To pay a visit; to meet; to have an interview.

ملاقاتی *mulāqāti, n.m.* A visitor; an acquaintance.

ملاقی *mulāqi* (A) *adj.* Meeting; visiting.

ملاقی هونا *mulāqī honā, v.* To meet; to have interview with.

ملاگیر *malāgir* (H) *n.m.* The best sandal-wood; a mountain or mountain range from which the best sandal-wood is brought.

ملاگیری *malāgiri* (H) *adj.* Of the colour of sandal-wood.

ملال *malāl* (A) *n.m.* Sadness; grief; anguish; langour; vexation; dejection of mind; melancholy; fatigue; weariness; displeasure.

ملال آنا *malāl ānā, v.* To be seized with sadness; to be dejected; to be afflicted; to be grieved.

ملا لینا *milā lenā* (H) *v.* To draw over; to win over; to annex.

ملامت *malāmat* (A) *n.f.* Reproach; rebuke; reproof; blame; accusation; reviling; reprehension.

ملامت کرنا *malāmat karnā, v.* To rebuke; to reprove.

ملامتی *malāmati* (A) *adj.* Reproached; reprehensible; blamable.

ملانا milānā (H) v. To mix; to blend; to bring together; to join; to unite; to harmonise; to adjust; to compare; to reconcile; to assimilate, to make partisans of; to act as a pimp.

ملاوٹ milāwaṭ (H) n.f. Agreement; concord; harmony; adultration.

ملائک، ملائکہ malā'ik, malā'ikah (A) n.m. (plu. of ملک malak). Angels.

ملائم mulā'im (A) adj. Soft; tender; gentle; mild; affable; placid; moderate; calm.

ملائمت mulā'amat (A) n.f. Softness; tenderness; gentleness; mildness; meekness; moderation.

ملائی malā'i (H) n.f. Cream; rubbing down a horse; price paid for rubbing.

ملبا malbā (H) n.m. Rubbish; dirt; debris.

مل بانٹ کے mil bānṭ ke (H) adv. Conjointly; by mutual agreement.

ملبوس malbūs (A) adj. Clothed; in ordinary wear. n.m. Clothes; garment; suit; wearing apparel.

مل بیٹھنا mil baiṭhnā (H) v. To live together in harmony.

ملت millat (A) n.f. Religion; belief; faith; nation.

ملت millat (H) n.f. Society; friendship.

ملت کا آدمی millat kā ādami, adj. Familiar; friendly; sociable.

ملتانی multāni (H) n.f. Name of a راگنی rāgnī or musical mode. adj. Of Multan.

ملتانی مٹی multānī matṭi, n.f. Armenian bole.

ملتجی multaji (A) adj. Fleeing (to); taking refuge with; having recourse (to). n.m. Supplicant; a petitioner.

ملتزم multazim (A) adj. Compelled; convicted; constrained; necessarily following. n.m. A toll gatherer.

ملتفت multafit (A) adj. Paying regard to; showing respect to; turning the head to look at; inclined towards; having regard.

ملتمس multamis (A) adj. Beseeching; requesting. n.m. A petitioner; an applicant.

ملتوی multawi (A) adj. Postponed; adjourned; delayed; pending; bent; crooked; spinning out; protracted.

ملتوی رکھنا، کرنا multawī rakhnā, karnā, v. To put off; to postpone.

ملٹھی mulaṭhı. See ملیٹھی muleṭhı.

ملجا maljā (A) n.m. An asylum; a retreat; place of refuge.

مل جانا mil jānā (H) v. To come together; to unite; to mix up; to be obtained or found.

مل جل کر mii jul kar (H) adv. Unitedly; jointly; mutually.

ملح milḥ (A) n.m. Salt; saltpetre; beauty; agreeableness.

ملحد mulḥid (A) n.m. A heretic; an infidel; an unbeliever; a free thinker; an apostate; athiest.

ملحق، ملحقہ mulḥaq, mulḥaqah (A) adj. Joined; added; annexed; adhering; adjunct.

ملحق ہونا mulḥaq honā, v. To be annexed; to be contiguous; to be adjoining (to).

ملحوظ malḥūẓ (A) adj. Contemplated; considered; regarded; viewed with affection.

ملخ malakh (P) n.m. Locust; propeller.

ملخص mulakhkhaṣ (A) n.m. Abstract; epitome.

ملذذ mulazẕaẕ (A) adj. Delicious.

ملزم mulzam (A) adj. Convicted; confuted; blamable. n.m. An accused; a convict.

ملزوم malzūm (A) adj. Inseparable; belonging to; affixed; necessitated.

ملعون *mal'ūn* (A) *adj.* Cursed· accused; execrated; excommunicated; driven out of society.

ملغوبا *malghūbā* (T) *n.m.* Emitting saliva; entrails; rubbish; a heap of broken things; filth; purulent matter; a thick infusion; foulness; contamination.

ملفوظ *malfūz* (A) *n.m.* Saying of a spiritual guide; that which is spoken or expressed (by); annals; (*plu.* ملفوظات *malfūzāt*).

ملفوف *malfūf* (A) *adj.* Wrapped up; enveloped; enclosed; collected; gathered; involved; folded.

ملقب *mulaqqab* (A) *adj.* Entitled; surnamed; nicknamed.

ملک *malak* (A) *n.m.* An angel; a divine messenger.

ملک‌الموت *malak-ul-maut, n.m.* The angel of death.

ملک *malik* (A) *n.m.* A king; a sovereign; a monarch.

ملک‌التجار *malik-ut-tujjār, n.m.* A great merchant; a merchant prince.

ملک‌الشعرا *malik-ush-shu'arā, n.m.* A prince among poets, a poet-laureate.

ملک *mulk* (A) *n.m.* A country; realm; region; territory; dominion.

ملک بدر *mulk badar, adj.* Banished; exiled; turned out of one's country.

ملک گری *mulk giri, n.f.* Conquest; annexation.

ملک *milk* (A) *n.f.* Property; possession; dominion; right; landed property; rent free land.

ملکات *malakāt* (A) *n.m.* (*plu.* of ملکہ *malakah*) Qualities; endowments.

ملکات ردیہ *malakāt-ĕ raddiyyah, n.m.* Pernicious qualities which are: ضد *zid*, persistence; بغض *bughz*, malice; بخل *bukhl*, niggardliness; بے حیائی *be hayā'ī*, shamelessness; حرص *hirs*, greed; غضب *ghazab*, wrath; کذب *kizb*, lying; کبر *kibr*, arrogance.

ملکات فاضلہ *malakāt-ĕ fāzilah, n.m.* Good qualities which are حکمت *hikmat*, wisdom; شجاعت *shujā'at*, valour; عفت *'iffat*, chastity; عدالت *'adālat*, justice.

ملکوت *malakūt* (A) *n.m.* The world of angels; empire; dominion.

ملکوتی *malakūti* (A) *adj.* Angelic; spiritual.

ملکہ *malikah* (A) *n.f.* A queen.

ملکہ *malakah* (A) *n.m.* Quickness of perception; strength of intellect; power; genius; proficiency.

ملکہ ہونا *malakah honā, v.* To be efficient; to be quick to perceive.

ملکی *mulki* (A) *adj.* National; political; civil; imperial, royal; belonging to one's country; indigenous.

ملکی *milki* (A) *n.m.* A farmer; a landlord. *adj.* Proprietory.

ملکیت *milkiyyat* (A) *n.f.* See ملک *milk*.

ملگجا ، ملگجی *malgajā, malgaji* (H) *adj.* Black and blue; brackish.

ملل *milal* (A) *n.f.* (*plu.* of ملت *millat*) Nations; religions.

ملمع *mulamma'* (A) *adj.* Plated; covered with gold or silver; bright; gilt; electroplated.

ملمع ساز ، گر *mulamma' sāz, gar, n.m.* A gilder; a plater, a dissembler; a hypocrite.

ملمع سازی *mulamma' sāzi, n.f.* Gilding; coating; plating; speciousness; imposition.

ململ *malmal* (H) *n.f.* Muslin.

ملن *milan* (H) *n.m.* Meeting; relationship; association.

ملن سار *milan sār, adj.* Civil; affable; sociable; friendly; familiar; convivial.

ملن ساری milan sārī, n.f. Affability; sociableness.

ملنا milnā (H) v. To be mixed, mingled or amalgamated; to be joined; to be blended; to meet; to embrace; to associate with; to have an interview with; to be reconciled to; to tally; to suit; to coincide; to resemble; to come to hand.

ملنا جلنا milnā julnā, v. To meet cordially; to have unrestricted intercourse with. n.m. Intimacy; association.

ملنا malnā (H) v. To tread on; to trample on; to rub.

ملنگ malang (H) n.m. A kind of Muslim dervish, who keeps long hair and leaves them uncombed; a dervish in ecstasy; a careless and inconsiderate person.

ملنی milnī (H) n.f. Meeting; reception; reception of the marriage procession at the bride's house.

ملوانا milwānā (H) v. To cause to be joined or united; to cause to be reconciled.

ملوانا malwānā (H) v. To cause to rub.

ملوث mulawwaṣ (A) adj. Polluted; contaminated; befouled.

ملوک mulūk (A) n.m. (plu. of ملک malik) Kings.

ملول malūl (A) adj. Sad; dejected; melancholy; tired; weary; languid; vexed; bored; depressed; grieved; fatigued; affected.

ملہار malhār (H) n.f. See ملار malār.

ملہم mulhim (A) adj. Inspiring; inspirer.

ملہم mulham (A) adj. Inspired.

ملی millī (A) adj. National.

ملی بھگت milī bhagat (H) n.f. Plot; conspiracy.

ملیٹھی maleṭṭhī (H) n.f. A medical root; liquorice.

ملیچھ malichh (H) n.m. An unclean person or race; an infidel; a miscreant.

ملیح malīh (A) adj. Salty; nut brown; of dark brown colour; agreeable; sweet; charming; beautiful; graceful.

ملیدہ malīdah (P) n.m. Pounded meal cakes mixed with butter and sugar; a kind of fine woollen cloth made of Kashmir lamb's wool.

ملین mulaiyyin (A) adj. Softening; emollient; laxative; lenitive; aperient; mollifier.

ممات mamāt (A) n.f. Death.

مماثل mumāṣil (A) adj. Similar; alike.

مماثلت mumāṣalat (A) n.f. Similarity; resemblance.

ممارست mumārasat (A) n.f. Practice; experience.

مماس mamās (A) n.m. Place of contact; tangent.

مماست mumāsat (A) n.f. Touch; contact.

ممالک mamālik (A) n.m. (plu. of مملکت mamlukat) Countries; states; provinces; dominions; kingdoms.

ممالک غیر mamālik-ĕ ghair, n.m. Foreign countries.

ممالک محروسہ mamālik-ĕ mahrūsah, n.m. Protected states.

ممالک مفوضہ mamālik-ĕ mufawwazah, n.m. Ceded provinces.

ممالیک mamālīk (A) n.m. (plu. of مملوک mamlūk) Possessions; slaves.

ممانعت mumāna'at (A) n.f. Prohibition; hindrance.

ممانعت کرنا mumāna'at karnā, v. To prohibit; to forbid.

ممانی mumānī, n.f. Maternal aunt; wife of the mother's brother.

ممتا mamtā (S) n.f. Affection; egotism; pride; arrogance; avarice.

ممتاز mumtāz (A) adj. Exalted; distinguished; illustrious; eminent; chosen.

ممتحن mumtaḥin (A) n.m. An examiner; a tester.

ممتد mumtadd (A) adj. Extended; prolonged; continued.

ممتنع mumtana' (A) adj. Prohibited; forbidden; impossible.

ممثل mumaṣṣil (A) n.m. Actor; a stage player.

ممثله mumaṣṣilah (A) n.f. Actress.

ممد mumidd (A) adj. Helper; protector.

ممدوح ' ممدوحه mamdūḥ, mamdūḥah (A) adj. Praised; lauded; celebrated.

ممدود ' ممدوده mamdūd, mamdūdah (A) adj. Extended; prolonged.

ممزوج mamzūj (A) adj. Mixed; tampered.

ممسک mumsik (A) adj. Miser; niggard; retentive; stingy.

ممکن mumkin (A) adj. Possible; practicable; feasible.

ممکن الحصول mumkin-ul-ḥuṣūl, adj. Procurable; obtainable.

ممکن الدخول mumkin-ud-dukhūl, adj. Accessible.

ممکن الوجود mumkin-ul-wujūd, adj. Liable to exist.

ممکن الوقوع mumkin-ul-wuqū', adj. Liable to happen.

ممکنات mumkināt (A) n.f. (plu of ممکن mumkin) Possibilities.

مملکت mamlakat, mamlukat (A) n.f. Sovereignty; do minion; country; region; kingdom; grandeur; empire.

مملو mamlū (A) adj. Filled; full.

مملوک mamlūk (A) adj. Possessed; in one's power. n.m. A purchased slave or captive.

مملوکه mamlūkah (A) adj. Possessed; purchased.

مملوکه و مقبوضه mamlukah-ŏ maqbūẓah, adj. Owned and possessed (by).

ممنوع ' ممنوعه mamnū', mamnū'ah (A) adj. Forbidden; prohibited; illicit, contraband; out of bounds.

ممنون mamnūn (A) adj. Obliged; favoured; thankful; grateful.

ممولا mamolā (H) n.m. A wagtail.

ممیا ساس mamiyā sās, n.f. Husband or wife's maternal aunt.

ممیا سسر mamiyā susar, n.m. Husband or wife's maternal uncle.

ممیانا mimiyānā (H) v. To bleat.

ممیرا ' ممیری mamerā, mamerī, adj. Relating to the maternal uncle.

ممیرا mamirā, n.m. (corr. of مامیراں māmirāṅ) A medicine useful for eyesight.

ممیز ' ممیزه mumaiyiz, mumaiyizah (A) adj Distinguishing; discriminating; separating.

من man (H) n.m. Mind; heart; soul; inclination; spirit; conscience; attention; intellect; understanding; will; purpose; character; disposition; temper; a maund; forty seers; a gem; a precious stone (said to be found in the head of a snake).

من اٹکنا man aṭaknā, v. To fall in love with.

من اٹھنا man uṭhnā, v. To be estranged; to be tired (of).

من اکتانا ' اکتا جانا man uktānā, uktā jānā, v. To be tired or sick of; to be fed up (with).

من بھاتا man bhātā, adj. Liked; agreeable to the mind; pleasing to the mind.

من بھاتا کھاجا man bhātā khājā, n.m. Desired food; cherished food.

من بھاری کرنا ' برا کرنا man bhārī karnā, burā karnā, v. To grieve over, to be displeased.

من بهر man bhar, adj. To one's satisfaction; as much as one desires; about one maund.

من بهر جانا man bhar jānā, v. To be satisfied; to be sated.

من بہلانا man bahlānā, v. To amuse oneself with; to divert the mind.

من چلا ، من چلی man chalā, man chalī, adj. Assiduous; intent, eager; zealous; bold; brave; courageous; generous; liberal; distracted.

من سمجھوتی man samjhautī, n.f. Comforting or consoling oneself; submission; resignation.

من کا کپٹی ،کھوٹا ، میلا man kā kapṭī khoṭā, mailā, adj. Of bad or evil mind; deceitful; crafty; cunning.

من کچا کرنا man kachchā karnā, v. To lose heart; to droop; to break the heart (of another).

من کرنا man karnā, v. To desire; to wish.

من کھٹا ہونا man khaṭṭā honā, v. To be offended; to be displeased.

من کے لڈو پھوڑنا man ke laḍḍū phoṛnā, v. To build castles in the air.

من کی مَن میں رهنا man kī man meṅ rahnā, v. Remaining of desire unsatisfied.

من لگنا man lagnā, v. To have the heart set upon; to take delight in.

من للچانا man lalchānā, v. To long for; to hanker after.

من مار کے بیٹھ رهنا ، مار رهنا man mār ke baiṭh rahnā, mār rahnā, v. To suppress one's desire and remain quiet, to suffer grief with patience; to suffer grief or loss with patience.

من مارنا man mārnā, v. To repress desire; to restrain oneself, to abstain; to be grieved or troubled in mind; to resist one's own inclination; to suffer patiently.

من مانی man mānī, n.f. Heart's desire; according to one's wish; self-will; wilfulness.

من مانی کرنا man mānī karnā, v. To do as one likes; to be head-strong; to act according to one's wishes.

من ملنا man milnā, v. To be at one (with); to be of the same mind as another; to be in full agreement (with).

من موجی man maujī, adj. Conceited; full of conceit: fanciful; capricious; whimsical; merry; jovial.

من موہ لینا man moh lenā, v. To captivate; to fascinate; to charm.

من موهن man mohan, adj. Fascinating; captivating; charming; delighting. n.m. Sweetheart; beloved.

من میں man meṅ, adv. In or into the mind.

من میں آنا man meṅ ānā, v. To enter the mind; to occur; to commend itself to; to find a place in the heart.

من هی من میں man hī man meṅ, adv. In one's heart of hearts.

من mann (A) n.m. Manna; favour; kindness; good offices; beneficence.

من و سلوئ maun-ŏ salvā n.m. Manna and quails (with which the Israelites were fed in the wilderness).

من man (P) pron. I; me; mine.

من mim (A) prep. From; of; out of; on.

من بعد mim ba'd, adv. After; hereafter; afterwards.

من اوله الی آخره min awwalihi ila ākhirihī, adv. From beginning to end.

منجانب min jānib, adv. Form (theside of); by.

من جانب الله min jānib illah, adv. From God.

من جمله min jumlah, adv. From among; in all; totally.

من و عن min-ŏ 'an, adv. As it was; to the very letter; circumstantially.

منا munnā (H) n.m. Darling; pear; pet.

منابر manābir (A) n.m. (plu. of منبر mimbar). Pulpits.

مناجات munājāt (A) n.f. Prayer; supplication; hymns.

مناجات پڑھنا munājāt paṛhnā, v. To sing hymns; to implore God; to supplicate.

منادی munādi (A) n.m. A proclaimer; herald; crier.

منادی manādi, n.f. A proclamation.

منادی کرنا manādi karnā, v. To proclaim; to promulgate.

منار ، مناره manār, manārah (A) n.m. A minaret; a turret; a watch-tower; a light-house.

منازعت munāz'at (A) n.f. Contest; controversy; litigation; altercation.

منازل manāzil (A) n.f. (plu. of منزل manzil) Stages; resting places; rest houses.

منازل قمر manāzil-ĕ qamar, n.f. Mansions of the moon; phases of the moon.

مناسب munāsib (A) adj. Proper; suitable; becoming; fit; convenient; meet; expedient; pertinent; congruous; correspondent; apposite.

مناسبت munāsabat (A) n.f. Suitability; fitness; expediency; consistency; relevancy; analogy; comparison; proportion; connection; relation.

مناسک manāsik (A) n.m. (plu. of منسک mansak) Rites or ceremonies performed by pilgrims at Mecca; the places where the pilgrims perform their duties.

مناصب manāṣib (A) n.m. (plu. of منصب manṣab) Posts; ranks; offices.

مناظر munāẓir (A) n.m. A critic; an arguer; a disputant.

مناظر manāẓir (A) n.m. (plu. of منظر manẓar) Views; scenes; phenomena.

مناظر قدرت manāẓir-ĕ qudrat, n.m. Natural sceneries; natural phenomena.

مناظره munāẓarah (A) n.m. Disputation; dispute; contest; discussion; argumentation; argument; debate; inspection.

منافرت munāfarat (A) n.f. Disgust; detestation; hatred; contempt.

منافع manāfi' (A) n.m. (plu. of منفعت manfa'at) Profits; advantages; gains.

منافق munāfiq (A) n.m. An infidel; a hypocrite; an atheist; an enemy at heart; a dissembler.

منافقت munāfaqat (A) n.f. Hypocrisy; false profession; pretence; dissimulation; show; affectation.

منافی munāfi (A) adj. Contrary; negative; prohibitory; against; opposite of.

مناقب manāqib (A) n.f. (plu. of منقبت manqabat) Virtues; abilities; praises.

مناقبت munāqabat (A) n.f. Virtue; ability; praise.

مناقشه munāqashah (A) n.m. Contention; dispute; wrangling.

مناکحت munākaḥat (A) n.f. Marriage contract.

منال manāl (A) n.m. Profit; manner; way; disposition; gain; ways or means of gain; place of gain; mode; substance.

منان mannān (A) n.m. A great benefactor; God.

منانا manānā (H) v. To persuade; to conciliate; to propitiate; to coax; to assuage; to bring round; to appease; to prevail upon; to celebrate.

مناهج manāhij (A) n.m. (plu. of منهج manhaj) Highways; roads; routes.

مناهی manāhi (A) n.f. (plu. of منهی manhi) Prohibited things; prohibitions.

منبت munabbat (A) adj. Inlaid; embossed.

منبت کاری munabbat kāri, n.f. Inlaying; embossing.

منبر mimbar (A) n.m. A pulpit; a rosturm; a high chair; a reading desk.

منبع *mamba'* (A) *n.m.* Source; fountain; spring; origin.

منت *minnat* (A) *n.f.* Humble and earnest supplication; entreaty; obligation; kindness.

منت آٹھانا *minnat uthānā*, *v.* To be under obligation.

منت پذیر *minnat pazir*, *adj.* Acknowldging or confessing kindness.

منت کرنا *minnat karnā*, *v.* To beg; to make earnest supplication.

منت کش *minnat kash*, *adj.* Under obligation; obliged.

منت *mannat* (H) *n.f.* Acknowledgment; a vow; a promise.

منت چڑھانا *mannat charhānā*, *v.* To fulfil a vow.

منت ماننا *mannat mānnā*, *v.* To make a vow.

منتج *muntaj* (A) *adj.* Deduced; inferred; concluded. *n.m.* Consequence; result; inference; conclusion.

منتخب *muntakhab* (A) *adj.* Chosen; selected.

منتخب کرنا *muntakhab karnā*, *v.* To choose; to select; to elect.

منتخب ہونا *muntakhab honā*, *v.* To be chosen; to be selected or elected.

منتر *mantar* (H) *n.m.* A spell; a charm; an incantation; a mystical or magical formula; spiritual instruction; a holy text; an advice; a passage of the Vedas.

منتر پڑھنا *mantar parhnā* *v.* To recite a passage of the Vedas; to enchant.

منتر پھونکنا *mantar phūnknā*, *v.* To cast a spell.

منتر جنتر *mantar jantar*, *n.m.* Incantation; exorcism; sorcery.

منتری *mantari* (H) *n.m.* An adviser; a counsellor; a minister of state; an enchanter.

منتشر *muntashir* (A) *adj.* Published; disorderly; divulged; dispersed; diffused; distracted; propagated; issued.

منتظر *muntazir* (A) *adj.* Looking out for; waiting for; expecting with impatience; waiting.

منتظر *muntazar* (A) *adj.* Awaited; expected.

منتظم *muntazim* (A) *n.m.* A manager; a superintendent.

منتفع *muntafi* (A) *adj.* Profiting; enjoying; gaining.

منتقل *muntaqal* (A) *adj.* Transported; carried; transferred.

منتقل کرنا *muntaqal karnā*, *v.* To transfer; to alienate; to negotiate (a bill after acceptance).

منتقم *muntaqim* (A) *adj.* Taking revenge; avenging; avenger.

منتقم حقیقی *muntaqim-ĕ haqiqi*, *n.m.* The real avenger; God.

منتقم مجازی *muntaqim-ĕ majāzī*, *n.m.* Punishing authority; officer; king.

منتہیٰ *muntahā* (A) *n.m.* The end; conclusion; extremity; boundary; climax.

منتہی *muntahi* (A) *adj.* Learned; accomplished; proficient; finished.

منثور *mansūr* (A) *n.m.* An unbored pearl; prose. *adj.* Scattered.

منجذب *munjazib* (A) *adj.* What can be absorbed.

منجلاب *manjalāb* (P) *n.m.* A sewer; a sink; a cesspool.

منجم *munajjim* (A) *n.m.* An astronomer; an astrologer; an almanac-maker.

منجمد *munjamid* (A) *adj.* Congealed; frozen: concreted; solid.

منجن *manjan* (H) *n.m.* Tooth-powder; dentifrice; cleaning the person (by wiping, bathing or rubbing it with oil or fragrant unguents).

منجنا ' منجهنا *mańjnā, mańjhnā* (H) *v.* To be polished; to be cleaned; to be trained.

منجنيق *mańjaniq* (A) *n.m.* A battering-ram; a catapult; a sling; a large crane.

منجھ *mańjh* (H) *n.m.* Middle.

منجھ دھار *mańjh dhār, n.f.* Mid-stream.

منجھلا ' منجھلی *mańjhlā, mańjhli* (H) *adj.* Intermediate; middle; between the eldest and the youngest.

منحرف *munḥarif* (A) *adj.* Changed; turned; disaffected; crooked; inverted; declining or turning from.

منحرف ہونا *munḥarif honā, v.* To revolt; to be disaffected; to rebel (against).

منحصر *munḥaṣir* (A) *adj.* Surrounded; besieged; restricted; dependent on; resting on.

منحنی *munḥani* (A) *adj.* Lean; thin; flexible; crooked; bent; curved; decrepit; humpbacked.

منحوس *manḥūs* (A) *adj.* ill-omened; unlucky; unfortunate; abominable; bad; dismal.

مند *mańd* (A) A suffix signifying *full of*, as دولت مند *daulat mańd*, wealthy; عقل مند *'aql mańd*, wise; سودمند *sūd mańd*, profitable.

مندا *mańdā* (H) *adj.* Abated; dull; mild; gentle; little, alloyed; low tone; cheap; slow; affable; tardy.

مندا ہونا *mańdā honā, v.* To be cheap; to fall down in price; to be dull (market); to be slow; to go down.

مندر *mandar, mandir* (H) *n.m.* A house; a temple; a pagoda.

مندرا *mundra* (H) *n.m.* A ring; a collar.

مندرج ' مندرجه *mundarij, mundarijah* (A) *adj.* Contained; inserted; comprised; included; comprehending; containing.

مندرجه ذیل *mundarijah zail, adv.* As under; as stated below; as follows.

مندری *mundri* (H) *n.f.* A ring; a finger-ring.

مندنا *mundnā* (H) *v.* To be shut; to be closed.

مندمل *mundamil* (A) *adj.* Healing up.

مندوب *mandūb* (A) *n.m.* A delegate.

مندیل *mindil* (A) *n.f.* A napkin; a towel; a turban woven with silk and gold thread; a table cloth.

منڈ *muńd* (H) *n.m.* The head; a chief; a headman. *adj.* Blunt; dull; leafless.

منڈا *muńḍḍā* (H) *n.m.* A kind of shoe; a branchless and leafless tree. *adj.* Shaven; bald; uncovered; harmless; not pointed (shoe).

منڈاسا *muńḍāsa* (H) *n.m.* A kind of small turban.

منڈانا *muńḍānā* (H) *v.* To get oneself shaven.

منڈائی *muńḍā'i* (H) *n.f.* Wages for shaving.

منڈپ *mańḍap* (S) *n.m.* A temporary building or shed; a temple.

منڈل *mańḍal* (H) *n.m.* A circle; circumference; sphere; orb; disc (of the sun or moon); halo; a round tent or house; the sky; an officer employed in village; excise-man; the headman of a village.

منڈلانا *mańḍlānā* (H) *v.* To make a circuit; to hover (as birds or clouds); to move about near.

منڈلی *mańḍali, mańdlī* (H) *n.f.* An assembly; a company; a congregation, a flock; a church; a sect; corporation.

منڈن *munḍan* (H) *n.m.* Shaving the head; the first shaving ceremony of a child.

منڈنا *munḍnā* (H) *v.* To be shaved; to be swindled.

منڈوا *mańḍwā* (H) *n.m.* A bower; a shed; an arbour; a house of entertainment; a theatre; a kind of small grain.

منڈوانا muṅḍwānā (H) v. To cause to be shaved; to get oneself shaven; to cause to be swindled.

منڈھا manḍhā (H) n.m. A temporary building or shed; an open shed or hall adorned with flowers; a shed erected on festive occasions; a nuptial bower.

منڈھنا manḍhnā (H) v. To cover with parchment; to coat over; to encase; to impose.

منڈی manḍī (H) n.f. A market; a mart; an emporium; a particular market for any one thing.

منڈی munḍḍī (H) n.f. Name of a medicinal plant; head; extremity; adj. Shaven.

منڈیر ، منڈیری muṅḍer, muṅderi (H) n.f. The caping of a wall; the ridge of a wall.

منزل manzil (A) n.f. A day's journey; a stage; destination; a storey of a house; lodging; house; a hotel; a sarai.

منزل بہ منزل manzil bah manzil, adv. From stage to stage; by stages.

منزل پر پہنچانا manzil par pahuṅchānā, v. To take to destination; to convey one to his last resting place; to perform the obsequies of.

منزل طے کرنا ، منزل کاٹنا manzil ṭai karnā, manzil kāṭnā, v. To complete journey; to reach the journey's end; to get over a stage.

منزل کٹنا manzil kaṭnā, v. To complete journey.

منزل کرنا manzil karnā, v. To halt; to go one stage in a journey.

منزل کو پہنچنا manzil ko pahūṅchnā, v. To gain one's object, to reach one's destination.

منزل کھوٹی ہونا manzil khoṭi honā, v. To be getting late for one's destination.

منزل مارنا manzil mārnā, v. To take journey; to solve a difficulty; to finish a difficult task.

منزل مقصود manzil-ĕ maqsūd, n.f. Destination; the goal.

منزل munzal (A) adj. Sent down; caused to descend, discharged (sexual intercourse).

منزل munazzal (A) adj. Sent down.

منزلت manzilat (A) n.f. Dignity; rank; station; step; post of honour; condition.

منزلہ manzilah (A) n.m. Dignity; station; a storey of a house.

بمنزلہ ba manzilah, adv. In the degree or position (of); in the place of; instead (of); as.

منزہ munazzah (A) adj. Kept apart from all impurities; pure; blameless; holy; exempted from; free.

منسلک ، منسلکہ munsalik, munsalikah (A) adj. Threaded; strung together; attached; annexed; appended. joined; connected.

منسوب ، منسوبہ mansūb, mansūbah (A) adj. Related; allied; betrothed; attributed; surnamed; referred to; belonging to.

منسوخ mansūkh (A) adj. Cancelled; obliterated; abolished: annulled; erased; broken; repealed; abrogated.

منسوخی mansūkhi (A&P) n.f. Abolition; cancellation.

منش manush (H) n.m. Man.

منش manish (P) n.f. Mind; soul; heart; greatness of soul; magnaminity; gravity; temperament; cheerfulness; arrogance; pride.

منشاء manshā' (A) n.m. Allusion; origin; principle source; beginning; intention; design; tenor; object; meaning; motive; purport.

منشور manshūr (A) n.m. A royal mandate; a diploma; a charter; potent; prism. adj. Divulged; published.

منشور مثلثی manshūr-ĕ muṣallaṣi, n.m. Triangular prism.

منشی *munshi* (A) *n.m.* A writer; a scrivener; a Persian teacher; a title of respect; a secretary; a clerk; amanuensis; a tutor; a language master.

منشی خانہ *munshi khanah*, *n.m.* Vernacular office.

منشی فلک *munshi-ĕ falak*, *n.m.* The planet Mercury.

منشی گری *munshi gari*, *n.f.* Clerkship; teachership; secretaryship.

منشیانہ *munshiyānah*, *adj.* Clerk-like; clerical. *n.m.* Fee of a clerk.

منصب *manṣab* (A) *n.m.* Dignity; office; post; station.

منصب دار *manṣab dār*, *n.m.* An officer or official of rank; a functionary; a magistrate.

منصب سرکاری *manṣab-ĕ sarkāri*, *n.m.* A government post; an official position.

منصرف *munṣarif* (A) *adj.* Turned back; converted; deviating; rebellious; (in *Gram.*) inflected; declined.

منصرم *munṣarim* (A) *n.m.* A manager: an administrator; a head clerk of a settlement or other important court.

منصف *munṣif* (A) *n.m.* A judge; a subordinate judge; an arbitrator. *adj.* Equitable; just; fair.

منصف مزاج *munṣif mizāj*, *adj.* Just; fair; upright; discreet, just minded; just in temperament.

منصفانہ *munṣifānah* (A) *adv.* Equitably; justly; fairly; candidly.

منصفی *munṣifi* (A) *n.f.* Justice; equity; a *munṣif's* court or office; arbitration; judgment; decision.

منصوب *manṣūb* (A) *adj.* Appointed; nominated; constituted; erected; fixed; established; marked with the vowel point نصب *naṣb*; set up; determined.

منصوبہ *manṣūbah* (A) *n.m.* Contrivance; project; scheme; plan; design; determination; intention; will; desire.

منصوبہ باز *manṣūbah baz*, *adj.* Foreseeing; prudent; designing; conspiring; planning; plotting; aspiring; scheming.

منصوبہ باندھنا *manṣūbah bandhna*, *v.* To resolve; to contrive; to conspire; to determine; to plan.

منصوبہ بندی *manṣūbah bandı*, *n.f.* Planning.

منصور *manṣur* (A) *adj.* Aided; protected; defended; victorious; conquering; triumphant; succoured.

منصه *manaṣṣɔh* (A) *n.m.* The tent or chamber of the bride; place of exhibition; a bedstead with curtains.

منصه شهود *manaṣṣɔh-ĕ shuhūd*, *n.m.* Place of exhibition of evidences.

منطبق *munṭabiq* (A) *adj.* Coinciding (with); conforming (to); fitting.

منطق *manṭiq*, *manṭaq* (A) *n.f.* Logic; oration; reasoning.

منطق چھانٹنا ، بگھارنا *manṭiq chhānṭna*, *bagharnā*, *v.* To chop logic.

منطقه *minṭaqah* (A) *n.m.* A zone; a belt; a girdle.

منطقة البروج *minṭaqa-tul-burūj*, *n.m.* The zodiac.

منطقه بارده *minṭaqah-ĕ bāridah*, *n.m.* The frigid zone.

منطقه حاره *minṭaqah-ĕ ḥarrah*, *n.m.* The torrid zone.

منطقه معتدله *minṭaqah-ĕ muʻtadilah*, *n.m.* The temperate zone.

منطقی *manṭiqi* (P) *adj.* Logical; dialectic. *n.m.* A logician.

منظر *manzar* (A) *n.m.* Countenance; face; visage, aspect; a sight; spactacle; theatre: a landscape; a scene.

منظر عام manẕar-ĕ 'ām, n.m. A conspicuous place or object.

منظم munnazzam (A) adj. Regular; annexed; added; strung; fixed; arranged.

منظور manẕūr (A) adj. Admired; chosen; approved of; admitted; accepted; sanctioned; granted; agreeable; designed; intended; seen; looked at; visible.

منظور خاطر manẕūr-ĕ khāṭir, adj. Desired; accepted; chosen; admitted.

منظور نظر manẕūr-ĕ naẕar, adj. Agreeable to the sight of; chosen; approved; a favourite; an object of regard or affection; a beloved object; a sweetheart; a mistress.

منظوری manẕūrī (A) n.f. Sanction; approval; consent; permission; choice; admissibility.

منظوری دینا manẕūrī denā, v. To accord sanction (to).

منظوم manẕūm (A) adj. Versified; in verse; metrical; poetic; joined; threaded; arranged in order.

منع mana' (A) n.m. Prohibition; refusal; hindrance; prevention; forbidding; dissuasion.

منع کرنا mana' karnā, v. To prohibit; to forbid; to hinder; to dissuade.

منع هونا mana' honā, v. To be forbidden; to be prohibited.

منعدم muna'dim (A) adj. Destroyed; annihilated; extinct.

منعطف muna'ṭif (A) adj. Returning; paying attention (to); attending to.

منعقد muna'qid (A) adj. Held; celebrated; bound (by contract); tied; covenanted; established; taking place.

منعقد هونا muna'qid honā, v. To be held; to be celebrated; to take place.

منعکس muna'kis (A) adj. Inverse; inverted; reversed; turned downward; topsy-turvy; reflected (as a figure in a mirror or water).

منعم mun'im (A) adj. Liberal; generous; beneficent. n.m. A benefactor.

منعم حقیقی mun'im-ĕ ḥaqīqī, n.m. The true benefactor; God.

منغض munaghaẓ (A) adj. Disturbed (in mind); miserable; sad; melancholy.

منفذ manfaẕ (A) n.m. A passage; an orifice.

منفرجه munfarijah (A) adj. Open; wide; extended.

منفرد munfarid (A) adj. Solitary; isolated; unique.

منفصل ، منفصله munfaṣil, munfaṣilah, (A) adj. Separated; divided; disjointed; decided; agreed upon.

منفعت manfa'at (A) n.f. Emolument; profit; gain; advantage.

منفعت اٹھانا manfa'at uṭhānā, v. To derive a benefit.

منفعل munfa'il (A) adj. Abashed; ashamed; afflicted; put to shame; disturbed; affected; bashful; performed; done; made.

منفی manfī (A) adj. Negative; minus; repulsed; rejected; separated; subtracted; deducted.

منقاد munqād (A) adj. Obedient; docile; submissive.

منقار minqar (A) n f. A bird's bill; a beak.

منقبت manqabat (A) n.f. Praise; virtue; glory; praise of the Prophet and his companion.

منقسم munqasim (A) adj. Divided; distributed; classified.

منقش munaqqash (A) adj. Painted; coloured; printed.

منقضی munqaẓī (A) adj. Elapsed; past; expired; terminated.

منقطع munqaṭi' (A) adj. Broken or cut off; terminated; finished; exterminated; disjointed; conclusive.

منقلب munqalib (A) adj. Inverted; turned upside down.

منقوش manqūsh (A) adj. Painted; carved.

منقوط ، منقوطه manqūt, manqūtah (A) adj. Dotted; spotted; a species of composition in which all letters used have dots.

منقول manqūl (A) adj. Copied; translated; transferred; transcribed; narrated; related; recounted; adapted.

منقولات manqūlāt (A) n.m. Things related or recounted; traditions; personal property; things transferable.

منقوله manqūlah (A) adj. Transferable; movable.

منقّٰی munaqqā (A) adj. Clarified; pure; cleaned; purged; purified. n.m. A Species of raisins.

منکا mankā (H) n.m. A rosary; a bead; the vertebrae of the neck.

منکا ڈھلکنا mankā ḍhalaknā, v. To be dying; to be at the point of death.

منکر munkir (A) adj. Rejecting. n.m. One who denies; an atheist.

منکر نکیر munkar nakir (A) n.m. The names of two angels who, according to Muslims, examine the souls of the departed in the grave.

منکسر munkasir (A) adj. Broken; poor; miserable; humble.

منکسرالمزاج munkasir-ul-mizāj, adj. Humble; spiritless; despondent.

منکشف munkashif (A) adj. Disclosed; discovered; displayed; revealed; published; illustrated.

منکوحه mankūhah (A) n.f. A lawful wife; a married woman.

منگانا maṅgānā (H) v. See منگوانا maṅgwānā.

منگتا maṅgtā (H) n.m. A beggar; a mendicant; a borrower.

منگتی maṅgtī (H) n.f. A beggar woman.

منگسر maṅgsar (H) n.m. The name of the eighth Hindu month.

منگل maṅgal (H) adj. Lucky; fortunate; prosperous; auspicious; propitious; pleasing; good; beautiful. n.m. Pleasure; happiness; prosperity; welfare; good luck; a happy or auspicious event; festivity; revelry; burnt offering; a good omen; blessing; benediction; the planet Mars; Tuesday.

منگل چار maṅgal chār, n.m. Benediction; prayer for the success of something; pronouncing a blessing; wishing joy; a marriage song; festivity; rejoicing; preface.

منگل گانا maṅgal gānā, v. To sing a song of joy or congratulation; to sing in praise or honour (of).

منگنی maṅgni (H) n.f. Betrothing; asking in marriage; betrothal; a thing borrowed; a loan; a thing obtained for the asking or for nothing.

منگوانا maṅgwānā (H) v. To cause to bring; to cause to be asked for.

منگیتر maṅgetar (H) n.m./f. One to whom a man or woman is betrothed.

منمن minmin (H) n.f. Murmuring; speaking indistinctly.

منمن کرنا minmin karnā, v. To be very slow; to be awfully considerate.

منمنانا minmināna (H) v. To murmur; to speak through the nose; to eat slowly.

مننا mannā (H) v. To be soothed; to be propitiated; to be pacified; to agree (with).

منوا manuā (H) n.m. Mind; soul; life.

منوانا manwānā (H) v. To cause to mind; to cause to agree to; to cause to trust.

منوتی manauti (H) n.f. Satisfaction; acceptance.

منور munawwar (A) adj. Brilliant; illuminated; enlightened; splendid.

منوهر manohar (H) adj. Heart ravishing; beautiful; pleasing; lovely.

منه muṅh (H) n.m. Mouth; face; countenance; presence; aspect; power; fitness; pretence; ability; strength.

منہ آنا munh ānā, v. To be or become alivated; to have the thrush; to taunt; to be insolent.

منہ اپنا سا لیکر رہ جانا munh apnā sā lekar rah jānā, v. To be disappointed; to feel ashamed; to be dejected; to lose hope.

منہ آترنا munh utarnā, v. To have the face thinned by weakness; to become thin; to be reduced.

منہ آٹھانا munh uṭhānā, v. To prepare for journey; to undertake a journey.

منہ آٹھائے چلے جانا munh uṭhā'e chale jānā, v. To proceed without fear; to go forward bravely.

منہ آجلا ہو جانا munh ujlā ho jānā, v. To come off with flying colours; to be saved from disgrace.

منہ اندھیرے munh andhere, adv. At dawn; early in the morning.

منہ اوندھا کر لینا munh aundhā kar lenā, v. To lie down with face downward (out of grief or sorrow or anger).

منہ باندھ کے بیٹھنا munh bāndh ke baiṭhnā, v. To sit silent; to keep tongue tied; to hold one's tongue.

منہ برا بنانا munh burā banānā, v. To express displeasure.

منہ بسورنا munh basūrnā, v. To pull or wear a long face; to be distressed; to sob.

منہ بگاڑنا munh bigāṛnā, v. To make a wry face; to make faces; to frown; to scoul; to look sulky.

منہ بنا لینا munh banā lenā, v. To look angry; to sulk.

منہ بنانا munh banānā, v. To make mouths or faces; to mock; to fashion the face; to pull a face.

منہ بند کر دینا munh band kar denā, v. To cork; to seal; to make silent; to put a stop; to fill the gap; to close the mouth.

منہ بند کلی munh band kali, n.f. A bud; a virgin.

منہ بنوانا munh banwānā, v. To show one's suitability for a thing; to be fit oneself with the requisite qualifications for doing a thing.

منہ بولا ، منہ بولی munh bolā, munh boli, adj. Nominal; by word of mouth only; adopted.

منہ بولتی munh bolti, adj. Life-like; living.

منہ بولتی تصویر munh bolti taṣwir, n.f. A life-like picture.

منہ بھر آنا munh bhar ānā, v. To feel nausea.

منہ بھرائی munh bharā'i, n.f. A bribe; a sop.

منہ بھر کے کوسنا munh bhar ke kosnā, v. To heap curses (on).

منہ پر munh par, adv. In the face; before the face; in the presence of.

منہ پر بات لانا munh par bāt lānā, v. To disclose a secret.

منہ پر تھوک دینا munh par thūk denā, v. To disgrace; to spit on the face (of).

منہ پر ٹھیکری رکھ لینا munh pār ṭhikṛi rakh lenā, v. To throw modesty aside; to be shame proof.

منہ پر جانا munh par jānā, v. To regard; to observe; to attend; to pay respect; to side with.

منہ پر چڑھنا munh par chaṛhnā, v. To face; to confront; to oppose; to be ready to quarrel; to be impudent; to become a favourite.

منہ پر خاک آڑنا munh par khāk uṛnā, v. To look blank.

منہ پر شفق پھولنا munh par shafaq phūlnā, v. To be flushed with joy.

منہ پر قفل لگ جانا munh par qufl lag jānā, v. To be dumb-founded.

منہ پر کہنا munh pār kahnā, v. To say in the presence of; to speak face to face.

منہ پر لانا munh par lānā, v. To tell; to relate; to say.

منه پر ناک نه هونا munh par nāk nah honā, v. To be shameless.

منه پر هوائیاں آڑنا munh par hawā'iān uṛnā, v. To change colour; to become confused; to show perplexity.

منه پهٹ munh phaṭ, adj. Abusive; fearless; a vain babbler.

منه پهلانا munh phulānā, v. To make a wry face; to frown; to look angry.

منه پهیرنا munh phernā, v. To abstain from; to turn one's face from one.

منه پهیلانا munh phailānā, v. To desire much; to gape.

منه پیٹنا munh piṭnā, v. To slap one's own face.

منه تکنا munh taknā, v. To be astonished; to gaze at one; to look for; to hope for; to look blank or foolish; to be afflicted.

منه توڑنا munh toṛnā, v. To break one's jaw-bone; to harass.

منه چاٹنا munh chāṭnā, v. To lick the face (of); to caress.

منه چڑانا munh chiṛānā, v. To make or pull a face or faces; to make mouths (at).

منه چڑھا ، منه چڑھی munh chaṛhā, munh chaṛhī, adj. Favourite.

منه چڑھانا munh chaṛhānā, v. To be rude or insolent; to be overbearing and haughty.

منه چڑھنا munh chaṛhnā, v. To become favourite or intimate with; to be insolent; to confront.

منه چلانا munh chalānā, v. To chew the cud; to bite or to be inclined to bite; to abuse.

منه چومنا munh chūmnā, v. To kiss; to caress.

منه چهپانا munh chhipānā, v. To hide one's face.

منه خراب کرنا munh kharāb karnā, v. To have the taste blunted; to abuse; to spoil the tongue.

منه در منه munh dar munh, adv. Face to face.

منه دکهانا munh dikhānā, v. To show one's face; to appear with confidence and satisfaction; to appear.

منه دکهائی munh dikhā'ī, n.f. A present given to a bride by female relatives on seeing her face for the first time after marriage.

منه دیکهتے ره جانا munh dekhte rah jānā, v. To be lost in astonishment; to stare at one with surprise.

منه دیکھ کر بات کرنا munh dekh kar bāt karnā, v. To flatter; to behave in a way as one would seem to deserve.

منه دیکهنا munh dekhnā, v. To look up to (for help); to have regard for one; to be astonished or helpless.

منه دیکهے کی محبت munh dekhe kī maḥabbat, n.f. A show of friendship or affection at meetings only.

منه دینا munh denā, v. To make familiar; to favour; to countenance; to put one's lips to.

منه ڈالنا munh ḍālnā, v. To beg; to request; to bite; to mouth.

منه رکهنا munh rakhnā, v. To keep on good terms with.

منه زبانی mūnh zabānī, adj. Verbal.

منه زور munh zor, adj. Headstrong; obstinate; hard-mouthed.

منه سنبهالنا munh sambhālnā, v. To hold one's tongue.

منه سی دینا munh sī denā, v. To seal one's mouth; to silence one; to give hush-money.

منه سے بات نه نکلنا munh se bāt nah nikalnā, v. To be unable to speak.

منہ سے دودھ ٹپکنا *muṅh se dudh ṭapaknā*, *v*. To be yet a child; to have little or no sense.

منہ سے پھول جھڑنا *muṅh se phūl jharnā*, *v*. Falling of the flowers of rhetoric from the lips (of); to rate in round terms; to abuse; to reproach.

منہ فق ہونا *muṅh faq honā*, *v*. To change colour from fear.

منہ کالا کرنا *muṅh kālā karnā*, *v*. To incur dishonour; to bring disgrace on; to punish; to disgrace.

منہ کا نوالہ *muṅh kā niwālah*, *adj*. Anything easily attained; mouthful.

منہ کرنا *muṅh karnā*, *v*. To confront; to side with; to regard; to be greedy; to burst open; to make the first attempt at seizing game; to turn one's face; to direct one's steps towards any particular object or place.

منہ کھلوانا *muṅh khulwānā*, *v*. To provoke one and cause unpleasant things to be uttered.

منہ کھولنا *munh kholnā*, *v*. To speak; to abuse; to open the mouth; to reveal.

منہ کے بل گرنا *muṅa ke bal girnā*, *v*. To fall face foremost; to fall headlong.

منہ کی کھانا *muṅh ki khānā*, *v*. To suffer a blow on the face; to suffer disgrace.

منہ لال ہونا *muṅh lāl honā*, *v*. Reddening of the face (with anger); to be honoured; to get a good name.

منہ لٹکانا *munh latkāna*, *v*. To hang down the head; to make a long face.

منہ لگانا *munh lagānā*, *v*. To be on good terms with; to be familiar with; to be intimate.

منہ لگنا *muṅh lagnā*, *v*. To have the mouth affected by some pungent substance; to become used to; to suit the palate of; to become a favourite of; to be intimate with; to bawdy words with.

منہ لے کے رہ جانا *muṅh le ke rah jānā*, *v*. To remain silent through shame.

منہ مارنا *muṅh mārnā*, *v*. To shut one's mouth up; to silence; to feed; to fall upon; to bite.

منہ مانگا ، منہ مانگی *muṅh maṅgā*, *muṅh māṅgi*, *adj*. Demanded; requested or asked for; prayed for.

منہ مانگی مراد پانا *muṅh māṅgı murād pānā*, *v*. To attain one's prayed for wish.

منہ موڑنا *muṅh moṛnā*, *v*. To turn away; to abstain from; to revolt; to desist from; to disregard; to be averse to; to avoid or shun; to give the cold shoulder (to).

منہ میٹھا کرنا *muna mīṭhā karnā*, *v*. To give (one) a treat; to give a bribe; to sweeten the mouth (of).

منہ میں پانی بھر آنا *munh men pāni bhar ānā*, *v*. Watering of the mouth; to be tempted; to feel eager desire for.

منہ نال ، منہنال *muṅh nāl*, *n.m.* The mouth-piece (for the *ḥuqqah*).

منہ ہی منہ میں *muṅh hi muṅh meṅ*, *adv*. To one's self.

منہا *minhā* (A) *adj*. Deducted; subtracted.

منہاج *minhāj* (A) *n.m.* Highway or road.

منہار *manhār* (H) *n.m.* A person who makes or sells glass bangles.

منہاری *manhāri* (H) *n.f.* The wife of a منہار *manhār*.

منہائی *minhā'i* (A) *n.f.* Abatement; reduction; decrease.

منہدم *munhadim* (A) *adj*. Demolished.

منہدی *meṅhdī*. See مہندی *mehṅdi*.

منہزم *munhazim* (A) *adj*. Put to flight; discomfited; defeated.

منہضم munhaẓim (A) adj. Digestible.

منہمک munhamik (A) adj. Absorbed; engaged; engrossed.

منہی manhi (A) adj. Forbidden; prohibited.

منہیات manhiyyāt (A) n.f. Unlawful things.

منی muni (S) n.m. A holy man; an inspired saint; an asectic; a devotee; a recluse who has taken a vow of silence.

منی manı (P) n.f. Egotism; boasting; presumption.

منی manı (A) n.f. Semen; sperm; animal seed.

منیا muniyā (H) n.f. The female amadavat.

منیب munib (A) n.m. A master; a patron; an agent; a client.

منیر munir (A) adj. Splendid; brilliant; shining; illuminating; illustrious.

منیم munim (H) n.m. A Hindu accountant or head clerk; an agent.

منیمی munımi (H) n.f. The office of an accountant.

مو mau (H) n.f. Prime; bloom; perfection; pleasure; will.

مو mū (P) n.m. Hair.

موباف mū bāf, n.m. A hair fillet.

مو بمو mu bamu, adv. Hair by hair; exactly; with precision; nicely; minutely.

موشگافی mu shigafi, n.f. Hair-splitting; criticism; minuteness of detail.

مو قلم mū qalam, n.m. A hair brush.

موئے زہار mū-ĕ zihār, n.m. The pubes; pubic hair.

موا، موئی mūa, mū'i (H) adj Dead; lifeless; dull.

موا بادل mua badal, n.m. Sponge.

مواثیق mawāṣiq (A) n.m. (plu. of میثاق miṣāq) Promises; agreements.

مواج mawwāj (A) adj. Waving; boistrous.

مواجب mawājib (A) n.m. (plu of موجب mujlb) Salaries; pensions; wages.

مواجہہ muwājahah (A) n.m. Presence; confronting; comparison; collation; meeting.

مواخات muakhāt (A) n.f. Brotherhood.

مواخذہ muakhazah (A) n.m. Calling to account; accountability; responsibility; amends; explanation; punishment; impeachment.

مواخذہ کرنا muakhazah karnā, v. To call to account; to call an explanation.

مواد mawādd (A) n.m. (plu. of مادہ māddah) Articles; matter; humours; materials; ingredients; pus; arguments; points.

مواد فاسد mawādd fāsid, n.m. Bad humours.

موازنہ muāzanah (A) n.m. Balancing; equipoising; comparing in weight; counterbalancing.

موازی muāzi (A) adj/ v. Parallel; being exactly opposite to and resembling one another; equal; nearly; about. n.m. A sum; a total.

مواشی mawāshi (A) n.m. (plu. of ماشیہ māshiyah) Quadrupeds; cattle.

مواصلت muwāṣalat (A) n.f. Conjunction; coming together; adhesion; interview; connection; copulation.

مواضع mawāẓi' (A) n.m. (plu. of موضع mauza') Places; villages; habitations.

مواظبت muwāẓabat (A) n.f. Assiduity; attention; carefulness; doing the same thing repeatedly.

مواظبت کرنا muwāẓabat karnā, v. To take care of; to do repeatedly.

مواعظ mawā'iz (A) n.m. (plu. of موعظت mau'iẓat) Lectures; sermons.

مواعید mawā'id (A) n.m. (plu. of میعاد mī'ād) Agreements; time-tables.

موافق muwāfiq (A) adj. Suitable; favourable; propitious; conformable; congruous; consonant; apt; analogous; concordant.

موافقت muwāfaqat (A) n.f. Conformity; analogy; agreement; accord; concord; affinity; propitiousness.

مواقع mawāqi' (A) n.m. (plu. of موقع mauqa') Situations; occasions; places.

موالات muwālāt (A) n.f. Friendship; affection; co-operation; pursuing a business steadily or without intermission.

موالی mawālı (A) n.m. (plu. of مولیٰ maulā) Lords; masters; friends; slaves; servants.

موالید mawālid (A) n.m. (plu. of مولود maulūd) sons; children; descendants; race; progeny.

موالید ثلاثہ mawalid-ĕ ṣalaṣah, n.m. The three kingdoms of nature (viz. animal, vegetable and mineral).

موانست muwānasat (A) n.f. Companionship; fellowship; society; familiarity; intimacy.

موانع mawāni' (A) n.m. (plu. of مانع māni') Impediments; obstacles; hindrances.

موبد mūbid, mūbad (P) n.m. A doctor; a philosopher; a counsellor of state; a worshipper of the sun; a priest of the guebres.

موت maut (A) n.f. Death; mortality.

موت آنا maut ānā, v. To come to one's death; to die.

موت پڑنا maut pạrna, v. To take ill; to fear; to be afraid of.

موت چاہنا maut chāhnā, v. To prefer death to life; to be tired of life; to pray for death (for someone else).

موت کا بازار گرم ہونا maut kā bāzār garm honā, v. To be having many people dying; to have wide-spread mortality.

موت کے دن پورے کرنا maut ke din pure karnā, v. To make two ends meet with difficulty; to be very poor.

اپنی موت مرنا apni maut marna, v. To die a natural death.

موت mut (H) n.m. Urine; piss.

مؤتمر mu'tamar (A) n.m. A conference; a consultative committee.

موتنا mutna (H) v. To make water; to urinate.

موتھا mothā (H) n.m. A kind of grass, the root of which is used in medicine.

موتی moti (H) n.m. A pearl.

موتی پرونا moti pirona, v. To string pearls; to talk nicely; to speak eloquently; to shed tears.

موتی چور moti chūr, n.m. A sweetmeat; n.f. Sparkling eyes (of pigeons of Kabul).

موتی چھیدنا moti chhednā, v. To pierce pearls; to deflower; to ravish.

موتی رولنا motī rolnā, v. To collect pearls; to hoard wealth.

موتی کی آب moti ki āb, n.f. The lustre of a pearl.

موتی کی سی آب moti ki sì āb, n.f. Lustre like that of a pearl.

موتی کی سیپی moti kī sipı, n.f. Mother of pearl.

موتی کی لڑی moti ki laṛı, n.f. A pearl string.

موتیوں کا ہار motiyon kā hār, n.m. A necklace of pearls.

موتیوں میں تولنا motiyon men tolna, v. To weigh one with pearls; to do a person great honour.

موتیا motiya (H) n.f. A jasmine; the name of a flower; a kind of small-pox.

موتیا بند motiyā band, n.m. A kind of blindness; cataract.

موٹا ، موٹی moṭā, moṭi (H) adj. Fat; corpulent; thick; coarse; large; big; rich; wealthy; bulky; plump; stout; great.

موٹا اناج moṭā anāj, n.m. Coarse cereals; grains of inferior kind.

موٹا تازہ moṭa tazah, adj. Plump and fat; well-conditioned.

موٹا جھوٹا moṭā jhoṭā, adj. Of inferior kind.

موٹی اسامی moṭi asāmı, n.f. A rich man; a heavy purse.

موٹی بات moṭi bāt, n.f. Straight talk; plain speaking.

موٹی گالی moṭi gali, n.f. Obscene language; gross abuse.

موٹھ moṭh (H) n.m. A kind of pulse; vetches; lentils.

موٹھ mūṭh (H) n.f. Handle; a fist; package; bale; a load; sorcery; a game.

موٹھ چلانا mūṭh chalānā. v. To cast a spell (over); to charm.

موٹھ مارنا mūṭh mārnā. To catch a pigeon in one's hand; to cast a spell (over); to grip; to commit self-abuse; to masturbate.

مؤثر mu'aṣṣir (A) adj. Penetrating; making an impression; striking; effecting; efficacious; touching.

مؤثر ہونا mu'aṣṣir hona, v. To have effect; to prove efficacious.

موج mauj (A) n.f. A wave; surge; a whim; emotion; enjoyment; ecstasy; abundance; carpice; plenty.

موج خیز mauj k͟hez, adj. Stormy; producing waves.

موج زن mauj zan, adj. Waving; boisterous; raging; agitated; billowy; tumultuous.

موج کرنا mauj karnā, v. To enjoy oneself.

موج مارنا mauj mārnā, v. To billow; to wave; to enjoy oneself without restraint.

موج میں آنا mauj men ānā, v. To be overjoyed; to be emotional; to be capricious.

موج نسیم mauj-ĕ nasım, n.f. A cooling squall.

موجب mūjib (A) n.m. Cause; reason; motive; account.

موجد mūjid (A) n.m. One who invents; inventor; causer; author.

موجل mu'ajjal (A) adj. Payable at a later time.

موجود ، موجودہ maujud, maujūdah (A) adj. Present; existing; at hand; ready; found; existent.

موجودات maujūdāt (A) n.f. (plu. of موجودہ maujūdah) Things found or present; assets; existing things; creatures; beings; effects; muster of troops; created things.

موجودگی maujūdagī (A&P) n.f. Presence; existence.

موجودگی میں maujūdagi men, adv. In the presence of; during the existence of

موجہ maujah (A) n.m. A wave; billow; surge.

موجہ muwajjah (A) adj. Agreeable; acceptable; valid; plausible; reasonable.

موجی mauji, adj. Cheerful; an easy-go-lucky sort of fellow.

موچ moch (H) n.f. Sprain; twist; strain.

موچ آنا moch ānā, v. To sprain.

موچرس mochras (H) n.m. Gum of the *semal* tree.

موچنا mūchnā, mochnā (H) n.m. Pincers; tweezers; nippers.

موچھ mūchh (H) n.f. Moustaches; whiskers.

موچھ پر تاؤ دینا mūchh par tāo denā, v. To twirl one's whiskers; to boast; to brag; to act the fop or swell.

موچھ مروڑا روٹی توڑا mūchh maroṛā roṭi toṛā, prov. One who is proud of eating the bread of idleness.

موچھل mūchhal (H) adj. Having large whiskers.

موچی mochī (H) *n.m.* A saddler; a shoemaker; a cobbler.

موحد muwaḥḥid (A) *adj.* Believing in one God. *n.m.* One who believe in the unity of God; a unitarian; theist.

موحش muwaḥḥish (H) *adj.* Shocking; horrible: frightful; bewildering.

موخر mu'akhkhar (A) *adj.* Posterior; consequent; delayed; procrastinated.

موخرالذکر mu'akhkhar-uz-zikr, *adj.* Last mentioned; the latter.

موءدب mu'addab (A) *adj.* Well-mannered; civil; polite; disciplined; courteous; modest.

مودت muwaddat (A) *n.f.* Friendship; love; affection.

مودھو modhū (H) *adj.* Simple; foolish; guileless; artless.

مودی mūdi (H) *n.m.* A grocer; a shop-keeper; a grain merchant; a steward; provider.

مودی خانہ mūdi khānah, *n.m.* A pantry; a store-house.

موءذن mu'azzin (A) *n.m.* One who calls Muslims to prayer.

موذی mūzi (A) *adj.* Noxious; troublesome; importunate; vexatious; pernicious; tyrant; wicked; miser.

موذی کا مال mūzi kā mal, *n.m.* A miser's property.

مور mor (P) *n.f.* The ant.

مور و ملخ mor-ŏ malakh, *n.f.* Ants and locusts; *adj.* Innumerable.

مور mor (H) *n.m.* A peacock.

مور پنکھی mor pankhi, *n.f.* A pleasure-boat; a barge; a hand-fan made of peacock feathers.

مور چال mor chāl, *n.f.* Walking on the hands with the feet in the air; a kind of dance.

مور چھل mor chhal, *n.m.* A kind of brush or fan of peacock feathers for driving away flies.

مور کی سی گردن mor kī sī gardan, *n.f.* Long and beautiful neck.

مور مکٹ mor mukat, *n.m.* A crown or crest like that of the peacock.

مور maur (H) *n.m.* The blossom of a tree, especially of the mango tree.

مور آنا maur ānā, *v.* To bloom; to bud; to blossom (mango tree).

مورت ، مورتی mūrat, murati (H) *n.f.* A statue; an idol; a picture; body; a portrait; a figure; a form.

مورتی پوجن mūarti pūjan, *n.f.* Idol-worship; idolatry.

مورث mūris (A) *n.m.* A legator; a person from whom an inheritance is derived. (P) *n.m.* A cause; a reason.

مورچا morchā, *n.m.* A line of entrenchment; a fortification; a battery.

مورچا بندی کرنا morchā bandi karnā, *v.* To entrench; to erect fortifications.

مورچہ morchah (P) *n.m.* Rust of iron.

مورخ mu'arrikh (A) A historian; a biographer; a chronologer; an annalist.

مورخہ mu'arrakhah (A) *adj.* Written on a particular date; dated.

مورد maurid (A) *n.m.* Proper place; the place of arrival, of descent, of halting or appearing; station; object sought.

موردالزام maurid-ĕ ilzām, *n.m. & adj.* The target of indictment; blameworthy.

مورکھ mūrakh (H) *adj.* Foolish; stupid; illiterate; ignorant.

مورنی morni (H) *n.f.* A pea-hen.

موروثی maurūsi (A) *adj.* Hereditary; ancestral; patrimonial.

موری mori (H) *n.f.* A drain; a gutter; underground passage for water; an orifice; a hole.

موڑ *moṛ* (H) *n.m.* A bend; a turn; twist; convulsion; writhe; sprain; fistula; winding (of a river).

موڑنا *moṛnā* (H) *v.* To twist; to turn; to bend; to screw; to plait; to pervert; to drive back.

موڑھا *mūṛhā*, *moṛhā* (H) *n.m.* A reed or cane chair; a stool.

موزون *mauzūn* (A) *adj.* Well-balanced; well-adjusted; fit; symmatrical; rythmical; agreeable; well-measured; of just quantity; weighed.

موزون کرنا *mauzūn karnā*, *v.* To correct a verse; to fit; to adjust.

موزونیت *mauzūniyat* (A) *n.f.* Agreeableness; fitness; correctness.

موزہ *mozah* (P) *n.m.* A stocking; a boot; a glove.

موسا *mūsā* (H) *n.m.* A mouse; a rat.

موسائی *musā'ī*. See موسوی *mūsavī*.

موسس *mu'assis* (A) *adj.* Founder; laying foundation.

موسل *mūsal* (H) *n.m.* A wooden pestle.

موسلا *mūslā* (H) *n.m.* A pestle; a taproot; root; staff; a rod; a bolt.

موسلادھار *mūslā dhār*, *adj.* Heavy or pelting (rain).

موسلی *mūslī* (H) *n.f.* A small pestle; root of a plant.

موسم *mausim* (A) *n.m.* Season; time.

موسم برشگال *mausim-ĕ barshagāl*, *n.m.* Rainy season.

موسم بہار *mausim-ĕ bahār*, *n.m.* Spring season.

موسم خزاں *mausim-ĕ khazāṅ*, *n.m.* Autumn.

موسم سرما *mausim-ĕ sarmā*, *n.m.* Winter season.

موسم گرما *mausim-ĕ garmā*, *n.m.* Summer season.

موسمی *mausimī*, *adj.* Seasonal; in season.

موسنا *mūsnā* (H) *v.* To pilfer; to steal; to filch; to defraud; to snatch; to seize by force.

موسوم *mausūm* (A) *adj.* Marked; named; signed; called; impressed; entitled; noted; stigmatised.

موسوم کرنا *mausūm karnā*, *v.* To name.

موسوی *mūsavī* (A) *adj.* Jewish. *n.m.* Followers of Moses; Jews; Hebrews.

موسیٰ *Mūsā* (A) *n.m.* Moses, the prophet.

موسیقار *mūsīqār* (P) *n.m.* A shepherd's pipe; a singing bird.

موسیقی *mūsiqī* (A) *n.f.* Music.

موش *mūsh* (P) *n.m.* A mouse.

موصوف *mauṣūf* (A) *adj.* Named; praised; celebrated; before-mentioned; a noun qualified by an adjective.

موصول *mauṣūl* (A) *adj.* Joined; connected; related; received; (in *Gram.*) the antecedent to the relative.

موصی *mūṣī* (A) *n.m.* Making a will; a testator.

موضع *mauẓā'* (A) *n.m.* A place; village; district; occurrence; conjuncture.

موضوع *mauẓū'* (A) *n.m.* A subject; object; a postulate. *adj.* Placed; situated; established.

موطن *mauṭin* (A) *n.m.* Birth-place; dwelling; house.

موعظت *mau'izat* (A) *n.f.* Advice; exhortation.

موعود *mau'ud* (A) *adj.* Promised; predicted; pre-destined.

موفور *maufūr* (A) *adj.* Copious; abundant; plentiful; numerous; many; full.

موقت *muwaqqat* (A) *adj.* Fixed or restricted to a certain definite time; temporary; provisional.

موقر muwaqqar (A) adj. Honoured; respected; revered; esteemed.

موقع mauqa' (A) n.m. A place; a situation, an occasion; an opportunity; a place where anything happens; a fit place; a contingency.

موقع بہ موقع mauqa' bā mauqa', adv. In season and out of season; in time of need.

موقع پر mauqa' par, adv. At the proper time; at the right place and time; on the spot.

موقع نکل جانا mauqa' nikal jānā, v. To let slip an opportunity.

موقع واردات mauqa'-ē wārdāt, n.m. Place of occurrence.

موقع ہاتھ سے نہ دینا mauqa' hāth se nah denā, v. To take time by the forelock; not to let an opportunity slip.

موقف mauqif (A) n.m. A place to stop; post; position; stand; a place to take a stand.

موقوف mauqūf (A) adj. Stopped; ceased; abolished; dismissed; fixed; dependent on; rested; bound.

موقوف الیہ mauqūf ilaih, n.m. A trustee.

موقوف رکھنا mauqūf rakhnā, v. To suspend; to postpone.

موقوف علیہ mauqūf 'alaih, adj & n.m. A person depended upon; a judge; a mediator.

موقوف کرنا mauqūf karnā, v. To stop; to leave off; to abolish; to dismiss.

موقوف ہونا mauqūf honā, v. To be stopped; to be dismissed; to depend on.

موقوفی mauqūfī (A&P) n.f. Dismissal; stoppage; suspension.

موکد mu'akkad (A) adj. Emphasized; confirmed; emphatic; corroborated; efficacious.

موکل muwakkal (A) n.m. A guardian; a superintendent; vicegerent; a trustee; a delegate.

موکل muwakkil (A) n.m. One who appoints a وکیل vakil; one who delegates power to another; a client.

موکھا mokhā (H) n.m. A small hole in a wall; an air hole; an aperture; an opening.

موگرا mogrā (H) n.m. A mallet; a hammer; a rammer; a double jasmine.

موگری mogri (H) n.f. A mallet for beating clothes with; a club to take exercise with.

مول mūl (H) n.m. Origin; root; race; generation; principal or capital sum of money; stock; text of a book.

مول mol (H) n.m. Purchase; purchase money; price; value.

مولا ، مولیٰ maulā (A) n.m. Master; lord; God.

مولانا maulānā (A) n.m. (Lit. Our master) A title given to persons respected for their learning.

مولائی maulā'i (A) n.f. Lordship; judgeship.

مولد maulid (A) n.m. Nativity; birth-place; native land.

مولسری maulsari (H) n.f. Name of a tree and its fruit.

مولف، مولفہ mu'allif, mu'allifah (A) n.m/n.f. A compiler of a book; editor.

مولف، مولفہ mu'allaf, mu'allafah (A) adj. Compiled; edited; composed.

مولود maulūd (A) adj. Born; generated. n.m. A son; celebration of the anniversary of the Holy Prophet's birth.

مولوی maulawi (A) n.m. A learned man; a professor; a Muslim doctor of law.

مولی mūli (H) n.f. A radish.

موم mom (P) n.m. Wax.

موم بتی mom batti, n.f. A wax-candl ; wax-light.

موم جامہ mom jāmah, n.m. Wax-cloth; cerecloth,

موم دل *mom dil, adj.* Tender-hearted.

موم کی گڑیا *mom kī guṛyā, n.f.* A wax doll; a delicate woman.

موم کی ناک *mom kī nāk, adj.* Fickle-minded; of fickle disposition.

موم ہونا *mom honā, v.* To soften; to tone down.

مومن *momin* (A) *n.m.* A believer; a follower of the Shia sect; a Muslim weaver. *adj.* Orthodox; faithful; believing.

مومی *momī* (P) *adj.* Waxen; waxy; soft as wax; of the colour of wax; pasty; adhesive.

مومی کاغذ *momī kāghaz, n.m.* Wax-paper.

مومی کپڑا *momī kapṛā, n.m.* Wax-cloth.

مومی موتی *momī motī, n.m.* Imitation pearls made of glass and filled with wax.

مومیا *momiyā* (P) *n.f.* A mummy.

مومیانا *momiyānā, adv.* To mummify.

مومیائی *momiya'ī* (P) *adj.* Of or like a mummy, *n.f.* A medicine, as soft as wax and used for wounds and hurts.

مومیائی نکالنا *momiyā'ī nikālnā, v.* To beat to a mummy.

مونث *mu'annas* (A) *adj.* Faminine; effeminate; of the feminine gender.

مونج *mūnj* (H) *n.f.* A kind of rush or grass of which ropes are made.

مونچھ *mūnchh* (H) *n.f.* See موچھ *mūchh.*

موندنا *mūndnā* (H) *v.* To shut; to cover; to close; to imprison.

مونڈن *mūnḍan* (H) *n.m.* The Hindu ceremony of shaving a child's head for the first time.

مونڈنا *mūnḍnā* (H) *v.* To shave; to make a disciple of; to impose upon; to cheat; to instruct; to convert; to wheedle out of anything.

مونڈھا *monḍhā* (H) *n.m.* A stool made of reeds and ropes; the shoulder; a gusset on the shoulder of native coat.

مونس *munis* (A) *n.m.* An intimate friend; a companion; a consoler; Thursday (so called, because on that day the ancient Arabs used to incline to places of pleasure).

مونس تنہائی *mūnis-ĕ tanhā'ī, n.m.* A friend in loneliness or solitude; a book.

مونگ *mūṅg* (H) *n.m.* A kind of pulse.

مونگ پھلی *mūṅg phalī, n.f.* Ground-nut or pig-nut of the West Indies.

مونگا *muṅgā* (H) *n.m.* Coral.

مونگے کا جزیرہ *mūṅge kā jazīrah, n.m.* A coral island.

مونگیا *mūṅgiyā* (H) *n.m.* Dark green colour.

مونہ *mūṅh* (H) *n.m.* See منہ *muṅh.*

موہ *moh* (H) *n.f.* Fascination; charm; love; affection; sympathy; compassion; pity; kindness; allurement; fainting; senselessness.

موہ لینا *moh lenā, v.* To fascinate; to charm; to captivate; to allure; to atttact.

موہن *mohan* (H) *n.m.* A sweetheart; a name of Krishna. *adj.* Fascinating; charming; captivating; depriving of sense.

موہن بھوگ *mohan bhog, n.m.* A kind of sweetmeat.

موہن مالا *mohan mālā, n.m.* A necklace of gold beads and corals.

موہنا *mohnā* (H) *v.* To fascinate; to enchant; to charm; to allure; to attract; to captivate.

موہنی *mohanī* (H) *adj.* Fascinating; captivating; charming; winning. *n.f.* A beautiful woman; a sorceress; charm; beauty.

موہوم *mauhūm* (A) *adj.* Imagined; fancied; imaginary.

مؤید *mua'yyid* (A) *adj.* Corroborative; conformatory.

مؤید *mua'iyyad* (A) *adj.* Strengthened; aided; confined; corroborated.

مویز mawez (P) n.m. Raisins; dried grapes.

مویز منقیٰ mawez-ĕ munaqqā, n.m. Raisins, cleared of seeds.

مویشی maweshī. See مواشی mawāshī.

مہ mih (P) adj. Great; chief; principal.

مہ تر mih tar, adj. Greater; superior. n.m. A prince.

مہ mah (P) n.m. (contr. of ماہ māh); the moon; a month.

مہ پارہ mah pārah, n.m. A beauty; a mistress.

مہ جبیں ، طلعت ، لقا mah jabīn, ṭal'at, liqā, adj. Beautiful as the moon; a beloved person.

مہ وش mah wash, adj. Like the moon; sweetheart; beloved.

مہا mahā (S) adj. Great; illustrious; high; mighty; strong; ample; excessive; supreme. adv. Very; extremely.

مہا اوت mahā ūt, adj. A big fool; egregious fool.

مہا بلی mahā balī, adj. Exceedingly strong; very powerful or mighty. n.m. A very strong person.

مہا بھارت mahā bhārat, n.m. A great war; a great epic poem in Sanskrit, describing the war between *Kurus* and *Panḍus*.

مہا بیر mahā bir, n.m. A very strong person.

مہا پاپ mahā pāp, n.m. A great crime or sin.

مہا پرش mahā purush, n.m. A great man; an eminent personage; a great saint; a consummate; knave.

مہا پرشاد mahā parshād, n.m. A great present of food; meat.

مہا پرلے mahā parlai, n.f. The great deluge.

مہاتما mahā tamā, adj. Holy; virtuous. n.m. A pious man.

مہاجن mahā jan, n.m. A merchant; a banker; a reliable person.

مہاجنی mahā janī, n.f. Banking business.

مہا دیو mahā dev, n.m. An epithet of Siva.

مہاراج mahā rāj, n.m. A supreme lord or sovereign; a prince; a superior.

مہا راجا mahā rājā, n.m. Sovereign; emperor.

مہاراج ادھیراج mahārāj adhirāj, n.m. King of kings; a great emperor.

مہا راشٹر mahārāshtar, n.m. A great kingdom; the land of Marhattas.

مہارانی mahā rānī, n.f. The principal wife of a *rājā*.

مہاسبھا mahā sabhā, n.f. The royal council.

مہا منتری mahā mantrī, n.m. A prime minister.

مہابت mahābat (A) n.f. Majesty; greatness; reverence; fear; dread; awe; authority.

مہاجر muhājir (A) n.m. Emigrant; evacuee; refugee.

مہاجرت muhājarat (A) n.f. Separation; distance; desertion; flight; migration; abandoning one's country or friends; fleeing.

مہار mahār, muhār (P) n.f. A nose-string; reins; a bridle (of a camel).

بے مہار be muhār, adj. Unbridled; unrestrained; loose.

مہارت mahārat (A) n.f. Practice; experience; skill; expertness; subtlety; acuteness; genius; excellence; proficiency.

مہاسا muhāsā (H) n.m. A pimple or mole on the face.

مہال muhāl (H) n.f. A bee-line.

مہاوت mahāwat (H) n.m. An elephant driver or keeper.

مہاوٹ mahāwaṭ (H) n.f. Rain which falls in the month of ماگھ māgh.

مہبط mahbaṭ (A) n.m. A landing place; a place of descent.

مہبل mahbal (A) n.m. The vagina.

مہتا mahtā (H) n.m. A chief; the headman of a village; a clerk; an agent or man of business.

مہتاب mahtab (P) n.m. The moon; the moonlight; a kind of fireworks.

مہتاب کا کھیت کرنا mahtāb kā khet karna, v. Rising of the moon.

مہتابی mahtābi (P) adj. Belonging to the moon; like the moon; of moonshine. n.f. A kind of fireworks; an open high terrace; a brocade.

مہتدی muhtadā (A) adj. Directed; guided; steered (to the right or left); rightly guided; aright.

مہتدی muhtadi (A) adj. Leading; guiding.

مہتر mihtar (P) n.m. A prince; a sweeper. adj. Greater; superior; chief.

مہترانی mihtarānı, n.f. A female sweeper; sweepress.

مہتمم muhtamim (A) n.m. A manager; a superintendent; an inspector; an overseer; a supervisor.

مہجور mahjūr (A) adj. Separated; cut off; left; forsaken; rejected.

مہجوری mahjūri (A&P) n.f. Separation.

مہد mahd (A) n.m. A cradle; a swing.

مہدی muhdi (A) adj. Leading; directing.

مہدی mahdi (A) adj. Guided; led to the right direction.

مہذب muhazzab (A) adj. Well-mannered; civil; civilised; polite; well behaved.

مہر mahr (A) n.m. A marriage portion; a gift settled upon the wife; alimony; jointure.

مہر باندھنا mahr bandhna, v. To settle a dower on a wife.

مہر بخشنا mahr bakhshna, v. To give up a jointure.

مہر شرعی mahr-ĕ shara'ı, n.m. A dower approved by the Muslim law.

مہر مثل mahr-ĕ misl, n.m. A dower in force in the family.

مہر معجل mahr-ĕ mu'ajjal, n.m Marriage portion payable at the time of marriage.

مہر موجل mahr-ĕ muwajjal, n.m. Marriage portion payable at the fixed time.

مہر نامہ mahr namah, n.m. A deed of alimony or jointure.

مہر muhr, muhur (P) n.f. A seal; a gold coin; a stamp.

مہر بلب muhr balab, adj. Silent.

مہر کرنا ، لگانا muhr karna, lagāna, v. To seal; to put a seal on; to close.

مہر کن muhr kan, n.m. A seal-engraver.

مہر mihr (P) n.m. The sun. n.f. Kindness; favour; affection.

مہربان mihr bān, adj. Loving; affectionate; kind.

مہربانی mihr bani, n.f. Favour; kindness.

مہرا mahra (H) n.m. A pālki bearer; a servant who carries water for his master.

مہرہ muhrah (P) n.m. A natural protuberance of the bone in the neck joint; a vertebrae; a shell; a chess-man; a bead.

مہرہ پشت muhrah-ĕ pusht, n.m. Spinal vertebrae.

مہرہ شطرنج muhrah-ĕ shatranj, n.m. A piece in chess.

مہری mahrı (H) n.f. The wife of a مہرا mahra a pālki bearer; a maid-servant.

مہری muhri (H) n.f. The end of a sleeve or of the leg of a pair of trousers; the bore of a gun; a drain; a gutter; aqueduct; conduit.

مہک mahak (H) n.f. perfume; odour; fragrance.

مہکنا mahakna (H) v. To exhale an agreeable smell; to emit odour; to smell; to perfume.

مہکیلا mahkilā (H) *adj.* Odoriferous; fragrant; spicy; aromatic.

مہلت muhlat (A) *n.f.* Retarding; deferring; delay; respite; time; leisure; intermission; cessation; armistice.

مہلت دینا muhlat denā, *v.* To allow time; to postpone; to defer.

مہلک ، مہلکہ mahlik, mahlakah (A) *n.m.* A place of destruction or danger; a danger spot.

مہلک muhlik (A) *adj.* Fatal; destructive.

مہم muhimm (A) *n.f.* An urgent matter; momentous business; important affair; exigence; exploit; enterprise; expedition; attack. (*plu.* مہمات muhimmāt).

مہمان mihmān (P) *n.m.* A guest;.

مہمان خانہ mihmān khānah, *n.m.* A guest-chamber; a guest-house.

مہمان دار mihmān dār, *n.m.* A host; an entertainer.

مہمان داری mihmān dāri, *n.f.* Hospitality; entertainment.

مہمان نواز mihmān nawāz, *adj.* Hospitable.

مہمان نوازی mihman nawāzi, *n.f.* Hospitality; entertaining; reception of a guest.

مہمانی mihmāni (P) *n.f.* Entertainment; hospitality; feast; banquet.

مہمل muhmal (A) *adj.* Meaningless; obsolete; not in use.

مہملات muhmalat (A) *n.f.* (*plu.* of مہملہ muhmalah) Absurdities; senseless things.

مہملہ muhmalah (A) *adj.* Without points or dots (a letter); Meaningless.

مہموز mahmūz (A) *adj.* Marked with ہمزہ hamzah; defective.

مہمیز mahmez (P) *n.f.* A spur.

مہنا mihnā (H) *n.m.* Sarcasm; taunt, ridicule.

مہنا پھینکنا ، دینا mihnā phainknā, denā, *v.* To sneer; to revile; to taunt,

مہنت mahant (H) *n.m.* The head of a religious order; a monk; on abbot.

مہندس muhandis (A) *n.m.* One well-versed in Geometry or Mathematics; an engineer.

مہندی mehndi (H) *n.f.* Myrtle; the henna plant.

مہنگا، مہنگی mahngā, mahngi (H) *adj.* Dear; expensive; high priced.

مہنگائی mahngā'i (H) *n.f.* Dearness; a time of dearness or scarcity.

مہوا mahvā (H) *n.m.* A tree bearing sweet flowers from which spirituous liquor is distilled.

مہورت mahūrat (H) *n.f.* A division of time equal to forty-eight minutes; an auspicious omen.

مہوس muhawwis (A) *adj.* Greedy. *n.m.* An alchemist.

مہوسی muhawwisi, *n.f.* Alchemy; greed.

مہیا muhaiyyā (A) *adj.* Prepared; got ready; arranged; supplied.

مہیب muhib (A) *adj.* Formidable; dreadful; tremendous; grim; awful; abominable.

مہین mahin, *adj.* Fine; thin; not coarse; feeble.

مہینا mahinā (H) *n.m.* A month; salary; monthly pay.

مہینے سے ہونا mahine se honā, *v.* To menstruate.

مہینے کے مہینے mahine ke mahine, *adv.* Monthly; every month.

مے mai (P) *n.f.* Wine; spirituous liquor.

مے آشام ، پرست ، خوار ، کش ، گسار ، نوش mai āshām, parast, khwār, kash, gusār, nosh, *n.m.* A wine-drinker; a sot; a drunkard.

مے پرستی mai parasti, *n.f.* Love of wine.

مے خانہ ، مے کدہ mai khānah, mai kadah, *n.m.* A tavern; a wine cellar; a liquor-shop.

مے خوری mai khori, *n.f.* Wine-drinking; drunkenness.

مے فروش mai farosh, n.m. A wine-merchant; a tavern-keeper.

مے کشی mai kashī, n.f. Wine-drinking; carousal; a jovial feast; drinking-bout.

مے گوں mai gūṅ, adj. Auburn; reddish; brown; light-red; fair; wine-coloured.

مے ناب mai nāb, n.f. Pure wine.

میا maiyyā (H) n.f. Mother.

میاں miyāṅ (H) n.m. Master; husband; lord; father; a title by which eunuchs are addressed.

میاں آدمی miyāṅ ādamī, n.m. A good natured man; a respected person; a gentleman.

میاں بیوی miyāṅ bīwi, n.m. Husband and wife.

میاں جی miyāṅ jī, n.m. A mediator; a school-master; a pedagogue; a go-between; an arbitrator.

میاں مٹھو miyāṅ miṭhū, n.m. A sweet talker; a parrot; a simpleton.

میان miyān (P) n.m. A scabbord; a sheath; waist; loins; the middle; centre; axis. adv. Between; among; in the midst of.

میان بستہ miyān bastah, adv. Ready; prepared; with the loins girt.

میان سے باھر ھونا miyān se bāhir honā, v. To be transported with rage; to pass all bounds.

میان سے کھینچنا miyān se kheṅchnā, v. To unsheathe; to be ready to fight.

میان میں کرنا miyān meṅ karnā, v. To sheath e; to stop quarrelling.

میانا miyānā (H) n.m. A planquin; a kind of sedan or palki.

میانہ miyānah (P) adj. Middling; moderate; n.m. Center; axis.

میانہ روی miyānah rawī, n.f. Moderation.

میانہ قد miyānah qadd, adj. Of medium stature.

میانی miyānī (H) n.f. A gusset between the legs of a pair of trousers; a cad-piece.

میت maiyyit (A) n.f. A dead body.

میت mit (H) n.m. A friend; a lover.

میتھی methī (H) n.f. The plant fenugreek.

میتھی کا ساگ methi kā sāg, n.m. A pot-herb.

میٹھا mithā (H) n.m. Name of a fruit; lemon; a general name for sweets, as sugar, molasses, etc.

میٹھا، میٹھی mīṭhā, miṭhi (H) adj. Sweet; slow; lazy; cunning; forbearing; patient; mild; tolerant.

میٹھا برس mīṭhā baras, n.m. The eighteenth year of life.

میٹھا تیل miṭhā tel, n.m. The sesamum oil.

میٹھا تیلیا miṭhā teliyā, n.m. A poisonous drug; aconite.

میٹھا درد miṭhā dard, n.m. Light pain.

میٹھا موسم miṭhā mauṣim, n.m. Temperate season.

میٹھا میٹھا mithā mithā, adj. Very light; slow; sweet.

میٹھا ھونا miṭhā honā, v. To be sweet; to be a little; to be light in colour; to be tolerable; to be endurable.

میٹھی بات miṭhī bāt, n.f. Sweet speech.

میٹھی بولی miṭhi boli, n.f. Mild talk; sweet dialect.

میٹھی چھری miṭhi chhuri, n.f. A foe in the guise of a friend; a snake in the grass.

میٹھی عید miṭhī 'id, n.f. 'Id-ul-Fitr.

میٹھی مار miṭhi mār, n.f. Internal hurt; contusion.

میٹھی مراد miṭhi murād, n.f. Sweet wish.

میٹھی نظر miṭhi nazar, n.f. Affectionate look.

میٹھی نیند miṭhi nīnd, n.f. Sound sleep.

میٹھی miṭhi (H) n.f. A kiss.

میثاق **mis̤āq** (A) *n.m.* A promise; an agreement; a bargain; a compact; a confederacy; alliance; league.

میثاق ملی **mis̤āq-ĕ millī**, *n.m.* National covenant.

میچنا **michnā** (H) *v.* To close (the eyes); to wink; to shut.

میخ **mek͟h** (P) *n.f.* A nail; a wedge; a peg; a tent-peg; a hook.

میخ چو **mek͟h chū**, *n.m.* A mallet; a hammer.

میدان **maidān** (A) *n.m.* A plain; an open field; an area; a battlefield; ground; a race course; a parade ground; a war; a battle; a conflict.

میدان جنگ ، میدان کارزار **maidān-ĕ jang, maidān-ĕ kārzār**, *n.m.* Battlefield.

میدان مارنا **maidān mārnā**, *v.* To win a battle.

میدان میں آنا **maidān meṅ ānā**, *v.* To come out in the open; to come out and fight.

میدان ہاتھ ہونا **maidān hāth honā**, *v.* To come out of the battlefield with flying colours.

میدانی **maidānī** (A) *adj.* & *n.m.* Level; open level country; a soldier of fortune; a kind of *huqqah* used by *faqirs*; dough made ready for the preparation of sweetmeats; a person who precedes an officer and proclaims his titles. *n.f.* A kind of big lentern.

میده **maidah** (P) *n.m.* Flour; meal; the finest flour.

میده کرنا **maidah karnā**, *v.* To grind very fine.

میر **mīr** (P) *n.m.* Chief; leader; a title by which Saiyyids are addressed; the king in cards.

میر آتش **mīr-ĕ ātish**, *n.m.* The chief of the fireworks or artillery; master of the ordnance.

میر آخور **mīr-ĕ āk͟hūr**, *n.m.* Master of the Stable.

میر بحر **mīr-ĕ baḥr**, *n.m.* A collector of post duty; an admiral.

میر بخشی **mīr bak͟hshī**, *n.m.* The paymaster general.

میر حاج **mīr-ĕ ḥājj**, *n.m.* A leader of pilgrims.

میر دیہہ **mīr-ĕ dih**, *n.m.* Headman of a village.

میر سامان **mīr-ĕ sāmān**, *n.m.* Head steward; major-domo.

میر شکار **mīr-ĕ shikār**, *n.m.* A game warden; a huntsman.

میر عرض **mīr-ĕ ʻarẓ**, *n.m.* An usher; an officer who presents letters and representations.

میر قافلہ ، کاروان **mīr-ĕ qāfilah, kārwān**, *n.m.* Leader of a caravan.

میر کلام **mīr-ĕ kalām**, *n.m.* An eloquent speaker.

میر مجلس **mīr-ĕ majlis**, *n.m.* A presiding officer; president; chairman; the master of ceremonies.

میرمحلہ **mīr-ĕ muḥallah**, *n.m.* Headman of a محلہ *muḥallah*, a division or a quarter of a city.

میرمحرر **mīr muḥarrir**, *n.m.* Head clerk.

میرمحکمہ **mīr-ĕ maḥkamah**, *n.m.* Head of department.

میر مشاعره **mīr-ĕ mushāʻirah**, *n.m.* President of the meeting of poets.

میر مطبخ **mīr-ĕ maṭbak͟h**, *n.m.* One who has charge of the kitchen.

میر منشی **mīr munshī**, *n.m.* A secretary; a head clerk.

میرا ، میری **merā, merī** (H) *pron.* Mine; belonging to me.

میراث **mīrās̤** (A) *n.f.* Patrimony; hereditary estate; a bequest; ancestral property; legacy.

میراثن **mirāṣan**, *n.f.* A singing girl who sings only before women.

میراثی **mirāṣi**, *n.m.* A singer by hereditary profession.

میرزا **mirzā** (P) *n.m.* See مرزا *mirzā*.

میری **miri**, *n.f.* Leadership; chiefship; richness. *n.m.* A winner at play; he that first comes to the teacher to say his lesson.

میری و فقیری **miri-ŏ faqiri**, *n.f.* Wealth and poverty.

میز **mez** (P) *n.f.* A table.

میزبان **mez bān**, *n.m.* A host; an entertainer.

میزبانی **mez bāni** *n.f.* Hospitality; entertainment; house-keeping.

میزان **mizān** (A) *n.f.* A balance; a pair of scales; measure; metre; rhyme; verse; prosody; total; addition; the sign Libra.

میزان کل **mizān-e kul**, *n.f.* Grand total.

میزانیه **mizāniyah** (A) *n.m.* Budget; estimates of income and expenditure.

میسر **muyassar** (A) *adj.* Attained; obtained; facilitated; favourable; easy; procurable; possible; feasible; practicable; available.

میسره **maisarah** (A) *n.m.* Left wing of an army.

میش **mesh** (P) *n.m.* A sheep; a ram; the sign Aries.

میش چشم **mesh chashm**, *adj.* Sheep-eyed; shy.

میعاد **mi'ād** (A) *n.f.* The limit of a promise; term; period; duration.

میعاد پوری هونا **mi'ād pūri honā**, *v.* To expire (a term or period allowed).

میعاد کاٹنا **mi'ād kāṭnā**, *v.* To undergo imprisonment for the full term.

میعادی **mi'ādi**, *adj.* Limited; terminable; Intermittent.

میعادی بخار **mi'ādi bukhār**, *n.m.* Intermittent fever; typhoid fever.

میعادی هنڈی **mi'ādi hunḍi**, *n.f.* A bill payable at a fixed time.

میقات **miqāt** (A) *n.m.* Appointed time; a place in Mecca where the pilgrims make a vow of pilgrimage, preparatory to entrance in Mecca.

میکا **maikā** (H) *n.m.* Kindred; relation; mother's family; the bride's paternal home.

میکروب **macrob** (A) *n.m.* Bactarium.

میکروب شناسی **macrob shināsi**, *n.f.* Bacteriology.

میل **mail** (A) *n.m.* Inclination; tendency; bias; bent; desire; wish; affection; regard; partiality; fondness; attachment; aptitude.

میل خاطر **mail-ě khāṭir**, *n.f.* Full attention.

میل **mail** (H) *n.m.* Dirt; filth; rust; scum.

میل خورا **mail khorā**, *n.m.* An undervest; an apron; a saddle-cloth; a cloth of brown colour.

میل کا بیل بنانا **mail kā bail banānā**, *v.* To make a mountain of a mole-hill.

میل **mil** (A) *n.m.* A pencil, style for collyrium; a rod; an axle; the barrel of a gun; a mile; a milestone.

میل **mel** (H) *n.m.* Connection; relationship; agreement; combination; intimacy; concern; union; concord; association; a meeting or assemblage of people.

میل جول ، میل ملاپ **mel jol, mel milāp**, *n.m.* Association; friendly intercourse; familiarity.

میل رکھنا **mel rakhnā**, *v.* To be intimate with; to be on good terms with.

میل کھانا **mel khānā**, *v.* To unite or mix with; to accord; to be in harmony.

میلا **mailā** (H) *n.m.* Filth, dirt.

میلا، میلی mailā, maili (H) adj. Dirty; nasty; foul; defiled.

میلا melā (H) n.m. Meeting; company; a fair.

میلا تماشا، میلا ٹھیلا melā tamāshā, melā thelā, n.m. A concourse of people for religious or commercial purposes.

میلاد milād (A) n.m. Birthday.

میلان mailān (A) n.m. Inclination; bent; affection; respect; regard; love.

میمنا memnā (H) n.m. A kid; a ram.

میمنت maimanat (A) n.f. Fortune; prosperity; happiness

میمنہ maimanah (A) n.m. The right wing of an army.

میمون maimūn (A) adj. Fortunate; auspicious; prosperous.

میمون maimūn (P) n.m. A monkey; a baboon.

میں meṅ (H) prep. In; within; between; among; at.

میں main (H) pron. I.

میں پنا main panā, n.m. Egotism; arrogance.

میں میں کرنا main main karnā, v. To be egotistical; to talk nothing but self.

مین min (S) n.f. A fish; the sign Pisces.

مین میکھ نکالنا min mekh nikālnā, v. To criticise.

مینا minā (P) n.m. A decanter; a goblet; a glass enamel; blue-stone; a colour; the azure vault; blue vitriol; caustic; heaven; paradise.

مینا بازار mina bazār, n.m. A fancy fair.

مینا کار minā kār, n.m. An enameller.

مینا کاری minā kāri, n.f. Enamelling.

مینا mainā (H) n.f. Starling; a term of endearment used for children.

مینڈھی meṅdhi (H) n.f. See مہندی mehndi.

مینڈ meṅḍ (H) n.f. A bank; a boundary; a mound of a field; a border; a dam; a landmark; dyke.

مینڈک meṅdak (H) n.m. A frog; a toad.

مینڈکی meṅḍaki (H) n.f. The feminine gender of مینڈک meṅḍak.

مینڈکی کو زکام ہونا meṅḍki ko zukām hona, v. To display pride; to assume consequential airs.

مینڈھا meṅḍhā (H) n.m. A ram.

مینگنی meṅgni (H) n.f. The dung of sheep, goats and camels.

مینو minu (P) n.m. Paradise; heaven.

مینہ meṅh (H) n.m. Rain.

مینہ برسنا meṅh barasnā, v. To rain.

میوہ mewah (P) n.m. Fruit.

میوہ دار mewah dār, adj. Fruit bearing; fruitful; fructiferous.

ن nūn, is the twenty-fifth letter of the Arabic, the twenty-ninth of the Persian and thirty-second of the Urdu alphabet. It is one of the dental letters having a more nasal sound than the English n. It stands for fifty in abjad.

نا nā (P&H) No; not; a negative prefix to nouns or participles; the termination of the infinitive or gerund of Urdu verbs.

ناآزمودہ، ناآزمودہ کار nā āzmudah, na azmudah kār, adj. Untried; inexperienced; unproved; raw; ignorant.

نا آشنا nā āshnā, adj. Unacquainted; unknown; friendless; a stranger.

نا آگاہ nā āgāh, adj. Uninformed; unaware; in the dark.

نا اتفاق nā ittifāqi, n.f. Disagreement; discord.

نا اُمید nā ummid, adj. Hopeless; despairing; despondent.

نا آمیدی nā ummidi, n.f. Hopelessness; despair; frustration.

نا اندیش nā andesh, adj. Short-sighted; improvident; thoughtless.

نا انصاف nā insāf, adj. Unjust; unfair.

نا انصافی nā insāfi, n.f. Injustice.

نا اهل nā ahl, adj. Incapable; unfit; unworthy.

نا بالغ nā bāligh, adj. Underage; unripe; immature.

نا بالغی nā bālighi, n.f. Nonage; minority.

نا بکار nā bakār, adj. Useless; worthless; vile; good for nothing; wicked.

نا بلد nā balad, n.m. A foreigner; a stranger; a clown; ignorant; inexpert; artless.

نابود nā būd, adj. Non-existent; annihilated; destroyed; vanished; extinct.

نا بینا nā binā, adj. Blind.

ناپاک nā pāk, adj. Polluted; dirty; unclean; filthy; impure; defiled; lewd.

نا پاکی nā pāki, n.f. Impurity; uncleanliness; defilement; pollution; lewdness.

نا پائدار nā pā'idār, adj. Unstable; frail; unsteady; fickle; transitory; inconstant; not durable or lasting; momentary.

نا پائداری nā pā'idāri, n.f. Inconstancy; instability; frailty.

ناپدید nā padid, adj. Invisible; concealed; private.

نا پسند ٬ نا پسندیده nā pasand, nā pasandidah, adj. Disliked; unacceptable; disapproved; offensive; disagreeable; rejected; unwholesome.

نا پسندیدگی nā pasandīdagi, n.f. Dislike; disapproval; rejection.

نا پید ٬ نا پیدا nā paid, nā paidā, adj. Unborn; non-existent; extinct; lost; missing; not evident; invisible; not to be found; not available.

نا پیدا کنار nā paidā kinar, adj. Expansive; wide; extending far and wide; limitless.

نا تجربہ کار nā tajribah kār, adj. Inexperienced; untrained.

نا تراشیده na tarāshīdah, adj. Not pared; not smoothed; unshaved; impolite; unpolished; unlicked; uncivilised.

نا تربیت یافتہ nā tarbiyat yāftah, adj. Uneducated; untrained; rude; raw; uncultured; uncivilised.

نا ترس nā tars, adj. Fearless; pitiless; hard-hearted; severe; tyrant; unfeeling; merciless.

نا تمام nā tamām, adj. Incomplete; imperfect; deficient; unfinished.

نا توان na tawan, adj. Weak; feeble; frail; impotent; infirm; powerless; decrepit.

ناتوانی nā tawāni, n.f. Weakness; impotence; inability.

نا جائز nā jā'iz, adj. Unlawful; contraband.

نا جنس nā jins, adj. Of another sort or species; heterogeneous; strange in kind.

نا چار na char adj. Without remedy; constrained; helpless; destitute; distressed; forlorn

نا چاری na chari, n.f. Helplessness; impotence; necessity; constraint; destitution.

نا چاقی nā chaqi, n.f. Disagreement; indisposition; discord; coolness; lukewarmness; displeasure.

نا چیز nā chiz, adj. Of no account; of no consequence; trifling; insignificant; worthless; contemptible; of no earthly use.

ناحق na haqq, adj. Unjust; improper, wrong; illegal; undeserved; false; untrue; injurious. adv. Unjustly; improperly; falsely; in vain; wrongfully.

نا خدا ترس *nā khudā tars, adj.* Not fearing God; ungodly; cruel; stone-hearted; godless.

نا خلف *nā khalaf, adj.* Degenerate; undutiful (son); wicked; vicious.

نا خوانده *nā khwāndah, adj.* Uneducated; illiterate; unread; uninvited.

نا خوانده مهمان *nā khwāndah mihmān, n.m.* An uninvited guest.

نا خوش *nā khūsh, adj.* Displeased; unhappy; disgusted; disagreeing; indisposed; ill; sick.

نا خوشگوار *nā khūshgawār, adj.* Unpleasant; disgusting; undesirable.

نا خوشی *nā khūshī, n.f.* Disagreeableness; displeasure; fretting; disagreement; unpleasantness.

نادار *nā dār, adj.* Insolvent; poor; pauper; indigent; having no possession.

نا داری *nā dārī, n.f.* Poverty; insolvency; pauperism.

نادان *nā dān, adj.* Ignorant; silly; innocent; foolish.

نا دانستگی *nā dānistagī, n.f.* Ignorance.

نا دانسته *nā dānistah, adv.* Unknowingly; unwittingly; ignorantly.

نادانی *nā dānī, n.f.* Ignorance; foolishness.

نادرست *nā durust, adj.* Not right; incorrect; wrong; false; untrue; crooked; improper; imperfect.

نا دهند *nā dihand, adj.* Stingy; not paying; close-fisted. *n.m.* A bad pay-master.

نا دهندی *nā dihandī, n.f.* Non-payment.

نا دیدنی *nā dīdanī, adj.* Unfit to be seen; not possible to bear the sight (of); invisible.

نا دیده *nā dīdah, adj.* Unseen; greedy; glutton.

نا راست *nā rāst, adj.* Dishonest; wrong; unjust; unfair; fake; not straight forward; adulterated; false; untrue.

ناراستی *nā rāstī, n.f.* Dishonesty; injustice.

ناراض *nā rāẓ, adj.* Dissatisfied; discontented; unwilling; displeased; offended.

ناراضی *nā rāẓī, n.f.* Discontent; displeasure.

نارسا *nā rasā, adj.* Incapable of reaching (the destination); unworthy; unfit; ill-bred; unmannerly.

نارسائی *nā rasā'ī, n.f.* Unworthiness; unfitness; incapacity; failure; inability; ill-breeding; unmannerliness; unskilfulness.

نارسته ، نارسیده *nā rustah, nā rasīdah, adj.* Immature; not arrived (at maturity, perfection or puberty); unripe; raw.

ناروا *nā rawā, adj.* Unworthy; improper; unsuited; unlawful; not current; not allowed; inadmissible; prohibited; intolerable.

نازیب، نازیبا *nā zeb, nā zebā, adj.* Unbecoming; ill-shaped; unseemly; misfit; unsuitable.

نا ساز *nā sāz, adj.* Indisposed; out of sorts; out of tune; discordant; dissonant; discrepant; disagreeing; uncivil; absurd.

نا ساز گار *nā sāz gār, adj.* Unfavourable; absurd; out of tune; unfortunate.

نا ساز گاری *nā sāz gārī, n.f.* Discordance; misfortune; dissention.

نا سازی *nā sāzī, n.f.* Discordance; dissension; indisposition.

ناسپاس *nā sipās, adj.* Ungrateful; disagreeable; unthankful.

نا سزا وار *nā sazā wār, adj.* Unmerited; unworthy; indecent; impertinent; foolish; improper; undeserved.

ناسفته *nā suftah, adj.* Unbored; unstrung.

ناسمجھ *nā samajh, adj.* Unintelligent; dull; silly; foolish.

ناسمجھی *nā samajhī, n.f.* Ignorance.

ناشادؔ nā shād, adj. Cheerless; low-spirited; dull; dissatisfied; joyless; displeased; unfortunate.

ناشائستگی nā shā'istagi, n.f. Impropriety; injudiciousness; indecency.

ناشائستہ nā shā'istah, adj. Unbecoming; indecent; ill-mannered; illicit; bad; improper; unworthy; unfit; indecorous; unmannerly; inexpedient; injudicious; uncouth.

ناشدنی nā shudanī, adj. Not fit to exist; worthless; unpromising; impossible; bad; ill-fated; impracticable.

نا شکر ، ناشکرا nā shukr, nā shukrā, adj. Ungrateful; discontented.

نا شکری nā shukri, n.f. Ungratefulness; unthankfulness; discontent.

ناشکیب ، ناشکیبا nā shakeb, nā shakebā, adj. Impatient; restless; unsteady.

ناشکیبائی nā shakebā'ī, n.f. Impatience.

ناشناس nā shinās, adj. Ignorant.

ناشنو nā shanau, adj. Not hearing; inattentive.

ناصاف nā ṣāf, adj. Impure; unclean; unchaste; uneven.

ناصبور nā ṣabūr, adj. Impatient; restless.

ناصبوری nā ṣabūri, n.f. Impatience; restlessness.

ناطاقت nā ṭāqat, adj. Feeble; infirm; weak.

ناطاقتی nā ṭāqati, n.f. Weakness; feebleness; inability.

نافرجام nā farjām, adj. Unfortunate; indiscreet; short-sighted; thoughtless.

نافرمان nā farmān, adj. Disobedient.

نافرمانی nā farmānī, n.f. Disobedience.

نا فہم nā fahm, adj. Stupid; unintelligent; unwise.

ناقابل nā qābil, adj. Unfit; incapable; insignificant; unable; undeserving; unqualified; unworthy.

ناقابل استعمال nā qābil-ĕ isti'māl, adj. Unserviceable.

ناقابل اصلاح nā qābil-ĕ iṣlāh, adj. Irreclamable; incorrigible.

نا قابل اعتبار nā qābil-ĕ i'tibār, adj. Unreliable; unstable; untrustworthy; undependable.

نا قابل انتقال nā qābil-ĕ intiqāl, adj. Inalienable.

ناقابل برداشت nā qābil-ĕ bardāsht, adj. Intolerable.

ناقابل تردید nā qābil-ĕ tardīd, adj. Irrefutable; unanswerable; unassailable; uncontrovertible.

ناقابل ترمیم nā qābil-ĕ tarmīm, adj. Unamendable.

ناقابل تسخیر nā qābil-ĕ taskhīr, adj. Impregnable; unconquerable.

نا قابل تلافی nā qābil-ĕ talāfī, adj. Irremediable; irreplaceable; irretrievable.

ناقابل عمل nā qābil-ĕ 'amal, adj. Impracticable; inexecutable; unworkable.

ناقابل فہم nā qābil-ĕ fahm, adj. Unintelligible; uninterpretable; unfathomable; unapprehensible; intangible.

ناقابل قبول nā qābil-ĕ qubūl, adj. Inadmissible; unplausible.

ناقابل کاشت nā qābil-ĕ kāsht, adj. Uncultur-able; uncultivable.

نا قابلیت nā qābiliyyat, n.f. Inability; unworthiness; helplessness.

ناقدر ، ناقدرا nā qadr, nā qadrā, adj. Having no just appreciation for anything; unappreciative; ungrateful.

ناقدری nā qadri, n.m. Disgrace; low-estimation; non-recognition of merit.

ناکارہ nā kārah, adj. Unserviceable; useless; worthless.

ناکام nā kām, adj. Unsuccessful; hopeless; failing; disappointed; discontented; useless.

ناکامی nā kāmi, n.f. Failure; discontent; disappointment.

نا کتخدا ، نا کدخدا nā katkhudā, nā kadkhudā, adj. Bachelor; unmarried.

ناکردنی nā kardani, adj. Not worth doing or trying.

ناکرده گناه nā kardah gunāh, adj. Innocent; not guilty; faultless.

ناکس nā kas, adj. Of no importance; unworthy; worthless; base; mean.

ناگاه ، ناگه ، ناگہاں nā gāh, nā gah, nā gahān, adv. Suddenly; unexpectedly; abruptly; all of a sudden.

ناگہانی nā gahāni, ādj. Unexpected; accidental.

ناگزیر nā guzīr, adj. Indispensable; inevitable; unavoidable; necessary.

ناگفتنی nā guftani, adj. Unspeakable; unutterable.

ناگفته nā guftah, adj. Unsaid; untold.

ناگفته به nā guftah bih, adj. Better unsaid.

ناگوار ، ناگوارا nā gawār, nā gawārā, adj. Unpleasant; unpalatable; unwholesome; irksome.

نالائق nā lā'iq, adj. Unworthy; unfit; inconvenient; improper; unsuitable.

نامانوس nā mānūs, adj. Unfamiliar; stranger.

نامبارک nā mubārak, adj. Unfortunate; unlucky; ill-omened; unauspicious.

نامتناهی، نامحدود nā mutanāhi, nā maḥdūd, adj. Endless; unending; *ad infinitum*; infinite; boundless.

نامحرم nā maḥram, n.m. A stranger; one who is not permitted to enter women's apartments.

نامراد nā murād, adj. Disappointed; unfortunate; dissatisfied; unsuccessful; unlucky.

نامرادی nā murādi, n.f. Disappointment; dissatisfaction; bad luck.

نامربوط nā marbūṭ, adj. Unconnected; impertinent; ungrammatical.

نامرد nā mard, adj. Unmanly; cowardly; impotent; imbecile. n.m. A coward; an impotent person.

نامرد کرنا nā mard karnā, v. To emasculate.

نامردی nā mardi, n.f. Cowardice; impotency; unmanliness.

نامساعد nā musā'id, adj. Unfavourable; unhelping.

نامشخص nā mushakhkhaṣ, adj. Undefined; inconstant; variable.

نامشروع nā mashrū', adj. Illegal; unlawful.

نامطابق nā muṭābiq, adj. Inconsistent.

نامطبوع nā maṭbū', adj. Unpleasant; disagreeable; unprinted; unpublished.

نامعتبر nā mu'tabar, adj. Untrustworthy; unreliable.

نامعقول nā ma'qūl, adj. Unreasonable; improbable; absurd; impertinent; improper; irrational.

نامعلوم nā ma'lūm, adj. Unknown; uncertain.

نا ملائم nā mulā'im, adj. Hard; rough; uncivil.

ناممکن nā mumkin, adj. Impossible.

نا مناسب nā munāsib, adj. Improper; unbecoming; unfit; inconsistent.

نا منظور nā manẓūr, adj. Disallowed; refused; rejected; inadmissible; disapproved.

نا منظوری nā manẓūri, n.f. Disapproval; rejection.

نا موافق nā muwāfiq, adj. Unsuitable; contrary; unwholesome; adverse.

نا موافقت nā muwāfaqat, n.f. Disagreement; unsuitableness; unwholesomeness; dissimilarity; want of adaptation.

نا موزوں nā mauzūn, adj. Misfit; unsuitable.

نا مہربان nā mihrbān, adj. Unkind; unfriendly.

ناواجب nā wājib, adj. Improper; unsuited.

نا واقف nā wāqif, adj. Unacquainted; ignorant; unskilled; inexperienced.

نا وقت nā waqt, adj. Unseasonable; out of time.

نا ہموار nā hamwār, adj. Uneven; irregular; improper; unworthy; ill-mannered.

نا هنجار nā hanjār, adj. Ill-behaved; mean; good-for-nothing; worthless.

نایاب nā yāb, adj. Scarce; rare; unprocurable.

ناب nāb (P) adj. Pure; genuine; unadulterated; clear; sincere.

ناپ nāp (H) n.f/ m. Measurement; measure.

ناپنا nāpnā (H) v. To measure.

ناتا nātā (H) n.m. Relationship; kin; alliance; affinity.

ناتا توڑنا nātā toṛnā, v. To sever relations; to break an alliance.

ناتا جوڑنا nātā joṛnā, v. To form an alliance.

ناتھ nāth (S) n.m. Patron; master; lord; husband, a nose-string a nose-ring.

ناتھنا nāthnā (H) v. To thread the nose of an animal with string; to bring under control; to have complete contol.

ناٹا ، ناٹی nāṭa, nāṭī (H) adj. Short; dwarfish.

ناٹک nāṭak (S) n.m. A dramatic performance; a play; a pantomime a drama; a theatre; a mimic;

ناٹکیا nāṭakiyā (H) n.m. An actor; a dancer.

ناثر nāṣir (A) n.m. A prose writer.

ناج nāj (H) n.m. Grain; corn.

ناجی nājī (A) adj. Escaped; saved; elect; liberated; excused; free.

ناچ nāch (H) n.m. Dance; entertainment.

ناچ رنگ nāch raṅg, n.m. Dancing and singing; a dancing entertainment; revelry; merriment.

ناچ گھر nāch ghar, n.m. A dancing hall; a ball room; theatre; a play house.

ناچ نچانا nach nachānā, v. To make one dance; to tease; to worry; to harass.

ناچ نہ جانے آنگن ٹیڑھا nāch nah jāne āṅgan ṭeṛhā, prov. A bad workman quarrels with his tools

ناچنا nāchnā (H) v. To dance; to caper or frisk about.

ناخدا nākhudā (P) n.m. The master or commander of a ship; a captain; a seaman; a supercargo; a leader.

ناخن nākhun (P) n.m. Nail; talon; claw.

ناخن تراش ، ناخن گیر nākhun tarāsh, nākhun gīr, n.m. A nail parer; a nail-cutter; a nail clipper.

ناخن سے گوشت جدا کرنا nākhun se gosht judā karnā, v. To cause Separation between dear and near ones.

ناخن شمشیر nākhun-ĕ shamshīr, n.m. The edge of a sword.

ناخن گڑنا nākhun gaṛnā, v. To have access; to succeed; to have possession (of).

ناخن لینا nākhun lenā, v. To pare the nails; to trip or stumble (as a norse),

ناخنہ nākhunah (P) n.m. An instrument used to strike the strings of a guitar; a plectrum; a guitar quill; a haw or web in the eye.

ناخون nākhūn, n.m. See ناخن nākhun.

ناد nād (H) n.m. Sound; song; roar.

نادر nādir (A) adj. Rare; wonderful; choice; uncommon; singular; precious; unusual; curious.

نادر روز گار nādir-ĕ rūzgār, adj. The wonder of the world; unequalled.

نادری nādarī, n.f. A kind of jacket. adj. Belonging to Nadir Shah.

نادری حکم nādarī ḥukm, n.m. A tyrannical order; a Nadir Shah's order.

ناد علی nād-ĕ 'alī (A) n.f. Stone, on which are inscribed verses from the Quran, brought by pilgrims from Mecca and hung as charms round the necks of children.

نادم nādim (A) adj. Repenting; penitent; sorry; ashamed; abashed; bashful.

نار nār (A) n.f. Fire; hell.

نار **nār** (H) *n.f.* A woman; wife.

نارائن **nārā'in** (S) *n.m.* The Supreme Being.

نارجیل **nārjīl** (P) *n.m.* A cocoanut; the cocoanut tree.

نارنج **nāranj** (P) *n.m.* An orange.

نارنجی **nāranjī** (P) *adj.* Orange-coloured.

نارنگی **nārangī** (H) *n.f.* A small orange.

ناری **nārī** (A) *adj.* Fiery; full of fire; hellish.

ناری **nārī** (H) *n.f.* See نار *nār*.

ناریل **nāriyal** (H) *n.m.* The cocoanut-tree and its fruit; a *huqqah* made of cocoanut; a kind of firework.

ناریل کا تیل *nāriyal kā tel, n.m.* Cocoanut-oil.

ناڑا **nāṛā** (H) *n.m.* Tape; trouser-string.

ناڑا کھولنا *nāṛā kholnā, v.* To have sexual intercourse; to untie the trouser-string.

ناز **nāz** (P) *n.m.* Blandishment; coquetry; toying; whims; pride; airs; playfulness; gracefulness; elegance; soothing; fondling; amorous playfulness; softness; delicacy.

ناز اُٹھانا *nāz uṭhānā, v.* To bear with the whims and airs of another.

ناز برداری *nāz bardārī, n.f.* Praising the coquetry (of).

نازپروردہ *nāz parwardah, adj.* Delicately nurtured or brought up; a spoiled child.

ناز کرنا *nāz karnā, v.* To take airs; to be full of pride.

ناز نخرہ ، نازونیاز *nāz nakhrah, nāz-o niyāz, n.m.* Blandishments; airs and graces; affectations; toying; coquetry; dalliance.

ناز و نعمت *nāz-o ni'mat, n.m.* The good things of the world; the blessings of life; wealthiness.

نازاں **nāzāṅ** (P) *adj.* Proud; conceited; toying; strutting; swaggering; sporting.

نازبو **nāzbū** (P) *n.m.* Name of a herb; basil; wild rue.

نازش **nāzish** (P) *n.f.* Pride; boasting; haughtiness; arrogance.

نازک **nāzuk** (P) *adj.* Thin; light; delicate; nice; fragile; gracious; slim; sensative; subtle; tender; brittle; elegant; facetious; genteel.

نازک اندام ، نازک بدن *nāzuk andām, nāzuk badan, adj.* Delicate of body or form.

نازک خیال *nāzuk khayāl, adj.* Of delicate perception; of fine thought; having a fine perception.

نازک خیالی *nāzuk khayālī, n.f.* Delicacy of idea or perception.

نازک دماغ *nāzuk dimāgh, adj.* Of sensitive mind; of touchy disposition.

نازک زمانہ ، وقت *nāzuk zamānah, waqt, n.m.* A critical moment; a crisis.

نازک مزاج *nāzuk mizāj, adj.* Of delicate habit or complexion

نازک معاملہ *nāzuk mu'āmalah, n.m.* A delicate matter.

نازکی **nāzukī** (P) *n.f.* Delicacy; nicety; softness; tenderness.

نازل **nāzil** (A) *adj.* Descending; dismounting; alighting; arriving at.

نازل ہونا *nāzil honā, v.* To descend; to alight; to fall or come down.

نازلہ **nāzilah** (A) *n.m.* A misfortune; disorder; calamity; a disaster from heaven.

نازنین **nāznīn** (P) *n.f.* A delicate woman; a belle; a sweetheart. *adj.* Delicate; lovely.

ناس **nās** (H) *n.m.* Destruction; ruin. *n.f.* Snuff.

ناس کر دینا *nās kar denā, v.* To destroy; to ruin.

ناس کی چٹکی *nās kī chuṭkī, n.f.* A pinch of snuff.

ناستک nāstik (S) n.m. An athiest; an unbeliever; an infidel; one who denies a future state of rewards and punishments.

ناسخ nāsikh (A) n.m. A scribe; a copier of a book; an amanuensis one who cancels or repeals or abolishes a rule. adj. Abolishing; erasing; cancelling the previous order.

ناسک nāsik (A) adj. Devoted to God or to virtue.

ناسوت nāsūt (A) n.m. Humanity; human kind; human nature.

ناسور nāsūr (A) n.m. A fistula; an ulcer; a running sore.

ناسور بهرنا nāsūr bharnā, v. Healing of an ulcer or a fistula.

ناسور پڑنا nāsūr parṇā, v. To ulcerate; to become a running sore.

ناشپاتی nāshpāti (P) n.f. A pear.

ناشتا nāshtā (P) n.m. Breakfast; repast; meal.

ناشر nāshir (A) n.m. Exposer; announcer; broadcastor; a publisher.

ناصب nāṣib (A) adj. Erecting; setting up; fixing; placing. n.m. One who erects; the particle in grammar which admits of the use of زبر zabar for the word after it.

ناصح nāṣiḥ (A) n.m. An adviser; a sincere friend; a monitor; a counsellor; a faithful minister. adj. Giving good counsel; giving sound advice.

ناصر nāṣir (A) adj. Helping; assisting. n.m. A defender; an assistant; a helper; an ally.

ناصیه nāṣiyah (A) n.f. The forehead; the forelock over the head.

ناصیه سائی ، فرسائی naṣiyah sā'ī, farsā'ī, n.f. Imploring humbly.

ناطق nāṭiq (A) n.m. Speaker; a rational being. adj. Decisive; rational (quantity); definite.

ناطقه nāṭiqah (A) n.m. The faculty of speech.

ناطقه بند کرنا nāṭiqah band karṇā, v. To tease; to silence.

ناظر nāẕir (A) adj. Having sight; seeing; observant. n.m. An inspector; spectator; beholder; reader; a supervisor; a bailiff; a nāzir, a superintendent; a keeper; a sheriff in a civil court.

ناظر ضلع nāẕir-ĕ ẕila', n.m. District inspector.

ناظر تعلیم ضلع nāẕir-ĕ ta'līm-ĕ ẕila', n.m. District inspector of schools.

ناظره nāẕirah (A) n.m. The eye; sight; vision; reading; studying. n.f. An inspectress; a lady superintendent.

ناظره پڑھنا nāẕirah parhnā, v. To read (in opposition to repeating by heart).

ناظرین nāẕirin (A) n.m. (plu. of ناظر nāẕir) Beholders; readers; spectators.

ناظم nāẕim (A) n.m. An administrator; a manager; a director; a controller; a governor; a ruler; a poet; a composer of verses; a composer; adjuster; arranger.

ناغه nāghah (T) n.m. Close day; leave; absence; respite.

ناف nāf (P) n.f. The navel; the centre; the hub of wheel. adj. Middle; umbilical; navel-shaped.

ناف ٹلنا nāf ṭalnā, v. To be displaced (navel muscle).

ناف زمین nāf-ĕ zamīn, n.f. Centre of the earth; the Ka'abah.

نافذ nāfiẕ (A) adj. Having effect; issued; passed; in force; operative; valid; penetrating; reaching to.

نافذ کرنا nāfiẕ karnā, v. To enforce; to issue (orders); to give effect to.

نافذ هونا nāfiẕ honā, v. To penetrate or reach to; to have effect (on); to be issued.

نافع nāfi' (A) *adj*. Salutory: profitable; advantageous; useful; beneficial; good; wholesome.

نافلہ nafilah (A) *n.f.* Over and above the obligation; in excess of what is due; supererogatory devotion.

نافہ nafah (A) *n.m.* A pad of musk; a musk bag.

نافی ' نافیہ nafi, nafiah (P) *adj*. Rejecting; denying; negative; forbidding; prohibiting; refusing; abandoning.

ناقد naqid (A) *n.m.* An assayer; a critici a reviewer; a fault-finder.

ناقص nāqiṣ (A) *adj*. Defective; imperfect; deficient; mutilated; inexpert; wanting (in); unsound; bad; worthless; vicious.

ناقص الخلقت nāqiṣ-ul-khilqat, *adj*. Defective by birth; deformed.

ناقص العقل nāqiṣ-ul-'aql, *adj*. Deficient in understanding; of unsound mind; foolish; ignorant; silly; stupid.

ناقل nāqil (A) *n.m.* A reporter; a narrator; a copyist; delineator; a transcriber.

ناقوس nāqus (A) *n.m.* A conch; a marine shell.

ناقوس پھونکنا nāqūs phūnkna, *v*. To blow a conch (at divine worships to summon the congregation).

ناقہ naqah (A) *n.f.* A she-camel, a dromedary.

ناقہ سوار naqah sowar, *n.m.* A camel rider or driver; a messenger who comes on a camel.

ناک nāk (H) *n.f.* The nose; a prominent person or thing; honour; grace; ornament; a conspicuous person.

ناک آنا ' بہنا nāk ānā, bahnā, *v*. To have a running at the nose; flowing of mucus from the nose.

ناک اونچی ہونا nāk unchi honā, *v*. To be honoured; to be exalted; to succeed.

ناک بند nāk band, *n.m.* Nose-band; the ornamental part of a horse's bridle over the mouth.

ناک بند ہونا nak band honā, *v*. To suffer from cold; to catch cold; to suffocate owing to an attack of catarrh.

ناک بھوں چڑھنا nak bhaun charhana, *v*. To turn up the nose and knit the brows; to frown; to scowl; to be displeased.

ناک بیٹھنا ' پچکنا nak baithna, pichakna, *v*. Flattening of the nose; to be pressed (the nose.)

ناک بیندھنا nāk bindhnā, *v*. To bore the nose.

ناک پر انگلی رکھ کر بات کرنا nāk par ungli rakh kar bāt karnā, *v*. To speak like a woman or an eunuch; to employ blandishments.

ناک پر رکھ دینا nāk par rakh denā, *v*. To make prompt payment.

ناک پر غصہ ہونا nāk par ghuṣṣah honā, *v*. To be very irascible: to be easily provoked; to be quickly irritable.

ناک پر کی مکھی تک نہ اڑانا nak par ki makhkhi tak nah urānā, *v*. To be very slow or sluggish; to be easy going; to be happy-go-lucky sort of fellow.

ناک پر مکھی نہ بیٹھنے دینا nāk par makhkhi nah baithne denā, *v*. To be high-minded; to be proud.

ناک چڑھانا ' سکوڑنا nāh charhana, sakorna, *v*. To frown; to be displeased.

ناک چڑھی رہنا nāk charhi rahnā, *v*. To be ill-natured; to be ill-tempered.

ناک چنے چبوانا nāk chane chabwānā, *v*. To worry; to harass; to torment; to tease.

ناک چوٹی کاٹنا nāk choṭi kaṭnā, *v*. To punish severely; to disgrace (a woman).

ناک رکھنا nāk rakhnā, *v*. To preserve one's honour.

ناک رگڑنا nāk ragaṛnā, v. To beseach very humbly; to be humbled.

ناک سے لکیریں کھینچنا nāk se lakīren khenchna, v. To admit one's fault and promise to refrain from repeating it.

ناک کا بال nak ka bal, adj&n.m. Beloved; favourite; respected; one who is respected or honoured; one who has influence over another.

ناک کا بانسا nāk kā bānsā, n.m. The bridge of the nose.

ناک کا بانسا پھر جانا nāk kā bansā phir jānā, v. To be at the point of death.

ناک کاٹنا ، ناک کان کاٹنا nāk kātnā, nāk kān kāṭnā, v. To dishonour; to disgrace.

ناک کٹانا ، کٹنا nāk kaṭānā, kaṭnā, v. To be disgraced; to be dishonoured.

ناک کی سیدھ میں nāk kī sidh men, adv. Just in front; in a straight line.

ناک مارنا nāk mārnā, v. To spurn; to contemn.

ناک میں بولنا nāk men bolnā, v. To speak through the nose.

ناک میں دم آنا nāk men dam ānā, v. To be greatly worried or harassed.

ناک میں دم کرنا nāk men dam karnā, v. To worry; to tease; to harass.

ناک والا، والی nāk wālā, wālī adj. Honour able.

ناک nāk (P) (used as suffix). Affected with; inflamed with; full of; laden with (as in خوفناک khofnāk, fearful).

ناکا nākā (H) n.m. Entrance or extremity of a road; cross roads; boundary; eye of a needle; a gap in a bank or hedge or fence; a passage; a lane; an avenue; a waterway; an alligator.

ناکا بندی nakā bandi, n.f. Shutting up a passage; placing a picket at the extremity of a road; to stop traffic; blockade.

ناکے میں سے نکالنا nake men se nikālnd. v. To pass a thread through the needle hole; to bring under the yoke; to subjugate; to coerce; to tease.

ناکح nakiḥ (A) adj. One who marries

ناگ nāg (S) n.m. A snake; a hooded snake, a cobra (regarded as secred by Hindus); a serpent.

ناگا nāgā (S) n.m. An aboriginal tribe of Assam; an ascetic; a jogi.

ناگر موتھا nagar motha (H) n.m. Name of a sweet smelling grass.

ناگری nāgrī (S) n.f. The most common Hindi character of writing.

ناگن ، ناگنی nāgan, nāgni (S) n.f. A female serpent.

ناگیسر nāgesar (S) n.m. Name of a flower.

نال nal (H) n.f. A tube; a barrel; a pipe; a hollow tubular stock; any tubular vessel; the bore of a gun; the navel string; throat; neck; a hollow reed; the threads or pith inside a writing reed; a weavers shuttle.

نالا nālā (H) n.m. A rivulet; a brook; a canal; a gutter; a furrow; a ravine; a water course; a drain tape; string for trousers or drawers; red thread.

نالاں nālān (P) adj. Lamenting; moaning; groaning.

نالش nālish (P) n.f. Complaint; lamentation; groan; charge; accusation; an action; a suit.

نالش کرنا nālish karna, v. To complain against; to bring an action; to prosecute; to sue.

نالشی nālishī (P) n.m. Complainant; plaintiff; suitor; prosecutor.

نالکی nalki (H) n.f. A sort of open palanquin, used by aristocratic ladies.

نالہ nalah (P) n.m. Complaint; lamentation, weeping.

نالہ کش nālah kash, adj. Lamenter.

نالہ کرنا nālah karnā, v. To lament; to sigh; to moan; to groan; to complain.

نالہ و زاری nālah-ŏ zārī n.f. Lamentation; moan.

نالی nālī (H) n.f. A drain; a vein; a tubulated tile; a sinuous ulcer or fistula.

نام nām (P) n.m. Name; designation; appellation; title; honour; fame; reputation; character; renown; good name.

نام آور nām āwar, adj. Famous; renowned.

نام آوری nām āwarī, n.f. Fame; renown; reputation.

نام اچھالنا nām uchhālnā, v. To expose a person; to defame.

نام باقی رہنا nām bāqī rahnā, v. To leave a successor; to leave only the name.

نام بدنام کرنا nām badnām karnā, v. To defame; to accuse.

نام بدنام ہونا nām badnām honā, v. To be accused; to be defamed.

نام بڑا ہونا nām baṛā honā, v. To have a name; to be renowned; to belong to a noble family.

نام بکتا ہے nām biktā hai, Saying. The name sells; when an article gets established in market its name is sufficient guarantee for its sale.

نام بگاڑنا nām bigāṛnā, v. To defame; to nickname a person; to speak ill of.

نام بہ نام nām bah nām, adv. Per head; after each name.

نام پانا nām pānā, v. To win a great name; to be honoured.

نام پر nām par, adv. In the name of.

نام پر جان دینا nām par jān denā, v. To be prepared to sacrifice one's life over one's good name.

نام پر حرف آنا nām par ḥarf anā, v. To become unpopular.

نام پڑ جانا nām paṛ jāna, v. To be called by another name.

نام پکارنا nām pukārnā, v. To call by name; to call over the names of.

نام پیدا کرنا nām paidā karnā, v. To make a name; to become famous.

نام جو nām jū, adj. Fame-hunter.

نام خاک میں مل جانا nām k͟hāk men mil jānā, v. To suffer in reputation.

نام خدا nām-ĕ k͟hudā, intj. Bravo! Good heavens !

نام خراب کرنا nām k͟harāb kārnā, v. To defame; to dishonour.

نام دار nām dār, adj. Famous; celebrated; renowned; noted.

نام داری nām dārī, n.f. Fame; renown; celebrity.

نام دھرنا nām dharnā, v. To give a name (to); to blame; to accuse.

نام ڈبونا nām dabonā, v. To lose one's honour or reputation.

نام رکھنا nām rakhnā, v. To name; to blame; to accuse; to criticie.

نام روشن ہونا nām roshan honā, v. To become famous.

نام زد nām zad, adj. Named; nominated; noted; destined; declared; appointed; famous; renowned; dedicated; betrothed.

نام زد کرنا nām zad karnā, v. To nominate; to dedicate, to betroth; to name.

نام زدگی nām zadagī, n.f. Nomination.

نام سے nām se, adv. In the name of; on behalf of.

نام سے بیزار ہونا nām se bezār honā, v. To hate one; to be tired of; to be sick of; to be fed up with.

نام سے دم نکلنا nām se dam nikalnā, v. To be afraid of.

نام سے واقف ہونا nām se wāqif honā, v. To know by name.

نام کر جانا nām kar jānā, v. To leave a good name behind.

نام کرنا nām karnā, v. To become famous; to name a child.

نام کو nām ko, adv. In name only.

نام کو دھبا لگانا nām ko dhabbā lagānā, v. To get a bad name; to defame.

نام کو نہ چھوڑنا nām ko nah chhoṛnā, v. Not to leave a thing worth the name.

نام کو نہ ہونا nām ko nah honā, v. Not to be worth the name.

نام لگانا nām lagānā, v. To accuse; to charge.

نام لگنا nām lagnā, v. To be accused (of); to be charged (with).

نام لے کر nām le kar, adv. In the name of.

نام لینا nām lenā, v. To praise; to tell one's beads; to call by name; to accuse falsely.

نام لیوا nām lewā, n.m. An heir; a descendent.

نام نکلنا nām nikalnā, v. To become famous or notorious; to discover the name of the guilty; to become a by-word.

نام نہاد nām nihād, adj. Called; so-called; nominated; dedicated; nominal; assumed; not real or essential.

نام ور nām war, adj. Celebrated; famous.

نام وری nām warī, n.f. Fame; renown; celebrity.

نام و نشان nām-ŏ nishān, n.m. Name and address or particulars; sign; trade mark.

نام ہونا nām honā, v. To be conspicuous; to be famous or renowned.

ناموس nāmūs (A) n.f. Reputation; fame; renown; chastity; honour; disgrace; the female part of a family.

ناموس اکبر nāmūs-ĕ akbar, n.m. The angel Gabriel.

نامہ nāmah (P) n.m. A letter; writing; history; treatise; book; principle.

نامہ اعمال nāmah-ĕ a'māl, n.m. Conduct; register; register of deeds.

نامہ بر nāmah bar, n.m. A letter-carrier; messenger.

نامہ نگار nāmah nigār, n.m. News writer; correspondent.

نامہ و پیام nāmah-ŏ payām, n.m. Correspondence.

نامی nāmī (P) adj. Illustrious; celebrated; famous; notorious.

نامیاتی nāmiyātī (A) adj. Organic.

نامیہ nāmiyah (A) n.f. The power of growth or vegetating.

نان nān (P) n.f. Bread; a loaf.

نان بائی nān bā'ī, n.m. A baker; a bread-maker.

نان پاؤ nān pā'o, n.f. A kind of leavened bread.

نان جویں nān-ĕ jawīn, n.f. Barley bread; simple and coarse diet.

نان خواہ nān khwāh, n.m. A seed of the plant of dill kind used as digestive medicine (اجوائن ajwā'in); a beggar.

نان و نفقہ nān-ŏ nafqah, n.m. Maintenance allowance.

نان و نمک nān-ŏ namak, n.m. Simple diet.

نانا nānā (H) n.m. Mother's father; maternal grandfather.

نانڈ nāṅd (H) n.f. A large earthen pan; vat.

نانی nānī (H) n.f. Maternal grandmother.

ناؤ nā'o (H) n.f. A boat; a ship; anything long and hollow within; a ferry.

ناوک nāwak (P) n.m. An arrow; a tube; the sting of a bee.

ناوک انداز nāwak andāz, n.m. An archer.

ناو نوش nāo nosh (P) n.m. Feasting; eating and drinking; carousing; banquetting.

ناہار nāhār (S) n.m. Lunch; breakfast.

ناہید nāhīd (P) n.m. The planet Venus.

نائب nā'ib (A) n.m. A deputy; delegate; vicegerent; attorney; assistant.

نائب مناب nā'ib manāb, n.m. A locum tenens; a successor; vicegerent.

نائک nā'ik (S) n.m. A chief; a leader; a man; a lad; a youth; a native officer; a person well-versed in dancing, singing &c.

نائکہ nā'ikah (S) n.f. Female of نائک nā'ik; a damsel; a lass; the mistress of a house; the mistress of a brothel; a bawd.

نائن nā'in (H) n.f. A barber's wife.

نائی nā'ī (H) n.m. A barber.

نبات nabāt (A) n.f. Vegetation; herb; vegetable; plant; grass.

نباتات nabātāt (A) n.f. (plu. of نبات nabāt) Vegetables; plants.

نبات nabāt (P) n.f. Sweetmeat; crystallised sugar.

نباتاتی nabātāti (A) adj. Botanical.

نباش nabbāsh (A) n.m. A plunderer of the dead.

نباض nabbāẓ (A) n.m. One who is expert at feeling the pulse; a physician.

نباہ nibāh (H) n.m. Accomplishment; carrying on or through; accomplishing; performance; accommodation; constancy.

نباہ کرنا nibāh karnā, v. To keep a promise; to accommodate; to live together; to endure; to pull on.

نباهنا nibāhnā (H) v. To accomplish; to perform; to guard; to behave; to conduct; to endure for a long time.

نبٹانا nibṭānā (H) v. To settle; to decide; to conclude; to discharge an account.

نبٹ جانا ، نبٹنا nibaṭ jānā, nibaṭnā (H) v. To be finished; to be settled; to be concluded.

نبرد nabard (P) n.f. Battle; engagement; war.

نبرد آزما nabard āzmā, adj. Brave; warrior; warlike.

نبردگاہ nabard gāh, n.f. Battlefield.

نبڑنا nibaṛnā (H) v. To be accomplished; to be finished or spent; to be ended; to be separated or divided.

نبض nabẓ (A) n.f. The pulse.

نبض دیکھنا nabẓ dekhnā, v. To feel the pulse (of).

نبضیں چھوٹنا nabẓeṅ chhūṭnā, v. To cease beating (the pulse); to have no pulse; to be dying.

نبوت nabuwwat (A) n.f. The office of a prophet; divining.

نبولی niboli (H) n.f. Fruit of نیم nim tree.

نبوی nabavi (A) adj. Of the prophet; prophetical.

نبھانا nibhānā (H) v. See نباهنا nibāhnā.

نبھاؤ nibhā'o (H) n.m. See نباہ nibāh.

نبھنا nibhnā (H) v. To serve; to succeed; to live together; to last; to be accomplished; to pass.

نبی nabi (A) n.m. A prophet.

نبیذ nabīẕ (A) n.f. Beer.

نبیرہ nabīrah (P) n.m/f. A grandson; a son's son; a daughter's son; a grand-daughter.

نبیڑنا nabeṛnā (H) v. To end; to put an end to; to complete; to finish; to spend; to perform.

نبیسہ nabbisah (P) n.m./f. Grandson; granddaughter.

نپاتلا napā tulā (H) adj. Measured and weighed; limited; fixed; determined.

نپان napān (H) n.f./m. Measure; meassurement.

نپٹانا nipṭānā (H) v. See نبٹانا nibṭānā.

نپٹنا nipaṭnā (H) v. See نبٹنا nibaṭnā.

نپنا napnā (H) v. To be measured; to be surveyed; to have a quarrel with.

نت nit (H) adj. Always; ever; continually; eternally.

نت‌نیا ، نت نئی nit nayā, nit na'i, adj. Everyday fresh; extraordinary.

نتائج natā'ij (A) n.m. (plu. of نتیجہ natijah) Results; issues; consequences.

نتھ nath (H) n.f. A large nose ring worn by women.

نتھارنا nithārnā (H) v. To purify; to distil; to draw off.

نتھرنا nitharnā (H) v. To be distilled; to be purified.

نتھنا nathnā (H) n.m. A nostril; a ring for the nose (of an animal). v. To have the nose bored and threaded.

نتھنے پھلانا ، چڑھانا nathne phulānā, charhānā, v. To be furious; to be angry.

نتھنی nathnī (H) n.f. A small nose-ring.

نتھنی آتارنا nathnī utārnā, v. To have a sexual intercourse with a virgin; to deflower.

نتھی naththi (H) n.f. A file; the thread with which papers are strung together.

نتھی شدہ naththī shudah, adj. Strung together and placed on the file; placed on record.

نتھی کرنا naththī karnā, v. To place on record.

نتیجہ natījah (A) n.m. Result; consequence; end; issue; reward; inference; deduction; conclusion; offspring; birth.

نٹ naṭ (S) n.m. The name of a tribe of jugglers; a rope-dancer; a tumbler; a mimic; an actor; a cheat; a knave.

نٹ کھٹ naṭ khaṭ (H) adj. Shrewd; naughty; roguish; artful.

نٹنی naṭnī (H) n.f. The wife of a naṭ; the woman of the naṭ tribe.

نثار niṣār (A) n.m. Scattering; throwing; strewing; dispersion; sacrifice; money which is thrown to the poor people on festive occasions.

نثار کرنا niṣār karnā, v. To scatter; to strew; to throw over the head (money etc.); to sacrifice.

نثار ہونا niṣār honā, v. To be sacrificed.

نثار naṣṣār (A) n.m. A prose writer; one well-versed in prose writing.

نثر naṣr (A) n.f. Prose.

نج nij (H) adj. Own; personal; particular; individual.

نج کا nij kā, adj. Private; personal; peculiar; unofficial.

نجابت najābat (A) n.f. Nobleness; gentility; nobility; high-mindedness.

نجات najāt (A) n.f. Liberation; salvation; absolution; escape; deliverance.

نجار najjār (A) n.m. A carpenter.

نجاری najjāri (A) n.f. Carpentry.

نجاست najāsat (A) n.f. Dirtiness; impurity; filth; dirt.

نجد najd (A) n.m. High ground or land; name of the higher part of Arabia.

نجس najis, najs (A) adj. Impure; dirty; filthy; nasty; unclean.

نجس العین najis-ul-a'in, adj. Impure by nature.

نجف najaf (A) n.m. High ground; a hillock; uncommanded area; place of Hazrat Ali's tomb.

نجم najm (A) n.m. A star; a planet; fortune; a prediction from observation of the stars; horoscope.

نجم الثاقب najm-uṣ-ṣāqib, n.m. A shining star.

نجوم nujūm (A) n.m. (plu. of نجم najm) Stars, astronomy; astrology.

نجومی nujūmi (A) n.m. An astrologer.

نجی niji (H) See نج کا nij kā.

نجیب najib (A) adj. Excellent; noble; generous; praise-worthy; of noble birth; honourable.

نجيب الطرفين najib-uṭ-ṭaraffain, adj. Noble on both sides (father and mother); of noble birth.

نچا کهچا nuchā khuchā (H) adj. Scratched and torn.

نچان nichān (H) n.f. Lowness; depression; depth; cavity; hollow; bottom; valley; slope; declinity.

نچانا nachānā (H) v. To make one dance; to spin.

نچڑنا nichuṛnā (H) v. To be pressed out; to be squeezed.

نچلا ، نچلی nichlā, nichlī (H) adj. Lower; silent; inactive; motionless; quiet.

نچلا نہ بیٹھنا nichlā nah baiṭhnā, v. Not to sit quiet; to be moving about; to be making a noise.

نچنا nuchnā (H) v. To be scratched or plucked.

نچنت nichant (H) adj. Free from thought or anxiety or care; unconcerned; leisured.

نچوانا nachwānā (H) v. To make one dance.

نچوانا nuchwānā (H) v. To cause one to scratch or pluck.

نچوڑ nichoṛ (H) n.m. The end or termination of an affair; essence; pith; gist; summary.

نچوڑ لینا ، نچوڑنا nichoṛ lenā, nichoṛnā (H) v. To rinse; to wring; to squeeze; to press out; to extort; to exact; to strain.

نچویا nachwaiyyā (H) n.m. A dancer.

نچهاور nichhāwar (H) n.m. Sacrifice; victim; money thrown to the poor on festive occasions; propitiatory offering.

نچهاور کرنا nichhāwar karnā, v. To sacrifice.

نچهتر nachhattar (H) n.m. A lunar mansion or constellation in the path of the moon; a star or asterism.

نحر naḥr (A) n.m. Cutting the throat (of a camel); slaughtering; sacrificing.

نحس naḥs (A) adj. Unlucky; inauspicious; ill-fated.

نحل naḥl (A) n.f. The bee.

نحو naḥv (A) n.f. Way; path; manner; mode; syntax (grammar); inflection.

نحوست naḥūsat (A) n.f. Bad presage; ominousness; portent; abomination; misfortune; evil; an unhappy accident.

نحوی naḥwī (A) n.m. A grammarian; a teacher of syntax. adj. Grammatical; syntactical.

نحیف naḥīf (A) adj. Meagre; weak; slender.

نخاس nakhkhās (A) n.m. A market for slaves and cattle; a slave market; a cattle market.

نخاس چڑهنا nakhkhās chaṛhnā, v. To go to the market for sale; to be ill-famed.

نخالص nikhāliṣ, adj. Impure; adulterated; mixed.

نخچیر nakhchīr (P) n.m. The chase; game; prey; hunting.

نخرا ، نخره nakhrā, nakhrah, n.m. Trick; artifice; coquetry; show; pretence; blandishment; lofty or disdainful airs; swagger.

نخرے باز nakhre bāz, adj. Pretender; an affected person; a prude; coquettish.

نخشب nakhshab (P) n. prop. Name of a city in Turkistan, where the imposter Muqanna' caused moon to ascend from a pit.

نخل nakhl (A) n.m. A date-tree; a palm-tree; a plant.

نخلستان nakhlistān (A&P) n.m. An oasis; a date grove.

نخوت nakhwat (A) n.f. Pride; haughtiness; pomp; magnificence.

نخود nukhūd (P) n.m. Grams; chick-pea.

نخود آب nukhūd āb, n.m. Gram water.

ند nad (S) n.m. Ocean; river; rivulet; stream.

ندا nidā (A) n.f. Sound; voice; call to prayer; proclamation; calling; vocative; edict; bid at auction.

نداف naddāf (A) n.m. A cotton dresser; a carder.

ندامت nadāmat (A) n.f. Repentance; regret.

ندرت nudrat (A) n.f. Oddness; singularity; rareness.

ندماء nudamā' (A) n.m. (plu. of ندیم nadīm) Companions.

ندوہ nadwah (A) n.m. Association; society; body.

ندی nadī, naddī (H) n.f. A river; a rivulet.

ندیم nadīm (A) n.m. A companion; a courtier.

نڈر niḍar (H) adj. Fearless; dauntless; intrepid; daring.

نڈھال niḍhāl (H) adj. Still; motionless; tired; weak.

نذر naẕr (A) n.f. A vow; a gift; an offering; an interview.

نذر و نیاز naẕr-ŏ niyāz, n.f. Gifts and oblation.

نذرانہ naẕrānah (P) n.m. A tribute; a present.

نذیر naẕīr (A) n.m. One who frightens or terrifies or threatens.

نر nar (P & S) n.m. A male; a man; mankind. adj. Masculine; male.

نر مادہ ، نر مادین nar mādah, nar mādin, n.m. Male and female.

نر ناری nhr nārī, n.m. Man and woman.

نر nir (S). A negative prefix; without.

نراس ، نراسا nirās, nirāsā, adj. Having no hope; despaired, despondent.

نربدھ nir budh, adj. Destitute of reason; stupid; fool.

نربل nir bal. Without strength or power.

نرپھل nir phal, adj. Fruitless.

نرجل nir jal, adj. Without water; waterless; waste.

نرجلا nir jalā, n.m. A fast during which drinking of water is prohibited.

نرجیو nir jīv, adj. Lifeless; inanimate. n.m. Lifelessness; death.

نردوش nir dosh, adj. Without defect or blemish; innocent.

نردھن nir dhan, adj. Poor; needy.

نرمل nir mal, adj. Spotless; stainless.

نرموھی nir mohī, adj. Wanting in affection; cold; heartless.

نروان nir wān, n.m. Disappearance; extinction (as fire); emancipation (of soul); highest bliss.

نرا ، نری nirā, nirī (H) adj. Mere; pure; only; unalloyed; simple.

نرالا ، نرالی nirālā, nirālī (H) adj. Aloof; unequalled; rare; strange; odd.

نرخ nirkh (P) n.m. Market rate; current price; tariff; assize.

نرخ بندی nirkh bandī, n.f. Fixation of rates.

نرخ نامہ nirkh nāmah, n.m. Price list; catalogue of prices.

نرخرا narkharā, n.m. The throat; windpipe.

نرد nard (P) n.f. A counter; a chessman; draughts; backgammons.

نرد بان nardbān (P) n.m. A stair case; flight of steps; a ladder; a scaling ladder.

نرسل narsal (H) n.m. See نرکل narkal.

نر سنگھا nar singhā (H) n.m. A horn; a wind instrument.

نرغا ، نرغہ narghā, narghah n.m. Encirclement; besieging; trouble; difficulty; crowd; mob.

نرغے میں آ جانا narghe meṅ ā jānā, v. To be surrounded (by troubles).

نرک nark (S) n.m. Hell; the infirnal regions.

نرکل narkal (H) n.m. A kind of reed of which mats are made.

نرگس ***nargis*** (P) *n.f.* Narcissus; the eye of a mistress.

نرگس شهلا ***nargis-ĕ shahlā***, *n.f.* The narcissus which is black instead of being yellow; the eye of a mistress.

نرگسی ***nargisi*** (P) *adj.* Like the narcissus; of the narcissus; a kind of garment.

نرگسی کباب ***nargisi kabāb***, *n.m.* Boiled eggs covered with cooked mince meat.

نرم ***narm*** (P) *adj.* Smooth; plastic; tender; simple; soft (tone); moderate (price); dull (market); slow (speed); easy (digestion); slack; mild; defective (coin). *adv.* Softly; gently.

نرم دل ***narm dil***, *adj.* Tender hearted; gentle.

نرم رو ***narm rau***, *adj.* Easy-going; considerate.

نرم گرم ***narm garm***, *adj.* Lukewarm; new and old; good and bad; the ups and downs of life; the vicissitudes of time.

نرم گرم سہنا ***narm garm sahnā***, *v.* To put up with the ups and downs of life; to endure; to bear up.

نرم لگام ***narm lagām***, *adj.* Tender mouthed (a horse).

نرم‌نرم ***narm narm***, *adj.* Very soft.

نرما ' نرمه ***narmā, narmah***, *n.m.* The silk cotton plant; a kind of grass.

نرمانا ***narmānā***, *v.* To soften; to relax; to abate; to soothe; to pacify; to reduce; to lower.

نرماهٹ ' نرمائی ***narmāhaṭ, narmā'ī***, *n.f.* Smoothness; softness; delicacy.

نرمی ***narmī*** (P) *n.f.* Softness; smoothness; tenderness; delicacy; sycophancy; abatement; mildness; easiness; fluency.

نری ***narī*** (P) *n.f.* Tanned leather of a goat; skin.

نرینه ***narinah*** (P) *adj.* Male; masculine.

نزار ***nazār*** (P) *adj.* Thin; slim; lean; slender; subtle.

نزاع ***nizā'*** (A) *n.m.* Dispute; contention; altercation; controversy; law-suit; subject of dispute; point of issue; litigation.

نزاکت ***nazākat*** (P) *n.f.* Delicacy; neatness; elegance; politeness; softness.

نزد ' نزدیک ***nizd, nazdīk*** (P) *adj.* Near; close; contiguous; neighbouring; in the opinion of; in the possession of.

نزدیکی ***nazdīkī***, *n.f.* Nearness; proximity; approach; vicinity; approximation; neighbourhood.

نزع ***naza'*** (A) *n.f.* The agonies of death; the last breath; expiration.

نزله ***nazlah*** (A) *n.m.* Catarrh; rheum.

نزله بر عضو ضعیف می ریزد ***nazlah bar 'uẓw-ĕ ẓa'īf mī rezad***, *prov.* The weaker always gets it in the neck.

نزول ***nuzul*** (A) *n.m.* Descent; alighting; sojourning; catarrh; cataract of the eye; hydrocele; hernia; humoralis; government lands; confiscated land.

نزول وحی ***nuzūl-ĕ waḥī***, *n.m.* Divine revelation; inspiration.

نزهت ***nuzhat*** (A) *n.f.* Verdure; freshness; pleasure; delight; cheerfulness; purity.

نژاد ***nazhād*** (P) *n.f.* Origin; root; race; family; descent; extraction.

نس ***nas*** (H) *n.f.* A vein; a muscle; a nerve; a sinew; a tendon.

نس دار ***nas dār***, *adj.* Sinewy.

نس مرنا ***nas marnā***. To have weak muscles.

نس ***nis*** (S) *n.f.* Night.

نس دن ***nis din***, *n.m.* & *adv.* Night and day; always.

نساء ***nisā'*** (A) *n.f.* (*plu.* of امرأة *imra'at*) Women; ladies; the female-sex.

نسب **nasab** (A) *n.m.* Geneology; family; lineage; race; caste.

نسب نامہ **nasab nāmah**, *n.m.* Pedigree; geneological tree; account of descent.

نسب نما **nasab numā'** *n.m.* Denominator.

نسبت **nisbat** (A) *n.f.* Relation; affinity; attribute; reference; alliance; connection; betrothal; relationship by marriage; ratio; comparison. *adv.* With reference (to); in respect (of); in proportion (to).

نسبت تناسب **nisbat-ĕ tanāsub**, *n.f.* Ratio-proportion.

نسبت رکھنا **nisbat rakhnā**, *v.* To bear relation (to); to have to do (with).

نسبت کرنا **nisbat karnā**, *v.* To refer; to attribute; to betroth; to form a matrimonial alliance.

نسبتی **nisbatī**, *adj.* Related; having reference to.

نسترن **nastaran** (P) *n.f.* A kind of white rose; the dog-rose; name of a kind of cloth.

نستعلیق **nasta'līq** (P) *n.m.* A kind of Persian script; a fine round hand. *adj.* Well-behaved; gentlemanly.

نسخ **naskh** (A) *n.m.* Abolition; transcribing; transformation; abrogation; repeal; a kind of Arabic character.

نسخ کرنا **naskh karnā**, *v.* To cancel; to abolish; to repeal; to reject; to abrogate.

نسخہ **nuskhah** (A) *n.m.* A prescription; a copy or model; an edition: a writing book; a treatise; a recipe; a prototype; an exemplar.

نسر **nasr** (A) *n.m.* A vulture; an eagle.

نسرین **nasrīn** (P) *n.m.* A wild rose; the jonquil.

نسق **nasaq, nasq** (A) *n.m.* Order; series; arrangement; style; manner.

نسل **nasl** (A) *n.f.* Race; pedigree; geneology; descent; breed; caste; origin; family; offspring; lineage; progeny.

نسل بڑھانا **nasl baṛhānā**, *v.* To progenerate; to breed.

نسلاً **naslan** (A) *adv.* By descent.

نسلاً بعد نسلٍ **naslan ba'da naslin**, *adv.* In succession; generation after generation.

نسلی **naslī**, *adj.* Of or relating to family or breed.

نسوار **naswār** (H) *n.f.* Snuff; powdered tobacco.

نسواں **niswāṅ** (A) *n.f.* (*plu.*) Females; ladies.

نسوانی **niswanī** (A&P) *adj.* Pertaining to females; effaminate.

نسیاً منسیاً **nasiyan mansiyan** (A) *adj.* Forgotten and obliterated.

نسیان **nisyān** (A) *n.m.* Oblivion; forgetfulness;

نسیم **nasīm** (A) *n.f.* Zephyr; fragrant air; breeze.

نشا **nashā**, *n.m.* See نشہ **nashshah.**

نشاۃ **nasha't** (A) *n.f.* Creation; growing; anything produced; universe.

نشاۃ اولیٰ **nasha't-ĕ ūlā**, *n.f.* Gensis; origination.

نشاۃ ثانیہ **nasha't-ĕ ṣāniyah**, *n.f.* Renaissance.

نشاستہ **nishāstah** (P) *n.m.* Starch; paste; pottage; thick gruel.

نشاط **nasāṭ** (P) *n.f.* Gladness; joy; pleasure; cheerfulness; sprightliness.

نشان **nishān** (P) *n.m.* Mark; sign; signal; proof; type; emblem; note; device; trace; scar; impression; armorial bearings; coat of arms; badge; an ensign; flag; standard; a clue; seal; stamp; address of a person; target.

نشان بردار ، نشانچی **nishān bardār, nishānchī**, *n.m.* Standard bearer.

نشانہ **nishānah** (P) *n.m.* A mark; a target; a butt; an aim.

نشانہ باندھنا **nishānah bāndhnā**, *v.* To take aim.

نشانہ خطا ہونا *nishānah khaṭā honā*, *v.* To miss the mark; to misfire.

نشانہ کرنا ' لگانا ' مارنا *nishānah karnā*, *lagānā*, *mārnā*, *v.* To hit the mark.

نشانی *nishānī* (P) *n.f.* A mark; sign; token; model; a keepsake, a souvenir; a book mark.

نشتر *nishtar* (P) *n.m.* A lancet; a fleam.

نشٹ *nishṭ* (H).*adj* Lost; destroyed; annihilated.

نشر *nashr* (A) *n.m.* Spreading; extending; deffusing; publishing; scattering; reviving; restoring of life; resuscitation.

نشرالصوت *nashr-uṣ-ṣaut*, *n.m.* Broadcast.

نشر *nashar* (A) *adj.* Scattered; spread out.

نشست *nishast*, *nashast* (P) *n.f.* Sitting; seat; society; symmetry.

نشست برخاست *nishast barkhāst*, *n.f.* Manners; etiquette; posture; politeness.

نشست گاہ *nishast gah*, *n.f.* A drawing room; a parlour.

نشو *nashv* (A) *n.m.* Growth; vegetation.

نشوونما *nashv-ŏ namā*, *n.f./m.* Growth; development.

نشور *nushūr* (A) *n.m.* Raising of the dead; resurrection.

نشہ *nashshah*, *nashah* (P) *n.m.* Intoxication; pride; arrogance; perception.

نشہ آترنا *nashah utarnā*, *v.* To come to one's senses.

نشہ پانی *nashah pānī*, *n.m.* Intoxicating liquors or drugs.

نشہ چڑھنا *nashah chaṛhnā*, *v.* To become intoxicated.

نشہ کرکرا کرنا *nashah kirkirā karnā*, *v.* To interrupt; to disturb; to upset a feast.

نشہ کرنا *nashah karnā*, *v.* To be addicted to intoxicating drinks.

نشہ ہرن ہونا *nashah haran honā*, *v.* To come to one's senses; disappearing of intoxication.

نشے باز *nashe bāz*, *n.m.* A drunkard; one addicted to intoxicating drinks.

نشے میں چور ہونا *nashe meṅ chūr honā*, *v.* To be dead drunk.

نشیب *nasheb*, *nisheb* (P) *n.m.* Descent; declivity; slope; low ground; a hallow.

نشیب و فراز *nasheb-ŏ farāz*, *n.m.* Ups and downs of life; descent and ascent; declivity and acclivity; good and bad; profit and loss; advantage and disadvantage of an affair; vicissitudes of fortune.

نشیلا ' نشیلی *nashīlā*, *nashīlī*, *adj.* Intoxicating.

نشیمن *nasheman* (P) *n.m.* Seat; residence; nest; resting place; bench; stool.

نشین *nashīn* (P) *adj.* Sitting (used in *comp.* as گوشہ نشین *goshah nashīn*, retired; recluse).

نشینی *nashīnī* (P) *n.f.* Sitting (used in *comp.* as in گوشہ نشینی *goshah nashīnī*, retirement; reclusion).

نص *naṣṣ* (A) *n.f.* Search; investigation; definite; decisive or final order; anything apparent and clear.

نص قرانی *naṣṣ-ĕ qurānī*, *n.f.* A verse of the Quran which is clear and definite in its meanings, or which states clearly what is right and what is wrong.

نصاب *niṣāb* (A) *n.m.* What is fixed or established; a root; origin; principle; principal; capital; property; stock; a certain estate or number of cattle for which tax is paid; course; curriculum; syllabus; fulcrum.

نصاری *naṣārā* (A) *n.m.* Nazarenes; Christians.

نصائح *naṣā'iḥ* (A) *n.f.* (*plu.* of نصیحت *naṣīḥat*) Advices; good counsels; admonitions.

نصب *naṣb* (A) *n.m.* Erection; establishment; fixing; planting; (Grammar) the vowel point زبر *zabar* (َ).

نصب العين naṣb-ul-'aīn (A) n.m. Ideal; a model of perfection.

نصب کرنا naṣb karnā, v. To establish; to fix; to erect; to plant.

نصر naṣr (A) n.f. Succour; help; aid; assistance; victory; support; friendship.

نصرانی naṣrāni (A) n.m. A Christian.

نصرانیت naṣrāniyat (A) n.f. Christianity; the Christian religion.

نصرت nusrat (A) n.f. Victory.

نصف niṣf (A) adj. The half; middle.

نصف النہار niṣf-un-nahār, n.m. Midday; noon; meridian.

نصف دائرہ niṣf dā'irah, n.m. Semicircle.

نصف قطر niṣf qutr, n.m. Radius of a circle.

نصفا نصف niṣfā-niṣf, adv. Half an half; by halves; in halves.

نصوح naṣūḥ (A) adj. Sincere; honest; unfeigned; free from disguise, pretence or hypocrisy.

نصوص nuṣūṣ (H) n.f. (plu. of نص naṣṣ) See نص.

نصیب nasib (A) n.m. Fortune; position; destiny; chance; lot; luck; part; fate.

نصیب آزمانا ، لڑانا naṣib āzmānā, larānā, v. To try one's luck or chance.

نصیب اعدا ، دشمناں naṣib-ĕ a'dā, dushmanāṅ. intj. Be it the lot of your enemies!

نصیب بگڑنا ، پھوٹ جانا nasib bigarnā, phūṭ jānā, v. To be unlucky or unfortunate.

نصیب جاگنا ، چمکنا ، کھل جانا naṣib jāgnā, chamaknā, khul jānā, v. To be great favoured by fortune; to be in the ascendant (one's stars.)

نصیب کا لکھا naṣib kā likhkhā, n.m. What is destined; fate; destiny.

نصیب لڑنا naṣib laṛnā, v. To have a turn of luck.

نصیب ہونا naṣib honā, v. To gain; to fall to the lot of.

نصیبا ، نصیبہ naṣibā, naṣibah, n.m. Lot; fortune.

نصیبہ ور naṣibah war, adj. Fortunate.

نصیبوں جلا ، نصیبوں جلی naṣiboṅ jalā, naṣiboṅ jali, adj. Unfortunate.

نصیحت naṣiḥat (A) n.f. Advice; counsel; precept; admonition; chastisement.

نصیحت آمیز naṣiḥat āmez, adj. Saturated with good advice.

نصیحت پذیر naṣiḥat pizir, adj. Listening to good advice.

نصیحت دینا ، کرنا naṣiḥat denā, karnā, v. To advise; to admonish; to reprove; to chastise; to counsel; to exhort; to reprimand.

نصیحت گر ، گو naṣiḥat gar, go. adj. & n.m. Adviser; counsellor; admonisher.

نصیحت ہونا naṣiḥat honā, v. To understand; to learn a lesson; to be warned by experience.

نصیر naṣir (A) n.m. An assistnnt; a defender; a friend; helper; ally.

نصیری nuṣairi (A) n.m. A Muslim sect which believe in the divinity of Hazrat 'Ali; a follower of Nusair. adj. Lover; devoted; sacrificing one's life.

نضارت naẓārat (A) n.f. Freshness; verdure; beauty; lustre; brightness; floridness.

نضج nuẓj naẓj (A) n.m. Ripening; cooking; suppuration (of a wound).

نطفہ nuṭfah (A) n.m. Seed; spermahominis; sperm; semen; clear water.

نطفۂ بے تحقیق ، نطفہ حرام nuṭfah-ĕ be taḥqiq, nuṭfah-ĕ ḥarām, adj. Illegitimate; bastard; rascal; mischievous.

نطفہ ٹھہرنا ، قرار پانا nuṭfah ṭhahrnā, qarār pānā, v. To be conceived; to be pregnant.

نطق nuṭq (A) n.m. Speech; power of speech; language; discourse; articulation; reasoning faculty.

نظارت nazārat (A) n.f. Supervision; observation.

نظارہ nazārah, nazzārah (A) n.m. Sight; view; show, inspection; vista; panorama.

نظارہ بازی nazārah bāzī, n.f. Ogling; amorous glance.

نظارہ کرنا nazārah karnā, v. To view; to look; to enjoy looking at; to cast amorous glance.

نظافت nazāfat (A) n.f. Purity; cleanliness; neatness.

نظام nizām (A) n.m. Order; disposition; arrangement; custom; habit; system; a string of pearls.

نظام الاوقات nizām-ul-auqāt, n.m. Time-table.

نظام بطلیموس nizām-ĕ batlimūs, n.m. Ptolemaic system of astronomy, that the earth was stationary and other bodies revolved round it.

نظام تعلیم nŏzām-ĕ ta'līm, n.m. System of education.

نظام شمسی nizām-ĕ shamsī, n.m. The solar system.

نظام فیثاغورث nizām-ĕ fisāghoras, n.m. Pythagorean system of astronomy, that the sun was stationary and the earth revolved round it, (in fact the astronomical system of Caperni-cus has been erroneously attributed to Pythagoras).

نظامت nizāmat (A) n.f. Arrangement; government; administration; department; the office of an administrator.

نظامی nizāmī (A) n.m. A soldier. adj. Pertaining to military; martial.

نظائر nazā'ir (A) n.m/f. (plu. of نظیر nazir) Examples; instances.

نظر nazar (A) n.f. A look; a glance; an eye; vision; sight; favour; consideration; regard; point of view; motive; view; reference; discretion; countenance; supervision; care; viewpoint; inspection; observation; the influence of an evil eye.

نظر التفات nazar-ĕ iltifāt, n.f. Favourable view; kind attention.

نظر انداز nazar andāz, adj. Rejected; disregarded; thrown out of favour.

نظر انداز کرنا nazar andāz karnā. To cast off from favour.

نظراندازی nazar andāzī, n.f. Rejection; casting off; disfavouring.

نظر باز nazar baz, adj. An ogler; a juggler.

نظر بازی nazar bāzī, n.f. Ogling; casting amorous glances.

نظر باینکہ nazar ba inkih, adv. With this fact; in view.

نظر بچانا nazar bachānā, v. To avoid the looks or sight (of).

نظربد nazar-ĕ bad, n.f. Evil eye.

نظر بند nazar band, adj. Strictly watched; under surveilance.

نظر بندی nazar bandi, n.f. Confinement; arrest; fascination.

نظر پڑنا nazar parnā, v. To come into view.

نظر ثانی nazar-ĕ sānī, n.f. A review; revision; second inspection; second reading.

نظر چڑھنا nazar charhnā, v. To take fancy; to begin to like a person.

نظر ڈالنا nazar dālnā, v. To fix the gaze on; to see.

نظر رکھنا nazar rakhnā, v. To keep an eye on; to set eyes upon; to have in view; to contemplate; to intend; to cast a wistful eye.

نظر سے گرا دینا nazar se girā denā, v. To look down upon; to disgrace; to degrade.

نظر سے گرنا nazar se girnā, v. To be disgraced; to fall in the estimation of.

نظر کرنا nazar karnā, v. To see; to look; to behold.

نظر لگانا nazar lagānā, v. To cast a malignant look (on); to regard one with evil intent.

نظر لگنا nazar lagnā, v. To be under the influence of an evil eye.

نظر ملانا nazar milānā, v. To compare; to meet the gaze of.

نظر میں رکھنا nazar meṅ rakhnā, v. To keep in view; to keep under control.

نظم nazm (A) n.f. Poetry; verse; a string. n.m. Order; arrangement.

نظم سنج ، نظم گستر nazm sanj, nazm gustar, n.m. A poet; a versifier.

نظم و نسق nazm-ŏ nasq, n.m. Order and arrangement; organisation; administration; management.

نظیر nazīr (A) n.f. Example; instance; precedent. adj. Alike; resembling; equal to.

نظیر دینا nazīr denā, v. To quote an instance or a precedent.

نظیف nazīf (A) adj. Pure; clean; neat; legal.

نعت na'at (A) n.f. Praise (especially of the Holy Prophet); enlogium; an epithet.

نعره na'rah (A) n.m. Slogan; shouting; clamour; crying.

نعره زن na'rah zan, adj. One who shouts or cries out; exclaiming; shouting.

نعره لگانا ، مارنا na'rah lagānā, mārnā, v. To shout; to raiseslogan; to exclaim; to cry.

نعش na'sh (A) n.f. A bier; a coffin; a corpse; a litter on which a dead body is carried.

نعل na'l (A) n.m. Shoe (of a horse or man); the ferrule at the end of a scabbard; a hoof.

نعل بند na'l band, n.m. A farrier; a blacksmith who shoes horses.

نعل بندی na'l bandī, n.f. Shoeing; giving a horse new shoes; a light tributes.

نعلین na'lain (A) n.m. A pair of shoes with wooden soles; sandals; slippers.

نعم ni'am (A) n.f. (plu. of نعمت ni'mat) Favours; benefits; pleasure; comforts; affluence; ease or blessings (of life).

نعم ni'm (A) adj. Very good; nice.

نعم البدل ni'm-ul-badal, n.m. Change for the better.

نعمت ni'mat (A) n.f. Favour; graciousness; benefit; delight; joy; affluence; ease; wealth; good things or comforts of life; blessings or favours of heaven; a delicacy.

نعمت خانہ ni'mat khānah, n.m. Home or abode of affluence; a palace; a paradise; a meat safe.

نعمت عظمیٰ ni'mat-ĕ-'uzmā, n.f. A great blessing.

نعمت غیر مترقبہ ni'mat-ĕ ghair mutaraqqabah, n.m. An unexpected piece of good fortune; a wind-fall.

نعوذ na'ūzo (A) We flee for refuge to (God).

نعوذ باللہ na'ūzo billah, intej. We seek refuge of God; Heaven preserve us! God forbid!

نعوظ nu'ūz (A) n.m. Erection of the penis.

نعیم na'īm (A) n.f. Pleasure; benefits; goods; ease; tranquility.

نغز naghz (P) adj. Beautiful; excellent; good; sincere; swift; nimble; rare; wonderful.

نغم ، نغمہ nagham, naghm, naghamah, naghmah (A) n.m. Melody; song; modulation; a musical note or sound or tone; a sweet voice; a soft voice; trill; shake.

نغمہ پرداز ، ریز ، زن ، سرا ، سنج ، طراز naghmah pardāz, rez, zan, sarā, tarāz, sanj, n.m. A singer; a warbler; a musician.

نغمہ پردازی، ریزی، سرائی، سنجی، طرازی naghmah pardāzī, rezī, sarā'ī, sanjī, tarāzī, n.f. Singing.

نغمات naghmāt, naghamāt (A) n.m. plu. of نغمہ naghmah or naghamah.

نفاخ naffākh (A) adj. Flatulent.

نفاذ nifāz (A) n.m. Penetrating; pervading; promulgation; piercing; being issued; going forth.

نفاس nifās (A) n.m. Child-birth; labour; bringing forth; forty days (of a woman) after child's birth; discharge of blood of the child-birth.

نفاست nafāsat (P) n.f. Refinement; purity; exquisiteness.

نفاق nifāq (A) n.m. Hypocrisy; fallacy; double dealing; deceit; guile; differences; disagreement; enmity; rancour; malice.

نفت naft (P) n.m. Crude oil; petroleum.

نفحہ nafhah (A) n.f. Perfume; odour; fragrance; (plu. نفحات nafhat).

نفخ nafkh (A) n.m. Flatulence; inflammation; swelling.

نفر nafar (A&P) n.m. A groom; a servant; one person; an individual; one hand.

نفرت nafrat (A) n.f. Fright; terror; aversion; disgust; flight; abomination; abhorrence.

نفرت انگیز nafrat angez, adj. Disgusting; loathsome; horrible.

نفری nafari, n.f. Service; trade; profession; number of persons employed; daily wages; daily work.

نفرین nafrin (P) n.f. Detestation; abhorrence; curse; imprecation; approbrious words; reproach.

نفس nafas (A) n.m. The breath; respiration; a draught of water; the voice or sound from the breath; moment; time.

نفس واپسیں nafas-ĕ wapasin, n.m. The last breath.

نفس nafs (A) n.m. Soul; spirit; self; person; body; flesh; blood; sensuality; lust; substance; concupiscence; ravity; sperm; penis; animal life; essence.

نفس الامر nafs-ul-amr, n.m. The essence; soul, the reality; the fact of the matter; the basis of a thing.

نفس امارہ nafs-ĕ ammārah, n.m. Inordinate appetites; ardent desire; concupiscence.

نفس پرست nafs parast, adj. Sensual; sensualist; selfish.

نفس پرستی nafs parasti, n.f. Sensuality; selfishness.

نفس کشی nafs kushi, n.f. Self-denial; self-mortification; penance; temperance.

نفس لوامہ nafs-ĕ-lawwāmah, n.m. Accusing soul; conscience.

نفس مارنا nafs mārnā, v. To restrain the passion; to mortify the sensual appetites.

نفس مطمئنہ nafs-ĕ-mutma'innah, n.m. Benevolence; the satisfied soul.

نفس ملہمہ nafs-ĕ-mulhimah, n.m. The inspiring spirit.

نفس ناطقہ nafs-ĕ-nātiqah, n.m. Reason; the rational soul; spokesman; mouth piece of a body.

نفس نفیس nafs-ĕ-nafis, adv. By oneself. n.m. God.

نفسا نفسی nafsā-nafsi, See نفسی نفسی nafsi nafsi.

نفسانی nafsāni (A) adj. Sensual; voluptuous; luxurious; carnal; lustful.

نفسانیت nafsāniyat (A) n.f. Sensuality; luxury; pomp; pride; conceit; egotism; anger; carnality; stateliness.

نفسی nafsi (A) adj. Of or relating to the soul; carnal; sensual; psychological; psychic.

نفسی نفسی nafsi nafsi, n.f. selfishness. each one for himself.

نفسیات nafsiyāt (A) n.f. Psychology.

نفسیاتی nafsiyāti (A) adj. Psychological.

نفع nafa' (A) n.m. Profit; gain; advantage; interest.

نفع رساں ، بخش nafa' rasāṅ, bakhsh, adj. Conferring benefits; beneficent.

نفع و نقصان nafa'-ŏ nuqṣān, n.m. Profit and loss.

نفقہ nafaqah (A) n.m. The expenditure on maintenance; maintenance; allowance.

نفل nafl (A) n.m. A voluntary act of religion, the observance of which is not prescribed; the work of supererogation; gift.

نفوذ nufūz (A) n.m. Penetrating; piercing; pervading; influence; penetration.

نفور nufūr (A) n.m. Fleeing; abhorrence; smelling (of the skin).

نفور nafūr (A) adj. Fleeing from; abhorring.

نفوس nufūs (A) n.m. (plu. of نفس nafs); Souls spirits; men; people.

نفی nafī (A) n.f. Forbiding; prohibition; rejecting; refusing; denial; negation; subtraction; the negative; refusal.

نفی و اثبات nafi-ŏ iṣbāt, n.m. Negative and affirmative.

نفیر ، نفیری nafir, nafirī (P) n.f. A brazen trumpet; a pipe; a clarionet.

نفیس nafīs (A) adj. Precious; choice; exquisite; delicate; refined; pure.

نقاب niqāb (A) n.m./f. A veil.

نقاد naqqād (A) n.m. A critic; an assayer; a reviewer; a person who examines money to ascertain its genuineness.

نقارچی naqqārchi (P) n.m. A drummer.

نقار خانہ naqqār khānah (P) n.m. The porch of a palace where the drums are beaten at stated intervals.

نقار خانے میں طوطی کی آواز کون سنتا ہے naqqār khāne meṅ ṭūṭī kī āwāz kaun suntā hai, prov. Who listens to a poorman against his rich opponent.

نقارہ naqqārah (P) n.m. A kettle-drum.

نقارے کی چوٹ naqqāre kī choṭ, adv. Openly; without restraint.

نقاش naqqāsh (A) n.m. A painter; a drawer; a draughtsman; an embroider; engraver; sculptor.

نقاشی naqqāshi (A) n.f. Painting; drawing; embroidery; engraving; sculpture statuary.

نقاط niqāṭ (A) n.m. (plu. of نقطہ nuqṭah) Points; dots.

نقال naqqāl (A) n.m. A mimic; an actor; a player; a clown.

نقالی naqqālī, n.f. Acting; mimicry.

نقاہت naqāhat (A) n.f. Weakness; debility; feebleness; imbecility; convalescence; recovery from disease.

نقائص naqā'iṣ (A) n.m. (plu. of نقیصہ naqīṣah) Defects; blemishes; flaws.

نقب naqb (A) n.f. House-breaking; a hole made by a burglar; a subterraneous excavation; a rabbit's burrow.

نقب زن naqb zan, n.m. A house-breaker; a burglar.

نقب زنی naqb zanī, n.f. Burglary.

نقد naqd (A) n.m. Ready money; cash; assay; examination; criticism.

نقد جان naqd-ĕ jān, n.m. Soul; spirit.

نقد مال naqd māl, n.m. Choice articles; dainties.

نقد و جنس naqd-ŏ jins, n.m. Money and goods; money and commodities.

نقدا نقد naqdā naqd, adv. Promptly; in cash.

نقدی naqdi (P) n.f. Cash, ready money.

نقرس niqris (A) n.m. A kind of gout.

نقرہ nuqrah (A) n.m. Silver; a white colour (in horses).

نقرہٴ خام nuqrah-ĕ khām, n.m. Pure silver.

نقرئی nuqra'ī (A) *adj.* Made of silver; silver; white (in colour, as a horse).

نقش naqsh (A) *n.m.* Painting; colouring; drawing; embroidery; a picture; print; an engraving; a carving; a stamp; a mark; a charm; delineation; map; portrait.

نقش بٹھانا *naqsh biṭhānā, v.* To make a strong impression; to establish one's authority.

نقش بدیوار *naqsh badīwār, adj.* Like a picture on the wall; like a statue; thunderstruck; confounded; motionless.

نقش بند *naqsh band, n.m.* A painter; a designer; a creator; an adorner; embroider; imaginer; a charm; a sect of ṣūfī.

نقش بندی *naqsh bandī, n.f.* Painting; creating; designing.

نقش پا *naqsh-ĕ pā, n.m.* Footprints; tracks; footseps.

نقش کرنا *naqsh karnā, v.* To imprint; to stamp; to engrave; to adorn with designs; to impress.

نقش و نگار *naqsh-ŏ nigār, n.m.* Decoration; embellishment; paintings; ornaments; pictures.

کالنقش فی الحجر *kannaqsh fīl ḥajar, adj.* Like an engraving in stone; indelible.

نقشہ *naqshah* (A) *n.m.* A portrait; model; pattern; map; plan; chart; sketch; design; example; a blank form; a table; a register; a muster roll; visage; feature; cast of countenance; state of affairs.

نقشہ بگڑنا *naqshah bigaṛnā, v.* To be put out of countenance; upsetting of plan.

نقشہ جمانا *naqshah jamānā, v.* To lay the foundation of; to work out a plan of; to have an intercourse; to set-out the main features of a plan.

نقشہ حاضری *naqshah-ĕ ḥāẓirī, n.m.* Attendance chart.

نقشہ حد بست *naqshah-ĕ ḥadd bast, n.m.* A boundary map.

نقشہ نویس *naqshah nawīs, n.m.* A draughtsman.

نقشہ کشی کا کاغذ *naqshah kashī kā kāg̱haẕ, n.m.* Drawing paper.

نقشہ نگار *naqshah nigār, n.m.* A cartographer.

فن نقشہ کشی *fann-ĕ naqshah kashī, n.m.* Cartography.

نقشی ، نقشین *naqshī, naqshīn, adj.* Ornamented with designs; engraved.

نقص *naqṣ* (A) *n.m.* Defect; diminution; detriment; fault; blemish; injury; harm; mischief; decrease; flaw.

نقص جسمانی *naqṣ-ĕ jismānī, n.m.* Bodily defect; infirmity.

نقص قطعی *naqṣ-ĕ qaṯa'ī, n.m.* A vital defect.

نقص نکالنا *naqṣ nikālnā, v.* To pick out faults; to point out defect; to condemn.

نقصان *nuqṣān* (A) *n.m.* Loss; defect; deficiency; detriment; injury; damage; blemish; prejudice; mischief.

نقصان اٹھانا *nuqṣān uṭhānā, v.* To suffer a loss.

نقصان پہنچانا *nuqṣān pahunchānā, v.* To injure; to harm; to damage.

نقصان دہ ، رساں *nuqṣān dih, rasāṅ, adj.* Detrimental; injurious; harmful.

نقصان کرنا *nuqṣān karnā, v.* To inflict injury; to harm; to do mischief.

نقض *naqẓ* (A) *n.m.* Demolishing; undoing; dissolution; breach.

نقض امن *naqẓ-ĕ amn, n.m.* Breach of peace.

نقض عہد *nuqẓ-ĕ 'ahd, n.m.* Breach of contract.

نقط *nuqaṯ* (A) *n.m.* (*plu. of* نقطہ *nuqṯah*) Dots; points; drops; spots.

نقطہ nuqṭah (A) n.m. A point; a dot; a spot; a stain; a vowel.

نقطہ آغاز nuqṭah-ĕ āghāz, n.m. A geometrical point; starting point.

نقطہ موہوم nuqṭah-ĕ mauhūm, n.m. Imaginary point; the mouth of a beloved.

نقطہ نظر nuqṭah-ĕ naẓar, n.m. View point.

نقل nuql (A) n.m. That which is eaten with wine or tea (as fruits or sweetmeats); a dessert; a sort of sweetmeat.

نقل naql (A) n.f. History; narrative; tale; story; fable; anecdote; copying; mimicking; acting; aping; transporting from one place to another; removing; changing; translating.

نقل اڑانا naql uṛānā, v. To copy by unfair means.

نقل در نقل naql dar naql, n.f. A copy of a copy.

نقل کرنا naql karnā, v. To relate; to narrate; to copy; to act; to play; to perform or represent a character; to imitate; to mimic; to move.

نقل مطابق اصل naql muṭābiq aṣl, n.f. A true copy; an exact counter-part of the original.

نقل مکان naql-ĕ makān, n.f. Moving from a place; migration; transmigration; emigration; removal; dying; the first stage of journey.

نقل نویس naql nawis, n.m. Copyist.

نقل وطن naql-ĕ waṭan, n.f. Migration.

نقلی naqlī (A) adj. Artificial; fictitious; spurious; counterfiet.

نقوش nuqūsh (A) n.m. (plu. of نقش naqsh) Paintings; engravings; writings; marks.

نقول nuqūl (A) n.m. (plu. of نقل naql) Copies.

نقی naqī (A) adj. Pure; clean; excellent

نقیب naqib (A) n.m. A herald; a chief; a leader; an intelligent person; an adjutant or aide-de-camp; a proclaimer.

نقیض naqiẓ (A) adj. Adverse; contrary; opposite. n.f. An enemy; opposition; contrariety.

نقیہ naqih (A) adj. Faint; feeble; weak.

نک nak (H) n.f. (contraction of ناک nāk) Nose.

نک بال nak bāl, adj & n.m. Favourite; respected; one who exercises influence over another.

نک چڑھا ، نک چڑھی nak charhā, nak charhī, adj. Ill-tempered; ill-natured; fastidious; proud; angry; fretful; passionate; having the nose turned up.

نک چھکنی nak chhiknī, n.f. A kind of medicine which is used as a sternutatory (causing to sneeze); sneezewort.

نک سک سے ٹھیک یا درست nak sak se ṭhīk yā drust, adj. Beautiful from head to foot; without any defect or deformity; tip top.

نک کٹی nak kaṭi, n.f. Defame; dishonour; disgrace; infamy.

نک گھسنی nak ghisnī, n.f. Rubbing the nose on the ground by way of humiliation.

نکا nikkā (H) adj. Small; short; delicate; incomplete; small-sized; pigmy; dwarf; little.

نکا nukka (H) n.m. The pointed part of anything.

نکات nikāt (A) n.m. (plu. of نکتہ nuktah) Nice points; phrases; witticism; epigrams.

نکاح nikāḥ (A) n.m. Matrimony; marriage; nuptials.

نکاس nikās (H) n.m. Outlet; issue; discharge; vent; sale; source; spring; origin; transit duties; skirts; the outer boundaries of a town or village; suburbs; adjustment of accounts; accomplishment.

نکاسی nikāsī (H) n.f. Taxes collected on goods; passing out of town; duties; produce; income; profit; assets.

نکالا nikālā (H) n.m. Banishment; extradition; withdrawal.

نکالا ملنا nikālā milnā, v. To be banished; to be turned out.

نکال دینا nikāl denā (H) v. To bring out; to expel; to drive out; to take out; to deduct; to banish; to eject; to discard; to exclude.

نکال لانا nikāl lānā (H) v. To bring off; to elope with; to run away with.

نکالنا nikālnā (H) v. To pull out; to draw out; to take out; to turn out; to extract; to distill; to pick out; to select; to deduct; to expel; to issue; to publish; to work out; to solve (as a problem); to accomplish; to discover; to strike a balance; to break in or train (as a horse); to let out; to invent; to hatch.

نکائی nikā'ī (H) n.f. The act of weeding; the cost of weeding out a field.

نکبت nakbat (A) n.f. Adversity; calamity; misfortune.

نکتہ nuktah (A) n.m. A point; a subtle or quaint conceit; point of wit; wise or pitty saying; a mystical significance.

نکتہ بین nuktah bīn, adj. Critical; hypercritical.

نکتہ پرداز nuktah pardāz, adj. Acute; subtle; ingenius; sagacious.

نکتہ چین nuktah chīn, adj. Captious.

نکتہ چینی nuktah chīnī, n.f. Captiousness; caviling.

نکتہ دان nuktah dān, adj. Sagacious; understanding; subtle.

نکتہ دانی nuktah dānī, n.f. Sagacity; discernment; wisdom.

نکتہ رس ، شناس nuktah ras, shīnās, adj. Sagacious; discerning; of penetrating intellect.

نکتہ گیر nuktah gīr, adj. Critical; captious.

نکتی nukti (H) n.f. A kind of sweetmeat.

نکٹا naktā (H) adj. & n.m. Having a cut nose.

نکٹی naktī. The feminine form of نکٹا.

نکرہ nakirah (A) n.m. An indefinite noun; a common noun.

نکڑ nukkaṛ (H) n.m. A corner; end; turning; projection.

نکسیر naksīr (H) n.f. A vein of nose; bleeding at the nose.

نکسیر پھوٹنا naksīr phūṭnā, v. To bleed at the nose.

نکل آنا nikal ānā (H) v. To come out; to come forth; to appear; to rise (as the sun etc.)

نکل بھاگنا nikal bhāgnā (H) v. To run away; to get off; to be off.

نکل پڑنا nikal paṛnā (H) v. To come out from; to be drawn forth.

نکل جانا nikal jānā (H) v. To disappear; to surpass; to escape; to go away.

نکلنا nikalnā (H) v. To issue; to go forth or out; to be extracted or taken out; to come out; to exceed; to be uttered; to appear; to result; to prove; to turn out; to begin; to escape; to slip; to spring; to be pulled or drawn out; to be hatched (as eggs); to germinate; to shoot; to depart; to secede; to proceed.

نکلوانا nikalwānā (H) v. To cause to come out or go out; to cause to issue; to cause to turn out or dismiss; to cause to expel.

نکما ، نکمی nikammā, nikammī (H) adj. Unserviceable; worthless; unprofitable; without work; base; poor; not fertile; good for-nothing.

نکو niko yā nikū (P) adj. (contraction of نیکو neko) Good; well-behaved; fair; beautiful.

نکوکار niko kār, adj. Good; pious; beneficent.

نکو کاری niko kārī, n.f. Beneficence.

نکو نام niko nām, adj. Reputed; well spoken-off; having a good name.

نکو نامی niko nāmi, n.f. Reputation; good name; credit.

نکو nakkū (H) adj. Big nosed; disgraced; infamous; low; wile; degraded; base.

نکو بنانا ، کرنا nakkū banānā, karnā, v. To disgrace; to make one a laughing stock.

نکوا nakwā (H) n.m. The nose.

نکوسنا nakosnā (H) v. To grin.

نکوہش nikohish (P) n.f. Spurning; rebuke; threat.

نکوئی niko'ī (P) n.f. Goodness; kindness; benevolence.

نکھار nikhār (H) n.m. Cleanliness; neatness; elegance.

نکھارنا nikhārnā (H) v. To str ain; to bleach; to clear; to wash; to clean.

نکھرنا nikharnā (H) v. To be clean to be bleached; to be settled.

نکہت nakhat (A) n.f. Perfume; odour; scent.

نکھٹو nikhaṭṭū (H) adj. Idle; unearning; without work; good for nothing.

نکھد nikhadd (H) adj. Worthless; worst; ominous; pernicious.

نکیر nakīr (A) n.m. Name of an angel (see منکر نکیر munkar nakīr).

نکیل nakel (H) n.f. A camel's bridle or halter; nose-string.

نکیل هاتھ میں هونا nakel hāth men honā, v. To lead by the nose-string; to get hold of.

نکیلا ، نکیلی nukīlā, nukīlī (H) adj. Sharp-pointed; pointed; conical; showy;

نگ nag (P) n.m. (contraction of یا نگینہ نگین nagīn yā nagīnah). The stone of a ring; a jewel; a gem; a precious stone.

نگ جڑنا nag jaṛnā, v. To set a gem.

نگار nigār (P) n.m. Painting; picture; portrait; effigy; idol; a beloved; a sweetheart.

نگار آلودہ nigār ālūdah, adj. Painted; beautiful as a painting.

نگار خانہ یا نگارستان nigār k͟hānah yā nigāristān n.m. A picture or portrait gallery.

نگارش nigārish (P) n.f. Writing; description.

نگاری nigārī (P) n.f. (in comps). Painting; writing.

نگاریں nigārīn (P) adj. Beautiful; lovely; beautified.

نگاہ nigāh (P) n.f. A look; glance; sight; view; the aspect; observation; watching; consideration; attention; custody; care.

نگاہ اٹھا کر نہ دیکھنا nigāh uthā kar nah dekhnā, v. Not to care to look at; to be very proud.

نگاہ بان nigāh bān, n.m. Watchman; guard; keeper; protector.

نگاہ بانی nigāh bānī, n.f. Watching; guarding; custody; care.

نگاہ بد nigāh-ĕ bad, n.f. Bad or evil eye.

نگاہ بدلنا ,پھیرنا nigāh badalnā, phernā, v. To give a cold shoulder to; to become unfavourable (to).

نگاہ چرانا nigāh churānā, v. Not to confront; not to be able to look one in the face.

نگاہ دار nigāh dār, adj. n.m. Guardian; a keeper; a watcher.

نگاہ داشت nigāh dāsht, n.f. Care; watch; enlistment; enlisting.

نگاہ رکھنا nigāh rakhnā, v. To take care; to lay by; to guard; to look after; to watch.

نگاہ کرنا nigāh karnā, v. To observe; to look at; to view; to inspect; to see.

نگاہ ملانا nigāh milānā, v. To look a person full in the face; to confront.

نگاہ میں رکھنا nigāh men rakhnā, v. To keep an eye on; to watch; to keep in view.

نگاہ ناز nigāh-ĕ nāz, n.f. Blendishments.

نگاہ نہ ٹھہرنا *nigāh nah ṭhahrnā*, *v.* To be very brilliant; to be dazzling.

نگر *nagar* (H) *n.m.* A city; a town.

نگر *niggar* (H) *adj.* Heavy; solid; weighty.

نگر *nigar* (P) *adj.* (*in comp.*) Beholding.

نگران *nigarān* (P) *adj.* Watching; beholding; guarding. *n.m.* A guard; a supervisor.

نگران حال رہنا *nigrān-ĕ ḥāl rahnā*, *v.* To keep a watch (over); to be watchful (of).

نگرانی *nigarānī* (P) *n.f.* Watch; care; custody; supervision.

نگرانی کرنا *nigarānī karnā*, *v.* To look after; to see a thing done; to supervise.

نگری *nagrī* (H) *n.f.* A town; a village.

نگلنا *nigalnā* (H) *v.* To swallow; to gulp down.

نگندا *nigaṅdā* (H) *n.m.* A long ornamental sewing.

نگندے ڈالنا *nigaṅde ḍālnā*, *v.* To quilt; to sew with long stitches.

نگندنا *nigaṅdnā* (H) *v.* To sew with long stitches.

نگوڑا، نگوڑی *nigoṛā, nigoṛī* (H) *adj.* Wretched; ruffian; devil; without feet; a helpless and unfortunate person.

نگوں *nigūṅ* (P) *adj.* Hanging down; adverse (used in compos).

نگہ *nigah* (P) *n.f.* (Contraction of نگاہ *nigāh*) Sight; glance; look.

نگین ، نگینہ *nagīn, nagīnah* (P) *n.m.* The stone of a ring; a gem; a jewel; what fits or sits well.

نگینہ جڑنا *nagīnah, jaṛnā v.* To set a stone.

نگینہ ساز *nagīnah sāz*, *n.m.* A polisher of precious stones; a lapidary.

نل *nal* (H) *n.m.* A species of reed; a joint of a bamboo; tube; pipe; a conduit; cylindrical case; pump; tap.

نلا *nalā* (H) *n.m.* A large pipe or tube; a bone; the urinary ducts; the radius of the arms; a kind of firework.

نلانا *nalānā* (H) *v.* To weed out.

نلائی *nalā'ī* (H) *n.f.* Act of weeding; wages for weeding.

نلی *nalī* (H) *n.f.* A hollow reed; a small pipe; a tube; the wind-pipe; barrel; marrow bone.

نم *nam* (P) *n.m.* Moisture; dampness; humidity. *adj.* Moist; damp; wet.

نم خوردہ، دیدہ، رسیدہ *nam khūrdah, dīdah, rasīdah, adj.* Destroyed by moisture; moist.

نم روک *nam rok, adj.* Damp proof.

نم گیرہ *nam gīrah, n.m.* A canopy; an awning.

نم ناک *nam nāk, adj.* Moist; damp.

نما *numā* (P) *adj.* Showing; exhibiting; like; resembling; pointing out; appearing (in *comps.* as جزیرہ نما *jazīrah numā*, like an island; a peninsula).

نماز *namāz* (P) *n.f.* Prayer; (especially as prescribed by the Muslim Law); adoration; divine service.

نمازی *namāzī* (P) *adj.* One who says his prayers regularly; devout; clean; pure. *n.m.* A person who prays.

نمائش *numā'ish* (P) *n.f.* Show; display; form; figure; face; vision; sight; spectacle; exhibition; affectation.

نمائش گاہ *numā'ish gāh, n.f.* Exhibition hall.

نمائشی *namā'ishī* (P) *adj.* Spectacular; apparent; for display or show; ostensible.

نمائندگی *numā'indagī* (P) *n.f.* Representation; deputation.

نمائندہ *numā'indah* (P) *n.m.* A representative; a deputy.

نمائی *numā'ī* (P) *n.f.* (*in compos.*) Display; show; exhibiting.

نمایاں *numāyāṅ* (P) *adj.* Appearing; apparent; evident; conspicuous; bold (a picture); prominent.

نمٹانا **nimṭānā (H) v. See** نبٹانا **nibṭānā.**

نمٹ جانا ، نمٹنا **nimaṭ jānā, nimaṭnā (H) v. See** نبٹنا **nibaṭnā.**

نمد ، نمدہ **namad, namdah (P) n.m. Felt cloth; woollen cloth formed without weaving; a felt carpet.**

نمد پوش **namad posh, adj. Clothed in felt cloth. n.m. A poor fellow; a beggar.**

نمسکار **namaskār (S) n.m. Salutation; adoration; reverential address; obeisance.**

نمک **namak (P) n.m. Salt; savour; flavour; grace; beauty.**

نمک پاشی **namak pāshī, n.f. Pouring salt on.**

نمک پروردہ **namak parwardah, adj. & n.m. A domestic servant; a favourite; a confidential servant.**

نمک چشی **namak chashī, n.f. The first feeding of a child.**

نمک چکھنا **namak chakhnā, v. To taste (food).**

نمک حرام **namak ḥarām, adj. Disloyal; disobedient; wicked; evil; perfidious; ungrateful.**

نمک حرامی **namak ḥarāmī, n.f. Disloyalty; perfidy; treason; treachery; ingratitude.**

نمک حلال **namak ḥalāl, adj. Grateful; loyal; true; submissive; obedient; dutiful.**

نمک حلالی **namak ḥalālī, n.f. Gratitude; fidelity; loyalty.**

نمک خوار **namak khwār, adj.&n.m. A dependent; servant; slave.**

نمک دان **namak dān, n.m. A saltcellar.**

نمک کا تیزاب **namak kā tezāb, n.m. Muriatic acid; hydrochloric acid.**

نمک کا حق ادا کرنا **namak kā ḥaqq adā karnā, v. To discharge one's obligation.**

نمک کی کان **namak kī kān, n.f. A salt mine.**

نمک لگانا **namak lagānā, v. To salt; to pickle with salt.**

نمک مرچ لگانا **namak mirch lagānā, v. To give a relish; to impart a flavour; to season; to colour highly; to excite; to exaggerate.**

نمکین **namkīn (P) adj. Saltish; saline; brackish; witty; sarcastic; animated; poignant; handsome; beautiful; of a nut-brown colour.**

نمکینی **namkīnī, n.f. Saltiness; saltishness; agreeableness; a brown complexion.**

نمو **numū (A) n.m. Vegetation; growth; increase.**

نمود **namūd (P) n.f. Conspicuousness; show; display; celebrity; appearance; sight; look; sign; boasting; vanity; pomp and show; fame.**

نمود بے بود **namūd-ĕ be būd, n.f. Outword show or display.**

نمودار **namūdār (P) adj. Apparent; visible; conspicuous; noted; famed; showy; manifest.**

نمودی **namūdī, adj. Famous; notorious.**

نمودیا **namūdiyā, adj. One given to display; a boaster.**

نمونہ **namūnah (P) n.m. Sample; specimen; pattern; model; example; type; form.**

نمونہ دان **namūnah dān, n.m. A show case.**

نمی **namī (P) n.f. Moistness; dampness; humidity.**

ننا **nannā (H) adj. Small; diminutive; tiny; little; young; petty; low. n.m. A mere child; a wee thing; a darling; a pet.**

ننا کاتنا **nannā kātnā, v. To spin very fine; to be frugal.**

ننامنا **nannā munnā, adj. Very small.**

ننانوے **ninānawe (H) adj. Ninety-nine.**

ننانوے کے پھیر میں پڑنا **ninānawe ke pher meṅ paṛnā, v. To be involved in difficulties; to be wholly absorbed in the acquisition of wealth.**

نند *nand, nanad* (H) *n.f.* A sister-in-law; husband's sister.

نندا *nindā* (H) *n.f.* Censure; reproach; scorn; defamation reproof; abuse; insult, blasphemy; blame.

نندوئی *nando'ī* (H) *n.m.* Husband of the husband's sister; a brother-in-law.

ننگ *nang* (P) *n.m.* Honour; esteem; reputation; shame; disgrace; infamy; ignominy.

ننگ خاندان *nang ĕ- khāndān, adj.* A disgrace to one's family.

ننگ خلائق *nang-ĕ khalā'iq, adj.* A disgrace to mankind.

ننگ و نام، ننگ و ناموس *nang-ŏ nam, nang-ŏ nāmūs, n.m.* Honour; esteem; shame.

ننگ *nang* (H) *n.f.* Nakedness. *adj.* Naked; penniless; destitute.

ننگ دھڑنگ *nang dharang. adj.* Stark naked.

ننگا ، ننگی *nangā, nangī* (H) *adj.* Naked; shameless; unarmed.

ننگا کرنا *nangā karnā, v.* To make naked; to strip off clothes; to uncover; to lay bare; to disclose; to expose.

ننگی تلوار *nangī talwār, n.f.* A naked sword; a drawn sword; a fearless person; an outspoken person; one who speaks his mind freely and without reserve.

ننگے پاؤں ننگے سر *nange pāon, nange sir, adj.* Bare-footed and bare-headed; perplexed; distracted; confused; harassed; rendered crazy.

ننھا *nannhā* (H) See ننا *nannā.*

ننھی ، ننی *nannhī, nannī* (H) *adj.&n.f.* The faminine form of ننھا یا ننا *nannhā* or *nannā.*

ننھیال *nanhiyāl* (H) *n.f.* Maternal grandfather's house or family.

نو *nau* (P) *adj.* New; young; fresh; raw; newly.

نو آباد *nau ābād, adj.* Newly settled, peopled, colonized or cultivated; newly arrived.

نو آبادی *nau ābādī, n.f.* Colony; settlement; colonisation.

نوآبادیات *nau ābādiyat, n.f.* Colonies.

نو آموز *nau āmoz, adj. & n.m.* A novice; an inexperienced person; a beginner; an apprentice.

نو بنو *nau banau, adj.* Quite new or fresh; up-to-date. *adv.* Again and again.

نو بہار *nau bahār, n.f.* The dawn of spring; early spring in full bloom or splendour.

نوجوان *nau jawān, adj.* In the bloom of youth; in the prime of life; fresh and young. *n.m.* A lad; a youth; a young man.

نوجوانی *nau jawānī, n.f.* Youth; prime of life; bloom or flower of youth.

نو چندی *nau chandī, adj.* Relating to the new moon.

نو خاستہ ، نوخیز *nau khāstah, nau khez, adj.* Newly risen; adolescent.

نوخیزی *nau khezī, n.f.* Raising up; springing up; shooting forth; youth.

نو دولت *nau daulat, adj.* New to wealth; one who has suddenly become rich; mean; base minded.

نورس *nau ras, adj.* Young; fresh; tender; recent.

نورستہ *nau rustah, adj.* Newly grown; recently sprung up.

نوروز *nau roz, n.m.* The new year's day (Persian Calendar).

نوشہ *nau shah, n.m.* Bridegroom, a young monarch.

نوعمر *nau 'umr, adj.* Young; inexperienced; beginner; minor.

نوگرفتار *nau giriftār, adj.* Newly captured; newly caught.

نومسلم *nau muslim, n.m.* A new convert to Islam.

نومشق *nau mashq, adj.* Inexperienced; a novice.

نونہال *nau nihāl, n.m.* A young plant; a sapling; shoot; a young man.

نو وارد *nau wārid, n.m.* A new comer.

نو *nau* (H) *adj.* Nine.

نورتن *nau ratan, n.m.* A bracelet consisting of nine jewels; nine great men at the court of Akbar and Vikramaditya.

نو سو چوھے کھاکے بلی حج کو چلی *nau sau chūhe khā ke billī ḥaj ko chalī, prov.* Sinning six days in the week and going to church on the seventh.

نولکھا *nau lakkhā, adj.* Of the value of nine lakhs of rupees.

نو میں نہ تیرہ میں *nau meṅ nah terah meṅ.* Having no value or respect.

نو نقد نہ تیرہ آدھار *nau naqd nah terah udhār, prov.* A bird in hand is better than two in the bush.

نوا *nawā* (P) *n.f.* Voice; sound; modulation; song; air (music); opulence; wealth; subsistence; goodness or splendour of circumstances.

نواب *nawwāb* (A) *n.m.* A nabob; a ruler of a territory; a governor of a district or town.

نواب *nuwwab* (A) *n.m.* (*plu.* of نائب *nā'ib*) Vicegerants; deputies; lieutenants; governors.

نوابی *nawwābi* (A) *n.f.* The office of a nabob; misrule. *adj.* Relating to a nabob.

نواح٬نواحی *nawāḥ, nawaḥī* (A) *n.m.* (*plu.* of ناحیہ *nāḥiyah*) Environs; district; tract; coast; shore.

نوادر *nawādir* (A) *n.m.* (*plu.* of نادر *nādir*) Rarities; things rare and singular; miracles; curiosities.

نوادر روزگار *nawādir-ĕ rūzgār, n.m.* Wonders of the world; curiosities of the world.

نوار ٬ نواڑ *niwār, niwāṛ* (H) *n.f.* Tape (of th coarse kind).

نواز *nawāz* (P) *adj.* Cherishing; caressing, soothing; playing on music; performer; (used in *compos.* as بندہ نواز *bandah nawāz*, cherisher of servants, ستار نواز *sitār nawāz*, a player on guitar).

نوازش *nawāzish* (P) *n.f.* Caress; kindness; politeness; favour; patronage; courtesy; (*plu.* نوازشات *nawāzishāt*).

نوازش نامہ *nawāzish nāmah, n.m.* A polite letter; complimentary letter; a letter.

نوازنا *nawāznā, v.* To caress; to favour; to patronise; to cherish; to comfort.

نواس *nivās* (S) *n.m.* Dwelling; residence.

نواسہ *nawāsah* (P) *n.m.* A daughter's son.

نواسی *nawāsi, n.f.* A daughter's daughter.

نواسی *nawāsi* (H) *adj.* Eighty-nine.

نوافل *nawāfil* (A) *n.m.* (*plu.* of نفل *nafl*) Acts of devotion not prescribed by law; supplementary prayers; supererogation.

نوال *nawāl* (A) *n.f.* A gift; present; benefit; kindness.

نوالہ *niwālah* (P) *n.m.* A morsel; a mouthful.

نواہی *nawāhi* (A) *n.f.* (*plu.* of ناھیہ *nāhiyah*) Prohibitions; interdicts.

نوائب *nawā'ib* (A) *n.m./f.* (*plu.* of نائبہ *nā'ibah*) Accidents; vicissitudes; unfortunate occurrences.

نوبت *naubat* (A) *n.f.* Period; time; turn; intermission; opportunity; occasion; stage; degree; pitch; accident; misfortune; calamity; sounding of kettle-drum at the residence of a great man at certain intervals; kettle-drums.

نوبت خانه ***naubat khānah***, *n.m.* A house where kettle-drums are beaten; a guard house.

نوبت کو پهنچنا ***naubat ko pohuṅchnā***, *v.* To reach a (certain) stage; to come to (such) a pass.

نوبتی ***naubatī*** (P) *n.m.* One who beats the kettle-drum. *adj.* Peridoical; intermittent.

نوج ***nauj*** (H) *n.f.* An expression of repulion (among women). *intj.* God forbid.

نوچا ناچی ***nochā nāchī*** (H) *n.f.* Mutual scratching and tearing.

نوچ کهسوٹ ***noch khasoṭ*** (H) *n.f.* Plundering; taking by force.

نوچنا ***nochnā*** (H) *v.* To pinch; to scratch; to claw.

نوچی ***nochī*** (H) *n.f.* A young girl kept by a bawd; a harlot.

نوح ***nūḥ*** (A) *adj.* Lamenting; weeping. *n.m.* The name of a prophet (Noah), known in history for the deluge.

نوحه ***nauḥah*** (A) *n.m.* Lamentation; moaning; mourning over the dead.

نوحه گر ***nauḥah gar***, *adj.* A mourner; a lamenter.

نوحه گری ***nauḥah garī***, *n.f.* Lamentation; mourning.

نور ***nūr*** (A) *n.m.* Light; splendour.

نور افزا ***nūr afzā***, *adj.* Light increasing; illuminating.

نورافشاں ***nūr afshāṅ***, *adj.* Light diffusing.

نور باف ***nūr bāf***, *n.m.* A weaver.

نور بافی ***nūr bāfī***, *n.f.* Weaving.

نورچشم ، نوردیده ***nūr-ĕ chashm***, ***nūr-ĕ dīdah***, *n.m.* Light of the eye; a son.

نورانی ***nūrānī*** (A) *adj.* Of or relating to light; composed of light; luminous; resplendent.

نورد ***noward*** (P) *adj.* Travelling over (used in *comps.* as صحرانورد *saḥrā noward*, travelling over a desert).

نوری ***nūrī***, *adj.* Of light; splendid; luminous; resplendent.

نوش ***nosh*** (P) *n.m.* Water of life; a draught. *adj.* Drinking (in *comps.* as, بادہ‌نوش *bādah nosh*, wine drinker).

نوش جان فرمانا ، کرنا ***nosh jān farmānā***, ***karnā***, *v.* To eat; to drink; to sup; to swallow; to devour.

نوش دارو ***nosh dārū***, *n.m.* Antidote; wine.

نوشابه ***nūshābah*** (P) *n.m.* Water of life; elixir.

نوشادر ***nūshādar***, ***naushādar*** (P) *n.m.* Salammoniac.

نوشت ***nawisht*** (P) *n.f.* Writing; a document; a letter; an epistle.

نوشت و خواند ***nawisht-ŏ khwāṅd***, *n.f.* Writing and reading; a written engagement.

نوشته ***nawishtah*** (P) *adj.* Written. *n.m.* A letter.

نوشته تقدیر ***nawishtah-ĕ taqdīr***, *n.m.* Destined; ordained.

نوشتنی ***nawishtanī*** (P) *adj.* Worth writing.

نوشیں ***noshīṅ*** (P) *adj.* Sweet; pleasant; agreeable.

نوع ***nau'*** (A) *n.f.* Kind; species; sort; manner; mode.

نوع انسان ***nau'-ĕ insāṅ***, *n.f.* Mankind.

بهر نوع ***bahar nau***, *adv.* At any rate; anyhow; at all events.

نوعیت ***nau'iyyat*** (A) *n.f.* Specific difference; special character; speciality.

نوک ***nok*** (P) *n.f.* A bill; beak; nib; point; tip; angle; end.

نوک جهوک (جهونک) ***nok jhok***, (***jhoṅk***) *n.f.* Tugging and putting; exchange of stinging allusions and sarcastic observation.

نوک دار **nok dār**, *adj.* Pointed.

نوک دم بھاگنا **nok dum bhāgnā**, *v.* To decamp; to show a clean pair of heels.

نوک زبان **nok-ĕ zabān**, *adv.* By heart; on the tip of the tongue.

نوکر **naukar** (P) *n.m.* A servant; a dependant; a retainer.

نوکر چاکر **naukar chākar**, *n.m.* Domestics in general; servants.

نوکرانی **naukarānī**, *n.f.* A maid-servant.

نوکری **naukarī**, *n.f.* Service; employment; pay; reward; post.

نوکری پیشہ **naukarī peshah**, *n.m.* A servant by profession; one whose means of livelihood are employment.

نوم **naum** (A) *n.f.* Sleep.

نومی **naumī** (H) *n.f.* The ninth day of a lunar fortnight,

نومید **naumīd** (P) *adj.* Hopeless.

نومیدی **naumīdī** (P) *n.f.* Hopelessness; despair; disappointment.

نون **non, nūn** (H) *n.m.* Salt.

نون تیل **non tel**, *n.m.* Salt and oil; small necessaries of life.

نونا **nūnā** (H) *v.* To bend down; to bow; to incline downwards; to submit; to be obedient; to stoop.

نوے **nawwe** (H) *adj.* Ninety.

نوید **navīd** (P) *n.f.* Good news; glad tidings; invitation to a wedding (to kinsfolk and brethren).

نویس **nawīs** (P) *adj.* Writing; (used in *comps.* as in عرضی نویس *'arzī nawīs*, a petition writer).

نویسندہ **nawīsandah** (P) *n.m.* A writer; a clerk; an accountant.

نویسی **nawīsī** (P) *n.f.* Writing. (*in compos*).

نویلا ، نویلی **nawelā nawelī** (H) *adj.* New; young; rare; singular; beautiful.

نہ **nah** (P) *adv.* Not; neither; nor; no; nay.

نہ **nuh** (P) *adj.* Nine.

نہاد **nihād** (P) *n.f.* Nature; disposition; essence; quality; mind; heart; family.

نہار **nahār** (A) *n.m.* Day; diffusion of light.

نہار **nahār** (P) *adj.* Without food since morning; hungry.

نہار منہ **nahar mūṅh**, *adv.* On an empty stomach.

نہاری **nahārī** (P) *n.f.* Breakfast; a kind of bit or bridle; a kind of soup taken with leavened bread; raw sugar mixed with spices given to horses.

نہال **nihāl** (P) *n.m.* A young plant; shoot; sucker; sapling.

نہال **nihāl** (H) *adj.* Exalted; pleased; happy; prosperous.

نہالچہ **nihālchah** (P) *n.m.* A quilt; wrapper; coverlet; mattress; cushion.

نہالی **nihālī** (P) *n.f.* A young plant; a quilt; a small carpet; a cushion.

نہاں **nihāṅ** (P) *adj.* Latent; hidden; concealed; clandestine; secret.

نہاں خانہ **nihāṅ khānah**, *n.m.* A private room; an underground store-room.

نہان **nahān** (H) *n.m.* Bathing; ablution.

نہانا **nahānā** (H) *v.* To bathe; to wash; to perform ablution.

نہانا دھونا **nahānā dhonā**, *v.* To wash; to bathe; to perform ablutions.

نہانا **nihānā** (H) *n.m.* To tie the legs of a cow when milking.

نہانی **nihānī** (P) *n.f.* Concealment. *adj.* Secret; private; privy.

نہایت **nihāyat** (A) *n.f.* Extreme; extremity; end; goal; limit; boundry; excess. *adj.* Very much; extreme; excessive; remarkable. *adv.* At the utmost; extremely; exceeding; very.

نہتا ، نہتی *nihattā, nihattī* (H) *adj.* Unarmed; empty-handed.

نہج *nahj* (A) *n.m.* Road; path; way; manner; mode.

نہر *nahr* (A) *n.f.* A stream; riverlet; brook; a canal (of running water).

نہرنا *naharnā* (H) *n.m.* A nail paring instrument.

نہرنی *naharnī* (H) *n.f.* A chisel; a nail parer.

نہضت *nuhẓat* (A) *n.f.* Marching; departure; rising up; movement.

نہفتہ *nihuftah* (P) *adj.* Concealed; hidden; private.

نہلا *nahlā* (H) *n.m.* The nine at cards.

نہلانا *nahlānā* (H) *v.* To bathe; to cause to bathe.

نہلوانا *nahlvānā* (H) *v.* To cause to be bathed or washed.

نہم *nahum* (P) *adj.* Ninth.

نہنگ *nahang* (P) *n.m.* A crocodile; alligator; shark; a water dragon or other similar monster.

نہنگ *nihang* (S) *adj.* Naked; free from care; unconcerned.

نہوڑانا *nahuṛānā* (H) *v.* To bend downward; to bow down.

نہی *nahī* (A) *n.f.* Prohibition; an interdict.

نہیں *nahiṅ* (H) *adj.* No; not; nay.

نہیں تو *nahiṅ to, adv.* Otherwise; else.

نے *nai* (P) *n.f.* A reed; a tube; a pipe; a flute; a cane.

نے ستاں (نیستاں) *nai sitāṅ, (naistān), n.m.* A sugar plantation; field of sugar-cane; a bed of seeds; a place where canes or reeds grow.

نے شکر *nai shakar, n.m.* Sugar-cane.

نے نواز *nai nawāz, n.m.* One who plays on a flute; a piper.

نے *nai, ne* (P) *adv.* No; not; neither; nor; nay.

نے *ne* (H) A particle affixed to the name of the agent with a transitive verb in the past tense.

نیا ، نئی *nayā, na'ī* (H) *adj.* New; modern; recent; fresh; strange; novel.

نیا پرانا ہونا *nayā purānā honā, v.* To become somewhat old.

نیا جنم *nayā janam, n.m.* Regeneration; new birth; complete recovery.

نیا راگ الاپنا *nayā rāg alāpnā v.* To sing a new song; to do something novel or extraordinary; to cause fresh trouble.

نیا رنگ لانا *nayā rang lānā, v.* To take a new turn; happening of a new or a strange thing.

نیا فتنہ آٹھانا ، نیا گل کھلانا *nayā fitnah uṭhānā, nayā gul khilānā, v.* To raise fresh dissensions; to create fresh trouble.

نیا نوکر ھرن مارتا ھے *nayā naukar hiran mārtā hai, prov.* New broom sweeps well.

نیا نویلا ، نئی نویلی *nayā nawelā, na'ī nawelī, adj.* Absolutely new; young; beautiful.

نئی جوانی *na'ī javānī, n.f.* Budding youth; beginning of youth.

نئی روشنی *na'ī raushanī, n.f.* New light; modern civilization.

نئے سرے سے *nae sire se, adv.* Anew; afresh; all over again.

نئے نواب آسمان پر دماغ *nae nawwāb āsmān par dimāgh, prov.* An upstart is always arrogant.

نئے نئے حاکم نئی نئی باتیں *nae nae ḥākim na'ī na'ī bātiṅ, prov.* New masters new laws.

نیا *naiyyā* (H) *n.f.* A boat.

نیابت *niyābat* (A) *n.f.* Deputation; representation; vicegerancy.

نیابتاً *niyābatan* (A) *adv.* As an agent; by proxy.

نیار *niyār* (H) *n.m.* Fodder; food for cattle; forage.

نیارا ، نیاری *niyārā, niyārī* (H) *adj.* Apart; aloof; separate; uncommon; distinct; different; extraordinary.

نیاریا *niyāriyā* (H) *n.m.* One who extracts metals from the scoria. *adj.* Prudent; cautious; not easily imposed on.

نیاز *niyāz* (P) *n.f.* Desire; supplication; poverty; a thing dedicated; an offering. *n.m.* Acquaintance; meeting.

نیاز چڑھانا *niyāz charhānā, v.* To make an offering; to dedicate.

نیاز حاصل کرنا *niyāz ḥāṣil karnā, v.* To attain one's desire; to pay one's respects (to).

نیاز دلوانا *niyāz dilwānā, v.* To give alms; to distribute food to the poor.

نیاز رسول *niyāz-ĕ rasūl, n.f.* Alms given in the name of the Holy Prophet.

نیاز کیش *niyāz kesh, adj.* Humble; obedient.

نیاز مند *niyāz mand, adj.* Supplicating; humble; obedient; indigent; needy.

نیاز مندی *niyāz mandī, n.f.* Supplication; humble; prayer; request; humility; want; indigence.

نیام *niyām* (P) *n.f.* Sheath; a scabbard; a case.

بے نیام *be niyām, adj.* Unsheathed; uncovered (a sword).

نیاؤ *niyāw* (S) *n.m.* Justice; equity; right; just decision.

نیایک *niyāyak* (S) *n.m.* A judge; a logician; a sophist.

نیبو *nībū, n.m.* The lime; the lemon.

نیت *niyyat* (A) *n.f.* Intention; design; will; purpose; desire; wish; aim.

نیت باندھنا ، کرنا *niyyat bāndhnā, karnā, v.* To repeat the prayer formula; to determine; to intend.

نیت بدل جانا، بد ہونا ، پھرنا *niyyat badal jānā, bad honā, phirnā, v.* To change one's mind; to change intention.

نیت ثابت رکھنا *niyyat ṣābit rakhnā, v.* To adhere firmly to one's intention.

نیت لگی رہنا *niyyat lagī rahnā, v.* To bear in mind.

نیت ، نیتی *nīt, nītī* (S) *n.f.* Conduct; guiding; morality; manners; ethics; moral philosophy.

نیچ *nīch* (H) *adj.* Low; base; vile; mean; vulgar; insignificant; short; small. *n.f.* Descent; declivity; slope; deepness.

نیچ آونچ یا آونچ نیچ *nīch ūnch yā ūnch nīch, n.f.* Inequality; unevenness; the high and low; the ups and downs of life.

نیچ ذات *nīch ẕāt, n.f.* A low caste; a depressed class.

نیچا ، نیچی *nīchā, nīchī* (H) *adj.* Low; sloping; low in position; depressed.

نیچا آونچا *nīchā ūnchā, adj.* Uneven; rugged; up and down; high and low.

نیچا دکھانا *nīchā dikhānā, v.* To bring one down; to disgrace.

نیچا کرنا *nīchā karnā, v.* To bend; to lower.

نیچی نظر کرنا *nīchī naẕar karnā, v.* To look downward, out of respect or shame.

نیچی نیچی نظروں سے دیکھنا *nīchī nīchī naẕroṅ se dekhnā, v.* To cast downcast looks; to throw side glances; to look askance.

نیچا *naichā* (H) *n.m.* A ḥuqqā snake; a ḥuqqā tube.

نیچا بند *naichā band, n.m.* One who prepares and sells ḥuqqā tubes.

نیچری nechri, n.m. A materialist; atheist.

نیچے niche (A) adv. Below; under; beneath; down.

نیچے سے اوپر تک nīche se ūpar tak, adv. From head to foot; from top to bottom.

نیر nīr (S) n.m. Water.

نیر naiyyir (A) adj. Luminary; shedding light. n.m. A bright star.

نیر اصغر naiyyir-ĕ aṣghar, n.m. The moon.

نیر اعظم ، تاباں naiyyir-e a'ẕam, tābān, n.m. The sun; the greater luminary.

نیرنگ nairang (P) n.m. Fascination; bewitching arts or wiles; deceit; trick; pretence; evasion; magic; sorcery; a miracle; anything new or strange.

نیرنگی nairangī (P) n.f. Magic; sorcery; deceitfulness; trickery; fickleness.

نیرنگی زمانہ ، عالم nairangī-ĕ-zamānah, 'ālam, n.f. The vicissitudes of time; fickleness or changefulness of the world.

نیرو nerū, nirū (P) n.m. Strength; power; force; troops.

نیز nīz (P) conj. Also; likewise; again; even.

نیزہ nezah (P) n.m. A spear; a lance; a javelin; a dart; a pike; reed from which pens are made.

نیزہ باز nezah bāz, n.m. A spearman; a a lancer; jouster.

نیزہ بازی nezah bāzī, n.f. Spear throwing; tilting.

نیسان naisān (P) n.m. Name of the seventh Syrian month corresponding to April—May.

نیست nest (P) adj. Non-existing; naught.

نیست و نابود کرنا nest-ŏ nābūd karnā, v. To demolish; to destroy; to ruin.

نیستی nestī (P) n.f. Non-existence; annihilation; ruin; destruction; poverty; misfortune.

نیستی چھانا nestī chhānā, v. Overshadowing of ruin and destruction.

نیستی کا مارا ، نیستی کی ماری nestī kā mārā, nestī kī mārī, adj. Unfortunate; wretched; abominable; disgusting.

نیش nesh (P) n.m. A sting; a puncture; a lancet; a probe.

نیش دار nesh dār, adj. Possessing a sting.

نیش زنی nesh zanī, n.f. Stinging; backbiting; tale-bearing; exciting of quarrels.

نیفہ nefah (P) n.m. Part of the trousers through which the string passes; a breeches' belt.

نیک nek (P) adj. Good; lucky; virtuous; pious; mannerly.

نیک اختر nek akhtar, adj. Lucky; fortunate.

نیک انجام nek anjām, adj. Of happy end; having a good end of life.

نیک اندیش nek andesh, adj. Well-disposed; benevolent; meaning well.

نیک اندیشی nek andeshī, n.f. Good intention.

نیک بخت nek bakht, adj. Lucky; well-behaved; well-disposed; true; dutiful; fortunate; of good disposition.

نیک بختی nek bakhtī, n.f. Good fortune; happiness.

نیک چلن nek chalan, adj. Of good conduct; virtuous.

نیک چلنی nek chalanī, n.f. Good conduct.

نیک خصال ، خصلت ، خلق ، خو nek khiṣāl, khaṣlat, khulq, khū, adj. Of good dispositions or habits; good-natured.

نیک خواہ nek khwāh, adj. Well-wisher; affectionate; faithful; grateful; benevolent.

نیک ساعت nek sā'at, n.f. A fortunate moment; auspicious time.

نیک سیرت nek sīrat, adj. Well-disposed; well-conducted; well-mannered.

نیک طینت nek ṭinat, adj. Of good disposition.

نیک فال nek fāl, n.f. Good omen.

نیک فرجام nek farjām, adj. Of happy end; having successful end.

نیک قدم nek qadam, adj. Welcome.

نیک کردار nek kirdār, adj. Of good habits or disposition; of good character.

نیک گھڑی nek ghaṛi, n.f. An auspicious moment.

نیک مزاج nek mizāj, adj. Well-mannered; well-behaved.

نیک نام nek nām, adj. Good repute; renowned; famous.

نیک نامی nek nāmī, n.f. Good character; renown; praise; fame.

نیک نہاد nek nihād, adj. Of good disposition; of good nature.

نیک نیت nek niyyat, adj. Well-meaning; well-intentioned.

نیک نیتی nek niyyati, n.f. Benevolence; goodness of intention.

نیک و بد nek-ŏ bad, n.m. Good and evil.

نیکو neko (P) See نکو niko.

نیکی nekī (P) n.f. Goodness; piety; beauty; virtue; probity; good.

نیکی اور پوچھ پوچھ nekī aur pūchh pūchh. prov. Do not be weary of doing good.

نیکی بدی nekī badī, n.f. Good and evil; weal or woe.

نیکی برباد گناہ لازم nekī barbād gunāh lāzim, prov. A good turn repaid by evil or wickedness.

نیکی کر دریا میں ڈال nekī kar daryā meṅ ḍāl, prov. Do good and forget about it; good deeds are always rewarded.

نیگ neg (H) n.m. Established custom; usage; exclusive right; presents made on festive occasions.

نیل nil (S&P) n.m. Indigo; the gem; the sapphire; blue colour.

نیل بگڑنا nīl bigaṛnā, v. To tell a unimaginable tale; to tell lies; to suffer a great loss; to turn mad; to be unfortunate; a vat of indigo being spoiled.

نیل پڑ جانا nīl paṛ jānā, v. To be beaten black and blue.

نیل ڈھلنا nīl ḍhalnā, v. Sliming of a dying man's eyes; to become shameless.

نیل کا ٹیکا nīl kā ṭikā, n.m. Blame; disrepute; a brand; stigma; slur.

نیل کنٹھ nīl kanṭh, n.m. The blue-necked jay; a peacock; a wag-tail; name of a plant.

نیل کنول nīl kanwāl, n.m. The blue lotus or water-lily; stain; slur.

نیل گاؤ nil gāo, n.f. A species of deer; the white antelope.

نیل گوں nīl gūṅ, adj. Azure; dark-blue.

نیل nail (A) n.m. Acquiring; attaining; taking.

نیل مرام nail-ĕ-marām, n.m. Obtaining one's object; success.

بے نیل مرام be nail-ĕ-marām, adj. Unsuccessful; defeated; dejected.

نیلا ، نیلی nīlā, nīlī, adj. Blue; dark-blue; azure.

نیلا پیلا ہونا nīlā pīlā honā, v. To become very angry.

نیلا پتھر nīlā patthar, n.m. The sapphire.

نیلا تھوتھا nīlā thothā, n.m. Blue vitriol; sulphate of copper.

نیلام nīlām (corr. from Portg.) n.m. Auction; public sale.

نیلام گھر nīlām ghar, n.m. Auction house.

نیلاہٹ nīlāhaṭ n.m. Buleness.

نیلم nīlam (P) n.m. A gem of the blue colour; sapphire.

نیلوفر nīlofar (P) n.m. The lotus; water-lily; nenuphor.

نیم nīm (H) n.m. Name of a tree; a margosa tree.

نیم nīm (P) adj. Half; middle.

نیم باز nīm bāz, adj. Half-open; intoxicated.

نیم برشت nīm barisht, adj. Half-boiled; half-fried; half-roasted.

نیم پخت ' پز nīm pukht, paz, adj. Half-cooked; per boiled; half-baked; soft-boiled.

نیم بسمل nīm bismil, adj. Half-slaughtered; half-killed; half-dead.

نیم پختہ nīm pukhtah, adj. Half-ripe.

نیم جان nīm jān, adj. Half-dead.

نیم جوش nīm josh, adj. Half-boiled.

نیم حکیم nīm ḥakīm, n.m. A quack; an untrained doctor.

نیم خوابی nīm khwābi, n.f. Drowsiness; dozing.

نیم خوابیدہ nīm khwābidah, adj. Half-asleep.

نیم خوردہ nīm khūrdah, adj. & n.m. Half-eaten; the remains of victuals; refuse of food.

نیم راضی nīm rāẓi, adj. Half-satisfied.

نیم رسمی nīm rasmī, adj. Demi-official.

نیم روز nīm roz, n.m. Midday.

نیم شب nīm shab, n.f. Mid-night.

نیم کش nīm kash, adj. Half-drawn; agonizing.

نیم کشتہ nīm kushtah, adj. Half-killed.

نیم گرم nīm garm, adj. Lukewarm; half-hearted.

نیم مردہ nīm murdāh, adj. Half-dead.

نیم ملا nīm mullā, adj. Half-learned; not well educated. n.m. A quack.

نیمچہ nīmchah (H) n.m. A small sword; a scimiter; a dagger.

نیمہ nīmah (P) n.m. Half; middle; side; direction; small trousers; a garment.

نیمہ آستین nīmah āstīn, n.f. Short under-garment; a half-sleeved jacket.

نین ' نینا nain, nainā (H) n.m. The eye.

نین سکھ nain sukh, n.m. A kind of white cotton cloth; Indin muslin; a kind of flower.

نین گنوانا nain ganwānā, v. To lose sight by constant weeping; to weep bitterly.

نین متنا nain mutnā, adj. Weeping at the smallest excuse.

نیند nīṅd (H) n.f. Sleep.

نیند آنا nīṅd ānā, v. To feel sleepy; to sleep.

نیند اچٹ جانا ' نیند اڑ جانا nīṅd uchaṭ jānā, uṛ jānā, v. To be unable to sleep; to have one's sleep driven off.

نیند بھر سونا nīṅd bhar sonā, v. To sleep soundly; to enjoy a full sleep; to be at ease.

نیند حرام کرنا nīṅd ḥarām karnā, v. To disturb one's sleep.

نیند کا ماتا ' نیند کی ماتی nīṅd kā mātā, nīṅd kī mātī, adj. Sleepy; drowsy.

نینو nainū (H) n.m. A kind of embroidered cloth; sprigged muslin.

نیو neo (H) n.f. The foundation (of a building); foundation.

نیو ڈالنا neo ḍālnā, v. To lay the foundation (of); to found.

نیوتا neyotā (H) n.m. Invitation.

نیوش niyūsh (P) adj. (used in compos). Hearing; listening.

نیولا newlā (H) n.m. A weasel; a mungoose; a ferret.

نیہا nehā (H) n.m. Effection; kindness; friendship; love.

و

و vao, vaw, is the twenty-sixth letter of the Arabic, thirtieth of the Persian and thirty-third of the Urdu alphabet. According to *abjad* it stands for number six. In Arabic and Persian it is generally used as a conjunction in the sense of "and" and "with" (implying society; connection; partnership) and when it connects two words, it sounds as "ŏ," as in شب و روز *shab-ŏ-roz*, day and night. In Arabic it is also used in swearing e.g. واللہ *wallah*, by God.

وا **wā** (P) *adj.* Open. *adv.* Again; back. *prep.* With. *interj.* An expression of pain; ah! oh!

وابستگان *wā bastagān*, *n.m.* Dependents; relation; adherents; domestics.

وابستگی *wā bastagi*, *n.f.* Adhesion; dependence; relationship.

وابستہ *wā bastah*, *adj.* Bound together; related; connected; depending on. *n.m.* An adherent; a dependent; an attache.

وابستہ ہونا *wā bastah honā*, *v.* To be attached; to be connected; to adhere to; to be dependent on; to depend upon.

واپس *wā pas*, *adj.* Behind; back; returning again; afterwards.

واپسی *wā pasī*, *n.f.* Withdrawal; return.

واپسین *wā pasīn*, *adj.* The last; latter; hindmost; posterior.

وارستگی *wā rastagi*, *n.f.* Deliverance; freedom; salvation; liberation.

وارستہ *wā rastah*, *adj.* Delivered; saved; escaped; free; carefree.

وارفتگی *wā raftagi*, *n.f.* Relaxaton; remissness; distraction; infatuation; madness.

وارفتہ *wā raftah*, *adj.* Wandered; lost; gone astray; distracted; mad.

واسوخت *wā sokht*, *n.m.* Aversion; disgust; an impassioned style in poetry.

واسوختہ *wā sokhtah*, *adj.* Inflamed; impassioned.

واکرنا *wā karnā*, *v.* To open.

واگذار *wā guẕār*, *adj.* Released.

واگذار کرنا *wā guẕār karnā*, *v.* To release.

وا گذاشت *wā guẕāsht*, *n.f.* Leaving behind; making over, cession; release; giving up; ceding.

وامانده *wā māṅdah*, *adj.* Fatigued; remaining behind.

واماندگی *wā māṅdagi*, *n.f.* The remaining behind; inability.

وا ہونا *wā honā*, *v.* To become open; to be opened; to open; to be freed; to be liberated; to become cheerful; to be relieved of sorrow.

واثق **wāṣiq** (A) *adj.* Strong; firm; binding; confident; secure; confiding.

واجب **wājib** (A) *adj.* Necessary; obligatory; binding; proper; worthy; just; right; expedient; fit; meet; reasonable; deserving; due.

واجب الادا *wājib-ul-adā*, *adj.* Payable; necessary to be discharged.

واجب الاذعان *wājib-ul-iẕa'ān*, *adj.* Fit to be complied with; worthy of compliance.

واجب الاظہار *wājib-ul-iẓhār*, *adj.* Fit to be disclosed; worthy of representation.

واجب التسلیم *wājib-ut-taslīm*, *adj.* Acceptable.

واجب التعزیر *wājib-ut-ta'zīr*, *adj.* Punishable.

واجب التعظیم *wājib-ut-ta'ẓīm*, *adj.* Worthy of respect; venerable; respectable.

واجب الرحم *wājib-ur-raḥm*, *adj.* Pitiable.

واجب الرعایت wājib-ur-ri'āyat, *adj.* Pardonable; excusable; remissable.

واجب العرض wājib-ul-a'rz, *adj.* Fit to be represented. *n.f.* A written representation or petition; an agreement; an adminstration paper.

واجب العمل wājib-ul-a'mal, *adj.* Necessary to be acted upon.

واجب القتل wājib-ul-qatl, *adj.* Deserving death.

واجب الوجود wājib-ul-wujūd, *adj* & *n.m.* Self-existent; God.

واجب الوصول wājid-ul-wuṣūl, *adj.* Realisable; recoverable.

واجب جاننا wājib jānnā, *v.* To regard as obligatory.

واجب و لازم wājib-ŏ lāzim, *adj.* Necessary; unavoidable.

واجبات wājibāt (A) *n.m.* (*plu.* of واجب wājib) Duties; essentials; expedients; important things.

واجبی wājibi (A) *adj.* Necessary; expedient; admissible; allowable; proper.

واجبی بات wājibī bāt, *n.m.* Reasonable thing.

واجبی معلومات wājibi ma'lūmāt, *n.f.* A workable knowledge.

واجد wājid (A) *adj.* Possessor; creater; finder.

واحد wāḥid (A) *adj.* One; alone; sole; individual; single; unique.

واحدالعین wāḥid-ul-'ain, *adj.* One-eyed.

واحد حقیقی wāḥid-ĕ ḥaqiqi, *n.m.* The only Being; God.

واحد شاہد wāḥid shāhid. (*Lit.*) God is my witness. *adj.* Giving; bestowing; knowing.

وادی wādı (A) *n.f.* Valley; vale; a low land; the channel of a river; a river; a desert.

وادی wādi, *n.f.* Habit; obstinacy; perverseness; disobedience.

وادی پر آنا wādı par ānā, *v.* To revert to one's bad habits; to be obstinate.

وار wār (H) *n.m.* A blow; wound; gash; attack; a knock; a stroke; a cut; turn; leisure.

وار خالی جانا wā khālī jānā, *v.* To lose an opportunity; to miss the aim.

وار کرنا wār karnā, *v.* To assault; to attack.

وار نہ لینے دینا wār nah lene denā, *v.* To allow no recess or leisure.

وار wār (P) Like; resembling; endowed with; having; possessing; (used in *comp.* such as امید وار ummīd wār, hopeful; candidate).

وار wār (S) *n.m.* Any day of the week; time; a moment.

وارا wārā (H) *n.m.* Blessing; benefit; wealth; gain; saving; thrift; victim; a sacrifice; an offering.

وارے نیارے wāre niyāre, *n.m.* Great benefit.

وارے نیارے ہونا wāre niyāre honā, *v.* To prosper; to flourish.

وارث wāriṣ (A) *n.m.* An heir; a master; a lord; an owner; a successor.

وارث بعید wārṣ-ĕ-ba'īd, *n.m.* A distant successor.

وارث شرطی wāriṣ-ĕ sharṭi, *n.m.* Stipulated successor.

وارث صلبی wāriṣ-ĕ ṣulbi, *n.m.* Heir-apparent.

وارث قانونی wāriṣ-ĕ qānūni, *n.m.* Heir-at-law.

وارث قیاسی wāriṣ-ĕ-qiyāsi, *n.m.* Heir presumptive.

وارث ہونا wāriṣ honā, *v.* To inherit.

وارد wārid (A) *adj.* Coming; arriving; approaching; alighting; decending; happening; being present.

وارد ہونا wārid honā, *v.* To come; to arrive; to alight; to befall; to enter; to be imported.

واردات wāridāt (A) n.f. (plu. of وارده wāridah) Imports; event; accident; incident; occurrence; affrays; crime; a catastrophe.

وارنا wārnā (H) v. To wave anything round or over another as a votive offering; to offer in sacrifice.

واری wārī (H) adj. Oblate; sacrificed.

واڑ، واڑی wāṛ waṛī (H) n.f. An enclosure; an enclosed piece of ground; an enclosed garden (used in *comps.* such as پھلواڑ *phul-wāṛ or* پھلواڑی *phulwāṛī*, a flower garden).

واڑا wāṛā (H) n.m. A quarter; a part of a city.

واژگون، واژوں wāzhgūn wāzhūn (P) adj. Inverted; overturned; reversed; preposterous; contrary; unfortunate; unlucky; backward.

واسطه wāsṭah (A) n.m. Account; sake; connection; relation; cause; réason; means; medium; motive; a mediator; agent; broker.

واسطه پڑنا wāsṭah paṛnā, v. To be concerned with; to come into contact (with).

واسطه پیدا کرنا wāsṭah paidā karnā, v. To find out ways and means; to find means of approach.

واسطه دینا wāsṭah denā, v. To cry for justice or help.

واسطه رکھنا wāsṭah rakhnā, v. To have relation with.

واسطه ھونا wāsṭah honā, v. To have concern; to be related to.

واسطی wāsṭī (P) adj. Belonging to *wāsiṭ*, a city in Iraq. n.m. A reed; a pen.

واسطے wāsṭe, prep. For; for the sake of; on behalf of; on account of; because of; in order to.

واسکٹ wāskaṭ (corr. of English) n.f. A waistcoat.

واسع wāsiʻ (A) adj. Capacious; wide; ample.

واصل wāṣil (A) adj. Joined; connected; coupled; arrived.

واصل باقی wāṣil bāqī, n.f. Collection and balances; account of payments.

واصل باقی نویس wāṣil bāqī nawīs, n.m. An account keeper for collections and payments.

واصل بحق ھونا wāṣil ba ḥaqq honā, v. To die; to give up the ghost.

واصلات wāṣilāt (A) n.f. (plu. of واصله wāṣilah) The proceeds of an estate; usufruct; account of collected money.

واضح wāẓih (A) adj. Evident; manifest; obvious; clear; apparent.

واضح رھے wāẓiḥ rahe. Be it known that; whereas.

واضح کرنا wāẓiḥ karnā, v. To clarify.

واضع wāẓiʻ (A) adj. Placing; establishing. n.m. Inventor; founder; establisher.

واضع قانون wāẓiʻ qānūn, n.m. Law-maker; law-giver; legislator

واعظ wāʻiẓ (A) n.m. A preacher; an adviser; a teacher; a monitor.

وافر wāfir (A) adj. Plentiful; abundent; wealthy; large; vast; copious; ample; opulent.

وافی wāfī (A) adj. Complete; just; sufficient; plentiful; entire; adequate; enough.

واقع wāqiʻ (A) adj. Happening; appearing; befalling; occuring; arriving.

واقع میں wāqiʻ meṅ, adv. In reality; in fact; actually; really.

واقع ھونا wāqiʻ honā, v. To happen; to occur; to befall.

واقعات wāqiʻāt (A) n.m. (plu. of واقعه wāqiʻah) Accidents; events; occurrences; intelligence; news; facts.

واقعه wāqiʻah (A) n.m. Event; incident; intelligence; accident; news; death.

واقعه نویس wāqiʻah nawīs, n.m. A news-writer.

واقعی wāqiʻī (A) adv. Really; in reality; actually; certainly; truly; in fact. adj. True; real; due; right; proper.

واقف wāqif (A) *adj.* Acquainted; aware of; experienced; conversant with; knowing; learned; sensible.

واقف حال wāqif-ĕ ḥāl, *adj.* Experienced; expert; intelligent. *n.m.* A connoisseur.

واقف کار wāqif-ĕ kār *adj.* Experienced; knowing; expert.

واقفیت wāqifiyyat (A) *n.f.* Experience; knowledge; information; intelligence; acquaintance.

واقفیت پیدا کرنا wāqifiyyat paidā karnā, *v.* To acquire a knowledge of; to form acquaintance with.

وال ، والا ، والی wal, wālā, wāli (H) *adj.* (used in *comp.*) Keeper; inhabitant; doer.

والا wālā (P) *adj.* Exalted in dignity; sublime; high; eminent; respectable; superior.

والا جاه ، مرتبت wālā jāh, martabat, *adj.* Of exalted rank or station.

والا شان wālā shān, *adj.* High in dignity.

والا قدر wālā qadr, *adj.* Highly esteemed.

والا نژاد wālā nazhād yā nizhād, *adj.* Of high family; of high origin.

والا نگاه wālā nigāh, *adj.* Of high thoughts.

والا همت wālā himmat, *adj.* Audacious; bold; daring.

والد wālid (A) *n.m.* Father.

والده wālidah (A) *n.f.* Mother.

والدین wālidain (A) *n.m.* Parents; father and mother.

والله wallah (A) By God.

والله اعلم wallah-ŏ a'lm. None but God knows.

واله wālah (A) *adj.* Distracted; mad with love; stupified; confounded; driven to despair.

والهانه wālihānah (A&P) *adv.* In madness with love.

والی wālī (A) *n.m.* A prince; a chief; superior; sovereign; ruler; master.

وام wām (P) *n.m.* Debt; creait; lending; borrowing.

وام و اجاره wām-ŏ ijārah, *n.m.* Lend and lease.

واں wāṅ (H) *adv.* (*contraction of* وهاں *wahāṅ*) That place; there.

وان wān (H) Possessing; endowed with; (used in *comp.* as دهن وان *dhan wān*, possessing wealth).

وا ویلا wāwailā (A) *n.m.* Lamentation; bewailing. *interj.* Alas! ah!

واه wāh (P) *interj.* Bravo; well done; excellent; alas.

واه واه wāḥ wāh, *interj.* Bravo! excellent!.

واهب wāhib (A) *adj.* Liberal; generous.

واهمه wāhimah (A) *n.m.* Fancy; imagination; whim; the faculty of imagination.

واهی wāhī (A) *adj.* Crazy; ill-founded; vagrant; a loose character.

واهی تباهی wāhī tabāhī, *adj.* Absurd; nonsensical; meaningless.

واهی تباهی بکنا wāhī tabāhī baknā, *v.* To talk nonsense; to use foul language.

واهیات wāhiyyāt (A) *n.f.* (*plu.* of واهیه *wāhiyah*) Absurdities; nonsense; fiddle faddle.

وائے wā'e (A) *interj.* Alas! fy! woe to you.

وبا wabā (A) *n.f.* Plague; pestilence; epidemic; pest.

وبال wabāl (A) *n.m.* Burden; anything painful or distressing; plague; epidemic; misfortune; a crime; fault; punishment for a crime; divine vengeance. *adj.* Unwholesome; burdensome; painful; vexatious.

وبائی wabā'ī (A) *adj.* Epidemic; epidemical.

وبائی امراض wabā'ī amrāẓ, *n.m.* Epidemic or infectious diseases.

وبائیات wabā'iyāt (A) n.f. Epidemiology.

وبائیاتی wabā'iyātī, adj. Epidemiological.

وتد watad, watid (A) n.m. A peg; a pin; a three-lettered word (prosody).

وتر watar (A) n.m. The hypotenuse of a right-angled triangle; sinew; tendon; diagonal of a quadrilaterel; the string of a bow.

وتیرہ watīrah (A) n.m. A path; way; manner; habit; custom.

وثائق waṣā'iq (A) n.m. (plu. of وثیقہ waṣīqah) Bonds; written agreements; pronote.

وثوق wuṣūq (A) n.m. Strength; firmness; obligation; steadfastness; confiding in; trusting.

وثیقہ waṣīqah (A) n.m. Firmness; solidity; confidence; faith; bond; obligation; endowment; a written agreement; a pronote; promissory note.

وثیقہ ضمانت waṣīqah-ĕ ẓamānat, n.m. A bail bond.

وثیقہ نویس waṣīqah nawīs, n.m. A deed writer.

وجاہت wajāhat (A) n.f. High position; dignity; comeliness; respect; respectability; appearance; aspect.

وجب wajab (A) n.f. A span; nine inches.

وجد wajd (A) n.m. Ecstacy; rapture; transport; frenzy; excessive love; discovering; procuring.

وجد میں آنا wajd meṅ ānā, v. To get a religious fit; to be enraptured.

وجدان wijdān (A) n.m. Rapture; ecstasy; intuition.

وجدانی wijdānī (A) adj. Intuitive.

وجع waja' (A) n.m. Disease; pain; application; malady; ailment; complaint; mourning.

وجع المفاصل waja'-ul-mafāṣil, n.m. Rheumatism.

وجوب wujūb (A) n.m. Necessity; expediency; obligation.

وجود wujūd (A) n.m. Existence; essence; being; body; substance; invention; penis.

وجوہ wujūh (A) n.m./f. (plu. of وجہ wajh) Faces; manners; reasons.

وجہ wajh (A) n.f. Cause; reason; argument; mode; manner; way; means; face; visage; appearance; semblance; shape.

وجہ تسمیہ wajh-ĕ tasmiyah, n.f. Reason for giving a particular name; the etymology of words.

وجہ موجہ wajh-ĕ muwajjah, n.f. A strong reason.

وجیہ wajīh (A) adj. Of a good appearance; handsome; respectable.

وحدانی waḥdānī (P) adj. Showing oneness.

وحدانیت waḥdāniyyat (A) n.f. Unity (of godhead); the belief in the oneness of God.

وحدت waḥdat (A) n.f. Unity; the being one; oneness.

وحش waḥsh (A) n.m. A wild beast.

وحش و طیر waḥsh-ŏ ṭair, n.m. Beasts and birds.

وحشت waḥshat (A) n.f. Solitude; dreariness; grief; wildness; barbarism; timidity; terror; horror; fright; fear; dread; sadness; loneliness; savageness; ferosity.

وحشت انگیز ، آلودہ ، ناک waḥshat aṅgez, ālūdah, nāk, adj. Frightful; terrible; shocking; horrible; desolate; dreary; bewildering.

وحشت برسنا waḥshat barasnā, v. Prevailing of wilderness.

وحشت زدہ waḥshat zadah, adj. Terrified; struck with loneliness; aghast; awe-struck.

وحشت ہونا waḥshat honā, v. To be frightened; to be terrified; to be aggrieved.

وحشی **waḥshi** (A) *adj.* Wild; untamed; shy; ferocious; uncivilised; cruel; barbarous. *n.m.* A wild beast; a brute; a savage.

وحوش **wuḥūsh** (A) *n.m.* (*plu.* of وحش *waḥsh*) Wild beasts.

وحی **waḥī** (A) *n.f.* Divine revelation; inspiration.

وحید **waḥīd** (A) *adj.* Unique; singular; unparallel; alone.

وحیدالعصر *waḥīd-ul-'aṣr*, *adj.* Non-parallel of his age.

وحیدالدھر *waḥīd-ud-dahr*, *adj.* The phoenix of his age.

ود ، وداد **wudd, widād** (A) *n.f.* Love; friendship; affection.

وداع **widā'** (A) *n.m.* Forewell adieu; bidding farewell.

ودود **wadūd** (A) *adj.* Loving; friendly; an epithet of God.

ودھوا **widhwa** (H) *n.f.* A widow.

ودیا **widdyā** (S) *n.f.* Knowledge; learning; science; philosophy.

ودیعت **wadī'at** (A) *n.f.* Deposit; trust.

ور **war** (P) Possessing; having; enjoying (used in *comp.* as نامور *nāmwar*, having a name; famous).

ورا ، ورائے **warā, warāi** (A) *adv.* Behind; beyond; besides.

وراثت **wirāṣat** (A) *n.f.* Heritage; heirship.

وراثت نامہ *wirāṣat nāmah*, *n.m.* Deed of inheritance.

وراثتاً **wirāṣatan̲** (A) *adv.* By inheritance.

ورثاء **wuraṣā'** (A) *n.m.* (*plu.* of وارث *wāriṣ*) Heirs; successors.

ورثہ **wirṣah** (A) *n.m.* A heritage; a bequest.

ورد **ward** (A) *n.m.* A rose; a flower; the leaf of a flower; a rose petal.

ورد **wird** (A) *n.m.* Access; approach; daily use; practice; talk; a portion of the Quran fixed for reading at a certain time.

ورد زبان *wird-ĕ zabān*, *adj.* Knowing by heart.

ورد زبان ہونا *wird-ĕ zabān honā*, *v.* To have by heart.

ورد کرنا *wird karnā*, *v.* To repeat.

وردی **wardī** (H) *n.f.* Uniform; livery.

ورزش **warzish** (P) *n.f.* Athletic exercise; habit; custom.

ورزش گاہ ، ورزش خانہ *warzish gāh, warzish k̲h̲ānah*, *n.f./m.* Gymnasium; polaestrar; a wrestling school; an athletic field.

ورزشی **warzishī** (A) *adj.* Athletic. *n.m.* An athlete.

ورطہ **warṭah** (A) *n.m.* Labyrinth; a maze; a whirlpool; embarrassment; any danger or difficulty.

ورع **wara'** (A) *n.f.* Apprehensiveness of doing wrong; fear of God; temperance; continence; chastity; timidity.

ورغلانا **warg̲h̲alānā**, *v.* To decieve; to decoy; to seduce; to tempt; to actuate; to provoke; to exasperate.

ورق **waraq** (A) *n.m.* A leaf; a card; a slice; a foil; silver or gold or tin leaf.

ورق الخیال *waraq-ul-k̲h̲ayāl*, *n.f./m.* Hemp, from which an intoxicating juice is extracted.

ورق اُلٹیے *waraq ulṭiye.* Please turn over.

ورق بازی *waraq bāzī*, *n.f.* Card-playing.

ورق تراشنا *waraq tarāshnā*, *v.* To cut cards.

ورق دار *waraq dār*, *adj.* Laminate; laminose; laminar.

ورق ساز *waraq sāz*, *n.m.* A leaf-beater (gold, silver etc.).

ورق کوٹنا *waraq kūṭnā*, *v.* To beat leaves (of a metal).

ورق گردانی کرنا *waraq gardānī karnā*, *v.* To turn leaves (of a book); to read a book.

ورق گل *waraq-ĕ gul, n.m.* Petal.

ورقہ *waraqah, n.m.* A leaf.

ورقی *waraqī, adj.* Leaf-like.

ورم *waram* (A) *n.m.* A swelling; tumour.

ورم کرنا *waram karnā, v.* To swell.

ورنہ *warnah* (P) *adv.* And if not; otherwise; although.

ورود *wurūd* (A) *n.m.* Arrival; coming; appearing; descending; alighting; approaching.

ورے *ware* (H) *adv.* On this side; near.

وزارت *wizārat* (A) *n.f.* The office of a minister; ministry.

وزارت امور خارجہ *wizārat-ĕ umūr-ĕ khārijah, n.f.* Ministry of foreign affairs.

وزارت تجارت *wizārat-e tijārat, n.f.* Ministry of trade and commerce.

وزارت تعلیم *wizārat-ĕ ta'līm, n.f.* Ministry of education.

وزارت پیشہ و ہنر یا صناعت *wizārat-ĕ peshah-ŏ hunar yā ṣanā, n.f.* Ministry of industries.

وزارت‌داد گستری یا عدل *wizārat-ĕ dād gushtari, 'adl, n.f.* Ministry of justice.

وزارت داخلہ *wizārat-ĕ dākhilah, n.f.* Ministry of the interior.

وزارت دفاع *wizārat-ĕ difā' n.f.* Ministry of Defence.

وزارت مالیات *wizārat-ĕ māliyāt, n.f.* Ministry of finance.

وزارت مواصلات *wizārat-ĕ muwāṣilāt, n.f.* Ministry of communication.

وزراء *wuzarā'* (A) *n.m.* (*plu.* of وزیر *wazīr*) Ministers of State.

وزن *wazn* (A) *n.m.* Weight; weighing; measure; metre; rhyme; verse; rhythm, reputation; esteem; honour; examination; estimation.

وزن دار ، وزنی *wazn dār, waznī, adj.* Weighty; heavy.

وزنہ *waznah* (P) *n.m.* Paper-weight.

وزیر *wazīr* (A) *n.m.* A minister of state.

وزیراعظم *wazīr-ĕ a'ẓam, n.m.* Premier.

وزیر اعلیٰ *wazīr-ĕ a'lā, n.m.* Chief minister.

وساطت *wasāṭat,* (A) *n.f.* Means; medium; mediation; inter-position.

وساوس *wasāwis* (A) *n.m.* (*plu.* of وسوسہ *waswasah*) Doubts; evil suggestions.

وسائل *wasā'il* (A) *n.m.* (*plu.* of وسیلہ *wasīlah*) Mediations; means.

وسط *wasṭ* (A) *n.m.* Middle; the centre.

وسطی *wasṭi* (A) *adj.* Middle; average; intermediate; moderate; central.

وسطیٰ *wusṭā* (A) *adj.* Middling.

وسع ، وسعت *wusa', wus'at* (A) *n.f.* Wideness; breadth; span; range; measurement; dimensions; area; latitude; amptitude; space; extent; leisure; convenience; opportunity; ease.

وسمہ *wasmah* (A) *n.m.* The leaves of indigo, which yield blue colour.

وسمہ لگانا، کرنا *wasmah lagānā, karnā, v.* To stain one's beard or head with indigo colour; to stain blue.

وسواس *waswās* (A) *n.m.* The temptation of the devil; distraction of mind; doubt; suspense; hesitation; suspicion; apprehension; dread; perplexity; superstition; scrupulousness.

وسواسی *waswāsī* (A) *adj.* Doubtful; distracting; scrupulous; apprehensive.

وسوسہ *waswasah* (A) *n.m.* Temptation; evil suggestion.

وسیع *wasī'* (A) *adj.* Extensive; large; spacious; roomy.

وسیع‌الاختیار *wasī'-ul-ikhtiyār, adj.* High-powered; having wide powers.

وسیع النظر *wasī'-un-naẓar, adj.* Far-sighted.

وسیلہ *wasīlah* (A) *n.m.* Affinity; cause; occasion; support; means; prop; mediation.

وسیله پیدا کرنا *wasīlah paidā karnā, v.* To find out means or support.

وسیله نا جائز *wasīlah-ĕ nājā'iz, n.m.* Illegal means.

وسیم *wasīm* (A) *adj.* Of a fine countenance; handsome; comely.

وش *wash* (P) (a particle affixed) Like; resembling.

وشواش *wishwāsh* (H) *n.m.* Trust; faith; belief.

وصال *wiṣāl* (A) *n.m.* Meeting; interview; connection; union; intercourse; society; enjoyment; confederacy; death.

وصال هو جانا *wisal ho jānā, v.* To meet; to die.

وصایا *waṣāyā* (A) *n.m.* (*plu.* of وصیت *waṣiyyat*) Legacies; bequests.

وصف *waṣf* (A) *n.m.* Praise; description; encomium; merit; virtue; worth; quality; attribute; epithet.

وصل *waṣl* (A) *n.m.* Meeting; union; conjuction; connection; copulation; sexual union.

وصل کرنا *waṣl karnā, v.* To unite; to attach; to copulate.

وصل هونا *waṣl honā, v.* To be united; to be connected; to be attached.

وصلت *waṣlat* (A) *n.f.* See وصل *waṣl*.

وصلی *waṣlī* (A & P) *n.f.* Two pieces of paper etc. pasted together for the purpose of practising writing on.

وصول *wuṣūl* (A) *n.m.* Arrival; conjunction; acquisition or enjoyment of anything desired; recovery; collection; realisation (of revenue etc.); receipt.

وصول باقی *wuṣūl bāqī, n.m.* Uncollected or unrealized balance.

وصولی *wuṣūlī, adj.* Recoverable. *n.f.* Recoverable dues.

وصی *waṣī* (A) *n.m.* An executor, administrator (of a will); preceptor.

وصیت *waṣiyyat* (A) *n.f.* Command; injunction; charge; a last will or testament; a legacy; bequest; precept; mandate; making a will.

وصیت کرنا *waṣiyyat karnā, v.* To bequeath; to advise; to leave by will.

وصیت نامه *waṣiyyat nāmah, n.m.* A last will or testament.

وضاحت *waẓāḥat* (A) *n.f.* Explanation; vivid description.

وضاحت کرنا *waẓāḥat karnā, v.* To make manifest; to make known; to explain.

وضع *waẓa'* (A) *n.f.* State; condition; manner; mode; way; conduct; behaviour; fashion; situation; procedure; giving birth; delivery; deduction.

وضع حمل *waẓa'-ĕ ḥaml, n.m.* Delivery; giving birth to a child.

وضع دار *waẓa' dār, adj.* Stylish; elegant; of good appearance or form.

وضع داری *waẓā' dārī, n.f.* Style; manner; elegance.

وضع کرنا *waẓa' karnā, v.* To deduct; to subtract; to found.

وضع نا گوار *waẓa'-ĕ nāgawār, n.f.* Intolerable behaviour.

وضو *wuẓū*, & (A) *n.m.* Ablution.

وضوح *wuẓūḥ* (A) *n.m.* Evidence; proof; clearness.

وضیع *waẓī'* (A) *adj.* Ignoble; base; low; plebian.

وطن *waṭan* (A) *n.m.* Native country; residence; abod; home; country.

وطن پرست، دوست *waṭan parast, dost, n.m.* A patriot.

وطن دشمن *waṭon dushman, n.m.* A traitor.

وطنی *waṭanī* (A) *adj.* Belonging to one's country; home-made.

وظائف *waẓā'if* (A) *n.m.* (*plu.* of وظیفه *waẓīfah*) Functions; scholarships.

وظيفه **wazīfah** (A) *n.m.* Scholarship; stipend; pension; salary; a daily performance or task; daily worship; duty; function; anything agreed on; land bestowed in gift for past service.

وظيفه دار **wazīfah dār**, *n.m.* Stipendiary; a scholarship holder; pensioner.

وعده **wa'dah** (A) *n.m.* A promise; agreement; bargain; assignation; appointment.

وعده آ پهنچنا **wa'dah ā pahunchnā**, *v.* Approaching of the time of death.

وعده ٹالنا **wa'dah ṭālnā** *v.* To procrastinate; to dilly-dally; to evade fulfilment of a promise.

وعده خلاف **wa'dah khilāf**, *adj.* One who does not keep his word; a defaulter.

وعده شكن **wa'dah shikan**, *adj.* A promise breaker.

وعده فراموش **wa'dah frāmosh**, *adj.* One who forgets his promises.

وعده معاف گواه **wa'dah mu'āf gawāh**, *n.m.* An approver.

وعده وعيد **wa'pah wa'hid**, *n.m.* Evading a promise; chicanery.

وعده وفا **wa'dah wafā**, *adj.* Punctual; true to one's words.

وعظ **wa'z** (A) *n.m.* Advice; admonition; sermon; preaching; homily.

وعيد **wa'id** (A) *n.m.* Threat; denunciation; predicting anything bad.

وغا **waghā** (A) *n.f.* War; battle; tumult; clamour.

وغيره **waghairah** (A) *adv.* Et cactera; and so forth; and others.

وفا **wafā** (A) *n.f.* Fulfilling a promise; observation of faith; fulfilment; sincerity; fidelity; sufficiency.

وفا بيگانه **wafā begānah**, *adj.* Faithless.

وفا پرست **wafā parast**, *adj.* Faithful; sincere.

وفا پيشه ' كيش ' شعار **wafā peshah, kesh, shi'ār**, *adj.* Faithful; sincere; loyal.

وفا دار **wafā dār**, *adj.* Faithful; sincere; constant.

وفا دارى **wafā dari**, *n.f.* Allegiance; constancy; sincerity; faithfulness.

وفا كرنا **wafā karnā**, *v.* To fulfil a promise; to keep faith (with); to be faithful (to); to be loyal; to be true; to suffice.

وفات **wafāt** (A) *n.f.* Death; demise.

وفاق **wifāq** (A) *n.m.* Concord; harmony; unanimity; federation.

وفاقى **wifāqi** (A) *adj.* Federal.

وفاقى حكومت يا وفاقيه **wifāqi ḥukūmat, wifāqiyah**, *n.f.* Federal government.

وفاقيت **wifāqiyat** (A) *n.f.* Federalism.

وفد **wafd** (A) *n.m.* Deputation; delegation.

وفق **wafq** (A) *n.m.* Sufficiency; concord; congruity.

وفور **wufūr** (A) *n.m.* A multitude; plenty; abundance.

وقار **waqar** (A) *n.m.* Dignity; estimation; steadiness; constancy; modesty; gravity; mildness; honour; reputation; prestige.

وقائع **waqā'i'** (A) *n.m.* (*plu. of* وقيعه *waqi'ah*) News; events; accidents; occurrences.

وقائع نگار **waqa'i' nigar**, *n.m.* A news writer; an intelligencer; a correspondent.

وقت **waqt** (A) *n.m.* Time; term; fixed time; season; hour; duration; opportunity; adversity.

وقت بوقت **waqt bawaqt**, *adv.* From time to time.

وقت بے وقت **waqt bewaqt**, *adv.* In season or out of season; constantly; perpetually; at all times.

وقت پر كام آنا **waft par kām ānā**, *v.* To stand by in time of need.

وقت پر گدھے كو بھی باپ بنا ليتے هيں **waqt par gadhe ko bhī bāp benā lete hain**, *prov.* Bow down before the fox in season.

وقت پڑنا *waqt paṛnā*, *v.* To suffer misfortunes; to be distressed; to stand in need of.

وقت پڑے پر جانیے کو بیری کو میت *waqt paṛe par jāniye ko bairy ko mit*, *prov.* Adversity is the best judge of a friend and foe.

وقت تنگ ہونا *waqt taṅg honā*, *v.* To be very short (time).

وقت کاٹنا *waqt kāṭnā*, *v.* To pass away the time; to pass days in difficulty and trouble.

وقت کا پابند *waqt kā pāband*, *adj.* Punctual; observant of the proper time.

وقت کے وقت *waqt ke waqt*, *adv.* At the nick of the time; just at the proper time.

وقت نازک *waqt-ĕ nāzuk*, *n.m.* Delicate time; critical moment.

وقت نکالنا *waqt nikālnā*, *v.* To find time (for); to reserve time (for).

وقتاً فوقتاً *waqtan̲ fawaqtan̲* (A) *adv.* From time to time.

وقتی *waqtī* (A&P) *adj.* Provisional.

وقتی طور پر *waqtī ṭaur par*, *adv.* For the time being.

وقر *waqr* (A) *n.m.* Dignity; honour; character.

وقعت *waqa't* (A) *n.f.* Weight; force; respect; regard; consideration.

وقعت رکھنا *waqa't rak̲h̲nā*, *v.* To have weight; to command respect.

وقعت کھونا *waqa't khonā*, *v.* To lose respect; to have no weight.

وقف *waqf* (A) *n.m.* Legacy; endowment for pious uses; dedication or foundation for public charity; trust; standing; stopping; stoppage; understanding; tranquility; firmness; constancy.

وقف لازم *waqf-ĕ lāzim*, *n.m.* A necessary stop.

وقف نامہ *waqf nāmah*, *n.m.* A deed of endowment; a trust deed.

وقفہ *waqfah* (A) *n.m.* Delay; pause; stopping; retarding; respite; vacancy; interval

وقوع *wuqū'* (A) *n.m.* A contingency; an accident; an event; incidence; occurrence; happening; coming to pass.

وقوع جرم *wuqū'-ĕ jurm*, *n.m.* Commission of a crime.

وقوع میں آنا *wuqū' men ānā*, *v.* To occur; to happen.

وقوعہ *wuqū'ah* (A) *n.m.* An event; occurrence.

وقوف *wuqūf* (A) *n.m.* Understanding; information; sense; experience; wisdom; knowledge; skill; discernment; awareness; cognition; standing; stopping.

وقوف دار *wuqūf dār*, *adj.* Experienced; imformed; aware of; skilled.

وقیع *waqi'* (A) *adj.* Lofty; weighty; wise; forceful.

وکالت *wakālat* (A) *n.f.* Pleadership; advocacy; practice at the bar; attorneyship; embassy; agency; commission; proxy.

وکالت کرنا *wakālat karnā*, *v.* To plead; to advocate the cause of; to practise at the bar; to practise as a pleader or advocate; to carry on a law suit.

وکالت نامہ *wakālat nāmah*, *n.m.* Power of attorney.

وکالتاً *wakālatan̲* (A) *adv.* By proxy.

وکیل *wakīl* (A) *n.m.* A counsellor; an attorney; a pleader; an agent; an ambassador; a commissioner; counsel; a lawyer.

وگر *wagar* (P) *conj.* And if.

وگر نہ *wagar nah*, *conj.* And if not.

ولا *wilā* (A) *n.f.* Nearness; affinity; friendship.

ولادت *wilādat* (A) *n.f.* Nativity; birth.

ولایت *wilāyat* (A) *n.f.* An inhabited country; dominion; a foreign country; abroad; realm; possession; being master of anything; sovereignty; control; government; jurisdiction; guardianship; friendship; union (specially with God); sanctity; prophecy; the office of a saint.

ولایت پانا *wilāyat pānā*, *v.* To become a friend of God; to become a saint.

ولایتاً *wilāyatan̲* (A) *adv.* On behalf of.

ولایتی *wilāyatī* (H) *adj.* Foreign. *n.m.* A foreigner.

ولد *walad* (A) *n.m.* A son; offspring.

ولدالزنا ، ولدالحرام *walad-uz-zinā*, *walad-ul-ḥarām*, *n.m.* Illegitimate son; son of whore; a bastard.

ولدالحلال *walad-ul-ḥalāl*, *n.m.* A legitimate son.

ولدیت *waladiyyat* (A) *n.f.* Patronage; pedigree; descent.

ولوله *walwalah* (A) *n.m.* Fervour; ardour; spirit; noise; outcry; a tumult; uproar.

ولی *walī* (A) *n.m.* A prince; lord; master; friend; governor; guardian; helper; friend of God; saint.

ولی‌الله *walī ullah*, *n.m.* A friend of God; a saint.

ولی جائز *walī jā'iz*, *n.m.* Lawful guardian.

ولی عہد *walī a'hd*, *n.m.* An heir to the throne; successor; heir-apparent.

ولی نعمت *walī ni'mat*, *n.m.* Patron; benefactor; a title of respect by which a father or a master or a governor is addressed.

ولے *wale* (P) *adv.* But; yet; however.

ولیک ، ولیکن *walek*, *walekin* (P) *conj.* But; yet; however.

ولیمہ *walīmah* (A) *n.m.* A marriage feast.

وہ *wuh* (H) *pron.* He; she; it; that; them; they; those.

وہاب *wahhāb* (A) *adj.* (*sup.* of واہب) Bestower; generous; an epithet for God.

وہابی *wahhābi* (A) *n.m.* A follower of Sheikh Abdul Wahhab, an Arabian reformer; a staunch Muslim.

وہاں *wahāṅ* (H) *adv.* There; thither; yonder.

وہب *wahb* (A) *n.f.* Giving; bestowing.

وہبی *wahbi* (A) *adj.* Bestowed, granted.

وہم *wahm* (A) *n.m.* Imagination; idea; fancy; opinion; conjecture; anxiety; apprehension; whim; doubt; suspicion; fear; superstition.

وہمی *wahmī* (A) *adj.* Whimsical; imaginary; suspicious; apprehensive; superstitious; visionary; fanciful; ideal.

وہن *wahn* (A) *n.f.* Sluggishness; indolence.

وہی *wuhī* (H) *pron.* He himself; that very.

وہیں *wahīṅ* (H) *adv.* Then and there; at that very time or place; immediately.

وے *we* (H) *pron.* They; those.

وید *wed* (S) *n.m.* Knowledge; science; a religious book of Hindus.

وید *waid* (S) *n.m.* A native physician; a medical man.

ویدانت *wedānt* (S) *n.m.* A philosophical and theological system of the Hindus.

ویدانتی *wedānti* (S) *n.m.* One who is conversant with the Hindu philosophy.

ویدک *vedak* (H) *n.m.* A Brahman well-versed in Vedas. *adj.* Relating to Vedas.

ویدک *waidak* (H) *n.m.* The practice or science of medicine.

ویر *vīr* (S) *n.m.* A hero; a friend; a brother. *adj.* Heroic; brave; powerful.

ویراگ *wairāg* (S) *n.m.* The act of renouncing the pleasures of the world; austerity; penance.

ویراگی *wairāgi* (S) *n.m.* Ascetic; devotee; recluse.

ویران *wīrān* (P) *adj.* Desolate; laid waste; depopulated; ruined.

ویران کرنا *wīrān karnā*, *v.* To ruin; to lay waste; to depopulate.

ویرانہ *wīrānah* (P) *n.m.* A ruined or desolate place; a solitude; ruins.

ویرانی *wīrānī* (P) *n.f.* Desolation; destruction; depopulation; ruin.

ویسا ، ویسی *waisā, waisī* (H) *adv.* & *adj.* In that manner; so; in such a way; like that; of that kind.

ویسا ہی *waisā hī*. In the same manner; in the same state or condition; in *status quo.*

ویسے *waise* (H) *adv.* In that manner; though; thus; freely; without cost.

ویسے کا ویسا *waise kā waisā*, *adv.* The same as before; as just before.

ویسے ہی *waise hī*, *adv.* Without cost; by chance; in the same manner.

ویش *vaish* (S) *n.m.* Ornament; dress; decoration; guise; a man of the mercantile class.

ویشنو *vaishnū* (S) *adj.* Relating to or belonging to Vishnu. *n.m.* A follower of Vishnu; a vegetarian.

ویشنو بھوجن *vaishnū bhojan*, *n.m.* Vegetarian diet.

ویل *wail* (A) *n.m.* Calamity; misfortune; revenge; punishment; hell; reprisal.

ہ

he, called ہائے ہوز *hā-e hawwaz* and ہائے مدورہ *hā-e mudawwarah*, is the twenty-seventh letter of the Arabic, thirty-first of the Persian and thirty-fourth of the Urdu alphabets. According to *abjad* it stands for 5.

ہا *hā* (H) *interj.* Ah! alas! oh! fie! shame!

ہات *hāt* (H) *n.m.* See ہاتھ *hāth.*

ہاتف *hātif* (P) *n.m.* An angel; a voice from heaven.

ہاتف غیب *hātif-ĕ ghaib*, *n.m.* A voice from heaven; a voice from an invisible speaker.

ہاتھ *hāth* (H) *n.m.* The hand; arm; a cubit (measure); half a yard; possession; reach; power; clutches; slap.

ہاتھ آنا *hāth ānā*, *v.* To fall into one's possession; to come to hand; to be gained; to be obtained.

ہاتھ آٹھا بیٹھنا *hāth uṭhā baiṭhnā*, *v.* To keep the hands off; to leave off; to relinquish; to beat; to oppress.

ہاتھ آٹھا کر دعا دینا *hāth uṭhā kar du'ā denā*, *v.* To raise the hands and pray (for).

ہاتھ آٹھا کر کوسنا *hāth uthā kar kosnā*, *v.* To raise the hands and curse a person; to call down curses on.

ہاتھ آٹھا لینا *hāth uṭhā lenā*, *v.* To give up; to withdraw oneself; to abandon; to desist (from).

ہاتھ آٹھانا *hāth uṭhānā*, *v.* To pray; to salute; to give alms; to curse; to abandon; to slap; to beat.

ہاتھ اونچا رہنا *hāth ūnchā rahnā*, *v.* To be well off; to be in a position to give.

ہاتھ باندھنا *hath bāndhnā*, *v.* To join the hands in a supplicating posture; to beg with folded hands; to render one unable to do a thing; to tie one's hands.

ہاتھ باندھے کھڑے رہنا *hāth bāndhe khaṛe rahnā*, *v.* To wait upon; to stand in attendance (on).

ہاتھ بٹانا *hāth baṭānā*, *v.* To extend a helping hand; to help; to lend a hand.

ہاتھ بڑھانا *hāth baṛhānā*, *v.* To stretch out the hand; to endeavour to get anything; to encroach upon; to gain possession of the property of others.

هاتھ بکنا *hāth biknā, v.* To be sold or made over.

هاتھ بند ھونا *hāth band honā, v.* To be poor or helpless or indigent; to have no leisure; to be much engaged in business.

هاتھ بھر *hāth bhar, adv.* Two cubits long.

هاتھ بھر جانا *hāth bhar jānā, v.* To be stained or smeared (the hands); to have the hand wearied or fatigued.

هاتھ بھر کی زبان ھونا *hāth bhar kī zabān honā, v.* To be insolent; to be cheeky; to be talkative.

هاتھ بھیجنا *hāth bhejnā, v.* To send through some one; to send by hand.

هاتھ پاؤں *hāth pā'oṅ, n.m.* A hard-working servant; hands and feet.

هاتھ پاؤں پڑنا *hāth pā'oṅ parṇā, v.* To supplicate; to extract; to implore.

هاتھ پاؤں پھول جانا *hāth pā'oṅ phūl jānā, v.* To become distress or confounded.

هاتھ پاؤں پھیلانا *hāth pā'oṅ phailānā, v.* To extend one's business or schemes; to begin taking bribes.

هاتھ پاؤں ٹوٹنا *hāth pā'oṅ ṭūṭnā, v.* To suffer breaking pains in limbs (as in fever).

هاتھ پاؤں ٹھنڈے ھونا *hāth pā'oṅ ṭhaṅḍe honā, v.* To swoon; to be dying.

هاتھ پاؤں چلنا *hāth pā'oṅ chalnā, v.* To have the ability to work; to be strong enough to work.

هاتھ پاؤں چومنا *hāth pā'oṅ chūmnā, v.* To supplicate; to entreat.

هاتھ پاؤں رہ جانا *hāth pā'oṅ rah jānā, v.* To lose courage; to be paralysed.

هاتھ پاؤں سنبھالنا *hāth pā'oṅ sambhālnā, v.* To begin to show off; to become well-developed.

هاتھ پاؤں مارنا *hāth pā'oṅ mārnā, v.* To sprawl; to swim; to endeavour; to strive; to toil; to struggle; to use all available means.

هاتھ پاؤں هلانا *hāth pā'oṅ hilānā, v.* To set oneself to work; to labour hard; to earn one's livelihood.

هاتھ پٹھے پر نہ رکھنے دینا *hāth puṭhe par nah rakhne denā, v.* To be very clever; to be insolent.

هاتھ پر سرسوں جمانا *hāth par sarsoṅ jamānā, v.* To show one's dexterity; to do a difficult task astonishingly, quickly and easily.

هاتھ پر طوطا پالنا *hāth par ṭoṭā pālnā, v.* To have the hand wounded; to have a boil on one's hand.

هاتھ پر قرآن رکھنا *hāth par Qurān rakhnā, v.* To make one swear by the Quran.

هاتھ پر هاتھ دھر کر بیٹھنا *hāth par hāth dhar kar baiṭhnā, v.* To do nothing; to sit idle.

هاتھ پر هاتھ رکھنا *hāth par hāth rakhnā, v.* To put one's hand into that of another; to promise; to bet.

هاتھ پر هاتھ مارنا *hāth par hāth mārnā, v.* To wring the hands in grief or despair; to make a promise; to wager.

هاتھ پڑنا *hāth parṇā, v.* To come to hand; to be plundered.

هاتھ پسارنا *hāth pasārnā, v.* To ask; to beg; to be ready to accept.

هاتھ پکڑنا *hāth pakaṛnā, v.* To shake hands; to take by the hand; to protect; to aid.

هاتھ پورا پڑنا *hāth pūrā parṇā, v.* To attack with full force.

هاتھ پہنچنا *hāth pahuṅchnā, v.* To have access; to have admittance.

هاتھ پھیرنا *hāth phernā, v.* To caress; to coax; to feel; to rob; to deceive; to cheat.

هاتھ پھیلانا *hāth phailānā, v.* To extend the hand; to beg; to pray.

ہاتھ پھینکنا hāth pheṅknā, v. To wield a sword etc.; to fence.

ہاتھ پیلے کرنا hāth pīle karnā, v. To get one married.

ہاتھ تکنا hāth taknā, v. To depend on another for subsistence.

ہاتھ تنگ ہونا hāth tang honā, v. To be hard up; to be penniless.

ہاتھ جوڑ کر کہنا hāth joṛ kar kahnā, v. To say with folded hands.

ہاتھ جوڑنا hāth joṛnā, v. To entreat earnestly; to supplicate.

ہاتھ جھاڑنا hāth jhāṛnā, v. To strike the blow; to empty the hands of money; to bestow; to give.

ہاتھ جھٹکنا hāth jhaṭaknā, v. To twitch; to give a jerk to the hand.

ہاتھ جھلانا hāth jhulānā, v. To wave the hands sideways in walking.

ہاتھ جھلائی hāth jhulā'ī, n.f. Plundering; the money charged by robbers from way-farers passing through their jurisdiction.

ہاتھ چالاکی hāth chālākī, n.f. Expertness; sleight of hand; skilfulness; thievishness.

ہاتھ چٹھی hāth chiṭṭhī, n.f. A letter in one's own hand-writing; a receipt; a certificate.

ہاتھ چڑھنا hāth chaṛhnā, v. To come into the hands.

ہاتھ چلانا hāth chalānā, v. To strike; to attack; to raise one's hand.

ہاتھ دکھانا hāth dikhānā, v. To show the hand to a fortune-teller; to let the physician feel the pulse.

ہاتھ دھو بیٹھنا hāth dho baiṭhnā, v. To lose something; to be relieved of something; to be hopeless; to despair.

ہاتھ دھو رکھنا hāth dho rakhnā, v. To give up all hopes (of).

ہاتھ دھو کے پیچھے پڑنا hāth dho ke pīchhe paṛnā, v. To pursue a matter in spite of stiff opposition; to persecute.

ہاتھ دھونا hāth dhonā, v. To wash hands; to take ablution; to despair; to be disappointed; to relinquish.

ہاتھ دیکھنا hāth dekhnā, v. To tell the fortune (of); to feel the pulse.

ہاتھ دینا hāth denā, v. To lend a hand; to support; to assist; to pledge oneself; to undertake.

ہاتھ ڈالنا hāth ḍālnā, v. To lay hands on; to violate the chastity of a woman; to meddle; to encroach upon; to interfere with.

ہاتھ رکھنا hāth rakhnā, v. To protect; to shield; to support.

ہاتھ رنگنا hāth raṅgnā, v. To take bribes; to earn by unfair means.

ہاتھ رواں ہونا hāth rawāṅ honā, v. To become expert; to practise a craft.

ہاتھ روکنا hāth roknā, v. To prevent; to refrain (from); to keep back; to withhold.

ہاتھ سر پر رکھنا hāth sir par rakhnā, v. To swear by the head (of); to patronize.

ہاتھ سے hāth se, adv. Through; by hand.

ہاتھ سے جاتا رہنا hāth se jātā rahnā, v. To lose an opportunity; to be helpless.

ہاتھ سے ہاتھ ملانا hāth se hāth milānā, v. To shake hands.

ہاتھ سے ہاتھ ملنا hāth se hāth malnā, v. To repent.

ہاتھ شل ہوجانا hāth shal ho jānā, v. To become tired; to be unable to do any work (through fear or shock).

ہاتھ صاف کرنا hāth ṣāf karnā, v. To cut down;to plunder; to slay; to dismiss from service; to practise; to attain perfection.

ہاتھ قبضے پر ڈالنا hāth qabẓe par ḍālnā, v. To be about to draw sword.

ہاتھ کا دیا ḥāth kā diyā, n.m. Alms; charity; a gift; a donation.

ہاتھ کا سچا hāth kā sachchā, adj. Honest; a trustworthy man.

ہاتھ کا میل hāth kā mail, n.m. Cash; money; wealth.

ہاتھ کانوں پر رکھنا hāth kānoṅ par rakhnā, v. To deny vehemently; to refuse point blank.

ہاتھ کنگن کو آرسی کیا hāth kaṅgan ko ārsi kiyā, prov. The thing is as plain as a pikestaff; self-evident facts need no justification.

ہاتھ کی لکیریں نہیں مٹتیں hāth ki lakireṅ nahīṅ miṭṭiṅ, prov. Fate does not change; changing destiny is beyond human endeavour.

ہاتھ (ہاتھوں) کے طوطے اڑ جانا hāth (hāthoṅ) ke ṭoṭe uṛ jānā, v. To be stunned; to be confounded; to be flabbergasted.

ہاتھ گھسانا hāth ghisānā, v. To waste time and energy.

ہاتھ گھنگولنا hāth ghaṅgolnā. To stir up (water); to shake water by the hand and make it muddy.

ہاتھ لپک hāth lapak, adj. A light-figured knave.

ہاتھ لگانا hāth lagānā, v. To handle; to touch; to lay hands on; to meddle; to lend a hand; to wager; to slap.

ہاتھ لگائے کملانا hāth lagāe kumlānā, v. To be very delicate.

ہاتھ لگائے میلا ہونا hāth lagāe melā honā, v. To be very beautiful; to be very fair and bright.

ہاتھ لگنا hāth lagnā, v. To get at; to come to hand; to be touched; to have an experience (of); to be aided; to be wagered (upon).

ہاتھ مارنا hāth mārnā, v. To acquire; to pilfer, to plunder; to capture illegally what is another's property; to wound with a sword; to slay; to promise; bo bet.

ہاتھ ملانا hāth milānā, v. To shake hands with; to claim equality; to prepare for a wrestling match; to close a bargain.

ہاتھ ملنا hāth malnā, v. To repent; to lament; to regret; to wring hands.

ہاتھ میں آنا hāth meṅ ānā, v. To win; to obtain; to get.

ہاتھ میں ٹھیکرا دینا hāth meṅ ṭhikrā denā, v. To make one a beggar; to reduce one to extreme poverty.

ہاتھ میں ٹھیکرا لینا hāth meṅ ṭhikrā lenā, v. To become a beggar.

ہاتھ میں رکھنا hāth meṅ rakhnā, v. To possess; to hold one in subjection; to hold one in reserve to get the benefit of his connections with persons in authority.

ہاتھ میں لے پات میں دھر کھانا hāth meṅ le pāt meṅ dhar khāna, v. To live from hand to mouth; to practise extravagance; to be profane.

ہاتھ میں لیے پھرنا hāth meṅ liye phirnā, v. To be over powered with sexual desire (spoken of a male).

ہاتھ میں لینا hāth meṅ lenā, v. To undertake; to take up; to take in hand.

ہاتھ میں ہاتھ دینا hāth meṅ hāth denā, v. To marry one's daughter; to give into the charge of.

ہاتھ میں ہنر ہونا hāth meṅ hunar honā, v. To be knowing an art; to be an artisan.

ہاتھ نہ آنا hāth nah ānā, v. To lose; to miss.

ہاتھوں hāthoṅ, adv. Hand to hand; with hand; by; on account of; owing to; through one's own actions; by the hands.

ہاتھوں ہاتھ hāthoṅ hāth, adv. Hand to hand; quickly; privately; stealthily; secretly.

ہاتھوں ہاتھ اڑ جانا hāthoṅ hāth uṛ jānā, v. To find a ready sale.

ہاتھوں ہاتھ اڑا لینا hāthoṅ hāth uṛā lenā, v. To take away stealthily.

ہاتھوں ہاتھ لینا hāthoṅ hāth lenā, v. To receive one with all respects.

ہاتھا پائی hāthā pā'i (H) n.f. Scuffling; fighting.

ہاتھا پائی کرنا hāthā pā'ī karnā, v. To scuffle; to fight; to struggle.

ہاتھی hāthi (H) n.m. An elephant.

ہاتھی پاؤں hāthi pā'oṅ, n.m. Elephantiasis.

ہاتھی جھولنا hāthi jhūlnā, v. To possess an elephant; to be very rich.

ہاتھی جھومنا hāthi jhūmnā, v. To have an unmarried grown up daughter.

ہاتھی دانت hāthi dāṅt, n.m. Ivory.

ہاتھی کے پاؤں میں سب کے پاؤں hāthī ke pā'oṅ meṅ sab ke pā'oṅ, prov. A rich man's contribution cover the contribution of the poor people.

ہاتھی کے دانت دکھانے کے اور کھانے کے اور hāthī ke dāṅt dikhāne ke aur khāne ke aur, prov. All that glitters is not gold.

ہاتھی وان hāthī wān, n.m. An elephant keeper; a mahout.

ہاٹ hāṭ (H) n.f. A market; a movable market or fair; a shop.

ہاجی hāji (A) n.m. A satirist.

ہادی hādi (A) n.m. A director; a leader; a guide.

ہار hār (S&P) n.m. A necklace of pearls; a wreath; a chaplet of flowers (worn as a necklace); garland.

ہار سنگار hār siṅgār n.m. Beauty; elegance; name of a tree from the flowers of which yellow and golden colour is obtained; the weeping nyctanthes.

ہار گوندھنا hār gūndhnā, v. To string a garland of flowers.

ہار hār (H) n.f. Loss; forfeiture; discomfiture; defeat; fatigue.

ہار جیت hār jit, n.f. Gambling; hazarding.

ہار جیت کرنا hār jit karnā, v. To gamble; to bet.

ہار بیٹھنا ، ہار جانا hār baiṭhnā, hār jānā, v. To be defeated; to lose a game; to be fatigued; to become old or feeble.

ہار ماننا hār mānnā, v. To accept defeat; to give up in despair; to submit; to bow; to feel tired; to give up a dispute.

ہار، ہارا hār, hārā (H) (in comp.) It means the performer of an action as in پالن ہار pālan hār, nourisher, cherisher; لکڑ ہارا lakaṛ hārā, wood cutter.

ہارنا hārnā (H) v. To be overcome; to be defeated; to be unsuccessful; to lose; to be tired.

ہاڑنا hāṛnā (H) v. To examine the correctness of a pair of scales; to equipoise; to balance.

ہاضم hāẓim (A) adj. Digestive; stomachic; peptic; digestible.

ہاضمہ hāẓimah (A) n.m. The digestive power; digestion.

ہال hal (H) n.f. The tire of a wheel; a plough; rudder.

ہالہ hālah (A) n.m. A circle round the moon; a halo; a nimbus.

ہالہ باندھنا hālah bāndhnā, v. To form a halo.

ہالی hāli (H) n.m. A ploughman.

ہامون hāmūn (P) n.m. A desert; a plain; a level ground.

ہامی hāmī (H) n.f. Assurance; guarantee; assent; confirmation; ratification.

ہامی بھرنا hāmi bharnā, v. To give consent; to confirm; to promise; to acknowledge; to confess; to avow; to give assurance (to); to be responsible (for).

ہاں hāṅ (H) adv. Yes, indeed; by the by; veriely.

هاں جی hāṅ jī, *adv.* Yes, sir.

هاں جی کا نوکر ہونا hāṅ jī kā naukar honā, *v.* To say always "yes, sir", to be a yesman.

هاں کرنا hāṅ karnā, *v.* To say "yes"; to approve (of); to accept.

هاں کہنا hāṅ kahnā, *v.* To assent; to yield.

هاں میں هاں ملانا hāṅ meṅ hāṅ milānā, *v.* To agree with another's opinion thoughtlessly.

هاں ہوں کرنا hāṅ hūṅ karnā, *v.* To say 'yes, yes'; to dilly-dally.

هانپنا hāṅpnā (H) *v.* To pant; to be out of breath; to breathe heavily

هانڈی hāṅḍī (H) *n.f.* A pot; a small cauldron; a hanging lamp.

هانک hāṅk (H) *n.f.* Cry; call; calling aloud; howling; driving.

هانک پکار hāṅk pukār, *n.f.* Uproar; outcry; hue and cry.

هانک مارنا hāṅk mārnā, *v.* To howl after; to call aloud; to cry out.

هانکنا hāṅknā (H) *v.* To drive; to urge on; to bawl.

دون کی هانکنا dūn kī hāṅknā, *v.* To boast.

هاون hāwan (P) *n.m.* A mortar.

هاون دسته hāwan dastah, *n.m.* Pestle and mortar.

هاو هو hā-ŏ-hū *n.f.* Noise; cry; tumult; uproar.

هاویه hāwiyah (A) *n.m.* The lowest region of hell.

ها ها hā hā (H) *n.f.* Flattery; earnest request; supplication; boisterous laugh.

هاهاکار hā hā kār (H) *n.f.* Consternation; a general or great lamentation; wailing; exclaiming.

هائل ، هائله hā'il, hā'ilah (A) *adj.* Terrible; horrible.

هائے hāe (H) *interj.* Alas! ah! *n.f.* A sigh.

هائے هائے کرنا hāe hāe karnā, *v.* To groan; to moan; to be afflicted.

هبوط hubūṭ (A) *n.m.* Decline, downfall; descent; coming down.

هبه hibah (A) *n.m.* A gift; a bequest; a grant; a present.

هبه کرنا hibah karnā, *v.* To bequeath; to execute a deed of gift; to make a present.

هبه نامه hibah nāmah, *n.m.* A deed of gift.

هپ hap (H) *n.f.* The act of snatching with the mouth and swallowing something; the sound made by a compression of the lips.

هپ جهپ hap jhap, *adv.* Greedily; quickly.

هپ کرجانا hap kar jānā, *v.* To gulp down; to swallow all at once; to gobble up.

هپا happā (H) *n.m.* Pap; soft food.

هت ، هت تریکی hat, hat tereki (H) *interj.* Begone! away! be off with you!

هتک hatak (A) *n.f.* Levity; affront; disrespect; defamation.

هتک آمیز hatak āmez, *adj.* Disrespectful; defaming; defamatory.

هتک عزت کا دعویٰ hatak-ĕ 'izzat kā da'wā, *n.m.* Defamation case; a suit for libel.

هتک عزت کرنا hatak-ĕ 'izzat karnā, *v.* To disgrace; to defame.

هتوڑا، هتهوڑا hatauṛā, hathauṛā (H) *n.m.* Sledgehammer.

هتوڑی ، هتهوڑی hatauṛī, hathauṛī (H) *n.f.* A small hammer.

هته hath (H) *n.m.* (*contrac. of* هاته hāth) Hand.

هته ادهار hath udhār, *n.m.* A loan for a short time.

هته باندها غلام hath bāndhā ghulām, *n.m.* A faithful servant.

ہتھ پھول **hath phūl**, *n.m.* A kind of firework; an ornament.

ہتھ پھیری **hath pherī**, *n.f.* Sleight of hand; trickery; manipulation.

ہتھ چکی **hath chakkī**, *n.f.* A small hand-mill.

ہتھ چھٹ **hath chhuṭ**, *adj.* A striker; a beater; one inclined to beat at the slightest provocation.

ہتھ رسی **hath rasī**, *n.f.* Amorous dalliance; toying; self-pollution; self-abuse; onanism.

ہتھ کٹی **hath kaṭī**, *n.f.* Name of a cut with the sword or club.

ہتھ کڑی (ہتکڑی) **hath kaṛī**, *n.f.* Handcuff; manacles for the wrist.

ہتھ کنڈا **hath kanḍā**, *n.m.* Cleverness; cunningness; an art; habit; manual dexterity; custom; knock; style. *adj.* Hand-made.

ہتھا **hatthā** (H) *n.m.* A handle; a shovel; a sleeve; a baker's peel; hand; handful; a large bunch of plantains.

ہتھے چڑھنا **hatthe chaṛhnā**, *v.* To gain power or control (over); to find an opportunity (for).

ہتھے سے اکھڑنا **hatthe se ukhaṛnā**, *v.* To be out of gear; to be uprooted; to be separated.

ہتھنی **hathnī** (H) *n.f.* A female elephant.

ہتھی **hatthī** (H) *n.f.* A small handle; a hair bush.

ہتھیا **hathyā** (H) *n.f.* The hand; a small handle; the thirteenth mansion of the moon; the end of the rain.

ہتھیار **hathyār** (H) *n.m.* A tool; a weapon; an instrument; arms; implements; apparatus.

ہتھیار بند **hathyār band**, *adj.* Equipped; armed; accoutred.

ہتھیار باندھنا **hathyār bāndhnā**, *v.* To arm; to wear arms.

ہتھیار ڈال دینا **hathyār ḍāl denā**, *v.* To surrender.

ہتھیار گھر **hathyār ghar**, *n.m.* An arsenal.

ہتھیا لینا ، ہتھیانا **hathyā lenā**, **hathyānā** (H) *v.* To seize; to pocket; to obtain by fraud.

ہتھیلی **hathelī** (H) *n.f.* Palm of the hand.

ہتھیلی پر سر رکھ لینا **hathelī par sir rakh lenā**, *v.* To be a dare-devil; to be playing with one's life.

ہتھیلی پر سرسوں جمانا **hathelī par sarsoṅ jamānā**, *v.* To do something very quickly; to astonish; to surprise; to perform wonders.

ہتھیلی پر لیے پھرنا **hathelī par liye phirnā**, *v.* To be overpowered with sexual desire (spoken of a female).

ہتھیلی کھجانا **hathelī khujānā**, *v.* Itching of the palm of the hand (a superstition that some money will come to hand).

ہتیا **hattiyā** (H) *n.f.* Murder; slaughter; the sin of killing an animal.

ہتیارا **hatyārā** (H) *n.m.* A murderer; an assassin; a wretch; a villain. *adj.* Inhumane; bloody; murderous; bloodthirsty.

ہٹ **haṭ** (H) *n.f.* Obstinacy; stubborness; perverseness.

ہٹ دھرم **haṭ dharm**, *adj.* Obstinate; tyrant; ungrateful; unjust; dishonest.

ہٹ دھرمی **haṭ dharmī**, *n.f.* Dishonesty; ungratefulness; unjustice; obstinacy.

ہٹ کرنا **haṭ karnā**, *v.* To be obstinate; to be peevish; to resist; to disobey obstinately.

ہٹا کٹا ، ہٹی کٹی **haṭṭā kaṭṭā**, **haṭṭī kaṭṭī** (H) *adj.* Stout and strong; robust; vigorous.

ہٹانا **haṭānā** (H) *v.* To repel; to foil; to remove; to drive backward; to push back; to put off; to put back.

هٹنا haṭnā (H) v. To fall back; to be driven back; to retire; to recede; to shrink; to be repulsed; to retreat; to be defeated.

ہٹکنا haṭaknā (H) v. To be repulsed; to be driven back; to retreat; to move; to stop.

ہٹی haṭṭī(H) adj. Peevish; obstinate; perverse. n.f. Market; shop.

ہٹیلا ، ہٹیلی haṭṭīlā, haṭṭīlī (H) adj. Teasing; pettish; perverse; obstinate.

هجا hijā (A) n.m. Spelling.

هجر hijr (A) n.m. Separation; absence from one's country and friends.

هجراں hijrāṅ (A&P) n.m. Separation; cutting off connections.

هجرت hijrat (A) n.f. Separation; migration; desertion of country and friends; flight; flight of the Holy Prophet from Mecca to Madina.

هجری hijrī (A) adj. Of the Hijrat. n.m. Muslim era.

ہجڑا hijṛā (H) n.m. An eunuch.

هجو hajv (A) n.f. A satire; a lampoon; blame; disrepute; infamy.

هجو گو hajv go, n.m. A satirist.

هجو مليح hajv-ĕ maliḥ, n.f. Irony; apparent praise but in reality a satire.

هجوم hujūm (A) n.m. A crowd; a mob; concourse; throng; an assault; attack; impetuosity.

هجوم کرنا hujūm karnā, v. To rush upon; to make an unexpected attack.

هجے hije, hijje (P) n.m. See هجا hijā.

ہچر مچر hichar michar (H) n.f. Dispute; cavil; excuse; hesitation.

ہچر مچر کرنا hichar michar karnā, v. To hesitate; to falter; to draw back; to make excuses.

ہچکا hichkā (H) n.m. A jolt; a shock; a jerk; concussion.

ہچکچانا hichkichānā (H) v. To doubt; to hesitate, to be in suspense; to falter.

ہچکچاہٹ ، ہچکچی hichkichāhaṭ hichkichī (H) n.f. Hesitation; doubt; wavering.

ہچکنا hichaknā (H) v. To draw back from; to recoil; to decline; to waver; to boggle; to shrink from.

ہچکولا hichkolā (H) n.m. A jolt; a shake; a jerk.

ہچکی hichkī (H) n.f. The hiccough; convulsive sobbing or breathing.

ہچکی بندھ جانا hichkī bandh jānā, v. To hiccough for long.

ہچکی لگنا hichkī lagnā, v. To suffer from hiccough.

هدا ، هدى hudā (A) n.m. Guidance towards the right direction; the right path; instruction.

هدايا hadāyā (A) n.m. (plu. of هديه hadiyah) Presents; gifts.

هدايت hidāyat (A) n.f. Instruction; guidance; righteousness; injunction.

هدايت پانا hidāyat pānā, v. To be guided; to accept instruction.

هدايت نامه hidāyat nāmah, n.m. A book of instructions; a guide; a directive.

هدف hadaf (A) n.m. A mark; butt or aim; object goal; target.

هدف مارنا hadaf mārnā, v. To hit the mark; to hit the nail on the head.

هدهد hudhud (A) n.m. The wood-pecker; pewit.

هدی hadī (A) n.f. Sacrificial cattle taken to Mecca for sacrifice; giving as an offering; a bride conveyed to her husband's home; anything honourable.

هديه hadiyah (A) n.m. An offering; a gift; a present; the present to the reciter of the Quran on completing the reading of it; the price of a copy of Quran.

هدیه کرنا *hadiyah karnā, v.* To make an offering; to dedicate; to sell a copy of the Quran; to make a present.

هڈا ، هڈ *haḍ, haḍḍā* (H) *n.m.* A big bone; spavin.

هڈی *haḍḍi* (H) *n.f.* A bone; the hard part in the centre of a carrot etc.

هڈی پسلی توڑنا ، هڈیاں توڑنا *haḍḍī paslī toṛnā, haḍḍiyāṅ toṛnā, v.* To beat severely; to beat black and blue.

هڈیوں کی مالا هو جانا *haḍḍiyoṅ kī mālā ho jānā, v.* To be very weak; to be emaciated; to be a bag of bones.

هڈیلا ، هڈیلی *haḍīlā haḍīlī* (H) *adj.* Bony; hard.

هذا *hazā* (A) *pron.* This.

هذیان *hazyān, hizyān* (A) *n.m.* Raving; delirium; useless talk.

هر *har* (S) *n.m.* A name of Mahadeva; a name of Vishnu; God; water; a frog; a snake.

هر بهجن *har bhajan, n.m.* Worshipping Har; devotion to God.

هر بهگت *har bhagat, n.m.* A worshipper of Har.

هر هر مهادیو *har har mahādev n.m.* The war-cry of the Hindus.

هر *har* (P) *adj.* Every; any; each; all.

هرآن *har ān, adv.* Constantly; whenever; every moment; continually.

هرآئینه *har ā'īnah, adv.* Indeed; certainly; by every law and rule; in every way; at all events; undoubtedly.

هر ایک *har ek, adj.* Every one; every body; each.

هربابی *har bābi, adj.* Master of knowledge of every kind; master of every art; jack of all trades.

هر بار *har bār, adv.* Every time.

هر جائی *har jā'i, adj.* Vagabond; stroller, faithless; a harlot, a strumpet.

هر جائی پن *har jā'ī pan, n.m.* Faithlessness; cleverness.

هر چند *har chaṅd, adv.* Although; how-much-so-ever; as often as; even if.

هر چند که *har chaṅd kih, adv.* Notwithstanding.

هرچه *har chih, adv.* Whatever.

هر چه بادا باد *har chih bādā bad.* Whatever the consequence; come what may.

هر دل عزیز *har dil 'aziz, adj.* Popular; loved by every body; liked by all.

هر دم *har dam, adv.* Every moment.

هر دیگی چمچه *har degī chamchah, adj.* A hanger on, one who sponges on others.

هر فن مولا *har fan maulā, adj.* Master of every art; jack of all trades.

هر کاره *har kārah, n.m.* Running footman; a courier; a spy; a messenger; an emissary; a peon.

هر کاری *har kārī, n.f.* Attending to all sorts of business.

هر کس و ناکس *har kas-ŏ-nā kas, n.m.* Everyone (noble and plebeian, gentle and simple, high and low).

هر کهیں *har kahīṅ, adv.* Everywhere.

هر گاه *har gāh, adv.* Whenever; whereas; always; everywhere; since; if; in case.

هر گنی *har gunī, adj.* Skilful; clever.

هرا *harrā* (H) *n.m.* Sound; voice; shout; name of an astringent nut, myrobalan.

هرا ، هری *harā, harı* (H) *adj.* Green; fresh; verdant; unripe.

هرا بهرا ، هری بهری *harā bharā, harī bharī, adj.* Luxuriant; fruitful; prosperous; happy.

هراس *hirās* (P) *n.m.* Fear; terror; confusion; sorrow; disappointment.

هراساں *hirāsāṅ* (P) *adj.* Frightened; alarmed; disappointed; confounded; overcome by grief.

هرانا harānā (H) v. To defeat; to foil; to worst; to tire.

هراول harawal, hirāval (T) n.m. The vanguard; the advance guard of an army; a herald; a running footman.

هر پھر کے hir phir ke (H) adv. At length; at last; after all investigation; time and again.

هرج harj (A) n.m. Tumult; sedition; confusion; trouble; loss; interruption; harm; injury.

هرج کرنا harj karnā, v. To obstruct; to harm; to interrupt; to waste.

هرج مرج harj marj, n.m. Trouble; bustle; agitation; tumult; chaos; confusion; disorder; anarchy; hurly-burly; sickness; delay.

هرجانه harjānah, n.m. Compensation; demurrage.

هرجه harjah, n.m. Damages; demurrage; compensation.

هرجه تشخیص کرنا harjah tashkhiṣ karnā, v. To assess damages (for).

هردا hirdā (S) n.m. Heart; breast.

هر زگی harzagī (P) n.f. Nonsense; frivolous talk; absurdity; babble; prate.

هر زه harzah (P) adj. Absurd; frivolous; nonsensical; vain; idle.

هرزه سرائی harzah sarā'ī, n.f. Talking nonsense.

هرزه گو harzah go, adj. An idle talker; a foolish prater.

هرزه گوئی harzah go'ī, n.f. Idle talk.

هرس haris (S) n.f. The tail of a plough.

هرسا hursā, n.m. A stone on which sandalwood is ground.

هر گز hargiz (P) adv. Ever; on any account.

هرم harim (A) adj. Old; decrepit. n.m. Pyramid of Egypt.

هرمزی hirmizī (P) n.f. Name of a red earth.

هرن haran, hiran (H) n.m. A deer; an antelope; hart.

هرن کاچوکڑی بھرنا haran kā chaukaṛī bharnā, v. Leaping or bouncing of a deer.

هرن کا چوکڑی بھول جانا haran kā chaukaṛī bhūl jānā, v. Forgeting of the bound on the part of a deer; to be confounded.

هرن هوجانا haran ho jānā, v. To run away; to flee.

هرنا hirnā (H) n.m. A stag; a buck; a male antelope; a pommel (of a saddle).

هرنا harnā (H) v. To seize; to take by force; to steal; to lose.

هرنی harnī, hirnī (H) n.f. A doe; a hind.

هری harī (S) n.m. Name of Hindu deity, Vishnu.

هریا haryā (S) adj. Green.

هریالا haryālā (H) adj. Verdant; green; grassy; young.

هریالی haryālī (H) n.f. Greenness; freshness; verdour; grass.

هریسه harīsah (A) n.m. A kind of thick pottage made of bruised wheat and meat, butter, cinnamon etc.

هریل haryal (H) n.m. A green pigeon.

هڑ haṛ (H) n.f. A Myrobalan; a tassel or ornament; the stocks.

هڑ بڑا کر haṛbaṛā kar (H) adv. Hurriedly; in hot haste.

هڑبڑانا haṛbaṛānā (H) v. To be confused; to start up from a troubled dream or sleep; to hurry; to confuse.

هڑبڑی haṛbaṛī (H) n.f. Flurry; alarm; uproar; tumult; riot; disorder; hubbub.

هڑبونگ haṛbong (H) n.f. Disorder; anarchy; confusion; name of Rajah of Jhansi who is renowned for his stupidity and misrule.

هڑبونگ مچانا haṛbong machānā, v. To make an uproar; to create a disturbance or commotion.

هڑبڑیا *haṛbaṛyā* (H) *adj.* Hasty; easily agitated; irritable; irascible.

هڑپ *haṛap* (H) *n.f.* Swallowing food without masticating it.

هڑپ کرنا *haṛap karnā*, *v.* To gulp down; to embezzle.

هڑپا *haṛappā* (H) *n.m.* A jump; gulping down; embezzlement.

هڑتال *haṛtāl* (H) *n.f.* Closure of all shops in a market as a protest against oppression or other causes; sulphurate of arsenic.

هڑ جوڑا *haṛ joṛā* (H) *n.m.* Name of a medicinal plant, used for joining broken bones.

هڑدنگا ، هڑدنگی *huṛdaṅgā*, *huṛdangī* (H) *adj.* Turbulent; troublesome.

هڑک *huṛak* (H) *n.f.* Hydrophobia; carving; hankering.

هڑکا *huṛkā* (H) *n.m.* Pining of children separated from parents; bar of a door.

هزار *hazār* (P) *adj.* A thousand. *adv.* However much; as much as. *n.m.* A nightingale.

هزار پا *hazār pā*, *n.m.* Milliped; centipede; a vanomous reptile.

هزارچشمه *hazār chashmah*, *n.m.* Cancer (the disease).

هزار داستان *hazār dāstān*, *n.m.* A kind of nightingale.

هزار میخی *hazār mek͟hī*, *n.f.* A common strumpet; a vixenish old woman.

هزارها *hazārhā*, *adj.* Thousands.

هزاری *hazārī* (P) *n.f.* The command of a thousand men. *n.m.* Commander of a thousand.

هزل *hazl* (A) *n.m.* A jest; a joke; buffoonery; pleasantries; (*plu.* هزلیات *hazliyāt*).

هزل گو *hazl go*, *n.m.* A joker; a satirist; an idle talker.

هزیمت *hazīmat* (A) *n.f.* Flight; rout; defeat.

هزیمت اٹھانا *hazīmat uṭhānā*, *v.* To be defeated.

هست *hast* (P) *n.f.* Being; existence.

هستنی *hastinī* (S) *n.f.* The lowest and the worst of the four classes into which women are divided; a very undesirable woman; a female elephant.

هستی *hasti* (P) *n.f.* Existence; life; entity; world.

هش *hush*, *intj.* The sound made to drive away birds or make camels sit down.

هشاش ، هشاش بشاش *hashshāsh*, *hashshāsh bashshāsh*, *adj.* Glad; jolly; happy.

هشت *hisht*, *husht*, *intj.* Pish! avount! away!

هشت *hasht* (P) *adj.* Eight.

هشت پهلو *hasht pahlū*, *adj.* An eight-sided figure; an octagon.

هشت گوشه *hasht goshah*, *adj.* Octangular; octagon.

هشتاد *hashtād* (P) *adj.* Eighty.

هشتم ، هشتمیں *hashtum*, *hushtumiṅ* (P) *adj.* Eighth.

هشکارنا *hushkārnā*, *v.* To halloo (set the dogs on); to incite.

هشیار *hushyār* (P) *adj.* (Contraction of هوشیار *hoshyār*) Intelligent; prudent; alert; awake.

هشیاری *hushyārī* (P) *n.f.* (Contraction of هوشیاری *hoshyārī*) Prudence; sobriety; caution.

هضم *hazm* (A) *n.m.* Digestion; misappropriation; embezzlement.

هضم کرنا *hazm karnā*, *v.* To digest; to misappropriate; to embezzle.

هضم هونا *hazm honā*, *v.* To be digested; to be embezzled.

هفت *haft* (P) *adj.* Seven.

هفت اقلیم ، هفت کشور *haft iqlīm*, *haft kishwar*, *n.f.* The world.

هفت‌اندام *haft andām, n.f.* The great vein that runs through the arm.

هفت پشت *haft pusht, n.f.* Seven generations.

هفت پہلو *haft pahlū, adj.* Seven-sided. *n.m.* Septagon.

هفت رنگی *haft rangī, adj.* Capricious; cunning; artful; versatile.

هفت زبان *haft zabān, n.m.* Master of seven languages.

هفت قلم *haft qalam, n.m.* Seven styles of handwriting; one who writes in seven styles.

هفت هزاری *haft hazārī, n.m.* One having the command of seven thousand men; the commander of seven thousand.

هفتاد *haftād* (P) *adj.* Seventy.

هفتم *haftum* (P) *adj.* Seventh.

هفته *haftah* (P) *n.m.* A week; seven days; the seventh day; Saturday.

هفته مختتمه *haftah-ĕ mukhtatimah, n.m.* Week eding.

هفته وار *haftah wār, adv.* Weekly

هفوات *hafwāt* (A) *n.f.* Idle talks; nonsense talks.

ہکا بکا *hakkā bakkā* (H) *adj.* Confused; aghast; confounded; struck dumb.

ہکا بکا رہ جانا *hakkā hakkā rah jānā, v.* To be confounded.

هكذا *hakazā* (A) *adv.* Similarly.

ہکلا *haklā, adj. & n.m.* A stammerer.

ہکلا پن *haklā pan, n.m.* Stammer; stutter.

ہکلانا *haklānā, v.* To stammer; to stutter; to falter.

ہکلی *haklī, adj. & n.f.* A female stutter.

ہگاس *hagās* (H) *n.f.* Desire or inclination to go to stools; tenesmes.

ہگانا *kagānā* (H) *v.* To cause t o go to stools.

ہگنا *hagnā* (H) *v.* To go to stools; to evacuate foeces.

ہگوڑا ، ہگوڑی *hogoṛā, hagoṛī* (H) *adj.* Going to stools very often; coward.

ہل *hal* (H) *n.m.* A plough.

ہل جوتا *hal jotā, n.m.* A tiller; a ploughman.

ہل جوتنا، چلانا ، پھیرنا *hal jotnā, chalānā, phernā, v.* To plough.

ہل چلنا *hal chalnā, v.* To be ploughed.

ہلا *hallā* (H) *n.m.* An assault; an uproar; attack; tumult.

ہلا بولنا *hallā bolnā, v.* To attack; to assault.

ہلا کرنا *hallā karnā.* To make a noise; to make an attack; to work vigorously.

ہلا دینا *hilā denā* (H) *v.* To shake; to move; to give a jerk.

ہلاس *hulās* (H) *n.f.* Alacrity; joy; gladness; snuff.

ہلاس دانی *hulās dānī, n.f.* Snuff-box.

ہلاس لینا *hulās lenā, v.* To take snuff.

ہلاک *halāk* (A) *adj.* Being lost; destroyed; fatigued. *n.f.* Perdition; destruction; ruin; slaughter; death.

ہلاک کرنا *halāk karnā, v.* To kill; to destroy; to fatigue; to distress; to drive to destruction; to overwhelm.

ہلاک ہونا *halāk honā, v.* To be killed; to be destroyed; to be tired; to be fatigued; to perish.

ہلاکت *halākat* (A) *n.f.* Death; destruction.

ہلاکو *halākū, adj.* Deadly; destructive; killer.

ہلاکی *halākī, n.f.* Perdition; ruin; destruction.

ہلال *hilāl* (A) *n.m.* The new moon; the cresent.

هلالی hilāli (A) *n.f.* A kind of bow; a segment of a circle. *adj.* Relating to the new moon.

هلانا hilānā (H) *v.* To shake; to move; to jerk; to agitate; to tame; to domesticate; to cause to swim.

هلاهل halāhal (P) *n.m.* A species of deadly poison.

هل جانا hil jānā (H) *v.* To move; to shake; to be tamed.

هل چل hal chal (H) *n.f.* Motion; confusion; alarm; commotion; bustle; fright; tumult; anarchy.

هل چل پڑنا hal chal paṛnā, *v.* To be panic-stricken.

هلدی haldī (H) *n.f.* Turmeric.

هلدی لگا کے بیٹھنا haldī lagā ke baiṭhnā, *v.* To presume a great deal.

هلدی لگے نہ پھٹکڑی haldī lage nah phiṭkarī. Without any expense; quiet easily.

انبا هلدی ambā haldī, *n.f.* Zedoary.

هلدیا haldiā (H) *n.m.* A kind of poison; the jaundice. *adj.* Of yellow colour.

هلڑ hullaṛ (H) *n.m.* Alarm; tumult; uproar; commotion; bustle; disturbance; riot; row.

هلڑ مچانا hullaṛ machānā, *v.* To create disturbance; to kick up a row.

هلکا ، هلکی halkā, halkī (H) *adj.* Light (in weight or character); debased; mean, silly; easy; soft; cheap; unimportant; gentle; easy of digestion.

هلکا پھلکا ، هلکی پھلکی halkā phulkā, halkī phulkī, *adj.* Very light; very lean.

هلکا جاننا halkā jānnā, *v.* To disdain; to disesteem; to despise.

هلکا رنگ halkā rang, *n.m.* Light colour.

هلکا کرنا halkā karnā, *v.* To lighten; to ease; to abate; to assuage; to debase; to abase; to depreciate.

هلکا هونا halkā honā, *v.* To become light; to be relieved of burden.

هلکا پن halkā pan (H) *n.m.* Lightness; vanity; levity; despicableness.

هلکان halkān (A) *adj.* Confounded; confused; tired; wearied.

هلکورا hilkorā (H) *n.m.* A wave; billow; surge.

هل کے پانی نہ پینا hil ke pānī nah pīnā, *v.* To be very lazy and sluggish.

هلگانا hilgānā (H) *v.* To hang; to suspend.

هلگنا hilagnā (H) *v.* To be hung on; to be entangled; to adhere; to stick to; to be constant.

هلنا hilnā (H) *v.* To shake; to move; to be moved; to be agitated; to be tamed; to be familiarized; to take to.

هلهل hulhul (H) *n.m.* Name of a plant.

هلیله halelah (P) *n.m.* The fruit myrobalan.

هم ham (H) *pron.* We; us.

هم hamm (A) *n.m.* Grief; care; solicitude; turning a thing over anxiously in the mind.

هم ham (P) *conj. & adv.* Also; even; same; likewise; in the same manner; equally; (in *comp.*) together; with; mutual; mutually; similar.

هم آغوش ham āghosh, *adj.* Embracing; locked in each other's arms.

هم آواز ، هم آهنگ ham āwāz, ham āhang, *adj.* Harmonious; concordant; consonant; of the same tone or voice; homophonic; homophonous; united; agreeing; consenting.

هم آهنگی ham āhangī, *n.f.* Harmony; agreement; tune; homophony.

هم اصل ham aṣl *adj.* Homogenitic.

هم بزم ham bazm, *adj.* Of the same society; associating together.

هم بستر *ham bistar, adj.* Sleeping together; lying on the same bed; bed-fellow.

هم بستر هونا *ham bistar honā, v.* To sleep together; to cohabit.

هم بستری *ham bistarī, n.f.* Cohabitation; sleeping together; coition.

هم بطن *ham baṭn, adj.* Related by blood; akin; intimate. *n.m.* A blood-relation; a close ally.

هم پایه *ham pāyah, adj.* Equal in rank or dignity.

هم پله *ham pallah, adj.* Of the same scale; of equal weight; equally matched.

هم پہلو *ham pahlū, adj.* Adjacent.

هم پیاله *ham piyālah, adj.* A pot-companion; a chum.

هم پیالهوهم نواله *ham piyālah-ŏ ham niwālah, adj.* Very intimate friend; a bosom-friend.

هم پیشه *ham peshah, adj.* Of the same trade or profession; similar in practice.

هم تا ، همتا *ham tā, adj.* Equal; alike. *n.m.* A peer.

همتائی *ham tā'ī, n.f.* Equality; likeness.

هم جلیس *ham jalis, adj. & n.m.* A close-friend; a constant companion.

هم جماعت *ham jamā'at, n.m.* A class fellow; one of the same party.

هم جنس *ham jins, adj.* Of the same kind; of the same species; homogeneous; of the same nature; congenial. *n.m.* A fellow-creature.

هم جولی *ham jolī, n.f. & n.m.* Playmate; equal; peer; a friend.

هم چشم *ham chashm, adj.* An equal; a rival.

هم خانه *ham k͟hānah, adj.* A fellow lodger; a spouse; an intimate friend.

هم داماں ، هم زلف *ham dāmān, ham zulf, n.m.* Wife's sister's husband.

هم درد *ham dard, n.m.* A sympathiser; a fellow sufferer; partner in adversity; condoler. *adj.* Sympathetic.

هم دردی *ham dardī, n.f.* Sympathy; condonlence.

هم درس ، هم سبق *ham dars, ham sabaq, n.m.* A class-fellow.

هم دگر *ham digar, adv.* Together.

هم دوش *ham dosh, adj.* Shoulder to shoulder; equal; like; close together.

هم دیوار *ham dīwār, n.m.* Next-door neighbour.

هم ذات *ham ẕāt, adj.* Of the same caste or class.

هم راز *ham rāz, adj.* Confident.

همراه *ham rāh, n.m.* Companion, a fellow-traveller. *adv.* With; along with; together with.

همراهی *ham rāhī, n.m.* A companion; a fellow passenger. *n.f.* companionship; company; society in travelling; fellow-travelling.

هم رتبه *ham rutbāh adj.* Of the same rank or dignity.

هم رکاب *ham rakāb, adj.* A fellow-rider; an attendant.

هم رنگ *ham raṅg, adj.* Of the same colour or disposition.

هم زاد *ham zād, n.m.* Born together; a twin; a contemporary; a familiar spirit said to be present at the moment of the birth of a child and accompanies him through life.

هم زبان *ham zabān, adj.* Unanimous; of the same language; conversing together; speaking the same language.

هم ساز *ham sāz, adj.* Friendly; unanimous; according.

هم سایگی *ham sāyāgī, n.f.* Neighbourhood; residing under the same shade.

هم سایه *ham sāyah, n.m.* Neighbour.

هم سر *ham sar, adj. & n.m.* Spouse; a match; a rival; an associate; contemporary; equal in rank; comrade; consort.

هم سری ham sarī, n.f. Rivalry; equality; evenness; matching; equalling.

هم سفر ham safar, n.m. A fellow-traveller.

هم سن ham sinn, adj. & n.m. Of the same age; a play-fellow.

هم شکل ham shakl, adj. Of the same appearance; alike; resembling; analogous; homotype; homomorphic.

هم شہری ham shahrī, n.m. A fellow-citizen.

هم شیر ، همشیره ham shir, ham shīrah, n.f. A sister.

هم صحبت ham ṣoḥbat, n.m. Companion; intimate; of the same society; associate.

هم صفیر ham ṣafīr, n.m. Fellow-songster; intimate friend.

هم طالع ham ṭāli, adj. Of like fortune.

هم عصر ham 'aṣr, adj. & n.m. Contemporary; living at the same period or time.

هم عمر ham 'umr, adj. Of the same age; coeval.

هم قدم ham qadam, n.m. An attendant.

هم قسم ham qism, adj. Of the same kind or species.

هم قوم ham qaum, adj. Of the same tribe or race.

هم قیمت ham qīmat, adj. Equivalent in value or price.

هم کار ham kār, adj. & n.m. A fellow-workman; co-operator.

هم کسب ham kasb, adj. Of the same trade or profession.

هم کفو ham kufw, adj. Of the samefamily.

هم کلام ham kalām, adj. Conversing together; having intercourse.

هم کلامی ham kalāmī, n.f. Conversation; intercourse.

هم کنار ham kinār, adj. Embracing.

هم مجلس ham majlis, adj. Of the same assembly or party.

هم مذهب ham maẕhab, adj. Of the same religion; coreligionist.

هم مرتبه ham martabah, adj. Equal in rank.

هم مرکز ham markaz, adj. Concentric.

هم مشرب ham mashrab, adj. Of the same creed or religion, or faith or disposition.

هم معنی ham ma'nī, adj. Synonimous.

هم مکتب ham maktab, adj. & n.m. Of the same school; a school-fellow.

هم نام ham nām, adj & n.m. A namesake; homonym.

هم نسل ham nasl, adj. Of the same breed; homogeneous.

هم نشین ham nashīn, n.m. A play-mate; an associate.

هم نفس ham nafas, adj. & n.m. A friend; harmonious; in concord.

هم وار ham wār, adj. Level; even; equable; smooth.

هم واری ham wārī, n.f. Evenness; consistency; equability; levelness; flatness; smoothness.

هم وطن ham waṭan, n.m. A fellow-country man; a compatriot.

هما humā (P) n.m. An eagle; a phoenix; a bird of Paradise; a bird of happy omen; a fabulous bird.

همارا ، هماری hamārā, hamārī (H) pron. Our; of us.

هما شما hamā shumā, adj. every body; all.

همالہ ، همالیه himālah, himāliyah (S) n.m. The abode of snow; the Himalaya mountains.

هما همی hamā, hamī n.f. Bragging; boasting; tall talk.

همایوں humāyūn (P) adj. Fortunate; august.

همایونی humāyūnī (P) adj. Imperial; royal.

همت himmat (A) n.f. Spirit; mind; inclination; resolution; bravery; liberality; courage; magnanimity; purpose; design; thought; care; desire; power.

همت باندهنا، کرنا himmat bāndhnā, karnā, v. To muster courage; to be bold; to take courage.

همت بندهانا himmat bandhānā, v. To encourage.

همت پڑنا himmat parnā, v. To take courage; to dare.

همت مردان مدد خدا himmat-ĕ-mardān madad-ĕ-khudā, prov. God help those who help themselves.

همت والا، والی himmat wālā, wālī, adj. High-minded; courageous.

همت هارنا himmat hārnā, v. To lose heart or courage.

همزه hamzah (A) n.m. The orthographical mark (ء).

همکنا humaknā (H) v. To assault; to stretch forward.

همه hamah (P) adj. All; the whole; every one.

همه تن hamah tan, adv. Wholly; entirely.

همه دان hamah dān, adj. Knowing everything; experienced; wise; all-wise; omniscient.

همه دانی hamah dānī, n.f. Omniscience; pantology.

همه صفت موصوف hamah ṣifat mauṣūf, adj. Endowed with every good quality.

همه گیر hamah gīr, adj. All comprising.

همه نگار hamah nigār, n.m. Pantograph.

همیان، همیانی himyān, hamyānī (P) n.f. A purse.

همیشگی hameshagī (P) n.f. Eternity; perpetuity.

همیشه hameshah (P) adv. Always; ever; continually; perpetually; incessantly.

همیں hamen (H) pron. Us; to us.

همیں hamīn (H) pron. (corrup. of هم هی ham hī) We ourselves.

همیں hamīn (P) adj. & pron. Even this; this very.

هن hun (H) n.m. A gold coin of the Deccan, usually called pagoda.

هن برسنا hun barasnā, v. Showering of the wealth; to have great income.

هنجار hanjār (P) n.m. A straight road; a true method; a mason's rule; a plumb-line; a level; a by-path; a short-cut.

هند hind (P&S) n.m. India.

هندبا hindbā (P) n.m. Name of a white seed; endine.

هندسه hindsah (P) n.m. Geometry; figures; arithmetic.

هندسه دان hindsah dān, n.m. A geometrician; an arithmetician; an accountant.

هندنی hindnī n.f. A Hindu woman.

هندو hindū (P) n.m. A native of India; a negro; a black Arabian, Indian or Ethiopian; a Gentoo (Hindu); a slave; a thief. adj. Black.

هندوانه hindwānah (P) n.m. A water-melon. adj. Indian; relating to Hindus.

هندوستان hindustān (P) n.m. India; the country of Hindus.

هندوستانی hidustāni, adj. Belonging to India; Indian.

هندی hindi (P) adj. Indian; relating to India. n.f. The Hindi language.

هندی کی چندی کرنا hindī ki chindī karnā, v. To explain a every obvious fact which does not admit of any explanation.

هنڈ کلهیا hanḍ kulhiyā (H) n.f. A small earthen pot.

هنڈول hinḍol (H) n.m. Name of a rāg or musical mode.

هنڈولا hinḍolā (H) n.m. A swing; a cradle; the song sung on a swing.

هنڈی، هنڈوی hunḍī, hunḍwī (H) n.f. A bill of exchange; cheque.

هنڈی درشنی huṅḍī darshani, n.f. A bill payable at sight.

هنڈی سکارنا huṅḍī sakārnā, v. To honour a bill.

هنڈیا haṅḍyā (H) n.f. A small eathen cauldron.

هنڈیا پکانا haṅḍyā pakānā, v. To cook; to gossip; to conspire.

هنر hunar (P) n.m. Excellence in any art; art; skill; accomplishment; cleverness; knowledge; attainment; virtue.

هنر فروش hunar farosh, adj & n.m. Pedantic; a pedant.

هنر مند ، هنر ور hunar mańd, hunar war, adj. Skilful; clever; excellent.

هنر مندی hunar mańdī, n.f. Skilfulness.

هنس hańs (H) n.m. A duck; a goose; life; soul.

هنسا ḥinṣā (H) n.f. Injury; hurt; malice; robbery; killing

هنسانا hańsānā (H) v. To cause to laugh; to tickle; to please.

هنسائی hansā'ī (H) n.f. Ridicule; fun.

هنسلی hanslī (H) n.f. Collar-bone; clavicle; a collar (of gold or silver) worn round the neck as an ornament.

هنس مکھ hans mukh (H) adj. Cheerful; merry; laughing; facetious; jocular; jolly; jovial; blithesome; blithe.

هنسنا hansnā (H) v. To laugh; to deride; to laugh at; to smile; to be merry.

هنسوڑ hansoṛ (H) adj. Jocular; merry; cheerful.

هنسوڑ پن hansoṛ pan, n.m. Jocularity; facetiousness.

هنسی hańsī (H) n.f. Sport; fun; mirth; laughter; laugh; ridicule; jesting.

هنسی آڑانا hansī urānā, v. To ridicule.

هنسی ٹھٹھا hansī thathā, n.m. Jesting; joking; laughter.

هنسی خوشی hansī khushī, adv. Gladly.

هنسی سمجھنا hansī samajhnā, v. To take as a joke.

هنسی کھیل hansī khel, n.m. Laugh; jesting; an easy task.

هنسی میں آڑا دینا hansī meṅ urā denā, v. To turn off with a joke.

هنسی هنسی میں hansī hansī meṅ, adv. In jest; humorously.

هنسیا hańsiyā (H) n.f. A sickle.

هنکارا، هنکاری huṅkārā, huṅkārī (H) n.m. n.f. Saying 'yes'; assent.

هنکارا یا هنکاری بھرنا huṅkārā yā huṅkārī bharnā, v. To say 'yes'; to assent.

هنکارنا huṅkārnā (H) v. To say yes; to assent; to halloo after.

هنکالنا ، هنکانا hankālnā, hankānā (H) v. To drive away (cattle etc.)

هنگام haṅgām (P) n.m. Season; time; period.

هنگامه haṅgāmah (P). n.m An assembly; a crowd; tumult; uproar; riot; sedition; disturbance; disorder; confusion; assault.

هنگامه پرداز haṅgāmah pardāz, adj. Riotous; tumultous.

هنگامه پردازی haṅgāmah pardāzī, n.f. tumult or riot.

هنگامه خیزی haṅgāmah khezī, n.f. Assaulting; causing disorder and confusion; rioting.

هنگامی haṅgāmī (P) adj. Accidental; provisional; temporary; make-shift.

هنود hunūd (A) n.m. (plu. of هندو) Hindus.

هنوز hanūz (P) adv. Yet; hitherto; still; just now; not yet.

هنوز دلی دور است hanūz Dillī dūr ast, prov. Delhi is a long way off yet; the end of the matter is still far off.

هنومان hanūmān (S) n.m. The monkey god of the Hindus; a baboon; a monkey; a miser.

هنهنانا hinhinānā (H) v. To neigh.

هو hū, howā (A) pron. He, e.g. God.

هو حق کرنا hū ḥaqq karnā, v. To remember God; to make a noise; to enjoy; to revel.

هو حق هو جانا hū ḥaqq ho jānā, v. To be ruined; to be annihilated.

هو کا عالم hū kā 'ālam, n.m. A desert (where none except God exists).

هو ho (H) A vocative particle; ho!

هو آنا ho ānā (H) v. To go and come back; to have gone and returned.

هوا hawā (A) n.f. Wind; air; atmosphere; breeze; space; flight; evil spirit; rumour; good name; worthless thing; lust; desire; greed; love; affection.

هوا آڑانا hawā uṛānā, v. To fart; to defame.

هوا آڑ جانا' آکھڑنا hawā uṛ jānā, ukharnā, v. To lose credit.

هوا باز hawā bāz, n.m. Aerostat, a pilot (of an airship); airman.

هوا بازی hawā bāzī, n.f. Airmanship; aeronautics.

هوا بدلنا hawā badalnā, v. To undergo a change of condition; to change climate; changing of condition.

هوا بسته hawā bastah, adj. Air tight.

هوا بگڑنا hhwā bigaṛnā, v. To be adversely affected (reputation); to lose credit; to get a bad name.

هوا بندھ جانا hawā bandh jānā, v. To win a name.

هوا بھر جانا hawā bhar jānā, v. To be inflated; to be puffed up with pride.

هوا بھی نه دینا hawā bhī nah denā, v. Not to disclose a secret; not to expose.

هوا پر دماغ هونا hawā par dimāgh honā, v. To be vain-glorious.

هوا پر سوار هونا hawā par sowār honā, v. To hurry; to be in haste.

هوا پھانکنا hawā phāṅknā, v. To go without food; to have nothing to eat.

هوا پھر جانا hawā phir jānā, v. Changing of conditions.

هوا تکیه hawā takyah, n.m. Air-cushion.

هوا توشک hawā toshak, n.m. Air-bed.

هوا چکی hawā chakkī, n.f. A wind-mill.

هوا چلنا hawā chalnā, v. To blow (wind).

هوا چھوڑنا hawā chhoṛnā, v. To fart; to break wind.

هوا خلاف هونا hawā khilāf honā, v. Blowing of the wind in the opposite direction; changing of conditions against (oneself).

هوا خواه hawah khwāh, adj. Wellwisher; lover.

هوا خواهی hawā khwāhī, n.f. Good-will; friendship.

هوا دار hawā dār, adj. Open; airy; ventilated; n.m. A movable throne on which kings took a ride; a lover.

هوا داری hawā dārī, n.f. Airiness; love.

هوا دان hawā dān, n.m. Ventilator.

هوا دینا hawā denā, v. To blow the cool; to excite or foment a quarrel; to aeriate.

هوا سا hawā sā, adj. Light as air.

هوا سنج hawā sanj, n.m. Barometer.

هوا سے آڑ جانا hawā se uṛ jānā, v. To be very lean; to be very thin; to be so light as to be blown away by the wind.

هوا سے باتیں کرنا *hawā se bāteṅ karnā*, *v.* To rival the wind in speed; to be very fast; to brag; to boast.

هوا سے بچ کر نکلنا *hawā se bach kar nikalnā*, *v.* To keep oneself aloof; to shun; to avoid; to hate.

هوا سے لڑنا *hawā se laṛnā*, *v.* To quarrel with the wind; to be ready to quarrel; to seek occasion for a quarrel.

هوا کا تھپیڑا *hawā kā thapeṛā*, *n.m.* A blast of wind; a gust of wind.

هوا کا رخ بتانا *hawā kā ru<u>kh</u> batānā*, *v.* To tell the direction of the wind; to tell how the things move.

هوا کا رخ دیکھنا *hawā kā ru<u>kh</u> dekhnā*, *v.* To look for one's opportunity; to notice how things are moving.

هوا کرنا *hawā karnā*, *v.* To fan; to broach; to divulge; to disclose; to publish.

هوا کھانا *hawā khānā*, *v.* To take an airing; to walk about idly; to go away.

هوا کے دوش پر *hawā ke dosh par*, *adv.* On the wings of the air; by wireless.

هوا کے گھوڑے پر سوار هونا *hawā ke ghoṛe par sawār honā*, *v.* To be in a great hurry; to be very proud.

هوا لگ جانا *hawā lag jānā*, *v.* To have rheumatism; to have one's head turned.

هوا کش *hawā kash*, *n.m.* An air pump.

هوا گزار *hawā guzār*, *n.m.* Airway.

هوا مٹھی میں بند کرنا ، هوا میں گرہ دینا *hawā muṭhī meṅ baṅd karnā, hawā meṅ girah denā*, *v.* To attempt the impossible.

هوا نکلنا *hawā nikalnā*, *v.* To be punctured; to be perforated; to be exposed; to lose honour.

هوا نہ رهنا *hawā nah rahnā*, *v.* To lose beauty; to lose splendour; to lose flourishing state.

هوا نہ لگنے دینا *hawā nah lagne denā*, *v.* To keep closed; to keep hidden; to keep off.

هوا و هوس *hawā-ŏ hawas*, *n.f.* Lust; sensuality; luxury; vanity; ambition; envy; greediness.

هوا هو جانا *hawā ho jānā*, *v.* To scamper off; to disappear; to vanish; to run away as fast as the wind; to evaporate (as water).

هوا *hawwā* (H) *n.m.* A bugbear; a hobgoblin.

هوائی *hawā'ī* (P) *n.f.* A sky-rocket; a rumour. *adj.* Aerial; airy; windy; pneumatic; swift.

هوائی اڑانا *hawā'i uṛānā*, *v.* To spread rumours.

هوائی بندوق *hawā'ī baṅdūq*, *n.f.* Air-gun; pop-gun.

هوائی جهاز *hawā'ī jahāz*, *n.m.* Aeroplane; airplane; air-craft.

هوائی جهاز بردار *hawā'ī jahāz bardār*, *n.m.* Aircraft carrier.

هوائی حمله *hawā'ī ḥamlah*, *n.m.* Air raid.

هوائی خبر *hawā'ī <u>kh</u>abar*, *n.m.* Rumour; a gossip.

هوائی صدری *aawā'i ṣadrī*, *n.f.* Air jacket.

هوائی قلعه *hawā'ī qila'h*, *n.m.* Castle in the air; cloud castles.

هوائی قلعے بنانا *hawā'ī qila'e banānā*, *v.* To build castles in the air.

هوائیاں اڑنا *hawā'iyāṅ uṛnā*, *v.* To lose colour; to become suddenly pale through fear.

هو به هو *hū ba hū*, *adv.* Exactly; quite; perfectly.

هو به هو نقل *hū ba hū naql*, *n.f.* A facsimile.

هوت *hot* (H) *n.f.* Ability; means; wealth; power. *interj.* Ho! halo!

هوتا سوتا *hotā sotā* (H) *n.m.* Living and dead; relations; helpers.

ہوتی آئی ہے hoti ā'ī hai (H). It is an old custom; it happens like that.

ہوتے hote (H) *adv.* In the presence of.

ہوتے ہوتے hote hote (H) *adv.* Gradually; slowly; by and by.

ہوتے ہی hote hī (H) *adv.* As soon as one is born; as it happened.

ہو جانا ho jānā (H) *v.* To become; to be born; to have happened.

ہودج haudaj (A) *n.m.* See ہودہ *haudah.*

ہودہ haudah (H) *n.m.* A litter (used on an elephant or camel, in which the ladies travel); on open seat on an elephant.

ہودہ hūdah (P) *adj.* Correct; proper; just; right.

ہوس hawas (A) *n.f.* Desire; lust; ambition; curiosity; inordinate desire.

ہوس پیشہ hawas peshah, *adj.* Covetous; greedy; lusty.

ہوس پرور hawas parwar, *adj.* Desirous; lustful; wishful; lascivious.

ہوس کرنا hawas karnā, *v.* To desire eagerly; to endeavour to procure.

ہوس کیش hawas kesh, *adj.* Desirous; ambitious; lascivious.

ہوس ناک hawas nāk, *adj.* Full of desire; curious; lustful.

ہوس نکالنا hawas nikālnā, *v.* To satisfy one's desire.

ہو سکنا ho saknā (H) *v.* To be possible.

ہوش hosh (P) *n.m.* Sense; judgment; understanding; discretion; mind; soul.

ہوش آنا hosh ānā, *v.* To come to oneself; to understand.

ہوش اُڑنا، اُڑجانا، باختہ ہونا، پراگندہ ہونا، جاتے رہنا hosh uṛnā, uṛ jānā, bā*kh*tah honā, parāgandah honā, jāte rahnā, *v.* To be or become confounded; to lose one's senses.

ہوش پکڑنا، سنبھالنا hosh pakaṛnā, sambhālnā, *v.* To recollect; to bethink of one's self; to arrive at the age of discretion.

ہوش مند hosh mand, *adj.* Intelligent; prud[illegible]t; sensible.

ہوش مندی hosh mandi, *n.f.* Intelligence; understanding; wisdom.

ہوش میں آنا hosh men ānā, *v.* To come to one's senses; to recover one's senses; to come to one's self.

ہوش و حواس hosh-ŏ ḥawās, *n.m.* Sense and understanding.

ہوشیار hoshyār, *adj.* Intelligent; attentive; prudent; discreet; careful; alert; awake; accurate; sensible; clever; learned; wise; cautious; watchful.

ہوشیار باش hoshyār bāsh, *intj.* Be cautious! take care!

ہوشیار کرنا hoshyār karnā, *v.* To warn; to give notice; to caution; to make acquainted.

ہوشیار ہو جانا hosayār ho jānā, *v.* To be alert; to be on the guard; to be careful; to be cautious; to be prudent.

ہوشیاری hoshyārī, *n.f.* Intelligence; cleverness; learning; prudence; wisdom; carefulness; accuracy; sobriety; caution; discretion; watchfulness; alertness.

ہوک hūk (H) *n.f.* Pain; ache; shooting pain; stitch; twitch.

ہوک اٹھنا hūk uṭhnā, *v.* To feel acute pain; to suffer from shooting pain.

ہوکا haukā (H) *n.m.* Greediness; cupidity; covetousness.

ہوکا کرنا haukā karnā, *v.* To be greedy; to be covetous.

ہول haul (A) *n.m* Terror; horror; fright.

ہول آنا haul anā, *v.* To be frightened; to be terror-stricken.

ہول بیٹھ جانا haul baiṭh jānā, *v.* To be terror-stricken.

ہول دل haul-ĕ dil, *n.m.* Melancholy; depression of spirits.

ہول زدہ haul zadah, *adj.* Terrified; aghast; frightened.

ہول کھانا haul khānā, v. To be afraid; to be frightened.

ہولناک haul nāk, adj. Frightful; terrible; terrific; dreadful; horrid; dismal; dreary; fearful.

ہولناکی haul nāki, n.f. Frightfulness; terror; direness; dreadfulness.

ہولا holā (H) n.m. Green gram parched in the pad.

ہولنا haulnā (H) v. To thrust; to goad; to drive an elephant; to urge forward.

ہولی holi (H) n.f. A Hindu festival.

ہولے haule (H) adv. Slowly; gradually; gently.

ہولے ہولے haule haule, adv. Patientlly; gently; slowly.

ہوں hūṅ (H) adv. Too; also; yes; well; very well; exactly.

ہوں ہاں کرنا hūṅ hāṅ karnā, v. To say yes; to assent; to dilly-dally.

ہوں ہوں کرنا hūṅ hūṅ karnā, v. To evade giving a clear answer; to dissuade.

ہونا honā (H) v. To exist; to be; to belong; to become; to serve; to happen; to accrue; to do; to stand; to be born; to come; to be accomplished; to come to pass; to be exhausted.

ہونٹ honṭ (H) n.m. The lip.

ہونٹ چبانا honṭ chabānā, v. To press or bite the lips; to repent; to be enraged.

ہونٹ سی دینا honṭ sī denā, v. To keep silent.

ہونٹ نکالنا honṭh nikālnā, v. To be angry; to be out of temper; to disdain.

ہونس hauṅs (H) n.f. Desire; wish; want; ambition; lust; envy.

ہونق hawannaq, adj. A fool; a simpleton.

ہونکنا hauṅknā (H) v. To pant; to puff and blow; to breathe hard.

ہونہار honhār (H) adj. That which must happen; possible; hopeful; promising; budding; intelligent.

ہونہار بروا کے چکنے چکنے پات honhār birwā ke chikne chikne pāt, prov. A thriving plant has tender leaves; a precocious child shows the man inside him.

ہو نہ ہو ho nah ho (H) adv. It may or may not be; right or wrong; undoubtedly.

ہونی honī (H) n.f. Fate; destiny; what is to happen.

ہویدا huwaidā (P) adj. Clear; manifest; evident; open.

ہی hī (H) adv. Very; exactly; even; indeed; truly; only.

ہے hai (H) v. Is.

ہے hai, interj. Alas! strange! wonderful.

ہے ہے hai hai, interj. Alas; alack-a-day; pity! wonderful!

ہیبت haibat (A) n.f. Fright; perturbation; panic; horror; dread; awe; fear; severity.

ہیبت زدہ haibat zadah, adj. Aghast; appalled.

ہیبت ناک haibat nāk, adj. Dreadful; awful; frightful; terrible; tremendous; appalling.

ہیٹا heṭā (H) adj. Indolent; cowardly; low: pusillanimous; inferior.

ہیٹی heṭī (H) n.f. Disgrace; insult; infamy; contempt.

ہیجان haijān (A) n.m. Rising of dust or of anger; exciting of anger, tumult or war; excitement; commotion; impulse.

ہیجڑا hijṛā See ہجڑا hijṛā.

ہیچ hech (P) adj. Nothing; a trifle; insignificant; worthless; good for nothing; any; anything.

ہیچ مدان hech madān, adj. Ignorant; knowing nothing; ignoramous.

ہیرا hirā (H) n.m. Diamond; adamant.

هيرا آدمی hīrā ādamī, n.m. A sincere and true friend.

هيرا هرن hīrā hiran, n.m. A black deer.

هيرا من hīrā man, n.m. A kind of parakeet.

هيرا پهيری herā pherī (H) n.f. Coming and going; buying a thing and then returning it; wangling.

هير پهير her pher (H) n.f. Changes; turnings; default; tricks; dodging.

هيزم hezum (P) n.f. Firewood; fuel; faggot.

هيزم فروش hezum farosh, n.m. A wood-merchant.

هيزم کش hezum kash, n.m. A wood-cutter; a woodman.

هيضه haiẓah (A) n.m. Cholera; a flux and vomit.

هيضه پهيلنا haiẓah phailnā, v. Breaking out of cholera.

هيضه کرنا haiẓah karnā, v. To suffer from cholera.

هيضے کا ٹيکا haiẓe kā ṭīkā, n.m. Cholera inoculation.

هيکڑ hekaṛ (H) adj. Strong; robust; wealthy; blockhead; hector.

هيکڑی hekṛī (H) n.f. Violence; oppression; powerfulness.

هيکڑی جتانا ' کرنا hekṛī jatānā, karna, v. To show violence; to oppress; to boast; to threaten.

هيکل haikal (A) n.f. Any great building; a palace; a temple; an ornament worn round the neck (of men as well as beasts); a necklace; a figure; face; form; statue or shape of body; appearance; person.

هيں haiṅ (H) v. Are. intj. What! why!

هينگ hiṅg (H) n.f. Assafoetida.

هينگ هگنا hiṅg hagnā, v. To void by stools involuntarily; to pine.

هيولا hayūlā (A) n.m. Matter; mass; chaos; appearance; the first sketch of a picture.

adj. Uncivilized; thin; lean; weak; fickle-minded.

هيهات haihāt (A) interj. Alack-a-day; begone!

هيئت hai'at (A) n.f. Astronomy; the aspect of the heavens; face; outward form; appearance; figure; countenance; aspect; manner; a body of men; a council; a board; a mission.

هيئت اصلی hai'at-ĕ aṣlī, n.f. Original form.

هيئت پکڑنا hai'at pakaṛnā, v. To take a form.

هيئت دان hai'at dān, n.m. An astronomer.

هيئت کذائی hai'at-ĕ kaẕā'ī, n.f. The present outward form (not good).

هيئت مجموعی hai'at-ĕ majmū'ī, n.f. Collective form or mass.

ی ' ے yā, ye, is the twenty-eighth letter of the Arabic, thirty-second of the Persian and thirty-fifth of the Urdu alphabet. According to ابجد abjad it stands for 10.

يا yā (A) vocative particle. O!

يا yā (P) conj. Or; either.

ياب yāb (P) adj. (in comps.) Finding; discovering; receiving.

يابس yābis (A) adj. Dry; arid; costive.

يابنده yābindah (P) n.m. A recipient; a finder; payee.

يابو yābū (P) n.m. A pony; a galloway; a nag.

ياترا yātrā (H) n.f. Pilgrimage of the Hindus; visit to a holy place; departure; journey.

ياجوج ماجوج yājūj mājūj (A) n.m. Gog and Magog.

ياد yād (P) n.f. Memory; recollection; remembrance.

ياد آنا yād ānā, v. To come to mind; to recure; to come to recollection.

یاد الله *yād allah, n.f.* A form of salutation between *faqīrs*; intimacy; acquaintance.

یاد آوری *yād āwarī, n.f.* Calling to mind; remembrance.

یاد داشت *yād dāsht, n.f.* A note; a memorandum; memory.

یاد دلانا *yād dilānā, v.* To remind.

یاد دهی ' یاد دهانی *yād dihī, yād dihānī, n.f.* Putting in mind; reminder; reminding.

یادش بخیر *yādish bakhair, adv.* May he be in peace; an expression used when mentioning an absent friend.

یاد فرمانا *yād farmānā, v.* To call; to send for.

یادگار *yād gār, n.f.* A memorial; a monument; a valuable present.

یادگار زمانه *yād gār-ĕ zamānah, adj.* Unparalleled; matchless; memorable.

یادگاری *yād gārī adj.* Worthy to be remembered; memorable.

یاد هونا *yād honā, v.* To be committed to memory; to learn by heart.

یار *yār (P) n.m.* A friend; a lover; a paramour; a companion.

یار باز *yār bāz, n.f.* A prostitute; a whore; a wanton woman.

یار باش *yār bāsh, adj* Voluptuous; sensual; jolly.

یار باشی *yār bāshī, n.f.* Sensuality; jollity.

یار بنانا *yār banānā, v.* To make friends; to form a friendship.

یار جانی *yār-ĕ jānī, n.m.* A bosom friend.

یار شاطر *yār-ĕ shāṭir, n.m.* A clever friend; a wise friend.

یار غار *yār-ĕ ghār, n.m.* A companion in the cave (has a reference to the flight of the Holy Prophet from Mecca with Hazrat Abu Bakr and their hiding in a cave); a sincere friend.

یار دوست *yār dost, n.m.* Friends.

یار مار *yār mār, adj.* One who betrays a friend.

یار وهی جو بهیڑ میں کام آئے *yār wohī jo bhīṛ meñ kām āe, prov.* A friend in need is a friend indeed.

یارا *yārā (P) n.m.* Strength; courage; power.

یارانه *yārānah (P) n.m.* Friendship. *adv.* Friendly.

یاری *yārī (P) n.f.* Friendship; love; assistance; intrigue.

یازده *yāzdah (P) adj.* Eleven.

یازدهم *yāzdhum (P) adj.* Eleventh.

یاس *yās (A) n.f.* Despair; fear; terror.

یاس کلی *yās-ĕ kullī, n.f.* Utter despair.

یاسمن ' یاسمین *yāsaman, yāsamīn (P) n.m.* Jasmine.

یاغی *yāghī (T) n.m.* Rebel; enemy.

یافت *yāft (P) n.f.* Income; profit; gain; advantage; earnings; emoluments.

یافتنی *yāftanī (P) n.f.* That which is to be received; dues; balance.

یافته *yāftah (P) adj.* (in comps.) Found; got; discovered.

یاقوت *yāqūt (A) n.m.* Ruby; a precious stone; a garnet.

یاقوت لب *yāqūt lab, adj.* Ruby-lipped; red-lipped.

یاقوتی *yāqūtī (A) adj.* Ruby-coloured. *n.m.* A medicine of which ruby forms a constituent.

یال *yāl (T) n.f.* A horse's mane.

یاں *yāṅ (H) adv.* (*contr. of* یہاں *yahāṅ*) Here (generally used in poetry).

یاور *yāwar (P) adj.* Aiding; friendly. *n.m.* An assistant; coadjutor; companion; friend.

یاوری *yāwarī (P) n.f.* Aid; assistance; friendship; favour.

یاوہ **yāwah** (P) *adj.* Absurd; vain; futile; lost; ruined.

یاوہ گو **yāwah go**, *adj.* An absurd talker.

یاوہ گوی **yāwah goi**, *n.f.* Absurdity; talking nonsense; babble.

یبوست **yubūsat** (A) *n.f.* Dryness; aridity; constipation; costiveness.

یتامیٰ **yatāmā** (A) *n.m.* (*plu.* of یتیم *yatim*) Orphans.

یتیم **yatīm** (A) *n.m.* An orphan; fatherless child.

یتیم الطرفین **yatim-ut-tarafain**, *n.m.* Parentless; orphan.

یتیم خانہ **yatim khānah**, *n.m.* Orphanage.

یتیمی **yatimī** (A) *n.f.* The state of an orphan; orphange.

یثرب **yasrib** (A) *n.m.* The holy city of Madinah.

یحییٰ **yahyā** (A) *n. prop.* John, the apostle.

یخ **yakh** (P) *n.f.* Ice; frozen water. *adj.* Very cold.

یخ بستہ **yakh bastah**, *adj.* Frozen.

یخنی **yakhnī** (P) *n.f.* Gravy; sauce; stew; hash.

یخنی پلاؤ **yakhnī pulā'o** *n.m.* Rice cooked with gravy.

ید **yad** (A) *n.m.* Hand; power; authority; aid; assistance; vigour; benefit; service; a handle; succour; protection.

ید اللہ **yad ullah**, *n.m.* The authority of God.

یدبیضا **yad-ĕ baizā**, *n.m.* A white hand; a miracle given to Moses.

ید طولیٰ **yad-ĕ tūlā**, *n.m.* Very long hand; approach; dexterity; skill.

یدھ **yuddh** (H) *n.f.* War; battle; fight.

یرغمال **yarghamāl** (P) *n.m.* A hostage.

یرقان **yarqān** (A) *n.m.* The yellow jaundice.

یزدان **yazdān** (P) *n.m.* God; the god of goodness of the Persians.

یزدانی **yazdānī** (P) *adj.* Divine.

یزدی **yazdi** (P) *n.f.* A kind of cloth made at Yazd (a cily in Persia).

یسار **yasār** (A) *n.m.* Left; left hand; plenty; opulence; affluence.

یسر **yusur** (A) *n.m.* Prosperity; wealth.

یسیر **yasir** (A) *adj.* Little; easy; soft; motherless.

یشب **yashb** (P) *n.m.* Agate; jasper.

یعسوب **ya'sūb** (A) *n.f.* The queen bee.

یعقوب **ya'qūb** (A) *n. prop.* Jacob, the apostle.

یعنی **ya'nī** (A) *adv.* That is to say; namely; videlicet.

یغما ، یغمان ، یغمہ **yaghmā, yaghmān, yaghmah** (P) *n.m.* Plunder; booty; spoil; pillage;

یقین **yaqīn** (A) *n.m.* Certainty; assurance; truth; confidence; belief; trust.

یقیناً **yaqinan** (A) *adv.* Certainly; assuredly; verily; indeed; as a matter of fact.

یقینی **yaqīnī**, *adj.* True; indisputable.

یقینی ثبوت **yaqīni subūt**, *n.m.* Convincing proof.

یک **yak** (P) *adv.* One; a; an.

یک انار و صد بیمار **yak anār-ŏ sad bīmār**, *prov.* See ایک انار اور سو بیمار *ek anār aur sau bīmār.*

یک بارگی ، یک بیک **yak bārgī, yak bayak**, *adv.* All of a sudden; at once.

یک بام و دو ہوا **yak bām-ŏ-do-hawā**, *prov.* To apply not one but different sets of rules to identical cases.

یکتارا **yak tārā**, *n.m.* An instrument like a guitar with one string; a fine muslin.

یک جا **yak jā**, *adv.* At one place; in one place; together.

یک جان **yak jān**, *adj.* One soul; fast friends.

یک جان دو قالب **yak jān do qālib**, *adj.* Intimate friends.

یک جدی **yak jaddī**, *adj.* Of the same stock; descended from one common ancestors; collateral.

یک جہتی **yah jihatī**, *n.f.* Unanimity; friendship.

یک چشم **yak chashm**, *adj.* Blind of one eye.

یک دل **yak dil**, *adj.* Unanimous.

یک دلی **yak dilī**, *n.f.* Unanimity; accord.

یک ران **yak rān**, *adj.* A thorough-bred (horse).

یک رخی **yak ruk͟hī**, *adj.* One-sided. *n.f.* Partiality; a kind of bow.

یک رنگ **yak rang**, *adj.* Of one colour; sincere; simple; uniform.

یک رنگی **yak rangī**, *n.f.* Sincerity; simplicity; uniformity; monotony.

یک روزہ **yak rozah**, *adj.* Of one day; for a day; ephemeral.

یک زبان **yak zabān**, *adj.* With one voice or tongue; uniform of opinion or speech.

یک ذات **yah ẕāt**, *adj.* Of the same tribe or sect or caste; well-mixed.

یکساں **yak sāṅ**, *adj.* Equal; alike; even; in the same manner; the same; ditto; conformable; uniform; plain; level; parallel.

یکسانیت **yak sāniyat**, *n.f.* Uniformity; identity; sameness; parity.

یک سر **yak sar**, *adj.* All at once; all together.

یک سو **yak sū**, *adj.* On one side; aside; together; fixed; settled.

یک سوئی **yak sū'ī**, *n.f.* One-sidedness; full attention.

یک شنبہ **yak shambah**, *n.m.* Sunday.

یک صد **yak ṣad**, *adj.* One hundred.

یک ضربی **yah ẕarbī**, *adj.* Of one shot (gun or pistol).

یک طرف **yak ṭaraf**, *adv.* Aside.

یک طرفہ ڈگری **yak ṭarafah ḍigrī**, *n.f.* Ex-parte decree.

یک قلم **yak qalam**, *adj. & adv.* Consistent (a writer); all; total; at once; entirely; altogether; all at once.

یک گز دو فاختہ **yak gaz do fāk͟htah**, *prov.* To kill two birds with one shot.

یک لخت **yak lak͟ht**, *adv.* All at once; suddenly; altogether; entirely; wholly.

یک مشت **yak musht**, *n.f.* A handful; prompt payment. *adv.* All at once; full payment; in one instalment.

یک منزلہ **yak manzilah**, *adj.* One storeyed; in single-decker.

یک نہ شد دو شد **yak nah shud do shud**, *prov.* One misfortune on the heels of another.

یکا ، یکہ **yakā, yakkah** (P) *adj.* One; alone; single; solitary; unequalled. *adv.* All at-once; together. *n.m.* A conveyance drawn by one horse; one horse carriage; the ace at cards.

یکایک **yākā yak** (P) *adv.* All at once; immediately.

یکتا **yaktā** (P) *adj.* Single; unique; singular; incomparable; matchless.

یکتائے زمانہ **yaktā-ē zamānah**, *adj.* Singular in one's time; unparalleled.

یکتائی **yaktā'ī** (P) *n.f.* The being unique, singular or unequalled; matchlessness; unity.

یکم **yakum** (P) *adj.* The first day of a month; the first.

یگانگت ، یگانگی **yagānagat, yagānagī** (P) *n.f.* Singularity; excellence; unity; concord; unanimity; union; conjunction.

یگانہ **yagānah** (P) *n.m.* Kinsman; kindred; *adj.* Single; sole; singular; agreed; unanimous; unique; unequalled; incomparable.

یل *yal* (P) *n.m.* A hero; a brave man; a wrestler. *adj.* Corpulent; robust.

یلغار *yalg͟hār* (T) *n.f.* The sudden assault of an army on the enemy; forced march of an army; sudden incursion.

یم *yamm* (P) *n.m.* Sea; occan; river.

یم *yam* (S) *n.m.* The regent of the worlds below; the angel of death.

یمن ، یمانی ، یمنی *yamān, yamānī, yamanī* (A) *adj* Belonging to Yaman (a country).

یمن *yumn* (A) *n.m.* Felicity; prosperity; good luck.

یمین *yamīn* (A) *n.m.* The right hand; an oath.

یمین و یسار *yamīn-ŏ yasār, n.m.* The right and left wings of the army.

یورش *yūrish* (T) *n.f.* Assault; storm; invasion.

یوسف *yūsuf* (A) *n. prop.* The patriarch Joseph.

یوم *yaum* (A) *n.m.* A day.

یوم الحساب ، یوم الحشر *yaum-ul-ḥisāb, yaum-ul-ḥashr, n.m.* The day of reckoning; the day of judgement; the day of resurrection.

یوماً *yauman* (A) *adv.* Per day; daily.

یوماً فیوماً *yauman fa-yauman, adv.* From day-to-day.

یومیہ *yaumiyah* (A) *adj.* Daily. *n.m.* Daily food or allowance or pay or wages.

یوں *yūṅ* (H) *adv.* Thus; in this manner.

یوں توں *yūṅ tūṅ, adv.* In various ways; somehow or other.

یوں ھی *yūṅ hī, adv.* In this manner; thus; accidentally; by chance; causelessly; easily; cursorily.

یونان *yūnān* (A) *n. prop.* Ionia; Greece.

یونانی *yūnānī* (A) *n.m.* A Grecian; Greek. *adj.* Belonging to Greece.

یونانی طبابت *yūnānī ṭabābat, n.f.* The native practice of medicine.

یونانی طبیب *yūnānī ṭabib, n.m.* A native physician, practising Greek science of medicine.

یونس *yūnus* (A) *n. prop.* Jonah, the apostle.

یہ *yih* (H) *pron.* This; he; she; it; these.

یہاں *yahāṅ* (H) *adv.* Here; hither; at the abode; near.

یہاں تک *yahāṅ tak, adv.* Upto this; upto this place; to this degree; thus for; hitherto.

یہاں سے *yahāṅ se, adv.* Hence; from this place.

یہاں کہیں *yahāṅ kahīṅ, adv.* Here abouts.

یہودی *yahūdī* (A) *n.m.* A Jew; a Hebrew. (*plu.* یہود *yahūd*).

یہی *yihī* (H) *adv.* This very; the very same.

یہیں *yahīṅ* (H) *adv.* Here; in this very place; this very.

یہیں کہیں *yahīṅ kahīṅ, adv.* Here about; in this place; hither and thither.

THE END

Printed & Published by Abdus Salam at Ferozsons (Pvt.) Ltd.
Lahore - Rawalpindi - Karachi